THE CAMBRIDGE HISTORY OF CLASSICAL LITERATURE

General Editors
Mrs P. E. EASTERLING
Fellow of Newnham College, Cambridge
E. J. KENNEY
Fellow of Peterhouse, Cambridge

Advisory Editors
B. M. W. KNOX
The Center for Hellenic Studies, Washington
W. V. CLAUSEN
Department of the Classics, Harvard University

THE
CAMBRIDGE HISTORY
OF
CLASSICAL LITERATURE

I
GREEK LITERATURE

Edited by
P. E. EASTERLING
Fellow of Newnham College, Cambridge

and

B. M. W. KNOX
The Center for Hellenic Studies, Washington

CAMBRIDGE UNIVERSITY PRESS
CAMBRIDGE
LONDON   NEW YORK   NEW ROCHELLE
MELBOURNE   SYDNEY

Published by the Press Syndicate of the University of Cambridge
The Pitt Building, Trumpington Street, Cambridge CB2 1RP
32 East 57th Street, New York, NY 10022, USA
10 Stamford Road, Oakleigh, Melbourne 3166, Australia

First published 1985

Printed in Great Britain by the University Press, Cambridge

Library of Congress catalogue card number: 82-22048

British Library Cataloguing in Publication Data

The Cambridge history of classical literature.
Vol. 1: Greek literature
1. Classical literature—History and criticism
I. Easterling, P. E. II. Knox, Bernard M. W.
880'.09   PA 3001

ISBN 0 521 21042 9

CONTENTS

List of plates   *page*   x

Preface   xi

Abbreviations   xiii

1   Books and readers in the Greek world   1
    1   From the beginnings to Alexandria   1
       by B. M. W. KNOX, *Director of the Center for Hellenic Studies, Washington*
    2   The Hellenistic and Imperial periods   16
       by P. E. EASTERLING, *Fellow of Newnham College, Cambridge*

2   Homer   42
    by G. S. KIRK, *Regius Professor Emeritus of Greek, University of Cambridge*
    1   The poet and the oral tradition   42
    2   The *Iliad*   52
    3   The *Odyssey*   74

3   Hesiod   92
    by J. P. BARRON, *Professor of Greek Language and Literature in the University of London, at King's College, London,* and P. E. EASTERLING

4   The epic tradition after Homer and Hesiod   106
    1   The cyclic epics   106
       by J. P. BARRON and P. E. EASTERLING
    2   The Homeric Hymns   110
       by G. S. KIRK

5   Elegy and iambus   117
    1   Archilochus   117
    2   Early Greek elegy: Callinus, Tyrtaeus, Mimnermus   128
       by J. P. BARRON and P. E. EASTERLING

CONTENTS

3 Theognis 136

4 Solon 146
by B. M. W. KNOX

5 Semonides 153
by P. E. EASTERLING

6 Hipponax 158
by B. M. W. KNOX

6 Archaic choral lyric 165
by CHARLES SEGAL, *David Benedict Professor of Classics and Professor of Comparative Literature, Brown University*

1 The nature of early choral poetry 165

2 Alcman 168

3 Stesichorus 186

7 Monody 202
by DAVID A. CAMPBELL, *Professor of Classics, University of Victoria, British Columbia*

1 Sappho 203

2 Alcaeus 209

3 Ibycus 214

4 Anacreon 216

5 Skolia 220

8 Choral lyric in the fifth century 222
by CHARLES SEGAL

1 Introduction 222

2 Simonides 223

3 Pindar 226

4 Bacchylides 235

5 Women poets: Corinna, Myrtis, Telesilla, Praxilla 239

6 Choral lyric to the end of the fifth century 242

9 Early Greek philosophy 245
by A. A. LONG, *Professor of Classics at the University of California, Berkeley*

1 Philosophical poets and Heraclitus 245

2 Anaxagoras, Democritus and other prose philosophers 253

10 Tragedy 258

1 The origins of tragedy 258
by R. P. WINNINGTON-INGRAM, *Emeritus Professor of Greek Language and Literature in the University of London, at King's College, London*

CONTENTS

2 Tragedy in performance   263
  by JOHN GOULD, *Professor of Greek, University of Bristol*

3 Aeschylus   281
  by R. P. WINNINGTON-INGRAM

4 Sophocles   295
  by P. E. EASTERLING

5 Euripides   316

6 Minor tragedians   339
  by B. M. W. KNOX

11 The satyr play   346
   by DANA F. SUTTON, *Professor of Classics, University of California, Irvine*

12 Comedy   355
   by E. W. HANDLEY, *Regius professor of Greek, University of Cambridge*

   1 Introduction   355
   2 Structural patterns in Old Comedy   358
   3 The earliest comic drama   362
   4 Epicharmus and others   367
   5 Myths and myth-making   370
   6 Political comedy   374
   7 Adventure and fantasy   379
   8 The life of the mind   384
   9 The social scene   391
   10 From Aristophanes to Menander   398
   11 Menander and the New Comedy   414

13 Historiography   426
   1 Herodotus   426
   2 Thucydides   441
   3 Common elements of fifth-century historiography   456
     by HENRY R. IMMERWAHR, *Distinguished Alumni Professor Emeritus, University of North Carolina at Chapel Hill*
   4 Historical writing in the fourth century B.C. and in the   458
     Hellenistic period
     by W. R. CONNOR, *Andrew Fleming West Professor of Classics, Princeton University*

14 Sophists and physicians of the Greek enlightenment   472
   by GEORGE A. KENNEDY, *Paddison Professor of Classics, University of North Carolina at Chapel Hill*

CONTENTS

15   Plato and the Socratic work of Xenophon   478
by F. H. SANDBACH, *Emeritus Professor of Classics, University of Cambridge*
    1   Xenophon   478
    2   Plato   480

16   Oratory   498
by GEORGE A. KENNEDY
    1   The beginnings of literary oratory   498
    2   Oratory in the fourth century   505

17   Aristotle   527
by A. A. LONG
    1   His life and writings   527
    2   Rhetoric   533
    3   Poetics   534

18   Hellenistic poetry   541
by A. W. BULLOCH, *Associate Professor of Classics at the University of California, Berkeley*
    1   Introduction   541
    2   Philetas and others   544
    3   Callimachus   549
    4   Theocritus   570
    5   Apollonius Rhodius   586
    6   Minor figures   598

19   Post-Aristotelian philosophy   622
by A. A. LONG
    1   The Later Academy and the Peripatos (Lyceum)   622
    2   Epicurus and Philodemus   625
    3   The Stoa and Stoic writers   631
    4   Sceptics, Cynics, and other post-Aristotelian philosophers   636

20   The literature of the Empire   642
    1   The early Empire   642
        Strabo   642
        Dionysius of Halicarnassus   643
        by G. W. BOWERSOCK, *Professor of Ancient History, Institute for Advanced Study (Princeton)*
        'Longinus' and others   646
        by D. C. INNES, *Fellow of St Hilda's College, Oxford*

CONTENTS

2 Poetry   649
   Poetic miniatures   649
   The hexameter poems ascribed to Oppian   653
3 Philostratus and the Second Sophistic   655
   Aelius Aristides   658
4 Science and superstition   662
   Galen   662
   Artemidorus   663
   by G. W. BOWERSOCK
5 Between philosophy and rhetoric   665
   Plutarch   665
   by G. W. BOWERSOCK
   Dio of Prusa   669
   Maximus   672
   Lucian   673
   Alciphron   679
   Aelian   680
   Athenaeus   682
   by E. L. BOWIE, *Fellow of Corpus Christi College, Oxford*
6 The Greek novel   683
   The genre   683
   The surviving texts   688
   by E. L. BOWIE
7 The fable   699
   by P. E. EASTERLING
8 Historical writing of the High Empire   703
   Arrian   703
   Appian   707
   by E. L. BOWIE
   Pausanias   709
   Cassius Dio and Herodian   710
   by G. W. BOWERSOCK

21 Epilogue   714
   by B. M. W. KNOX

Appendix of authors and works   719
edited by MARTIN DRURY

Metrical appendix   893
by MARTIN DRURY

Works cited in the text   900

Index   919

PLATES

(between pages 272 and 273)

Ia Boy reading from a papyrus roll. Fragment of a red-figure cup by the Akestorides Painter, about 460 B.C. Greenwich, Connecticut. Walter Bareiss 63. Photo: Courtesy of Alexander Cambitoglou.

Ib Girl reading. Marble funerary relief. British Museum Catalogue of Sculpture 649. Photo: Courtesy of the Trustees of the British Museum.

II Part of a papyrus roll. British Museum Papyrus 115, cols. 27–34. Reproduced by permission of the British Library. Photo: British Library.

III Leaf of an open papyrus codex. British Museum. Reproduced by courtesy of the Egypt Exploration Society. Photo: Egypt Exploration Society.

IVa Epidaurus: the theatre from the air. Photo: R. V. Schoder, SJ.

IVb *Auletes* and figures in oriental costume. Fragments of a hydria found in Corinth. Corinth T 1144. Photo: American School of Classical Studies.

Va Actors dressing and rehearsing. Red-figure pelike from Cervetri, *c.* 430 B.C. H. L. Pierce Fund 98.883. Courtesy of the Museum of Fine Arts, Boston. Photo: Museum.

Vb Actors dressing and rehearsing. Red-figure bell-krater, from Valle Pega, *c.* 460 B.C. Museo Archeologico Nazionale, Ferrara T 173C (V.P.). Photo: Biancolli.

VIa Painted backdrop for a play. Fragment of a polychrome vase from Tarentum, *c.* 350 B.C. Würzburg, Martin von Wagner Museum inv. H 4696 and H 4701. Photo: Museum.

VIb An actor and his mask. Wall-painting from Herculaneum. Naples, National Museum no. 9019. Photo: Anderson no. 23415, courtesy of The Mansell Collection.

VIIa Mask of a tragic heroine. Fragment of a red-figure jug from Athens, *c.* 470–460 B.C. Agora Museum inv. P 11810. Photo: American School of Classical Studies.

VIIb Female tragic mask. Fragment of a red-figure vase from Athens, *c.* 400 B.C. Würzburg, Martin von Wagner Museum inv. H 4781. Photo: Museum.

VIIc Actor holding his mask. Fragment of a polychrome vase from Tarentum, *c.* 340 B.C. Würzburg, Martin von Wagner Museum inv. H 4600. Photo: Museum.

VIII Actors, satyr chorus, *auletes*, playwright and lyre-player. The Pronomos Vase: red-figure volute-krater from Athens, *c.* 400 B.C. Furtwängler-Reichhold (1921).

PREFACE

'Ancient Greek literature' is not easily defined. There is no difficulty in placing its starting point in the archaic period, but the choice of closing date is bound to be arbitrary, since literary production in Greek continued for centuries after the ancient world ceased to be in any sense classical. No attempt is made here to deal with Christian literature, which would warrant a volume of its own, or with the classicizing works of early Byzantine authors; it has seemed best to close the volume with the end of the period of stable Graeco-Roman civilization in the third century A.D. Even with this comparatively early terminal date the period covered is a very long one – over a thousand years – and there is a wealth both of surviving material and of information about the much larger body of literature now lost. The emphasis of the present survey is mainly on works that are still extant, have intrinsic literary interest, or have exercised an influence on later literature. Within this general scheme particular attention has been paid to texts discovered in recent years: it is an important feature of ancient Greek literature that it is growing all the time. Quotations in the original are unevenly distributed: more extensive samples are given of texts not yet widely available, and more poetry than prose is cited in Greek. The background of historical events and the development of ideas over so long and diverse a period have had to be treated only incidentally, in order to keep the volume within bounds, but the reader who follows its roughly chronological thread should gain some sense of the changing tastes and literary values of educated Greeks over the centuries.

Fuller documentation of the lives and works of the authors discussed is to be found in the Appendices, where details are given of editions, collections of fragments, translations and critical studies. The List of Works Cited in the Text and List of Abbreviations together supply in full the references cited in abbreviated form in the footnotes.

The spelling of Greek names is an intractable problem, since current English practice is to use a mixture of transliterated Greek, latinized and anglicized forms. Latin and English have generally been preferred on grounds of familiarity, but some inconsistency has been unavoidable.

PREFACE

A collaborative enterprise of this kind owes much to a large number of people. The Publishers and Editors would like to make special acknowledgement for help, on behalf of the contributors to be mentioned, to Professor Christian Habicht, Professor C. P. Jones (G. W. Bowersock); Mr E. L. Bowie, Miss J. M. Reynolds, Professor R. P. Winnington-Ingram (P. E. Easterling); Professor B. R. Rees (A. A. Long); Professor Hugh Lloyd-Jones (R. P. Winnington-Ingram). Mr Martin Drury deserves particular appreciation for his work as editor of the Appendix of Authors and Works and author of the Metrical Appendix. Jenny Morris compiled the index.

The Editors wish to thank the contributors most warmly for their patience in the face of frustrating delays, which bedevilled the production of this volume, and the Publishers for their constant and imaginative support.

P.E.E.
B.M.W.K.

ABBREVIATIONS

BT	Bibliotheca Scriptorum Graecorum et Romanorum Teubneriana (Leipzig & Stuttgart)
Budé	Collection des Universités de France, publiée sous le patronage de l'Association Guillaume Budé (Paris)
Bursian	Bursian's *Jahresbericht über die Fortschritte der klassischen Altertumswissenschaft* (Berlin, 1873–1945)
CAF	T. Kock, *Comicorum Atticorum Fragmenta* (Leipzig, 1880–8)
CAH	*The Cambridge Ancient History* (Cambridge, 1923–39)
CAH[2]	2nd ed. (Cambridge, 1961–)
CHCL	*Cambridge History of Classical Literature* (Cambridge, 1982–5)
CGF	G. Kaibel, *Comicorum Graecorum Fragmenta* (Berlin, 1899)
CGFP	C. F. L. Austin, *Comicorum Graecorum Fragmenta in papyris reperta* (Berlin, 1973)
CIL	*Corpus Inscriptionum Latinarum* (Berlin, 1863–)
CVA	*Corpus Vasorum Antiquorum* (Paris & elsewhere, 1925–)
Christ–Schmid–Stählin	W. von Christ, *Geschichte der griechischen Literatur*, rev. W. Schmid and O. Stählin (Munich, 1920–24) 6th ed. (Cf. Schmid–Stählin)
Diehl	E. Diehl, *Anthologia Lyrica Graeca* I (2nd ed. 1936); II (3rd ed. 1949–52)
DTC	A. W. Pickard-Cambridge, *Dithyramb, tragedy and comedy*. 2nd ed., rev. T. B. L. Webster (Oxford, 1962)
DFA	A. W. Pickard-Cambridge, *The dramatic festivals of Athens*. 2nd ed., rev. J. Gould–D. M. Lewis (Oxford, 1968)
DK	H. Diels–W. Kranz, *Die Fragmente der Vorsokratiker*. 6th ed. (Berlin, 1951–2)
EGF	G. Kinkel, *Epicorum Graecorum Fragmenta* (Leipzig, 1877)
FGrH	F. Jacoby, *Fragmente der griechischen Historiker* (Berlin, 1923–)

FHG	C. Müller, *Fragmenta Historicorum Graecorum* (Berlin, 1841–70)
FYAT	(ed.) M. Platnauer, *Fifty years (and twelve) of classical scholarship* (Oxford, 1968)
GLK	H. Keil, *Grammatici Latini* (Leipzig, 1855–1923)
GLP	C. M. Bowra, *Greek lyric poetry*, 2nd ed. (Oxford, 1961)
Gow–Page, *Hell. Ep.*	A. S. F. Gow–D. L. Page, *The Greek Anthology: Hellenistic Epigrams* (Cambridge, 1965)
Gow–Page, *Garland*	A. S. F. Gow–D. L. Page, *The Greek Anthology: The Garland of Philip* (Cambridge, 1968)
Guthrie	W. K. C. Guthrie, *A history of Greek philosophy* (Cambridge, 1965–81)
IEG	M. L. West, *Iambi et Elegi Graeci* (Oxford, 1971–2)
IG	*Inscriptiones Graecae* (Berlin, 1873–)
Kai	G. Kaibel, *Comicorum graecorum fragmenta*, I fasc. I *Doriensium comoedia mimi phylaces* (Berlin, 1899)
KG	R. Kühner–B. Gerth, *Ausführliche Grammatik der griechischen Sprache: Satzlehre.* 4th ed. (Hannover, 1955)
Lesky	A. Lesky, *A history of Greek literature*, tr. J. Willis–C. de Heer (London, 1966)
Lesky, *TDH*	A. Lesky, *Die tragische Dichtung der Hellenen*, 3rd ed. (Göttingen, 1972)
LSJ	Liddell–Scott–Jones, *Greek–English Lexicon*, 9th ed. (Oxford, 1925–40)
Loeb	Loeb Classical Library (Cambridge, Mass. & London)
*OCD*²	*Oxford Classical Dictionary*, 2nd ed. (Oxford, 1970)
OCT	Scriptorum Classicorum Bibliotheca Oxoniensis (Oxford)
Ol	A. Olivieri, *Frammenti della commedia greca e del mimo nella Sicilia e nella Magna Grecia* (Naples, 1930)
Paravia	Corpus Scriptorum Latinorum Paravianum (Turin)
PLF	E. Lobel–D. Page, *Poetarum Lesbiorum Fragmenta* (Oxford, 1963)
PMG	D. L. Page, *Poetae Melici Graeci* (Oxford, 1962)
PPF	H. Diels, *Poetarum Philosophorum Graecorum Fragmenta* (Berlin, 1901)
Pfeiffer	R. Pfeiffer, *A history of classical scholarship* (Oxford, 1968)
Powell	J. U. Powell, *Collectanea Alexandrina* (Oxford, 1925)
Powell–Barber	J. U. Powell–E. A. Barber, *New chapters in the history of Greek Literature* (Oxford, 1921), 2nd ser. (1929), 3rd ser. (Powell alone) (1933)
Preller–Robert	L. Preller, *Griechische Mythologie*, 4th ed., rev. C. Robert (Berlin, 1894)

ABBREVIATIONS

RAC	*Reallexikon für Antike und Christentum* (Stuttgart, 1941–)
RE	A. Pauly–G. Wissowa–W. Kroll, *Real-Encyclopädie der klassischen Altertumswissenschaft* (Stuttgart, 1893–)
Roscher	W. H. Roscher, *Ausführliches Lexikon der griechischen und römischen Mythologie* (Leipzig, 1884–)
SEG	*Supplementum Epigraphicum Graecum* (Leyden, 1923–71; Alphen aan den Rijn, 1979–)
SH	P. J. Parsons and H. Lloyd-Jones, *Supplementum Hellenisticum* (Berlin & New York, 1983)
SLG	D. L. Page, *Supplementum Lyricis Graecis* (Oxford, 1974)
SVF	H. von Arnim, *Stoicorum Veterum Fragmenta* (Leipzig, 1903–)
Snell	B. Snell, *Tragicorum Graecorum Fragmenta* (Göttingen, 1971–)
Schmid–Stählin	W. Schmid–O. Stählin, *Geschichte der griechischen Literatur* (Munich, 1929–48)
Spengel	L. Spengel, *Rhetores Graeci* (1853–6); I ii rev. C. Hammer (Leipzig, 1894)
TGF	A. Nauck, *Tragicorum Graecorum Fragmenta*, 2nd ed. (Leipzig, 1889)
Walz	C. Walz, *Rhetores Graeci* (Stuttgart, 1832–6)

1

BOOKS AND READERS IN
THE GREEK WORLD

I. FROM THE BEGINNINGS TO ALEXANDRIA

The Greeks, who gave us the names, forms and classic models of tragedy, comedy, epic, lyric and pastoral poetry, and, in fact, of almost every literary genre known to the West, did not develop a system of writing adequate for the recording of literature until late in their history. When, towards the end of the eighth century B.C., they finally did so, Egyptian literature, religious and secular, had been transmitted on papyrus scrolls for over two millennia; the literature of the Mesopotamian civilizations, inscribed on clay tablets, went back to a similarly remote antiquity. There had, of course, been a period of literacy, of a very restricted nature, in the great centres of Mycenaean civilization; inscribed clay tablets, dating from the last half of the second millennium, have been found at Pylos, Thebes and Mycenae on the mainland and at Cnossus in Crete. The script – known as Linear B – seems to have been a rough and ready adaptation for Mycenaean Greek of the Cretan Linear A script (still undeciphered but almost certainly non-Greek); the new writing system was used, as far as our evidence goes, mainly for lists of property and simple bureaucratic and legal records – 'long lists of names, records of livestock, grain and other produce, the account books of anonymous clerks'.[1] No text of an even faintly literary quality survives. In any case the script's inefficiency as an instrument for literary purposes is clear at first glance: it lacks both economy and clarity. Since it is a syllabary, not an alphabet, the number of signs to be memorized – eighty-seven – is burdensome. And the script does not distinguish between the sounds we represent by *r* and *l*, it omits initial *s* and *l* as well as *m*, *n*, *r* and *s* at the end of a syllable – and so on. The signs for *pa-ka-na*, for example, represent what in later Greek is *phasgana*, *ka-ko* is *chalkos*, *ku-ru-so chrusos*, *pe-ma sperma*; *pa-te* may be either *pater* or *pantes*. Obviously, it would be almost impossible to interpret the script without the possibility of error unless the meaning were indicated by the context, as, in this case, it is – by easily recognizable ideograms for sword, bronze, gold, etc.

---

[1] Chadwick (1976) ix.

Even so, modern scholarly disagreement over interpretation of the signs is far from rare. When, towards the very end of the second millennium B.C. the Mycenaean palaces were destroyed by fire, the clay tablets with their strange markings were buried in the ruins; baked to brick-like hardness by the fire, they remained hidden until the excavator's spade uncovered them in the twentieth century. In Greece all memory of this earlier literacy was lost, unless Homer's 'baleful signs' (the message carried by Bellerophon which said 'Kill the bearer' in *Iliad* 6.168) are a faint reminiscence of it, preserved uncomprehendingly by the oral tradition.

When, many centuries later, the Greeks learned how to write again, they did so by adapting, as before, a script designed for a foreign language: a Phoenician (North Semitic) system in use in Syria. But this time the adaptation was a brilliant success: not only did it produce a sign system fully adequate for Greek sounds, it also improved on the original. The Semitic script did not indicate vowels; this left much room for misunderstanding and, in any but the most obvious context, demanded skilled readers and interpreters. To represent their vowels the Greek adaptors assigned some of the Semitic consonantal symbols which were, for them, redundant and thus created the first genuine alphabet: a system of writing which, because of its economy and clarity, could become a popular medium of communication rather than, what it had always been in the Near-Eastern civilizations (and almost certainly in Mycenaean Greece), the exclusive province of trained specialists.[1] The Phoenician provenance of the script is reflected in legend (Cadmus, king of Tyre, is supposed to have brought letters to the city of Thebes, which he founded) and the letters were known to later ages as *phoinikeia* (Hdt. 5.58). But the real as opposed to the mythical date of its appearance in Greece is problematical. The earliest extant examples of Greek writing in the new alphabet (or rather, alphabets – since there were significant local variations) are all incised or painted on pottery and, although dating of such fragments is largely a matter of inference from the history of decorative style, there is fairly general agreement that they all combine to suggest a date in the last half of the eighth century B.C. They come from all over the Greek world: from Attica, Boeotia, Corinth on the mainland, from Rhodes in the east and Ischia, off the coast of south Italy, in the west.[2]

Since writing on more perishable materials, leather, for example, or papyrus (if indeed it was available in Greece so early) could not have survived, it is theoretically possible that writing had been in use in the Greek world much earlier than the date suggested by these objects; the texts so recorded might have been longer and more elaborate than the graffiti on pots and could even

---

[1] On the importance of the Greek innovations, see Havelock (1976) 44ff.
[2] Jeffery (1961) 12ff.; cf. Heubeck (1979), with very full bibliography; Pfohl (1968).

have been literary in character. But, although two of the inscriptions, those from Attica and Ischia, contain hexameter verses (and the Ischian inscription seems to indicate acquaintance with Homeric epic),[1] the scripts themselves do not encourage such speculation. The letters are crude and unwieldy; the run of the letters, still following the Semitic model, is from right to left. It also seems likely that if writing had been available for a considerable period before the last quarter of the eighth century, potters and sculptors would have made use of it earlier; the first appearance of lettering on so many objects of such scattered provenance suggests that the technique became general knowledge at just about this time.

It is one more paradoxical feature of the Greek literary achievement that in the late eighth century, when they devised a system of writing suited to their language, they already possessed a literature. The date at which the Homeric epics were given the form in which we know them, and the role which writing may have played in this process, are still matters of controversy (see pp. 47ff.) but the work of Milman Parry has demonstrated one thing beyond any doubt: the poems display, in significant proportion, many of the characteristics of oral, pre-literate composition. The magnificent architecture of these two great poems is almost certainly, in each case, the creation of a single poet, whether oral or literate, but a considerable proportion of the basic material is traditional, the refined product of experimentation by many generations of oral composers. Before there were books and readers in Greece, there were poets and audiences. And this is true for types of poetry other than epic; the so-called Homeric hymns and the didactic poems of Hesiod show the same signs of oral origin.

In the work of Hesiod, however, a new phenomenon suggests the possibility that these poems were written down in the lifetime of their author: Hesiod identifies himself, gives biographical details and expresses personal opinions on moral and social problems. It is the nature of fully oral poetry that the singer recreates the song at each performance; he does so as the anonymous servant of the Muse, who is the repository of age-old knowledge and the techniques of the oral tradition. Hesiod's solid presence in his work (the *Theogony* begins with an account of his meeting with the Muses on Mount Helicon and the *Works and days* is addressed to his lazy, greedy brother Perses) suggests that he expected the poems to be handed on in the form he had given them, securely identified as his work. The most reasonable explanation for such confidence seems to be that the poems were fixed in writing.

For the next great figure in Greek literature, Archilochus of Paros, who was active in the first half of the seventh century, writing seems assured; the variety of his metres, the intensely personal tone of many of his poems, the

---

[1] Meiggs and Lewis (1969) no. 1.

wide range of subject matter and above all the freedom from formula make it unlikely that his work could have survived the centuries by any other means than through written copies of the poet's own manuscripts. And the same holds, even more strongly, for the poems of Sappho and Alcaeus, who composed on the island of Lesbos around the turn of the sixth century. Some of their songs could have achieved universal popularity and so have been preserved by memory. But writing must have played a role in the transmission of the complete poems of Sappho, which the Alexandrians arranged in nine books, the first containing 333 four-line Sapphic stanzas.

This does not mean of course that the work of these poets was 'published' nor even that many copies were in existence. The poems were composed for performance (most of them to musical accompaniment); the written text must have been intended as a support for the memory of the performer, whether it was the poet or another. In a cultural milieu where poetry was a public medium, there would be little incentive to multiply copies. In any case wide circulation of copies at this early period may not have been possible; it depended on the availability of a relatively cheap writing material, Egyptian papyrus. This plant was native to the marshes of Lower Egypt and from the fibres of its stalk, triangular in cross-section and reaching to ten feet or more in height,[1] the Egyptians had for more than a millennium manufactured a 'paper' (it is the same word) which was smooth-surfaced, strong, flexible and, if kept dry, remarkably durable. From the pith of the stalk vertical strips were peeled or sliced off; a number of these were placed side by side on a hard surface and a second set superimposed at right angles to the first. Under pressure, perhaps applied with a wooden mallet, the two surfaces were almost indissolubly bonded by the natural gum of the plant itself; the edges were then trimmed to produce sheets (κολλήματα, kollēmata) which varied considerably in size – extant specimens suggest that for literary texts the norm was somewhere near nine by nine inches, though sheets higher than they are wide are not at all uncommon. These sheets (usually about twenty of them) were then made into a roll (χάρτης, chartes) by pasting the lateral edges together with the fibres running horizontally along the surface; the edge of each sheet was imposed on its neighbour to the right so that the pen, moving from the left, would cross the join smoothly. On this inside, protected surface the scribe would write from the left in vertical columns, their width determined by the line length in the case of regular verse metres, and usually, in the case of prose, varying between fifteen and twenty-five letters (see Pl. II).

There is no agreement about the date at which papyrus was introduced into Greece, but little doubt that it was in common use early in the sixth century.

---

[1] Lewis (1974) 22ff.

4

It is in this century that evidence for close connexions between the two countries is first attested: the names of the Greek mercenaries carved on the left leg of the Colossus of Pharaoh Rameses II at Abu Simbel around 590 B.C.; the establishment, at the end of the seventh century, of a Greek trading station at Naucratis on the Nile delta.[1] From this time on, multiplication of copies must have been much easier but our sources are silent on the subject. For the whole of the archaic period, down to the early years of the fifth century, there is no firm evidence for books and their circulation among readers. What few glimpses we are given refer in fact not to circulation but to unique texts. Pausanias, in the second century A.D., says that on Mount Helicon he was shown a copy of Hesiod's *Works and days* inscribed on lead and 'much defaced by time' (9.31); Heraclitus of Ephesus, we are told by a late source, dedicated his 'book' in the temple of Artemis (Diog. Laert. 9.6). Nevertheless, when, in the last quarter of the fifth century, evidence for a book trade does appear in Athens, the sheer bulk of earlier literary production which was available for reproduction suggests that these texts had been circulating in a respectable number of copies. When the Alexandrians came to edit and arrange in 'books', i.e. papyrus rolls, the poetry which had come down to them from the seventh and sixth centuries B.C., they produced six books of the Spartan choral poet Alcman, two of the Ionian poet Mimnermus and seven of the Spartan Tyrtaeus, ten books of Alcaeus and nine of Sappho, seven books of Ibycus of Rhegium in south Italy, seven books of Anacreon of Teos, five thousand lines, elegiac and iambic, of Solon of Athens, and no less than twenty-six books of the Sicilian poet Stesichorus of Himera. This is an argument from survival which must be balanced against the argument from silence; it suggests that there was a certain circulation of texts and multiplication of copies in the archaic period. For otherwise it is hard to understand why more archaic and classical literature was not already lost without trace (as some in fact was)[2] when the Alexandrian scholars began their work of collection, correction and interpretation.

Though the archaic period yields no explicit evidence of books and readers, there is evidence of the essential precondition for their existence, widespread literacy. Public inscriptions recording laws, for example, are found all over the Greek world; Solon's famous *Axones* ('noticeboards') are known to us only from the literary tradition, but surviving stones record complicated legal instructions from Chios which date from the first half of the sixth century and, from the last quarter, an involved set of legal stipulations about landed

---

[1] Meiggs and Lewis (1969) no. 7; Austin (1970) 22–33.

[2] Not all of Euripides' plays, for example, reached Alexandria: satyr plays in particular were likely to disappear (cf. the *Medea hypothesis*). The *hypothesis* to Aristophanes' *Acharnians* notes the loss of Cratinus' *Cheimazomenai*, produced in the same year. The Alexandrian formula is οὐ σώʒεται 'not preserved'.

property and many other matters in the script of Ozolian Locris, a remote and backward area of the Greek world.[1] Inscriptions on vases became steadily more elegant, informative and versatile. The François Vase, made in the early sixth century, identifies, in an exuberant display of literacy, twenty-seven heroes and hounds of the Calydonian hunt, sixteen of the figures in the scene showing Theseus at Delos, six of the racers in the games for Patroclus, thirteen figures in the Centauromachy, thirty divine characters in the procession at the wedding of Peleus and Thetis and twelve in the return of Hephaestus, twelve heroes in the death of Troilus – the vase even identifies objects (altar, pitcher, fountain, chair) as well as announcing the name of potter and painter. A black-figure Athenian *pelike* from later in the century shows, in two scenes, a transaction between an oil dealer and a client whose jar he is filling with oil. The dealer is given the words 'Father Zeus, if only I could become wealthy' and in the facing scene he tells the customer, whose gesture signals dissatisfaction, 'now, now it's too much – it's run over'.[2] In addition to inscriptions added by the artist we have specimens of private messages scratched on broken potsherds. Three sixth-century graffiti from the Athenian agora clearly suggest that writing was a commonplace accomplishment. 'Put the saw under the threshold of the garden door' says one; a second, which gives orders for bringing some household furniture (plausibly restored as 'couches') is remarkable because it opens with a vocative address, *pai*, which in normal Athenian context means 'slave'; a third says simply 'Titas – Olympic victor – pervert'.[3] A recent discovery suggests a similar level of common literacy for the same period at the extreme frontier of Greek expansion: a private letter written in Milesian dialect on a thin strip of lead which was found near the Greek trading post of Olbia on the Russian shore of the Black Sea.[4]

It is not until the fifth century that we begin to hear of a necessary prerequisite for general literacy, the existence of elementary schools. These may well be much older, at least in Athens, where we are told (Aeschines 1.9ff.) that Solon, archon in 594 B.C., enacted laws governing their operation. But in the fifth century their existence is established by three casual references to them, recording, in each case, the violent death of the children: on the island of Chios (Hdt. 6.27 – 494 B.C.), in the Boeotian town of Mycalessos (Thuc. 7.29 – 413 B.C.) and on the small island of Astypalaea (Pausanias 6.9.6 – 496 B.C.). From a late source (Plutarch, *Them.* 10) comes the detail that when the Athenians, in 480, evacuated their families to Trozen, the Trozenians voted to hire teachers for their children. During the early years of the century the red-figure vases begin to picture school scenes with boys learning to read

[1] Meiggs and Lewis (1969) nos. 8, 13.
[2] Hirmer and Arias (1962) plates 40–6; Guarducci 465–6.
[3] Lang (1976) nos. B1, B2, C5.
[4] Chadwick (1973) 35–7.

or reading; scenes of adults reading also occur but, surprisingly enough in view of the minor role women play in all our literary accounts of fifth-century Athens, the figures are usually women. In nearly all cases where the artist has given any indication of the text which is being read, the book contains poetry.[1]

Since we do not possess even one specimen or fragment of a Greek book written earlier than the late fourth century B.C., it is from these vase paintings that we have to form our idea of books and reading during the great centuries of Athenian literature. The books look very much like those which, as we know from surviving fragments and even rolls, were in common use in Ptolemaic Egypt two centuries later. This is not surprising since Egypt was the unique source of processed papyrus and it was presumably exported early (as we know it was later) in the form of ready-made rolls. From these paintings it is clear that reading was a communal affair; the solitary reader hardly appears: books were read aloud. This does not necessarily imply, as it was once fashionable to believe, that silent reading was an accomplishment so rare in antiquity that its exceptional appearance proves the rule,[2] but it does emphasize the fact that, early and late, ancient reading was predominantly reading aloud, performance in fact – before a smaller audience than at the Dionysia or at Olympia but still performance. The book, at this early stage of transition from a fully oral to a fully literate society, serves as a script for recital rather than as a text for individual study; though now written, literature is still a communal experience and its direct, powerful impact on the emotions of its audience, so vividly described in Plato's *Ion* (535e), must be kept in mind if we are to understand the vehement attack on poetry with which Plato ends the *Republic*.[3]

The books in the paintings are papyrus rolls as we know them from actual specimens found in Egypt; the readers unfold the roll with the right hand and re-roll the portion already read with the left. Naturally the few letters the artist can paint on what is visible of the scroll are not a realistic representation; the letters are magnified so as to be legible. Most of the books contain verse, though one, in a school-scene, has the beginning of what seems to be a mythological handbook (see Pl. Ia).[4] The letters are a mixture of the local Attic alphabet and the Ionic alphabet which, increasingly favoured during the fifth century, was finally adopted for official documents at Athens in the archonship of Euclides, 403/2 B.C.

Parallel with this artistic representation of reading, the language of the poets, the only literature we have for the first half of the century, reflects the increasing importance of the written word. Metaphors from writing and reading

---

[1] Immerwahr (1964) and (1973); Beck (1975) plates 9–15, 69–75. Cf. Harvey (1978); Turner (1965).
[2] Knox (1968).   [3] Havelock (1963) 145ff.   [4] Immerwahr (1973) 143.

make their appearance: Pindar (*Ol.* 10.1ff.) opens a victory ode with a command to himself to 'read aloud the Olympic victor's name ... where it is
written down on my heart' and Aeschylus writes of the 'tablets of the mind'
(Aesch. *P.V.* 789, cf. Soph. fr. 597), and the tablets on which the gods record
human misdeeds (Aesch. *Eum.* 275, fr. 530 Mette, cf. Eur. fr. 506). And,
though the dramatic time of Aeschylean tragedy is the remote mythic past,
writing is presented as a normal feature of the heroic world. Three of the
Argive champions in the *Septem contra Thebas*, for example, have writing on
their shield blazons (434, 468, 646–8); the letters proclaim the Argive warriors'
violent threats against the city and, in the longest inscription of all, Polynices'
claim that Justice brings him home. The king of Argos, in the *Suppliants*
(946ff.), announces the people's decision to the Egyptian herald as the words
of a 'free-speaking tongue' – not 'written in tablets or sealed within the folds
of papyrus'. And Prometheus, listing his contributions to human civilization,
proudly includes 'combinations of letters, memory of all things, the Muses'
mother...' (460–1). Memory, mother by Zeus of the Muses, whom Hesiod
addresses in the proem of the *Theogony* and who had personified the vast
resources of formula, theme and myth drawn on by the oral poet, is here
identified with the written word.

In Athens the annual performances of tragedy, and later of comedy, at the
festivals of Dionysus must have stimulated the demand for books. Not everyone in Athens could attend, and for those who could not as well as for the rest
of the Greek world, which admired Athenian drama as much as it feared
Athenian imperialism, written copies of the plays must have been in demand;
although there is evidence for performances in the Attic demes in the last years
of the fifth century,[1] theatrical companies travelling outside Attica do not
seem to appear until much later. Circulation of books can be inferred also
from the growing importance of prose writing. Though we have accounts of
Herodotus reading his work aloud to audiences at Athens, the sheer bulk of
the *Histories* makes it unlikely that this was the only medium in which the
public came to know it. Other types of prose writing, the philosophical
treatise of Anaxagoras, for example, the rhetorical handbooks of the sophists,
the quasi-biographical writings of Ion of Chios and Stesimbrotus,[2] were not
suitable for oral presentation. The last quarter of the fifth century saw the
production of a work, the *History* of Thucydides, which was clearly intended
for the reader rather than the hearer; the crabbed syntax of many of the
speeches – the effort of a powerful intellect to express abstract concepts for
which the language was as yet hardly adequate – must have demanded, as it
still does, careful reading and reflection. Thucydides is conscious of the

---

[1] *DFA* 45ff.
[2] Momigliano (1971) 30ff.

difference; his work, he says, is not a prize-contest piece for an immediate audience but a possession for ever – 'he was already thinking of his future readers'.[1] In a fragment of Euripides' *Erechtheus* (412 B.C.) we find our first reference to a reader who, unlike those pictured on the vases, is alone. The soldier yearns for peace, to let his spear lie for spiders to weave their webs round it, to hang up his shield ... 'and may I unroll the voice of the tablets (δέλτων τ' ἀναπτύσσοιμι γῆρυν), the voice wise men give tongue to' (369 *TGF*). Clearly he is thinking of reading aloud, but without an audience.

Another solitary reader appears in Aristophanes' *Frogs* (52–3): the god Dionysus tells Heracles that while sailing with the Athenian war-fleet, he read the *Andromeda* of Euripides to himself (it had been produced eight years before). This is the only specific reference to a book-text of a tragedy, though our text of one Aristophanic comedy, *Clouds*, is a revised version which was never performed and seems to have been intended for a reading public.[2] But the availability of tragic texts is implied by the chorus' encouraging words addressed, later in the *Frogs*, to the two tragic poets as they prepare to cite chapter and verse in their mutual criticism. 'If this is what you are afraid of – that the audience may suffer from ignorance, so as to miss the fine points of your arguments – dismiss those fears. That's not the case any more. For they are veterans and each one has his book and understands the witticisms' (1109ff.). Whatever that much-disputed phrase about the book may mean,[3] the scene which follows does seem to expect a reading knowledge of tragedy and certainly demonstrates it for Aristophanes himself; his abundant citation and parody of Aeschylean and Euripidean drama strongly suggests that he possessed a collection of texts. From a late source (Athenaeus 3a) comes the information that Euripides had a book collection; this has been doubted, but is confirmed by two passages in the *Frogs*. 'Euripides' boasts of his recipe for rejuvenating tragedy, a recipe which includes a dash of 'book-juice' (943) and later, when the rival poets weigh individual lines on a balance, 'Aeschylus' contemptuously offers to pit two lines of his poetry against the weight of 'Euripides' and his whole family – 'and let him bring his books with him, too' (1409). Xenophon tells us of Socrates' pursuit of a young man called Euthydemus, who had 'assembled many writings of poets and the most celebrated sophists' and who announces that he will continue to collect books until he has 'as many as possible' (*Mem.* 4.2.1). All this suggests that books must have been produced in late fifth-century Athens in some quantity, even commercially; it is in fact in this period that we first hear (Eupolis fr. 304 K) of a place 'where books are for sale' (it is in the market, among the stalls dispensing garlic, incense and perfumes) and the word for booksellers

---

[1] Pfeiffer 29. [2] Dover (1968a) xcviii.
[3] For a thorough (and sceptical) discussion of both passages in the Aristophanic play, see Woodbury (1976).

(βιβλιοπῶλαι) turns up in the texts of comic poets writing around the turn of the century (Aristomenes fr. 9 K, Theopompus fr. 77 K, Nicophon fr. 19.4 K).

Socrates once heard someone reading from a book by Anaxagoras (*Phaedo* 97b) and was so excited by what he heard that he 'seized the books enthusiastically and read as fast as he could' – only to be disappointed with the result. Years later – when accused, at his trial, for impiety, of teaching the very doctrine he had found inadequate, he turned on his accuser.

> Do you think it is Anaxagoras you are accusing? . . . Do you think the gentlemen of the jury are illiterate and don't know that the books of Anaxagoras of Clazomenae are packed full of these doctrines? So this is what the young men learn from me, is it? Things they can buy, sometimes for a drachma at most, in the orchestra and then laugh at Socrates if he claims they are his own. (*Apol.* 26d–e)

Even with due allowance made for Socratic irony and the rhetorical compliment to the jurymen's literary expertise, the words used (ἀπείρους γραμμάτων) still suggest easy availability of, and wide acquaintance with, books, and difficult philosophical books at that. The price at which a copy of Anaxagoras could sometimes be picked up in the 'orchestra' (an area of the market-place, not the theatre) was once thought impossibly low; a contemporary inscription gives the price of two *chartai* of papyrus (which were once taken to be single sheets) as two drachmas four obols – more than twice the price of the book. But an authoritative study of the history of papyrus in antiquity has established the fact that *chartai* were not sheets but rolls – so that, if the copy of Anaxagoras were a small or second-hand volume, 'the price of the book and that of the paper would no longer be inconsistent'.[1]

The book trade was not, however, confined to Athens; the city was an exporter of books. So much might have been surmised from the fact that it was the literature produced in Athens, especially tragedy, which was eagerly sought after by the rest of the Greek world; a random piece of evidence brings some confirmation. On the dangerous shore of Salmydessus, Xenophon tells us, where the local Thracians fought each other over the cargo washed up from wrecked ships, the Greeks found 'many beds, many small boxes, many written books and many of the other things that merchants transport in wooden cases' (*Anab.* 7.5.14).

It is in this period that evidence begins to accumulate for the use of books in education. For what actually went on in the primary schools we have practically no evidence; what little we have suggests that the boys (girls' schools do not seem to have existed) were taught athletics by a *paidotribes*, music, performance on the kithara and singing, by a *kitharistes* and their letters by

[1] Lewis (1974) 74.

a *grammatistes*, who then, according to Plato (*Protagoras* 325e), 'put down beside them on the benches the poems of excellent poets to read ... and learn by heart'. Alcibiades, Plutarch tells us, asked a schoolmaster for his copy of Homer and beat the man when he found he did not possess one; another schoolteacher, who claimed to have a copy 'which he had corrected himself', was told that if he had the competence to edit Homer he should be teaching not boys but young men (*Alcibiades* 7). Xenophon gives us a glimpse of Socrates at a school sitting shoulder to shoulder with a handsome boy as they both 'hunted something down in the same book roll' (*Symp.* 4.27). Plato's Lysis (he appears to be about fourteen years of age) admits to acquaintance with 'the writings of very wise men – those who debate and write about nature and the universe' (214b οἱ περὶ φύσεώς τε καὶ τοῦ ὅλου διαλεγόμενοι καὶ γράφοντες). Xenophon's Socrates speaks of reading together with young men 'the precious stores wise men of old have bequeathed to us, writing them down in books, I unroll (ἀνελίττων) and read through with my friends, and if we find something good, we extract it' (ἐκλεγόμεθα, *Mem.* 1.6.14).

These schools do not seem to have been state institutions ('the children of the rich' according to Plato's Protagoras 'are the earliest to begin study in the schools and the latest to leave'), nor was elementary education compulsory; and yet by the closing decades of the fifth century literacy, at varying levels of competence it is true, seems to have been general in Athens.[1] Two passages in Aristophanes suggest that even the poorest citizens, though they might not study music and poetry under the *kitharistes*, somehow learned their letters. In Aristophanes' *Knights* (189ff.) the sausage-seller, acclaimed as perfectly fitted for high public office by his low birth, ignorance and effrontery, objects that he has no knowledge of 'music' – 'only my letters, and I don't know them too well'. In the *Wasps*, when Labes the dog is accused of stealing the Sicilian cheese, his advocate finally admits his guilt but pleads for pardon: 'Forgive him. He doesn't know how to play the kithara.' 'I wish' says the judge in reply 'he didn't even know his letters – so he couldn't have falsified the account' (958–60). And there is a scene in Euripides' (lost) *Theseus*, imitated by two other tragic poets, which presented an illiterate herdsman who described, one by one, the shapes of the letters forming the hero's name; it was clearly designed to intrigue and flatter an audience which knew its letters (Eur. fr. 382, Agathon 4, Theodectas 6 *TGF*).

At a higher level of education – the training offered by the sophists – books, very often those written by the teacher, played a part; the great sophist teachers Protagoras, Gorgias, Prodicus and Hippias wrote prose treatises. A fragment of a lost Aristophanic comedy announces that someone has been ruined 'by a book or by Prodicus ...' (fr. 490 K). Prodicus' book *Horae* is mentioned in

[1] Harvey (1964) and (1966).

11

Plato (*Symp.* 117c) and the famous allegory of Heracles' choice between Virtue and Vice which it contained is reproduced by Socrates, from memory or so he claims, in Xenophon's *Memorabilia* (2.1.21). The long mythical account of the origins of human civilization which Plato puts into the mouth of his Protagoras in the dialogue named after him must be based to some extent on the famous book *On primitive conditions* (Περὶ τῆς ἐν ἀρχῆι καταστάσεως) which was written by the real man. And his notorious book *On the gods*, of which only the uncompromising first sentence survives, was, according to one tradition, read aloud in the house of Euripides; according to another, it must have circulated as a written book, for after Protagoras had been expelled from Athens for impiety 'his books were burned in the agora after being collected from their owners by a herald' (Diog. Laert. 9.52).[1]

There were also in circulation books of lesser importance. Both Plato (*Symp.* 177b) and Isocrates (10.12) mention with contempt a treatise in praise of salt, evidently a rhetorical showpiece, and Phaedrus, in Plato's dialogue, produces a copy of what purports to be Lysias' cynical plea for the non-lover. In the same dialogue we hear of rhetorical handbooks (τὰ γ' ἐν τοῖς βιβλίοις τοῖς περὶ λόγων τέχνης γεγραμμένοις 266d) – Socrates goes on to mention those of Theodorus of Byzantium, Euenus of Paros, Gorgias, Tisias, Prodicus, Hippias, Polus, Licymnius, Protagoras and Thrasymachus – and later (268c) of medical treatises, a type of book which, as we learn from Xenophon (*Mem.* 4.2.10), was fairly common.

With Plato we are, of course, in the fourth century, though the fictional background of most of the dialogues is the lifetime of Socrates, who was executed in 399 B.C. Poetry continued to be written and performed, but this is pre-eminently an age of prose writing, much of it technical and most of it designed for circulation in book form. The dialogues of Plato, for example, are the work of an exquisite prose stylist, whose strictures against books, so forcefully expressed by Socrates in the *Phaedrus* (274dff.) are hardly consonant with the care he obviously devoted to his own compositions. Dionysius of Halicarnassus (*De comp. verb.* 208) speaks of Plato's devotion to taking pains and the way he continued to 'comb and curl and rework' his dialogues all his life (κτενίζων καὶ βοστρυχίζων καὶ...ἀναπλέκων...). The story that after his death there was found a wax tablet with many different versions of the opening of the *Republic* may be apocryphal but it rings true for all those who have admired the severe but graceful simplicity of that opening phrase. That the dialogues circulated as books in Plato's lifetime we know from the fact

---

[1] Dover (1976) 34ff. suspects that this story was invented by Demetrius of Phalerum but shows that 'the idea of invalidating certain types of written utterance by destruction of the material on which it was written was established by the time of Protagoras himself'.

that one of his pupils, Hermodorus, sold copies of them in Sicily; his activities gave rise to a proverbial phrase 'Hermodorus trades in tracts' (λόγοισιν Ἑρμόδωρος ἐμπορεύεται), which Cicero quotes in a letter to Atticus about the circulation of his own writings (*Att.* 13.21a).[1]

Plato's Academy must have had a library; the Alexandrian biographer Satyrus (Diog. Laert. 3.9) tells us that Plato commissioned his friend and pupil Dion to buy, for the sum of 100 minas, the three volumes of the Pythagorean philosopher Philolaus. We hear, in Isocrates, of a collection of prophetic books, which, received as a legacy, set the recipient up in business as a prophet (*Aeginiticus* 5) and a comic fragment (Alexis 135 K) introduces us to an unusual school library. The mythical poet Linus instructs an unlikely pupil – Heracles. 'Go up and take out any book you like and then you'll read it; take your time, look over the titles. There's Orpheus there, Hesiod, tragedy, Choerilus, Homer, there's Epicharmus, all kinds of writings . . .' Heracles, however, chooses a cookery book, the work of one Simon. With the establishment of Aristotle's philosophical school, the Lyceum, we come to the first serious institutional library, in the modern sense of the word – a tool for research; this is probably why Strabo (13.608) calls Aristotle 'the first whom we know of who collected books'. He is reported to have bought the books of another philosopher, Speusippus, for the immense sum of three talents (Diog. Laert. 4.5). And evidence of wide reading and frequent consultation of books meets us at every turn in his writings and in the work of his school. 'We ought to make extracts also from written works' he says, when discussing the collection of 'propositions' (ἐκλέγειν. . .ἐκ τῶν γεγραμμένων *Top.* 105b), and the fact that he did so is clear from his constant citation from earlier writers: the more than thirty philosophers and poets cited in the *Metaphysics*, the stream of quotations from tragic, comic and epic poets, from orators and rhetorical treatises in the *Rhetoric*. It is in this work that for the first time we are presented with critical remarks which refer specifically to the text visualized as a written page rather than conceived of as something heard; Aristotle evidences Heraclitus as an author 'difficult to punctuate' (διαστίξαι *Rhet.* 1407b) and there are other passages in which problems raised by word-division, accent and punctuation are discussed in terms of the written as well as the spoken text (e.g. *Soph. El.* 166b, 177b, 178a). There are indications that by the late fourth century public performance had lost its predominant, almost exclusive position as the medium of literary communication; Aristotle, for example, says (*Poet.* 1462a11ff.) that 'tragedy may produce its effect without movement, just like epic poetry; for from reading the quality of the play emerges clearly' (cf. also 1450b18, 1453b6). He even speaks of tragic poets like Chaeremon and dithyram-

---

[1] The translation is Shackleton Bailey's (1966) 213. Incidentally, Cicero's words imply that Hermodorus was acting with Plato's permission.

bic composers like Licymnius who write with readers in mind (ἀναγνωστικοί) and whose books are 'in wide circulation' (βαστάζονται). And, of course, the research activities of Aristotle and his associates, the collection of no less than 158 constitutions of cities and tribes, of the dramatic records of Athenian tragedy, as well as of the lists of Olympic and Pythian victors, attest the existence of what a modern historian of ancient scholarship has called 'the stupendous treasures of his collections'.[1]

Though it is possible, even likely, that Aristotle and his pupils read much of the material on which they based their research swiftly and silently, it must not be forgotten that any book which had even the slightest claim to literary merit was written to be read aloud. This was obviously true of those writers Aristotle refers to as 'writing with readers in mind'; the context makes clear that the difference between reading and performance was simply the absence of spectacle, movement and gesture – the poems would still in either case be heard. Even Isocrates, who did not deliver his speeches because, he says, he lacked the two things which most powerfully affected the Athenian assembly, a loud voice and a bold front, even Isocrates wrote for the ear, not the eye. He is a master of euphony (the avoidance of hiatus – of clashing vowels – is one of his stylistic innovations) and he even went so far as to write into his speeches passages which look like directions to the readers who were to recite them (e.g. *Antidosis* 12).

Clearly the late fourth century was a period in which books were written and circulated, but we have no information about how or by whom they were produced: not one aspect of the phenomenon we know as 'publication' is attested. Isocrates, who continued the sophistic tradition of rhetorical teaching, preferred to circulate written copies of his discourses rather than deliver them; some of them, in fact, are too long to have been delivered to any but a captive audience. But he does not mention a 'publisher'; his words suggest personal distribution of copies on request (διαδοτέος τοῖς βουλομένοις λαμβάνειν, *Panath.* 233) – a process which has been compared to a modern scholar's distribution of offprints of his articles.[2] Nevertheless, his speeches were circulated in quantity, even some he might have liked to recall – the forensic speeches of his early career. When his son claimed that Isocrates wrote no such speeches Aristotle replied that 'plenty of bundles of Isocratean law-court speeches were carted around by the book-sellers' (δέσμας πάνυ πολλὰς δικανικῶν λόγων Ἰσοκρατείων περιφέρεσθαι...ὑπὸ τῶν βυβλιοπωλῶν Dion. Hal. *Isocrates* 18).

Once an author circulated copies of his work, it was out of his control; and the practice, referred to by Xenophon's Socrates and Aristotle,[3] of 'making

---

[1] Pfeiffer 70.   [2] Turner (1952) 19.
[3] Cf. Isocr. 2.44, Plato, *Laws* 811a.

extracts' (ἐκλέγειν) almost certainly meant that it might appear in strange contexts and truncated or extended form. Some such process may be the genesis of the collection which has come down to us under the name of Theognis; it contains, besides passages which may well be the work of the sixth-century Megarian poet who addresses his remarks to a young man called Cyrnus, lines which are elsewhere attributed to other poets (Solon, Tyrtaeus), drinking songs, short hymns to the gods, and gnomic passages on politics and ethics many of which directly contradict each other. The texts of the tragic poets ran especially high risks, for the liberties which theatrical companies will take with a script are notorious, even in modern times. The fourth-century performers of the classic plays seem to have been so high-handed that in 330 B.C. the Athenian statesman Lycurgus introduced a law to control their excesses – in Athens, for he could not do it elsewhere. A transcript of the work of the three great poets was to be deposited in the archives; the city's secretary was to read it to the actors and departures from this text were forbidden (Plut. *Vitae dec. or.*, *Lycurgus* 841 f). This official copy is presumably the one which Ptolemy Euergetes I borrowed (and kept) for the Alexandrian library (see p. 31); and since it was specifically designed as a substitute for the actors' copies, the text was presumably that of the book-copies in commercial circulation.

That there was such circulation is clear enough from our evidence but the mechanics and economics of the process are unknown. We do not know very much either about what the books looked like. The arrangement of text on the papyrus rolls which appear on the vase-paintings is clearly determined to a large extent by pictorial exigencies, but the vase-paintings in question, all of them from the fifth century, are almost certainly true to the reality in two respects: the use of separate capital letters and the absence of word division, accentuation or punctuation. These are features of inscriptions on stone which survive for the same period and they are present also in the only fragment of an ancient book which has been found on Greek soil, the carbonized papyrus from Derveni, as well as in the fragments of the *Persians* of Timotheus, the only literary papyrus of Egyptian provenance which antedates the foundation of Alexandria (331 B.C.). Both are easily legible, written in the firm strokes characteristic of the Greek reed pen (the Egyptians used a soft reed for their hieroglyphic script which was painted rather than drawn); in both the letters have something of the monumentality of those carved in the marble of Attic inscriptions. The lyric verse of the Timotheus poem is written as if it were prose, regardless of metrical units, in columns much wider than those found in later books; but the columns of the Derveni papyrus, a prose text, are more regular. This is the upper half of a roll which was burned when it was placed on a funeral pyre; it contains a prose commentary on an Orphic religious poem, a type of book mentioned by Plato (*Rep.* 364e) and Euripides (*Hipp.* 954). The writing is small, neat and easily legible – 'the hand of a skilled calligrapher'; dating the hand is a difficult problem since the manuscript is unique, but archaeological evidence (the date of objects found in neighbouring tombs) suggests some time in the late fourth century.[1]

These two specimens are all the evidence we have for the appearance of the books which were shipped to Alexandria to form the library and to be catalogued, edited and explained by the great scholars of the next century. We have only the vaguest idea how they were produced and distributed; but we do know that they were available and in quantity. In such quantity, in fact, that in the third century A.D. Athenaeus of Naucratis could put in the mouth of one of his loquacious dinner guests the claim, which he could evidently have made for himself, that he had read and excerpted 'more than 800 plays of the so-called Middle Comedy' – that is to say, the comedies produced in Athens between the end of the Peloponnesian War (404) and the battle of Chaeronea (338).

2. THE HELLENISTIC AND IMPERIAL PERIODS
The evidence

For later antiquity there is a profusion of direct evidence. Among the innumerable papyri that have come to light in the excavations of the last hundred years there are Greek texts of all kinds, copied at all periods from the third century B.C. onwards. Scholars can now tell much more precisely what the books looked like and how they were made, and with the aid of the many dated official documents among the finds they can trace the changing style of handwriting over the centuries. The papyri also reveal a great deal about the intellectual level and the tastes of readers, but this is more equivocal evidence which needs to be treated with caution.

The difficulty arises because the evidence comes overwhelmingly from a single corner of the Greek-speaking world, Egypt, where climatic conditions have most favoured the survival of papyrus books. Papyrus decomposes in a damp atmosphere, but buried in dry sand it will survive for many centuries in a remarkably good state of preservation. Sometimes whole rolls have been found in caves or in the remains of houses, stored in jars for safe-keeping, but much greater numbers of fragmentary texts have been recovered from the excavation of rubbish mounds and cemeteries. In the mounds the papyri are simply waste paper; in the cemeteries they are found as cartonnage, the papier-mâché which the Egyptians used in making mummy cases. Outside Egypt and neighbouring areas, such as the desert round the Dead Sea, the survival

---

[1] Kapsomenos (1964) 5. Illustration in Turner (1971) 93.

of papyri has depended on the much rarer accidents of history. After the eruption of Vesuvius in A.D. 79 a library of philosophical books was submerged under the volcanic ash at Herculaneum and preserved in a carbonized state. This was a more substantial find than the half-burnt roll at Derveni in Macedonia (see pp. 15f.), but both are tiny exceptions to the general pattern of discoveries: Egypt remains the only area for which we have extensive documentation, and the question that must always be asked is how far it can be considered typical.

In some respects Egypt was closely comparable with other areas conquered by Alexander and settled by his Successors: Greek was the language of government, trade and education throughout the Ptolemaic and even the Imperial period, and Greek immigrants formed a quite important part of the population. But the political organization of the Ptolemies was much more centralized and bureaucratic than that of the other kingdoms, and Egypt had fewer Greek cities, the real focus of Greek intellectual life. On the other hand in Alexandria it could boast the most distinguished of all ancient centres of literature and scholarship. Another atypical feature is probably the degree of literacy in Egypt; we know from extensive evidence in the papyri that there were large numbers of minor officials who could at least read and write stereotyped documents. Egypt was by tradition a country of scribes, and the Ptolemies' complex administration increased the need for written records. This no doubt explains why literacy seems to have been fairly widespread even in the villages and why the native demotic managed to survive – though not to flourish – as a written language, whereas in most other areas Greek became the only language of literacy.[1]

The provenance of many of the papyri is modest up-country villages and small towns, where the intellectual climate cannot have been that of sophisticated Alexandria. We do not know how closely the picture we have of provincial Egyptian reading-tastes would be paralleled if the evidence came from, say, the Peloponnese or Cyprus or Antioch (or how much it would differ in each of these areas). The papyri must be considered alongside whatever other historical information is available, such as inscriptions, representations in art, or the testimonies of ancient writers themselves about such matters as books and education.

Books and the book trade

At least there is less difficulty in extrapolating from the Egyptian evidence for the material and make-up of books. It is a known fact that for most of antiquity the other parts of the Greek world used papyrus as the standard material for books (see p. 4) and that papyrus had to be imported from

---

[1] For the use of Latin in Egypt see Turner (1968) 75.

Egypt. The roll format was also international, as literary references and vase paintings and sculpture show. This was no doubt because the papyrus factories of Egypt exported the papyrus already made into rolls; the process of gluing together the component sheets (κολλήματα) was carried out in the factory, and the roll (χάρτης), not the single sheet, was the unit of sale.[1] Even for letter writing the normal practice was to buy a roll and cut pieces from it as they were needed.

A new development in the make-up of books, the highly significant change from roll to codex (σωμάτιον, the modern book form), began taking place about the second century A.D. and by the end of antiquity the new form had established itself as the standard vehicle for literary texts. There was no essential link between format and material; even if (as seems likely) the idea of the codex came from the wax or wooden tablet by way of the parchment notebooks which we know to have been in common use at Rome, there was a period of several centuries during which papyrus was by far the commonest material for the new kind of book (see Pl. III). The codex form has practical advantages which to a modern reader are obvious and overwhelming: it is much easier to handle and consult than the long roll, which must be rewound at each reading, it can be protected by binding, and since the pages are written on both sides it makes more economical use of the material. Even so, with the exception of one important branch of non-classical literature, it was slow to establish itself as the standard format. The exception is the texts of the Christians, which from the start show a strong preference for the codex form. C. H. Roberts has suggested that it was in fact first used in Christian circles and only gradually became accepted as a viable alternative to the roll for ordinary pagan texts.[2] This view is reinforced by the fact that the earliest examples of non-Christian works in codices are technical texts such as manuals of grammar and medicine for which an 'inferior' format would be acceptable. But the codex inevitably gained ground, and since it is even better suited to parchment and paper than to papyrus it became the standard medieval and modern book form.

Another important change was taking place in later antiquity, a change in the public's attitude to the material appropriate for books. The technique of parchment making was by now well developed, and the potentialities of parchment as a fine and durable writing material were fully appreciated, at the latest by the fourth century A.D., as the great surviving biblical codices testify, and certainly much earlier in some areas.[3] The early history of the

---

[1] The technical terms are discussed by Lewis (1974) 70–83.

[2] Roberts (1954) 169–204 and (1970) 53–9. But see now Roberts and Skeat (1983).

[3] At Dura-Europos, a Macedonian settlement on the Euphrates, all the earlier documents found in the excavations are on parchment, and papyrus does not appear until well into the Roman period (Welles, Fink and Gilliam (1959) 4).

industry is notoriously unclear; the story that parchment was invented by Eumenes of Pergamum in response to an embargo placed on papyrus by 'the king of Egypt',[1] probably Ptolemy Epiphanes (205/4–181/0 B.C.), is an obvious fiction, but some connexion with Pergamum is suggested by the late term for parchment, περγαμηνή (first used in Diocletian's price edict, 7.38 Lauffer). This came to replace the vaguer διφθέρα 'skin', which might connote either leather, i.e. skin treated with tannin, or parchment, i.e. skin treated with alum and chalk. Possibly some refinement of the technique was developed at Pergamum, or perhaps parchment making was simply undertaken on a larger scale there than elsewhere; it would not be surprising if centres of book production outside Egypt felt some incentive to perfect a material other than papyrus. At all events parchment was increasingly esteemed and brought into use, and papyrus gradually yielded place to it as the material for book texts, though papyrus continued in common use for documents and was still being manufactured and exported as late as the tenth century and even beyond.[2] The old view that parchment developed because papyrus was an unsuitable material for use in codex form is becoming less popular nowadays as more papyrus codices are discovered; the reasons for the change must have been more complex, though without detailed economic information we cannot hope to reconstruct them.

So far as we can tell, and admittedly the conclusion depends on a fair amount of guesswork, the economic organization of the Greek book trade underwent no fundamental change during the period of antiquity. Certainly the trade expanded greatly from the late fifth century onwards; and equally certainly authors could now write with the expectation that there would be a reading public for their work. But the phenomenon of publishing as a profession seems not to have existed; at least there is no evidence which even implies it. How then did authors and books become known, particularly outside their own city? It is easy to see how anything composed for performance, such as a play, or an epic poem to celebrate some civic occasion, would have immediate local publicity which (if favourable) might stimulate a demand for copies; eminent teachers – philosophers or rhetoricians – will have circulated works among their friends or pupils which would easily become more widely disseminated; and for the non-academic author at the beginning of his career one can guess that the notice of a patron or the distinction of winning a poetry competition may have been a vital first step towards a wider circulation.

No one, at any rate, seems to have thought of employing a middleman to promote the sales of a composition in return for a monopoly over its reproduction. This is no doubt largely because once a work had been made known

---

[1] Pliny, *N.H.* 13.11, citing Varro. See Turner (1968) 9–10.
[2] Lewis (1974) 90–4.

in even one written copy it was outside its author's control: there was no practical or legal means of safeguarding the text or limiting the number of copies made. Thus the terms ἐκδιδόναι and ἔκδοσις, which are regularly used for making a book known to the public, have nothing to do with publication, in the modern sense. The application of these terms has been well defined by van Groningen: 'They imply the activity not of a publisher or a bookseller, but of the author himself, who "abandons" his work to the public; he gives them the opportunity to read it, to recopy it, to pass it on to others. From that moment the text goes off at random . . .'[1] This was clearly a source of frustration to authors: Diodorus (1.5.2) attempts to warn off those 'pirates' who make books by compiling material from other writers; and Galen ruefully describes how the working notes he gave his pupils for their private use were subjected to wholesale distortion and alteration and circulated commercially as genuine works of the master (19.9–10 Kühn).

The fact that professionally produced books were in common use shows that there was money to be made from the trade, but the authors themselves can hardly have written for direct profit from sales: their financial support must normally have come from patronage or from the fees they could earn by giving public readings or lectures, a very important feature of intellectual life throughout later antiquity. The copyists, on the other hand, were professional craftsmen whose living depended on writing book hands. Many of them must have been slaves; and the profession as a whole never achieved social prestige, except perhaps at the village level where a scribe might be the only literate member of the community.[2] The best opportunities for making profit must have been reserved for the booksellers, who might, for example, commission multiple copies of a popular text for rapid sale, or use their commercial talents to inflate the prices of locally rare items.

The papyri show clearly that the professional scribes followed quite standardized practices in the copying of texts. They evidently computed their payment by the hundred lines of text, as we can tell from the 'stichometrical' letters placed in the margins and the sum total of lines given at the end of a work.[3] The script is usually a formal book hand without abbreviations; there is some evidence that different rates were charged for handwriting of different qualities.[4] In general the textual accuracy of these professionally made copies does not seem to have been high: Strabo writing at Rome in the first century B.C. complains of the negligence of the commercial copyists there and at Alexandria (13.1.54), and the papyri tend to bear him out. Some careful copies survive, with marks indicating that they have been checked against other texts, but these are in the minority and are more likely to have been

[1] van Groningen (1963) 25.
[2] Cf. Turner (1968) 83, on Egypt.
[3] Ohly (1928) *passim*; Turner (1971) 19.
[4] Ohly (1928) 88–9; Turner (1968) 87–8.

produced for scholars than for the general public.[1] Perhaps for the ordinary market what mattered most was handsomeness of presentation and material and general legibility; readers of ancient books may have been as much accustomed to correcting trivial slips as readers of modern newspapers. (It is a striking fact that throughout antiquity Greek readers unquestioningly accepted texts without word-division and largely without punctuation.) Dictation may have been used in some scriptoria as a device for rapid dissemination when only one exemplar was available;[2] but very often copies must have been made one at a time, as customers commissioned them. It is probably right to think of copying enterprises as mainly quite small-scale, as most craftsmen's establishments were in antiquity.

The relations between copyists and booksellers are not well documented. Clearly some copyists worked directly for authors, as members of their staff,[3] and many must have been employed by the major libraries; others copied texts at piece-rates for individual customers without the intervention of booksellers. But there were certain roles that only the booksellers could fulfil: they seem to have travelled to areas where library resources were limited, offering texts that were not available locally;[4] and they established regular shops in the great intellectual centres where they could count on an educated clientele: wherever there were important libraries the stimulus to the trade must have been considerable. It is difficult to tell from the very inadequate sources how widespread bookshops were outside these obvious centres, and since the demand for ordinary necessities like school texts could presumably often be met by orders placed direct with copyists there is no reason to suppose that the existence of a school or even of a gymnasium (see p. 25) argues for a regular bookshop. Many school texts must have been passed from one generation of pupils to the next, as they still are, and the fewer the bookshops the greater must have been the scope for an informal second-hand market.

There was certainly a trade in books as articles of luxury, to be displayed rather than read. Lucian (*Adv. ind.* 7) makes fun of the ignorant book collector who cares only about the trimmings: the purple vellum wrapper and the gilt knob. (This was the projecting knob (*omphalos*) of the roller, made of wood or bone, on which the more lavish kind of roll was fixed.) The ancient world seems to have had its share of 'experts' who could manufacture fakes: Dio Chrysostom describes a process – burying the rolls in grain – by which newly produced books were made to look old (21.12) and Lucian mentions the prestige of so-called autograph copies, laughing at the would-be collector

---

[1] Turner (1968) 92–4.   [2] Skeat (1956) *passim*; Turner (1971) 19–20.
[3] Cf. Diog. Laert. 7.36 (Zeno); Norman (1960) 122 (Libanius).
[4] Cf. Dion. Hal. *Isocr.* 18 (cited above, p. 14) and the story of Hermodorus (above, p. 13). Dziatzko (1899) 976.

who is willing to believe that Demosthenes copied Thucydides 'eight times over' (*Adv. ind.* 4). Elsewhere he accuses an enemy of forging the handbook of Tisias on rhetoric and charging an outrageous price for it (*Pseudolog.* 30). Of course, serious and knowledgeable collectors existed too; we know the names of several authors who wrote guides to the collection and arrangement of books which must have interested bibliophiles as well as librarians.[1] Some ancient books carried illustrations, though our extant papyri yield little direct evidence. Not surprisingly, certain types of work attracted illustration: technical treatises on botany or medicine or mathematics, which could be clarified with the aid of pictures and diagrams, and popular literary genres such as epic, romance and drama, which offered the illustrator plenty of scenes of action.[2] Presumably illustration, however modest, raised the price, and anything approaching the sumptuous illumination we find in some medieval codices would put a book into the category of luxury goods.

Little more is known in detail about book prices than about the distribution of bookshops. The high sums mentioned for special rarities – Lucian says the pseudo-Tisias fetched 750 drachmas – are no guide to ordinary prices for ordinary books; and such evidence as we have is too scattered to give more than the roughest of impressions. There are records of the prices of papyrus rolls, mainly from Egypt, which suggest that the norm was two to four drachmas, the equivalent, as N. Lewis points out,[3] of anything from one to five or six days' pay at the very lowest point on the economic scale, that of the unskilled labourer. But the level of affluence rose fairly steeply, and the more prosperous classes, even at a socially quite modest level, must have been able to take papyrus for granted as a not particularly expensive commodity. At copying rates as recorded in Egypt in the second century A.D. a short work, inclusive of the price of material, might not have cost more than say five or six drachmas. But how far these would be standard prices outside Egypt we cannot determine. Evidently some users of papyrus needed to make economies, as we can tell from the fact that the rolls were sometimes re-used and a second text written on the verso. Most often this was non-literary matter such as accounts, but there are famous exceptions: Aristotle's *Constitution of Athens* and Euripides' *Hypsipyle* both survive as opisthograph texts.

The spread of Greek culture

The interrelated questions of the circulation of books, education, scholarship and taste cannot be considered without taking into account the remarkable spread of Greek culture prompted by the conquests of Alexander the Great.

[1] Kleberg (1967) 20.   [2] Weitzmann (1959) *passim* and (1970) esp. 225–30.
[3] Lewis (1974) 129–34.

The implications of this movement were easily as important for the history of Greek literature as the impact of the Homeric poems themselves. Alexander's policy, continued by his Successors, of planting cities all over the East led to the establishment of Greek, in the modified form of Attic known as the *koine* (ἡ κοινὴ διάλεκτος), as the language of government and culture far beyond its old boundaries. As a result many non-Greeks came to contribute directly to the development of Greek literature: Zeno of Citium was probably of Phoenician origin; Lucian of Samosata was a native Aramaic speaker. Alexander's most significant foundation was Alexandria in Egypt, which the Ptolemies established as an intellectual centre to rival and indeed surpass Athens (in all branches of learning except philosophy). It was men of letters working at Alexandria in the third century B.C. who rescued a great deal of past Greek literature for posterity, laid the foundations of classical scholarship, and through their own creative output gave the Roman authors some of their most influential models. Another important long-term effect of Hellenization was the continuity of ancient and Byzantine education. Because the early Christians chose Greek as the vehicle for their proselytizing literature there was a strong reason for the basic character of the ancient educational system to be preserved into the Byzantine world and with it a demand, however limited, for pagan texts.

(*a*) *The demand for books*. It seems clear that the process of Hellenization depended to quite a large extent on the easy availability of books. What is striking about the Greek world in the Hellenistic and Roman periods is its cultural homogeneity despite its enormous geographical range. Writers from all over this vast area share the same literary attitudes and quote the same authors; and a long list could be compiled of distinguished intellectuals who came from quite insignificant cities: Alexander of Cotiaeum, Metrophanes of Eucarpia, Heraclitus of Rhodiapolis, Strabo of Amasia, Herodorus of Greek Susa (Seleucia on the Eulaeus).[1] All this suggests a uniform educational system and a common stock of literature, at least of 'the classics'.

There is a fair amount of evidence from the Hellenistic period onwards for the foundation of libraries, and the sort of figures that are quoted for their holdings support the view that books were plentiful. Quite apart from the book collecting on a vast scale financed by the early Ptolemies at Alexandria, where it seems to be no exaggeration to speak of many thousands of rolls,[2] or the rival activity at Pergamum, there is epigraphic evidence for more modest institutions which perhaps can be taken as more typical. An inscription of the

[1] Cf. Jones (1940) 283.
[2] The evidence is discussed by Pfeiffer 100–2; cf. Blum (1977) cols. 140—4, 156–61.

second century B.C. from Cos records the endowment of a library by several benefactors, of whom some give sums of 200 drachmas, some give 100 books, and others give both books and money.[1] It is true that the term 'books' (βίβλοι, βιβλία) can be misleading, since it more often connotes rolls than whole works, and a long work would fill a sizable number of rolls, but even when due allowance is made for inflated totals it seems hardly conceivable that books were a scarce commodity. No doubt they were to be found in greatest concentration at major cultural centres (as they still are nowadays): at Athens, for example, the library of the gymnasium founded by Ptolemy Philadelphus was officially entitled to receive 100 books (or rolls) from each outgoing year of ephebes, which can hardly have been typical of ordinary cities.[2] But the very existence of libraries in other places suggests that the demand for books was widespread, and the evidence of the papyri points the same way. Even if Egypt was not representative of the Greek world as a whole, the sheer abundance of written texts found at quite unimportant Egyptian sites argues for a general availability of reading matter in other areas with some pretension to Greek culture.

This culture (*paideia*) was evidently very highly esteemed, by Greeks and non-Greeks alike, as the essential qualification for positions of prestige and influence. The status accorded to literary men and intellectuals generally was high, as we can tell from the proliferation of such people in the Hellenistic period. Along with social standing might go influence with a royal patron or even direct responsibility in the role of ambassador; the Successors of Alexander all thought it worth while to enlist the support of the intellectuals, and the pattern was followed by the Roman emperors, most strikingly in the second century A.D., the 'grand baroque age'[3] when the sophists came fully into their own. It would no doubt be wrong, though, to suggest that culture was all-pervasive in the sense that it extended very far beyond the cities or even within them reached all levels of society. In 'old Greece' it was probably more widely diffused than in the new foundations, and there is evidence from some places that primary education was provided at the expense of a local benefactor.[4] The new cities were interested in higher education, which they subsidized by paying the salaries of teachers of grammar and rhetoric, but they do not often seem to have paid for elementary teaching although the lessons might be held at the civic gymnasium. The very lowest classes, who were too poor to take advantage of anything that was not completely free, probably had their only taste of *paideia* at the theatre, when some leading citizen provided the show.

It was essentially through the gymnasia and the theatres that the inhabitants

---

[1] Robert (1935) 421–5. [2] Delorme (1960) 331–2; Marrou (1965) 572.
[3] Bowersock (1969) 16. [4] Marrou (1965) 176–7, 221.

of the new cities expressed their consciousness of Greek identity, whether inherited or adoptive. These were the centres of all the activities most closely associated with the Greek way of life: physical training, education, competitions in athletics, poetry, music, drama. Education in Greece itself had shown signs of becoming more institutional from the latter part of the fourth century onwards,[1] and thanks to a development at Athens in the 330s there was a convenient pattern for the new cities to follow, at least for the highest age-group. This was the new system of training the ephebes, which seems to have been introduced in response to the great defeat at Chaeronea and was certainly designed in the first place as a military measure, to improve the quality of Athenian national service training. It soon developed into something more broadly educational, though at the same time socially more exclusive: we hear of the ephebes going to lectures at the philosophical schools and of professors lecturing at the gymnasium; mention has already been made of the ephebic contribution to the library. In adopting this system the new cities put less emphasis on military preparation, but naturally enough took over the curriculum and educational aims of mainland Greece; enthusiasm for Greek culture in general was so strong that individuals gave themselves Greek names and cities looked for heroic figures from Greek myths who could plausibly be counted as their founders.

The desire to preserve the essential character of Greek culture has been strikingly illustrated by recent finds at Aï Khanoum in Afghanistan.[2] The French excavators of this remote city of the third century B.C. have found not only a gymnasium but also, in a sanctuary dedicated to the probable founder of the city, the base of a pillar on which was once inscribed a large collection of Delphic maxims (there is a parallel text from another Greek city, Miletopolis in the area of Cyzicus).[3] The particular interest of the find is the dedicatory epigram which records that the maxims were set up by one Clearchus after he had copied the text at Delphi: 'these wise sayings of the men of old, words of the famous, are displayed at holy Pytho; there Clearchus carefully copied them and has set them up for all to see in the sanctuary of Cineas'. This shows how closely the new settlers maintained their links with the old centres, even from a distance of 5,000 km or more. L. Robert has identified Clearchus as the Peripatetic philosopher of that name, pointing to the travelling habits of men of letters, scientists and performers of all kinds. But even if it did not boast anyone so distinguished, society in these remote parts was not so barbarous that it could not appreciate a quite elegant epigram elegantly inscribed; and the maxims themselves were no doubt regarded as the very essence of Hellenism.

[1] Marrou (1965) 163–80.　　　　　　　　[2] Robert (1968) 421–57.
[3] Ed. H. Diels in Dittenberger, Sylloge[3] 1268.

(*b*) *The educational system.* For the detail of the educational system most of the evidence comes from Egypt, where the sands have preserved vast numbers of school exercises. There is a remarkable sameness in these texts throughout the whole period from early Ptolemaic to early Byzantine times; so far as we can tell from the much patchier evidence relating to other areas this basic pattern seems to have been common to the whole Greek world.

Apart from athletics, and to a lesser degree music and mathematics, which were always part of Greek education, the major focus of attention was correct understanding and correct use of the language. This illustrates the enormous prestige that was accorded to fluency in Greek; it is worth noting that there was never any general interest in learning foreign languages, and even Latin in the Imperial period had a very restricted role in the Greek world. Great importance was attached to correctness of form: it was not enough for an educated person to master the current *koine*; one must also be able to read classical poetry with its different dialects, and from the end of the first century B.C. onwards more and more stress was laid on imitation of Attic authors.[1]

The procedure for acquiring fluency was laborious, but we may guess so thorough as to be quite effective. Children spent the first five years being taught reading and writing by the elementary schoolmaster, the *grammatistes*. He made them learn first the alphabet, then syllables, then whole words, then scansion and correct syllable division: dozens of papyri and ostraca survive to illustrate the various copying and dictation exercises that all this involved.[2] The texts chosen for the copying exercises were simple but morally instructive: maxims, fables, little stories about famous people from history or myth. There is some evidence for girls sharing at least this elementary stage; but we do not know how widespread the practice was, or what proportion of girls went on to the more advanced schools.[3]

These were for pupils between the ages of (roughly) twelve and fifteen, under the direction of the *grammatikos* ('language teacher' is a less misleading translation than 'grammarian'). The emphasis was on reading and composing, the subject matter mainly poetry, which was studied in an elaborately analytical way, giving pupils a knowledge of mythology, geography and history as well as correct understanding of grammar and style. Work on the chosen authors seems to have been narrow and artificial but relentlessly systematic: reading aloud and recitation, 'construes' of the text (for the dialect, vocabulary and style would differ widely from those of the *koine*), study of the poet's

[1] Browning (1969) 49–55.
[2] Listed by Zalateo (1961); specimens in Milne (1908).
[3] Marrou (1965) 174–5.

allusions so that the pupil could locate every mountain and river, give the genealogy or exploits of every hero, retail all manner of precise and curious detail – a preoccupation shared by the writers of later antiquity. These literary studies were accompanied by lessons in the rudiments of composition and, after the time of Aristarchus and his pupils (see pp. 32f.), in formal grammar (morphology but not syntax). The purpose of exercises in composition was to inculcate correctness and fluency rather than to stimulate original expression. In the more elementary of these so-called *progymnasmata* or preparatory exercises (the rest were the province of the teacher of rhetoric) the pupil was asked to retell a fable, or write a little narrative based on characters from history or myth, or take the saying of some famous person and develop it, according to strictly formal rules, into a short essay – this last was called a *chria* (χρεία).

Such was the crucial training in literary culture which gave a person a claim to be called Greek. It was more widely influential than the more advanced and technical teaching of rhetoric and philosophy which came later; like the Classics as taught in the public schools of Victorian England it was a shared basis for all educated people. Even though our evidence (school manuals and exercises) does not suggest that much attention was paid to the 'judgement of poems' (κρίσις ποιημάτων) which according to Dionysius Thrax (*Ars grammatica* 1) is the finest part of the grammarian's craft, we can tell from the writings of the educated – from Strabo, Galen, Plutarch, Lucian – that such intensive reading of the poets did have its effect. Educational theory might not be able to claim anything more than rather limited moral lessons or a superficial interest in curious erudition as the benefits of the system, but the material itself must often have made a more direct and exciting appeal.

The final stages of education were the special province of the gymnasia, which regularly maintained teachers of rhetoric (*rhetores, sophistai*)[1] and sometimes had resident *grammatikoi* and philosophers as well (clearly the teaching of 'grammar' might be carried on at a higher level with older pupils: there was no hard and fast demarcation which ruled it out beyond the age of fifteen). The ephebes of most cities could expect to be given at least an introduction to rhetoric, but the most serious students would stay on for further study after the short period of ephebic training. The regular courses given by the local rhetorician might be supplemented by lectures or performances given by visiting virtuosi: the line between intellectual and artiste seems to have been difficult to draw. The heyday of the great rhetoricians was the second century A.D., when to be a 'sophist' was to be a person of the utmost consequence and influence, political as well as intellectual. Particularly notable

---

[1] Bowersock (1969) 12–14 discusses the different nuances of these terms.

figures could earn very high fees for their public appearances and private teaching, and their status is reflected in the honours and civic commissions pressed upon them by their fellow citizens and in the immunities from local obligations granted by the imperial government.[1] This is very striking evidence for the high value set on eloquence and its real importance in public life.

The surviving handbooks of rhetorical exercises combine with the evidence of the papyri to illustrate a highly developed and long-lasting system, which strikes the modern reader as narrow and formalistic, but seems at least to have been remarkably efficient. From the more elementary types of composition: fable, narrative and *chria*, the student proceeded by the way of maxim, refutation and confirmation, enkomion ('Thucydides', 'wisdom'), vituperation ('Philip'), comparison, speech written in character ('Niobe after the death of her children') and so on, to the most advanced, the introduction of an imaginary law. Aelius Theon (who wrote in the second century A.D.) in a section of his *Progymnasmata* entitled *On the training of the young*[2] gives advice to the teacher on the examples from the classics to choose for each exercise. As one would expect, he repeatedly cites the orators; he also draws on Herodotus, Thucydides, Ephorus, Theopompus and Philistus, Xenophon and Plato, and for the speech in character he recommends using Homer and Menander as well as Plato's Socratic dialogues. Reading Theon one can detect the same principles as have traditionally underlain the teaching of Greek and Latin 'composition' in English schools: the end is not merely technical fluency but also sympathetic contact with the authors and their styles. Both in their earnest concern for 'purity' of style and in their insistence on the use of classical models the rhetoricians furthered the sense of a common culture which was founded on the study of the poets. Their stylistic notions could lead to absurdities of exaggerated Atticism and may all too often have stifled originality and experiment, but at least they helped to sustain the cosmopolitan character of the Greek world through its most important medium, a universal educated language.

The philosophers had a less pervasive effect on general literary culture, partly because in the ancient world the study of philosophy beyond the elementary stages tended to imply a way of life, almost like a religious calling, which marked a man off from his fellows and might require him to reject the values implicit in the rest of the educational system. But the scholarly study and exegesis of the works of the masters that was carried on in the philosophical schools of Athens (and later at other centres) must have done a great deal to preserve and protect their doctrines. Moreover, systematic book collecting

[1] Bowersock (1969) 30ff.; Millar (1977) 493ff.
[2] *Prog.* 2, Spengel II 65–72.

had first developed in the Peripatos under Aristotle and the antiquarian researches of his school had a great influence on the history of scholarship.

(c) *Scholarship*. Scholars writing about scholarship are always tempted to exaggerate its importance; but the particular phase associated with Alexandria under the patronage of the early Ptolemies can fairly be called decisive for the survival and interpretation of quite a large proportion of the Greek literature that remains to us. This is not to claim that the scholars of Alexandria had much direct effect on literacy or the educational system, or that some major texts would not have been preserved without them: Homer, at least, was never in danger of being lost. But time has a filtering effect on literature even in the era of the printed book; it was all the more vital when works circulated only in manuscript that positive steps be taken to salvage the output of the past, particularly for the Greeks of the third century B.C. with an astonishingly creative period of literature behind them. Otherwise there was a grave risk that some of the more recondite texts would disappear altogether because not enough people were interested in having them recopied, and even the texts that did get transmitted were liable to degenerate into ever worsening states of corruption if nothing more scrupulous than the normal book-copying procedures were followed. Besides, the older a work became, the more it called for exegesis, of words or ideas or institutions that had ceased to be current.

The large-scale promotion of book collecting and the development of scholarship at Alexandria in the third century can be traced to several causes. Evidently Ptolemy I (Soter) himself was a key figure: he wanted to do as Greek tyrants and princes had traditionally done and patronize men of letters – this was one obvious way of giving Alexandria the prestige of a royal capital – but instead of confining his support to creative writers who would praise his regime he did something more original. He established[1] a research centre where his poets, who were also scholars, could work secure from financial worries and surrounded by the finest materials for study known to the Greek world. This was the Museum (τὸ Μουσεῖον), formally the cult centre of a religious organization, which was dedicated to the Muses and presided over by a priest. In some respects it could be compared with older institutions called *mouseia*, shrines of the Muses at which literary societies met and worshipped, and particularly with the great philosophical schools of Athens, the Academy and the Peripatos, each a learned community with a Muses' shrine;[2] but in all essentials it was a new sort of establishment. Philosophy was not one of its major concerns (Pergamum was closer to Athens in this respect), although the influence of

---

[1] If this is the correct interpretation of Plutarch, *Non posse suaviter vivi secundum Epicurum* 13.1095d. The alternative is to ascribe the foundation to Ptolemy Philadelphus. Cf. Pfeiffer 96–8; Fraser (1972) II 469.

[2] Diog. Laert. 4.1, 5.51.

Aristotle must certainly be seen in the manifold interests of its scholars – literary, historical and scientific – and Strabo indeed claims that 'Aristotle taught the kings of Egypt the arrangement of a library' (13.608). This must mean that Aristotle's methods as used by the Peripatetics were applied at Alexandria when the Library was established,[1] and it seems reasonable to see the link as Demetrius of Phalerum, who is known to have been in Ptolemy's entourage from 297 and (according to Tzetzes)[2] had a role to play in the setting up of the Library; but beyond this our evidence does not go and cannot be pressed.

Another influence on Alexandrian scholarship in its early days must have been the tradition represented by the Atthidographers. These were chroniclers of Athenian history, active in the fourth and third centuries, whose preoccupation with local events was combined in some cases with an interest in festivals, cult or antiquities: titles like *On the Eleusinian Mysteries* (Melanthius) and *On sacrifices* (Demon) clearly come into this category. The most significant of these writers was Philochorus, who died in the 260s; Jacoby gives him a place of honour as 'the first scholar of the Atthidographers' in view of the range and variety of his titles and the ambitious enterprise implied by such works as *Attic inscriptions*.[3] He wrote books *On the contests in Athens*, *On Delos*, *On divination* as well as works on literary subjects which recall the interests of the Peripatetics (*On tragedies*, *On Alcman*, for instance). All this finds an unmistakable echo in Alexandrian scholarship: the style of the Museum must have been affected at least to some extent by these Athenian traditions.

Important as such 'academic' influences were, it seems to have been the creative poets themselves who gave the new institution its distinctive character. Among the poets of the late fourth and early third centuries there were a few who saw that if poetry was to be rescued from the decline of the past century the great literature of earlier times must be preserved and studied with a new self-consciousness: the poets must train themselves through a most attentive study of the masters, but out of this study must come something fresh and individual. This was a highly significant stage in Greek literary history, the direct forerunner of Roman *ars* and *imitatio*. Philetas of Cos (see pp. 544ff.) is the most important figure at the beginning of the new movement. He wrote a book of glosses on rare words, as well as composing elegiac poetry which was seen by his successors as the first major example of the 'lean' (λεπτός) style that ultimately dominated Hellenistic poetry. Philetas must have been educated at Cos, a well established intellectual centre with a distinguished medical school,[4] but he was drawn into the Alexandrian orbit through his appointment as tutor to Ptolemy Philadelphus. This connexion between

---

[1] Pfeiffer 98–102.   [2] *Prolegomena de comoedia* = *CGF* 1.19.
[3] *FGrH* 3b, 227.   [4] Fraser (1972) I 343–4.

scholars, poets and the court continued for several generations: the head of the Library was normally also tutor in the royal household, and the kings provided the supply of funds necessary for gathering the essential tools of scholarship, the books.

The rescue of previous Greek literature could not be left to chance. Galen records (17a606 Kühn) that the early Ptolemies systematically sought out texts from all over the Greek world and even impounded books that arrived in Alexandria as cargo, had copies made of them and returned the copies, not the originals, to their owners. He goes on to tell a famous story (17a607): how the texts of the great Attic tragedians, which were officially kept in the public record office at Athens as a guard against actors' interpolations, were borrowed by 'Ptolemy' (i.e. Euergetes I) against an indemnity of fifteen talents; once safely at Alexandria the originals were kept for the Library, handsome new copies made for the Athenians, and the indemnity forfeited. The first task of the scholars was to sort out and identify all this material, which certainly included a good deal of spurious writing falsely attributed to famous authors. But even the first generation of scholars working in the 280s and 270s – Zenodotus, the first librarian and a pupil of Philetas, and the poets Lycophron and Alexander Aetolus – seem to have gone beyond mere classification. They are said to have 'corrected' (διώρθωσαν/διωρθώσαντο)[1] the works of the comic poets (Lycophron), the tragedians (Alexander) and the epic and lyric poets (Zenodotus); this suggests that they used their newly gathered material to produce editions, though we know almost nothing about their methods or the nature of their textual work; the evidence for Zenodotus' criticism of Homer is the least shadowy, but still controversial.

For the scholar working on Homer the most pressing need was for some kind of standardization: there was a very wide discrepancy in the number of verses from one text to another, and a bewilderingly large number of texts available from all over the Greek world. Athetesis, the condemnation of spurious matter, seems to have been one of the first critical procedures applied to the Homeric text, and Zenodotus probably invented the obelus for this purpose.[2] How extensively and on what principles he compared manuscripts cannot be determined; perhaps after a preliminary scrutiny of the material he chose a particular existing text to use as the basis of his 'edition'. The term 'edition' conjures up for the modern reader the idea of a large number of identical copies carrying the editor's version of a text, complete with apparatus criticus – Page's Aeschylus, for example – but in the ancient context the ἔκδοσις (the same word as for the publication of a new work) might be no more than a

[1] Tzetzes (n. 36 above); Pfeiffer 105–22; Blum (1977) cols. 161–7.
[2] Pfeiffer 115. The obelus was a horizontal stroke placed in the left-hand margin to indicate a suspected verse.

31

single copy which the scholar has made available for consultation and annotated with signs indicating his view of particular passages. Perhaps for a start the notation went no further than the simple use of the obelus to indicate spurious lines.

As might be expected in such a context, where intellectual activity was extremely intense and the facilities for advanced work were unrivalled, there was a continuous succession of gifted scholars and poets drawn by the prestige of Alexandria, each learning from his predecessors and building on their work. Three great names must be singled out from successive generations. Callimachus (c. 305–c. 240 B.C.) used the classifying work of the first 'correctors' as the basis for his ambitious bibliographical enterprise, greater even than a catalogue of the Library, which was known as the *Pinakes* (*Tables*), a series of registers of all available Greek authors listed by genre, with essential biographical data for each entry together with titles of works and notes on their length and genuineness.[1] This was far more exhaustive than anything previously attempted; it laid the foundation for extensive scholarly work, and although it has not survived it has had an enormous indirect influence on our knowledge of ancient literature.

Aristophanes of Byzantium (c. 255–c. 180 B.C.) is credited with a vast amount of significant textual work – on Homer, Hesiod, many of the dramatists, the lyric poets – and also with technical contributions to scholarship which have had a lasting impact on our texts. He seems to have introduced the written system of accentuation, the habit of arranging lyric texts according to metrical cola (previously they had been written out like prose), and the use of a developed system of critical signs – the obelus, the asteriscus, the diple and others[2] – to convey his views on doubtful passages in the texts. He did fundamental work on the lyric poets, establishing terminology, classification into different types, and metrical analysis, and for the large number of plays that he edited he provided 'hypotheses', prefaces which gave historical information such as date of first performance as well as brief notes on subject matter.

Aristarchus (c. 216–c. 144) took the use of critical notation to its logical conclusion, composing written commentaries (ὑπομνήματα)[3] to explain the reasoning behind his textual recommendations and also to give other sorts of exegesis: notes on rare words or points of myth or history. The earliest examples of such commentaries may have been notes taken at lectures: we

---

[1] Blum (1977) Chapters 4 and 6.

[2] Pfeiffer 178; Turner (1968) 114–18, 184; (1971) 17. The signs were not always used with the same significance. In the system as finally developed by Aristarchus the asteriscus ✻ indicated lines incorrectly repeated elsewhere; the diple > marked anything noteworthy in language or content.

[3] Pfeiffer 160–1 notes that Euphronius had anticipated Aristarchus as the author of a written commentary.

must certainly allow for oral *explication de texte* as one of the activities of these scholars (who were teachers at least to the extent that other scholars were their pupils). Aristarchus concerned himself mainly with the same range of authors as Aristophanes, but he broke new ground by writing a commentary on Herodotus. His work on Homer was particularly celebrated and influential: luckily we possess a good deal of information about it embedded in the scholia of a famous medieval manuscript of the *Iliad*, 'Venetus A'.[1] His work on Homeric usage was an essential foundation for informed judgement of individual passages; outside his textual studies he made important contributions to lexicography and grammar.

To a modern reader accustomed to tools of scholarship which have been perfected over centuries of sophisticated study the methods and attitudes of these scholars may sometimes seem naive or arbitrary, but it would be wrong not to recognize this as an era of distinguished intellectual activity, rarely matched in later times. Some of the stimulus to produce work of such ambitious range must have come from the contact of the men of letters with the scientists who were their colleagues in the Museum: Eratosthenes, librarian and authority on Attic comedy who was also a student of chronology, mathematics and astronomy, exemplifies the close links between the disciplines. This was clearly a period of great intellectual confidence and creativity, with the excitement of new discoveries in the air. Apollonius Rhodius, whose poetry is full of implicit literary and philological comment, also shows that he has responded to the scientific advances of the time.[2]

The persecutions of Ptolemy VIII (Euergetes II) after 145 caused a dispersal of scholars, and although Alexandria remained a major intellectual centre until the end of antiquity its greatest days were past. Pergamum with its library, its antiquarian scholarship and its distinguished Stoics was a serious rival to Alexandria in the second century B.C., and some of the old centres – Athens and Rhodes, for example – remained important, but in the end the appeal of Rome as the source of patronage outweighed that of any of the Greek cities. It was only at Alexandria, however, that there was such a sustained period of work at a high level on literary texts, and none of the work of the Imperial period showed the same originality.

It is easy to assess the importance of the Alexandrians for modern scholarship; but how well can we gauge the impact of their work on the ancient world?

In the field of book production the influence of the Library must have been considerable.[3] Here was an institution which required a copying service on an unprecedentedly large scale; and the size of its collections must have guaranteed

---

[1] Ven. Marcianus gr. 822 (A). See now Erbse I (1969) xiii–xvi.
[2] E.g. at 3.761–5. Cf. Solmsen (1961) 195–7.
[3] Fraser (1972) I 472–8.

a regular demand from outsiders for copies of works that were not easy to find elsewhere. Since Alexandria was also the headquarters of the papyrus trade any tendency towards standardization which was fostered in the Library (e.g. in the size of books) could also become regular practice in a wider context. In the presentation of texts, too, it looks as though several of the conventions introduced by the Alexandrian scholars were gradually adopted as the norm when texts were reproduced. We find Aristophanes' colometry dominating lyric texts from now on, widespread use in the papyri of the critical notation and orthography employed by the scholars, and most striking of all the tendency of Homeric papyri from about the middle of the second century B.C. onwards to conform to a regular pattern, the so-called 'vulgate'. Whereas the earlier texts very often include many lines which have disappeared from later texts, the vulgate shows a general conformity in the matter of length which is difficult to explain if it does not represent the influence of Aristarchus and his predecessors. The fact that by contrast the emendations proposed by the scholars had remarkably little effect on the texts circulating after their time – either in the papyri or in the medieval manuscripts – need not surprise us: one can understand that the general public and the booksellers who supplied them might be more interested in a certain standardization of length and layout and conventional signs than in the niceties of textual criticism.[1]

It has often been pointed out that only a very small amount of Alexandrian exegetical literature survives and that even in antiquity these scholarly works do not seem to have had a long life. But this need not mean that they were not influential. A commentary, being a series of discrete notes, perhaps originating in a record of oral discussion, did not have the same status as a continuous literary work and did not demand faithful re-copying *in extenso*: the form lends itself easily to excerpting or recasting, as the history of modern commentaries shows. The scholia in our extant medieval manuscripts seem, in fact, to reach back across the centuries to early Alexandrian exegesis. When, for example, they cite Didymus (*c.* 65 B.C.–A.D. 10) citing 'the commentators' they are preserving traces of the work of this period; and for Homer there is the more extensive evidence in the scholia of Venetus A. It is easy to imagine scholars and schoolmasters taking what they needed from whatever commentary was available, so that instead of wholesale recopying of the earliest commentaries there was a continuous process of excerpting, simplification or adaptation according to different needs. The local distribution of this scholarly material is worth taking into account; D. A. Russell writing of Plutarch's time makes a point which must also be valid for earlier centuries:

Apart from the acknowledged classics, few books existed in many copies. Instead, we should envisage countless different titles, each circulating in a small range, and

[1] S. West (1967) 11–18; Reynolds–Wilson (1974) 8–9, 12.

many more or less duplicating one another. With few exceptions, we can hardly speak of a standard history or commentary. Quite small local groups would each have their own. It follows that an individual scholar could only hope to see a few of the books that he had heard of...[1]

(*d*) *The classics.* One of the major achievements of the scholars seems to have been to provide the reading public with an authoritative definition of 'classical literature'. This no doubt reflected the popular preferences that assert themselves when literature is exposed to the test of time (even in the fifth century Aeschylus, Sophocles and Euripides clearly towered above their fellow dramatists, as the *Frogs* demonstrates), but the corpus of 'best authors' was given official recognition in the classifications made by the scholars of Alexandria and perhaps of Pergamum,[2] and came to exercise a very powerful effect on Greek culture. Aristophanes of Byzantium is credited with dividing literature into what modern scholarship calls 'canons' (there is no equivalent Greek term, but we may follow Pfeiffer in using the Suda's ἐγκριθέντες 'the included' for the chosen authors (Latin *classici*)).[3] So the nine lyric poets became firmly established, the ten orators, the three tragedians, and so on. The scholars tended to concentrate their work in these selected areas, which in those days were in any case very extensive (the three tragedians had written about 300 plays between them); the evidence from the papyri and from quotations suggests that the public increasingly confined their reading to the same authors and to a decreasing selection within those authors' works. Naturally the demand for a work not 'included' would fade as fewer and fewer copies circulated and the text became almost unknown. It is interesting to see that the definition of classical literature was by no means rigid: some of the major writers of the third century soon became 'included', among them Apollonius Rhodius and Callimachus, fragments of whose *Aetia* with a very detailed running commentary have recently been published from papyri of the third century B.C.[4]

The inclusion of new authors must often have been compensated for by the loss of older ones; and it is not surprising that with so vast a literary heritage the readers of later antiquity liked their classics in the form of various kinds of selection or digest or anthology. There are plenty of parallels in the modern world: how many members of the educated public read, say, Elizabethan sonneteers except in anthologies; how many of the works of even Shakespeare are read in schools and generally well known?

We ought to envisage a long and probably rather desultory process of narrowing down: in the case of tragedy, for example, the number of plays

[1] Russell (1973) 42–3.   [2] Cousin (1935) 565–72.   [3] Pfeiffer 203–8.
[4] Meillier (1976).

that were commonly read and performed must have been a good deal smaller even in the fourth century than the total output of the three tragedians, and it is easy to see how it would shrink further as time went on. The more famous and popular plays – *Oedipus tyrannus* for example, particularly after its canonization in Aristotle's *Poetics* – would be the ones that were most easily available; and presumably the Alexandrian scholars did not write commentaries on the whole corpus, though they possessed most of the texts. Schoolmasters would naturally set their classes to read works that were well known, easily come by and supplied with commentaries, thus perpetuating the popular selection. This looks more plausible than anything more clear-cut, such as a deliberate choice by a particular individual of the seven surviving plays of Aeschylus, the seven of Sophocles and the ten 'select' plays of Euripides to form the standard selections for use in schools. So far as we know there was never any state control of school curricula or any equivalent of modern examining boards to impose a standard pattern on education: this makes it all the more likely that the choice of works read in school reflects the choice of society at large.[1]

Our extant 'selections' may in fact never have been firmly fixed until the time when the contents of rolls were being transferred to codices (the third and fourth centuries A.D.). A codex could accommodate a number of plays from separate rolls, and it would be natural if the most familiar plays were grouped together in a single codex. Once the practice of incorporating the commentary in the same volume had established itself[2] – and the codex form lent itself to annotation in the margins – there was a very strong likelihood that the tradition would become standardized: 'Aeschylus' now becomes a single book.

Survival

A great deal of ancient Greek literature vanished during antiquity itself or in the course of the Middle Ages; some of it has reappeared dramatically in the papyrus finds of the last hundred years: Menander, Bacchylides, Callimachus, Hyperides, Aristotle's *Constitution of Athens*. But it was never in danger of being completely forgotten or destroyed, because the continuity of culture on which it depended was never wholly severed, and there was no widespread lapse into barbarism.

The language was one of the most important factors in this story of survival. Greek has been slow to change in the course of its long history. Unlike Latin it never broke into a series of separate languages; and from the end of the

[1] Roberts (1953) 270–1; Barrett (1964) 50–3; Reynolds–Wilson (1974) 46–7.
[2] This seems to have been a gradual process stretching over several centuries; cf. Turner (1968) 121–4; Reynolds–Wilson 46.

Hellenistic period until very recent times Greek-speaking societies have tended to maintain a classicizing literary language more or less distinct from ordinary speech. This has made possible a very striking continuity, as R. Browning points out: 'From that date [the sixth century B.C.] until the present day there has been a continuous and uninterrupted literary tradition, maintained by schools, by a body of grammatical literature, by the continuous study of a limited number of literary texts, whose linguistic form came to differ more and more from that of current speech.'[1] Homer, in fact, has always been part of the curriculum in Greek-speaking lands. But why did Virgil never supplant Homer once the Roman empire had established itself? And why was Homer not banned by the Christians, who had far more reason to take exception to him than Plato had?

The answer to the first of these questions is obvious enough from what has already been said about the value universally set on Greek *paideia*. The Romans of the later Republic, for all their belief in the superiority of things Roman, had absorbed along with Greek literature and philosophy the assumptions on which Greek education was based. Admittedly they made a literature of their own out of their response to the Greek, but they never tried to impose their culture on the Eastern provinces.[2] This is hardly surprising considering that the Greek educational system had been established at Rome before Rome had a fully fledged literature to use for the purpose (see *CHCL* II, pp. 5–6); Homer was studied in Roman schools, and those Romans who could afford it finished their education by studying Greek rhetoric and philosophy. Rome became as important a centre of the Greek book trade as Athens or Alexandria, and Roman libraries had large Greek holdings; far from being a threat to Greek civilization the Roman empire in fact sustained and consolidated it over a very wide area. There was an exceptional period at the end of the third century A.D. and in the fourth century when the emperors at Constantinople knew either very little Greek or none at all, and preferment in the higher reaches of the civil service, at court, or in a legal career depended on a knowledge of Latin even in the Greek-speaking East.[3] But the pattern did not last and in any case the demand for Latin never imposed itself at the crucial level of elementary teaching.

It might have been expected that when the Roman empire became officially Christian a new educational system would be created, replacing the old authors with biblical texts and using Christian precepts instead of pagan maxims. After all, there was a model ready to hand in the Jewish schools, which provided the faithful with an exclusively Jewish training.[4] But nothing of the kind developed within the Greek-speaking world; only outside it do we find

[1] Browning (1969) 13.   [2] Jones (1963) 4; Momigliano (1975) 7–8, 17.
[3] Jones (1963) 13.   [4] Marrou (1965) 454–5.

distinctively Christian establishments using Coptic and Syriac as the vehicle for their teaching.[1] It is true that as the monastic system grew a special form of religious education was devised for the children destined for the monasteries. But for society at large the old patterns remained, partly perhaps because they were so efficient, and now that the state had become more elaborately bureaucratic, particularly since the time of Diocletian, there was a greater need for trained men for the civil service. Training meant fluency in composition, and the power of the common culture was so great that no one conceived of a fluency that would have different stylistic and formal criteria. The early Fathers might in theory have imitated the Hebrew elements in the Christian heritage, or at least have fostered a more popular development of the *koine*; but they too had been educated in the common culture and wrote for an audience which shared it.

The Christians certainly disapproved in principle of pagan literature, but since they found themselves in practice using the pagan educational system they had to think of ways of making the classics harmless. St Basil, in his little work addressed to the young on how to profit from pagan authors (*Homily* 22), lays great stress on the way these can be used to teach virtue: the point of the Phaeacian episode in the *Odyssey*, for example, is to present Odysseus as a pattern of upright behaviour who converts the Phaeacians from their decadent ways (5.25–42). In moralizing the classics and particularly in giving them allegorical interpretation Christian teachers had plenty of pagan forerunners: allegories of Homer had been well known since at least the fifth century B.C.

St Basil, like Clement of Alexandria, evidently enjoyed classical literature, but he was not writing as an apologist of Hellenism so much as offering practical advice in the interests of a good Christian education. 'We must not admit everything indiscriminately, but only what is useful' (8.2–3) is his advice; it was left to later ages, particularly the Italian Renaissance, to interpret his work as a manifesto of humanism. In the early Middle Ages there seems to have been very little interest outside the context of the schools in the whole heritage of classical literature; the severe losses that must be dated to some time between the third or fourth century and the ninth were probably due more to sheer neglect than to any positively hostile policy. The systematic burning of books seems to have been reserved for heretical Christian sects,[2] and it would not be surprising if after the period of transition in the fourth century outright paganism never posed a serious threat of the kind that required such a violent response.

Within the range of 'included' authors of antiquity the Byzantine schools

[1] Marrou (1965) 456–8.
[2] Reynolds–Wilson (1974) 44, 220.

could find plenty of material to meet their needs while shedding some of the less 'useful' authors. Even if there is little trace of wholesale suppression we can certainly discern changing patterns of taste, most striking in the case of Menander,[1] who shrank in the Middle Ages to a series of one-line maxims taken out of context and preserved in various gnomic anthologies. This was a poet who in antiquity enjoyed overwhelming popularity and very wide-spread circulation, as we know from papyri, records of performances, quotations, adaptation by Roman playwrights, mosaics representing scenes from his plays and the explicit testimony of ancient writers. 'In the theatre,' says Plutarch, 'in the lecture-room, at the dinner-party, his poetry provides reading, study and entertainment for a wider public than that commanded by any other Greek masterpiece . . .'[2] Here perhaps is a clue to the disappearance of Menander from the tradition, his popularity on the stage. The theatre was regarded by the Christians as a dangerously immoral place; and the world of hetaerae and illicit liaisons which forms the background to Menander's plays cannot have been condoned either (though Plautus and Terence survived in Latin Christendom: perhaps like Aristophanes they seemed linguistically more remote and therefore safer). In the end the only acceptable role for Menander was as author of edifying maxims in company with the sages and the Fathers.

The converse process can be seen in the rise to popularity of the pseudo-Homeric *Batrachomyomachia* or *Battle of frogs and mice*. This unfunny parody of epic battle narrative is first mentioned in antiquity by Martial (14.183) and probably belongs to the Hellenistic period.[3] It never once turns up in the papyri, despite the fact that so many Homeric texts survive from the Imperial period. But in the Middle Ages and particularly in the Renaissance it had a distinct vogue; about seventy-five manuscripts are extant, of which a dozen are as early as the eleventh century, and it had the distinction of being one of the first Greek texts to be put into print. No doubt it was a useful text in the schoolroom, but even in post-classical times the fact that it was believed to be genuine Homer must have been what gave it prestige.

Something analogous to the shift in educational attitudes seems to have taken place in the creative writing of the early Byzantine period. Theology rather than literature was what now attracted the ablest minds, but radical as the break was from the content of classical prose and poetry, it did not entail a parallel change of form. The rhetorical patterns and the poetic dialects of antiquity persist well into the Byzantine period, so that one finds, for example, in Book 1 of the *Greek Anthology* a series of poems on Christian churches,

---

[1] Dain (1963), but cf. Reynolds–Wilson (1974) 221.
[2] *Ar. et Men. comp.* 854a, tr. Russell (1973) 53.
[3] Wolke (1978) 46–70.

martyrs, figures from the Old Testament and stories from the life of Christ, all in classical elegiacs and iambics. This kind of composition tells us something about the taste of the intelligentsia – we should be thinking now of small concentrations of educated people in a few centres such as Constantinople, Antioch or Alexandria – and reminds us that this was a crucial factor in the survival of classical literature. These were after all the people who could afford to have books copied, and in a world in which the classics were becoming increasingly alien and remote there was little scope for a popular market. The nearest thing to widespread demand was presumably whatever was regularly required by the elementary school teachers, which can hardly have amounted to much beyond a few extracts from Homer. Secondary schools would need more texts, but they must have been a good deal more thinly spread than the elementary schools, and even before the 'dark age' from the mid-seventh to the mid-ninth century the overall numbers of classical books in circulation must have been pitifully small by comparison with, say, the second century A.D.[1]

The abstruseness of some texts no doubt contributed to their dwindling popularity: the lyric poets, for example, whose work had formerly had a place in the school curriculum, must have seemed increasingly obscure and irrelevant; only Pindar's *Epinicians* passed into the tradition. Many long works suffered because once excerpts or epitomes had been made there was less demand for the original versions: we can see this happening in the case of Books 6–18 of Polybius. But chance must very often have been the decisive factor as soon as the extant numbers of any work had become very small. All kinds of hazard threatened survival: loss or decay through neglect, destruction by fire, particularly during the upheavals of wartime, as when the Crusaders sacked Constantinople in 1204. Often we can tell from lacunae in our existing texts, the beginning of Aeschylus' *Choephori* for instance, that part of a book – a leaf or a whole quire – must have become accidentally detached and lost. And the other side of the coin, the recovery of rare works, must have been a matter of chance too, in each of the periods when scholars deliberately searched out classical texts and had them recopied: in the ninth century, at the end of the thirteenth century, and again, with the impetus now coming from Italy, in the fifteenth. So the *Hecale* of Callimachus probably survived until the Fourth Crusade but then disappeared, whereas a happy accident preserved Aristophanes' *Thesmophoriazusae* in a single copy.

The fact that revivals of serious interest in classical literature and learning were possible at all suggests that there was never a complete break in continuity.[2] Even in the dark age, when scholarship was dead and higher education

---

[1] Wilson (1975) 4–8.
[2] Irigoin (1962).

had lapsed, the pattern of secondary education seems to have persisted: at least the curriculum of the ninth and tenth centuries (so far as it can be reconstructed) did not differ significantly from that of the sixth and seventh, and the most natural explanation is that it continued in being throughout the period. The function of the schools was essentially to train future civil servants,[1] who were needed all the time in the Byzantine administration, whatever the intellectual climate. But if the movement inspired by Leo the Philosopher and Photius in the ninth century had not come when it did the loss of Greek literature would undoubtedly have been much greater. During the eighth century a new kind of script, minuscule, had established itself for book texts in place of the capitals which had been used since the earliest times. Once this became standard, as it very rapidly did (it was quicker to write and took up less space), texts written in the old script must have looked unfamiliar and therefore have had less chance of being preserved; and since it was expensive to have a transliteration made no one would order new copies of works that were not of special interest to him. So the 'second Hellenism' (ὁ δεύτερος ἑλληνισμός) of the ninth century was the most crucial event for the survival of Greek texts.[2]

Comparatively little has been lost since; the Fourth Crusade wiped out some rare works, but it was followed at the end of the thirteenth century by a revival of learning, when scholars once more took an interest in recovering old texts.[3] The impetus of this second 'renaissance' had not completely faded when a demand for Greek books began to come from the West. By one of the more fortunate accidents of history a very large number of the Greek texts available in Constantinople had already found their way to Italy before the Turkish conquest in 1453, a virtual guarantee that they would ultimately reach the safety of print.

[1] Lemerle (1969).
[2] See Lemerle (1971) *passim*; Reynolds–Wilson (1974) 51–8, 222.
[3] Browning (1960).

2

HOMER

I. THE POET AND THE ORAL TRADITION

What would the world be like if the *Iliad* and *Odyssey* had utterly perished, or been preserved only in fragments? The question hardly bears thinking about. Yet only a fraction of Greek tragedy has survived – why then are we so fortunate in the case of Homer, who lived and worked some three hundred years earlier than the great tragedians, long before the era of libraries and a developed book-trade, probably even before writing itself was seriously applied in Greece to the composing and recording of works of literature? The main reason is that Homer was from the beginning the most admired poet of Hellenic and Hellenized antiquity, and remained so until near its end. He seemed to embody the spirit of an age of heroes, yet never looked old-fashioned like Aeschylus or morally dubious like Euripides. Learning his poetry by heart was an essential part of ordinary education, and that, more than anything, is what saved it from fragmentation and decay in the first centuries after his death. Once consigned to writing, the text gradually achieved a standard form. The written versions ran wild at first, but were slowly reduced to order by scholars and librarians in Athens, Alexandria and Pergamum from the fifth to the second centuries B.C.[1] For hundreds of years even after that, as is shown by the ruins of Graeco-Roman settlements along the Nile, on the dry escarpments where papyrus books happen to survive, the *Iliad* and *Odyssey* were still widely read, more popular even than the lowbrow and more modern works of Menander. Many of the papyrus fragments of Homer come from school copies, but many are from finely-written rolls that were the treasured possession of educated men. Six or seven hundred years before, closer to the time when the poems were made, things were not very different. Even the philosophers Plato and Aristotle dropped quotations from Homer into their lectures and treatises, perpetuating (and in Plato's case also criticizing) the traditional idea of him as fountain-head of wisdom and expert on such diverse matters as medicine, military affairs and popular morality. If their quotations were not always quite accurate, that was

[1] Mazon (1948) 7–38; J. A. Davison in Wace and Stubbings (1962) 221–5; Kirk (1962) ch. 14.

not because the epics were obsolescent or no reasonable texts available. Rather they were too available for their own good; one carried much of the text in one's head and did not bother to unwind the awkward papyrus volumes to check a reference or an exact context.

This orality of Homer is of prime importance not only as a factor in the transmission and survival of his work but also in determining its true quality. For it is imperative to understand about the *Iliad* and *Odyssey* that they were composed wholly or substantially without the help of writing, by a poet or poets who were effectively illiterate, and for audiences that could not (or at least for literary purposes did not) read. So much can be discovered simply on internal evidence from the style of the poems, and in particular from their dependence on a great mass of standardized phrases or 'formulas' that could be fitted together to cover many of the common actions and events of heroic experience. Both the broad scope of this coverage and its surprising economy (for there was usually just one phrase for the expression of a single idea within the limits of a given portion of the hexameter verse) are proof that Homer made use of a *traditional* diction, evolved over several generations by a whole sequence of singers. In other words, his was a special kind and degree of what most poets employ, an artificial – because a poetical – language. His verses were sung, with some help from the lyre, and as an *aoidos* or singer he had to be able to produce them fluently – not exactly spontaneously, but by a kind of instinctive yet controlled release of phrases, verses and ideas that he had absorbed from other singers and made part of his own artistic personality. 'Memorizing' and 'improvising' are misleading, if much-used, terms for what he and the other heroic singers did, although his activity entailed elements of both. For the oral poet has heard many songs in his time; he assimilates their form and substance and much of their exact expression, adjusting them continuously to his own special repertory of favourite plots, phrases and motifs. When he sings a song he has heard before, it tends to emerge always slightly differently, stamped with his immediate range of theme and vocabulary, lengthened or shortened or otherwise varied according to audience and circumstance, as well (of course) as to his personal capacities, ambitions and inclinations.

The consequence is that each singer was at the same time a representative of the tradition of heroic poetry – and therefore a transmitter – and a unique shaper of the songs, language and ideas he had acquired from the tradition – and therefore an innovator. Many singers must have been less than brilliant, and their innovations would be neutral at best; at worst they would tend to corrupt the songs learned from others, either by truncating and deforming them or by relatively tasteless and incompetent elaboration. Other singers would be able to combine and extend their acquired materials in ways that amounted to important new creation. Homer must have been one of these; and yet *his* mode of creation obviously went far beyond what was normal, or ordinary. It was, in a valid sense, unique.

This can be clearly demonstrated in at least one respect. For oral poetry works fairly strictly within certain functional limitations, and one of these is length – a limitation imposed by what an audience can reasonably absorb and enjoy on a single occasion. Most oral heroic poems could surely be heard in an afternoon or evening, or part of one. The singers Phemius and Demodocus who are shown in action in the *Odyssey* sing songs that occupy some, but only some, of the time after the evening meal. We may guess that most ordinary songs varied from about a hundred verses (the length of the self-contained and apparently unabbreviated song about the unfortunate love-affair of Ares and Aphrodite that is placed in the mouth of Demodocus in *Odyssey* 8) to about five or six hundred verses – the extent, say, of many of the twenty-four books into which each great epic is divided. This was something like the norm of length, determined by what an audience would tolerate and a singer could perform. Now clearly each of the great Homeric epics vastly exceeds this norm: by a factor of something approaching twenty-four, if it is indeed the case that many of their single books approximate to the functional length. Therefore Homer (if he may be allowed for the time being to be the indisputable composer of both) was an absolutely *abnormal* oral poet. We know of none other like him. Even his imitators in the post-oral period, for instance the almost unknown composers of the 'Epic Cycle' who wrote poems designed to fill the gaps or exploit the omissions of Homer's narration of the war against Troy and its aftermath, operated on a far smaller scale. As for possible predecessors, we know of none by name or repute. At the same time it is certain that many predecessors existed, precisely the founders and developers of the oral heroic tradition; and we have no reason to suspect any of them of inordinate scale or ambition. There is every likelihood that the *Iliad* was the first very long, or monumental, poem and the *Odyssey* the second. The *Iliad*, then, would be Homer's own invention and conception, and in elaborating and agglomerating many of the ordinary songs from his repertoire and making them into a unified whole he would have been exemplifying a kind of monumental aspiration that seems to have been in the air in the eighth century B.C., and was paralleled in the appearance at precisely that period of colossal temples and enormous funerary vases. As for his audiences, they would just have had to tolerate the inconvenience of several performances in sequence, and would perhaps be most likely to do so in response to a unique reputation and genius – as much as through the provision of some specially suitable occasion like a religious festival, as has often been supposed.

Virtually all the lesser hexameter poetry vanished into thin air, destroyed in different ways by mediocrity and by literacy. Everything that was not an *Iliad* or *Odyssey* must have seemed, by comparison, both brash and thin. It was both the special *réclame* of the two great epics and their persistent orality that probably maintained them until they were first written out in a complete form (although no doubt with many inaccuracies) for the purposes of the 'rhapsodic' contests that became popular as part of the Panathenaic Games in the sixth century B.C. Yet one of the curious things about Homer is his appearance on the scene just at the end of the oral period – at the exact epoch in which writing, through the introduction from the Levant of a practicable alphabetic system in the ninth or early eighth century B.C., began to spread through Greece. The earliest alphabetic inscriptions to be found there (as distinct from the vague and cumbrous syllabic documents of the Mycenaean age) date from shortly after 750 B.C. and are both brief and informal.[1] A verse or two of poetry could be scratched or painted on a perfume-pot or drinking-cup, but it is improbable that writing was used for the recording, let alone the composing, of anything resembling continuous literature until almost a century of further development both of the script itself and of the form and material of books. The first distinguishable figure of the era of literacy is Archilochus, the warrior-poet of Paros and Thasos, who referred to an eclipse of the sun in 648 B.C. and certainly composed his poems in writing, replete though they still were with the diction of the old epic.[2]

It is tempting to wonder whether Homer was able to assemble his complicated and monumental poems simply because of the recent availability of writing. The idea cannot be excluded that he somehow made use of written notes or written lists of themes and episodes. Yet it would be surprising if the new technique were to be applied so quickly as an essential element of such a massive undertaking. Scholars differ about this. Those who feel that Homer must have been literate in some sense (if only by dictating to a literate assistant) are motivated by their conviction that such long and subtle poems could not be composed by heart and ear alone. Close examination of the techniques of oral diction and analogous thematic construction suggests that their incredulity could be misplaced. But in any event there are important considerations of a different kind that are regularly overlooked. The primary one seems to be this: that Greece acquired a fully practicable writing-system uniquely late in its cultural development. Admittedly Egypt and Mesopotamia were technically quite advanced when they developed the art of writing ages before, back in the third millennium B.C. But the Achaean kingdoms of the second millennium, if they lagged behind in engineering and building (through the accidents of geography for the most part), were little less sophisticated in most other cultural matters than their Near-Eastern contemporaries and neighbours. In politics and religion, indeed, they clearly outstripped them. Yet they still lacked a script suitable for literature;

[1] Heubeck (1979) 109ff.; Kirk (1962) 69f.
[2] Kirk (1976) 197–9.

the Linear B syllabary was evidently confined to basic documentary uses, whereas cuneiform and hieroglyphs had long been used for historical, religious and even purely artistic literature.

In many respects, obviously, this strange backwardness of the Greeks over writing, their insistence on clinging to the worst available system – and then dropping it without immediate replacement – was disadvantageous to them. It must have been largely responsible, for example, for their historical naivety down to the time of Thucydides. In respect of poetry, however, it had some paradoxical merits. For the oral tradition (and such traditions are normally killed off by widespread literacy) continued and expanded far beyond the stage at which the requirements of either village or baronial entertainment might still be quite modest. Admittedly the heroic tradition (already well established, in all probability, in the late Bronze Age) ran into the 'Dark Age' that followed the Mycenaean collapse, but it was nevertheless still going strong in the new expansionist era of the tenth, ninth and eighth centuries B.C. – the era of colonizing and of political, social and economic stabilization. How far the range and techniques of oral poetry benefited is a matter for speculation. It is a likely guess that they did so considerably, and that the heroic poetry of the eleventh century (for example) had been much simpler, and in particular consisted for the most part of short sentences confined, as in other oral cultures, to the whole verse. If so, then the 'Dark Age' may not have seriously inhibited the development of relatively sophisticated techniques, like that of the expanded simile, in traditional poetry.

Even the creation of the monumental poem, more or less without warning, was now made possible. What had hitherto kept heroic poems short had presumably been not one but two main causes: not only function but also tradition itself. The functional desirability of shorter poems still applied, but tradition had already been broken in many important aspects of the cultural environment. Oral poetry originates, and is most conservatively maintained, in a traditional society – but Greek society in the eighth century B.C. was no longer that. Economic change, colonizing and exploration, the growth of urban life and the decline of kingship: these and other factors must have seriously disrupted a traditional way of life that had persisted (with some interruption at the end of the Bronze and beginning of the Iron Age) for many centuries. Largely through the failure to develop the technique of writing, traditional poetical methods survived into an age when traditional restraints on the scope and form of oral verse had virtually disappeared.

Thus the monumental epic was made feasible through a spirit of cultural experimentation that was still compelled to operate within the limits of non-literacy. In an important sense, therefore, the alphabet and Homer are likely to have been not so much cause and effect as parallel products of the new expansionism. A generation or so later the impulse had gone. Writing had spread too far for the creative oral genius to flourish much longer; one result was the derivative Cyclic poems and the *Homeric Hymns* (on which see pp. 110ff.), even the earliest and best of which, like the *Hymn to Demeter* or the *Hymn to Apollo*, show signs of self-consciousness and laboured imitation. The eighth century B.C. was exactly the period during which conditions were best for the production of a monumental epic; and that is the century to which the *Iliad* and *Odyssey* – the former near its middle, the latter near its end – most probably belong.[1]

How can one be so confident over this question of chronology? There is little enough help to be had from the ancient biographical tradition itself. The Greeks remained excessively vague about the person of Homer. Admittedly Herodotus got his date roughly right, for he placed Homer and Hesiod not more than ten generations before his own time, his source presumably being some genealogical tradition; yet we cannot expect too much accuracy from people who, even after Herodotus, persisted in ascribing the poet's birth to a river-nymph.[2] One consoling feature is that there existed in the Ionian island of Chios a guild of rhapsodes, or professional reciters, who called themselves the Homeridae or 'Descendants of Homer' and can be traced back into the sixth and perhaps even the seventh century B.C.[3] They failed to convince their contemporaries either that Homer was certainly a Chiote or that they had special rights to the correct text of his poems. Yet the claims of Chios over most of its ancient competitors are considerable, and the Homerids were perhaps not so much fraudulent as naive in thinking they could continue to control an oral tradition in an age of literacy. In any event Homer must have lived before the mid-seventh century, when we find unmistakable allusions in Callinus, Semonides and the *Hymn to Apollo* and when the spread of writing was putting an end to oral poetry as a living tradition.[4] At the other end of the scale he must have worked after the date of the Trojan War that provided his subject, and that took place, in one form or another, in the thirteenth century B.C.

The earliest and latest conceivable dates for Homer are, say, 1200 and 650 B.C., but several factors combine to suggest a date closer to the end than to the beginning or even the middle of this long period: the lifetime of Hesiod, for instance, who is probably later than Homer but not by much, and who seems to fit best, by other criteria, into the early seventh century. More specific indicators are the objects, practices and beliefs described in the Homeric poems themselves. Admittedly the poems are an artificial amalgam, both in language and in cultural content, of elements derived from different periods: from the poet's own time, from that of his closer predecessors in the oral tradition, and indeed from all the

---

[1] Kirk (1962) 282–7.   [2] Herodotus 2.53; *Certamen* 10.
[3] Pindar *Nem.* 2.1f., with scholium; Kirk (1962) 272 and (1976) 140f.; Wade-Gery (1952) 19–21.   [4] Kirk (1962) 283; Mazon (1948) 264.

centuries back (in theory at least) to the Trojan War itself. If we can identify some of the latest of these elements then we have an approximate lower limit for the composition of the poems – provided always that the elements are integral and not later accretions. A few are probably datable after about 900 B.C.: the pair of throwing-spears as standard armament (conflated in the *Iliad* with the single Mycenaean thrusting-spear), the use of large tripod-cauldrons (described among the Phaeacians' gifts to Odysseus), Phoenician ships trading widely in the Aegean (in the *Odyssey* again, prominently in Odysseus' false tales and Eumaeus' account of his childhood). Still fewer elements point to the eighth century, including perhaps the occasional description of what amounts to 'hoplite tactics', that is, fighting in close-packed ranks as opposed to the heroic system of duel and free-for-all. One or two objects, especially in the *Odyssey*, can be paralleled by archaeological finds from the early seventh century and not from the eighth: for example the gorgon-head as decorative motif. All this suggests about 700 B.C., or conceivably just a decade or two later for the *Odyssey*, as *terminus ante quem*. The development of language points in the same direction; for example the *w*-sound represented by the old letter digamma had disappeared from spoken Ionic Greek by the seventh century but was still observed more often than not by the Homeric singers. This is a precarious criterion, admittedly, for an oral tradition; so is the appearance on vases of figure-scenes apparently derived from one or other of the poems – they occur increasingly from about 675 B.C. onward, but that could be the result of new artistic fashion as much as of the spread of the Homeric epics.

Only a handful of passages prevent one from arguing Homer back into the late ninth century rather than the middle to late eighth; but those passages look organic, and in any event that would be the furthest one could reasonably go. Naturally, since his poetry was largely traditional, it contained elements that were created long before that: archaic phraseology (βοὴν ἀγαθός 'good at the war-cry', ἀνὰ πτολέμοιο γεφύρας 'along the bridges of war', ἐν νυκτὸς ἀμολγῷι 'in the milking-time of night'), archaic names of people and places, archaic objects (silver-studded swords, a boar's-tusk helmet – this in an episode developed relatively late, the night-expedition of *Iliad* 10).[1] Indeed a fair amount of both the incident and the expression of each poem could be derived from centuries before Homer's own time. Parts could go back close to the time of the Trojan War itself, and fragments to an even earlier period of the late Bronze Age. A recent linguistic argument suggests that the Homeric modes of separating adverbial and prepositional elements that were later combined into compound verbs belong to a stage of language anterior to that represented in the Linear B tablets.[2] If so, that would take elements of Homer's language back

---

[1] Swords, e.g. *Il.* 2.45, 14.405; helmet, *Il.* 10.261–71.
[2] Horrocks (1980) 148–63.

more than 500 years before his time – not impossible in an oral tradition, but unlikely for more than sporadic relics of morphology or syntax. The contribution of, say, the tenth and ninth centuries B.C. remains even more problematical. It was probably considerable, presumably larger than that of the late Mycenaean age. Even so Homer himself, as monumental composer, can plausibly be credited with everything that accompanies great scale. That may include the more highly elaborated similes, much of the more complex (and often more felicitous) language, including the longer and more complicated sentences, and most of the crucial and elaborate episodes: for example the deaths of Patroclus and Hector in the *Iliad* and the careful plotting against the suitors in the *Odyssey*.

Chios, Smyrna, Colophon, Ephesus: the cities that seriously claimed Homer for their own were at least all in Ionia, directly across the Aegean from mainland Greece. Moreover the dialect of the poems is predominantly Ionic (although there is a substratum of Aeolic forms, from the region just to the north of Ionia, that were retained for primarily metrical reasons); and there are a few signs in the *Iliad* of personal knowledge of the country round Troy and of the whole east-Aegean seaboard.[1] That all adds up, at any rate for the *Iliad*, to the conclusion that Homer was an Ionian singer, that he lived and worked primarily in Ionia. One is reluctant to conclude anything strikingly different for the *Odyssey*. Admittedly its main scene, the island of Ithaca, lies over on the far western side of Greece, and Telemachus' journey takes him down into the southern Peloponnese, still a good way from Ionia and Troy. Yet such geographical details as are provided, for example about the exact position and terrain of Ithaca itself, contain just that mixture of fact, distortion and fancy that we might expect of a tale whose elements had been widely diffused – right across the mainland and to the further side of the Aegean in this case, to be developed and elaborated there by the Ionian school of singers.[2] Moreover the dialect of the poem is no less strongly Ionic in colouring than that of the *Iliad*. That might conceivably be the result of literary convention, which ensured that all subsequent epics should approximate to the dialect of Homer; but such a convention is unlikely to have worked so strongly within the oral period itself.

The regional affiliations of the two poems raise directly at last the question of the specific authorship of the *Iliad* and *Odyssey*, one that has proved notoriously beguiling and intractable over the ages – although it is hardly one of the more productive questions either about the poems or about Homer, whose biography remains remarkably bare in any event. Even the purely poetical questions that might be thought to depend on authorship can be almost as well answered by the assumption of earlier and later stages in the working life of a single main

---

[1] *Il.* 2.144ff., 459ff., 9.5, 13.12f.; cf. Kirk (1962) 272f.
[2] E.g. *Od.* 9.21–7, 13.344–51.

composer as by that of separate composers. At least it seems probable that the earlier poem was known to the composer of the later one.

More interesting are the differences between the poems themselves, whatever their external implications. The first task is to distinguish differences that could be caused merely by different subjects. The predominantly martial poem will obviously be rich in martial vocabulary and, in spite of occasional scenes by the ships or in Troy, short of domestic language. The *Odyssey*, on the other hand, being a combination of picaresque or fantastic adventure with the peacetime life of Ithaca, and to a lesser extent of Pylos and Sparta, will be short of martial language and have much more about travelling, storms at sea, palace life and so on. Actually the language, which in broad terms is remarkably consistent between the two poems, varies in certain detailed respects quite independently of subject, and this may be significant. The *Odyssey* has a number of exclusive formulas, among them the following: κακὰ βυσσοδομεύων 'pondering evils', τετληότι θυμῶι 'with steadfast spirit', μεταλλῆσαι καὶ ἐρέσθαι 'to question and ask', κατεκλάσθη φίλον ἦτορ 'dear heart was broken', δύσετό τ' ἠέλιος σκιόωντό τε πᾶσαι ἀγυιαί 'the sun set and shadowed were all the streets'. All these occur five times or more. The last instance, a whole verse, is admittedly inappropriate to all except the Troy-scenes of the *Iliad*, but the rest are of general application. One can add the whole verses that occur frequently in the *Odyssey* but only rarely in the *Iliad* – and then in parts (like Book 24) that are least traditional and show some degree of relatively late development: ἀλλ' ἄγε μοι τόδ' ἔειπὲ καὶ ἀτρεκέως κατάλεξον 'but come, tell me this and truthfully declare it' (thirteen uses against four) and the famous ἦμος δ' ἠριγένεια φάνη ῥοδοδάκτυλος Ἠώς 'when early-born rosy-fingered Dawn appeared' (twenty uses against two). Conversely the following among others are exclusive to the *Iliad*: ἐρεβεννὴ νύξ 'dark night', μοῖρα κραταίη 'mighty destiny', ὄσσε κάλυψε 'covered his eyes', and (only four times, but useful as one might think for describing Odysseus) φρεσὶ πευκαλίμηισι 'with subtle mind'. As expected, there are fewer exclusive general phrases in the earlier and therefore imitable poem, but some exclusive Iliadic single words, even though subject-conditioned in varying degrees, are striking: χραισμεῖν 'to help' (19 times), λοιγός, λοίγιος 'destruction, destructive' (25 times), κλόνος 'rout' (28 times), ἕλκος 'wound' (22 times). The *Odyssey* can counter with δέσποινα 'mistress' (10 times) as its most strikingly exclusive word – again subject-conditioned to some extent, but a conspicuous absentee from the *Iliad* none the less.

Changes in vocabulary, especially in formular vocabulary, are more suggestive in an oral than in a literate context. They tend to imply a different repertoire, and hence a different singer or even a different regional tradition. This last possibility cannot apply in the Homeric case; the similarities and interdependence of the two poems are too conspicuous for that. Different singers are a stronger possibility, and nothing in particular, except perhaps the phenomenon of two such great poets so close together, excludes it. Yet we still cannot over-look 'Longinus'' conception of the *Odyssey* as the work of Homer's old age (*Subl.* 9.13), for the same singer can develop or curtail his formular apparatus to a limited extent over a period of years, not least with poems of differing tone or genre.

In general the language and style of the two poems are not dissimilar. It is important to recognize, nevertheless, that broad stylistic differences do exist and may be significant. They can be summed up as amounting to a decline in vigour of expression in the later poem – again, that is not inconsistent with 'Longinus'' judgement. Even more significant, perhaps, is what appears to be a subtle but important alteration in the view taken of the gods: not so much that their messenger is Iris in the *Iliad*, Hermes in the *Odyssey* (although the com-pleteness of that change is odd in itself) as that the gods of the later poem care for overall justice among mortals and not simply for the preservation of heroic decorum and the natural order as in the *Iliad*. The Zeus of the *Odyssey* begins (1.28–47) by expressing concern because men blame the gods for evil, whereas it is really their own fault, and he is periodically envisaged as sending blessings on the virtuous and punishment on sinners. The seeds of that attitude are admittedly present in the *Iliad*, but in the later poem they have grown into something more like a developed theology.[1] Again, the subject of the *Odyssey* might be held to lead more naturally to moral reflection, what with the wicked suitors and the paradigm of Orestes as avenger. Yet on the whole it seems reasonable to conclude that the theological presuppositions of the *Odyssey* are indeed the more developed, and imply a rather more sophisticated stage of the whole oral heroic tradition. Its language, even apart from formular vocabulary, is consistent with that, being slightly freer of archaisms and more generous with developed forms from the era of monumental composition itself. Other differences, especially in the redeployment, with slight variation, of basic characters and themes, will emerge in the pages that follow. On the specific question of authorship the most probable conclusion is perhaps that the *Odyssey* is the product of a separate main composer, although one cannot be certain that it is not indeed the work of 'Homer's' old age. In any case his name will con-tinue to be used in the following pages for the monumental composer of each epic. But what really matters is that two poems of genius, so complementary and yet so distinct, appeared in the eastern half of Greece at the very dawn of the full historical age, to impose their stamp on almost every aspect of culture in the splendid civilization that followed.

[1] Lloyd-Jones (1971) ch. 2.

2. THE *ILIAD*

This grand and complex composition, surely the greatest of all epics, can be treated by the critic on many levels. Present readers will probably have read much of the poem for themselves, so that a mere paraphrase would be otiose. Yet in the end it has seemed best to base the discussion on a critical survey of the poem's main themes, book by book, and on translated passages chosen to illustrate the interlocking aspects of action and language. For the basic structure of the *Iliad*, though straightforward in itself, is often obscured by massive elaborations and digressions; and one must experience the whole in due order if the resulting impression is to be unified and monumental rather than merely chaotic. In the pages that follow the aim is gradually to build up a view not only of the narrative plan and its implications but also of the qualities of expression, style and feeling on which any refined appreciation of the poem must depend.

The epic opens with a short invocation to the Muse to sing of the 'wrath of Achilles'. That, with its immediate consequences, is to be the central narrative theme, although in different ways the entire *geste* of Troy, and the tensions inherent in the heroic code itself, are no less important. Prince Achilles' wrath is provoked by his quarrel with Agamemnon, leader of the Achaean – the Greek – forces encamped before Troy. Indirectly it is started by the god Apollo; he has sent a plague on the besieging army because, as the seer Calchas reveals, Agamemnon refuses to restore his prize of war, the girl Chryseis, to her father Chryses who is Apollo's priest. Already the poem has moved from its lapidary prologue to the heart of a tense debate among the Achaean leaders; already it displays the scale and detail of a work that is to be uniquely long and ambitious. Agamemnon is regally annoyed and insults first Calchas and then, more dangerously, Achilles who comes to the seer's defence. Achilles replies in vicious terms that challenge the honour and authority of the king to whom the expeditionary force has sworn allegiance – both as elder brother of Menelaus and so responsible for avenging Helen's abduction by the Trojan prince Paris, and as the uniquely powerful ruler of 'Mycenae of much gold'. In his disaffected words to Agamemnon Achilles already reveals the envy and discontent that were implicit not only in his particular role but also in the whole heroic scale of values:

'Yet my prize never equals yours, whenever the Achaeans sack a populous city belonging to the Trojans. It is my hands that perform the greater part of grievous fighting, but if ever a share-out is made then your prize is much greater, and I have to be content with something small to rejoice in when I return to the ships, exhausted though I am by fighting. But now I shall go back to Phthia, since it is obviously better by far to return home with my curved ships. I do not propose to win affluence and riches for you, here, while I myself suffer dishonour!' Agamemnon, lord of men, answered him: 'Be off, then, if that is your heart's wish. I do not ask you to stay for my sake; I have others to pay me honour, counsellor Zeus most of all. Of all the god-reared kings you are the most hateful to me; quarrelling, wars and battles are what you always like. Strong as you may be, it is a god, I imagine, that has made you so. Be off with your ships and comrades and rule over the Myrmidons; I care nothing for you, and do not mind if you *are* in a rage. But I give you this warning: since Phoebus Apollo wants to take my Chryseis, I shall send her back with my ships and comrades; but I shall go in person to your hut and fetch fair-cheeked Briseis, *your* prize, so that you can appreciate to the full how much more powerful I am than you – and anyone else may recoil from claiming to be my equal, and setting himself up against me as my peer!' These were his words, and grief came upon Achilles son of Peleus, and inside his shaggy chest his heart debated two separate courses; whether to draw the sharp sword from his thigh and stir up the others and kill the son of Atreus, or to put a stop to his rage and restrain his anger. While he pondered this in his heart and mind, and was drawing the great sword from its scabbard, Athena came from the sky; for white-elbowed goddess Hera despatched her, because she loved and cared for both men alike in her heart. And Athena stood behind Peleus' son and seized him by his brown hair, appearing to him alone. None of the others saw her, but Achilles was amazed, and turning round he instantly recognized Pallas Athena, and her eyes looked terrible to him...(1.163–200)

Agamemnon is to display a curious lack of confidence later in the poem, but here he is dangerously assertive of his rights and the honour due to him. He has been accepted by all the others, for the purposes of the expedition at least, as supreme *basileus* or king, and Achilles had better not go back on that. For a *basileus* derives his authority direct from Zeus – Zeus who asserts his own power over the other gods by right of ancestry and sheer strength and who supports an analogous but infinitely lesser power in human 'Zeus-reared kings'. The concept is ultimately derived from ancient Mesopotamia, where kingship was 'lowered from heaven' and devolved on the first generation of priest-kings on earth. Its logic is far from clear in the derivative and slightly confused Greek version, but the existence of a kind of divine right of kings is most plainly expressed in Book 2, where Agamemnon's sceptre, the symbol of kingly office (and, at the king's will, of a hero's right to speak in assembly), is described as having been made by the smith-god Hephaestus for Zeus, who gave it to the messenger-god Hermes to pass on to Pelops of Argos; and from Pelops it descended to his Argive successors, Atreus, Thyestes and then Agamemnon himself, who was also king of Mycenae (2.100–8).

The gods' involvement in the human quarrel is confirmed by the intervention of Athena. Naturally Achilles could not be allowed to kill the great king. That would have led to anarchy, and in any case the traditional tale made it plain that Agamemnon lived to sack Troy and be murdered on his return home by

Clytemnestra. Equally naturally, it is a god that has to prevent the chaotic deed – although as it happens Athena acts not as the agent of her father Zeus protecting the institution of kingship, but rather as the dedicated supporter of the Achaean army and implacable enemy of Paris (who had earlier offended her by his famous Judgement) and the other Trojans. No other passage in the *Iliad* describes a theophany so starkly. Usually the gods, when they intervene in human affairs, do so either invisibly or disguised as humans. Here Athena comes as a goddess, but acts with human tangibility by pulling Achilles' hair; she is invisible to the others but concretely and frighteningly deterrent to Achilles himself (1.193–200). And yet her intervention, although striking, is not especially stressed. It is just one of many ways (decisions taken in divine assembly on Olympus being the commonest) in which the singers of the Homeric tradition express the extreme interest they envisage the gods as taking in human affairs.

Chryseis is escorted back to her father by ship – the description is an exceptionally conventional one, formular almost to the point of staleness – and Apollo calls off the plague. Agamemnon reacts by depriving Achilles of Briseis, although he does so by sending heralds to fetch her and not, as he had threatened, in person. Achilles prays for revenge to his mother, the sea-goddess Thetis; she appears before him on the sea-shore in another remarkable epiphany and promises to try and persuade Zeus to favour the Trojans, and so make Achilles' withdrawal from the fighting all the more disastrous for Agamemnon. Her supplication of Zeus, his solemn oath of approval as he nods his great brow and shakes Olympus, and Hera's rage as she spies on the scene and guesses what it portends for the Achaeans, bring this exceptionally varied and dramatic book to a close.

At the beginning of the second book Zeus decides to send a misleading dream to Agamemnon, promising him imminent victory. Before joining battle the king has the bizarre idea of testing morale by proposing that his troops give up and go home – which they instantly try to do, being restrained with the greatest difficulty by Odysseus and the other leaders. No wonder the bitter and unheroic Thersites, 'the ugliest man to come to Troy', rails against authority; but the Achaeans only laugh delightedly as Odysseus lays into him with his staff – weakness and deformity were proper causes for heroic amusement, which is partly why the gods themselves had laughed at 1.599f. as they watched the crippled Hephaestus hobbling around in emulation of young Hebe or Ganymede. A great march-out from the naval camp is made both vivid and portentous by a string of no less than six successive similes that illustrate the gleam of weapons, the noise of thundering feet and hooves, the size of the Achaean army and the proficiency of its leaders (2.455–83). The march-out is also the pretext for a long poetical muster of contingents from the different regions of Greece – the 'Catalogue of Ships', so called by ancient scholars, which is seemingly based on an old list of the naval forces that assembled at Aulis at the start of the campaign and carefully records how many ships each leader had with him. This Achaean catalogue fills no fewer than two hundred and sixty-six verses (thereby revealing a good deal about the capacity of oral audiences) and is followed by a list of Trojan allies that is much shorter – a relief in a way, for it also betrays a certain jejune quality in both artistic and historical terms.

The flavour of the Achaean catalogue, with its careful recording of sometimes obscure settlements (which are probably never fictitious, however) and its imperfect fit here and there with the rest of the poem, is given by the description of Agamemnon's contingent centred on Mycenae:[1]

> Those who possessed Mykenai the well-built town
> and rich Korinthos and well-built Kleonai
> and who dwelt in Orneai and lovely Araithurea
> and Sikyon, where Adrastos was once king,
> and those who possessed Hyperesia and steep Gonoessa
> and Pellene, and who dwelt round Aigion
> and all along Aigialos and around broad Helike –
> of their hundred ships Agamemnon was commander,
> son of Atreus. With him by far the most numerous and best
> host followed; and among them he himself had donned flashing armour,
> exulting, and stood out among all the heroes
> because he was best and led by far the most numerous host. (2. 569–80)

The plain and factual, if slightly repetitious, style is relieved by the euphony of the place-names themselves. Their epithets sometimes seem derived from a different poetical tradition from that of the main poem, and a similar independence may account for the eulogy of Agamemnon, which is in sharp contrast with the ambivalent picture of him elsewhere as indecisive, torn by doubt, an erratic warrior. At least this extract deals with an important commander and some well-known cities; others, for example those listing the Thessalian contingents, contain few familiar names or none at all. And yet they have their own fascination, not only an antiquarian one but also through the impression they give of an utterly diverse yet ultimately Panhellenic army.

Book 2 ends with the list of Trojan allies, and Book 3 resumes the general description of the approaching armies. The book-division, incidentally, is fairly typical – organic in a way, a convenient enough place for a mild break, but no necessary indication that Homer himself composed in these book-units, or that they were not systematized and extended to twenty-four by later scholars

---

[1] Here and elsewhere, where it seems appropriate, I have varied the translation by dividing it into verse-lengths corresponding closely with the Greek, and also retained a closer transliteration of proper names.

and librarians. The expected clash of armies does not, however, take place. It is prevented when Paris (whose other name in the poem is Alexandros) runs ahead of the Trojans and issues a challenge to single combat. The challenge is instantly accepted by Menelaus, the prince whose wife Paris had enticed away. Helen herself joins King Priam and the Trojan elders on the wall above the Scaean gate of the city to watch the ensuing duel. The old men comment on her almost divine beauty, and the king asks her to identify for him some prominent Achaeans – a request notoriously more apt to the first than to the tenth year of fighting, but one that can be accepted in the loose framework of an ambitiously compendious poem. He begins by enquiring about Agamemnon himself:

'Come here, dear child, and sit by me, so that you can see your former husband and your relations by marriage and your friends – I don't blame you, but rather the gods, for bringing grievous war upon me from the Achaeans; and name for me this mighty man – tell me who this Achaean is, so noble and great. Others are taller in stature, but I never yet saw with my eyes anyone so handsome or dignified. He looks like a king.' Helen, divine among women, answered him: 'What reverence and awe I have for you, father-in-law! I wish I had been content to die in dishonour, when once I followed your son here and left my marriage-chamber and relatives and new-born child and delightful friends of my own age. But that did not happen, and I waste away in tears because of it. But I shall tell you what you ask and enquire about. This is the son of Atreus, Agamemnon ruler of broad domains, both good king and strong spearsman, and again, brother-in-law of my bitch-faced self – if these things ever really happened!' (3.162–80)

It is important for the *Iliad* that both Priam and Helen should be sympathetic figures, even though neither can have been entirely so in the ordinary heroic tradition. This passage serves to establish them as civilized and humane, as well as to restore, temporarily, the more imposing aspect of Agamemnon. Some of its plethoric phraseology ('saw with my eyes', 'ask and enquire') literally reproduces the Greek. These are formulas, standardized phrases, in this case probably quite ancient ones deriving from a stage when the diction was not so highly refined as it came to be by Homer's time – although he, of course, still retained much of the traditional language. The concluding phrase, εἴ ποτ' ἔην γε, is also a formula, but a more brilliant one; its literal meaning, 'if I ever was', conveys in so few words the mixture of incredulity and nostalgia with which Helen suddenly sees her own strange circumstances.

In the remainder of the episode known to the ancients as the 'Viewing from the Walls' she identifies for Priam first Odysseus, then Ajax and Idomeneus. Ajax is dismissed in a summary and off-hand way, even though he is an important and striking figure and Priam had specifically asked about him. Perhaps this is a rare piece of psychological subtlety (since Homer normally depicts the heroic character with broader strokes); for Helen seems to become increasingly distracted as she searches the battlefield for her own brothers, the Dioscuri, and concludes that they must either have stayed behind in Greece or be ashamed to appear among the others on account of their sister. But in reality, as the poet comments in a famous couplet, 'the life-giving earth already held them, back in Lacedaemon, in their own dear country' (3.243f.).

Paris and Menelaus now begin their duel in the space left clear for them between the two seated armies. Paris is soon in great danger, but Aphrodite snatches him away and hides him in a thick mist, then sets him down in his bedchamber back in Troy and summons Helen to join him. He is quite beautiful, she tells Helen, as he sits there on the fine bed, as if fresh from a dance rather than from the battlefield. But Helen sees through Aphrodite's disguise – she had taken the shape of Helen's old serving-woman – and accuses her of ruthlessly manipulating her in order to gratify the goddess's own wishes. '*You* go and sit by his side', she says; 'abandon the paths of the gods and never again return with your feet to Olympus, but fuss round him and take care of him till he makes you his wife – or his slave! As for me, I refuse to rush into his bed; it would be shameful, and the women of Troy would reproach me for it later. I have a heap of troubles already in my heart' (406–12). That is too much for a goddess to tolerate, even a Homeric one, and Aphrodite warns Helen not to make of her as violent an enemy as she had formerly been friend and protector. Helen is afraid, and follows meekly as the goddess leads her to make love with her paramour – the scene is a brilliant and extraordinary one, not only for its clarity and concision but also for its violent juxtaposing of love and war, of male voluptuousness and complacency and female indignation and subjection, and for its startling suggestion, more Mesopotamian than typically Greek, of the uses to which gods might put their mortal worshippers.¦

In the fourth book another and less mockable goddess, Athena, descends like a comet to the battlefield and takes the form of a warrior who persuades the archer Pandarus to shoot at Menelaus and so violate the truce made with solemn oaths before the duel. He inflicts a bloody but superficial wound which breaches the agreement and therefore allows the preparations for full-scale fighting to continue. In a formal and rhetorical episode King Agamemnon rallies his contingents and dispenses praise and blame to his princes. Rebuke, even if un-deserved, is part of the heroic posture, but Agamemnon, true to his ambiguous status in the poem, turns out to be unusually bad at it; Diomedes especially has to show great patience with his tactlessness. After all the delays, battle is at last joined. A short generic account of the collision of armies is brought to life by an elaborate simile, and the poet passes to the first of the long series of individual encounters that form the constant background and typical material of the poem:

. . . Then at once came groaning and boast of men
slaying and slain, and the earth ran with blood.
As when winter torrents running down the mountains
throw together their heavy water into a valley bottom
from great springs, within a hollow gorge,
and from far in the mountains a shepherd hears their roaring,
so as they joined battle was their shouting and toil.
Antilochus was first to take a helmeted Trojan warrior,
a good man among the front fighters, Thalysias' son Echepolus.
He got in first with a blow to the ridge of the horse-plumed helm
and pierced his forehead, and the bronze spear-point
penetrated the bone; and darkness covered his eyes
and he toppled like a tower in the strong turmoil.
Powerful Elephenor seized him by the feet when he fell,
Chalcodon's son, leader of the great-hearted Abantes,
and dragged him out from beneath the missiles, keen to hasten
and plunder his armour, but his effort was short-lived;
great-hearted Agenor saw him dragging the body
– saw his flanks showing outside his shield as he bent over –
and struck him with bronze-tipped spear-shaft and loosed his limbs.
So the life-spirit left him, and over him grievous action was wrought
of Trojans and Achaeans. Like wolves
they sprang at each other, and man toppled man. (4.450–72)

The simile of the mountain torrents is typically Homeric in its leisurely development of detail, but also in its subtle complexity. The explicit point of comparison
is sheer noise and confusion; of mass fighting on the one hand, thunderous
water on the other. The roar of the torrent comes from far off in the hills, yet is
heard by a man, a solitary shepherd, who makes a poignant link between the
world of raw nature and that of men but who also leads on ingeniously from
mass fighting to the first individual combat of the poem. Admittedly the
Homeric style only rarely needs such devices; usually it moves from scene to
scene with simple directness; but here the simile serves this special purpose as
well as others. The fight itself contains elements that we shall see to be standard
in such individual encounters, although the elements are almost never used
in exactly the same combination. The mortal blow is traced in detail, the
victim's fall is marked by a striking phrase or simile, he is carefully identified by
patronymic and city. In the present episode there is, as often, a secondary victim
on the other side, and we are told precisely how he made himself vulnerable
and was killed. The sequence is rounded off by a reversion to general
fighting, less abstract than before only in that the Trojans and Achaeans are
now likened to wolves.

The series of individual fights is instantly resumed, first by an encounter whose obscure young victim acquires an anecdotal pathos that renders him temporarily heroic, something more than a routine target for the irresistible Ajax:

> Then Telamonian Ajax struck Anthemion's son,
> handsome young Simoeisios, to whom his mother
> gave birth by the banks of Simoeis as she came down
> from Ida – she had accompanied her parents there to watch over the flocks.
> That was why they called him Simoeisios; but he did not pay back
> to his dear parents the cost of upbringing, but his lifetime was short,
> subdued as he was with the spear by great-hearted Ajax.
> For as he first came on, Ajax struck him in the chest by the right
> breast, and straight through his shoulder the bronze spear
> went, and he fell to the ground in the dust like a poplar
> that grows in a broad water-meadow,
> smooth, but with branches growing out from its top;
> a chariot-maker with shining iron
> has cut it down to bend a wheel-rim for a fine chariot
> and it lies weathering by the river's banks.
> Such was Anthemion's son Simoeisios, slain
> by Ajax of divine ancestry . . . (4.473–89)

Simoeisios' unusual name is explicated in progressive and lingering verses. Not much is disclosed apart from these details of his birth, but they, with the rustic naturalism of his mother's going up into the hill country with the family flocks and the pathetic comment about his frustrated upbringing, make the occasion a touching one. The fight itself is over almost as soon as begun; youngsters like Simoeisios make easy victims for great professionals like Achilles, Hector or Ajax. The wound is simple but immediately fatal, and he falls, not like a tower this time, but with stronger pathos like a tall and elegant tree that takes shape before our eyes in an image that is also a little confused (is it the falling or the fallen tree that matters most?) as detail after detail is added by the singer with effortless but also relentless virtuosity. And so the man-slaying continues, more rapid now, for a further sixty verses to the book's end.

By this point the modern reader is tending to look for relief from the bare fighting, for some further diversification by speeches at least, or by an episode at the ships or in the beleaguered city. He will have to wait until the sixth book for that; meanwhile the fifth opens with Athena inspiring Diomedes to special deeds of valour and destruction, and the whole of this very long book of over nine hundred verses continues to explore the theme of fighting, with only the encounters with gods, Ares and Aphrodite, to provide a lighter tone quite near the end. For the *Iliad* is as much a massive celebration of heroic struggle as anything else; and the delays over opening the battle were not because the poet kept putting off an evil but necessary moment and dwelling on more interesting matters, but in part, at least, to make an appropriately portentous preparation for the central business of warfare.

Diomedes is the dominant figure, but the impression of violent and widespread battle is reinforced by typical encounters between lesser fighters. Here are two of them:

> Meriones slew Phereclus, son of the joiner
> Harmonides, who knew how to make all cunning things
> with his hands; for he was a special favourite of Pallas Athena;
> it was he that made the balanced ships for Alexandros,
> the ones that began the trouble, that were an evil for all the Trojans
> and for himself, since he paid no heed to the divine decrees.
> Meriones pursued and overtook him,
> struck him in the right buttock, and the spear-point
> went right through under the bone and into the bladder;
> and he fell to his knees groaning, and death covered him over.
> Then Meges killed Pedaeus, Antenor's son –
> his bastard, but lady Theano carefully brought him up
> equally with her own dear children to please her husband.
> Phyleus' son, famed with the spear, came close to him
> and struck him with sharp spear on the bone behind the head,
> and the bronze cut through, along by the teeth and under the tongue,
> and he collapsed in the dust, gripping the cold bronze with his teeth. (5.59–75)

Again these two deaths illustrate several of the standard and recurrent devices and motifs of the minor battle poetry: the brief but often poignant biographical detail of the victim or his parents, the graphic and sometimes horrifying description of the wound, the conventional but not entirely monotonous phrases for the death itself. In these two encounters (as indeed in the one that follows) there is an additional motif, for in each case the father surpasses his son in interest – the builder of the fatal ships that carried Paris to Lacedaemon, then Hector's brother Antenor, an important Trojan prince. Pedaeus' stepmother, moreover, is the very Theano that appears as Athena's priestess in Troy in the next book. The audience is pretty well acquainted with heroic genealogy, so an allusive patronymic like 'Phyleus' son' presents no difficulty; it simply adds another piece of information about Meges, not essential but comforting to have, as well as permitting the singer to name him in a different part of the verse. As for the wounds, their description is alarming and heroic, as often, rather than clinically precise, even though in these two cases the anatomical details, including Pedaeus' teeth clenching on the spear-point, are just possible. It is an odd fact that the Cretan princes, of whom Meriones is second to Idomeneus, inflict crueller deaths than almost any other warrior on either side, as upon Phereclus here – something that might reflect the special taste of specifically Cretan poems that were then absorbed into the general heroic repertoire.

Even the war-god Ares, an almost barbaric import who remained an awkward appendage to the Olympian family, is wounded by Diomedes in the end. The wound is healed by Apollo and the blood thickens like curds; undismayed by his degrading position or Zeus's obvious dislike he sits by his father's side exulting, as complacent among the gods as Paris among mortals. So the fifth book ends. The sixth continues with no organic break as the fighting in the plain continues, but Diomedes' *aristeia*, his interval of special glory and invincibility, peters out on a recurring note of mild levity when he challenges the Lycian Glaucus to fight, but then discovers him to be an old family friend. The tale, with its detailed personal reminiscences and its parody of heroic boast and counter-boast, is told at length and may be a version of a once-independent song.

Meanwhile Hector returns to the city to organize prayers to Athena for the hard-pressed Trojans. Most of this sixth book consists of scenes in Troy brought about by this convenient, if slightly improbable, device; first with his mother Hecuba, then with Paris whom Hector rebukes for his slackness, then with Helen to whom he is kind and understanding, and at greatest length with his own wife Andromache. She implores him to be prudent, to play safe, not to risk her and her son as well as himself; Hector replies with full heroic severity, but also with unusual compassion and vivid imagination:

> 'I too am concerned about all this, Andromache; but I am terribly ashamed of what the Trojans and their wives with trailing gowns will think if I skulk like a coward away from the fighting. Moreover my own spirit forbids me to do so, since I have learned to be always valiant and to fight among the first of the Trojans, winning great glory for my father and myself. Well I know in my heart and mind that a day will come when holy Ilios is destroyed, and Priam of the strong spear and all his host. Yet I am not so concerned for the suffering of the Trojans... as I am for you, and the time when one of the bronze-corsleted Achaeans will lead you away in tears, depriving you of the day of freedom; and you will be in Argos, working at the loom under another woman's orders, and carrying water from some spring, some Messeis or Hypereia, much against your will, but strong necessity will lie upon you. And some day someone will say as he sees you weeping, "This is the wife of Hector, who used to be champion among the horse-rearing Trojans when they were fighting around Ilios."...But may the earth be poured over my dead body and conceal me, before I hear your cries as you are dragged away!' (6.441–65, with omissions)

Shortly afterwards compassion is replaced by sheer domestic tenderness, for as Hector stretches out to pick up his baby son Astyanax the child is frightened by his father's flashing helmet and waving plume and leans back into his nurse's bosom, 'and his dear father and lady mother burst out laughing, and at once glorious Hector took the helmet from his head and placed it shining on the ground...' (6.471–3). Stricter heroic standards are restored as Hector prays to

Zeus for the child to grow up to be even better than his father, 'and may he bring back bloody armour after slaying an enemy, and may his mother rejoice in her heart' (480f.). The whole scene is an extraordinary mixture of tragic irony – for the audience knows the child is to be brutally murdered when the Achaeans break into the city – and heroic cruelty and magnanimity. Hector shows no weakening of his resolve, but his words and actions illustrate the terrible confusion at the heart of the heroic ideal: the belief that a warrior's honour is paramount, that wife and even son must be risked for it, even if one recognizes as wrong the public opinion on which heroic honour depends. The moral balance of the whole epic is affected by the deliberate ambiguity and destructive undertones of this unusual scene. The note of domesticity is rarely sounded in this poem; here it is conspicuous, and not only renders Hector himself more solid as a foil for the stronger but harsher Achilles but also emphasizes for the listener the life of the beleaguered city and its impending doom, to give point and poignancy to the battle surging over the plain below.

Until now everything in the poem has been germane to the development of the wrath-plot or the purpose of displaying widespread warfare; moreover, there has been an engrossing variety of episodes, from the quarrel itself to the catalogue and march-out and eventual joining of battle, leading to Hector's brief return to Troy. Through the seventh and eighth books, by contrast, the intensity of poetic imagination and the sense of formal unity both decline. There are magnificent details, even whole scenes, but Book 8 in particular carries the action almost no further and seems to lack purpose, except as mere elaboration. It is true that oral poets are always concerned with that, and the gradual development of a basic narrative is what ultimately led to the great poem we possess. Even Homer, its monumental composer, must occasionally have succumbed to elaboration of a more or less routine kind. Pointless embroideries would usually, no doubt, be censored soon enough – dropped, that is, from the poet's working repertory and excluded from the plan of the larger poem to which that repertory was leading. At any rate the seventh book opens with Athena and Apollo agreeing, untypically, to stop the general fighting by inspiring Hector to issue a challenge to a duel. This has all happened before, or something very like it, in Book 3. The present duel is between different principals – it is Ajax that draws the lot for the privilege of standing up to Hector – and considerably more elaborate than before. No reference is made to its predecessor or its awkward consequence in the treacherous breaking of the earlier truce, an omission curious in itself. Yet it is not inconsistent with a probability that emerges on other grounds: that the second duel is a more detailed and deliberately different elaboration of the first – or of some simpler archetype of both.

The sequence of blow and counter-blow is certainly more ambitious than elsewhere. Hector throws his spear first (by a common Homeric confusion over armament, for the single spear should properly be used for thrusting and not for throwing); it almost but not quite penetrates Ajax's massive and unique shield; Ajax in turn pierces Hector's shield and breast-plate but just fails to touch flesh as Hector swerves aside; they regain their spears and Hector thrusts at Ajax, but once again the great shield frustrates the blow. Again Ajax's spear penetrates, this time to graze Hector's neck – he can nevertheless hurl a huge stone, but Ajax's shield (seven ox-hides thick, tower-like and faced with bronze) once again wards off the missile. Ajax replies with an even bigger stone and lays his opponent flat. Apollo intervenes and sets him on his feet – 'and they would have smitten each other at close quarters with swords had the heralds not come, messengers of Zeus and men, Talthybius and Idaeus, the one Achaean, the other Trojan...' (7.273–6); and in such bland innocuous terms the heralds stop the fight. On what excuse? On the ground that 'night is already coming on; it is good to obey night' (282)! It seems an abrupt and pointless anticlimax, and the exchange of gifts that follows makes the episode resemble even more closely an almost playful encounter like that of Glaucus and Diomedes in Book 6, or an event in a warrior's funeral games like the contest-in-armour in Book 23; which may indeed be where part of the elaboration originated. Admittedly the heralds have a point when they declare that Zeus loves both men; and the poet, of course, loves his plot and cannot have the war brought to a premature end. But he could have arranged things differently and ended the duel in some other way – even the way adopted in Book 3, where the losing party is rescued by a god. It is a role that is hinted at for Apollo, but perhaps at the last moment the poet recoiled from the repetition.

Nothing else in the duel is strikingly unusual. Ajax's impenetrable shield is the decisive factor, but in other important combats, too, the dice are loaded, unfairly by modern standards, against one or other fighter. Yet the dénouement *is* unsatisfactory as it stands, and no amount of stress on the inevitable untidiness of oral poetry (which is particularly prone, and even more so when it is on a monumental scale, to minor inconsistencies) can adequately explain the anomaly. This is not to claim that the episode is an interpolation or post-Homeric addition, or that its inclusion was the responsibility of any but the main poet. Rather it seems to demonstrate that the re-use of standard themes, elaborated or otherwise deliberately varied, can sometimes lead even a great poet into temporary difficulties. Yet there are fine things, too, in this book. Ancient Nestor, survivor of an older generation of heroes, indulges at length in one of his famous reminiscences ('Would that I were young as I was when Pylians and Arcadians fought by swift-flowing Celadon...', 133f.) when he tells of a local war in which he killed Ereuthalion, who wielded the unconventional club of mace-man Areïthous – events and people derived from some minor regional tradition of heroic, or near-heroic, warfare. It is Nestor's plan, too, that dominates the end of the seventh book: to call a truce for the cremation of the dead and during it to build a great trench, protected by a wall, in front of the naval camp (327–43; 433–41). This major military obstacle is sometimes over-looked in the remainder of the poem, and both ancient and modern critics have been tempted to call it an intrusion. Yet it was probably Homer's own idea, after all – or the theme was an ancient one that was only sporadically observed in the developing tradition. The book ends unusually and vividly with the arrival of wine-ships from the neighbouring island of Lemnos.

The eighth book opens with a divine assembly at which Zeus bans the gods from helping either side. On the battlefield Diomedes rescues Nestor in a not very powerful episode. Hector carries all before him, but Zeus, contrary to his main purpose of helping the Trojans, accedes to Agamemnon's prayer for relief. The archer Teucer has a brief run of success but cannot hit Hector, and Zeus sets the Trojans on the offensive once more. Hera and Athena prepare to defy the ban, but are deterred by savage threats from Zeus. Night falls with the Trojans encamped in the plain threatening the ships, and so rounds off a book that is replete with divine decision and counter-decision, with rapid changes of fortune on the battlefield, but is formless and confused in its total effect.

The ninth book, by contrast, provides one of the central pivots of the wrath-plot. An embassy is despatched to Achilles to convey Agamemnon's change of heart and offer lavish gifts, with the intention of inducing Achilles to come to the rescue of the hard-pressed Achaeans. But he violently rejects the offer – threatens to leave for home forthwith, but later softens this by declaring that he will not lift a finger till Hector attacks his headquarters and sets fire to the ships. This second threat, which is quoted below, foreshadows the series of attacks by Hector that dominates the central part of the epic. The whole proceedings, both the preparations for the embassy and the speeches of persuasion and re-jection that follow, are described with great virtuosity. Agamemnon begins charac-teristically by publicly urging the immediate abandonment of the expedition (in a variant of a theme already used of him in Book 2); Diomedes censures him firmly, though without the provocative insolence that Achilles had dis-played: 'Zeus gave you contradictory gifts: he gave you honour above all others because of your sceptre, but fortitude in battle he gave you not' (9.37–9) – let him leave if he wishes, the rest will stay and complete their task. Nestor tactfully intervenes and suggests a dinner and a council of war for the chieftains; only then, when Agamemnon has had time to calm down, does he suggest that the moment has arrived for an apology. The king agrees and suggests generous compensation: treasure, slaves, his daughter for bride, whole cities. But when Odysseus repeats all this to Achilles, word for word in the oral manner, he is almost swamped by a long speech of rejection that is pathetic and near-hysterical by turns. Its argument is logical enough: why should he, Achilles, do the lion's share of the fighting and see Agamemnon keep all the best prizes? And why should the king and his brother be allowed to love their women, and not Achilles to love Briseis and resent her being snatched away out of pique? This suggestion of romantic attachment for a concubine is in itself rather unheroic, stimulated, no doubt, by the demands of rhetoric; but the underlying concern is with *timē*, honour:

> My heart is swollen with rage whenever I remember
> how the son of Atreus has made me look foolish
> among the Argives, as though I were some migrant devoid of honour.
> But go off and give him this message:
> I shall not for a moment turn my mind to bloody war
> until god-like Hector, martial Priam's son,
> reaches the huts and ships of the Myrmidons,
> killing Achaeans, and sets the ships ablaze. (9.646–53)

Phoenix tries to moderate his charge's anger with a parable about the Prayers healing the damage done by Infatuation, and by the more enthralling cautionary tale (which looks like a summary version of a complete song) about Meleager, who took umbrage and withdrew from his martial duties after killing the Calydonian boar. All is of no avail, and Odysseus and Ajax return alone to report Achilles' obduracy to their anxious comrades.

The fulfilment of Achaean fears is delayed by another independent episode during the same night: the spying expedition in which Odysseus and Diomedes first seize the Trojan spy Dolon, then slaughter the Thracian king Rhesus, newly arrived to help the Trojans, and capture his horses. These events occupy the tenth book, which has often been suspected of being a post-Homeric addition made, perhaps, by a brilliant and ambitious rhapsode – a professional reciter – in the seventh century B.C. The suspicion may be unjustified, although the events of the book, which are not referred to elsewhere in the poem, are sometimes odd in themselves and are expressed in language that occasionally seems to lie outside the usual formular repertoire. The behaviour no less than the clothing of the protagonists is certainly untypical; yet a night patrol does not call for day-time tactics or indeed apparel, and many readers, at least, find this book especially dramatic and enjoyable. As for language, we may be surprised (for example) by the simile at 5–8, in which Zeus flashes lightning 'making either an awful rainstorm or hail or snow...*or in some place the great mouth of piercing war*' (ἠέ ποθι πτολέμοιο μέγα στόμα πευκεδανοῖο). The oddity here is confined to a single verse which could be an intrusion; but then Agamemnon is said to groan as frequently as these lightning-flashes 'from the bottom of his heart, and his lungs trembled within' (τρομέοντο δέ οἱ φρένες ἐντός, 10), a unique phrase; and a little later he 'drew many hairs by the roots from his head to Zeus on high' (πολλὰς ἐκ κεφαλῆς προθελύμνους ἕλκετο χαίτας | ὑψόθ' ἐόντι Διί, 15f.), again a bizarre expression far from the regular epic language for signs of grief. And yet the following, eleventh book, which is crucial to the main plot and is certainly by Homer, opens with a no less unique idea whereby Zeus, wishing to inspire the Achaean chieftains, 'sent grievous Strife to the swift ships of the Achaeans *holding a portent of war in her hands*' (πολέμοιο τέρας μετὰ χερσὶν ἔχουσαν, 11.3f.). The expression of the idea is admittedly more felicitous than that of the simile in Book 10, but even so we are reminded that Homer can sporadically and at any time use language and concepts unparalleled in the rest of the poem. That is especially so where the general circumstances of the action are irregular or unusual. It is only in a normal or regular context that unusual language and the apparent abandonment of the formular style give good grounds for suspicion of post-Homeric elaboration.

Book 11 brings a critical change in Achaean fortunes with the wounding of Agamemnon (after an interval of unusual martial prowess on his part) and then of Odysseus and Diomedes, and begins a sequence of no less than seven books devoted with great severity to the description of tense and desperate fighting. The delays and diversions over joining battle in the open plain lie far behind. If the reader had begun to expect that the monotony of hundreds of individual combats would be constantly relieved for him by viewings from the walls, scenes in Troy, night expeditions and the like, then his expectations must now fade almost away as he is driven to understand that warfare, subtly varied but relentless and massive in effect, is a dominant theme of the poem. It is true that close attention to language and detail reveals this poetry of warfare as brilliant and enjoyable in its own way; Homer is a master of variation, and the endless extension of formular situations brings its own pleasures. Nor is the poetry heartless; the succession of victories and victims, of turns of fortune as the battle moves to and fro, has its regular moments of pathos, sympathy, profound insight, even satire. Yet ancient listeners – ordinary people, surely, to a large extent, and not just an audience of military-minded aristocrats – must have had special motives and interests to enable them to follow attentively and appreciatively over the long hours of singing that this huge and austere central section required. The cardinal considerations may be these: that many men (not women) enjoy descriptions of fighting for its own sake; that this was a national epic in which every village and city in Greece could share (although it remains odd that the Athenian contingent had such a feeble role); that the audience must have known something about many of the families and individuals mentioned, and could appreciate sheer invention when it occurred; that in any event the poem could only be rendered in separate sections, over several days or parts of days; and that its remarkable author must have had a unique reputation, as well as unique gifts, and could thus compel attention to material that might have seemed too gargantuan and repetitive when presented by a lesser singer.

Of course there are still occasional diversions – several lesser ones and one major one. The wounded chieftains worry and confer behind the fighting, and that forms a new theme for variation, with much carrying of messages to and from and within the Achaean camp. The gods are repeatedly revealed in conclave, their minds on the progress of the war, either on Olympus or more frequently now on Mount Ida overlooking the battlefield itself. Poseidon and Apollo descend to inspire either side; among the human contestants there are special phases of triumph, for Agamemnon before he is wounded, for Idomeneus the Cretan leader, for Ajax as he dourly defends the ships, and for Hector almost throughout. The major diversion is the Deceiving of Zeus in the latter part of 14 and the beginning of 15: Hera, in order to give Poseidon greater freedom to help the Achaeans, and with the aid of Sleep and the girdle of Aphrodite, overwhelms Zeus with desire so that he makes love to her and then falls into a deep slumber. The episode is light-hearted and amusing (as Zeus recites to Hera a list of his mistresses whose charms she seems to him at that moment to surpass), but also touching and lyrical in tone:

> ...and the son of Kronos took his wife in his arms
> and the divine earth made fresh grass grow beneath them,
> and dewy lotus and crocus and hyacinth,
> thick and soft, which kept them high above the ground.
> In that they lay, and clothed themselves in a cloud
> that was fair and golden, and glistening drops of dew fell from it.
> So the Father slept, quite still, on the ridge of Gargarus
> subdued by sleep and love, and held his wife in his arms. (14.346–53)

Meanwhile Poseidon inspires Ajax to wound Hector, and the Trojans are driven back across the trench; but then Zeus wakes up, is furious at what he sees and decisively asserts just what is to happen. Apollo is to revive the stunned Hector and fill the Achaeans with panic, so that

> in flight they fall among the well-benched ships
> of Peleus' son Achilles; and he shall send into action his comrade
> Patroclus; and glorious Hector shall slay him with the spear
> in front of Ilios, once Patroclus has destroyed many young men
> – others, too, but among them my son, divine Sarpedon.
> In anger for Patroclus, divine Achilles shall slay Hector...(15.63–8)

We are reminded sharply by these words that, despite the occasional unexpected twist in the action, the general outcome of the war is not the object of suspense and was perfectly known to the audience. It is the exploration of detail, of exact motive and circumstance, that maintained the intensity of interest needed to carry listeners on through the dense concentration of this poetry – that, together with the progressive unfolding of the wrath-plot itself, which now takes a crucial step forward in the sixteenth book, perhaps the finest of the whole poem.

Book 15 had ended with Hector about to fire the ships. Ajax resists desperately, and then at the opening of 16 Patroclus carries the news to Achilles and begs to be allowed to join the fighting. Achilles not only consents but even lends him his own armour; Patroclus marches out with the Myrmidons and brings swift relief, then surges to the very walls of Troy, borne on against Achilles' instructions by triumph and destiny. First he kills Sarpedon, as Zeus had predicted or rather ordained – he was tempted when the time came to overrule destiny, but was dissuaded by Hera and the other gods (16.432–58). The encounter with Sarpedon is told at greater length than any of its predecessors (save for the formal duels of 3 and 7); it is important because it establishes Patroclus as truly magnificent and renders his own death at Hector's hands more awful, but also because the ascending series of tragic and exceptional deaths – Sarpedon, then Patroclus in 16, finally Hector in 22 – shows the special art and taste of Homer, the monumental composer, himself.[1] Each has significant elements of language and content in common with one or both of the others; each is an essential component of the monumental wrath-plot. Sarpedon, admittedly, is only preparatory in this respect, but he introduces a continuing note of pathos, accentuated by Zeus' grief and the shower of bloody rain he sends to do macabre honour to his son before he dies. Patroclus with his first throw hits Sarpedon's charioteer, not Sarpedon himself, just as he is later to hit Hector's charioteer Cebriones; here is no fighting over the charioteer's body, but Cebriones will be the object of a bitter struggle presaging the fight over Patroclus' own corpse that will occupy the whole of Book 17. The second spear-throw mortally wounds Sarpedon, whose concern that his body shall not be mutilated foreshadows that of Hector later. These three death-scenes are the only ones in which dying men speak, and the same verse is used in each instance: 'when he had thus spoken the end of death covered him'. So too the idea of the release of the *psyche* or life-spirit is common to all three; with Patroclus and Hector, and nowhere else, the soul is described as flitting mournfully down to Hades, but Sarpedon's body is to be carried to his homeland in Lycia by Sleep and Death, since as son of a god his soul might be expected to have a special fate.

The three scenes are closely related, and Homer seems to be developing them serially until he reaches the great climax of Hector's death. But the death of Patroclus is dramatically almost as important; in its preliminaries it is linked with that of Hector both by its strong pathos and by the fact that a god joins in on the other side and makes defeat inevitable. Patroclus as he faces Hector is

[1] Kirk (1976) 209–17.

struck from behind and dazed by Apollo, who remains invisible, and then his armour is stripped from him to render him helpless before a minor assailant and then Hector (16.787ff.). Hector, too, will be deceived by Athena, who will disguise herself as his brother Deiphobus and so persuade him to stand up to Achilles, and then will return Achilles' spear to him after his first throw has missed (22.226–77). Here, indeed, divine intervention seems gratuitous, for the audience knows that, strong as Hector may be, Achilles is the better man. Yet Homer is not so much interested in skill and physique and the actual exchange of blows (which are described in a standardized and almost perfunctory way) as in whether one or other combatant has been made irresistible by an upsurge of valour and heroic self-confidence that is the direct reflection of divine favour and even destiny. For Patroclus must die to bring back Achilles to the fight, and Hector must die to restore Achilles' bruised honour and make way for the fall of Troy, itself the punishment for Helen's abduction and the violation of the laws of hospitality that were Zeus's special concern.

A bitter struggle for possession of Patroclus' body occupies the 761 verses of the seventeenth book and marks the exceptional importance of his death. The tenseness of fighting as it surges back and forth, with first one side and then the other gaining the upper hand, is both emphasized and relieved by similes that reach a climax as the Achaeans finally prevail:

> Thus they eagerly carried the body out of the fighting
> toward the hollow ships; and war was stretched over them
> like fierce fire that speeds upon a city of men
> and, suddenly springing up, sets it burning, and the houses crumble
> in a great flame; and the force of the wind makes it roar.
> Just so, as they made their way, the unceasing din
> of chariots and fighting men beset them;
> but like mules that exert mighty strength
> and drag from the mountain over a rugged track
> either a beam or a great ship's timber, and their spirit
> is worn down by toil and sweat as they make haste,
> just so eagerly did they carry the body. And behind them
> Ajax and his brother held back the foe, as a wooded promontory
> holds back water by projecting into the plain
> and restrains the destructive streams even of mighty rivers
> and at once directs all their flow into the plain,
> baulking them, and the force of their stream makes no impression on it –
> just so did Ajax and his brother always hold off in the rear
> the Trojan attack... (17.735–53)

The almost abstract points of comparison, the naturalism of the scenes of power or violence in nature or in peacetime life and the piling of one comparison on another are typical of the Homeric use of developed similes, often imitated but never equalled. Each simile stands up to careful consideration in its accurate observation and brilliant expression, and in the comment it implicitly makes on the main action. Even the river-and-promontory simile, which seems to be drawn on and on in an effort to elicit the precise effect from an obdurate vocabulary, reproduces by its leisurely emphasis the solid and unremitting resistance of Ajax and Teucer.

Patroclus' corpse is firmly in Achaean hands, and now at last, at the start of the eighteenth book, Achilles learns the bitter news and rolls in the dust in his agony of heart. His mother Thetis arrives with her nymphs to try and comfort him; she can at least see to the making of new armour by Hephaestus to replace that of Achilles that had been wrenched from the body of his friend; meanwhile Hera sends Iris to persuade him to paralyse the Trojans with fright by appearing and shouting terribly by the trench. The poet turns for a significant interval to show Hector heroically but imprudently rejecting Polydamas' advice to retreat within the walls. The last 130 verses of the book are devoted to a splendid diversion, the description of the armour made by Hephaestus, above all of the great shield decorated with scenes of peace and war, all depicted in a compressed but evocative style akin to that of the similes, with dancing and harvesting, judgement in the market-place, ambushes and, as a sinister echo, the dragging away of corpses slain in battle.

Before Achilles can return to the fight there must be a formal reconciliation with King Agamemnon. It occupies much of the nineteenth book and is complemented and a little weakened by an argument about whether or not Achilles shall take food before going into action. From now until Hector's death there is a series of deliberate delays and diversions, comparable with those at the beginning of the poem, whose purpose is to heighten the audience's sense of Achilles' anger and determination and of the close concern of all the gods with what is happening. As Achilles drives out in his chariot, his horses, by a rare mixture of natural and supernatural, predict his death (19.397–424). Then in Book 20 the gods (apart from Zeus, who is too august for such sport) descend to the plain and prepare to fight each other in support of Trojans or Achaeans. The divine battle is abruptly broken off, and Achilles engages Aeneas after some lengthy and curiously rhetorical preliminaries; but Aeneas, like Hector a little later, is divinely whisked out of harm's way. In the next book, 21, the Theomachy or Battle of the Gods is resumed, but fizzles out without result; Poseidon and Apollo see that it is undignified, and an episode that is never handled with much confidence, and has surely been heavily distorted at some stage in the process of composition and development, is gradually allowed to rest (21.385–514).

Earlier in the twenty-first book, and before the resumption of the interrupted Theomachy, come two far more powerful scenes. The second is Achilles' fight with the river Scamander who resents being blocked and defiled with the corpses of his victims, and it is developed by Homer into a chilling and fantastic *tour de force*. The first is briefer and more ordinary in that it is simply another killing, but it brings out to an extraordinary degree the ruthlessness and pathos of heroic action as the poet focuses on the details of a single hopeless encounter (21.34–135). Achilles intercepts young Lycaon, one of Priam's many sons, whom he had captured not many days before and sent across to Lemnos to be ransomed. He expresses ironical surprise at seeing him back so soon, and then as the boy clutches Achilles' great spear with one hand and his knees, in a ritual gesture of supplication, with the other, addresses him in these words:

'You fool, do not speak to me of ransom or mention it. Before Patroclus drew on himself the day of destiny, then it was more congenial to me to spare Trojans, and I took many alive and despatched them across the sea. But now there is no one that shall escape death, of those that god casts in my hands before Ilios – of all the Trojans, but especially Priam's children. But you, too, friend, must die now; why do you lament so? Patroclus also died, and he was far better than you. Do you not see the kind of man I am in beauty and stature – son of a valiant father, and a goddess bore me and was my mother? But death and strong fate stand over me too; a dawn or evening or midday will come when someone will take away my life-spirit, too, in war, hitting me either with spear or with arrow from the bow-string.' So he spoke, and Lycaon's knees and dear heart were dissolved. He let go of the spear and sat with both arms spread out, and Achilles drew his sharp sword and struck him on the collar-bone beside the neck, and the two-edged sword sank right in, and he lay stretched out, face down on the earth, and the black blood flowed and wet the earth. (21.99–119)

At the end of 21 Apollo has disguised himself as Agenor and lured Achilles into chasing him, so allowing the Trojan army to retreat to the safety of the walls. Only Hector, driven by pride and destiny, remained out there in the plain, and the twenty-second book, in the great climax of the poem, describes his death, with the events leading up to it, on a larger scale than any other heroic encounter. His parents beseech him from the walls, and their despairing words are given in full. Hector remains adamant, and when Achilles draws near he tries to steel himself to face him – but fails, and starts running (22.90–144). Zeus pities him, not least as a faithful and regular sacrificer, but is deterred from sparing him by Athena in words similar to those used earlier by Hera about Sarpedon. Three times they circle the walls with Achilles close behind. Some of the landmarks they pass are described with painful and dramatic realism, like the hot and cold springs that are mentioned now for the first and last time. They run like race-horses, although the prize is no casual one but Hector's life; Zeus weighs the fates and Hector's sinks downward (22.208–13). Apollo abandons the doomed man, and Athena is sent exulting to help Achilles – as if he really needed it! She does so in two ways, both of them unfair by chivalrous standards: she appears at Hector's side as his brother Deiphobus, so that Hector thinks he has an ally, and then she gives back Achilles' spear to him when he misses with his first throw. Hector's return shot strikes Achilles' shield but bounces off (naturally, since the shield was made by Hephaestus); he calls for Deiphobus' spear, but the bogus ally has disappeared and Hector understands his true predicament:

'Alas! Assuredly the gods have called me toward death,
for I said that hero Deiphobus was by my side –
but he is within the walls, and I am deceived by Athena.
Now evil death is close by me, no longer distant,
and there is no avoiding it. In the past my safety was of concern
to Zeus and his far-shooting son, who, before,
were eager to protect me; but now destiny has come upon me.
Yet let me not perish without effort and without glory,
but after accomplishing some great deed for future men to hear of.' (22.297–305)

So Hector draws his sword and rushes at Achilles, who, however, has his spear back and is thus able to pierce his enemy's throat almost at leisure. The 'great deed' of Hector's words has amounted to little or nothing in effect, but it is the words themselves and the spirit behind them that matter most. Dying though he is, he still can speak; once again he implores Achilles not to maltreat his body – it is his special obsession – but hears in reply the reiterated cruelty of the threat to throw him to the dogs and birds. Once again Hector is forced to recognize the bitter reality, and he faces it with courage and a final threat:

'I recognize you well as I look upon you, and would never
have persuaded you. Truly your heart in your breast is made of iron.
Now is the time for you to consider whether I may not be a cause of
    divine anger against you
on the day when Paris and Phoebus Apollo
destroy you, good fighter though you are, at the Scaean gates.'
As he spoke these words the end of death covered him
and his life-soul sped from his limbs and went toward Hades
groaning over his fate, leaving his manliness and youth.
God-like Achilles addressed him, even though he was dead:
'Die! My own doom I shall receive at the moment when
Zeus and the other immortal gods wish to accomplish it.' (22.356–66)

With these assertions of inexorability and resignation, of divine control over men and the future fate of Achilles and of Troy, the martial part of the *Iliad* is done. Hector's is the last death in battle of the entire poem; what follows is concerned with the glorification, through proper burial, of Patroclus and Hector himself and with the resolution of Achilles' unnatural anger. But first comes the mutilation of his enemy's corpse as Achilles pierces Hector's ankles and drags him round the walls behind his chariot in an unparalleled parade of savagery that reduces Hecuba and Priam to total despair (22.395–415). In the twenty-third book Achilles turns to the overdue burial of his friend, whose ghost appears before him and demands to be released to the world below. Prisoners are sacrificed at his pyre in another act of pathological barbarism, but after that the singer turns to gentler pursuits, the funeral games held by Achilles to honour the dead man. The chariot-race and its consequences are lavishly evoked in over four hundred verses whose vivid detail and humour brilliantly suggest the lighter side of the heroic character, and are free from the ponderous touch of other partly humorous set-pieces – the chastisement of Thersites, the abortive Theomachy, or even the love of Ares and Aphrodite in the eighth book of the *Odyssey*. Subsequent contests in the funeral games are entertaining on a smaller scale, except for two or three (the fight in armour and the archery-contest in particular) that must have been elaborated by plodding rhapsodes.

The final, twenty-fourth book turns from Patroclus back to Hector and resolves the remaining issues, both narrative and moral, of the poem. Achilles is still periodically dragging the corpse behind his chariot, and the gods as they see it are affronted; not always Sunday-school characters in Homer, they are nevertheless determined guardians of the basic rules of order and respect. Zeus decides that Thetis shall instruct her son to surrender the corpse to King Priam, and Iris, the gods' messenger who is also the rainbow, is sent to tell Priam to set off at dead of night, with a cart and much ransom, for Achilles' hut. This strange adventure, which has sometimes been seen as a symbolic representation of a descent to the world of the dead, becomes less dangerous when he encounters Hermes, the god who escorts both travellers and souls, disguised as a young Myrmidon; he leads the old man across the battlefield and toward Achilles' encampment (24.349–447). Achilles receives the king magnanimously and looks after him (though not without moments of dangerous impatience) for much of the night in a hut that is now seen almost as a palace. The corpse has been divinely preserved from decay; it is placed on the cart and driven back to Troy, where the proper laments are sung for it by the women. A truce is made for the gathering of wood for the funeral pyre, and 'thus they saw to the funeral of Hector, tamer of horses', the closing verse of the poem.

It is in many ways an extraordinary ending. The whole book is punctuated by phraseology that reminds one of the *Odyssey* rather than the *Iliad* – partly because the events are closer to those of the non-martial poem and partly, perhaps, because these closing episodes, like those of the opening book, were favourite ones with audiences and singers, including Homer himself, and so acquired a veneer of more highly developed, or at least slicker, language. The events of the book, too, have something of the fantastic and mysterious quality of parts of the *Odyssey*, with the night journey, the divine young helper in disguise, the other-worldliness (Odysseus landing in Ithaca), the intimate conversations (as in the swineherd's hut) between Achilles and the old man who reminds him of his father. Yet all this complexity serves as a perfect culmination of the whole poem: a pathetic yet noble end to all the fighting, an unsentimental restitution of Achilles to the more admirable side of hero-hood with the final obliteration of his destructive wrath, and an overwhelming demonstration of the respect owed by men to destiny, to death and to the gods.[1]

3. THE *ODYSSEY*

The *Odyssey* belongs to the same epic tradition as the *Iliad* and shares with it much in the way of formular language and thematic material. But it is a different kind of poem, and for this and other reasons it warrants a rather different treatment – an attempt not to analyse it progressively, but rather to isolate its methods of construction and its unifying poetical aims. The two approaches complement each other, and the reader who engages directly with either poem will find himself applying both at once. If he starts with the *Odyssey*, he will be tempted to judge it independently and not in comparison with the *Iliad*. That has its advantages, but it remains true that a reasonable understanding of the *Odyssey* – which as we saw is likely to be subsequent in composition to the *Iliad* – can only come if the other poem is seen as its model in certain formal respects (for example scale, and the use of speeches and similes), and as an illustrious predecessor to be emulated or, at times, studiously ignored.

It is helpful, therefore, even if it might seem unimaginative, to consider how the *Odyssey* differs from the *Iliad* and in what respects it falls short of it or surpasses it. Clearly the subjects of the two poems impose their own special qualities. The *Iliad* is relentlessly martial in tone and detail; it contains, as we saw, important digressions, some of them with their own peculiarities of language, but the style as a whole, together with the treatment of situations and characters, remains severe and dignified, as might be considered appropriate to a heroic age and a heroic standard of values. The *Odyssey*, on the other hand, concerns a time of uneasy peace – the near aftermath of the Trojan War, admittedly, when some of the heroes have only recently reached home and when Odysseus himself is still lost and wandering, but when the main issue is personal, political and economic survival rather than mass fighting, public heroism, the acquisition of booty or manifest loyalty to friends and class. And there are other quite different issues that hardly belong at all to a nostalgically heroic conception of life: issues of love and respect between men and women, of devotion on the part of son, wife or servants, of hospitality in its less ostentatious forms, of the proper retribution for crime, even of the apportioning of divine and human responsibility for hardship and misfortune. None of these is

---

[1] Griffin (1980) is illuminating on the underlying concerns and emphases of both poems.

entirely unforeshadowed in the *Iliad*, but none becomes a dominant theme there as it does in the slightly later poem.

These broader and indeed more abstract topics do not of themselves require the hard concentrated language of Iliadic combat and endurance. Much of the formular phraseology remains common to the two poems, but the *Odyssey* extends the range of standardized phrases to cover fresh subjects. It also has several new and conspicuous locutions for common events or sequences, as was shown on p. 50. Somehow the language of the later poem is not only more relaxed but also blander and less vivid, more fluent but also occasionally more flaccid than that of the *Iliad*. Direct speech is no less important than before, but the speeches tend to be less dramatic, more leisurely and wordy, sometimes rather insipid even when no effect of that kind can have been intended. At their best, it is true, the conversations of the *Odyssey* achieve a degree of civilized subtlety that exceeds anything in the *Iliad*. When the gods decide to bring about Odysseus' release from the island of Calypso they send Hermes to instruct her, and as a consequence the nymph, reluctant but resigned, brings up the subject after dinner with her desirable guest:

> But when they had enjoyed food and drink, then Calypso, lady goddess, began their conversation: 'Lordly son of Laertes, Odysseus of many devices, so it is your desire to go home this very moment to your dear native land? Well, I wish you joy of it. Yet if you knew in your heart how many cares you are destined to fulfil before you reach your native land, you would stay here with me and keep to this house and be immortal, even though you long to see your wife for whom you yearn all your days. Yet I know that I am not her inferior in either body or stature, since it is in no way fitting for mortal women to vie in body and appearance with immortal goddesses.' Then in answer Odysseus of many counsels addressed her: 'Mistress goddess, do not be angry with me. I, too, am well aware that prudent Penelope is less than you in appearance and in stature when one looks upon her; for she is mortal, and you are deathless and free from old age. But even so I wish and yearn all my days to go home and see the day of my return. If once again some god strikes me down in the wine-dark sea, then I shall endure it and keep in my breast a steadfast spirit. For I have already suffered much grief and toil in waves and war; let this, too, be added to them.' These were his words, and the sun set and darkness came over them, and the two of them went into the inner part of the hollow cave and enjoyed themselves in love and stayed by each other's side. (5.201–27)

There is so much here that is lightly touched on and yet left inexplicit: the nymph's disappointment and surprise, Odysseus' tact and homesickness and determination to stick to what is properly human. The poet has already shown him as tired of Calypso, yet here at the end the passion revives itself as dutiful affection – well outside the range of normal heroic lust and proprietary interest in beautiful, efficient and valuable women. There is a quiet philosophy in this passage, a resigned insistence on human values, that is not uncommon in the *Odyssey* but that strips the gentle verses of taut heroic vigour as surely as it fills them with an insistent and almost urbane melancholy.

Speeches in the *Iliad* are hurled to and fro like weapons; in the *Odyssey* they are the ingredients of strangely placid conversations that surprise us only occasionally and then, for the most part, through the accidents and limitations of oral technique. In the opening book, which sets out the position in Odysseus' palace in Ithaca, with Penelope resigned and beset by suitors and Telemachus immature and powerless until he is stiffened by the disguised Athena, Penelope hears the court-singer Phemius as he sings of the return of various heroes from Troy. She is distressed because it reminds her of her own husband, apparently lost for ever, and asks the singer to choose another song. She is at once rebuked by her son, who treats her with a quite unexpected sternness that is the product (as the audience is meant to feel) of the new grown-up determination the goddess is instilling into him. That sternness raises the conversation above the usual unemphatic level and gives an urgency to the proceedings which, even with Athena's presence, they have strikingly lacked so far. Yet the tone of the boy's words is somehow odd, too bitter and sneering to be easily understood – precisely because they are not created for this particular occasion, but adapted from other contexts and compounded with minor motifs about the technique and status of singers (a recurring subject in this poem) and the proper place of women in the home:

'It is no reproach for this man to sing of the evil doom of the Danaans, for men assign greater glory to the song that is newest to its hearers. Let your heart and spirit endure hearing it; for Odysseus was not the only one to lose in the land of Troy the day of his return, but many other men perished. Go into the house and see to your own business, the loom and distaff, and tell the servants to get on with their work. Talking shall be the concern of men – of all of us, but of me most of all; for a man has the power in the home.' She was dumbfounded and went back into the house, for she took to heart her child's wise saying. She ascended to the upper storey with her serving-women and then wept for Odysseus, her dear husband, until grey-eyed Athena cast sweet sleep upon her eyelids. But the suitors made a din through the shadowy halls, and all of them desired passionately to sleep by her side in bed. Wise Telemachus began to address them as follows: 'Suitors of my mother, you whose arrogance is un-bridled, now let us take our pleasure at dinner; and let there be no shouting, since it is fine to listen to a singer such as this one, god-like in his utterance. And at dawn let us all go to the place of assembly and take our seats, for me to tell you this message outright – to get out of my halls! Concern yourselves with different kinds of feast; eat up what belongs to you, taking turns in each other's houses! But if this seems to you preferable and better, for one man's livelihood to be consumed without payment, then go on and devour it; but I shall call upon the eternal gods to see if Zeus may in the end grant that works of vengeance come to pass. Then would you perish, likewise without payment, in my house.' These were his words, and they bit their lips with their teeth as they marvelled at how confidently Telemachus addressed them. (1.350–82)

'Talking shall be the concern of men', says Telemachus to his mother here, adapting Hector's statement to Andromache in the sixth book of the *Iliad* (492f.) that warfare shall be the concern of men. Penelope retires with surprising meekness, not so much because the poet wants to make her into an enigmatic figure (which she nevertheless becomes, through similar manipulations, as the poem progresses) as because the stage must be left clear for a further demonstration of the young man's new confidence. But is it part of the poet's design that Telemachus should now speak out so spasmodically in an uneasy succession of threats against the suitors, a plea for better table-manners and renewed praise of singers before he comes to the real point – that he will give them an important message the next day? And is his anticipatory summary of this message, with its apparently mistimed threat of counter-action, a telling sign of passion and immaturity, or is it the result of a complicated adaptation of motifs and formulas that slightly outstrip the singer's complete control at this point? Perhaps the disjunction is unjustified and both causes are at work simultaneously; for part at least of the effect of an impassioned young man is presumably deliberate. But in this kind of context one can never be entirely sure; for if the Nausicaa-conversations of Book 6 show how delicate are the effects the poet of the *Odyssey* can achieve, there are many other cases where the inherited language and thematic material prove mildly intransigent, so as to impose a complexity that was probably not initially intended.

Not only speech but also narrative is generally smoother and less strongly expressive than in the earlier epic – unless what needs expressing is something outside, or on the edge of, the ordinary range of heroic language and tradition, like the delicate feelings of a young girl. It is significant that the *Odyssey* has far fewer similes than the *Iliad*. Admittedly its action is so complex and varied that it rarely calls for the diversionary element that similes, in one of their roles, can supply. When it does drag or falter it is usually because conversation has run riot (as it does between Odysseus and Eumaeus in the fourteenth book), and similes can do nothing to help. Where they occur is often in passages of Iliadic tone, as at the end of Book 21 where Odysseus, still disguised as a beggar, is handling the great bow that the suitors have failed to string:

But Odysseus of many counsels weighed the great bow and closely examined it. As when a man expert in the lyre and in singing easily stretches a string about a new peg, fitting the twisted sheep-gut from both sides, so without effort did Odysseus stretch the great bow. Then he took it and with his right hand tested the string, and it gave forth a beautiful singing note like the voice of a swallow. Great grief came upon the suitors, and all of them changed colour. Zeus thundered loudly, revealing signs of what was to come; then much-enduring noble Odysseus rejoiced, because the son of crooked-counselled Kronos had sent him a portent; and he took a swift arrow that lay ready uncovered on the table – but the others lay inside the hollow quiver, and the Achaeans were destined soon to test them. He took the bow by the handgrip and drew the string in the arrow-notches, there from the seat where he sat, and shot the arrow, aiming straight ahead, and did not miss any of the axes – the first part of their shaft – and the arrow with its heavy bronze tip went right through them to the doorway. He said to Telemachus: 'Telemachus, your guest does not bring you disgrace in your halls, seated though he is; I neither missed the target nor took time or effort to string the bow. My strength is still firm, and not as the suitors disparage it to dishonour me.' (21.404–27)

The details of this scene, with its careful description of the act of drawing the bow-string (which is not exactly paralleled even in scenes concerning the archers Teucer and Pandarus in the *Iliad*), and of the row of axes and the shot itself, are peculiar to the *Odyssey*, as indeed is the subject of the brilliant simile that typically concerns a singer once again; but the tone and style are nevertheless Iliadic, and they accord perfectly with the suddenly martial and heroic subject matter.

Sometimes that kind of Iliadic energy is released in a scene that is not martial but domestic and almost lyrical, and there the effect, 'Odyssean' now at its best, is remarkable:

But when Nausicaa was about to turn back home again after yoking the mules and folding the fair clothes, then grey-eyed goddess Athena had another idea, that Odysseus should wake up and see the lovely girl, who should lead him to the town of the Phaeacians. Then the princess threw a ball to one of her attendants; she missed the attendant but threw it into the deep swirling water, and the women gave a great shriek, and noble Odysseus awoke and sat up and debated in his heart and spirit: 'Ah me, whose land have I come to this time? Are they violent and fierce and without justice, or hospitable and with a god-fearing mind? For a female cry came about my ears, as though of maidens – nymphs that possess the steep mountain peaks and streams of rivers and grassy meadows. Or am I perhaps close to men with human speech? Come, let me make trial and see for myself.' So saying noble Odysseus emerged from the bushes, breaking off with his thick hand a leafy branch from the dense undergrowth to keep from sight his bare male genitals. And he went like a mountain-reared lion, confident in his prowess, that goes through rain and through wind, and his eyes flash out, and he comes upon the cattle or sheep, or goes after wild deer, and his belly urges him to make trial of the flocks even to the point of entering a well-made fold. Just so was Odysseus about to come among the fair-haired girls, naked though he was, for necessity beset him. Terrifying he appeared to them, befouled with brine, and they ran in panic in every direction over the jutting headlands. Alcinous' daughter was the only one to stand firm, for Athena put courage in her mind and took the fear from her limbs. And she stood facing him; and Odysseus wondered whether to grasp her knees and beseech the lovely girl, or to stand apart as he was and beseech her with soothing words to point out the town and give him clothes. (6.110–44)

There is so much here that is typical of the *Odyssey*: Athena determining the course of events, the charming accident with the ball, Odysseus' suspicions and tactful prudence in a fresh situation of potential danger. Yet as he rushes out like a ravenous lion he assumes an Iliadic role and posture, and Nausicaa, too, becomes heroic in her god-given imperturbability; and it is just this tension of roles and styles that gives the scene its special power and magic.

Yet the *Odyssey* as a whole is not really a heroic poem, and that tells us much about its limitations, especially in style and language, when compared with the *Iliad*. It has important qualities the *Iliad* does not possess, but if one wants to understand it properly then its diction, relaxed and at times almost nerveless, at other times strangely prosaic, has to be taken into account – not least because it is used in the service of an unusually complex and carefully constructed plot. An important consideration here is that the oldest parts of the narrative tradition to have left their mark on the language of Homer were probably martial and heroic in character. The system of standardized poetical phraseology that permitted the tradition to spread so widely in time and space grew up in the first instance to describe the actions, words and interests of aristocratic fighting men, on the battlefield or on raids or encamped round plunderable cities. This cannot be proved, but it is some indication that the most archaic-looking phrases (those for example with clustered Mycenaean elements) tend to be martial rather than domestic or picaresque in reference. 'Martial' is perhaps too narrow; among these older materials of oral poetry would be descriptions of seafaring, feasting and sacrifice, concomitants of fighting and the heroic life-style. Even the scenes behind the lines or in Troy could be based on archaic materials. Their assumptions and the language used to express them are still heroic, although one has a sense at this point of brilliant new singers carrying the old poetical equipment into fresh territories. In the *Odyssey* the exploration is carried still further. The scenes of conversation and feasting, of singers at work and of the finer nuances of encounters between men and women, depend on a vocabulary and phraseology that, although still formular, are sophisticated extensions rather than direct descendants of the severer language of strictly heroic poetry.

It is, of course, a mistake to treat the *Iliad* as a very ancient poem and the *Odyssey* as a very modern one. Little more than a generation's span, if that, separates them, and they might still be the work of the same main composer. That cannot be excluded. Yet they are different in essence, the one inclining to be archaistic and conservative, the other innovative and eclectic. The extension of its hero's (in the modern sense) values from honour, courage, success and love of showy possessions to resignation, endurance, plotting and humble disguises; of its lesser characters from minor warriors to magicians, one-eyed monsters, herdsmen and serving-women; of its locations from camp, battlefield and besieged city to Peloponnesian palaces, Ithacan countryside and the fantastic lands of Odysseus' adventures, does much for the variety of possible feeling and action, but at the same time stretches the resources and slightly dims the vigour of the oldest language of poetry. The capacity for adapting formulas to new uses can be carried almost too far, and the tight concrete phrases and verses of the *Iliad* tend to become abstract and imprecise in many parts of the *Odyssey*. That can be seen even from some of the passages which have been selected for translation in this account (although their primary function is to illustrate different and more positive qualities); and particularly from the description of the islet off the land of the Cyclopes (pp. 83f. below), where the subject is pastoral and lyrical but the language becomes at times curiously vague and repetitive, relying too heavily on conventional epithets (or other standardized devices) for the rich texture such a description needs. It is far superior to most oral poetry, and indeed most written narrative poetry; most oral poetry tends, like the Yugoslav, to be redundant and drab; but it falls below the exceptional standard of the *Iliad*, whose traditional timbre and constantly varied exploitation of a limited range of actions are particularly well suited by the taut expressiveness of familiar verse-components.

The widening of the traditional heroic ambience leads to a complementary result in a different sphere. For those Iliadic characters that recur in the *Odyssey* tend to become a little lifeless and indefinite, as if the poet did not quite know what to make of them. That does not apply to Odysseus himself, whose bravery and resourcefulness are developed in the later poem into a touching and often witty amalgam of trickster-like ingenuity and over-confidence. But Nestor, Menelaus and Helen, as they are described at length in the third and fourth books when young Telemachus visits them in their palaces at Pylos and Lacedaemon, turn out to be disappointingly awkward and undramatic. Their chief interest lies in their accounts of the aftermath of the *Iliad* – the fate of Agamemnon, the Trojan horse, adventures in Egypt on the way home. Nestor is even wiser and more fatherly than in the other poem, but his modified prolixity is matched by that of too many other characters to be (as it was in the *Iliad*) both idiosyncratic and amusing. Menelaus is proud of his rich palace in an almost humble and completely unheroic way (4.78–99); his wife Helen, her ambivalent past glossed over by unconvincing professions of mixed feelings while in Troy, assumes some of the less dangerous characteristics of Circe as she spikes the drinks with an anodyne drug (4.219ff.). These are figures that are the product not of the heroic age of which they are the ostensible survivors, nor even of any depressed and diminished successor, but rather of poetic imaginations moving a little unsurely in what has become an artificial, almost a patchwork landscape.

To counterbalance these weaknesses the *Odyssey* possesses strong positive qualities peculiar to itself. The variety of its action, the simple but effective transitions from place to place, the ingenuity with which the main components of a complicated plot are interwoven – these required elaborations of planning greater than those needed for the *Iliad*, skilful and complicated though the manoeuvres of the poetic battlefield had to be. Then there are special supernatural elements beyond the activities of the anthropomorphic gods themselves – who, although slightly different in character from those of the *Iliad*, for instance in their heightened moral sensibility and the increased role of the guardian deity, still belong to the same genre. The *Iliad* is almost free of complex omens once the famous manifestation at Aulis has been recalled by Odysseus in the second book. The *Odyssey* is full of them. Along with Odysseus' fictitious tales and the songs of Demodocus and Phemius they constitute the characteristic diversion of this poem, much as the developed simile and Nestor's reminiscences are typical diversions of the *Iliad*. Sometimes, as with the early appearances of the fugitive seer Theoclymenus, they are cursory and thin. If the monumental composer was aiming at a sense of the numinous and mysterious, then he achieved it more successfully in the fantastic and atmospheric passages to be mentioned shortly. And yet the idea of gods sending special signs to men – Odysseus at one point asks for, and gets, two kinds of sign at once, both a divine clap of thunder and a propitious saying by a human bystander (20.98–121)– accords well with the magical adventures that are an essential component of the poem, and even with Athena's almost doting protection of her favourite Odysseus. In its turn that protection seems consequently less pantomime-like when she transforms him back and forth from his own shape to that of a battered old beggar, or beautifies him at a touch to impress Nausicaa or Penelope. There are supernatural tricks by gods in the *Iliad* – Poseidon flicks Aeneas through the air at one point (*Il.* 20.325–9) – but they are rare and alluded to only in passing. The poets of the Odyssean side of the tradition evidently liked this sort of thing better, or, a fairer statement perhaps, found it more appropriate to the aura of fantasy that can surround even the most realistic scenes of the *Odyssey*.

This combination of fantasy and naturalism gives the poem one of its most powerful and unusual qualities. The minute detail of Odysseus shooting a stag in Circe's island is closely associated with an odd passage in which he surveys the landscape from a peak and (as later transpires) is mysteriously lost, so much so that he cannot distinguish east from west (10.145–97). When he awakes in Ithaca after being landed there from the Phaeacian ship he finds everything shrouded in mist by Athena so that he cannot recognize where he is (13.187ff.).

His subsequent encounter with the goddess is charming and etherial, until she suddenly discloses the familiar landscape and they settle down at the foot of an olive-tree, like a couple of peasants, to plan Odysseus' revenge. And as he sets off for that last journey home – last, except for the mysterious trip predicted by Tiresias to the place where men use no salt and mistake an oar for a winnowing-fan – his Phaeacian hosts carry both gifts and provisions down to the seashore:

> But when they came down to the ship and the sea
> immediately the illustrious escorts received the things
> and stowed them in the hollow ship, all the food and drink.
> Then they spread for Odysseus a rug and a sheet
> on the platform of the hollow ship, where he might sleep without waking,
> at the stern. He himself boarded and lay down
> in silence, while they sat each on his thwart
> in order, and loosed the stern cable from the pierced stone.
> Then they leant forward and churned the sea with their oars,
> and sweet sleep descended on Odysseus' eyelids,
> unwaking sleep, sweetest of all, nearest to death.
> The ship – as in a plain four-yoked stallions
> all leap forward together under the blows of the whip
> and rearing high swiftly accomplish their course,
> so did the ship's stern rear up, and behind it the wave
> seethed, the great purple wave of the boisterous sea.
> And the ship ran on very surely and steadily, nor would a hawk
> have kept pace with it, swiftest of flying creatures.
> So it ran on swiftly, cleaving the waves of the sea,
> carrying a man possessed of god-like intelligence
> who earlier had suffered very many griefs in his heart
> cleaving his way through wars of men and waves of the sea;
> but now he slept without stirring, forgetful of all he had suffered. (13.70–92)

The transition is from the distant and magical country of Scheria back to the realities of the suitors in Ithaca, and the poet creates an entrancing effect of timelessness as the hero lies on the stern-platform in the sleep that is almost indistinguishable from death, while the ship (which in truth needs no rowing, as the poem reveals elsewhere) cuts majestically through the waves – in unmistakable contrast to Odysseus' earlier struggles with storms and shipwreck. The close of this remarkable passage, which deliberately recalls the words of the poem's prologue, forms a coda to the foreign adventures of the 'man of many turns', and the death-like sleep imposes a kind of sacral interlude between them and the trials to come in Ithaca.

This particular sense of the mysterious is not entirely novel – one recalls Priam's nocturnal journey in the last book of the *Iliad*, which has, admittedly, been worked over here and there with the *Odyssey* in mind – but is sharpened by the poet's preoccupation with the idea of place. There is nothing quite like it in the *Iliad*, although its similes can evoke a scene in nature with spectacular economy and force. The poet of the *Odyssey*, on the other hand, evidently enjoyed the elaborate description of palaces (those of Odysseus, Menelaus and Alcinous), countryside (Scheria, Circe's island, Ithaca) and seascapes (Odysseus' shipwrecks, the voyage back from Scheria). In particular he developed the theme of the *locus amoenus* or 'delightful spot' that was to become so important in Latin and European pastoral. Calypso's cave is beset with verdant trees that are carefully named, and with water flowing from springs that nourish the wild vines there (5.63–71). When Odysseus goes to see his father Laertes in the last book of the *Odyssey* he finds him tending his garden out in the country, and its plants and trees are lovingly noted in the course of the complex recognition-scene (24.241ff.). The shape and feeling of Ithaca itself are conveyed as Odysseus walks over the rough tracks from the harbour of Phorcys to Eumaeus' hut, near Raven Rock and the spring Arethusa, and then back into the city past another spring surrounded by poplars.[1] The exotic places he visits in his wanderings are sometimes dealt with more cursorily, but Circe's island, as well as Calypso's, and the seashore scene with Nausicaa at the river's mouth are carefully evoked; and so are the harbours, sanctuary and market-place of the city of Scheria as Odysseus enters it in disguise.[2]

Landscape is not a naturally heroic topic – it is too liable to be inhabited by peasants and other mundane creatures – yet the singer of the *Odyssey* has made it into an important ingredient of his poem. 'The sun set and shadowed were all the streets' – even this repeated phrase, peculiar to the *Odyssey*, suggests a kind of visual imagination which, if it works sporadically through the whole heroic tradition, finds its fullest expression in the romantic and mysterious settings of this poem. Consider the leisurely detail of the description, not so much of the land of the Cyclopes itself, but rather of the small island that lies just off its coast where Odysseus and his companions beach their ship in the depths of night:

> From there we sailed onward, grieved in our hearts.
> We came to the land of the Cyclopes, overbearing
> and lawless, who trusting in the immortal gods
> neither plant anything with their hands nor plough
> but everything grows for them without sowing or ploughing –
> wheat and barley and vines which produce
> wine from fine grapes, and rain from Zeus gives them increase.
> They have neither laws nor decision-making assemblies
> but dwell on the peaks of high mountains
> in hollow caves, and they each make laws
> for children and wives, and take no heed of each other.

[1] *Od.* 13.345, 14.1–4; 13.408; 17.204–11.
[2] *Od.* 6.291–4, 7.43–5.

Then there is an island stretched out beyond the harbour
of the land of the Cyclopes, neither near nor far,
a wooded one. In it live numberless goats,
wild ones; for the tread of human feet does not keep them away
neither do hunters track them down, who suffer hardships
in the thickets as they roam over mountain crests.
Nor is the land given over to flocks or ploughed fields,
but unsown and unploughed for all its days
it is bare of men, but nurtures bleating goats.
For the Cyclopes have no crimson-cheeked ships,
neither are there ship-builders among them who could build
well-benched ships which could produce all those things,
by travelling to the cities of men, that in profusion
men carry to each other across the sea in ships.
Ship-builders would have made that island a prosperous possession;
for it is not a bad one, and would bear all things in season,
for there are meadows by the shores of the grey sea
that are soft and well watered; vines there would never fail.
There is smooth ground for ploughing; they would always reap
a deep harvest in season, since the soil beneath is very fertile.
And there is a safe harbour where there is no need of cable,
neither of casting out anchor-stones nor of tying on stern-ropes,
but only of beaching the ship and remaining for as long as the sailors'
spirit urges them and the winds blow.
But at the head of the harbour runs shining water,
a spring from the foot of a cave, and poplars grow round;
there we sailed in, and some god was leading us
through the dark night. . . (9.105–43)

Sometimes an important episode is marked out at its beginning by an elaborate description, of armament or locality for instance; but that does not entirely account for the depiction of the island at such length. The mainland that needed 'no planting or ploughing' seems to have triggered off the description of an ideal landscape awaiting development, but also solitary and therefore a little mysterious, because undefiled by men. Certainly the verses are cumulated one upon another almost too casually, and the sense begins to falter with those non-ships of the Cyclopes. It steadies itself again with the development of the ideal-harbour theme that recurs elsewhere and must have been a persistent dream of Homeric audiences and their colonizing predecessors; and the cave seems to prefigure the cave of the Nymphs at the head of the harbour of Phorcys in Ithaca, where Odysseus stores his treasure and where likewise a deity leads the way.

That kind of redeployment and careful variation of themes leads back to a question that has already been touched on. How can a poem so long and complex as this have been composed orally, without the aid (except perhaps in a minor way) of writing? Part of the answer is undoubtedly given by the observation that Homeric verses are made to a considerable extent out of standardized phrases designed to fill the three or four main segments of the hexameter verse. That gives the clue to the effortless composition of verses and distinct passages; but how were the passages put together to form such a large and complicated whole, and in general with such impressive consistency? Here the answer must be that the large-scale narrative is for the most part composed out of standardized narrative elements analogous to the small-scale formulas or fixed phrase-units. These larger components are motifs or themes, and they range from minor sequences of action or concept (as at the beginning of the passage just quoted, where 'we sailed on, and then came to another landfall' is a repeated motif of the sea-adventures) to broader topics like that of the unknown island in the same passage, or throwing oneself on the mercy of strangers as in the passage on pp. 78f., and basic narrative patterns like that of a human loved by a god or goddess who is rejected by him, as in the Calypso passage on p. 75. Themes of varying scope and content can of course be detected in the *Iliad* also; but the overall action is more restricted there, and the wide proliferation of themes is less important than the variation of a limited number, notably those concerned with single combat (including the hurling of weapons that miss or hit in turn) or the fortunes of massed battle. In the *Odyssey* the greater complexity and variety of action depend on an even more highly developed deployment of themes, together with a more sophisticated application of the arts of repetition and variation – or, to express it more accurately, repetition disguised by variation. It is by such means that the main poet of the *Odyssey* was able to build up his enormous structure, which can now be more easily seen to lie within the capacities of a single gifted singer – and later, and in a rather different way, of substantially illiterate reproducers. Determining these means is more than a merely technical or historical matter, for the poetry can be more exactly appreciated as the poet's resources, both in language and in his power to repeat, extend and vary a limited range of narrative themes, are better understood. This is the kind of approach (rather than by the establishment of the special 'oral poetics' that some critics hanker after) by which we can reach a fuller appreciation of the shape and construction of the *Odyssey*.

Above the level of minor motifs, the poem's major themes can be divided into several overlapping categories. First, in an arbitrary order, are the folktale themes. It is obvious to everyone who reads them that Odysseus' sea-adventures, which occupy from the fifth to the twelfth book or nearly a third of the poem, belong to the genre of popular story-telling known as folktale; and that many of their narrative ideas (like escaping from a one-eyed or blind giant, or the bag of winds, or the beautiful princess who helps the hero as Nausicaa helped Odysseus) are common to different popular traditions the world over. Folktales overlap myths and take many forms. Certainly this class of theme operates outside, as well as within, the strict limits of the sea-adventures. Success against apparently impossible odds is a conspicuous element of folktales, and is exemplified not only in Odysseus escaping from the Cyclops but also in his triumph over the suitors back in the everyday world. A popular folktale figure is the trickster, and Odysseus, more than Hermes, Sisyphus or Autolycus, is the main Greek exemplar. Ingenious ideas, like the No-man motif of the Cyclops episode or, more feebly, that of concealing the death of the suitors by pretending that a dance is in progress in the palace, are one speciality of the trickster, while disguise, which plays so prominent a part in the second half of the *Odyssey*, is another. The wife beset by suitors when her husband is thought to be dead is a popular folktale theme; it is often elaborated by the idea of putting off the suitors by a trick, as Penelope does with the shroud she weaves by day and unweaves by night, or alternatively by a test (here, of the bow and axes) or a quest. Finally the husband returns in the nick of time and deals with the suitors in various ways; this central theme belongs to many different cultures, and is so popular because it is piquant and dramatic and yet has a footing in real life, as well as because of its capacity for elaboration by the attachment of various ingenuity-motifs.

An important way of deploying these folktale themes, which applies to other types as well, is by repeating them in different forms and with varying degrees of elaboration. Many of the themes of the *Odyssey* are used over and over again in slightly different guises – we can see that most easily in some of the character-doublets. The good swineherd Eumaeus has a lesser male counterpart in the good cowherd Philoetius, and a female counterpart in the nurse Eurycleia, who in turn has a lesser shadow, Eurynome the keeper of the bedchamber. But Eumaeus also has an opposite counterpart in the form of the evil goatherd Melantheus, who has a sister of almost the same name, Melantho, who is equally evil and balances the good female servants, Eurycleia among them. For the principle of theme-duplication includes that of reversal; so Odysseus has a guardian angel in Athena and a corresponding divine enemy in Poseidon, who in turn is briefly paralleled by Helios, the sun, when Odysseus' companions slaughter his cattle. The theme of the nymph or goddess who detains the hero in her island and makes love to him is used first with Calypso and then with Circe, and the poet applies his arts of variation to make their episodes seem distinctively different, although they are in fact structurally almost identical.

Another category of Odyssean themes consists of universally dramatic actions or sequences of action; in a sense this category subsumes the folktale one, but without laying special stress on fantasy or ingenuity. The surmounting of apparently insuperable difficulties is such a theme (to put it in its most general and abstract form), and Odysseus exemplifies it repeatedly. Sometimes it is preferable to talk of narrative devices rather than themes, as when the singer inserts a long diversion at a critical moment (as Eurycleia's recognition of her master is tantalizingly interrupted for no less than seventy verses by the tale of how Odysseus got the revealing scar in the first place, 19.392–466) or turns unexpectedly to a different scene of action, for example from the palace in Ithaca back to Telemachus in the Peloponnese. Recognition in the broad sense is another narrative idea of wide application. It is at the heart of *Oedipus tyrannus*, but equally underlies the thoughts and behaviour of Telemachus and Penelope in their confusion about Odysseus, of Menelaus and Alcinous as they wonder on different occasions who their unknown guest might be, or of the suitors as they face the former beggar and discover their destiny.

A third overlapping category contains themes that doubtless came in other oral poems but were specially developed for the purposes of the *Odyssey*. Telling a false tale to keep one's identity concealed must have been used elsewhere, but with Odysseus it is almost a fetish, and his fictitious wanderings as Cretan refugee, or a Phoenician captive or passenger, become an important and recurrent element of the poem. Complementing this is the theme of disbelief in the face of his claims to know that the 'real' Odysseus is on his way home or already in Ithaca. Eumaeus in the fourteenth book (115–408) and Penelope in the nineteenth (508ff.) carry caution and incredulity to almost irritating extremes. Of course they have been misled by false claimants before, and Penelope's scepticism is in addition an aspect of the distrust she has to show toward the suitors; but clearly the singer of the *Odyssey* found this idea very much to his taste as a subject for variation and elaboration, and used it in the service both of suspense and of character-drawing.

Arrival in a strange land is another common theme, one bound to occur in folktales like the sea-adventures but developed in a special way in the *Odyssey*, where arrival in disguise is repeatedly followed by careful attempts to establish one's worth and gain status before the final revelation of identity is made. The theme occurs both when Odysseus reaches the land of the Phaeacians (with both Nausicaa and her father Alcinous) and in Ithaca itself (with both Eumaeus and Penelope); but in a truncated form it determines the delay in establishing Telemachus' identity when he arrives at the palace of Menelaus and Helen in the fourth book (20–170) – a scene that cannot be properly understood without knowledge of this general theme and its overall deployment. In this case it seems to be shyness rather than cunning that prevents him from saying who he is; when his father is mentioned he covers his face with his cloak to hide his tears, and that again is a motif that is re-used, not once but twice, when Odysseus is obstinately concealing his identity from the Phaeacians. As a final example of this category, the poet constantly uses the idea of individuals disclosing their steadfast loyalty to the lost Odysseus by breaking into a lament for him as soon as he is mentioned; that happens with Telemachus in the presence of Athena, and with Eumaeus, Telemachus and Philoetius, each in different ways, in the presence of the disguised Odysseus himself.[1]

It is precisely by using and re-using such themes as these that the main composer of the poem succeeded in constructing an apparently very complex plot out of a relatively small number of elements constantly varied and re-deployed. As a further kind of theme-ingredient he had at his disposal the whole tradition of the fall of Troy and its immediate aftermath – a kernel of historical fact, probably, remembered with increasing inaccuracy and then elaborated in prose stories and, soon enough no doubt, in short poems. The poet of the *Odyssey* carefully avoids repeating any of the content of the *Iliad* itself, but uses tales of Odysseus' spying expedition to Troy, of the city's fall, of the quarrel of Ajax and Odysseus and of the varying fortunes of the Achaean survivors as they return home. Above all, the death of King Agamemnon at the hands of Clytemnestra and Aegisthus is mentioned in detail both early and late in the poem (although the context in Book 24 involves one of the rare instances of post-Homeric elaboration).[2] Orestes is repeatedly held up to Telemachus as an example of youthful steadfastness and determination, just as Odysseus is warned not to return home openly and risk the fate of Agamemnon. The *exemplum*, the cautionary tale, is a recurring motif of the *Iliad* (notably in the story of the wrath of Meleager told to Achilles, *Il.* 9.527–605) as well as the *Odyssey*, and was doubtless a common element of much or most oral heroic poetry.

The practice of thematic variation could be an encouragement to secondary expansion as well as an aid to large-scale composition in the first place. There are sections of the *Odyssey* that are more certainly the result of rhapsodic elaboration than anything (beyond the occasional single verse) in the *Iliad*. Odysseus' journey to the world of the dead in the eleventh book embodies a probably familiar and traditional theme; but his meeting with Tiresias, his mother and certain dead companions takes a distinctly peculiar turn when he is envisaged as strolling in the underworld itself and watching its great sinners undergoing punishment (*Od.* 11.568–600) – and that is preceded by a catalogue of famous heroines that is highly inappropriate if not definitely suspect (11.225–329). The underworld theme is used again, once more probably by an imitator, in the curious 'Second Nekyia' that opens Book 24, when the souls of the dead suitors are led down by Hermes past scenery that is wholly alien to the usual Homeric view of Hades. But then most of that twenty-fourth book has evidently been heavily reworked and expanded from a smaller nucleus, probably by rhapsodes in the seventh or early sixth century B.C., who unleashed

---

[1] *Od.* 1.158–68, 14.61–71, 16.112–20, 20.185–210.
[2] *Od.* 1.35–43, 298–302; 24.19–22, 96 f., 191–202.

their virtuoso abilities on the most popular parts of the text before it was recorded complete in writing, at some time in the sixth century, to control the competitions in recitation at the Panathenaic games.

So much for the mechanics of construction and progressive elaboration. What can be said of the poem as a whole, considered as a work of the imagination – for that, whatever its pre-existing materials and techniques of repetition, it undoubtedly remains? It can be judged on two levels. On the first and more superficial one it is clearly a rich and engaging story, fluent and adroit in expression and rising at times to high poetry. Occasionally the momentum falters, especially in the conversations and plottings of the second half; but the skilful varying of basic themes and the combining of folktale adventures with Trojan memories and special ideas like Telemachus' trip to the Peloponnese enable the central plot of Odysseus' return and vengeance to sustain the weight of its massive treatment. On a second and deeper level the poem is sharply focused on its central character, Odysseus. That is what it professes in its opening words:

> Tell me, Muse, of a man, a man of many turns, who underwent many wanderings when once he had laid waste Troy's sacred city; he saw the towns and learned the mind of many men, and many were the griefs he suffered in his heart at sea, striving for his own life-soul and his comrades' return.

His release from Calypso is the first topic to be discussed among the gods, directly after this prologue, and although he is formally absent from the scene until the fifth book he is present in everyone's thoughts and words. Thereafter he is almost continuously the centre of attention.

'Seeing the towns and learning the mind of many men' has sometimes persuaded critics that the main composer is claiming Odysseus' experience to be both spiritual and intellectual. Actually the expression probably means no more than that between Troy and Ithaca he visited many places and often had occasion to ask himself whether the inhabitants were 'arrogant, wild and unjust or hospitable and of god-fearing mind' (for example at 6.120f.). Yet the poem does, in the end, reveal things about him that raise him above the level of a determined, resourceful and picaresque character. Admittedly some of its episodes do no more than that; whoever was hero of the sea-adventures in earlier versions, or of simpler tales of the return home of a long-lost king, we can be fairly sure that his role was simply to succeed – to be heroic but little more. The impression given by our *Odyssey* in its entirety is rather different. Is it simply the multiplicity of his successes that raises him to another plane? Surely not; it is something to do, rather, with the interplay of the different circumstances in which he finds himself, together with his responses to them and the effects he thereby has on others.

For it is a sign of the strong central conception of the monumental poem that all its characters (except for a few probable additions in the underworld scenes) are so powerfully affected by Odysseus. None of them is otiose in this respect, and none is treated as a mere mechanism for triggering off new events. Telemachus' journey is prompted by his determination to discover his father's fate, and his hosts, Nestor and Menelaus, are themselves almost obsessed with memories of the man. The suitors repeatedly try to convince themselves that he is dead, and the whole situation in the palace, not least the despondency and confusion of Telemachus and Penelope, depends on the dilemma created by Odysseus' long absence. Calypso 'the concealer' is necessary to initiate that dilemma; Odysseus himself is bored, but she is nonetheless devastated by the thought of losing him. In rejecting her offer of immortality Odysseus prudently decides in favour of common sense and humanity; but even being offered the choice makes him a little more than human, as we should remember when he finally does return, almost too coolly, to the wife and home and possessions he had claimed to love beyond all else. The Phaeacians, a half-magical people related to the gods and remote from ordinary men, are no less strongly affected by their shipwrecked guest. Nausicaa is fascinated by him, and so in a different way is her father Alcinous, a model of hospitality but also at times bluff, bumbling and comically obtuse. The eliciting of Odysseus' reminiscences is one purpose of the episode, but another is surely the placing of the hero in a kind of limbo between the open fantasy of Circe and Calypso and the erratic but intense realities of Troy and Ithaca. In that limbo he, and the audience with him, draws together the strands of past and future as the disparate elements of the plot are cunningly connected.

Once again Odysseus emerges larger than before, not only materially (he had arrived in Scheria naked, battered, a suppliant, and left with gifts worth more than his lost share of the booty from Troy) but also – much as one hesitates to use the expression – spiritually. Odysseus' spirit is not only his *thymos*, that part of him that is the passionate will to survive and that also suffers grief, and that in Greek literally means 'breath' or 'spirit'; it is also something for which Greek had no proper expression, the whole of man's experience reflecting itself in his personality and behaviour. Are we meant to sense that special aspect of Odysseus, his experience of most things human and some divine, once he has regained the familiar landscape of his native island? One wonders – for in some ways the action of the second half of the poem is too concentrated to let this side of him appear with great clarity, at least after his revelation of himself to Eumaeus and Telemachus. Those conversations of the fourteenth and fifteenth books were the obvious opportunity for the poet to make his point about Odysseus, if it were a point to be openly made; either then, or when Penelope is finally permitted to accept him as her husband. The poet certainly did not take the first opportunity. Caution, and repeated false tales including hints that Odysseus is close at hand, are the main elements of those former scenes. As soon as the hero reveals his identity, and after a brief moment of hugging and rejoicing, the plotting continues. With Penelope it is almost the same, at least to begin with. But then, as they go to bed, he summarizes all his hardships and adventures and outlines Tiresias' prediction of a last journey to be made and a peaceful death from the sea (23.248–343).

That, perhaps, is the clue we need. For in most of his behaviour, both before and after his triumph, he has resembled an ordinary hero, fierce and cruel with the suitors and disloyal servants, generous and just with his friends. So far, then, an Iliadic figure. It is in his private demeanour with his wife, in the emphasis on his wanderings and sufferings, his encounters with divine beings, his happy but indefinite future, that Odysseus' role as the man of more than human experience is underlined. Boastful, erratic, morose and unfaithful he had been, at one time or another in the twenty years since he left home; but also brave, resourceful and passionate, a connoisseur of circumstances and of persons, of women no less than men; above all god-guided by Athena, with the blessing of all the Olympians save Poseidon (whose anger against Odysseus had been aroused by the blinding of his son Polyphemus) – not because he was of divine descent like Aeneas, Achilles or Sarpedon in the *Iliad* but because in the last resort he was *polymetis*, 'of many counsels'. Resourcefulness, the ability to assess and deal with things as they are, were qualities admired and rewarded by the gods, by Athena above all. In allowing Odysseus to experience grief, frustration and minor successes without for a moment being distracted from his ultimate aim, in making him the omnipresent figure who, whether lost or disguised or completely revealed, brings both truth and fantasy to the heroic past and the unsettled present, the poet of the *Odyssey* exhibits the touch of genius that his traditional materials did not necessarily contain or indicate.

3

HESIOD

'Who could speak highly enough of training in the art of writing?' asks the historian Diodorus (12.13.2). 'By this means alone the dead speak to the living, and through the written word those who are widely separated in space communicate with those remote from them as if they were neighbours.' The quarter-millennium from *c.* 730 to *c.* 480 in Greece was a period in which literacy came to have far-reaching effects on literature, making possible an infinitely complex network of relationships between authors remote from one another in time or space or both, and allowing the development of a single unified literary culture, to which local differences only added richness. For it is no coincidence that as literacy spread there came a growing consciousness of national identity, the universal Greekness of all who spoke and wrote the common tongue. This capital event, the re-invention of writing, was itself, moreover, only one element among many in the great renaissance of Greece which came from the rediscovery of the wider world after centuries of isolation – centuries in which, following the collapse of the literate Mycenaean culture between 1200 and 1100, all the fine arts and delicate skills of the Bronze Age had been forgotten and all that remained was the memory of great deeds and great heroes, enshrined in the traditional forms of oral poetry and chanted to precarious settlements of refugees on the coastal fringe of Asia Minor.

It makes sense to begin a discussion of the period of Greek literacy with Hesiod, not because there is any certainty that he was a literate poet – in fact there is much to be said for the view that he worked in a tradition of formular oral poetry which was fairly closely akin to Homer's – but because he was doing something new and individual which pointed the way that subsequent Greek poetry was to take. For while Homer keeps his own personality entirely separate from his poetry and gives no clue to any datable event with which he might be associated, Hesiod is the first European poet who introduces himself into his work as an individual with a distinctive role to play. And in *Works and days* he takes the important step of abandoning traditional narrative with its stock of set themes and scenes in favour of a poem with an argument, perhaps using models from Near-Eastern culture as his inspiration (though we cannot be sure that Greek poets had not already taken to composing wisdom literature of this kind). In combining traditional form and style with a highly individual 'tone of voice' and in extending the range of the poet's functions Hesiod set the pattern for what we misleadingly call 'archaic' Greek poetry, the literature of a period of territorial expansion through colonization, of rapid social change and of sophisticated artistic experiment.

The date of Hesiod's poetic activity is disputed, but there can be little doubt that this was some time in the latter part of the eighth century. He tells us himself[1] how he won a prize for poetry in a competition in Chalcis at the funeral games of Amphidamas, a Chalcidian killed in a naval battle in the Lelantine War. This famous war, which drew so much of Greece into alliance that it is excepted from Thucydides' general disparagement of the campaigns of archaic Greece (1.15.3), was fought between the Euboean cities Chalcis and Eretria for the possession of the plain of Lelanton which lies between them. An upper limit for its date should therefore be provided by the presumably amicable colonial enterprises on which the two cities embarked jointly in Chalcidice and in the west at Pithecusae and Cumae, c. 750. The lower limit is indicated by the fact that it is said by Aristotle to have been an old-fashioned cavalry war (*Pol.* 1289b36–9); it must therefore predate the coming of hoplites and the tactics of the phalanx, c. 700–680. There is now archaeological confirmation of this date: the settlement on the ridge of Xeropolis, near Lefkandi in Euboea at the eastern (Eretrian) end of the plain of Lelanton, was destroyed without reoccupation shortly before 700, after continuous habitation since the Late Bronze Age. Amphidamas' funeral and Hesiod's victory belong therefore to the last third of the eighth century.

His father, he tells us, left the Aeolian city of Cyme for mainland Greece:

> Your father and mine, foolish Perses, used to go to sea in search of a good livelihood. One day he came here over a great expanse of sea, leaving Aeolian Cyme in a black ship. What he fled was not riches, wealth and prosperity, but evil penury, which Zeus gives to men. And he settled near Helicon in a miserable village, Ascra, which is bad in winter and unpleasant in summer, never any good. (*W.D.* 633–40)

That Hesiod's father should have left Asia for the less fertile and apparently overpopulated mainland is unexplained. But it is to be noticed that the date of his removal, which must have been about 750 or a little later, falls within the very period when others, themselves sea-going merchants, were leaving Cyme to share with Euboeans in the colonization of Cumae in Campania. Hesiod's father evidently became a farmer, for the poet and his brother fell out over an agricultural inheritance. The scale of their farming has sometimes been romantically disparaged. In fact the *Works and days* presupposes yeomen rather than

---

[1] *W.D.* 654–9 with schol.; Plutarch, *Mor.* 153f.

peasants. The farmer does not work alone but can employ a friend (370), as well as servants (502, 573, 597, 608, 766), has a lively forty-year-old free labourer to follow the plough and a slave-boy to turn in the seed (441–6, cf. 469–71), together with a female servant at home (405, 602). Of draught animals he has plough oxen and mules (405, 607f.). On the other hand he cannot afford merely to oversee the work of others: he must take his share too (458–61). For all Hesiod's harping on poverty (638, cf. 376f.), life at Ascra cannot have been too uncomfortable.

Three poems survive in Hesiod's name, together with a host of fragments of other works attributed to him in antiquity; all are composed in dactylic hexameters and in the conventional language of epic. Of the three survivors, one, the *Shield of Heracles*, is undoubtedly spurious and probably belongs to the sixth century.[1] Of the other two, the severest of ancient critics allowed only the *Works and days* to Hesiod (cf. Pausanias 9.31.3). But the poet is named in *Theogony* 22, and it requires some perversity to interpret the context in such a way as to deny that the author is here naming himself. Moreover, despite the general disparity of their subject matter the two poems offer versions of the Prometheus myth which, as Vernant has shown,[2] interlock with one another, and their close relationship in language, metre and prosody sets them apart from Homer on the one hand and the *Shield* on the other.

If both are indeed the work of Hesiod, the priority of the *Theogony* is easily established. For the opening of the *Works and days*, 11–23, appears explicitly to modify a doctrine of the *Theogony*: there is not after all only one kind of Eris (contention), as had been said at *Theog.* 225f.; there are two, beneficial competition as well as destructive strife. The same conclusion is suggested by Hesiod's treatment of the story of Prometheus and Pandora in the two poems. In the *Theogony* we read in detail of the sin of Prometheus and of the creation and adornment of Pandora (501–616), whereas in the *Works and days* Hesiod passes over the early part of the story in two lines (47f.), and dwells at length on the subsequent history of Pandora and the jar[3] (49–105). In the *Works and days*, in fact, Hesiod seems to presuppose knowledge of the *Theogony*. The latter may indeed be the very poem to which Hesiod looks back in *W.D.* 654ff., the prize-winning entry at Amphidamas' funeral. For the competition-piece was a *hymnos*, and the prize tripod was dedicated by the poet to the Muses of Helicon on the very spot where they had inspired him first. The *Theogony*, addressed to the Muses of Helicon, describes that first inspiration (22–35), and is itself characterized as a *hymnos* (33, cf. 11, 37, 51).

[1] Cook (1937) discusses its possible date.
[2] Vernant (1980) 184–5.
[3] A jar (*pithos*), not the box familiar in later European tradition, which derives from Erasmus; cf. Panofsky (1962) and West (1978a) on *W.D.* 94.

The poem begins with a long invocation of the Muses (1–115), itself of the nature of a 'Homeric' hymn, celebrating their power as well as their piety in singing of the generations of the gods. They are the daughters of Zeus by Memory, a parentage which recalls the long tradition of oral recitation, when a bard's skill did indeed depend on memory, his own and his forerunners'. It was they who 'once taught Hesiod beautiful song, as he tended his sheep under holy Helicon' (22–3) and 'they gave me a staff, plucking a fine branch of flourishing bay, and breathed in me a divine voice, so that I might sing of what was to come and what had been. And they commanded me to hymn the race of the blessed immortals and always to sing of themselves first and last' (30–4).

So Hesiod begins his account of creation and of the succession of divinities who have presided over it since the beginning. Partly a narrative of development, partly an account of the theological *status quo*, it is constructed loosely, with passages in which some three hundred gods are classified according to genealogy, interspersed with a number of more leisurely stories. The Creation itself is given no cause: Chaos, the yawning void, merely 'came into existence', followed by Earth, Tartarus and Eros (Love). From Chaos came Erebus and Night to become the parents of Aether (the clear upper air) and Day; from Earth came Heaven (Uranus), Mountains and the Sea. Then creation is filled with three main lines of descent, from Night, from Earth and Heaven, from the Sea. The main line is that of Earth and Heaven, leading through the generations of the Titans and Cronos to Zeus himself. The first extended myth (154–210) describes the dethronement of Uranus, castrated by Cronos, and the birth of Aphrodite from his severed genitals; the second (453–506), after another long section of genealogies, tells the story of Cronos, who determined to eat the gods, his children, in order to forestall his overthrow by one of them, but was tricked into swallowing a stone instead of Zeus and was supplanted in his turn.

By this time Hesiod has lost interest in cosmogony, and says no more of the way in which things came to be. The remainder of the poem is concerned to explain the world as it is rather than to identify stages in its development. So the rise of Zeus is followed by a list of the sons of the Titan Iapetus, which serves as an introduction to the story of Prometheus and Pandora[1] and the invention of woman, and the phenomena of sacrifice and fire (507–616). Here the scene is broadened again to present a resurgence of the Titans and their final overthrow by Zeus (617–720). There follows an account of Tartarus, where Zeus imprisoned them, the haunt of Sleep, Death, Cerberus and Styx (721–819). This is a prelude to the struggle between Zeus and the monster Typhoeus, the youngest child of Earth (820–80); when Zeus is victorious he

---

[1] For the fundamental significance of this myth see Vernant (1980) 168–85.

95

HESIOD

is elected king of the gods and gives to each of the immortals his or her sphere (881–5). From this point the poem tails off into an extended series of marriages and love-affairs, beginning with those of Zeus himself, then those of the other gods, goddesses, and nymphs, and ending with a transition to the *Catalogue of women*, a long poem of which only fragments survive.

In the *Theogony* there is much that successive editors have regarded as spurious,[1] but they disagree fundamentally in their choice of suspect passages, and it is hard to find safe criteria for judging interpolation in an author like Hesiod. Both his extant poems show a certain diffuseness, a tendency to be side-tracked from the matter in hand, which leads one to doubt whether they ever possessed any logical or rigorous arrangement. Nevertheless it may be agreed that the end of the *Theogony* is not as Hesiod left it: we might after all expect it to close with an invocation of the Muses, as promised at the beginning (34). There are some indications that the end of the poem was remodelled in order to smooth a transition to the *Catalogue of women*, which follows without a break in some of the manuscripts.

Herodotus regarded Homer and Hesiod as the founders of Greek theology (2.53), and the *Theogony* is the only coherent account of it to have survived from this early period. To the modern mind Hesiod's theology is bewildering: powers of nature are now conceived as geographical entities, as when Heaven's children are concealed in a hollow of the Earth (157f.), now made wholly anthropomorphic, as when Heaven himself suffers castration (178ff.). The Olympian gods, by contrast, are always anthropomorphic. Homer's beliefs were evidently similar. His gods are unfailingly human, but he alludes to the older powers in making Oceanus and Tethys the progenitors of the gods (*Il.* 14.201ff.). The creation myths of Homer and Hesiod soon came to seem unsatisfactory, and impersonal causes were adduced instead – either abstract, as when Alcman (*c.* 600) explained all in terms of End and Means (*Tekmor* and *Poros*, fr. 5.2.ii; fr. 1.14 schol.), or concrete, as when the sixth-century Ionian philosophers sought a primary substance among the four elements. Though the Olympians never lost their simple anthropomorphic nature, ridiculed as it was by Xenophanes as early as *c.* 530 (cf. frs. 21B 10–16 DK), the ambiguity of Hesiod's view of the powers of creation remained characteristic of much Greek religious thought even in the classical period, most obviously in relation to the powers which were essential to human life, Mother Earth as well as the river-gods and fountain-nymphs. In Hesiod these divinities rub shoulders with more abstract powers such as Toil, Famine, Sorrow and the other children of Strife, as well as with purely fantastic monsters, Chimaera, Sphinx and so on, any literal belief in whom was certainly abandoned by the Greeks of later days.

[1] Cf. Edwards (1971) 4–6.

Theological notions of such disparate kinds, it is clear, must have reached Hesiod from more than one tradition, to say nothing of his own invention. To what extent the cosmogony and theology which are unfolded in this poem would have appeared novel or exceptional to an eighth-century audience is hard to say; certainly, despite a general similarity of approach, not all is consistent in detail with Homer, and part of the material of the *Theogony* in fact shows close affinities with the theology of Egypt and the Near East. Striking parallels have been found in Hittite and Babylonian texts for the succession myth of Uranus–Cronos–Zeus and for Zeus's fight with Typhoeus.[1]

Hesiod's second poem, the *Works and days*, is like the *Theogony*, a celebration of the power of Zeus, to whom the Muses are invited to contribute a hymn. Zeus is the source of justice, and Hesiod will undertake to instruct his brother Perses in the truth (1–10). Though the instructions and the reflections which follow are mostly of very general application, Hesiod continually calls his brother to order with some sharply pointed moral.[2] The first truth is that there are two kinds of Contention (Eris): constructive competition and destructive rivalry (11–26). From this spring two of the poem's important themes, that Perses should give up the destructive strife which has marred relations between the two brothers – here Hesiod takes the opportunity to dilate upon the virtues of justice – and should instead let the spirit of competition direct him towards a life of honest labour on the farm. That it is a hard world, with toil and suffering as man's appointed lot, is illustrated by two myths. In the first, Hesiod resumes the story of Pandora, begun in the *Theogony* – her creation and adornment, and the jar out of which all evils flew to harass the world leaving only Hope imprisoned (42–105). It looks like a traditional tale, slightly clumsy in that no real reason is advanced for Hope's failure to escape. But what matters is the ambiguity of Hope's position: it expresses the essential ambiguity of human life, in which good and bad, happiness and unhappiness are inextricably intermingled.[3] The motif of the jar as prison is also found at *Iliad* 5.385–91, where Otus and Ephialtes are held in a bronze jar, but the closest parallel with Hesiod is at *Iliad* 24.527ff., where Achilles speaks of the two *pithoi* which stand at the entrance to Zeus's palace, the one containing good and the other evil, from which the god ladles out to men their combination of good and bad fortune in life. The second of Hesiod's myths designed to illustrate the hardness of life is that of the metallic ages of mankind, a gloomy tale of degeneration from Cronos' day, when the men of the golden race lived like gods without a care in the world, through silver and bronze to Hesiod's own race of iron (106–201). Here again we have an evidently traditional tale,

[1] Details in West (1966) 19–30, 106f., 379f.
[2] On the question whether Perses was real or fictitious see West (1978a) 33–40.
[3] Vernant (1980) 184–5.

somewhat crudely adapted. For Hesiod could not square this doctrine of progressive decline with his picture of the Seven against Thebes or the Achaeans before Troy. He therefore intercalated an age of heroes or demigods, non-metallic, between the bronze and the iron. A further, and surely conclusive indication that this myth is adapted from an alien source is its inconsistency with the *Theogony*, in which the time of Cronos is not at all paradisal, merely a stage on the road of progress towards the reign of Zeus.

His account of the iron race moves quickly from description of the present to prophecy of an even grimmer future:

> I wish that I had never belonged to the fifth race, but had either died earlier or been born later. For truly now it is a race of iron. Neither by day will men cease from toil and woe nor from suffering by night. And the gods will give them troubles hard to bear. None the less, even they will have some good mixed with their woes. But Zeus will destroy this race of mortal men too, when they come to have grey hair at birth. A father will not be in harmony with his children, nor the children with their father, nor guest with host, nor comrade with comrade, and a brother will not be dear to his brother as they were in the past. Men will dishonour their quickly ageing parents and will reproach them with harsh words of abuse, wicked men who do not understand the vengeance of the gods. They will not repay their aged parents the cost of their nurture, for might is their right, and one man will sack another's city. There will be no respect for the man who keeps his oath or for the just or the good; instead they will praise the man who does evil, insolence incarnate. And right and reverence shall depend on might. The bad man will harm the better, telling lies about him and confirming them with with an oath. And ugly Envy, that causes uproar and delights in evil, will keep company with the whole of miserable mankind. Then Aidos and Nemesis[1] will wrap their fair bodies in white robes, and go from the earth with its broad paths to Olympus to join the race of immortals, forsaking men, and bitter sorrows will be left for mortal men, and there will be no help against evil. (174–201)

Hesiod now develops the theme of Justice, introduced by its opposite Hybris, the doctrine that might is right, which is embodied in the fable of the hawk and the nightingale. This, the earliest fable in extant Greek literature, points the path to be avoided by Perses, and by princes upon the seat of judgement, and the way of Justice to be followed (202–92). It is noteworthy that the somewhat radical view of the lawlessness and dishonesty of princes developed here runs counter to the favourable view of princes to be found in the *Theogony* (e.g. 80–93). It may be that Hesiod by now was older and wiser; it may be only that the flattery of princes matched the occasion of Amphidamas' funeral. Either way, it raises the question of the kind of occasion for which the *Works and days* was composed. Hesiod's preoccupation with ethics and with the justice of Zeus is a whole world away from the old aristocratic view of the

---

[1] Aidos = 'shame', 'reverence'; Nemesis = 'awe', 'public disapproval'.

divine right of kings, which is unquestioned in the *Iliad* and still largely prevails in the *Odyssey*, even if the self-condemning behaviour of Penelope's princely suitors marks the beginnings of doubt. In particular, it is noteworthy that in Hesiod's view injustice leads ultimately to war as the worst of evils (276ff.). War, of course, is the sport of princes, and in this passage above all Hesiod turns his back on Homer and the heroic tradition.

From Justice Hesiod turns to the broader theme of work: the attitude as well as the equipment of the farmer and householder is prescribed in the greatest detail, a calendar of the yearly round of toil (293–617). This whole section, the longest part of the poem, is of course invaluable for the insight it gives into the life and outlook of an ordinary Greek of the eighth century. There is no romantic view of country life such as Virgil was to import into his *Georgics*: the romantic approach is characteristic not of the countryman but of the city-dweller, and it is no accident that we first find it in the Hellenistic period, when truly urbanized society first began to emerge. Hesiod has no illusions about life on the farm. Here is his account of winter:

> Avoid the month of Lenaeon [late January/early February], wretched days, all fit to flay an ox, and the frosts, which are severe when Boreas blows over the earth. He blows across horse-breeding Thrace and on the broad sea and stirs it up, and the earth and woodlands roar. Often he falls upon oaks with their lofty foliage and thick pines in the mountain glens and brings them down to the bountiful earth, and then all the immense wood groans. And the beasts shiver and put their tails between their legs, even the ones whose hide is covered with fur. But his cold blasts blow through them despite their shaggy breasts. And he goes even through oxhide and it cannot resist him, and through the thin-haired goat. But the strength of Boreas does not penetrate the sheep, because their wool is abundant; yet it makes the old man bent like a wheel. (504–18)

And he goes on to give advice about the kind of boots and jerkin and felt cap that the farmer should wear against the bitter weather.

Farming, however, is not the only career Hesiod envisages. If, instead, the life of the merchant seaman seems to offer attractions, as it did to Hesiod's father, then words of warning and advice are in place (618–94). Whatever the means of livelihood, the indispensable basis is the family – even if financial prudence demands its strict limitation (376f.) – and this necessitates the choice of a wife. For Hesiod this seems to have been a matter for regret, and in his misogyny he anticipates Semonides (see pp. 153ff.). In the *Theogony* the creation of woman was the worst Zeus could do to plague mankind (570–612), and Love (*Philotes*) and Deceit are linked among the children of Night (224). In the present poem the need to choose a good wife and to treat her well serves largely as an occasion to warn of the havoc a bad wife can wreak (cf. 373ff.):

Bring a wife to your house when you are the right age, neither far short of thirty nor much older: this is the right age for marriage. The woman should be four years beyond maturity and marry in the fifth. Marry a virgin so that you can teach her proper conduct, and make a point of choosing someone who lives near, but take care not to make a marriage that will be a joke to your neighbours. For there is nothing a man can win that is better than a good wife, and nothing worse than a bad one – a parasite who scorches her husband without fire, however strong he is, and brings him to cruel old age. (695–705)

Finally, a few lines on friendship bring this part of the poem to a close (706–23).

The remainder of the *Works and days* has been thought spurious by many critics. Interesting as it is to the historian of religion, the detailed list of taboos it contains (724–64) has seemed to express a primitive narrowness of vision at odds with the broad and elevated concept of the justice of all-seeing Zeus. Yet it is common experience that in unsophisticated societies the most religious standards of probity in commercial dealings are in no way incompatible with the most elaborate web of superstition. A similar controversy has been waged over the last section of the poem – the *Days*, in fact (765–828) – which gives a list of days that are propitious or unpropitious for various undertakings. But the burden of proof is upon those who would declare the verses spurious.[1]

There is no doubt that as a whole the poem is lacking in that architechtonic quality which strikes every reader of the *Iliad* and *Odyssey*. Those poems may sometimes seem to digress, sometimes dwell too long on one scene, sometimes repeat a theme a little tediously, but that they have a beginning, middle and end in the full sense of Aristotle's famous definition no one can doubt. About the *Works and days*, on the other hand, doubts have been expressed since Pausanias in the second century A.D. stated that according to the Boeotians the text of the poem began with our line 11 (9.31). One modern critic after another has condemned the end of the poem and even in the middle the apparatus criticus bristles with such words as *suspecta, damnavit, delevit, proscripsit, seclusit* – scholars have for years tried to make a logical discourse of the poem by cutting, rearranging and rewriting. The trouble is, they are asking too much of it. They are asking it to be a logical progression (as each of the Homeric poems is a narrative progression); they are treating it as if it were a practical handbook on agriculture or a poem about justice, with a continuous argument. Judged by that criterion it fails to live up to elementary standards of logic, consistency and structural coherence.

It must be judged, of course, by quite other standards. It is the first attempt in western literature to compose a large-scale work without the armature of a given narrative line. It is, in fact, an extraordinarily bold venture. In the

[1] For a review of the problems see West (1978a) 346–50.

Theogony Hesiod had a genealogical line to follow which was itself a sort of narrative thread; in the *Catalogue of women* he (or whoever was its author) simply added one story to another. The alternative title of the poem is Ἦ Οἶαι (*Ehoiai*); each fresh episode begins with ἢ οἶαι 'like those women who . . .' (or the singular ἢ οἴη 'like that woman who . . .'), followed by the tale of their loves, usually with a god, and the birth of heroes. Such a poem needed no structure and could obviously go on as long as anyone wanted to hear it; the episodes could be arranged in any order. But the *Works and days* has a purpose: to explain why life is a ceaseless round of labour and to offer advice which will make that labour profitable and tolerable. And it does this in a dramatic framework: Hesiod's quarrel with his brother Perses.

If the *Theogony* were not so plainly a farrago of Greek and oriental elements, the oriental character of much of the *Works and days* might have passed without notice, since it is in so many ways the fountain-head of an essentially Greek view of life. Yet it too has its antecedents in the east and in Egypt. The myth of the metallic ages of man, it has been noted, was not of Hesiod's own invention; exact parallels are wanting, but the closest analogies are with Zoroastrian myths.[1] The poem as a whole has many counterparts in Egypt and in the Near East, didactic works about life and behaviour which, however, typically enshrine the advice of a father to his son.[2] Hesiod's variant, the advice of brother to brother, is perhaps original, and no motive for the change need be sought beyond the poet's own circumstances. The Egyptian texts in this genre extend from the Old Kingdom to the Saïte dynasty beyond the lifetime of Hesiod, and include exhortations to agricultural toil in the context of a relationship between man and god that is not at all far removed in spirit from Hesiod's view of Zeus. Similar texts are found in the Near East, at Ugarit and elsewhere, and it is clear that the Sumerians (who loved animal fables similar to Hesiod's tale of the hawk and the nightingale), Hurrians and Babylonians all succumbed to the human temptation to seek to order the lives of others. In such a universal theme one must be careful not to rule out coincidence. Argument from such texts as the *Instructions of Ninurta* to his son, a Sumerian farmer's almanac, are particularly dangerous in view of the uniform demands of agricultural life. Yet there is enough in the Sumerian *Instructions of Šuruppak*, the Babylonian *Counsels of Wisdom*, and the Egyptian *Instructions* to locate Hesiod in the mainstream of a current of literature which enjoyed popularity in the orient (though not enough to identify a particular source or to establish a date for the arrival of this genre in Greece).

Some features of Hesiod's poetry may strike a modern reader as curiously quaint and 'archaic', by comparison even with Homer's. M. L. West has noted

[1] West (1978a) 172–7.
[2] For a survey of Near-Eastern wisdom literature see West (1978a) 3–15.

the difference between the expansiveness and eloquence of speeches in Homer and the brief, rather stiff utterances that Hesiod gives his characters: 'curt little affairs, devoid of Homeric rhetoric, and quaintly formal'.[1] So Hesiod's story-telling often seems comparatively naive and lacking in Homer's psychological depth, while his tendency to repetitiveness, and some tricks of style like his use of kennings (the 'boneless one' = the octopus, ἀνόστεος, *W.D.* 524; the 'five-branched thing' = the hand, πεντόζοιο, *W.D.* 742) may contribute to a certain impression of primitivism. But against this we should set the energy and vitality of his poetry and the authoritativeness of its tone, sometimes solemn, sometimes almost sardonic. There is an attractive robustness and absence of sentimentality even in his most idyllic passages, like the description of high summer in his directions for seasonal activities:

> When the golden thistle is in flower, and the chirping cicada sits in a tree and incessantly pours out its shrill song from under its wings in the time of exhausting summer heat, then goats are fattest and wine sweetest and women most wanton and men at their feeblest, for Sirius burns their heads and their knees and their skin is parched in the heat. Then is the right time for the shade of a rock and Bibline wine and milk bread and late-season goat's milk, and the meat of a heifer that has been put out to graze and has not calved, and of firstling kids. Drink the bright wine sitting in the shade when you have had your fill of food, turning your face towards the fresh Zephyr, and pour in three parts of water from a perpetually running, unmuddied spring, and the fourth part of wine. (*W.D.* 582–96)[2]

(This should be read without forgetting 500–3: 'Hope is not a good companion for a poor man, who sits around where people meet to chat when he has no decent livelihood. Tell your servants while it is still midsummer, "It won't always be summer: build yourselves shelters".'.)

There is real dignity in many passages: in the proem to the *Theogony*, or the picture of the just and unjust cities in *W.D.* (225–47), or the account of Hecate's honours in the *Theogony*, a passage which well illustrates how effective a rather simple use of repetition can be:

> ἣ δ' ὑποκυσαμένη Ἑκάτην τέκε, τὴν περὶ πάντων
> Ζεὺς Κρονίδης τίμησε, πόρεν δέ οἱ ἀγλαὰ δῶρα,
> μοῖραν ἔχειν γαίης τε καὶ ἀτρυγέτοιο θαλάσσης·
> ἣ δὲ καὶ ἀστερόεντος ἀπ' οὐρανοῦ ἔμμορε τιμῆς,
> ἀθανάτοις τε θεοῖσι τετιμένη ἐστὶ μάλιστα.
> καὶ γὰρ νῦν, ὅτε πού τις ἐπιχθονίων ἀνθρώπων
> ἔρδων ἱερὰ καλὰ κατὰ νόμον ἱλάσκηται,
> κικλήσκει Ἑκάτην· πολλή τέ οἱ ἕσπετο τιμὴ
> ῥεῖα μάλ', ὧι πρόφρων γε θεὰ ὑποδέξεται εὐχάς·
> καί τέ οἱ ὄλβον ὀπάζει, ἐπεὶ δύναμίς γε πάρεστιν.

---

[1] West (1966) 74.
[2] This passage is imitated in the *Shield of Heracles* 393–7 and by Alcaeus (fr. 347).

HESIOD

ὅσσοι γὰρ Γαίης τε καὶ Οὐρανοῦ ἐξεγένοντο
καὶ τιμὴν ἔλαχον, τούτων ἔχει αἶσαν ἀπάντων·
οὐδέ τί μιν Κρονίδης ἐβιήσατο οὐδέ τ’ ἀπηύρα
ὅσσ’ ἔλαχεν Τιτῆσι μετὰ προτέροισι θεοῖσιν,
ἀλλ’ ἔχει ὡς τὸ πρῶτον ἀπ’ ἀρχῆς ἔπλετο δασμός·
οὐδ’, ὅτι μουνογενής, ἧσσον θεὰ ἔμμορε τιμῆς,
[καὶ γέρας ἐν γαίηι τε καὶ οὐρανῶι ἠδὲ θαλάσσηι,]
ἀλλ’ ἔτι καὶ πολὺ μᾶλλον, ἐπεὶ Ζεὺς τίεται αὐτήν.   (411–28)

And she [Asterie] became pregnant and gave birth to Hecate, whom Zeus son of
Cronos honoured above all. He gave her splendid gifts, a portion to have as her
own of the earth and the unharvested sea. She received honour too from the
starry heaven, and she is exceedingly honoured by the immortal gods. For to
this day whenever any mortal offers fine sacrifices and prays according to custom
he calls upon Hecate; and great honour comes easily to him whose prayers the
goddess receives favourably, and she grants him prosperity, for she has the power.
For she has a portion among all those who were born of Earth and Heaven and
obtained honour. The son of Cronos did her no violence and took nothing from
her, of all the privileges that fell to her lot among the Titans, the former race of
gods, but she continues to hold them just as she did when the distribution was
first made. Nor, because she was an only daughter, did the goddess obtain a
smaller share of honour [and privileges on land and in heaven and in the sea],
but much more still, since Zeus honours her.

The individuality and power of Hesiod's imagination can best be seen from
comparison with a work by one of his imitators, the short epic known as the
Shield of Heracles (Scutum or Aspis), which is transmitted along with Theogony
and Works and days in the medieval manuscripts. This is a weak and muddled
account of the fight between Heracles and Cycnus, containing a long ecphrastic
passage, modelled on Homer's accounts of the shields of Achilles (Il. 18.478–
607) and Agamemnon (Il. 11.32–40), in which the shield of Heracles is described.
It wholly lacks the strength and wit of Hesiod and depends for its effects on
sheer accumulation of detail, preferably detail of a sensational kind:

By them stood Achlys [Woe, literally the mist that covers the eyes in death],
gloomy and dreadful, pale, shrivelled, shrunken with hunger, with swollen knees
and long fingernails. Mucus flowed from her nose, and blood dripped from her
cheeks to the ground. She stood grinning horribly, and much dust, damp with
tears, covered her shoulders. (264–70)

This is one of the less derivative passages; other less spine-chilling scenes are
rather clumsily adapted from Homer. The work has no claim to be by Hesiod,
though it shows close familiarity with his genuine work and was designed to
fit into the Catalogue of women: it opens with a section on Heracles' mother
Alcmena beginning ἢ οἵη (see above, p. 101).

Two main issues of Hesiodic scholarship remain unsettled: his relationship to Homer and his mode of composition. Although it now seems clear that Hesiod was active in the latter part of the eighth century, there is no consensus on the question of the relative dates of Hesiod and the *Iliad* and *Odyssey* respectively. All that can be demonstrated is that Hesiod and Homer are very closely comparable in language and manner: in essence they share the same dialect, and they have a large proportion of their vocabulary and formulaic phrases in common, though there are also notable differences,[1] and some of Hesiod's peculiarities of dialect are particularly hard to explain. G. P. Edwards, on the basis of a close study of Hesiod's language, arrived at the following conclusion:

Ionian epic poetry was known on the mainland in the time of Hesiod and was recited in its Ionic form even by mainlanders. The Homeric poems suggest themselves as the most obvious representatives of this Ionian tradition, but clearly they need not have been the only Ionian poetry which Hesiod could have known, nor can we assume that Hesiod knew them in the form in which they have survived in our written texts. At the same time, the most economical hypothesis may be that the *Iliad* and the *Odyssey* already existed and were known on the Greek mainland by Hesiod's time in a form recognisably the same as that in which we know them today...[2]

M. L. West, on the other hand, has argued that the *Theogony* is quite likely to be 'the oldest Greek poem we have',[3] on the grounds that both the *Iliad* and the *Odyssey* in their present form admit elements that cannot be dated earlier than *c.* 700 B.C. It is probably too risky to demand such precision from archaeological evidence, and in the end it may not matter that we cannot precisely date any of these poems; more important is the growing recognition by modern scholars that there was a common Ionian tradition of hexameter poetry in which both poets worked, despite their geographical separation.

Whether Hesiod was an oral or a literate composer is an equally controversial question; but here again there is an important area of agreement, namely that however Hesiod himself may have proceeded[4] the tradition in which he learned his craft was an oral one. It is probably impossible to prove one way or the other whether he used writing to compose his poetry, but there is perhaps some force in the consideration that a highly personal poem like the *Works and days*, which has no narrative thread to help the reciter, stood a better chance of surviving if it was committed to writing at a fairly early stage, that is, during the poet's lifetime. This is not to suggest that there was such a thing as a regular reading public at this date: the normal mode of communication

[1] West (1966) 77–91 and (1978a) 31f.; Edwards (1971) especially 140–65.
[2] Edwards (1971) 202f.
[3] West (1966) 46.
[4] West (1978a) 40–8 makes some interesting suggestions. Cf. Edwards (1971) 190–3.

between poets and their audiences was surely that of oral performance, whether at festivals or at some other kind of social gathering. But the wide acquaintance with *Works and days* that we can demonstrate for the archaic period[1] is difficult to account for without supposing that some use was made of written texts. As with the work of Archilochus and the early elegists and lyric poets, the possibility of long-term survival must have been enormously enhanced by the development of writing in Greek society.

[1] Tyrtaeus 12.43 may be an echo of *W.D.* 291; Semonides 6 is a reworking of *W.D.* 702f.; Alcaeus fr. 347 echoes *W.D.* 582–9; Ibycus 282 *PMG*, 18–24 may make use of *W.D.* 646–62.

4

THE EPIC TRADITION
AFTER HOMER AND HESIOD

I. THE CYCLIC EPICS

Homer and Hesiod, as the sole survivors of the earliest age of Greek literature, have conveyed such an impression of uniqueness that it requires some effort to recall that they were by no means without rivals and imitators. The formulaic nature of their verse, which implies a common bardic tradition, the recitations of Phemius and Demodocus in the *Odyssey*, and the occasion of Hesiod's competition at Chalcis all suggest that the eighth century was a period of lively poetic activity. When at *Od.* 12.70 the good ship *Argo* is said to be 'of interest to all', that surely alludes to some well-known treatment of the story of the Argonauts; and the brief résumé of Oedipus' story at *Od.* 11.271–80 must recall a more extended treatment elsewhere. We know that many early epic poems in fact survived from the archaic period alongside the works of Homer and Hesiod; at some (unknown) stage they were grouped into a sequence or 'cycle' starting at the remotest of beginnings with a *Theogony* and a *Battle of the Titans* and running through the legends of Thebes[1] and the Trojan War. They were performed by professional reciters (rhapsodes) in competitions at festivals, and must have been widely known until at least well into the fifth century. Probably the term 'cycle' was originally used of most epic narrative poetry, Homeric and non-Homeric alike; it was only after the time of Aristotle that 'cyclic' meant something essentially different from 'Homeric'.[2]

Of this enormous body of verse only a few brief quotations have survived – a mere 120 or so lines – but we have a helpful summary of the Trojan part of the Cycle (excerpted from a work of the fifth century A.D.,[3] the *Chrestomathia* of Proclus). This gives the whole story of the Trojan War, from the initial plan of Zeus to relieve the earth of excess population down to the death of Odysseus (and the final bizarre marryings-off: Penelope and Odysseus' son

---

[1] The Theban epics were *Oedipodeia*, *Thebais* and *Epigoni*.
[2] Pfeiffer (1968) 43f. and 230.
[3] Unless a different Proclus is involved; cf. Severyns (1963).

Telegonus, Circe and Telemachus). The myths themselves must have been mainly very old, as we can tell from allusive references to them within the *Iliad* and the *Odyssey* (e.g. *Il.* 3.243f.: the Dioscuri, cf. *Cypria*; *Od.* 4.271–84: the Wooden Horse, cf. *Iliou persis*), but it is certain that many of the poems in the Cycle were composed later than the Homeric epics, probably in the seventh and sixth centuries, and many authors other than Homer are named (see Appendix).[1] According to Proclus the Trojan Cycle comprised *Cypria* (11 books); *Iliad*; *Aethiopis* (5 books); *Little Iliad* (4 books); *Iliou persis* 'Sack of Troy' (2 books); *Nostoi* 'Homecomings' (5 books); *Odyssey*; *Telegonia* (2 books). A glance at Proclus' summary at once suggests the importance of these epics for later Greek literature. The *Cypria*, for example, dealt with the following episodes: the judgement of Paris, the rape of Helen, the gathering of the Greek host, Achilles on Scyros, Telephus, the quarrel of Achilles and Agamemnon, Iphigenia at Aulis, Protesilaus. As Aristotle says in a critique of the formlessness of the cyclic poems, there is material here for many tragedies (*Poet.* 1459b1–7), and the same is true of most of the other works in the Cycle; their influence on lyric poetry, too, and on the visual arts must have been immense.

If our fragments were less meagre it would no doubt be possible to differentiate more sharply between the individual epics, which must have varied to some extent in quality and interest, as they did in date. A valuable attempt has been made by J. Griffin to characterize the cyclic poems by contrast with the *Iliad* and the *Odyssey*, with strong stress on the idea that the Homeric poems must have survived because they were better than the rest – more coherent and more amply detailed, more consistently serious, less sensational and romantic.[2] For example, the fantastic seems to have been more freely allowed by these authors: folk-tale motifs like the invulnerability of a hero (Ajax in the *Aethiopis*) or magic objects (Philoctetes' bow in the *Little Iliad*, the Palladium in the *Iliou persis*) and romantic incidents, like Achilles meeting Helen in the *Cypria* (a rendezvous arranged by Thetis and Aphrodite), suggest a very different tone from the severe world of the *Iliad*. The cyclic poets seem to have relished such pathetic and shocking episodes as the sacrifices of Iphigenia (*Cypria*) and Polyxena (*Iliou persis*) and to have been less discreet than Homer in the use of horrific stories of incest or kin murder. Of course such sensational material could be handled with great dignity and seriousness, as we know from plays like *Agamemnon* or *Oedipus tyrannus*, but from what little we have of the cyclic poems it does not seem likely that most of the authors had adequate poetic resources; certainly in later antiquity they are dismissed as formless, conventional, repetitive and flat. Aristotle's strongly expressed views in the

[1] Cf. Griffin (1977) 39 n. 9 for references.
[2] Griffin (1977).

Poetics (1459a30–b16) no doubt set the pattern for later criticism and ensured that the Cycle was no longer read: 'after Aristotle, compared with the two selected poems of Homer, everything "cyclic" was regarded as inferior, which meant at least conventional and often trivial'.[1] However, the tendency to neglect the cyclic poems may have begun earlier: we find Plato confining his quotation of epic to the *Iliad* and the *Odyssey*.[2] But by this time they had fertilized tragedy and provided the visual artists with an extremely rich and important body of source material.

Some of the epics composed in early times seem not to have been included in the Cycle (though our evidence is too meagre for certainty). Eumelus of Corinth, who was active in the latter part of the eighth century, may have been the author of the cyclic *Battle of the Titans* as some sources claim, but the rest of his work does not seem to have been treated as part of the Cycle. He is an interesting example of an epic poet who apparently chose and adapted his material with patriotic ends in view. He equated Corinth, which had no great past enshrined in legend, with the heroic but unidentifiable Ephyre, accounting for the change of name by a typical piece of invented genealogy (fr. 1). Thus armed with a corpus of mythology which included the tales of Sisyphus and Bellerophon, he proceeded to annex the Argonautic legend itself for Corinth under her new guise. To do this he made Aeetes an Ephyrean who ventured off into the unknown and settled in Colchis (fr. 2) and there received the Argonauts and Jason, whose adventures included the sowing of the dragon's teeth (fr. 9). We do not know the title of Eumelus' poem or poems: a later prose summary was entitled *Corinthiaca* or *History of Corinth* (Paus. 2.1.1). However named, Eumelus' work was one of the chief sources on which Apollonius of Rhodes drew for his *Argonautica* (see p. 588), and it is in the scholia on Apollonius that the most notable fragments are preserved. The whole tenor of Eumelus' treatment of Ephyre and the Argonautic saga seems to have been propagandist, evidently designed to enhance the esteem of Corinth by giving her a rich epic tradition, and perhaps also providing in the story of Aeetes' emigration from Corinth an implicit historical argument which could be used to justify a Corinthian claim to territories on the Black Sea.

We can tell from the fragments of Eumelus, from what little is recorded about the work of the Cretan Epimenides, and from the allusive manner of Apollonius' epic that the Argonautic story continued to be a favourite subject for poetry. Another important corpus was the group of poems associated with Heracles, the most popular and most widely revered of all Greek heroes. Of these poems the oldest on record was the *Capture of Oechalia* (Οἰχαλίας ἅλωσις) attributed to Homer himself or to Creophylus, though not, it seems, an original part of the Cycle. Peisander of Rhodes was the author (in the seventh or sixth century) of a more ambitious epic on the saga of Heracles which covered his whole career; this was followed by the much admired *Heraclea* of the Halicarnassian Panyassis, a cousin (or uncle) of Herodotus. Panyassis was active in the first half of the fifth century, and in the Alexandrian period he was esteemed as one of the finest epic writers; clearly ancient taste did not equate 'late' with 'bad' in the manner of modern scholarship.

Not all epic verse was devoted to heroic narrative: the form was clearly used also for classificatory, catalogue poetry: genealogies of the gods like Hesiod's *Theogony*, or the *Theogony* that stood at the beginning of the Cycle, or collections of human biographies like the *Catalogue of women* (see p. 101). And although *Works and days* seems to have been a poem of great originality, Hesiod was evidently not the only early Greek composer of didactic poetry. Among works doubtfully attributed to him we hear of the *Great works (Megala erga)*, presumably another poem about farming, and the *Precepts of Chiron*, the advice purportedly given to Achilles by Chiron the Centaur. No doubt Hesiod, as the greatest poet in this field, attracted attributions of similar poems, just as Homer was reputed to have composed the *Thebais*, *Epigoni*, *Cypria*, and *Capture of Oechalia*, among others. In fact we should think of a large number of reciters, some of them composers as well, who performed and thereby helped to preserve a very substantial body of hexameter poetry.

There were also, it seems, attempts at self-parody within the tradition. Homer himself was credited with a curious piece of levity, the *Margites*. Its hero, if that is the word, is an archetypal village-idiot, unable to dig or plough or even to count beyond five. How, then, would such a simpleton fare amid the perils of matrimony? Not even knowing whether he was born from his mother or his father, afraid to sleep with his wife lest she complain to her mother of his inadequacy, he was at length tricked into it by her, and an account of their sexual relations evidently provoked great hilarity. A papyrus fragment, *P.Oxy.* 2309, may well preserve part of the poem; the scene is a bedroom equipped with chamberpot, and the action takes place in the 'black night'. The whole tale was evidently made more amusingly incongruous by being put into the mouth of a grave singer of epic in the manner of Homer's Demodocus or Phemius (fr. 1):

> ἦλθέ τις εἰς Κολοφῶνα γέρων καὶ θεῖος ἀοιδός,
> Μουσάων θεράπων καὶ ἑκηβόλου Ἀπόλλωνος,
> φίλην ἔχων ἐν χερσὶν εὔφθογγον λύραν.

> An aged, divine minstrel came to Colophon,
> a servant of the Muses and Apollo the far-shooter,
> with his own tuneful lyre in his hands.

In Greek these three lines consist of two epic hexameters followed by an iambic trimeter, and the ancient metricians indicate that the poem as a whole consisted of blocks of hexameters alternating with blocks of trimeters in no discernible pattern. This is also the form of *P.Oxy.* 2309. A similar mixture of metres may already be intended in the light-hearted three-line inscription on a cup of the late eighth century found at Pithecusae,[1] where two hexameters are preceded by a line which can be scanned as an iambic trimeter. Although the attribution of *Margites* to Homer can be given no weight there is no reason to treat the poem as a late forgery; it could well belong to the seventh or sixth century and was widely quoted from the fourth century onwards.[2]

Another piece of epic parody, the *Battle of frogs and mice* or *Batrachomyomachia* (which seems to have been a great favourite as a school book in the middle ages and the Renaissance), is demonstrably later than the archaic period and most likely to be Hellenistic.[3] The main interest of this otherwise unexciting poem is that it does not seem to have been an isolated phenomenon but to have belonged to a genre of 'beast epics' – we hear of Battles of Cranes, Spiders and Starlings,[4] which may all have been in the same burlesque tradition.

2. THE HOMERIC HYMNS

Among the minor works often ascribed to Homer in antiquity were certain hymns, hexameter poems addressed to various deities. Thus Thucydides (3.104), citing Homer as the 'best evidence' for a historical judgement, quotes ll.145–50 of the *Hymn to Apollo* as from 'the prelude of Apollo'. The term 'prelude', *prooimion*, was a standard one for these hymns and probably implies that on occasions they were given as a preliminary to a longer epic recitation. At some time in later antiquity all the hexameter hymns not associated with other famous hymnodists (especially Orpheus, Musaeus, Olen and Pamphos) were gathered with those specifically attributed to Homer to form the corpus of 'Homeric Hymns' that has survived from the end of the medieval period. The truth is, however, that not a single one of these hymns, even the more imposing ones, can be by Homer, for their language and style are derivative, 'sub-epic', and in places clearly Hesiodic. The practice of ascribing to Homer a whole variety of poems in epic metres began quite early, whether through ambition, ignorance, piety or a sense of tidiness. It included a poem about Thebes, the *Thebais*, as well as unclaimed components of the 'Epic Cycle', those shorter and derivative epics that were designed to fill in gaps left by the *Iliad* and *Odyssey* and of which only plot-summaries and a few uninspired

---

[1] Page (1956).
[2] Testimonia in Allen (1912), *IEG* s.v. 'Homerus', West (1974) 190.
[3] See Wolke (1978) 46–70.
[4] Suda s.v. Ὅμηρος 45, 103.

fragments survive. So it is not surprising that Thucydides believed the Apolline hymn to be by Homer, or that other similar works were uncritically regarded as his. It is more puzzling, perhaps, that Hesiod was not occasionally chosen as their author, since at *Works and days* 656f. he claims to have won a contest with a hymn at the funeral games of Amphidamas in Euboea; and there was a well-known tradition that he and Homer sang a hymn to Apollo at Delos.

The corpus includes four long hymns (to Demeter, Apollo, Hermes and Aphrodite), of between 293 and 580 hexameter verses, and twenty-nine short ones, varying from three verses to fifty-nine in the case of Hymn 7, to Dionysus, which is probably truncated as it stands and looks relatively early on stylistic grounds. Hymn 1, also to Dionysus, may once, to judge by its position in the collection, have been a 'long' hymn, but only a twenty-one verse fragment, unimpressive in quality, survives. The long hymns and the short ones differ radically in intention and quality as well as in length; the latter are cursory eulogies addressed to a god or goddess with little or no narrative element, whereas the former narrate in a leisurely manner some central episode from the deity's mythical biography (so with the Hymns to Demeter, Hermes and Aphrodite) or attempt a broader coverage of his main aspects (*Hymn to Apollo*). There is another important difference: the long hymns seem to date from between 650 and 400 B.C. (to give broad but still ultimately conjectural limits), whereas many of the short ones are likely to be later. Indeed the latter are for the most part feeble and unimpressive, whatever their date, and it would hardly be an exaggeration to say that their chief interest is that, whether through sectarian zeal or through efficient libraries, they managed to survive at all. In fact even the long ones, judging by ancient references and quotations, seem to have made a rather slight impact in antiquity itself. Of these the Thucydidean quotation already noted is by far the most spectacular; otherwise there is a possible reference to the same hymn in Aristophanes (*Birds* 574), and Antigonus of Carystus in the third century B.C. quotes *Hymn to Hermes* 51. Other direct quotations are considerably later than that, but several echoes, at least, of the *Hymn to Demeter* are to be found among Hellenistic poets with their interest in the Mysteries.[1] This suggests that the Alexandrian Homerists did not consider the bulk of the corpus to be by Homer. Curiously enough the *Hymn to Demeter*, in spite of its relatively early though post-Homeric date, its superior poetical quality and its intrinsic religious interest, nearly passed into oblivion in the medieval period and survives only in a single manuscript (the early fifteenth-century Mosquensis, now in Leiden); whereas the remainder of the corpus was evidently much favoured by monks and copyists. The *editio princeps* by Demetrius Chalcocondyles, which appeared in Florence in 1488, was one of the earliest Greek texts to be printed.

---

[1] Richardson (1974) 68ff.

The *Hymn to Demeter* has considerable charm as well as religious and antiquarian appeal. It opens with the abduction, as she gathers flowers, of the young Persephone by Hades king of the underworld, who emerges from beneath the earth with his chariot. Her mother Demeter is heart-broken at the loss, and when she discovers from Helios, the Sun, that Zeus had condoned the abduction she abandons Olympus in disgust – the theme is an ancient Meso-potamian one – and wanders over the earth disguised as an old woman, until eventually she meets the daughters of King Celeus at Eleusis and is engaged to nurse the baby prince Demophon. She holds him in the fire each night to make him immortal, but is discovered by the child's mother; her identity revealed, she commands the building of a temple for herself there at Eleusis. Meanwhile the abandonment of her normal fertility functions has caused a famine, and Zeus is compelled to order Persephone's release from the under-world – where, however, she has been tricked into eating a single pomegranate seed and so is bound to return to Hades' realm for a third of each year (the time when the soil is infertile). But for the moment she is re-united with her mother and fertility returns to the stricken earth. Demeter instructs the Eleusinian princes in her rituals, which confer a better lot after death.

Little is revealed, or could be, about the secrets of the Mysteries themselves, but the Hymn is nevertheless a powerful piece of propaganda for Eleusis and the cult of the two goddesses. Athens, which took over Eleusis before 550 B.C., is not mentioned, which suggests that the poem was composed before this date. Other omissions, like the absence of reference to Iacchus, to the clan of Kerykes and to Triptolemus in his role of agrarian hero, are also unlikely to result from deliberate archaizing, and confirm that the hymn is indeed earlier than the mid-sixth century. Diction and style, which are still oral or nearly so, suggest a date toward the end of the seventh century, but here (as always with these poems) one is largely guessing. In any event the Hymn is no empty or artificial performance, but a religious document that provides an august aetiology of the foundation of the cult at Eleusis, as well as being a charter for the priestly administration of the Mysteries by the main noble families. In its emphasis on the fertility powers of Demeter and her daughter, specifically through Persephone's alternation between Olympus and the world below, it contrives to suggest a valid escape for initiates from the horrors of contem-porary eschatology:

> And all the broad earth was weighed down with foliage
> and flowers; and Demeter made her way and revealed to the law-giving kings
> – to Triptolemus and Diocles, smiter of horses,
> and mighty Eumolpus and Celeus leader of the people –
> the performance of her sacred rituals, and declared her rites to all of them,
> her solemn rites, which are in no way to be transgressed, or learned by others,

or declaimed; for great reverence for the goddesses restrains the voice.
Blessed among men who dwell on earth is he who has seen these things;
but whosoever is uninitiated into the rituals, and has no share in them, nevermore
has a similar portion when he is dead, beneath the dank darkness. (472–82)

The *Hymn to Apollo* is artistically uneven, but only slightly less important than the Demeter-hymn from a historical and religious point of view. It is commonly regarded as a blend of two originally separate hymns, one to the Delian, the other to the Pythian Apollo. The view has been disputed, but in essence is probably correct.[1] Verses 1 to 178 tell of the goddess Leto's search for a birthplace for Apollo, and of her eventually giving birth to the god in the infertile little island of Delos. A rather odd prologue, perhaps added after the main composition was complete, depicts the mature Apollo and the almost excessive reverence paid him by the other Olympians. At the end of this portion comes a *sphragis* or 'seal', a kind of signature by the composer, who declares himself to be a blind man from rugged Chios (172). 177f. are a clearly terminal formula: 'But I shall not cease from hymning Apollo of the silver bow, to whom fair-tressed Leto gave birth.' The three inconsequential verses that immediately follow in our version connect the god with Lycia, Maeonia and Miletus as well as with Delos (179–81); their purpose seems to be to widen his range beyond the cult-place associated with his birth, and to provide a transition to a distinct episode from which Delos is entirely absent. They are followed, with no greater coherence, by the beginning, at least, of a loose description of his progress down from Olympus to Pytho, the later Delphi. Next the poet asks what aspect of the god he is to sing (207ff.); rejecting the theme of his female conquests, he decides to relate how he passed through many places in search of a site for his oracle.

This all looks like the start of a fresh hymn, or at least a separately-composed episode designed to extend the Delian part. There is an obvious parallel with the main theme of that part (the search for a site for his birth), which is reinforced by the catalogues of places visited in each case (216ff. and 30ff.). Such themes presumably occurred in other hymns, too, but in the present case there are signs of deliberate imitation and expansion, with the Delian part providing the starting-point. For example the rhetorical enquiry about which aspect of the god to celebrate appears in a simpler form in the Delian section (19–25), and the more elaborate Pythian version (207ff.) also seems the more contrived. Other thematic parallels are to be seen in Hera's wrath (95–101 and 305–55, the latter an insertion of some kind) and in the barrenness of the chosen site and the ability of the priests to live off sacrifices (54–60, developed in 529–37).

[1] Disputed most recently by West (1975) 161ff.; see further Kirk in Brillante, Cantilena and Pavese (1981) 163–81.

Not even the Delian portion is a consistent and completely coherent composition; like most sub-epic poetry it uses pre-existing materials quite loosely at times. Its catalogue of places, for instance, begins as a list of Apollo's chief worshippers and turns into a gazetteer of Aegean promontories and islands; moreover, verse 81, with its mention of an oracle that can surely never have been an important feature of the early cult on Delos, is probably an intrusion from the Pythian part. Nevertheless the most probable conclusion is that the Delian part has provided the idea, and to a certain extent the model, for the Pythian.

Linguistically the Hymn is fairly homogeneous, except that the Pythian part observes the effects of the lost letter digamma more scrupulously than does the Delian.[1] That in itself suggests separate authorship, and on a simple view of linguistic and stylistic development could be held to indicate priority not for the Delian but for the Pythian hymn. But archaizing and imitative poems, which all the Homeric Hymns are in some degree, do not respond to this simple view, and the digamma criterion has been shown to be erratic in other respects also.[2] A broader and more important difference in style and intention appears in the emphatic interest of the Pythian composer in aetiology: the explanation of the curious ritual involving newly-broken horses at Poseidon's sanctuary at Onchestus (230–8); the origin of Apollo's association with Telphousa, implied in his traditional epithet Telphousios (244–77 and 375–87); the name of Pytho itself, emphatically connected with the rotting, *puthein*, of the corpse of the dragon slain by Apollo at the site of his oracular shrine (363–74); the explanation of Apollo's epithet Delphinios and the establishment of his priesthood, which occupies the last 150 verses of the poem and involves Apollo turning into a *delphis*, dolphin, and in this form diverting a Cretan ship to Cirrha, the port of Pytho – it being apparently known on the mainland that the god was worshipped as Delphinios in Crete. Several of these aetiological excursuses are in a crabbed and prosaic style distinct from the relaxed and ample expression of the Delian poem, with its simpler structure and more carefully limited intentions. Whether or not this suggests specifically priestly intervention, it is hard to believe that the Delian part would not have a much stronger aetiological tinge if it were the copy, in some sense, with the Pythian part as model.

There are at least three internal indications of date in the aggregated Hymn. First, the lively description of the festival at Delos is earlier not only than Thucydides (who as we saw quotes a part of it), but also than the Persian Wars, which interrupted this sort of gathering for a generation or so. Second, the informative scholium on Pindar, *Nemeans* 2.1 asserts that the blind Chian

---

[1] Janko (1982) examines this and other linguistic characteristics in detail.
[2] Allen, Halliday and Sykes (1936) xcviff.; Richardson (1974) 53f. and 334f.

singer of the Delian hymn was Cynaethus of Chios, a rhapsode who according to the same source was the first to perform Homer to the Syracusans in
504 B.C.[1] Third, the apparent prophecy after the event in verses 540–3 looks
like a further reference to the re-organizing of the cult and games by the
neighbouring states at the end of the First Sacred War in 586 B.C. The reference
at 295–7 to the stone temple-floor of Trophonius and Agamedes might also
be adduced, since that temple was burned in 548 (according to Pausanias
10.5.5); on the other hand deliberate archaizing is more likely with this well-
known event than with the other and less conspicuous instances. Together,
at least, these internal clues may be held to suggest a date later than 586 for
the Pythian part. They do not, however, preclude a somewhat earlier date for
the Delian portion, once we assume that the blind Chiote was not in fact
Cynaethus (who may still have had something to do with the Pythian part)
but, perhaps, the product of a pious effort to credit the hymn to Homer himself.
On stylistic grounds it is tempting to push the Delian hymn back to the
beginning of the sixth century, or less plausibly to the end of the seventh.

The *Hymn to Hermes* and the *Hymn to Aphrodite* must be dealt with more
summarily, although they, too, are of interest for the history both of religion
and of literature. The former relates how Hermes was 'born at dawn, was
playing the lyre at midday and stole far-darting Apollo's cattle in the evening'
(17f.). By far the greater part of the hymn is devoted to the theft of Apollo's
cattle by the infant Hermes (68–507). It ends with Zeus and the now mollified
Apollo agreeing on the young god's future prerogatives, but the tone throughout is one of ponderous irreverence and rustic humour rather than aetiological
investigation. The language is more crabbed and difficult, containing fewer
purely Homeric elements, than that of the other long hymns; it is notable for
some conspicuous Attic and Boeotian forms. The tale of Apollo's cattle is at
least as old as Hesiod's *Ehoiai*, but the style of humour (in which there is little
that appears genuinely naive) and the obviously literate pastiche suggest as
the general period of composition the late archaic or full classical age – some
time, that is, between the late sixth and early fourth century B.C.

The *Hymn to Aphrodite* is shorter and structurally simpler, relating as it
does the goddess' seduction of the young Anchises followed by her prediction
of the birth and future of their child Aeneas. Linguistically it is the most
Homeric of the long hymns – that is to say, of all of them; it is replete with
Homeric verses, half-verses and formulas, very conventionally used, although
like all the long hymns it also shows the influence of the Hesiodic tradition.
Of itself that reveals little about the date of composition, but the sharing of a
few unusual expressions with the *Hymn to Demeter*, together with at least one
probable doublet-verse at 98 (which is more compatible with rhapsodic than

[1] West (1975).

with more fully literate techniques), suggests a relatively early date, say the early sixth century. Yet no period down to the end of the fifth century can be excluded; after that the production of this kind of straightforwardly archaizing imitation (at least at this relatively high poetical level) becomes improbable. For the Hymn is quite charming in places, especially in the sexual encounter itself (particularly 143–75) and in Aphrodite's description of the fate of Tithonus, which she adduces as reason for not making her own lover immortal. This last passage gives a taste of the Hymns at their best and may fittingly conclude the present brief account:

> Again, golden-throned Dawn ravished Tithonus away,
> another of your family, and like the immortal gods.
> She went to ask Kronos' son, of the dark clouds,
> for him to be immortal and live for the sum of days,
> and Zeus nodded and fulfilled her prayer.
> Foolish she was, lady Dawn, for she did not think in her heart
> of asking for youth, and stripping off destructive old age.
> So Tithonus, for as long as lovely youth possessed him,
> rejoiced in early-born, golden-throned Dawn
> and dwelt by the streams of Okeanos at the ends of the earth;
> but when the first grey hairs poured down
> from his beautiful head and noble beard
> the lady Dawn kept away from his bed –
> but cosseted him still, keeping him in her halls,
> with food and ambrosia, and gave him fair clothing.
> But when hateful old age hastened fully upon him,
> and he could not move or raise up any of his limbs,
> this seemed to her in her heart to be the best plan:
> she placed him in a chamber and closed the shining doors.
> His voice flows on unending, but there is no strength,
> such as was present before, in his gnarled limbs. (218–38)

5

ELEGY AND IAMBUS

Archilochus is in many ways the focal point for any discussion of the development of literature in the seventh century, since he is the first Greek writer to take his material almost entirely from what he claims to be his own experience and emotions, rather than from the stock of tradition.

By a happy coincidence this central figure is also precisely datable. He was a contemporary of Gyges, king of Lydia c. 687–652 (fr. 19).[1] He alludes to the destruction of Magnesia by the Cimmerian Treres in or about the latter year (fr. 20), and seems himself to have been of military age at the time. In fr. 122 he speaks of the recent wonder of a total eclipse of the sun, which (despite recent attempts to revive the claims of 711 or 557) must be the eclipse of 6 April 648.

Archilochus the Parian presents himself as a man of few illusions, a rebel against the values and assumptions of the aristocratic society in which he found himself. A plausible explanation of this tension, to which we owe much of the interest of Archilochus' work, is to be found in the circumstances of his life. He came of a notable family. His grandfather (or great-grandfather?) Tellis had joined in taking the cult of Demeter to Thasos towards the end of the eighth century, and was to be immortalized in a great painting at Delphi by the Thasian Polygnotus (Paus. 10.28.3). The poet's father, Telesicles, also won distinction, as the founder of the Parian colony on Thasos. But if we may believe a passage (fr. 295) in which the fifth-century writer Critias is quoted as criticizing Archilochus for revealing damaging information about himself in his poetry, his mother was a slave, Enipo, and Archilochus was compelled by poverty to leave Paros and seek his fortune abroad. So Archilochus went to Thasos and served there as a soldier – we do not know whether he was actually a mercenary – and later, back in Paros, he helped to defend the island against attacks from neighbouring Naxos. In one such engagement he was killed by a Naxian named Calondas.

---

[1] Jacoby (1941) 99. All fragments in this chapter are numbered as in *IEG*.

For all we know, Archilochus was a turbulent and even disreputable figure in his lifetime; but after his death his memory was treated with the religious veneration the Greeks gave to their writers of genius. There is ample evidence in the many references to him in later literature that he had achieved the status of a classic,[1] fit to be mentioned in the same breath as Homer and Hesiod, and from a text discovered on Paros in 1949 we now have detailed information about the kind of hagiography he inspired. The Inscription of Mnesiepes was set up in the mid-third century B.C. to record how Mnesiepes, on the instruction of Apollo's oracle, built a *temenos* (sacred precinct) for the worship of the Muses, Apollo, Dionysus and other deities, and in honour of Archilochus.[2] 'We call the place the Archilocheion and we set up the altars and we sacrifice both to the gods and to Archilochus and we pay him honour, as the god instructed through his oracle.' The text continues with the story of Archilochus' life and quotations from his works. Much is made of his miraculous meeting with the Muses, who gave him a lyre; in its essentials the story is reminiscent of Hesiod's encounter on Mt Helicon (see above, p. 94), but there is nothing to suggest that he told it himself.

Archilochus writes so vividly that critics have been inclined to treat his poetry as essentially autobiographical, on the assumption that the first person singular will normally refer to the poet himself 'in real life'. But we have the clear evidence of Aristotle (*Rhet.* 1418b23ff.) that he sometimes used dramatic *personae* – Charon the carpenter in fr. 19, a father speaking about his daughter in fr. 122 – and in any case, as K. J. Dover has pointed out, it is true of songs in general, and particularly of songs in pre-literate societies, that the first person may refer to any personality the composer chooses.[3] It is characteristic of songs to deal with the 'I' and the here and now, but there is no reason why they should be confined to the persons and situations of documentary reality. And M. L. West has argued that it may have been a particular feature of the type of poetry the ancients called 'iambus' to use imaginary characters and situations.[4] Since all the surviving work of Archilochus is in a fragmentary state it is difficult in many cases to be sure of the dramatic context of the poems; some of the apparently autobiographical avowals may well have been made by fictitious characters, and even when 'Archilochus' is the speaker there is no certainty that he was not assuming a role – Archilochus the mercenary soldier, the boon companion, the sexual adventurer, etc. On the other hand his addressees Glaucus and Pericles appear to have been real people,[5] and it would be absurd to claim that a poet composing songs for performance

[1] Cf. the list given by Tarditi (1968) 232–8.
[2] Text in Lasserre (1958); Tarditi (1968).
[3] Dover (1964) 199–212.
[4] West (1974) 22–39.
[5] For the monument on Thasos to Glaucus son of Leptines see Pouilloux (1964) 20f.

in a small community in which everyone knew everyone else would not exploit his audience's knowledge of that society and its relationships. For the literary critic, the historical questions are not the most important ones; it is possible to study – and enjoy – Archilochus' poetry without being able to ascertain the connexion between the poet's life and the picture he presents of it in the poems. But there may be great significance in the fact that he chose to make the individual's feelings and experiences the main subject matter of his poetry.

Formally Archilochus is an interesting mixture of the traditional and the radically new. In diction and phrasing he relies heavily on the epic,[1] but he also introduces a range of modern words and idioms, some of them quite earthy, and while he can hardly have invented his various metres from nothing – it is surely right to think of a flourishing tradition of popular song behind him – he seems to have been the major innovator who turned these every-day forms into an important literary medium. For, like Catullus, Archilochus makes a serious claim on our attention even when his subject matter is slight and trivial; his control over language and metre is so powerful that he forces us to respect his choices. Perhaps there is a special relevance to his times in the particular gestures he elects to make: the abandonment of grandly heroic attitudes in favour of a new unsentimental honesty, an iconoclastic and flippant tone of voice coupled with deep awareness of traditional truths. One of the most famous fragments (5) is his claim that he threw away his shield, a provocative rejection of one sort of image of 'the hero', but not in fact alien to some strands of thought in Homer (Odysseus might well have done the same):[2]

> ἀσπίδι μὲν Σαΐων τις ἀγάλλεται, ἢν παρὰ θάμνωι,
> ἔντος ἀμώμητον, κάλλιπον οὐκ ἐθέλων·
> αὐτὸν δ' ἐξεσάωσα. τί μοι μέλει ἀσπὶς ἐκείνη;
> ἐρρέτω· ἐξαῦτις κτήσομαι οὐ κακίω.

Some Saian prides himself upon my shield, a splendid piece of equipment, which I left by a thorn-bush – and I didn't leave it willingly. But I saved myself. Why should I mind about that shield? Let it go: I'll get another just as good.

Another piece (fr. 13), one of his most serious and dignified passages, which is usually cited as an example of the strong epic influence on his elegiac poems, still shows his distinctive qualities of directness and 'plain speaking', what G. S. Kirk has well described as his 'passionate and sardonic self-control':[3]

> κήδεα μὲν στονόεντα Περίκλεες οὔτέ τις ἀστῶν
> μεμφόμενος θαλίηις τέρψεται οὐδὲ πόλις·
> τοίους γὰρ κατὰ κῦμα πολυφλοίσβοιο θαλάσσης
> ἔκλυσεν, οἰδαλέους δ' ἀμφ' ὀδύνηις ἔχομεν

---

[1] Page (1964) 125–62.
[2] Lloyd-Jones (1971) 38–41; Seidensticker (1978).
[3] Kirk (1977) 41. For a similar ethos cf. frs. 11, 16, 17, 128, 131, 132.

πνεύμονας. ἀλλὰ θεοὶ γὰρ ἀνηκέστοισι κακοῖσιν   5
  ὦ φίλ᾽ ἐπὶ κρατερὴν τλημοσύνην ἔθεσαν
φάρμακον. ἄλλοτε ἄλλος ἔχει τόδε· νῦν μὲν ἐς ἡμέας
  ἐτράπεθ᾽, αἱματόεν δ᾽ ἕλκος ἀναστένομεν,
ἐξαῦτις δ᾽ ἑτέρους ἐπαμείψεται. ἀλλὰ τάχιστα
  τλῆτε, γυναικεῖον πένθος ἀπωσάμενοι.   10

No man in all our city, Pericles, will take pleasure in festivities as he mourns these sad sorrows. Such were the men drowned by the waves of the surging sea; and our lungs are swollen with grief. But, friend, the gods have given us a remedy for desperate ills – endurance. First one man has trouble and then another: now we are afflicted and grieve over the bleeding wound, but tomorrow it will be someone else's turn. So now endure and put away feminine tears.

The thoughts as well as their expression are all traditional, but the image of lungs swollen with grief is particularly telling in a context of men drowned at sea, and the paradox of man's situation is finely brought out by 5–7, in the contrast between the 'incurable' evils that he must suffer and the 'remedy' the gods offer for them, which is entirely dependent on man's own will; the enjambment of τλῆτε makes the point strongly.

The fragments of Archilochus are arranged by editors according to their metrical form, the main divisions being elegy, iambic trimeter, trochaic tetrameter catalectic, and 'epodes' or repeating combinations of various iambic, trochaic, and dactylic units in which the characteristic pattern is one longer line followed by one (or two) shorter (e.g. iambic trimeter plus hemiepes, iambic trimeter plus iambic dimeter).[1] This is convenient and orderly, but it may imply greater distinctions between the different metrical patterns than were felt by Archilochus and his contemporaries. In fact it makes sense to group all the non-elegiac metres under the general heading 'iambus',[2] which seems to have been the ancients' term for poetry of an informal every-day kind which was designed essentially to entertain. The occasions on which iambus might be performed must have overlapped to some extent with those thought appropriate for elegy, but the elegists seem to have sought some degree of decorum in the poems they composed for performance at parties, on campaign, or in public gatherings; they apparently avoided both obscene language and the sort of topic that later belonged to the world of comedy – sex, food, violent abuse of individuals – all of which are regular ingredients of iambus. In Archilochus' rather scanty elegiac fragments we find no obscenity (though this could be a matter of chance); what we do find is as much wit, vigour and realism as in his other poems, and the homogeneity of tone and outlook throughout his work is more striking than differences corresponding to

---

[1] See Metrical Appendix.
[2] West (1974) 22–39.

formal variations. Probably there was some difference in performance between elegy and iambus: elegy was commonly sung to the accompaniment of the pipe, *aulos*, whereas the iambic trimeters and trochaic tetrameters would be recited (or chanted?) and the epodes sung, presumably to an instrument, though we do not know which. Since for us as modern readers the similarities are greater than the differences, the poems will be considered by theme rather than according to formal criteria.

One important *persona* adopted by Archilochus is that of the professional soldier, full of the hard-bitten cynicism of his calling. There is little romance in the profession of a mercenary; he is valued only while the fighting lasts, as Archilochus tells his friend Glaucus (fr. 15: elegiacs). He has no time for the kind of commander whose pride is in his good looks: better a short, bow-legged figure so long as he has a stout heart (fr. 114: tetrameters). He looks at the casualty list with a knowing eye: seven dead, a thousand claiming the credit (fr. 101: tetrameters). For all we know some of the stray remarks quoted from Archilochus about Paros and Thasos could come from similar contexts: the tone is equally disenchanted and forthright. 'Goodbye to Paros and its figs and seafaring' (fr. 116); 'the woes of all the Greeks have come together in Thasos' (fr. 102); 'Thasos, thrice miserable city ....' (fr. 228); 'it stands like a donkey's back, clad in wild forests' (fr. 21, a view of Thasos).

The soldier must be tough, self-reliant, living for the present: this is the tone of several fragments which seem to come from songs designed for the military drinking party. In fr. 2 (elegiacs) he celebrates his self-sufficiency:

> In my spear is my kneaded bread, in my spear is my wine of Ismarus, and on my spear I lean to drink it.

Fr. 4 (again elegiacs) is more boisterous:

> Come on, take your cup; go over the swift ship's benches and wrench off the lids of the casks, take the red wine off the lees. We shan't be able to stay sober on this watch.

But the soldier could also offer exhortations to his comrades in more serious vein, as in fr. 128 (tetrameters), which though addressed to his own heart has obvious relevance for his audience. Its advice is 'nothing too much' – neither excessive exhilaration in victory nor excessive grief in defeat: 'understand the rhythm that controls men's lives' (γίνωσκε δ' οἷος ῥυσμὸς ἀνθρώπους ἔχει). Another tetrameter fragment (130) expresses the same traditional idea of mutability, again with Archilochus' distinctive vigour: 'often the gods raise up men prostrated on the black earth by their troubles, and often they knock flat on their faces men who've stood firm, on a sure footing – and then there is plenty of trouble for them and they wander, needy and robbed of their wits'. It may well be that the many fragments which refer to contemporary events come from similar poems of advice or exhortation to companions, pieces like fr. 105, which is quoted as a political allegory:

> See, Glaucus. Already the deep sea is troubled with waves, and around the peaks of Gyrae the cloud stands upright, a storm-signal. From the unexpectedness of it, fear seizes me.

Many of the other fragments in tetrameters refer to the conflicts of the times (cf. 88, 89, 91, 93, 94, 96, 98), but they are too mutilated to give us a clear knowledge of the details. One common feature is clearly traceable: the poet is always committed, always expressing feelings and opinions about events, in a way that will influence an audience. Fr. 20 (iambic trimeters) is typical: 'I weep for the troubles of the Thasians, not for the Magnesians.'[1]

Fr. 1 sums up what is most remarkable about Archilochus, the fact that he presents himself as both man of action and poet: there is no suggestion that his poetic activity is a mere pastime for his moments of leisure.

> εἰμὶ δ' ἐγὼ θεράπων μὲν 'Ενυαλίοιο ἄνακτος
> καὶ Μουσέων ἐρατὸν δῶρον ἐπιστάμενος.

> I am a servant of Lord Enyalios [Ares] and I understand the lovely gift of the Muses.

As Denys Page remarked, 'a social revolution is epitomised in this couplet':[2] it is inconceivable in Homer that the fighting man and the poet could be one and the same person. And it is typical that in expressing so novel an idea Archilochus should use language that is very closely modelled on the epic. He says very little elsewhere about his role as poet, though perhaps there is a hint of artistic self-consciousness in fr. 120: 'I know how to strike up the dithyramb, the lovely song of Lord Dionysus, when my wits are thunderstruck with wine.'

Archilochus the lover is another familiar figure in the poems (though 'lover' is too narrow a term for this frank celebrant of sex). The fragments on sexual themes range from the delicate and sensuous ('she rejoiced in the myrtle and the fair flower of the rose', fr. 30, cf. 31) to the coarsely explicit ('. . . as a Thracian or a Phrygian sucks his barley beer through a tube; and she was leaning forward, working', fr. 42; cf. 43, 119, 152, 252). Often his choice of expression is traditional: desire is the 'liquefier of the limbs' as *eros* is in Hesiod (*Theog.* 121) and it 'overpowers' him as *eros* conquered Zeus in the *Iliad* (14.315f.): ἀλλά μ' ὁ λυσιμελὴς ὦταῖρε δάμναται πόθος (fr. 196). His descriptions of the physical symptoms of passion owe their phrasing to the epic, but their intensity foreshadows Sappho's:

[1] For the historical background cf. Jacoby (1941) 104–7.
[2] Page (1964) 134.

δύστηνος ἔγκειμαι πόθωι,
ἄψυχος, χαλεπῆισι θεῶν ὀδύνηισιν ἕκητι
πεπαρμένος δι' ὀστέων.   (fr. 193)

I'm a helpless victim of desire, the life gone out of me, pierced through the
bones by the gods' bitter pains.

τοῖος γὰρ φιλότητος ἔρως ὑπὸ καρδίην ἐλυσθεὶς
πολλὴν κατ' ἀχλὺν ὀμμάτων ἔχευεν,
κλέψας ἐκ στηθέων ἁπαλὰς φρένας.   (fr. 191)

For such is the craving for love that has coiled itself up in my heart and dimmed
my eyes, robbing my breast of its tender senses.[1]

But he is very different, too, from Sappho and the other lyric poets – in form
(see p. 202), in range of subject matter and vocabulary, and in his apparently
exclusive concentration on heterosexual activity. The choice of a sexual theme
by Archilochus certainly does not imply a 'love poem': some of the verses
seem to come from the sort of entertaining narratives of low-life erotic adventure that we find in Hipponax (see pp. 158ff.), others evidently belong to poems
of violent invective, the lampoons which brought Archilochus his greatest
fame (or notoriety, cf. Pindar, *Pyth.* 2.54–6, where he is described as 'fattening
himself on hate and heavy words').

According to ancient tradition his favourite targets were a Parian called
Lycambes and his daughters, Neobule and her younger sister. The story went
that Lycambes promised Neobule to Archilochus as his wife, but then insulted
him by breaking the contract, and the poet retaliated with abuse so virulent
that the family (or some of them) committed suicide.[2] The evidence is bafflingly
difficult to assess, and the discovery of a new papyrus fragment which dramatizes the seduction of the younger daughter only adds to the complexity of the
problem.[3] The best known piece is fr. 172, the opening of a long attack on
Lycambes:

πάτερ Λυκάμβα, ποῖον ἐφράσω τόδε;
τίς σὰς παρήειρε φρένας
ἧις τὸ πρὶν ἠρήρησθα; νῦν δὲ δὴ πολὺς
ἀστοῖσι φαίνεαι γέλως.

Father Lycambes, what's this you've thought up? Who has relieved you of your
wits, which used to be so sound? Now you've made yourself a great laughing-
stock for the townsfolk.

In this poem (probably frs. 172–81) Archilochus used an animal fable, the
story of the fox and the eagle, to abuse the faithlessness of Lycambes, who

---

[1] The translation supplies the first person; the Greek does not make clear whose the feelings are.
[2] Evidence in West (1974) 26f.; *IEG* I, 15 and 63f.
[3] *P.Colon.* 7511 = *SLG* 5478, West fr. 196A.

like the eagle has betrayed a friend and deserves the same hideous retribution. Evidently the poet shamed the daughters by describing in obscene detail an orgy in which he claimed they had taken part; some of the extant fragments (e.g. 48, 49, 51–4) may belong to this poem (or series of poems), but we have only teasing scraps of papyrus and very short quotations to judge from. The new fragment, the longest surviving piece of Archilochus, combines abuse of Neobule with a rather delicate description of how the younger daughter was seduced; it is difficult to see this as a purely defamatory poem,[1] though some degree of insult is clearly intended. An interesting approach to the story of Lycambes and his daughters has recently been made by M. L. West, who raises the possibility that they were 'not living contemporaries of Archilochus but stock characters in a traditional entertainment'.[2] The poet's freedom to assume different *personae* and to create fictitious situations needs always to be remembered; on the other hand we should avoid making the assumption that invective was never used by Archilochus in a direct and personal way. We know after all that the victims of Hipponax (and in a later age those of Catullus) were real enough.

The new fragment deserves quotation in full:[3]

πάμπαν ἀποσχόμενος·
ἴσον δὲ τολμ[

εἰ δ' ὦν ἐπείγεαι καί σε θυμὸς ἰθύει,
ἔστιν ἐν ἡμετέρου
ἣ νῦν μέγ' ἱμείρε[ι   5

καλὴ τέρεινα παρθένος· δοκέω δέ μι[ν
εἶδος ἄμωμον ἔχειν·
τὴν δὴ σὺ πένθ[

τοσαῦτ' ἐφώνει· τὴν δ' ἐγὼ ἀνταμει[βόμην·
'' Ἀμφιμεδοῦς θύγατερ   10
ἐσθλῆς τε καὶ [περίφρονος

γυναικός, ἣν νῦν γῆ κατ' εὐρώεσσ' ἔ[χει,
τ]έρψιές εἰσι θεῆς
πολλαὶ νέοισιν ἀνδ[ράσιν

παρὲξ τὸ θεῖον χρῆμα· τῶν τις ἀρκέσε[ι.   15
τ]αῦτα δ' ἐπ' ἡσυχίης
εὖτ' ἂν μελανθη[

---

[1] As Merkelbach thinks it is (1974) 113.

[2] West (1974) 27. West also suspects (28) that Archilochus' presentation of himself as a bastard is similar role playing, noting that the name Enipo (see above, p. 117) 'with its connotation of ἐνιπαί ['abuse'] is suspiciously apt for an iambographer's mother'.

[3] Text from *SLG*; see Appendix for bibliography.

ἐ]γώ τε καὶ σὺ σὺν θεῶι βουλεύσομεν·
π]είσομαι ὥς με κέλεαι·
πολλόν μ' ε[20

θρ]ιγκοῦ δ' ἔνερθε καὶ πυλέων ὑποφ[
μ]ή τι μέγαιρε, φίλη·
σχήσω γὰρ ἐς ποη[φόρους

κ]ήπους. τὸ δὴ νῦν γνῶθι· Νεοβούλη[
ἄ]λλος ἀνὴρ ἐχέτω·   25
αἰαῖ πέπειρα δ .[

ἄν]θος δ' ἀπερρύηκε παρθενήιον
κ]αὶ χάρις ἣ πρὶν ἐπῆν·
κόρον γὰρ οὐκ[

. .]ης δὲ μέτρ' ἔφηνε μαινόλις γυνή·   30
ἐς] κόρακας ἄπεχε·
μὴ τοῦτ' ἐφοῖτ' αν[

ὅ]πως ἐγὼ γυναῖκα τ[ο]ιαύτην ἔχων
γεί]τοσι χάρμ' ἔσομαι·
πολλὸν σὲ βούλο[μαι πάρος·   35

σὺ] μὲν γὰρ οὔτ' ἄπιστος οὔτε διπλόη,
ἡ δ]ὲ μάλ' ὀξυτέρη,
πολλοὺς δὲ ποιεῖτα[ι

δέ]δοιχ' ὅπως μὴ τυφλὰ κἀλιτήμερα
σπ]ουδῆι ἐπειγόμενος   40
τὼς ὥσπερ ἡ κ[ύων τέκω.'

τοσ]αῦτ' ἐφώνεον· παρθένον δ' ἐν ἄνθε[σιν
τηλ]εθάεσσι λαβὼν
ἔκλινα, μαλθακῆι δ[ὲ μιν

χλαί]νηι καλύψας, αὐχέν' ἀγκάληις ἔχω[ν,   45
δεί]ματι π . . [.] . μένην
τὼς ὥστε νέβρ[

μαz]ῶν τε χερσὶν ἠπίως ἐφηψάμην
ἧιπε]ρ ἔφηνε νέον
ἥβης ἐπήλυσις χρόα·   50

ἅπαν τ]ε σῶμα καλὸν ἀμφαφώμενος
λευκ]ὸν ἀφῆκα μένος
ξανθῆς ἐπιψαύ[ων τριχός.

'. . . but if you're in a hurry and can't wait for me
there's another girl in our house who's quite ready
to marry, a pretty girl, just right for you.'
That was what she said, but I can talk too.
'Daughter of dear Amphimedo,' I said,
'(a fine woman she was – pity she's dead)
there are plenty of kinds of pretty play

125

young men and girls can know and not go all the way
– something like that will do. As for marrying,
we'll talk about that again when your mourning
is folded away, god willing. But now
I'll be good, I promise – I do know how.
Don't be hard, darling. Truly I'll stay
out on the garden-grass, not force the doorway
– just try. But as for that sister of yours,
someone else can have her. The bloom's gone – she's coarse
– the charm too (she had it) – now she's on heat
the whole time, can't keep away from it –
damn her, don't let anyone saddle me with that.
With a wife like she is I shouldn't half
give the nice neighbours a belly-laugh.
You're all right, darling. You're simple and straight
– she takes her meat off anyone's plate.
I'ld be afraid if I married her
my children would be like the bitch's litter
– born blind, and several months too early.'
But I'd talked enough. I laid the girl
down among the flowers. A soft cloak spread,
my arm round her neck, I comforted
her fear. The fawn soon ceased to flee.
Over her breasts my hands moved gently,
the new-formed girlhood she bared for me,
over all her body, the young skin bare;
I spilt my white force, just touching her yellow hair.

(tr. Martin Robertson)

The nearest parallel is fr. 23, another narrative (with reported conversation)
of what appears to be a seduction scene; unfortunately the context here is not
clear in detail.[1]

The aggressive tone adopted against Lycambes and Neobule is often heard in
Archilochus' poetry directed against other (or no longer identifiable) targets:
'The hated babbler prowled about the house' (fr. 297); 'I long to fight you,
as a man thirsts to drink' (fr. 125); 'One great principle I hold, to requite evil
with terrible evil' (fr. 126); 'O Lord Apollo, do you also punish the guilty,
destroy them as you know how' (fr. 26). The papyrus from Cologne that
preserves fr. 196A also contains a short piece which amplifies fr. 188 and
evidently was an important model for Horace (*Epod.* 8, *Odes* 1.25 and 4.13).
It is an attack on an ageing woman (who may or may not be Neobule):

οὐκέ]θ᾽ ὁμῶς θάλλεις ἀπαλὸν χρόα, κάρφετα[ι γὰρ ἤδη
ὄγμοι]ς, κακοῦ δὲ γήραος καθαιρεῖ
.....], ἀφ᾽ ἱμερτοῦ δὲ θορὼν γλυκὺς ἵμερος π[ροσώπου

¹ Discussed by West (1974) 118–20.

πέπτω]κεν· ἦ γὰρ πολλὰ δή σ' ἐπῆιξεν
πνεύμ]ατα χειμερίων ἀνέμων ⟨   ⟩ πολλάκις δε[

You don't bloom any more: your skin isn't soft, it's dried up with furrowing wrinkles, and the . . . of nasty old age overpowers (you), and the sweet allure has taken a leap and left your once alluring face. Yes, you've been the target for the blasts of winter wind, and often . . .

Friends, too, were attacked, but without knowing the full context we cannot tell how seriously. Some of these fragments could come from poems of fairly light-hearted banter, like fr. 124 to Pericles, who is berated for coming to a party 'like a man from Mykonos', uninvited and without a present, but none the less having plenty to drink: 'Your belly perverted your mind and your wits into shameful behaviour.' Fr. 185, which announces to one Cerycides that it will tell the story of the fox and the monkey, sounds more threatening, as though the addressee might have to be identified with the vain and foolish ape.

It would be particularly interesting to know more about the poems in which the speaker is someone other than 'Archilochus'; fr. 19 and fr. 122 are identified as such by Aristotle (see above, p. 118), but there could well be others. As they stand these fragments are cryptic – we have to guess the dramatic context – but in each the tone is clear enough. In fr. 122, a father's remarks about his daughter on the theme of 'wonders will never cease', the hyperbole is witty and striking:

Nothing can be surprising any more or impossible or miraculous, now that Zeus, father of the Olympians, has made night out of noonday, hiding the bright sunlight,[1] and . . . fear has come upon mankind. After this men can believe anything, expect anything. Don't any of you be surprised in future if land beasts change places with dolphins and go to live in their salty pastures, and get to like the sounding waves of the sea more than the land, while the dolphins prefer the mountains.

Fr. 19, which rejects the riches of the great Gyges of Lydia, presents a perfectly traditional sentiment – on the lines of 'nothing too much' and 'think mortal thoughts' – but the use of a 'man in the street', Charon the carpenter, as speaker suggests that Archilochus gave it an original twist:

'οὔ μοι τὰ Γύγεω τοῦ πολυχρύσου μέλει,
οὐδ' εἷλέ πώ με ζῆλος, οὐδ' ἀγαίομαι
θεῶν ἔργα, μεγάλης δ' οὐκ ἐρέω τυραννίδος·
ἀπόπροθεν γάρ ἐστιν ὀφθαλμῶν ἐμῶν.'

'I have no interest in the property of golden Gyges. Envy has never taken hold of me, and I don't begrudge what is the work of the gods or have any longing to be a mighty tyrant. For these things are far beyond my sights.'

[1] The reference is to the total eclipse of the sun in 648 B.C. (see above p. 117).

Most scholars believe that Archilochus was a literate composer; but whether he was or not, more significant is the fact that literacy was established in Greece by his time (though we have no evidence for actual book production so early) and there was therefore more chance that his work could be recorded and widely disseminated. This is not to suggest that the initial 'publication' and much subsequent reiteration of the poems would not be oral; but it is hard to imagine Archilochus' being so popular in fifth-century Athens without the existence of a written tradition at some stage in the intervening generations. It is disappointing (though no surprise) that there was no place for so fine and important a poet in the Byzantine school curriculum, but the fact that he was read by the Alexandrian scholars makes possible the discovery of new texts in the papyri. After what has happened in the last decade it would be too pessimistic to suggest that we know as much of Archilochus now as we ever shall.

2. EARLY GREEK ELEGY: CALLINUS, TYRTAEUS, MIMNERMUS

The contemporaries of Archilochus whose work has survived confined themselves to elegy. The elegiac metre at first glance appears a hybrid, and has been regarded as an adaptation of the epic in the direction of lyric. Misleadingly described as an alternation of dactylic hexameters and pentameters to form a couplet, the metrical unit in fact consists of hexameter followed by two hemiepes with word division between each of the three elements; and it was the Romans who abridged the freedom of the earlier Greek poets by insisting that the end of the unit should coincide with the end of the sentence (see Metrical Appendix). Distinctions of genre are often clearer musically than metrically. Elegy was normally accompanied on the pipe, and is therefore quite distinct from the epic, which was chanted to the deep-voiced *cithara*, and from lyric, sung to the *lyra* or *barbitos*: of these only the elegy necessarily required two performers. The use of the pipe on campaign or at a party is known from Homer (*Il.* 10.13, 18.495), and the earliest elegiac specialists whose work has survived – Callinus, Tyrtaeus, Mimnermus – composed for precisely such occasions. From our knowledge of its later development we tend to think of elegy as above all the vehicle of lamentation and of short commemorative epigrams, funerary, dedicatory and so on. There is no evidence that these were among its primary functions at an early date. Archilochus used the form so variously that it may be doubted whether his occasional use of it in the context of grief (cf. fr. 13) is of any great significance. For the elegiac epigram our evidence is clear: the earliest elegiac inscriptions are of the sixth century, and in the seventh both dedications and commemoration of the dead were, if metrical, most commonly expressed in continuous hexameters.

Ancient scholars argued fruitlessly over the inventor of elegy, Archilochus, Callinus and Tyrtaeus all having their champions.[1] All that it clear is that the ancients possessed no earlier elegy than we ourselves possess, for the simple reason, no doubt, that these were the first elegists whose verses were committed to writing.

Callinus the Ephesian was an exact contemporary of Archilochus, whose experience of the Cimmerians and their 'heavy deeds' he shared (fr. 5A). He spoke of Magnesia at war with Ephesus before the Cimmerian sack (fr. 3) – that sack which moved Archilochus less than did the troubles of Thasos (above, p. 122); and he knew the Cimmerian tribe of the Treres who killed Gyges and burned Sardis in 652 B.C. His only substantial fragment is of twenty-one lines. It is a military song which strikes a discordant note amid the feasting, an appeal to the youth of Ionia to raise themselves from idleness and face the enemy (fr. 1):

μέχρις τέο κατάκεισθε; κότ' ἄλκιμον ἕξετε θυμόν,
ὦ νέοι; οὐδ' αἰδεῖσθ' ἀμφιπερικτίονας
ὧδε λίην μεθιέντες; ἐν εἰρήνηι δὲ δοκεῖτε
ἧσθαι, ἀτὰρ πόλεμος γαῖαν ἅπασαν ἔχει...

How long will you go on lounging? When will you show a bold spirit, young men? Do you not fear the scorn of neighbours round about, in your excessive idleness? You think you are sitting at peace, when war grips the whole land...

There is a lacuna at this point. The text resumes,

...and let each man as he dies make one final javelin-cast. For it is honourable and glorious for a man to fight against the enemy for his land and children and wedded wife. Death will come whenever the Fates spin their decree. But each man must go forward with spear upraised and stout heart covered by his shield, the moment war begins. There is no way a man can escape the destiny of death, not even if he were a child of immortal ancestors. Often a man avoids the fighting and the thud of spears, and comes home to meet the death that is his fate. But the people do not regard him as their special friend or grieve over him. But the warrior, if anything happens to him, is mourned by great and small. For the whole people feels grief when a brave man dies, and while he lives he is reckoned the equal of heroes. For they see him as a tower before their eyes, since all alone he does the work of many.

It is a stirring piece, evoking the world of Homer in a more straightforward manner than Archilochus. The appeal is direct and unadorned. The one simile in the passage, the comparison of a brave man to a tower, was already traditional (cf. Od. 11.556, of Ajax). In the context of patriotism and self-sacrifice we think of Hector; and there is a reminiscence of Hector's words to Andromache in Il. 6.487ff., that Death awaits the brave man and the coward alike, and of Sarpedon's similar remarks to Glaucus in 12.322ff. The diction is as traditional

[1] Didymus ap. Orion, Et.Mag. p. 57, and schol. on Ar. Birds 217; cf. Horace, A.P. 77.

as the sentiments it conveys. The vocabulary is taken almost entirely from the epic, and the structure is formulaic, of phrases constructed in an Homeric mould or actually Homeric, some of them slightly adapted to fit the 'penta-meter' line. The whole effect is to remind the Ionians of the heroes whose descendants they claimed to be, and to induce in them a spirit of emulation of their famous ancestors. What is remarkable and makes Callinus a poet of quality is his ability to strike an unmistakable note of freshness and directness through the use of such wholly traditional and formulaic material.

Across the Aegean, in rich Laconia, Tyrtaeus sang of political and military themes in elegies no less 'Homeric' than those of his contemporary Callinus – a measure of the extent to which the Ionian epics had by now created among the Greeks a cultural unity which transcended dialect and ethnic rivalry. The name of Tyrtaeus' father, Archembrotus, is preserved; everything else about the poet's life is at best deduction from his verses, at worst mere fiction. The supposed incongruity of Ionic dialect in Dorian Sparta prompted a rumour of Milesian origin, and Plato (echoed by many later writers) even claimed him for Athens. But the authoritative tone he adopts in teaching the Spartan warrior-class its business seems to tell against a foreign origin; and the occasional Dorisms of his diction – first declension accusatives in -ᾰς, a future in -εῦμεν – perhaps betray the accents of one to whom Ionic was unac-customed.

For a hundred years from the latter part of the seventh century Sparta was to enjoy a heyday of cultivated living which has left its traces in ivory and gold, in bronze vessels of surprising workmanship, in pottery of the finest quality, and in the odes of Alcman. This prosperity had been dearly purchased by Tyrtaeus' generation, who fought and died to suppress a revolt of the rich land of Messenia, which, first conquered by their grandfathers in the last third of the eighth century, had become the foundation of the Spartan economy. This military crisis about the middle of the seventh century, and the political discontent to which the loss of Messenian holdings gave rise, inspired the whole of Tyrtaeus' poetic production, so far as we can tell from what has survived. The political crisis took a form which was to become a regular feature of Greek history: the demand for redistribution of land. Those whose income had fallen or ceased with the loss of Messenia were driven to the verge of revolution; their demands were the more pressing among a people uneasily holding down a population of serfs; and they were, moreover, citizen-warriors of a state in which political rights were virtually confined to the soldiery. Tyrtaeus rallied their loyalty by appealing to the divine origin of the existing order, and at the same time castigated their defeatism and breathed into them the spirit to fight and recover what had seemed lost.

His poem *Eunomia*, 'Good order', which survives in only a few fragments, seems to have recapitulated the history of Sparta, emphasizing the part played by divine providence in the development of the Spartan constitution (frs. 1, 2, 4). Perhaps this religious propaganda sufficed, perhaps the successful outcome of the war and the economic recovery which followed victory removed the pressure for political change. At any rate, the Spartan constitution survived the test.

The Messenian revolt can hardly have come as a surprise. Tyrtaeus describes the bitter twenty-year war which the Spartan king Theopompus waged to win that rich territory (fr. 5) – no doubt as an example of endurance to be emulated – and there is no hint of pity in his description of the conditions to which its inhabitants were reduced (frs. 6–7):

ὥσπερ ὄνοι μεγάλοις ἄχθεσι τειρόμενοι,
δεσποσύνοισι φέροντες ἀναγκαίης ὕπο λυγρῆς
ἥμισυ πάνθ' ὅσσων καρπὸν ἄρουρα φέρει.

δεσπότας οἰμώζοντες, ὁμῶς ἄλοχοί τε καὶ αὐτοί,
εὖτέ τιν' οὐλομένη μοῖρα κίχοι θανάτου.

...like asses weighed down by huge burdens, under bitter compulsion paying their lords half of all crops their soil produces...groaning at their masters – themselves and their wives alike – till the terrible fate of death claimed them.

The rising was inevitable, and Tyrtaeus' became the voice of repression.

We are fortunate in having three poems called forth by the war which may be complete, or virtually so, in twenty-two, nineteen and sixteen couplets respectively. Probably chanted on the march, to a flute accompaniment, they vividly express the Spartan military ethic, the limited concept of the 'good man' (ἀνὴρ ἀγαθός) and of 'virtue' (ἀρετή) which undervalues all but the steadfast soldier, a concept notorious from its revival in the fifth century. In Tyrtaeus' day the concept was new. In Homer men are 'good' (ἀγαθός), but *good at* some particular skill – the war-cry, perhaps, or boxing, or healing (e.g. *Iliad* 2.408, 3.237, 2.732) – not simply good in the abstract. Similarly *arete* in Homer, as in Hesiod, is the quality of being good at something, in fact a word generally denoting success. The transformation of a particular skill into the sole criterion of moral worth was the achievement of Tyrtaeus' propaganda. He develops the definition in fr. 12. The very reflective nature of this piece, which contains none of the poet's usual exhortation to battle, has led some to think it spurious. But the language and sentiments are entirely characteristic of Tyrtaeus, and it is absurd to suppose him incapable of composing anything but martial elegies. What makes a man manly? the poet asks. Not skill at athletics nor the strength of the Cyclopes, not if he were swifter than the North Wind, fairer than Tithonus, richer than Midas, more kingly than Pelops, more eloquent than Adrastus: no matter what, if he has not courage.

> No one is a 'good man' in war if he cannot stand the sight of blood and slaughter, or come up and reach out for the enemy. This is 'goodness' (*arete*), this is the best and fairest prize among mankind for a young man to win.

The theme is elaborated, the fruits of courage identified in terms of achievement and reputation – reputation which even makes immortality the recompense for death in action – together with the possibility of survival to enjoy the deference of young and old, in lines which recall in sharp contrast Callinus' descriptions of the man who avoids death in battle only to earn the contempt of all (fr. 1.14–17).

This concept of military virtue inspired the two other more or less complete poems which have come down to us, poems of exhortation. 'Be bold, for you are the race of Heracles the unconquered. Zeus has not yet turned his head away' (fr. 11). In this poem a general statement of the advantages of standing fast, the disadvantages of flight, the shame of a soldier dead from a wound in the back, leads to a demand for action, the first couplet of which (21–2) is repeated verbatim in the other poem (fr. 10. 31–2) and paraphrased elsewhere:

> One must take up a proper stance, feet apart and both firmly planted on the ground, and must wait, biting one's lip.

There follows a compelling picture of the battle, the clash of opposing hoplite lines (lines 29–34):

> Go close and get the enemy, hand to hand, with a wound of your great lance or your sword. Set foot to foot, push shield on shield, tangle crest in crest, helmet on helmet, breast on breast, and fight your man, gripping hilt of sword or long spear.

The other poem (fr. 10) has been regarded by some critics as a combination of two separate fragments, but it is cited by the fourth-century orator Lycurgus as a continuous text. It begins with the bleak doctrine that it is a fine thing for a 'good man' to fall and die in the front line, fighting for his country. Tyrtaeus goes on to contrast the result of failure to fight (lines 3–12):

> To abandon one's city and rich fields for the life of a beggar is the most miserable thing of all – wandering with dear mother and aged father, little children and wedded wife. Hateful will be his company to all when he approaches, giving in to need and wretched poverty: he shames his family, belies his good looks, and dishonour and disrepute of every kind attend him. So then a displaced person has no consideration, no respect – neither he nor his descendants to come.

The conclusion is inevitable. 'With spirit let us fight for this land and for our children: let us die and no longer hesitate to give our lives.' The poet then turns to address specifically the young men, calling on them to fight stead-fastly, and not to fly and desert their older comrades who can no longer run so fast as they. Another vivid picture follows, the sight of an old soldier killed in battle (lines 21–7):

αἰσχρὸν γὰρ δὴ τοῦτο, μετὰ προμάχοισι πεσόντα
  κεῖσθαι πρόσθε νέων ἄνδρα παλαιότερον,
ἤδη λευκὸν ἔχοντα κάρη πολιόν τε γένειον,
  θυμὸν ἀποπνείοντ' ἄλκιμον ἐν κονίηι,
αἱματόεντ' αἰδοῖα φίλαις ἐν χερσὶν ἔχοντα –   25
  αἰσχρὰ τά γ' ὀφθαλμοῖς καὶ νεμεσητὸν ἰδεῖν –
καὶ χρόα γυμνωθέντα· νέοισι δὲ πάντ' ἐπέοικεν,
  ὄφρ' ἐρατῆς ἥβης ἀγλαὸν ἄνθος ἔχηι,
ἀνδράσι μὲν θηητὸς ἰδεῖν, ἐρατὸς δὲ γυναιξὶ
  ζωὸς ἐών, καλὸς δ' ἐν προμάχοισι πεσών.   30

This is indeed shameful, for an older man to lie fallen among the front rank, out in front of the young men, his hair already white, his beard grey, breathing out his brave spirit in the dust, clutching his blood-drenched genitals – a shame-ful sight for the eyes, a reproach – and naked flesh. To the young everything is becoming as long as they have on them the bright bloom of lovely youth – they attract the admiration of men and loving glances of women while they live, and are a fine sight if they die in the front line.

The poem ends with the couplet already quoted from fr. 11 (21–2).

This poem employs the common archaic device of ring-composition; within it, twice repeated, a general statement with which no one could disagree – the horror of beggary, the shame of allowing an older man to be killed – which is the cue for a call to action. The language is largely that of the epic tradition. Indeed all of Tyrtaeus' poems show close knowledge of the vocabu-lary of the *Iliad* and *Odyssey*, with a sprinkling of words otherwise known from the Homeric Hymns and from Hesiod. That the Ionian Callinus owed a debt to Homer is not remarkable, though the contrary would have been. The extent of Homeric influence as far afield as Sparta ought not to surprise, but it is certainly very striking. For all that, there is one important difference. There is no aristocratic celebration of battle in Tyrtaeus, only a stern devotion to duty and an awareness of what misery awaits an individual if his community is destroyed. His poems are the martial hymn-book of that discipline and devotion to the state which held Spartan ranks steady in the face of certain death at Thermopylae and became one of the enduring legends of western history.

Tyrtaeus and (for all we know) Callinus were amateurs, prompted by national crisis to use the only medium of propaganda they knew. That alone is enough to rule them out as inventors of elegy, against the claims of Archi-lochus the lifelong poet. A generation later another professional of outstanding skill was at work, Mimnermus of Colophon.[1] He lived in the latter part of the seventh century: the traditional date is confirmed by the knowledge of his works displayed by others (see below, pp. 136, 153). His *oeuvre* appears to have comprised at least two books (many, according to the Suda), containing a series of separate poems, evidently quite short, as well as a longer production later entitled *Nanno*, after a flute-girl whom the poet loved. Mimnermus was remembered primarily as a love poet (cf. Propertius 1.19.11); but the extant fragments of *Nanno* have little to say about love. This may be pure accident, and several of the fragments (4, 5, 12) could quite easily be associated with a larger erotic context. But it is more puzzling to find also attributed to *Nanno* the earliest surviving account of the Ionian migration, the settlement of Colophon and Smyrna from Pylos (frs. 9 and 10).

The opening of fr. 5 (a passage which also found its way into the *Theognidea*, see p. 137) recalls Sappho's account of her feelings at the sight of her beloved (fr. 31 LP) and could possibly have been known to her:

αὐτίκα μοι κατὰ μὲν χροιὴν ῥέει ἄσπετος ἱδρώς,
πτοιῶμαι δ' ἐσορῶν ἄνθος ὁμηλικίης
τερπνὸν ὁμῶς καὶ καλόν· ἐπὶ πλέον ὤφελεν εἶναι·
ἀλλ' ὀλιγοχρόνιον γίνεται ὥσπερ ὄναρ
ἥβη τιμήεσσα· τὸ δ' ἀργαλέον καὶ ἄμορφον   5
γῆρας ὑπὲρ κεφαλῆς αὐτίχ' ὑπερκρέμαται,
ἐχθρὸν ὁμῶς καὶ ἄτιμον, ὅ τ' ἄγνωστον τιθεῖ ἄνδρα,
βλάπτει δ' ὀφθαλμοὺς καὶ νόον ἀμφιχυθέν.

A river of sweat floods my flesh, and I tremble at the sight of the flower of youth, delightful and fair. I wish it would last longer. But precious youth is fleeting as a dream, and from the start painful and ugly old age hangs over its head, hateful and dishonoured. It makes a man unrecognizable, and shed over his eyes and his wits it does them harm.

These lines have an engaging immediacy, but they are not as artless as they appear at first glance. The rhetorical antithesis of τερπνὸν ὁμῶς καὶ καλόν (3) and ἐχθρὸν ὁμῶς καὶ ἄτιμον (7) and the vigorous use of words and images make this much more than a reworking of Homeric material.

In frs. 11 and 11a Mimnermus gives a version of the story of the Golden Fleece in which Aeetes' palace lies on the banks of Ocean, where Helios stores his rays in a golden chamber. And fr. 12, the lavish and imaginative description of the golden 'bed' in which the Sun travels from west to east, could also be part of his account of the story of Jason and Medea. All this could have been told to adorn or diversify the theme of a contemporary love affair, but we have no certain clues, and a quite different case can be plausibly argued.[2] Fr. 8,

---

[1] Or Smyrna; see Appendix.
[2] West (1974) 74–6.

which is also ascribed to *Nanno*, tempts the guess that part at least of the poem dealt directly with a relationship between two people: 'May there be truth between you and me, of all things the most just.'

Of the other poems the two best known (frs. 1 and 2) are on identical themes (and could even be part of a single work). Fr. 1 speaks of the 'desirable flowers of youth', asking 'What is life, what is joy without golden Aphrodite? May I die when these things no longer mean anything to me.' The poet goes on to lament the indignity and deprivation of old age. Fr. 2 is rather more elaborate:

> ἡμεῖς δ᾽, οἷά τε φύλλα φύει πολυάνθεμος ὥρη
> ἔαρος, ὅτ᾽ αἶψ᾽ αὐγῇς αὔξεται ἠελίου,
> τοῖς ἴκελοι πήχυιον ἐπὶ χρόνον ἄνθεσιν ἥβης
> τερπόμεθα, πρὸς θεῶν εἰδότες οὔτε κακὸν
> οὔτ᾽ ἀγαθόν· Κῆρες δὲ παρεστήκασι μέλαιναι,   5
> ἡ μὲν ἔχουσα τέλος γήραος ἀργαλέου,
> ἡ δ᾽ ἑτέρη θανάτοιο· μίνυνθα δὲ γίνεται ἥβης
> καρπός, ὅσον τ᾽ ἐπὶ γῆν κίδναται ἠέλιος.
> αὐτὰρ ἐπὴν δὴ τοῦτο τέλος παραμείψεται ὥρης,
> αὐτίκα δὴ τεθνάναι βέλτιον ἢ βίοτος.   10

Like the leaves which the flowery season of spring puts forth, when stirred to sudden growth by the sun's rays, so we enjoy the flowers of youth for a span, learning neither good nor ill at the hands of the gods. But the black Fates are at hand, the one with grievous old age as the end, the other with death. The fruiting of youth is brief, only as long as the sun shines over the earth. But when this season is ended, to die at once is better than to live.

And then he enumerates the miseries of old age, the common lot of all mankind, poverty, childlessness, disease. This poem indicates a mind not only stored richly with the inheritance of epic formulas (cf. also 6.2 and Tyrtaeus 7.2, 13a.2 and Tyrtaeus 19.7) but inclined also to dwell upon Homeric contexts. The use of the simile of the leaves, from *Iliad* 6.146, contributes much to the effect of the first four lines. Equally Homeric is the ensuing reference to the two Fates, *keres*, founded upon *Iliad* 9.411ff., in which Achilles discusses his own alternative *keres*, to die gloriously in battle or to survive in obscurity to a ripe old age. Mimnermus has been criticized for posing false alternatives, in that old age is not an alternative to death. But the Homeric context, and indeed Mimnermus' own, shows that it is death in one's prime that is meant. More starkly than Homer, Mimnermus declares that beyond youth nothing good awaits. Yet the tone is not always gloomy: in fr. 7 the poet's voice is jauntier. 'Please yourself: your fellow citizens have no mercy, and one will blame you while another praises.'

If the *Nanno* contained an account of the founding of Colophon and Smyrna, the poem entitled *Smyrneis* recalled events within living memory, the defence of Smyrna against Gyges of Lydia, *c*. 680. The elegy began with an invocation of the Muses, which distinguished the Muses as daughters of Zeus from their predecessors the children of Earth and Heaven. Little is preserved of the narrative, but enough to gauge its temper. A Smyrnaean warrior's charge is described (fr. 14): 'Pallas Athena found no fault with the keen strength of his spirit when he rushed forward with the front line in the bloody battle, forcing his way against the enemy's bitter shafts. For never was there among the foe a better man than he at doing the work of mighty war, as he ran forward, carried[1] by the rays of the swift sun.' No prosaic history, this, such as Tyrtaeus or Solon would have composed, however vividly; for Mimnermus, the life of battle is still heroic, the gods still watch upon the side-lines.

Mimnermus' poetry quickly won a wide circulation, as we can tell from allusions in other writers. The deep pessimism with which he repeated Homer's comparison of the life of man to that of leaves whose brief sprouting is soon ended (fr. 2) perhaps stung a later poet to the more bracing reflection that, since the comparison holds, one must be unstinting in enjoyment of the good things of life for as long as possible ('Simonides', see p. 157). Mimnermus' hope for survival in good health to the age of sixty (fr. 6), already perhaps ambitious in terms of the expectations of his time, seemed unduly modest to Solon, who would add a further score of years to the term (Solon, fr. 20). One of his rare and idiosyncratic pieces of mythology, the slaughter of Ismene by Tydeus (fr. 21, mentioned by no other writer), was illustrated on an early Corinthian amphora of *c*. 625–600. Nor does his fame seem to have faded in later centuries: there must be some significance in the fact that Callimachus singles him out in the famous programmatic prologue to the *Aetia* (see below, pp. 553ff.) as a practitioner of the kind of poetry most admired by the *avant-garde*.[2] It is easy to understand Callimachus' enthusiasm: here was poetry that was brilliantly vivid and in its own way elegant and sophisticated.

3. THEOGNIS

Theognis is one of the few Greek poets (and the only poet of the archaic age) whose work has come down to us not as a small selection made by some anthologist, not in fragments quoted by late authors or on scraps of papyrus, but as a complete corpus preserved through late antiquity and the Byzantine period. Unfortunately the corpus is more than complete: we have too much. The text preserved in the medieval manuscripts consists of some 600 elegiac couplets;

---

[1] The text of this line is uncertain.

[2] The interpretation of *Aetia* fr. 1.10–12 is uncertain, but Callimachus seems either to be praising all of Mimnermus' poetry as 'small-scale' (*kata lepton* – a key phrase in Callimachus' critical vocabulary) or contrasting his more pleasing 'small-scale' poems with a long composition (the *Nanno*? the *Smyrneis*?).

one manuscript, the oldest and the best, adds another hundred or so under the superscription 'Book 2'. The verses are written in unbroken sequence but there is no overall structure, no logical continuity which holds for very long. On the contrary, abrupt changes of subject, theme and even person addressed meet us at every turn; repetition – verbal (e.g. 853–4 = 1038ab, 571–2 = 1104ab, etc.) and thematic (cf. 527–8 with 1131–2, 585–6 with 1075–6, etc.) – incoherence (e.g. 1128ff.) and outright contradiction (813–14 ≠ 1181–2, etc.) are far from uncommon. The conclusion is hard to avoid that we are faced with a miscellaneous collection of elegiac poems, most of them very short, some of them incomplete; that they are not all from the same hand is clear from the fact that many short runs of verse found in 'Theognis' are elsewhere securely assigned to Solon, Mimnermus and Tyrtaeus. How much more of the work of these poets lies still unrecognized in the Theognidean corpus we do not know since we have only fragments of their work; we shall never know, either, how many other poets, now anonymous, have been drawn on to swell the muster.

The so-called second book harps on the same theme throughout – boy-love; it consists of a series of short units (one or two couplets for the most part) many of which begin ὦ παῖ . . . 'Boy . . .'. But the rest of the miscellany contains such diverse items as short addresses to divinities (Apollo, Artemis and the Muses, 1–18), poems addressed by Theognis (named only once, l. 22) to Cyrnus, son of Polypas (a fairly solid block, 19–254, with others strung out through the remainder, including Book 2), poems addressed to other men (Simonides and Onomacritus, for example, who may be the well-known figures mentioned elsewhere, but who equally well may not), gnomic moral exhortations of a general not to say banal character and drinking songs of the type in favour among the revellers at aristocratic symposia. It looks as if an original collection of poems by Theognis, addressed to Cyrnus, a much younger man, has grown over the course of many years of transmission, to its present shape and size by the addition of parallel (and contrasting) material, perhaps by the process of excerpting (ἐκλέγειν, cf. pp. 14f.).

Exactly when the anthology was fixed in its present form we do not know. The poets whose work we can identify (Solon, Mimnermus, Tyrtaeus) all predate the fifth century and (as far as we can tell) fifth-century poets who did use the elegiac couplet (Ion of Chios, for example, Simonides, Critias) are not represented.[1] The latest historical event referred to is the Persian invasion of

[1] Lines 467–96, 667–82 and 1341–50 are often assigned, in modern editions, to Euenus of Paros (active in the latter half of the fifth century). The basis for this attribution is the fact that Aristotle (*Metaph.* 1015a28) cites 472 (with one word changed) as a line of Euenus; Camerarius assigned the whole sequence 467–96 to Euenus and since these lines are addressed to one Simonides, gave Euenus the other two passages which contain that name. This structure is obviously shaky; everything depends on Aristotle's attribution of one line. But that line is not a very original observation

Greece in 480 B.C.; lines 773–82, an eloquent appeal to Apollo to save Megara, clearly refer to a present, not a far-off, danger and also deplore Greek disunity in the face of the invader.

> Lord Phoebus, it was you in person who built the towers on our city's high place, as a favour to Pelops' son Alkathoos. Now in person keep the savage army of the Medes away from this city, so that in gladness, when spring comes on, the people may bring you glorious animal sacrifices in procession, rejoicing in the sound of the harp and the lovely banquet, the cries and dance-steps of the hymns in your honour performed at your altar. Save us, I beseech you – for I am terrified when I see the mad folly and the destructive disunion of the Greek people. Be gracious to us, Phoebus, and watch over this our city.

These powerful lines are clearly the work of a Megarian poet, but most critics today agree that they cannot be the work of Theognis, who was probably a younger contemporary of Solon; their inclusion in a collection which seems otherwise to have confined itself strictly to poets of the archaic age can be easily explained: an anthology which went under the name of Theognis of Megara was the obvious place to put them.

The lines which are addressed to Cyrnus all bear the stamp of a particular strong personality. We know nothing about him except what we are told in the poems: that his name was Theognis, his city Megara. His voice is that of an embittered aristocrat, a loser in the social upheavals of archaic Greece, warning his beloved Cyrnus against the violence and vulgarity of the lower orders and later, perhaps in exile, lamenting his poverty and calling for revenge.

A suitable historical context for this poet could be found in almost any Greek city of the archaic age – in mainland Megara as well as Megara Hyblaea, its colony in Sicily, to which Plato (*Laws* 630a) assigns him. But there is fairly general agreement today that the mother-city is the more likely candidate. It suffered in the late seventh century under the regime of a particularly vicious tyrant, Theagenes, whose overthrow was followed by many decades of political turbulence; a democracy which seems to have been notorious for its extreme measures against the wealthy was brought to an end, we are told by Aristotle (*Pol.* 1304b34), when its confiscations had driven so many into exile that they were numerous enough to come back in force and establish an oligarchy.[1]

Theognis is the first poet in Greek literature to voice concern over the eventual fate of his productions; in fact he announces that he has taken measures to protect them.

> Cyrnus, as I compose my poems for you, let a seal be placed on the verses; if stolen they will never pass undetected nor will anyone exchange their present

---

– 'For everything forced on one by necessity is painful' – and even if the lines depend on each other, Euenus may be quoting Theognis, just as in fr. 1 (West) he quotes a 'παλαιὸς λόγος'.

[1] West (1978*b*) collects the ancient evidence for archaic Megara: 'Testimonia historica' pp. 4–6.

good content for worse – but everyone will say: 'They are the verses of Theognis of Megara, a name known to all mankind.' (19–23)

Unfortunately, we do not know what this 'seal' was; the single occurrence of the poet's own name could hardly serve to protect the integrity of his text and even the frequently recurring mention of Cyrnus would not be a barrier against interpolation. Perhaps a copy of the poem was entrusted under seal to a temple; we are told that Heraclitus of Ephesus deposited a copy of his book in the temple of Artemis there. Whatever the 'seal' may have been, it was obviously ineffective; disputes about how much of our present text should be attributed to Theognis have continued ever since Welcker made the first systematic attempt to separate the grain from the chaff in 1826. A recent editor, confining himself to those sequences which contain the name Cyrnus and those which are quoted as the work of Theognis by fourth-century authors (Plato and Aristotle), prints 306 lines, and although, as he says, the collection may contain still more genuine verses, this selection constitutes an acceptable core.[1] The traditional text opens with four invocations of divine beings, two addressed to Apollo, one to Artemis, and one to the Muses and Graces (Χάριτες). The lines addressed to Artemis are identified by Aristotle as the work of Theognis (*Eth. Eud.* 1243a18); they may well be the prologue of the original book, for they have a conciseness and a touch of wit – characteristics of Theognis at his best.

"Αρτεμι θηροφόνη, θύγατερ Διός, ἣν 'Αγαμέμνων
εἵσαθ', ὅτ' ἐς Τροίην ἔπλεε νηυσὶ θοῆις,
εὐχομένωι μοι κλῦθι, κακὰς δ' ἀπὸ κῆρας ἄλαλκε·
σοὶ μὲν τοῦτο, θεά, σμικρόν, ἐμοὶ δὲ μέγα.   (11–14)

Artemis, killer of wild beasts, daughter of Zeus, you whose sanctuary Agamemnon founded when he was about to sail for Troy in his swift ships, listen to my prayer and protect me from the evil death-spirits. Goddess, this means little to you, but much to me.

The form Theognis' original book may have assumed can be surmised from a phrase in the Suda entry: Θέογνις… ἔγραψεν… πρὸς Κύρνον… γνωμολογίαν δι' ἐλεγείων καὶ ἑτέρας ὑποθήκας παραινετικάς…'Theognis … wrote … addressed to Cyrnus … a collection of maxims in elegiac verse, and other ethical prescriptions.' This word ὑποθῆκαι occurs in a didactic poem ascribed to Hesiod, the 'prescriptions of Chiron' Χίρωνος ὑποθῆκαι – Chiron the centaur gives ethical advice to his pupil Achilles. And the cognate verb ὑποθήσομαι 'I shall prescribe' occurs in Theognis' first announcement that he will take young Cyrnus' education in hand.

[1] West (1978b).

With your interest at heart, Cyrnus, I shall pass on the precepts (ὑποθήσομαι) which, still a child, I learned from good men and true. Be prudent; and do not try to win honour, prestige or wealth by actions which are shameful and unjust... Do not associate with bad men, but hold fast always to the good – with *them* drink and eat, sit with *them*... (27–34)

The end of the sentence makes it crystal-clear what Theognis means by 'good' men: '... try to please those whose power is great'.

Many of the 'prescriptions' are neatly phrased couplets which encapsulate traditional Greek morality: respect for the gods (1179–80), parents (131–2, 821–2), and strangers (143–4). It was lines like these which earned Theognis his reputation as a moralist – Isocrates, for example, (*Ad Nicoclem* 43) lists him among 'the best advisers for the conduct of human life' (ἀρίστους ... συμβούλους τῶι βίωι τῶι τῶν ἀνθρώπων...). But the teacher also urges on his young pupil the old aristocratic code which enjoined full requital for benefits and injuries received.

May Zeus grant me this, Cyrnus: to repay my friends who love me and to have greater power than my enemies. If this were so I would seem like a god among men – if the destined day of death found me fully paid up. (337–40)

Another version clarifies the veiled menace in the words 'have greater power than my enemies'.

May the thing feared by all men who walk the earth happen to me, may the great, wide, brazen sky fall on my head – if I do not give aid and comfort to those who love me, and become a torment and great affliction to my enemies. (869–72)

Though he assumes the role of tutor, he does not blithely assume that education is always effective. 'It is easier to beget and raise a human being than to put a sound mind in it... If understanding could be made and implanted in a man, a son of a good father would never turn out bad – he would be ruled by his father's words of wisdom. But by teaching, you will never turn a bad man to good' (429–33, 435–8). This pessimistic estimate was apparently just; Theognis has cause later, at the end of the famous lines which claim that he has made Cyrnus' name immortal, to reproach the young pupil whom he loved for deceit and ingratitude.

σοὶ μὲν ἐγὼ πτέρ' ἔδωκα, σὺν οἷσ' ἐπ' ἀπείρονα πόντον
  πωτήσηι, κατὰ γῆν πᾶσαν ἀειρόμενος
ῥηϊδίως· θοίνηις δὲ καὶ εἰλαπίνηισι παρέσσηι
  ἐν πάσαις πολλῶν κείμενος ἐν στόμασιν,
καί σε σὺν αὐλίσκοισι λιγυφθόγγοις νέοι ἄνδρες
  εὐκόσμως ἐρατοὶ καλά τε καὶ λιγέα
ἄισονται. καὶ ὅταν δνοφερῆς ὑπὸ κεύθεσι γαίης
  βῆις πολυκωκύτους εἰς Ἀΐδαο δόμους,

240

οὐδέποτ' οὐδὲ θανὼν ἀπολεῖς κλέος, ἀλλὰ μελήσεις   245
ἄφθιτον ἀνθρώποισ' αἰὲν ἔχων ὄνομα,
Κύρνε, καθ' Ἑλλάδα γῆν στρωφώμενος, ἠδ' ἀνὰ νήσους...

.   .   .

πᾶσι δ', ὅσοισι μέμηλε, καὶ ἐσσομένοισιν ἀοιδή   251
ἔσσηι ὁμῶς, ὄφρ' ἂν γῆ τε καὶ ἠέλιος.
αὐτὰρ ἐγὼν ὀλίγης παρὰ σεῦ οὐ τυγχάνω αἰδοῦς,
ἀλλ' ὥσπερ μικρὸν παῖδα λόγοις μ' ἀπατᾶις.   (237–47, 251–4)

I have given you wings with which to fly aloft over the boundless sea and the whole earth effortlessly; at banquets and festivals you will be there, at all of them, your name on the lips of many, as, to the sound of high-pitched pipes, handsome lads sing your praises loud and clear in lovely harmony. And when you go down under the depths of the gloomy earth to the mournful house of Hades, not even then, not even in death, will you lose your glory; you will be a theme of men's song, Cyrnus, your name immortal forever as you range the mainland of Hellas and the islands... For all those now and in time to come who love to sing you will be there as long as earth and sun shall last. But as for me, you have not the least consideration for me; you cheat me with words as if I were a little child.

In style and vocabulary, as this specimen shows, Theognis differs little from other archaic poets who wrote in elegiac couplets; like them, he is heavily indebted to Ionian epic. This address to Cyrnus is hardly Homeric in tone and content; yet, except for the Theognidean coinage πολυκωκύτους, the vocabulary is entirely Homeric. The passage, in fact, is a mosaic of Homeric phrases and formulas, some unchanged, some subtly varied. The ending of the first line, for example, ἐπ' ἀπείρονα πόντον comes from *Il.* 1.350; the end of 243 ὑπὸ κεύθεσι γαίης is a recurrent Homeric formula, like εἰς Ἀίδαο δόμους (244) γῆ τε καὶ ἠέλιος (252) and ῥηϊδίως as a line opening (239). The rest of line 239 echoes *Il.* 10.217 with θοίνηις substituted for δαίτησι and the striking phrase ἐσσομένοισιν ἀοιδή in 251 comes from *Od.* 8.850. Tyrtaeus could use the epic language for a situation and in a tone Homer (at least the Homer of the *Iliad*) would have recognized; but Theognis adapts it for a new world of thought and feeling – the celebration of a young man's fame and beauty, the reactions of an aristocrat to social innovation and turbulence.

Cyrnus is to be a theme for song in feasts and festivals but especially in those aristocratic, male drinking parties we know so well from the vase paintings. Many of the poems of the collection develop themes appropriate for such gatherings: the joys of wine, of male companionship, the exquisite short season of youth.

As for us, let us devote our hearts to feast and celebration, while they can still feel the joy of pleasure's motions. For glorious youth passes by swift as a thought, swifter than the burst of speed shown by horses as they take a chieftain and his spear to the battle line, galloping furiously as they take their joy in the flatness of the wheatfields. (983–8)

The love poems which were at some point concentrated in the second book[1] (though a few remain in the first) are of course typical of this masculine world and in the last couplet of Theognis' claim to have made Cyrnus' name immortal there is a clear hint that Theognis sees himself in that love relationship between older and younger man which was characteristic of such milieux. 'You cheat me with words, as if I were a little child.' Elsewhere, using an image common in Greek erotic poetry, he even begs Cyrnus not to make him fall too deeply in love: 'Do not with your violent goading drive me, against my will, under the yoke, drawing me into excessive love' (371–2). And a recurrent theme is the complaint, familiar from other Greek sympotic song, that love and friendship are unstable, the protest against infidelity and, above all, deceit. 'Don't give me words of love as you turn your mind and heart elsewhere .. either wipe your mind clean and love me, or reject and hate me, picking a quarrel openly. The man whose one tongue conceals two minds is a dangerous comrade, Cyrnus, better your enemy than your friend' (87–92).

Perfidy, of course, is not confined to love relationships; in the wider world of commerce and politics it is just as prevalent, and Cyrnus is warned against it. He must choose the good, not the bad, as friends and these two words, ἀγαθός and κακός, as so often in archaic Greek literature, denote social as well as moral categories.

Let no man persuade you to love a bad man, Cyrnus; what use to have a base man as your friend? He will not rescue you from toil and trouble or from ruin and if he has anything good he will not be willing to share it. (101–4)

The social import of these words comes out clearly in the aristocrat's protest against marriages made for money; he views unions between well-born and *nouveaux riches* as tantamount to miscegenation.

When it comes to rams, donkeys and horses, Cyrnus, we search for thoroughbreds (εὐγενέας) and we get mates of good stock (ἀγαθῶν) for them to mount. But a fine man (ἐσθλός) does not refuse to marry the lowest of the low (κακὴν κακοῦ) if she brings him lots of money. And a woman doesn't spurn the bed of a low born man (κακοῦ) if he's rich; she'd rather have a wealthy man than a good one (ἀγαθοῦ). Money is what they care about; noble (ἐσθλός) marries a base man's (κακοῦ) daughter, the base man (κακός) the noble's (ἀγαθοῦ). Wealth crosses the breeds. So don't be surprised, son of Polypas, that the purity of our citizens' stock is blurred; for good is being mixed with bad. (183–92)

---

[1] It seems fairly certain that the contents of Book 2 were once distributed throughout the collection, and were extracted to form a separate unit during the Byzantine period.

One of the most potent solvents of the old aristocratic order was the intro-duction of coinage, which made possible depths of indebtedness and rapid accumulations of wealth unknown in the earlier economy; it also brought into existence a class of newly-rich men who pressed for admission, by marriage, bribery or political agitation into the hereditary ruling circles. Theognis sees money as the destructive agent which has shattered the whole heroic mythic tradition, the sacred book of aristocratic ethics. This trenchant assessment is made in a poem which deliberately imitates the structure of Tyrtaeus' celebration of martial courage as the only form of excellence (ἀρετή) – more to be admired than the strength of the Cyclopes, the speed of Boreas, the beauty of Tithonus, the wealth of Midas and Cinyras, the kingly power of Pelops or the honey-sweet tongue of Adrastus (cf. pp. 131f.). Tyrtaeus' poem uses the device known as priamel – a series building up towards the climactic component, martial valour, which far outshines its predecessors. Theognis, however, begins with a stark declaration of his bitter thesis and names his highest virtue at once.

> In the eyes of most men (πλήθει) there is only one form of excellence (ἀρετή): this one, to be rich. Nothing else, it turns out, is any good (τῶν δ'ἄλλων οὐδὲν ἄρ' ἦν ὄφελος) not even if you had the sober wisdom (σωφροσύνην) of Rhadamanthys, not even if you were cleverer than Sisyphus son of Aeolus, who won over Perse-phone with lying speeches and came back up from Hades by his cunning... not if you could make false things sound true, had, in fact, the skilful tongue of god-like Nestor, not even if you were faster on your feet than the swift Harpies or the fast-running sons of Boreas. No, everyone must get this firmly in mind: money has most power for all men. (699–704, 713–18)

Another bitter poem defines more clearly the upstarts whose wealth prevails over noble birth in the marriage market; it also gives a vivid impression of the tense atmosphere of the period, the frustration of the propertied class in a time of revolution.

> Cyrnus, the city is still a city, but the people are changed. Once they knew nothing of rights or laws; they wore out their goatskins against their flanks and grazed, like deer, outside the city. And now, Cyrnus, *they* are the good men and true (ἀγαθοί)! And those who once were noble (ἐσθλοί) are now low. Who can bear to see it? (53–8)

The situation is so fluid and confusing that old standards are no sure guide; a man does not know how to avoid censure.

> I cannot read the mind of my fellow citizens, know what is in their thoughts. Whether I do them good or harm, no matter – I cannot please them. (367–8)

It is a world in which the poet has lost his bearings; he even comes to doubt the justice of Zeus and the Olympian gods.

Dear Zeus, I wonder at you. For you rule all, you alone have the great power and the glory, you know the mind and heart of every man, and your strength, O Lord, is highest of all. How then...can you be so hard of heart, to treat the wicked and the just man alike? (373–8)

This despairing mood reached its ultimate expression in some lines which became the classic formulation of Greek pessimism, echoed in Bacchylides (5.160) and a famous Sophoclean ode (*O.C.* 1225ff.):

> πάντων μὲν μὴ φῦναι ἐπιχθονίοισιν ἄριστον
> μηδ᾽ ἐσιδεῖν αὐγὰς ὀξέος ἠελίου,
> φύντα δ᾽ ὅπως ὤκιστα πύλας ᾿Αίδαο περῆσαι
> καὶ κεῖσθαι πολλὴν γῆν ἐπαμησάμενον.   (425–28)

Not to be born is best of all for men, never to see the dazzling rays of the sun. Once born, to go as fast as may be through the gates of death, and lie under a heap of earth.

In the unpredictable world of political and social change one can no longer afford the traditional aristocratic virtue of loyalty.

> θυμέ, φίλους κατὰ πάντας ἐπίστρεφε ποικίλον ἦθος,
> ὀργὴν συμμίσγων ἥντιν᾽ ἕκαστος ἔχει·
> πουλύπου ὀργὴν ἴσχε πολυπλόκου, ὃς ποτὶ πέτρηι,
> τῆι προσομιλήσηι, τοῖος ἰδεῖν ἐφάνη.   (213–16)

My heart, in your dealings with all your friends, be versatile of character, vary according to the mood each one may have. Adopt the temper of the subtly-coiling octopus, who takes on the appearance of the rock to which he intends to cling.

But even this pliant attitude will hardly ensure survival in the catastrophe which Theognis foresees – the tyranny which was all too often the end result of Greek civil strife.

> Κύρνε, κύει πόλις ἥδε, δέδοικα δὲ μὴ τέκηι ἄνδρα
> εὐθυντῆρα κακῆς ὕβριος ἡμετέρης.   (39–40)

Cyrnus, this city is big with child and I fear it may give birth to a man who will chastize our wicked pride.

This admission of general responsibility – '*our* wicked pride' – is an unusually objective formula for Theognis but it is soon abandoned; the fault lies not with the citizens or the 'good' but with the 'leaders', who are of course *kakoi*.

For our citizens are still of sound mind, but their leaders are set on a course towards much mischief – and a fall. No city, Cyrnus, was ever yet ruined by good men (ἀγαθοί), but when the bad men (κακοῖσιν) take to insolence (ὑβρίζειν), corrupt the masses (δῆμον) and give judgement in favour of the lawless in order to win power and private gain, then, you may be sure that the city, though it lies deep in tranquillity now, will not enjoy peace for very long – when this is what the bad men find dear to their heart: profit at the expense of the public good. For it is from things like this that factions are born and civil murders and a dictatorship. May this city never choose that way. (41–52)

In another couplet Theognis seems to be issuing a call to action rather than voicing the usual impotent complaint.[1]

Cyrnus, with those friends we have, let us scotch the evil at its source, seek remedy for this sore before it comes to a head. (1133–4)

But a lament for his lost estates suggests that whether or not he took any action, Theognis became one of the many casualties of Greek political life, one of those 'who told their lies too late | caught in the eternal factions and reactions | of the city-state'.[2] The voice of the migratory crane, on its way to Africa, was the signal, Hesiod tells us (*W.D.* 448ff.), to begin the late autumn ploughing. But for Theognis it is bitter reminder of his losses.

I heard the voice, son of Polypas, the high-pitched cry of the bird which comes to tell men: 'Plough in season'. And my heart was struck dark with anger, to think that other men possess my fertile acres now; it is not for me that the mules pull at the curved yoke...(1197–1201)

These lines sound the nostalgic note characteristic of the exile and some other lines (which contain no mention of Cyrnus) speak of travels to foreign cities.

For I have been in my time to the land of Sicily, and to the plains of Euboea with their vines, I have been to Sparta, the glorious town on the reedy Eurotas river – and everywhere I went I found hearty welcome and friendship. But from all of it no joy came to my heart; it is true, after all, that there is no place like one's homeland. (783–8)

Whether he was in fact exiled or suffered only confiscation we do not know (though if he went overseas late in life to settle in Sicilian Megara, Plato's description of him as a Sicilian becomes more intelligible) but we can be sure that like most losers in Greek faction fights, he was reduced to poverty. He is eloquent in his diatribes against it.

Poverty, Cyrnus, brings a good man (ἀγαθόν) to his knees more than anything else, more than grey old age or fever; to get away from it, throw yourself into the ocean's hollow deeps or down from precipitous rocks. (173–6)

The loss of his estates and the pain of exile must have been the fuel which fired a savage prayer for vengeance, a reformulation, in grim terms, of one aspect of the heroic code he had taught Cyrnus.

[1] See the note to no. 49 in West (1978*b*).
[2] Louis MacNeice, *Autumn Journal*, London 1939, IX.

Olympian Zeus, fulfil at least my prayer in season; grant me some experience of good to balance the evil. I would wish to die, unless I can find some relief from sad cares and give back pain for pain. For here stands my fate: I see no vengeance coming on those men who stripped me of my property and hold it still – I am the dog that crossed the flooding river in the gorge – he shook everything off. May it be mine to drink their dark blood...(341–9)

As far as we know he never lived to see the day of restoration and revenge. His enemies were no doubt as unforgiving and unforgetting as he was. And for all his calls to moderation in the gnomic passages of his poems, he reveals his true feelings in four lines which sum up the bitter contempt for the common people which brought him and his fellow aristocrats, in Megara, and elsewhere to disaster.

Drive the empty-headed vulgar herd with kicks, jab them with sharp goads and put a galling yoke on their neck; you will not find, among all the men the sun looks down on, a people that loves a master more than this one. (847–50)

4. SOLON

In Athens, Megara's next-door neighbour and her rival for the possession of Salamis, the same social and economic problems faced the old aristocracy, but Athens was more fortunate in the political outcome. She was saved from the worst excesses of *stasis* by a statesman whose reforms prevented civil war and who was regarded by the later democracy as one of its forerunners. But Solon was also a poet and his poems present us with an extraordinary phenomenon: a political leader using poetry as his principal means of communication, to agitate, to warn, to announce and defend his policies.

As usual, most of his work is lost. Diogenes Laertius tells us that his elegiac verses totalled 5,000 and that he wrote iambics and epodes as well. No trace of the epodes remains, but we have some 20 lines of trochaic tetrameter, 47 or so of iambic trimeter, and 219 of the 5,000 elegiac lines. This is a pitifully small remnant; yet it is enough to conjure up an unforgettable personality: a statesman and poet who is not only the first of an illustrious line of Athenian writers but also the first Athenian to emerge from the historical obscurity of illiterate ages. Plutarch's Athenian *Lives* begin with Theseus, the mythical founder of Attic unity; the next in time is Solon – the only historical figure before the fifth century for whom oral tradition and written documents had preserved material enough for a biography. Cylon, who made the first attempt to found an Athenian tyranny, and Draco, who wrote the laws in blood, are historical figures, but for us they are little more than names; the Solonian fragments give us glimpses of a many-sided individual and also of the context in which he lived – that sixth century which in literature, the arts and social experimentation laid the foundations for Athens' golden age.

He was known to later ages as ὁ νομοθέτης 'the Lawgiver', and Athenian orators of the fourth century never tire of invoking his name as the criterion of traditional legality. But his career began with a defiance of the spirit, if not the letter, of the law. An indecisive war with Megara (late seventh century) over the possession of the strategically vital island of Salamis had so disgusted the Athenians that they ceased fighting and decreed the death penalty for anyone who should speak or write in favour of renewing hostilities. Solon (pretending insanity and wearing the cap of an invalid on his head) came into the agora and declaimed his hundred-line elegiac poem, *Salamis*, a call for winning the island at all costs. 'I have come in person, a herald from lovely Salamis,' it began, 'delivering a song, a pattern of verse, instead of a speech' (ἀντ' ἀγορῆς, fr. 1). The burden of his song was reproof, a forcible expression of the ignominy that would follow the abandonment of Salamis. If we do not win it, one of the extant fragments goes on to say, 'in that case, I would rather change my homeland, instead of an Athenian be a man from Pholegandros or Sikinnos. For all too soon this word would be on all mens' lips: "He is from Attica, this man, one of the Salamis-losers"' (fr. 2):

εἴην δὴ τότ' ἐγὼ Φολεγάνδριος ἢ Σικινήτης
ἀντί γ' Ἀθηναίου πατρίδ' ἀμειψάμενος·
αἶψα γὰρ ἂν φάτις ἥδε μετ' ἀνθρώποισι γένοιτο·
"Ἀττικὸς οὗτος ἀνήρ, τῶν Σαλαμιναφετέων.'

He turns from reproach to exhortation. 'Let us go to Salamis, to fight for the lovely island and cast off the burden of disgrace' (fr. 3). They did go to Salamis and, though it was not done overnight, Salamis was won for Athens in the end; the threat to Eleusis and the harbours of Athens was removed.

This episode (which does not rest on Plutarch's authority alone, for a passage in Demosthenes (19.252, 255) shows that it was accepted history in the fourth century B.C.) is a vivid reminder of the fact that in the archaic age poetry was not a written text to be read but a performance to be watched and heard; *Salamis* is poetry in action. Tyrtaeus' elegies were, in later times, sung to Spartan troops to raise their morale (and perhaps were composed for this purpose) but Solon's performance is not only unofficial, indeed subversive propaganda, it is also, with its assumed identity (a herald) and disguise (the cap of the invalid), a fully dramatic performance.

The lines are remarkable also in that they present us with the first reference to Athens and Attica by an Athenian poet; they are informed by a fierce pride in the city's greatness and an assumption that Athenian citizenship imposes great obligations – the salient features of Pericles' ideal vision of Athenian democracy, the Funeral Speech of some two hundred years later.

Not all of Solon's poetry was addressed to the immediate political situation, in fact the longest poem we possess (fr. 13: 76 lines of elegiacs) is a leisurely reflection on moral issues and the vicissitudes of human life and the justice of Zeus. In its rather rambling discursiveness it is often reminiscent of Hesiod's *Works and days* and there are correspondences in thought as well as in structure and style. It is, in form, a prayer to the Muses: the poet asks for prosperity (ὄλβον) and good reputation (δόξαν...ἀγαθήν) in the eyes of all men. This last phrase seems to be defined by the couplet which follows: 'let them say that I am honey to him that loves me, bitter gall to him that hates me, respected by the one, feared by the other.'

> εἶναι δὲ γλυκὺν ὧδε φίλοις, ἐχθροῖσι δὲ πικρόν,
> τοῖσι μὲν αἰδοῖον, τοῖσι δὲ δεινὸν ἰδεῖν.　　　　　　(5–6)

Solon then returns to his first theme, prosperity, which is developed as the real subject of the poem as a whole. He wants prosperity but not to win it by injustice (ἀδίκως). The wealth given to a man by the gods stands on a firm foundation and will last, but wealth won by violence and wickedness will be destroyed by Zeus whose wrath is described in an impressive simile drawn from the storm winds (of which Zeus is the dispenser). His wrath, however, is not swift, like ours; punishment may come late, and it may fall on the next generation of the wrongdoer's family, or even on their children's children. There follows a long and detailed catalogue of the vanity of human wishes, the vain hopes (κούφαις ἐλπίσι, 36) of mankind, their different ways to wealth – as sailor, farmer, craftsman, poet, seer, doctor – all beset with uncertainty; only the seer, if the gods are with him, knows what the future will bring. For it is Fate (Μοῖρα, 63) which brings good or evil to mankind; the gifts of the immortal gods cannot be avoided. The poem returns to its earlier theme – wealth, and here the focus seems to move from the individual to the social level: 'There's no limit set to wealth for men to see. For those of us who now hold the greatest resources, struggle to double their possessions; and who could satisfy them all?'

Not only is the structure loose and the sequence of thought muddy; the style is careless – ἰδεῖν used as a line ending three times (6, 22, 24), the colourless adjective ἀργαλέος three times (37, 45, 61). But, outside of the long simile (18–25) and the catalogue of professions (43–62), the language is less dependent on Homer than anything seen in elegiac poetry so far and many individual linguistic traits appear – the use of the adverb πάντως in line 8 (a favourite word of Solon's), the first use of an adjective very common in later Attic, φλαῦρος (15).

There is nothing particularly new in the moral formulation, indeed lines 5–6 (see above) remind us forcibly that Solon, descended from the mythical King Codrus, was of aristocratic stock, for this attitude towards friends and enemies is the standard heroic ethic. But Solon, unlike Theognis, realized that this same personal code of martial honour, elevated to the level of political programme and blindly followed in the factions of the body politic, was a recipe for disaster. In a fragmentary elegy (quoted by Demosthenes in a fourth-century oration) Solon warns his fellow citizens against Δυσνομίη 'anarchy', for so, he tells us, 'my heart tells me to instruct the Athenians' (4.30).

> ἡμετέρη δὲ πόλις κατὰ μὲν Διὸς οὔποτ' ὀλεῖται
> αἶσαν καὶ μακάρων θεῶν φρένας ἀθανάτων·
> τοίη γὰρ μεγάθυμος ἐπίσκοπος ὀβριμοπάτρη
> Παλλὰς 'Αθηναίη χεῖρας ὕπερθεν ἔχει·
> αὐτοὶ δὲ φθείρειν μεγάλην πόλιν ἀφραδίηισιν
> ἀστοὶ βούλονται χρήμασι πειθόμενοι...　　　　　　　　(4.1–6)

Our city shall never perish by the destiny of Zeus and the will of the blessed immortal gods – such is the power of our protector, great-hearted Pallas Athena, daughter of mighty father, who holds her arm over us. But the citizens themselves, in their madness, want to bring to ruin our great city – and all for money's sake...

The poem gives a graphic description of the evils brought on by the unrestrained pursuit of riches, the plundering of the city's wealth by her leaders, the disregard of justice, the conspiracies of warring factions, with, as the crowning calamity, the lot of the poor – sold into slavery abroad. This is Δυσνομίη, bad government; its consequences no man, rich or poor, can escape.

So the communal evil comes home to every man alike, the gates of his housecourt will no longer keep it out; it leaps high over the enclosure wall and finds its man no matter where – even hidden in the recesses of the bedroom. (4.26–9)

The greed of the rulers and the violence of partisans release forces of destruction which cannot be controlled; this is what had happened in Megara and was to happen again, much later, in Corcyra.

Solon's praise of the opposite state of affairs, Εὐνομίη 'good government', rises, in a highly skilled rhetorical arrangement, to lyrical heights.

> Εὐνομίη δ' εὔκοσμα καὶ ἄρτια πάντ' ἀποφαίνει,
> καὶ θαμὰ τοῖς ἀδίκοις ἀμφιτίθησι πέδας·
> τραχέα λειαίνει, παύει κόρον, ὕβριν ἀμαυροῖ,
> αὐαίνει δ' ἄτης ἄνθεα φυόμενα,
> εὐθύνει δὲ δίκας σκολιὰς, ὑπερήφανά τ' ἔργα
> πραΰνει· παύει δ' ἔργα διχοστασίης,
> παύει δ' ἀργαλέης ἔριδος χόλον, ἔστι δ' ὑπ' αὐτῆς
> πάντα κατ' ἀνθρώπους ἄρτια καὶ πινυτά.　　　　　　　(4.32–9)

The goddess Good Rule makes everything well-ordered and sound; and often she puts the wrongdoers in irons. She makes the rough smooth, checks excess, dims violence; she withers the flowers of ruinous madness on the stalk, straightens crooked judgements, tames the works of insolence, stops the working of faction. She checks the anger of deadly dissension; under her governance everything in the human world is sound and sensible.

But Solon's warnings went unheeded and affairs came to the critical stage which in so many other Greek cities resulted in civil war or tyranny. The Athenians managed to avoid civil war and, for the moment, tyranny as well; they appointed Solon archon with full power for one year, to act as διαλλάκτης 'conciliator' – an office which under various titles had been created in more than one faction-riven Greek city (Mytilene, for example, see p. 209) as a last resort. Solon, once in office, told both sides to curb their demands and inaugurated a series of reforms (known as the Seisachtheia – 'shaking off of burdens') which included remission of debts, prohibition of debt-slavery, the return to Athens of men who had fled abroad because of debt, a code of laws to replace the fierce punitive code of Draco and many other measures besides. But they were all compromises; none of them a complete victory for either side.

> To the people I gave the portion that was theirs; I took nothing from them in the way of honour, offered nothing more. As for those who already had power and were respected for their wealth, I took measures to protect them from outrage. I took my stand with my strong shield thrown over both sides; I would not allow either side an unjust victory. (fr. 5)

To the rich, his own class, he counselled moderation: 'You who have driven on to overabundance of all good things, quiet your strong hearts in your breasts, set your proud mind on moderate aims.' (fr. 4c). Aristotle, who quotes these lines, tells us that Solon blamed the rich for the civil discord. But he had no illusions about the other side; in an account of his actions written after his year of office he is just as hard on the leaders of the popular party, who had raised the classic revolutionary cry for a redistribution of the land.

> They came to plunder, with high hopes of riches; each one thought he would find great wealth and that I was coaxing with smooth speech but would reveal a ruthless mind. Their hopes were liars and now they are angry with me, give me black looks as if I were an enemy... (fr. 34)

He is proud to boast that he disappointed both sides, above all that he disregarded demands from both sides for the punishment of their adversaries.

> If someone else had taken the goad in hand, some man of evil intent and grasping hand, he would not have held the people back. If I had agreed to do what the people's opponents wanted or on the other hand to what the people had in mind for them, this city would have been full of widows... (36.20–5)

His loyalty was not to either side but to Athens. Aristotle tells us that the poem which induced the two factions to give him the supreme authority began with the lines: 'I know, and pain builds up in my heart, as I see the oldest land of

Ionia in decline...' (4a). He went on, Aristotle tells us, 'to champion each side against the other, argue their case, and then recommend an end to the continuing faction-fighting'.

Solon's love for Athens embraces not only the people but the land itself; there is a tender note in his famous boast that he removed the mortgage stones from Attic soil.

> συμμαρτυροίη ταῦτ' ἂν ἐν δίκηι Χρόνου
> μήτηρ μεγίστη δαιμόνων Ὀλυμπίων
> ἄριστα, Γῆ μέλαινα, τῆς ἐγώ ποτε
> ὅρους ἀνεῖλον πολλαχῆι πεπηγότας,
> πρόσθεν δὲ δουλεύουσα, νῦν ἐλευθέρη.   (36.3–7)

Let my witness in the court of Time be the great mother of the gods on Olympus, black Earth; I pulled up the mortgage markers that were fixed in her far and wide – she was enslaved and now is free.

He loved the language too, the dialect which stamped a man as Athenian; his remission of debts brought home men who had been sold abroad or had left 'by sheer necessity, to escape debt' and now 'no longer spoke the Attic tongue, since they had wandered far and wide':

> γλῶσσαν οὐκέτ' Ἀττικὴν
> ἱέντας, ὡς δὴ πολλαχῆι πλανωμένους.   (36.10–12)

This is the first mention of that Attic dialect which, because of the unrivalled greatness of those who later wrote in it, was to become the literary language of Greece, relegating all other dialects to provincial status and exerting its powerful influence on writers of Greek all through antiquity and even beyond.

The dialect in which Solon writes is not Attic, however; his language is the modified Ionic of the elegiac and epic tradition, though he is less closely tied to Homeric diction than some of his predecessors and he introduced into the elegiac vocabulary words which later became common in Attic writing (φλαύρη 13.15 for example, λατρεύει 13.48). But it is in his iambic poems, trimeter and tetrameter, that his real originality as a poet stands revealed. The iambic trimeter had been employed for violent personal abuse by Archilochus and Hipponax, for satiric abuse of the whole female sex by Semonides; in all these cases the identity of the speaker was not necessarily, sometimes not possibly, that of the poet. But Solon speaks in his own name about his own actions, the voice of a statesman offering a defence of the measures taken during his year as ruler of Athens. The long passage preserved by Aristotle (fr. 36) which contains the lines cited above – the claim to have removed the mortgage stones and the reference to the Attic dialect – is couched in the metre which later will be used by the speakers in Attic tragedy; the style and pace of these lines, as a modern scholar has pointed out, make them an entirely new phenomenon in archaic literature. 'The flow of the verses...rolls on like a great speech in classical tragedy...Even the grammatical structure is different; the sentences are long and carry one subject after another to completion...Surely and steadily, the discourse presses forward without pause in a consistent and solid stream.'[1] Another scholar has claimed that it was Solon who in iambic poems like these created the model which enabled the epic hero, when he later became the tragic hero, to speak 'a language to which the men of the sixth century could respond in living terms'.[2]

Solon could vary the tone, however; the solemn dignity of the statesman could be leavened by sardonic humour, as when, in a tetrameter passage, he writes a speech for a critic who despised him for not holding on to office at the end of the year, to establish that tyranny which was the usual solution of the political dilemma.

> Solon was no deep thinker, it seems, but a man lacking in sense, for the gods offered him blessings and he simply refused. He had the catch inside his big net but just stood there agape, unable to pull it tight – a failure of spirit as well as lack of wits. Now I would have been willing – just to hold power, to get wealth without limit, and be despot of Athens for one single day – I'd have been willing to be flayed alive to make a wineskin, my whole line wiped out. (fr. 33)

The temptation to retain power, and the advice of his friends that he should do so may have been hard to resist, but his refusal was uncompromising. 'I spared the land of my fathers, held my hand back from tyranny and harsh violence...' (fr. 32). Yet he was intelligent enough to know that others would be more ambitious than he; the strains in the body politic were relieved, not removed, and Solon warned his fellow citizens to beware.

> From a cloud comes the force of hail and snow,
> From the lightning flash the rolling thunder
> And from great men comes the city's destruction.
> And the poor, in their ignorance,
> Stumble into slavery, under the rule of a despot. (fr. 9)

His warnings were dismissed by the Pisistratid faction as madness and he replied: 'Time will show the Athenians whether I am mad or no; it will not be long, as the truth comes to plain view' (fr. 10). And later, with Pisistratus in the saddle, he reproaches his fellow citizens for not seeing through the classic manoeuvre of the would-be tyrant, the request for a bodyguard: 'Do not attribute any share of these things to the gods; you yourselves built these men up by assigning them protection...' (fr. 11).

---

[1] Fränkel (1975) 226f.
[2] Else (1965) 45.

These and other bitter comments may have been addressed to his fellow citizens from abroad, for we are told that after his year as archon he left Athens, so that he would not be the object of pressure to repeal his laws. He seems to have travelled to Egypt; one line (fr. 28) mentions the Canopic mouth of the Nile, and Plato, much later, has Critias claim that Solon brought back from his Egyptian travels the story of Atlantis (*Ti.* 21c). A stay in Cyprus is attested by six elegiac lines addressed to a king on that island (fr. 19) but there is nothing in the fragments to support Herodotus' famous story of his visit to Croesus of Lydia.

Some of the smaller fragments show us a Solon who was not always obsessed by affairs of state. Plato quotes a couplet which sounds like a short aristocratic credo: 'Happy the man who has loving sons, horses with uncloven hoof, hunting dogs and a guest from abroad' (23). Another (25) celebrates the joys of boy-love and a surprising group of iambic fragments (38–40) deals in considerable detail with food. A rather dull elegiac poem (27) divides the life of man up into ten seven-year periods, with remarks on the virtues of each phase: the fourth (age 22–8) is the height of physical strength and the seventh and eighth (age 43–56) the best for 'mind and tongue'. 'And if anyone duly reaches the end of the tenth, it would not be untimely if he came to the end of his days.' Later, presumably, he saw fit to revise this estimate. In a poem addressed to Mimnermus of Colophon (see pp. 134ff.) he takes issue with that poet's wish to die at sixty. 'If you will still take my advice now, erase that line. Don't take it ill that I have a better idea than you, revise the line, Mimnermus, and sing this: when I am eighty let death come for me' (fr. 20). We do not know whether he reached that age himself but the insecure dates we are given for his life suggest that he went most of the way. And of his old age he said, in a line that has been quoted with admiration ever since: 'I grow old learning many things'

γηράσκω δ' αἰεὶ πολλὰ διδασκόμενος.   (fr. 18)

5. SEMONIDES

Semonides of Amorgos is one of our earliest representatives of a perennial literary mode – informal, humorous, down-to-earth – which manifests itself now in lampoon or parody, now in comedy, now in satire. As a writer of iambics he belongs to the same tradition as Archilochus and Hipponax, but in later antiquity he was often confused with his distinguished near-namesake, the lyric poet Simonides of Ceos (see pp. 223ff.).[1] Modern scholars have been able to disentangle what remains of the two poets' work with reasonable confidence, but a few pieces are likely to remain in doubt, particularly since they shared

---

[1] Only Choeroboscus (*Et.Magn.* 713, 17c) preserves the correct spelling of his name; in all our other sources he is called Simonides.

at least one metre, elegiacs, and many of the fragments are too short to yield much decisive evidence.

Semonides was probably a Samian who settled in Amorgos and may indeed have been a leader of colonists on the island, as one of the sources claims;[1] otherwise we know nothing about his family or personal circumstances. Even his date is uncertain, though the latter half of the seventh century seems plausible. The attitude he strikes in the poems is that of the 'ordinary man' (e.g. in fr. 7, his account of the mare-woman, quoted below), but no doubt that is a tone of voice dictated by the choice of genre. He is said to have written poems of invective: Lucian (*Pseudolog.* 2) mentions the name of his alleged *bête noire*, one Orodoecidas,[2] but the surviving fragments (which may be quite unrepresentative) give very few clues. Most of the scraps that have come down to us were quoted by grammarians to illustrate points of usage, not to characterize Semonides. Some of these snippets may possibly come from lampoons on individuals, like fr. 13 on a dung-beetle ('there flew up to us the creature with the worst life-style of all beasts'), which could easily be part of an attack on some offensive enemy, but there is no means of telling. All we can say for certain is that he frequently wrote in iambics, the appropriate metre for light-hearted, informal or abusive poetry, and that his style and subject matter are correspondingly 'low', though there is little obvious obscenity in what happens to survive, and at least one fragment (1) is quite serious and dignified. Food seems to be a favourite topic (fr. 15 mentions tunny, squid and gudgeon, fr. 23 a 'wonderful cheese'); so too are animals (heron, buzzard and eel, fr. 9; hawk, fr. 12; pig, fr. 28). In fr. 24 the speaker is a cook, another sure sign of comic intent in an ancient poet.

His longest and most celebrated piece, fr. 7, clearly belongs to the same mode. It is a 118-line fragment on women, preserved for us in the anthology of Stobaeus (fifth century A.D.). The poem was undoubtedly meant to be funny (though Stobaeus may not have thought so), and it must be seen as an early example of a favourite theme in western literature, the attack on women written by men for men in a male-dominated society.[3] It is close to Hesiod in its general attitude to women (as in the story of Pandora, *Theog.* 570ff., where women are said to be a 'great bane for mortal men, companions not of poverty but of excess', cf. *W.D.* 54ff., 702ff.), but Semonides' purpose is more obviously to entertain. He purports to account for women's natures by telling of their creation from ten different sources, seven animals, two elements and one insect, in the order sow, vixen, bitch, earth, sea, donkey, ferret, mare, monkey, bee. All but the bee are highly unflattering images: the animal associations suggest women who

---

[1] Suda IV 363.1 and 360.7, discussed by Lloyd-Jones (1975) 15–18.

[2] Or Orodoecides. West (*IEG* II) 97, thinks the name is corrupt, but see Lloyd-Jones (1975) 14 n. 13.

[3] Cf. Hodgart (1969) ch. 3; Hipponax 68.

are lazy, dirty, greedy (sow), unscrupulous and too clever (vixen), inquisitive, nagging (bitch), inert and stupid (earth), fickle (sea), stubborn, promiscuous (donkey), lecherous, dishonest (ferret), extravagant and luxurious (mare), ugly, malevolent (monkey), but there is a good deal of overlapping in the detail given to the different types, and some of the satirical effect depends precisely on the vehement and 'unfair' exaggeration. The cumulative impression given by the insistent list – the technique is the same as Juvenal's – is that *almost all* feminine traits are inherently bad: both the dirty sow and her opposite, the elegant mare, and both the clod-like earth-woman and the mercurial sea-woman, are equally objectionable.

The description of the mare-woman exemplifies Semonides' vivid use of everyday detail, his outspokenness and wit – and his straightforwardness by comparison with writers of more decadent times:

> τὴν δ᾽ ἵππος ἁβρὴ χαιτέεσσ᾽ ἐγείνατο,
> ἣ δούλι᾽ ἔργα καὶ δύην περιτρέπει,
> κοῦτ᾽ ἂν μύλης ψαύσειεν, οὔτε κόσκινον
> ἄρειεν, οὔτε κόπρον ἐξ οἴκου βάλοι,
> οὔτε πρὸς ἰπνὸν ἀσβόλην ἀλεομένη
> ἵζοιτ᾽. ἀνάγκηι δ᾽ ἄνδρα ποιεῖται φίλον·
> λοῦται δὲ πάσης ἡμέρης ἄπο ῥύπον
> δίς, ἄλλοτε τρίς, καὶ μύροις ἀλείφεται,
> αἰεὶ δὲ χαίτην ἐκτενισμένην φορεῖ
> βαθεῖαν, ἀνθέμοισιν ἐσκιασμένην.
> κᾶλὸν μὲν ὦν θέημα τοιαύτη γυνὴ
> ἄλλοισι, τῶι δ᾽ ἔχοντι γίνεται κακόν,
> ἢν μή τις ἢ τύραννος ἢ σκηπτοῦχος ἦι.   (57–69)

Another was produced by a dainty mare with a flowing mane. She shirks menial tasks and anything painful: she wouldn't put her hand to a mill or lift up a sieve or throw dung out of the house or sit by the stove dodging the soot. She makes her husband a friend of Necessity; and she washes the dirt off herself twice, sometimes three times, every day, and rubs on scents, and always wears her thick hair well combed and garlanded with flowers. A woman like this is very nice for other people to look at, but a terrible bane to her husband – unless he's a tyrant or a king.

If the mare-woman has a certain charm, the ferret and the monkey conjure up more repulsive pictures, the woman who is 'crazy for sex but makes the man she has with her sick' (53–4), and one who is 'short in the neck and moves awkwardly, and has no bottom but is all legs' – and is a nasty character into the bargain (75–9). But unlike most of his successors in the genre, Semonides allows the possibility of good in womankind and ends his list with a picture of the virtuous bee-woman, devoted wife and mother, beautiful, chaste and sensible. This interesting if unromantic picture recalls Hesiod, who also thought good women could exist and saw the practical advantages of marriage as well as its drawbacks (*Theog.* 603ff.; *W.D.* 695ff.), though he too emphasizes the bad side and in fact uses the bee image to bring out the laziness of women: they are the drones for whom the men work all day long (*Theog.* 596ff.). Semonides moves on from the picture of the bee-woman to some generally condemnatory sentiments on women as the greatest evil given to men by Zeus (l.96 is closely echoed by l.115, the familiar device of ring-composition used to mark off a section). This passage seems to have been designed as a bridge to a part of the poem now lost, on disastrous women in legend: the last two lines of our extant fragment run 'some have gone to Hades fighting for a woman' (117–18), and it seems best to suppose that a series of *exempla* followed. Helen is the notorious case, but the myths could supply many more *femmes fatales*.

Even in its incomplete state this is a lively and arresting poem. Semonides has a sharp eye for detail and a suitably knowing and cynical tone, but there is a lack of density in the writing that makes it intellectually undemanding; Archilochus, working in a similar medium, achieved altogether more brilliant effects.

Semonides' poetry feels close to popular life, though our evidence for that life is of course very slight. As well as using homely detail he may have incorporated beast fables into his verses (e.g. perhaps frs. 9 and 12), and there may be some link between his notion of women created from animals and a fable by Aesop about men with the souls of beasts. Perhaps, too, he knew and drew upon folk-tale;[1] but it would be quite wrong to set him apart from the mainstream of archaic literature with its shared values and its all-pervading use of epic language. Commentators have noted that his pictures of the donkey and the mare, for example, have links with famous Homeric similes (*Iliad* 11.557ff.; 6.506ff.) as well as with 'real life', and his language consistently reveals its debt to Homer and Hesiod. His tone, salty and unheroic, is particularly reminiscent of Hesiod; like Alcaeus (fr. 347), he seems to have made a point of reworking a Hesiodic passage in his own metre:

γυναικὸς οὐδὲν χρῆμ' ἀνὴρ ληίζεται
ἐσθλῆς ἄμεινον οὐδὲ ῥίγιον κακῆς.　　　　　　　　　　(fr. 6)

a man carries off no prize better than a good woman or more horrid than a bad one.

(Cf. Hesiod, *W.D.* 702f. οὐ μὲν γάρ τι γυναικὸς ἀνὴρ ληίζετ' ἄμεινον | τῆς ἀγαθῆς, τῆς δ' αὖτε κακῆς οὐ ῥίγιον ἄλλο 'for a man carries off no prize better than the good woman, nor any more horrid than the bad'.)

When he chooses, Semonides can write quite seriously, as in fr. 1 on man's helplessness and vulnerability. Here the poet uses themes familiar in Mimnermus,

[1] Lloyd-Jones (1975) 20–2.

Solon and the lyric poets – the way man clings to hope, and the many disasters he is heir to – but there is a characteristic touch of wit in the expression of these 'great commonplaces':

> Some people wait for another day to come, others for a whole year to pass; but there's not a single mortal who doesn't think that next year he will make friends with wealth and prosperity. (7–10)

The poem seems to be leading up to an exhortation to enjoy the present moment, but it has been cut short by the anthologist who quotes it, and breaks off before the climax.

There is no certainty that any of Semonides' elegiac work has been preserved, though he is said to have composed an 'elegy in two books'. We know nothing of his alleged history of Samos (ἀρχαιολογία τῶν Σαμίων); conceivably this was in elegiacs. One fine poem in this metre has often been attributed to him because of its closeness in sentiment to fr. 1, although others have preferred on stylistic grounds to assign it to Simonides. The most recent editor, M. L. West, cautiously treats it as a 'doubtful' fragment (= Simonides fr. 8), typical of the younger poet's period, but not certainly identifiable as his. Whoever its author was, it deserves to be quoted as a felicitous expression of archaic Greek feeling; its elegance perhaps tells against Semonides, though he would surely have endorsed its tone and message:

> ἒν δὲ τὸ κάλλιστον Χῖος ἔειπεν ἀνήρ·
> 'οἵη περ φύλλων γενεή, τοίη δὲ καὶ ἀνδρῶν'·
> παῦροί μιν θνητῶν οὔασι δεξάμενοι
> στέρνοις ἐγκατέθεντο· πάρεστι γὰρ ἐλπὶς ἑκάστωι
> ἀνδρῶν, ἥ τε νέων στήθεσιν ἐμφύεται.
> θνητῶν δ' ὄφρά τις ἄνθος ἔχηι πολυήρατον ἥβης,
> κοῦφον ἔχων θυμὸν πόλλ' ἀτέλεστα νοεῖ·
> οὔτε γὰρ ἐλπίδ' ἔχει γηρασέμεν οὔτε θανεῖσθαι,
> οὐδ', ὑγιὴς ὅταν ἦι, φροντίδ' ἔχει καμάτου.
> νήπιοι, οἷς ταύτηι κεῖται νόος, οὐδὲ ἴσασιν
> ὡς χρόνος ἔσθ' ἥβης καὶ βιότου ὀλίγος
> θνητοῖς. ἀλλὰ σὺ ταῦτα μαθὼν βιότου ποτὶ τέρμα
> ψυχῆι τῶν ἀγαθῶν τλῆθι χαριζόμενος.

The finest thing the man of Chios [Homer] said was this: 'Like the generation of leaves, so is that of men.' Few mortals taking this in with their ears have stored it in their hearts; for each man is attended by hope, which grows in young people's breasts. And while he has the lovely bloom of youth a mortal man is light-hearted and full of impossible ideas: he doesn't expect to grow old or die, and while he is healthy he has no thought of being ill. They are fools who think this way and don't understand that for mortals the time of youth – and life – is short. So be aware of this and bear up as you near life's end, indulging yourself with good things.

6. HIPPONAX

It was presumably the approving references in Plato and Aristotle to Theognis as a moralist which guaranteed the survival of his book through the Byzantine era. No such protective label was or possibly could be attached to the work of Hipponax of Ephesus; even though he was a favourite of the Alexandrian poets and scholars (who seem to have neglected Theognis entirely) he survives only in fragments. His abusive tone and unedifying subject matter could hardly have been expected to win the approval of the Christian fathers, but they were also displeasing to the last aggressive representative of paganism, the emperor Julian. He wanted his priests to 'abstain not only from impure and lascivious acts but also from speech and reading of the same character...No initiate shall read Archilochus or Hipponax or any of the authors who write the same kind of thing...' (*Ep.* 48). The fact that the poet's Ionic dialect and polyglot vocabulary were unsuitable for an educational system which emphasized Attic purity is one more reason why our text of Hipponax, apart from recent papyrus discoveries, is a miserable collection of fragments, none containing more than six complete consecutive lines and many only a short phrase or a single word.

Our sources mention two 'books'; these are probably the books of the Alexandrian edition. If they were anything like the *Iamboi* of Callimachus, who in his introductory poem brings Hipponax back from Hades to give the Alexandrian *literati* a piece of his mind, the contents were separate poems on a variety of subjects and in a wide range of metres. Our fragments contain iambic trimeters, trochaic tetrameters, hexameters and a combination of iambic trimeter with a shorter dactylic line.

Most poets of the archaic period, no matter what their provenance or the genre in which they worked, were strongly influenced by the Ionian epic tradition and particularly by its main representative, Homer. The dependence is most clearly marked in the poems of Hesiod the Boeotian, who composed in the same hexameter metre as Homer, and in the closely related elegiac couplets of poets whose origins are as diverse as Ionia (Mimnermus and Callinus), the Aegean islands (Semonides of Amorgos and Archilochus of Paros) and the Greek mainland (Tyrtaeus of Sparta, Theognis of Megara and Solon of Athens). The Lesbian poets, too, though they write in unhomeric metres and dialect, adapt his themes and techniques, while Archilochus, in his iambic as well as in his elegiac verse is, as Denys Page put it, 'seldom for long free from the influence of the traditional language of the epic'.[1] Hipponax, however, who came from one Ionian city, Ephesus, and went to another, Clazomenae, writes for the most part, to judge from the pathetically few fragments we have left, as though Homer had never existed. There is one significant exception: a

[1] Page (1964) 159.

hexameter passage satirizing a glutton which is a ludicrous travesty of Homeric style:

Μοῦσά μοι Εὐρυμεδοντιάδεα τὴν ποντοχάρυβδιν, ·
τὴν ἐν γαστρὶ μάχαιραν, ὃς ἐσθίει οὐ κατὰ κόσμον,
ἔννεφ᾽, ὅπως ψηφῖδι 〈 〉 κακὸν οἶτον ὀλεῖται
βουλῆι δημοσίηι παρὰ θῖν᾽ ἁλὸς ἀτρυγέτοιο. (fr. 128)

Muse, sing of Eurymedontiades, sea-swilling Charybdis,
his belly a sharp-slicing knife, his table manners atrocious;
sing how, condemned by public decree, he will perish obscenely
under a rain of stones, on the beach of the barren salt ocean.

This is the only intelligible hexameter fragment we possess; we have also some trochaic tetrameters, but the bulk of Hipponax' extant work is couched in the metre he may have invented but which in any case he made his trademark: the 'limping' (*skazon*) or 'lame' (*choliambos*) iambic. It is the iambic trimeter we know from Archilochus, except that it ends with a spondee; the three long final syllables produce a dragging, breaking effect.

ἐμοὶ δὲ Πλοῦτος – ἔστι γὰρ λίην τυφλός –
ἐς τὠικί᾽ ἐλθὼν οὐδάμ᾽ εἶπεν ''Ἱππῶναξ,
δίδωμί τοι μνέας ἀργύρου τριήκοντα
καὶ πόλλ᾽ ἔτ᾽ ἄλλα᾽· δείλαιος γὰρ τὰς φρένας. (fr. 36)

It never happened to me. The god of wealth's stone blind.
He never came into my house and said to me: 'Hipponax,
Here's money for you, thirty minae of pure silver
And a lot more besides.' No, he's too hard-hearted.

The tone of that fragment is characteristic; with Hipponax we are in an unheroic, in fact, a very sordid world.

There is a remarkable (and rather suspect) parallel between the biographies and poetic activity of the two most famous writers of iambics, Hipponax and Archilochus. Archilochus, spurned by Lycambes, turned his satiric rage against father and daughters, who, we are told, hanged themselves for shame: Hipponax, insulted by two sculptors, Bupalus and Athenis of Chios, who made caricatures of his ugly features, drove them to suicide with his iambic onslaughts. We know nothing more about Lycambes and his daughters than what Archilochus tells us, but Bupalus and Athenis are known from other sources; they were active on the Aegean islands in the middle and late years of the sixth century B.C. Pliny dismisses the story that they hanged themselves – *quod falsum est* – and mentions a statue signed by them on Delos (*N.H.* 36.5.11–13); Pausanias tells us there was a statue of the Graces by Bupalus in the art collection of the Hellenistic kings of Pergamon (9.35.6). Athenis is rarely mentioned in our fragments (fr. 70.11 and possibly fr. 1); but Bupalus' name recurs again and again (three times in fr. 95, for example). It appears in what was probably the first line of Hipponax' book (fr. 1); elsewhere Bupalus is accused of sleeping with his mother (ὁ μητροκοίτης, fr. 12) and in another fragment Hipponax imagines a confrontation with him: 'Hold my coat; I'll knock Bupalus' eye out' λάβετέ μεο ταἰμάτια, κόψω Βουπάλωι τὸν ὀφθαλμόν (fr. 120), a line which possibly connects with another; 'For I can swing with left and with right and I land them on target' ἀμφιδέξιος γάρ εἰμι κοὐκ ἁμαρτάνω κόπτων (fr. 121).

In addition to the two sculptors, a painter, one Mimnes, also figures among the victims of Hipponactean invective. He is reproved for painting a serpent on a war ship wrong way round – facing back towards the pilot at the stern instead of forward towards the enemy.

> Mimnes, you lousy pervert, when you paint the serpent on the trireme's full-oared side, quit making it run back from the prow-ram to the pilot. What a disaster it will be and what a sensation – you low-born slave, you scum – if the snake should bite the pilot on the shin. (fr. 28)

Another figure in this low-life saga (whether it has any basis in fact we do not know) is a woman whose Homeric and programmatic name is singularly at odds with her conduct and surroundings. She is associated with some deceitful scheme of Bupalus in fr. 12 but elsewhere appears in intimate association with Hipponax. 'Bending down to me over the lamp Arete...' κύψασα γάρ μοι πρὸς τὸ λύχνον 'Αρήτη (fr. 17) clearly comes from an erotic context and may be from the same poem in which Hipponax says:

> ἐγὼ δὲ δεξιῶι παρ' 'Αρήτην
> κνεφαῖος ἐλθὼν ῥωδιῶι κατηυλίσθην. (fr. 16)

At dark I came to Arete's place, with a heron – lucky sign – on the right hand, and there I settled in.

A drinking party seems to have ensued, of a vulgarity which reminds one irresistibly of François Villon and his *grosse Margot – en ce bordeau ou tenons nostre estat.*

> ἐκ πελλίδος πίνοντες· οὐ γὰρ ἦν αὐτῆι
> κύλιξ, ὁ παῖς γὰρ ἐμπεσὼν κατήραξε,
>
> ἐκ δὲ τῆς πέλλης
> ἔπινον· ἄλλοτ' αὐτός, ἄλλοτ' 'Αρήτη
> προύπινεν. (frs. 13, 14)

...drinking from a milk pail since she didn't have a goblet, a slave had fallen on it, smashed it...now I would take a drink and then Arete would drain it dry.

There is another line of dialogue which may fit into this context: 'Why did you go to bed with that rogue Bupalus?' τί τῶι τάλαντι Βουπάλωι συνοίκησας; (fr. 15).

Other fragments give us more glimpses of life in the *bas-fonds* of Clazomenae. A papyrus fills out two already known fragments to produce an enigmatic but fascinating description of a quarrel which is interrupted by the appearance of the god Hermes and followed by what sounds like a legal manoeuvre of some kind.

> ...beaten up...this madness...the jaw...crapped on...with gold-blazing wand...near the foot of the bed...Hermes followed to Hipponax' house... the dog stealer...hisses like a viper...He went right away, with three witnesses to where the blackguard peddles vino and found his man sweeping out the shop – no broom, though, he was using the stock of a thorn bush. (fr. 79)

It is not a very comfortable world, this; someone 'never stops warming his chilblains by the coal fire' (fr. 59) and Hipponax prays to Hermes for some warm clothing:

'Ερμῆ, φίλ' 'Ερμῆ, Μαιαδεῦ, Κυλλήνιε,
ἐπεύχομαί τοι, κάρτα γὰρ κακῶς ῥιγῶ
καὶ βαμβαλύзω...
δὸς χλαῖναν 'Ιππώνακτι καὶ κυπασσίσκον
καὶ σαμβαλίσκα κάσκερίσκα καὶ χρυσοῦ...   (fr. 32)

> Hermes, dear Hermes, Maia's son, born on Cyllene, I beseech thee, for I am damnably cold, my teeth are chattering...Grant Hipponax a cloak and a dolman and alpergatas, fur-lined boots and gold...

The foreign words in this translation are an attempt to represent a conspicuous feature of Hipponax' style: his use of words drawn from the non-Greek languages of the Ionian hinterland and the orient in general. The 'vino' the blackguard is peddling in the first fragment quoted above is in Hipponax an Egyptian word ἔρπιν and in the prayer to Hermes the names of the items of clothing and footgear are all from Anatolian languages. One fragment (125) uses a word for 'bread' – *bekos* – which we know from a famous story in Herodotus (2.2) was Phrygian.

Hipponax can even address Zeus with a foreign title, *palmys*: 'Oh Zeus, father Zeus, shah of the Olympian gods, why haven't you given me any money...?' (fr. 38). So Hermes is addressed with a title – Kandaules – which Hipponax specifies as 'Maeonian' (fr. 3a) and we hear also of Zeus's daughter Kubebe (fr. 127). Such linguistic borrowings were almost certainly typical of the Greek spoken in the Ionian cities; their appearance in the poems reinforces the vivid local colour which is one of the charms of these somewhat disreputable fragments – the glimpses (the only ones we are given) into the everyday life of the Eastern Greek cities. A very corrupt fragment (42) seems to be giving directions to a traveller going west through Lydia towards Smyrna; he will pass the tombs, monuments and columns of Lydian kings (Gyges is the only one we can be sure of). Another fragment (50) speaks of someone 'who lives by the back of the city, in Smyrna, between Roughroad and Cape Decay' μεταξὺ Τρηχέης τε καὶ Λεπρῆς ἀκτῆς. (Smyrna, we are told by Strabo, who cites these lines, is not the great city of that name but a part of Ephesus.) One line reminds us that the prosperity of these cities was based on sea-borne commerce: 'caulking the keel with pitch and wax' ἔπειτα μάλθηι τὴν τρόπιν παραχρίσας (51), and another passage that the Asia Minor littoral was one of the reservoirs of supplies for the slave market:

καὶ τοὺς σολοίκους ἢν λάβωσι περνᾶσι,
Φρύγας μὲν ἐς Μίλητον ἀλφιτεύσοντας. (fr. 27)

...and if they catch any barbarians, they put them up for sale: the Phrygians to work the grain mills in Miletus...

The presence of many such slaves in the Ionian cities may account for the frequent references in the poems to non-Greek people: a woman dressed in a Koraxian robe (fr. 2), an obscure (and obscene) mention of the Sindoi on the Black Sea – 'Sindic slit' Σινδικὸν διάσφαγμα (fr. 2a), a woman speaking Lydian (fr. 92).

Not all of the characters of these low-life sketches live in the city; we have one fragment which seems to be the voice of a man reduced to peasant fare by the profligacy of one of his sons:

For one of them spent whole days at ease at table
swilling down tunafish and cheese in a steady stream
for all the world like a eunuch from Lampsacus
and so ate up the family fortune. I have to dig
rocks on the mountainside, munch medium-sized figs
and barley-wheat loaves – slave fodder. (fr. 26)

Another fragment may be a partial list of what this disgruntled speaker no longer gets to eat:

...not chewing on partridges and hares,
not seasoning the pancakes with sesame,
not dipping the fritters in honey...(fr. 26a)

But if eating plays a large role in the Hipponactean world, so does the opposite process, evacuation; not until Aristophanes do we encounter so varied a scatological vocabulary again. Fully worthy of Aristophanes is the compound μεσσηγυδορποχέστης (fr. 114c) which is quoted with the explanation: 'a man who goes to the toilet often during the meal so that he can fill up again'. Elsewhere somebody is 'croaking like a raven in a privy' (fr. 61) and in fr. 155 somebody is doing something almost indecipherable (but certainly reprehensible) 'like a lizard in a privy'. The Aristophanic verb τιλάω and its compounds turn up frequently (frs. 73.4, 79.6, 86.2).

It is only to be expected that such a poet would be equally uninhibited in matters sexual but it is only in recent years that papyrus fragments have confirmed what the few book fragments with erotic content (mostly lexicographical entries) seemed to suggest – that Hipponax is a grand master of obscene fiction. One damaged papyrus gives us a tantalizing but lacunose portrayal of what seems to be a love encounter rudely interrupted.

> ...on the floor...undressing...we were biting and kissing...looking out through the door...so they wouldn't catch us...naked...she was hurrying things up...and I was doing my part...

An obscure (and certainly obscene) passage about a sausage is followed by 'telling Bupalus to go to hell...' and two lines later 'and just when we were on the job...' καὶ δὴ 'πὶ τοῖς ἔργοισιν εἴχομεν...(84). Another fragment (92) manages to combine two of Hipponax' themes, sex and evacuation, in one wild scene which may well have been the model for the Oenothea episode in Petronius' *Satyricon* (138). The papyrus, once again, is fragmentary; the right-hand end of the lines is missing, and interpretation is difficult. But clearly a woman, who is introduced as 'speaking Lydian' λυδίζουσα, carries out some magical and obscene rite on the narrator (it includes, besides some obscure anal operation, beating his genitals with a fig branch); the object, presumably, is, as in the *Satyricon*, to restore his lost virility. In Hipponax, however, all this takes place in a privy (its smell is singled out for mention); the protagonist gets spattered with excrement and this provokes an invasion of dung-beetles – they come 'whirring, more than fifty of them' – to provide a Rabelaisian finale.

The fig branch (κράδη) with which the narrator is stimulated in this passage turns up in another context, the religious rite of expelling the scapegoat, the *pharmakos*. The late Byzantine scholar Tzetzes, who quotes the passages in question (they amount to ten lines = frs. 5–10) tells us that in time of famine or plague the 'ancients' chose 'the ugliest man of all' and after various ceremonies mentioned by Hipponax, burned him and scattered his ashes in the sea. These last two details, however, are not derived from Hipponax and in fact the fate of the *pharmakos* in such ceremonies is still a controversial matter – it may have been merely a ceremonial expulsion. In any case the Hipponax passages are not descriptions of the rites but allusions to them, often for purpose of comparison. 'Beating in winter and thrashing with fig branches and squill-stalks, like a *pharmakos*...figs and cereal and cheese, the sort of things the *pharmakos* eats...' One passage – 'And on the genitals let the *pharmakos*, led away, be seven times thrashed' – recalls the Lydian lady's formula for restoring virility in the obscene fragment. What all this has to do with the lives of Hipponax' characters we do not know; perhaps they are parts of imprecations against Bupalus and Athenis, perhaps Hipponax sees himself in the role of victim; in one fragment (fr. 37) someone 'was giving orders to beat and stone Hipponax' ἐκέλευε βάλλειν καὶ λεύειν Ἱππώνακτα.

The tone of the fragments is not always abusive or obscene, nor is its background always sordid. One beautiful line, as clear, melodious and spare as a line of Sappho, tells of yearning for a girl: 'If only I had a maiden, fair and soft of skin' εἴ μοι γένοιτο παρθένος καλή τε καὶ τέρεινα (fr. 119); another (a Homeric reminiscence for once) has an epic quality:

> ἐπ' ἁρμάτων τε καὶ Θρεϊκίων πώλων
> λευκῶν †ὀείους κατεγγύς† 'Ιλίου πύργων
> ἀπηναρίσθη 'Ρῆσος, Αἰνειῶν πάλμυς... (fr. 72. 5–7)

He came on his chariot and white Thracian horses; but in his sleep, near the towers of Troy, he was slain, Rhesus, the shah (*palmys*) of the Aeneans...

But of course we do not know the context, which may have been decisive for the effect of these lines. One papyrus fragment (fr. 102), for example, contains elements which suggest a similar epic tone but soon belies it by adding incongruous details. The phrases '...hydra at Lerna...he crushed the crab...' obviously celebrate one of the labours of Heracles but a few lines later we read the name Kikon, a character known to us from other fragments (4,78,102,118) as one of the cast of disreputable characters who haunt not the heroic but the Hipponactean world.

Hipponax remains a mystery. We have lost the matrix of these fascinating but puzzling fragments; ripped from their frame they leave us in doubt whether to take them seriously as autobiographical material (unlikely, but it has been done), as complete fiction (but there is no doubt that Bupalus and Athenis were real people), as part of a literary adaptation of some ritual of abuse (a *komos* or something similar), or as dramatic scripts for some abusive proto-comic performance. Whatever they were, they are a pungent reminder of the variety and vitality of archaic Greek literature and of how much we have lost.

6

ARCHAIC CHORAL LYRIC

1. THE NATURE OF EARLY CHORAL POETRY

From Alcman in the seventh century to Timotheus at the beginning of the fourth, choral lyric remains an important literary form. Performed by citizen choruses – men, boys, women, or girls – as well as by guilds of professionals,[1] these poems were sung by a dancing chorus at public religious festivals or at important family events like weddings or funerals. Because the festivals in honour of the gods also celebrated the civic life of the polis, choral song played a major role in affirming the values and solidarity of the community. The connexion between music and ethical values, in fact, remains strong through the archaic and classical periods. Like much of early Greek poetry, choral lyric is public rather than personal in outlook, expression and orientation. In this respect it differs from monodic lyric, which is much more an expression of personal emotion.

The basic forms and sub-genres of choral lyric are already attested in Homer and doubtless reach back long before the literary evidence.[2] The Shield of Achilles in the *Iliad* describes a marriage song (*hymenaios*, *Il.* 18.491–6), a harvest song accompanied by dancing (18.569–72), and an elaborate perform-ance of dance and song by youths and maidens at Cnossus (18.590–606). In the *Odyssey* the bard Demodocus sings the famous song about the illicit love of Ares and Aphrodite while all around him the young Phaeacians dance to its rhythm (8.262ff.). These passages imply a close interconnexion of music, dance and poetry in choral lyric. The lament for Hector in *Iliad* 24.720–76 illustrates the *threnos* or dirge and also reflects its formal structure: a 'singer' (*aoidos*) 'leads off' (ἐξάρχει, ἔξαρχος); he or she is followed by the collective voice of the chorus joining in some kind of refrain (*Il.* 24.720, 723, 747, 761, 776; cf. also *Il.* 18.51 and 314). The formulaic phrase ἀμειβόμεναι ὀπὶ καλῆι 'answering with lovely voice' (*Il.* 1.604, *Od.* 24.60, *Hymn to Apollo* 1.189) may also indicate the division of such songs into strophes, that is, stanzas whose set

---

[1] E.g. the Onitadai in Miletus and the Euneidai at Athens: see Schmid–Stählin 1 1.452.
[2] Webster (1970a) 46–55.

metrical and probably choreographic form is repeated to different words. Only later, possibly with Stesichorus in the early sixth century, does triadic composition develop. This is a more complex stanzaic arrangement, consisting of a strophe, corresponding antistrophe, and an epode, the last in a related but slightly varied metre.

Besides the marriage-song, dancing song, dirge and paean (*Il.* 1.472–4, a song in honour of Apollo), choral lyric also includes the maiden-song (partheneion), processional song (prosodion), hymn, dithyramb (in honour of Dionysus). Slightly later and of more secular character arise the enkomion (song in praise of men, not gods) and skolion (popular song sung at banquets and symposia).[1]

The division between choral and monodic lyric is convenient, but artificial, for many poets composed songs of both types. Alcman, chiefly a choral poet, composed love songs, some of which may have been monodic. The monodists Sappho, Alcaeus and Anacreon composed choral works: marriage-songs, hymns and partheneia. The elegist and iambist Archilochus may have composed dithyrambs (77 Diehl) and paeans (76 D).[2]

The numerous local and religious festivals – the Carneia and Hyacinthia at Sparta, the Adrasteia at Sicyon, the Iolaia at Thebes, the Adonidia on Lesbos – provided the public occasions for choral song. Choral lyric also played an important part at the great cosmopolitan celebrations, like those at Delphi and Olympia or the Delian festival in honour of Apollo vividly described in the *Homeric Hymn to Apollo* (146–73). With the Greeks' typical love of competition, poets and choruses often competed against one another for prizes.

The poet (*aoidos*) composed both music and words. He also directed a chorus, led by a chorus-leader (*choregos*) and varying from seven to fifty members, which sang and danced the words to an instrumental accompaniment of lyre and flute. As surviving fragments attest, the richness of festal attire – robes, jewellery, hair-style, elaborately adorned musical instruments – was an important feature of the performance (cf. Alcman 1.64ff. *PMG*; *Hymn to Apollo* 182–5). Alcman's poetry makes frequent allusion to the dance-movements of the singer-performers (e.g. 3.9, 3.70 *PMG*).

Because archaic choral lyric developed especially in the Dorian-speaking areas of the Peloponnese and west Greece, its dialect remained Doric, unlike monody, which followed the poet's local dialect. There are a few exceptions: Alcman, our earliest preserved choral poet, composed in his local Laconian dialect; and some sixth- or early fifth-century Boeotian poets composed in their own dialects also (*PMG* 692–4). From Stesichorus on, however, and even in some poems of Alcman, choral poetry tends to be written in a more or less

---

[1] For more detailed discussion of the individual genres see *GLP* 4–9; Smyth (1900) Intro. xxiii–cxxxiv.

[2] Cf. Ibycus 296 *PMG*; Anacreon 500, 501, 502b *PMG*. In general *GLP* 6f.; Webster (1970a) 63–5, 79.

conventional literary Doric, which admits many borrowings from the old Ionic language of Homeric epic and a certain mixture of Aeolic forms, the latter more frequent in Boeotian Pindar than elsewhere. The dialect, in other words, was an artificial literary language, a '*Kunstsprache*'. Its conventional nature enabled the genre to transcend local or regional boundaries and stress the Panhellenic aspect of the festivals at Olympia or Delphi.

Despite changes over time and the different spirit and conventions of different types of cult songs, much in choral lyric remains constant: mythical narrations of gods or heroes; gnomic reflections on moral behaviour, the limitations of mortality, the nature of the human condition; comments on the art of song, predecessors, the poet's skill; a certain religious aura, even in the secularized forms of the sixth and fifth centuries.[1] Expressions of personal feelings, though not uncommon, tend to be more stylized and less emotional than in monody. Recent research has shown how misleading it may be to take first-person state-ments, even when not in the *persona* of the chorus, as reflections of the poet's sentiments.

Mythical narration forms a particularly important part of these poems, not only as ornament, but also as illustration of moral norms and precepts, often reinforced by a concluding ethical maxim. The poet could exploit a rich mythic tradition, confident that an audience brought up on Homer, Hesiod, the Cyclic epics would grasp and appreciate his allusions to or departures from earlier versions. Rapidity, selectivity of detail, elaborate compound adjectives, decorative richness, epithets borrowed or adapted from Homer are the most constant features of the style. There is also a tendency toward density of syntax, the isolation of vivid moments of action, powerful and often audacious meta-phors, tightly phrased and weighty gnomic pronouncements.

The demands of cult and worship did not severely constrain the exuberance of choral lyric. Here, as elsewhere in Greek art, aesthetic brilliance counted for more than pious solemnity. Human emotions, pathos, the physical beauty of men and nature, the city and its legends are generally in the foreground. Celebration of the gods is a joyous affair; the more movement, colour, sensuous detail the better. Even in Pindar, the most religious in spirit of those poets, the religious element is personal and meditative rather than cultic.

The extant poetical fragments and the depiction of choral celebration on vases and sculpture attest to the concern with the beauty of the singers, the grace of their dance, the importance of both the vocal and instrumental music, incense, the altar, the crowd (cf. *Hymn to Apollo* 152ff.; Sappho 2, 44.24ff., 141, 154 *PLF*). For us only the bare words survive, and we must make an effort of imagination to supply the other elements, which were at least of equal import-ance for the ancient audience.

---

[1] See *GLP* 12f.; Schmid–Stählin I 1, 452–7; Fränkel (1975) 159f.

The poets of early choral lyric are shadowy figures. They are more closely associated with the history of music than with literature. Much of our information about them, in fact, comes from the treatise *On music* attributed to Plutarch. Corinth and Sparta are particularly important. Of Eumelus of Corinth, a contemporary of Archias who founded Syracuse in 734 B.C., we have two lines in dactylic metre, part of a prosodion (processional song) written for the Messenians at the Delian festival (fr. 13 *EGF*, 696 *PMG*). The practice of commissioning foreign poets at the great international festivals clearly has a long history. Figures like Olympus of Phrygia, inventor of the musical scale, Pamphos and Olen of Lycia, early writers of hymns (cf. Hdt. 4.35) possibly in hexameter rather than lyric metres, are scarcely more than names.

Terpander of Lesbos is a little more substantial. A few fragments survive, of doubtful authenticity (697–8 *PMG*). He is celebrated for converting the older four-stringed instrument into the seven-stringed cithara or lyre, capable of a wider and subtler range of melodies. He established the 'first school of music' at Sparta, won a victory at the first festival of the Carneia in 676 B.C., and invented the skolion (see below, pp. 220f.; Ps.-Plut. *De musica* 28). Still partly in the realm of myth too is another Lesbian poet, Arion of Methymna, whose miraculous rescue by a dolphin is recounted by Herodotus (1.23f.). The Suda and Eusebius agree in placing his *floruit* in the last quarter of the seventh century. In Corinth, under the tyrant Periander, he seems to have raised dithyrambic choral song to the level of artistic composition. These early choral songs, involving satyrs with speaking parts and probably some mythical narration, are sometimes considered to have been one of the early influences on the development of tragedy (see below, pp. 258ff.).[1] The fragments attributed to him (Diehl vol. 1.5f.) are of doubtful authenticity.

2. ALCMAN

Only with Alcman does early choral lyric have a literary reality. He is the first choral poet of whom anything substantial is preserved. Both dates and origins are controversial. Traditional dates vary between early and late seventh century; recent evidence suggests the end rather than the beginning of the seventh century (see Appendix). Whether he was a native Laconian or a Lydian has also been disputed from antiquity on (13a, *PMG*). Fragment 16, *PMG*, 'He was no rustic fellow nor gauche...nor a Thessalian by race nor a shepherd from Erysiche [in Acarnania], but from lofty Sardis', was interpreted autobiographically, probably wrongly (see Appendix). The bias against believing that Sparta could have produced a native poet like Alcman may also have contributed to the notion of Lydian birth (cf. Aelian, *Var. Hist.* 12.50). Alcman's

[1] See Else (1965) 14–17; Webster (1970a) 68f.; Lesky 225; *DTC* 10–13, 97–101.

use of the local dialect, intense familiarity with local customs, and his burial near the shrine of Helen in Sparta (Pausanias 3.15.3) favour Spartan or at least Laconian birth. It is, of course, possible that he was born in Sardis of parents who were Laconian or emigrated in his early years to Sparta. The question remains unsolved.

The Sparta of Alcman was a very different place from the austere militaristic society that it became in later times. In the late seventh and early sixth century Sparta and Corinth, not Athens, were the cultural centres of mainland Greece. The British School excavations at the sanctuary of Artemis Orthia near Sparta have amply documented the vigorous flourishing of the arts there, particularly between 650 and 550.[1] The success of the Second Messenian War, whose martial spirit Tyrtaeus sang, brought a period of prosperity, expansiveness, enjoyment of life. Alcman's Sparta was adorned with large temples and statuary in marble, ivory, bronze and terracotta. The shrine of Artemis Orthia contained numerous votive offerings of elegant design, elaborate jewellery in gold and silver, and imports from Egypt and the Near East. The pottery, sculpture and ivory plaques show the imaginative figures of Orientalizing art: vivid mythical scenes, inventive geometric designs, and fabulous creatures of all sorts. The simple elegance, gaiety, bold energy, vigour, and originality of the Laconian pottery of this time parallel in spirit the poetry of Alcman.

In the later seventh and early sixth century Sparta continued to attract poets and musicians: besides Alcman we hear of Terpander, Thaletas of Gortyn, Clonas of Thebes or Tegea, Xenocritus of Locri, Polymnastus of Colophon and Sacadas of Argos. They sang at festivals like the Carneia, Hyacinthia, Gymnopaidiai, and others. Even in its more austere period later, Sparta retained the reputation for brilliant choruses (see Pindar, fr. 199 Snell = 189 Bowra). Near the end of the fifth century Aristophanes reproduced a Laconian choral song in *Lysistrata* of 411 B.C. (1306ff.).

Like the early monodists, Sappho and Alcaeus, but unlike most later choral poets, Alcman composed in his local dialect; he also borrowed freely from the common storehouse of epic diction. He probably composed a few poems in Ionic, possibly as preludes (*prooimia*) to longer works, a practice vaguely attested for Terpander and other early lyricists (Ps.-Plut. *De mus.* 3 and see below, p. 182). His works were collected into six books of Lyrics (Μέλη), and a puzzling work, Κολυμβῶσαι 'The women diving', now confirmed as a separate poem by the discovery of the end of Book 6 on *P.Oxy.* 3209. Its character remains a problem: guesses range from a poem about Leda to some kind of marriage-song.

Alcman was especially celebrated for his love-poetry, not all of which was

[1] See Dawkins (1929) *passim*; Huxley (1962) 61–3; Forrest (1968) 71–3; Tigerstedt (1965) 39–44; Calame (1977) II 33ff.; Janni (1965) 25ff.

necessarily personal. Erotic themes were doubtless prominent in his marriage-songs or hymenaia, for which he was also famous (see 159 *PMG*), and in his partheneia or maiden-songs, as we can see from the extant fragments. Of these last we have two major examples: his most important surviving work, the Louvre Partheneion so called from the present location of the papyrus, discovered at Sakkara in 1855 and published at Paris in 1863, and substantial portions of a second Partheneion from Oxyrhynchus, published in 1957 (fr. 3 *PMG*). The Oxyrhynchus papyri have also enriched our knowledge of Alcman with a cosmogonic poem, important scholia on the Louvre Partheneion, and other fragments. Many short fragments, sometimes only a word or a phrase, quoted by lexicographers or metricians for their formal anomalies, are tantalizing, but mysterious.

The grace, liveliness, and range of Alcman's choral style are best seen in the Louvre Partheneion (fr. 1 *PMG*). This work was composed for a chorus of Spartan girls, to be sung at a local religious festival whose exact nature is uncertain.[1] The goddess to whom the girls offer the song and a *pharos* (generally a sacred tapestry or robe, but here glossed by the scholia as a plough) is called Aotis and, as her name suggests, may have some connexion with the dawn and possibly with marriage and fertility. (Attempts to elicit a reference to Artemis Orthia from ὀρθρίαι in line 61 are, for metrical and linguistic reasons, invalid.) Our ignorance of the cult, the obscurity of many of the allusions, and the lacunose state of the text leave many problems unsolved. Even so, we have a good overall picture of the whole work and can appreciate the general limpidity and richness of Alcman's style.

The scale of the poem was ample. There were probably ten stanzas of fourteen lines each, probably not in triadic composition. Thirty-five lines, or two-and-a-half stanzas have been lost from the beginning. These contained the invocation and part of a myth. A diacritical sign (a coronis) preserved on the papyrus and marking the end of the poem indicates the loss of the last four lines. We are also fortunate to have a number of scholia from Hellenistic commentaries, some in the margins of the Louvre papyrus, some found later on papyri from Oxyrhynchus.

Our text begins near the end of a myth about the defeat of the sons of Hippocoon. In other versions of this Laconian legend Heracles has an important role, restoring the exiled Tyndareus and thus helping to establish the line of Spartan kingship. There is no trace of Heracles in the preserved fragments, so that the exact version which Alcman is following is still a matter for speculation.[2]

---

[1] See Calame (1977) II 103ff.; Burnett (1964) 30–4; Garvie (1965) 185–7; Gentili (1976) *passim*; Griffiths (1972) 24ff.; Page (1951a) 72–4; Treu (1968a) 28.

[2] The presence of Heracles here rests on the indirect evidence of Sosibius *ap.* Clement Alex., *Protrept.* 36 with schol. *ad loc.* Other versions which include Heracles: Apollod. 2.7.3, Diod. 4.33.5f.; Paus. 3.15.4f. See Page (1951a) 30ff.; *GLP* 40ff.; Davison (1968) 148–53; Garvie (1965) 186; Griffiths (1972) 14.

The mention of 'Destiny and Resource, Aisa and Poros, eldest of the gods', at this point (13f.) suggests that the victory illustrated the triumph of the moral order, a function of myth familiar from Pindar. The warning against trying to wed Aphrodite (μηδὲ πηρήτω γαμῆν τὰν Ἀφροδίταν, 17) suggests that the myth had something to do with marriage, possibly the Tyndarids' defence of Helen, their sister, or possibly the Hippocoontids' rival suit for the future brides of the Tyndarids. The listing of the fallen Hippocoontids by name shows a fondness for local detail that we find elsewhere in choral lyric. A second myth, more briefly told and also extremely fragmentary (22–35), seems to have recounted the punishment of a crime against the gods, also of an amorous nature, perhaps committed by the Giants or the Aloadae, Otus and Ephialtes.[1]

Both myths were rounded off by gnomic statements about respecting the due limits of the mortal condition:

> μή τις ἀνθ]ρώπων ἐς ὠρανὸν ποτήσθω
> μηδὲ πη]ρήτω γαμῆν τὰν Ἀφροδίταν
> Ϝάνασσαν...

(16–18)

Let no mortal fly to the heavens nor attempt to marry goddess Aphrodite...

> ἄλαστα δὲ
> Ϝέργα πάσον κακὰ μησαμένοι·
> ἔστι τις σιῶν τίσις.

(34–6)

Devising evil deeds they suffered unforgettably; there is some requital from the gods.

As in Pindar and Bacchylides such 'gnomic bridge-passages' serve as a transition to a new subject, in this case the chorus' playful dispute about the beauty of two of their members, Agido and Hagesichora, the latter called the chorus-leader (36–43):

> ἔστι τις σιῶν τίσις·
> ὁ δ' ὄλβιος, ὅστις εὔφρων
> ἀμέραν [δι]απλέκει
> ἄκλαυτος· ἐγὼν δ' ἀείδω
> Ἀγιδῶς τὸ φῶς· ὁρῶ   40
> Ϝ' ὥτ' ἄλιον, ὅνπερ ἅμιν
> Ἀγιδὼ μαρτύρεται
> φαίνην...

There is some requital from the gods. But he is happy who in joy of mind weaves a day through to its end without lamentation. But my song is Agido's radiance. I see her shine as the sun whom Agido summons to shine for us [or, to whose shining for us Agido bears witness]...

[1] See Page (1951a) 42f.; Janni (1965) 68–71.

The changefulness of mortal life defines man as *ephemeros*: even his precarious happiness must be measured within the limits of the 'single day' (cf. Pind. *Ol.* 2. 33–8). The poet's song both describes and exemplifies the necessity of staying within the norms of mortal life. Here implicitly, as far more explicitly and programmatically in Pindar, the poet places his art in a large moral framework and makes poetry itself part of the struggle for order and beauty against what is aesthetically and morally formless and chaotic. Not only the evil-doing in the preceding stanza, but also the recognition that mortal life is rarely without grief form the foil to this sun-like beauty in the festal joy of celebration.

As in choral lyric generally, the structure of the poem tends to be discontinuous, but the imagery of light is prominent throughout. If, as seems highly probable, the song was part of a *pannychis*, or 'all night festival', performed shortly before dawn, the movement from darkness to light underlined by the imagery would also have symbolic value, particularly in a cult concerned with fertility, marriage, growth and passage to maturity. The comparison of Agido to the sun may have religious or cultic significance too, but that does not exclude the note of playful exaggeration which dominates the next section of the poem, in sharp contrast to the more serious regal and martial themes of the first two strophes.

The chorus goes on (43–72):

ἐμὲ δ᾽ οὔτ᾽ ἐπαινῆν
οὔτε μωμήσθαι νιν ἁ κλεννὰ χοραγὸς
οὐδ᾽ ἁμῶς ἐῆι· δοκεῖ γὰρ ἤμεν αὔτα   45
ἐκπρεπὴς τὼς ὥπερ αἴτις
ἐν βοτοῖς στάσειεν ἵππον
παγὸν ἀεθλοφόρον καναχάποδα
τῶν ὑποπετριδίων ὀνείρων·

ἦ οὐχ ὁρῆις; ὁ μὲν κέλης   50
Ἐνετικός· ἁ δὲ χαίτα
τᾶς ἐμᾶς ἀνεψιᾶς
Ἁγησιχόρας ἐπανθεῖ
χρυσὸς [ὡ]ς ἀκήρατος·
τό τ᾽ ἀργύριον πρόσωπον,   55
διαφάδαν τί τοι λέγω;
Ἁγησιχόρα μὲν αὔτα·
ἁ δὲ δευτέρα πεδ᾽ Ἀγιδὼ τὸ ϝεῖδος
ἵππος Ἰβηνῶι Κολαξαῖος δραμήται·
ταὶ Πεληάδες γὰρ ἇμιν   60
ὀρθρίαι φᾶρος φεροίσαις
νύκτα δι᾽ ἀμβροσίαν ἅτε σήριον
ἄστρον ἀυηρομέναι μάχονται·

οὔτε γάρ τι πορφύρας
τόσσος κόρος ὥστ᾽ ἀμύναι,   65

οὔτε ποικίλος δράκων
παγχρύσιος, οὐδὲ μίτρα
Λυδία, νεανίδων
ἰανογ[λ]εφάρων ἄγαλμα,
οὐδὲ ταὶ Ναννῶς κόμαι,   70
ἀλλ' οὐ[δ'] 'Αρέτα σιειδής,
οὐδὲ Σύλακίς τε καὶ Κλεησισήρα...

But the glorious chorus-leader in no way allows me either to praise or to blame her (Agido). For she herself (Hagesichora) seems outstanding, just as if one should set among cattle a well compacted horse, winner of prizes, of ringing hooves, a horse of winged dreams [or, a horse of dreams which lie beneath rocks].[1]

Do you not see her? The one is a Venetic pony; but the hair of my cousin, Hagesichora, blooms like gold unalloyed. Silver her face. Is my speech clear? Here she is, Hagesichora herself. But she who is second after Agido in beauty will run as a Colaxaean horse against an Ibenian. For the Pleiades early in the morning, rising like the star Sirius through the ambrosial night, fight against us as we bear the plough [robe?].

Nor is there such an abundance of purple to defend us, nor the dappled snake, all-gold, nor the Lydian cap, joy of soft-eyed girls, nor Nanno's tresses, no, nor Areta the godlike, nor Sylacis nor Cleësisera (can defend us)...

Agido's beauty is now balanced by Hagesichora's. The rivalry has a stylized, mock-serious character. The agonistic mood may be related to the cult setting. Some scholars have suggested rival choruses or a bridal serenade like Catullus 61, but there is no clear evidence for either. Cultic function, in any case, does not preclude playfulness. The repetition of 'see' (ὁρῶ, 40; ὁρῆις, 50), the language of brightness and clarity (54–6, 60–3), the comparison to horses, the playful military imagery (63, 65) and the comparison to precious metals (54f., cf. 67) maintain a certain formal unity; but the dominant tone is one of banter, rapid colloquial interchange, familiarity. The chorus' reference to Hagesichora as 'my cousin' (52) may indicate a relationship of a cultic as well as a familial nature. The listing of the girls' names in 70ff. is part of this atmosphere of friendly intimacy. The concreteness of detail, characteristic both of Alcman and choral lyric generally, both presupposes and celebrates the solidarity of this society. The girls named by Alcman in other poems are of high social standing: Timasimbrota, a king's daughter (5, fr. 2, col. i *PMG*) and Astymeloisa in 3.73f.; we may assume that these girls too are of good family or noble birth.

The lines on the Pleiades (60–3) are the poem's most notorious crux.[2] The

---

[1] 'Winged dreams' favoured by Page (1951a) 87; see also Calame (1977) II 67, with n. 40; 'dreams under (shady) rocks': West (1965) 195 and Marzullo (1964) 193f. The ancient lexicographers attest the meaning 'winged' (e.g. *Et.Gen.* s.v.; *Et.Magn.* 783.20ff. The linguistic objections to this meaning, though serious, are not perhaps decisive.

[2] See Page (1951a) 52ff., 75ff. Recent discussion and bibliographical surveys in Gerber (1967/8) 325–7 and (1975/6) 95–7; Puelma (1977) 53f.; Calame (1977) II 179–86; Gianotti (1978) 257–71.

scholiast says that the Pleiades ('doves') are Agido and Hagesichora, and it is probably safest to follow that view. An alternative, that 'Pleiades' is the name of a rival chorus, is widely assumed, but has no evidence to support it. The comparison to Sirius confirms that, whatever else the Pleiades may refer to, they are also the constellation and form part of the imagery of light in the poem. The two outstanding members of the chorus are now said to 'rise like Sirius through the ambrosial night' (the last phrase is a Homeric formula), possibly to contrast their joint beauty with that of the rank and file, the eight girls listed in the next stanza. In that case the comparison to the bright and generally baleful light of Sirius would be part of the tone of playful exaggeration and mock-combat between chorus and its two leading members. Other interpretations stress local connexions (one of the Pleiades is the Laconian nymph, Taygeta) or reference to the season or to the approach of daylight (the girls are racing to beat the dawn).[1] Scholarly consensus on the passage is still remote.

The list of the girls' charms in 64ff. makes clear the erotic colouring of the playful banter. This is implicit also in the comparison to horses (cf. Anacreon 346, 360, 417 *PMG* and Ibycus 287 *PMG*) and in the language of combat. The references to the chorus-members' hair, jewellery, and robes also serve to call attention to the festive brilliance of the present celebration. These erotic overtones may have some relation to the cult as well, particularly if Aotis is a goddess of fertility and marriage, like the Spartan Helen, or, if, as some have suggested, the song formed part of a marriage-celebration or an initiatory ritual of girls approaching marriageable age.

The erotic elements become stronger as the chorus concludes the listing of its own members and turns back to Hagesichora (73–7):

οὐδ' ἐς Αἰνησιμβρ[ό]τας ἐνθοῖσα φασεῖς·
'Ασταφίς [τ]έ μοι γένοιτο
καὶ ποτιγλέποι Φίλυλλα 75
Δαμαρ[έ]τα τ' ἐρατά τε Ϝιανθεμίς·
ἀλλ' 'Αγησιχόρα με τείρει.

Nor if you go to the house of Aenesimbrota will you say, 'May Astaphis be mine; may Philylla cast her glances at me and Damareta and the lovely Vianthemis'; but rather will you say, 'Hagesichora wears me down'.

Most recent interpreters have welcomed M. L. West's excellent suggestion that Aenesimbrota is a dealer in love-charms, a *pharmakeutria* like the old woman of Theocritus' second *Idyll*.[2] Vianthemis' epithet, ἐρατά 'lovely', is obviously erotic, as are Philylla's 'glances'; we may recall the Graces, ἐρογλεφάροι 'with

---

[1] Erotic associations of 'Pleiades': Calame (1977) II 75ff. and also 86–97; Gentili (1976) 63; cf. also Puelma (1977) 34f., n. 65. A 'race with the dawn' in a night festival or *pannychis*: Griffiths (1972) 17ff.; Burnett (1964) 30–4; Gianotti (1978) 268–71.
[2] West (1965) 199; see Puelma (1977) 40f.

love in their eyes', earlier (20f.) and the related epithet, ἰανογλεφάρων 'soft-eyed', in 69. The erotic sense of τείρει, 'wears me down', is now confirmed by a new papyrus fragment of a scholium (schol. B), as well as usage elsewhere in early Greek poetry (Hesiod fr. 298 M–W; cf. Telestes 805 *PMG*).

The poet now skilfully brings the ode back to its unifying figures, Hagesichora (77) and soon Agido (78–101):

> οὐ γὰρ ἀ κ[α]λλίσφυρος
> Ἀγησιχ[ό]ρ[α] πάρ' αὐτεῖ,
> Ἀγιδοῖ .... ἀρμένει   80
> θωστήρ[ιά τ'] ἄμ' ἐπαινεῖ.
> ἀλλὰ τᾶν [..]... σιοὶ
> δέξασθε· [σι]ῶν γὰρ ἄνα
> καὶ τέλος· [χο]ροστάτις,
> ϝείποιμί κ', [ἐ]γὼν μὲν αὐτὰ   85
> παρσένος μάταν ἀπὸ θράνω λέλακα
> γλαύξ· ἐγὼ[ν] δὲ τᾶι μὲν Ἀώτι μάλιστα
> ϝανδάνην ἐρῶ· πόνων γὰρ
> ἇμιν ἰάτωρ ἔγεντο·
> ἐξ Ἀγησιχόρ[ας] δὲ νεάνιδες   90
> ἰρ]ήνας ἐρατ[ᾶ]ς ἐπέβαν·
>
> τῶ]ι τε γὰρ σηραφόρωι
> ..]τῶς εδ..........
> τ[ῶι] κυβερνάται δὲ χρὴ
> κ[ἠ]ν νᾶϊ μάλιστ' ἀκούην·   95
> ἀ δὲ τᾶν Σηρην[ί]δων
> ἀοιδοτέρα μ[ὲν οὐχί,
> σιαὶ γάρ, ἀντ[ὶ δ' ἕνδεκα
> παίδων δεκ[ὰς ἄδ' ἀείδ]ει·
> φθέγγεται δ' [ἄρ'] ὤ[τ' ἐπὶ] Ξάνθω ῥοαῖσι   100
> κύκνος· ἀ δ' ἐπιμέρωι ξανθᾶι κομίσκαι...

For is not the lovely-ankled Hagesichora present here? She remains beside Agido and praises our festival: Do you receive their [prayers], O gods; for in the gods lies fulfilment too.
Leader of the chorus, I would speak; yet I myself, a girl, cry in vain, like an owl from the rafters. Yet it is my desire to be pleasing to Aotis most of all. For to us she has been the healer of toils, and from Hagesichora have the girls entered upon (the paths of) lovely peace.
For...the trace-horse...and in a ship one must especially heed the steersman. She [Hagesichora], to be sure, is not more songful than the Sirens, for they are goddesses; but we, ten instead of eleven girls, sing as the swan at the stream of Xanthus, while she with her desirable yellow hair...

The appeal to present vision earlier in the comparison of Agido and Hagesichora ('Do you not see', 50) is now echoed in the appeal to Hagesichora's visible presence as Agido returns (78–80). Instead of mock-rivalry for praise between girls (cf. 43f.), the praise is now for the festival itself. The gnomic statement about the gods (83f.) recalls the generalization about the gods' 'requital' that led into the rivalry of the two girls at the end of the mythic section (36–40). 'Singing' is now re-established as a main theme, and the emphasis falls on Hagesichora's superiority in art rather than in beauty. The humour remains, however, in the self-deprecating simile of the owl, the foil to Hagesichora's swan in 100f. Possibly the bird-similes have some connexion with the Pleiades, 'doves', in 60ff. The homely comparison to the 'owl from the roofbeam' contrasts with the highly poetical language of divine grace (87–9) and the Sirens. The 'lovely peace' that girls have from Hagesichora (90f.) may be part of the erotic colouring or the competitive setting; it may also be an allusion to the *topos*, common in lyric, of the joyful calm that comes from song.[1] In any case it forms a strong ending to the strophe. Despite the fragmentary condition of 92ff. we can still recognize the rhetorical figure known as the priamel in the lines about obeying a knowledgeable leader, the transition to another implicit praise of Hagesichora's artistry. Physical beauty and choral skill, however, are still being interwoven as our poem breaks off: Hagesichora has the voice of a swan and the golden hair of a desirable woman.

The shifting between Hagesichora and the chorus in these lines is confusing, and the reference to 'ten girls instead of eleven' is not entirely clear. The scholiast says that the chorus was sometimes of ten, sometimes of eleven, and ten girls have here been named. The rapid colloquial style, the plethora of connectives, and the companionable acknowledgement of Hagesichora's superiority continue the mood of gaiety, familiarity and girlish admiration. The style moves easily from proverb to mythical allusion, from local detail to Homeric reminiscence (the swan at the Xanthus, cf. *Iliad* 2.459ff. and 2.877).

Choral lyric, even at this early date, is still far from primitive. Despite the incompleteness of the text and the difficulties caused by our ignorance of the goddess, the cult and the context of the song, we can still recognize sophisticated structural devices like gnomic transitions, verbal echoes and parallelism.[2] There are also rhetorical figures: the developed simile, *praeteritio*, priamel, *adynaton*. Mythical narration is carried to some length, imagery is sustained, and diction is rich with compound adjectives in such phrases as 'prize-winning ringing-hoofed horses' (47f.), 'soft-eyed girls' (69), 'love-glancing Graces' (20f.). Alcman also enhances the atmosphere of playful exaggeration and mock-rivalry by using Homeric formulas in new contexts (e.g. the horses in 47–9, the 'ambrosial night' in 62, the swan in 100f.). Both song and singers must manifest the presence of beauty, symbolized, as in Pindar, by the superlative radiance of gold and the

---

[1] See Pavese (1967) 127. The epinician parallels to rest after toil in athletic contests in *GLP* 62 are not entirely apt. See also Puelma (1977) 21f. with n. 50.

[2] Puelma (1977) *passim*; Pavese (1967) *passim*; Rosenmeyer (1966) 353.

sun. Alcman achieves a wide and rapid variation of tones, from narratives of heroes and gods to proverbial commonplaces, from gnomic moralizing to lively personal exchanges in direct address (e.g. 50, 'Do you not see?'). There is also a trace of the 'kenning' that one finds in Pindar in a phrase like ποικίλος δράκων παγχρύσιος 'the dappled all-gold snake' (66f.), used to describe a bracelet.

The language itself, however, is clear and straightforward. Sentences tend to be brief and paratactic. The leaps and abrupt transitions characteristic of the genre, like the unintroduced proper names, include the audience in an assumed intimacy and communal spirit. Phrasing is sometimes conventional, like 'lovely-ankled Hagesichora' (78f.), but Alcman is also capable of bold expressions, like the girls 'walking upon the paths of lovely peace' (ἰρήνας ἐρατᾶς ἐπέβαν, 91) or the happy mortal 'weaving the day through to the end' (ἀμέραν διαπλέκει, 38), framed by two familiar but emphatic and contrasting adjectives, one positive, one negative (εὔφρων and ἄκλαυτος, 37 and 39). He can use striking contrasts too, like that between the 'solid horse' and the horse 'of dreams' (whether 'winged' or not) in 47–9. As in Pindar, figures of speech and comparisons tend to accumulate in progressions, like that from metals to horses to stars in 54–63 or that from owl to Siren to swan in 86–101. This figurative language sometimes creates sharp juxtapositions of prosaic reality and remoter mythical elements, as in the horses of 47–9 or the priamel of 92ff. which builds up from horsemanship to seamanship to the Sirens.

The poet's concern with his art and the nature of his song has moral as well as aesthetic significance. Proud of his expertise, he takes himself and his song as a microcosm of the world-order (cf. 13–23, 35–40), a nascent form of one of Pindar's most important themes (cf. *Pyth.* 1 and below, pp. 228–30). The mood of levity, perhaps characteristic of partheneia generally, is dominant; but beneath the lightness and play appears the deep moral seriousness which characterizes most of Greek choral poetry.

The recently published second partheneion (3 *PMG*) provides valuable perspective on the Louvre poem. Here the proem, lost in Partheneion 1, is partially preserved. The chorus calls on the Olympian Muses who have filled their hearts with desire for song. The inspiration for the new song takes the form of an awakening from sleep; it 'will scatter sweet sleep from the lids' ὕπνον ἀπὸ γλεφάρων σκεδασεῖ γλυκύν. . ., 3. 7); we may recall the awakening of song in the proem of Pindar's seventh *Isthmian*. The chorus then calls attention to their movements 'as the song [?] leads me to come to the dancing place where most of all I shall toss my yellow hair. . .and my soft feet [may dance]. . .'.

]ς δέ μ' ἄγει πεδ' ἀγῶν' ἴμεν
ἆχι μά]λιστα κόμ[αν ξ]ανθὰν τινάξω·
. . .ἀπαλοὶ πόδες. . .   (3.8–10 *PMG*)

After a gap of some fifty lines (which, on the analogy of Partheneion 1, may have held a myth), the text resumes with the theme of sleep again, but now with a mixture of erotic colouring and ritual action that closely parallels the Louvre Partheneion:

λυσιμελεῖ τε πόσωι, τακερώτερα
δ᾽ ὕπνω καὶ σανάτω ποτιδέρκεται·
οὐδέ τι μαψιδίως γλυκ . . ήνα·

'Α[σ]τυμέλοισα δέ μ᾽ οὐδὲν ἀμείβεται
ἀλλὰ τὸ]ν πυλεῶν᾽ ἔχοισα   65
[ὥ] τις αἰγλά[ε]ντος ἀστήρ
ὠρανῶ διαιπετής
ἢ χρύσιον ἔρνος ἢ ἀπαλὸ[ν ψίλ]ον
. .̂]ν
] . διέβα ταναοῖς πο[σί·]   70
-κ]ομος νοτία Κινύρα χ[άρ]ις
ἐπὶ π]αρσενικᾶν χαίταισιν ἴσδει·

'Α]στυμέλοισα κατὰ στρατόν
] μέλημα δάμωι...

· · ·

]α ἴδοιμ᾽ αἴ πως με . . ον φίλοι
ἄσ]σον [ἰο]ῖσ᾽ ἀπαλᾶς χηρὸς λάβοι,   80
αἶψά κ᾽ [ἐγὼν ἱ]κέτις κήνας γενοίμαν·

νῦν δ᾽ [   ]δα παῖδα βα[.]ύφρονα...

(3.61–74, 79–82 PMG)

...and with desire that looses the limbs, but she looks glances more melting than sleep and death; nor in vain she...sweet.
But Astymeloisa makes me no answer; but, like a star that falls through the radiant sky or a branch of gold or soft plume, holding the garland... she passed on slender feet; and on the tresses of the girls sits the lovely-haired dewy grace of Cinyras.
Astymeloisa (moves) among the gathering, an object of care to the people...
If she should come near and take me by the soft hand, at once would I become her suppliant.
But now...a girl of deep [?] thought...

As in the Louvre Partheneion, the chorus of girls are lost in admiration for an outstanding member of their group. Astymeloisa, like Hagesichora, may be the chorus-leader, a position suggested also by the pun on her name in 74, μέλημα δάμωι, 'a concern to the people', a double pun, perhaps, if the first word, *melema* also alludes to *melos* 'song', which in fact occurs in the proem, καλὸν ὑμνιοισᾶν μέλος 'girls hymning lovely song'.

The erotic overtones of this admiration are even more overt than in the Louvre Partheneion. The helplessness of the girl if the object of her love should take her hand (79f.) recalls the chorus of the longer poem 'worn down' with love for Hagesichora (1.77). The celestial brightness of Astymeloisa's beauty

(3.66–8) reminds us also of the sun- and star-imagery of that poem (cf. 1.40–3, 60–3). Here too that beauty slips briefly into mythical allusion, the charm of Cinyras, darling of Aphrodite (3.71f.; cf. 1.96ff.). The love-motif is also treated with a certain playfulness and perhaps deliberate exaggeration. Lines 61–8 and 79–81 offer a glimpse of the same kind of personal exchange as in the Louvre Partheneion: the chorus casts itself in the role of a helplessly smitten lover before an overpoweringly beautiful beloved whom they praise with rather conventional details of physical grace and images of light and gold. Taken together, the two poems show a lively freshness, set in a rather stylized frame. That stylized character may be due to the ritual occasion of the song, possibly initiatory, possibly involving a goddess of sex, marriage, or fertility, like Helen or Aphrodite (cf. Cinyras in 3.71).

A very different area of Alcman's poetry has been revealed by another new papyrus, also published in 1957, a fragment of a commentary on a cosmogonic poem (*P.Oxy.* 2390 = 5, fr. 2, col. ii *PMG*). Only a few of Alcman's own words are quoted, but the commentary enables us to restore the general outline. Alcman seems to have posited the original condition of the world as an undifferentiated mass, akin to what later philosophers termed ὕλη, unformed matter. The goddess Thetis came into being and gave form to this matter as a craftsman forms metal (cf. 17–19). With this act appear the two ordering principles, Poros and Tekmor, 'Path' ('Resource') and 'Limit', or, as H. Fränkel suggests, 'Open Possibility' or 'Accessibility' and 'Binding Definition'.[1] With them the primal matter is differentiated into day and night, light and darkness (cf. 25f.). The process of differentiation has some affinity with the cosmogonic process in Hesiod (cf. *Theogony* 123–5); but the non-anthropomorphic agents, Poros and Tekmor, are quite unhesiodic and resemble the non-personal, non-sexualized elements, water, air, fire, in the Milesians Thales and Anaximander. Thetis' role is striking. Sea-goddesses elsewhere in early Greek literature, as Vernant has shown, serve as cosmogonic deities,[2] but Alcman may also owe something to Near-Eastern notions of a 'waste of waters' ruled by a female deity of the deep, like Tiamat in the Babylonian *Enuma Elish*.[3] In any event, the fragment is a precious piece of evidence for a far more advanced intellectual atmosphere in seventh-century Sparta than had ever been suspected and a valuable indication that philosophical speculation and Near-Eastern influences were not confined to Ionia in the early archaic period. It suggests too the artificiality of the sharp break sometimes assumed between poets and philosophers or between 'mythic' and 'philosophical' thought in this formative period in the intellectual history of early Greece.

The new fragment also enables us to put a number of hitherto unrelated scraps

---

[1] West (1967) 2f; Fränkel (1975) 164. See also Penwill (1974) 13–39; West (1963) 154–6.
[2] Vernant–Detienne (1974) 136–9. See also Hdt. 4.180.5.   [3] West (1967) 3–7.

of Alcman's work into perspective. First, we can recognize the same cosmogonic concerns in the gnomic generalization at the end of the myth in the Louvre Partheneion (1.13f.), for here Aisa and Poros, 'Destiny' and 'Path', called 'the oldest of the gods', have an important role as embodiments of the moral order. We can now make better sense of the scholiast's comment on this passage, 'By Poros (Alcman) means the same being as that represented by Chaos in Hesiod's mythology', for he is doubtless referring to the cosmogonic function of Poros in the poem of fragment 5. We can also better appreciate Alcman's interest elsewhere in connecting his poetry with the mythical beginnings of the world-order. In one fragment, for instance, he calls the Muses the daughters of Ouranos and Ge, Sky and Earth (67 *PMG*) not Zeus and Mnemosyne as in Hesiod. In another Erse, Dew, a fertilizing principle, appears as daughter of Zeus and Selene (57 *PMG*). He calls Akmon the son of Ouranos because of the sky's 'untiring' (*a-kamatos*) movement (61 *PMG*). Tyche, Chance, is the sister of Eunomia and Peitho, 'Lawfulness' and 'Persuasion', and the daughter of Prometheia 'Forethought' (64).[1]

From the sparse quotations by late grammarians and metricians it has long been clear that Alcman treated epic themes, often drawing upon Homeric language and showing a predilection for dactylic metres. His subjects, mostly mentioned only by name, include the fall of Troy (68–71 *PMG*), Heracles (72), Niobe (75), Tantalus (79) and Odysseus. On the last we have an interesting line and a half in dactyls telling how 'Circe once smeared (with wax) the ears of the companions of Odysseus, enduring in spirit' (80 *PMG*):

καί ποκ' 'Οδυσσῆος ταλασίφρονος ὦατ' ἑταίρων
Κίρκα ἐπαλείψασα.

Alcman has modified the Homeric narrative by having Circe actually perform what she only advises the hero to do in Homer.

That modification of Homeric detail is now substantiated at greater length by an important new papyrus fragment (*P.Oxy.* 2443, fr. 1, +3213).[2] Where the papyrus becomes intelligible there is a brief reference to Poseidon and a description of someone coming to 'a shrine of the Nereids':

]εφ.[....]ουδεις.[
]φρασάμαν μονὄς [
]ε Ποσειδᾶνος χα[.].
].ος   10
μα.Λευκοθεᾶν ἐρατὸν τέμενος
ἐκ Τρυγεᾶν ἀνιών, ἔχον
δὲ σίδας δύω γλυκήας.

[1] Lloyd-Jones, in West (1963) 156, suggests that fr. 65 *PMG*, on the prerogatives of the gods, may come from the same cosmogonic poem as the Poros–Tekmor fragment. Still, we must recognize the rather light and humorous tone of this fragment; see Campbell (1970) *ad loc.* and Perrotta–Gentili (1965) *ad loc.*   [2] See West (1977) 38f.; Brown (1978) 36–8.

180

ALCMAN

ταὶ δ' ὅτε δὴ ποταμῶι καλλιρρόωι
ἀράσαντ' ἐρατὸν τελέσαι γάμον   15
καὶ τὰ παθῆν ἃ γυναιξὶ καὶ ἀνδρά[σιν
φίλτ]ατα κωριδίας τ' εὐνᾶς [τυ]χῆν[,

...No one... (?)
...I took thought alone (?)...
Poseidon...Coming from Trygeai to the lovely grove of the Leucotheai
(= Nereids); and they held two sweet pomegranates.
And, when they prayed to the river of beautiful streams to accomplish lovely
marriage and to have experience of the endearments between men and women
and to enjoy the bed of wedlock...

The passage is possibly to be associated with fr. 81 *PMG*, Ζεῦ πάτερ, αἰ γὰρ
ἐμὸς πόσις εἴη 'O father Zeus, may he be my husband'. The scholiast on *Odyssey*
6.244, who cites this passage, notes that Alcman has substituted several girls
for the single maiden, Nausicaa, who speaks a similar prayer in the Homeric
passage. This situation would suit the new fragment, although the transition
from Odysseus and the sea (if such it is) to the girls' prayer for marriage is abrupt.
In Homer too, though a single Leucothea helps Odysseus to escape from the
sea, we hear nothing of a 'grove of Leucotheai' (glossed by Hesychius and the
Etymologium Magnum as 'Nereids'). Difficult too is the long dependent 'when-'
clause, uncharacteristic of Alcman's style. Still, the coincidences seem too great
to be fortuitous. Some of these difficulties would be resolved by supposing the
fragment to be a first-person narrative (cf. φρασάμην, 8) by Odysseus of his
landing on the Phaeacians' island. It is interesting to see Alcman's addition of
the characteristically concrete detail of the 'sweet pomegranates'. The passage
is further evidence for the knowledge of the Homeric poems on mainland
Greece in the late seventh century. This elaboration of and variation upon
Homeric myth in dactylic metres will be carried farther, as we shall see, in
Stesichorus.

In dactyls too, this time in hexameter, is one of Alcman's most celebrated
passages (26 *PMG*):

οὔ μ' ἔτι, παρσενικαὶ μελιγάρυες ἱαρόφωνοι,
γυῖα φέρην δύναται· βάλε δὴ βάλε κηρύλος εἴην,
ὅς τ' ἐπὶ κύματος ἄνθος ἅμ' ἀλκυόνεσσι ποτήται
νηδεὲς ἦτορ ἔχων, ἀλιπόρφυρος ἱαρὸς ὄρνις.

No longer, O maidens, honey-songed, holy-voiced, can my limbs bear me up.
Ah, would that I were the *kerylos* (male halcyon bird) who skims above the
wave's bloom (of foam) with the halcyons, fearless of heart, sea-purple sacred
bird.

The passage is an early expression of the nostalgia for 'escape' that recurs in
the lyrics of Greek tragedy, especially in Euripides. The note of romantic

longing and wistfulness, actually rather rare in early Greek poetry, shows us another side of Alcman, one that easily matches his interest in the passions of love. The accumulation of compound adjectives in the first line and the bird imagery are both familiar from the Partheneia. The poet is presumably addressing the girls who perform his choral songs, perhaps in a half-playful way, as he contrasts his age and feebleness with their vigour and beauty. If this is the situation, it may be compared with that of the maidens in the Delian *Hymn to Apollo* 166–73. Other early choral poets, like Terpander and Arion, are said to have written 'preludes' for the cithara in dactylic hexameter, and a similar context is probably to be imagined for Alcman's fine lines as well.[1]

The expressive use of natural phenomena characterizes another famous fragment (89 *PMG*):

εὕδουσι δ' ὀρέων κορυφαί τε καὶ φάραγγες
πρώονές τε καὶ χαράδραι
φῦλά τ' ἑρπέτ' ὅσα τρέφει μέλαινα γαῖα
θῆρές τ' ὀρεσκῷοι καὶ γένος μελισσᾶν
καὶ κνώδαλ' ἐν βένθεσσι πορφυρέας ἁλός·
εὕδουσι δ' οἰωνῶν φῦλα τανυπτερύγων.

Asleep are the mountains' peaks and the gulleys and the headlands and the torrent-beds and the creeping tribes, all that the black earth nurtures, and the mountain-dwelling beasts and the race of bees and the beasts in the depths of the darkling sea. Asleep are the tribes of the long-winged birds.

This cosmic sleep may have been the foil to the turmoil in the speaker's breast, as in later poets from Theocritus to Goethe.[2] Alcman's lines are remarkable both for the haunting beauty of sound and for the impression of objective clarity and inclusiveness. The accumulation of five strong nouns in the first two lines sets forth the massive, rocky face of nature, softened by the appearance of the first living creatures and the 'black earth' in line 3, and then in rapid sequence the other living beings, increasingly individualized as the austere phrasing of the opening changes to a more ornate, though still solemn, grandeur ('depths of the darkling sea', 'tribes of long-winged birds'). The poet makes a step-by-step visual survey of all of nature as he traverses the distance from the peaks of the mountains to the bottom of the sea and then looks back upward again to the birds.[3] The polysyndeton and the bareness of adjectives (until the general and Homeric 'black earth', 3) reinforce the impression of largeness and grandeur. There are more adjectives in the second group of three lines, but they are all generic, and the generalizing effect is reinforced by the repetition of φῦλα, 'tribes' and γένος, 'race' in 3, 6 and 4. For all the apparent simplicity and natural-

---

[1] See Plut. *De mus.* 3; Suda, s.v. 'Arion'; *GLP* 23; Gerber (1970) 99.
[2] Ancient and modern parallels in Perrotta–Gentili (1965) *ad loc.*
[3] Dawson (1966) 59f.

ness of movement, there is a studied repetition of word and sound in 1 and 6, εὕδουσι δ' ὀρέων...εὕδουσι δ' οἰωνῶν and in φῦλα τ' ἑρπέτ'...φῦλα τανυπτερύγων in 3 and 6.

We can trace this feeling for the mysterious beauty of nature in the star similes of the two Partheneia (cf. 1.62f. and 3.66ff.). It is present too, though in a different setting, in a fragment presumably addressed to a nymph or a bacchant, possibly in a dithyrambic chorus (56 *PMG*):

> πολλάκι δ' ἐν κορυφαῖς ὀρέων, ὅκα
> σιοῖσι ϝάδηι πολύφανος ἑορτά,
> χρύσιον ἄγγος ἔχοισα, μέγαν σκύφον,
> οἷά τε ποιμένες ἄνδρες ἔχοισιν,
> χερσὶ λεόντεον ἐν γάλα θεῖσα
> τυρὸν ἐτύρησας μέγαν ἄτρυφον Ἀργειφόνται.

Often on the peaks of mountains when the festival of many torches is pleasing to the gods, you, holding in your hands a golden vessel, a great tankard, such as shepherd men have, put into it lioness's milk and for Hermes Argus-Slayer made a great whole cheese.

The last line of this fragment illustrates another, quite different quality of Alcman: a hearty interest in food, often enumerated in loving detail (frs. 19, 20, 56, 95, 96, 98 *PMG*). 'All-devouring Alcman' (ὁ παμφάγος Ἀλκμάν, 17.4 *PMG*), the poet calls himself playfully in a poem where, as in Catullus 13, the dinner guest is expected to supply the more substantial part of the meal. Although on the one hand Alcman can follow conventional epic phraseology ('black earth', 'ambrosial night', 'yellow hair', etc.), he can also write with a keen, all-embracing sense of concrete particulars. In almost Aristophanic vein he can move from delicate, flower-like jewellery (91 *PMG*) to porridges and partridges, from sleeping mountains to tables and cheeses (cf. 17, 19, 39, 56, 96 *PMG*).

Alcman's wide range and diverse sources of poetic inspiration appear also from a series of fragments dealing with distant, semi-mythical peoples and places (frs. 131, 148–57 *PMG*), somewhat after the manner of Aristeas of Proconnesos, whose *Arimaspeia* could conceivably have influenced him.[1] Two lines are especially noteworthy for their imaginative and suggestive poetry (90 *PMG*):

> Ῥίπας, ὄρος ἀνθέον ὕλαι,
> νυκτὸς μελαίνας στέρνον.

Rhipean range, mountain blooming with forest, breast of black night.

We may recall the evocative descriptions of mountains in fragments 89 and 56 cited above. Closer to home, Alcman also wrote about the local customs, history and myths of Sparta. One of his poems included a genealogy of legendary

---

[1] See *GLP* 27; West (1965) 193f.

Spartan kings (5, fr. 2, col. i *PMG*), and the Louvre Partheneion gave a leisurely enumeration of the slain sons of Hippocoon (1.2–12). Other poems, all lost, described minor Laconian divinities (62 *PMG*), localities in Sparta (52, 92 *PMG*) and the Spartan *syssitia* or men's eating-club (98 *PMG*).

Alcman took a self-conscious pleasure in language. We have noted his puns on the names of Hagesichora and Astymeloisa (1.84, 3.73f.) and his etymology of Akmon-*akamatos* (61). This interest also appears in the curious hexameter line (107) Πολλαλέγων ὄνυμ᾽ ἀνδρί, γυναικὶ δὲ Πασιχάρηα 'Say-much the man's name, Rejoicing-in-all the woman's'. The line may be a wry erotic joke about excessive compliance.[1] Equally well, it might be a condensed version of the traditional contrast between the hard-working man, 'Much-caring' (πόλλ᾽ ἀλέγων), and the beautiful, but idle woman, 'Pleasing-to-all', but useless, like Hesiod's Pandora: χάρις δ᾽ ἐπὶ πᾶσιν ἄητο 'and upon all was breathed grace' *Theog.* 583; cf. 590ff. and *W.D.* 373f. Beside the occasional 'kenning' (cf. 1.66f. above), Alcman also enjoys pithy proverbial statements, like the 'owl screeching from the roofbeam' (1.86f.), 'neighbour for neighbour is a big thing' (123), 'trial the beginning of learning' (125), 'narrow the path, pitiless Necessity' (102).

This interest in words has a possibly deeper significance in two short but important fragments (39 and 40 *PMG*):

ϝέπη τάδε καὶ μέλος Ἀλκμὰν
εὗρε γεγλωσσαμέναν
κακκαβίδων ὄπα συνθέμενος.

These words and this song Alcman invented, understanding the tongued speech of partridges.

ϝοῖδα δ᾽ ὀρνίχων νόμως
παντῶν.

Of all birds I know the tunes (ways).

Elsewhere keenly interested in birds, Alcman may be serious when he speaks of deriving his song from them. The first fragment looks like the poet's *sphragis* or personal 'seal' and reflects his pride in his art as intellectual discovery, not a gift of the Muses.[2] The fragment also, as Gentili suggests, may reflect the importance of imitation and mimicking in the oral context of early Greek poetry.[3] In many passages Alcman calls upon the Muses for divine inspiration (14, 27, 30, 67; cf. also 28, 43, 59b *PMG*). He also associates the power of song with the divine power of love and desire (e.g. 3.1ff.; fr. 27 *PMG*). The awareness of the intellectual side of his craft in fr. 39, however, is a small intimation of the self-

---

[1] See *GLP* 24f.; McKay (1974) 413f.
[2] For the implications see Gianotti (1975) 43–7.
[3] See Gentili (1971) 59–67.

conscious artistry which becomes important later in Pindar's pride in his *sophia* or poetic skill.

There is another trace of this poetic self-consciousness in an important new fragment (4, fr. 1.4–6 *PMG* = *P.Oxy.* 2388) in which Alcman seems to be commenting on his predecessors, who 'showed to men wondrous new songs, delicate, full of delight':

θαυμαστὰ δ' ἀνθ[ρώποισι
γαρύματα μαλσακὰ
νεόχμ' ἔδειξαν τερπ[

These lines are among the earliest indications in Greek lyric of a poet directly criticizing what has gone before. The generosity of Alcman's judgement is particularly interesting. The recent Oxyrhynchus fragment that confirms the existence of the sixth book of poems may also contain a reference to the *topos* of the poet's immortality of fame or κλέος (*P.Oxy.* 3209, fr. 1; cf. Sappho fr. 55 and 147 *PLF;* Ibycus fr. 282.47f. *PMG*).

In antiquity Alcman was famous for his treatment of love. Later writers characteristically construed as autobiographical professions of desire statements which were in fact part of the conventions of choral poetry. Thus Athenaeus (13.600f) interpreted the following fragment to mean that Alcman was madly in love with the poetess Megalostrata (59b *PMG*):

τοῦτο ϝαδειᾶν ἔδειξε Μωσᾶν
δῶρον μάκαιρα παρσένων
ἁ ξανθὰ Μεγαλοστράτα.

This gift of the sweet Muses did yellow-haired Megalostrata, happy among maidens, show forth.

Indeed, playfulness rather than passion seems to characterize Alcman's love-poetry, whether of heterosexual or of homosexual love. Two other verses which Athenaeus cites in the same context show the gentler rather than the impassioned side of love (59a):

Ἔρως με δηῦτε Κύπριδος ϝέκατι
γλυκὺς κατείβων καρδίαν ἰαίνει.

Sweet Eros, then, for the Cyprian's sake, drips down and warms my heart.

Another brief fragment on Eros suggests the playful inventiveness with which Alcman may have treated male homosexual love (58).[1]

Although we have lost much of the poetry that would justify Athenaeus' title, 'leader in the songs of love' (13.600f, 59 *PMG*), fortune has been kinder in preserving enough to document another epithet conferred on him by a later poet, 'graceful Alcman', τὸν χαρίεντ' Ἀλκμᾶνα (*Anth. Pal.* 7.19, 159 *PMG*).

[1] See Easterling (1974) 37–41.

3. STESICHORUS

Stesichorus of Himera, regarded in antiquity as the successor to Alcman in lyric, is best known for his retelling of epic themes in lyric metres. In this extended lyric narration Stesichorus seems not to have been unique. Sacadas of Argos, active in Sparta at the end of the seventh century, composed a *Sack of Troy* with even more detail than Stesichorus (Athenaeus 13.610c). Xanthus of Lydia, another rather shadowy predecessor of Stesichorus, composed an *Oresteia* which may have influenced Stesichorus (Athenaeus 12.512f; Aelian, *V.H.* 4.26; 699–700 *PMG*). The popularity of mythic subjects on contemporary vases parallels this interest in casting myths into new and vivid forms.

The sands of Egypt and the patient skill of papyrologists have spectacularly enhanced our knowledge of Stesichorus' poetry. Recently published papyri have added to our knowledge of the *Nostoi* (209 *PMG*), the *Palinode* for Helen (193), the *Oresteia* (217), and the *Hunt for the Calydonian Boar* (222); and the last ten years have brought to light major fragments of the *Geryoneis* (s7–87 *SLG*), *The Sack of Troy* (s88–132), the *Eriphyle* (s148–50), and, perhaps most important, a hitherto unknown poem on the fortunes of the house of Oedipus and the quarrel of Polynices and Eteocles (*P.Lille* 73 and 76). These new discoveries have substantiated the high value which ancient critics placed on Stesichorus' work, confirmed his role as a link between epic and lyric narrative, and demonstrated his importance for the representation of myths in sixth-century art.[1] A word of caution, however, is necessary. There is not total unanimity that all the new Trojan and Theban fragments belong to Stesichorus. In particular, some metrical features of the Lille Papyrus (below, pp. 197ff.) diverge from attested Stesichorean practice.[2] Subject matter and style afford a high degree of probability, but not absolute certainty.

The biographical tradition gives Stesichorus' dates as 632/29–556/53 B.C. (Suda), making him roughly contemporary with Sappho and Alcaeus (see Suda s.v. 'Sappho') and a generation later than Alcman.[3] He is associated both with Locrian Matauros in southern Italy and Himera in Sicily and is said to have been buried at Catane where his tomb was celebrated for its architecture. Most ancient writers connect him with Himera, but in Matauros too he would have encountered that mixture of Doric and Ionic in both language and literature that stamps his poetry. The synchronization of his death with Simonides' birth

---

[1] See *GLP* 119ff.; Robertson (1969) *passim*; Vallet (1958) 281ff. (on the metopes from the Heraion at the Foce del Sele now in the Paestum museum).

[2] Parsons (1977) 12. Parsons's point about the repetitiveness and slackness of the style (p. 7), however, tends to support rather than weaken the case for Stesichorean authorship.

[3] There seems to have been a later 'Stesichorus', perhaps even two poets of that name, with predictable confusion in biography and the attribution of certain works. For the chronology see Vallet (1958) 257–63; West (1971a) 302–14, esp. 302–7.

(556/53) may be taken as signifying a major division between older and newer styles. Simonides himself cites Stesichorus as an established authority, ranked with Homer (564 *PMG*). Eupolis in the *Helots* of *c.* 424 B.C. joins Stesichorus' songs with those of Alcman and Simonides as 'old-fashioned' (ἀρχαῖος, fr. 139 *CAF* = Stesich. 276b *PMG*).

The new fragments demonstrate Stesichorus' importance for the development of extended lyrical narrative in Bacchylides and odes of Pindar like *Pythian* 4. His poems, it appears, were probably more leisurely in their movement and closer to the flow of epic than to the highly selective techniques of late sixth- and early fifth-century lyric.

The new texts also raise a major problem. How were these poems sung and performed? Were they choral? The *Geryoneis*, for example, appears to have contained at least 1,500 lines, which would make it three and a half times as long as Pindar's fourth *Pythian*, our longest extant choral ode. This work, on a rough estimate, would require some four hours to perform, longer than a chorus could reasonably dance.[1] The freedom and flexibility of metre suggest that Stesichorus sang such poems to his own lyre, without choral accompaniment.[2] Such poetry, a spin-off of epic or rhapsodic recitation, is called 'citharodic'.[3] Unlike the rhapsode's work, it is original composition; unlike the monodist's, it is narrative and lengthy, not personal and relatively brief. Sacadas' *Sack of Troy* and Xanthus' *Oresteia*, mentioned above, would seem to fall into this same category.

At this point, however, a second problem arises. Stesichorus' name indicates some connexion with the chorus; it should mean 'he who sets up the chorus'. The Suda, in fact, says that the poet's real name was Teisias, and 'he was called Stesichorus because he first established a chorus of song to the lyre' (κιθαρωιδίας χορὸν ἔστησεν). It is possible that 'Stesichorus' was a title like 'choirmaster', an assumption made the more plausible by the reference to 'Stesichorus' in the *Marmor Parium* at two later dates.[4] There is, of course, no necessary contradiction between a Stesichorus/Teisias who composed choral poetry similar (say) to Alcman's and a Stesichorus/Teisias who also, possibly at a later point of his career, developed or perfected the long citharodic narrative poems, blending lyric metre with epic themes, for which he is celebrated. Still, the fact remains that the name suggests strong connexions with choral poetry, whereas the new texts point to poems which, on the face of it, do not look as if they were choral.

Be this as it may, Stesichorus' work wins high praise from the ancient critics, mainly for epic rather than strictly lyrical virtues. Horace places his

[1] Pavese (1972) 243f.; West (1971a) 307–9.
[2] See Haslam (1974) 33 with n. 53; West (1969 and 1971a) *passim*.
[3] See Pavese (1972) 239, 266f.; West (1971a) 313f. *Od.* 8.256–67 suggests that dances might be performed in accompaniment to rhapsodic narrative poetry. Cf. also *DTC* 11.
[4] See West (1970a) 206; Pavese (1972) 245.

'severe Muses' (*graues Camenae*) close behind Homer (*Odes* 4.9.8–11). Dionysius of Halicarnassus agrees (*De comp. verb.* 24) and commends his 'grandeur of subject matter' (*megaloprepeia*) and his attention to the 'character and rank of his personages' (*Vet. cens.* 2.7), qualities which we can now see amply attested in the new fragments. To 'Longinus' he is 'most Homeric' (*Subl.* 13.3). Quintilian places him second to Pindar for his 'strength of genius' (*ingenio ualidus*). He singles out his lofty epic themes of battles and heroes (*maxima bella et clarissimos canentem duces et epici carminis onera lyra sustinentem*) 'singing vast wars and glorious leaders and lifting on his lyre the full weight of epic song' (10.1.62), but criticizes his diffuseness:

> For he gives his characters their appropriate dignity in action and in speech; and, if he had exercised restraint, he could have been a close rival to Homer. But he is too abundant and spreads out (*redundat atque effunditur*), a flaw which, though worthy of blame, is yet a fault of his very fluency and copiousness.

The leisurely pace of the *Geryoneis* and the poem on the sons of Oedipus confirm Quintilian's judgement. Hermogenes found his abundant use of adjectives 'very pleasing' (σφόδρα ἡδύς, *Id.* 3.322 Walz).

This descriptive fullness characterizes most of Stesichorus' poetry. In the *Geryoneis* the Centaur Pholus offers Heracles a cup of wine (181 *PMG*):

σκύφιον δὲ λαβὼν δέπας ἔμμετρον ὡς τριλάγυνον
πῖ' ἐπισχόμενος, τό ῥά οἱ παρέθηκε Φόλος κεράσας.

Taking a cup-like tankard of three-bottles' measure, he held it up and drank, the cup which Pholus mixed and set beside him.

Nearly everything is said twice. Yet the accumulation of modifiers is not without structure. There are four nouns or adjectives and one verbal form in the first line and just the reverse proportion in the second. The profuseness seems to serve the narrative better in the account of the remote west where Geryon's herdsman, Eurytion, was born (184 *PMG*):

σχεδὸν ἀντιπέρας κλεινᾶς Ἐρυθείας
Ταρτησσοῦ ποταμοῦ παρὰ παγὰς ἀπείρονας ἀργυρορίζους
ἐν κευθμῶνι πέτρας.

...nearly across from famed Erytheia, by the limitless, silver-rooted streams of the river Tartessus in the hollow of the rock.

The richness of compound adjectives, a stylistic trait developed even further in the lyric narrative of Bacchylides, is not only decorative. The continuous narration in the new fragments, as we shall see, illustrates how this fullness of detail can also serve to awaken pathos.

In diction Stesichorus is indeed 'most Homeric'. His language is a literary Doric, with a strong predilection for Homeric formulas. His heavily dactylic metres facilitate the Homeric borrowings. He adapts Homeric phraseology, however, with considerable freedom and flexibility, as this fragment of the *Nostoi* shows (209 *PMG*):

θε[ῖ]ον ἐ[ξ]αίφνας τέρας ἰδοῖσα νύμφα
ὧδε δε[..]. ῾Ελένα φωνᾶι ποτ[ὶ] παῖδ᾽ ᾽Οδύσειο[ν·
῾Τηλέμαχ[..]τις ὅδ᾽ ἁμὶν ἄγγελ[ο]ς ὠρανόθεν
δι᾽ αἰθέρο[ς ἀτ]ρυγέτας κατέπαλτο βαδ[
                    ].ε φοιναι κεκλαγγω[
]...ς ὑμετέρους δόμους προφα.[.......]υς
               ].....αν.υς ἀνὴρ
βο]υλαῖς ᾽Αθάνας
           ].ηις αυτα λακέρυζα κορώνα
           ].μ᾽ οὐδ᾽ ἐγώ σ᾽ ἐρύ[ξ]ω
Παν]ελόπα σ᾽ ἰδοῖσα φίλου πατ[ρ]ὸς υἱὸν...᾽

> ...Helen the bride, suddenly seeing the divine omen, and thus did she speak to the son of Odysseus: 'Telemachus, whatever messenger this is that has come to us hurtling down through the unharvested aether...shrieking...(Odysseus?) appearing in your halls...by the counsels of Athena...a screeching crow. Nor will I keep you back; but Penelope, on seeing you, the son of your dear father...'

Stesichorus is closely following the Homeric scene of Telemachus' departure from Sparta in *Odyssey* 15.113ff. In Homer the gifts come first and in much more detail (*Od.* 15.113–29); then, as Telemachus makes a parting speech, the omen appears (*Od.* 15.160–3):

ὣς ἄρα οἱ εἰπόντι ἐπέπτατο δεξιὸς ὄρνις,
αἰετὸς ἀργὴν χῆνα φέρων ὀνύχεσσι πέλωρον,
ἥμερον ἐξ αὐλῆς· οἱ δ᾽ ἰύζοντες ἕποντο
ἀνέρες ἠδὲ γυναῖκες.

> Thus as he spoke a bird flew by on the right, an eagle bearing in its claws a huge white goose, tame, from the yard; and they all followed shouting, the men and the women.

As all cry out with rejoicing, young Pisistratus asks Menelaus to interpret, but Helen anticipates him (171–8). Telemachus briefly prays for the fulfilment of the prophecy and departs (180–4). Stesichorus has obviously greatly condensed the scene while following the main outline as given in Homer. He puts the omen earlier and from the first makes Helen the one who sees, describes and expounds its meaning. The omen itself is different: to the Homeric eagle Stesichorus has added a lowly crow, borrowing a phrase which occurs in Hesiod (*W.D.* 747) but not in Homer. We should note especially the dramatic use of direct discourse, a feature of lyric style prominent in Pindar and Bacchylides. An additional small fragment (col. ii) shows that Stesichorus has changed Menelaus' gift of a silver and golden mixing bowl (*Od.* 15.115–19) to a vessel taken as booty from Priam's palace, again a colourful embroidering of Homeric detail.

An even more telling comparison emerges from this recently published fragment of the death of Geryon from the *Geryoneis* (S15.14–17 *SLG*):

> ἀπέκλινε δ' ἄρ' αὐχένα Γαρ[υόνας
> ἐπικάρσιον, ὡς ὅκα μ[ά]κω[ν
> ἅτε καταισχύνοισ' ἁπαλὸν [δέμας
> αἶψ' ἀπὸ φύλλα βαλοῖσα...

And Geryon leaned his neck to one side, as when a poppy...befouling its soft body suddenly throwing off its petals...

The passage echoes the death of Gorgythion in *Iliad* 8.306–8:

> μήκων δ' ὡς ἑτέρωσε κάρη βάλεν, ἥ τ' ἐνὶ κήπωι
> καρπῶι βριθομένη νοτίηισί τε εἰαρινῆισιν·
> ὡς ἑτέρωσ' ἤμυσε κάρη πήληκι βαρυνθέν.

And as a poppy casts its head to one side, a poppy in a garden, weighed down with fruit and the rains of the spring, so did he droop to one side his head weighed down with his helmet.

Stesichorus, it seems, omits the spring rains (kept by a later imitator, Virgil, *Aen.* 9.436) and increases pathos by making his flower 'soft' and 'defiled' as it loses its petals. 'Blameless Gorgythion' in Homer is the son of King Priam and a beautiful mother, 'in form like the goddesses' (*Il.* 8.303–5); Stesichorus' Geryon has three bodies and wings to match, an improvement over the Hesiodic monster who has only three heads (*Theogony* 287).[1] The Homeric echo, if pressed, might seem bizarre; a poppy with 'soft body' (if δέμας is the right supplement) is a potentially grotesque point of comparison for a dying monster. Stesichorus presumably adopted this Homeric detail as part of his compassionate portrayal of Geryon. He seems unaware of the possible unsuitability of the comparison. In the high seriousness of the heroic style a monster exterminated by Heracles can also be a victim with whom we can sympathize.

The problem of the poppy simile is symptomatic of the dangers and limitations involved in perpetuating the Homeric style. Transferred to a different structure, the Homeric frame at a certain point seems strained, becomes overburdened and cracks. Other poets – Archilochus, Sappho, Alcaeus – turned Homeric language to new, entirely non-epic situations. At the same time we must not underestimate the sheer delight which the Greeks of the seventh and sixth centuries took in these stories for their own sake, as vase-painting and a monumental representation like the François Vase (*c.* 570 B.C.) indicate. Stesichorus may well have shared his contemporaries' growing malaise about the

---

[1] See *GLP* 91f.; Robertson (1969) 209.

epic as the norm for measuring human experience. His recasting not only of the form, but also of the substance of epic material is an indication of his awareness that the epic mould was not entirely satisfying.

His boldest innovations appear in his *Palinode* for Helen. 'This tale is not true', he recanted, 'nor did you go in the well-benched ships nor reach the citadels of Troy' (192 *PMG*). He developed the motif, possibly already in Hesiod's *Catalogue of women*, that not Helen herself, but a wraith or *eidolon* went to Troy.[1] As there is now evidence for not one but two *Palinodes*, it is probable that Stesichorus told two different versions of the *eidolon* story, one in which the real Helen never went anywhere (Dio Chrys. 11.40) and another in which she was protected by Proteus, as in Euripides' *Helen* (193.15ff. *PMG*).[2] The heroine of his original *Helen* seems to have resembled the figure of Aeschylus' *Agamemnon*, a dangerous, immoral, licentious woman (190 *PMG*). To this poem may also belong a fragment about Aphrodite's curse on the daughters of Tyndareus (223 *PMG*), a story already in Hesiod's *Catalogue* (176 M–W = 93 Rz). In this version, prior to Helen's marriage with Menelaus she is abducted by Theseus and bears him a child; the child is none other than Iphigenia (191 *PMG*). In his *Iliou persis* too Stesichorus may have given Helen a bad character, but the exiguous fragments do not admit of certainty (s104 *SLG*). Such a view of Helen was certainly widespread among his Lesbian contemporaries (cf. Sappho 16.6–10 and Alcaeus B 10 *PLF*).[3] The *Palinodes*, it has been suggested, made the poet's amends in Sparta or one of the Dorian colonies in Magna Graecia where Helen was an important cult-figure. The revision of the myth may be compared with Pindar's reworking of the story of Neoptolemus in *Paean 6* and *Nemean 7* (see below, p. 232 n. 1).

Stesichorus went blind, the story goes, as a result of Helen's wrath (presumably at the version of her character in the *Helen*); but he regained his sight when he sang the *Palinode*. This tale, already well established in the fourth century B.C. (cf. Plato, *Phdr.* 243a; Isocrates, *Helen* 64), may have arisen from a metaphorical statement about darkness and illumination, misunderstood as literal fact. The Oxyrhynchus commentary which cites the beginnings of the two *Palinodes* reports that Stesichorus criticizes Homer in the one and Hesiod in the other (193 *PMG*). This detail receives some support from Plato, who contrasts Homer's blindness with Stesichorus' restored vision (*Phdr.* 243a = 192 *PMG*):

For those who err in telling myths there is an ancient purification which *Homer* did not perceive, *but Stesichorus did*. Deprived of his sight because of his

---

[1] Hesiod 458 M–W = 266 Rzach; but the evidence for this motif as Hesiodic rests only on a late scholium to Lycophron (*Alex.* 822), of dubious value: see Sisti (1965) 307f.

[2] Scholars have remained reluctant to accept the notion of two separate palinodes, but the new evidence makes this conclusion almost inescapable: see Vallet (1958) 273–7; Sisti (1965) 301–13; Woodbury (1967), 157–76; Davison (1968), 196–225; Treu (1968*b*) 1254f.; Podlecki (1971) 313–27.

[3] See Page (1955) 280f.; Kirkwood (1974) 267 n. 75.

vilification of Helen, he did not fail to learn this, *as Homer did*, but, being musical, discovered the cause and at once wrote, 'This tale is not true...'

Not only is the relation of the two *Palinodes* to one another obscure, but there is also a question whether either was entirely separate from the *Helen*.[1] The way in which the ancients refer to these works, however, suggests separate poems.

Stesichorus' narratives are full of colourful detail, and it is not surprising that vase-painting in the sixth century drew heavily on them. His Cycnus, for instance, builds a grisly temple from the skulls of his victims (207 *PMG*).[2] He is probably the first poet to represent Athena leaping 'shining with arms' from the head of Zeus (223 *PMG*).[3] He graphically depicted Artemis' punishment of Actaeon by having her throw a stag's skin over him (236 *PMG*).[4] Sympathy for the defeated, grotesque monster though he be, appears not only in the *Geryoneis*; there is probably a touch of compassion in his picture of the Calydonian boar, 'hiding the tip of its snout beneath the ground', presumably in terror (221 *PMG*).

Innovation in genre as well as theme is suggested by the tradition that Stesichorus sang bucolic songs, like those of the neatherd Daphnis (280, 281 *PMG*), possibly drawing on the folklore of his native Sicily, but there is a question of authenticity.[5] Popular currents may appear too in a number of Aesop-like animal fables with a strongly moralizing point. Two on politics are attested by Aristotle; another, cited at length by Aelian, is more doubtful (281 *PMG*).[6] Two poems dealing with unhappy love, the *Calyce* and *Rhadine* (277, 278 *PMG*), are also attributed to him; but these stories have the look of a later age and may well be the work of the fourth-century Stesichorus mentioned by the *Marmor Parium*.[7] The same suspicion attaches to the above-mentioned *Daphnis*. On the other hand Stesichorus was celebrated as a poet of erotic themes (276 *PMG*). Evidence for these now appears in some of the new fragments, particularly a longish poem, erotically coloured, to a handsome youth, attributed by Page to Ibycus, but very possibly the work of Stesichorus (S166–219 *SLG*).

The list of Stesichorus' known works reveals a strong interest in the myth of Heracles, a favourite subject in Magna Graecia, as that hero's far-flung adventures included those distant colonies in the cycles of famous myths.[8] The *Cerberus*,

---

[1] See *GLP* 112; Davison (1968) 219.   [2] See *GLP* 81; Dawe (1972) 28–30.

[3] See *GLP* 123–6; Vallet (1958) 279 with n. 2 points out, however, that the motif occurs on a shield band at Olympia at the end of the seventh century.

[4] See *GLP* 99f.; Nagy (1973) 179f.   [5] See West (1970a) 206; Vürtheim (1919) 73–6.

[6] On the Aelian passage Vürtheim (1919) 79 remarks, 'Dass Stesichoros solch albernes Zeug geschrieben habe, ist kaum denkbar': Vallet (1958) 284–6 is more sanguine.

[7] See West (1970a) 206; *GLP* 87; Rose (1932) 88–92; Vallet (1958) 285 is more positive.

[8] See Vallet (1958) 263ff., who also suggests possible western connexions for the *Oresteia* (266ff.) if Stesichorus' Apollo sent Orestes to the west for purification.

Cycnus, Geryoneis, possibly the *Scylla*, all involve Heracles. The Trojan cycle is represented by his *Nostoi, Sack of Troy* and *Helen*; the Theban cycle in the *Eriphyle* and the new poem about Thebes (*P.Lille* 73, 76). His *Oresteia, Calydonian Boar hunt* and *Funeral games of Pelias* show his interest in other traditions, both Peloponnesian and north Greek.

Thanks to the recent discoveries, we can see Stesichorus' imagination at work over the large part of a whole poem, the *Geryoneis*.[1] An already existing fragment, quoted by Athenaeus, told of the Sun's journey in a golden cup across Ocean 'to the depths of dark sacred night to his mother and wedded wife and dear children', while Heracles proceeded 'on foot to a grove shadowy with laurel trees' (185 *PMG*). It is not certain whether Heracles is here entering or leaving the western lands of his encounter with Geryon. The former view, maintained by Barrett and Gentili against Page, is somewhat more probable.[2] The fantasy-geography, reminiscent of *Odyssey* 10–12, in any case pervades the mood of this work. This mythical geography and the ample scope of the poem are clear from the details about Geryon's herdsman, Eurytion (184 *PMG*, cited above). Eurytion's mother, one of the Hesperids, took him in infancy 'over the waves of the deep sea...to the most lovely island of the gods, where the Hesperids have their homes, all-golden' (s8 *SLG*). This geographical expansiveness and insistence on the genealogy of even secondary characters indicate the poem's broad scale. A stichometric sign in the papyrus marks line 1300, and this is not the end.

The most important new fragments depict the death of Geryon. Instead of describing a rousing victory over a terrible monster, Stesichorus shows a remarkable sympathy for Heracles' doomed enemy. Geryon delivers a long speech, possibly to Heracles, which is closely modelled on Sarpedon's speech to Glaucus in *Iliad* 12.310–28.[3] The epithets introducing the speech (of which 'immortal' is fairly certain) serve the function both of ennobling him and of stressing the contrast with his approaching mortal end (s11.1–12, 16–26 *SLG*):

τὸν
δ' ἀπαμ[ειβόμενος
ποτέφα [κρατερὸς Χρυσάορος ἀ-
θανάτοιο [γόνος καὶ Καλλιρόας·

'μή μοι θά[νατον προφέρων κρυόεν-   5
τα δεδίσκ[ε' ἀγάνορα θυμόν,
μηδεμελ[

[1] See especially Page (1973a) 138–54; Robertson (1969) 207–21; Webster (1968) 1–9. For an interesting interpretation of the myth, connecting Geryon with the herdsman of the dead, see Burkert (1977) 273–83; also Adrados (1978) 266.

[2] Gentili (1976) 745f., on the basis of Apollod. 2.5.10.

[3] Page favours Menoites as the interlocutor (s11 *SLG*); Gentili (1976) 747 argues for Heracles on the analogy of Achilles' speech to Lycaon in *Il.* 22.

αἰ μὲν γὰ[ρ γένος ἀθάνατος πέλο-
μαι καὶ ἀγή[ραος ὥστε βίου πεδέχειν
ἐν ᾽Ολύμπ[ωι,   10
κρέσσον[ἐ-
    λέγχεα δ[12
        . . .
αἰ δ᾽ ὦ φί[λε χρὴ στυγερόν μ᾽ ἐπὶ γῆ-   16
ρας [ἰκ]έσθαι,
ζώ[ει]ν τ᾽ ἐν ἐ[φαμερίοις ἀπάνευ-
θε θ[ε]ῶν μακάρω[ν,
νῦν μοι πολὺ κά[λλιόν ἐστι παθῆν   20
ὅ τι μόρσιμ[ον

καὶ ὀνείδε[
καὶ παντὶ γέ[νει
ὀπίσω Χρυσ[άο]ρο[ς υ]ίόν·
μ]ὴ τοῦτο φ[ί]λον μακά[ρε]σσι θε[ο]ῖ-   25
σι γ]ένοιτο᾽

Answering him so spoke the mighty son of immortal Chrysaor and Callirhoe:
'Do not hold chill death before me and try to frighten my manly spirit...
But if I am ageless and immortal in race (and partake of?) life on Olympus,
better (to fight than leave behind) shameful reproaches...But if, dear friend,
I must come to hateful old age and live among men creatures of a day far from
the blessed gods, better by far is it for me now to suffer whatever is my fated
portion; (not endurable) that the son of Chrysaor should leave behind reproaches for his whole race in aftertime. Let this not be pleasing to the blessed
gods...'

The Homeric situation and language is adapted with a poignant clarity. Against
the formulaic diction of the heroic ethos Stesichorus sounds a more vibrant
note of pathos in the repetition of 'blessed gods' (19, 25), in contrast with the
'chill death' facing the speaker.

That pathetic contrast between the concern of loved ones and the firmness of
the doomed warrior is even stronger in the scene between Geryon and his
mother, Callirhoe. This scene of warrior and *mater dolorosa* draws heavily on
the exchanges between Thetis and Achilles in *Iliad* 18 and Hector and Hecuba
in *Iliad* 22. Unfortunately we have only a few lines of Callirhoe's entreaty
(s13.1–5 *SLG*):

ἐγὼν [μελέ]α καὶ ἄλασ-
τοτόκος κ]αὶ ἄλ[ασ]τα παθοῖσα
Γ]αρυόνα γωνάζομα[ι,
αἴ ποκ᾽ ἐμ]όν τιν μαζ[ὸν] ἐ[πέσχεθον...

I who am unforgettably wretched, in my motherhood, in my suffering, Geryon, I
supplicate you, if ever I held out my breast to you...

194

These scenes prepared the way for the pathos of Geryon's end. Grotesque monster though he is, Geryon's situation and suffering are thoroughly human-ized. We have already noted the poppy-simile of his death (s15. col. ii. 14–17 *SLG*). The earlier part of this fragment describes how Heracles poisons his arrows with the Hydra's venom (ὀλεσάνορος αἰολοδείρου ὀδύναισιν Ὕδρας 'with the agonies of the Hydra, man-destroying, of glittering neck', col. ii.5f.). Heracles takes advantage of tricks and guile to kill his foe (λάθραι, col. i.8; σιγᾶι...ἐπικλοπάδαν, col. ii.6f.). The death itself is painful:

διὰ δ' ἔσχισε σάρκα [καὶ] ὀ[στ]έα δαί-
μονος αἴσαι·
διὰ δ' ἀντικρὺ σχέθεν οἰ[σ]τὸς ἐπ' ἀ-
κροτάταν κορυφάν,
ἐμίαινε δ' ἄρ' αἵματι πορφ[υρέωι
θώρακά τε καὶ βροτόεντ[α μέλεα.   (col. ii.8–13)

The arrow split through the flesh and bones, in accordance with the destiny of the god; and it drove through to the topmost part of the skull and fouled with dark-red blood the breast-plate and the bloody limbs...

The addition, 'in accordance with the destiny of the god', keeps pity within the larger perspective of the divine plan and divine justice. Shortly before the battle, in fact, the gods met in council to discuss the outcome, and Athena and Poseidon somehow resolved their conflicting sympathies, possibly with the help of Zeus (s14 *SLG*). Unfortunately there is not enough left to determine whether the issue at stake was just a choice between favourites or some principle of order and justice. On the analogy of the deaths of Patroclus and Hector in the *Iliad*, the latter is the more likely.

Geryon's death formed the climax, but not the end of the poem. After his victory Heracles returns with Geryon's stolen cattle and on his journey meets the Centaur Pholus (181 *PMG*), possibly the encounter where he wounds Chiron with the incurable Hydra's venom. Pausanias mentions Pallanteum in Arcadia (181 *PMG*), the probable site of this adventure.

The other numerous papyrus fragments are too small to do more than offer tantalizing hints. Even with this small fraction of the work, we can still glimpse its richness of style set off against familiar motifs of heroic poetry, its blend of vivid action and evocative geographical fantasy, its imaginative plot, its mixture of traditional phraseology and 'occasional strokes of almost Pindaric boldness' (Page), as in the description of the Hydra's poison cited above.[1] The new fragments justify Dionysius of Halicarnassus' admiration for Stesichorus' 'grandeur' of subject and attention to 'the character and rank of his personages' (*Cens. vet.* 2.7).

[1] Page (1973*a*) 152.

Similar in scope, episodic character, and epic borrowings is the *Iliou persis* or *Sack of Troy* (s88–132 *SLG*) of which some fragments have recently been recovered. To judge by the remains, this poem must have had a leisurely tempo not unlike that of the *Geryoneis*. Unity seems not to have been among its virtues: it related the invention and deployment of the Trojan horse, the prophecy of Cassandra and her rape by Ajax, the death of Astyanax, Menelaus' pardon of Helen, and so on.[1] The existing quotations show us Stesichorus' innovating spirit. He has Hecuba carried off to Lycia by Apollo (198 *PMG*) and presents Athena pitying Epeius, inventor of the wooden horse, as he performs his lowly task of carrying water for the Atreids (200 *PMG*):

$$\text{ὤικτιρε γὰρ αὐτὸν ὕδωρ}$$
$$\text{αἰεὶ φορέοντα Διὸς κούρα βασιλεῦσιν.}$$

For the daughter of Zeus pitied him as he was always carrying water for the kings.

Stesichorus may have drawn this rather unheroic detail from folklore motifs (divine aid to the clever underdog); we may contrast the very different setting of Athena's help to Bellerophon in Pindar's thirteenth *Olympian* (66–86).

The new fragments of the *Iliou persis* show us Stesichorus 'lifting on his lyre the full weight of epic song', as in Quintilian's phrase. We have a bit of an energetic debate among the Trojans about bringing the horse within the citadel and the dramatic appearance of omens from the sky at a crucial moment (s88 *SLG*). As the Greeks attack from the horse, the city seems helpless and its gods of no avail (s105*b* *SLG*). This and a number of other fragments about a battle for Troy (s133–47 *SLG*), however, come from a different papyrus (*P.Oxy.* 2803), and Page assigns them to a separate poem specifically on the Trojan Horse.[2]

The *Oresteia*, in two books, must also have been of considerable length. Surely we must think here of citharodic recitation rather than choral performance. The extent of this poem's influence on the iconography of the myth in sixth- and fifth-century vase-painting is controversial, but there is little doubt of its influence on Attic tragedy.[3] Agamemnon's appearance to Clytemnestra in the form of a snake with bloodied head (219 *PMG*) may have suggested the Aeschylean Clytemnestra's vision of Orestes as a snake drawing blood from the breast. Stesichorus' version already contained the nurse and, according to a

[1] If the late relief sculpture known as the *Tabula Iliaca* owes its iconography to Stesichorus, as many believe (cf. 205 *PMG*), Stesichorus may have been the first to depict Aeneas leaving Troy with Anchises on his shoulders, but suspicion on this point, given the later celebrity of the tale, is justified. Vallet (1958) 270–3, however, believes that this story of Aeneas was included in the *Iliou persis*. See also Galinsky (1969) 106–13.

[2] Page (1973*b*) 47–65; *contra*, West (1971*b*) 262–4.

[3] See Davies (1969) *passim*, esp. 248–51; *GLP* 116f.; Vallet (1958) 266–70. On Clytemnestra's dream in Stesichorus see Devereux (1976) 171–9.

recent papyrus fragment of a commentary (217 *PMG*), also the recognition by the lock of hair and Apollo's support of Orestes against the Furies, though in a more purely martial form than in Aeschylus' *Eumenides*. As Stesichorus, following Hesiod, identified Iphigenia with 'the figure now called Hecate' (215 *PMG*), his version presumably included the death and transformation of Iphigenia (cf. also Paus. 1.43.1).

The most sensational find so far is the new fragment about Thebes (*P.Lille* 73 and 76). The papyrus begins a little after line 200 and ends shortly after line 300 (a stichometric mark for the latter is preserved); the middle portion is scrappy, but a good deal is preserved, particularly a virtually complete text of a speech by the Theban queen, perhaps Jocasta. Where the text becomes intelligible, she is desperately trying to find a solution to Tiresias' prophecy that Oedipus' two sons will kill one another (lines 26–56). The brothers seem to agree to divide Oedipus' kingdom and the property (60–76). Then, in a more legible portion of the papyrus, Tiresias is foretelling how Polynices will go to Argos and marry King Adrastus' daughter; the result will be 'grief' (πένθος, 112) for himself and the city. Polynices departs to Argos via Cithaeron, Athens, Corinth and Lerna. As in the *Geryoneis* Stesichorus does not stint on geographical detail.

The best preserved section of the text is, fortunately, the queen's speech. It may be compared with the speech of Geryon to Menoites and the exchange between Geryon and his mother in the *Geryoneis* (above, p. 194). The full characterization, the pathos, the situation of strong emotions in a mother's love for her children are all similar (26–59 = 201–34):[1]

> 'ἐπ' ἄλγεσι μὴ χαλεπὰς ποίει μερίμνας,   26 = 201
> μηδέ μοι ἐξοπίσω
>   πρόφαινε ἐλπίδας βαρείας.
>
> οὔτε γὰρ αἰὲν ὁμῶς
>   θεοὶ θέσαν ἀθάνατοι κατ' αἶαν ἱρὰν   30 = 205
> νεῖκος ἔμπεδον βροτοῖσιν
> οὐδέ γα μὰν φιλότατ', ἐπὶ δ' ἀμέραι ἐν νόον ἄλλον
> θεοὶ τιθεῖσι.
> μαντοσύνας δὲ τεὰς ἄναξ ἑκάεργος Ἀπόλλων
> μὴ πάσας τελέσσαι.   35 = 210
>
> αἰ δέ με παῖδας ἰδέσθαι ὑπ' ἀλλάλοισι δαμέντας
> μόρσιμόν ἐστιν, ἐπεκλώσαν δὲ Μοῖρα[ι],
> αὐτίκα μοι θανάτου τέλος στυγερο[ῖο] γέν[οιτο,
> πρίν ποκα ταῦτ' ἐσιδεῖν
>   ἄλγεσ⟨σ⟩ι πολύστονα δακρυόεντα[– –,   40 = 215
> παίδας ἐνὶ μεγάροις
> θανόντας ἢ πόλιν ἁλοίσαν.

---

[1] The text is that of Haslam (1978) 32f., which is a slightly modified version of Parsons's (1977). See also Bollack, Judet de la Combe, and Wismann (1977) *passim*. Adrados (1978) 274–5 assigns the Lille fragments to the first book of *Eriphyle*.

ἀλλ' ἄγε παῖδες ἐμοῖς μύθοις, φίλα [τέκνα, πίθεσθε·
τᾱΐδε γὰρ ὑμὶν ἐγὼν τέλος προφα[ίνω·
τὸν μὲν ἔχοντα δόμους ναίειν πα[ρὰ νάμασι Δίρκας,   45 = 220
τὸν δ' ἀπίμεν κτεάνη
   καὶ χρυσὸν ἔχοντα φίλου σύμπαντα [πατρός,
κλαροπαληδὸν ὃς ἂν
   πρᾶτος λάχηι ἕκατι Μοιρᾶν.

τοῦτο γὰρ ἂν δοκέω   50 = 225
   λυτήριον ὔμμι κακοῦ γένοιτο πότμο[υ,
μάντιος φραδαῖσι θείου,
αἴ γε νέον Κρονίδας γένος τε καὶ ἄστυ [σαώσει
Κάδμου ἄνακτος,
ἀμβάλλων κακότατα πολὺν χρόνον [ἃ βασιλείαι   55 = 230
πέπρωται γενέ[θ]λαι.'

ὣς φάτ[ο] δῖα γυνὰ μύθοις ἀγ[α]νοῖς ἐνεποῖσα,
νείκεος ἐν μεγάροις π[αύο]ισα παῖδας,
σὺν δ' ἅμα Τειρ[ε]σίας τ[ερασπό]λος· οἱ δ' [ἐ]πίθο[ντο...   59 = 234

P. Lille 73 and 76, *ZPE* 26 (1977) 7–36

'... Upon (existing) griefs do not set harsh cares nor show forth hard expectations for me in aftertime.

For not always have the immortal gods established equally for mortals strife firm-fixed upon the holy earth, no nor love either, but a mind changing to other moods do the gods set upon men; and do not, O lord far-shooter Apollo, accomplish all your prophecies.

But if it is my fated portion to see my children slaughtered by one another and the Fates have spun that out, let me have at once the fulfilment of chill death before seeing these things, amid griefs full of lamentation, full of tears, my children dead in the halls or the city taken.

But come, my sons, dear (children), (be persuaded) by my words, for I am showing you an end (of hostility) in this way: one of you keep the house and dwell in Thebes, and the other go away possessing the chattels and all the gold of his dear father, making the choice by lot, whoever first through the Fates draws the winning lot.

This, I think, would be a release for you from evil destiny in accordance with the thoughts of the divine prophet, if perchance Zeus (may save) the race afresh and the city of lord Cadmus, postponing for a long time the evil (which) is fated for the (royal family).'

So she spoke, regal lady, addressing them with gentle words to stop her sons from strife in the halls. And at the same time Tiresias..., and they obeyed...

The context of the narrative is rather obscure. The absence of Oedipus is particularly striking, and we do not know whether he is dead, exiled, or still alive but without power in Thebes. (The distribution of his property in 45–9 suggests that he is dead, but this is not certain.) We cannot even be sure that the speaker is Jocasta. In one early tradition the incestuous wife, Jocasta or

Epikaste, ostensibly childless, commits suicide when she learns that Oedipus is her son; a second wife, Euryganeia, then bears the children of Oedipus (*Odyssey* 11.271–80, *Oedipodeia*, fr. 1 Allen).[1] Stesichorus' emphasis on the family curse makes it likely that the sons are born from an incestuous union and that the speaker is therefore Oedipus' mother-wife, Jocasta or Epikaste. If so, the situation resembles that of the *Phoenissae* of Euripides, who also followed a Stesichorean variant of a myth in the case of Helen. The queen's intervention between the quarrelling brothers also resembles the *Phoenissae*. Her prayer at lines 38ff. may be a foreshadowing of her suicide, another detail which would strengthen the resemblance with Euripides and also square with the tradition of Jocasta's suicide elsewhere in epic and tragedy. For the sake of convenience we shall call the queen Jocasta, with the reservation that the identification is unproven. Here, as with Helen, Stesichorus may be following an unfamiliar early variant of the story of Oedipus. It may also be that some or all of the narrative details are his own innovation: making Jocasta the mother of Oedipus' children, postponing or omitting her suicide, and having her mediate between the rival brothers.

Jocasta speaks partly in gnomic utterances that recall Homeric situations like the speech of Priam in *Iliad* 24.211ff. The gnomic generality adds weight and dignity to a mother's intense concern for her children. The passage is heavy with a brooding sense of the ill-omened destiny of the house which Jocasta understands all too well but still hopes to avert. Her apostrophe to Apollo not to fulfil '*all* his prophecies' (34f.), her direct address eight lines later to her sons with the simple παῖδες (43), her reference to Zeus in 53 all express her anguish and her hopes somehow to fit the oracles to a 'release from evil destiny' (51). Yet this Jocasta is not just a mother distraught by love and fear, like Hecuba in *Iliad* 22, or one bitterly resigned, like Hecuba in *Iliad* 24.209–12. She has practical proposals to offer, in lucid detail and in sharp antithetical clauses, τὸν μέν...τὸν δέ (45f.), and she is emphatic about the mechanism of the lottery to implement her solution (48f.). This is a strong woman, who well deserves the heroic epithet δῖα γυνά in 57. Her 'gentle words' take effect and end the quarrel, but there must have been an even greater pathos in the sequel as the respite proves only temporary and the house falls to its terrible doom after all.

The fullness of detail for which Quintilian criticizes Stesichorus is here not without its literary effectiveness. The repetitions of the theme of fate and prophecy (34, 37, 52, 56) and of the references to 'children' (παῖδας...παῖδας... παῖδες, 36, 41, 43) hammer home both the mother's concern and its ultimate futility. The repetition of the idea of prophecy in 37, 'If it is fated and the Fates have spun it out', and of the words for 'grief' in 40 all contribute to the intensity of her suffering. Stesichorus takes her through a complex emotional movement

---

[1] See Gostoli (1978) 23–7.

as she wishes for death at the idea of 'seeing' (ἰδέσθαι, ἐσιδεῖν, 36, 39) her sons
dead, but comes back with practical and energetic measures as she addresses the
living sons in a more positive mood (ἀλλ' ἄγε παῖδες, 43), to forestall that image
of those 'sons dead in the halls' (παίδας ἐνὶ μεγάροις | θανόντας, 41f.). Likewise
to her prayer to Apollo not to 'fulfil' the doom (τελέσσαι, 35) and to her im-
pulsive wish for a 'fulfilment of chill death' (θανάτου τέλος στυγεροῖο, 38) she
opposes a realistic and immediate 'end' or 'fulfilment' (τᾶιδε γὰρ ὑμὶν ἐγὼν τέλος
προφαίνω, 44) that may bring release from this 'evil' (cf. also πρόφαινε, 28 and
προφαίνω, 44). Passion calms to a quieter and more hopeful closure; and yet her
'belief' (δοκέω, 50) that the 'release from evil destiny' may be in accordance
with 'the thoughts of the divine prophet' (52) leaves open the possibility of
tragic self-delusion.

Taken as a whole the passage is remarkable for its combination of great
emotional power and the dignity of traditional epic diction. There is an
emotional vibrancy that goes beyond epic forms. Even better than the speeches
of Geryon in the *Geryoneis*, this text reveals Stesichorus' full mastery of his
technique, handling epic situations and characters with the flexibility and
poignancy of lyric.

The new fragments are particularly interesting for their documentation of the
diverse interests of early sixth-century poets. The epic form of leisurely heroic
narrative continues side-by-side with the monodists' personal and occasional
short poems on contemporary politics or love-affairs. Stesichorus' mythical
narratives remind us that the 'Lyric Age' of Greece was not all bent on self-
expression and the discovery of the individual. Heroic values and epic themes
remain a constant concern. It would probably be wrong to view this continuity
as the conservatism of the provincial west or as a self-conscious opposition to
new developments.[1] Rather, Stesichorus' citharodic narrative points to the
simultaneous coexistence of different literary genres and currents in an age of
great artistic energy and experimentation. It is one of the exciting qualities of
early Greek culture that forms continue to evolve, but the old traditions still
remain strong as points of stability and proud community, unifying but not
suffocating.

Looking ahead from Stesichorus to Simonides, Bacchylides and Pindar, we
can discern many changes: greater departures from epic language, freer and
more complex metrical structures, bolder metaphors, even more emotional
expressiveness, and, so far as the fragmentary state of the evidence allows,
greater artistic self-consciousness on the part of the poet. Yet this distance
between Stesichorus and Bacchylides is, in some ways, less than that between
Homer and Archilochus or between Hesiod and Sappho. The generic similarities
within large-scale choral lyric between 600 and 450 are perhaps greater than

[1] For these questions see Treu (1968*b*) 1256.

the differences. Stesichorus, however, as 'Longinus' perceived, is far more 'Homeric' than any of his three great successors in choral lyric. In this delight in objective narrative for its own sake and (so far, at least) the absence or relative unimportance of reflectiveness on his art, his true successor is Bacchylides.

7

MONODY

Monody or solo song was the product of sixth-century poets living in the Aegean islands. The most remarkable were Sappho and Alcaeus of Lesbos and Anacreon and Ibycus at the court of Polycrates in Samos. The poetry was distinguished by its metre, dialect and subject matter and by the conditions of its performance from elegiac and iambic verse on the one hand and choral lyric on the other. The poets used short stanzas in a variety of metres, and sang the songs to their own accompaniment on the lyre, presumably repeating the melody for each stanza. They composed for the most part in their own dialects, Sappho and Alcaeus in Aeolic,[1] Anacreon in Ionic, whereas the writers of choral lyric used an artificial language distinguished by some characteristic features of the western dialect group. The audience was presumably a small circle of friends who shared the poet's literary or political interests or lived at the court of his patron.

The poetry of Sappho and Alcaeus is the oldest monody to survive, but it had its antecedents in the earlier music and poetry of Lesbos and in the compositions of Archilochus. Seventh-century Lesbos was famous for its musicians Terpander and Arion (see above, p. 168), and although they wrote poetry of different types from Sappho and Alcaeus and gained their fame in other parts of the Greek world, they bear witness to the musical and literary prowess of the island. Archilochus mentions the Lesbian paean (fr. 121 *IEG*), and Sappho calls Lesbian singers superior to those of other lands (fr. 106).[2] Archilochus was influential in a different way: his themes were often amatory, sympotic or political, and his poetry has the intensity and direct forcefulness that mark the work of Sappho and Alcaeus. It is only his metres and musical accompaniment that exclude him from the genre of lyric poetry. Whether it was Sappho or some other who first sang songs in repeated stanzas we cannot say: perhaps earlier examples failed to survive because writing was not yet in common use or because they were inferior to the later poetry.

---

[1] For the dialect of the Lesbian poets see Lobel's introductions (1925, 1927), Page (1955), Gomme (1957), Hamm (1958).

[2] The poems and fragments of Sappho and Alcaeus are numbered by the marginal numeration of *PLF*, which is used as far as possible by Voigt (1971). The text is not invariably that of *PLF*.

I. SAPPHO

Sappho was probably born about 630 in the town of Eresus on the western shore of Lesbos, but seems to have spent most of her life in Mytilene, the principal city of the island. She went to Sicily in exile at some time in the period from 604/3 to 596/5, and so it is likely that her family or her husband's family was involved in the political life of Lesbos; in fr. 71 she appears to speak with hostility of the noble family of Penthilus into which the statesman Pittacus married. She may refer to her own old age in fr. 58, and Rhodopis, the courtesan with whom her brother Charaxus became entangled, was said to have flourished in the reign of Amasis of Egypt, who came to the throne in 568. The Suda says that her husband, Cercylas, was a wealthy trader from Andros, but it has been thought that his odd name and his provenance are due to some comic writer.[1] She certainly had a daughter, of whom she speaks with affection in her poetry.

Love was her main theme, and she often expressed strong homosexual feelings. Her audience must usually have been her circle of women and girls: in fr. 160, where she says, 'I shall now sing these songs beautifully to delight my companions', the term for 'companions' indicates that they are female. She may have taught her poetic and musical skills to members of her group: the Suda lists three 'pupils', all from overseas, and a commentator on her poetry (s261A *SLG*) says that she educated the best of the local girls and also of those from Ionia; her reference to 'the house of those who serve the Muses' (fr. 150) suggests some kind of literary association, however informal. Her friends were singers, and we hear of rival groups. Only a small amount of her work seems to have been intended for a wider audience: her epithalamia (frs. 27, 30, 103–17, perhaps 44) must have been written for actual weddings and fr. 140a for the worship of Adonis. Some Alexandrian scholar allocated her collected poems to nine books on metrical principles, Book 9 containing epithalamia which were excluded by their metre from other books. Book 1 alone had 1,320 lines, i.e. 330 Sapphic stanzas, perhaps 60–70 poems, but Book 8 was only one-tenth as long. Only one complete poem, her prayer to Aphrodite, survives, but we have substantial parts of a dozen others.

The complete poem (1) is preserved in the text of Dionysius of Halicarnassus (*De comp. verb.* 173–9) as an example of the 'polished and exuberant' style:

ποικιλόθρον᾽ ἀθανάτ᾽Ἀφρόδιτα,
παῖ Δίος δολόπλοκε, λίσσομαί σε,
μή μ᾽ ἄσαισι μηδ᾽ ὀνίαισι δάμνα,
πότνια, θῦμον,

---

[1] Six comedies called *Sappho* are known, the earliest by Ameipsias, the latest by Diphilus; two plays called *Phaon* and five *The Leucadian* may also have dealt with her.

ἀλλὰ τυίδ' ἔλθ', αἴ ποτα κἀτέρωτα   5
τὰς ἔμας αὔδας ἀίοισα πήλοι
ἔκλυες, πάτρος δὲ δόμον λίποισα
χρύσιον ἦλθες
ἄρμ' ὐπασδεύξαισα· κάλοι δέ σ' ἆγον   10
ὤκεες στροῦθοι περὶ γᾶς μελαίνας
πύκνα δίννεντες πτέρ' ἀπ' ὠράνω αἴθε-
ρος διὰ μέσσω,
αἶψα δ' ἐξίκοντο· σὺ δ', ὦ μάκαιρα,
μειδιαίσαισ' ἀθανάτωι προσώπωι
ἦρε' ὄττι δηὖτε πέπονθα κὤττι   15
δηὖτε κάλημμι,
κὤττι μοι μάλιστα θέλω γένεσθαι
μαινόλαι θύμωι· 'τίνα δηὖτε πείθω
ἄψ σ' ἄγην ἐς Ϝὰν φιλότατα; τίς σ', ὦ
Ψάπφ', ἀδίκησι;   20
καὶ γὰρ αἰ φεύγει, ταχέως διώξει·
αἰ δὲ δῶρα μὴ δέκετ', ἀλλὰ δώσει·
αἰ δὲ μὴ φίλει, ταχέως φιλήσει
κωὐκ ἐθέλοισα.'
ἔλθε μοι καὶ νῦν, χαλέπαν δὲ λῦσον   25
ἐκ μερίμναν, ὄσσα δέ μοι τέλεσσαι
θῦμος ἰμέρρει, τέλεσον· σὺ δ' αὔτα
σύμμαχος ἔσσο.

Ornate-throned immortal Aphrodite, wile-weaving daughter of Zeus, I entreat you: do not overpower my heart, mistress, with ache and anguish, but come here, if ever in the past you heard my voice from afar and acquiesced and came, leaving your father's golden house, with chariot yoked: beautiful swift sparrows whirring fast-beating wings brought you above the dark earth down from heaven through the mid-air, and soon they arrived; and you, blessed one, with a smile on your immortal face asked what was the matter with me this time and why I was calling this time and what in my maddened heart I most wished to happen for myself: 'Whom am I to persuade this time to lead you back to her love? Who wrongs you, Sappho? If she runs away, soon she shall pursue; if she does not accept gifts, why, she shall give them instead; if she does not love, soon she shall love even against her will.' Come to me now again and deliver me from oppressive anxieties; fulfil all that my heart longs to fulfil, and you yourself be my fellow-fighter.

Dionysius commended the smoothness of the composition: 'Word follows word inwoven according to certain natural affinities and groupings of the letters'. He gave no examples, but we can see that Sappho showed a strong preference for the liquids, *l*, *m* and *n*, and avoided the hard consonant *b* completely, and that she devoted equal care to the vowel sounds, e.g. *a* and *o* in the first stanza. Alliteration is frequent, but obtrusive only in l. 22, where it underlines the antithesis of refusing and giving gifts and emphasizes the finality of Aphrodite's answer, as does the rhyming effect of ll. 21-3.

Sappho's poetic skill can be seen also in her handling of the Sapphic stanza, which seems to have been her favourite. In the sixth stanza, the climax of the poem, Aphrodite's promises are emphasized by the strong stops, by the fact that the stanza is the first to be self-contained, and by the short final line with its crushing κωὔκ ἐθέλοισα 'even against her will'. She exploits the structure of the stanza also at ll. 11-12 to illustrate the swoop of the chariot.

The prayer-form gives a tight structure to the poem: the framework, similar to that of a Homeric prayer, begins, 'I beseech you, come to me, if ever you came before': Sappho describes the previous coming, and finishes in l. 25 with 'Come again now', a clear example of ring-composition. The verbs ἔλθ' (5), ἦλθες (8) and ἔλθε (25) hold the poem together. Sappho's prayer, however, takes some interesting turns: the mention of the previous epiphany of the goddess leads into a leisurely narrative which occupies almost all of the five central stanzas, finishing with the words of Aphrodite, which move from indirect to direct question at l. 18 and to bluntly direct statement at l. 21.

Recent criticism has been concentrated on the tone of Sappho's poem. Page saw it as an expression of 'the vanity and impermanence of her passion', composed in a spirit of self-mockery; in his view, Aphrodite teased Sappho with the inconsistency of her passion and indicated that her suffering would soon pass. But this is not the most obvious interpretation of the poem, and it does not explain the emphasis which is laid throughout on the divinity and power of Aphrodite: everything leads up to her final words, 'even against her will'; Aphrodite is a goddess, child of Zeus, and she will have her way. She did not come to laugh and preach on the mutability of love, but smilingly gave proof of her divinity by helping Sappho.

It is just possible that a second poem (31) is complete: the author of Περὶ ὕψους, *On the sublime*, quotes four stanzas which form a satisfactory whole; but they are followed by six puzzling words which are almost certainly the beginning of a fifth stanza:

φαίνεταί μοι κῆνος ἴσος θέοισιν
ἔμμεν' ὤνηρ, ὄττις ἐνάντιός τοι
ἰσδάνει καὶ πλάσιον ἆδυ φωνεί-
σας ὐπακούει

καὶ γελαίσας ἰμέροεν, τό μ' ἦ μὰν   5
καρδίαν ἐν στήθεσιν ἐπτόαισεν·
ὠς γὰρ ἔς σ' ἴδω βρόχε', ὤς με φώναι-
σ' οὐδὲν ἔτ' εἴκει,

ἀλλὰ †κὰμ† μὲν γλῶσσα †ἔαγε†, λέπτον
δ' αὔτικα χρῶι πῦρ ὐπαδεδρόμηκεν,   10

205

ὀππάτεσσι δ' οὐδ' ἒν ὄρημμ', ἐπιβρό-
μεισι δ' ἄκουαι,
† ἔκαδε† μ' ἴδρως κακχέεται, τρόμος δὲ
παῖσαν ἄγρει, χλωροτέρα δὲ ποίας
ἔμμι, τεθνάκην δ' ὀλίγω 'πιδεύης 15
φαίνομ' ἔμ' αὔται.
ἀλλὰ πὰν τόλματον, ἐπεὶ † καὶ πένητα†

That man seems to me to be the equal of the gods who sits opposite you and close by hears your sweet words and lovely laughter: this, I swear, makes my heart pound in my breast; for when I glance at you for a moment, I can no longer speak, my tongue (is fixed in silence?), a thin flame at once runs under my skin, I see nothing with my eyes, my ears hum, sweat flows down me, trembling seizes me all over, I am paler than grass, and I seem to be not far short of death. But all can be endured, since...

The poem depends for its effect on the list of physical reactions which occupies ll. 9–16: the directness of these two stanzas is in contrast with the greater syntactical complexity of the first two. Sappho uses enjambment freely, and there are scarcely any strong stops in the poem, so that everything leads up to the climax of ll. 15–16, climactic whether or not the poem ended there. She makes little use of imagery, although the expression 'thin fire' and the comparison 'paler than grass' are striking. Again it is Sappho's emotional state that occupies critical attention: Page identified it as jealousy, caused by the sight of a man, 'fortunate as the gods', enjoying the company of a girl she loves; according to others, Sappho is contrasting the reactions of the man, 'strong as the gods', with her own lack of self-control.

Two stanzas of an incomplete poem (16) found on papyrus are among the finest examples of Sappho's composition. She begins with a priamel, in which she lists the views of others only to reject them for her own:

οἱ μὲν ἰππήων στρότον, οἱ δὲ πέσδων,
οἱ δὲ νάων φαῖσ' ἐπὶ γᾶν μέλαιναν
ἔμμεναι κάλλιστον, ἔγω δὲ κῆν' ὄτ-
τω τις ἔραται.

Some say that a host of cavalrymen is the fairest thing on the black earth, some a host of infantry, others of ships: I say it is what one loves.

In the space of one stanza she sets out the contrast between three other views and her own, and she unerringly positions the word ἔραται 'loves' at the end. After the bravado of this opening she reduces the intensity with the leisurely introduction of her proof: Helen, she says, was the most beautiful of women, but she left husband, daughter and parents for Paris. The intensity returns when she speaks of the absent Anactoria, of whom she has been reminded by the story of Helen:

τᾶ]ς κε βολλοίμαν ἔρατόν τε βᾶμα
κἀμάρυχμα λάμπρον ἴδην προσώπω
ἦ τὰ Λύδων ἄρματα κἀν ὅπλοισι
πεσδομ]άχεντας.   20

Her lovely walk and the bright sparkle of her face I would rather see than those
chariots of the Lydians and infantry in armour.

The chariots and infantry clearly recall the soldiery of the opening stanza,
and the description of the girl is remarkable for the adjective ἔρατον applied
to her walk – the word has stronger erotic connotations than the English
'lovely' – and for the noun ἀμάρυχμα, a rare, melodious word used of flashing
eyes.

Two poems are concerned with absent friends. In one (94) Sappho reminds
the departed girl of their happy times together, and recalls garlands of violets
and roses, perfume, shrines, groves, and soft couches. In the other (96) she
uses the Homeric technique of expanded simile:

...(she thought) you like a goddess manifest, and in your song she took most
pleasure. Now she shines among Lydian women, as the rose-fingered moon
surpassing all the stars when the sun has set: it extends its light over salt sea and
flowery fields alike, dew is spread in beauty, roses flourish and delicate chervil
and blossoming clover. Often as she goes to and fro, remembering gentle Atthis
with longing, her tender heart is consumed...

Loneliness is the theme of four famous lines (976 *PMG*), the authorship of
which has been called in question by Lobel and Page among others:

δέδυκε μὲν ἀ σελάννα
καὶ Πληΐαδες· μέσαι δὲ
νύκτες, παρὰ δ' ἔρχετ' ὤρα,
ἔγω δὲ μόνα κατεύδω.

The moon has set and the Pleiads; it is midnight; time passes by; and I sleep
alone.

The lines are effective for the graceful rhythm, the simple paratactic structure,
similar to that of the first stanza of fr. 16, the enjambment at the end of the
second line, and above all the directness of the statement.

Writers like Pausanias and Himerius who knew all her work confirm the
impression created by the fragments that most of it was love poetry. Sometimes no more than a brief image survives in the debris: 'Love shook my heart,
like the wind falling on oaks on a mountain' (47), or 'Once again Love, the
loosener of limbs, shakes me, that sweet-bitter, irresistible creature' (130).
There are traditional elements here, for example, the epithet λυσιμέλης 'loosener
of limbs', but γλυκύπικρον 'sweet-bitter' is astonishing, particularly when

applied to ὄρπετον, a 'creature' or even a 'monster'. A substantial fragment (2) takes the form of an invitation to Aphrodite to visit a shrine:

> ...Come hither, I pray, from Crete to this holy temple, where your lovely apple orchard is, and altars smoking with frankincense. In it cold water gurgles through the apple branches, the place is all shadowy with roses, and from the quivering leaves sleep comes down. In it a meadow where horses graze blossoms with spring flowers, and the breezes blow sweetly... There, Cyprian goddess, take... and in gold cups gracefully pour nectar that mingles with our festivity...

In this poem as in others Sappho lingers over detail and in some of her most melodious lines creates a dream-like picture of an earthly paradise. The imagery of apples, flowers, gardens and horses is strongly erotic, and all the senses are involved, sight, smell, touch, hearing, even taste in the mention of nectar.

Domestic themes of various kinds are found in the fragments. She says of her daughter in 132, 'I have a beautiful child who looks like golden flowers, my darling Cleis, for whom I would not (take) all Lydia or lovely ...' Her brother distressed her by paying a large sum of money to buy the freedom of a famous courtesan of Naucratis: Herodotus (2.134–5) says that Sappho ridiculed him in one of her poems, but we also have parts of a poem (5) in which she prays for his safety and well-being.

The scraps of epithalamia which have survived vary greatly in tone. Some are strongly lyrical, for example, the address to Hesperus (104a), or the comparison of the bride to the hyacinth, trodden underfoot by shepherds (105c), or to an apple (105a):

> οἶον τὸ γλυκύμαλον ἐρεύθεται ἄκρωι ἐπ᾽ ὕσδωι,
> ἄκρον ἐπ᾽ ἀκροτάτωι, λελάθοντο δὲ μαλοδρόπηες·
> οὐ μὰν ἐκλελάθοντ᾽, ἀλλ᾽ οὐκ ἐδύναντ᾽ ἐπίκεσθαι.

As the sweet-apple reddens on the bough-top, on the top of the topmost bough; the apple-gatherers have forgotten it – no, not forgotten it: they could not reach it.

The boisterous comedy and lyric metre of 110a are in sharp contrast: 'The door-keeper's feet are seven fathoms long, and his sandals are made from five ox-hides; ten cobblers worked hard to make them.' The humour of 111 is similar: 'On high raise up – Hymenaeus! — the roof, you carpenters – Hymenaeus! The bridegroom is coming, the equal of Ares, much larger than a large man.' Sappho may be mocking the convention that the bridegroom is of epic build: elsewhere she compares him to Achilles. At any rate the fondness for comparison is well attested: bridegrooms are likened to slender saplings or prize-winning horses, brides to roses. One long papyrus fragment (44)

ALCAEUS

describes with lively detail Hector's return to Troy with his bride, Andromache, and it may well have been performed at a real wedding.

A few passages refer to her literary skill and to her confidence that it will bring her immortality, and in 55 she speaks harshly of a woman who has no such skill:

κατθάνοισα δὲ κείσηι οὐδέ ποτα μναμοσύνα σέθεν
ἔσσετ' οὐδὲ πόθα εἰς ὕστερον· οὐ γὰρ πεδέχηις βρόδων
τὼν ἐκ Πιερίας, ἀλλ' ἀφάνης κἀν Ἀίδα δόμωι
φοιτάσηις πεδ' ἀμαύρων νεκύων ἐκπεποταμένα.

But when you die you will lie there, and afterwards there will never be any recollection of you or any longing for you, since you have no share in the roses of Pieria; unseen in the house of Hades also, flown from our midst, you will go to and fro among the shadowy corpses.

2. ALCAEUS

Dionysius of Halicarnassus, commenting on the style of Alcaeus, says that often if one removed the metre one would find political rhetoric (*Imit.* 422), and Horace, looking for a single epithet for Alcaeus' songs, called them *minaces* 'threatening' (*Odes* 4.9.7). The turbulent politics of Lesbos were the immediate source of inspiration for perhaps half of his surviving poetry. A full generation before his birth the ruling aristocratic family, the Penthilidae, who traced their ancestry through Penthilus to Orestes and Agamemnon, were overthrown, and the tyrants who succeeded them, Melanchrus, Myrsilus and Pittacus, are all mentioned in the fragments of Alcaeus' poems.[1] He himself belonged to a noble family which competed unsuccessfully for political power in Mytilene; he was exiled three times, and was finally forgiven by Pittacus. The date of his birth was *c.* 620 B.C., perhaps as early as 630, and his reference to his 'grey chest' (50) suggests that he did not die young.

One of the longest surviving passages of his poetry (129) gives an idea of the forceful style attested by ancient critics: Alcaeus, in exile somewhere on Lesbos, appeals to Zeus, Hera and Dionysus for help:

ἄγιτ' εὔνοον
θῦμον σκέθοντες ἀμμετέρας ἄρας   10
ἀκούσατ', ἐκ δὲ τῶνδε μόχθων
ἀργαλέας τε φύγας ῥ[ύεσθε·
τὸν Ὕρραον δὲ παῖδα πεδελθέτω
κήνων Ἐ[ρίννυ]ς ὥς ποτ' ἀπώμνυμεν
τόμοντες[15
μηδάμα μηδ' ἔνα τὼν ἑταίρων
ἀλλ' ἢ θάνοντες γᾶν ἐπιέμμενοι
κείσεσθ' ὑπ' ἄνδρων οἳ τότ' ἐπικ[άν]ην

[1] For the politics of Lesbos see Page (1955) 149–243, Andrewes (1956) 92–9.

209

ἤπειτα κακκτάνοντες αὔτοις
δᾶμον ὑπὲξ ἀχέων ῥύεσθαι.   20
κήνων ὁ φύσγων οὐ διελέξατο
πρὸς θῦμον ἀλλὰ βραϊδίως πόσιν
ἔμβαις ἐπ' ὀρκίοισι δάπτει
τὰν πόλιν ἄμμι...

Come, with gracious spirit hear our prayer, and rescue us from these hardships and from grievous exile; and let their Avenger pursue the son of Hyrrhas, since once we swore, cutting (a lamb's throat?), never (to abandon?) any of our comrades, but either to die at the hands of men who came against us then and to lie clothed in earth, or else to kill them and rescue the people from their woes. But Pot-belly did not talk to their hearts; he recklessly trampled the oaths underfoot and devours our city...

Not all of the detail is clear, but it seems that Pittacus, 'son of Hyrrhas', had conspired with Alcaeus and others against Myrsilus and had defected from the alliance. Alcaeus' abuse of him is written with a sure touch: the alternatives of death and victory are neatly set out, two lines to each, in ll. 17–20, and the expressions 'clothed in earth', 'trampled the oaths underfoot', and 'devours our city', are effective. 'Pot-belly' is only one of several opprobrious epithets he applied to Pittacus: Diogenes Laertius lists also σαράπους and σάραπος 'splay-footed', χειροπόδης 'with chapped feet', γαύρηξ 'boaster', γάστρων 'big-belly', ζοφοδορπίδας 'diner in the dark' and ἀγάσυρτος 'filthy'.

The allegory of the storm-tossed ship of state is found in two fragments: in one (6) Alcaeus speaks of waves pouring into the ship, and appeals to his fellows to shore up the ship's sides and race for a secure harbour. Then, moving from allegory to reality, he tells them to avoid soft fear, remember previous hardship, show steadfastness and not disgrace their ancestors by cowardice. Three stanzas later the word μοναρχίαν 'monarchy' appears in the text and a marginal comment refers to Myrsilus. There is little doubt that Heraclitus, the Homeric scholar who quotes the opening lines as an example of allegory, was correct in his interpretation.

Heraclitus quotes the other piece (326) for the same purpose, declaring that in spite of appearances the poem is about Myrsilus and his tyrannical conspiracy against the Mytileneans:

ἀσυννέτημμι τὼν ἀνέμων στάσιν·
τὸ μὲν γὰρ ἔνθεν κῦμα κυλίνδεται,
τὸ δ' ἔνθεν, ἄμμες δ' ὂν τὸ μέσσον
νᾶϊ φορήμμεθα σὺν μελαίναι
χείμωνι μόχθεντες μεγάλωι μάλα·   5
πὲρ μὲν γὰρ ἄντλος ἰστοπέδαν ἔχει,
λαῖφος δὲ πὰν ζάδηλον ἤδη,
καὶ λάκιδες μέγαλαι κὰτ αὖτο,
χόλαισι δ' ἄγκυρραι...

I fail to understand the direction of the winds: one wave rolls in from this side, another from that, and we in the middle are carried along in company with our black ship, much distressed in the great storm. The bilge-water covers the masthold; all the sail lets the light through now, and there are great rents in it; the anchors are slackening...

The lines show Alcaeus' craftsmanship at its finest: he begins the poem, as often, with a verb, an unfamiliar one here and impressively long; the word στάσις fits both the storm description and the political allegory, since it can denote either the set of the winds or civil strife. Alcaeus makes cunning use use of the Alcaic stanza in ll. 3–4, where the jerky rhythm of the third line is followed by the rapid movement of the fourth in illustration of the head-long rush of the ship. Assonance in l. 1 and alliteration in ll. 2 and 5 are effective, and the paratactic construction makes for great clarity.

In another long political poem (298 Voigt, s262 *SLG*) Alcaeus devotes several stanzas to the myth of Locrian Ajax, who raped Cassandra in Athena's temple when the Greeks captured Troy. Alcaeus appears to tie the myth to contemporary affairs in his introduction: '... we must put (a noose?) on their necks and (kill them) by stoning. It would have been far better for the Achaeans if they had killed the man who did violence to the gods.' After devoting some nine stanzas to his account of the crime of Ajax, Alcaeus reverts to the politics of his own day with a mention of Pittacus: presumably it was he and his associates who, like Ajax, ought to have been stoned for their crimes.

The symposium must have provided the occasion for these poems, and wine is the theme of many of the surviving fragments. Athenaeus, who quotes most of our convivial pieces, comments that Alcaeus is found drinking in all seasons and circumstances. One scrap (367) mentions springtime: 'I heard the flowery spring coming ... mix a bowl of the honey-sweet wine as fast as you can.' The heat of the dogdays is given as the excuse for drinking in several poems, in one of which (347) Alcaeus recasts lines of Hesiod (*W.D.* 582–8) in lyric metre and Lesbian dialect: the detail is Hesiod's except for the opening flourish, which may be a popular turn of phrase or a colourful invention:

τέγγε πλεύμονας οἴνωι, τὸ γὰρ ἄστρον περιτέλλεται,
ἀ δ' ὤρα χαλέπα, πάντα δὲ δίψαισ' ὑπὰ καύματος.

Wet your lungs with wine: the dogstar is coming round, the season is harsh, everything thirsts under the heat.

A winter poem (338) may have provided inspiration for Horace's Soracte ode (1.9):

ὖει μὲν ὁ Ζεῦς, ἐκ δ' ὀράνω μέγας
χείμων, πεπάγαισιν δ' ὑδάτων ῤόαι...
κάββαλλε τὸν χείμων', ἐπὶ μὲν τίθεις

πῦρ, ἐν δὲ κέρναις οἶνον ἀφειδέως
μέλιχρον, αὐτὰρ ἀμφὶ κόρσαι
μόλθακον ἀμφιβάλων γνόφαλλον.   (3–8)

Zeus sends down the rain, a great storm comes from the heavens, flowing streams are frozen solid... Down with the storm! Stoke up the fire, mix the sweet wine without sparing it, and put a soft pillow about your head.

The short phrases, the placing of the verbs at the beginning of the clauses, the paratactic structure and the skilful handling of the metre are all typical features of Alcaeus. They may be seen also in the following vigorous exhortation (346):

πώνωμεν· τί τὰ λύχν' ὀμμένομεν; δάκτυλος ἀμέρα.
κὰδ δάερρε κυλίχναις μεγάλαις, ἄϊτα, ποικίλαις·
οἶνον γὰρ Σεμέλας καὶ Δίος υἶος λαθικάδεον
ἀνθρώποισιν ἔδωκ'. ἔγχεε κέρναις ἔνα καὶ δύο
πλήαις κὰκ κεφάλας, ἀ δ' ἀτέρα τὰν ἀτέραν κύλιξ
ὠθήτω...

Let's drink! Why do we wait for the lamps? A finger's breadth of daylight is all that remains. Take down the great decorated cups, my friend; for the son of Zeus and Semele gave man wine to make them forget their worries. Pour it in brim-full, mixing one part of water to two of wine, and let one cup elbow the next...

The first line is remarkable for containing an exhortation, a rhetorical question and a statement of justification. We cannot say whether the striking phrase δάκτυλος ἀμέρα 'a finger's breadth of daylight' was a commonplace or an invention of Alcaeus: it was certainly proverbial after his time. The jostling of the cups is another happy idea, and Alcaeus exploits the Asclepiad rhythm for an amusing effect in ἀ δ' ἀτέρα τὰν ἀτέραν.

As in the political songs, myth can be pressed into service in a convivial context: Alcaeus exhorts a companion, Melanippus, to drink on the grounds that we have only one life to enjoy, and he makes his point by alluding to the story of Sisyphus, who cheated Death into releasing him from the underworld but had to return and undergo punishment; such exploits are not for us, he says, and we must make the most of our youth (38A).

We have considerable knowledge of some of the hymns written by Alcaeus, and it is clear that the loss of the originals is one of the saddest in the field of Greek lyric poetry. The Homeric Hymns, at least some of which belong roughly to the same period as Alcaeus, are similar in that they record the attributes and exploits of individual gods and were intended as entertainment for a secular audience rather than as religious cult-hymns. The longest Homeric Hymns, however, run to several hundred lines and use epic metre and technique, whereas Alcaeus wrote short songs in the same metres and dialect as

ALCAEUS

his other poetry. We can gain some impression of their form and scale from a poem such as Horace's hymn to Mercury (*Odes* 1.10), based according to the commentator Porphyrio on Alcaeus' hymn to Hermes (308), and from a few references in ancient writers. The opening of the Hermes hymn survives:

χαῖρε, Κυλλάνας ὁ μέδεις, σὲ γάρ μοι
θῦμος ὕμνην, τὸν κορύφαισ' ἐν αὔταις
Μαῖα γέννατο Κρονίδαι μίγεισα
παμβασίληϊ.

Greetings, ruler of Cyllene – for it is of you that I wish to sing, you whom Maia bore on the very mountain-tops, having lain with Cronos' son, the king of all.

There are resemblances here to the opening of the *Homeric Hymn to Hermes*, but these are probably due simply to the genre, and in any case we cannot say which poem is the earlier. Alcaeus uses the short fourth line of the Sapphic stanza to stress the majesty of Hermes' paternity. He seems to have continued with references to the midwifery of the Graces and the nursing of the Horae, material which is not in the Homeric hymn. Pausanias tells us that Alcaeus described Hermes' theft of the cattle of Apollo, and Porphyrio adds that in the poem Hermes capped this by stealing Apollo's quiver. The poem may have comprised no more than Horace's five stanzas.

The hymn to Apollo (307) was given pride of place by the Alexandrian editor, who made it the first poem of Book 1. Alcaeus used his favourite Alcaic stanza: ὦναξ Ἄπολλον, παῖ μεγάλω Δίος 'Lord Apollo, son of great Zeus'. Scarcely anything else survives of the text, but the sophist Himerius gives a paraphrase of the contents: Zeus equipped his son with golden headband, lyre and swan-drawn chariot and sent him to Delphi to declare justice to the Greeks; but Apollo went instead to the land of the Hyperboreans and spent a year there before going to Delphi. Himerius describes Alcaeus' account of the god's arrival as follows: 'what with the blaze of summer and the presence of Apollo the poet's lyre also adopts a summer wantonness . . .: nightingales sing for him the sort of song that one might expect birds to sing in Alcaeus, swallows too and cicadas, not proclaiming their own fortunes in the world but telling of the god in all their songs. Castalia flows in poetic fashion with waters of silver, and Cephisus rises in flood . . .' This hymn too, which need not have been longer than seven stanzas, differs fundamentally from the Homeric Hymn in its account of Apollo's coming to Delphi.

The love songs of Alcaeus are lost, but Horace tells us (*Odes* 1.32.9–12) that among the themes of his poetry were 'Venus and the boy who ever clings to her, and Lycus, handsome with his black eyes and black hair'. He was thus one of the first poets to sing of male homosexual love. A tantalizing fragment

213

(10B) formed the opening of a poem in which a girl speaks of her misery: ἔμε δείλαν, ἔμε παίσαν κακοτάτων πεδέχοισαν 'Wretched me, who share in all ills!' If Horace's poem in the same rare Ionic rhythm (*Odes* 3.12) was based on it, the girl's miseries were the tortures of love.

The political faction or *hetaireia* must have provided the audience for Alcaeus' poetry: it seems likely that he sang his verses to his friends and allies at the symposium at the end of the day. The political poems with their personal invective are obviously at home in these surroundings: a famous one, echoed by Horace, begins, 'Now we must get drunk and drink with all our strength, since Myrsilus has died' (332). Alcaeus' emphasis on friendship (71), broken promises (67, 129, 306 fr. 9) and deceit (68, 69) suggests a circle in which loyalty was all-important. The Ajax-fragment indicates that even poems with considerable mythological content may have been essentially political. The drinking itself was not only a means of forgetting military setbacks, betrayals or the hardships of exile (73, 335): it was seen as an opportunity to test a man's true feelings, and fragments such as 'wine, dear boy, and truth' (366) and 'wine is a peep-hole into a man' (333) should be seen in this context. The love-poetry also belongs here: 'if I am to enjoy the symposium, I request that charming Menon be invited' (368). We can add that his companions must have shared his enthusiasm for poetry, since the very existence of hundreds of elaborate short poems and hymns is evidence for a willing and informed audience.

3. IBYCUS[1]

Ibycus belonged like Stesichorus to Magna Graecia: he was born at Rhegium and was buried there, but he left the west for the court of Polycrates, tyrant of Samos from *c.* 533 to *c.* 522. It is not certain that he wrote monody. He is known to have composed narrative poems on the same themes and in the same manner as Stesichorus, and the long papyrus fragment which is ascribed to him (282a) has the triadic structure of choral poetry. But the strongly personal and erotic nature of the best-known fragments (286, 287) and the fact that Ibycus' colleague in Samos was Anacreon, most of whose work is monodic, leave room for the possibility that some of his work was for solo performance.

Fr. 286 may be regarded as an elaboration of Sappho's comparison of love to a gale-force wind:

ἦρι μὲν αἵ τε Κυδώνιαι
μαλίδες ἀρδόμεναι ῥοᾶν
ἐκ ποταμῶν, ἵνα Παρθένων
κᾶπος ἀκήρατος, αἵ τ' οἰνανθίδες
αὐξόμεναι σκιεροῖσιν ὑφ' ἔρνεσιν   5

---

[1] The poems and fragments of Ibycus and Anacreon are numbered by the marginal numeration of *PMG*, but the text sometimes differs.

οἰναρέοις θαλέθοισιν, ἐμοὶ δ' ἔρος
  οὐδεμίαν κατάκοιτος ὥραν.
†τε† ὑπὸ στεροπᾶς φλέγων
Θρηίκιος βορέας ἀίσ-
σων παρὰ Κύπριδος ἀȝαλέαις μανί-   10
αισιν ἐρεμνὸς ἀθαμβὴς
  ἐγκρατέως πεδόθεν τινάσσει
ἀμετέρας φρένας.

In the spring flourish Cydonian quince-trees, watered from flowing rivers, where stands the inviolate garden of the Maidens, and vine-blossoms growing under the shady vine-branches; but for me Love rests at no season: like the Thracian north wind blazing with lightning, rushing from the Cyprian with parching fits of madness, dark and shameless, he powerfully shakes my heart from the roots.

Ibycus contrasts the seasonal regularity of nature with his ever-present love which knows no seasons, and makes a further contrast between the tranquillity of nature, which he illustrates by the repeated vowel sounds of the first six lines, and the harshness of love's attack. The image of κατάκοιτος is apt: Love 'goes to bed' at no season. In describing the wind of love Ibycus interweaves his epithets: ἐρεμνός 'dark' suggests the clouds carried by the wind, whereas ἀθαμβής 'shameless' belongs rather to a personified Love.

The imagery of fr. 287 is equally striking:

Ἔρος αὖτέ με κυανέοισιν ὑπὸ
βλεφάροις τακέρ' ὄμμασι δερκόμενος
κηλήμασι παντοδαποῖς ἐς ἄπει-
ρα δίκτυα Κύπριδος ἐσβάλλει·   5
ἦ μὰν τρομέω νιν ἐπερχόμενον,
ὥστε φερέȝυγος ἵππος ἀεθλοφόρος ποτὶ γήραι
ἀέκων σὺν ὄχεσφι θοοῖς ἐς ἄμιλλαν ἔβα.

Again Love, looking at me meltingly from under his dark eyelids, hurls me with his manifold enchantments into the boundless nets of the Cyprian. How I fear his onset, as a prize-winning horse still bearing the yoke in his old age goes unwillingly with swift chariot to the race.

The metaphor of the hunt, in which Eros drives the prey into Aphrodite's nets, is smoothly succeeded by the imagery of the racecourse, and there is humour as well as pathos in the picture of the old horse, successful in earlier days but now reluctant to compete. In fr. 288 Ibycus addresses a youth in equally rich language, reminiscent of choral poetry rather than monody:

Εὐρύαλε γλαυκέων Χαρίτων θάλος, ⟨'Ωρᾶν⟩
καλλικόμων μελέδημα, σὲ μὲν Κύπρις
ἅ τ' ἀγανοβλέφαρος Πει-
θὼ ῥοδέοισιν ἐν ἄνθεσι θρέψαν.

Euryalus, offshoot of the blue-eyed Graces, darling of the lovely-haired Horae, the Cyprian and soft-lidded Persuasion nursed you among rose-blossoms.

No other early Greek poet expressed his love with this hymnal elaboration.

The choral poem written for Polycrates (282a) is insipid by comparison. The first 35 lines of the fragment tell of the fall of Troy and list Trojans and Greeks of whom the poet will not or cannot speak; one of the Greek warriors, we are told, rivalled the Trojan Troilus in beauty; and the poem ends in Pindaric manner with the assurance that Polycrates will have undying fame, thanks to the poetic ability and fame of the writer. This puzzling work has been seen as a sample of the poet's wares offered to his potential patron, as a *recusatio* in which he declares his intention of avoiding epic themes in favour of love-poetry, and as simple glorification of Polycrates' son of the same name. Ibycus may have made his purpose clear in the beginning of the poem, now lost.

4. ANACREON

Anacreon was born in the Ionian city of Teos in Asia Minor, and when Harpagus, Cyrus' general, attacked the Greek coastal cities, he sailed with the rest of the Teians to Thrace, where they founded Abdera c. 540 B.C. He is next heard of at the court of Polycrates of Samos, whose tyranny is dated c. 533–522, and after the murder of his patron he was taken to Athens by Hipparchus, son of Pisistratus, who during the tyranny of his brother Hippias was responsible for cultural affairs. Anacreon may have lived on in Athens after Hipparchus' assassination in 514, or he may have gone to Thessaly: epigrams written for the Thessalian ruler Echecratidas and his wife Dyseris are attributed to him (frs. 107, 108 Diehl). If he did visit Thessaly, he must have returned to Athens and may have spent much of his later life there: he is said to have sung the praises of Critias, grandfather of the Athenian politician of that name, and to have enjoyed the poetry of Aeschylus. He may have been born c. 570 and died c. 485: he was said to have lived 85 years.

Most of his poetry was concerned with love and wine: Maximus of Tyre (37.5) summed up its content as 'the hair of Smerdies and Cleobulus, the pipes of Bathyllus and Ionian song', but Cicero (*Tusc. Disp.* 4.71) exaggerates when he says it was all erotic. The symposium must have provided the occasion for its performance; Critias indeed called him συμποσίων ἐρέθισμα 'the excitement of the drinking-party' (Athen. 13.600d). Samian politics appear twice in the fragments, one satirical poem remains and more is attested, and we hear also of choral poetry, although nothing remains except a doubtful fragment of the Maiden-songs.

Anacreon does not write in the rich, sensuous style of Ibycus, but relies for his effect on careful craftsmanship, elegance and wit. These qualities may be seen in his address to a young girl, written in a lilting trochaic rhythm which contributes much to the gaiety (417):

πῶλε Θρηικίη, τί δή με λοξὸν ὄμμασι βλέπουσα
νηλέως φεύγεις, δοκεῖς δέ μ' οὐδὲν εἰδέναι σοφόν;
ἴσθι τοι, καλῶς μὲν ἄν τοι τὸν χαλινὸν ἐμβάλοιμι,
ἡνίας δ' ἔχων στρέφοιμί σ' ἀμφὶ τέρματα δρόμου·
νῦν δὲ λειμῶνάς τε βόσκεαι κοῦφά τε σκιρτῶσα παίζεις·
δεξιὸν γὰρ ἱπποπείρην οὐκ ἔχεις ἐπεμβάτην.

Thracian filly, why do you look at me out of the corner of your eye and run pitilessly from me, and suppose that I have no skill? Let me tell you, I could neatly put a bridle on you and holding the reins turn you round the limits of the course; as it is, you graze the meadows and play, skipping lightly, for you have no clever horseman to ride you.

The imagery is common in Greek poetry and is sometimes used coarsely, as by Aristophanes, sometimes delicately, as here and in Alcman's Maiden-songs. Thracian horses were famous, but if the poem was addressed to a Thracian girl, there would be added point. There is a pleasant touch in the adverb νηλέως 'pitilessly', which belongs to the language of epic and is used with mock-heroic effect.

Another encounter with a girl forms the material for one of Anacreon's wittiest poems, in which much is stated and much suggested in very short space (358):

σφαίρηι δηῦτέ με πορφυρῆι
βάλλων χρυσοκόμης Ἔρως
νήνι ποικιλοσαμβάλωι
    συμπαίζειν προκαλεῖται·
ἡ δ', ἐστὶν γὰρ ἀπ' εὐκτίτου
Λέσβου, τὴν μὲν ἐμὴν κόμην,
λευκὴ γάρ, καταμέμφεται,
    πρὸς δ' ἄλλην τινὰ χάσκει.

Once again golden-haired Eros hits me with a purple ball and challenges me to play with the girl with the fancy shoes; but she, coming as she does from Lesbos with its proud cities, finds fault with my hair, since it is white, and gawps after another girl.

Anacreon sets the scene of this miniature drama in his first stanza: he has fallen in love, this time with a girl distinguished by her elaborate footwear; the description, like 'the Thracian filly', no doubt served to identify her for the audience. The pictorial quality of the stanza is remarkable, each noun being accompanied by a colour-epithet, so that the whiteness of the poet's hair is in contrast. In the second stanza Anacreon misleads his listeners more than once before revealing the truth of the matter: Lesbos is distinguished by an epic adjective εὐκτίτου which draws attention to its fine ancient cities, and the suggestion is that a girl from such a background might consider Anacreon's social status too mean for her; but the reason she actually gives for her rejection is Anacreon's age. The sad truth is reserved for the last line of the poem: the proclivities of Sappho and her friends were not forgotten, and this girl like them comes from Lesbos. She has eyes only for some other girl, and she concentrates, open-mouthed in her single-mindedness, on her.[1] The poem, which began with bright colours and gay imagery, finishes with mutual fault-finding and the harsh hiss of the verb χάσκει.

Love, the ball-player in this poem, has other roles, as boxer (396), dice-player (398), blacksmith (413). In another poem it is not Love but the beloved boy himself who is a charioteer (360):

> ὦ παῖ παρθένιον βλέπων,
> δίζημαί σε, σὺ δ' οὐ κοεῖς,
> οὐκ εἰδὼς ὅτι τῆς ἐμῆς
> ψυχῆς ἡνιοχεύεις.

Boy with the virgin glance, I pursue you, but you pay no attention, not realizing that you hold the reins of my soul.

This short stanza is a fine example of Anacreon's technique: l. 1 is notable for the alliteration, ll. 2–4 for the rhyme and near-rhyme which tighten the structure of the stanza. He creates a neat antithesis in l. 2 by juxtaposing the pronouns σέ, σύ. The stanza moves surely to the impressive epic verb ἡνιοχεύεις with its unexpected metaphor.

One poem (357) takes the form of a prayer to Dionysus, who is asked to advise Cleobulus to accept the singer's love. Dionysus was not the obvious addressee for such a prayer, but Anacreon, like Alcaeus, probably sang his song with a wine-cup before him. There is no sharp distinction between the erotic and the convivial poetry. One imagines the typical setting as an all-male drinking-party given by Polycrates or Hipparchus: the content of Ibycus' poems suggests that Polycrates' court appreciated poems about homosexual love,[2] and Thucydides (6.54.3ff.) tells us that it was homosexual passion that led to the assassination of Hipparchus.

Anacreon and other poets from the second half of the sixth century onwards display two attitudes towards wine-drinking. There is still the straightforward exhortation to unrestrained revelry, but a small group of Anacreon's poems preaches moderation: Scythian-style carousal with clatter and shouting is forbidden in favour of moderate drinking and beautiful hymns (356b); and

---

[1] Most recent studies take ἄλλην τινά to refer to a κόμη other than the hair on Anacreon's head: see Woodbury (1979a) for full bibliography.

[2] Athenaeus, presumably arguing from the content of Anacreon's poems, says (12.540e) that Polycrates was 'passionately devoted to the company of males'; cf. Aelian, V.H. 9.4.

in elegiac couplets, the usual medium for reflective poetry and prescriptive writing, he says (fr. eleg. 2 West):

οὐ φιλέω ὃς κρητῆρι παρὰ πλέωι οἰνοποτάζων
νείκεα καὶ πόλεμον δακρυόεντα λέγει,
ἀλλ᾽ ὅστις Μουσέων τε καὶ ἀγλαὰ δῶρ᾽ Ἀφροδίτης
συμμίσγων ἐρατῆς μνήισκεται εὐφροσύνης.

I don't love the man who while drinking his wine beside the full mixing-bowl talks of quarrels and tearful war, but the man who by mixing the splendid gifts of the Muses and Aphrodite keeps lovely festivity in mind.

Love-song, the poetry for which Anacreon himself was most renowned, is what the civilized drinker should sing, not poetry on epic themes or Alcaeus' songs of violent politics.

When Anacreon does choose a political theme, he writes a hymn in his customary lyric metre (348):

γουνοῦμαί σ᾽, ἐλαφηβόλε,
ξανθὴ παῖ Διός, ἀγρίων
   δέσποιν᾽ Ἄρτεμι θηρῶν,
ἥ κου νῦν ἐπὶ Ληθαίου
δίνηισι θρασυκαρδίων   5
ἀνδρῶν ἐσκατορᾶις πόλιν
χαίρουσ᾽, οὐ γὰρ ἀνημέρους
   ποιμαίνεις πολιήτας.

I beseech you, deer-shooter, fair-haired child of Zeus, Artemis, queen of wild beasts, who now somewhere by the eddies of the Lethaeus look down on a city of bold-hearted men and rejoice, since the citizens whom you shepherd are not untamed.

The poem must have continued with a request that Artemis preserve the people of Magnesia, the city on the river Lethaeus, near which was a temple of Artemis Leucophryene. Anacreon speaks of them as courageous and civilized as a reminder that they are Greeks, citizens of a Greek city (πόλιν . . . πολιήτας), although they are at present under Persian rule and Magnesia is the head-quarters of a Persian satrap. As always, Anacreon writes with a firm touch, making his point by the alliteration of l. 8 and the metaphor of the shepherdess, appropriate for Artemis.

Satirical themes are attested by an isolated line about an effeminate who 'did not marry but got married' (424), and by the lines, possibly a complete poem, on the social upstart Artemon (388), who once wore shabby clothes, had wooden dice in his ears, kept low company and was often in trouble with the law:

νῦν δ᾽ ἐπιβαίνει σατινέων χρύσεα φορέων κατέρματα
παῖς ⟨ὁ⟩ Κύκης καὶ σκιαδίσκην ἐλεφαντίνην φορεῖ
γυναιξὶν αὔτως ⟨ἐμφερής⟩.   (10–12)

> But nowadays the son of Cyce rides in a carriage wearing gold ear-rings, and he carries an ivory parasol exactly like the ladies.

It is not only Artemon's social advancement that is satirized but the effeminacy of his accoutrements.

Solemnity is rare in Anacreon, but in one poem (395) the theme is the finality of death:

πολιοὶ μὲν ἡμὶν ἤδη
κρόταφοι κάρη τε λευκόν,
χαρίεσσα δ' οὐκέτ' ἥβη
πάρα, γηραλέοι δ' ὀδόντες,
γλυκεροῦ δ' οὐκέτι πολλὸς   5
βιότου χρόνος λέλειπται·
διὰ ταῦτ' ἀνασταλύζω
θαμὰ Τάρταρον δεδοικώς·
Ἀίδεω γάρ ἐστι δεινὸς
μυχός, ἀργαλῆ δ' ἐς αὐτὸν   10
κάτοδος· καὶ γὰρ ἑτοῖμον
καταβάντι μὴ ἀναβῆναι.

My temples are already grey and my head is white; graceful youth is no more with me, my teeth are old, and no long span of sweet life remains now. So I often weep in fear of Tartarus: the recess of Hades is grim, and the road down to it grievous; and it is certain that he who goes down does not come up again.

The short clauses and paratactic structure are an effective medium for this catalogue of woes, and the chiasmus of ll. 1–2 and the frequent enjambment prevent any sense of monotony. Word-position is particularly striking in ll. 3 and 5, where the adjectives χαρίεσσα 'graceful' and γλυκεροῦ 'sweet' are immediately cancelled out by the negative οὐκέτι 'no more'. The rare verb ἀνασταλύζω 'I weep' stands impressively at the beginning of the second half of the poem, and the repetition of the prefix κατα- in the last two lines emphasizes the message. Although the thought is gloomy, Anacreon expresses it in his slight, frivolous anacreontic lines, giving what Kirkwood has called 'a somewhat macabre air' to the poem.[1] Here as elsewhere we find the grace in which Anacreon took pride: χαρίεντα μὲν γὰρ ᾄδω, χαρίεντα δ' οἶδα λέξαι 'for I sing graceful songs, and I know how to speak graceful words' (402c).

5. SKOLIA

Some of the drinking-songs of the monodists were current in fifth-century Athens under the title 'skolia'. A fragment from Aristophanes' *Banqueters* (223 K) runs, 'Take one of the skolia of Alcaeus or Anacreon and sing it for me', and in the *Wasps* the ability to sing skolia is represented as the mark of the civilized guest at a drinking-party.

---

[1] Kirkwood (1974) 173.

SKOLIA

Athenaeus preserves a collection of twenty-five 'Attic skolia', most of which must have been composed in Athens in the late sixth or early fifth century. The majority are in four-line stanzas in aeolic rhythm, and they were presumably sung to one or two standard tunes. The best-known have a political content:[1] the austere lament for comrades who died at Leipsydrion (907) clearly belongs to Alcmaeonid circles, whereas the Harmodius-song, known in several versions, may have belonged to factions which refused to give the Alcmaeonids credit for the establishment of democracy (893):

ἐν μύρτου κλαδὶ τὸ ξίφος φορήσω
ὥσπερ Ἁρμόδιος κ' Ἀριστογείτων
ὅτε τὸν τύραννον κτανέτην
ἰσονόμους τ' Ἀθήνας ἐποιησάτην.

I shall carry my sword in a myrtle-branch, as did Harmodius and Aristogeiton when they killed the tyrant and made Athens a city of equal rights.

Loyal friendship, a favourite topic of Alcaeus, is commended in four songs (889, 892, 903, 908), and there are prayers to Athens and to Demeter and Persephone to protect the city (884, 885). The two-line stanzas are more light-hearted in tone (900):

εἴθε λύρα καλὴ γενοίμην ἐλεφαντίνη
καί με καλοὶ παῖδες φέροιεν Διονύσιον ἐς χορόν.

Oh that I might become a handsome ivory lyre, and that handsome boys might carry me to the choir of Dionysus.

Athenaeus says that the skolia might be sung in chorus or in succession round the table or by the best singers present, and he derives the name σκόλια 'crooked songs' from their irregular course among the guests. In Aristophanes' *Wasps* (1222ff.) old Philocleon is asked to 'take up' skolia from his fellow-guests and does so by improvising the second line after being given the first. Whatever their origin, Athenaeus' collection had become traditional, by reason either of their political content or of their high quality as concise lyric utterance.

[1] The skolia are numbered by the marginal numeration of *PMG*.

8

CHORAL LYRIC IN THE FIFTH CENTURY

I. INTRODUCTION

The development of monodic lyric in the sixth century toward greater variety, expressiveness and flexibility in poets like Sappho, Alcaeus, Ibycus and Anacreon cannot be documented for choral lyric. Whether because of historical accident, the popularity of monody, or an actual decline in the genre, very little choral poetry is preserved between Stesichorus and Simonides. We have a few lines of Lasus of Hermione (702–6 *PMG*), who is said to have introduced dithyrambic competitions into Athens under Pisistratus and competed against Simonides (cf. Aristophanes, *Wasps* 1410f.).[1] He also wrote an asigmatic poem, *Centaurs* (704 *PMG*), and a poem on the death of the children of Niobe (706 *PMG*). A paean by one Tynnichus of Chalcis, perhaps in the sixth century, won the admiration of both Aeschylus and Plato (*Ion* 534d, 707 *PMG*), but only a small phrase survives.

Certainly the religious and social occasions for choral poetry did not diminish. On the contrary, musical performances and competitions continued to hold an important place in the cultural life of sixth- and fifth-century Greece, both at public festivals, whether local or Panhellenic, and at the courts and houses of individual tyrants and nobles, an important source of patronage for travelling poets. Hymns, paeans, dithyrambs and partheneia continued to be performed at religious celebrations, while enkomia, dirges, marriage-songs and victory-odes were commissioned by rulers or nobles for private festivities. Many of these latter, as we shall see in the case of Pindar, would be public in nature, a display of munificence affirming the donor's high standing in the community.

Helped by the expansion of the great public festivals like the Athenian Dionysia and Panathenaea in the sixth century and stimulated by the stirring historical events of the early fifth – the rise of the powerful Sicilian tyrant-states, the defeat of the Persians and Carthaginians, the resultant affirmation of the

---

[1] On Lasus of Hermione see *GLP* 318; Else (1965) 73f.; *DTC* 13–15; Privitera (1965) *passim*. For choral lyric generally between Alcman and Simonides see Schmid–Stählin 1. 1, 468f.

Greek polis and its traditions – choral lyric reached a new flowering in the first half of the fifth century in the work of Simonides, Pindar and Bacchylides.

Beside the numerous local festivals for which choral poets like Alcman or Stesichorus composed their songs, the four great international festivals, Olympian, Pythian (at Delphi), Nemean and Isthmian become particularly important for choral lyric in the fifth century. Athletic victories here were celebrated with elaborate care, the glory preserved for all time in an imperishable monument of song. Most of Pindar's victory odes or epinikia, the largest single body of choral lyric extant, celebrate victories at these four festivals. Since Hellenistic times the poems have been divided into four books according to the festival in question (in the citations below *O.* = *Olympian Odes*, *P.* = *Pythian*, *N.* = *Nemean*, *I.* = *Isthmian*). Commissioned by the victor or his family, these odes were performed at the festival or, more commonly, at the celebration in the victor's home city on his triumphant return. If the victor was a ruler, like Hieron of Syracuse, Theron of Acragas, or Arcesilaus of Cyrene, the celebrations could have the status of major state festivals (this seems to have been the case for *Pythian* 1 and possibly *Pythian* 4), and the poet would aim at a grandeur and solemnity appropriate to the occasion. Though choral lyric in this period continues to reflect the religious themes and mood of its beginnings, i.e. song celebrating the gods, there is a more self-conscious interest in literary artistry, the moral seriousness of poetry, and intellectual, political or aesthetic concerns.

2. SIMONIDES

Simonides of Ceos is a good example of how the humanistic spirit of late sixth- and early fifth-century choral lyric operates within its religious frame. His long lifetime (557/6 to 468) witnessed both the flowering of late archaic art and the turbulence and change that led into the classical period. Widely travelled, at home in the courts of tyrants as well as in democratic Athens, commissioned to compose important dedicatory epigrams on the Persian Wars, celebrated for his wisdom in practical affairs as well as for his skill in his art, Simonides is not only a major influence on the poetry of Bacchylides (his nephew) and Pindar, but also has a fair claim to being considered a precursor of the sophistic enlightenment.

No complete poem survives. The most important fragment is part of an ode for Scopas of Thessaly (542).[1] Plato quotes large portions of the poem as a showpiece of Protagoras' interpretative skill (*Protag.* 339a–46d). Because of the nature of the citation and our ignorance of the genre to which it belongs (enkomion and dirge are the likeliest possibilities) there are many uncertainties. The most widely held view (largely supported by the new Oxyrhynchus frag-

[1] For further discussion see Appendix. The fragments of Simonides are numbered by the marginal numeration of *PMG*.

223

ment, 541) is that Simonides is criticizing the traditional definition of the 'good', 'noble', or 'successful' man (*agathos*, *esthlos*). Such 'goodness' or 'nobility' depends upon external achievements and possessions (wealth, honour, prowess in battle) which are too insecure to form a real basis for human excellence. Instead Simonides stresses intention, justice that benefits the city, acknowledgement of the fragility of life:

> I praise and embrace everyone who willingly does nothing base (*aischron*), but with necessity not even the gods fight...A man not too helpless (*apalamnos*) suffices for me, one who knows the justice that benefits the city, a sound and healthy man. I will not lay blame, for the generation of fools is limitless. Everything is noble (*kala*) with which base deeds (*ta aischra*) are not mingled. (542.27–40)

To the heroic absolutes of the aristocratic tradition Simonides opposes a tolerant, flexible ethic which takes fuller account of the tension between inner probity and the uncertainty of fortune. For this reason the poem may have appealed to Protagoras. Pindar too can challenge a patron's values, as in his admonitions to Hieron in *Pythians* 1 and 2. Yet Pindar still identifies with the heroic ethic, whereas Simonides adopts its vocabulary only to analyse and revalue it, as he does in the case of words like *agathos*, *kakos*, *aischros* ('goodly', 'mean', 'shameful'). His sharply antithetical style expresses this same tension between the new and the traditional. We may note the contrast between the Homeric phrasing of 'all of us who enjoy the fruit of the wide-seated earth' (...εὐρυεδέος ὅσοι καρπὸν αἰνύμεθα χθονός) and the almost breezy colloquialism of 'when I find him [*sc.* the faultless man], I'll send you back news' (ἐπὶ δ' ὑμῖν εὑρὼν ἀπαγγελέω, 24–6).

'Sadder than the tears of Simonides' (Catullus 38.8): this proverbial expression reflects the celebrity of Simonides' dirges (*threnoi*) and his power of pathos. Dionysius of Halicarnassus (*De comp. verb.* 26) quotes a twenty-seven line fragment describing Danae adrift with her infant son Perseus (543). Dionysius admires the fluency and unity of the rhythms, but the passage is equally remarkable for its fine contrasts between the wild, dark sea and the sleeping child and between the elaborately described setting (lines 1–12) and the simplicity of Danae's opening words (7–9):

> ὦ τέκος οἷον ἔχω πόνον·
> σὺ δ' ἀωτεῖς, γαλαθηνῷ
> δ' ἤθεϊ κνοώσσεις...

O my child, what suffering I have. But you sleep and drowse like the tender infant you are...

We find a similar pathos in a two-line fragment (perhaps from a dirge) in which the followers of the mythical king Archemorus of Nemea 'wept at the infant child of the violet-crowned (Eurydice) that breathed out its sweet life' (ἰοστεφάνου γλυκεῖαν ἐδάκρυσαν | ψυχὰν ἀποπνέοντα γαλαθηνὸν τέκος, 553). It is this ability to present basic human situations with affecting simplicity and yet with just the right admixture of poetic detail that earned Simonides his great acclaim as a writer of funeral epigrams.

With Simonides the epinician or victory ode comes into its own as a full-fledged literary form, coinciding with the increasing importance of athletic contests in the sixth century. Of Simonides' epinikia, however, only the tiniest scraps remain (including some recent papyrus finds, 511, 519). The pun on the 'shearing' of Krios, 'Ram' (507), and the claim that a victor surpasses even Polydeuces and Heracles suggest a less solemn and less reverent tone than Pindar's.[1] Simonides also composed choral poems on historical subjects relating to the Persian Wars, including the *Battle at Artemisium* (532–5), *Battle at Salamis* (536) and *Dirge for the fallen at Thermopylae* (531); nine lines of the last survive. Some recently published scraps of the Oxyrhynchus papyri provide small additions to our scanty evidence for the *Paeans*. One fragment seems to describe the birth of Artemis and Leto's 'shout as the august birth-pangs weighed her down' (519, fr. 32), a scene with which we can compare two passages in Pindar (*O.* 6.43 and *N.* 1.35).

The extant fragments reveal a rich repertory of mythical subjects, ranging from familiar heroic legends like those of the Argonauts, Theseus, perhaps the sacrifice of Iphigenia (544, 550–1, 608), to the fantastic: Talos guarding Crete (568) or the daughters of Anius who change whatever they touch into wine, olives, and grain (537). We have a few glimpses of what must have been brilliant and moving scenes. 'Longinus' compares Simonides' description of Achilles' ghost at Troy to the finale of the *Oedipus at Colonus* (557); Pindar's description of the Muses singing at Achilles' burial perhaps gives some idea of what such a scene might be (*I.* 8.62–6). There survive some splendid verses describing the birds and fish following the singing Orpheus (567) and a haunting dactylic passage spoken by a deserted woman like Danae (571): ἴσχει δέ με πορφυρέας ἁλὸς ἀμφιταρασσομένας ὀρυμαγδός 'the roar of the heaving sea dashing all around holds me'.

Though Simonides uses the compound adjectives and decorative, colourful epithets that characterize late archaic lyric poetry, he is equally remarkable for his restraint and balance. Ancient critics admired his 'sweetness and elegance' (Cicero, *Nat. deor.* 1.22) and his 'smooth and decorative composition' (Dion. Hal. *De comp. verb.* 230; cf. Quintilian 10.1.64). Beside the sensuous details of passages like 597, 'Dark-blue swallow, glorious messenger of sweet-smelling spring', or the description of the 'halcyon days' (508), there stands the austere gnomic style of the ode on the dead at Thermopylae (531), with its succession

---

[1] See Page (1951*b*) 140–2.

of short antithetical clauses and heavy nouns, its sparsity of adjectives and almost total absence of figurative language. Fragment 521 can illustrate Dionysius' praise of Simonides for his 'choice of words and his accuracy in combining them':

ἄνθρωπος ἐὼν μή ποτε φάσῃς ὅ τι γίνεται αὔριον
μηδ' ἄνδρα ἰδὼν ὄλβιον ὅσσον χρόνον ἔσσεται·
ὠκεῖα γὰρ οὐδὲ τανυπτερύγου μυίας
οὕτως ἁ μετάστασις.

Being human never say what will happen tomorrow nor how long a happy man will remain so. For not even of a long-winged fly is the change so swift.

The only decorative word in the passage is 'long-winged' (τανυπτέρυγος.) Standing out in the otherwise unadorned generalization, it forms a suggestive 'objective correlative' for the fragility of the human condition.

The fifth-century choral poets often reflected on their craft and its significance. Like Pindar, Simonides asserts the power of song over the violent forces of nature (595; cf. Pindar fr. 94b.11–20 Snell). Like Pindar too Simonides quotes and comments on the earlier poetic tradition (542, 564, 579), and he may have defended himself against his younger rival (602; cf. Pindar, O. 9.48–9). Two fragments relating to his art are especially interesting: 'Seeming does violence even to truth' (598) and 'Painting is silent poetry, poetry is painting that speaks' (Plut. De glor. Ath. 3.346f). Following a tradition which can be traced back to Homer, Hesiod and Solon (cf. Odyssey 19.203; Hes. Theog. 27–8, Solon fr. 29 West), Simonides stresses the power of poetic art to create illusion or even falsehood, unlike Pindar who solemnly emphasizes Truth (see below).[1] Simonides was notorious for charging high fees, but his apparently mercenary attitude also reflects a different conception of his art: it is the professional practice of a craft of words, not the inspired gift of the Muses or the gods. In this secularization of his art he may have helped pave the way for the sophistic movement.[2]

3. PINDAR

Pindar is the most brilliant of fifth-century choral poets. He was born near Thebes, probably in 518, received some training in Athens, and wrote an early ode (P. 7) for the Alcmaeonid Megacles in the year of the latter's ostracism (486).[3] The medizing of Thebes in the Persian Wars must have been a strain for one whose sympathies were so strongly with the Greek values of order, discipline

[1] See Detienne (1967) 109ff.; Thayer (1975) 13–19.
[2] See Detienne (1967) 105–19; Gentili (1972) 77f.
[3] P.Oxy. 2438 adds some new details on Pindar's life and helps confirm the date of his death. For a searching critique of the ancient Lives and the biographical data in the scholia see Lefkowitz (1975b) 71–93 and (1978) 460–2.

and valour in battle. According to an anecdote in the *Vita* Thebes fined him a thousand drachmas (ten thousand in Isocrates, *Antid.* 166) for composing a dithyramb for Athens (fr. 76 Snell). A number of passages express his uneasiness in these years (*I.* 5.48ff., *I.* 8.10–16, frs. 109–10 Snell). Possibly these tensions led to his sojourn in Sicily between 476 and 474, where he composed *Olympian* 1 for Hieron of Syracuse and *Olympians* 2 and 3 for Theron of Acragas.

Pindar's work spans a half-century. He wrote his earliest ode (*P.* 10) in 498, his last (*P.* 8) in 446. The most majestic odes date from the two decades 480–460: *O.* 1–3, *O.* 6, 7, 13, *P.* 1–5, *P.* 9, *N.* 1, 9, *I.* 3–5, *I.* 8. Among the later odes *N.* 7 and 8, *I.* 7 (which may not be late), and *P.* 8, are especially impressive. The dates of the epinikia, however, are often uncertain. The scholia leave many undated, and where they do propose a date it is not always reliable.[1]

Although there are many fragments of lost poems,[2] especially the *Paeans*, the epinikia are Pindar's most important work and constitute by far the largest single body of Greek choral poetry to have been read continuously from classical antiquity to the Byzantine era and from the Renaissance to the present day. From Horace to Hölderlin and on to Ezra Pound they have strongly influenced the modern conception of the 'ode' and the high style of poetic inspiration.

For the ancient critics Pindar represented the 'severe' or 'rough' style (αὐστηρὰ ἁρμονία), difficult because of his bold collocations, abrupt transitions, loftiness of thought and expression. Horace compares him to a soaring eagle and a rushing stream (*Odes* 4.2); 'Longinus' likens him to a vast fire (*Subl.* 33.5). Athenaeus speaks of 'the great-voiced Pindar' (13.564c).

Despite the conventional 'programme' which the epinician poet must follow (praise of the victor and his family, his generosity, ancestors, mention of previous victories, friendship and obligation between poet and victor),[3] he has still a wide range of flexibility. He can vary ornamental epithets, invocations, rhythm and metre; he can contract or expand images or myths.

For a hundred and fifty years the major issue of Pindaric scholarship has been the question of the unity of the ode.[4] Of those who believe that the ode has a unity there are essentially two camps: the one side finds unity in content, a unifying thought or idea (*Grundgedanke*) or a single pervasive image; the other finds it in external criteria. The latter approach has come to the fore recently in the work of Bundy and Thummer, who have concerned themselves with the formal conventions governing the movement of the ode.[5] But if unity of

[1] See Fränkel (1961) 385–97; Lefkowitz (1975a) 173–85.
[2] Fragments are cited from Snell and Maehler (1975). There is a useful discussion of the new papyrus fragments in Lesky 177–208 and in Griffith (1968) 65–82.
[3] This aspect of the Pindaric ode has been studied by Schadewaldt (1928); see also Hamilton (1974), esp. 3–25.
[4] See Young (1964) for an excellent survey of the question, also Köhnken (1971) 1–18, 227–32.
[5] Bundy (1962); Thummer (1968–9); Hamilton (1974).

'thought' or 'idea' is too abstract and conceptual, the formulaic approach of Bundy is too rigid. The Pindaric epinikion is more than a carefully structured sequence of encomiastic motifs. Although it clearly utilizes formulaic sequences and traditional themes and expressions, its unity is organic rather than mechanical. The progression of thought and meaning in an ode depends not merely on the 'horizontal' linear unfolding of certain programmatic topics, but also on a 'vertical' metaphorical association of images and symbols and a parallelism between metaphor and actuality, myth and historical present.

While Norwood's view that each ode is given its unity by a single symbol is too narrow and often rather arbitrary,[1] Pindar does seem to weave myth and imagery together more or less densely in different odes, developing resonances between parallel myths or clusters of related images within an ode. In *Olympian* 1, for example, the parallels and contrasts between Pelops and Tantalus and between Hieron and Pelops, the imagery of light and darkness, eating and starvation, festivity and isolation, upward and downward movement all interlock into a complex pattern which cannot be encompassed in a single 'idea' or 'image', but is nevertheless vital to the poem's structure and movement. The themes of water, gold, light out of darkness in the proem recur in the two mythical narratives of Pelops and Poseidon (26–7, 71–87). The 'brilliance' and 'far-shining glory' of the victor, Hieron, find resonances in Pelops' cult at Olympia (compare 14 and 22–4 with 90–5).

The first *Pythian* provides an especially clear and powerful instance of how parallelism and contrast interlock within a complex unified structure. The extended analysis which is offered here is meant to be exemplary rather than exhaustive.

Written as a kind of coronation hymn for Hieron's foundation of his new city Aetna, *Pythian* 1 moves through a series of ever-expanding analogies between the political order of well-ruled cities, the aesthetic and moral order of dance, music and poetry, the governance of the universe by Olympian Zeus and the physical order of nature. The hymnic invocation to the 'Golden Lyre, rightful and joint possession of Apollo and the violet-tressed Muses' (1–2), establishes a parallelism between the music and dance of the present moment, 'the step which begins the festive brilliance' (2), and the music of the gods on Olympus. Thus the Muses connected generally with the lyre in 1–2 recur in a more specifically Olympian setting at the end of the antistrophe (13). The lyre which leads the dance among men (1–4) also calms the violence of Zeus's thunder, of the eagle, and of harsh Ares on Olympus (5–13). This symbolical and emblematic statement of the triumph of order over chaos is then developed both in myth and in historical reality, both in local and remote settings. Aetna, mentioned three times in the ode, is simultaneously part of the present festal

[1] See Norwood (1945) chs. 5–7.

context, a manifestation of the divine order in the punishment of the monster Typhon (19b–28), and an expression of political order in Hieron's new foundation (60–6). As the 'heavenly pillar' (κίων οὐρανία, 19b) which confines the monster, the volcano is also the physical link between Tartarus below (cf. 15) and Olympus above. It is thus itself a visible sign of an ordered world: the spatial coherence parallels the moral coherence.

In the large temporal context of historical events this same order finds realization in the Greek victories over Persian, Carthaginian, and Etruscan foes (71–80b), the equivalents on the human and political plane to the monstrous Typhon. They have a closer and more human mythic analogue also in the Greek defeat of the Trojans, alluded to in the myth of the ailing Philoctetes, a paradigm for the unwell Hieron (50–7). Hieron's two great achievements, the founding of Aetna (60) and the defeat of the Etruscans at Cumae (72), assure the political order in complementary ways: the former action, in peace, creates a Greek polis with 'god-built freedom' (61); the latter, in war, preserves Greeks from 'heavy slavery' (75). Aetna and Cumae, therefore, embody the order created by Hieron as king. It is significant that on the mythic plane Aetna and Cumae are also combined in the cosmic order established by Zeus (17–19), the sceptred king of gods and men (cf. 6), in his repression of Typhon, symbol of cosmic disorder. The flaming lava which Aetna hurls into the sea (21–2, 24b) parallels Hieron's hurling the Etruscan youth into the sea at Cumae (74) to check hubris (72). The constraint (cf. συνέχει, 19b) of Typhon whom the volcano 'presses down' (πιέзει, 19), on the other hand, contrasts with the soft rise and fall of Zeus's eagle asleep on Olympus, lulled by the magic of Apollo's lyre (6, 8–9). The slumbering eagle 'raises his liquid back' (ὑγρὸν νῶτον αἰωρεῖ, 9), whereas the monster, 'bound' in the depths of Tartarus beneath Aetna's 'black-leaved summit and plain' has his 'whole back' (ἅπαν νῶτον, 28) scratched and torn by this harsher manifestation of Zeus's order.

The beautiful description of Aetna as 'all-year nurse of sharp snow, from whose depths there belch forth the most holy springs of unapproachable fire' (20–2), not only incorporates the fearful 'wonder' (26) of a volcanic eruption into the framework of Olympian order, but also makes explicit the almost Heraclitean tension of opposites which that order encompasses. Beneath the physical contrasts of earth and sky (cf. 19b), fire and water, heat and cold (20–2), darkness and light (23–4) lies a more complex polarity of force and gentleness. Aetna is the cold snow's 'nurse' (20b), as well as the source of the blazing and smoking lava (22–3). These fiery streams are 'most holy' (21) and are associated with the Olympian Hephaestus (25): that is, they are a manifestation of fire and force in the service of order, not the *uis consili expers* of the monster. Yet in the proem Zeus's fire is something to be 'quenched' by the peaceful harmony of the Golden Lyre (5–6). The Lyre also calms the violence of Zeus's eagle, with his dangerously hooked beak (cf. 8), and charms the heart of 'Ares the violent' (10–11). The Zeus who protects the mountain of Aetna, 'brow of the fair-fruited land' (30), and the Apollo who 'loves Parnassus' Castalian spring' (39b, in contrast to Aetna's 'springs' of fire in 22) exemplify the gentler side of this Olympian order, just as Hieron's foundation of Aetna is the gentler side of the regal and martial force exhibited at Cumae.

The symbolical music of the lyre has these two aspects from the very beginning: its sound calms and enchants (1–13), but is also a 'shout' (*boa*) which can affright those 'whom Zeus holds not in his love' (13). On the plane of historical actuality, the 'harmonious calm' (σύμφωνος ἡσυχία, 70) which the poet invokes for Hieron's son, Deinomenes, ruler of Aetna, contrasts with the war cry and groans of the defeated Etruscans at Cumae (ἀλαλατός, ναυσίστονον, 72). More distantly, but still in history rather than myth, the allusion to the Sicilian tyrant Phalaris, notorious for roasting his victims in a bronze bull (95), may suggest the screams which cruelly simulated the animal's bellowing. In any case Phalaris' 'evil reputation' contrasts with the good name of King Croesus' 'kindly excellence' (93–6). The lyres at festal gatherings refuse honour to Phalaris (97–8). These lyres take us back to the symbolical Golden Lyre of the invocation (φόρμιγξ 1 and φόρμιγγες 97). Here too the present festal occasion becomes transparent to all those occasions for song whose task (*inter alia*) it is to distinguish virtue and evil, celebrate and perpetuate the fame of the noble and condemn the vicious; hence the close parallel between the 'lyres' which do not receive Phalaris and the 'Golden Lyre' which leads the 'festive brilliance' (2) of the present celebration of Hieron (cf. 1–4 and 97–8).

The fire with which the 'pitiless' Phalaris roasted his victims (95) also contrasts with the metaphorical fire which will flash forth from the anvil of Hieron's tongue (86–7) and thus resumes the antithesis between the violent and creative aspects of Zeus and Aetna's fire (5f., 21ff.). Likewise the evil fame which 'holds down' Phalaris (κατέχει, 96) echoes the effect of the Golden Lyre which 'holds down' the eagle in sleep (κατασχόμενος, 10) and the armed might of Hieron which forced the Etruscan war cry to stay at home (κατ' οἶκον...ἔχηι, 72), or, with a different punctuation, 'to keep its violence at home'. In keeping with the importance of harmonious or discordant sound in the ode, 'war cry' is virtually personified.

The relation between Croesus and Phalaris, however, reverses the ode's consistent opposition of Greek and barbarian. Now the oriental monarch is the exemplar of 'kindly excellence', the Greek of cruel despotism. We have also moved, with Phalaris, from gold to bronze (1 and 95). The bronze anvil of Hieron in the metaphor of 86f., therefore, has an ominous resonance in the behaviour of his Sicilian predecessor (95). Pindar may be hinting at the destructive violence inherent in all absolute power, be it Zeus's thunder or Hieron's kingship.

Beginning and ending with music and the importance of a 'good name' (99b; cf. 96–8), Pindar also underlines the fact that poetry too has its power. Its 'enchantments' are also 'arrows' (κῆλα in 12 has both meanings), just as the Muses' song can both calm and terrify (6ff. and 13f.). In a certain sense all of Pindar's odes celebrate the power of poetry as well as the prowess of the victor. The poet who sings the 'due measure' (*kairos*, 81; cf. 57) and joins together the 'limits of many things in small compass' (81f.) holds the balance between potentially dangerous extremes, between destructive and ordering power. He teaches the *kairos* of this force which may be released for good or for ill.

Pythian 1 shows Pindar in his most expansive conception of his poetic role. He moves between present and past, myth and history, Olympus and Tartarus, Greek and barbarian, to reveal the universal paradigms in which the present achievement must take its place in order to be fully meaningful. His lyre, like the king's sceptre or Zeus's thunder, unlocks the hidden analogies between the cosmic, political, moral, and natural order. The poet fashions on earth the 'harmonious calm' (70) which the Golden Lyre creates on Olympus.

In praising the victor the poet is not merely glorifying a particular successful athlete. Through metaphor, gnomic generalization and mythic paradigm the epinikion seeks to link the present victory with the timeless world of myth and to place it within the common realm of values, the *Wertewelt* (to use H. Fränkel's term), of aristocratic society.[1] The 'purpose' of the ode, therefore, transcends its immediate encomiastic function, for it is the poet's task to relate the victory to the ultimate issues of life: change, suffering, the gods, the rhythms of nature, old age and death. The victor exemplifies the highest ideals of discipline, energy, generosity, beauty, grace. His *arete* or excellence is not merely a matter of the competitive virtues or technical skill, but involves the quieter 'cooperative virtues' (Adkins's term[2]) of 'justice', 'restraint', 'lawfulness', 'calm' (*dike, sophrosyne, eunomia, hesychia*). Through disciplined form and creative effort the ode, like the victory itself, enacts man's conquest of 'darkness', chaos and death (cf. *O.* 1.81–4, *N.* 7.11–16, *P.* 8.92–7).

Bundy's study of the formulaic elements in Pindar has had one important consequence. References to envy, danger, silence, and the gnomic formulas which frequently break off the myth and effect a transition to a new topic (*Abbruchsformel*) cannot be read as certain allusions to events in the lives of the victor or the poet. Hence the historical and biographical allegorization of Pindar, which reached its acme in Wilamowitz's *Pindaros* (1922), must be critically re-examined. Pindar often alludes openly to historical events (*P.* 1, *I.* 5, *I.* 8 are the clearest examples) and sometimes to personal experiences (*P.* 8.56–60; *N.* 7 is

---

[1] See Fränkel (1962) 559–67 (488–96 of Engl. tr. 1975).   [2] Adkins (1960).

still a matter of controversy).[1] But we must now be more cautious about finding covert allusions to the waning of Theban power and the advance of Athens in poems like *I.* 7, *N.* 8, *P.* 8.

Grandeur and sublimity are the hallmarks of Pindar's style. He states it almost as a principle of his art to make an impressive beginning (*O.* 6.1–4). Hence he opens his odes with monumental architectural or sculptural imagery (*O.* 6, *P.* 7, *N.* 5) or with a ponderous gnomic statement framed in dynamic antitheses (*O.* 1, *N.* 6) or with a ringing invocation to a place (*O.* 14, *P.* 2, *P.* 12) or a goddess ('Kindly Quietude, daughter of Justice, you who make cities of greatest might and hold the highest keys of councils and of war', *P.* 8).

Though Pindar excels in the rich decorative language and florid compound adjectives of his contemporaries, he is especially effective in his vivid flashes of detail or touches of pathos: the sons of Boreas 'their backs ashiver with purple wings' (*P.* 4.182f.); the tears falling from old Aeson's eyes as he looks upon his long-lost son, now 'handsomest of men' (*P.* 4.120–4); Alcmena leaping nude from her bed of childbirth to save her new-born children from Hera's serpents while Amphitryon brandishes his great sword (*N.* 1.50–2); Bellerophon on Pegasus shooting at the Amazons 'from the cold bosom of the empty aether' (*O.* 13.88). There are wide variations of mood, from the pathos of Polydeuces' grief over his dying brother in *N.* 10 to the sensuousness of Zeus's union with Aegina in *Paean* 6 where 'the mist's golden tresses covered in shadow the spine of the land', or the flamboyant brilliance of the advent of spring in a dithyramb, where, amid the mingling of roses, violets, flutes and dancing, 'at the opening of the chamber of the crimson-robed Seasons the nectarous flowers usher in sweet-smelling spring' (fr. 75 Snell).

Pindar's myths unfold through a few grand, majestic gestures which stand out against a backdrop of large, often symbolical elements: sea, sky, or mountain, darkness or fire. Thus Iamus, like Pelops in *O.* 1, calls to the god in the night from the river (*O.* 6.57–63); fire surrounds Apollo's rescue of the infant Asclepius from his mother's body on the flaming pyre (*P.* 3.36–46); Ajax drives the sword through his breast 'in the late night' (*I.* 4.38–40). Even the massive fourth *Pythian*, which contains Pindar's most expansive, 'Bacchylidean' narrative, jumps back and forth between the various stages of the myth, tells prophecy within prophecy, and emphasizes the vast sweep of time and the succession of generations (cf. 54–65) rather than the single strand of continuous event. Sometimes Pindar pulls back abruptly from a myth which he thinks unworthy of a god or hero, as in the story of the gods eating Pelops (*O.* 1.51f.) or the tale of Phocus' murder by his half-brothers Peleus and Telamon (*N.* 5.9–18). A

---

[1] See Lloyd-Jones (1973) 127–37; Köhnken (1971) 37–86. Woodbury's careful study (1979*b*) of the historical and geographical bases of the Neoptolemus myth tends to support the scholiasts' connexion of *Paean* 6 and *Nemean* 7.

number of odes lack a fully developed myth, and in some a weighty gnome or apophthegm serves as the chief poetical embellishment (e.g. *O.* 11, *N.* 6, *N.* 11).

Pindar's boldness of metaphor rivals that of his contemporary, Aeschylus. Occasionally a violent metaphor is almost a kenning. 'The fruit of olive in fire-scorched earth' carried in 'all-adorned enclosures of vessels' describes the oil-filled amphora won in the Panathenaic games (*N.* 10.35–6); a cloak won as a prize is 'warm medicine against cold breezes' (*O.* 9.97). He does not use such expressions, as a Hellenistic poet might, to demonstrate erudition or to tease the reader with riddling obscurity. Such metaphors, rather, serve to transfigure and exalt everything connected with the victory. Pindar's mixed metaphors have a similar purpose: they intensify the effect of sensuous concreteness and exuber-ance by crossing between different realms of experience. Thus they heighten the festive joy of the occasion and even add a certain playfulness, as in the enkomion for Theoxenus (fr. 123 Snell).

Pindar is the most concrete of poets. Even what we would consider abstrac-tions or psychological processes have a physical tangibility: 'the cloud of forgetfulness' (*O.* 7.45); 'the leaves of strife' (*I.* 8.47); 'the flowers of lawful-ness' (*Paean* 1.10); 'hammer-welded necessities' (fr. 207 Snell). Excellence, *arete*, can 'blossom' like a flower and (within the same ode) 'scale a tower' (or, in another interpretation, 'fortify a tower' *I.* 5.17 and 44f.); honours are 'planted' (τιμαὶ φυτευθέν, *P.* 4.69).

Possibly attacking Simonides' secular conception of his art (see above, p. 226), Pindar protests strongly against the idea that he works for hire (*I.* 2). He is a 'prophet of the Muses' and the servant of Truth, Aletheia, herself the child of Zeus (*O.* 10.3–6, *Paean* 6.6, fr. 205 Snell).[1] Poetry teaches, confers fame and gives pleasure. But poetry for him is not all a matter of honey, garlands, sweet liquids. It has associations also with the mystery of the sea and the violence of wind (*N.* 7.79, fr. 94b.13ff. Snell), with arrows and the javelin (*O.* 2.83–5, *P.* 1.43–5, *N.* 7.71f.), with the eagle who seizes his bloody (or tawny) prey in his claws (*N.* 3.80–2; cf. *N.* 5.21). Song can be a healing, medicinal 'charm' or drug (*N.* 4.1–5), but it is also a dangerous siren luring men to their death (*Paean* 8.70–9). In *Pythian* 12 he traces the origin of flute music to the painful death-wail of Medusa.[2] The 'grace' or 'charm' (*charis*) of song fashions all that brings joy to mortals (*O.* 1.30; cf. *O.* 14.5ff.); yet the shifting play of crafted words can also obscure the truth with meretricious falsehood (*O.* 1.28–9; cf. *N.* 8.25, where we may contrast the 'variegated falsehood' that leads to Ajax' death with the positive significance of Pindar's 'varied art' or *poikilia* in *N.* 8.15). As a 'craft' or 'skill' (*sophia, mechane*), poetry, like any art, can be misused to distort the true worth of men and their achievements. The true poet will use his

---

[1] See Bowra (1964) ch. 1; Davison (1968) 289–311; Svoboda (1952) 108–20.
[2] See Schlesinger (1968) 275–86; Köhnken (1971) 117–53.

art for truth, not for gain or *kerdos*: the latter is a concept which Pindar frequently associates with the wily, dangerous aspects of 'craft' (cf. *N.* 7.14–24, *I.* 2.5–12, *P.* 3.54 and 113–14). The poet's *logos* serves the gods, life, rebirth; over against it stand the envy and calumny which cut off the 'life' or 'bloom' of great achievements or, in mythical terms, bring death to the great Ajax (*N.* 7.23–32, *N.* 8.25–34; contrast *I.* 4.36–46).

In Pindar the Olympian religion of the early classical period finds its full majesty of expression. He studiously portrays the gods as dignified and solemn, maintaining order and suppressing injustice (*O.* 1, *P.* 1–3, *P.* 8), compassionate (*N.* 10) and even forgiving (*O.* 7.45ff.), helpful guardians of civilization and morality. Pindar celebrates Apollo for his omniscience (*P.* 3.27–30, *P.* 9.44–9) and for the art of healing, music and prophecy (*P.* 5.63–9), Athena for inventing the flute (*P.* 12), Heracles for exploring the sea and land (*N.* 3.23–6) and planting trees to shade the Olympian games (*O.* 3). He suppresses or reinterprets myths which show the gods' violence, lust, or meanness (*O.* 1.46ff.; *O.* 9.35–9). The loves of Zeus and Apollo are orderly and lead to the foundation of great cities and families (*O.* 6, *O.* 9, *P.* 9, *Paean* 6).

Yet the gods retain an element of inscrutable force. As the proem of *Nemean* 6 puts it, sheer power, *dynamis*, sets the gods apart from mortals in their remote 'brazen sky'. Anthropomorphic features, like the gods' loves, remain, but are often given a new meaning. Zeus and Poseidon are conquered by lust for Ganymede and Pelops respectively (*O.* 1.40–5), but the passion of Poseidon plays a major role in the foundation of rites at Olympia (*O.* 1.75–96). 'Eros gripped' both Zeus and Poseidon, but they obey the prophecy of 'wise-counselling Themis' (*I.* 8.29–37). Apollo's wrath nearly destroys the innocent along with the guilty, until he reverses his decision and saves the unborn Asclepius (*P.* 3.34–42). 'Golden-throned Hera, queen of the gods' can implement her bitter anger against the infant Heracles (*N.* 1.37–40), but this too is part of Zeus's 'solemn law' (*N.* 1.72).

Though not a religious innovator, Pindar seems to have been impressed by the south Italian belief in the afterlife and the purgation and transmigration of souls. These ideas inspire some of his richest poetry (*O.* 2; frs. 129–34 Snell; cf. fr. 94a). Pindar, however, may here be reflecting the beliefs of his Sicilian patrons rather than his own.[1] The controversy about what Pindar really believed may never be settled, but it is clear that at the least he could respond to such conceptions with deep sympathy.

That sympathy is all the more likely as he seems to have been susceptible to visionary experiences (*Vita Ambrosiana* p. 2.1ff. Drachmann) and incorporated them into his poetry (*P.* 8.56–60, frs. 37 and 95 Snell). More important still is his conviction that the 'Zeus-given gleam' (*P.* 8.96–7) or the 'clear light of the

[1] Good discussion in Bowra (1964) 92ff.; Zuntz (1971) 83–9.

melodious Graces' (*P.* 9.89–90) can illuminate the brevity and darkness of mortal life. Like Plato, he is concerned with the moments when the present life becomes transparent to a more lasting reality, the eternal beauty of the gods. At such moments the Muses or Graces are present among men (*N.* 5.22ff., *P.* 3.88ff., *I.* 8.61ff.; cf. *O.* 1.30ff.; *O.* 14.5ff.). The famous passage at the end of his last ode comes as close as any single statement can to presenting this vision of his art (*P.* 8.95–7):

> ἐπάμεροι· τί δέ τις; τί δ' οὔ τις; σκιᾶς ὄναρ
> ἄνθρωπος. ἀλλ' ὅταν αἴγλα διόσδοτος ἔλθῃ,
> λαμπρὸν φέγγος ἔπεστιν ἀνδρῶν καὶ μείλιχος αἰών.

Creatures of the passing day. What is any one? What is any one not? Shadow's dream is man. But when the radiance given of Zeus comes, there is a bright light upon men, and life is sweet.

4. BACCHYLIDES

Until 1897, when F. G. Kenyon published a papyrus containing substantial portions of fourteen epinikia and six dithyrambs, Bacchylides was little more than a name. Few discoveries have been more sensational in restoring to us a virtually unknown poet of high quality. The dates of Bacchylides' birth and death are uncertain. Younger than Pindar and nephew of Simonides, he was born on Ceos perhaps around 510 B.C.[1] Most of his works seem to fall between *c.* 485 and 452, the latest date we can establish (*Odes* 6 and 7).

Ever since 'Longinus' made his unflattering comparison between the flawless smoothness of Bacchylides and the all-encompassing blaze of Pindar (*Subl.* 33.5), Bacchylides has suffered by comparison with his great contemporary. But it is perhaps fairer to consider Bacchylides as the successor to Stesichorus' tradition of extended lyrical narrative than as the rival of Pindar. He is more concerned than Pindar with storytelling *per se*; and the characteristics of oral recitation are rather more evident in his poetry: his narrative is marked by a graceful leisureliness, a fullness and clarity of detail, and a heavy reliance on ring composition (verbal repetition which signals the resumption of a theme after a digression in a kind of *da capo* effect). The art of the rhapsode, we may recall, flourished vigorously in Bacchylides' lifetime.

Bacchylides' myths are distinguished not only for their fluidity and grace of movement, but also for their pathos, their high proportion of direct discourse, and especially for the richness and lushness of their epithets. There is no appreciable difference in style between his epinikia and dithyrambs, save that the latter have a higher proportion of narrative. His virtues appear at their best in *Odes* 3,

[1] For the evidence see Severyns (1933) 15–30, who argues unsuccessfully for an earlier birthdate of 518/17. Apollodorus' date is 507.

5 and 17, which relate respectively the stories of Croesus on the pyre, Heracles' encounter with Meleager in Hades, and Minos' challenge to Theseus. Of special interest also are *Odes* 11 (the madness of the daughters of Proetus), 13 (the Trojan burning of the Greek ships), 15 (Odysseus and Menelaus in Troy to plead for Helen's return) and 16 (Deianira's plan to anoint Heracles' robe with the magical philtre of Nessus' blood). *Ode* 18 is interesting for its form: a dialogue between Aegeus and the chorus relates the early deeds of young Theseus as he approaches Athens.[1]

Bacchylides' epinikia share many of the conventions and motifs of Pindar's. There are brilliant invocations (5.1ff.), a vivid sense of place (cf. 14B.4–8), rich mythic narration. Both poets dwell on the dangers of envy offset by the value of the lasting glory which the poet confers (cf. 13.199–225), the generosity of the victor and his proper display and use of wealth (cf. 3.13f.), the poet's tie of friendship or hospitality (*philia, xenia*) with the victor (3.16, 5.49), the limits of human happiness. Both poets use similar imagery for the victor's success: flowers, growth, bloom, brightness, sweetness.

The scholiasts to Pindar find allusions to a rivalry between him and Bacchylides. The most famous instance is *O.* 2.86–8: 'Wise is he who knows much by nature; but those who learn, like a pair of raucous ravens, chatter in vain in their fulness of tongue against Zeus's divine bird.'[2] The 'twin ravens' are explained as Simonides and Bacchylides; but, of course, birds do chatter in pairs, and Hellenistic scholars tend to interpret conventional motifs or metaphors in biographical terms. In several passages, however, Bacchylides does seem to be 'imitating' Pindar, but this imitation is more like creative adaptation of the kind frequent in ancient poetry, and one must also reckon on the possibility of a conventional motif used by both poets independently. Pindar's collocation of water, gold and sky in the proem to *O.* 1, for example, which Bacchylides is thought to imitate in 3.86f., may be such a motif.[3] Like Pindar, Bacchylides draws heavily on the earlier poetic tradition: Homer, Hesiod, the *Cypria*, the epic *Capture of Oechalia* (for *Ode* 16), Sappho, Alcaeus, Solon, Theognis, Stesichorus.

Bacchylides has little of Pindar's brilliant density of metaphor or abrupt transitions. He generally gives more attention to details of the victory itself, and he effects more obvious connexions between the mythical paradigm and the victor. He is a master of the rich sensuous vignette, like 'young men, their hair teeming with flowers' (6.8–9) or the 'brilliant moon of the mid-month night' which outshines the 'lights of the stars' (9.27–9), a Sapphic reminiscence. At

[1] This use of dialogue is sometimes compared, rather inaccurately, with the dialogue between chorus and chorus-leader in the early dithyramb from which, according to Aristotle, tragic dialogue arose. For critical discussion see *DTC* 28f.

[2] For the quarrel see Gentili (1958) 24–9.

[3] Cf. Simonides 541 P; Wind (1971/2) 9–13.

his worst, he can be blandly conventional (cf. *Ode* 10). His open, limpid style favours simile over metaphor. Pindar offers no simile quite so extensive as the long Homeric simile of 5.6–30 or 13.124–32. His metaphors are milder than Pindar's too, but he can also experiment with the striking phrase: τόθεν γὰρ | πυθμένες θάλλουσιν ἐσθλῶν 'from song bloom the foundations of noble deeds' (5.198); δνόφεόν τε κάλυμμα τῶν | ὕστερον ἐρχομένων 'a dark veil of things later to come [destroyed Deianira]' (16.32–3), an expression which brilliantly foreshadows the poisoned robe.

Though Bacchylides prefers to trace out the whole line of the narrative rather than highlight details, as Pindar does, nevertheless his technique is far from naive or simplistic. *Ode* 5 exploits a striking collocation of the tales of Meleager and Heracles; *Ode* 11 sets the madness of the Proetides in a rich temporal and spatial framework which encompasses the dynastic quarrels of Argos, the founding of Tiryns, and the establishment of a cult of Artemis in Arcadia. *Ode* 13, the most Homeric of the poems, uses a striking simile of a storm at sea to effect a skilful transition between the two Aeacid heroes, Achilles and Ajax, and to strengthen the unifying effect of the marine setting (cf. 13.105, 125–32, 149–50). *Ode* 17 systematically exploits verbal and thematic repetitions to create a series of parallels and contrasts between its two mythical events, Minos' insult and Theseus' underwater quest.[1] In the case of this latter myth, as also in the case of the story of Croesus on the pyre in *Ode* 3, there are close parallels between Bacchylides' version and contemporaneous vase-painting, a fact which suggests not only that Bacchylides follows the traditional version of a legend, but also that he has an eye for its graphic aspects.[2]

Bacchylides uses direct speech in his myths more abundantly than Pindar; like Pindar he reserves it for moments of great emotional intensity (cf. 5.160–9, Heracles' weeping at Meleager's tale of woe). He can use brevity of quotation to effect. Croesus ends his speech with the clipped, 'Things once hateful are now dear; sweetest to die' (τὰ πρόσθεν ἐχθρὰ φίλα· θανεῖν γλύκιστον, 3.47). There are effective silences, too, like Daedalus' when Pasiphae reveals her love for the bull: 'When he learned her tale he held back in thought' (26.14–15).

Bacchylides shares with the other lyric poets a predilection for colour and light. Of the ninety-odd compound adjectives which occur only in Bacchylides, a large proportion are compounded of elements denoting these properties ('dark-', 'crimson-', 'shining-', κυανο-, φοινικο-, ἀγλαο-). Like earlier lyric poets, Bacchylides borrows a number of epithets directly from Homer, but he often gives them a new twist. 'Rose-fingered' describes not the Dawn, as always in Homer, but the daughter of Inachus, Io (ῥοδοδάκτυλος κόρα 'rose-fingered maid', 19.18). His Dawn is not 'rose-fingered', like Homer's, but 'of golden arms' (χρυσόπαχυς Ἀώς, 5.40).

[1] See Stern (1967) 40–7; Segal (1977). [2] See Smith (1898) 267–80.

These Homeric echoes can sometimes add an epic grandeur or reflective breadth to the narrative, as in the description of the sack of Sardis (cf. 3.31–2 and 44–6) or the quotation of Homer's famous comparison of men to leaves at the beginning of Heracles' encounter with Meleager in the Underworld (5.64–7). The frequent borrowings from the Homeric underworld of *Odyssey* 11 in this latter passage also evoke the melancholy shadowiness of the Homeric dead and point up a contrast between the active heroic quality in epithets like 'gate-wrecking', 'bold-enduring', 'spear-brandishing' and the futility and emptiness in the setting.[1]

Bacchylides' use of the noun–epithet combination, however, is totally different from Homer's. Whereas the Homeric epithet generally occurs in metrically fixed formulas and stresses the generic, universal quality of the object or person within an established literary tradition, Bacchylides' epithets highlight particular details and thereby enhance the emotional vibrancy and the pathetic contrasts sought by the lyric style. The mood of austerity produced by the functional repetition of the fixed noun–epithet combination in Homer becomes in Bacchylides a decorative, individualizing lushness. Yet Bacchylides' epithets have a thematic as well as a decorative function.[2] They sometimes effect contrasts and parallels between related sections of an ode or a myth. In *Ode* 3, for example, the 'bronze-walled court' and 'well-built halls' of Croesus (3.30–1, 46, reinforced also by the image of Hieron's 'towered wealth', 13) create a grandiose architectural foil to Croesus' near-death on the humbler 'wooden house' of his pyre (ξύλινον δόμον, 49).

Even where Bacchylides follows Homer closely, the tone is utterly different. *Ode* 13, for example, builds the Homeric materials of battle, cloud, sea, shore, into a rich figurative interplay of light and dark, nearness and distance, human valour and impersonal natural forces (cf. 62ff., 127, 153, 175ff.). And in the midst of the martial narrative the brief two-line description of 'the yellow-haired woman, Briseis of the lovely limbs' stands out with a sharpness of detail that is distinctively lyrical (ξανθᾶς γυναικός, | Βρισηΐδος ἱμερογυίου, 13.136–7). *Odes* 5 and 17 exploit a deliberate movement from heroic themes to a gentler, more wistful, more personal mood: compassion and marriage in 5, the sensuous richness of the Nereids after the scenes of heroic challenge in 17.

Though Bacchylides calls himself 'the divine prophet of the violet-eyed Muses' (9.3), he exhibits less of Pindar's deep commitment to his art as a god-given mission. Indeed, this less intense moral earnestness may have helped Bacchylides against his rival: Hieron commissioned Bacchylides alone for his Olympian victory of 468, possibly out of uneasiness with Pindar's sternness and insistent warnings on tyranny, violence, outrage in earlier odes (*O.* 1, *P.* 1–3). Bacchylides' narrative grace probed less deeply and was less threatening.

[1] See Lefkowitz (1968) 69f., 84f.   [2] See Segal (1976).

For Bacchylides poetry is a matter of brightness, joy, open exuberance. For Pindar it is also something dark and mysterious, in touch with strange forces and hidden powers. It is instructive to juxtapose two descriptions of the Muse: 'Like a skilful pilot, O Cleo, ruler of hymns, do you guide now my heart if ever before you have done so' (Bacch. 12.1–4). 'To weave garlands is easy. Strike up the tune. The Muse joins together gold and white ivory and the lily-flower which she lifts from beneath the sea's dew' (Pind. *N.* 7.77–9). Bacchylides' lines have a lucid confidence, Pindar's a poetic depth and a rich allusiveness of diction and symbol.

It would be mistaken, however, to exaggerate too much the differences between the two poets. They share a common repertory of motifs, images, conventions, diction; and they affirm and celebrate the heroic values of an ancient aristocracy. Both seek to bridge the gap between the fleeting present in its glorious display of beauty and energy and the eternal world of the gods. Pindar, however, grasps the contrast between the extremes of mortality and divinity with greater intensity than Bacchylides and for this reason seems the more philosophical and meditative, more concerned with ultimate questions of life and death, transience and permanence. Bacchylides prefers to observe the gentler play of shadow and sadness over the sensuous surface of his brilliant world. Pindar's bolder, more steadfast vision takes in the 'power set apart' that separates men from the gods in their 'brazen heaven' (*N.* 6). Bacchylides characteristically lingers over the freshness of youth and the charm and infatuation of 'golden Love' in the dark realm of the insubstantial dead (5.171–5):

> ψυχὰ προσέφα Μελεά-
> γρου· 'λίπον χλωραύχενα
> ἐν δώμασι Δαϊάνειραν,
> νῆϊν ἔτι χρῦσέας
> Κύπριδος θελξιμβρότου.'

The shade of...Meleager addressed him: 'I left in my halls Deianira, throat fresh with the green life of youth, still ignorant of golden Aphrodite, enchantress of mortals.'

5. WOMEN POETS: CORINNA, MYRTIS, TELESILLA, PRAXILLA

We possess fragments of four Boeotian or Peloponnesian poetesses: Corinna of Tanagra, Myrtis of Anthedon, Telesilla of Argos, Praxilla of Sicyon.[1] Of these the most important and the most puzzling is Corinna, whose work is represented by significant portions of three poems surviving in papyrus fragments (654–5). These poems, in Boeotian dialect, seem from their orthography to belong to the third century B.C., and there is no reference to Corinna in any writer earlier

---

[1] The fragments are numbered by the marginal numeration of *PMG*.

than the first century B.C. On the other hand a late tradition makes her a contemporary of Pindar. If the latter is correct she was presumably ignored by the Alexandrian scholars on account of the provincial character of her language and subject matter, but was rediscovered and copied for local reasons in Boeotia in the third century. The alternative is to believe that she actually wrote in the third century and was much later added as a tenth poet to the Hellenistic canon of nine.

Scholars are still divided between the early and the late date, although there is a tendency, especially in England, to place her late. Not only are the circumstances of the alleged transcription suspicious, but the reference to secret balloting (654.i.20ff.) suggests familiarity with an institution which, so far as we know, developed only in Athens around the middle of the fifth century.[1] Plutarch, however, reports a celebrated anecdote in which she appears as an older mentor of Pindar (*De glor. Ath.* 4.347f), and the Suda has her defeat Pindar five times. Pausanias saw a painting at Tanagra depicting her being crowned in victory over Pindar (Paus. 9.22.3). These legends, however, may have arisen when Boeotia experienced a new period of political and cultural self-consciousness in the third century. The question of Corinna's date remains open.

It is not absolutely certain that all of Corinna's poetry is choral, but references to choruses of girls in the most recently discovered poem suggests that it probably is (655.i.2–3 and 11; cf. 690.12).[2] In the first part of the so-called Berlin papyrus, the longest text, Corinna describes a singing contest between the mountains Helicon and Cithaeron. The latter sings the Hesiodic tale of the concealment of Zeus from Cronos. He wins, and Helicon, in childish frustration, hurls a boulder into the air, smashing it into a thousand pieces. On a recent reconstruction, however, the two contestants are mythical heroes, Helicon and Cithaeron; Helicon hurls himself, not a boulder, down the mountainside; and from his death Mount Helicon takes his name.[3] An aetiological myth of this sort has a Hellenistic rather than an archaic look.

After a long gap of badly mutilated text the papyrus resumes with a dialogue between the river god Asopus, grieving for his daughters, and the prophet Acraiphen, who reassures Asopus about his daughters' fate and tells the history of Apollo's oracular shrine on Mt Ptoon near Thebes. In the third and most recently discovered fragment (655) Corinna speaks in the first person and tells of the pleasure she gave her city with her legends of Boeotian heroes like Cephalus and Orion. She seems to have restricted herself to Boeotian myths. Even her *Orestas* (if the few lines remaining can be assigned to her, 690) seems to have had a Theban setting, probably Orestes' presence at a spring rite of Apollo at Thebes.

[1] See Boegehold (1968) 368 n. 6; Bolling (1956) 285f.; Segal (1975) 1–8.
[2] See West (1970b) 280, 283; Kirkwood (1974) 192.   [3] Ebert (1978) 5–12.

Despite the unfamiliar Boeotian vernacular, Corinna's style is lucid and simple. She uses short clauses and paratactic sentences. There are few metaphors and few tropes of any kind. The narrative has a certain vividness and fresh charm suggestive of folk poetry. There are touches of humour: the elaborate voting procedures on Olympus (654.i.19ff.) or possibly the grotesque anthropomorphization of Mount Helicon 'held by harsh pains' as he hurled his rock, groaning 'piteously'. She uses a few compound epithets of the type familiar from Bacchylides; but apart from λιγουροκωτίλυς 'coaxing in high tones' (655.5), they are not especially recherché ('crafty-minded', 'gold-shining', 'white-robed'). Her metres are simple and regular, a fact which may suggest archaism or, conversely, the metrical simplification of the later period. Given the simplicity of Corinna's style and the restrictions of her material, it is interesting, not to say puzzling, that she could have won five victories (or, with Pausanias, one victory) over her brilliant fellow-Boeotian.

Of Myrtis we have almost nothing. She is best known from a fragment of Corinna who criticizes her, a woman, for venturing to compete with Pindar (664a):

μέμφομη δὲ κὴ λιγουρὰν
Μουρτίδ' ἰώνγ' ὅτι βανὰ φοῦ-
σ' ἔβα Πινδάροι πὸτ ἔριν.

I blame too the clear-voiced Myrtis because born a woman she went to contest against Pindar.

Like Corinna she too seems to have related local legends like the love of Ochne for the Tanagran hero Eunostos, a variation on the Potiphar's wife motif.

Telesilla wrote poems, perhaps choral, for Apollo and Artemis. A lost poem told the story of Niobe (721). Of Praxilla a little more is preserved. She wrote a 'hymn' to Adonis of which three melodious lines survive and gave rise to the proverb, 'sillier than Adonis' (747). Asked in Hades what he most regretted, Adonis answered,

κάλλιστον μὲν ἐγὼ λείπω φάος ἠελίοιο,
δεύτερον ἄστρα φαεινὰ σεληναίης τε πρόσωπον
ἠδὲ καὶ ὡραίους σικύους καὶ μῆλα καὶ ὄγχνας.

Loveliest of what I leave behind is the light of the sun
Next the bright stars and the moon's face
And the ripe cucumbers and apples and pears.

These lines, however, are in dactylic hexameters, not in any of the usual choral metres. Praxilla also wrote a dithyramb on Achilles, whose sole remaining line suggests close adherence to Homer: 'But never did they (I?) persuade the spirit within your breast' (ἀλλὰ τεὸν οὔποτε θυμὸν ἐνὶ στήθεσσιν ἔπειθον, 748). Some bits of proverbial wisdom have also survived (749–50); and, like Telesilla, she gave her name to a type of metre (717, 754).

6. CHORAL LYRIC TO THE END OF THE FIFTH CENTURY

Although the odes of Pindar and Bacchylides mark the end of the great period of Greek choral poetry as an independent form, it continues to be written to the end of the fifth century (fragments in *PMG*, pp. 359–447). The competition among dithyrambic choruses at the Dionysiac festivals in Athens assured a steady production of dithyrambs. Most of the scanty fragments that survive, therefore, are from dithyrambs. There are also scraps of a paean by Sophocles (737), an epinikion for Alcibiades by Euripides (755), and notices of hymns, prosodia, enkomia. Ion of Chios, Sophocles' contemporary, wrote a dithyramb narrating the death of Antigone (740) in a version quite different from Sophocles'. Among the earliest pieces are fifteen lines (708) by Pratinas (*fl.* 500), known chiefly for his satyr plays. This lively fragment (which may well be from a chorus in a satyr play)[1] uses outlandish compounds in a way that anticipates Timotheus at the very end of the century. It complains that the instrumental accompaniment of the flute players has begun to dominate the vocal part of the chorus. This predominance of music over words becomes more marked in the choral lyric of the fifth century, especially the dithyramb, perhaps under the influence of the tragic performances.

The period from 450 on saw a general loosening of the old forms, both of music and of verse, and an increasing tendency toward exaggerated diction. The strict strophic composition of the earlier period (strophe, antistrophe, epode) gives way to free or 'loosened' verse (ἀπολελυμένα). Philoxenus of Cythera (436/4–380/79) is said to have introduced monodies into the choral songs of the dithyramb (Plut. *De mus.* 1142a; Aristophanes, fr. 641 K). In the comic poet Pherecrates (145 K) Music appears on stage denouncing Melanippides (*fl. c.* 440) to Justice for taking the lead in making her 'looser' (χαλαρωτέραν); and she then goes on to list Cinesias, Phrynis and Timotheus, the worst of all with his trills and arpeggios like the twisting paths of ants (ἄιδων ἐκτραπέλους μυρμηκιάς, line 23). Aristophanes provides a delicious parody of Cinesias (*Birds* 1373ff.), suggesting that this etherial bard would find wings especially appropriate to his 'air-whirling and snow-driven' poems:

κρέμαται μὲν οὖν ἐντεῦθεν ἡμῶν ἡ τέχνη.
τῶν διθυράμβων γὰρ τὰ λαμπρὰ γίγνεται
ἀέρια καὶ σκότιά γε καὶ κυαναυγέα
καὶ πτεροδόνητα.

Why our whole trade depends upon the clouds;
What are our noblest dithyrambs but things
Of air, and mist, and purple-gleaming depths,
And feathery whirlwings? (*Birds* 1387–90, tr. Rogers)

[1] See Garrod (1920) 129–36, especially 134f.; *DTC* 17–20, with bibliography; Lloyd-Jones (1966) 11ff.

The choral lyrics of late Euripidean tragedy show parallel tendencies and also drew Aristophanes' fire in the brilliant parody of the *Frogs* (1301–63). On the other hand the new style had its admirers. Aristodemus in Xenophon's *Memorabilia* (1.4.3) puts Melanippides' excellence in the dithyramb on a par with the art of Sophocles, Polyclitus, Zeuxis. The comic poet Antiphanes has a character praise Philoxenus for his inventions of new words and his shifting rhythms and melodies (207 K). Philoxenus and Timotheus were still popular in the schools of Arcadia in Polybius' day (Polyb. 4.20).

Most of these poets seem to have carried on the literary dithyramb as we have seen it in Bacchylides, *Odes* 17–20; they relate mythical tales in a decorative style and with a certain amount of dialogue (e.g. Melanippides 758). Athena and Marsyas, Persephone, Peleus and Thetis, the Danaids, Asclepius' resurrection of Hippolytus, Endymion are some of the subjects. Licymnius of Chios wrote on a quasi-historical subject recalling Bacchylides 3, the betrayal of Sardis to Cyrus by Croesus' own daughter, Nanis (772).

The most extensive piece of later choral lyric to survive, once more thanks to the luck of a papyrus discovery, is the *Persians* of Timotheus (*c.* 450–360). This work is a 'nome', an ancient form developed by Terpander in the seventh century, but in Timotheus' time a rather free composition without strophes and dominated by the music.[1] Its style and narrative technique closely resemble the 'literary' dithyramb of Bacchylides and later.[2] But Timotheus' pomposity and bombast are a far cry from either the grandeur of Pindar or the grace of Bacchylides. They look forward to the worst traits of Hellenistic poetry. Wine mixed with water is 'the blood of Dionysus mixed with the fresh-flowing tears of the nymphs' (from the *Cyclops*, 780). Teeth are 'the mouth's light-flashing children' (*Pers.* 91ff.). There are occasional touches of solemnity and pathos: the lament of the Persian women (100ff., 120ff.) and Xerxes' heroic decision (189ff.); but the pidgin Greek of the Persian women (150ff.) sinks to comical bathos that is hard to imagine in an earlier poet. Yet the abrupt break-off from the myth (202), the poet's defence of his own art and closing prayer for the city (206–28) illustrate the continuity of traditional motifs even in this late and florid style.

The work of Timotheus and his contemporary, Philoxenus of Cythera, who wrote a humorous version of the loves of Galatea and Polyphemus that anticipates Theocritus, reveals one of the reasons for the decline of choral lyric. The poet no longer regarded his art with the high seriousness of a Simonides or a Pindar. Rather than a 'prophet of the Muses' who seeks to interpret the ways of

[1] See Wilamowitz (1903) 79ff., 89ff.

[2] This 'literary' dithyramb is a lyrical narrative in honour of gods and heroes, not a poem in honour of Dionysus, as the term originally implied. All of Bacchylides' preserved dithyrambs are of the former, 'literary' type except 19, which ends with the birth of Dionysus.

the gods and to understand the limitations of mortality, the choral poet becomes merely an entertainer. Aesthetic novelty and ingenuity are demanded rather than moral depth or religious power; or, as Plato charges in the *Laws*, taste formed by aristocratic values has given way to taste formed by the mob and the 'theatocracy' (3.700c, 701a, cf. *Gorgias* 501e).

More than almost any other literary form, choral lyric is bound up with the values of city and clan in a world where things changed slowly. By 450 the tyrants and aristocratic families which had commissioned the odes of Pindar and Bacchylides were gone or endangered, their values threatened by the fast-rising power of Athenian democracy. By the last quarter of the century the festivals which provided the occasion for choral song were losing their religious basis. The power politics of the latter half of the fifth century, the scepticism and rationalism brought by the sophistic enlightenment, the disruptions of the Peloponnesian War, and the rapid social and cultural changes which these movements precipitated were all inimical to the old poetry. With the exception of Pindar's very last ode (*P*. 8), all the significant choral poetry that we have predates 450. Choral lyric implied a stable community founded on universally shared religious and moral beliefs, well established rituals and firm traditions. By the midpoint of the century these old values were no longer unquestioned. Tragic drama rather than the genre of lyric poetry *per se* expressed the forces and tensions of greatest concern to the thinking and feeling men of the day.

9

EARLY GREEK PHILOSOPHY

Three early Greek philosophers were poets, Xenophanes, Parmenides and Empedocles. Heraclitus, who lived at about the same time, was a philosopher whose prose is stylistically unique in Greek literature. These are the earliest philosophical writers whose work, though fragmentary, has been preserved in some quantity. It would have been possible for them to express their thought in a 'simple and economical' prose, as Anaximenes, who was older than any of them, is reputed to have done (Diog. Laert. 2.3). But Anaximenes is one of the first Greeks who is known to have written a book in prose. His philosophical predecessor at Miletus, Anaximander, did so too, and Theophrastus commented on the 'somewhat poetical' style of his single extant fragment (DK 12 A 9). There is no reason to suppose that the philosophical poets surprised their contemporaries by declining to follow a prose tradition of such recent origin.

Equally, however, their use of verse rather than prose was deliberate. Each of the philosopher poets must be considered as an individual writer, but it may be significant that Parmenides and Empedocles (and Xenophanes during his later years) belonged not to Ionia but to the western Greek world of southern Italy and Sicily. Parmenides 'wrote as a philosophical pioneer of the first water'[1] and probably confined his recognition of the prose philosophers of Ionia to critical rejection of their views. The Ionian philosophers (excluding Xenophanes) differentiated themselves from traditional authorities by writing in prose. As hexameter poets Xenophanes, Parmenides and Empedocles placed themselves in a line which had Homer and Hesiod as its illustrious founders. But to do this was not to express approval of their epic and didactic forerunners. Xenophanes attacked Homer and Hesiod explicitly for giving men an immoral account of the gods (fr. 11). The debts of Parmenides and Empedocles to these poets are formal and stylistic rather than conceptual. In appearing to imitate Homer and Hesiod, the philosopher poets borrow what suits their

---

[1] Owen (1960) 101.

needs; the form of their poems tells the reader or hearer to expect a subject matter of the greatest general significance. The claims they make for its truth reveal Homer, Hesiod and other poets as possessing a reputation for wisdom which they do not deserve.

The early writers of Ionian prose cannot have expected a wide readership for their work. In composing accounts of cosmology they must have written for an interested minority. The philosopher poets, it is reasonable to think, were aiming at a larger audience.[1] Homer and Hesiod held pride of place as educative writers, and Xenophanes, Parmenides and Empedocles may all be assumed to challenge their authority. (Nor is it coincidence that Heraclitus, in his idiosyncratic prose, attacked Homer and Hesiod and also some of his contemporaries including Xenophanes.) The poetic tradition, moreover, provided them with an acceptable means of emphasizing their own insight into the true nature of things. All three poets have their own way of asserting a wisdom which sets them apart from other men. Xenophanes does so directly (fr. 2); Parmenides' poem ostensibly reports the revelation of a goddess, and Empedocles invokes a muse as his helper. Such motifs do not in the least undermine the philosophical significance of the poems. But they give the writer an additional authority which calls to mind what earlier poets have said.

Xenophanes has been spoken of so far in company with Parmenides and Empedocles. He is in fact a writer who in many respects belongs in a class by himself. Some of his statements, and views attributed to him, were unmistakably influenced by the Milesian philosophers and associate him with the Ionian enlightenment. But Xenophanes also wrote elegies which make social and moral comments in the manner of Solon and Theognis. He was the inventor of *Silloi*, satirical verses, a genre later adopted by Timon of Phlius (see pp. 636f.), and his activities in southern Italy and Sicily, where he spent much of his later life, gave rise to the tradition that he initiated the Eleatic movement in philosophy.

It is not surprising that such a many-sided figure has prompted a host of different opinions from modern scholars[2] and misconceptions about him can be traced back to antiquity. Aristotle, following Plato, tried to make Xenophanes · the progenitor of Eleatic monism and rated him of little account (*Metaph.* A5 986b22).[3] Theophrastus did not consider that his ideas fell under the study of natural philosophy (Simplicius, *Phys.* 22.26), and a comment by Diogenes Laertius (9.18) has sometimes been wrongly interpreted to mean that Xenophanes was a rhapsode who gave public recitations of Homer. Most difficulties disappear once it is recognized that he lived at a time when no firm boundary existed between poetry and philosophy. Theological and cosmological specu-

---

[1] Jaeger (1939) 169f.   [2] Guthrie (1962) 361f.

[3] Reinhardt (1916) was the first scholar who conclusively showed the implausibility of this tradition. But his attempt to make Xenophanes the follower of Parmenides has been universally rejected.

lation was not an invention of 'philosophers': it is found as early as Hesiod and there are traces of it even in Alcman (see above, pp. 179f.).[1]

Xenophanes' surviving work is too fragmentary to permit firm generalizations about the aim and methods of all his poetry. Like other elegists he took social festivities and behaviour over wine as one of his themes (cf. Ion of Chios fr. 26, Anacreon fr. eleg. 2 West): his longest poem (fr. 1) combines vivid and charming description of preparations for a party with rules for host and guest, including a ban on false and immoral statements about the gods. Criticism of current values appears more prominently in another elegy (fr. 2) where the rewards accorded to victorious Olympic athletes are contrasted with the recognition which he, Xenophanes, deserves for his art and its benefits to his city. In six tart lines he condemns the luxurious tastes of the people of Colophon before their conquest by the Lydians (fr. 3), and his elegies also included personal anecdotes (fr. 7 refers to Pythagoras) and autobiography (fr. 8).

Some if not all of the hexameter lines are fragments from the *Silloi*. It was here that Xenophanes revealed his radical theology, and strongly condemned the Homeric and Hesiodic accounts of the gods (frs. 10–12). He went on to extend his criticism, it seems, to all existing theological beliefs. In a mock-serious fashion he argues that if animals had gods they would make them in their own image (fr. 15), just as Ethiopians worship gods who are black and snub-nosed, while those of the Thracians have grey eyes and red hair (fr. 16). No one has any clear view of the gods (fr. 34, cf. fr. 18) but, in spite of this, Xenophanes advanced a theology quite remarkable for its time. Completely rejecting the traditional plurality of anthropomorphic gods, he wrote of 'one god, greatest among gods and men, unlike mortals in form or thought' (fr. 23). This 'one god' is completely immobile (fr. 26): he thinks and perceives 'as a whole' and makes 'all things shake with his thought' (frs. 24, 25). Later writers attributed to Xenophanes a spherical god identical with the world, but we cannot be sure that this was his own view.[2]

The few cosmological fragments are of much less general interest. Xenophanes regarded earth and water as the source of all living things (frs. 29, 33). He had views about meteorology (frs. 31–2) but none of the fragments suggests that his science represented a significant advance on Milesian cosmology. Like his other work, however, it shows him to have been an acute observer of the world, who was far ahead of the main currents of thought in his times.[3] Xenophanes was not a sceptic in any technical sense, but his comments on the

[1] Cf. West (1963) 154–6 and (1967).
[2] Guthrie (1962) 376–83 advances positive arguments against the scepticism of Kirk and Raven (1957) 170–2 and Jaeger (1947) 43.
[3] Hippolytus (DK 21 A 33) reports that he drew geological inferences from the discovery of fossils.

limitations of human understanding (fr. 34) are an integral part of his critical and innovative attitudes.

As a poet he is not easy to assess, since much of the surviving material is severely factual and descriptive. The vocabulary and structure of his verse call for no particular comment, but rhythmical fluency and lucidity of thought are notable features of all his lines. The *Silloi*, fragmentary though they are, show that he could temper his polemic with wit, and as an original genre they provide further evidence of his independent mind. Whether they included parody of Homer, as in Timon of Phlius and the Cynics (see pp. 636ff.), it is not possible to say.

Too little of Xenophanes' work survives to warrant precise assessments of his intellectual significance. The poem of Parmenides presents no such problem. Large sections of it are preserved, and scholars are unanimous in regarding Parmenides as the outstanding figure in early Greek philosophy. The detailed interpretation of his arguments is controversial and falls outside the scope of this survey. But there is no disagreement about their originality and their remarkable logical coherence.

Parmenides is the first Greek philosopher who presents his views about the world in a series of formal arguments. In its structure, however, his poem is not a philosophical treatise but a work which belongs to the epic tradition of Homer and Hesiod. The Muses met Hesiod on Mount Helicon and told him what to sing (*Theog.* 29–35). Parmenides begins his poem with the narrative of a journey which he made to the gates of the paths of Night and Day on a horse-drawn chariot escorted by the daughters of the Sun.[1] On passing through these doors, whose keys are kept by 'avenging Justice', he is warmly greeted by an unnamed goddess. She tells the poet that he is to learn 'both the unshaken heart of well-rounded Truth and the opinions of mortals in which true belief is not present' (fr. 1.28–30). The main parts of the poem now follow, in which the goddess in her own person fulfils her dual revelation.

Parmenides' journey to the goddess symbolizes the philosopher's quest for knowledge. At the beginning of her discourse the goddess continues with the language of travelling: she proposes to reveal the only two 'routes' of 'enquiry'. One of these, which the first part of the poem pursues to its destination, is the 'path of persuasion', the Way of Truth; the other is a 'track completely closed to enquiry'. Taken together the two ways are contradictory. The first is 'that it is and that it cannot not be'; the second 'that it is not and that it must not be' (fr. 2). Once the validity of the first way has been established, the goddess uses it (and the consequential exclusion of the second way) to establish charac-

---

[1] The journey has generally been interpreted as 'into the light', but several scholars have recently given strong arguments for treating its destination as the 'House of Night' through whose gates both Day and Night emerge alternately; cf. Furley (1973) 1–5.

teristics of 'what is', ungenerated, imperishable, whole, unique, immovable, without end (the line containing these last four predicates is textually uncertain), eternally present, all together, one, and continuous (fr. 8.2–6). She calls these 'signposts' (*semata*), and we are to think of them as markers on the Way of Truth or, in philosophical language, the conclusions of deductive arguments.

Having concluded her 'reliable account and thought about truth', the goddess passes next to a 'deceptive arrangement of words' on the subject of mortal opinions (fr. 8.50–2). This part of the poem is very imperfectly preserved and its purpose has been much debated. It is certain, however, that Parmenides made the goddess give an account of the very phenomena whose separate existence is disproved in the previous part, and prefaced her remarks by revealing the error from which all acceptance of contrary 'forms' (e.g. Night and Light) proceeds.

As a poet Parmenides has won little praise from most historians of literature. Their assessments have perhaps paid too little regard to the logical rigour of his arguments and the strains this imposed on composition in the epic manner. Mourelatos has shown how very closely Parmenides adhered to the metrical conventions of Homer and Hesiod.[1] From an analysis of the poet's vocabulary he concludes that less than ten per cent of his language is absent from early epic and that many of the apparently new words are imitations of epic forms. But for the most part Parmenides does not read like Homer or Hesiod. This is due both to his subject matter and, more significantly, to his much greater use of subordinate clauses, especially those introduced by the inferential conjunction γάρ 'for'. With the exception of the prooemium, which contains many ornamental phrases and amplification of concrete details, the style of the poem is subordinated to the logical development of the argument. But this is not to deny Parmenides' skill as a poet. He is capable of vivid and original phrases: mortals are 'carried about, deaf and blind alike, bemused, undiscerning tribes' (fr. 6.6–7); 'Justice does not allow *what is* to be born or to perish, loosening it in her fetters, but holds it fast' (fr. 8.13–15). Part of the importance and achievement of Parmenides is the fact that he developed a wholly new philosophical methodology within the conventions of traditional poetry.

Through his arguments concerning the nature of 'what is' and his uncompromising dismissal of the phenomena perceived by the senses, Parmenides had enormous influence on all philosophers of the next generation. Empedocles was probably the first of these to offer a complete explanation of the world which took account of his predecessor's work, and he is the only other Greek philosopher of outstanding significance who wrote as a hexameter poet. His closeness to Parmenides in time and place must have been one of the factors responsible for this, but his versification is far too accomplished and his feeling

[1] Mourelatos (1970).

for language much too sensitive to justify Aristotle's assertion that Homer and Empedocles have only 'metre' in common (*Poet.* 1447b18). For an adequate judgement on Empedocles we must go to another philosopher poet of genius, Lucretius, who praises the 'songs of his godlike heart' (1.731) and whose whole poem *On the nature of things* is an imitation of Empedocles as well as an essay on Epicureanism.

On nature, whether or not it is Empedocles' own title, well describes the subject of his principal work. Enough of this poem survives for us to see that it gave a comprehensive account of the world, starting from basic principles whose behaviour explains the origin and present state of the universe and also the structure of living things. The basic principles of Empedocles' universe are presented as divine beings, the 'four roots' of everything – earth, air, fire and water – and Love and Strife, which act in opposite ways upon and through them. The use which Empedocles makes of these principles is of the greatest philosophical and scientific interest, but the manner in which he presents them, particularly Love and Strife, is not dispassionate but coloured by emotive and evaluative language. Love is sometimes 'love', *philotes,* but she is also described as Kypris or Aphrodite, 'she by whom mortals think friendly thoughts and accomplish peaceful deeds'(fr. 17.23). Strife too has a variety of synonymous names; he 'leapt to take office in the fulfilment of time' (fr. 30) and is presented as a grim power of destruction and division. The history of the universe at its simplest is the combination and separation of the 'four roots', which Love and Strife bring about respectively.

Like Parmenides Empedocles is greatly indebted to Homer in style and language, and he has affinities with epic which Parmenides does not share. It is not simply that Empedocles has greater gifts as a poet. His poem, unlike that of Parmenides, is a dynamic narrative: it tells us what Love and Strife did and are doing. Empedocles accepted the full reality of movement and this is reflected in his style.

But within and outside this narrative, which seems to have been his main theme, Empedocles has a variety of other styles. The poem probably began in the first person, as an address to a disciple called Pausanias (fr. 1). Such a beginning associates Empedocles with Hesiod's address to his brother in *Works and days.* The poet appeals for assistance to a muse who is 'a much remembering white-armed maiden' (fr. 3.3), and he has many lines which might be called methodological, setting out the misunderstandings of 'mortals' and laying down his own fundamental principles.[1] His narrative is embellished and enlivened by descriptive phrases and epithets some of which appear to be original – 'wing-going' birds (fr. 20.7), 'water-nurtured' fish (fr. 21.11), 'gentle-

---

[1] Frs. 12–14 and certain other passages are 'deliberate echoes' (Guthrie (1965) 158) of Parmenides.

thinking' Love (fr. 35.13), 'mild-shining' moon (fr. 40) – while others are taken from epic or are modelled on epic forms. Like Homer he uses extensive similes, comparing the mixtures of the four 'roots' to the living creatures represented on temple offerings by painters who have mixed pigments of different colours (fr. 23). This simile takes up nine lines and Empedocles has another which is equally elaborate to illustrate respiration, likening the process to a girl playing with a *klepsydra* (a kitchen utensil for collecting water, fr. 100). Vivid imagery and acute observation of everyday life are characteristics of Empedocles' poetry which particularly attracted Lucretius.

Empedocles accounted for phenomena by postulating four ungenerated and indestructible 'roots', which are under the alternating control of changeless powers, Love and Strife. Thus he maintained some of Parmenides' requirements for 'what is' while abandoning unity and absence of movement. He also wrote a poem, *Purifications* (*Katharmoi*), the main antecedents of which are ideas about man's fall from a condition of primal bliss and the means of his redemption.

It probably began with a remarkable address to the citizens of Acragas (fr. 112), in which Empedocles describes himself as (or as regarded as) an 'immortal god, no longer mortal', who is sought after by thousands as a seer and healer. Our knowledge of the whole poem is very defective and its relationship to *On nature* is a problem which has never been finally settled. It seems likely that the six principles of the 'scientific' poem also provided the structure of the universe in the *Purifications*. But here Empedocles' interest was not to explain phenomena but to offer an account of the soul's destiny in concrete, allegorical terms. The cause of the soul's exile from happiness is its destruction of life, and in punishment for this it has to be born and re-born in different animal (and even vegetable!) forms. Eventually, it seems, the soul regains its purity and is restored to its original divine condition. The eschatological myth in Pindar's second *Olympian* ode cannot be far in date from Empedocles, and it is highly likely that the *Purifications* influenced Plato's mythical presentations of the soul's destiny which conclude the *Gorgias*, *Phaedo* and *Republic*.

Neither the style nor the subject matter of Empedocles' *Purifications* can have been entirely his own invention. From the fourth century B.C. until much later we have considerable evidence of hexameter poetry, much of it jejune and derivative, which expresses a religious system analogous to Empedocles'.[1] It has been supposed that such beliefs formed part of a systematic mystery cult of Orpheus predating Empedocles,[2] and whatever the conditions of Orphism may have actually been, it is reasonable to suppose that Empedocles knew of a number of religious poems with similar intent to his own. But if the

---

[1] Most of the material is collected in Kern (1922).
[2] Cf. Lesky 190–3.

Purifications belongs to a tradition which maintained its own life alongside prose writing of philosophy, his greater poem *On nature* had no imitators in the Greek world. Writers of comedy and tragedy could include philosophical reflections in their work and have been placed by ancient or modern historians in lists of philosophical writers (Epicharmus, and Critias the uncle of Plato). Much later, philosophical poetry was written by Cleanthes the Stoic, Timon of Phlius the Sceptic, and Crates the Cynic; but the true successor of Empedocles was Lucretius.

Though not a poet, Heraclitus is most naturally discussed in company with Xenophanes, Parmenides and Empedocles. He was familiar with the work of Xenophanes whom he names after Hesiod and Pythagoras as someone whom 'much learning has not taught intelligence' (fr. 40). As an Ionian Greek, almost certainly unacquainted with any other philosophical tradition, Heraclitus is generally considered in his chronological position following the philosophers of Miletus. Like them he expressed his thought in prose but a prose which, after making due allowance for its early date, has qualities of style and rhythm that are without parallel. As a thinker Heraclitus has equal claims to Parmenides for originality. His fundamental ideas were not primarily a development of Milesian cosmology; they give a new picture of the world, which he describes in sentences whose structure seems designed to exhibit the structure of reality.[1]

It is difficult to reproduce the effect of Heraclitus' style in translation. He saw the world as a continuous cycle of change in which the oppositions expressed by such pairs of words as 'up/down', 'day/night', 'war/peace' form a unity: 'immortals mortals, mortals immortals, living their (mortals') death and dying their (immortals') life' (fr. 62); 'sea – water purest and most polluted, for fish drinkable and healthful, for men undrinkable and destructive' (fr. 61); 'a road, upwards downwards, one and the same' (fr. 60). Such statements coordinate opposites and draw attention to their underlying unity; or, to put it another way, unity consists of co-existing opposites: 'one thing, the only wise, is unwilling and willing to be spoken by the name of Zeus' (fr. 32); 'God – day night, winter summer, war peace, excess want, – and he changes as fire, when it is mixed with fumes of incense, is named according to each man's pleasure' (fr. 67).

Such statements, complete in themselves, are characteristic of Heraclitus. Antithesis, word-play, paradox and imagery help him to express underlying truths about the world which are obscured by ordinary language and everyday judgements: 'Nature is accustomed to hide herself' (fr. 123), 'unapparent harmony is stronger than apparent' (fr. 54). Consistently with this conception of things he prefers to use hints and symbols to arouse his audience rather than discursive reasoning. The 'bow' and the 'lyre' symbolize the harmony

---

[1] Cf. Hussey (1972) 59.

of opposites (fr. 51); 'Time is a boy playing, playing draughts' (fr. 52), and 'it is not possible to step into the same river twice' (fr. 91), a saying which does not necessarily express the universal flux attributed to Heraclitus by Plato and later writers. The thought of such a philosopher cannot be summarized in a word or two. But his view of the world was focused upon unity, law-like regularity and order, what he called *Logos*, even if his manner of expression suits that of a poet and visionary.

Heraclitus' reputation and influence were greater in later antiquity than in his own time. Neither Plato nor Aristotle grasped his full significance, but the Stoics gave a new life to some of his ideas, which they interpreted as supports to their own system.[1] Cleanthes' *Hymn to Zeus* reflects Heraclitus at many points; Marcus Aurelius is never tired of likening change to a river and there are many more examples of his indebtedness. Clement of Alexandria, one of the earlier Christian Fathers, excerpted many of Heraclitus' aphorisms for their educative value. His influence persists in modern writers, witness the quotation of fragments 2 and 60 by T. S. Eliot in introducing his *Four Quartets*.

2. ANAXAGORAS, DEMOCRITUS AND OTHER PROSE PHILOSOPHERS

The Ionian prose of Anaxagoras is more representative of early Greek philosophical writing than are the aphorisms of Heraclitus. We are fortunate in possessing a good number of extensive quotations from his treatise, which beguiled but eventually disappointed Socrates, if Plato may be trusted (*Phd.* 97c–99d). Though much of his adult life was spent in Athens, Anaxagoras belongs to the Ionian tradition of philosophy initiated by Anaximander of Miletus. But his cosmology, like that of his Sicilian contemporary Empedocles, is to be understood principally as a critical reaction to the work of the south Italian Parmenides. Both Empedocles and Anaxagoras accepted the full reality of movement and plurality. But whereas Empedocles explained phenomena in terms of the mixture and separation of four changeless elements, Anaxagoras maintained that 'everything has a share of everything' (fr. 6) and that anything which exists is infinitely divisible (fr. 3). What distinguishes one thing from another is the different proportion of the same ingredients which constitute each substance. Hair and flesh can be nourished by bread and water because our food contains 'shares' of everything that is needed for nutrition (DK 59 A 46). So Anaxagoras reacted to Parmenides' ban on generation and destruction by reducing both of these to rearrangements of pre-existing material.

The most remarkable feature of Anaxagoras' cosmology was his postulation of Mind (*nous*) as the principal cause of change and cosmic order.

[1] Cf. Long (1976).

It is the finest of all things and the purest, and it possesses all understanding about everything and has the greatest power. Whatsoever has life (*psyche*), both the greater and the smaller, Mind controls them all...And Mind controlled all the rotation, so that it started to rotate at the beginning...And all things that were to be, and all things that were but are not now, and whatsoever things are now and will be, Mind arranged them all, both this rotation in which the stars and the sun and the moon now rotate and the air and the aether which are being separated off. And this rotation made them separate...(fr. 12)

In the same passage Anaxagoras states that Mind, unlike everything else, is entirely homogeneous, infinite, and autonomous. Though said to be 'unmixed with anything' it is omnipresent and eternal (fr. 14). Within the differentiated world Mind 'is in some things' (fr. 11) and may plausibly be identified with the vital principle of living things (DK 59 A 100).

Plato and Aristotle found an unhappy blend of rationality and mechanism in Anaxagoras' philosophy (Plato, *Phd.* 97c–99d, Arist. *Metaph.* 985a18). In the last sentence of the long extract quoted above (fr. 12), Anaxagoras refers to the 'rotation' which caused things to separate out of the undifferentiated state of matter which existed before the formation of the world. Thus, it seemed, Anaxagoras made only limited use of Mind as a causal principle and stopped short of any full-scale teleological explanation; and Socrates is made to say, 'I found the man making no use of Mind ... but finding causes in things like air and aether and water' (Plato, *Phd.* 98b).

It is difficult to assess the fairness of this criticism on the evidence of the existing fragments. Anaxagoras however makes it quite plain that Mind has organized as well as initiated the formation of the world; rotatory movement is not a second, independent principle but a consequence of Mind's own cosmological activity. Anaxagoras' philosophical predecessors regarded their cosmic principle(s) as divine, and it seems likely that he would have accepted god as a predicate of his cosmic Mind. His descriptions of Mind have affinities with traditional hymns in praise of a divinity.[1] The syntax is simple, the language plain and dignified, the thought clear and elevated. He expressed himself 'attractively and solemnly' (Diog. Laert. 2.6), and in the same context we are told that Anaxagoras came to be nicknamed Mind.

Focus upon the single word and also upon Anaxagoras' style is not out of place in assessments of his philosophy. He was charged with impiety for denying the divinity of the heavenly bodies, but his concept of Mind, and the language in which he describes it, suggest that he wished, like Xenophanes, to replace traditional religious beliefs with a unitary power of cosmic rationality whose name, *Nous*, connects the world order with human consciousness. (Some support for Anaxagoras' interest in educational innovations may be

[1] Deichgräber (1933) 347–53.

found in the report (Diog. Laert. 2.11) 'that he was the first to declare that the poetry of Homer is concerned with virtue and justice'.) Anaxagoras was not the first to conceive an analogy between cosmic processes and mental activity. The Milesians had already thought of the divine power in the universe as like the *psyche* in the body.[1] But Anaxagoras' *Nous* has stronger links with the divine craftsman of Plato's *Timaeus* than with the self-activating material of Anaximander and Anaximenes. It would be unhistorical to regard Anaxagoras as an idealist and a dualist but he helped to prepare the way for those important tendencies in later Greek thought.

Throughout the fifth century B.C. most of the leading philosophers continued to come from the Ionian cities of Asia Minor and the Greek colonies of Sicily and southern Italy. As a result of Pythagoras' emigration from Samos to Croton towards the end of the sixth century, it seems correct to think of a Pythagorean community there. But there is no evidence of Pythagorean literature before Philolaus of Croton (b. *c.* 450 B.C.) none of whose 'fragments' is attested by any writer earlier than the third century A.D. Alcmaeon of Croton, who is said to have 'heard Pythagoras' (Diog. Laert. 8.83), wrote a book which allegedly began: 'Alcmaeon of Croton spoke as follows to Brotinus and Leon and Bathyllus. Concerning things unevident and concerning things mortal, gods have clarity, but as for men conjecture (alone is possible?)' (fr. 1). These words recall Xenophanes' remarks on the difference between divine and human understanding (frs. 23, 24). Alcmaeon's book treated human physiology and advanced the influential doctrine that health is due to the 'equal balance' of opposite powers – dry wet, cold hot, etc. (fr. 4).

Support for the philosophy of Parmenides came both from the west and from the east. Zeno, an Eleatic citizen like Parmenides, wrote a series of extremely subtle arguments against plurality and motion in about the middle of the fifth century. Little of his own words survives, though a fair idea of his methodology – demonstrating paradox and self-contradiction in common-sense assumptions – can be recovered from Aristotle and Simplicius.

At about the same time, or perhaps some years later, Melissus of Samos reinforced and modified Parmenides' deductions about 'what is' in a treatise composed in Ionian prose. Thanks to quotation by Simplicius enough of this work has survived to permit comparison of Melissus' style with that of Anaxagoras. The changelessness and inactivity of Melissus' unitary 'being' make it an inappropriate subject for stylistic flourishes. But if Melissus' philosophy lacked anything comparable to the *Nous* of Anaxagoras (it is impossible to know whether Anaxagoras read Melissus or vice versa) their style in other respects is similar. We do not find narrative or description in Melissus since,

---

[1] Hussey (1972) 139.

unlike Anaxagoras, he has no cosmogony to relate. But both philosophers show the same clarity and simplicity in their methods of argument. One may even detect traces of wit in Melissus' proofs that 'what is' does not feel pain or distress (fr. 7). Melissus' arguments, derivative as they are in part from Parmenides, do not generate the same intellectual excitement as the poem of his great predecessor. But his writing makes us aware that Greek prose, as a medium for expressing philosophy, had developed with remarkable speed by the middle of the fifth century.

It is uncertain whether Melissus registered his support for Parmenides before Leucippus (whose native city is variously reported, Diog. Laert. 9.30) initiated the atomic theory. But there is no doubt that Leucippus and the much greater thinker associated with him, Democritus, developed their philosophy as an attempt to explain plurality and movement without challenging Parmenides' principal arguments against genesis and destruction. According to atomism, all phenomena are to be explained by the combination and separation of wholly solid, ungenerated, indestructible and discrete bodies (atoms) moving in empty space. Thus early Greek atomism, subsequently extended by Epicurus (see pp. 625ff.), is comparable in its purposes and some of its assumptions to the theories of Empedocles and Anaxagoras.

Leucippus is a shadowy figure, whose existence Epicurus, probably out of polemic, is said to have denied (Diog. Laert. 10.13). He was almost certainly the author of a work known as *The great world system* (ibid. 10.46), and one sentence survives from a further treatise, *On mind*: 'nothing comes to be without grounds, but all things from a reason and by necessity' (fr. 2).

Democritus, in spite of the loss of his writings, must certainly be regarded as the most versatile and constructive philosopher of the later fifth century B.C. The range of his interests was enormous, covering science, mathematics, art, and anthropology, and foreshadowing the universal researches of Aristotle, Theophrastus, and Posidonius. In later antiquity Democritus was highly esteemed as a moralist, and most of the many quotations attributed to him are ethical maxims. These, together with some other fragments, show him as a polished and forceful writer. His style has many of the qualities of early Ionian prose in its liking for balanced phrases, repetition, and emphatic placing of particular words, but these devices do not conceal an individual voice which can be wry and acerbic and at other times benign.

Some examples:

> The man who intends to be good humoured should not engage in many things either in private or in public, nor in what he does should he choose things that exceed his own power and character. But he should so keep guard that when fortune falls upon him and leads him on to excess by her appearance he lays

her aside and does not grasp at things beyond his powers. For good size is safer than great size. (fr. 3)

(The words 'good size' (εὐογκίη) and 'great size' (μεγαλογκίη) appear to be Democritean neologisms.) Here we find traditional wisdom about the dangers of excess expressed in a form which looks forward to the Epicurean recipe of the 'quiet' life. More characteristic of the epigrammatic style of the ethical fragments are fr. 185: 'The hopes of the educated are better than the wealth of the unlearned', and fr. 188, 'Limit of expedient and inexpedient things is pleasure and its absence', an equally Epicurean sentiment.

In positing atoms and empty space as the two constituents of the universe, Democritus expressed himself sceptically about the objective truth of sense experience. Several fragments refer to the 'dark' understanding derived from the senses, or the 'depth' in which truth is situated (frs. 9–11, 117), and one of these is expressed dramatically: 'Unhappy mind, after taking your proofs from us do you try to overthrow us? The overthrow will be your downfall' (fr. 125, where Galen, our source, reports that Democritus 'thus made the senses converse with the reason'. Much later, the Stoic Cleanthes wrote a dialogue between Reason and Passion, *SVF* 1 570, and Plato liked to represent divisions within the soul in dramatic terms).

Democritus admired Homer (fr. 21) and claimed that divine inspiration is the source of the 'finest' poetry (fr. 18). He wrote a book, cited by later commentators on Homer, which seems to have explained points of epic language and to have discussed various passages in a moralizing fashion (frs. 20a–25). He was interested in linguistics and grammar, and sided with the conventionalists against the naturalists in the debate about the origin of names, claiming that four features of language – homonymy, polyonymy, changes of proper names, and absence of a name – supported his view (fr. 26, a difficult text of Proclus, which should not be accepted as verbatim Democritus). His view of language as a changing phenomenon in human evolution is consistent with what we know about his general approach to the development of society. While it is possible to exaggerate Democritus' influence on later Greek approaches to anthropology, there is enough evidence to show that he supported, and doubtless encouraged, the notion that civilization is to be explained in empirical and materialist terms. Plato, who never names Democritus, had no sympathy for his atomism, but it has been thought that the prehistory in *Laws* 677aff. (cf. *Epinomis* 974e–976c) loosely reflects Democritus.[1] Cicero sets Plato and Democritus together for their qualities of rhythm and 'most brilliant flashes of language' (*clarissimis uerborum luminibus*), adjudging them closer than the comic poets to poetry (*De or.* 1.49, DK 68 A 34).

[1] Cole (1967) 97–130.

10

TRAGEDY

I. THE ORIGINS OF TRAGEDY

The documented history of Greek tragedy begins in 472 B.C. with Aeschylus' *Persae*. Of his earlier career we know little; we know something but not much about one or two of his contemporaries; we have a date (536/533) for the institution of a competition in tragedy at the Great Dionysia. The origins of tragedy lie in the sixth century. So complex, however, and so obscure is the evidence, so various are the theories advanced, that the hardened scholar approaches this subject with dismay.[1]

The surviving plays of Aeschylus tell us what needs to be explained. There is a chorus, dramatized as the play demands. Their songs are elaborate and bulk large and, in pre-Aeschylean tragedy, may have bulked larger, since Aristotle informs us that Aeschylus reduced the choral element and 'gave the leading role to the spoken word'.[2] For the earlier plays two actors are required (either of whom could, with a change of mask and costume, take more than one part). Aeschylus is said himself to have added the second actor and either he or Sophocles the third, and Aeschylus uses three in his later plays.[3] The actors deliver speeches, often of considerable length and formality, but also enter into dialogue with the coryphaeus (chorus-leader) or with the other actor. Particularly characteristic are passages of line-by-line interchange (stichomythia) which, like the narrative speech, remains a formal convention of tragedy as long as we know it and may well go back to its earliest beginnings. The plays (except *Agamemnon*) are of moderate length, rather over 1,000 lines. In what kind of performances did plays like these originate?

It is easy to list contributory influences. (i) Tragedy took its stories, with few exceptions, from mythology. These stories had been treated by the epic poets, Homer and the Cycle and other epics now lost; and Aristotle, with a sure instinct, regarded the Homeric handling of myth as a prototype of tragedy.[4] But myth

---

[1] For bibliography see Appendix.   [2] *Poetics* 1449a17f.
[3] *Poetics* 1449a18 (with note in D. W. Lucas's edition).
[4] *Poetics passim*. A famous Aeschylean trilogy now lost clearly followed the plot of the *Iliad* very closely.

had also been treated by lyric poets. It seems that, from an early stage, it had been characteristic of hymns and other types of choral lyric poetry to contain a narrative; and Stesichorus had developed lyric narrative on a big scale. One could say that the stories came to the tragedians rough-shaped for drama by epic and lyric poets. (ii) The choral songs of tragedy, metrically complex and linguistically rich, written in a literary dialect which is not pure Attic (using, for instance, the α of the lyric *koine* for Ionic-Attic η),[1] are clearly indebted to the choral lyric tradition of the Peloponnesian and western Greeks: Attica had no great tradition of the kind. (iii) For a noble rhetoric in spoken iambic trimeters we must look elsewhere. Aristotle thought – it may or may not have been a guess – that the original dialogue metre of tragedy was the trochaic tetrameter.[2] Both the tetrameter and the trimeter had developed in Ionia, at the hands of Archilochus and his successors, but tragic trimeters may have owed most to Solon who, at the turn of the seventh and sixth centuries, had elevated the metre to be a medium of political exhortation.

It is easy to list these influences: but on what were they brought to bear? Few today would agree with Murray in deriving tragedy from a ritual passion play.[3] Aristotle, on what evidence we do not know, believed that it originated by extemporization on the part of 'those who led the dithyramb'; and the dithyramb was a choral hymn to Dionysus, which is likely to have included a narrative. Ignorant as we are about early dithyramb, it seems likely that the burden was carried by the leader and the main function of the chorus was to utter conventional refrains. But how does a choral performance, even with mimetic dancing (the extent of which we cannot judge), become a drama? There was a tradition, known apparently to Aristotle (though not mentioned in his extant works), current in the Hellenistic period and adopted by Horace in his *Ars poetica* (275–7), which ascribed this development to a certain Thespis from the country-deme of Icaria in Attica. There are many obscurities in the various accounts, but we must suppose that he separated himself from the chorus which he led (what kind of chorus we are not told), assumed a dramatic role and addressed speeches to the chorus: in other words, he stopped singing a story and began to act it. He brought his new invention to Athens, in mid-sixth century or later, where he acted before and after the institution of competitions.

The role of the actor was at first strictly relative to the chorus. The word for actor is *hypokrites*, the sense of which is debated. Some scholars think that it means 'interpreter': the actor elucidated the complexities of the mythical story, partly perhaps through a spoken prologue. (Whether early tragedy had a prologue is itself debated, since two of the surviving plays of Aeschylus, including the earliest, open with the entry of the chorus.) There is still, how-

---

[1] Cf. Björck (1950).   [2] *Poetics* 1449a21.
[3] For criticism of this and other theories see *DTC* 174ff.

ever, much to be said for the view that *hypokrites* means 'answerer'. He answers the questions of the chorus and so evokes their songs. He answers with a long speech about his own situation or, when he enters as messenger, with a narrative of disastrous events; or else he submits to a catechism in stichomythia. Naturally, the transformation of the leader into an actor entailed a dramatization of the chorus, which was easy enough if a citizen-chorus became the spokesmen of a city. The process envisaged, if rather vague, is plausible enough. The problem, however, is complicated in several ways, all controversial.

Thespis was an Athenian, and tragedy was generally regarded as an Attic product. But Aristotle tells us that some of the Dorians in the Peloponnese laid claim to tragedy.[1] There is indeed elusive evidence bearing on tragedy from just those parts of the Peloponnese which were nearest to Attica: from Corinth, Sicyon and Phlius. At Corinth Arion was a notable figure in the days of Periander; that he helped to turn a primitive extemporized dithyramb into an elaborate form of art is beyond doubt. Herodotus tells us this, and only this, but a later writer gives Solon, in his elegies, as the authority for saying that Arion put on 'the first drama of tragedy'. Solon cannot have used the phrase but must have said something to evoke it. The Suda-lexicon mentions Arion's work on dithyramb (clearly following Herodotus), but also says that he was the discoverer of the tragic mode or style (*tropos*), whatever that may mean, and that he brought on the stage 'satyrs speaking verse'.[2] Obscure though this all is (the last words sound like a quotation from comedy),[3] the combination of dithyramb, tragedy and satyrs in one notice is bound to be suggestive. At neighbouring Sicyon, Herodotus tells us that the tyrant Cleisthenes, at war with Argos, wishing to suppress the worship of the Argive *heros* Adrastus whose sufferings were honoured with 'tragic choruses', gave them over to Dionysus.[4] What was it about these choruses that caused the friend of Sophocles to call them tragic? Finally, Pratinas of Phlius is said to have been the first to write satyr plays; and the presumption is that he introduced them from his native city to Athens, where he also practised as a tragedian in the early fifth century. One problem leads into another.

The evidence of Aristotle's *Poetics* is not lightly to be disregarded. Not only does he tell us that tragedy arose from the 'leaders of the dithyramb' but he also uses, mysteriously, the adjective 'satyric' (*satyrikos*): he says that tragedy, beginning with short 'myths' (plots or stories) and ridiculous language, was late in attaining dignity through a change out of a 'satyric' state (or performance), and he adds that the tetrameter was used first because the 'poetry' was 'satyric' and 'more danceable'.[5] Aristotle may, but need not, have meant that tragedy

---

[1] *Poetics* 1448a29–b2.
[2] Herodotus 1.23; Joannes Diaconus, *Comm. in Hermogenem*, ed. H. Rabe, *Rh.M.* 63 (1908) 150; Suda s.v. 'Arion'.
[3] An anapaestic tetrameter? [4] Herodotus 5.67. [5] *Poetics* 1449a20, 22.

developed out of a dithyramb sung and danced by a satyr chorus; if he did, he could have been right or wrong. There is little or no independent evidence for a satyric dithyramb, but naturally we think of the notice which associates Arion with dithyramb, tragedy and satyrs. At this point in the argument looms up the grotesque shadow of a goat. The members of a tragic chorus were 'goat-singers' (*tragoidoi*). Were they so called because they sang in goatskins or for a goat-prize or in connexion with a goat-sacrifice? Or because they were masque-rading as goat-like demons? This sounds attractive but encounters the difficulty that Attic satyrs or *silenoi* had horses' tails. But they were conceived as shaggy and lustful; nor need we rule out this association simply because tragedy became sober and serious. Not only is the evidence on satyrs complex and disputed (see pp. 346ff.), but we are confronted with a basic dilemma. The fact that, in the competition, three tragedies were followed by a satyr play, that satyr plays were written by the same poets as tragedy, on stories drawn from the same fount, and were governed broadly by the same conventions, strongly suggests, if it does not prove, that there was a genetic connexion between the two forms. On the other hand, the members of a satyr chorus are already masked and 'drama-tized' as satyrs – a serious obstacle to their re-dramatization as elders (or what-ever it might be); and it can be argued that out of a satyr chorus no kind of drama could develop other than a satyr play, which did in fact so develop, perhaps at Phlius. *Non liquet*: neither the degree to which choral performances had approximated to drama in the Peloponnese nor the question whether dithyramb and tragedy shared a satyric background with satyr play can be determined on the evidence.

All three forms, along with comedy, were from the beginning, and remained, part of the cult of Dionysus. The myths sung in dithyramb and then acted in tragedy may originally have been taken from Dionysiac legend, but of these there was a limited supply. The proverbial expression 'nothing to do with Dionysus' (οὐδὲν πρὸς τὸν Διόνυσον) may suggest that the introduction of non-Dionysiac myths gave rise to protest, but this is likely to have happened fairly early in both contexts. In point of theme, tragedy moved away from Dionysus. But was its nature and character, its emotional impact, still in any degree determined by its Dionysiac associations? That there was a political factor is fairly clear. The cult of Dionysus was popular and may have been encouraged by tyrants seeking popular support, as a counterpoise perhaps to established cults under aristocratic control. We have seen some hint of this at Corinth and Sicyon; and at Athens the establishment of tragedy clearly owed much to Pisistratus and his sons (under whom Lasus of Hermione was active in the field of dithyramb). To suggest that their motives were purely political, that they had no concern to promote these new developments of that traditional choral art so intimately bound up with the cultural life of archaic Greece, might be unfair. It is likely, however, to have been under the Cleisthenic democracy that tragedy attained the greater dignity and seriousness of which Aristotle speaks; and one may speculate, if hazardously, about the effect on tragedy of a new social climate in which responsibility for grave decisions was placed upon the body of citizens meeting in the assembly – citizens who would then, at the festivals, meet in the theatre of Dionysus to hear and watch the tragedies.

Certainly, by 472 tragedy had become highly serious, political (in some sense) – and religious. Religious it had always been as part (like comedy) of a cult; and it was no doubt to cult that it owed those masks which became progressively less appropriate to the kind of plays which were written. It cannot be too strongly insisted, however, that tragedy was not itself a ritual,[1] having none of that rigid repetitive character by which ritual is marked, though tragedies did incorporate ritual features if the action so demanded (and choral odes often take the form of hymns and use hymn-language). Nor should we attribute to Dionysus both a hypothetical early grotesquerie and the later seriousness, which tragedy will have owed far more to the fact that it used and interpreted myths that were themselves impregnated with religion and had been treated lyrically in religious contexts, and to a tradition of thought upon great issues of human destiny and divine government which descended to the tragic poets from thinkers such as Hesiod and Solon. The tradition runs from them to Aeschylus.

How much tragedy owed to the sheer genius of Aeschylus, with what truth Murray called him 'the creator of tragedy', is not demonstrable, since we know so little of his predecessors and contemporaries.[2] It is just possible that four mythological play-titles (including *Pentheus*) attributed to Thespis are genuine, but nothing secure can be said about the character of his plays. Choerilus is little more than a name: he is said to have competed with Pratinas and Aeschylus in 499/496. Of Pratinas it is said that 32 of his 50 plays were satyric, which, if true, means that he cannot have operated entirely within the normal fifth-century Attic scheme. There is one substantial and very interesting fragment under his name, in which a chorus of satyrs protest that their words are being drowned by the *aulos*-accompaniment. That this comes from a satyr play rather than a lyric is pure surmise, and it has recently been suggested, with great plausibility, that the fragment really belongs to the late fifth century and has been wrongly attributed to this Pratinas.[3] Of Phrynichus, who won his first victory 511/508 and must have been senior to Aeschylus, we know a little more and get the impression of a considerable figure. In 493, during the archonship of Themistocles, he produced 'The capture of Miletus' (Μιλήτου ἅλωσις), as a result of which he was fined, says Herodotus, by the Athenians for 'having reminded the citizens of their own misfortunes'.[4] In 476 (probably), with

---

[1] Cf. Vickers (1973) 41f.   [2] For bibliography see Appendix.
[3] Cf. Lloyd-Jones (see Appendix) 15–18.   [4] Herodotus 6.21.

Themistocles as *choregos*, he won a victory with *Phoenissae*, on the theme of Salamis. He also wrote on normal mythical subjects, about the Danaids, about Actaeon, and others. From Aristophanes we learn that his songs were still famous and sung in the late fifth century.[1] That is, however, no ground for asserting that his plays were more lyrical than dramatic. What kind of plays he wrote, and with what tragic content, we simply do not know,[2] except that he twice used contemporary themes and showed the way for Aeschylus' *Persae*.

2. TRAGEDY IN PERFORMANCE

Anyone who asks: What was Greek tragedy like? What was its effect, in performance? will find the business of answering these questions somewhat frustrating. For we are the prisoners of our evidence, which is everywhere slighter than we could wish, often much later than the period we are chiefly concerned with (the fifth century B.C.), and almost always difficult to interpret. There are all too many vital questions which we cannot answer without some measure of guesswork and speculation, nor without relying on *a priori* assumptions whose validity we can never adequately test. And yet it is essential that we do raise these questions, or else the texts of Greek tragedy must remain inert, like musical scores which we cannot and do not even try to perform. For the texts are essentially scripts for performance, and the style and context of that performance are fundamental to our understanding of the texts themselves.

We can roughly classify our evidence under three heads: the discoveries and conclusions of archaeological research, later tradition about the theatre, and the play texts themselves. Each kind of evidence has its own pitfalls. The evidence of archaeology is itself of two rather different kinds. The first depends on the conclusions to be drawn from the excavation of theatre sites, the second upon the interpretation of visual imagery drawing on the theatre which appears in the painted pottery of fifth-century Attica (and to a lesser extent in other pottery) and also in the relief sculpture and terracotta figures of the late fifth and fourth centuries.

The first stone-built theatre in Athens was the work of the late fourth century, in the decade which saw Athens fall under the domination of Macedon: the site was almost totally reworked in later centuries. Earlier performances, and thus all those in the period which most interests us, relied largely on temporary constructions in wood, which have left little or no trace in the archaeological record. Late tradition connected the earliest performances of tragedy at Athens

---

[1] *Wasps* 220; *Birds* 748ff.

[2] Unless we attribute to him a papyrus fragment containing part of a tragedy based on the story of Gyges (cf. Herodotus 1.8ff.). Scholars are not agreed whether this is a work of the early fifth century or of the Hellenistic period. For bibliography see Appendix.

with the *agora*: we have no reason to doubt the tradition, but the raised plat-forms for the performers and tiers of wooden seating for the audience have left no mark behind. For most of the fifth century the performances took place in the theatre of Dionysus at the foot of the southern cliff of the Acropolis, where an acting area had been terraced up with a stone retaining wall, but the theatre 'building', the *skene*, at the end of the century was still of wood on a stone foundation, and we can learn very little for certain from what is left of those foundations about the nature of the wooden building above. The evidence of vases and other representations is somewhat better, even if it is thin. Theatre scenes, which characteristically represent actors and chorus-men seen off-stage, before or after performance, occur as early as the first surviving plays of Aeschylus (perhaps earlier), and we have a number of such scenes covering most of the fifth century. But there is a problem of deciding what is relevant: it is never easy to distinguish between pictures of actors presenting roles from the heroic repertory of Greek tragedy and scenes showing the heroic figures themselves, with the artist influenced perhaps by dramatic performance in his imagining of the scene. Before we can be sure that what is being presented to us is a scene of actors and not of mythical figures, we have to have undeniably 'theatrical' features present (dressing scenes, unmistakable masks, or the figure of the *auletes*, the musician who played the double pipe that accompanied sung scenes in Greek tragedy). And even then we have always to reckon with the play of the artist's imagination and with the conventions within which he worked.

With the evidence of later tradition our problems are different again. Here, with the exception of Aristotle, we are dealing with antiquarians, men of the Hellenistic or Roman periods assembling a miscellany of information, almost entirely from their reading, in order to produce encyclopaedias and commentaries which would make intelligible a vanished past. For the most part we can assume that their first-hand knowledge, even of the contemporary theatre, is nil, and we cannot read their sources and assure ourselves of their reliability: often we do not even know to what period their information refers, and this last point is crucial since theatrical productions and indeed the actual pieces performed had changed radically by, say, the second century B.C., let alone by the second or third century A.D. Their evidence can never be used to contradict the evidence of archaeology; it can sometimes fill gaps in that evidence.

Our last category of evidence, that of the play texts themselves, raises problems that are like those we encounter when we try to interpret the painted scenes on pottery: how do we separate the theatrical experience presented solely through the playwright's imaginative use of language from what was there, in concrete fact, before the audience's eyes? In a masked drama, as Greek drama was, it is obvious enough that some things evoked in the play text, such as tears or smiles, existed only in language and in gesture, and did not, in the literal sense, 'happen'. But how are we to decide, for example, how much of the scene evoked by the chorus in the Parodos of Euripides' *Ion*, the temple sculpture of Delphi to whose detail they respond with such emotion, or of the complex cave setting in Sophocles' *Philoctetes*, was actually represented in the stage construction of the late fifth-century theatre? What of the presentation of dramatic events such as the earthquake in *Prometheus vinctus*, or Orestes' shooting his arrows at the Furies in the mad scene of Euripides' *Orestes*?[1] As we shall see, these are not easy questions to answer.

The first thing we have to take account of in trying to assess the impact of Greek tragedy as it was experienced in performance is the context of that experience, the place of tragic drama in the life of the Athenian community. Though it was not itself a liturgical, ritual act (see p. 262 above), it was nevertheless part of the worship of divinity, a sacred event with its place fixed in the religious calendar of Athens, and marked as sacred by the actual rituals which surrounded it (such as the torchlight procession in which Dionysus' statue was brought from the altar on the road to Eleutherae to his theatre in Athens, the great phallic procession on the first day of the Dionysia, and the sacrificial rites of purifying the theatre), as well as by the suspension of profane activities of the community during the festival. A second important aspect of the dramatic experience also derives from its social context: it is the analogy with the great religious contests of the Greek world, such as the Olympic and Pythian 'games'. In both, the endemic and potentially disruptive competitiveness of ancient Greek society was validated and sanctified by dedicating conspicuous display of competitive achievement to the worship of the gods. The dramatic performances of Athens, like the athletic contests, took much of their meaning for those who witnessed them from being contests in achievement before the eyes of the community. Playwrights, actors and *choregoi* (Athenians who displayed their wealth by paying lavishly for the costs of performance) were all taking part in competition with one another and the 'victories' of each were publicly proclaimed and attested in the records of the Athenian polis and in conspicuous private monuments alike. The role of the audience, thought of as both 'the Athenians' and 'the Greeks', is to give its recognition to the triumphant prowess of the victor, and, conversely, to deride unmercifully the humiliation of the defeated.

The very size of the audience at Athens (perhaps 15,000) made it natural and indeed accurate to think of the performances as an expression of the Athenian people's solidarity and as an act of the community, with two aspects; the first an act of celebration honouring the gods, and the second the provision of an arena for the acknowledgement of prestige and standing within the community.

[1] Eur. *Ion* 184ff.; Soph. *Phil.* 15ff.; Aesch. *P.V.* 1080ff.; Eur. *Orestes* 253ff.

Both aspects are reflected in the fact that, as we learn from Aristotle, the organization of the festival, the processions and the dramatic performances, was one of
the major responsibilities of the archon, the chief magistrate of Athens.[1] The
same two aspects of the dramatic performances also mean that, though they
represented something radically new in form and presentation, the tragic
competitions were rooted in tradition. The plays themselves not only draw
heavily on traditional stories and on the traditions of religious imagery which
gave those stories much of their significance, but also, in enacting heroic
struggle both of man against man and of men against all that is alien to man,
contribute to the reinforcing of the traditional values of ancient Greek society,
even though the traditional values are at the same time subjected to scrutiny
through the constant reshaping of myth. For the whole community, represented
in the audience, the performances of tragedy constitute a fusion of the traditional
past with a new, innovating present.

This is to put the double-sidedness of past and present, tradition and change,
in sociological terms. We can see it equally clearly expressed in the concrete
realities of the place and circumstances of performance. The centre of the
performance space is the level circular area of the *orchestra*, the dancing-floor,
now vanished at Athens in the re-ordering of the theatre of Dionysus for later
styles of performance, but present and unaltered in the best preserved of Greek
theatres, the theatre of Epidaurus (Pl. IV*a* and Fig. 1). This was built probably
no earlier than the third century B.C., to plans by an otherwise unknown architect, Polyclitus, but was already famous in later antiquity for the beauty and
symmetry of its architectural composition.[2] The *orchestra* is the focal point of
the whole design. It measures some twenty metres in diameter (the *orchestra* at
Athens was probably a little larger), and is almost two-thirds enclosed by the
rising tiers of the auditorium, in the shape of a cone, inverted and truncated.
The origins of the *orchestra* are very much earlier than those of drama; in all
probability they are to be found in the circular threshing-floors, often terraced
out of the hillside, which are dotted in large numbers over the Greek landscape.
As well as being the place for threshing grain or drying grapes and figs, such
threshing-floors were a place for dancing. Dancing upon a circular floor, with a
crowd of spectators surrounding it, is figured in the design of the shield of
Achilles in the *Iliad*: 'a dancing-floor like the one Daedalus made in the wide
town of Cnossus', on which the dancers circle effortlessly 'like the wheel of a
potter when he crouches and works it with his hands to see if it will run'
(18.590ff.). Upon such a floor the chorus of tragedy moves: it is the fixed and
essential element in the construction of a theatre for dramatic performances. By
contrast the ground for spectators might vary considerably in shape and siting.
After the abandonment of temporary wooden stands, spectators were almost

[1] Aristotle, *Ath. Pol.* 56.2–5.   [2] Pausanias 2.27.5.

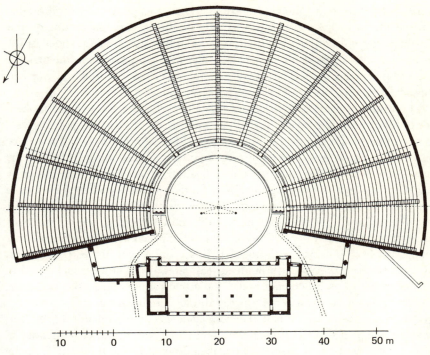

Fig. 1 The theatre of Epidaurus.

always placed on a hillside, usually curving but often far from the symmetrically graded and curving auditorium at Epidaurus: at Athens the curve is noticeably flatter, hardly more than half enclosing the *orchestra*, with acoustics that can never have been as good as those at Epidaurus, while local village theatres, such as the late sixth-century theatre at Thoricus in Attica, might be wholly lacking in symmetry.[1] Orientation also varied very widely: the theatre at Athens faced roughly south-south-east, while that at Epidaurus was almost diametrically opposed, facing north-north-west. In every case the orientation of the most appropriate hillside determined that of the theatre: at Athens the theatre overlooked the sacred precinct of Dionysus and his archaic temple, while at Epidaurus the sanctuary of Asclepius lay only some 500 metres away below the theatre.

The circular form of the *orchestra* is related to the ring-dances of early Greek folk celebration, and the traditional dance pattern was retained in the circling dance of the fifth-century dithyramb. Dithyrambic competitions for choruses of men and boys, each fifty strong, representing the ten tribes of Attica, also formed part of the celebrations in honour of Dionysus, and seem to have taken

[1] For the date of the theatre at Thoricus, see T. Hackens in Mussche et al. (1965) 75–96.

267

place in the theatre of Dionysus on the same days as performances of drama. But the chorus of tragedy characteristically moved in line, like a military unit parading, and did not, except rarely, reflect the traditional plan retained in the *orchestra* circle. It was also very much smaller (probably twelve in the plays of Aeschylus; fifteen in the later plays of Sophocles and Euripides), and had consequently a relatively much larger space in which to move.

The sense of openness of space pervades the performances of tragedy; open, not only to the light of the sky, with a total absence of walls or roof to give a feeling of enclosure, but also with open sight lines which converge from every angle on the huge, uncluttered *orchestra* and what lay beyond it. It is with the question of what lay beyond that our difficulties of interpretation begin. At a tangent to the *orchestra* circle but set back a little from its edge there was, by the time of the *Oresteia* at least (458 B.C.), the theatre building called the *skene*, and on either side of it, in the space between it and the forward edge of the half-circle of spectators, two open passage ways by which actors could enter the acting area from outside the theatre. These are the *eisodoi*, the entry passages, and at Epidaurus they pass through formal gateways of stone which stand at right-angles to the supporting wall of the auditorium. Since the late fifth-century *skene* at Athens was built of wood, there are questions we cannot very well answer as to its height and external appearance, the number of doors and other openings in it, and its painted decoration. It was a solid construction, of fairly substantial timbers, but could be taken down between festivals;[1] it seems to have had a flat roof, strong enough to support several actors upon it, and at least one double doorway facing the spectators. It is probable that from the first some such building served as a store-room for masks, costumes and props, and as a green room for actors preparing to make their entries. But we cannot be certain how early it came to be part of the fixed and accepted design of a theatre area or how it was at first interpreted. In Aeschylus' earliest surviving play, *Persae*, it has been convincingly argued that the action of the first part of the play is to be somewhat loosely imagined as taking place inside, not in front of, a building: this is certainly the most obvious and least strained interpretation of the words of the chorus of Persian elders in council with Xerxes' mother, Atossa: τόδ' ἐνεζόμενοι στέγος ἀρχαῖον 'sitting in (near? on?) this ancient building' (140f.). In that case, the *skene* was presumably either not yet in a position behind them as the spectators viewed the scene, or at least not thought of as part of the imagined scene of action, but rather as a non-dramatic piece of theatre equipment, like the banks of spotlights and floods in a modern theatre. But by the early 450s at least the *skene* is thought of as bounding the scene of action and in certain moments part of it. It may represent a building (commonly a palace or a temple) or the background of a scene of seashore or of mountainside. Entrances

---

[1] Xenophon, *Cyropaedia* 6.1.54.

are made from it and the scene of action is now clearly marked as being out of doors: interior scenes can be shown only in tableau.

It is convenient and natural to speak of the 'acting area', but as soon as we ask where it was, and how if at all it was distinguished from the *orchestra*, controversy intensifies. There is some slight evidence, partly in the plays themselves, partly in tenuous traces in the theatre of Dionysus and the fifth-century theatre at Eretria in Euboea, that the space in front of the *skene*, between it and the *orchestra*, was raised a little above the latter, at Athens probably on a low wooden platform with one or two steps down into the *orchestra*. We cannot be certain of this but it seems the most plausible interpretation of our slight evidence. What we can be confident of is that there was no high stage, lifting the actors a metre and a half or more above the level of the chorus, such as was imagined in the last century when reconstructions of the Greek theatre were attempted. Not only do the texts of the plays (such as the scene in Sophocles' *Oedipus at Colonus* (822ff., esp. 856–7) in which the chorus try physically to intervene as Oedipus and Antigone are carried off by the ruthless Creon and his armed men) tell strongly against it, but it is far more convincing to connect the high stage with the much later Hellenistic and above all Roman elaboration of the wooden *skene* into a stone-built façade of several stories. Such structures threatened to dwarf the actors and this effect was countered by raising them above the audience (the chorus having now effectively vanished from the theatre) and then, as we shall see, by elongating their figures with new kinds of mask and footwear which gave added height to suit the new perspective. For the fifth-century Athenian theatre we have to imagine the actors for the most part speaking and moving in front of the *skene* and close to it, on a low platform. One of the functions of the *skene* will thus have been to project the actor's voice forward towards the spectators and lessen the vocal demands made by the scale of the auditorium and theatre space.

The scene displayed before the spectators will thus have been one in which their eyes could travel across the breadth of the acting area and beyond it, into the side passages. The figures in that area will have been relatively few in relation to the space available and their movements therefore the more significant in spatial terms. There are important implications to this. The fact, for example, that entrances and exits, other than through the doorway of the *skene*, had measurable duration for the spectator and were made in full view, means that they had added dramatic weight. They were not instantaneous passages from the invisibility of the wings to the visibility of the stage, but extended happenings with considerable dramatic potential. It is only when we appreciate this that we can understand the dramatic strategy of the scene, for example, in *Oedipus at Colonus* in which Ismene enters. Her long approach is heralded and accompanied by an ecstatic account from Antigone, her sister, who describes to her blind father, in a controlled unfolding of detail, the appearance of the approaching figure, the mare she rides on, her broad Thessalian traveller's hat, until she is within the range of speech, and finally of touch (310ff.). Such moments of intense acceptance contrast with the silent, unacknowledged approach, equally visible, of characters whose arrival is, as it were, rejected and denied and who have to force themselves past the barrier of silence into the world of the play. An example of such entrances is given by the several arrivals of Jason in Euripides' *Medea*: he comes and goes in silence, addresses no greetings and receives no farewells. The dramatic weight of comings and goings is proportional to the openness of space that the Greek theatre presented to the playwright, who was also the producer, for exploitation.

In its function as part of the scene of imagined action, the *skene* is the place where those dramatic events which occur, as we should say, 'off-stage' are imagined as happening. Though it is not true that death is an event which, in Greek tragedy, can never occur in view of the spectators (the deaths of Alcestis and, more disputably perhaps, of Ajax in Sophocles' play are obviously exceptions),[1] nevertheless violent death characteristically occurs within, that is, inside the *skene*, and has its dramatic impact through the death-cries of the victim and the controlled passion of the messenger-speech. But there is another way also open to the playwright to give weight to violent death in his plays, through the use of the interior tableau. Late tradition provides evidence for the existence of a theatrical device known as the *ekkyklema*, most probably a low trolley which could be thrust forward towards the spectators through the doors of the *skene*, and several passages in Aristophanes, parodies in which its use is transferred to tableaux of the domestic interiors of tragic playwrights, make it certain that the device was used in the fifth-century theatre.[2] We can form some idea of its dramatic effect by looking at two scenes. In Aeschylus' *Agamemnon*, the death-cries of the king are followed almost at once by the opening of the *skene* doors and the first words of Clytemnestra's speech of triumph. At line 1379 she says 'I stand where I struck, over the work that I have done', and in the light of the other evidence, it is clear that we are to imagine Clytemnestra standing within the palace over the bodies of Agamemnon and Cassandra, the tableau revealed by the thrusting out of the *ekkyklema*. The scene is hauntingly repeated in the second play of the *Oresteia*, where (*Choephori* 973) the doors open again and this time Orestes stands over his mother's body and that of Aegisthus. In Euripides' *Heracles*, at line 1029, the doors of his palace open, revealing the scene of slaughter and havoc within, which the appearance of Iris and Lyssa (815ff.) had predicted and the messenger-speech (909ff.) described: Heracles is seen slumped unconscious over the bodies of his own children

---

[1] Eur. *Alc.* 387ff.; Soph. *Aj.* 815–65 with 891–9.
[2] Ar. *Ach.* 395–479; *Thesm.* 95–265.

whom he has murdered, then gradually returns to consciousness. In scenes such as these the device of the interior tableau is used to powerful effect.

Another piece of theatrical equipment is also best attested in use in the fifth-century theatre by Aristophanic parody. In *Peace* (154ff.) the hero Trygaeus flies up to heaven on an enormous dung-beetle to interview Zeus, and as with the *ekkyklema* dramatic illusion is suddenly abandoned with a panic-stricken address to the crane-operator (the *mechanopoios*). The *mechane* is a device also attested in later tradition about the theatre, and the scene in *Peace* looks like a parody of one in Euripides' lost play *Bellerophon*, in which Bellerophon flies to heaven on Pegasus. In extant tragedy it may have been used for the appearance of divinities who are described as winging their way through the air, as with Oceanus in *Prometheus vinctus* (284ff.), or Thetis in Euripides' *Andromache* (1228ff.), Athena in his *Ion* (1549ff.) and the Dioscuri in his *Electra* (1233f.): Euripides attained some notoriety for his use of the 'god from the machine'.

It was customary in the theatre of a generation ago, and in the West End commercial theatre of domestic comedies and farces still is customary, for the acting area to be occupied not only by actors but by a proliferation of objects, furniture, ornaments and the like, whose function is to give a naturalistic impression of lived-in space. By contrast the theatre space of Greek tragic drama was starkly bare: the actors were not lost in, nor their movements confined and determined by, a profusion of things defining and occupying space. Stage properties were certainly used, but for their dramatic quality, not to create an ambient illusion. Those of which we can be most certain are the focus of continuing and powerful dramatic emotion: thus, for example, the robe in which Agamemnon is killed in the *Oresteia*. Related to the purple cloths upon which Agamemnon walks to his death, it figures constantly as an image (often as a 'net') in the language of the first play, linking the death of Agamemnon to the fall and sack of Troy; and in the second it is displayed to the spectators by Orestes after the killing of his mother (*Choephori* 980–1020). It is spread out before their eyes ('stretch it out and standing in a circle display the thing that trapped a man') and insistently referred to in the sequel ('this robe', 'this fabric') as the visible symbol of Orestes' right action in killing his mother.[1] Sophocles has a particular inclination towards the use of such powerfully emotive properties: the sword of Ajax, the bow of Philoctetes, the urn in which the ashes of the supposedly dead Orestes are brought to his sister Electra. In Aeschylus stage properties have something of the uncanny force of an object with the power to cause of itself death and destruction, and are analogous in their use to the stage

[1] A recently published red-figure vase in Boston, without evident theatrical connexion but dating from the same period as the production of the *Oresteia*, gives a good idea of how Agamemnon's death-robe was imagined, as an almost transparent ankle-length garment without holes for neck or hands: cf. Vermeule (1966) 1–22 and plates 1–3; Davies (1969) 214–60.

events of an eerie strangeness, such as the ghost-raising scene in *Persae* or the Cassandra scene in *Agamemnon*, from which Aeschylus derives much of his theatricality. In Sophocles, on the other hand, they are felt more as the focus of powerful human attachments and feelings, and around these feelings much of the stage action revolves. Their use in Euripides seems more attenuated, even ironical (the shield of Hector in *Troades* 1136ff. or Apollo's bow in *Orestes* 268ff. are slight instances beside the Sophoclean examples: the latter even may be imaginary, the product of Orestes' insane hallucinations), but in all three dramatists their effect in the theatre derives from the spareness of the use of properties in general.

Another kind of property, the appurtenances of splendour and power, seems also to have been used. Such are the chariot in which Agamemnon returns with Cassandra from Troy (*Agamemnon* 906), or that in which Clytemnestra visits her daughter, supposedly in childbirth, at the peasant cottage to which she has been exiled (Euripides, *Electra* 966, 998ff., 1135ff.). They too have a dramatic point to make and underline the ironies of splendour in a context of violent death: they are very different from the illusionistic properties of later theatres. It is much more difficult to be sure about the use of properties, and of painted scenery generally, whose function is largely or solely to create a specific sense of place, the illusion of a scene designated by objects. How, for example, was the raising of Darius' ghost in *Persae* actually staged? Our difficulties in interpreting the contemporary archaeological evidence are well illustrated by a fifth-century Attic vase-painting which has, unconvincingly, been used to answer this particular question. Fragments of a hydria found in Corinth (Pl. IV*b*) show a scene which is seemingly marked as theatrical by the presence of the *auletes* playing his double pipe; five or more Oriental, probably Persian, figures are depicted in trousered costume with a flapped headdress, and in attitudes of horror or amazement, but without any attempt to suggest that they are wearing masks. The central figure is a king, to judge from a wooden pyre, constructed of logs with each row laid at right angles to the one below. The pyre is alight and flames are licking about it. What are we to make of this? It seems unlikely, though on purely *a priori* grounds, that burning pyres formed part of the stage properties of a fifth-century tragedy: perhaps the combination of the *auletes* and the horrific scene presented was meant to evoke a dramatic moment described in a messenger-speech or even in a dithyramb. Perhaps, though, our assumptions are false and such a scene could have been staged literally as depicted. The question is an open one.

The problem of such properties and of scenery inevitably brings in the evidence of later tradition: our earliest source is Aristotle who records laconically that Sophocles introduced *skenographia* ('painting the *skene*') into performances of tragedy (*Poet.* 1449a18f.). A much later source, the Roman architect

Ia Boy reading from a papyrus roll. Fragment of a red-figure cup by the Akestorides Painter, about 460 B.C. As often in such paintings, the text on the roll is represented unrealistically in order to be legible: the letters are enlarged and the writing runs across the roll rather than in columns down its width (as in Plate II). The text appears to be from a mythological handbook.

Ib Girl reading: marble funerary relief commemorating Avita (Ἀβεῖτα), who died at the age of ten. She holds a tablet on her lap, and there is an open roll on the reading stand beside her.

II Part of a papyrus roll, showing the characteristic division of the text into columns. This is the famous copy of the speeches of Hyperides, dating from the second century A.D., which is the main source for the text of this

III A leaf of an open papyrus codex, showing the binding string in the centre of the leaf. The text is part of a glossary, copied in the sixth century A.D.

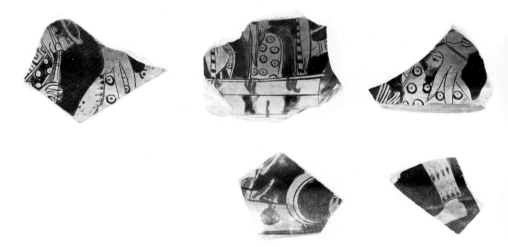

IVa Epidaurus: the theatre from the air.
IVb Fragments of a hydria found in Corinth, showing an *auletes* and figures in oriental costume.

Va Red-figure pelike from Cervetri showing actors dressing and rehearsing, *c.* 430 B.C.
Vb Red-figure bell-krater showing actors dressing and rehearsing, *c.* 460 B.C.

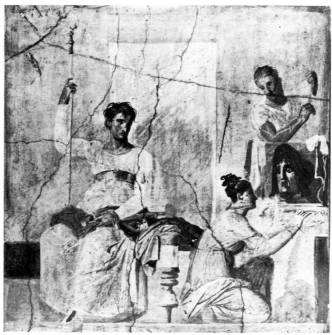

VIa Vase-painting in several colours, *c.* 350 B.C., from Tarentum. This seems to show a painted backdrop for a play, rather than a stage building.

VIb Wall-painting from Herculaneum, probably a copy of a Greek model of *c.* 300 B.C., showing an actor and his mask.

VIIa Red-figure jug from Athens, *c.* 470–460 B.C., showing the mask of a tragic heroine.

VIIb Red-figure vase-painting from Athens, *c.* 400 B.C., showing a female tragic mask.

VIIc Vase-painting in several colours, *c.* 340 B.C., from Tarentum, showing an actor holding his mask.

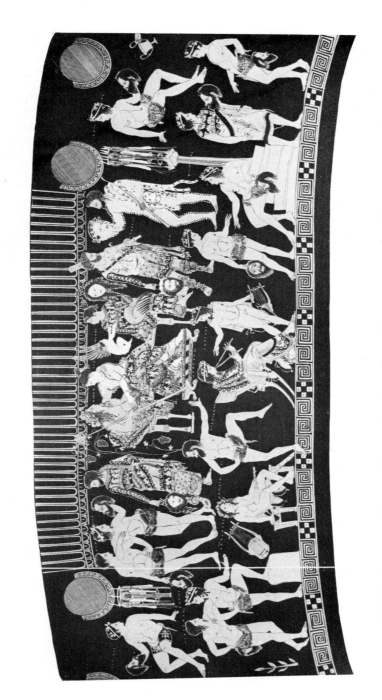

VIII The Pronomos Vase: red-figure volute-krater from Athens, c. 400 B.C., showing actors, a satyr chorus, an *auletes*, the play-wright and a lyre-player.

Vitruvius, asserts that Aeschylus adopted the idea from the painter Agatharchus of Samos.[1] Like the introduction of a third actor, this development seems to have been attributed to the decade in which the theatrical careers of Aeschylus and Sophocles overlapped, with some uncertainty about which of the two was responsible. But how are we to interpret the assertion? Tragedies were performed at the Athenian City Dionysia in sequences of three, followed by a satyr play, and it was normal for the three tragedies to have no continuity of setting: even Aeschylus, who alone seems frequently to have written connected sequences of three plays presenting different stages in the unfolding of a single story, did not seek to place his plays within a single setting. Indeed the third play of the *Oresteia* itself involves a change of setting, from before the temple of Apollo at Delphi to the Areopagus at Athens. Another of Aeschylus' plays, the *Women of Aetna*, seems to have had a setting which was imagined to shift five times within the play.[2] But here (the play is lost and the assertion occurs in the ancient *hypothesis*) the inference must be from the language of the play and we may be dealing with an action very loosely anchored in spatial terms, as we are in *Persae*, where the relationship between the 'ancient building' of line 141 and the tomb of Darius later in the play is left entirely open and the setting almost freely variable. There is a world of difference between this and the opening, for example, of Sophocles' *Electra*, where the evocative landmarks of Argos are pointed out one after another by the *paidagogos* to Orestes on his return as a young man from exile since childhood. The introduction of 'painting the *skene*' almost certainly falls between these two plays. Indeed we have already seen that in the earliest plays there may have been no *skene*-building placed so as to focus the acting area immediately in front of it. In the early plays of Aeschylus (*Persae, Septem contra Thebas, Supplices*) it is noticeable that the setting is either left without precise locality or imagined as an open space: there are several references to a rocky crag or mound (*Persae* 659f., the tomb-mound of Darius; *Supplices* 189; the crag recurs in the probably somewhat later *Prometheus vinctus*, lines 20, 130, 272 etc.); moreover in the theatre of Dionysus at Athens the ground beyond the *orchestra* from the spectators was almost two metres lower than the *orchestra* terrace itself. Thus the placing of a *skene* in that area may have been a development of the middle or late 460s and 'painting the *skene*' may have occurred very shortly after the building itself was first constructed so as to close the spectators' view.

As to what was painted we have no contemporary evidence and are left to guess: the most plausible guess is that it represented a building or buildings or a landscape-setting painted in a kind of primitive perspective with multiple

---

[1] Vitruvius, *De architectura* 7.1.11; cf. 1.2.2. For Agatharchus' date, which is disputed, see also Plutarch, *Alcibiades* 16.5; *Pericles* 13.3 and the discussion in Pollitt (1974) 236–47.

[2] Aesch. fr. 287 Lloyd-Jones.

vanishing points. This tradition of painting was connected with Agatharchus and found its fullest expression considerably later, in the Hellenistic wall-paintings which were the source for the painted 'theatrical sets' used to decorate the houses of southern Italy, at Pompeii, Herculaneum and Boscoreale. Our earliest evidence for this tradition comes from a vase of the mid-fourth century from Tarentum in southern Italy which shows (on Erika Simon's interpretation),[1] not a stage-building, but a painted theatre set of a building, with projecting porticoes at either end, each crowned by a pediment with gilded *akroteria* and ceiling panels, and with two double doors, one at the end of each portico (Pl. VI*a*). But the relevance of this painting to the fifth-century Athenian theatre is highly uncertain.

When we turn to the question of actors and acting styles, we are to begin with on firmer ground. The first, essential fact is that all actors and chorus-men in Greek tragedy were male: that is, that female parts were acted, not by boys as in the Shakespearian theatre, but by adult men, often of middle age or older. For acting careers in the tragic theatre seem to have been long.

The actor Mynniscus who acted for Aeschylus (that is before 456 B.C.) won first prize in a play by Menecrates in the competition of 422 and in the late fourth century the actor Polus was still performing eight tragedies in four days at the age of seventy.[2] It is tempting to suggest that the part of Clytemnestra in the *Oresteia* was played by Aeschylus himself, then in his late sixties: tradition recorded that it was Sophocles who was the first playwright to abandon acting the leading part in his own plays, and that was not at the beginning of his career (he almost certainly acted in his early plays *Thamyras* and *Plyntriai*). Thus we have to imagine not merely female roles that convey an almost aggressively masculine feeling, such as that of Clytemnestra or of Euripides' Medea, played by men, but also highly 'feminine' roles such as those of Io in *Prometheus*, Deianira in *Trachiniae* or Euripides' Creusa (in *Ion*), Iphigenia or Helen: the only comparable theatrical experience available to us is perhaps the same tradition in the Japanese No and Kabuki theatres. The parts of children were indeed played on stage by children, but as silent mimes: children are never given spoken lines in Greek tragedy, and it is noticeable that the brief snatches of sung lamentation, which is all the utterance that they are given, are always so placed that there is a male actor available to sing them off-stage.

In his account of the development of tragedy, Aristotle records the introduction of a second actor by Aeschylus, and of a third by Sophocles: at this point, in Aristotle's view, tragedy had 'attained its natural form' and no further changes took place (*Poet.* 1449a14f.). Correspondingly, the series of nouns 'protagonist', 'deuteragonist', 'tritagonist' does not continue beyond its third member. It follows that, down to Aristotle's time, only three actors were avail-

---

[1] Simon (1972) 35.   [2] Plutarch, *Moralia* 785b.

able to the playwright in writing and casting his plays. Silent walking-on parts might be used: hence the unspeaking figures such as Pylades in the Electra plays of Sophocles and Euripides. The explanation for this limitation may have been financial but is more likely to have been aesthetic and practical. It will not have been easy to find large numbers of trained voices capable of meeting the vocal demands of text and theatre. In addition, masked drama makes it difficult to identify the source of speech, so that if a considerable number of speakers are all engaged together in dialogue the audience may become confused: it is very noticeable that even with three actors a genuinely free-flowing three-cornered dialogue is extremely rare in Attic tragedy. Usually, if two speakers are engaged in dialogue, the third is silent until one or other has fallen out of the exchange: a carefully patterned sequence of utterances is the norm, as in the scene between Oedipus, Creon, Jocasta and the chorus in *Oedipus tyrannus* (512ff.). An important consequence of the limitation, of course, is the doubling of parts by a single actor; occasionally, even, the splitting of a single part between two actors. We cannot in the nature of things be certain which actor played which parts in a given play (a subject on which we have no direct evidence), but sequences of entrances and exits, speech and silence, often suggest inferences, and the likely doubling of parts is sometimes striking in its histrionic possibilities. The probability that the parts of Deianira and Heracles (in *Trachiniae*), of Phaedra and Theseus (in *Hippolytus*) or of Pentheus and Agave (in *Bacchae*) were played by the same male actor gives an idea of the challenge to an actor's technical skills, and a messenger-speech will often have been delivered by an actor who in the same play also acts the part of one of the central figures in the scene he is describing: again *Bacchae* produces an example, since the messenger is likely to be the same actor as he who played the part of Dionysus.

The extreme case of doubling and splitting parts is that of Sophocles' *Oedipus at Colonus*, where on a strict interpretation of the three-actor limit the role of Theseus must be played by two, perhaps even three, actors and Ismene is present but silent for almost a third of the play, played by an 'extra' (in the technical language of the theatre a *kophon prosopon*, a silent mask), because no fourth actor was available. The story of Oedipus' death, involving his two daughters, his son, Creon and Theseus in a shifting pattern of conflict and loyalty, presented a fifth-century dramatist with major problems of dramatic construction.

Soon after the introduction of the third actor, acting as such, as a skill distinct from that of play-writing, became a sphere of achievement in its own right, and from 449 B.C. actors, as well as playwrights, were ranked in competition and awarded prizes. The entry into the theatre of the new specialism is perhaps reflected in the extent to which sung passages (not unlike operatic recitatives and arias) are given to actors of the later fifth century: already in the *Oresteia* such sung passages are important (the Cassandra scene of *Agamemnon* is the most striking example: the part of Cassandra was perhaps played by Mynniscus, the recently introduced third actor), and in Euripides actor-arias figure from the first and play a steadily increasing and important part in his later productions. The actor's apprenticeship in the chorus may be one of the factors lying behind this development.

Before we turn to the question of acting techniques, we must look at the evidence for the actor's theatrical appearance, his costume and mask. All actors, whether playing speaking or silent parts, and the members of the chorus, were masked: indeed the word *prosopon* means not only 'face' and 'mask', but also 'character' in the theatrical sense. Only the *auletes* (who played throughout in view of the spectators) was unmasked. Masks were full face and covered the whole of the front half of the head, including the ears, with wigs attached. Fifth-century masks seem to have been made of linen or other flexible material, stuccoed over with plaster and painted: none has survived. Vase paintings are our best evidence. The earliest certain example of a theatrical mask appears depicted on fragments of a red-figure jug found in the *agora* at Athens and dating from 470/460 B.C. (Pl. VII*a*). It is the mask of a female character, painted white in the conventional way in which female skin colour was shown in all Greek art, with hair cropped short and held in with a head-band; the eyes are fairly wide-set, almond-shaped not circular, and the mouth is small in proportion to the breadth of the face and the lips only slightly parted. There is no striving after intense emotional expression in the painting of forehead, eyebrows or mouth; rather a certain openness of regard. The style is reminiscent, as has been pointed out, of the so-called 'severe style' of the temple sculptures of Olympia, which date from around 460 B.C., and there seems to be nothing specifically 'theatrical' in its presentation. The general impression of clarity and simplicity of expressive means is confirmed by other paintings of masks on Attic pottery in the decades from 460 to 430 or a little later, such as the dressing scenes on a bell-krater in Ferrara (Pl. V*b*) and on a pelike in Boston (Pl. V*a*), and a more imaginatively treated scene of a chorus-man who has become the maenad whose role he is playing, with theatrical reality retained only in the mask and in the figure of the *auletes* who faces him: in the last two, the mask is shown in profile and we can form a clear impression of its relationship to the actor's own head and hair, which is commonly cut short and held in by a sweat-band. To the last decade of the fifth century probably belong two vases (Pl. VII*b* illustrates one of them), perhaps by the same painter, and a relief from the Piraeus. From all three we can see that the mask mouth is now somewhat larger and more widely open, though still very far from the gaping, almost trumpet-like mouths of Hellenistic and Roman masks: the effect of emotional strain in the painting of the face is also rather more marked, with the forehead and the area of the mouth heavily lined.

One of the two vases, the so-called Pronomos vase in Naples (Pl. VIII), is our most detailed and magnificent depiction of a scene of actors: it figures three, perhaps four actors carrying masks and in costume, and a complete satyr chorus, as well as the *auletes* (the central figure, who must have commissioned the painting), the playwright and a lyre-player, all three named on the vase. One of the actors is dressed to play the part of Papposilenus, the stock old man who accompanies the satyr chorus, wearing neck-to-ankle tights of white fleece flocked with tufts of wool, with a leopard-skin over his left shoulder and carrying a mask of grotesque and sad old age: his role in extant satyr plays makes it clear that he is not the chorus-leader. This is presumably the figure to the right of the altar bearing the victory tripod, who holds a satyr mask (indicated by its snub nose, wrinkled forehead and animal ears) but wears an elaborately decorated *chiton*. The other satyr chorus-men wear only bathing-trunk shaped tights of animal skin with a large, erect phallus and animal tail attached: they too have their human names on the vase. There is continuing argument over the three figures dressed as actors and carrying masks, two of whom flank the central couch in the upper bank while the third is perched on its foot: are they actors from the cast of a tragedy or from a satyr play? Happily there is no need to pursue the argument here, since the silence of all our sources makes it virtually certain that, apart from Papposilenus, the actors in a satyr play (as distinct from the chorus) were not distinguished by mask or dress from those in a tragedy. The actor who faces Papposilenus is playing Heracles, as his club and lion-skin (worn with a breastplate over it) make clear, while the figure who balances him at the other end of the couch has a mask with an oriental tiara attached: his part is not that of a Greek. The third figure with a mask (also with tiara) has the face of a woman, not a male actor: we are perhaps to think of her as the image of an abstraction, perhaps Tragedy or *Paidia*, the burlesque personification of the satyr play, dressed as though an actor. Interpretation is difficult, since in the artist's eye these last three figures have become fused with their parts and have taken on a heroic and distant dignity: none is named on the vase. The latest (and persuasive) suggestion of a subject for the play in which these actors appeared is the story of Heracles and Omphale.[1]

Two other representations of actors come from later centuries and from outside Athens, but are still of interest. The first is a fragment from Tarentum (Pl. VIIc), like the *skenographia* painting we have already discussed, and is of much the same date in the second half of the fourth century. The mask, again seen in profile, is not very different from those on the Pronomos vase of half a century earlier, the eyebrows and forehead perhaps more strongly marked but the mouth-opening no greater, the forehead no higher: it suggests that there had been little change in masking designs. The piece is particularly interesting for a new, sociological point that it makes in the eloquent contrast between actor and

[1] Simon (1971) and (1972) 30.

part: the actor is stocky, balding and greying, square-faced and flat-nosed, with the stubble of a beard strongly marked on his chin and jaws; beside his mask he is palpably ordinary. Conversely, on a wall painting from Herculaneum but drawing probably on a Hellenistic picture of around 300 B.C. (Pl. VI*b*), the actor appears as matinée idol, handsome, tall and slim with delicate hands and hair elegantly ruffled. The painting of his mask is in equally striking contrast with its vast, staring sunken eyes, mouth hugely open and towering pointed forehead and peak of hair, the *onkos* of theatre handbooks. It belongs to the new theatre of the Hellenistic world, in which as we have seen the actor has to compete with the towering stone façade behind him, and will serve as a classic reminder of what the fifth-century mask was *not* like.

Besides giving us, at least in general terms, a fair idea of the look of fifth-century masks, the pottery scenes we have considered also remove another widespread misunderstanding about the actor's appearance. In the Hellenistic and Roman theatres actors wore shoes and boots with blocked soles and heels to give them extra stature by perhaps as much as six inches. The pottery scenes make it absolutely clear that footwear of this kind was never worn in the fifth-century theatre. What we find on the vases is actors either barefoot or wearing shoes or boots (it is not always possible to tell which, but in some cases certainly they are calf-length) made of soft, pliable leather with a thin sole and a marked turning up of the toes. Such shoes appear on the pottery scenes from the 460s right through to the end of the century, sometimes elaborately decorated, sometimes plain: they seem to be early established as the traditional actor's footwear. If the actor's boot was, in the fifth century, called a *kothornos* (and there is no contemporary evidence that it was), then passages in Herodotus, Aristophanes and Xenophon make it clear that its associations were not with added stature but with women (Dionysus in actor's gear is even more effeminate than usual) and with a degree of looseness of fit that ruled out distinctions of left and right.[1] The tradition that connects Aeschylus with the platform-soled boots of the Hellenistic theatre is certainly the result of some misunderstanding, which goes back at least to Horace, probably to the third century B.C., and presumably arose when the word *kothornos* had come only to refer to what was by then the characteristic footwear of the actor.[2]

Our evidence for costume is somewhat confusing. If we take the pottery scenes as our guide, the picture is of a dress that becomes markedly more elaborate and stylized as the century proceeds, though interpretation is complicated by the fragmentary state of some of the pots and the fact that while some of the scenes can be firmly identified as representations of chorus-men and others

[1] Herodotus 1.155.4; 6.125.3–4; Ar. *Frogs* 47; *Lys.* 657; *Eccl.* 313ff.; Xenophon, *Hellenica* 2.3.30f.
[2] Horace, *Ars poetica* 280.

of actors, some remain uncertain. The earlier scenes show actors or chorus-men generally in a long, ankle-length *chiton* with a heavier *himation* over it: decoration consists largely of borders and there are no sleeves, any more than there were in contemporary dress outside the theatre. But by the end of the century, on the Pronomos vase, for example, and on other scenes that seem to have at least heavily theatrical overtones, the actor appears wearing costumes of elaborately decorated and heavy material, with sleeves that stretch to the wrist: an example is an Attic krater found at Capua showing the captive Andromeda surrounded by figures some of whom have a distinctly theatrical air. From now on, sleeves seem to be an unchanging and characteristic feature of costume in the theatre as they never were in the world outside. At all periods, of course, distinctive costume can be used to identify characters (such as Heracles, Hermes or Dionysus) or groups (the Persians on the pyre scene from Corinth (Pl. IV*b*) wear trousers, like the Ethiopian girl on the Andromeda krater). But rich and elaborately patterned fabrics made up into sleeved garments are the mark of the actor dressed to play a part. It seems likely enough that the sleeved *chiton* came into the theatre through being worn by the *auletes*, who is shown wearing it from the first, in a garment of almost standardized patterning of black circles with a central dot and a long stripe running from shoulder to ankle. We could be fairly confident of recognizing the late fifth-century actor by the richness and stylization of his costume if it were not for a string of jokes in Aristophanes about Euripides' repeated use of actors dressed in rags (*Acharnians* 412ff.).

Aristophanes' jokes seem to suggest that we are wrong, about Euripides at least, but perhaps a simple inference as to theatrical fact would be a mistake: Aristophanes has a habit of making comic capital out of treating the metaphors of tragic language as statements of literal fact (for example, the stage business with the chopping-block in *Acharnians* when Dicaeopolis offers his head as guarantee of his words, 355ff.) and this may be merely another example. Certainly Euripidean characters do talk of themselves as tattered, dishevelled and sometimes filthy (his Electra or the shipwrecked Menelaus of *Helen* are good examples), but already in Aeschylus' *Persae* the defeated Xerxes is described as returning with his clothing torn to shreds.[1] Faced with this contradiction between the evidence of the pottery and that of comedy, we can only back a hunch: it seems most likely that the vases show what the spectators actually saw in the theatre, and that Aristophanes' jokes do no more than exploit Euripides' intensification of the language of degradation in his plays. The nearest we get to 'rags' in the pottery evidence is the rather muted brown fringed *chiton* of the actor on the Tarentum fragment (Pl. VII*c*).

From the evidence we have been discussing we can form a good impression of an actor's visual impact in the theatre. But what of his acting? We have to

---

[1] Eur. *El.* 184ff., 304ff.; *Hel.* 415ff., 554; Aesch. *Pers.* 834ff., 1017ff.

make do here with generalized accounts of the emotional effect that acting could have on an audience, with scrappy references to voice production and to gesture, and with what we can infer from the play texts and from the actor's costume and mask. Descriptions of an actor's performance in terms of the emotional experience involved are certainly important, but they can tell us almost nothing of the technique that produced that experience. Descriptions of Japanese actors in the No and Kabuki theatres, of actors in the Shakespearian theatre from those of his own day through to Garrick, Kean and Irving are all evidence for the sense of 'life' displayed and for the emotions aroused in the audience, but where we can compare these accounts with more technical descriptions or with present-day representations of the same tradition, we can readily perceive the stylization involved and the extent to which it is the audience's acceptance of a particular stylization which leads to the experience of 'naturalness' and to a strong, direct emotional response. That there was such a response to the performance of Greek tragedy is clear enough: it is attested in stories such as that of the great fourth-century actor Polus moving an entire audience to tears by his playing, under the impact of his own son's death, the part of Electra in the recognition scene of Sophocles' *Electra* (Aulus Gellius 6.5). That is a late story: other similar stories refer to fifth- and fourth-century actors such as Callippides, Theodorus and Satyrus. A near-contemporary analogy is Ion's account in Plato (*Ion* 535c–e) of his solo performances of the Homeric poems: the audience weep, their faces filled with anger, while his own eyes well with tears and his heart pounds. But references to the actor's technique are more often concerned with qualities of voice, and many of them refer to dieting and to vocal training and exercises that suggest the world of opera rather than the spoken theatre. Actors, of course, might have to sing, but it is clear that vocal control, the capacity to vary tone and colour as well as dynamic range, was a prime requirement for delivery of the spoken as well as the lyric portions of the complex texts of Greek tragedy in a large, open-air theatre space.

As for style in movement and gesture, there are traces of changes in the fifth century. Aeschylus' third actor Mynniscus is reported by Aristotle (*Poet.* 1461b26ff.) as having described his younger contemporary Callippides as an 'ape' for his excessively emotional and extravagant style of gesture and movement: Callippides won a victory at the Lenaea of 418 B.C. It is a reasonable guess that the development of sleeves in the actor's costume and the increasingly striking decoration was partly at least a response to the need to make gesture more expressive and more clearly visible, so that an actor's 'line' (to use a ballet term) was more marked. On the other hand, both the thin soled shoe and what we hear in later tradition about the movements of the chorus suggest that a smooth and gliding movement of the body was more typical of tragedy than angularity and muscular tension, a sinuous continuity rather than explosive staccato movements. The construction of the plays themselves, the formality of long speeches on the one hand, and of such exchanges as stichomythia on the other, must have inhibited the development of a wholly naturalistic delivery and movement. It would be contrary to what we know of theatre history elsewhere to assume a divorce between styles of writing and styles of acting since the playwright was himself very much of the theatre, and it is not until the fourth century, when revivals become a feature of the dramatic festivals, that the question of 'interpreting' in the theatre an existing body of classic plays can have arisen. An increasingly 'expressive' use of voice and gesture in the last quarter of the fifth century would be exactly what we should expect from changes in the writing of plays, particularly in the later theatre of Euripides. In his plays, along with a spoken line that becomes steadily freer and more flexible in its metrical patterning goes a rapid adoption of the new possibilities of expressiveness offered by developments in music. In the hands of composer-poets such as Melanippides and Timotheus, the tight structuring of sung passages by the demands of symmetrical responsion of stanzas and the harmonic discipline of modal composition gives way to a new astrophic use of long, highly flexible stanzas and to the abandonment of the strict demands of the musical mode. Euripides adopts these features as early as *Troades*, and late plays such as *Ion*, *Helen* and *Orestes* are marked by a quite new style of writing in which long, elaborate arias are given to actors as well as by increasing experimentation in the use of new versions of old forms, such as immensely extended passages of stichomythia and of whole scenes written in trochaic tetrameters. It is likely enough that all of this goes closely with developments in acting style aimed at a greater range of expressive possibilities. If we imagine Callippides in the role of the Phrygian slave in *Orestes* (1369ff.), we can well understand the reaction of an older generation of actors whose style had been moulded by the far more severely controlled writing of Aeschylean theatre.

3. AESCHYLUS

Aeschylus won his first victory in 484, which will be a firm date based on records; and it could throw some slight suspicion on 525/524 as the date of his birth (*floruit-* dating?), though, if he competed as early as 499/496, it may not be too far out. He was born to Euphorion, a eupatrid, at Eleusis. The known facts of his life are few. He fought at Marathon, where his brother Cynegeirus fell; doubtless at Salamis, which he describes; and perhaps also at Plataea. When he wrote of war, he wrote as one who knew its glory and its misery. He visited Sicily at least twice. Some time between 472 and 468 he was at the court of Hieron I at Syracuse, where he is said to have revived *Persae* and, in honour of the newly-founded city of Aetna, produced a play called *Aetnaeae* (part of the argument to which may be preserved on a papyrus).[1] In 458 or later, after the fall of the Sicilian tyrants, he went to Gela, where he died in 456. What part, if any, he played in Athenian politics is debated, but there is reason to suppose he was sympathetic towards Themistocles, who was in trouble when Aeschylus wrote his *Persae*; and it seems clear from *Eumenides* that he accepted the radical reforms of the Areopagus by Ephialtes, but scholars are not agreed whether it was with enthusiasm as an extreme democrat or with reserve as a 'moderate'. His importance to us is that he wrote plays. He wrote, acted and produced, devising new dance-movements for the chorus. His mastery of stage-effect is obvious.

The number of his victories is given both as 13 and as 28.[2] The latter figure must include victories won after his death, since we are told he was granted the unique honour that his plays might be entered in subsequent competitions; the lower figure in itself suggests a considerable pre-eminence. Some 80 of his titles are known to us, but only seven of his plays survive entire, three of which constitute the trilogy of the *Oresteia*. The trilogy was a striking feature of his dramatic art. It had become a rule of the competition (we cannot say when) that each poet should put on three tragedies followed by a satyr play. These plays could be, and after Aeschylus generally were, unconnected with one another, but it was clearly his practice, at least during his later career, to write three tragedies dealing with successive phases of the same myth, followed by a satyr play on a closely related story.[3] (It is to these linked plays that the terms trilogy and tetralogy are alone properly applied.) We have the rare good fortune that a complete Aeschylean trilogy has survived, since without it we could hardly have understood how he used this form to explore human destiny upon an extended time-scale or how he imposed architectonic unity so as to create, virtually, a single work of art. It follows that, where, as with *Septem contra Thebas*, *Supplices* and (probably) *Prometheus*, we possess only one play out of three, interpretation labours under a grave disability. Of the lost plays some can with certainty, and others with fair probability, be grouped in trilogies.[4] It is quite likely that Aeschylus invented the form (though others are known to have used it), but how early we cannot tell. Some titles are known, and others conjectured, to be satyric, about 15 in all, but, since we do not know when the rule of three tragedies and a satyr play came in, we have no idea how many

[1] Cf. Lloyd-Jones (1957) 593.

[2] Works: for references and bibliography see Appendix.

[3] E.g. the satyr play of *Oresteia* was *Proteus* (Menelaus and Helen in Egypt, cf. Homer, *Od.* 4.351ff.); of the Theban trilogy *Sphinx*; of the Danaid trilogy *Amymone*.

[4] A *Lycurgeia* is certain, cf. schol. *ad* Ar. *Thesm.* 134 (*Edoni, Bassarides, Neaniskoi*, satyr play *Lycurgus*), and an *Achilleis* virtually certain (*Myrmidones, Nereides, Phryges* or *Ransom of Hector*). A second Dionysiac trilogy (including *Semele* and *Pentheus*) is highly probable; also a trilogy on the Ajax-story (*Judgement of the arms, Threïssae, Salaminiae*); possibly trilogies on the Argonauts and on Odysseus. In some cases there may have been only two related plays. Cf. Metze (1959) and Lloyd-Jones (1957).

satyr plays Aeschylus had been required to write, though we know that his reputation in this line was great. His early career is thus quite obscure, and it is not until 472 that we reach firm ground, and that with a play which differs from the other extant plays in two respects.

Between *Persae* and the lost plays produced with it (*Phineus*, *Glaucus Potnieus*, and the satyric *Prometheus pyrkaeus*) there is no discernible link; it is the only extant tragedy on a subject taken from contemporary history. It might seem surprising that a tragedian could move from, say, Achilles to Xerxes, from Xerxes back to Agamemnon, but this is to misunderstand the twin facts that the Greeks regarded myth as history and that Aeschylus treated history as myth. If the emotions of a recent threat and triumph were vividly evoked (if Themistocles, and perhaps Aristides, were not forgotten), the Persians are not mocked, and patriotic exultation takes second place to a religious interpretation of events which has, to a degree, determined the form of the play. Stiff and archaic the form may seem. The play opens with the chorus of Persian counsellors: concerned that no news has come from the great expedition, they declaim and sing for 150 lines before the first character appears. It is the mother of Xerxes, who tells them of an ominous dream that the great king's chariot had been wrecked, when he tried to yoke two women, one in Persian dress, one in Greek. Then enters the second actor, a messenger, giving the news of Salamis to queen and chorus. Messenger-speeches are a staple feature of Greek tragedy: so also are *kommoi* or lyric-scenes between chorus and actor (or actors); and *Persae* ends with a long and tense lamentation between Xerxes and the elders. But the return of a humiliated Xerxes is postponed, while the ghost of Darius is raised from his tomb. Spectacular effects are found elsewhere in Aeschylus, who was held by ancient critics to aim at 'astonishment'; and this apparition, prepared by an incantation, must have been sensational enough. But Darius was introduced not merely to amaze but to instruct; not merely because he has foreknowledge of that other great disaster at Plataea, but because he alone (though a Persian) understands the significance of events and the moral order upheld by Zeus who 'is set as the chastener of minds that are over-proud, and heavy is the account which he exacts' (827f.). Earlier in the play the divine power is seen as cruel, fickle and unpredictable; so it is seen by Xerxes on his return. The final *kommos* – a ritual dirge with its music and dance-movements – may be the emotional climax of the piece, but by reverting to the religious notions and superstitious tone of the earlier phase it highlights the advanced morality of the Darius-scene, which is thematically and structurally the central feature.

In *Septem contra Thebas* five years later (467), if we find once more an austere simplicity of structure, we are confronted with far more complex problems of interpretation, and that not only because the plays which preceded it in the trilogy (*Laius*, *Oedipus*) are lost. In *Persae* the moral and religious issue is straightforward: Xerxes and his Persians offend and are punished. The Theban trilogy is, like *Oresteia*, the story of a doomed house; and *Septem* came at the end of a series of disasters – and doubtless crimes – in the royal house of Thebes, initiated by Laius and affecting the destinies of Oedipus and his sons. How the earlier events were distributed and handled in the lost plays we do not know with any certainty. The third play opens after the death of Oedipus and the quarrel of his sons; Polynices, in exile, has brought a foreign army against Thebes, and Eteocles leads the defenders. It opens with a speech by Eteocles, who is virtually the sole character in the play. That a play should be so dominated by a character is something new, and we shall not find it again except in *Agamemnon* and *Prometheus vinctus*. A word should be said at this point about characterization in Aeschylus.

It is austere and limited and in keeping with the archaic simplicity of the dramatic action. The extent to which Aeschylus was interested in character for its own sake is not easily defined. It has been said, with much truth, that the Aeschylean character is his role in the play and nothing more. What complicates the case of Eteocles is the fact that his role is twofold: he is at once 'lord of the Cadmeans', leading the defence of his native-city, and 'son of Oedipus', lying under his father's curse which he is bound to fulfil in the mutual fratricide; and he is thus the focus of a twofold issue, since the fates of family and city are both involved. When, at the climax of the play, he decides to fight his brother at the seventh gate, this has been seen as the instantaneous transformation of conscientious patriot into demon-haunted fratricide. It is less simple than that. The motivation of Eteocles is specifically explored, and a complex fabric is woven out of patriotic duty, personal honour, brotherly hatred, and paternal curse. If Aeschylus has not created a 'character' in the modern sense, he has imposed a notable figure on the stage, but how, exactly, we are meant to understand the relationship of the curse-Erinys to the human motives of Eteocles is hard to determine in the absence of the earlier plays.

We are left with a strangely gripping, if elusive, play. Once again, there is a big central scene, in which a spy describes the foreign champions at each gate and Eteocles posts a defender against each. The sombre rhetoric is magnificent; but what could be more static? Yet a tension is built up towards the moment of decision, when Eteocles finds his brother at the seventh gate. At the end of the play we are confronted with one of those textual problems which dog the study of Aeschylus. Enter Antigone and Ismene and a herald who forbids the burial of Polynices. But many scholars believe that all this was interpolated subsequent to the *Antigone* of Sophocles, that the authentic play ended with the young women of Thebes who form the chorus lamenting over the brothers.

If there is an archaic stiffness about *Persae* and *Septem*, what could be more archaic than *Supplices*? The play opens, like *Persae*, with the entry of the chorus, to which well over half the lines belong. There are still only two actors, and little use is made of the second; there is no dominant figure, but as it were a collective heroine; the dramatic interest is in their fate, the dramatic tension is generated by their songs. It is not surprising that this was long regarded as the earliest play, datable perhaps to the 490s. Perhaps scholars should have been more cautious, reflecting, among other things, on the leading role played by the chorus in *Eumenides*, on the function of choral odes in *Agamemnon*, and in general on that deep concern of the Aeschylean chorus with the action, and the interpretation of action, which is nowhere more evident than in *Oresteia*. In 1952, however, there was published a fragmentary didascalic notice on papyrus which indicates that the Danaid trilogy was victorious in competition with Sophocles, who first competed in 468 (or at the earliest 470); the plausible restoration of an archon-name would date the production to 463.[1] Rearguard actions have failed, and there is now general recognition that the early dating must be given up.

The story of the fifty daughters of Danaus, living in Egypt but descended from Argive Io, who fled to avoid marriage with their cousins, the fifty sons of Aegyptus, was a myth of great antiquity which had already been treated in tragedy (see pp. 262f. on Phrynichus). The surviving play was first in the trilogy. It opens with the Danaids newly arrived in Argos, their cousins in hot pursuit. They appeal to the king Pelasgus, who needs 'deep salutary thought that plunges, like a diver, into the depths, with seeing sober eye' (407–9). He is confronted with a dilemma between war with the Egyptians, if he protects the suppliants, and the wrath of Zeus Hikesios, if he rejects them; to which is added the prospect of pollution, if they carry out their threat to hang themselves from the images of the gods. Pelasgus decides that he will commend their case to the people of Argos, who have the final word. This word is favourable, but a herald lands from the Egyptian fleet and with barbarous violence seeks to drag the Danaids from the altars. They are saved by the king, but war seems inevitable.

The king's dilemma and decision are clearly a factor of dramatic importance, and his reference to the people adds to the play a political dimension which was doubtless taken up in the sequel. But Pelasgus does not emerge as an individual, while Danaus is merely characterized as the planner and plotter behind his daughters. Not even a tormented Pelasgus really takes the stage from the Danaids. It is their play and remains their trilogy – a trilogy of remarkable unity in point of place, time and theme, the events of the three plays following in quick succession at Argos, concerned with the fate of the same set of persons, who formed the chorus of two – and perhaps of all three – plays. *Aegyptii* and *Danaides* are lost, but, if we cannot work out their economies in detail, we know

---

[1] Cf. Lloyd-Jones (1957) 595ff. and *A.C.* 1964 (see App.).

some of the things that happened.[1] We know that the Danaids did marry their cousins and, on the instigation of their father, killed them on the wedding-night, the victims (and threatened suicides) of the first play becoming murderers in the sequel; that one Danaid, Hypermestra, spared her husband and so created the dramatic situation of the final play; that Aphrodite appeared and proclaimed her universal power in nature. There may or may not have been a trial, on stage or off stage, of somebody. There must have been a solution: but of what problem?

It is a remarkable fact that the whole trilogy seems to have been focused upon the relations between men and women and the place of marriage in the structure of society. The Danaids have an abhorrence of marriage which may have stemmed less from the cousinship than from the violence of their suitors. Yet women must marry, as their handmaidens (who are introduced as a subsidiary chorus at the end of *Supplices*) knew, and as Hypermestra accepted, and as Aphrodite will have proclaimed. How the trilogy ended we cannot be sure, but it may well have ended with a 'conversion' of the Danaids. If this is a social issue (becoming political through the involvement of the Argive democracy), it is also religious, not merely because of Aphrodite, but because Zeus presides, with his mysterious purposes, the protector of suppliants, who nevertheless are wedded against their will, and of strangers, whom nevertheless they kill, the god who, with Hera, presides over marriage.

With the Oresteian trilogy, produced in 458, we can at last survey an Aeschylean drama in all its sweep and intricacy. It consists of three plays (*Agamemnon, Choephori, Eumenides*), each with its own action, its own tone and character, but constituting a single dramatic exploration of a single tremendous theme. *Agamemnon* is the longest, as it is the most complex; yet in some ways its dramatic technique is the oldest. The action could not be simpler: Agamemnon returns from Troy and is killed by his wife. It receives, however, an elaborate preparation through the exposition of past events and an accumulation of foreboding, to both of which the chorus (of Argive elders) contributes. The choral odes, particularly the entrance-song, are long and highly elaborated. Though Aeschylus now has three actors at his disposal, scenes tend to be played between one actor and the chorus; genuine dialogue is rare: the more impressive, therefore, when Clytemnestra persuades her husband to enter the palace treading on scarlet draperies. The third actor provides a Cassandra who is silent, until, left alone with the chorus, the prophetess weaves past, present and future into a single fabric, in an astonishing scene of song and speech. But the play is dominated by the figure of Clytemnestra, the injured mother and wife, but also the man-woman who threatens the principle of male domination.[2]

[1] Cf. Garvie (1969) 163–233 for a careful examination of the problem.
[2] Cf. Winnington-Ingram (1948).

If the dramatic technique of *Agamemnon* is in several ways archaic, the play is full of colour and variety; its horizons are wide, since they embrace the earlier events in Argos and at Aulis and the Trojan War itself, all leading in their different ways to the fall of Agamemnon, the quality of whose vengeance upon Troy is revealed by chorus, Clytemnestra and Herald. By contrast, *Choephori* is sombre, narrowly concentrated upon the theme of vengeance through matricide: Orestes – a relatively colourless figure – has returned to avenge his father and restore male domination in Argos. Now we meet for the first time two more staple features of Greek tragedy: a recognition, when Electra recognizes her brother returned from exile, and an intrigue, when together they plot the killing of Aegisthus – and of their mother. In the second half of the play, the action moves rapidly, and the old nurse of Orestes plays her part, but perhaps the most striking feature of all is lyrical, a great *kommos* in the centre of the play, when son and daughter join with the chorus of palace-slaves to pay respect to the dead Agamemnon within the earth and invoke his aid. A tensely moving ritual, it is also a preparation (of Orestes and of the audience itself) for the bloody acts to come.[1]

Eumenides is a play of gods, even the chorus is divine; it is a play of brilliant variety and scenic effect. Orestes is pursued by the Erinyes – to Delphi, where he is disclosed in the shrine of Apollo surrounded by sleeping demons, and then (a change of scene rare in Greek tragedy) to Athens, where they dance round him singing their Binding Song. Athena empanels the Areopagus; Apollo enters to oversee the defence of Orestes; there is a trial and a ceremony of voting. Orestes goes free, and Athena persuades the Erinyes to accept his acquittal and a cult in Athens. The play ends with a procession: singing songs of good will, the Erinyes, now Eumenides, are escorted by torchlight to their new home in the rock.

The three plays are forged into a unity not only by the causal sequence of events but by the carrying through from play to play of themes – and above all of one paramount theme, which is justice, the justice of men and the Justice of Zeus; indeed the trilogy can well be seen as a vast dramatic exploration of the nature of justice human and divine. Which raises a problem, since at both levels justice first appears to be a matter of retaliation, of *talio*. It is characteristic of the earlier stages of the trilogy that, at every point, the issue is complicated. In *Agamemnon*, the just punishment of Troy involves, mysteriously, the sacrifice of Iphigenia, the dilemma – and the guilt – of Agamemnon. The stage is held far more, however, by Clytemnestra the avenger, who is studied and presented (so it has been held) as herself involved in a tragic situation, being a woman with the will and power to dominate within a man-dominated world; and if as an avenger she has her case, her menace lies within the context of a social situation.

---

[1] Cf. Lesky, *TDH* 125 and Appendix bibliography.

This social theme runs, like a counter-subject, throughout the trilogy. In *Choephori*, the dilemma is obvious: justice must be done, but it can only be done by Orestes and through an act of matricide, by a crime parallel to that of Clytemnestra, the parallelism being brought out in many ways. Orestes acts at the command of Apollo, but under threat of persecution by Erinyes, and he is pursued by Erinyes. In *Eumenides*, Apollo and Erinyes are in dispute before the court of the Areopagus; and a human jury is in its turn confronted with an apparently insoluble dilemma. The human votes are equal:[1] it is Athena who resolves the situation, giving her vote on preference for the male; and the arbitrary fiat of a prejudiced divinity may well convey what Aeschylus saw as a social necessity. But Athena does more than decide the case: she persuades the menacing Erinyes to accept a home and worship in Athens. To what extent the close of the trilogy can be said to resolve the complications of its earlier phases is a question to which we must return.

Prometheus vinctus raises special problems: even its authenticity has been impugned.[2] This hypothesis, based upon real peculiarities of language and technique (if not also of thought), needs to be taken very seriously. If a majority of scholars do not accept it, this is partly because some of the linguistic arguments have little cogency when so few Aeschylean plays have survived, more because of an unlikelihood that there were two poets alive, one of them anonymous, capable not only of the grand dramatic conception but of such an Aeschylean effect as the entry of Io. Perhaps the strongest argument for authenticity is the fact that the play demands a sequel and what we know of *Prometheus lyomenos* ('The loosing of Prometheus'), which is more than we had any right to expect, provides the kind of sequel required: in fact the *Prometheus vinctus* and the *Prometheus lyomenos* would seem to stand or fall together, and both were accepted as Aeschylean by Hellenistic scholarship. Since there is a good deal of linguistic evidence to associate the play more closely with *Oresteia* than either with earlier plays, it is likely, if Aeschylus wrote it, to be late and there are reasons for supposing that it could have been written in Sicily during the last years of his life. A third title remains to be considered: *Prometheus pyrphoros*, which may have been the third play of a Promethean trilogy. If so, it is more likely to have been the last play than the first, the title referring, not

---

[1] Some scholars believe that Athena cast a vote for Orestes as a member of the jury, so that a majority of human jurors found against Orestes. It depends on the interpretation of *Eum.* 734–41, which is controversial.

[2] The case for authenticity is well put by Herington (1970) but Griffith in a careful study (1977) suggests the opposite conclusion. (See also Taplin (1975) 184–6.) The present writer must confess that his faith in the traditional authorship has been severely shaken, but it seemed right in all the circumstances to discuss the play here as Aeschylean, not least because, if another wrote it, he did so under strong Aeschylean influence. Perhaps we assume too readily, thanks to Aristophanes and Aristotle, that there were three great tragedians only and the rest were indifferent performers.

to the bringing of fire to men, but to a torch-race cult of Prometheus at Athens. We cannot be quite sure, however, that there were more than two plays or that a trilogy, if planned, was ever carried to completion. We have to make what we can of the extant play, helped by some knowledge of the *Lyomenos*.

One of the puzzles of *Prometheus* has always been its presentation of Zeus, whose character, as seen by the hero and his friends, corresponds at every point to the traditional Greek picture of the tyrant. Prometheus is the persecuted friend of man. Taking the trickster-god of folk-lore (and Hesiod), who also bore a significant name ('Forethought') and had become the patron of Athenian potters, Aeschylus made of him a great symbol at once of goodwill to mankind and of practical intelligence. In a long speech which is an astonishing feat of historical imagination, Prometheus tells how he not only gave men fire but brought them out of a Hobbesian state of nature into the semblance of civilized life by teaching them the practical arts (*technai*). For this he is punished by that Zeus who, in *Oresteia*, 'set mortals upon the path of wisdom' (*Ag.* 176f.).

The shape of the play is determined by the situation: other heroes come and go, but Prometheus, crucified upon a rock in the Caucasus, abides and is visited. He is visited by the chorus of Oceanids and by their father Oceanus; he is visited – the entry is sensational and unprepared – by another victim of Zeus, the 'cow-horned virgin' Io, whose sufferings match his own but whose ultimate destiny foreshadows his own release. The hero remains for a brief span of dramatic time at a remote point in space, yet no play has broader horizons. The whole world is embraced, when Prometheus tells us of the journeyings past and future of Io (matched, apparently, by the journeys of Heracles in *Lyomenos*); and, brief though the traffic of the stage may be, the dramatist conveys the long process of development from the bestial state of primitive man to that settled community in which the story of Io is placed. Much of the play is taken up with long expository speeches. Where, then, does drama reside? It resides in the conflict between Prometheus and Zeus, the intensification of his obstinate resistance, and the fact that he holds a weapon against his oppressor, a secret. Zeus, whose lust appears to be victimizing Io, will one day lust after a goddess destined to have a son greater than his father, and so Zeus may fall from power.

Our knowledge of the sequel is limited. We know that Heracles, in *Lyomenos*, killed the eagle which came to devour the liver of Prometheus and, ultimately, released him from those bonds that Hephaestus had made so firm. Somehow the quarrel between Zeus and Prometheus must have been resolved. The secret was revealed, because Zeus did not marry Thetis; there was reconciliation, but on what terms, and at what level, we cannot easily judge. It has been suggested, with plausibility, that Zeus not only accepted the survival of the human race but to the material and intellectual gifts of Prometheus added his own gift of justice necessary to human society. To say that Zeus has 'developed' may go beyond the evidence; and perhaps the question we should ask ourselves is this: Under what other mode could the government of the world present itself to primitive man, as depicted by Aeschylus, than that of harshness and force?

This review of the extant plays may have given some impression of the power – and the range – of Aeschylean tragedy. To sum up the character of Aeschylus as dramatist and as religious thinker – the two roles are indissociable – is no easy task, and the difficulty resides partly in a combination of all but contradictory qualities. There is a traditional picture of Aeschylus – the stern moralist, prophet of a Zeus who is concerned with the inexorable punishment of offenders; master of a grand style, with an imagination so lofty as to set him apart from common humanity. The picture is both true and false.

His style is indeed grand, though not grandiloquent, since it is strikingly free of ornament applied for its own sake. Rich but disciplined, if at times it appears lavish, it is lavish with a density of meanings. Style cannot profitably be discussed without a degree of illustration which is impossible here, but some points can be made. If the wide vocabulary of Aeschylus owes a debt to his epic and lyric predecessors – a debt which, with the loss of most of the early poetry, cannot be particularized – he was doubtless a bold innovator in his own right, particularly perhaps in the coinage of those compound epithets which are so characteristic of his diction; and, like many great poets ancient and modern, he had a bold way with language. Not only in smaller matters of semantics and syntax did he strain normal usage but in metaphor, where he has no peer except Pindar, his combination of images seems sometimes to strain figurative language almost to breaking-point; when he wished, however, he could elaborate a single image with amazing skill. Of the Greeks who died before Troy, the Chorus of *Agamemnon* sing:

ὁ χρυσαμοιβὸς δ' Ἄρης σωμάτων
καὶ ταλαντοῦχος ἐν μάχηι δορὸς
πυρωθὲν ἐξ Ἰλίου
φίλοισι πέμπει βαρὺ
ψῆγμα δυσδάκρυτον ἀντ-
ήνορος σποδοῦ γεμί-
ζων λέβητας εὐθέτους.   (437–44)

But the money-changer War, changer of bodies,
Holding his balance in the battle
Home from Troy refined by fire
Sends back to friends the dust
That is heavy with tears, stowing
A man's worth of ashes
In an easily handled jar. (tr. Louis MacNeice)

The style is grand, in dialogue as well as in lyric, but he could also write very simply and give colloquial turns of speech to humbler personages.

For his minor characters are not to be forgotten or else we shall miss the wide range of his sympathies. In *Agamemnon*, for instance, alongside Clytemnestra (and her beacon speech) and a cold triumphant Agamemnon, we have the Watchman and the Herald, with their wry peasant humour and that concern for their own affairs which reveals the effects of high tragic events upon common people. These are 'character-parts'; and it could well be that it was through such figures that a degree of naturalness in characterization first found its way into Greek tragedy. The Nurse in *Choephori* harks back to the incontinence of the infant Orestes and to his dirty linen. Perhaps we should not have been surprised, when extensive fragments of some Aeschylean satyr plays came to light, to discover with what a light touch he could handle the traditional obscenities, what a charming song (in *Dictyulci*) Silenus sings to the infant Perseus, as the child plays with the monstrous phallus.[1]

Aeschylus combines with an intricate detailed art a mastery of overwhelming emotional effects, which are often produced by the sheer force – or poignancy – of language. All three tragedians, however, in their different ways, used spectacle as well as language for dramatic ends; and the visual effects of Aeschylus are particularly striking. Reference has already been made to the raising of Darius, the unprepared entry of the cow-horned Io, and to the whole sequence of spectacles in *Eumenides*; to these could be added the irruption of the terrified female chorus in *Septem*, not marching sedately but dancing in to the dochmiac metre, or the cries and contortions of Cassandra when, after her long silence, she enters into trance. This is the *ekplexis* 'astonishment' ancient critics spoke of. In *Agamemnon* Clytemnestra is disclosed standing over the bodies of her victims; in *Choephori* Orestes stands over his. The effect is visual and powerful, but the aim is different, since a comparison is invited between the two pictures and a question is thereby raised about the relationship of the two actions. There is a pattern; and such structural patterning is not rare in the art of Aeschylus.

A certain formality is characteristic of Greek art, literary as well as visual. Much has been written recently about ring-composition, which is found in Homer and may have originated as a convenient device of the oral bard, which we can observe in Pindar and infer from him for his lyric predecessors. A section, long or short, is concluded by returning to a word or theme with which it began. With a great artist, this is not a mere formal device for its own sake, but the word or theme when it reappears may carry more meaning than it had before: 'release from troubles' means more at the end of the first half of the Watchman's speech than it meant at the beginning (*Ag.* 1; 20); the words and

[1] Cf. Lloyd-Jones (1957) 531ff.

themes, images and symbols, picked up at the end of *Oresteia* mean more and other than they meant early in the trilogy. Ring-composition on every scale is all-pervasive in Aeschylus. Another device of emphasis concerns his imagery. It is characteristic of him to sustain an image or images throughout a play: in *Septem* the ship of state, in *Supplices* birds of prey, in *Oresteia* nets and snares, indeed a whole complex of metaphors from hunting and fishing. But these are only special cases of a much wider phenomenon. Words, or groups of words, carrying an important theme are repeated, often at points of emphasis. For instance, in *Oresteia* we find words of mastery and victory associated with the theme of male/female domination; words of heredity; words of justice and legal process. The polarities of good and evil, light and darkness, joy and sorrow, paeans and dirges, force and persuasion, run right through the trilogy. Scholars may dispute this or that interpretation, but there would be wide agreement that the texture *is* dense, that repetitions *are* deliberate, that themes *are* carried through. Similarly with those ambiguities which Aeschylus uses as a kind of compressed metaphor, often looking backwards or forwards to link the superficially disparate. Some scholars are more cautious than others in identifying ambiguity, but few would deny that the language of Aeschylus is often deliberately ambiguous, that references to parents and children in *Agamemnon* are made with thought of the matricide in *Choephori*, that references to legal process in the earlier plays look forward to a trial in *Eumenides*.

These are some of the resources of the art of Aeschylus, ranging from overwhelming, and often spectacular, effects to the intricate working-out of themes. To what dramatic ends are they applied? How did Aeschylus see the world, and see it as tragic? And here perhaps we come up against the most remarkable combination of all. The thought and art and language of Aeschylus are deeply rooted in an archaic past, in a world haunted by terrors and superstitions; and yet many have found in his drama a rational control, a power of general thought, a profound insight into fundamental problems of the human condition, a movement out of darkness into the light.[1] Disagreement is, however, fairly wide within this field, and no coherent statement can fail to be in some degree personal.

Aeschylean tragedy is concerned with human destiny, with the individual fate of an Eteocles or an Agamemnon. But the individual is part of a family, a cohesive kinship-group: Eteocles suffers under his father's curse, Agamemnon for the sins of his father. And the family is part of a wider kinship-group, the *polis*. All are closely bound together, as they still were in the contemporary Greek world: the relationship of *oikos* to *polis* is a fundamental theme in *Septem* and hardly less important in *Oresteia*. All the great issues are social, and they

---

[1] Cf. e.g. Dodds (1951) 40. Contrast the Introduction to Denniston–Page (1957). See also Lloyd-Jones (1956) and (1971).

touch the social life of the poet's own time. If, in the heroic context, the polis is rudimentary, neither could he speak nor his audience hear of the polis without thought of their own political experience; and it is indeed an essential feature of *Oresteia* that the action moves from the heroic monarchy of Argos to Athens and the Areopagus, to a court and a trial; and the Eumenides pray for blessings on an Athens that Aeschylus and his hearers knew. He wrote for his own time and for his fellow-citizens.

Individual, family and state, all are dependent on the gods, so that there is an integration of personal, social and religious issues. But what were these gods, and how did they operate in the world of men? It is generally, and rightly, held that Aeschylus, his thought centred upon Zeus, was greatly concerned with what is sometimes called theodicy, with the justice and the justification of the gods. But theodicy was not an invention of Aeschylus or of the fifth century. The more the Greeks felt gods about them (and within them) and the more dependent they felt, then the more concerned they were to understand how the gods worked. Were they jealous of human greatness and prosperity? Were they, as men wished to believe, just? Or were they themselves, by sending infatuation, the ultimate cause of the offences they punished? Was this the way offenders were punished through their descendants? Aeschylus had inherited these questions and, from Hesiod and Solon, some answers. To questions and answers he had given his own thought.

One does not look to a poet for the strict formulation and solution of philosophical and theological problems. On one issue, however, Aeschylus formulates clearly, when he makes the chorus of *Agamemnon* sing (*Ag.* 75off.) that it is not wealth and prosperity in themselves that cause woe, but impiety and outrage which breed after their kind. They breed, in this case, within the family; and we discover that Agamemnon dies not for his own offences only but for those of his father; and Clytemnestra claims to embody the avenging spirit which haunts the house. Here we get another formulation: because the *daimon* has lent its aid, she cannot therefore disclaim her own responsibility.

> ΚΛ. αὐχεῖς εἶναι τόδε τοὔργον ἐμόν,
> μὴ δ' ἐπιλεχθῆις,
> 'Αγαμεμνονίαν εἶναί μ' ἄλοχον·
> φανταζόμενος δὲ γυναικὶ νεκροῦ
> τοῦδ' ὁ παλαιὸς δριμὺς ἀλάστωρ
> 'Ατρέως χαλεποῦ θοινατῆρος
> τόνδ' ἀπέτεισεν
> τέλεον νεαροῖς ἐπιθύσας.
> Χο. ὡς μὲν ἀναίτιος εἶ
> τοῦδε φόνου τίς ὁ μαρτυρήσων;
> πῶ πῶ; πατρόθεν δὲ συλλή-
> πτωρ γένοιτ' ἂν ἀλάστωρ.   (1497–1508)

CLYT.   You say this is *my* work – mine?
        Do not cozen yourself that I am Agamemnon's wife.
        Masquerading as the wife
        Of the corpse there the old sharp-witted Genius
        Of Atreus who gave the cruel banquet
        Has paid with a grown man's life
        The due for children dead.
CHORUS That you are not guilty of
        This murder who will attest?
        No, but you may have been abetted
        By some ancestral Spirit of Revenge. (tr. Louis MacNeice)

It seems to be generally true that, in Aeschylus, while divine and human causes operate simultaneously, the divine justice accomplishes itself through human motivation; that, whatever the pressures of hereditary guilt and delayed vengeance, a responsibility does lie upon the human agents.

In the background there is a problem of freedom and compulsion of which the Greeks, who had slaves and oxen, were well aware. The metaphor of the yoke is common in tragedy, and so is the notion of *ananke*. Passionate for freedom, conscious at all points of the constraints put upon them by the gods, they may well have asked themselves how free in fact they were. When our own philosophers and theologians have got these matters straight, then will be the time to criticize the mental competence of ancient writers, but meanwhile there is perhaps something to be learnt from a poet who faced the questions of divine government and human responsibility with so much honesty. We shall not learn it, until we realize that, for Aeschylus, Zeus was not so much the solution of a problem as the problem itself (which is why he could present it through myths as disparate as those of *Oresteia* and the Prometheus-plays).

It is only in *Oresteia* that we can observe the full development of Aeschylean trains of thought. The main theme is justice in the mode of *talio*, human and divine. Human beings resent their wrongs and retaliate, but in doing so they are ministering to a divine justice. They are not wrong – neither the Atridae going against Troy nor Clytemnestra and Aegisthus – to claim this function, yet the result is a sequence of horrific events. Again and again there is a reference to Erinyes, those demons in whom Aeschylus found – or created – a symbol of rigid punitive justice, of an inflexible past. In the last two plays the issue is firmly focused on the case of Orestes, who commits matricide, at the command of Apollo but also in furtherance of a law cited by the chorus in the great *kommos*, which had already been proclaimed as an ordinance of Zeus by the chorus of *Agamemnon* – the law that doers must suffer for their actions.[1] Must Orestes suffer for his? He is pursued by the Erinyes of his mother; he is acquitted

---

[1] *Cho.* 306–14, 400–4; *Ag.* 1560–6.

at Athens, thanks to the vote of Athena, who endorses that preference for the male which had been part of Apollo's defence of Orestes. If the sociological problem admits an answer, the votes of the human jury were divided, and the Erinyes fume and threaten. There is still a problem to be solved; and the play – and the trilogy – end not with the acquittal of Orestes but with the persuasion of the Erinyes. Angry demons could not be left threatening Athens. If they acquire benevolence (without losing their punitive role), it could be said that Aeschylus has invoked, in the interests of Athens, another aspect of chthonian powers, as givers of fertility. One may doubt, however, whether this exhausts the significance of the closing scene.

No poet has presented tragic evil with less mitigation than Aeschylus. Yet *Oresteia* – and so far as we can judge both the Danaid and Promethean plays – end with reconciliation and the prospect of harmony, which is a kind of tragedy that has found few imitators. Clearly Aeschylus was no sentimental optimist. What, then, is it that makes reconciliation possible? Among the tools of Greek thought was a polar opposition between force (or violence) and persuasion. There is no more insistent theme in the later Aeschylus. In the Danaid trilogy force and persuasion are contrasted modes of sexual approach and Aphrodite will have come to persuade. The ministers of Zeus in *Prometheus* are Mastery and Violence, evoking an answering stubbornness in the hero, but already there are hints of that persuasion which must have brought about the ultimate reconciliation. The earlier stages of *Oresteia* are a story of recurrent violence, as the justice of Zeus is carried forward by Erinyes, making a mystery, if not a mockery, of the Hymn to Zeus in the Parodos of *Agamemnon*, in which the Chorus sings, in one breath, of the favour (χάρις) and the violence of the gods (*Ag*. 182f.). Apollo commands the matricide and, when it has been committed, threatens the Erinyes with his bow; Athena persuades them. In a context of democratic Athens, she brings persuasion to bear upon the very exemplifications of violent revenge. If this is a notion which dominates the last phase of Aeschylus, then perhaps it was his supreme religious insight that the Greek gods of power could also be seen to work persuasively.

4. SOPHOCLES

Sophocles' long life almost spans the fifth century B.C.: he was born *c.* 496 before the first Persian invasion and died *c.* 406 in the last years of the Peloponnesian War. He has often seemed to symbolize all that is Attic and classical: dignity, formal perfection, idealism. At the same time critics have found him in some ways the most elusive of the three great tragedians. No one disputes that he is a dramatist of the first rank; and in the surviving plays at any rate – a mere seven out of 123 – it is hard to find any trace of the 'unevenness' criticized by Plutarch;[1] but beyond this there is no critical consensus: now serene, pious and conventional, now passionately humanist or despairingly pessimistic, Sophocles undergoes transformations with every new book that is written about him. Paradoxically, the impact of his work on reader, actors, or audience, is one of striking lucidity, even of simplicity, but it is a lucidity like Virgil's, which gives expression to deep complexities of meaning, difficult to discuss except in the poet's own terms.

Interpretation is made all the harder because so few plays have survived and most of these cannot be securely dated. Thus it is impossible to give a reliable account of Sophocles' development; four plays and some fragments are all that is left to represent the first fifty years of his extremely productive career. 468 is the date given for his first contest, which was also a victory over Aeschylus, but none of the extant plays seems likely to be earlier than the 450s. Most scholars would put *Ajax* before *Antigone* (probably late 440s: see Appendix), though the evidence is not conclusive. *Trachiniae* is often placed next after *Antigone* and before *Oedipus tyrannus* (in the 420s), again on very insecure evidence. With *Electra* (between 418 and 410), *Philoctetes* (409) and *Oedipus at Colonus* (c. 406) we are at last on firmer ground, and some characteristics of 'late' Sophocles can be identified, but in general we simply lack the materials for a literary biography.

There is some record of what the ancients thought of his merits and of his place in the history of drama: this can help to fill some at least of the gaps in our knowledge, provided that it is treated with great caution and pruned of the more fanciful growths of anecdote. The biographical tradition is overwhelmingly enthusiastic: Sophocles was well born, handsome, accomplished, patriotic, outstandingly pious. The picture looks suspiciously roseate, but the warmth of contemporary references must count for something. Sophocles was treated very favourably by the comic poets, who normally missed no opportunity of making fun of tragedians, and his friend Ion of Chios told stories illustrating his gaiety and wit which give credibility to the picture drawn in the ancient *Life* of his magnetic charm of personality. He was by far the most successful, and therefore presumably the most popular, of the tragedians of his time: he won the first prize with about two thirds of his plays and was never placed lower than second. Moreover he was a well known public figure, and if our authorities are to be even partially believed he was entrusted with responsible public offices. He was certainly elected *strategos* at least once (441/0), and it was probably he and not a namesake who was *hellenotamias* in 443/2 and one of the *probouloi* after the Sicilian disaster; according to the ancient *Life* (1) he also served on embassies. He was deeply involved in the city's religious life: the role he played in establishing the cult of Asclepius at Athens

---

[1] *De recta ratione audiendi* 13; cf. 'Longinus', *Subl.* 33.5.

was so important that he himself received heroic honours after his death under the cult name of Dexion. Like Aeschylus, he founded a family of dramatists: his son Iophon and grandson Sophocles were both tragedians of some note.

The ancient sources have a good deal to say about Sophocles' place in the history of tragedy. Aristotle (*Poet.* 1449a18) gives him credit for introducing the third actor, presumably sometime between 468, the date of his first contest, and 458, when Aeschylus used a third actor in the *Oresteia*. It is easy to see how this gave scope for sophisticated dramatic effects (see p. 315), but it is harder to deduce what lay behind another Sophoclean innovation, the raising of the number of chorus men from twelve to fifteen. The same source (*Life* 4) says that he gave up the habit of acting in his own plays owing to the weakness of his voice, but changes in the organization of the Dionysia may in any case have discouraged dramatists from doubling as actors. According to the Suda it was he who began the practice of presenting plays on different subjects at the same contest rather than writing connected trilogies (or tetralogies, count- ing the satyr plays).[1] This cannot be quite true, since we know that Aeschylus presented unconnected plays at least once (*Phineus, Persae, Glaucus Potnieus* in 472), but it is likely that Sophocles deliberately broke with what had latterly become a regular Aeschylean habit. So he established the norm – the single play – that has prevailed throughout the entire European dramatic tradition.

Aristotle refers cryptically to Sophocles' introduction of *skenographia* (*Poet.* 1449a18). We know too little about the fifth-century theatre to be able to say for certain what this implies; probably *skenographia* refers to perspective painting of panels for the wall of the stage-building, which perhaps to begin with represented an architectural façade rather than anything more closely connected with a particular play (see pp. 273f.). Evidently there was still plenty of scope for pioneering work in the theatre, at any rate in the earlier part of Sophocles' career, and he must have influenced Aeschylus as well as following in his footsteps. We must certainly also allow for close interdependence between Sophocles and Euripides, as many parallel passages testify;[2] for nearly fifty years the two playwrights were in active competition at the Athenian festivals.

Sophocles appears to have been a highly self-conscious writer. The Suda records that he wrote a book *On the chorus*, but despite all the speculation this has prompted nothing is known for certain about it (even the title may mean something more like 'On tragedy'). The literary pronouncements attributed to him in various ancient sources could possibly be quotations from this book, but they are more likely to have been *bons mots* recorded in the memoirs of friends and contemporaries. He said of Aeschylus that he did the right thing

---

[1] This seems to be the correct interpretation of the Suda's confused text, cf. *DFA* 80–1.
[2] E.g. Soph. *Trach.* 899ff. and Eur. *Alc.* 157ff.

without knowing what he was doing, which has been taken to suggest a strong interest in technique on Sophocles' part (though the remark occurs in a gossipy passage in Athenaeus about Aeschylus' drunkenness, 1.22a–b). Euripides occasioned the famous dictum, preserved in the *Poetics* (1460b35), 'I portray men as they ought to be, Euripides as they are'. On his own development Sophocles is recorded as making a more detailed comment, which turns out to be extraordinarily difficult to interpret: 'Sophocles used to say that after practising to the limit the pomp of Aeschylus and then the harsh artificiality of his own manner of elaboration, he turned finally to the kind of style which was best and most expressive of character' (Plutarch, *De prof. in virt.* 7). With only seven surviving plays it is impossible to identify these three stages convincingly. Many scholars think that the early 'Aeschylean' stage is not represented, but whether we have an extant example of the second stage is less clear. All that the passage actually proves is Sophocles' literary self-awareness and his interest in character.

Portrayal of character is indeed singled out by the ancient critics as one of Sophocles' chief merits. One of the most interesting comments in the *Life* (21) runs as follows:

οἶδε δὲ καιρὸν συμμετρῆσαι καὶ πράγματα, ὥστ' ἐκ μικροῦ ἡμιστιχίου ἢ λέξεως μιᾶς ὅλον ἠθοποιεῖν πρόσωπον. ἔστι δὲ τοῦτο μέγιστον ἐν τῆι ποιητικῆι, δηλοῦν ἦθος ἢ πάθος.

> He knows how to arrange the action with such a sense of timing that he creates an entire character out of a mere half-line or a single expression. This is the essential in poetry, to delineate character or feelings.

Elsewhere (6, citing Istrus) the *Life* records that Sophocles composed his plays with the talents of his actors and chorus-men in mind. This may be further evidence of a special interest in character portrayal, but there is no certainty that it refers to acting rather than to musical talent: it could mean that Sophocles varied the proportion of lyric for solo performance according to the musical capabilities of his cast.[1]

Unanimously the ancient sources praise Sophocles, nicknamed 'the Bee' for his 'honeyed' style, the highest compliment that could be paid to poet or speaker. 'Sweetness' (γλυκύτης), which to the Greeks suggested flowing eloquence as well as charm, is noted in the *Life* (20) as one of Sophocles' prime qualities; the others are a sense of appropriateness and timing (εὐκαιρία), boldness (τόλμα), and intricacy of ornament (ποικιλία). This is praise of the kind that the ancients gave to Homer himself; and when they called Sophocles 'the tragic Homer' (Polemo, cited by Diogenes Laertius 4.20) or 'the only disciple of Homer' (*Life* 20) they were making a qualitative judgement, not just alluding to the strongly Homeric colouring of his style.

---

[1] Owen (1936) 148.

For Aristotle, whose work lies behind most of the ancient critical tradition, Sophocles plainly exemplified what was most to be admired in tragedy. This is clear from his repeated use of *Oedipus tyrannus* as a model example and from his generally very favourable comments on Sophocles, as at 1456a25 on the superiority of his handling of the chorus. It is no doubt the overwhelming influence of the *Poetics* as much as Sophocles' midway historical position that has led critics to treat him almost as the norm of Greek tragedy, by comparison with whom Aeschylus has often been judged primitive and Euripides decadent.

In one important respect there has been a marked shift away from the critical emphasis of Aristotle. For modern interpreters from the nineteenth century onwards the question of meaning, which was traditionally either ignored or taken for granted, has been a major concern. In its cruder forms, as the search for an explicit 'moral' or 'message' or 'philosophy', it is bound to lead to distortion and bafflement: the focus of Sophocles' plays is not on ideas, but on the doing and suffering of men and women, and although he shows his characters facing the fundamental problems of life the plays never offer unambiguous solutions. It would be simplistic to expect anything more clear-cut; but at least a remarkable consistency of attitude can be detected in the seven extant plays, despite the fact that they must span a period of forty years or more, and it is not misleading to speak of a distinctively Sophoclean treatment of certain tragic issues.

Fundamental to all the plays is the same two-sided view of man, in which his heroic splendour is matched by his utter vulnerability to circumstance. Of course this had traditionally been the way the Greeks looked at the human condition, as we can tell from Homer, the early elegists, and the lyric poets, but Sophocles gives it new expression in dramatic form. Like all these poets Sophocles seems to require an assumption that the human spirit has an ultimate dignity and value: man *can* be brave, clever, morally strong, humane (though filled at the same time with what Bernard Knox calls 'passionate self-esteem'),[1] and most of all he can face suffering with endurance, not the mere uncomprehending submission of an animal. These qualities are not negated and their value is not nullified by the presence of misfortune, suffering and wrong-doing in the world, what the Greeks called *to kakon* and we translate, for want of a better word, as 'evil'. This is always recognized by the poet as part of the way things are: alongside man's potentiality for greatness are set his helplessness and mortality. He may indeed be 'godlike' in his endowments or his achievements, but he is caught in the infinite web of circumstances outside his control, limited by time, by ignorance of past, present and future, by his passions which impede his judgement or undermine his will, always liable to

[1] Knox (1964) 57.

destroy himself and others through failure – or unwillingness – to understand.

This is the consistent Sophoclean background, though the emphases vary from play to play. In *Ajax* the dualism in man's condition is brought sharply into relief, particularly through the contrast between two different ethics, the heroic code and the fifth-century ideal of *sophrosyne*, though (as always) the centre of the play's interest is not a conceptual problem but human action and suffering: the disgrace, death and burial of Ajax. A great military hero, believing himself to have been grossly insulted because he did not receive the highest mark of honour, plans to take bloodthirsty revenge on his former associates, but he suffers from a delusion which causes him to butcher animals instead of his intended victims. The action of the play centres on his return to his senses, his shame and regret at finding that he has not after all killed his enemies, and his subsequent suicide. What is the meaning of these events, particularly of his self-chosen death? What kind of significance is there in this portrait of Ajax? Is it a case-study in abnormal psychology, a celebration of heroic ideals coupled with a recognition of their unsuitability in the modern world, an edifying example of the punishment of arrogance, or (more simply but also more subtly) an insight into a universal human predicament?

In bare outline Ajax's behaviour seems psychopathic, yet the play ends not with his dying curses but with his rehabilitation through burial accompanied by full heroic honours. Indeed, the audience's sympathy is so much directed towards Ajax (following the cue of Odysseus in the Prologue, then of the Chorus and Tecmessa) that critics have tended to overlook his brutality and to stress the heroism of the great man who refuses to compromise, choosing to sacrifice his life rather than abandon his view of what a hero should be. 'The well-born man should either nobly live or nobly die' (479–80). But this approach, too, is open to objection on the ground that it could not be honourable to intend the treacherous murder of the Atridae and the torture of Odysseus. Besides, Ajax has twice boasted that he does not need divine help in battle (774ff.): his behaviour has been either savage or inspired by the more-than-human thought that he is too special and too strong to need the gods' favour. One way of reconciling revulsion at his deeds and intentions with the strong sympathy generated for Ajax is to see him in historical rather than universal terms as representing the old heroic code which must make way for the new 'quiet' ethos of the fifth century typified by the *sophrosyne* of Odysseus. The trouble with this view is that the dramatic focus is not on Odysseus, who though admirable and sympathetic cannot command our attention in the way that Ajax does: it is Ajax who is the tragic figure, and we look for an interpretation which will not confine him so narrowly to a particular set of historical circumstances.

Ajax, superficially an improbable paradigm of humanity, acquires a universal significance by virtue of his suffering, which is caused by the sense of total disgrace and shame following a disastrously mistaken action. He has enjoyed a fantasy of revenge only to discover that his victims were simply animals. His first reaction is the deepest possible dismay that he should be the object of society's derision; all he wants is that the sailors should kill him (361). His relations with his crew and with his wife and son (towards whom he is tender and brutal by turns), and his thoughts about his parents are all part of his tragic situation: Ajax can only be fully himself if he is surrounded by his family and dependants, filling his place in society. But now he is hated by the gods (as he knows from the fact of his madness, which he can interpret only as a divine visitation), by the Greeks, and by the Trojans, and he cannot go home to face his glorious father in disgrace. The only escape from shame is by a 'noble' death, but it is hard to find room for nobility when a man is so humiliated. Then something happens to lift Ajax out of this state of despair, though not to deflect him from his intention to commit suicide. Hitherto he has seen only one side of the dual picture of man, the capacity for great achievement of the talented individual, with a corresponding sense of that individual's unique importance and of the total unacceptability of insult. Now in his great speech at 646ff. he sets himself in the context of unending time and sees that all men have to accept the reality of change; he too will learn to behave with a proper sense of his human limitations (*sophronein* 677).

This speech makes his wife and followers think he has given up his plan to kill himself, but the terms he uses are ambiguous, and the audience must at least fear that he is still intent on suicide. It is less important to answer the question how far Ajax is deliberately deceiving his hearers; what matters is our sense of the intensity of his insight. He is not recognizing that he has been wrong to hate the Atridae and Odysseus, or feeling sorry for it: a simple moral interpretation would be very wide of the mark. He is using his newly found awareness (which he says has been prompted by pity for Tecmessa, a new emotion for Ajax, 652) in order to come to terms with himself, instead of allowing his overwhelming shame to take possession of him and make his suicide another senseless killing. The suicide speech (835ff.) confirms that he still hates his enemies, even to the point of calling down curses on the entire army, and it is clear that the only gesture he can make towards change is through death, but there is no longer any word of his shame.

The end of the play after 973 is an emotional anticlimax until the final tableau of the funeral procession, but the issue on which the action turns – the burial and rehabilitation of Ajax – is important for the audience's response to his story. His last two speeches in particular have given us reason for believing that despite all his savagery he deserves honourable burial, no longer just in memory of his great achievements in the past, or because (as at the beginning of the play) he is an object of pity; and this feeling is confirmed by the final success of Odysseus in persuading the Atridae. *Their* meanness and lack of dignity confirm all the more strongly our sense of the grandeur of Ajax.

This play's appeal for an audience derives both from the reality of Ajax's suffering – as a man most acutely susceptible to feelings of shame – and from the moments of self-knowledge which he seems to experience: out of his despair he finally recognizes (though he cannot will himself to accept) that his view of himself has been mistaken. He has succumbed to the temptation, ever present to the competitive Greek mind, of thinking more-than-mortal thoughts; he has behaved in a way that has been more bestial than heroic and has been brought low, yet his fall itself is not what matters: it is his response to the fall that the play explores. *Ajax* tells us little about the gods and their purposes or the working of divine justice, but it profoundly illuminates the value and the fragility of man.

Ajax's speech at 646ff. says much about time and the rhythm of change. Sophocles often returns to the theme of time, as one of the great limiting and therefore tragic factors in human life. Time must be taken into account because it brings death, but even more because it brings change: how can a man ever be sure that what he believes is worth dying for will not be transformed or swept away? Is there anything permanent in this mortal world?

Both Ajax and Oedipus in the *Coloneus* (607ff.) emphasize that in the course of time friends become enemies and enemies friends. This might seem to suggest a relativist or cynical attitude, an assertion that there are *no* absolute values, but Sophocles is offering a deeper insight. The imagery in both these speeches is drawn from the natural rhythms of the universe: winter alternating with summer and night with day, the endless reciprocal relation of winds and sea, sleep and waking, decay and growth, death and life. One is reminded of the language in which he describes the mutability of human fortune, another aspect of the process of time and change. In the Parodos of *Trachiniae* the cycle of good and bad fortune is compared to 'the circling paths of the Bear' (131), the constellation which for the Greeks of antiquity never set, but was always visible in its rhythmic movement round the Pole. Similarly, Heracles experiences successes and reversals like a swimmer raised and thrown back by a succession of waves (112ff.). Tossing on the sea is a more violent image than the movement of the stars, but Sophocles makes the two essentially comparable: like the rhythms of the seasons and of natural life they suggest permanence in change. In every instance the stress is on regular alternation rather than on chaotic and unpredictable diversity. Hence time is a principle of order as well as an inescapable destructive force.

This sense of time and mutability is important in Sophoclean tragedy because it gives the essential context for man's endeavour. He must do and suffer in the awareness that nothing remains as it is, except the gods and their eternal laws; Knox was right to insist that Sophoclean man is heroic precisely because he resists 'time and its imperative of change'.[1] But there is an important gloss that needs to be added: the hero may defy time, but he can never ignore it; his defiance is made in full knowledge that he is bound to lose. Time's tragic lesson is that mortal creatures never win. For the advantage is always on the side of time, which is linear as well as circular: as it draws each man and woman nearer to death it makes them what they are. 'Accompanying time' (*O.C.* 7) may damage or embitter the sufferer's mind as irreversibly as old age affects his body. So Electra sees her chances of marriage and childbearing fading as she lives enslaved by her mother and stepfather, dedicated to keeping alive the memory of Agamemnon whom they murdered: '... the best part of my life is already gone leaving me without hope, and I have no strength left; I, who am pining away without children' (185–7). What the audience see is the tragic effect of this dedication on her personality, an effect which cannot be reversed when the vengeance is at last achieved. The Chorus in this play may call Time a 'soothing god' (179), but the action of *Electra* does not bear them out.

The process of arriving at an understanding of time and its power over man, and the ordeal of facing and enduring it, are central preoccupations of Sophoclean thought. A great part of all men's lives is lived in ignorance or rejection or evasion of the truth, particularly about their own natures and their mortality. Sophocles, like all great tragedians, is concerned with the attainment of knowledge; his characteristic emphases are on the ironic contrast between appearance and reality, on the climactic moment of revelation, and on how men come to terms with the truth about themselves. Two plays which give particular prominence to this theme are *Trachiniae* and *Oedipus tyrannus*, both of which explore the irony of human ignorance and show their characters arriving, through extremes of suffering, at knowledge which totally alters their lives.

Oedipus tyrannus makes a more explicit and insistent contrast between appearance and reality, most of all through its sustained use of the imagery of sight and blindness: Oedipus who has physical sight is blind to the truth about himself and puts out his eyes when he learns it; Tiresias who is physically blind is the true seer. In *Trachiniae* the stress is on the irony of finding out too late: Deianira, Hyllus and Heracles all discover too late the true nature of their situations, and Sophocles so designs the structure of the play that each discovery is given great prominence. Deianira tries to win back the love of her unfaithful husband with what she supposes to be a benign love charm; only when she has taken the risk and sent Heracles a robe anointed with it does she find out that it is a deadly poison. Their son Hyllus sees Heracles tortured in the robe and rushes home to denounce his mother as a murderess; but she kills herself

[1] Knox (1964) 27.

303

before he discovers her innocence. Heracles understands only when he is on
the point of death the meaning of an oracle told him long before, that he would
be killed by the hand of the dead: the poison that Deianira unwittingly administered came from the centaur Nessus, who was killed by Heracles himself.
Almost everything the characters say has an ironic import for the audience,
who know – or guess – better than they. But this use of irony is not easy
sensationalism; for Sophocles irony is a means of conveying profound insights
into the nature of man and his world.

Similarly, the climax of revelation is not a mere melodramatic thrill of
horror, but what John Jones has called 'the flash of perfect clarity' which
comes at 'the moment when a man perceives the operation of the powers that
are destroying him'.[1] At such moments there is a very strong sense that things
are as it were swinging into place: now at last the oracles are seen to be intelligible and true. ἰοὺ ἰού, cries Oedipus when the truth is out at last, 'everything comes out clearly!' (1182). So Heracles, who utters the same great cry
(*Trach.* 1143ff.), 'Now I understand ...' Knowledge is combined with a
strong sense of inevitability.

Acceptance of the revelation is the mark of the great human being, who
unlike the ordinary unheroic person, the average member of any audience,
does not evade or deny or seek to shift the blame. Jocasta's reaction in *Oedipus
tyrannus* to the discovery that her husband is also her son is to stifle the truth
and allow Oedipus to live on in ignorance. This is deeply understandable,
but for Sophocles the extreme of endurance is only met when like Oedipus
a man faces and accepts that truth, with whatever appalling implications it
may have. In effect this acceptance may be identical with the hero's 'defiance'
discussed above; when he refuses to ignore the implications of the truth he
does so because of the need to retain his integrity. The ordinary person runs
away and tries to forget, or patches up some compromise, but for the heroic
individual no such evasion is possible. Thus Ajax does not try to save himself,
as Tecmessa and the Chorus hope he may, and Oedipus both persists against
advice in making his discovery and when he has made it finds ways of coming
to terms with his new identity.

If knowledge of reality is endurable only through intense suffering, what
of the authors of this reality, the gods? Is it right, critics have asked, that men
should have to suffer these things, men like Oedipus, who committed his
terrible deeds without knowing what he was doing? In other words, are
Sophocles' characters justified in worshipping the gods and trying to live by
their laws, and does Sophocles himself endorse their attitudes, or present them
with ironic detachment?

Like almost all Greeks before them, Sophocles' men and women believe in

[1] Jones (1962) 170.

gods who are the source of everything in life, evil as well as good. The universe controlled by these gods is involved in a constant process of rhythmic change, but they themselves are outside time. 'Only to the gods comes neither old age nor death . . .' (*O.C.* 607f.); Zeus is 'unaged by time' (*Ant.* 608). Worship them as they must, men cannot expect unmixed blessing from the gods: it is the condition of mortals to experience pain as well as happiness (*Trach.* 126f.). The only sure event in any human future is death; 'tomorrow does not exist until today is safely past' (*Trach.* 943ff.). But men who are *eusebeis* should expect more divine favour than the *asebeis*, who are unfailingly punished, either in their own lifetimes or through their descendants. 'Pious' and 'impious' are inadequate translations of these terms: being *eusebes* means respecting the divine laws that are the foundations of human society, and hence it includes right behaviour towards others as well as proper worship of the gods. These are the 'unwritten and unfailing statutes' invoked by Antigone (*Ant.* 454f.) when she defends her burial of Polynices in defiance of Creon's decree; in *Electra* it is clear that for the Chorus as well as for Electra herself loyalty to Agamemnon's memory is in harmony with the eternal laws (1095f.). It is an affront to the gods to allow a corpse to remain unburied or to fail to respect parents; and if a man is guilty of this sort of insulting behaviour he is forgetting his place as a mortal and courting divine disfavour.

It used to be claimed that Sophocles' purpose was to justify the ways of these gods to men. 'Undeserved suffering', wrote S. H. Butcher in a sensitive essay published in 1891, 'while it is exhibited in Sophocles under various lights, always appears as part of the permitted evil which is a condition of a just and harmoniously ordered universe. It is foreseen in the counsels of the gods . . .'[1] Much was made of Sophocles' known personal piety to corroborate this reassuring view, and so to create the stereotype of the serene, conventional poet untroubled by the more disturbing aspects of life around him and of the stories he chose to tell. Many modern critics, reacting against what they see as wishful thinking in this approach, have preferred a Sophocles who is more humanist, more Euripidean, vastly more pessimistic. But there is a danger here, too, that a misleading stereotype will impose itself.

'Pessimism' after all seems to be a misplaced term for the traditional Greek attitude to human life. Men may be creatures of a day, but they are not abject, unworthy, valueless unless redeemed by god. And the gods are objects of worship, not of mere brute fear: Dodds was right to speak of the beauty as well as the terror of the old beliefs.[2] If human achievement at its greatest is thought to be 'godlike' and the humane virtues are believed to be enjoined by divine law, that is, to have absolute value, then there is a sense in which traditional Greek thinking is not pessimistic. The cosmos may be cruel, but it cannot be

---

[1] Butcher (1891) 127.   [2] Dodds (1951) 49.

simply meaningless. Against this background Sophocles creates a drama that explores unmerited suffering, without protest on the one hand or justification on the other, but with pity and respect. When he chooses Oedipus as the paradigm of human blindness – and human intelligence – he uses him as a *consolatio*, not to question why these horrors should happen to a man. They do happen, the play says, but we with our imperfect understanding cannot tell why; all we can do is try to come to terms with the strange necessities of being human. Even the most perceptive and intelligent of our kind, Oedipus, was hopelessly wrong, even about his own identity; but he endured the revelation of the truth.

It can of course be argued that *Oedipus tyrannus* shows the work of malicious gods playing with men's sufferings for their sport. But that is not how it is seen by Oedipus himself, or by the Chorus watching his ordeal. When all is revealed they reflect not on the unfairness of the gods but on the fragility of human success and the inexorable revelatory process of time: ἐφηῦρέ σ' ἄκονθ' ὁ πάνθ' ὁρῶν χρόνος 'time the all-seeing has found you out against your will' (1213). Even so, one might ask, are *we*, the audience, not to recoil with disgust at the cruelty of Apollo, who did not give Oedipus a straight answer to the question 'Who are my parents?' but simply told him that he would kill the one and marry the other? This no more undermines Apollo than the story of the oracle he gave to Croesus, told by Herodotus (1.53, 91): 'If you invade Persia you will destroy a great empire'. Men do not always know what are the important questions to ask, and when told the truth they are prevented by their human limitations from understanding it. As guardian of the truth Apollo is actively concerned to see it fulfilled and revealed, but he has no ultimate responsibility for what happens to Oedipus.

If Apollo, the play's presiding deity, cannot be made to carry the responsibility, what of the will of the gods generally? Sophocles nowhere illuminates the divine purpose by explaining why it had to be that Oedipus would kill his father and marry his mother, but he does lay stress on the idea that such was his destiny. How important, then, is the idea of fate in this play, or for that matter elsewhere in Sophocles? It would be anachronistic to think of fate as a detailed predestined programme of each man's life, an idea which only makes its appearance in Hellenistic thought.[1] Sophocles treats the notion of fate in a way much more appropriate to tragedy: in his plays fate is simply being mortal and being the person one is. A man's freedom to act is at every point limited by his circumstances and temperament, which are an inheritance from the past; about the future the only thing he knows for certain is that he will die; for the present he is compelled to act as if he knew all the things of which he is ignorant.

[1] Reinhardt (1947) 108.

Oedipus' act of parricide was freely chosen: it was his decision to take the road to Thebes, his choice to retaliate when Laius insulted him. But if we ask what lay behind these decisions we see the limitations of human knowledge and the complexity of human action. Oedipus' avoidance of Corinth and choice of the road to Thebes were prompted by the commendable wish to avoid harming his parents, but since he did not know who his parents were this was a misconstruction of the oracle and in fact he was leaving Corinth unnecessarily. Once on the road to Thebes he was more likely to meet Laius, though the timing of their meeting was a matter of coincidence – the coincidence that he and Laius should have chosen to travel when they did. The actual killing was provoked by Oedipus' natural resentment at the high-handed behaviour of Laius; this vigorous self-defence was characteristic of Oedipus' royal temperament, and of course the deed was done in ignorance of his own and Laius' identity. If Laius had been more gracious ... or Oedipus had been a milder man ... or if he had for a moment suspected that there could be any kinship between them ... then things might have turned out differently. But for the audience listening to the story of these events there is a strong feeling of inevitability, just as the actions of Oedipus within the play itself seem inevitable, though each is freely chosen and fully motivated. Thus the poet achieves that 'tension between freedom and necessity which seems essential to the tragic paradox'.[1] And the importance of the idea of fate lies in its power to convey the compulsions of the human condition.

Sophocles' characters and choruses describe these compulsions as supernatural forces, *daimones* like Ate and the Erinyes; this was traditional in Greek religious thought and may well have been part of the poet's own belief. But the question of what he personally believed is only marginally important; it is more interesting to study the use he makes of the traditional religious language. It is through this language that he expresses the mysterious, non-rational, frightening and awe-inspiring aspects of life, both the 'dark underpit' (to use Lattimore's phrase)[2] and the inscrutable orderliness of the cosmic design.

Antigone and *Oedipus at Colonus* illustrate very well how Sophocles uses the ambiguities of religious language to express his deepest insights. A crude analysis of the two plays might lead one to posit an historical development in his attitudes: in *Antigone*, one might say, he protests at the gods' arbitrariness; in *Oedipus at Colonus* he celebrates their making amends to one of their most notable victims. But it would be hard to find a more misleading formulation. In both plays Sophocles creates a powerful sense of the forces outside man's control and the emotions that they inspire; in neither does he take up attitudes or sit in judgement or find answers.

---

[1] Winnington-Ingram (1965) 50.   [2] Lattimore (1958) 102.

For many modern critics *Antigone* is one of Sophocles' darkest plays: 'the *Antigone* conceals vast potentialities of unreason and chaos';[1] 'the message of the Chorus in their odes is one of helpless bewilderment and dark despair; but it is fully consonant with the evils that we have witnessed on the stage'.[2] Creon the new ruler of Thebes issues an edict forbidding the burial of Polynices, who has committed treason by attacking his native city. Antigone disobeys the prohibition, claiming that she has a sacred and overriding duty to bury her brother; for this Creon punishes her with imprisonment in a rocky tomb and leaves her to die. But when the seer reports that Polynices' corpse is polluting the city Creon goes to release her, only to find that she has already hanged herself. A question that is often raised is why the gods allow Antigone to die if she is really upholding their laws. They show their displeasure quickly enough when Creon leaves Polynices unburied; why do they not intervene to keep Antigone alive so that she can be released when Creon changes his mind? Sophocles almost encourages his audience to expect – or hope for – a miracle by lavishing so much detail (998ff.) on the signs of divine displeasure at the unburied corpse, but no miracle happens: Antigone is dead by the time Creon arrives. She had freely chosen to risk death in order to bury her brother; when that death actually comes it tells us nothing about the gods, only about life as it really is in which actions have their consequences and the consequences have to be faced. The task of a tragedian is to confront the worst facts of life; in such contexts miracles can too easily seem like evasion or fantasy.

But a more subtle question can be raised about our view of Antigone's action. She belives that she is right to bury Polynices because this is in accordance with the eternal laws, a god-given and permanent moral order, whose validity she never doubts until her last pathetic scene in which she confronts the fact of death. 'Nor did I think', she says to Creon at 453ff., 'that your decrees were so compelling that a mortal could override the unwritten and unfailing statutes of the gods. For they endure not just today and yesterday, but eternally, and no one knows when they were ordained.' It is natural for an audience to approve Antigone's generous act of loyalty to her brother and her courage in dying for her beliefs; but for some critics there is only pathetic self-delusion in her claim that these beliefs are divinely sanctioned. How then are we to interpret the language used by the Chorus at the end of the episode in which Antigone makes her great speech?

τεάν, Ζεῦ, δύνασιν τίς ἀνδρῶν ὑπερβασία κατάσχοι;
τὰν οὔθ' ὕπνος αἱρεῖ ποθ' ὁ παντογήρως
οὔτ' ἀκάματοι θεῶν
μῆνες, ἀγήρως δὲ χρόνωι δυνάστας

---

[1] Torrance (1965) 300.   [2] Coleman (1972) 27.

κατέχεις Ὀλύμπου
μαρμαρόεσσαν αἴγλαν.
τό τ' ἔπειτα καὶ τὸ μέλλον
καὶ τὸ πρὶν ἐπαρκέσει
νόμος ὅδ'· οὐδὲν ἔρπει
θνατῶν βιότωι πάμπολύ γ' ἐκτὸς ἄτας.   (604–14)

Your power, O Zeus, what human transgression can limit? That power neither
Sleep the all-aging nor the gods' tireless months can master, but you dwell, a
ruler unaged by time, in the dazzling radiance of Olympus. And for the future,
near and distant, as for the past this law will be found true: nothing that is vast
comes to the life of mortals without ruin.[1]

It is true that this stasimon is full of irony: the Chorus are trying to explain
the frightful situation of Antigone in terms of the family curse of the Labdacids,
yet in doing so they use language of sin and punishment which is much closer
to Creon's case and foreshadows his fall. But these ironies do not reduce the
power of the lines on the unchanging certainty of Zeus's laws. If the poetry of
this passage carries conviction it is hard to feel so sure that Sophocles is denying
the existence of a suprahuman order.

But if protest is not a characteristic Sophoclean mode neither is the positive
assertion of divine benevolence. The nearest he comes to this is in the sense
of holiness and blessing which he evokes in *Oedipus at Colonus*, for instance
in his description of the sanctity of Colonus and the grove of the Eumenides
(16ff., 36ff., 54ff., 466ff., 668ff.), or in the intimacy with which the divine voice
summons Oedipus (ὦ οὗτος οὗτος Οἰδίπους, τί μέλλομεν | χωρεῖν; 'Oedipus,
Oedipus, why are we delaying to go?' 1627f.), most of all in the mystery of
Oedipus' favoured passing, which only Theseus was allowed to witness.
'... and we could no longer see Oedipus anywhere, but the king alone and
holding his hand over his face to shade his eyes, as if he had seen some terrible
sight that no one could bear to look upon' (1648ff.). In this play, indeed,
Sophocles places a miracle at the centre of the action, but even here he is so
reticent that we are given no illumination of the gods' purposes. Certainly
it would be wrong to interpret what happens to Oedipus as a sign of divine
recompense for his sufferings; perhaps even the view that the gods rejoice in
human heroism goes further than Sophocles suggests (though it is a natural
Greek idea). The most that can be claimed is that the sense of holiness conveyed
in this play implies something more than a purely humanist vision of the world.

The question of crime and punishment is not central to Sophoclean tragedy.
His characters are caught in complex destructive situations which – being
human – they have helped to create for themselves, but the issue never turns

[1] The text of 614 is not certain, but most editors interpret the passage in the sense given here.
Cf. Easterling (1978).

on the precise degree of their guilt: in tragedy as in life it is common for a man's suffering to go far beyond what he morally deserves. Even in *Ajax*, where some stress is laid on the hero's hubris, the sequence of pride and punishment is plainly not the main subject of the play. The function of the Messenger's report at 748ff., in which we are told of Ajax's arrogant behaviour and Athena's anger, is partly to create a sense of crisis (if only Ajax can be kept safe for one day the danger will pass), partly to give a fateful pattern to his story, not to spell out the moral 'message' of the play. In *Trachiniae* some critics treat the sins and punishment of Heracles as the real issue; but Heracles is more convincingly interpreted as a paradigm of man's helplessness. Even the greatest of Greek heroes 'the best of men' (177, 811) – the strongest, bravest, most successful – is a slave to his sexual passion (Sophocles makes much of the idea of 'slave' in this play) and no better able than anyone else to escape the limitations of his ignorance.

What matters, evidently, is the way the characters respond to their appalling predicaments; and here we meet the question of Sophocles' idealism. He notoriously represents men 'as they ought to be'; but in what sense can idealized characters exemplify the realities of human experience? If we compare the Electra plays of Sophocles and Euripides we find Euripides forcing us to see the implications that such a situation would have in real life; the social embarrassments and the jealousy of his Electra compel us to believe in the continuing and urgent reality of the old heroic tale. But the Sophoclean heroine, though more elevated, has no less power to convince; and particularly in her total commitment to the mother-murder and her absence of regret at the end of the play she is a more frightening example of man's capacity for self-destruction in the cause of preserving moral integrity. In Euripides the horror is to some extent mitigated by Orestes' hesitation before he does the deed and by the remorse of brother and sister after it. In Sophocles there is no irresolution; no regret; Electra from the stage calls out to the unseen Orestes as he kills their mother: 'Strike again if you have the strength!' (1415). After the tender scene of her reunion with Orestes the starkness and cruelty of the end of the play are almost unbearable, but they grow out of the earlier action of the play in a way which forces the audience to accept them as real.

This impression of reality is achieved because Sophocles presents the action with extreme psychological nicety and sureness of touch. It is only in a very limited and individual way that he can be said to idealize: he is quite ready to portray evil characters when the plot demands them, like the villainous Creon in *Oedipus at Colonus*, and he certainly does not sentimentalize his heroes (though many critics have written as if he did). Antigone's harshness towards Ismene, the brutal way Ajax treats Tecmessa, the virulence of Philoctetes' hatred of Odysseus, are all uncomfortable features which ought to warn us against taking a romantic view of Sophoclean heroism. And yet his characters do make a distinctively different impression from those of Euripides. It is partly a matter of style. Sophocles prefers to maintain the distance of the world of the epic stories, whereas Euripides is more insistent in his reminders of contemporary humdrum reality. But there is also a difference in the way they appeal to the audience's sympathy. In Sophocles' extant plays we are not asked to transfer our sympathies or make a fundamental reappraisal of a character in mid-action: there is nothing comparable to the shifts in response that we are required to make in *Medea* or *Bacchae*. Sophocles seems often to have been interested in exploring the limits of human endurance: man's capacity for asserting his belief in himself against all external pressures, including the promptings of good sense and the pull of ordinary emotional ties. The conversion or moral collapse of one of these intransigent heroes would profoundly alter the character of his drama.

But the term 'hero' must be used with caution, in case it leads us to adopt a formula too rigid for the fluidity of Sophoclean drama. The intransigent, isolated, suffering figure is clearly the most important of his symbols of mankind, but it is not the only one. Neither Deianira nor Heracles can be forced into such a mould, but this does not reduce their claim to be regarded as tragic characters; Creon in *Antigone*, too, who finally changes his mind, and Neoptolemus in *Philoctetes*, who undergoes a process of moral transformation, are also central figures who demand as much attention in their respective plays as Antigone and Philoctetes themselves. We should be rash to call *Trachiniae* an 'odd' play because it does not have the more familiar kind of hero: we have no reason for thinking that the limits of the poet's range coincide with what is offered in seven plays out of 123. Who would have thought that he made bold use of changes of scene if *Ajax* had not happened to survive?

There is another respect, too, in which the image of the isolated hero is liable to mislead. This is in its associations with specifically modern, post-romantic ideas of the outsider, the individual who rejects society or is permanently and profoundly alienated from it. Sophocles' men and women, it is true, reject the norms of ordinary behaviour, the safe compromises, the comfortable or corrupt evasions familiar in everyday life, which the dramatist illustrates in vividly contemporary detail, but they do not reject society as such, and they define themselves in relation to society.

Ajax cannot be truly Ajax without his *philoi* – his kin and dependants – to defend and his enemies to fight; Antigone dies as much for her brother as for her principles; Electra, who cuts herself off from all the normal life of the household, still values that life as the only meaningful context in which to exist. This is what gives pathos to the picture she draws for Chrysothemis of the rewards they will win if they murder Aegisthus singlehanded:

'Do you not see what fame you will win for yourself and me if you do as I say?
Everyone who sees us – citizen or stranger – will greet us with praises like these:
"See these two sisters, friends, who saved their father's house...all must love
them, all must reverence them; at festivals and wherever the people are gathered
all must honour them for their bravery."' (973 ff.)

Oedipus in *Oedipus at Colonus*, first an outcast from his own city, then himself
rejecting it, comes to find new citizenship in Athens; most of all Philoctetes,
who to the modern reader seems so clearly an archetypal outsider, set apart
by his wound and his bow from the rest of the world, in Sophocles is only
truly fulfilled when he consents to go to Troy as the comrade of Neoptolemus,
to be healed and win glory. Sophocles has not made his story sentimental by
suggesting that the world Philoctetes will rejoin is perfect, or glory something
worth having at any price: much of the play is concerned precisely with the
evaluation of ends and means; but it is so designed that although the world
(represented by the Greeks at Troy) is decadent, Philoctetes' going to Troy
is also the reintegration of the wild man into society and something which the
audience must endorse.

Sophocles' greatest strength is his mastery of the dramatic medium. Everything in his plays, plot structure, character drawing, language, spectacle, is
fully exploited to achieve that 'imitation of action and life' which Aristotle
sees as the essence of tragedy. The intense aesthetic pleasure given by Sophocles'
plays has been well compared to the effect of Mozart's music, the exhilaration
felt by an audience when the artist is superbly in control of his material. This
aesthetic impression demands to be taken into account when we try to grasp
the poet's meaning: it makes a significant difference to the way we respond
to his terrifying stories.

A major principle of Sophoclean composition is the use of contrast. This is
seen at all levels: contrasting themes, as in *Oedipus at Colonus* where the
behaviour of Oedipus' sons is repeatedly set against that of his daughters;
contrasting moods, as when a song of joy and hope is at once followed by the
climactic revelation of disaster (e.g. *Ajax* 693ff.); juxtaposition of contrasting
characters, as in *Antigone* and *Trachiniae*, where the central pairs are both
opposed and intimately interconnected. It is relevant to mention the use of
irony here, for irony draws attention to the fundamental contrast between
appearance and reality, to the distance between what the characters think and
what we the audience know to be true, and between what they intend and what
actually happens: *peripeteia* itself is dependent on the principle of contrast.
Thus Sophocles finds essentially dramatic means of expressing his sense of the
ambiguity of all experience, the two sides of the human picture and the corresponding antinomies in nature.

His language is less exuberant than Aeschylus', his imagery comparatively 'ordinary' and unobtrusive. This however is art that conceals art. His seemingly effortless verse depends on bold extensions of syntax and meaning and on great metrical virtuosity, and his imagery is often all the more effective for being understated. Stylistic reserve does not imply lack of inventiveness or complexity: themes are developed and interwoven, and the language shades from literal to metaphorical, with an intricacy which belongs only to the very greatest poets. At one of the high points in *Trachiniae*, when the Nurse has just burst in to tell the Chorus of Deianira's suicide (893ff.), they cry out ἔτεκ' ἔτεκε μεγάλαν ἁ | νέορτος ἅδε νύμφα | δόμοισι τοῖσδ' 'Ερινύν 'This new bride has given birth, given birth to a great Erinys for the house', meaning Iole, the girl for whom Heracles sacked Oechalia, the girl who is now ruining his family. It is natural to think of the bride bearing a child – Heracles' child – and the image gains weight from its literal appropriateness in the context. More than this, it specifically recalls the ironic scene where Deianira asks of Iole whether she is 'unmarried, or a mother' (308), and concludes that she must be 'without experience of all these things'. But the child is no human child; it is a 'great Erinys', a great avenging spirit: the Chorus recognize that the death of Deianira is the inevitable consequence of Heracles' bringing home Iole. The image thus advances one of the play's dominant themes, the inescapable power of sexual passion, and in representing a death in terms of giving birth it restates a connexion made twice before in the play. In the Parodos (94f.) night is said both to give birth to the Sun and to put him to death (imagery which is related in complex ways to Deianira and Heracles) and in the Third Stasimon (834) the poison of the Hydra, with which Heracles killed Nessus and which Deianira used as a love charm, is said to have been 'generated by death' (the Greek uses the same verb τίκτειν each time).

Because Sophocles (particularly by contrast with Euripides) is neither a theoretician nor an apologist, the intellectual content of his plays has often been minimized. But it is hard to see how he could have used language of such finesse, variety and sophistication if he had not been in touch with the important movements of thought of his time as well as deeply read in the poetry of his predecessors. As A. A. Long has emphasized, we find evidence in his plays of interest in Presocratic thought and sophistic argument, of medical knowledge, of concern with politics and political ideology, all exemplifying 'a mind which was completely involved in the intellectual life of fifth-century Athens'.[1] The terminology of the ethical debates in *Electra*, the sophistic attitudes of Odysseus in *Philoctetes*, the political programme of Menelaus in *Ajax* or of Creon in *Antigone* all have precise relevance to contemporary ways

[1] Long (1968) 167.

of thought, suggesting that 'remote' and 'detached' are not terms too readily to be used of Sophocles.

Boldness, intelligence, resourcefulness are all characteristics of his dramatic technique as much as of his use of language. He is daring in his manipulation of inconsistency, which gives him some marvellously concentrated and dramatic moments, though its purpose is subtler than just the creation of isolated brilliant effects. In *Philoctetes*, for example, there is notorious inconsistency in the treatment of Neoptolemus' knowledge of the prophecy that he and Philoctetes are destined together to take Troy: in the Prologue he knows hardly anything about it, but by the end of the play he can give Philoctetes a circumstantially detailed account. There is no satisfactory way of explaining this logically, as if we were dealing with the facts of history, but there are good dramatic reasons for releasing the crucial information piecemeal and for presenting Neoptolemus at the outset as wholly dependent on Odysseus, while the deeper significance of the inconsistency seems to be that it enables the audience to share with Neoptolemus a growing awareness of the true meaning of the prophecy.

Sophocles pays more attention than Aeschylus to the interaction of his characters. This is particularly a feature of his latest plays and may have been what he had in mind when he used the term ἠθικώτατον 'most expressive of character' to describe his mature manner (see p. 298). The effect of one person's words or actions on another's feelings is brought out in all kinds of ways: in *Trachiniae* the enigmatic Iole stands in silence while Lichas lies to Deianira about her and the Messenger challenges his lies; in *Electra* the false messenger speech on the death of Orestes, which was designed to disarm Clytemnestra, has a devastating effect on Electra, who is also there to listen; in *Philoctetes* the silences and ambiguous language of Neoptolemus make the audience suspect that he is under increasing strain as he comes to know and pity Philoctetes. Often the use of visual effects deepens this study of the relations between characters, as when Electra cannot be convinced that Orestes is alive and standing before her until she has been forced to put down the urn in which she thought she held his ashes (*El.* 1205ff.), or when Neoptolemus' action in supporting Philoctetes physically is at once followed by his own emotional breakdown (*Phil.* 889ff.).

It is easy to overlook the visual side of Sophocles' dramaturgy because we have only the text on the page without explicit stage directions; but readers who attempt to act the plays or imagine them in performance soon become aware of the unerring theatrical instinct that created them. His use of props – the sword of Ajax, the casket in *Trachiniae* that carried the poisoned robe, Philoctetes' bow – is both simple and sophisticated: each represents a fundamental theme in its play and is closely related to the verbal imagery, but there is nothing contrived in the prominence given to it. The stage action, too, often makes a strong visual impact, as in *Ajax* when the door of the stage building is opened and the hero is seen surrounded by the butchered animals (346f.), or later in the searching scene (866ff.) when the Chorus agitatedly look for the missing Ajax, and Tecmessa finds him where he fell on his sword. In *Oed'pus at Colonus* there is a remarkably violent scene (818ff.) when Creon seizes Antigone and very nearly comes to blows with the Chorus. Even more gripping is the final scene of *Electra* (1466ff.): Aegisthus lifts the cover from the corpse he believes to be the dead Orestes, sees with horror that it is Clytemnestra, and at once finds himself in a trap, facing the drawn swords of Orestes and Pylades. The same sense of theatre is evident in Sophocles' use of entrances and exits, such as the unexpected reappearances of Odysseus (*Phil.* 974, 1293), or the slow silent departure of Deianira after Hyllus has denounced her (*Trach.* 813ff.), or the great moment in *Oedipus at Colonus* (1540ff.) when the blind Oedipus leaves the stage, leading the way to the place where he is to die. Many scenes show how resourcefully he made use of the third actor, scenes like *El.* 660ff. when Electra and Clytemnestra listen to the story of Orestes' death, or *Phil.* 542ff. when the False Merchant purports to talk to Neoptolemus without letting Philoctetes overhear, or *O.T.* 1110ff., the brilliant scene in which Oedipus and the messenger from Corinth cross-question the Theban herdsman and elicit the truth he is trying to hide.

These effects ought not, of course, to be considered in isolation from their contexts, as if they were mere virtuoso displays: in each play they are part of the distinctive shape and emotional movement of the whole, a complex unity which can hardly be described without oversimplification. How, for example, can the critic, particularly the modern critic, who has no knowledge of Sophocles' music, do justice to the effects created by his handling of the different modes of delivery – speech, lyric dialogue and choral song? Some of the most exciting and intense sequences are formally very elaborate, with a symmetry which can more easily be paralleled in opera than in modern spoken drama. So Ajax' first appearance after the killing of the animals is marked by an elaborate exchange (348ff.) between him, the Chorus and Tecmessa. Ajax sings three pairs of agitated lyrics, each pair metrically different and each punctuated by responses, now by the Chorus, now by Tecmessa, in the iambic trimeters of spoken dialogue. The contrast strongly emphasizes their different emotional states: Ajax in a wild frenzy of despair, Tecmessa and the sailors begging him to be calm. Much of the power of this *kommos* comes from the words, but the formal patterning plays a significant and subtle part in conveying the emotional quality of the scene.

The plays of Sophocles strikingly confirm the truth of Eliot's claim that 'in genuine drama the form is determined by the point on the line at which a tension between liturgy and realism takes place'.[1] In the search to understand Sophocles we need to be sensitive not only to his realism – both in universal terms and in the context of fifth-century Greek life – but also to the 'liturgical' aspect of his language, rhythms and structures, for it is this in combination with his realism that gives his plays their particular distinction.

5. EURIPIDES

The relative abundance of surviving Euripidean drama (we have eighteen tragedies which have come down to us as his work) is not wholly a result of his continuing popularity in antiquity; like the other great dramatists, Euripides survived the early centuries of Byzantium in a selected edition, in his case one of ten plays. By some fortunate accident, however, part of what seems to have been a complete edition arranged in alphabetical order by title survived the later centuries in which so many classical texts vanished; it was available for reproduction in the revival of classical learning which marked the Byzantine recovery from the disaster of the Fourth Crusade. In addition, the papyrological finds of the last hundred years have given us extensive fragments of lost plays, which, combined with quotations found in ancient authors, often enable us to form a clear idea of the play as a whole.

Not only do we possess a large body of material, we also have a fair idea of the chronology of Euripidean production. Many of the plays are dated in ancient records; for many of them we have a *terminus ante quem* in the shape of an Aristophanic parody. For others an approximate date (or rather period) is suggested by the frequency of metrical resolution in the trimeter,[2] since this phenomenon shows a steady progression from the earliest dated plays to the latest. Of the extant plays, the earliest we possess is *Alcestis* (438). *Medea* is securely dated in 431; *Hippolytus* in 428. The decade 427–417 probably saw the staging of *Heraclidae, Hecuba, Electra, Andromache* and *Supplices*. *Troades*, with *Alexander*, is firmly dated in 415, and *Helen* in 412; *Phoenissae, Antiope, Heracles, Ion* and *Iphigenia in Tauris* belong to the next six years. *Orestes* was staged in 408 and *Bacchae* and *Iphigenia in Aulide* were produced at Athens after the poet's death in Macedon in 406 B.C.

When news of Euripides' death reached Athens, Sophocles had still some months to live, but Euripides was by far the younger man. His first production (which earned him a third prize) took place in 455 B.C., three years after the staging of Aeschylus' *Oresteia*; Sophocles' debut (a first prize) had preceded the *Oresteia* by ten years. This disparity in age was of great importance for the intellectual formation of the younger poet, for during the middle decades of the century sophistic teaching explored new critical attitudes towards politics and

---

[1] Eliot (1926) x.   [2] See below, p. 337.

morality, expressed in new rhetorical forms. Sophoclean drama shows familiarity
with the rhetoric and a sharply critical awareness of the ideas; but they are
viewed from a distance, as it were – the reaction of an older man whose vision
of the world is already formed. Euripides, though his critique of the ideas may
be just as incisive, is very much a man of the sophistic age; the language and
techniques of the new rhetoric come naturally to him and his plays fully reflect
the intellectual controversies of the time.

He is an intellectual dramatist and his career has a curiously modern look.
His unpopularity during his lifetime is clear from the rarity of his victories at
the Dionysia, the frequency of jibes at his tragedies and travesties of his person
on the comic stage, and his eventual withdrawal from Athens to Macedonia;
it was followed by overwhelming popularity with succeeding generations. In
the fourth and later centuries his plays, both in reading and performance,
eclipsed and almost extinguished the reputations of his competitor and predecessor. The late tradition that he composed his plays in a cave on Salamis is
certainly apocryphal but the story does symbolize a real situation – the isolation
which we have come to recognize as the usual fate of the intellectually advanced
artist in democratic society. And there are passages in his dramas which seem
to derive from consciousness of such a situation. Medea, for example, in
her attempt to reassure Creon sounds a contemporary, possibly a personal
note.

> 'This is not the first time...that my great reputation has injured me...No
> man of intelligence and judgement should ever have his sons educated so that
> they become excessively clever...If you introduce new, intelligent ideas to
> fools, you will be thought frivolous, not intelligent. On the other hand, if you do
> get a reputation for surpassing those who are supposed to be intellectually
> sophisticated, you will seem to be a thorn in the city's flesh. This is what has
> happened to me. I am a clever woman, and some feel envious spite toward me,
> others count me their adversary...' (292–305)

The dramatist's engagement with the intellectual, political and moral controversies of the day did not however result in a clear position on one side or
the other. Dramatists, who speak through the masks of their creations, are notoriously difficult to pin down, and Euripides more so than most. He was a
problem to his contemporaries and he is one still; over the course of centuries
since his plays were first produced he has been hailed or indicted under a
bewildering variety of labels. He has been described as 'the poet of the Greek
enlightenment'[1] and also as 'Euripides the irrationalist';[2] as a religious sceptic
if not an atheist, but on the other hand, as a believer in divine providence and
the ultimate justice of divine dispensation. He has been seen as a profound
explorer of human psychology and also a rhetorical poet who subordinated

---

[1] Nestle (1901).   [2] Dodds (1929).

consistency of character to verbal effect; as a misogynist and a feminist; as a realist who brought tragic action down to the level of everyday life and as a romantic poet who chose unusual myths and exotic settings. He wrote plays which have been widely understood as patriotic pieces supporting Athens' war against Sparta and others which many have taken as the work of the anti-war dramatist *par excellence*, even as attacks on Athenian imperialism. He has been recognized as the precursor of New Comedy and also as what Aristotle called him – 'the most tragic of the poets' (*Poetics* 1453a30). And not one of these descriptions is entirely false.

There have been attempts to frame these contradictions in schemes of artistic and intellectual development. A persuasive spiritual biography has been drafted along the following lines: an early period of what might be called high tragedy (*Medea, Hippolytus*), followed by the patriotic plays of the opening years of the Peloponnesian War (*Heraclidae, Supplices*); plays expressing disgust with the war as the fighting went on and became more senseless (*Hecuba, Troades*); a turning away from tragedy to romantic intrigue plays (*Ion, Iphigenia in Tauris, Helen*) and a final return to the tragic mood, more despairing and violent than before (*Orestes, Phoenissae, Bacchae*). But of course the procedure is hazardous if only because so many plays are missing and, although sometimes we can guess at their contents, we have no idea of their mood. And the last set of his plays included both *Bacchae* and *Iphigenia in Aulide* – one of the most violently tragic and one which contains scenes whose tone and technique seem to foreshadow New Comedy.

That there was development in Euripidean technique is undeniable, but if there was a similar development in his thought we do not have sufficient evidence to chart its course. And in any case some basic themes and attitudes are common to the latest and the earliest plays. The merciless Dionysus of *Bacchae* is cast in the same mould as the vindictive Aphrodite of *Hippolytus* and the revengeful Athena of *Troades*: all three gods wreak havoc to punish human disrespect for their divinity. Medea's ferocious revenge is very like that of Hecuba and Electra, not to mention the vicious reprisals planned by Orestes, Electra and Pylades in *Orestes*. The disturbance of the heroic atmosphere by realistic scenes which may even verge on the comic is constant throughout, from the degrading quarrel of father and son in *Alcestis*, through the burlesque arming of Iolaus in *Heraclidae*, all the way to the spectacle of two old men, one of them blind, dressed in fawn skins and trying to dance like Maenads, in *Bacchae*. Even the most harrowing of the tragic plays, *Troades*, has an incongruously comic line (Menelaus is advised not to take Helen home aboard his own ship and asks: 'Why? Has she got any heavier?' 1050) and the play which is the closest Euripidean approach to Menandrian comedy, *Ion*, contains Creusa's lament for her lost child (859ff.), one of Euripides' most poignant and bitter solo arias. The pattern of the extant work suggests not so much changing views as variation on persistent themes.

The characterization of Euripides as a spokesman for the new ideas and his responsibility for what were thought of as their destructive effects were first given pungent and exaggerated expression in his own lifetime by Aristophanes, the comic poet who was both fascinated and repelled by his work. A recurrent tactic of his assault is to identify Euripides with many of the subversive ideas which were felt to be typical of sophistic teaching, prominent among them a destructive scepticism about the Olympian gods. The widow of *Thesmophoriazusae* whose husband was killed on Cyprus and who feeds her five children by making wreaths for worshippers, complains that her business has been cut by more than half since Euripides 'in his tragedies, has persuaded men that the gods do not exist' (450–1) and in *Frogs*, while Aeschylus prays to Demeter, Euripides addresses his prayer to 'other gods' (889) among them 'upper air, my nourishment' and 'intelligence' (892–3). The result of such teaching, the comic poet claimed, was moral degeneration. Euripidean drama is blamed by 'Aeschylus' in the *Frogs* for converting noble, warlike Athenians into 'marketplace loungers, tricksters and scoundrels' (1015), for teaching 'ranting and blather which has emptied the wrestling schools' (1069–70). In modern times the case has been put seriously: Nestle's *Euripides, the poet of the Greek enlightenment* attempts to construct a Euripidean philosophical outlook – the poet's message 'of enlightenment about the real state of things as against the traditional belief, blindly accepted by the mass of mankind'.[1] Quite apart from the fact that Euripides is a dramatist, not a philosopher, the argument is insecurely based, for the passages used to support it are cited with little regard to context (many of the most important, in fact, are isolated quotations from lost plays). But in drama, context can modify or even contradict the surface meaning of a particular passage. Hippolytus' line ('My tongue has sworn an oath but my mind is free', 612) was often used against Euripides by his comic critic, and if the play had not survived we would never have known that in fact Hippolytus goes to his death precisely because he will not break his oath. Nevertheless Nestle's title can serve as a reminder that Euripidean drama gives us the clearest reflection of the intellectual ferment of fifth-century Athens, and unlike the Platonic retrospective (and partisan) reconstruction it is the reaction of a contemporary.

The plays reflect, more literally than those of Sophocles, the intellectual controversies of the time, sometimes in a manner incongruous with the mythical setting. One recurrent theme is the problem of education for civic life, the problem to which the sophists proposed a solution. In *Antiope*, a play with a

[1] Nestle (1901) 50.

violent revenge action, two sons, Amphion and Zethus, stage a celebrated debate about the value of the active as opposed to the artistic life.[1] Amphion champions the intellectual and artistic life, Zethus the military, agricultural and political. It is remarkable that Zethus' speech echoes many of the criticisms levelled at Euripides himself by the comic poets. Zethus reproaches his brother for his lack of manliness and inability to stand by his friends in war and council.

> 'Where is the cleverness in this, an art which receives a noble nature and makes it inferior? . . . A man who . . . lets his household affairs go to waste and pursues delight in song, will become remiss in both private and public duty . . . Put an end to your singing, practise the fair art of practical affairs. Sing its praises and you will be thought a sensible man, digging, ploughing the earth, watching the flocks. Leave to others these elegant, intellectual pursuits . . .' (frs. 186, 187, 188)

Amphion's reply rejects the active life.

> 'The quiet man is a source of safety for his friends and of great benefit to the city. Do not sing the praise of dangerous action. I have no love for excessive boldness in a ship's captain, nor in a statesman either . . . Your contempt for my lack of physical strength is misplaced. If I can think straight, that is better than a powerful right arm . . . It is by a man's brains that cities are well governed and households too, and therein lies great strength for war . . .' (frs. 194, 199, 200)

Education is not the only controversial issue of the day reflected in the plays; political theory, another speciality of the sophistic teachers, also bulks large. In a long scene early in *Phoenissae*, the brothers Eteocles and Polynices dispute their rights to the throne of Thebes; their mother Jocasta tries to mediate between them. To Polynices' reasonable offer of a return to the *status quo* Eteocles replies with an unashamed proclamation of his will to rule – words which are echoed in the Athenian speeches of the Melian dialogue and the arguments of Thrasymachus and Callicles in Plato.[2]

> 'Mother, I will speak out . . . I would go to the place where the stars rise or below the earth, if that were possible, so as to hold Absolute Power, greatest of the gods. This is a prized possession I have no wish to let pass to another; I will keep it for myself.' (503–8)

Jocasta rebukes them both equally but counters Eteocles' argument with democratic theory.

> 'Why do you pursue, my son, the most evil of divinities, Ambition? She is an unjust goddess. She comes into prosperous homes and cities and when she goes out leaves destruction for those who entertained her . . . It is better to honour Equality, who firmly links friends to friends, city to city, ally to ally . . . For it is

---

[1] Cf. Plato, *Gorgias* 485eff.
[2] Thuc. 5.105, Plato, *Rep.* 343bff., *Gorg.* 482cff.

Equality which has fixed for mankind its divisions of measures and weights, has defined number. The rayless eye of night shares the cycle of the year equally with the blaze of the sun and neither one feels hateful envy for the other as it gives way...' (531–45)

But Euripides reflects the negative as well as the positive aspects of sophistic thought; in particular the plays cast scorn on those prophecies which played so important a part in Greek life and which in Sophoclean drama are always, in the end, vindicated. The most explicit condemnation of prophecy is put in the mouth of the messenger in *Helen*; he has just learned that the woman the Greeks fought and died for at Troy was merely an image made of cloud – the real Helen was in Egypt all the time.

'I realize how contemptible...are all the words of the prophets. So there was nothing sound in the voices of the fire oracle or the birds. Birds indeed – it was simple-minded to think that they were any use to men. For Calchas gave no word or sign to the army as he saw his friends dying for a cloud, nor Helenus either – but his city was sacked, and all for nothing.' (744–51)

This is not the only radical opinion on religious matters to surface in Euripidean drama. Tiresias in *Bacchae* explains that the goddess Demeter is the earth – 'call her by either name' (276) – and similarly Dionysus, besides being the inventor of wine, *is* the wine, 'a god poured out in libation to the gods' (284). Similar theories of the nature of divinities are attributed to the sophist Prodicus. But Euripidean characters propose even more unusual religious formulas, such as those of Hecuba in *Troades*. 'O You who are the earth's support and have your throne upon it, whoever you may be, beyond our knowledge or conjecture, Zeus, whether you are natural necessity or human intelligence, hear my plea ...' (884–7). It is no wonder that Menelaus remarks on her 'innovative prayers' (889).

Some Euripidean characters go beyond philosophical reformulations of religious belief, they indulge in harsh criticism of the Olympian gods. Amphitryon in *Heracles* condemns Zeus for abandoning the family of Heracles, his own son, in scathing terms.

'So you were not the friend you seemed to be. You are a great god but I, a mortal man, surpass you in excellence: I did not betray the sons of Heracles. But you, you knew how to steal secretly into women's beds, to take another's bride... what you do not know is how to save your children. You are a callous, ignorant god (ἀμαθής τις εἶ θεός) – or else there is no justice in your nature.' (341–7)

A common motif in Euripidean plays is an appeal to a god for mercy, coupled with a reminder that gods should have higher standards of morality than men. So Cadmus in *Bacchae* appeals to Dionysus for forgiveness: 'Gods should not be like mortals in their passions' (1348). And the old servant of Hippolytus addresses Aphrodite in almost the same words. Both prayers are rejected; both gods merciless. These passages seem to suggest that gods are no better than men; in the case of Hippolytus, who does forgive the father who unjustly engineered his death, that they are perhaps worse. Such criticism may culminate in rejection of the whole mythological tradition. In *Heracles*, the hero is urged by Theseus to reject suicide and live with the consequences of his murderous action, just as the gods live on Olympus, though they have committed adultery and violence against each other. But he replies (1341–6): 'For my part I do not believe the gods have forbidden loves; that one of them could chain the other's hands I never accepted and will never believe. For a god, if he is rightly a god, needs nothing. These are the wretched tales of poets' (ἀοιδῶν οἵδε δύστηνοι λόγοι). This comes close to denying the existence of the Olympian gods altogether, for the adulteries of Zeus, to take only one example, were the genesis of Dionysus, Perseus, Helen and many another. It is true that Euripides seems never to neglect an opportunity to bring the gods on stage, but modern critics have found it easy to dismiss the divine appearances at the end of so many of the plays as a device to reassure the pious or a merely technical solution for the problems raised by the radical treatment of the myth. The juxtaposition of amoral gods and human beings who vainly expect justice or mercy is taken as an ironic denial of the existence of such gods; Euripides was 'attempting to show citizens bred on traditional views ... that such conceptions of the gods *should* offend them'.[1] Such gods cannot exist: they must be 'the wretched tales of poets'.

Yet such dramatic statements must be seen in context. Heracles' famous repudiation of divine wrongdoing, for example, refers specifically to adultery as unthinkable for a god. Yet he is himself the offspring of divine adultery, and the madness which has ruined his life is the vindictive reaction of Hera, the divine jealous wife. The audience has seen Iris and Madness, the ministers of Hera, at work, experienced the shock of their sudden appearance and sensed in the rhythm of the racing trochaics the pulse of the insane fit which before their eyes descends into the house to seize its innocent victim. Heracles can talk in the way he does because he has not seen Iris and Madness at work; but the audience has. And since in the theatre everyone who appears on stage is equally real, Heracles is quite surely wrong.

This qualification by context obtains for all manifestations of the new intellectual views in Euripides: they are the words of dramatic fictional characters and parts of an overall design. It is usually thought (and may very well be true) that in the argument between the brothers in *Antiope*, the case put by Amphion must have been dearer to Euripides' heart, but Amphion seems to have conceded defeat in the argument, and it is certainly Amphion who at the

---

[1] Conacher (1967) 51.

end of the play is about to kill the tyrant Lycus when Hermes arrives to stop him.[1] In *Phoenissae* Jocasta's eloquent praise of Equality falls on deaf ears; before the play is over the mother and the two sons lie together in the equality of death. In one play after another the 'rationalist' point of view is repudiated by the outcome of events.

On the other hand, Euripides shows concern with and knowledge of religious phenomena which many would regard as 'irrational'. His presentation of Hippolytus, for example, is an understanding and sympathetic picture of a religious abstention from the sexual life which must have been extremely rare in the ancient world. An almost monastic obsession with purity can be sensed in Hippolytus' first speech, his dedication of a crown of flowers to Artemis. It came from 'a meadow undefiled . . . where no shepherd dares to pasture his flocks, no blade of iron ever came; only the bee in springtime haunts this untouched meadow, and Modesty tends its garden with the river waters' (73–8). A similarly moving picture of piety in a young man appears in *Ion*; the monody with which the acolyte greets the dawn (82ff.) suggests what the religious atmosphere of Delphi must have been in its great days. In fact it is remarkable how often Euripides chooses a religious, ritual background for his great scenes: the death of Neoptolemus in the shrine at Delphi (*Andromache*), the temple of Artemis among the Taurians (*Iphigenia in Tauris*), the sacrifice Aegisthus offers in the grove of the nymphs (*Electra*), the sacrifice of Polyxena on the tomb of Achilles (*Hecuba*). And of course *Bacchae*, in its ferocious action and in the ecstasies of its choral odes, is the greatest portrayal of the Dionysiac spirit in all literature.

Whether this play is a celebration of the blessings of Dionysiac religion or a condemnation of its violence, one thing is sure: the poet who created this passion play was no 'rationalist'. It is the only Attic tragedy we know of which features a god as the protagonist; Dionysus, who in the prologue announces his assumption of human form as a votary of his own worship, dominates the central scenes and appears at the end in divine majesty. The play presents us with different reactions to his divinity: the mockery of Pentheus, the cynical adhesion of Cadmus, the political conversion of Tiresias; the ecstatic visions of the chorus alternating with their vengeful imprecations against the king who resists the new cult; the total possession of the women of Thebes, their paradisal peace and communion with nature, their ferocious reaction to interference and finally their frenzied dismemberment of Pentheus.

The dramatic centre of the play consists of three scenes in which man and god confront each other. In the first, the god, in the person of his votary, is bound, jeered at for his effeminate appearance, told he will be shorn of his hair, and imprisoned; he defends Dionysus with mock humility (the actor wore a

[1] Cf. Page (1942) 66–8.

smiling mask in this scene).[1] In the central scene, after an earthquake that wrecks the palace and releases Dionysus, the god begins to dominate the mind of Pentheus, persuading him to go and spy on the Maenads at what he imagines are their obscene revels. In the last scene the reversal is complete: Pentheus, his senses deranged, appears dressed as a woman, a Maenad with long hair. Now it is the god's turn to mock his victim; he congratulates him on his appearance, rearranges his wig, readjusts his waistline and skirt length before he sends him off to his hideous death. These scenes have a bizarre, deadly magic which has never been surpassed; Euripides here drew on some deep vein of primitive feeling which made his play unique in the annals of the theatre.

To the objection that the gods who end so many of the plays seem mechanical and lifeless, a dramatic convenience or a bow to convention rather than a religious epiphany, the obvious answer is that Euripides did not have to end his plays in this way, that, in fact, as far as our evidence goes, he is the inventor of this particular kind of ending. And not all of these gods are unimpressive figures; Dionysus at the end is the same terrifying relentless deity he has been all through the play, and Artemis at the end of *Hippolytus* is as credible in her pride and anger as her opposite number Aphrodite, who spoke the prologue. Further, these divine figures usually have specifically religious functions: instructions for the founding of a cult or a city, for the burial of the dead, for the administration of an oath and the attendant sacrifices. They also regularly predict the future, and these prophecies are evidently meant to be taken seriously; they range from confirmation of the further development of the legend through legitimization of contemporary dynasties to fully-fledged panegyrics of Athenian expansion or promises of protection for Athenian soil.

The passages which demand a higher standard of morality from gods than from men, and the portrayal of the Olympian gods as jealous, vindictive, merciless, unjust, do not necessarily imply a rationalistic viewpoint. These are Homeric gods; it is hard to imagine gods more unforgiving than Athena and Hera in the *Iliad*, Poseidon in the *Odyssey*. The centuries since Homer had seen incessant questioning of this pessimistic view, even attempts to reshape it along more moral lines, but Euripides recreates in all their fierce passions the gods of Homer's poems. The gods who rule the Euripidean universe are not like the Zeus of the *Oresteia*, who imposes suffering that is a step to wisdom, nor are they like the Sophoclean gods who seem to represent an assurance of divine order though it is one which can only be accepted not understood. Euripides' gods, Aphrodite, Artemis, Athena, Hera, Dionysus, are just like Homer's – which is to say, just like us. Torn by the same passions, pride and the vindictiveness of pride insulted, revengeful anger, jealousy and desire, they

[1] Dodds (1960) on l. 439.

are huge and awesome images of everything that is violent and uncontrollable
in man, and they order the universe according to their conflicting and changing
wills, bargaining for the fates of human beings as Athena does in *Troades* or
promising to take a life for a life as Artemis does in *Hippolytus*.

These are the gods to whom mortals, despairing of human nature, appeal as
representatives of something higher and better. 'You should be wiser than
mortals, you are gods', says the old servant in *Hippolytus* (σοφωτέρους γὰρ χρὴ
βροτῶν εἶναι θεούς, 120). The goddess he is addressing is Aphrodite, the personification of Eros, the most capricious and irrational of all human emotions. The
Euripidean gods are naked passion unrestrained by any sense of moderation.
Aphrodite engineers the deaths of two mortals to pay for Hippolytus' neglect
of her worship (and cynically admits that one of them is innocent); Athena
in *Troades* organizes the destruction of the Greek fleet because one Greek
hero insulted her divinity; Hera, acting from jealousy, sends the spirit of
Madness to wreck Heracles' life the moment he has finished his great labours
for mankind; Dionysus demands as payment for the denial of his divinity not
only the dismemberment of Pentheus but the exile of Cadmus and Agave as
well. The gods, in Euripidean tragedy, project on to the enormous scale of
the divine those passions which human beings struggle vainly to control in
themselves; these passions, in the shape of Olympian gods, self-absorbed,
unrelenting, rule the life of men and women.

It is not likely that Euripides believed in these gods with the literal acceptance and religious awe of the archaic time which gave them their shape. They
serve him as dramatic incarnations of the capricious, irrational forces which his
tragic vision saw as the determinants of the fate of mankind. They may sometimes be replaced in the prayers of his characters by abstractions such as those
formulas of Hecuba which so surprised Menelaus, or by the all-embracing
concept of *Tyche*, blind chance. Yet they are more than symbolic figures; they
have a terrifying vitality which betrays a religious imagination at work under
the sophisticated surface. Whatever else they are, they are not the creation of a
'rationalist'; rather, they are the dramatic expression of that bewilderment
the poet puts in the mouth of the chorus in *Hippolytus*.

ἦ μέγα μοι τὰ θεῶν μελεδήμαθ' ὅταν φρένας ἔλθηι
λύπας παραιρεῖ. ξύνεσιν δέ τιν' ἐλπίδι κεύθων
λείπομαι ἔν τε τύχαις θνατῶν καὶ ἐν ἔργμασι λεύσσων.   (1104–6)

When I think of the care the gods have for men, my heart is greatly relieved of
its sorrow. But though deep within me I hope to attain understanding, I fail to
reach it, as my eyes see what happens to men and what they do.

This haunted vision of irrational forces at work in the universe has its
counterpart in Euripides' exploration of the irrational in individual human

beings; he is the first of the dramatists for whose work the modern term 'psychology' does not seem out of place. This is not to deny (as some have done) consistency of character and subtlety of motivation to the dramaturgy of Aeschylus,[1] still less to that of Sophocles; it is merely to assert that Euripidean characters are less linear and monumental, more complicated, more changeable. They run the gamut of human emotions, change direction suddenly, reveal what seem to be contradictions which, though they violate the canons of Sophoclean classic art, make them more recognizably and compellingly human.

Such psychological reversals are a Euripidean trade-mark from the earliest plays on. In the *Alcestis*, Admetus, who has never for a moment questioned the propriety of accepting his wife's sacrifice, who over her dead body has abused his father Pheres for not taking his place and angrily rejected the old man's cruel (but justified) reply, mourns her death in terms which still emphasize nothing but his own loss and then suddenly realizes how he will appear to others. His wife's death is glorious 'while I, who was supposed to die, but eluded my fate, will live out a sorry life. ἄρτι μανθάνω. Now I realize the truth' (939–40). The realization is not prepared by any hint in the speeches of Admetus or the chorus, and yet it is not unexpected. For the home truths his ignoble father told him in the earlier scene are so forcibly expressed ('You enjoy living: do you think your father doesn't?' 691), so scandalous but irrefutable, that even Admetus must eventually look them in the face and see his real situation – from which however he is rescued by the fairy-tale restoration of Alcestis from the kingdom of death.

The action of *Iphigenia in Aulide* turns on a change of mind so sudden that Aristotle cites it as an example of failure to maintain consistency of character; it is Iphigenia's decision to offer herself as a sacrifice to ensure the Greek departure for Troy after previously begging her father to spare her life. Aristotle's criticism – 'the girl who makes the speech of supplication here bears no resemblance to the later one . . .' (*Poetics* 1454a32) – overlooks the fact that the audience has been subliminally prepared for this volte-face by the whole of the play's action so far; a series of swift and sudden changes of decision which is unparalleled in ancient drama. Agamemnon opens the play by sending a letter to Clytemnestra countermanding the instructions previously sent her to bring Iphigenia to the camp in Aulis. Menelaus intercepts this letter and taunts Agamemnon with his instability; but when Agamemnon expresses despair at the news that Iphigenia has arrived, Menelaus changes his mind and urges Agamemnon to disband the army and abandon the expedition rather than sacrifice his daughter. 'You will say I have changed, my words no longer fierce. This is true. But what has happened to me is natural. I have changed

---

[1] Easterling (1973).

over to feel love for my brother. And such shifts are by no means the mark of an evil man' (500–3). But Agamemnon has changed his mind again: he now sees no way out; the army will demand his daughter's sacrifice.

An even more striking change, which is in fact something of a psychological puzzle, is the eerie process by which Dionysus, in *Bacchae*, transforms the menacing tyrant Pentheus into a crazed victim. It is of course a presentation of Dionysiac possession but it is also rooted in a Euripidean perception of the obscure depths in the human soul. Dionysus persuades Pentheus not to lead his troops against the wild women on the hills; he appeals to Pentheus' fevered vision of their orgies, and Pentheus reveals the strength of his obsessive desire to see them with his own eyes. There is only one way to fulfil it, Dionysus tells him: disguised as a maenad. Pentheus goes into the palace to decide what to do, but he is now the prey of dark forces in motion in his own soul. The god-priest on stage calls on Dionysus to 'derange his wits, set loose a giddy madness' (850–1) and the god's full power, exerted from outside, now combines with the forces released inside Pentheus' mind by his surrender to temptation, to produce the macabre figure who comes on stage, 'a giggling, leering creature, more helpless than a child, nastier than an idiot . . .'.[1]

This scene is unique, but everywhere in Euripides a preoccupation with individual psychology and its irrational aspects is evident: Hermione's emotional breakdown and suicidal mood after the failure of her attempt to kill Andromache's child; Medea's soliloquy in which, after deciding to kill her sons, she alternately yields to and masters her maternal instincts; Electra's exultant speech over the corpse of Aegisthus, shot through with perverted sexual jealousy; Phaedra's delirium as she tries to conceal her guilty love and the account she later gives of the stages of her struggle to conceal her passion – these situations and reactions are characteristically Euripidean. In his hands tragedy for the first time probed the inner recesses of the human soul and let 'passions spin the plot'.

The originality of Euripidean psychological characterization has in recent years been given less than its due in the justified reaction against interpretations which, in nineteenth-century style, tried to reach behind the surfaces of the characters displayed by the action and construct a fully rounded personality, its past as well as its present. Against such probing below the surface, other critics urged consideration of the action and its demands and also of the rhetorical possibilities open to exploitation. We may get much nearer to Euripides' thinking, it has been suggested, if instead of asking ourselves in any dramatic situation 'What would . . . such a man be likely to say . . .?' we asked ourselves: 'How should he . . . best acquit himself? How gain his point? Move his hearers? Prove his thesis? . . .'[2]

[1] Dodds (1960) 192.   [2] Dale (1954) xxviii.

There is much truth in this observation; rhetoric was the principal offering of the sophistic teachers and Athenian audiences were expert judges of the oratorical skills demanded by assembly and law-court.[1] Aristophanes was not slow to seize on this aspect of Euripidean style; his Euripides in the *Frogs* claims that he taught the Athenians to 'chatter' by means of 'introductions of subtle regulations and angle measurements of verses' (956). And it is true that Euripides' characters all seem to have had at least an elementary course in public speaking; their speeches are sometimes self-consciously rhetorical. Electra, for instance, begins her arraignment of the dead Aegisthus with what sounds like textbook language:

εῖεν. τίν' ἀρχὴν πρῶτά σ' ἐξείπω κακῶν,
ποίας τελευτάς; τίνα μέσον τάξω λόγον;   (907–8)

'Let me see. What shall I express first as the beginning of the wrongs you have done, what as the end? And what discourse shall I arrange in the middle?'

Other Euripidean characters are less naively technical but they are just as anxious to put their case well; the characteristic Euripidean dialogue is a debate, with long speeches of more or less equal length, one on each side, followed by the cut and thrust of one-line exchanges. And they can make out a case for anything. In a fragment of the lost *Cretans* (Page (1942)), Pasiphae, haled before an outraged Minos after she has given birth to the Minotaur, pleads her case with virtuoso skill. Denial, she says, would be useless. But she is no adulteress, giving her body to a man in secret lust. It was madness sent from heaven; what else could explain her action? 'What could I see in a bull to sting my heart with shameful passion? Was he handsome? Well dressed? Was it the gleam from his tawny hair, his flashing eyes . . .?' (11–15). She goes on to put the blame on her husband: he had sworn to sacrifice the bull to Poseidon but failed to do so. 'The fault is yours, you are the cause of my sickness . . .' (34–5). It is no wonder Minos begins his reply by asking his guards: 'Has she been muzzled yet?' (44).

Pasiphae is pleading for her life before a judge, and this courtroom atmosphere, so familiar to the Athenian audience, is typically Euripidean. Hecuba and Polymestor plead their case in contrasted speeches before Agamemnon in *Hecuba*, as Hecuba and Helen do before Menelaus in *Troades*, Orestes and Tyndareus before Menelaus in *Orestes*; so Hippolytus defends himself against Phaedra's accusation before Theseus.

Yet though they use rhetorical techniques in formal debate the effect is not monotonous; the speeches are fully expressive of individual character and also designed for dramatic effect. Hippolytus, for example, proves the truth of his earlier assertion that he is not at home in a public assembly (986) by using

[1] Cf. Thuc. 3.38.7.

arguments which infuriate the father he is trying to convince; he even tries to prove lack of motive (a standard sophistic approach) by asking: 'Was her body pre-eminent in beauty over all other women?' (1009–10). It was not exactly the best thing to say to a sorrowing husband in the presence of his wife's body; it is, however, very much 'in character', for Hippolytus' almost pathological distaste for women (revealed in his speech to the Nurse) has now been concentrated on Phaedra who has falsely accused him of attempted rape.

Euripides' characters present their cases in the organized framework of rhetoric but they are driven by irrational forces working below the surface. His drama cherishes no illusion that mankind is capable of choosing the good; Phaedra sums up the human dilemma in a short but chilling sentence: 'We know what is right, we recognize it clearly, but we don't achieve it' (τὰ χρήστ' ἐπιστάμεσθα καὶ γιγνώσκομεν | οὐκ ἐκπονοῦμεν δ'..., 380–1). The mind is not strong enough to combat the weakness and violence of our nature. Phaedra is talking about her love for Hippolytus, and this, the most irrational of human passions, is a theme predominant in Euripidean drama – a point pressed home by Aristophanes' Aeschylus, who claims that he never brought 'whores like Phaedra' on stage nor for that matter 'any woman in love' (*Frogs* 1043–4). 'Eros', sings the chorus of *Hippolytus*, 'you that make desire flow from the eyes ... may you never ... come to me beyond due measure ... Eros, tyrant over men, who comes upon mortals with destruction and every shape of disaster' (525–42). It was this aspect of Eros, the destructive, which fascinated Euripides: the delirium of Phaedra and, later, her love turned to hate, the jealous rage of the barren wife Hermione, the unforeseen violence of Medea's revenge, the love of brother and sister in the lost *Aeolus*, the Potiphar's wife plot of the lost *Stheneboea*. Euripides in fact is the creator of that three-walled room in which the imprisoned men and women destroy each other by the intensity of their loves and hates, of that cage which is the theatre of Shakespeare's *Othello*, Racine's *Phèdre*, of Ibsen and Strindberg.

It was this preoccupation with women's loves and hates which won Euripides his reputation, widespread in antiquity, as a misogynist; a whole play of Aristophanes is devoted to the hilarious results of the decision taken by the women of Athens to punish him for his sins against them. This is of course comic exaggeration, but it may well reflect the feelings (at least the public feelings) of Athenian wives, for Euripides' characters shattered the polite fictions about female docility which both men and women paid lip service to. 'A wife's honour' Pericles is supposed to have said 'is – to be least talked about by men, for good or bad' (Thuc. 2.45.2); but Phaedra, to protect her honour, contrives the death of Hippolytus, and Medea, invoking the male code of honour, revenges herself by the murder of her sons. Yet, though it is not likely Athenian wives would have defended such extreme measures, the Euripidean plays are sympathetic rather than critical. Phaedra is the victim of Aphrodite and her account of her struggle to overcome her passion puts her in a noble light. And in the case of *Medea*, Euripides chose to emphasize the issue of women's social subordination; it is the argument Medea uses in her famous speech. 'Of all creatures that have life and intelligence, we women are the most afflicted stock' (πάντων δ' ὅσ' ἔστ' ἔμψυχα καὶ γνώμην ἔχει | γυναῖκές ἐσμεν ἀθλιώτατον φυτόν, 230–1). She touches on one sore point after another in what must have been the grievances of many an Athenian wife: the dowry with which women 'buy an owner of their body'; the risk involved (for if the husband turns out badly 'divorce does a woman's reputation harm'); their lack of preparation for marriage and a new household; the man's freedom to leave the house for distraction, the wife's obligation 'to keep her eyes fixed on a single human being'. The routine male justification of their privileges – that they fight the wars – is rejected: 'I'd rather stand in the battle lines spear in hand three times than give birth once' (230–51).

Medea is of course an extraordinary figure, an eastern princess, grand-daughter of Helios, but this speech cannot be discounted on the grounds that she is a barbarian and witch – it comes too close to home. The chorus of Corinthian women are won over; they welcome Medea's announcement that she plans revenge with an ode which rejects the male literary tradition on the subject of women. It was not to women that Apollo gave the gift of song, for if he had 'I would have sung a hymn to counter the male sex' (426–7). It is significant that this remarkable critique of the tradition occurs in a play which presents the revenge of a wronged wife in the heroic terms usually reserved for men and, in what must have been a very disturbing ending for the audience, shows her victorious over her enemies and, aided by Helios, escaping unpunished to Athens.[1] 'In my plays' says the comic Euripides in the *Frogs* 'the woman spoke ... and the young girl and the old woman ...' (949–50). It is in fact remarkable how important female roles are in Euripidean drama compared with that of his fellow dramatists. In play after play it is a woman who plays the principal part or, in a secondary role, makes an indelible impression.

It is typical of Euripides that he could take a figure as exotic as the princess from Colchis, the awesome priestess, prophet and magician of Pindar's fourth Pythian Ode, and present her in a context of domestic strife which is painfully realistic. 'One word will floor you' says Medea, countering Jason's claim that he is marrying the princess only to advance the family interest. 'If you were an honest man, you would have tried to persuade me and then married the girl, instead of concealing it ...' (585–7). The retort is quick and to the point. 'And you, of course, would be giving me a helping hand in the project – all I had to do was mention the word "marriage". Why, even now you can't

---

[1] Cf. Knox (1976).

bring yourself to renounce the huge rage in your heart' (588–90). It is all too human, it verges in fact on the sordid. And it is not a solitary example; Euripides' treatment of the mythical figures is often realistic in the extreme. Once again Aristophanes knew his man; his Euripides boasts that he introduced into tragedy 'domestic affairs, the kind we deal and live with' (οἰκεῖα πράγματ' εἰσάγων, οἷς χρώμεθ' οἷς ξύνεσμεν . . ., 959).

Euripides' treatment of some of the most prestigious myths suggests that he must have asked himself the question: 'How would these people act and speak if they were our contemporaries?' The results are often disconcerting, nowhere more so than in his handling of the figures of Electra and Orestes. His *Electra* is from start to finish a clear challenge to the canonical Aeschylean version; in fact it contains, among its many surprises, what can only be regarded as a parodic critique of Aeschylus' recognition scene (509ff.). The setting of the play is the house of a farmer in the countryside; he delivers the prologue and gives us the unexpected news that he is Electra's husband. The heroine herself carries a pot balanced on her head as she goes to draw water. Orestes acts like a fifth-century exile returning home in secret to conspire; instead of going to the palace, he comes just over the border to this remote farm, ready to run for safety if there is no local support for his plans. When the farmer invites Orestes and Pylades (their identity still cautiously concealed) into the house for a meal, Electra scolds him shrewishly for not realizing that his poor house is no place to entertain what are obviously high-class visitors. The effect of this domestic tone is to strip Electra and Orestes of the heroic stature conferred on them by the legends, so that we see the treacherous murder of Aegisthus and the cold-blooded killing of their mother not as the working of destiny or a curse, not even the fulfilment of a divine command, but rather as crimes committed by 'men as they are' – Sophocles' description of Euripidean characters.[1] In *Orestes* the realistic presentation is even more extreme. The hero, after the murder of Clytemnestra, is afflicted not by the Erinyes (in his delirium he takes Electra for one of them) but by sickness – and we are spared no detail. 'Take hold of me' he says to his sister 'and wipe the caked foam from my miserable lips and eyes' (219–20). Helen has put on mourning for her sister but 'she cut her hair just at the ends' Electra tells us 'so as not to spoil her beauty. She's the same old Helen still' (127–8). Menelaus is a cautious trimmer who according to Aristotle (*Poetics* 1454a) is 'an example of unnecessary baseness of character'. Tyndareus is a vindictive and violent old man, while Orestes, Electra and Pylades, as they enthusiastically discuss their plans to murder Helen and hold Hermione hostage, emerge as juvenile delinquents of a start-lingly modern depravity. The great moral and legal dilemma posed by the myth, Orestes' conflict of duties, is dismissed in cavalier fashion by Clytem-

---

[1] Aristotle, *Poetics* 1460b33.

nestra's father, Tyndareus, who condemns Orestes' killing of his mother in surprising terms. 'He took no account of justice, had no recourse to the universal Hellenic law ... Orestes should have charged his mother with murder ...' (494–500). To this reversal of the canonical order of events (in Aeschylus the law court was convened for the first time in history precisely to deal with Orestes' killing of his mother) no one in the play takes objection; Orestes answers Tyndareus on other grounds. Its effect, for the moral context of Orestes' action, is devastating; he is stripped of all justification except the command of Apollo, the god whom he accuses of deserting him.

These two plays are widely criticized as artistic failures in their unconvincing endings; in each case the god from the machine announces, in what seems to be a deliberately banal fashion, a bundle of future marriages, apotheoses, etc. which seem incongruous with the desperation portrayed in the body of the play. But it is hard to see what else Euripides could have done. His realistic treatment has destroyed the heroic and moral values underlying the myth and no ending which could re-identify the Orestes and Electra of these plays with their heroic prototypes is conceivable; perhaps he thought it best to underline, by the deliberate artificiality of the form of his ending, the irrelevance of its content.

In contrast to this realistic remodelling of central myths stands Euripides' exploitation of the romantic and exotic material offered by others which deal with the adventures and ordeals of heroes in far-off lands. The *Andromeda* was such a play; it opened (as we know from the hilarious parody in Aristophanes' *Thesmophoriazusae*) with the heroine bound to the rock awaiting the sea-monster and the arrival of Perseus, her rescuer. Two extant plays of this type suggest that Euripides is the inventor of a genre of romantic melodrama which turns on the rescue of the heroine from the clutches of backward foreigners by adventurers who take advantage of the natives' superstitions. Both *Iphigenia in Tauris* and *Helen* are built on this formula: Iphigenia, spirited away from the sacrificer's knife at Aulis by Artemis, now serves the goddess as a priestess presiding over the human sacrifices offered by the barbarians, while the real Helen (as opposed to the image of her which went to Troy) is in Egypt, resisting the demands for her hand made by the local king Theoclymenus. In both plays the recognition scenes are models of skilful dramaturgy; the Iphigenia scene, in the technical brilliance of its prolongation of suspense (it was singled out as exemplary by Aristotle, *Poetics* 1455a) and the Helen scene in its sophisticated wit. Both plays end with the appearance of gods from the machine: Athena in *Iphigenia* prevents the recapture of the fugitives, whose ship has been thrown back on the shore, and the Dioscuri in *Helen* prevent Theoclymenus from killing his sister Theonoe, who helped Helen and Menelaus escape. But these interventions are not a mere dramatic convenience. In

Iphigenia the failure of the attempt to escape is not necessary; it seems to have been deliberately contrived to motivate the divine intervention, which has the important mythical-religious function of linking the action with the foundation of the Artemis-cult at Brauron in Attica. In *Helen*, the assurance brought by the Dioscuri that Helen and Menelaus will be immortal is less urgent a motive, but their intervention does make possible the dramatic final scene of the action proper: Theoclymenus' attempt to vent his frustrated rage on Theonoe; in any case she is a fully developed and sympathetic character who cannot be left to suffer for the help she has given the heroine.

These 'romantic' plays come comparatively late in Euripides' career; the plays (*Heraclidae*, *Supplices*) which have been described as 'patriotic' (more recently and accurately as 'political')[1] date from the years of the Archidamian War. They deal with topics which recur in Athenian patriotic orations: the rescue of Heracles' children from their persecutor Eurystheus by Theseus' son Demophon, the intervention of Theseus himself to force the Thebans to allow burial of the seven fallen champions. In the *Heraclidae* a daughter volunteers herself for sacrifice to save her family; *Supplices* has no such sacrifice scene (though the widow of one of the Theban champions throws herself on to his funeral pyre) but its main theme is the same: the celebration of Athenian martial valour not in self-defence but to protect the rights of the helpless and oppressed elsewhere. Such plays were standard fare; Aeschylus had already in his *Eleusinii* dramatized Theseus' intervention on behalf of the Theban widows and had also produced a *Heraclidae*. But the two extant Euripidean examples of this genre are not simple-minded patriotic propaganda. In both cases the principal character representing the persecuted victims rescued by Athens is an ambivalent figure. Adrastus in *Supplices*, who asks for aid to get the bodies of his champions buried, is reproached by Theseus in harsh terms which must have made some in the audience think of their own involvement in the Archidamian War.

> 'You ruined your city, your wits disturbed by young men, who in their desire for glory promote the cause of war unjustly and bring ruin on their fellow citizens – one because he wants command, another to get his hands on power and use it harshly, another for profit – and not one of them considers what harm war brings to the masses of the people.' (231–7)

In fact Theseus refuses to risk a war on behalf of a man who acted so unwisely and consents to help the Argives only when his mother Aethra reminds him that Athens is the traditional champion of the weak and oppressed. And in *Heraclidae* Alcmena, the mother of the children, ends the play by ordering the execution of a captured Eurystheus who had been promised his life by the

[1] Zuntz (1955).

333

Athenian victors: worse still, she orders his dead body to be thrown to the dogs (1045ff.).

This emphasis on the ugliness and waste of war becomes a major theme in other plays which however lack the patriotic appeal; in *Hecuba* and especially in *Troades* the sack of Troy serves as a general symbol of war's destructiveness. In both plays the chorus consists of enslaved Trojan women, and in *Hecuba*, as they contemplate the sorrows of their queen, they recreate for us the terror of Troy's fall.

> 'My end came at midnight... The dances and sacrifices over, my husband lay at rest, his spear hung on the wall... I was arranging my hair... gazing into the fathomless light of the golden mirror... preparing to fall into bed, when a shout rang out in the city, a war-cry... I left my familiar bed, dressed in one robe like a Dorian girl... I saw my husband killed, was taken away over the sea, looking back at Troy...' (914–38)

But it is in *Troades* that the most vivid tableau of war's terror and cruelty is staged. Greek literature from the *Iliad* on had been much concerned with war, but war had been seen always from the point of view of the men who fought it – the Achaean heroes, the soldier of fortune Archilochus, the aristocratic partisan Alcaeus, the Spartan regular Tyrtaeus. This play presents it from the standpoint of the captured women; the characters are a royal grandmother Hecuba, who in the play learns of the death of a daughter and a grandson; an unmarried princess, Cassandra, who is taken as his mistress by the Greek commander; a mother, Andromache, who is assigned as concubine to the son of the man who killed her husband and whose infant son is thrown to his death from the walls. The chorus who brood desperately on what their individual fates will be, represent a whole female population sold into slavery after the slaughter of their men (a punishment which Athens had inflicted on the city of Scione six years earlier and on the island of Melos in the preceding winter).

That the play stems from concern over the plight of war-torn Greece there can be little doubt, but the position that it is specifically an attack on Athenian imperialism can be maintained only with difficulty. For one thing, the chorus, speculating on their eventual destination in Greece, pray that they may come to the 'blessed land of Theseus' (209) and not 'to the eddies of the Eurotas' (210), the river of Sparta. And, for another, the fundamental question raised by the debate between Hecuba and Helen, that of responsibility for the war, is left unanswered. Helen's case is that Troy was responsible since Hecuba bore Paris; Priam, though the gods warned that Paris would be a firebrand to burn Troy, failed to kill him. This case looks weak in the context of the suffering we see in the *Troades*; but the audience had seen, as the first of the sequence of plays in which this play came last, the *Alexander*, which was concerned with precisely this question and seems to have suggested that Helen was not entirely wrong. Like the 'patriotic' plays, the 'anti-war' plays of Euripides are complex and ambiguous.

No less ambiguous is the treatment of war in *Iphigenia in Aulide*. The action gives a picture of the moral cowardice and personal ambition of Agamemnon so vivid that many have taken Iphigenia's speech accepting self-sacrifice for the Panhellenic cause as Euripides' ironic symbol of the insanity of war – an innocent girl who gives her life for tawdry slogans in which no one but she can believe. Yet this theme, Panhellenic unity against the barbarians, is not only a leitmotiv of the play but was also a policy urged by many voices in the last years of the war which saw Athens and Sparta competing for Persian help.

The play is a sombre tragedy of war, but it contains one scene which shows an entirely different side of Euripides' genius, a scene which in its lightness of touch and its exploitation of the nuances of a social situation foreshadows the atmosphere of Menandrian comedy. It is the meeting of Clytemnestra and Achilles. The queen has brought her daughter to Aulis believing that Achilles is going to marry her. But Achilles has never heard of this proposed marriage; Agamemnon lied to Clytemnestra to get her to bring her daughter to be sacrificed. Clytemnestra and Achilles have never met, but, inside the royal tent, she hears him announce his name as he calls for Agamemnon; she comes out to make the acquaintance of her future son-in-law. He professes embarrassment in the presence of a beautiful woman (he does manage to pay her that compliment) and with the manners of a *grande dame* she puts him at his ease:

CLYT. No wonder you don't know who I am; we have never met. And my compliments on your modesty.
ACH. Who are you? Why have you come to the camp, a woman among men at arms?
CLYT. I am Leda's daughter, my name is Clytemnestra, my husband lord Agamemnon.
ACH. Thank you for telling me the facts in such compact form. But I am ashamed to be exchanging words with a lady... [*He moves off.*]
CLYT. [*Detains him*] Wait! Don't run away! Put your right hand in mine – a happy first step to a wedding.
ACH. My hand in yours? How could I face Agamemnon if I took hold of what I should not?
CLYT. But you *should* – since you are going to marry my daughter...
ACH. Marry? Marry whom? I am speechless, lady. But – perhaps this strange statement comes from a disturbed mind...
CLYT. It's a natural reaction in everyone to be embarrassed when they set eyes on new family connexions and discuss marriage. (823–40)

They finally realize that they are both under a misapprehension and the play resumes its prevailing mood of grim foreboding. But this scene alone would be enough to suggest that Euripides was a forerunner of Menander, a claim which is in fact made in a headless sentence from an Alexandrian *Life of Euripides*: '. . . towards wife, and father towards son and servant towards master, or the business of reversals – virgins raped, babies substituted, recognitions by means of rings and necklaces. For these are the sinews of New Comedy, and Euripides brought these dramatic means to perfection.'[1]

The forceful wooing of a maid by a god, the complications involved in bringing up (usually in secret) the resultant offspring, and the ultimate recognition of the child's high lineage – these were all commonplaces of heroic genealogy; Euripides seems to have used them as an intrigue formula for a series of plays (now lost) which exploited the possibilities with virtuoso skill. But there is one surviving play which is based on this formula and does in fact suggest, in clear outline, the shape of the New Comedy to come. The *Ion* presents us with a virgin princess overcome by a god (Creusa, in fear of her father, exposes Apollo's child), and on a lower level, a girl seduced by a human suitor (Xuthus remembers his affair with a local girl at Dionysiac revels in Delphi). The whole plot turns on substitution of children (Apollo foists his son by Creusa on Xuthus, persuading him, from his oracular shrine, that Ion is his own illegitimate child) and one of the signs by which Creusa recognizes Ion's identity is a golden snake collar. And though much of *Ion* is played on a serious note, there is one scene at least which is undeniably high comedy: the false recognition scene in which Xuthus, misled by the oracle, takes Ion for his son and Ion, appalled, takes Xuthus for a would-be seducer or perhaps insane. Like the Clytemnestra–Achilles scene, this depends on *agnoia*, ignorance of identity, the mainspring of New Comedy; in fact in Menander's *Girl who has her hair cut off* the goddess Agnoia delivers the Prologue. The poets of the New Comedy recognized their indebtedness; a character in Menander's *Arbitrants* proposes to recite a speech from the *Auge*, a Euripidean play, which, like that in which the speaker is appearing, turned on identifications through tokens left with a child.[2] And a character in a play of Philemon is given the line: 'If I were sure of life beyond the grave, I'd hang myself – to see Euripides.'[3]

But it is not only in the ingenuity of his intrigue-plots and the sophistication of his tone that Euripides foreshadows the drama of Menander and Philemon; he also developed a conversational style for his characters which was closer to normal speech than anything so far heard on the Attic stage. The dialogue of the Euripidean characters, though still subject to the demands of metre and the decorum of the tragic genre, creates an illusion of everyday speech, perfectly suited to the unheroic figures and situations of his drama. In fact in its avoidance of sustained metaphor, its striving for clarity, precision and point, the style sometimes verges on the prosaic. Yet this plain surface is cleverly contrived,

---

[1] von Arnim (1913) 5 (col. VII).   [2] Menander, *Epitrepontes* 1125.   [3] 130 K.

as Aristotle pointed out: 'the best concealment of art is to compose selecting words from everyday speech, as Euripides does, who was the first to show the way' (*Rhetoric* 1404b5).

One effective instrument for Euripides' purposes was his gradual loosening of the iambic trimeter which (as we saw above, p. 316) provides a rough guide for dating the plays. In the strict metre of the Aeschylean trimeter the appearance of two short syllables in succession (and *a fortiori* of three) was avoided as much as possible; in Euripides it is admitted more frequently as his style develops. Not only did this give his dialogue a much more natural sound (for in Greek conversation, as is clear from early Platonic dialogues where natural speech is the effect aimed at, runs of short syllables are frequent), it also allowed him to employ new syntactical combinations and to make extensive additions to the vocabulary of spoken dialogue. The list of such additions is long; two types predominate. The first consists of compound verbs made with prepositions, most of which, in Greek, consist of two short syllables – *apo, dia, meta* etc. The prepositional prefixes of these words limit and direct the action expressed by the main verb to a particular attitude or context; their precision allows Euripides to make logical distinctions, and also subtle psychological differentiations. The second type consists of nouns and adjectives which bring into tragic dialogue the new intellectual dialogue of sophistic debate on the one hand and on the other everyday words for household objects and situations of domestic life.[1] In the *Frogs*, 'Euripides' jeers at the heroic, metaphorical style of Aeschylus and claims that the poet should 'express himself in human terms' (*anthropeios* 1058); this is exactly what Euripides did.

It is characteristic of this paradoxical figure that he is also a great lyric poet. Plutarch tells us that some of the survivors of the Athenian disaster at Syracuse, wandering about the countryside after the battle, were given food and drink in exchange for singing some of his lyrics (*Life of Nicias* 29). And his *Life of Lysander* contains the story (immortalized by Milton) that in 404, when the fate of defeated Athens hung in the balance, the Peloponnesian generals were diverted from their projects of enslavement and destruction by the performance, at a banquet, of the Parodos of the *Electra* (167ff.): 'They felt' says Plutarch 'that it would be a barbarous act to annihilate a city which produced such men.' These stories may not be true but they are eloquent testimony to the strength of Euripides' reputation as a lyric poet.

In this area, too, he was an innovator. We can no longer assess the new-fangled musical style which he adopted from the dithyrambic poet Timotheus

---

[1] A few examples: *hypotithemi* (suggest), *anakalypto* (reveal), *epigameo* (marry a second wife), *metagrapho* (rewrite), *isotes* (equality), *anomia* (lawlessness), *philotimia* (ambition), *paradoche* (tradition), *sphagida* (meat-cleaver), *ochetos* (irrigation-ditch), *sanida* (plank), *diabrochos* (soaking wet), *mysaros* (disgusting), *kerkida* (shuttle).

(cf. p. 243); all we can say is that in a few passages of late Euripidean lyric, repetitions and syntactical vagueness suggest that the music has become more important than the words (the same impression emerges from the merciless parody in the *Frogs* 1309ff.). But two other innovations are perfectly clear: the transference of much of the musical performance of the chorus (*stasimon*) to individual actors (*monody*) and the comparative detachment of the choral odes proper from dramatic context.

Lyrical exchange between actor and chorus (*kommos*) had been a feature of tragic style from the beginning (cf. the great *kommos* of the *Choephori*, p. 287) and appears regularly in Euripides (often in the Parodos, e.g. *Troades* 121ff., *Orestes* 140ff., *Ion* 219ff.). But just as frequent are lyric arias of a single actor and lyric dialogues between two – both rarities in Sophocles and existent only in rudimentary form in Aeschylus. The lyric dialogue is frequently used for highly emotional moments such as recognition scenes (Iphigenia–Orestes in *I.T.* 827ff., Ion–Creusa in *Ion* 1445ff., Helen–Menelaus in *Helen* 625ff. – this last the target of a devastating parody in Aristophanes' *Thesmophoriazusae* 911ff.). The monodies display a rich variety of passions and dramatic reactions: Cassandra's mock marriage-hymn with its undertone of baleful prophecy (*Troades* 308ff.); the blinded Polymestor's curses and revengeful threats (*Hecuba* 1056ff.); Ion's 'work-song' as he performs his duties as a Delphian acolyte (*Ion* 112ff.) and, in the same play, Creusa's confession and her accusation of Apollo (859ff.); most innovative of all, the Phrygian slave's elaborate, ornate account of the attempt on Helen's life in *Orestes* (1369ff.).

The choral stasima are less firmly bound to their dramatic context than those of Sophocles and Aeschylus (though there is always an exception to any statement about Euripides – in this case it is the *Bacchae*). Sometimes, in fact, especially in the 'romantic' plays, the connexion seems tenuous and becomes a matter of scholarly debate; but the view that late Euripidean odes are musical interludes entirely unrelated to context goes too far. The connexion is usually one of mood rather than thought; in the *Troades* the choral odes are not linked directly with preceding or succeeding stage action but they are variations on a fundamental theme – the tragedy of Troy's fall. Similarly, the stasimon in *Electra* which celebrates the glories of Achilles' shield (432ff.) throws into sharp relief the unheroic nature of Orestes' return to Argos. Often the choral poems recreate a religious atmosphere and background which, missing in the action, is needed to give the final divine appearance authority (this is perhaps the function of the ode to the Great Mother in *Helen* 1301ff. and the celebration of the birth of Apollo in *I.T.* 1234ff.). The content of many of the choral poems is, like so much else in Euripides, a hint of the future. They are insistently pictorial: the evocation of the temple at Delphi (*Ion* 184ff.) as of the landscape traversed by the mourning Demeter (*Helen* 1801ff.), the account of the golden-fleeced lamb of Atreus in *Electra* (699ff.). All these passages, with their fullness of sensuous detail and colour, point the way to the genre pictures so dear to the hearts of the Alexandrian poets, especially Theocritus.

But it is as a tragedian that Euripides made his real mark on Greece and the world. In spite of his faults in other respects, Aristotle says, he is 'the most tragic of the poets'; the context suggests that this judgement refers specifically to a preference for unhappy endings, but it is valid in a wider sense. For in his representation of human suffering Euripides pushes to the limits of what an audience can stand; some of his scenes are almost unbearable. The macabre details of the death of Pentheus in *Bacchae*, of the princess in *Medea*, of Aegisthus in *Electra*, are typical of the Euripidean assault on the audience's feelings. And Hecuba's funeral lament over the shattered corpse of Astyanax is the work of a poet determined to spare us nothing. 'Poor child, how dreadfully your head was sheared by the walls your fathers built . . . the locks your mother tended and kissed; from them now comes the bright gleam of smashed bone and blood . . .' (*Troades* 1173ff.). In Euripidean drama man's situation is more helpless than in the tragic vision of the other poets; his plays give no hint of a divine purpose in human suffering and his characters are not so much heroes who in their defiance of time and change rival the gods, as victims of passion and circumstance, of a world they cannot hope to understand. The only useful virtue in such a world is silent endurance, and this is what Talthybius recommends to Andromache as he takes her child away. 'Let it happen this way . . . take your pain and sorrow with nobility (*eugenos*) . . . be silent, adjust yourself to your fate . . .' (*Troades* 726–7, 737).

This despairing tragic vision was prophetic; the world became Euripidean as the chaos of fourth-century Greece paved the way for Macedonian conquest and the great Hellenistic kingdoms. In that new world, where the disappearance of the free city-state reduced the stature of the individual, where the huge Hellenistic kingdoms waged their dynastic wars, locked, like Euripidean gods, in seemingly endless conflict, in that age of uncertainty, doubt and anxiety, Euripides won at last the applause and veneration which had eluded him during his life. And thanks to his adaptation by the Roman dramatist Seneca, who carried over into Latin in exaggerated form his psychological insight, his rhetorical manner, his exploitation of the shocking and the macabre and above all, his brooding sense of man as victim, it was Euripides, not Aeschylus or Sophocles, whose tragic muse presided over the rebirth of tragedy in Renaissance Europe.

6. MINOR TRAGEDIANS

For us, Greek tragedy begins with the *Persae* of Aeschylus (472 B.C.) and ends with the posthumous performances of Sophocles' *Oedipus at Colonus* and

Euripides' *Bacchae*, both just before the turn of the century; we have inherited from late antiquity and Byzantium a selection from the work of three tragic poets which represents, all too inadequately, the splendid flowering of this native Athenian art in the great period of imperial democracy. But of course there were other tragic poets, who competed with the canonical three in their lifetime. Most of them are known to us mainly or solely as targets of Aristophanic abuse; Morychus, whose passion was for the good life (βίον γενναῖον, *Wasps* 506) and especially eels (*Ach.* 887); Theognis, whose frigid verses are compared with the snows and frozen rivers of Thrace (*Ach.* 138ff.); and Morsimus, whose set pieces earned those unwise enough to have them copied out exemplary punishment in the next world – to lie in excrement together with the perjurers and father-beaters (*Frogs* 151ff.). But three fifth-century tragic poets, Ion, Critias and Agathon, achieved a certain eminence in their day and, though only fragments of their work survive, they stand out as distinct literary personalities.

Ion of Chios first competed at the Dionysia in the 82nd Olympiad (451–448 B.C.); he won third prize the year Euripides came first with the *Hippolytus* (428). On one occasion, when he was awarded first prize, he is said to have supplied the entire Athenian population with wine from his native island. He wrote prose memoirs, the *Epidemiae* (*Visits*); one fragment (*FGrH* 392 F 6) tells a delightful story of Sophocles at a banquet he attended on Chios while on his way, as one of the ten generals, to the Athenian fleet blockading Lesbos (441). The fragments of Ion's tragedies (which include an *Agamemnon*) are unfortunately all short; no extended passage gives us an idea of his style. But we do have an estimate of his poetic achievement by a much later critic – the author of the treatise *On the sublime* ('Longinus').

> Take lyric poetry: would you rather be Bacchylides or Pindar? Take tragedy: would you rather be Ion of Chios or Sophocles? Ion and Bacchylides are impeccable, uniformly beautiful writers in the polished manner, but it is Pindar and Sophocles who sometimes set the world on fire with their vehemence, for all that their flame often goes out without reason and they collapse dismally. Indeed, no one in his senses would reckon all Ion's works put together as the equivalent of the one play, *Oedipus*.[1]

An uncle of Plato, Critias, who, as the leading figure among the Thirty Tyrants, clamped a reign of terror on Athens after the surrender to Sparta in 404 and died fighting the resurgent democracy in 403, is credited in our sources with three plays which were also thought by some to be Euripidean. One other play, *Sisyphus*, is specifically cited as his; an important speech from it survives. His skill as a poet is clear from the impressive fragments of his elegiac poetry (*IEG* II 52–6) and since Plato, once in an early dialogue (*Charmides*

---

[1] 'Longinus' 33.5 tr. D. A. Russell in Russell and Winterbottom (1972) 493.

162d) and once in a late (*Critias* 108b), seems to hint at a career as a tragic poet, he may well be the author of the disputed plays: *Tennes, Rhadamanthys* and *Pirithous*. Some thirty fragments of the *Pirithous* remain. It dealt with Heracles' rescue of Pirithous and Theseus from Hades; Pirithous was punished with imprisonment in a stone chair for his attempt to kidnap Persephone, and Theseus loyally stayed with him. We have what seem to be the first sixteen lines of the play, a vigorous dramatic opening in which Aeacus, guardian of the gate of Hades, challenges Heracles, who proudly identifies himself and reveals that he has been sent on another impossible mission, the capture of Cerberus. From the *Sisyphus* comes the famous speech which caused Critias to be ranked by the later doxographical tradition among the atheists. Sisyphus himself, the trickster who cheated even death, describes the origin of religion. Man's life was at first anarchic (ἄτακτος) until laws and punishments were prescribed. But when wrongdoers began to break the law not violently but stealthily, then some wise man 'invented for mortals the fear of the gods ... introduced divinity ... a spirit everlasting ... that would hear every word spoken and see every deed done ... the most pleasant of doctrines ... concealing the truth with a false story ...' (fr. 19 Snell).

Agathon, whose victory-celebration in 416 B.C. was used, many years later, as the setting for Plato's *Symposium*, seems to have been a much more innovative poet than would appear from the surviving fragments of his works, which are, for the most part, rhetorical *jeux d'esprit* or cleverly turned moral clichés. According to Aristotle (*Poet.* 1451b19) he was the first poet to abandon mythical (and historical) subjects for wholly invented plots and characters and he was also (ibid. 1456a) the first to introduce choral lyrics which had nothing to do with the plot and could in fact fit into any tragedy – *embolima*, Aristotle calls them – 'interpolations'. Like Euripides, he left Athens for Macedonia in the last years of the long war, as the city, torn by internal faction and facing the prospect of defeat, resorted to ever more desperate measures. And in Aristophanes' *Frogs*, produced in 406, the god Dionysus delivers, with a pun on the poet's name, the city's regretful farewell: 'He has gone off and left me – an excellent (*agathos*) poet, and one much missed by his friends' (*Frogs* 84).

These lines come from a scene which, in spite of the comic situation – the effeminate Dionysus, dressed in the garb of Heracles, confronting his all-too-masculine model – sounds a serious note; it is a sort of comic requiem for fifth-century tragedy. Dionysus is going to Hades to bring Euripides back to life; he needs, he says, a 'clever poet'. Heracles asks him what is wrong with the living – with Iophon, Sophocles' son, for example? Dionysus admits some merit there, but suspects Iophon is still using his father's work – a reason for waiting a while and also for not bringing Sophocles, rather than Euripides, back to life. Agathon has gone, Xenocles (who won first prize in

415 against Euripides' *Troades*) is dismissed with a curse, Pythangelus is ignored and the host of 'young effeminates' who turn out talkative Euripidean-style tragedies by the ten thousand, are rejected in a characteristically salty Aristophanic metaphor: 'barbarous chatterbags, who, once they are awarded a chorus, just take a leak on tragedy and disappear – search as you may, you won't find a seminal (γόνιμον) poet any more . . .' (*Frogs* 93ff.).

This lugubrious estimate by the god of the tragic festival seems to have been prophetic. For the whole of the fourth century, new tragic poets competed at the Dionysia and Lenaea but, though they were extraordinarily productive (Astydamas, we are told, wrote 240 plays, the younger Carcinus 160), they did not make enough of an impression on later ages to ensure the survival of their work. Many of them are cited and some of them praised by Aristotle and in their own time they were generally admired; in fact, Astydamas (whose first victory was in 372) was honoured with a bronze statue in the theatre ten years before the Athenian statesman Lycurgus paid similar honours to Aeschylus, Sophocles and Euripides. Invited to compose the inscription for the statue, Astydamas produced something so boastful that his name became a proverb: 'you praise yourself, as Astydamas once did'. The meagre fragments do little to explain his great popularity. Plutarch singles out his *Hector* for mention but the one certain quotation from this play is far from reassuring. It clearly comes from a dramatic version of one of Homer's greatest scenes, the meeting of Hector and Andromache; Hector tells a servant 'Take my helmet so that the boy won't be frightened' (fr. 2 Snell) and this choice of subject, though it speaks volumes for Astydamas' self-confidence, raises doubts about his judgement.

Such a direct challenge to Homer on his own ground is something the great tragic poets of the fifth century seem to have been wary of; though they drew heavily on the epic poems of the cycle, tragic adaptations of material from the *Iliad* and *Odyssey* are rare.[1] But one play which has come down to us in the Euripidean corpus, the *Rhesus*, presents a dramatic version of the events of Book 10 of the *Iliad*: the capture of the Trojan spy Dolon by Odysseus and Diomedes and their successful raid on the Trojan camp to kill Rhesus, the newly-arrived Thracian ally of Troy. The ascription of this play to Euripides was questioned in antiquity and the debate continues into modern times. If it is Euripidean, the infrequency of resolution in the trimeter demands an early date (before the *Alcestis*). On the other hand many features of the style and stage action suggest that if it is indeed by Euripides it belongs to much later in his career. But it is more likely to be a product of the fourth century. The large number of speaking roles (eleven, cf. *Phoenissae*) in what is the shortest tragedy extant (996 lines), the rapid succession of short scenes, the complete

---

[1] The lost *Ransom of Hector* (Aeschylus) and *Nausicaa* (Sophocles) are among the exceptions.

absence of gnomic pronouncements, the complicated entrances and exits of ll. 565–681, the goddess Athena's assumption of the role of Aphrodite in order to deceive Paris, the fact that the whole of the action is supposed to take place at night – all this, and more besides, seems to bear witness to a post-classical phase of tragedy, one which has abandoned fifth-century ideals of artistic economy for a lavish, varied display of individually exciting scenes. The *Rhesus* seems to be striving for that ideal of 'variety' (ποικιλία) held up as the standard for the tragic poet in a fragment from a satyr play of Astydamas: 'the clever poet must offer the complicated bounty, as it were, of a luxurious dinner ...'.[1]

Aristotle's pupil and friend Theodectas was an orator as well as a tragic poet, the author of fifty plays: it is perhaps significant that three of the passages where Aristotle quotes him are in the *Rhetoric* and one in the *Politics*. About 65 lines have survived; since, unfortunately, most of them come from Stobaeus' collection of moral maxims, the overall impression is one of glib sentiment and skilful versification. Athenaeus, however, preserves a reworking of a Euripidean *tour de force*, which had already been imitated by Agathon – the description by an illiterate peasant of the letters spelling the name of Theseus (fr. 6 Snell); and Strabo quotes a passage in which Theodectas attributes the black skin and woolly hair of the Ethiopians to the action of the sun (fr. 17 Snell).

Carcinus, too, is cited in the *Poetics* (1455a26), but for writing at least one of his plays without visualizing the action; he seems to have written a scene which would have passed scrutiny if heard or read, but, seen on stage, contained a glaring contradiction. Aristotle also refers to his use of recognition tokens in his *Thyestes* (1454b23) and from the *Rhetoric* (1400b9) we learn that his Medea was tried for the murder of her children and put up a sophistic defence. Not much more than a score of his verses remain, but a recent papyrus discovery bears witness to his almost classical stature in the eyes of his contemporaries. In the *Aspis* of Menander, the slave Daos acts the part of a man overcome by despair at news of his master's mortal sickness; he rattles off a series of tragic clichés, in which a citation from Aeschylus is followed by 'Carcinus says: "For in one day a god makes the happy man unhappy"' (417ff.).

Daos quotes a line from another contemporary tragic poet, who is mentioned by Aristotle – Chaeremon (411). Aristotle cites him as one of the ἀναγνωστικοί, which has been taken to mean that his plays were written for reading or recitation rather than performance. The context, however (*Rhet.* 1413b8ff.), suggests that Aristotle means merely that Chaeremon, unlike some of his more rhetorical competitors, is as effective when read (ἐν ταῖς χερσίν)

---

[1] Fr. 4 Snell. The Eupolidean metre however seems to indicate a comic provenance.

as on the stage.[1] His style is characterized as ἀκριβής 'accurate, precise', and the fragments (some 75 lines) exhibit a richness of descriptive detail and a special emphasis on colour which seem almost Alexandrian. A celebrated description (fr. 14 from the *Oeneus*) of girls resting after Dionysiac dance (inspired by Euripides' *Bacchae* 678ff.) gives some idea of his pictorial, sensual quality:

> One lay down, her shoulder-strap undone, revealing a white breast to the moon-light. Another had exposed her left flank in the dancing – naked to the gazes of the air she made a living painting... Another bared the beauty of her forearm as she embraced a companion's tender neck. Still another, her robes ripped open, showed her thigh beneath the folds...

A note of comic relief is sounded by the tragic offerings of Dionysius, tyrant of Syracuse (not mentioned by Aristotle), who, we are told, won a victory at Athens in 367. Judging by the universal contempt expressed for his poetry by later writers, this award must have been a conciliatory political gesture on the part of the Athenians. Even though he purchased what purported to be the writing tablets of Aeschylus, he could get no better inspiration from them than whatever it was that inspired the pathetic line: 'Alas, alas, I've lost a useful wife' (οἴμοι γυναῖκα χρησίμην ἀπώλεσα, fr. 10 Snell). And one wonders what the audience thought when one of his characters announced: 'For tyranny is the mother of injustice' (fr. 4 Snell).

Also not mentioned by Aristotle (his debut may in fact have occurred after the philosopher's death) is a tragic poet called Moschion, about whom we would like to know more. He revived an old fashion – historical drama (see pp. 262f.): we have a three-line fragment of his *Themistocles* and one of his plays, the *Pheraioi*, dealt with the death of Jason, the cruel tyrant of Pherae in Thessaly. The most interesting fragment (6) is a speech, 33 lines long, which is the latest variation on a theme often exploited by Attic playwrights – the history of human progress; the speech of Prometheus (*P.V.* 436ff.), the famous first stasimon of the *Antigone*, Theseus' speech in the *Supplices* of Euripides (201ff.), even Critias' speech about the invention of religion, belong to this tradition. Moschion's *Kulturgeschichte* follows the usual patterns at first: men lived like beasts, in caves, without benefit of grain, wine or metals; but a new, sensational detail is added to his description of the primitive state – cannibalism. 'The weak was the food of the strong.' Finally, time brought the age of discoveries which transformed human life, whether this was due to the thought of Prometheus, to necessity or to 'long experience, with nature as instructor'. Among the marks of civilization is the custom of burying the dead; this is presumably the point of the speech in the dramatic situation exploited by this play (for which we have no title). The trimeters are regular, extremely so, for

---

[1] *IG*² v 2118 records a third-century performance of Chaeremon's *Achilles Thersitoktonos* by an athlete-actor.

the Euripidean innovations have been abandoned; in the 33 lines there are no resolutions.

Though tragedy lived on in Athens and elsewhere through the third century B.C. and even beyond (our latest inscription recording a victory with a 'new tragedy' belongs to the twenties of the first century B.C.),[1] we know nothing of it but names. From the whole of this period, from Athens and the theatres built all over the Greek world in the fourth and succeeding centuries, from the widespread activities of the guilds of 'the artists of Dionysus' in the Hellenistic world, even from Alexandria where the so-called Pleiad produced tragedies on a lavish scale (Lycophron is credited with 46 or 64, Philieus with 42) we have less than fifty lines that were thought worth preserving. 'Nothing in the history of the transmission of Greek drama', to quote Sir Denys Page, 'is much more remarkable than the earliness, totality and permanence of the eclipse of Hellenistic Tragedy.'[2]

[1] *Fouilles de Delphes* III 2, 67. 'Thrasycles the Athenian . . . competed in his own country with a new tragedy and was victorious . . .' (177 Snell).

[2] Page (1951c) 37.

11

THE SATYR PLAY

In classical dramatic traditions there seems to be a recurrent tendency to present serious drama and broad farce in immediate juxtaposition. Much as, for instance, Roman tragedy was followed by *exodia* (usually consisting of Atellan farce), Japanese No plays by *Kyōgen,* and Elizabethan tragedy by jigs, so for most at least of the fifth century B.C. the three tragedies of a trilogy were followed by a satyr play, composed by the same author, the only known exception being Euripides' *Alcestis* of 438 B.C., presented instead of a satyr play and therefore termed a 'prosatyric' play. Most satyr plays were lost in antiquity; only Euripides' *Cyclops* survives in the manuscript tradition. Modern papyrus discoveries, however, have greatly increased our knowledge of the genre.

The principal features of the satyr play were:

(1) Invariable use of a chorus of satyrs; these are small rustic creatures, half-goat, half-human, elemental and often comically grotesque. They are regularly accompanied by their father Silenus, who is a dramatic character in his own right but also functions as a choral spokesman.

(2) Use of mythological plots, with mythological travesty a principal source of humour.

(3) Absence of satire of contemporary people and events, overt or covert.

(4) Use of the same language, metres, and dramaturgic resources as tragedy, modified by special generic requirements: occasional colloquial and bawdy language, boisterous dances, etc. There is somewhat greater metrical freedom than in tragedy: Porson's Law is sometimes disregarded and cyclic anapaests outside the first place in the iambic line are admitted.

(5) Use of a relatively few stereotypes of situation, theme and characterization.

(6) A typically spirited tone, with occasional touches of slapstick and scurrility.

(7) Comparative shortness in length, as in Euripides' *Cyclops* (slightly more than 700 lines).

(8) The evidence seems to indicate that satyr plays occasionally parodied elements in the preceding tragedies.

Demetrius, *De elocutione* 169, describes the satyr play as 'tragedy at play', a fine aphorism for the specific nature of satyric humour, which largely derives from humorous re-employment of the language and dramaturgy of tragedy, from travesty of the same mythological world peopled by the same gods and heroes, and from the absurdity created by the intrusion of Silenus and the satyrs into this world. To a large extent, therefore, the humour of satyr plays consists of poking fun at tragedy, in order of course to provide comic relief.

This comically subversive assault on tragedy takes many forms. The satyr play features, above all, a comedy of incongruity. The satyrs are elemental creatures, at once fey and subhuman, perpetually interested in immediate gratification of their appetites, lazy, arrogant when sure of themselves, craven when they are not. In a satyric *Oeneus*, or perhaps *Schoeneus*, possibly by Sophocles, they present themselves for an athletic competition (the prize is the hand of the king's daughter) with the following self-description:

> We are children of the nymphs, devotees of Bacchus, and neighbours of the gods. Every worthwhile art is embodied in us: fighting with spears, wrestling, horsemanship, running, boxing, biting, crotch-grabbing; in us you will find musical song, knowledgeable prophecy with no fakery, discriminating knowledge of medicine, measuring of the heavens, dancing, lore of the Underworld. Hey, is this fund of learning fruitless? All of this is at your disposal – just give us your daughter.

Almost invariably these satyrs are introduced into a mythological situation in which they have no legitimate place, creating an incongruity that is initially absurd and funny, and that can be further exploited. An incident which in the *Odyssey* is characterized by a certain grimness and horror and by the suffering of sympathetic characters, and which serves as a parable of barbarism and civilization, is dramatized by Euripides in *Cyclops*. These values are preserved in the play, but the presence of Silenus and the satyrs provides a continuous comic counterpoint. Thus, for instance, when Odysseus is seeking to make Polyphemus drunk, Silenus keeps trying to steal the wine and the satyrs lend their comically feckless assistance to Odysseus when he is attempting to blind the ogre. The presence of the satyr chorus performs another function in this and similar plays. They give an aura of unreality to an otherwise distressing situation, thereby signalling to the audience that Odysseus' predicament need not be taken over-seriously. Thus when he first lands on the Cyclopes' island he sees the satyrs and rightly exclaims that he has stumbled upon a sort of Dionysiac Never-Never Land: 'we seem to have invaded the polis of Dionysus!' (99).

The satyr play's comic assault on tragedy takes other forms. One technique is to create a momentary mood reminiscent of tragedy, and then deliberately destroy it. In *Cyclops* Odysseus makes a dignified and altogether serious appeal to Polyphemus for mercy, and then Silenus chimes in with one of his typically idiotic remarks (313–15). Similarly, in Aeschylus' *Dictyulci* Silenus is seeking to bully Danae into a marriage (perhaps intended to parody a serious situation in the tragedy *Polydectes*), and she delivers herself of a miniature replica of a tragic heroine's lament (773–85). But then she ends with a distinctly off-key 'that's all I have to say'.

The heroes of tragedy are often treated comically. A hero or villain who appears as larger than life in tragedy reappears in satyr plays either as a serious figure surrounded by incongruous absurdity, whereby his own seriousness appears humorously inappropriate, or as himself a comical figure. The former technique is employed in *Cyclops*. Odysseus himself is treated with complete respect, but humour is generated by the fact that, despite his initial exclamation that he has stumbled upon the kingdom of Bacchus, he reacts in deadly earnest to a situation which we perceive to be less than wholly serious: the Cyclops is essentially no more than a mock-blustering bogeyman from a fairy tale. In other satyr plays the traditional Greek heroes might themselves be presented as ludicrous and grotesque. Thus in Sophocles' *Syndeipnon*[1] the Achaean warlords engaged in a comically degrading squabble at a banquet, and one of them, perhaps Odysseus, received the contents of a chamber-pot over his head. Heracles was a common character in satyr plays, and often was featured as a gargantuan eater, drinker, and wencher.

If the satyr play takes a humorous look at the heroes prominent in tragedy, and perhaps at tragedy's ideals of heroism in some more general sense, so too it displays a nose-thumbing attitude towards some of the characteristic attitudes of tragedy. In tragedy, for instance, cleverness and deception are presented with toleration, most notably in Euripides' rescue plays, *Iphigenia in Tauris* and *Helen*, which have other significant points of contact with the satyr play and may even themselves, like *Alcestis*, have been prosatyric (cf. p. 352). Otherwise, when a clever man appears in a tragedy, he is usually represented as unprincipled and dangerous. One thinks of the anonymous demagogue in Euripides' *Orestes*, and above all of Odysseus in such plays as Sophocles' *Philoctetes*, and Euripides' *Hecuba* and *Iphigenia in Aulide*. But in many satyr plays, such as Sophocles' *Ichneutae* and *Inachus*, and Euripides' *Autolycus*, *Cyclops*, and *Sisyphus*, the plot hinges on sly misrepresentation, and a clever man or trickster is often the hero. Many satyr plays deal with subtle plots for overcoming ogres, monsters, and other villains, and wily schemes for theft and deception, and there is every reason to think that these were presented as tolerable, or even admirable. The Greeks always liked a tale of a good piece of deception, and the satyr play seems frequently to have catered to this taste. Also, the hero of many satyr plays was some such trickster as Odysseus (who is a hero in satyr plays just as frequently as he is a villain in tragedies), Autolycus, Sisyphus, and the patron deity of trickery and theft, Hermes. Other mythological figures noted for their cleverness may have also been characterized as tricksters in satyr plays, such as

---

[1] Ancient evidence wavers between *Syndeipnon* and *Syndeipnoi*. If the play is satyric, *Syndeipnon* is the more likely title, since *Syndeipnoi* would imply a chorus not of satyrs but of Achaeans.

Oedipus in Aeschylus' *Sphinx* and Prometheus in his *Prometheus pyrkaeus*. (We know that Prometheus was presented as a trickster in some comedies: cf. Aristophanes, fr. 645 and Eupolis, fr. 456 K.) Similarly, the many moral shortcomings of Silenus and the satyrs seem to have at least been regarded with toleration rather than condemnation, a sharp contrast with the morality of tragedy.

This tendency to use the satyr play as a mock-tragedy, as a means of disarming the tension and anxiety tragedy creates, was carried to its logical conclusion in instances in which a satyr play was contrived to parody elements in the tragedies of the preceding trilogy. This is most evident in the satyr plays of Aeschylus, in which the principal character of the trilogy reappears in a comic situation in the accompanying satyr play. Thus Lycurgus appeared in both the *Lycurgeia* trilogy and the following *Lycurgus satyricus*, and Oedipus in the *Oedipodeia* and *Sphinx satyricus*. In a variant of this parodizing technique, the satyr play presents a humorous counterpart not of a tragic character but of a dramatic situation which in the tragedy or trilogy is treated seriously, as in *Amymone*, the satyr play produced with the Danaid trilogy which included the extant *Supplices*. Amymone, pursued by the satyrs wanting to reduce her to sexual bondage, appeals for aid and finds a protector in Poseidon (cf. Hyginus, *Fab.* 169, 169A Rose). This presents a parallel to the situation of the Danaids in *Supplices*. Similarly, *Dictyulci* may have been presented with a *Perseus* trilogy containing the tragedy *Polydectes*, and it has been suggested that Silenus' attempt to marry Danae parodies that of Polydectes in the tragedy.

It is possible that the writing of satyr plays parodying accompanying tragedies persisted after the time of Aeschylus. Sophocles' *Ajax* and *Ichneutae* are commonly assigned to the middle or late 440s, and several resemblances between these plays suggest they were written together and that *Ichneutae* parodies elements in *Ajax*. The description in *Ichneutae* of Apollo searching for his missing cattle and their thief distinctly recalls that of Odysseus searching for the killer of the Achaean herd; the divided chorus of searching satyrs (*Ichn.* 85ff.) seems to parody the divided chorus of searching sailors (*Aj.* 866ff.), and both plays conclude with a scene of reconciliation.

There are stronger grounds for thinking that Euripides wrote his *Cyclops* as a parody of *Hecuba*.[1] The blinding of Polyphemus parodies that of Polymestor even in detail of diction (cf. *Hec.* 1035ff., *Cyc.* 663ff.). Both plays are concerned with the problem of civilized behaviour, expressed in terms of *nomos*. Both contain a plea for mercy based on idealism turned aside with a cold lecture about expediency. If the two plays were performed together there is an ironic contrast between Odysseus' rejection of Hecuba's plea in the tragedy and his

[1] The dating of *Cyclops* is disputed, cf. Sutton (1974a). The arguments for a date substantially later than 424 (the probable date of *Hecuba*) are not compelling.

own plea to Cyclops in the satyr play. Polymestor appears to be an invention of Euripides, and his characterization seems modelled on that of the Cyclops. These correspondences suggest that *Cyclops* is a comic foil for *Hecuba*, and although no external evidence exists, it is an attractive idea that the correspondences are intentional, that is, that both plays were produced in the same year.

A notable feature of the satyr play is marked dependence on a limited repertoire of stereotyped themes, situations, narrative elements, and characterizations; *Cyclops* incorporates a number of these generic stereotypes. One of these, the frequent importance of trickery and trickster-figures, has already been noted. A second, perhaps the commonest of all, is the overthrow of ogres, monsters, and giants. As in *Cyclops*, and such other plays as Aeschylus' *Cercyon*, Sophocles' *Amycus*, Euripides' *Busiris*, and Sositheus' *Daphnis* or *Lityerses*, the villain is an ogre who molests wayfarers until he makes the mistake of practising his art on a passing hero who destroys him.

In many such plays the villain challenges passers-by to an athletic match or similar contest. Athletics and competition also figure frequently in satyr plays with other types of subject such as Aeschylus' *Theoroi* or *Isthmiastae*, in which the satyrs run away from Dionysus and decide to become competitors in the Isthmian Games, and the (possibly Sophoclean) *Oeneus* or *Schoeneus*, about an athletic contest for the hand of the protagonist's daughter.

Another theme frequently associated with this typical situation – the ogre who molests passers-by – is that of abused hospitality. This is explicit in *Cyclops* (cf. especially 299ff.), and probably in similar plays. But this theme of hospitality and its abuse also figured in satyr plays with other types of subject. In Sophocles' *Inachus*, for instance, Hermes apparently first comes to Inachus' kingdom disguised as a foreign stranger (he is described as a *karbanos aithos*, 'swarthy barbarian', *P.Oxy.* 2369 ii 26) and is received hospitably by Inachus.[1] Then he transforms Inachus' daughter Io into a cow, and Inachus and the satyrs, unaware of his benevolent motive, are naturally enraged: their indignation was probably all the greater because they thought he had abused hospitality. There may have been a similar disruption in Sophocles' *Iambe*, a dramatization of the *Homeric Hymn to Demeter*, if the play contained the incident where the king and queen of Eleusis find Demeter baptizing their son on the fire and misconstrue her motive.

Again, many plays, such as *Cyclops*, about the defeat of wayfarer-molesters featured the theme of escape or rescue. Like Odysseus, the hero would fall into the clutches of the villain and destroy him in order to regain his freedom. In such plays the satyrs could always be introduced plausibly as slaves of the

---

[1] Some think the stranger is Zeus himself, but this is unlikely if the stranger appeared on-stage in the early scenes: the tragic poets were reluctant to represent Zeus as an on-stage character. On the other hand, if Inachus and the stranger did not meet on stage it is hard to imagine what could have filled the first 280 lines of the play.

villain, to be released as part of the play's happy ending. This was presumably the case, for instance, in Euripides' *Sciron*. The evidence of vase paintings suggests that in Aeschylus' *Circe* they shared with Odysseus' crew a transformation into bestial shape and eventual release from it. Escape and rescue appeared in many forms: in the plays of Aeschylus, for example, one may mention escape from bestiality in *Circe*, from foreign lands in *Proteus*, from sexual bondage to Silenus and the satyrs in *Amymone* and *Dictyulci* and the Suitors in *Ostologoi*,[1] and from the Underworld in *Sisyphus drapetes*.

Usually, as in *Cyclops*, the satyrs have been forcibly separated from their natural master Dionysus 'whose service is perfect freedom', and are allowed to return to him at the end of the play. Aeschylus, however, sometimes reverses the normal process: in *Isthmiastae* the satyrs (temporarily – we do not know how the play ends) seek escape from Dionysus, and in *Amymone* and *Dictyulci* they are themselves the villains who threaten the heroine.

Another frequent narrative element is magic and the miraculous. Taking, for example, the satyr plays of Sophocles, one may note the appearance of the Cretan 'robot' Talus in *Daedalus*; the possible baptism by fire in *Iambe*; a magical flute, and headgear that confers invisibility, as well, of course, as Io's transformation into a cow in *Inachus*; Hermes' magical growth in *Ichneutae*; the cure of Orion's blindness in *Cedalion*; a magic philtre conferring immortality in *Kophoi*, etc. Similarly, witches such as Circe and Medea, wizards such as Proteus, and numerous monsters and similar fabulous beings appeared as characters in satyr plays.

All these satyric stereotypes may also be seen as aspects of a more general tendency to employ elements reminiscent of *Märchen* and fairy tales. For many of the narrative elements found in satyr plays can be related to familiar folklore motifs. Thus, to name a few, Aeschylus' *Sphinx* features a riddle contest, and his *Proteus* a 'shape-shifter'; Sophocles' *Iambe* and *Kophoi* present variants of the theme of loss of immortality through folly. Euripides' *Cyclops*, like other satyr plays about the destruction of wayfarer-molesting villains, dramatizes a variant of the 'Jack the Giant-Killer' situation: the defeat of an ogre by a plucky and clever hero.

Also, in *Cyclops*, which seems representative of plays of its type, the original viewpoint of a fairy tale is preserved intact. Odysseus is a simple hero, and Polyphemus a simple villain. The quality of Odysseus' revenge is scarcely called into question, either in respect of its brutality or its fraudulent nature. Even the gruesomeness of Polyphemus' cannibalism and of his blinding is presented with the comic exaggeration of a fairy tale, intended to evoke the same pleasurable *frisson* of horror as children derive from such stories. This, like the unreality conferred by the presence of the satyrs, keeps the play from

[1] There is no real reason for doubting that *Ostologoi* was satyric, cf. Sutton (1974*b*) 128.

having a distressing effect out of keeping with its function of providing comic relief.

Two other common characteristics of satyr plays may be noticed. The first is that many satyr plays are set either in the countryside or in exotically alien locales: Asia Minor, Egypt, Libya, etc. Second, almost by definition a satyr play must have a happy ending. In the few instances where the poet seems to have selected a plot that did not end happily, he must have adapted his material so as to minimize the unhappy aspects.

If tragedy affirms the existence of some kind of general world-order, so does the satyr play. Many satyr plays end with the defeat of villains of one kind or another, so that even if the satyr play is tolerant of the chorus' shortcomings and of cleverness, it is scarcely an amoral genre. It holds a comic mirror up to tragedy, but at the deepest level it affirms its values. For all its humour, for instance, one should not forget that *Cyclops* is no less cautionary in intention than is its Homeric prototype.

Euripides' *Alcestis* was presented in 438 B.C. instead of the usual satyr play, and a number of satyric stereotypes recur in this play: hospitality, rescue from bondage, use of folklore themes,[1] drunken carousal and gluttony (for comical banqueting scenes were not uncommon in satyr plays, e.g. Sophocles' *Syndeipnon* and Euripides' *Syleus*), and the appearance of Heracles, a frequent satyric character. Also, familiar satyric elements are found in Euripides' *Iphigenia in Tauris* and *Helen*: defeat of a villain, violation of hospitality, trickery (which is condoned rather than criticized), and exotic settings, and these are combined much as in *Cyclops*. The Euripidean romance was created by the introduction of satyric themes into the tragic performance. Indeed, since these plays resemble *Alcestis* in this respect, it is tempting to consider them prosatyric. This is especially true of *Helen*, since it seems to have parodied a tragedy in the same set, *Andromeda*, and since its treatment of Menelaus' heroism has a distinctly comic flavour. The length of these plays, particularly of *Helen*, might be deemed an objection to this theory. But *Alcestis* is already substantially longer than any known satyr play, and in view of the length of Euripides' later plays generally, this is probably not a fatal objection.

It is a striking fact that the typical subject matter and scenes of satyr plays are also those of the *Odyssey*: incidents involving the defeat of villains and ogres presented with the same simple, readily-identifiable polarization into good and evil; the theme of hospitality and its abuse, functioning, as in plays like *Cyclops*, as a litmus test for the identification of sympathetic and unsympathetic characters; use of cleverness and of a clever man as hero; situations of escape or rescue from actual or impending bondage; use of folktale narrative elements, magic and the miraculous, wonderful and terrible beings, and exotic settings to

[1] Schmid–Stählin I 3, 537 n. 5.

create a highly romantic universe. The *Iliad* is essentially grimly realistic, and by contrast the *Odyssey* is romantic. Though it is not itself escapist in intent, it may be regarded, since it contains these elements, as the ultimate ancestor of all western literature of escape, romance, and fantasy. It is precisely these elements which are carried over into the satyr play.

The satyr play provides comic relief by allowing us to escape from the universe of tragedy, which is realistic in the same sense as that of the *Iliad*, into a colourful and fabulous world of boundless possibility. At the same time, since this is a palpable fantasy world, and since a happy ending is obligatory by the rules of the game, we may be excited by the predicaments of satyric characters without being moved or distressed. So besides being a romantic universe, this is an optimistic one. The satyr play thus presents a roseate vision of life counterbalancing that of tragedy.

Tragedy is also realistic in that it reproduces the moral ambiguities of life. The unending debate over the rights and wrongs of Antigone and Creon is witness to the fact that the universe of tragedy is not peopled by simple heroes and villains. In imitating the *Odyssey* by adopting a simple and readily comprehensible polarization of heroes and villains, often in starkly agonic terms, the satyr play offers relief from the necessity of confronting a complex universe. This contrast is posed dramatically in the instance of *Hecuba* and *Cyclops*. Polymestor and Polyphemus are similar ogres destroyed by their victims, who wreak their vengeance with particular savagery. In *Hecuba*, by such devices as the final prophecy and the creation of a measure of sympathy for Polymestor when he genuinely grieves over the murder of his children, Euripides adds a moral complication by casting doubt on the quality of Hecuba's revenge, which in retrospect is made to seem barbaric and otiose. But in *Cyclops* a similar incident is recounted in the simple, unquestioning terms of a fairy tale. It is almost as if we view the same incident twice, through the eyes of an adult and a child. This release from the need to respond to complex moral issues must also have been experienced as a form of relief.

We have seen that clever men and tricksters are frequently cast as sympathetic central characters in satyr plays. Indeed, these are so common that the clever man, if anybody, may be characterized as the satyric hero. Again, this recalls the contrast between the *Iliad* and the *Odyssey*, for the tragic hero is notoriously a linear descendant of Achilles, and this satyric hero is equally descended from Odysseus. Like Achilles, the tragic hero who attains greatness because of his heroic self-assertion is guided by exalted and rather forbidding standards. Odysseus in the *Odyssey*, however, is great for entirely different reasons: persistence, shrewdness, self-reliance, industry, adaptability, and similar 'middle-class virtues'. After tragedy's presentation of exceedingly uncommon, often great, individuals, the satyr play's presentation of more ordinary virtues

353

may have been experienced by the audience as another form of relief. Moreover, the great problems posed by tragedy are genuine and genuinely terrifying, while the satyric hero is regularly confronted by nurseryroom monsters like Polyphemus who are mock-terrifying straw men to be sent down to routine and predictable defeat.

By 340 B.C. (cf. *IG* II² 22.2320) the dramatic festival of the Dionysia was re-organized, and satyr plays were thenceforth performed independently of tragedy. Thus they no longer served to provide comic relief after tragedy, and it is probably no coincidence that shortly after this date evidence appears for a new kind of satyr play, which retained the satyr chorus but gravitated into the orbit of contemporary comedy, abandoning mythological plots in favour of contemporary satire, and adopting the dramatic techniques and metres of comedy.

The two best known such plays are Python's *Agen* and Lycophron's *Menedemus*. *Agen* was written and produced at the behest of Alexander, to satirize and discredit his fallen minister Harpalus. It was probably produced in 324, when Harpalus was still alive and a potent threat to the internal security of Alexander's empire; if so, this is an interesting example of the use of literature as political propaganda. *Menedemus* seems to have been a good-natured lampoon on the notorious frugality of this philosopher.

There is evidence for other such plays. Although Sositheus is best known as a reviver of the classical mythological satyr play, perhaps in response to the rise of bucolic poetry (cf. Dioscorides' epigram *Anth. Pal.* 7.707), a satyr play ridiculing the philosopher Cleanthes is probably attested by Diogenes Laertius 7.173, and the Eupolidean metre of a fragment of Astydamas Minor's *Heracles satyricus* quoted by Athenaeus suggests that it may have been a similar play.

Wilamowitz's suggestion that Timocles' *Ikarioi satyroi* was a satyr play rather than a Middle Comedy is nowadays unpopular,[1] but Athenaeus 9.407d seems to say that Timocles the comic poet and Timocles the contemporary tragedian were one and the same, and there is nothing in this play's fragments uncharacteristic of other late satyr plays. More conclusively, titles consisting of plural nouns and *Satyroi* are otherwise reserved for satyr plays; comedies with satyr choruses, such as Cratinus' *Dionysalexandros*, received different types of title. Thus, if this was a satyr play, the common suggestion that Python invented this new kind of satyric drama must be wrong, for while *Agen* ridicules Harpalus for establishing a cult for his newly deceased mistress Pythionike, *Ikarioi* speaks of her as still living. Timocles, who was, in fact, virtually unique in writing both tragedies and comedies, and was quite possibly working at the time of the re-organization of the festival (his name appears on the inscription cited above), would be admirably situated to make this innovation.

---

[1] Wilamowitz-Moellendorff (1962) IV 688f.; the most recent argument to the contrary is that of Constantinides (1969) 49–61.

12

COMEDY

I. INTRODUCTION

'It was produced in the archonship of Euthynus at the Lenaea by Callistratus. Result, first; second, Cratinus with *Kheimazomenoi* (not preserved); third, Eupolis with *Noumeniai*.' So runs the record for our earliest surviving comedy, the *Acharnians* of Aristophanes, and it refers to an occasion in the year we call 425 B.C.[1] At that time Aristophanes and Eupolis were near the beginning of their careers, young men in their twenties; Cratinus had won his first victory at the festivals some thirty years before, and Aristophanes, on the way up, could portray his distinguished rival as a figure from literary history, now a neglected old has-been with a drink problem.[2] It happens that the first date in that literary history is some thirty years earlier still, in a year reckoned to be 486 B.C., when a competition for comedies was instituted at Athens as an official event at the Dionysia, and the winner was one Chionides, a man remembered by posterity for little else.

If Chionides and Magnes are the names to mention from the first generation of writers of Athenian Old Comedy, as they are for Aristotle in the *Poetics* (1448a34), then Cratinus and Crates represent the second generation; Eupolis and Aristophanes are of the third and last. What we know about Old Comedy still depends, in overwhelmingly large measure, on the selection of eleven plays by Aristophanes which survive in medieval copies together with an inheritance of interpretative commentary, a corpus of marginal scholia which has offered a perennial invitation to scholarly interest and may have been of decisive importance in keeping the text alive through times when so much other literature was lost.[3] As to the rest: papyrus fragments of plays or commentaries recovered by modern excavation, inscriptional records of productions, remains of theatres, works of art representing masks, actors, and choruses, quotations from lost plays and numerous statements of widely varying date and value about plays

---

[1] Ar. *Ach.* hyp. 1 Coulon: nothing else is known about either of the competing plays mentioned, and it has been suggested that 'not preserved' originally applied to both.

[2] Ar. *Knights* 526–36.

[3] See above, chapter 1, pp. 34f.

and their authors – all this catalogue of material contributes to the construction of a fuller and more balanced account than can be given from Aristophanes alone, but it is still an account with a strong Aristophanic bias. We cannot help seeing the rest in terms of similarities to Aristophanes and (more cautiously) differences from him; and it is good to have that in mind from the first. Menander is another part of the story. His first plays were produced more than sixty years after Aristophanes' last, when the mode of comedy, like so much else in the Athenian world, had been transformed. Yet a reference to Menander and the New Comedy is in place here because the very substantial accessions of text from papyri published in the twentieth century must be admitted to have some effect on our views of comedy's earlier age. The new discoveries suggest new comparisons and contrasts, but they also remind us, if we care to look back to the time before their making, how great can be the differences between whole, partial and fragmentary knowledge.

For all their variety of theme and incident, Aristophanes' plays have a common basic pattern: a revolutionary idea, a way to change a situation which the hero will not tolerate, is carried against opposition and pursued through some of its consequences, which are good for some and bad for others. In *Acharnians*, for instance, a man who has had enough of wartime life in Athens makes a personal treaty with Sparta and sticks to it through all accusations of traitorous behaviour to enjoy his monopoly of the benefits of peace – an open market for imports, feasting, celebration and the chance to go back home again to his farm. Or in *Plutus*: the hero takes charge of the blind god Wealth, and, despite opposition from Poverty, has Wealth's sight restored by a miraculous cure so that poor but honest men (like himself of course) can be prosperous. It is characteristic of this kind of comedy that the issues involved are those of the public world – peace against war, right and wrong distribution of wealth – and that those issues are simplified and made concrete by being transposed into the private world of individual people and their families. Among other things, the public world includes education, modern versus traditional, as in *Clouds*; and it includes the performing arts, especially tragedy, as in *Thesmophoriazusae*, *Frogs* and elsewhere.

As the themes of the plays are varied, so are their characters. Some, like Heracles and Dionysus, are familiar figures from myth, and probably appealed to many in the audience as old stage favourites: 'Heracles cheated of his dinner' is mentioned as a stock routine of comedy in the *Wasps* (60). Others represent real people of present or past (the latter can be seen in, or summoned from, the Underworld); and it is a good question how true to life the 'real people' are or were ever supposed to be. The art of Aristophanic portraiture is well compared to that of a modern newspaper cartoonist; it exploits, and indeed helps to create, the popular image of public figures, and (again like the modern cartoonist) it will sometimes present a satirical hybrid between the real person and a second imaginary identity, as when Cleon in the *Knights* becomes a Paphlagonian slave in the household of Demos of Pnyx Hill, the sovereign people. Demos, like John Bull or Uncle Sam, is an imaginative summation of the qualities of a senior member of the electorate. Here he serves to remind us that the very common tendency of the ancient Greeks to personify concepts, whether verbally or visually, can in comedy take the form of bringing the personified entity on stage: thus Reconciliation (Diallage) is thought of by the chorus of Acharnians as a fine young girl, just the one to set up house with in the country (*Ach.* 989); while in *Lysistrata* she actually appears in a walk-on part to bring Athenians and Spartans together (1114ff.). From the viewpoint of later comedy, and hence that of much modern drama, the specially interesting group of Aristophanic characters is the large one of fictional ordinary (and not so ordinary) people in their everyday social or professional relationships, ranging from leading characters like Strepsiades in the *Clouds* down to such as the lodging-house keeper and her friend in the *Frogs* (549ff.). Strepsiades interests us here not as the comic hero who has adventures with Socrates, but rather in the role he is given at the start of the play, a man with a teenage son whose life-style he cannot support. If such people often seemed like familiar contemporaries to their audiences, there were still ways in which their special identity as stage characters and their remote origins as part of a ritual were recalled. Comic actors, like all others, wore masks; but there was also a traditional comic costume, with padded paunch and posterior and (for males) a leather phallus worn outside their tights which showed under short clothes and, according to Aristophanes, could be used to raise a laugh from the small boys.[1] This costume, which is documented from representations contemporary with Aristophanes, can be traced back in art to a time long before we have any texts, as can the tradition of choruses made up of creatures of the wild (animals, birds, insects, fish), an inheritance which Aristophanes himself associated with early comedy in the person of Magnes, and was to exploit inventively in his own plays.[2]

The variety of visual effect is something that the reader of Aristophanes learns to recapture in imagination; the appeal of the music and dancing is irreparably lost, though the pattern and language of the lyrics can still evoke a response; and in his portrait of Cratinus in the *Knights* Aristophanes recalls two songs from the old master which were popular hits and became all the rage at parties (529ff.). From lyric writing to dialogue at a casual and unaffected level of everyday speech, the fifth-century comic poet has a whole vocabulary of

---

[1] *Clouds* 539: the phallus, like the padding (*Frogs* 200), could be referred to and used for comic by-play or taken for granted and ignored; on jokes for the boys, cf. Eupolis, *Prospaltioi* 244 K.

[2] Magnes: *Knights* 520ff. (see below, p. 364 with n. 2).

different modes of expression at his command, and within them, like a modern comic entertainer, he can be both mimic and creator; he can produce laughter and suggest criticism. One main line of development in comedy, which can be seen in Aristophanes in the contrast between his latest plays, *Ecclesiazusae* and *Plutus*, and the earlier ones, is the trend away from this highly colourful and 'poetic' writing to a much more uniform and naturalistic manner, to be perfected in the end by Menander. But for earlier comedy, the alternation between song and speech, between chorus and actors, is something vital and organic; and its nature cannot be properly appreciated without at least some consideration of the forms which that alternation takes.

2. STRUCTURAL PATTERNS IN OLD COMEDY

The simplest kind of pattern in Aristophanic comedy, and the one that is basic to its structure, is an alternation in the form A B A' B', where A and A' are lyrics in responsion to each other, and B and B' are blocks of lines either for the speaking voice or to be recited to some form of accompaniment in the manner loosely called 'recitative': the technical term is *iambic syzygy* when lyrics interlace with the iambic trimeter of regular soliloquy and dialogue; it is *epirrhematic syzygy* where the longer tetrameter lines, anapaestic, trochaic and iambic, are concerned.[1] Not all of Aristophanes is written in syzygies: for instance, in prologues, before the chorus arrives, there are sequences of scenes without intervening lyrics; episodic composition, in scenes marked off by non-linking lyrics or none, is specially favoured late in the plays; and these sequences do sometimes have balancing elements, if only because some comic effects are enhanced by repetition. But the four-part syzygy pattern is basic; it can be varied in order, prolonged, and variously embellished; a great volume of critical work centres on attempts to define and explain its different manifestations in relation to the content and dramatic design of the plays, and in particular to project backwards from those features which seem most genuinely traditional towards a proto-form of comedy or comic revel. This whole line of enquiry stems largely from research into the origins and development of Attic comedy by Zieliński (1885); some important successors are Mazon (1904), Pickard-Cambridge (*DTC*: 1927, rev. 1962), Gelzer (1960), Händel (1963) and Sifakis (1971). Discussion can usefully begin from the choral parabasis, a characteristic feature of the fifth-century plays of Aristophanes which is absent from the two surviving fourth-century plays, *Ecclesiazusae* and *Plutus*.

In full form, the choral parabasis has seven parts. It consists of an epirrhematic

[1] 'Recitative' means, in layman's language, something between speech and song; but, given that there was such a mode of delivery, it still is unclear how far this was varied, e.g. for different kinds of tetrameters or different styles within one kind: see for a brief discussion *DFA* 156ff., esp. 164.

syzygy prefaced by a block of lines in a long metre, commonly anapaestic tetrameter, with their own matching introduction and conclusion. The whole pattern can thus be written A B C D E D′ E′; but there are various ways in which it can be reduced, and it always is reduced when it is used for a second parabasis within one play. In the main parabasis of *Knights* (498–610) the correspondence between form and content is particularly close. In the syzygy, the two lyrics, D D′, are miniature hymns, in which the chorus of knights invokes first Poseidon, then Athena; the two epirrhemes, E E′, are each 16 lines of trochaic tetrameters (both the metre and the length, sixteen lines or twenty, both multiples of four, are canonical); the first subject is praise of the traditional valour and virtues of the knights, the second a euphoric account of their horses' novel and recent success in a landing of cavalry on an enemy shore. In this wartime play (424 B.C.) part of the appeal is the topical one to popular sentiment, but the chorus can be a comic chorus as well as representing the cavalry and the upper-class Athenians who served in it, and the victory they specially hope for is victory in the festival (591–4). In any case the dramatic action of the play is in suspense. The break with what has gone before is marked, here as elsewhere, in the short opening section we have called A, which sees the departing hero off the stage with a wish of good luck, and invites the audience to 'pay attention to our anapaests' (B C). The dramatic identity of the knights is not quite forgotten, for (507ff.): 'if any of the comic dramatists of old had tried to make us come forward (*parabainein*) to face the theatre and speak lines, he wouldn't have got his way easily' – but now, they continue, the poet deserves support as a brave outspoken man with whom they have enemies in common. Essentially, however, the lines are an advertisement for Aristophanes and an appeal for a favourable reception (end of B into C) which is hung on the peg of a defence: this is the first play, after a dramatic début three years ago, that Aristophanes has produced in his own name.[1] The *apologia* includes, among other things, Aristophanes' celebrated description of Cratinus and other comic poets which has been mentioned above already.

The reference to 'our anapaests' and the use of the term *parabainein* which we have just noted would of themselves suggest what is abundantly confirmed by the extant plays and recognizable fragments: namely that for the third generation of writers of Old Comedy and their audiences a parabasis such as we have described was an established component of a play, with certain familiar conventions. But the balance between convention and innovation was not always evenly poised, and there are some ways in which we can see it shift. The first five plays, *Acharnians, Knights, Clouds, Wasps, Peace*, were successively

---

[1] Aristophanes was not alone in having some of his plays produced by others, and he went on doing so (e.g. *Frogs*). We do not know why this was done, but can accept that rivals and critics might carp: see *DFA* 84–6, with Plato Com. 99–100 K and *P.Oxy.* 2737 fr. 1 ii 10ff. (= *CGFP** 56, 44ff.).

produced in the years 425–421, *Clouds* and *Peace* at the Dionysia and the others at the Lenaea. Of these, *Acharnians*, *Knights* and *Wasps* have a full parabasis, but in *Peace* there is one without epirrhemes (i.e. A B C D D'); in *Clouds*, where the other plays have their anapaests, the surviving revised version offers a single block of lines in another variety of parabasis metre, the Eupolidean (i.e. B for B C). Each time, with interesting consistency, the anapaests or their equivalent present a kind of literary discourse, an *apologia* for the poet, which can be spoken in the first person as if by him as well as in the way exemplified above from *Knights*; though in *Acharnians* (628f.) Aristophanes has the chorus claim that he has not previously seen fit to advertise himself. We can note here with the complete plays the evidence of a commentary on a lost play (?*Anagyros*) first published in 1968, which gives some quotations in sequence from anapaests and from the lyrics and trochaic tetrameters of a syzygy.[1] The four complete plays from the later fifth century are *Birds* (414 Dion.), *Lysistrata* (411, (?) Len.), *Thesmophoriazusae* (411, (?) Dion.) and *Frogs* (405 Len.). Of these, only *Birds* has the full form of parabasis; in *Thesmophoriazusae* the syzygy is reduced to a single epirrheme (E for D E D' E'); in *Frogs* there is simply a syzygy; in *Lysistrata* (614–705) there is a carefully balanced structure including two pairs of ten-line epirrhemes which looks like a special variant for a play with a chorus representing twelve men plus twelve women in two opposed halves.[2] The *apologia*, which was so prominent earlier, has now gone, even where, as in *Birds* and *Thesmophoriazusae*, there are the anapaests to accommodate it. Also absent from *Lysistrata*, *Thesmophoriazusae* and *Frogs* is the second parabasis, which, though shorter and more variable in form, is a regular feature of the earlier plays, granted that *Acharnians* is a special case.[3] We noted at the outset that *Ecclesiazusae* (produced in 393 or 392) and *Plutus* (388) have no parabasis at all.

The parabasis is sometimes thought of as a kind of fossil, a survival from remote origins in a ritual, which has preserved and somehow transmitted to other parts of the play as they evolved the patterning which its own precise balance marks so clearly. What we see in Aristophanes is then the end of a long story: this component of the play, which is exclusively choral and does nothing to further the dramatic action, is in decline as the interest in organized dramatic action grows and the role of the chorus diminishes. It is easier to subscribe to the second part of this view than to the first, though one should still beware of supposing that the process of decline was necessarily as tidy as the limited set of data we have makes it look. In fact there is another well-established claimant,

---

[1] *P.Oxy.* 2737 (see p. 359 n. 1 above).

[2] We know of other plays in which the chorus was similarly divided, as between rich and poor in Eupolis, *Marikas* (421 B.C.), but not enough survives to show the shape of their parabases: see Webster in *DTC* 160; and for *Marikas* (*P.Oxy.* 2741) *CGFP* no. 95, 29n.

[3] The choral performance at *Ach.* 971–99 can perhaps be seen as a hybrid between a second parabasis and the sort of ode which would be regular at such a place: Sifakis (1971) 35.

some say a still stronger one, to be an archetypal element of comedy. This is the formal debate, for which the name *agon*, like much other technical terminology, is a legacy of the nineteenth century. In its canonical form, the agon has balancing epirrhemes in tetrameters in which the two principals present their arguments (E); each of these runs into a conclusion, like the anapaests of the parabasis, for which the traditional name is *pnigos* 'choker' (P); each again is prefixed by a matching exhortation (*katakeleusmos*) from the chorus (K); each half of the debate, so constituted, has one of a pair of lyric odes (O), and the whole sequence is rounded off by a concluding section, like that of the anapaests of the parabasis, namely the *sphragis* or 'seal' (S). Thus the basic alternation of ode and epirrheme is elaborated to the form O K E P O' K' E' P' S. If we now recall the simplified statement of the basic pattern of a play which served us for a moment above, 'a revolutionary idea . . . is carried against opposition', then we can say that an *agon* in the first half of the play tends to accommodate the main dramatic issue. But from the first Aristophanes is master of the pattern, not its slave.

In *Acharnians*, the revolutionary idea of a personal peace treaty with Sparta arouses powerful opposition, and might have been expected to offer a suitable theme for an epirrhematic agon in full form, but it does not: Dicaeopolis' main defence of his actions, when we reach it, is a speech in iambic trimeters based on the famous long speech by Telephus in Euripides' lost play *Telephus* of 438 B.C., and the whole unit (490–625), which is sometimes called a quasi-agon, is in form a simple four-part syzygy, with two matching choral parts in dochmiac metre and a further iambic scene roughly in balance with that of the speech. Then *Knights* has two epirrhematic agons, one before the main parabasis and one after; *Clouds* has two, both in the latter part of the play; in *Peace* 'there is not, strictly speaking, an agon as regards either matter or form', and so on.[1] But however the definitions are drawn, the pattern verifiably persists, and is still recognizable in the fourth-century plays when reduced to half of itself or less: *Ecclesiazusae* 571–709 shows the form O K E P; and *Plutus* 487–618, the role of the chorus still further reduced, has simply K E P for the debate between Chremylus, in favour of restoring sight to Wealth, and the figure of Poverty. In spite of all the variations, such a structure in a regular simple form could be imagined as the core of a primitive drama for chorus and actors, and as the growth point for the symmetries and balances which are seen elsewhere in the plays. The problem with this exercise in imagination, even though the patterns found in Aristophanes can be traced to some extent in fragments, is given by the two generations of plays which are lost; and Dover, writing in 1954, put the point crisply when he said 'we cannot extrapolate from Aristophanes'.[2] But if the search for patterns of proto-drama must at present remain a speculative one, the study of relationships between form and content in the surviving plays can

---

[1] *DTC* 200.   [2] In *FYAT* 139.

be more rewarding, for the patterns are under pressure not only from the demands of subject matter within particular parts of plays, but from the trend towards an organized plot composed in the units we call 'acts' and away from a participating chorus. That trend we can to some extent follow by way of Aristophanes' later work to the *Dyskolos* of Menander and other plays of New Comedy. But there are still the missing generations in between.

3. THE EARLIEST COMIC DRAMA

If ever we recovered a series of comedies dating back to 486 B.C., it would still be an interesting question how much further the history of comedy could or should be pursued. What was the essential change which made the revel-songs of *komodoi* into comedy, and when did it occur? Aristotle confronted the problem, and much modern discussion takes off from the few remarks of his on early comedy which appear in the surviving part of the *Poetics*.

According to Aristotle, stages in the evolution of tragedy were marked by innovations associated with particular people (for example, Sophocles and the use of a third actor); but for comedy the innovators were generally unknown 'since in the beginning it was not taken seriously'.[1] The official recognition of comedy at Athens came 'quite late' (this is our date of 486 B.C.) and by then, when the names of the first comic poets are recorded, it had already 'certain formal characteristics'; before then, performances were by volunteers. Comedy, like tragedy, originated in improvisation.[2] The pattern of 'improvisation' Aristotle had in mind seems to be the one common to the Hellenic and many other cultures, with leader and responding chorus or group: the leader initiates the occasion and may 'improvise' or compose orally; the response of the group is previously composed or otherwise predictable; and there may, of course, be more than one leader and more than one group. Such a pattern can be illustrated from the lament for Hector in the *Iliad* (24.719ff.) where there are singers (*aoidoi*) to lead the lament; the women and then finally the whole people responding, while in turn Andromache, Hecuba and Helen intervene with speeches expressing their personal grief. Whether rightly or not, Aristotle saw the genesis of tragedy in 'the leaders of the dithyramb'; for comedy he thought of the leaders of the phallic songs (*phallika*) 'which still survive as institutions in many Greek cities'. But the claim to have originated comic drama came from more than one quarter. The mainland Megarians, notes Aristotle, claimed that comedy arose with them in the time of their democracy (i.e. in the period following the expulsion of the tyranny in the early sixth century); the Megarians of

---

[1] This paragraph quotes from chapters 3, 4 and 5 of the *Poetics*: here 1449a37ff., with 18f. on Sophocles, and continuing from 1449b1.

[2] 1449a9ff.

Megara Hyblaea in Sicily also put in a claim, on the ground that Epicharmus, who was 'much earlier than Chionides and Magnes' came from there; and there were some dubious etymological arguments about 'drama' and 'comedy' in support.[1] Not surprisingly, when he looked back from the comedy of his own time, Aristotle found the element of invective and personal abuse a striking feature of early comedy, which he seems to have thought of as the natural successor in this respect to the development represented by Archilochus and other writers of abusive personal poetry.[2] The start of a movement away from that concept of comic writing is the one development on which he is precise: 'plot-composition came first from Sicily; of the Athenians, Crates was the first to move away from the iambic convention and write plots with subjects of general [and not particular] reference'.[3]

When he derives comedy from *phallika* such as were known in his own day, Aristotle is in some way using surviving primitives to confirm an evolutionary hypothesis. Descriptions of performances by *phallophoroi*, *ithyphalloi* and others compiled by scholars of the Hellenistic age can be taken to indicate what he had in mind.[4] These traditional ceremonies, which have their parallels in other cultures, offer a number of points of contact with fully developed comedy: for instance, the performers are sometimes masked, and there can be a prominent element of invective and abuse which, as we have just noted, was something which struck Aristotle as characteristic of early comedy. What Aristotle found wanting, and what we lack also, is any record of the stages of development that may have intervened; and this is still true even if we make the most of the links between comedy and the hypothetical proto-comedy at the expense of their differences, and discount as far as possible the point that, by the time Aristotle and his successors made their observations, there was ample opportunity for the ostensibly primitive performances to have absorbed elements from formal comedy at a developed stage.[5] In short, Aristotle's derivation of comedy is a hypothesis which is interesting and possibly correct, but he does not offer, and we cannot adequately supply, the means by which it might be verified.

We do not know how far Aristotle, if pressed, would have extended a definition of *phallika*; but the picture we can form of *komoi* that are possibly related to comedy is of increasing interest and diversity as the evidence of vase

[1] 1448a29–b2.

[2] 1449a2ff.: in other words, comedy became the natural medium for those who would earlier have been writers of iambics. See also 1451b10ff. and *Eth.Nic.* 1128a16–31.

[3] 1449b5ff.: in mentioning Sicily, Aristotle no doubt had Epicharmus and Phormis in mind, whether or not their names were originally intended to be cited in some way.

[4] The principal texts are from Sosibius (*c.* 300 B.C.: *FGrH* 595 F 7) and Semus of Delos (2nd cent. B.C.: *FGrH* 396 F 24); these are quoted by Athenaeus 14, 621d–f, 622a–d, and translated and discussed with others in *DTC* 132–47.

[5] See *DTC* 132–47 with special reference to Webster's contributions to the revised version.

paintings and other works of art is exploited by intensive study and enhanced by new discoveries. Among the earliest to be quoted and the best known are the Attic vases which offer a line of ancestry for the theriomorphic choruses of Aristophanes and others: Sifakis (1971) includes an admirable discussion of previous interpretations. Examples are an amphora in Berlin (F 1830) and an oenochoe in the British Museum (B 509), both dated 500/480 B.C., which show a piper with two chorusmen dressed as cocks: the first one has them wrapped in mantles, and perhaps marching on, while on the second they are in a running dance-step. Another amphora in Berlin (F 1697) is dated as early as the mid-sixth century, and has a piper with three young beardless men in armour on the backs of three bearded men with horse masks and horse tails: Athenian knights, a century and a quarter before Aristophanes used them as a comic chorus.[1] Unfortunately (and this is generally true of the monuments which concern us here) there is nothing to show what occasion the representations recall, or with what cult it was connected. The vase with the knights was painted long before our date (486 B.C.) for the official recognition of comedy at the Dionysia, but could perhaps represent a performance there by the 'volunteers' mentioned by Aristotle. The two pictures of bird-dancers may be earlier than or just later than 486, but whether they are regular comic chorusmen, 'volunteers', or something else, they were painted in the lifetime of the first generation of Attic comic poets, and may therefore give a fair idea of the appearance of the chorus in the *Ornithes* of Magnes, whose flappings are mentioned by Aristophanes, the future author of plays called *Birds* and *Storks*.[2] Music, movement and colour were obvious elements to exploit in choruses of this kind, and the *Birds* is an outstanding example of what could be done. Such choruses could, like any others, have generated a patterned structure of composition by alternation with a leader; being very markedly special beings (even aristocratic young men on horseback) they might be expected to have something special to say to introduce themselves and dilate on their relationship – past, present or future – to the spectators; but something more is needed before a pattern of dramatic action appears.

Another important group of monuments consists of vases with padded or exaggeratedly fat (and sometimes phallic) dancers whose costume seems to relate them on the one hand to the human characters of classical Attic comedy in their conventional stage dress and on the other hand to satyrs and other semi-feral companions of Dionysus. Prominent among these are the Corinthian *komos-*

[1] These three vases are nos. 27, 26 and 23 in the List of Monuments in *DTC* 300ff.; they are illustrated in that book and often elsewhere, as in Sifakis (1971) plates i, vi, vii–viii; Bieber (1961) figs. 124, 123, 126; cf. Trendall and Webster (1971) under 1, 12 and 1, 9.

[2] Ar. *Knights* 520ff.: the other choruses referred to are *Barbitistai* 'Lyre-players', *Lydians*, *Psenes* 'Gall-flies' and *Batrachoi* 'Frogs'; the 'lyre-players' could be musical satyrs, the *Ornithes* (*pace* Aristophanes) could as well mean 'Cocks' as 'Birds', and in this instance chronology does not rule out the idea that the two vases actually commemorate the play. Cf. Muscarella (1974) no. 49, a terracotta statuette possibly recalling Aristophanes' *Birds*.

vases which are the subject of a special study by Seeberg (1971); they are the source of some scenes that have often been discussed, since a very influential article by Körte (1893), for the sake of the evidence they may give for early Dorian dramatic dances and hence for the claims by some Dorians to have originated comedy itself. Of special interest here are the elements of story or plot that have been recognized. An amphoriskos in Athens (NM 664), dated 600/575 B.C., shares with other vases a representation of the Return of Hephaestus: Hephaestus had imprisoned Hera by his magic, and now Dionysus and companions bring him home, fuddled with wine on a mule, to release her; two 'padded dancer' figures are present.[1] A fine (but notoriously puzzling) column-krater of the same period in the Louvre (E 632) has two scenes which are possibly to be read in sequence: in one, alongside a dancing padded figure with a companion who pipes for him, two figures named Eunos ('Kindly') and Ophelandros ('Helpmate') are carrying off a krater, watched by a third figure with two sticks, whose name is Omrikos ('Rainer' or 'Umbrian' or what?); while in the other scene two male figures are imprisoned next to a stack of kraters, and a female seems to be bringing them food.[2] The story of the Return of Hephaestus, a popular myth, can be seen as an ancestor, perhaps even as a prototype, of adventures like Dionysus' quest in Hades in Aristophanes' *Frogs*; it is known from Epicharmus, one of the first generation of comedy writers.[3] Eunos and Ophelandros are persuasively interpreted as satyr-like followers of Dionysus in an escapade of stealing wine and then suffering for it (Ombrikos is recorded as a title of Dionysus at Halicarnassus); or they have been taken as thieving slaves; or as part of the preparations for a party; and the story of crime and punishment (if that is what it is) is compared with that of the 'men stealing produce' which (we are told) was a theme of a traditional form of folk-drama in Sparta acted by players called *deikeliktai*.[4] But the party that leads from simple celebration to boisterousness, violence and then redress is a recurrent topic of comedy from Epicharmus onwards;[5] and the transforming effects of wine may be the link between the two scenes of an Attic black-figured cup of 530/510 B.C. in Thebes (BE 64.342), which was first published in 1971. This skyphos has on both sides a frieze of old men with large heads, well taken as representing masks, and long white hair and beard; both times they are accompanied by a piper, but

---

[1] Seeberg (1971) no. 227a (with 227b–c and 228); *DTC* no. 38 and fig. 5 (with nos. 39 and 47; and Attic versions, nos. 8 and 11); Bieber (1961) fig. 130; Trendall and Webster (1971) 1, 4.

[2] Seeberg (1971) no. 226; *DTC* no. 41; Bieber (1961) fig. 132; Trendall and Webster (1971) 1, 6.

[3] *Komastai or Hephaestos*: an entry in Photius confirms the subject that the title suggests, but the fragments (84–6 Kai, 47–9 Ol) add little: see further Webster (1959) 62–4 and in *DTC* 171–3, 265; *CGFP* under no. 85.

[4] The source is Sosibius, as cited above, p. 363 n. 4.

[5] Epicharmus 148 Kai, 175 Ol; Ar. *Wasps* 1253–5; and later Eubulus, *Semele or Dionysus* 94 K; Alexis, *Odysseus hyphainon* 156 K.

the first set stride or dance along in a decorous way, wearing large *himatia* and leaning on big sticks with white or woollen caps to them; the second set are standing on their heads waving their legs to the music, like Hippoclides half a century before, who did this in front of his prospective father-in-law, and 'danced away his marriage';[1] one recalls also Philocleon in Aristophanes' *Wasps*, and his progress from respectable (if obsessive) juryman to uninhibited reveller (1253–5; 1299ff.).

If the useful result of investigating the structure of fifth-century comedy proves to be the recognition of basic and potentially productive patterns rather than the extraction of a single archetypal proto-form, the study of pre-literary *komoi* may likewise be better directed towards those elements of myth and motif which we can see were productive rather than to a search for origins and development in an Aristotelian sense. Yet one of the most interesting circumstances (it may be) is revealed by Aristotle's remark that comedy 'was not taken seriously' from the first, and gained official recognition at Athens relatively late. There may have been many centuries of pre-history in which cult-ceremonies made no recognizable move in the direction of drama. Judged by the test of results, the most significant moves in that direction were made in sixth-century Attica, though one sees that cross-influences between different cities' institutions could easily occur, and rival claims easily arise over matters that often can have admitted no very precise definition. In time, tragedy and satyr play gained the measure of identity that organized festival competition presupposes; comedy could take, in response to them, a no-holds-barred attitude to conventions, and perhaps carried already, in the variety of forms its early constitution accommodated, the capacity to adapt and transform in the ways it so strikingly did. The mainstream became Attic, and possibly always had been.

As to the Megarians (returning to Aristotle for a moment) not much dependable information survives, but we can at least confirm that there was a local comic tradition from occasional – and of course condescending – references in Attic writers.[2] The claim from the Megarian side that comedy developed there in the time of their democracy seems to be asserting that comedy in the 'iambic' tradition was a Megarian invention. That claim is matched by, and possibly responsible for, the setting up of a founder of Attic comedy called Susarion, from Icaria (like Thespis, the founder of tragedy), and of a date, duly recorded in the third-century Parian chronicle, for the first comic performance (the date fell somewhere between 581 and 560 B.C.: the part of the inscription which gave it is now lost); nor are we astounded to find a tradition that Susarion was a

---

[1] Trendall and Webster (1971) 1, 13, referring *inter alia* to Hdt. 6.129 for Hippoclides and to Pollux 4.104 for a Laconian dance of *hypogypones*, old men with sticks.

[2] 'Laughter stolen from Megara', of stock routines, Ar. *Wasps* 57 (422 B.C.); other allusions by contemporaries in Eupolis 244 K (referred to above, p. 357 n. 1) and Myrtilus, *Titanopanes* 1 K; earlier, Ecphantides 2 K.

Megarian anyway.[1] What core of truth there is in all this will probably never be known. If there had been any substantial amount of information about sixth-century comic artists in the Athens of Aristotle's day, it is hard to credit that what we gather from him about the dispute over priorities would take the form it does; but the pointers to the earlier sixth century are interesting in view of the independent evidence from the *komoi* of the vases, which must have been organized by someone, 'volunteer' or whoever. Epicharmus, though we know much less of him than we should like, is of a different order of reality; and if Plato and Theocritus can rank him as the supreme writer of comedy and as its inventor, then the citizens of the Sicilian Megara, which claimed him as a favourite son, were not simply men labouring under delusions of local loyalty.[2] It is to Epicharmus and the west that we should now briefly turn our attention, before further exploration of the Attic mainstream.

4. EPICHARMUS AND OTHERS

Syracuse was a Corinthian colony; Corinthian influence has been seen in sixth-century representations of dancers produced in Sicily;[3] and there are reports from Hellenistic sources of *komoi* in the west similar to those of the Greek homelands and like them of indeterminable antiquity.[4] The early colonists could have been expected to transport and foster institutions from their mother-cities; but growth is often different under another sky. Epicharmus, by repute, lived to be 90 or more; he was perhaps born, as some think, as early as the mid-sixth century; in later ages, and possibly from his own lifetime onwards, he acquired a remarkable reputation as guide, philosopher and friend to everyman from the miscellaneous didactic poetry that circulated under his name. If we believe that he really was 'much earlier' than the Athenians Chionides and Magnes, we may wish to think of him as active at a date before 500 B.C.;[5] but for our purposes, he comes most clearly into focus as a comic writer in the Syracuse of Hieron I in the 470s, in a circle whose distinguished visitors included the lyric poets Simonides, Bacchylides and Pindar, and the tragedian Aeschylus, who wrote his *Aetnaeae* in honour of the foundation of a new city of Aetna and also gave the *Persae* its Sicilian première. In writings of this time Epicharmus

---

[1] Parian chronicle: *IG* XII.5, 444 ep. 39 = *FGrH* 239 A 39, quoted with other relevant texts in West (1972) 147–8; cf. West (1974) 183f.

[2] Plato, *Tht.* 152e; Theocritus, *Ep.* 18, an inscription for a statue set up in Syracuse.

[3] *DTC* nos. 67–8; cf. Payne (1931) 124.

[4] For *phlyakes* as the south Italian equivalent of the Spartan *deikeliktai* etc., see Semus of Delos (quoted above, p. 363 n. 4); and cf. *schol. in Theocr. vetera*, p. 2 Wendel, on a *komos* to Artemis Lyaea at Syracuse: *DTC* 135ff., with text p. 296.

[5] The three ways of escape from Aristotle's 'much earlier' (*Poetics* 1448a33: see above) are that it is corrupt, interpolated, or an exaggeration, and each has found advocates: perhaps most of the data are satisfied if E. was born about 530 and became known in the decade before the first (as opposed to the second) Persian War.

and Pindar both allude to one of Hieron's incursions into mainland Italo-Greek affairs, when he set himself up in 477 B.C. as the protector of the western Locrians;[1] Aeschylus met with the comic poet's mockery over a favourite word of his; but it is (unfortunately) no more than a possible conjecture from the title that Epicharmus' *Persians* is connected with its Aeschylean namesake.[2] References elsewhere to the iambic writings of Aristoxenus of Selinus and to the choliambic poet Ananius suggest that Epicharmus and at least some of those for whom he wrote were well enough acquainted with poetry in the 'iambic tradition'; but the abusive political topicalities of a Cratinus were not for him, and, one supposes, hardly could have been in the ambience of Hieron's court.[3]

Individual play-titles, when we have virtually no text, may only serve to remind us of what we should like to know and do not; but when studied collectively they can show something of the trend of a dramatist's interests. In lists and from quotations, we have some 40 titles of plays by Epicharmus (biographical sources give figures of 35, 40 and 52; but there is no saying in any case what proportion survived of those he wrote); of these, about half indicate subjects from myth, like the *Komastai or Hephaistos* which has been mentioned already in connexion with the Return of Hephaestus as a subject of sixth-century vase-painting. *Komastai or Hephaistos* and at least two other titles (*Bakchai, Dionysoi*) suggest themes from adventures of Dionysus; others who provided subjects for several plays each are Heracles and Odysseus, the hero of strength and the hero of resource. The context often seems to have been given by the story of a confrontation with a special trial, giant or monster, as for instance in *Heracles and the girdle* (of the Amazon Queen, or another?), *Odysseus the deserter* (in the army before Troy), *Bousiris* (Heracles and the king of Egypt who proposed to sacrifice him), *Cyclops*, *Sirens*; and similarly with other heroes, as in *Amykos* (Castor, Pollux and the pugilist king of the Bebrycians); *Pyrrha or Prometheus* (the Flood); *Skiron* (starring Theseus, presumably) and *Sphinx*. The take-off point can be a particular treatment in more serious poetry (and no doubt was, more often than we are sure): the Sirens sing to Odysseus' crew in a parody of a Homeric hexameter; but then, from a scrap of dialogue which survives, the temptation they offer is the typically comic one of feasts with a variety of delicious seafood.[4] The contrast between heroic occasion and unheroic behaviour is seen again in *Odysseus the deserter*, which has been thought

[1] Pindar, *Pyth.* 2.18ff., with Schol. *ad Pyth.* 1.98 (= Epich. 98 Kai, 121 Ol); it is anyone's guess if the play in question, *Nasoi* 'The Islands' also alluded to the Syracusans' attempt to colonize Pithecusae/Ischia after their famous naval victory over the Etruscans in 474 (Strabo 5.4.9; Livy 8.22.6).

[2] Schol. *ad* Aesch. *Eum.* 626 (= Epich. 214 Kai, 194 Ol); for Aeschylus' *Persae* in its Sicilian context, cf. Pindar, *Pyth.* 1.71–80, an ode written for Hieron's chariot victory of 470.

[3] Aristoxenus: *Logos kai Logina* 88 Kai, 112 Ol. Ananius: *Hebas gamos* 58 Kai, 22 Ol; note Pindar, *Pyth.* 2.54ff. on Archilochus; and for the abuse in *Megaris* (90 Kai, 114 Ol) cf. *Wasps* 1308ff.

[4] *Seirenes* 123–4 Kai, 70–1 Ol; *Odyssey* 12.184ff.

to take off from the story of Diomedes and Odysseus in *Iliad* 10; it has two characters, probably these two, in a scene where Odysseus seems to be preparing some kind of cover story for an operation that had gone by no means according to plan; in another snatch of text, a Trojan apparently says he has been accused of traffic with the Greeks because he accidentally lost a neighbour's piglet, and one can look ahead to Aristophanes' debunking of the emotions which cause war in the *Acharnians*, with his fiction of the contraband puppy that launches three hundred ships.[1] One of Heracles' gifts to the comedian was his legendary appetite for food and drink. There is a vivid description of him at the table in *Bousiris*, guzzling, champing, snorting and wagging his ears (21 Kai, 8 Ol); his wedding feast in *Hebas gamos* (revised as *Mousai*) called forth a virtuoso narrative, which, to judge from the surviving excerpts, must have catalogued a good number of the edible creatures of the Mediterranean as well as other delicacies.[2] But the flavour of the writing is not easy to catch, whether from short excerpts or gappy papyrus fragments; there is no evidence for the shape and structure of the plays, and no sign of the metrical variety of fifth-century Attic comedy; if the source which reports that two plays were written wholly in one metre really had whole plays and not abridgements, we have to think of a very different use of actors and chorus.[3] That said, there are in the non-mythological as well as in the mythological plays a number of motifs which had interesting developments elsewhere, and it could be among plays of this group above all that Aristotle found a trend towards the kind of comedy whose beginnings in Athens he associated with Crates. Perhaps the most often quoted is a figure with many descendants in fourth-century comedy and its derivatives, the professional sponger or parasite, from *Hope or Wealth* (35 Kai, 103 Ol) – a man who will dine anywhere given an invitation (or not), who flatters and sides with his host at every opportunity, eats and drinks well, and then goes home alone through dark and mud, facing a mugging, to a bed with no bedclothes.

Some other titles are of special interest because they point in two directions, both to Attic drama and to the much less well-documented tradition of the literary mime, which extends from Sophron (whose early years in Syracuse probably overlapped with Epicharmus' old age) to those Hellenistic writers whose work may have been specially influenced by Sophron, among them Theocritus and Herodas. Epicharmus' *Thearoi* 'Visitors to Delphi' (79 Kai, 109 Ol) has a description of dedications to Apollo which recalls Euripides'

---

[1] *Odysseus automolos* 99–100 Kai, 50–1 Ol, augmented in 1959 by text from *P.Oxy.* 2429, *CGFP* no. 84; Ar. *Ach.* 541ff.
[2] *Hebas gamos/Mousai* 41–75 Kai, 11–40 Ol; among unidentified fragments of Doric comedy is one which may be *Bousiris*: *P.Heid.* 181, *CGFP* no. 223.
[3] Hephaestion, *De metris* 26.10, on *Epinikios* and *Choreuontes*, wholly in anapaestic tetrameters. Some deny that Epicharmus had a chorus at all, probably unrealistically, given some of his plural play-titles; if he had, neither its size nor the distinction between actors and chorus need have been the same as in Attic comedy.

chorus in the *Ion* (184ff.) and Herodas' ladies in a temple of Asclepius in the fourth Mimiamb; to the same family belong Theocritus 15, the ladies at the Adonia, as well as lost works by Aeschylus (*Theoroi or Isthmiastae*), Sophron (*Tai thamenai ta Isthmia*) and a late comic poet Euphron (*Theoroi*, 7 K). Another literary family with representatives in Epicharmus is the dialogue or debate, as of *Land and sea* (23–32 Kai, 93–102 Ol) and *Logos kai Logina* 'His argument and hers' which immediately recalls the two *Logoi* in Aristophanes' *Clouds*, Right Argument and Wrong, as the other recalls a mime-title of Sophron's 'The Fisherman and the rustic'.[1]

There were other writers of comic plays in the Doric dialect besides Epicharmus: we have slight records and remains of Phormis, mentioned as a contemporary, and Deinolochus, of a younger generation. It is fairly easy, and sometimes of significant interest, to mark out common ground between these writers and Attic drama, much harder to be sure how far common developments speak for influence in one direction or the other. The plain story is that in the course of the fifth century, Attic drama became overwhelmingly dominant, and the Athenian festivals set the standard; where local and dialect drama survived, it was not to compete with established tragedy and comedy, but essentially to fill the gap in popular entertainment that full-dress plays left open. Some few names survive of people whose developments or recreations of these local traditions were thought worth remembering; among them is that of Rhinthon of Syracuse (or of Tarentum?) writing about 300 B.C. and blending, apparently, the literary tradition of tragic burlesque with that of the local festival performers whom the Italian Greeks called *phlyakes*.[2] Once Athenian comedy turned away from its involvement with the life of contemporary Athens and became universal (a movement which, as we have seen, Aristotle traced to Sicily), western Greeks could join others from all quarters in writing in the Attic mode, whether in Athens or elsewhere; but that is basically the story of the age after Aristophanes.

5. MYTHS AND MYTH-MAKING

Near the end of their journey through the Underworld in Aristophanes' *Frogs*, Dionysus and Xanthias hear a mysterious noise, and then see a most remarkable creature, large, frightening, and all shapes at once: now a cow, now a mule, now a beautiful woman; but then suddenly dog-like with a face lit by fire;

---

[1] On this kind of dialogue see Coffey (1976) 29f. Drama and non-dramatic discourse can be very much alike in it, as in a papyrus fragment which has been thought of both as a speech by a comic doctor in a play by Epicharmus and as part of a (?pseudo-)Epicharmean treatise, perhaps *Chiron*, spoken by the centaur Chiron himself: *P.Sak.* inv. 71/2 GP 6 5673, first published by Turner (1976) 48ff.

[2] See above, p. 367 n. 4. Rhinthon is later than the last of the so-called 'phlyax vases' which document performances of Attic and of local comedy in southern Italy from the late fifth century through the first three quarters of the fourth: see Trendall (1967) 9ff.

'it must be Empusa', says Dionysus (293); and it has, finally, one leg of bronze and the other of cow-dung. 'The cow-dung', notes Radermacher in his commentary, 'is probably comic invention.'

Comedy can be very interesting for the fragments it preserves of old myths and popular beliefs; and here indeed is a primitive-looking apparition, a sinister compound of animal and human, like a thing from a child's nightmare or a folk-tale. The opposite point, that comedy refashions and recreates its mythical material, is one that is rightly stressed in a valuable study by Hofmann (1976) of myth in comedy with special reference to Aristophanes' *Birds*; and this applies to a story of the creation like the one told in the *Birds* or to the gods and heroes and their adventures at large in just the way that it does to such a detail as the leg of an Underworld bogy.[1] If it is hard to define precisely what we mean by myth, it is not easy either to form a view of the various ways in which myth (in one sense or another) inspired the comic imagination. The possible importance of that source of inspiration has been indicated already by our rough reckoning that about half of Epicharmus' plays had themes from myth. When we come to stress, as we now must, the variety of use that comedy makes of mythological subject matter, Empusa and some kindred figures can open up the topic in a way that may be instructive.

With mythical material, as with anything else in comedy, the control to interpretation given by context is a vital complement to what can be learnt by static analysis and comparison. Empusa in her context in *Frogs* is part of a sequence designed to give the impression of a magical mystery tour through Hades. The leg of cow-dung (let us agree) is probably comic invention; it adds momentarily to the laughter. But whatever else, Empusa has two elements, sexual attractiveness and terror, which are present and emphasized precisely because Dionysus is to react to them: these emotions here and elsewhere in the play are part of the comic portrait (for the god of the *Frogs*, in matters of sex and courage, is a good step nearer those followers of his, the satyrs, than is the god of Euripides' *Bacchae*); and the traditional Empusa figure, with the emphases given by context and comic refashioning, plays its minor part in bringing this out. Later on in the *Frogs*, there is another interesting apparition, namely the dream from Hades which comes to the Girl in Distress in Aeschylus' parody of a Euripidean solo lyric (1331ff.). This is that well-remembered child of black Night, with a shiversome dreadful face, black-corpse-clad, looking bloody murder, and equipped with a soul that is no soul and big nails. From Rau, Barlow and others one can follow in detail the working of the parody and assess its validity as a reflection of Euripides' lyric style;[2] our point here is simply that this time Aristophanes has put a monster together which is something more than

[1] Hofmann (1976) 161ff.; and 177–96 on the creation story in Ar. *Birds* 685ff.
[2] Rau (1967) 132f.; Barlow (1971) 44f.

a denizen of the Underworld: it is part of a demonstration piece in musical and dramatic criticism. Similar components are found in the imagery of political attack. At *Knights* 75ff. Cleon is a relatively plain kind of monster, a giant, all-seeing, with one leg in Pylos and the other in the Assembly, as well as other parts in places chosen to suggest theft, venality and moral turpitude; but at *Peace* 751ff. Aristophanes looks back in anger, and imagines himself having attacked, in the spirit of a Heracles, a creature with a whole gallery of un-amiable characteristics, some of them borrowed from Hesiod's Typhoeus (*Theogony* 820ff.): there is a horrible smell; instead of snake-locks, the tongues of a hundred flatterers surround its head; it has snapping dog-teeth, a voice like a toxic torrent, and so on. In this final example, an element of story or action is just perceptible if we reflect that Aristophanes casts himself in the role of Heracles performing a labour. The unlovely portrait is perhaps something that gave Aristophanes special satisfaction: it is repeated in *Peace* almost word-for-word from *Wasps* (1029ff.).

Of course, more elevated figures still from the mythological pantheon can be pressed into service. For instance, Plutarch's *Life of Pericles* recalls from comedy not only Pericles and Aspasia being satirized as Heracles and Omphale, or Heracles and Deianira, but quotes from Cratinus' *Cheirones* a bogus Theogony in lyric, in which Stasis and Cronos unite to produce the supreme tyrant, Pericles Lord of the Dome (his head, not the sky), and Katapygosyne (Lady Lewdity) bears Aspasia to be his Hera.[1] More elaborately still, in the *Dionysalex-andros*, Cratinus involves Dionysus in a comedy of mistaken identity over the Judgement of Paris and the Trojan War and (we are told) 'Pericles is satirized very cleverly by indirect means as having brought the war on the Athenians'.[2] Perhaps these are enough instances to carry the point that the fifth-century Athenian's inheritance of myth and folk-tale could be exploited in comedy for anything from a passing allusion to a whole sequence of action or plot, and that sometimes complicated sets of overtones could be conveyed. Cratinus' lyric Theogony is being satirical about mythical genealogies and at the same time about certain personal qualities of Pericles and Aspasia, but he also chooses to present it in a manner which debunks the elevation of the high mode of choral lyric. The adventure story of the *Dionysalexandros* is amusing at one level because it makes a romp (and sometimes a decidedly down-to-earth romp) of a story of gods and heroes; but it also gives a kind of framework for reflecting on and criticizing contemporary politics which we can legitimately set alongside the framework from everyday life which Aristophanes provides for his fantasy of Demos and the politicians in the *Knights*.

[1] Plut. *Per.* 3 and 24 (Crat. *Cheirones* 240–1 K): Cratinus called Pericles *kephalegeretas* after *nephelegereta*, the Homeric epithet for Zeus Cloudgatherer.
[2] *P.Oxy.* 663, col. ii fin. = *CGFP* no. 70: see below, pp. 378, 383f.

What kinship (if any clearly traceable one) may exist between the comic poet's mode of creating figures like Demos or Right Argument and the process which created figures of myth is a question which needs to be opened here rather than discussed. The special case of mythological comedy which does need our attention is that of myth as reflected in tragedy, and conveyed to the comic stage by derivative and allusive treatments for which there are many varieties and names (travesty, parody, burlesque, quotation, imitation and so on). The full influence of early tragedy on early comedy is not likely to be well assessed without more texts of both than we have; but parody and tragic allusion in Aristophanes have been very carefully studied;[1] we have noted already in discussing structure that Aristophanes' interest in the *Telephus* of Euripides has certain possible implications for the composition of the *Acharnians*, and (little though we still know of the *Telephus*) there is something more to add if one also relates the sequence of incidents in that play to the *Thesmophoriazusae*.[2] Wholesale burlesque of tragedy, especially the thrilling kind of Euripides, is something that begins in the fifth century and is extremely popular in the first half of the fourth; unfortunately, our only complete specimen of this genre is the putative original of Plautus, *Amphitruo*, perhaps to be dated about 330 B.C. What we can sometimes trace is the way in which, in time, comedy absorbs from tragedy some of what might be called the grammar of dramatic composition: a motif or a piece of technique is taken over by way of parody or burlesque, and comes to stay as part of the comic dramatists' stock-in-trade. An example might be the recognition scene in Aristophanes' *Knights*, full of pointed parody, in contrast with that of Menander's *Perikeiromene*, where the fainter hints of a poetic tone are hardly more than a reminder to the audience that life is sometimes like literature.[3]

The words 'myth-making' in the heading to this section were put there to call attention to the point that, though comedy borrows so much of its mythical material, it often transmutes what it takes. There is, of course, quite another sense in which comedy can be said to make myths, and that will escape no one who has considered what the effect of Aristophanes' portraiture has been on the impression posterity has of Socrates, Cleon and Euripides. Further thought on the nature of these portraits must enter into our discussion of some other kinds of comedy; the entry of mythical elements into all of them will make it plain that any tight classification is out of the question.

[1] Rau (1967) with bibliography 220–3.

[2] Handley and Rea (1957), Rau (1967) 19–50, Webster (1967) 43–8.

[3] Ar. *Knights* 1232–52, with Rau (1967) 170–3; Menander, *Pk.* 349ff. (779ff. Sandbach), with *Entretiens Hardt* (1970) 126–8 and 41–2; and see below, pp. 385, 395, 420f.

6. POLITICAL COMEDY

The *Acharnians* opens with a scene in which Aristophanes faces the audience for a few moments with a man who, like themselves, is waiting for something to happen. He is thinking over, as perhaps they are, some past experiences of music and drama at the festivals. He specially liked 'the five talents that Cleon disgorged' (6). It is a guess (but a good one) that this is a reference to a recent comedy, probably Aristophanes' own play *Babylonians*, produced the year before. He will return to the topic of that play. What the man is waiting for, it soon appears, is an assembly of the people; but 'the Pnyx here is empty' (20) and he is the only one on time.[1] What he wants is a formal motion on peace with Sparta; all he gets is Reception of Delegates and Reports – or that would have been all, but for the fact that he is an Aristophanic hero, and there is one Amphitheus there, whose pedigree from Demeter (no less) plus a contribution of eight drachmas travelling expenses, makes possible a miraculous journey to Sparta and the personal peace-treaty, the hero's revolutionary idea, from which the rest of the action springs. The mixture of fantasy and realism is about to become more diverting still. There is violent opposition from the men of Acharnae, who form the chorus; their hatred of the enemy is sharpened by what they have lost themselves in the invasions of Attica, and our hero must defend himself. To do this, he borrows, in the way we have already noted, from the role of Euripides' hero Telephus, the king of Mysia who came to Agamemnon's palace in disguise, and found himself defending the Trojans against Greek demands for invasion and revenge.[2] But twice, briefly, yet another identity appears, that of the playwright, speaking with the actor's voice: 'And I know what happened to me with Cleon because of last year's play, when he dragged me into the Council and slandered me practically to death...' (377); 'Cleon will not slander me now for abusing the city in front of foreigners: this is the Lenaea, and we are on our own' (502ff.). This sequence of incidents illustrates as well as any single example can the diversity of elements which make up ancient political comedy. It was, as we gather, an exciting game for a good young player.[3] It is one where the play, at our distance of time, is not at all easy to follow.

We are far from knowing the full story of Cleon's action against Aristophanes. But it shows well enough that in fifth-century Athens, as in other societies which have taken pride in being free, there was still tension, sometimes aggravated into conflict, between those who pushed their freedom to its utter limits

---

[1] Line 20, as quoted here, gives the scene; the man's name, Dicaeopolis, becomes known much later (406).

[2] See above, pp. 361 and 373; and below, pp. 384f.

[3] This view assumes that Aristophanes personally was the object of Cleon's attack; the actor is then speaking for the writer (but need not have been Aristophanes himself); the matter is disputed because the play was officially in the name of Callistratus (above, p. 355; p. 359 with n. 1).

and those who, for various reasons, sought to draw those limits tighter. In or about 442 B.C., when Aristophanes was no more than a child, comic productions at the Lenaea gained the official status they had already had at the Dionysia for some forty-five years.[1] This must reflect some measure of growing public enthusiasm for comedy, even if we allow for the consideration that productions of tragedy were similarly recognized at the same time or soon after. The other side is given by the record of a decree of the year of the archonship of Morychides (440/439 B.C.: schol. *ad* Ar. *Ach.* 67) 'against attacking people by name in comedy'. One would like to know much more about the terms and effects of this measure, and not least who was supposed to be protected by it; it was repealed in the third year after its passing. 'They do not allow comic attacks and abuse directed against the People', says a critic of the Athenian democracy writing not far from this time, 'or they might suffer abuse themselves; but against individuals they encourage this.'[2] In the affair of the *Babylonians*, Cleon must have been able to argue that the production of Aristophanes' play had been contrary to public interest; and Aristophanes, for his part, can hardly have found the proceedings before the Council a pleasant experience. Yet within the year he was at work on the *Knights*, with Cleon cast as a rascally slave, with Demos, the Sovereign People, as a gullible old master (even if he is transformed at the end) and with an unflattering description of a debate in the Council thrown in for good measure.[3] The *Knights* won first prize. Within weeks, the villain of the piece was voted into office as one of the ten generals.

Plainly, in favourable circumstances, both comic poet and politician had a capacity to bounce back from blows which might have been expected to floor them. What happened when popular support was less sustaining is harder to say. What (for instance) did attacks in comedy contribute to the discredit and suspension from office of Pericles in 430?[4] How influential was opposition to the comedy of personal attack (in particular laws against it) in the movement away from that kind of comedy in the later fifth century and the early fourth?[5] The problem with such questions is not only the limited amount of contemporary evidence that bears on them; it is that the nature of comedy's image-making is in itself so infinitely varied. Plato, at all events, was someone who understood and did not underrate the comic poet's capacity to make his images live on in the mind, whether for evil effect or not. In the *Apology* (18b–d, 19c) Socrates

[1] *IG* ii² 2325; *DFA* 113 with 40f.
[2] Pseudo-Xenophon, *Ath.Pol.* 2.18.
[3] *Knights* in progress, cf. *Ach.* 301; debate in the Council, *Knights* 624ff.; see also *Wasps* 1284ff. with MacDowell (1971) *ad loc.*
[4] See Schwarze (1971) with Gomme (1956) on Thucydides 2.65.4 and de Ste Croix (1972) 231ff.
[5] Horace (*A.P.* 282ff.) and others treat the transformation of comedy by legislation as a fact of literary history; yet the only legislation we know of for sure is the decreee of 440–439 B.C. already mentioned; and its effect was transitory.

presents the *Clouds* as a prime example of the man-in-the-street's idea of him as an unscrupulous intellectual quack; and it could well be that the play fostered the prejudice which was to prove so powerful a weapon in his accusers' hands. Then in the *Symposium* (221b) Alcibiades is praising Socrates' behaviour as a member of a defeated and retreating army, and Plato (this time with a more benevolent recollection of Aristophanes) has him allude to a description, again in the *Clouds*, of Socrates stalking through the streets of Athens with an air of superiority to his surroundings, his eyes scanning the scene.

As to political policies, in the *Frogs*, written twenty years after the clash with Cleon, the chorus is still claiming the right to offer the state good advice (686ff.). Through his chorus, Aristophanes there advocates the restoration of full citizen rights to the disenfranchised and the dismissal of low-class politicians in favour of leaders with some of the traditional values and virtues. This does not perhaps at first sight seem like particularly stirring stuff; but one ancient scholar is quoted for the statement that the play was so much admired for its parabasis that it was actually given a repeat performance.[1] Whether or not that was so, the parabasis in which the advice was given begins with a spiteful allusion to a contemporary politician who could be taken, and was no doubt intended to be taken, as a type-specimen of the species that Aristophanes holds up for disapproval. The politician is Cleophon, with his voice like a Thracian barbarian's (675ff.); and it was the same man who gave his name to the play which came third to the *Frogs* in the festival competition, the *Cleophon* of Plato, the comic poet who was Aristophanes' slightly older contemporary. The years of war and revolution which have intervened since Aristophanes' youth still leave it possible, in 405 B.C., for politics to enter into comedy and even to be a foreground subject of it.

Wars with Sparta and her allies in fact went on almost continuously through Aristophanes' early life, from his teens to his forties; and in modern times, when war and fear of war have affected people universally, his expression of some of man's basic longings for peace is something which has had a special appeal. Yet if we slip into thinking of plays such as *Acharnians*, *Peace* and *Lysistrata* as if they were part of a political campaign, there is a danger of overlooking something more basic about the way in which Aristophanic comedy operates. The pains and problems of the complex, intractable world of political reality are transformed by Aristophanes into a simpler and more colourful world where they will yield to a man's wishes if he has pluck and luck enough. That is not to say that the portrait of a contemporary situation can simply take leave of reality. There would be no fun in a new fantastic solution to the real world's problems if the real world itself seemed to be being left behind. The comic poet can be an acute observer, and may be motivated by strong (and not necessarily system-

---

[1] Dicaearchus in Ar. *Frogs* hyp. 1 (= fr. 84 Wehrli).

atized) views of his own. But his selection of detail and his presentation of issues and arguments need only answer to the demands he sets himself within the medium of a comic play designed to amuse a large audience and capture the public imagination; he need not respond to the different demands which would be made of a documentary reporter or a propagandist.[1]

Wars bring death, mutilation and misery; but comedy does not dwell on these things. Its portrait of the effects of war, much like that in some wartime plays of later ages, is more of the ordinary man's frustrations, discomforts and longing for a better life. The painful depths remain unplumbed, just as the heights of courage or patriotic devotion are not scaled. But ordinary everyday things, on which most people focus for most of their lives, have more evocative power than is commonly admitted; and it would be wrong, if we return again for an example to the opening of the *Acharnians*, to see no more than an amusing allusive monologue in the words of the man who, as he says, hates the city and longs for the place where he belongs, his home in the country where he could produce basic necessities and not have to buy them from traders in the streets (33–5). The theme of peace and plenty and rustic bliss is a recurrent one in this play and the *Peace*, as well as in the fragments of *Georgoi* (so one would expect from a play with a chorus of farmers); and after several years of war, the audience can hardly have needed much prompting to respond to it.[2] But Aristophanes is often much more direct. 'How can you say you love the People?' Cleon is asked in the *Knights*, '– when for seven years now you've seen them living in barrels and turrets and places for vultures to nest in, and you don't care: you've got them shut up and you're taking all the honey'; and still (the accusation continues) you scorn and reject proposals for peace when we get them.[3] The 'No Peace, no Sex' campaign, the brilliant idea by which the women in the *Lysistrata* end the war, is a theme which allows Aristophanes to give something of a woman's-eye viewpoint. There is the wife who wants news (510ff.): 'Often enough, at home, we'd hear how you men had gone wrong over something big; and we'd smile and ask with a sinking feeling inside "What was it you decided to add to the treaty in the Assembly today?" "What's that to you?" he'd say, "Shut up!" And I did.' Then later (591ff.) Lysistrata points out that though she and the other wives miss their men in wartime, it is worse for the girls growing old without a husband. 'But don't men grow old too?' she is asked. 'Not the same thing at all. A man can come back from the war with grey hair, and he's married to a young girl in no time; but women are so soon past their best...' Naturally there were other sides to the picture of war: the young cavalrymen

---

[1] The point is well put by Gomme (1938) 102f.; on A.'s political outlook in general, see de Ste Croix (1972) 355–71.

[2] See for instance *Ach.* 247–79, 665ff., 989ff. (p. 357 above); *Georgoi* frs. 107, 109, 110 K; *Peace* 556ff., 571ff., 1140ff.

[3] Ar. *Knights* 792–6; for background see Thuc. 2.16–17, 52.2; 4.15–23, 41.4.

who form the chorus of *Knights* present themselves with plenty of panache; Dionysus recruited to the fleet can be drilled by Phormio like the rawest of raw recruits; early in the war, Pericles can be accused by a comic poet of down-right cowardice for not living up to his brave oratory.[1] But basically, war and comedy did not agree with each other; and if the Aristophanes of *Peace* and *Lysistrata* sometimes seems over-sentimental in his vision of the warring states working together for peace and rejoicing together when they get it, there is still no reason to deny him a core of sincere pacifist feeling beneath all that.

One thing which the comic poet shares with the common man is a realistic, not to say earthy, attitude to the motives on which people act, especially eminent people. Thus in the passage of *Knights* referred to above, it is not enough simply to charge Cleon with not caring about overcrowding in Athens; it is insinuated by the metaphor of taking honey from the bees that he is some-how using the situation to line his pockets as well. Bribery and corruption, with whatever truth or degree of truth, are constantly said to have been at work whenever a person or a policy earns strong dislike; personal idiosyncrasies, especially social and sexual behaviour, are freely admitted to a kind of relevance by association. Pericles 'the Olympian' and his Aspasia, as we have noted, lent themselves readily to translation into a number of mythological roles.[2] The insinuation in Cratinus' *Dionysalexandros* that Pericles somehow, like Paris, plunged the world into war from self-interest, for the sake of a woman, is akin to, and may in part have inspired, the notion in Aristophanes' *Acharnians* that the root cause of the whole embroilment was three brothel-girls, one kidnapped Megarian and two from Aspasia's house taken in retaliation: that was why the Olympian stirred up a certain local commercial friction with his Megarian decree worded like a drinking song (*Ach.* 515ff.). Looking back in the *Peace*, in a passage which has been called a 'malicious and quite unnecessary sideswipe at Pericles', Aristophanes has Hermes say that the trouble began with the trial of Phidias (he was accused of fraud over gold supplied for the making of the statue of Athena for the Parthenon); and then Pericles stirred up the flames of war to make a smoke screen for himself and avoid any similar attacks.[3] Fortunes change: inside ten years, in the *Demoi*, Eupolis is resurrecting Pericles as one of the great statesmen of the past who will scrutinize Athens' present condition and advise her.

The scope of ancient political comedy is wide. It ranges from passing

[1] Ar. *Knights* 498–610 (above, p. 359); Dionysus joins Phormio's fleet in Eupolis, *Taxiarchoi* (250ff. K, with *P.Oxy.* 2740 = *CGFP* 98; and cf. pp. 383ff. below; Pericles as 'King of the Satyrs', Hermippus, *Moirai* 46 K, cf. Schwarze (1971) 101–9.

[2] See above, p. 372 with n. 1.

[3] *Peace* 605ff.; the quotation is from de Ste Croix (1972) 371; for attacks on Pericles' friends, see Gomme (1956) on Thuc. 2.65.4.

allusions to contemporary people and events as far as the embodiment of a whole political situation in a play; and that situation can be transformed just as well into a setting from myth as it can into one of everyday life. But further, since the field of Athenian public affairs that might be called political is so extensive, a discussion of political comedy could take illustrations from many more passages and deal with many more topics than have been selected here – not least passages concerning the management of state finances and the administration of justice. In those areas, political comedy, especially as seen in the *Wasps*, shades over into what is more conveniently called social comedy. As to their political attitudes, comic poets, as critics of the present, are very easily labelled by turns as conservatives and as idealists; for they most naturally contrast what is bad now with what was good then or what would be good if... For Aristophanes, in so far as we can recognize the man beneath the work, there seems no reason to deny either label; yet for someone of Cratinus' generation, he was a smart young man, tarred with the same brush of intellectualism as Euripides.[1] One feature of the representation of public affairs in comedy, whatever selection we make, is so prominent in its importance both for a historical and for a literary approach that it deserves a final word of stress. That feature is the element of creative imagination or fantasy which dominates the design of a play, however true to the real world details and individual incidents or characters may be; for one good part of the effect of the well-conceived play is to offer an escape from that world into a fictional one where dreams (or at least some of them) come true.[2] It is that aspect of comic invention which must be our next main concern.

7. ADVENTURE AND FANTASY

The *Birds* of Aristophanes begins with the entry of two men who are on a journey. Popular fiction is fond of far away places; and fifth-century Greek comedy is no exception. The very idea that people are travelling, be it far or near, is one that can be relied upon to make reader or audience take notice. Three other plays of the eleven, *Thesmophoriazusae*, *Frogs* and *Plutus*, all begin with two people going somewhere. In *Birds* (as indeed in *Peace*) the journey is to the world above the earth; in *Frogs*, as in the *Demoi* of Eupolis and in other plays known only from fragments, a part of the action takes place in Hades. The dramatist enacts an escape from the world about us by physical transposition of the action into another.

The *Birds* missed the first prize in 414 B.C., but won second. One wonders if anyone asked Aristophanes, in the course of the celebrations, how he arrived at

---

[1] Cratinus 307 K kills two birds with one stone by coining the verb *Euripidaristophanizein*.
[2] This point is well taken by Connor (1971) 180f.

the idea that two people should leave Athens in search of peace and quiet and end up founding a new city in the sky, Nephelokokkygia – that Cloudcuckooland whose name has entered the English language as that of a specially insubstantial kind of Utopia. Perhaps he could have told his questioner, perhaps not: creating is one thing, reconstructing the process another. For readers of a remote age, there are still more hazards in the way; yet there is still some point in reflecting on certain of the elements in the creation and how they relate to each other, even if we do not presume to be drawing an Aristophanic mental map.

Why birds for a chorus? *Ornithes* was not a novel title; and Aristophanes had known as much for ten years and more (*Knights* 522: above, p. 364 with n. 2). But the non-human chorus, which we have taken (and Aristophanes himself may have taken) as a survival from a very primitive type of comedy, is something that still held its place in the later fifth century precisely because it continued to offer possibilities to the imagination. Not least, such a chorus, by challenging or inviting the audience to identify with it, offers a kind of transposition, not necessarily in physical space (though moving to the bird-world in the sky does this) but at any rate into a new non-conventional and perhaps purely escapist system of values. 'If you will follow our way' the argument tends to run 'you will have all these good things which you do not now have.' Accordingly, Aristophanes' chorus of birds, after more elaborate claims on the attention of mankind, which include asserting their role in the Creation,[1] at last come on to some very concrete benefits of being winged: with wings, a man could go home from the theatre for lunch and return; he could fly off and ease himself in comfort; or he could fit in a visit to another man's wife while her husband was safe in his front seat (785–96). Two variants of the same motif can be noted in passing. At *Clouds* 1115–30, the chorus of Clouds addresses the judges, promising them good weather if they favour the play, and bad if not (in the event they did not);[2] and in a fragment of the *Theria* of Crates the animals which gave the play its name are to be found arguing the benefits of men eating radishes and fish: this was in fact one of a series of plays with fantasies on the 'Land of Cockaigne' theme – free and effortless food, whether in an idealized past or somewhere else over the rainbow.[3]

One can of course have a fantastic plot without running to a non-human chorus, just as one can have a strikingly decorative chorus without imitating the creations of nature. But the choice of birds as a chorus gave Aristophanes some very special opportunities, visual and musical, and one can see from the text how eagerly he grasped both. It is a main function of the first two hundred lines of the play to build up to an elaborate sequence of song and choral

[1] See Hofmann (1976) quoted above, p. 371 with n. 1.
[2] The play came third, and Aristophanes did not conceal his disappointment (hyp. vi Coulon with 524f.); for the form of this appeal, cf. *Birds* 1101ff.
[3] On this theme see Baldry (1953).

parade.[1] The bird motif is present from the first, and in a form typical of the way in which Aristophanes creates stage spectacle from language. *Ornis* means both 'bird' and, by extension, 'omen'. Ordinary men might be expected to have an omen for their journey, but Aristophanes' two heroes have the literal thing, a bird each from the market. Their errand is to a bird-man, Tereus, the legendary king who became the hoopoe. Before they meet him, there is a preliminary routine with a bird-servant;[2] then dialogue with the Hoopoe leads to the idea of founding a new bird city, and the birds are to be called together to be persuaded. Music and song are natural to the occasion. The Hoopoe first calls to his mate, Procne, the nightingale, in an attractive little lyric (209ff.), to which the response is nightingale song in the form of a solo by the piper; and then he summons at large birds of field and garden, of mountain, marsh and sea (227ff.). The words ingeniously slip from bird-call to human speech and back again; the metrical structure hints, but hints clearly, at a virtuoso song and dance with changing mode and movements as each group of birds is summoned.[3] At last, when the birds do arrive, there are individual decorative costumes to excite comments and wonder. There were other plays in which members of the chorus had individual identities (Eupolis' play *Poleis*, for example, appears to have had a chorus of individually named cities, frs. 231–3 K), but it is hard to see that there can have been a better opportunity for show. Certainly for later ages the *Birds* represents the musical side of ancient comedy at its spectacular peak.

Less tangible, perhaps, but still significant as a constituent of the play, is the set of ideas which relate to air and the elevated setting in the sky. 'Elevated', *meteoros*, is a word which prompted one of Aristophanes' best-known visual jokes of all, when in the *Clouds* he presents Socrates elevating himself literally in a basket so that he can raise his mind (figuratively) to higher things and mix his thought with the air which (he asserts) is its like (227ff.); similarly, words for 'fly' and 'take wing' (as at *Clouds* 319) can refer to intellectual excitement as well as literal elevation. The relationship between *Clouds* and *Birds* in the use of this complex of imagery has been perceptively recognized;[4] and it is well represented in the long sequence with the men who want wings from the new bird city. Cinesias, the dithyrambic poet, wants wings to fly and collect material for preludes from the clouds, preludes full of air, snowflakes and heavenly chiaroscuro (1383ff.). An informer, who is the next applicant, is given a discourse on the power of words to make men's minds 'take wing' (1437ff.). There is a way in which the whole play can be seen as an imaginative take-off from reality into a world of air in which a man with nerve and a good gift of

[1] Gelzer (1976) gives a well-balanced discussion of the early part of *Birds*.
[2] Like master, like man: so with Euripides' servant at *Ach.* 395ff. and Agathon's at *Thes.* 39ff.
[3] Fraenkel (1950); Dale (1959).   [4] Gelzer (1956) esp. 79ff.

arguing can have things all his own way and end by bringing even the Olympian gods to make terms. Gilbert Murray (1933), for whom *Birds* is a type-example of a 'play of escape', gives a good sketch of the trials and tensions of Athenian home and foreign affairs at the time of the play, from which an escape would no doubt have been welcome. There were many things of pressing concern to contemporary Athenians which do not strike the surface in *Birds*. On the other hand, as Murray rightly emphasizes, there are still stinging references to some of Aristophanes' pet political hates – Cleonymus, Peisandros, Dieitrephes, Cleisthenes. Typically of the technique of political comedy, these men are mercilessly attacked for their real or exaggerated personal foibles, a godsend to the modern political cartoonist just as to the ancient comic poet: a fat figure, lack of a beard when most men wore one, the classic cowardice of throwing away one's shield in a retreat that has become a rout.

There is, for all that, in *Birds* as in other fifth-century comedy, another kind of engagement with reality which has a special role in relation to plays with fantastic situations. Somehow, it seems, the dream is only delectable if the real world keeps rearing its head. So if (as happens at 1035ff.) a professional drafter of decrees visits Cloudcuckooland, his offerings – which, be it noted, are in prose[1] – are not only amusing as a reflection of the ways of political legislators: we recognize the invasion of the real world into the clouds as having a function akin to those vividly realistic elements we sometimes meet in pleasant dreams. The mission of Poseidon, Heracles and a foreign god to negotiate a deal with the birds has both elements of fantasy and elements of satire against established (in so far as it can be called established) Olympian religion. But what is also interesting, not least with the perspective given by our knowledge of later developments in comedy, is the degree of character contrast between three individuals engaged in the same action: Poseidon, consciously senior; Heracles, tough and simple, ruled by appetite and mood; foreign god, the racially under-privileged element, with (among his other problems) broken Greek. At the beginning of the scene (1565ff.) an extra dimension is given by the fact that Our Hero, whom the gods have come to visit, is far too preoccupied with cookery (grilling birds, condemned rebels against the ornithocracy) to notice his visitors; as negotiations develop, points of Attic law (including a quotation from Solon, 1661ff.) come into the argument: these realistic details point up the fantasy, the satire and the component (in so far as we recognize it) of social commentary.

Of the play that was placed first over *Birds*, the *Komastai* 'Revellers' of Ameipsias, we know no more than that one fact. Third came a play of which just enough is known to make us wish, as so often, that we had more: namely, the *Monotropos* 'Solitary' of Phrynichus. 'I am called solitary –' (so runs a quotation, fr. 18 K) 'I live the life of Timon: no wife, no slaves, sharp temper,

---

[1] So is the law quoted at 1661ff., and the prayer at *Thes.* 295ff.

unapproachable, mirthless, speechless, my own man entirely.' Here was another way of escape – misanthropy, the conscious rejection of one's fellow men and their ways. A few years earlier, at the Lenaean festival of 420 B.C., Pherecrates had put on a play *Agrioi* 'Savages' whose chorus apparently gave a collective portrait of a similar sort, of life without its conventional values and encumbrances. Timon appears again as a type-example of misanthropy at *Birds* 1549, and once more when Aristophanes takes up the theme in 411 B.C. in a lyric of *Lysistrata* (805 ff.). Two points concern us here. Timon of Athens, thanks above all to Lucian and Shakespeare, is better known as a fictional personality than as a real one; but real he apparently was, and he is worth remembering as an example of the way in which real people do lend parts of their identities to imaginative creations. What begins as satirical portraiture of an individual sometimes persists and contributes to the establishment of a dramatic type. It does not of course follow that Pherecrates or Phrynichus was interested in the ethical motivation of their respective misanthropes in the way that Menander was interested in the hero of his *Dyskolos* or *Misanthrope* a century later (indeed it is most improbable that either was). But if Timon is first of all useful as a reminder of one more way in which reality becomes fantasy, a kind of comedy which turns on one or more of its characters' social behaviour is well worth observing as one of the fifth-century developments which was to have a long future.

If 'fantasy' in this discussion has seemed to be a somewhat elastic term, there are ways in which 'adventure' could be stretched even further. Merely to encounter a body of (let us say) Ant-men, a chorus of Goats or Fish, makes for an adventure as typical of Old Comedy as it is untypical of life or literature in general. Yet there is one kind of adventure story which deserves special mention here, however brief. That is the kind which involves adventures of the god of drama himself, Dionysus, of which the type-example is *Frogs*; other plays with Dionysus by Aristophanes' principal rivals have already been referred to above, namely *Dionysalexandros* by Cratinus and *Taxiarchoi* by Eupolis.[1]

Adventures of Dionysus are a theme common to tragedy, satyr play and comedy. From the point of view of comedy they have a particular interest, like that of the animal choruses, in representing what is very likely to be a primitive element with a very long history which still held its place in fifth-century competitions. A motif which is recurrent in Dionysus plays and which has a future in plots of adventure and mistaken identity, is that which can be conveniently called disguise (the precise application of this term to a god in one or more human roles is not something that need detain us here). In *Dionysalexandros*,

---

[1] *Dionysalexandros*, *P.Oxy.* 663, as cited above, p. 372 with n. 2, with quoted fragments 37 ff. K; it is arguable that *P.Oxy.* 2806 (*CGFP* *76) is from the play's parabasis: Handley (1982*a*). *Taxiarchoi*, see p. 378 n. 1.

Dionysus, for what reason we do not know, appears in the role of a shepherd on Mount Ida, no doubt a bungling novice, and finds himself standing in for Paris, judging the goddesses' beauty-contest, collecting Helen from Troy, vainly disguising himself as a ram and her as something else (perhaps a goose) in order to escape detection and revenge; then finally he is handed over to an imprisonment which – we are sure – he will escape. The chorus was of satyrs (though there may have been a subsidiary chorus of shepherds or herdsmen); the occasion of the play, for the sake of which we have referred to it already, was an elaborately contrived attack on Pericles. In *Taxiarchoi* (the chorus was presumably made up of officers of that rank), Dionysus is not a *soi-disant* shepherd, but a recruit to the fleet of Admiral Phormio, in which (among other things) he learns some drill and has a rowing lesson which Aristophanes very likely remembered when it came to the rowing scene of *Frogs*.[1]

Frogs, like *Birds*, is a play with a very full measure of music and poetry; and that is by no means solely because it has a contest between tragedians as a major theme. Like *Birds* with its re-embodiment of the creation myth, it refashions for its Dionysiac adventure plot a set of popular images of the Underworld. As with *Ornithes*, Aristophanes knew *Batrachoi* as a very old title.[2] The Frogs' chorus, which is a splendid extra, gives place to the chorus of Initiates in the Mysteries for the elaborate sequence of processional hymns which is the choral parodos. Dionysus, first playing Heracles, then as literary critic, has an air of the happy amateur such as we seem to recognize in him when he plays shepherd or sailor. Looking back from later comedy, we can see how this early comic tradition of adventure with mythical background is very heavily overlaid by the type of myth-burlesque which derives primarily from tragedy, especially the later and more adventurous kind of Euripidean tragedy. That, together with the part of *Frogs* which means most to most people, the literary debate, will be among the topics which concern us next.

8. THE LIFE OF THE MIND

In 438 B.C., when Euripides produced the tetralogy of plays which includes *Telephus*, Aristophanes was still a boy. He may have seen the production on his first or an early visit to the theatre; but whether or not, thirteen years later in *Acharnians*, we find him using one of the high spots of the play, its hero's major speech, as a model for a speech by the hero of his comedy, and taking over much of the context as well. Another fourteen years pass: in 411, in *Thesmophoriazusae*, the whole sequence is remade for a quite different dramatic context. In *Frogs*, in 405, the famous play of a generation ago is still fair game; even in *Plutus*

[1] Cf. Wilson (1974); Harrison (1976) 137; Handley (1982 *b*).
[2] See p. 364 with n. 2.

(we are by now fifty years on) there is still an allusion either to *Telephus* or to Aristophanes' own reminiscence of it in *Knights*.[1]

Many other illustrations could be chosen to show that Aristophanes' interest in forms of literature more elevated than the one he practised was not only early but lasting. But a point which the *Telephus* offers immediately is that being topical about politics and being topical about works of the creative mind can be two very different things from the viewpoint of the comic poet and his public. True, there are lasting political issues and there are matters which politicians are never allowed to forget; true also that some literary and intellectual movements are transitory. But in general the distinction suggested here seems to hold: in the life of the mind there is a certain timelessness, the creator living through his creation, and by most people strongly identified with it; this is something which it is useful to remember as a corrective to the simple idea of comedy as a mirror of the contemporary scene.

Literary allusions in Aristophanes range from Homeric epic to plays produced at the last dramatic festival. Commonest are allusions to the tragedians, and among them much the most prominent is Euripides, who is in fact a character in *Acharnians*, *Thesmophoriazusae* and *Frogs*. Here, as so often, we recognize Aristophanes as heir to a considerable comic tradition. The entertainment that comes from reinterpreting stories of the gods and heroes in new down-to-earth terms is, we find, effectively reinforced by a simultaneous downgrading into the new context of the poetic language of one or another of the previous versions of these stories. A similar verbal incongruity is created when the ordinary man in comedy rises above the everyday language which might have been appropriate to his situation and borrows elevation from a more highly-wrought poetic counterpart of the feelings he is to express. Under the terms allusion, parody and burlesque modern discussions of comedy include a whole galaxy of comic effects of this kind. Examples have been mentioned in other contexts above from early Doric comedy as written by Epicharmus as well as in Attic plays by Aristophanes' much older contemporary Cratinus.[2] Three more references to Cratinus will show that neither literary subject matter nor poets as characters were unexpected on the fifth-century stage. His *Archilochoi*, dated soon after 449 B.C., is a forerunner of the *Frogs* in the sense that it involved a contest between 'Archilochus and company' on the one hand and Homer, perhaps with Hesiod in support, on the other; the *Odysses*, a plural title of the same sort, brought on 'Odysseus and company' in a parody of the Cyclops story from the *Odyssey*; *Pytine* 'Wineflask', the play which won first prize over *Clouds* in 423, had Cratinus himself as a character, in contention between his wife Comedy and his mistress Liquor.

---

[1] *Plut.* 601, *Knights* 813 = Eur. fr. 713 *TGF*.
[2] Pp. 367ff., 372f.

It is often asked whether there was any more than sheer entertainment in the comic writers' representations of poets and poetry. In one way, perhaps, the question is a reaction against the studious pursuit and discussion of allusions by commentators: can an audience of thousands, one wonders, have shared *en masse* the educated man's reaction to a literary hit? Surely not all of them: but modern experience of satirical revue shows that it is not necessary for all of the people to see all of the jokes all of the time. Laughter is infectious; satire can have several levels; and in theatrical performance voice and gesture, sometimes allied with costume and staging, can add significantly to the effect of the words. A good example, not least because we have the whole of the text being parodied, is the take-off of Euripides' *Helen* in *Thesmophoriazusae* 846–928. The basic situation is clear and broadly comic. Euripides' kinsman (Mnesilochus, as he is often called) has been caught dressed up as a woman acting as his agent at the Thesmophoria. In hope of a rescue he takes on roles from Euripidean adventure plays, first sending a message by a device from *Palamedes*, then turning to last year's productions, *Helen* and *Andromeda*, for Euripides to play the hero to his heroine in distress. When we come to detail, not only is the mock-tragic elevation of the two principals brought down to earth time and time again by the presence and interventions of a third party, an uncomprehending guard, but there are extra nuances of criticism, direct or implied. For instance, the long prologue speech of the *Helen* is transacted in 16 lines, including interruptions, with a wickedly precise selection of quotations; there are elements of visual and musical parody (855, at Proteus' tomb; 914f., lyrical moment of recognition); and there are minor quirks and distortions of language which would puzzle no one amid the general amusement, but add to the refinement of appreciation by those who knew their Euripides well.[1]

The same multiplicity of appeal is surely to be recognized in the sequence of scenes which represents the peak of ancient literary comedy, the contest between Aeschylus and Euripides in the second half of *Frogs*. It is interesting that after the Dionysiac adventure story of the first half of the play, Aristophanes takes special care to build up to the agon between the poets (738–894, prefacing 895ff.); then immediately after their debate he sets out to anticipate, by sheer flattery of the audience, any lurking objection that the scenes of competition that follow will be too highbrow (1099–118).[2] Even lacking the music, we can make something of the caricature of Aeschylean lyrics by Euripides, and of Euripidean by Aeschylus: the Aeschylean parody is full of heroes' names and recalls epic or early choral poetry with its trailing dactylic rhythms; the specimens of choral writing and solo in the manner of Euripides are presided over by a muse who appears in the role of a castanet dancer and are represented by

[1] For detailed discussion see Rau (1967) 53–65.
[2] Not only are they clever; they even read books: cf. above, p. 9 and Turner (1952) 22.

Aeschylus as trivial, modern and debased below the standards of true tragic art.[1] There is a level at which all this can be appreciated as sheer ragging. There is another, potentially more serious level of appreciation if we respond not only to the portrayal of the two contrasted styles but to the technical criticisms of the metric of the lyrics, both explicit (as at 1323) and implied. But there are two other levels at which both the contrast of lyrics operates and the whole literary debate of which it is part. The individual arguments, jokes and illustrations are part of an antithesis between traditional and modern in tragedy, as it might be a clash of generations; and they are part of a further antithesis between traditional and modern morality, a clash of ideals. It is no accident that in the *Daitales* 'Banqueters' of 427 B.C., Aristophanes' first production, the Good Son has been reared on Homer and the Bad Son on rhetoric, or that Phidippides in the *Clouds* gives his father such grief by condemning Simonides and Aeschylus, and reciting a speech of Euripides about incest between brother and sister (1371).[2] The doctrine, to put it in Aeschylus' words from the *Frogs* (1054f.) is that 'little children have a schoolmaster to teach them; but the youth have the poets'. The idea that literature is to do with education is one that still causes deeply engaged argument; and it may well be that the *Frogs* was a force in its first formulation and eventual diffusion.[3]

If we ask what part the personalities of the two debating poets, Aeschylus and Euripides, have to play in this picture, it will be as well to remember that Aeschylus had been dead for more than 50 years, some years before Aristophanes was born, and neither the comic poet nor the vast majority of the audience could possibly have had any personal memory of him. Euripides could have been (though we have no reason to suppose he was) a familiar Athenian figure with personal idiosyncrasies recognizable to many; but even so, unless any feature could in some way be related to aspects of his dramatic technique, it could hardly be helpful to the overall comic effect and might even prove distracting. The scene in *Acharnians* (407ff.) of Euripides composing at home with his feet up, surrounded by the costumes of past productions, is one that at first sight might look like portraiture; but the portrait is very much more of the type of intellectual poet than of an individual; it is closely related to the purposes of the context and has close kin in the portrait of Agathon in *Thesmophoriazusae* (95ff.) and in a long series of works of art with portraits of poets composing.[4] If we can rely on the independence of the tradition that Agathon was a handsome man, then the scene in *Thesmophoriazusae* does exploit a personal characteristic in the course of a satirical portrait of the writer's poetry. The idea, interesting

---

[1] Rau (1967) 125ff.; cf. Barlow (1971) 44f.
[2] *Daitales* 198ff. K, esp. 198, 222 (= frs. 1, 28 Cassio (1977)); note also *Clouds* 964ff. on musical education old and new.
[3] Snell (1953) 113–35.   [4] Handley (1973) 106.

as part of the early history of the concept of mimesis, is that the beautiful write beautifully, that it is logical to dress up as a woman to write about women, and so on. But essentially the portrait is of the poetry, not of the person.[1]

The plain man's view of the intellectual is, as we have seen, a prominent ingredient in comedy's portraits of the literary scene. So it is, as would naturally be expected, when we come to philosophers and the comedy of ideas. The line is led by *Clouds*, with Socrates as a character; but Aristophanes was not alone in this genre: there are immediately to hand some interesting parallels with plays by contemporaries from which we may select. In *Clouds* (95ff.) the audience's first intimation of the topics which are discussed in Socrates' Reflectory is the idea that the cosmos can be understood in terms of a stove; this is noted by a commentator as having been used already by Cratinus in ridiculing the natural philosophy of Hippon of Samos.[2] Then in the *Konnos* of Ameipsias, the play that came second over *Clouds* in 423, Socrates is referred to as hungry and lacking a cloak, in a way which recalls the lines in the *Clouds* about 'the rogues, the pale shoeless men of the company of the miserable Socrates and Chairephon' (102ff.). Callias, and the sophists whose company he kept, were the target of satire in Eupolis' *Kolakes*, placed first over *Peace* in 421 (the setting of the house of Callias was used again by Plato in his *Protagoras*); finally, there is the famous quotation from an unidentified play by Eupolis, which goes: 'I hate Socrates too, the beggar, the idle talker, who has thought out everything else, but how to get food to eat is something he's neglected' (352 K: compare *Clouds* 175–9).

Forewarned as we are by now of the nature of comic portraiture and of the existence of a flourishing style of satire against the philosophers in fifth-century comedy, we need not be surprised either that the initial presentation of Socrates in the *Clouds* is of an old man talking airy nonsense while suspended in the air (218ff.), or that Plato in the *Apology* makes Socrates recall the incident and the part it played in prejudicing people against him (19c, 18b).[3] The basis of the joke is to be found in comedy's constant tendency to take metaphors literally and to translate abstract or intellectually recondite notions into concrete or familiar ones.[4] Socrates, in order to think about things above the mundane level (*meteora*), is literally *meteoros* or 'elevated' himself. But at the same time, the word *meteoros* has a range of meaning which will extend to suggest a variety of things including astronomical interests (Socrates claims to be 'thinking about the sun', 225) and supernormal brainpower (Socrates, as if god speaking to

---

[1] Cf. Bruns (1896) 156ff.; admittedly the joke is funnier because of Agathon's known effeminacy.
[2] Cratinus, *Panoptai* 155 K; DK 38 A 2.
[3] See above, pp. 375f., 381.
[4] This aspect of comic writing is well explored by Newiger (1957); cf. Handley (1959).

mortal, calls his visitor 'creature of a day'); or again, to be *meteoros* is to be in a state of excitement – no longer to have one's feet on the ground – of a kind which the plain man may find insubstantial and vaguely disreputable.[1] It is perhaps in the combination of a direct visual appeal with this periphery of verbal suggestiveness that the power of this comic image lies. But there is more to it than that. When Socrates claims to be mingling his thought with the air which is its like, and goes on to develop the point in quasi-scientific terms, he is parading a philosophical equation between mind or thought and air which was formulated by Diogenes of Apollonia.[2] The Socrates of the *Apology* (loc. cit.) explicitly denies all knowledge of such matters; yet it is possible to suppose that, as with other subjects in which he disclaimed expertise, the historical Socrates would have been willing to argue with the professed experts.

The search for a historical Socrates has been pursued with vigour from the philosophical as well as from the literary viewpoint. Though the fortunes of the Socrates of the *Clouds* have fluctuated in the debate, an approach from the side of comic portraiture makes one doubt, as with the poets of the *Frogs*, whether there is much of the personal and idiosyncratic that survives critical scrutiny, and whether in any case it could have had a primary comic function.[3] If the portraits of Aeschylus and Euripides are in essence portraits derived from a concept of their poetry, that of Socrates is in immediate contrast in having no body of writing on which it could be based. It has been claimed on the one hand that the emphasis on memory and endurance, and the technique of arguing with a pupil are Socratic features of the Socrates of the *Clouds*, but it can still be asked whether they were specifically so; and the figure who is head of a school of unwashed poverty-stricken idlers and teaches disreputable rhetoric is something which, on any reasonable account, is decidedly *un*-Socratic.[4] The verbal portrait of Socrates striding through the streets with an air of superiority to his surroundings does seem, from its recollection by Plato, to be an authentic detail (362; see above, pp. 375f.); but the supposed references to 'midwifery' (especially 137) are both of debatable allusive effect in the *Clouds* and open to question as a Platonic rather than a historical element in the Socratic tradition.[5] Aristophanes, it seems, is giving a portrait not from life, but from the popular image of an educator, which he chooses to hang on to Socrates; it is the worse as biography, but not necessarily the worse as comedy, for that.

[1] See LSJ, s.v. μετέωρος, not forgetting compounds and derivatives; on this group of ideas in *Clouds* and *Birds* especially, see Gelzer (1956) esp. 79ff.

[2] See Dover (1968a) on 230–3 for references and discussion.

[3] Basic to this approach (though I do not follow it wholly) is the discussion in Bruns (1896) 181–200 and 201–424 *passim*.

[4] See Schmid (1948) and Philippson (1932), together with the more sceptical view of Dover (1968a) xxxii–lvii.

[5] Burnyeat (1977).

By his own account, Aristophanes was pleased with himself when he had written the *Clouds* (521–4). *Acharnians* and *Knights*, in the two previous years, had won first prizes; but this time, notoriously, the result was a third. He made a revised version, which is the version we have. Though we are not clear about the circumstances or (in detail) the extent of the revision, he must have felt – and rightly, as events have proved – that it was a play with a statement to make, a play worth an author's second thoughts. One of the new features was the debate between the two personified Arguments, whether we call them the Worse Cause and the Better, or Wrong and Right, or whatever else (889ff.).

The conflict between generations which has been present as a theme from the first is now elaborated and developed in the form of a conflict of educational ideals; and there is a resemblance in type, as well as in structure, to the debate between the two poets in *Frogs*. Right describes the traditional way of education, painting a picture of decorously-behaved boys at music school and gymnasium learning what their fathers learnt and acquiring a certain gentlemanly athleticism. Wrong skirmishes with him in argument, then gives in his turn a prospectus for the new system, in which the technique of effective argument is supreme: once learn to talk your way out of a situation, and then you can 'indulge your nature, laugh and play, and think that nothing's shameful' (1078). Right defects: unable to beat the opposition, he joins it. From all this, Socrates is absent: 'Your son', he says, 'will learn for himself from the pair of them, and I shall not be there' (886f.). If we ask where Aristophanes' own sympathies lay, whether on these educational issues or on others, the normal (and probably basically correct) answer is that he was conservative, with a strong dash of wishful-thinking idealism about the past. But there are reservations to make. The obvious contrast with what one dislikes in the present is either a recollection of the past, however rose-tinted, or a dream of the future, however fantastic. Comic dramatists, as we have seen, naturally tend in these directions; and they know well what appeal the Good Old Days can have to an audience in a holiday mood. Thus there needs to be room to wonder how far Aristophanes, or any other writer of satirical comedy, is personally engaged in the attitudes which are recurrent in the genre. Secondly, in portraying a clash of ideals, no matter where his own sympathies lay, Aristophanes is much too good a writer to let the contest be too one-sided. In *Clouds*, Right's personality is not wholly sympathetic from the start: the aggressive old man who surrenders in the end to the educational – and sexual – ethics of his opponent's world has already shown a marked weakness for the physical attractions of the young boys whose up-bringing he idealizes; Wrong is a rogue, but at times we all admire the dash and cleverness that brings a rogue his success; and so, probably, we are intended to do here. But even so, the balance of appeal need not all be put down to dramatic contrivance. A man of vivid imagination who lived through the political and intellectual revolutions of the age of Aristophanes must have felt his own opinions constantly put under test and stress. It would not be surprising if, as many have with the technological advances of the twentieth century, he admitted the excitements of the new advances of his contemporaries while deploring the accompanying decay of the inherited standards of behaviour and belief. The basic impulse to satirical writing is after all, one suspects, that of a divided mind.

9. THE SOCIAL SCENE

The latter part of Aristophanes' *Wasps* is the occasion of an interesting social gathering. Old Philocleon, the play's hero, has at last been turned, by a trick, away from the passion for jury-service which has obsessed him. He is now to be re-educated. He is given smarter clothes and new shoes, and told how to behave himself in polite company. In the event, he turns out to be a grown-up version of everyone's horror-child. Eventually, he leaves his party, which we have had described to us, and appears as a tipsy reveller on his way home with a girl-friend by torchlight (1326ff.): 'And if you're not naughty, Piglet', he says, 'I'll set you free and make you my mistress when my son's dead.' He goes on to explain that he has no money of his own yet; his son is grumpy and mean, and afraid of his coming to ruin – 'for I'm the only father he's got' (1359). There is a cluster of motifs here that interest us.

The tradition that comedy ends with a revel is likely to be a very ancient one, going back remotely beyond any of our historical documentation.[1] When the revelling of a proto-comic chorus transformed itself to represent a celebration held by men or gods, a wide variety of comic possibilities must have been opened up. Food and feasting lend themselves readily to euphoric description; then, if the behaviour of the revellers is also portrayed in words or action, the way is open to a kind of social criticism. Historically speaking, we can claim that the description of Philocleon's behaviour at the party is in a line of descent from the description of the gluttonous Heracles in Epicharmus.[2] But the reflection of the fashionable world of fifth-century Athens gives another dimension, and raises questions about the qualities of Attic comedy as a mirror of the social scene. Is Aristophanes' representation of everyday life (for example, the language people spoke in conversation) in any sense truer than what we have seen of his treatment of some of the issues and personalities from the public world of contemporary politics or literature? To look at the scene yet again, does the comic exchange of roles between father and son ('for I'm the only father he's got') imply that fathers with young sons in love, so

[1] See, e.g., *DTC* 132ff., 301ff.; Ghiron-Bistagne (1976) 207ff.
[2] 21 Kai, 8 Ol: see above, p. 369, and also p. 365 with n. 5 and p. 366 with n. 1.

familiar from fourth-century comedy, were already familiar enough as stage figures for Aristophanes to raise an easy laugh from his audience by standing the convention on its head?[1] If so, is there more background to the Comedy of Manners in fifth-century comedy than one would happily suppose from the general trend of the surviving plays themselves?

One lost play which has a special interest in the context of these questions is the *Korianno* of Pherecrates, Aristophanes' older contemporary, whose *Agrioi* 'Savages' of 420 B.C. has already been noted as one of the fifth-century examples of the misanthrope theme in comedy.[2] *Korianno* takes its title from a woman's name, and we know that she was a woman with lovers, for the play is included by Athenaeus (13.567c) among examples of comedies with the names or nicknames of hetaerae as titles. As in the *Wasps*, comedy is created from the generation gap between father and son, but this time, instead of undergoing a transposition of roles, they seem to be rivals: 'Oh, no: for me to be in love is natural; you're past it ... you're an old man and you're crazy' (frs. 71–2); 'Lord Zeus, do you hear what this wicked son of mine says about me?' (fr. 73). There are also some fragments from a scene with women talking together, waited on by the young daughter of one of them. Fr. 70 reads as follows: 'Undrinkable, Glyke.' 'Mixed you a watery one, did she?' 'All water, I'd say.' 'What *have* you done? How did you mix it, blast you?' 'Two water, Mummy.' 'And wine?' 'Four.' 'Get to Hell: it's the frogs you should be serving.' It is a reasonable, though unverified, guess that Korianno is both the thirsty guest and the object of the rivalry in love.

With the hindsight given by our knowledge of later comedy, we can see what a bright future there was for plays with a love-interest and an ambience of family relationships. The genre-painting (if we may so call it) of the women's drinking-session at once calls to mind the famous opening scene of Menander's *Synaristosai* 'The hen party', adapted by Plautus in his *Cistellaria*.[3] Fathers and sons as rivals in love-affairs also appear in plays of the fourth century that were to become classics, for example in Diphilus, *Kleroumenoi* 'Taking the lot', which we know from Plautus' version in *Casina*;[4] Act III of Menander's *Samia* (206–420) develops to a high emotional peak the situation in which a man thinks that his mistress and his adopted son have betrayed him together and produced a child. It is important here not to outrun our evidence. Comparable extracts from the beginning of *Clouds* (assuming we had them as fragments) could be very temptingly disposed against Terence's *Adelphoe* to suggest that *Clouds* is much more concerned with the internal relationships

[1] Wehrli (1948) 24.
[2] See above, p. 383.
[3] See on this Charitonidis–Kahil–Ginouvès (1970) 41ff.; Oeri (1948) 61, 82ff., 86; and cf. below, p. 397 n. 1.
[4] Wehrli (1948) 56ff. (though 57 n. 2 dismisses *Casina* from its natural company).

of Strepsiades' family than is the case. Moreover, to remind us that *Korianno* is a fifth-century play, and that Pherecrates, like his contemporaries, and unlike his fourth-century successors, had a strong interest in the musical side of drama, we can quote a fragment from a parabasis which is written in the metrical unit which came to be called 'Pherecratean' after him (fr. 79): 'Audience, pay attention to a novel innovation, anapaests in syncopation.'

The problem of evaluation which these quotations present is typical of the difficulties of fragmentary texts. Yet some help with it can be sought from the direction of ancient literary theory. Aristotle, we recall (and indeed others after him) made a distinction in modes of comedy between the comedy of topical satire (that is to say, writing in the mode derived from Archilochus and the iambic poets) and the comedy of fiction (that is to say, making plots with invented characters and general, not particular, reference to the contemporary scene). We met this distinction above, in discussing Aristotle's account of the earliest comic drama (p. 363), and noted his remark that 'plot-composition came first from Sicily; of the Athenians, Crates was the first to move away from the iambic convention and write plots with subjects of general reference'. Crates, for all that Aristophanes looked up to him as one of the Old Masters, has not been kindly treated by posterity; and the few fragments and play-titles which survive do not offer a way to verify Aristotle's placing of him at the head of a literary trend.[1] The matter becomes somewhat more tangible when we are told of Pherecrates by one of the better informed treatises on comedy that he was an actor, that he set himself to follow the example of Crates, that he turned against abuse and made his reputation by introducing new subjects and being inventive in plots.[2] There is much here one could question, beginning, perhaps, with the nature and validity of the distinction there was supposed to be between satirical and fictional comedy, and ending with the notion that Pherecrates came into playwriting by way of acting, which is open to suspicion as a typical device of the ancient biographer to fill the vacuum he abhors.[3] What remains, however, after due scepticism has operated, is a set of observations by someone who knew Pherecrates' work and could link him with Crates as a poet who developed a style of comedy differentiable from that of the great triad of Cratinus, Eupolis and Aristophanes, the true heirs of Archilochus. Accordingly, though we may still not feel confident enough to speak with Gilbert Norwood of 'The School of Crates',[4] there are good reasons for taking seriously what signs we have in Aristophanes and elsewhere of the emergence of that mode of fictional comedy which was to prove dominant.

[1] Ar. *Knights* 537–40 and *Second Thesmophoriazusae* fr. 333 K.
[2] Anon. *De com.* II 32ff. Kaibel, III 29ff. Koster.
[3] The same is said of Crates (Anon. *De com.* II 28ff. Kaibel, III 26ff. Koster) and of others, sometimes perhaps rightly; yet the main point seems to be to provide a kind of theatrical lineage.
[4] Norwood (1931) ch. 4; and see Bonanno (1972).

We are concerned not simply with the quantity of the evidence, but with its quality and the circumstances in which it comes to us.

One of the pleasures of comedy that is sometimes undervalued is the pleasure of familiarity. We feel relaxed and at home with ourselves in the presence of what is recognizable from the world around us; we can then respond all the more readily when, in one of an untold number of ways, the representation transcends the reality. Even when Aristophanic comedy is at its most fantastic, it is justifiable to look for the points of contact between the fantasy and the audience's familiar experience; even when the representation seems to be at a level of unaffected realism we need to ask, if we do not wish to be deceived, what the dramatist's fictional purpose was. Since comedy commonly represents kinds of people and activities from everyday life which do not figure in more serious literature, it offers some specially interesting data for the social and economic historian; but he must be prepared to find that the comic poet's attitude to documentation does not have much in common with his own. None the less, when all is said about the distortions of comic fiction, where the portrayal of everyday life is concerned, there is a way in which the 'familiarity principle' that we have envisaged above can work to give some reassurance. The comic poet will distort reality for amusement, or to make propaganda; he will expect his audience to meet him half-way or further in matters of stage representation; and he will stretch reality in the direction of optimism, making people eat more, travel faster, be richer (and so on) than the corresponding man in the street – but the background detail must have a degree of verisimilitude which will convince audiences and not leave them puzzled or hostile. It is the Aristophanic Euripides in the *Frogs* (959) who uses a phrase which the comic poet can hardly have formed in mind without some thought of its applicability to himself: Euripides speaks of bringing familiar things (*oikeia pragmata*) on to the stage, things people knew by personal experience or from close association and on which they could successfully criticize him.

Our knowledge of classical Greek as a spoken language is a compound. We derive it from Aristophanes and the other dramatists and from prose authors, notably Plato, on occasions when they represent people talking naturally together; with the recovery of more Menander, there are even ways in which we can distinguish fifth-century idiom from fourth-century and so sharpen our knowledge of both. The resultant picture is far from perfect, not least in that the written word can never be quite like the spoken word, the composed dialogue not the same as the conversation overheard. One of the pleasures of seeing an Aristophanic comedy must have been, for contemporary audiences, that of hearing people talk as they talked themselves. Yet in fact, as anyone knows who has tried to translate any substantial amount of Aristophanes into modern English, the range of style or tone is wide, and a mood is rarely built up with consistency or sustained for long; the comedy breaks through.

At the lower end of the colloquial (or social) scale comes the broken Greek of such characters as the Triballian in the gods' embassy in *Birds* (1565–693), or the Scythian policeman in *Thesmophoriazusae* (1001ff.); vulgarisms in the speech of the politician Hyperbolus are picked on in a fragment of the *Hyperbolus* of Plato (168 K); at least a proportion of the copious vocabulary of obscenities would be likely to have been heard in the market or the wine-bar.[1] At the upper end of the scale, we might put parody of the talk of the bright young men in the perfume shop, their heads full of the language of their rhetoric teacher; and with this might go the reference in *Wasps* to the aristocratic Alcibiades' lisp.[2] People from outside Attica can be brought on speaking in dialect (it is a hard question how authentic Aristophanes' use of non-Attic dialects was): for example, the Megarian and the Boeotian in *Acharnians* (729ff., 860ff.), Lampito and the other Spartans in *Lysistrata*. A special case of Doric speech in comedy, and one with a lasting tradition, is the doctor, talking the Doric of his Sicilian medical school; there is one line surviving from such a character in a comedy by Crates, and he runs through Middle Comedy to Menander.[3] Realism is here shading into theatrical convention, and it does so in another way when at times of high emotion the language of characters is coloured with quotation, parody, and other borrowed plumage from high poetry.[4] The social portrait given by different kinds of speech easily blends with elements of social or literary satire, as can be seen from the examples given here and many others. When, in the fourth century, comedy strove for a more naturalistic effect, it tended to lose not only the bite but the variety of the age of Aristophanes.

A passage which brings together a number of the points made so far is at *Thesmophoriazusae* 279ff. It begins: 'Here now, Thratta; follow me. Oh, Thratta, look – the torchlight, and all the people coming up, and the clouds of smoke . . .' The genre is that which we have sampled in Pherecrates, the women's conversation piece: in fact a representation of someone going with her maid to the Thesmophoria. No great extent of text is needed to suggest that Aristophanes could write as much as he chose in this vein. But there is a twist to the representation, which saves it from the flatness of total familiarity. The character is in fact not a woman, but Euripides' kinsman dressed up as a

---

[1] Henderson (1975) 35ff. distinguishes 'primary obscenities' from metaphorical expressions which can be either current ('frozen wit') or literary.

[2] Bright young men: *Knights* 1375ff., cf. Radermacher (1951) XIII 1; Alcibiades, *Wasps* 44f., cf. Archippus 45 K (from Plutarch, *Alc.* 1).

[3] Crates: 41 K. Alexis, *Mandragorizomene* 142 K (from Athenaeus 14.621d, q.v.); Menander, *Aspis* 439ff. (a man pretending to be a doctor).

[4] See for instance *Knights* 1232ff. (mock-tragic recognition scene: above, p. 373 with n. 3) and *Lys.* 954–79, referred to below, p. 397.

woman, showing just how well he can carry it off; and no doubt the maid is imaginary, giving scope to the actor's talent for mime. The routine continues with an invocation of Demeter and Persephone, the offering of a cake which the maid is supposed to produce from its container; and then there is a prayer for a daughter to find a rich, stupid husband and for a son to grow up sensible – but they are referred to not as son and daughter, but in terms of their sexual organs. The kinsman is not, after all, quite the perfect middle-class housewife.

It has been said that Aristophanes sometimes cares more to have a remark made than who makes it. But the comic effect on such occasions is not simply that of the unexpected: the breaking of the image which was being built up coincides with the breaking of the normal social ban against verbal explicitness in matters of sex; and the appeal is suddenly not to our sense of realism but to our sense of fantasy, as Aristophanes lets the character say what the audience will enjoy hearing such a person say (like the stage bishop being driven to swear).

Women have major parts in both *Lysistrata* and *Thesmophoriazusae*; and there many times over, and on a much larger scale, we can examine the compounding of realistic and comic elements in the way that they and the social life around them are portrayed. They are not, of course, any more than Euripides' kinsman, the true image of the middle-class housewives they purport to be. Apart from the consideration that they are women as seen and acted by men, one of the strong features of their interest for dramatic purposes is that they are women taking on male roles. This is true whether we see them assembling at the Thesmophoria (because their ceremony is a transposition of a male one, and they make speeches like orators against Euripides) or gathering together and trying to force their husbands to political action – the making of peace – by an international 'Ban Sex' movement. But the very fact that women are so prominent in these plays, as opposed to the earlier ones, means that some kinds of relationships are explored in ways which there would have been no occasion to do with a differently oriented plot. We can take as an instance *Lysistrata* 870–979: Myrrhine has joined the Movement, and left Cinesias: 'What's wrong with you? No thought for the child, not fed or bathed for five days?' '*I* think of him, but he's got a feckless father ...' (88off.). 'You don't care that the hens have gone off with your spinning?' 'Good God, no' (896f.). 'But won't you come and – well – lie down with me just now?' 'No way – though I won't say I don't love you.' 'You do? Then why not, pet?' 'In front of the baby? – you must be joking' (904ff.). With these preliminaries Myrrhine leads Cinesias through a routine of teasing and partly undressing and breaking off to get cushions, perfume and the like; this appeals, of course, to the audience's sexual fantasies; but there is no extravagance in the style, which remains basically familiar and colloquial. Only when she finally breaks off and frustrates him is there a change, when Aristophanes moves to the level of mock-heroic, and has Cinesias complain about the agonies of his tension in dialogue with the chorus in a parody of tragic lament (954–79). We can class this episode as social comedy because, for all its other qualities, it is a depiction of a kind of personal relationship which is universal; it rests not on its comic effects alone, not on any satire of individuals, but on the author's observation of human nature in the world about him.

If it is hard to draw a clear picture of a comic poet's attitude to political events or any of the other affairs of the public world, it is perhaps harder still to pin down personal feelings in relation to the social scene. Often enough, for instance in his constant satire against homosexuals, or his propagation of the old comic theme that women are alcoholics, Aristophanes simply seems to be echoing or writing large what the man in the street holds as his own view or as an inherited prejudice.[1] Yet there are moments of subtler and keener perception. We have noticed already how, in *Lysistrata*, the war is portrayed from a woman's point of view, not least with a good verbal sketch of the wife who is anxious for news and is told to shut up (above, p. 377). A similar detail at the opening of *Acharnians* highlights the unhappiness of the country-man condemned to a wartime life within the city walls, when he has to buy everyday necessities like charcoal, oil and vinegar from street traders rather than enjoy his own produce at home (33ff.; above, p. 377). In *Peace*, when peace comes, the changes it can bring to people's circumstances are shown in two vivid instances: that of the sickle-maker and the dealer in earthenware jars, whose goods have leapt in price, and that of the arms-merchants, whose gear is a drug on the market (1197ff.). Some insight into the personal implications of a misfortune appears from the case of the old man in court, who is defeated by a smart young opponent and achieves a retort which has its elements of pathos as well as of rhetoric: 'I leave the court fined by the amount I'd saved for a shroud' (*Ach.* 691). Some of the realities of dealing with old people show through the scene in *Wasps* in which Philocleon is cosseted into agreeing to hold a trial in his own home, and, among other things, thoughtfully provided with a chamber-pot hung up on a peg (807ff.). These, and many passages like them, offer flashes of insight into people's social and economic affairs rather than studied portraiture. A passage where the portrait is some-what more sustained is the self-description by the chorus of flatterers in Eupolis' *Kolakes*, the play which, as we have noted (p. 388), competed successfully with the *Peace* in 421 B.C.: fr. 159 reads (in part) as follows:

---

[1] Homosexuals: see, e.g., the list of 42 people attacked by name for homosexuality in comedy given by Henderson (1975) 213ff. Women and wine: e.g. *Lys.* 194ff., *Thes.* 630ff., 690ff.; more passages in Oeri (1948).

'I have these two outfits of outer clothes, very elegant, and I put on one or the other and take a spin to the market. And then, when I see some simple-minded type with money, I'm all over him. If he has something to say, I praise it strongly, and show amazement, and pretend to be delighted – and then off we go to dinner, to eat someone else's bread, and to keep joking, on the spot, or it's "out". . . .'

The similar character in Epicharmus' *Hope or Wealth*, as we have noted, tells the same sort of story; and both the social type and the kind of portraiture have a developing future in later comedy.[1]

In its sharpness of description, whether hostile or sympathetic, and in its strong vein of interest in the life (and to some extent the relationships) of ordinary people, fifth-century comedy had two growth points of enormous potential. With the familiarity brought by centuries of later literary history, it is easy to underrate their importance. How it was that this side of comedy, rather than any of the others, was to prove to be so fruitful, is clearly a key question to be asked in any study of the comedy of the fourth century.

10. FROM ARISTOPHANES TO MENANDER

The gap in time between Aristophanes' *Plutus* and Menander's *Dyskolos* is just over seventy years, or two rather stretched generations. Of the comedy of that period, Gilbert Norwood writes:

Between the excitingly varied landscape of Old Comedy and the city of Menander stretches a desert: therein the sedulous topographer may remark two respectable eminences, and perhaps a low ridge in the middle distance, or a few nullahs, and the wayfarer will greet with delight one or two oases with a singing bird or so; but the ever-present foreground of his journey is sand, tiresome, barren and trickling. (Norwood (1931) 38)

Yet this is the period in which Attic comedy really became international. The popularity of its plays among the Doric-speaking Greeks of the west is in evidence from south Italian vase-paintings with comic scenes dating from the first quarter of the fourth century onwards; Attic terracotta statuettes and their replicas occur in places as far apart as Ampurias near Barcelona, Olynthos, Lindos and southern Russia.[2] It was in this period that actors came increasingly into prominence as famous personalities,[3] that Aristotle delivered in Athens the lectures represented by our surviving *Poetics*, and much theatrical

---

[1] See p. 369 above, and Handley (1965a) on 57ff.

[2] South Italian vases (the so-called 'Phlyax vases') are catalogued by Trendall (1967) and listed in appropriate places by Webster–Green (1978). Terracottas: e.g. the famous set of characters from a mythological comedy in the Metropolitan Museum, New York, with numerous far-flung replicas: Webster–Green (1978) no. AT 9–23.

[3] Ghiron-Bistagne (1976) 154ff., *DFA* 279ff.; there is firm evidence for organized guilds from the early third century onwards, though they may have been known by their professional name 'Artists of Dionysus' for half a century before that (Dem. 19.192; Arist. *Rhet.* 1405a23 et al.).

rebuilding and reorganization took place, not least in Athens under the financial administration of Lycurgus.[1] It is also clear that the public had its idols, some of whom wrote very prolifically; and that success at Athens was sought for, and won, by Greeks from quite different quarters of the world, some of whom eventually gained citizenship. Anaxandrides is an example from the first generation of fourth-century comic poets. An East Greek, by report, from Rhodes or Colophon, he scored brilliantly with first prizes at the Dionysia in successive years, 376 and 375, and won a first at the Lenaea at about the same time; he ended with ten firsts in all, and we have a record of him still producing (and winning a fourth prize) in 349. Antiphanes, another great name, was a close contemporary, another non-citizen (we are told that Demosthenes was responsible for making him one), and apparently another East Greek, with three places laying claim to be his home town. Alexis is said to have come from the west, from the Athenian colony of Thurii on the gulf of Taranto; he was a copious writer who lived to a great age; some ancient critics brought him into a specially close relationship with Menander, whose life he in fact overlapped at both ends. The fourth-century Athenian theatre freely drew in talent and freely exported plays, which were certainly written in some number: 617 were catalogued for the period called Middle Comedy – our period – according to the so-called Anonymus, *De comoedia*; and Athenaeus' figure, possibly differently based, is 'over 800'.[2] How is it that from all this activity the impression made on a modern scholar should be that of sand, 'tiresome, barren and trickling'? And can we, without prejudice to our answer, see anything of the shape of things to come in the last plays of Aristophanes?

The most tangible difference between the earlier plays and *Ecclesiazusae* and *Plutus* is the diminution of the role of the chorus. This we noted before in discussing structural patterns (pp. 358ff.). The parabasis is now gone, and the formally patterned agon reduced to half of itself or less than half; twice in the *Ecclesiazusae* and several times in the *Plutus* at places where a choral performance might have been expected the manuscripts have the heading XOPOY (as one might write CHORUS in English), a notation familiar from fragmentary texts of post-classical tragedy as well as from Menander. Though there is still room for discussion about the textual history and significance of this notation (we cannot claim to be certain in either play how many times the chorus performed or what it did),[3] the main points for our purpose are sufficiently clear. The element of poetry and song is diminished: even if, at all likely points, the chorus sang and danced, the effect must still have been weaker than what

---

[1] Pickard-Cambridge (1946) 134ff.
[2] Anon. *De com.* II 52ff. Kaibel, III 45ff. Koster; Athenaeus 8.336d.
[3] See Hunter (1979).

happens in (say) *Frogs*, since their lyrics were not specially composed for the play. At the same time, with the dramatist's mind no longer so clearly focused on his alternating patterns of scene or speech and lyric, the action will almost inevitably have fallen into sections or stages demarcated by the principal choral performances. These sections will then have tended to take on a compositional status akin to what one would recognize by the term 'act'; and that process is fully realized in Menander.[1] To take an illustration: the action of *Plutus* from 802 onwards, after a XOPOY, consists of a series of illustrations of the effects of the miraculous cure by which Wealth has had his sight restored. First Carion narrates the transformation within the house – the bin full of good barley, the jars full of wine and the well of olive oil, and so on. Then there arrives the Just Man, who had been scorned by the friends he had helped, but now that Wealth is no longer blind, he brings as a thank-offering the cloak in which he had shivered for thirteen years. They are joined by an Informer, who is pushed off in the old cloak to be a bath attendant, while the Just Man is taken in to meet Wealth in person. XOPOY again (958). The parallelism is obvious and traditional, but instead of being grouped into a pattern by interlacing choral odes (like the scenes with the Farmer and the Best Man in *Acharnians* 1000ff.), the three elements come together to form a kind of unit.

We should follow the fortunes of the chorus and of lyric in comedy somewhat further. After *Plutus*, Aristophanes wrote two more plays, very likely his last, which were produced by his son Araros, namely *Kokalos* and *Aiolosikon*; *Aiolosikon*, we are told, lacked parabasis and choral lyric. In this respect, and in being a mythological comedy without personal attacks, *Aiolosikon* is presented by our source as a type-example of Middle Comedy; while in *Kokalos* (it is said) 'he introduces rape and recognition and all the other things in which Menander followed him'.[2] When Cratinus' *Odysses* 'Odysseus and Co.' is mentioned together with *Aiolosikon* it appears to be thought of by our source not simply as a mythological play, but as one lacking abuse, parabasis and lyrics as well.[3] This could be so. If so, it is a useful reminder that Old Comedy was not necessarily as regular in development as simple extrapolation from Aristophanes would make it; but there remains the possibility that our information has been garbled in the course of passing from one ancient scholar to another, or that behind it all lies a later adaptation of Cratinus' original fifth-century composition. The one substantial piece of choral performance in the *Plutus* is the parodos (253ff.), in which the chorus of old farmers enters in trochaic tetrameters (not lyrics) in dialogue with Carion. They sing a parody of a

[1] This topic, including the definition of 'act', has been much discussed: see, e.g., *Entretiens Hardt* (1970) 12ff. and Blanchard (1970).
[2] Platonius, *De com.* I 1.24f., 29ff. Kaibel, 1.22ff., 27ff. Koster; the quotation is from *Vit. Ar.* XI 69ff. Dindorf–Dübner, XXVIII 54ff. Koster.
[3] Platonius, quoted n. 2 above.

dithyramb by Philoxenus, the *Cyclops*; this is in simple iambic stanzas (290ff.). They then return to their own role with a song indicated in the text by XOPOY.[1] The Philoxenus parody, though preserved as part of the text, is in fact completely inorganic to it, and could perfectly well have been performed in similar circumstances in any other play. But the notion that a chorus might have a special identity, or do a special performance at least on its first appearance, is one that persists. Four fragments of a marble relief in Athens dated to the third quarter of the fourth century show a dancing chorus of men in soldiers' caps with staffs;[2] from the same period, Eubulus' *Stephanopolides* 'Garland sellers' had, as its title suggests, a characterized female chorus which introduced itself in a lyric of which fragments survive (104–5 K). These instances, among others, allow us to trace a little of the story until it resumes in Menander, with a chorus announced on its arrival, either in the general character of tipsy revellers (as in *Perikeiromene*, for instance) or, on occasion, with a special function or description to suit the play (as in *Dyskolos*).[3]

Menander offers no evidence for specially written choral song. There is a little evidence for actors' lyric, which could still occur in special situations (a song at a temple, recalling Euripides' *Ion*; a song and dance in honour of the Great Mother);[4] recitative, in the sense of lines delivered to a musical accompaniment, is well illustrated in the lively scene of the ragging of Knemon at the end of the *Dyskolos*, which takes on a kind of poetic colour as it rises to the description of the party which the old misanthrope has refused to attend (see below, p. 423). But the basic mode of Menandrean comedy is the speech of everyday human relationships, and his basic metre correspondingly is that which Aristotle (*Poetics* 1449a24) thought of as closest to speech, namely the iambic trimeter.

If, then, the decline of the chorus and of lyric in general is not quite so sharp and simple as a crude contrast between early and late Aristophanes would make it, it is still to be seen as a major change in comedy, part of a trend of development well marked in *Ecclesiazusae* and *Plutus* which has consequences for the shape and structure of plays as well as for the nature of their appeal to audiences. The diminishing role of the lyrical and poetic elements must to some extent account for the impression of flatness of style given by the fourth-century fragments. These contributions towards the questions we set out to answer will be augmented as other general trends in fourth-century comedy are

---

[1] Cf. Handley (1953) 59 with n. 4.

[2] Webster–Green (1978), no. AS3 with pl. ix; cf. also AS4.

[3] 'Paean-singers', according to the papyrus, 'Pan-worshippers' by the generally accepted correction: see Handley (1965a) on 230–2.

[4] *Leukadia*, fr. 258 Kö; schol. *ad* Eur. *Andr.* 103, cf. Handley (1969) 96 and Gomme–Sandbach (1973) 400ff.

surveyed. But there remains, before we leave the present set of topics, a scene which merits mention here both for its own sake and as an indication of what could have happened but apparently did not.

It is part of the reversal of the normal order of things in *Ecclesiazusae* that sexual relationships shall be free, but on condition that the oldest and ugliest are satisfied first (611–34). Aristophanes illustrates this situation by constructing a comic routine around a young man, a girl, and a fearsome old hag, soon to be displaced by two even more hideous competitors (877ff.). In this way he creates an opportunity to introduce pairs of songs in which his actors can take turns to answer each other ('There's something pleasant and comic about this, even if the audience don't enjoy it', 888–9). The high point, so far as we are concerned here, is the duet of boy and girl – she, in pain and longing, begs her lover to come to her, while he, again in pain and longing, stands at the door and begs her to come down and open up. Perhaps, as has been suggested, Aristophanes is drawing on the idiom of contemporary popular song; but what the incident recalls, rather than anything else in Greek comedy, is the serenade sequence in Plautus, *Curculio* (96ff., esp. 147–57). The Aristophanic scene has, among its other elements, some of the basic ingredients of romantic comedy and of musical comedy in a much more modern sense than Aristophanes would have recognized; and it is perhaps even more significant from the historical point of view as an indication of potential than as an achievement. The convergence of theme and mode of performance with Plautus is interesting chiefly to remind us of what did in fact not (so far as we know) develop in fourth-century Greece. For although music and poetry were still admitted to comedy, they never seem to have regained the status they once enjoyed in Aristophanes, still less to have taken the interesting route which led to the musical comedy of Plautus.

Myth, we have seen, is a very primitive element in comedy; mythical scenes and characters, often based on a treatment in some more elevated form of literature, continued from Epicharmus onwards to lend themselves to many different comic purposes, including those of political comedy; myth, especially myth as found in tragedy, could provide patterns of character and action which transmuted themselves into part of the comic poet's own stock-in-trade. Though much is uncertain about the chronology and content of many plays, some picture of development can be formed from the results of an investigation by Webster.[1] According to this, in the last twenty years of the fifth century just under half of the dated plays are mythological; for the years 400–350 the fraction is between a half and a third, as opposed to only one tenth of the titles assignable to 350–320. 'Mythological' can, of course, apply to several different

---

[1] Webster (1952); see also Webster (1970*b*) 85, 259ff.

kinds of play. There is a sense in which the *Plutus* is a mythological comedy, having the mythical figures of Wealth and Poverty as characters; but the kind of play in which we are interested here is one which takes a whole fabric of plot and characters from myth, and is comic by virtue of exploiting the clash and contrast between the values and incidents of the 'parent' story and their counterparts in the world of men like ourselves or worse than ourselves. Euripides' lost *Antiope* presented, through the contrast between Antiope's sons, a conflict of ideals between the cultured intellectual and the practical man (see p. 320). In the *Antiope* of Eubulus there is a comic Boeotian speaking his own dialect (like the Boeotian of Aristophanes' *Acharnians*); and in a fragment from a messenger speech we hear that the ever-hungry Zethus is to be settled in the 'sacred plain of Thebes' (for the bread is better there), while the more etherial Amphion is sent to hungry Athens, where men drink the breezes and live on hopes. Eubulus' *Bellerophon* again recalls Euripides, it seems: in our one fragment, the hero calls for someone to steady him as his flying horse Pegasus rises; and once more we can compare Aristophanes, in his parody of Euripides' play in the *Peace*, where Trygaeus has a shaky start flying to Heaven on his dung-beetle (82ff.).[1] Examples can be multiplied;[2] but one story which is specially worth mention is that of Auge, for it involves the motifs of rape and recognition which were remarked on by ancient scholars as basic ingredients of the New Comedy of Menander and his contemporaries, and were notably present in Aristophanes, two of whose last plays, as we have seen, were taken as type-examples of what was to come in the age after him.[3] Euripides' play *Auge* is slightingly referred to in the *Frogs* (1080) for the sake of its heroine, who gave birth to her son by Heracles in the temple of which she was priestess. Comic plays entitled *Auge* are known from Philyllius and Eubulus. Philyllius' play could well have been written in the closing years of the fifth century, when *Auge* was new (it was one of Euripides' latest productions); and in that period, it seems, there originates a group of terracotta statuettes which include Heracles, a woman veiling her face in shame, an old nurse with a baby and others eminently suitable to have been souvenirs of the cast of such a comedy.[4] The continuing popularity of the terracotta types and the production of another comic *Auge* by Eubulus give some indication of the appeal this kind of story had. The fragments on food and feasting which we have in quotations by Athenaeus do something to show how the comic poets brought the story down to earth, and they remind us of Heracles' traditional comic role as a glutton; the food-and-drink motif has its visual counter-

---

[1] See also the texts quoted in *P.Oxy.* 2742, *CGFP* no. *74.
[2] See, e.g., Webster (1970*b*) 16ff., 82ff.
[3] See above, p. 400 with n. 2.
[4] Terracottas: see above, p. 398 n. 2.

part among the statuettes in the figures of a man carrying a shopping basket and a man carrying a jar.[1]

One can see how stories like that of Auge may have admitted comic innovations and distortions in the traditional manner; single lines from the tragedians could also still be picked up and twisted to good effect. Anaxandrides, it can be said, is being Aristophanic when he takes a famous line from the *Auge* of Euripides and parodies it to make a political witticism: 'Nature willed it: she cares naught for laws' (Eur. fr. 920 *TGF*) becomes 'The city willed it: she cares naught for laws' (Anax. fr. 67 K). But such stories had other qualities too, much less tangible from our evidence. They had been (and surely still could be) so shaped as to yield a satisfactory dramatic pattern, an organic whole; they could be (as they were by Euripides) so treated as to throw into question the divine and human motivation behind the plot, even if the comic poet's means and purposes were different; and they could be so handled as to involve the audience in sympathy with the characters and their attitudes from time to time, to promote a certain feeling of identification, to evoke the smile and not the laugh. In spite of the strong Roman colour of Plautus' writing, the *Amphitruo* probably still gives a good idea of the blend of different effects in comedies of this kind. We begin with the basic and farcical confusions of mistaken identity, when Zeus/Jupiter and Hermes/Mercury masquerade as Amphitruo and his servant, so that the king of the gods can have the pleasure of adultery with Amphitruo's queen Alcmena; we move on to the elements of human sympathy in the portrait of a woman who retains her dignity in spite of the way in which she is being deceived, and in this we can see something of the side of later Greek comedy which is other than sheer light entertainment. That is a side which Menander was to develop. But for the sake of the contrast, we can note now that when Menander recalls Euripides' line about Nature and laws, as Anaxandrides did, it is not in order to make an allusive political witticism, but to give an extra dimension to the everyday affairs of the people in his play from the situation of their mythical counterparts.[2]

It was in fact the decline in political and personal satire that gave Aristotle and other ancient critics one of the clearest contrasts they could make between the comedy of the age of Aristophanes and later comedy. But how sudden and how clear-cut was the change? For Aristotle, as we noted, the movement away from the iambic or satirical convention had already begun, as far as Athens was concerned, in the generation before Aristophanes, with Crates;[3] while on the other hand, the references to contemporary individuals and political events in

[1] Philyllius, *Auge* 3–6 K, Eubulus, *Auge* 15 K; Heracles, Ar. *Wasps* 60 (cf. above, p. 369).
[2] Men. *Epitr.* 765–7 (1123–5 Sandbach): see also below, pp. 420f.
[3] See above, p. 363 with nn. 2–3, p. 393 with nn. 1–2, and the texts referred to in p. 400 n. 2.

Ecclesiazusae, *Plutus* and later fragmentary plays of the fourth century show (to say the least) that there was no universal inhibition against such things. That is not to say that there was no tension between attackers and attacked of the kind we found when discussing political comedy in its prime. Isocrates, writing in 355 B.C., contrasts the difficulties faced by people with serious but unappealing policies to advocate (like himself) with the position of orators in the assembly, as unthinking as they are unscrupulous, and with that of comic poets in the theatre, who retain public favour while broadcasting their fellow citizens' mistakes to all Greece.[1] Isocrates was an old man at this time, turned eighty in fact, and one wonders if his mind was not on comic poets of the past, by whom he had himself been attacked, rather than on those of the immediate present.[2] Nevertheless, it is hard to divorce what he says completely from contemporary reality; and the same applies, though with different reservations, to the political theorizing of Isocrates' somewhat younger contemporary Plato, when he lays down his rigid rules in the *Laws* against personal attack in comedy or in any kind of iambic or lyric poetry (935e). From the comic poet's point of view, personal attack and political commentary were a traditional licence; and like many comic traditions, this one was preserved. For Menander, contemporary affairs are about as far in the background as the Napoleonic Wars are for Jane Austen, yet still (more than Austen) he embodies elements of social commentary in the words and actions of his characters, and still he allows himself an occasional nod in the direction of comedy's past, as in his allusions in the *Samia* and elsewhere to a notorious sponger and butt of the comic stage, Chairephon.[3]

Accordingly, with politics in comedy, as with its music and poetry, one can point to a declining trend, to a shift of interest elsewhere; and though a dramatist who ran against the trend might attract the necessary sponsorship and acceptance for an Athenian production, and might achieve success with it, we should beware of exaggerating the exceptions, particularly when we are arguing from fragments. One such exception seems to have been Timocles. There is a high incidence of personal and political references in what survives of him, and he is remarkable as a late exponent of this mode of comedy: a pro-Macedonian, who attacked, among others, Demosthenes and Hyperides, he was still writing after their deaths and during the dramatic career of Menander. The parallel with music and poetry perhaps has more to it than coincidence. The decline in quotable abuse might, one supposes, have an effect similar to that of the decline in music and poetry in making the general run of fragments of fourth-century comedy less exciting to read. But these two parallel

[1] Isocrates, *De pace* (8).14.
[2] Note for this point Aristophanes, fr. 700 K and Strattis, *Atalante* 3 K: Webster (1970*b*) 28.
[3] *Samia* 603 with other references given by Gomme–Sandbach (1973) ad loc.

phenomena have one more common feature. It is that, since Aristophanes' younger years, both music and politics had been growing increasingly more complicated, and therefore less readily exploitable in terms of popular entertainment. The musical developments which contributed to the decline of the tragic as well as of the comic chorus are those which are reflected in the *Frogs* in the contrast between traditional choral lyric in the Aeschylean manner and the modernisms of Euripides, seen at their most characteristic in virtuoso arias for actors, something quite alien to choral writing.[1] In politics it was less easy by the fourth century, and had perhaps become progressively less easy since the plays of Aristophanes' younger years, for the evils of the day to be summed up in terms of the wickednesses of a Cleon or a Hyperbolus. Both *Ecclesiazusae* and *Plutus* are political comedies in the sense that they offer a solution, albeit a typically comic one, to the problems of life in Athens; but in both the solution, and the ills it seeks to remedy, are conceived rather in social and economic terms than specifically in terms of politics: this applies almost equally to the quasi-communistic state set up by the women who take over the Assembly in *Ecclesiazusae* and to the redistribution which follows the miraculous cure of Wealth in *Plutus*.

Some impression of the political atmosphere of the 390s can be gathered from the speech which Praxagora, the heroine of the *Ecclesiazusae*, rehearses for delivery in the Assembly. She knows how to make a political speech, as she explains, because she and her husband set up house on the Pnyx Hill 'when we were refugees' (243), and so she heard the speakers there. The precise reference of some of her allusions escapes modern scholars, and it may be that even for Aristophanes' audience the overall picture was of more importance than the detail.[2]

The speech, including interruptions, runs from 171 to 240. It portrays a mood of disillusionment which seems to go beyond the comic poet's habitual attack on things as they are. There has been a succession of increasingly bad leaders ('even if a man is good one day, he's bad for ten', 177f.); but the Assembly in its turn has shown itself more moved by a man's attitude to the rate for attendance money than his true worth or worthlessness. The Athenians' judgement of politics (the argument continues) is as inconstant as their judgement of politicians: 'now take the alliance – when we were considering it, they said we'd be ruined without it; once we got it, they were furious, and the proposer instantly took flight' (193–6). Then again: 'We need ships: the poor are for, the rich and the farmers against' (197f.). The charge of fickleness comes again at 823ff., where the proposer of a new tax is said to have won a

---

[1] See above, pp. 386f.

[2] See Ussher (1973) xx–xxv for discussion and for the dating of the play to 393 B.C. and not 392 from these references.

golden reputation from his idea until (inevitably) there were second thoughts and he was vilified; the tension between rich and poor is reflected again and again in this play and the *Plutus*, not least in the scenes with the personified figure of Poverty herself (415–618).

The New Order set up by the women in *Ecclesiazusae* has some striking features in common with that of Plato in *The republic*, though the nature of their relationship (if the two are related) remains an open question. For example, both political systems envisage community of land, money and possessions, with maintenance provided by the state. Meals, women and children are all nationalized, and we may note with Murray that the objection 'How will a man know his own son?' is a problem posed and answered by both systems, and an advantage of both is the absence of lawsuits.[1]

Ecclesiazusae is traditional comedy in that its mainspring is the enactment and illustration of a fantastic solution to a contemporary problem. Such a solution can take the form of escape into a Utopian future just as well as into a place far away or an idealized past, as we remarked in discussing *Birds* (p. 380 with n. 3). Nephelokokkygia, the ideal city of the birds, is in a sense a forerunner of *Ecclesiazusae*; but this time the scene is in Athens and not in the sky, and the innovators, as in *Lysistrata*, are nothing more bizarre than housewives taking over where they think their menfolk have failed them.[2] On the other hand, as we saw above, *Ecclesiazusae* is modern like *Plutus* in its emphasis on social and economic problems rather than on specific political or personal attack. We can perhaps call it equally modern, as opposed to *Clouds*, in that its satire has moved away from verbal wit and from the cartoon-like portraiture of a comic Socrates and taken a step towards criticizing ideas in the more general terms of their content and consequences. Aristophanes, who was not backward in stressing the novelty of his ideas, does so with emphasis for *Ecclesiazusae* (577–87), but this need mean no more than that they had not had full-dress treatment in a comedy before. The difficulty of postulating a circulated version of Plato's ideas in *The republic* early enough for *Ecclesiazusae* to draw on it is matched by the lack of any clear reference to the play in Plato, who must at all events have known it. If we suppose that *The republic* and *Ecclesiazusae* are essentially independent elaborations of a common stock of ideas (perhaps we need not postulate a lost treatise by some person unknown) the central interest from our point of view is still that an early fourth-century comedy takes the theme it does and pursues it for amusement in comic terms.

[1] Murray (1933) 188. See particularly *Eccl.* 597ff. with *Rep.* 416d–e; 657, 673ff. with 464d; 610ff. with 423e, 457c–d; 635ff. with 461c–d: Ussher (1973) xv–xx.

[2] The theme of women's rule is known from other plays, and some see a forerunner of *Lys.* and *Eccl.* in Pherecrates, *Tyrannis*: Ussher (1973) xv.

COMEDY

The tradition of *Clouds* continues in fourth-century comedy after *Ecclesiazusae*, and can be recognized in references to Plato, the Academy and other philosophers and their pupils.[1] A scene which recalls the famous one of Socrates' Reflectory is narrated in a fragment of Epicrates:[2] in this, Plato conducts a seminar on the classification of living things – animals, trees and plants – in which the students have problems with a pumpkin and are patiently taken back to first principles when all have failed. The plain man's image of the intellectual is readily illustrated from some of the other references to Plato: the great man frowns in concentration, raising his eyebrows like a snail's horns; he walks up and down in thought, of course to no purpose; discussion with him is all idle talk, and he has a notion of the Good which can stand as proverbial for obscurity.[3] Pupils may be thin and wasted, like the half-dead associates of Socrates;[4] but the young or old Academician can also be thought of as an elegant, like the flatterers who waited on the great thinkers in Eupolis' philosophical comedy *Kolakes*, and he can be a smart young rhetorician, like the modern young of Aristophanes' day.[5]

The passage just cited on Plato's notion of the Good (Amphis 6 K) can be of further use to us in a more general aspect. It reads in full: 'But what good it can be that you are going to come by through her, master, is something that I understand less than I understand the Good of Plato.' 'Pay attention then', says the master. The context is the familiar one in which a man tells his slave or companion (and hence the audience) about his relationship with a woman, and meets with the incredulity, the worldly wisdom and the attempt to pass the whole thing off with a joke which are common human reactions (and hence good material for dramatists) in such situations.[6] As we have seen before, and can hardly recall too often, the status of allusions in comedy is vitally affected by their context, which in fragments is often much less easily inferred than in the present example. The element of satire against Plato in the reference to the Good is slight and good-humoured when it comes as part of a chat between slave and master, and when the emphasis of the scene is elsewhere. Two questions suggest themselves. Firstly: in considering allusions to tragedy in all their variety, we can see something of the process by which what began as satirical references stayed on and developed into part of the dramatic fabric

[1] For a survey, see Webster (1970*b*) 50–6.
[2] Epicrates 11 K, cf. Ar. *Clouds* 133ff.
[3] Amphis, *Dexidemides*, 13 K; Alexis, *Meropis* 147 K; Alexis, *Parasitos* 180 K; Amphis, *Amphikrates* 6 K – all quoted among other passages by Diogenes Laertius, *Vit. Platonis* (3).26–8; for 'idle talk', cf. Ar. *Clouds* 1485 with *Tagenistai* 490 K and Eupolis 352 K (quoted above, p. 388).
[4] Aristophon, *Plato* 8 K, with Ar. *Clouds* 103, 504, 1112; *Birds* 1553ff.
[5] Antiphanes, *Antaios* 33 K, with Eupolis, *Kolakes* 159 K (above, p. 397f.); Ephippus, *Nauagos* 14K, with Ar. *Knights* 1375ff., (above, p. 395 with n. 2).
[6] Examples are the opening scenes of Menander, *Dyskolos* and *Misoumenos* and of Plautus, *Curculio* and *Pseudolus*.

408

of comedy; to what extent (we ask) can something similar be said of satire against Plato, the Pythagoreans and other intellectuals? And secondly: how far does comedy itself respond during the fourth century to developments in thought about politics, ethics, the craft of literature and other humane subjects? To answer the first question, as our example suggests, we need to know what characters in what situations are given allusions to philosophers or express ideas with a recognizable philosophical background;[1] on one aspect of the second question something will be said later on.

But to return once more to Aristophanes; it is interesting, and perhaps genuinely indicative of a trend in the development of comedy, that *Ecclesiazusae*, in illustrating the concept of the community of all property also produces what has been pointed out as the earliest scene in comedy in which two old men are clearly contrasted. The contrast is between the man who loyally brings out his household goods and forms them for the state occasion into the order of a festive procession; and on the other hand the sceptic, who finds all reasons for hanging back, but is keen enough to go when there is to be a free state banquet: they are the forerunners of such pairs in Menandrean comedy as Demeas and Nikeratos in the *Samia*, or Demeas and Micio in the *Adelphoi* as adapted by Terence.[2]

Athenaeus, as we have remarked, read fourth-century comedies voraciously (p. 399 with n. 2). Even a rapid inspection of one of the editions of comic fragments will show what a dominant part in our knowledge of comedy between Aristophanes and Menander is played by the quotations which Athenaeus puts on the lips of the scholars whose dinner-party is the subject of his *Deipnosophistai*. The range of the diners' conversation, though wide, is by no means universal: so it comes about that we have relatively rich material for some topics which Athenaeus regarded as germane to academic party conversation, such as cooks, food in variety, wine, wine-cups and hetaerae; but (even adding in our other material) we do not have the random sample of characters, motifs and dialogue which would result if the same amount of text were recovered by papyrological discovery from small pieces of ancient copies of the plays owing their preservation to chance. The word 'fragment' can mean more than one thing. Two immediate considerations arise. On the one hand, the fact that Athenaeus has special interests in certain themes and puts together passages which display them is one more factor to take into account when questions of repetitiveness or monotony in fourth-century comedy are raised. On the other hand, we know well that Greek comic poets were aware, as popular entertainers in other ages have been, that familiarity (with just a dash of

[1] See Webster (1970*b*) 54–5 and (1950) 195 ff.
[2] *Eccl.* 728 ff.; Webster (1970*b*) 13.

something new) can be a powerful ingredient of success. With the help of Athenaeus' material we can explore some themes and their variants quite fully and attempt to mark out patterns of development which may illuminate the less well-documented areas that interest us. The figure of the *mageiros*, the professional caterer or cook, has been fully studied and can be quoted as an example.[1]

The cook, who is hired to cater for weddings and other special celebrations, is one of a group of characters who come together in plays with a love-intrigue theme. The theme itself and at least some of the character-types have fifth-century forerunners; but it is no doubt to the two generations after Aristophanes that we are to look for the basic development of what was to become, through Menander and the other writers of New Comedy in Greek and Latin, one of the most fruitful forms of fiction.

Young and old lovers and young and old hetaerae are characters we have met in earlier discussions.[2] The game of sexual pursuit can be complicated by rivalries within or across the age-groups; as helpers and confidants, there are available the household slaves, or the old dramatic type of boon companion, the parasite;[3] as hindrances, there can be stern fathers or domineering wives; the cook, the procurer and the moneylender all wait in the wings for their turn.[4]

In the formation of such fictional characters, the blend of fresh observation with literary inheritance is a fascinating one. Sometimes we may feel that the satirical portrait of a particular individual has been specially influential in forming a literary type. Needing an opponent in *Acharnians* for his hero's peace treaty with Sparta, Aristophanes brings on stage a contemporary military commander, Lamachus, in full hoplite gear with extravagantly plumed helmet; Lamachus rants and rages, but to no purpose, and he ends up with a battle and a wound for his efforts while Dicaeopolis enjoys women and wine. Here is a pattern both of a person and of a story which can be built on and transmuted. But of course, Lamachus is far from being the first soldier in literature. The Braggart Captain we all think of (taking our cue from Plautus and his *Miles gloriosus*) is not a regular officer like Lamachus, but a free-lance, a mercenary, corresponding in real life to those Greeks like Xenophon and many after him in the fourth century who sought their fortune in foreign wars, and looking back in literature to such ancestors as the wandering Orestes with his companion Pylades in Aeschylus, and perhaps as far as Archilochus.[5] One

[1] There are full studies by Giannini (1960) and Dohm (1964); see Handley (1965a) on 393 and index s.v. *cook*, and Berthiaume (1982).

[2] Above, pp. 391ff. on Ar. *Wasps*, Pherecrates, *Korianno* and other plays; p. 402 on *Ecclesiazusae* 877ff.

[3] Cf. above p. 398 with n. 1.

[4] Webster (1970b) 63–7 gives a brief survey with references.

[5] Cf. Webster (1970b) 64, 132: Archilochus 1ff. West, Aesch. *Cho.* 675 with Antiphanes, *Athamas* 16 K and the terracotta types listed by Webster–Green (1978) nos. AT 6–7.

attraction of service of this kind was the glamour of far away places and foreign despots' courts, and it is reflected in the tall story told by the soldier in Antiphanes' *Stratiotes* (202 K): 'Tell me, did you spend long in Cyprus?' 'All the time the war lasted.' 'Where, mostly?' 'In Paphos; and there was a remarkable piece of refinement to be seen there – you wouldn't have believed it.' 'What?' 'The King had pigeons to fan him at dinner, pigeons . . . .' (He wore perfume which attracted them, and had slaves scare them off and make them flap). The progress from satirical portrait to type was not, of course, necessarily regular or uniform. There are odd satirical references to contemporary soldiers (as to Lamachus) in fourth-century comedy, but satire against individuals is commoner in the case of hetaerae – perhaps not surprisingly, since they are part of the urban scene in the way that soldiers are not.[1] But the young girl with her lover in Aristophanes' *Ecclesiazusae* has her descendants in the girls who are cast as the fictional heroines of love-intrigue plots; and we hear of one in Antiphanes, *Hydria* (212 K):

> 'The man I'm talking about had a girl living next door to him, a hetaera, and he fell in love with her on sight; she was freeborn, but had no relations, no one to look after her – she was a good girl, one with a golden character, a hetaera in the true sense of "friend", when all the others spoil a good name with their bad ways.'

The typology of characters which can be built up from the fragments is complemented by representations of masks, actors and scenes in works of art, which give us much fuller evidence for fourth-century than for fifth-century comedy.[2] Having said much to bring out the continuity of comic traditions, we must also recognize that alongside their development of mythological comedy, the fourth-century dramatists were powerful innovators in the drama of everyday life, in the creation of comic fiction. Our difficulty in evaluating what they achieved is the inevitable one, that, for the lack of continuous Greek texts, we tend to think in terms of survivals from the age of Aristophanes and anticipations of Menander. There is a passage of Antiphanes which can be used to throw some light on the literary principles which comic fiction was developing, and it may help us to a conclusion.

Antiphanes' long dramatic career runs from within a year or so of the death of Aristophanes in the mid-380s until the Olympiad 334/331 B.C., ten years or more before the dramatic début of Menander in 321. Fragment 191, which is unfortunately undated, is part of a speech on the relative difficulty of composing tragedy and comedy; and it is plausibly suggested that the title of the play,

---

[1] Webster (1970*b*) 63f. See also above, p. 383, on Timon of Athens as the archetypal misanthrope.
[2] Webster–Green (1978) with supplements published at intervals in *B.I.C.S.*; cf. p. 398 n. 2 above.

Poiesis, indicates that the speech was a prologue-speech spoken by the personi-fied figure of Poetry herself. As a sign of the times, we can note in passing that a discussion of playwriting of this kind is something that a fifth-century poet would probably have handled, as Aristophanes does, by having the chorus speak for him in the parabasis.[1] Poetry (if it is Poetry) speaks for Antiphanes as follows:

> 'Tragedy is a lucky kind of writing in every way. Its plots, in the first place, are well known to the audience before a line is spoken; all the poet need do is remind them. Suppose I just say "Oedipus", they know the rest: father – Laius; mother – Jocasta; who his daughters and his sons were; what it is that he did, and what he will suffer. Or take the case of Alcmaeon... [which we here omit, partly be-cause the text is not properly elucidated]... then, when they have no more to say and their plays have completely run dry, they raise the crane (*mechane*) like a finger and the spectators are satisfied. We can't do this. Everything has to be invented: new names, what happened in the past, the present circumstances, the end and the beginning. If a Chremes or a Pheidon leaves any of this out, he gets hissed off the stage, but your Peleus and your Teucer can do that.'

In interpreting this passage, we shall beware of treating Antiphanes as if he were writing an article on theatre and audience in the fourth century. We need to take what he says about tragedy and comedy much more as advertising material for the kind of play he is presenting than as documentation. That said, it can be seen that he is writing for an audience which likes to feel at home with its drama. Theatrical realities are present, in the shape of tragedy resolved by the *deus ex machina* and unsuccessful comedy hissed off the stage. Oedipus, Alcmaeon and other tragic heroes are alluded to in familiar terms, as in our time Hamlet or Hedda Gabler might be; but we need not go on to believe, as Antiphanes chooses to suggest, that a call for the name of Oedipus' father (any more than for that of Hamlet's uncle) would necessarily have met with a hundred per cent response.[2] What interests us above all is the concept of comedy as artistically constructed fiction, with an invented story, which must in fact be more than a story: it must be a plot, with a beginning, a middle (or present state) and an end, coherent and coherently presented; for incoherence (such is Antiphanes' self-defensive compliment to the audience) will meet with vigorous critical disapproval; while the characters, however idiosyncratic their circumstances, are to be people with names 'invented' by the author – in practice, as the two examples show, the invention often involved no more than a choice from a familiar stock.

Antiphanes, as we have just recalled, was old enough to have begun writing

---

[1] E.g. *Knights* (p. 359 above); cf. Sifakis (1971) 38ff.
[2] Aristotle, *Poetics* 1451b25, has it that even the best-known subjects of tragedy are known only to a few, though they give pleasure to all.

plays at or near the end of the lifetime of Aristophanes; but his conception here of organically constructed comedy about fictional people is closely akin to some of Aristotle's principles of dramatic composition, and may have been influenced by them; it anticipates, at least in essentials, what we find in Menander. 'Poetry', says Aristotle, 'tends to express the universal, History the particular' (*Poetics* 1451b6ff.). The distinction which interests him is between the way in which a man of a certain type will act, according to probability or necessity, and the particular, 'what Alcibiades did or suffered'. 'In Comedy', he continues, 'this is already clear: for comic poets construct their plot from probable incidents and then add names as they chance to come to mind.' One wonders how far comic practice nourished Aristotelian theory before the formulated principles in their turn influenced comic dramatists.

The Anonymus *De comoedia*, who was quoted near the beginning of this whole discussion for the number of plays of Middle Comedy, has this to say of their quality: 'The poets of Middle Comedy did not pretend to poetic style; they proceeded through familiar speech, and their virtues are those of prose – there is in them little work of the poet. They are all careful with their plots.'[1] If this is so it is not surprising that they do not lend themselves well to the gathering of colourful literary flowers, and that they may seem to be dull writers, especially when one takes into account the consideration that the authors whose quotations and excerpts provide the bulk of our fragments are hardly ever concerned, except incidentally, to illustrate the strictly dramatic virtues of the plays they use. One basis for plot-construction, we have seen, is in mythological comedy, with its pre-existing stories and characters. But for the design of plays with typical fictional characters, we depend on reconstruction from Latin adaptations and from the more traditional side of Menander's comedy. Plautus' *Menaechmi*, with its constant comedy of mistaken identity, can be taken with *Amphitruo* and (say) Menander's *Aspis* to give an idea of the ways in which poets of our period learnt to work out comic situations; and the existence of titles like *Homoioi* ('Two alike', Antiphanes and others) and *Didymoi* or *Didymai* ('Twins' of either sex, Anaxandrides, Antiphanes, Alexis and others) suggests that we are not dealing with isolated cases.[2]

One of the most productive techniques of mythological comedy – already pioneered, it must be allowed, by Euripides – was to subject the mechanisms of plot and the motivations of characters to the harsh light of the world we live in, to the standards of ordinary people, or rather, as Aristotle has it, of 'people worse than ourselves'.[3] If the traditional story pattern and the inherited behaviour pattern, whether the product of external divine agency or inner

[1] Anon. *De com.* II.49–52 Kaibel, III.42–5 Koster.
[2] For discussion of *Menaechmi* in this aspect see Webster (1970*b*) 67ff.
[3] Aristotle, *Poetics* 1448a16ff.

conviction, were to suffer erosion or distortion, some reinforcement was needed, some new standard of probable or acceptable human behaviour. It came with the fourth century's growing interest in the human individual and his relationships – in a word, with the science that came to be known as ethics. Fine distinctions between motives and personal qualities are the common ground of later fourth-century philosophers and of the higher reaches of the Comedy of Manners, with the foundation of which we credit Menander.

II. MENANDER AND THE NEW COMEDY

Menander's *Perikeiromene* takes its title from the incident which begins the action. 'The girl who has her hair cut off' has it cut off by the man she is living with, a young Corinthian who is a professional soldier. He cuts it off in a fit of fury when he is told that she let another man kiss her. She then leaves him. Here is part of a conversation between the soldier, Polemon, and a friendly neighbour, Pataikos:[1]

POLEMON I've always treated her as my wife.
PATAIKOS Don't shout at me. Who gave you her?
POLEMON Gave me her? She did.
PATAIKOS Very good. Perhaps she fancied you then, and now she doesn't. She's left you because you're not treating her properly.
POLEMON Not treating her properly...?

Polemon is deeply hurt by this, and not at all reassured to be told that violence will get him nowhere. The girl is her own mistress, and if he wants her back all he can do is try to persuade her; the man, if he can be found, can be brought to face a legal action, but the use of force would put Polemon himself in the wrong. 'Glykera has left me, Pataikos; she's left me, Glykera' – that is still the overpowering fact for Polemon; and (he urges) Pataikos must go and plead with her. 'If I ever did her any wrong at all...if I don't love, honour and cherish her...if you could just see her things...' At that, Pataikos backs away, but he is persuaded. Among the girl's clothes and jewellery, which for Polemon are a proof of his generosity, Pataikos will find the trinkets which were given her as a baby, and so discover that she is his own daughter. He had abandoned her together with a twin brother when their mother died after childbirth and he lost his livelihood in a shipwreck. It is the twin brother who is the cause of all the trouble. He is the man who was seen kissing Glykera; they had been brought up separately, and though he did not know who she was, she had been told about him. From these complications, one can see, will eventually come reconciliation and marriage.

All this seems a long way from Aristophanes, with his Trygaeus in *Peace*

[1] *Pk.* 239–43 (489–93 Sandbach) and continuing in what follows.

flying to Heaven on a dung-beetle to put an end to the war, or Praxagora in *Ecclesiazusae* packing the Assembly with women dressed as men in order to create her social revolution. But time has moved on. If it is rightly reckoned that Menander's first play, the lost *Orge* 'Anger' was produced in 321 B.C., that is the hundredth anniversary of the production of *Peace*; his death at about 50 in 292/291 or a neighbouring year is – near enough – a century after *Ecclesiazusae*. It is typical of the genre of New Comedy, the comedy of Menander and his contemporaries, that the plot of a play should be set in the domestic world of family relationships, and that it should have, prominently, what the cliché calls a love interest – anything from the intrigue by which a young man secures a desirable woman to a quarrel and reconciliation, as in *Perikeiromene*, between partners who are already attached. It is typical of Menander to have seen in this domestic world, which occupies the thoughts and daydreams of so many people for so much of their time, the material for a form of entertainment which would prompt serious reflection in its audiences as well as amusement. The balance is delicate. The headstrong and self-centred Polemon may make us laugh as he meets his match in the calm and civilized Pataikos; but if so, we laugh quietly, for there is a sense in which we are laughing at ourselves, at feelings we could admit to having experienced or could recognize among family and friends. Glykera's position in law and by the standards of fourth-century society was different, as commentators explain, from what it would be in twentieth-century Britain or many another modern society; but we overload the comedy if we make it, in any terms, too much of a tract on women's rights: the serious point, as is typical of Menander, is not just verbally asserted but woven into the plot, and it is that there are standards of equitable behaviour in human relationships which may lie deeper than the surface reactions of one person to another.

The Cairo codex of Menander was published in 1907. It gave, for the first time, large parts of *Epitrepontes* 'The Arbitrants', *Perikeiromene* and *Samia* 'The Woman of Samos' – three plays which were (not untypically) known beforehand from a total of about 20 lines of text between them in the form of identified quotations – and for good measure the beginning of *Heros* 'The Hero' and some lesser items.[1] This body of text, amounting to some 1,600 lines, was the basis of work on Menander for the next half-century. Around it there clustered a number of interesting lesser discoveries, sometimes from plays which could not be securely identified and have in some cases been identified since. From this material it became possible for the first time in the modern world to form a first-hand impression of the dramatic art of the author in such matters as the handling of dialogue, the articulation of plot through

---

[1] Gomme–Sandbach (1973) 39ff. and 50ff. give descriptions and lists of papyri. There has since been a new photographic edition of the Cairo codex with a preface by Koenen (1979).

sequences of scenes, and the delineation of character.[1] At the same time, the recovery of substantial portions of continuous Greek text gave a new impetus to the comparative study of Menander and his contemporaries with Latin adaptations of their plays by Plautus, Terence and other authors less fortunate in their survival.[2] There were now fresh reasons for taking an interest in the rich visual material relating to New Comedy, in the shape of scenes from plays, actors and masks represented in a wide range of media – terracottas, bronzes, mosaics, paintings, sculptures, gems – and produced over a period of several centuries for admirers of Greek comedy in all parts of the Graeco-Roman world.[3] A second stage of this story is briefly told in terms of a single event – the publication in 1959 from the Bodmer codex in Geneva of a play that is virtually complete, the *Dyskolos* or 'Misanthrope'. The third stage, that of the following twenty years, has not so far yielded any more complete plays, but the first and last of the three in the Bodmer codex, damaged at beginning and end, proved to be *Samia* and *Aspis* 'The shield'. When these followed the *Dyskolos* into print in 1969, they went together with the previously known remains to yield the last three acts of *Samia*, with portions of the first two; and the first two acts of *Aspis* with the beginning of the third and some fragments from later in the play.[4] Among other discoveries of the sixties and seventies were large portions of *Misoumenos* 'The man she hated' (1965ff.),[5] *Sikyonios (-oi)* 'The man – or men – from Sikyon' (1965) and a hundred-odd lines of *Dis exapaton* 'The double deceiver' (1968), many of them in poor condition, but giving much the most extensive text to date which is available for direct comparison with its adaptation into Latin, namely a stretch of the *Bacchides* of Plautus, beginning at 494ff. While work on these texts was in progress, there became known a most remarkable series of mosaics of scenes from Menander which were found in a house of the latter half of the third century A.D. at Chorapha, Mytilene: they are a fascinating complement to what we have learnt from the papyri and have opened up possibilities for the recognition of more illustrations of famous scenes from particular plays among the growing stock of visual material which has come down to us.[6]

This outline of the progress of rediscovery will be in place here if it serves to show how much the basis of modern criticism of Menander has been chang-

[1] Of course, many good and interesting things were said about Menander and New Comedy before 1907: see (e.g.) Lefèvre (1979) quoting Goethe and A. W. von Schlegel, and Leo (1895) III.

[2] Fraenkel (1922) remains exemplary in this field.

[3] E.g. Robert (1911); Webster (1969) gives an extensive catalogue, of which a revised edition is currently (1983) in preparation.

[4] *Aspis* absorbed 87 lines first published in 1913, and previously quoted as *Comoedia Florentina*; line references to *Samia* in books published before 1969 are to the 341 lines from the Cairo codex.

[5] Gomme–Sandbach (cf. p. 415 n. 1) under the sigla I, O10, O11; and add O19–O22, which are, respectively, *P.Oxy.* XLVIII 3368–71; for discussion, see Turner (1973) 15–21, 48–50 and (1978).

[6] Charitonidis–Kahil–Ginouvès (1970).

ing.[1] The impact of sheer novelty is complemented by the challenge of revaluing what we previously knew or thought we knew. Three questions at once suggest themselves: one asks what proportion of Menander's work we now have; whether there are likely to be more discoveries; and whether there are implications for the study of other writers of New Comedy. A recent calculation by W. G. Arnott reckons that the amount of Greek text available to us is something less than eight per cent of Menander's total output.[2] That would give a figure of the same order as our sample of Sophocles; for Aristophanes we can probably reckon that we have as much as 25 % to 30 % of the total amount of text known to the librarians at Alexandria. But the reality of the matter is both better and worse than the raw figures suggest. It is worse, in that we still only have one complete play of Menander in Greek; better in that there are eight (perhaps more) Latin plays by Plautus and Terence which are adapted from him. The list, with Greek titles in brackets, is as follows:

Plautus: *Aulularia* (*Apistos* or another); *Bacchides* (*Dis exapaton*); *Cistellaria* (*Synaristosai*); *Stichus* (*First Adelphoi*)

Terence: *Andria* (*Andria*, with additions from *Perinthia*); *Heauton Timoroumenos* (same title); *Eunuchus* (*Eunouchos*, with additions from *Kolax*); *Adelphoe* (*Second Adelphoi*, with a scene from Diphilus, *Synapothneskontes*).[3]

By a prudent estimate (leaving out of count many texts of unproved identity) there are now known more than fifty ancient copies of plays by Menander. These range in extent from the Bodmer and Cairo codices to scraps of a few letters only; and they range in date from the third century B.C. to the sixth or perhaps the seventh A.D.: Menander is in fact one of the best-represented ancient authors among those that survive on papyri.[4] The chances are therefore good that if collections of papyri continue to be published Menander will continue to be represented; and new methods of taking apart mummy cases in order to recover written papyri offer promising prospects for the future.[5] It is noticeable that though there are among papyri of Later Greek Comedy a number which do not appear, on stylistic or other grounds, to represent plays by Menander, there is very little which is certainly identifiable as a copy of a play by another writer in the genre.[6] It could well be, if enough papyri of the Hellenistic and early Roman period are recovered, that we shall be lucky enough to find and identify

[1] For more detail, see Arnott (1975) and (1979) xxvi–xxx, xlvii–lii; Handley (1979); Luppe (1980).

[2] Arnott (1979) xxx.

[3] Some doubt *Aulularia* (but the likeness to *Dyskolos* seems decisive); several other plays, including *Miles gloriosus* and *Pseudolus*, have been claimed as Menandrean.

[4] See for instance on an unidentified papyrus Handley (1975b) and (1977).

[5] See Maehler (1980).

[6] Examples are *P.Heid.* 183, third/second century B.C., Posidippus, *Apokleiomene*; and *P.Oxy.* 427, third century A.D., Antiphanes, *Anthropogonia*: respectively *CGFP* nos. 218 and *3.

a specimen of the work of Philemon, Diphilus or another of Menander's rivals and successors; but on present evidence the chances must be rated much lower than for Menander himself. Latin adaptations by Plautus from Philemon and Diphilus and by Terence from Apollodorus of Carystus do something to fill out the picture that can be formed from the Greek fragments, but the texts on which we depend for our knowledge of Menander's work are so much greater in extent as to make a just comparison problematical. If, on the other hand, it were possible to set aside a large part of our Menandrean material and reduce him to the size of a Philemon or a Diphilus, how much that is now taken for granted should we have to unlearn? We noted in our approach to fifth-century comedy that the new discoveries of Menander can be useful as a reminder of the differences between whole, partial and fragmentary knowledge (above, p. 356), and the point is equally to be taken now that we have come to Menander's own time. It will therefore be well to resume our attempt to form an impression of his literary qualities before we try to see how far the writing of others can contribute to an overall picture of New Comedy.

There is in Plutarch a story about Menander and playwriting which, true or not, has become virtually canonical in modern writing about him, ever since it was used by Wilamowitz to open his much-admired discussion of 'The Art of Menander'.[1] A friend is said to have pointed out that the time of the Dionysia was approaching 'and you haven't composed your comedy for it, have you?' 'Composed my comedy?' said Menander, 'I most certainly have composed it: I have my treatment of the theme worked out – I just have to set the lines to it.' It is perhaps a pity that we do not have Aristophanes on record in a similar situation, for there is a sense in which the two stand at opposite poles of comic writing. With Aristophanes, brilliance of language is primary, and sometimes we can see how stage spectacle and action are actually generated by a verbal concept transformed into visual terms.[2] With Menander, it is not that the dialogue is dashed off anyhow (one need only read some to test that); simply that the overall design of the play comes first. That Menander should have been conscious of this principle, even (as it might seem) to the point of being able to turn it, half-jokingly, against himself, is something which accords well with what we have seen earlier of the development of organized dramatic composition in comedy.[3] A similar insight can be derived, perhaps, from the very well-known portrait-relief of Menander sitting looking at the mask of a young man, which he is holding up in front of him, with two more masks on a table nearby.[4] This is one of a long series of representations in art of poets with masks,

[1] Plutarch, *Moralia* 347e; Wilamowitz-Moellendorff (1925) 119; cf. Handley (1965a) 10.
[2] See above, p. 388 with n. 4 and p. 389 with n. 1.
[3] See above, p. 400 with n. 1 and p. 413.
[4] Two versions are known: Webster (1969) nos. AS6 and IS10; Bieber (1961) figs. 316–17; on the series see Webster (1965) and Handley (1973).

and in showing Menander looking at one of a group such as this, the artist may well have been thinking of him precisely in the act of 'setting the lines' to the scene he has now reached in his plan.

It should follow, unless our impressions so far are seriously at fault, that plot and character-drawing in a comedy of this kind will be integrally related. A central feature of the design of the *Dyskolos* can be used to show how this is so.[1] The play is fashioned around a single character, Knemon the misanthrope, the 'Angry Old Man' who gives it its title. He is in fact on stage for about a quarter of the time the play would take to act – hardly more – and half of that quarter is allotted to Acts IV and V. For the rest, he is in the background, dominating the play largely through what we learn from others of him and his extraordinary way of life, and being built up for his one great moment, the major speech in Act IV at 708ff., made as if from his deathbed. The main line of the action is given from the first by the attempts of young Sostratos to gain Knemon's consent to marry his daughter. It is through the lover's story, with its ups-and-downs of unreliable helpers and unexpected allies, that the portrait of Knemon is built up; and as it proceeds the audience see him through the eyes of other characters. Thus, the god Pan gives a prologue speech, and with it the outline of the man, a sketch which will accumulate details as the play goes on and in some ways look different as it does so.[2] We next see Knemon through the eyes of a frightened slave whom he has chased off his land, and can observe the reactions of Sostratos and his friend Chaireas to this (81–146); then at last Knemon himself makes a brief appearance, and Sostratos is seen in his first direct confrontation (147–88); a little more is added by what we see of and hear from Knemon's daughter, and the first act ends with a portrait of Knemon as he appears to the slave from next door who inclines, as slaves do, to see the worst of things (220ff.). This description could be continued further into the play, but perhaps enough has been said to suggest how the technique works. While the action itself flows in a plausibly motivated sequence (that is, we accept that the people we are seeing would probably or necessarily behave as they do if the given circumstances were real), the various characters are presented in such a way that we have a clue to the value of what they say about Knemon from what they themselves are shown to be; but in turn, by defining him, they also define themselves. Chaireas, for instance, is soon recognized by the audience as a specimen of a familiar dramatic type, the parasite, a man who makes friendship a profession. Of course he can help in a love-affair; of course he knows just what sort of man Knemon is; and of course, when the moment comes, he will deal with the matter 'first thing in the morning'.[3] In watching

[1] Cf. Handley (1965a) 11f.
[2] For references, see Handley (1965a) 23f. and index s.v. *prologue-speech*.
[3] See particularly 57ff., 125–34; and above p. 398 with n. 1.

the play, we see with a smile how hollow Chaireas is, but we also see how much more idiosyncratic a character Knemon is than Chaireas thinks. It happens that we have, in the hero of Plautus' *Aulularia*, a close dramatic relation of Knemon's, the self-centred old miser Euclio; and it also happens that in the broad structural terms with which we are dealing the plays are the mirror-image of each other, with Euclio very much in evidence at the beginning, and on stage in all for more than half, and possibly near three quarters of the play's acting time (to judge from Plautus' version as we have it); the lover's story, which corresponds to that of Sostratos, is correspondingly in the background until late on. The contrast in the presentation of the hero is very striking.[1]

It is sometimes said that there is no development of character in New Comedy, and it is perhaps useful to say so if the standard of comparison is the novel, or the kind of drama with an action extending over a considerable period of time. What does develop, and what gives a forward movement to plays with a serious interest in character, is the portrait which the audience is given, and the system of contrasts by which that portrait is built up and reinforced.[2] A character like Knemon differs from a real person in that he exists only in the linear dimension of the play's performance. For the purposes of the play, his character is what it is seen to be at a chosen moment; and a summation, such as we make for a programme note or an academic essay, is a creation which misses something of his essence. Just so, a retelling or summary of a plot made for the same purposes will easily trivialize and flatten action which was conceived in terms of a different medium than narrative.

If we now move a step away from the strategy of dramatic composition towards the tactics, narrative speeches can in fact be taken to illustrate some of the ways in which Menander varies his presentation of an incident. Our examples come from *Sikyonios*, *Misoumenos*, *Aspis* and *Dyskolos*. The action of the *Sikyonios* involves a slave and a young girl taking refuge at the sanctuary of Demeter at Eleusis. She will eventually prove to be freeborn and marry the hero, but at this point she and the slave are runaways, and in the narrative their status is being debated in front of a crowd which has gathered round. A debate of this sort can be presented by means of antithetical speeches from two actors, as is commonly done in drama: such a scene is the Arbitration from which *Epitrepontes* takes its title.[3] But by presenting a debate in narrative and not on the stage, as in *Sikyonios* 176–271, the dramatist exchanges the immediate impact of the speakers' presence for the ability to set a more elaborate scene in the audience's imagination; he can use more speakers, he can characterize them through the narrator's eyes, and – not least – he can abbreviate and select in a

---

[1] See p. 419 n. 1 above and *Entretiens Hardt* (1970) 100–1.

[2] See above, p. 409 with n. 2 and Webster (1950) 190ff.

[3] *Epitr.* 43–200 (219–376 S): the underlying pattern is that of the tragic agon, not the form we associate with Aristophanes.

way which would not work with direct presentation. On this occasion, a further dimension is given by echoing, in words and pattern, what was (and is) a classic example of its kind, Euripides' narrative in *Orestes* 866–956 of the debate in Argos which decided the fate of Orestes and Electra. The echo offers a kind of justification (if one were felt to be needed) for the unusual length and prominence – by Menandrean standards – of the narrative; but it also points the analogy between the slave and the girl in one perilous situation, and the tragic hero and heroine in another.[1]

The narrative which concerns us in *Misoumenos* is that of a quarrel. After a long search, Demeas has rediscovered his daughter, Krateia, a war-captive. He wants to ransom her from Stratophanes; Stratophanes wants to make her his wife; she utterly refuses, for he is at this time (in the words of the title) 'the man she hated': she had a special reason for doing so and – as it will prove – a mistaken one. All three parties are thus in a storm of conflicting emotions. Menander does not tackle the problems of managing this scene in direct presentation: it would have been a difficult peak to climb and to descend from. Instead, he brings on a slave, Getas, who has been there in the background, and is now reliving, quoting to himself and commenting on some of the high moments of the scene. He has an audience, in the shape of young Kleinias, who knows still less of what has been going on than the audience in the theatre; Kleinias paces up and down with the slave, listening, working things out for himself and eventually breaking in. The presentation thus exploits several different viewpoints at once, and blends almost the whole range of comic effects from high drama to farce. Something of this can perhaps be seen in a short excerpt:

> GETAS Lord help us, he couldn't just be reasonable about it, could he? It was pig versus mule, as they say. But that's not so bad as her – looks away, she does, while he's speaking. 'Oh, Krateia', he says, 'don't leave me, I beg you, don't. You'd never had a man when I took you, and I *was* your man, the first to love you and cherish you; and I do love you, Krateia, my dearest. What is there about me that pains you? I'll be dead, you'll see, if you leave me.' No answer, none.
>
> KLEINIAS What *is* all this?
>
> GETAS A barbarian, the woman is, a lioness.
>
> KLEINIAS Damn you, you *still* can't see me. How strange.
>
> GETAS Completely out of his mind. By Apollo here, *I'd* never have set her free...[2]

The interruptions to the narrative, which seem at first sight to reflect the randomness of real life, are in fact an integral part of its structure; and a similar technique

---

[1] See *Entretiens Hardt* (1970) 22f., and for more detail Handley (1965*b*) 47 with n. 10; on Menander and tragedy, Webster (1974) 56ff.; and cf. above p. 373 with n. 3 and p. 404 with n. 2.
[2] *Mis.* 302–15, taking for granted restorations etc. which do not affect the point being argued.

is used very effectively, if less elaborately, in the long narrative at the beginning of *Aspis*.[1]

The shield which gives *Aspis* its title is part of the spectacle that opens the play. It is broken; it is carried by the late owner's batman, and there follows a procession of captives with bundles and boxes, the spoils of a campaign. With the party, but somehow not of it, is an old man who for some time looks on in silence. The occasion is a sad one, strikingly so for the start of a comedy; the batman laments the loss of his young master, who had gone to war to provide a dowry for his sister and been killed. 'What an unexpected calamity, Daos.' 'Terrible.' 'Tell me, how did he die, what was the way of it?' The story proceeds, punctuated by comments from the old man. It was not a glorious campaign, but a tale of a force grown over-confident after easy success and good plunder; there was a surprise attack by night, and they were routed. The verse-rhythms are sombre, to match the mood of the story, and the manner is akin to that of tragedy, though without specific allusion or parody. The old man's interventions articulate the narrative, but they also gradually add a new colour to the scene. It becomes plain that his concern is no more than a mask for greed. He means to get his hands on the spoils, even if he has to marry his ward, the surviving child of the family, to do so. The plot proceeds through the intrigues by which he is frustrated, and comes to a peak with the return of the young soldier who had been supposed killed in battle: it was a case of mistaken identity, as Fortune, the prologue speaker, tells the audience immediately after the opening scene we have described. This is a remarkable piece of dramatic writing, and an interesting contrast with it is given by the narrative of a battle in Plautus' *Amphitruo*. Plautus makes a lyric of this, and there is a strong Roman colour to its language, but in Plautus we have war with 'the thunder of the captains and the shouting', not the death of a young mercenary after an ordinary military blunder.[2]

A further contrast is given by our last narrative, at the end of the *Dyskolos*, which looks back to the comic rather than to the tragic side of New Comedy's ancestry and is remarkable in being a musical scene – not, it is true, in any way resembling the full-blooded Plautine lyric of the *Amphitruo* narrative just mentioned, but at least with the accompaniment of a piper.[3] The slave Getas and the cook Sikon take revenge on Knemon, the old misanthrope, for the way in which he drove them from his door when they wanted to borrow a cooking-pot; and in a scene which is in effect a farcical reprise of the borrowing scenes of Act III they carry Knemon out from his house and go through a ballet-like routine of knocking at the door and shouting fantastic demands for party

[1] See Turner (1980) 9f. and 11, quoting Bozanic.
[2] *Amphitruo* 186–262, esp. 219–47, cf. Handley (1975a) 129f.
[3] *Dysk.* 880 (piper), 935–53 (narrative).

equipment. Finally Sikon forces the old man to listen to a recital of the pro-ceedings at the betrothal feast which he has insisted on missing, and they then carry him in to the party under threat of being made to dance with them instead. Comedy has an interesting tradition of euphoric elevated style for descriptions of feasts and the like, for which it borrows freely from the language of higher poetry, especially perhaps dithyramb, and in calling old wine 'the Bacchic grizzlehead' (to take one phrase), Menander is alluding to this tradition, just as he is conscious in constructing the whole scene that comedy can by tradition end with a revel (and if the revel avoids the problem of shaping any more serious end, so much the better). As before, the narrative is punctuated by interruptions, and its festive note is diversified by Knemon's misery and Getas' triumphant sarcasm.[1]

The four narratives which have just been described and contrasted can be offered as a token of Menander's dramatic range; but they can also perhaps be taken together to make a fundamental point about his playwriting. Here, as so often, he takes a basically familiar situation, and diversifies it by giving it a novel context, a new variant, an unexpected additional dimension, an artifice of structure. One could show these same broad principles at work in his treatment of characters, when he takes typical figures, often recognizable from the outset by their costumes, masks and even by standard names; and then, in the way we have seen, he builds up through the action of the play a portrait which shows that the typical is not, in this or that way, what it seems to be on the surface. Examples ready to hand are Polemon, Stratophanes and Thrasonides, the three soldiers of *Perikeiromene*, *Sikyonios* and *Misoumenos*, each of whom is fixed by type in the tradition of the 'miles gloriosus', but is shown by the play as an individual with characteristics that evoke a response of sympathy and interest rather than superiority and ridicule.[2]

An important consequence of this concept of playwriting for the critic is that it matters very much to have a full context for whatever it is in a play by Menander that one wants to interpret. That, in the fragmentary state of much of the author, is something we very often do not have, or have to achieve by conjecture. To take a single example, fr. 111 'Whom the gods love, dies young' is several times quoted as a moral maxim in antiquity (and known in English from Byron); but in the context given by Plautus' adaptation (*Bacchides* 816f.) it is said by a slave at the expense of his elderly master.[3] It is appropriate here to remember that Menander is a poet of the Hellenistic Age. Though approaching by a different route, from concepts in social anthropology, T. B. L. Webster's treatment of the plays in his last book in terms of armatures and codes rather

---

[1] Cf. Handley (1965a) on 946–58; and see above, p. 365 with n. 5, p. 366 with n. 1, p. 368 with n. 4, p. 369 with n. 2 and p. 391 with nn. 1–2.

[2] See above, p. 410 with n. 5, and for New Comedy Hofmann and Wartenberg (1973).

[3] Handley (1968) 6, quoting Webster.

than tradition and innovation is extremely revealing if viewed in this light; and in regard to more detailed matters of language and dramaturgy both Sandbach and Arnott (in a discussion entitled 'The Cleverness of the Hellenistic Poet') have mapped out some interesting new territory.[1]

A difficulty which criticism of this kind of writing always faces is that of seeming to be too clever in turn (or indeed of being too clever).[2] Whether Menander's rivals and successors were often equally subtle is, as will have been plain from the state of the evidence, something very much harder to judge. Greek fragments apart, we know Philemon from Plautus' *Mercator*, *Mostellaria* and *Trinummus*, and Diphilus from *Casina*, *Rudens*, the fragmentary *Vidularia* (probably) and a scene in Terence's *Adelphoe*.[3] It is eminently credible from the scale on which some motifs are treated in the fragments that both poets had a more relaxed, more traditional, and in a sense more comic attitude to comic writing;[4] and a story which may be well found if not true has Menander saying to his rival 'Tell me, Philemon, don't you blush when you beat me?'[5] Philemon, on the evidence of the Latin plays, excelled in comedy of situation; in the Greek that we have the pompous heavy-footedness of some of his writing, as opposed to Menander, reminds one of Plautus as opposed to Terence, and suggests a man with broader rather than subtler theatrical effects in mind.[6] Diphilus, judging from *Rudens*, had a colourful way with a romantic comedy in a remote setting. Though the extent of Plautus' modifications is (as ever) a problem, it is likely that the original was both more expansive and more comic than *Dyskolos*.[7] A certain sharpness has been seen in his writing, both in some of his verbal felicities and in the way in which (both in *Casina* and in *Rudens*) there are groups of black-and-white (as opposed to Menandrean pastel) characters in confrontation.[8] But it remains hard to be confident from what we have of these authors that one is not imagining more than one sees.

It happens that, with the loss of Menander at the end of antiquity, the world of New Comedy reached modern times through Plautus and Terence. The idea of amusing, civilized fiction based on ordinary people's everyday affairs has proved to be an immensely fruitful one, with its myriad descendants and influences from ancient times onwards, and now including not only drama on radio and cinema or television screen, but above all, the novel. Popular fiction

---

[1] Webster (1974); Sandbach in *Entretiens Hardt* (1970) 111ff.; Arnott (1979) xxxviii–xlv.

[2] Cf. *Entretiens Hardt* (1970) 7f.

[3] Webster (1970*b*) has well-documented chapters on Philemon, Diphilus and (from the next generation) Apollodorus of Carystus, from whom Terence took *Hecyra* and *Phormio*.

[4] E.g. long speeches by cooks, Philemon 79 K, Diphilus 43 K; and parasite, Diphilus 60–1 K; and compare Philemon 28 K with *Samia* 206ff., 98 K with *Georgos* 35ff., Diphilus 17 K. 11ff. with *Samia* 99f., 55 K with *Dyskolos* 402ff.

[5] Aulus Gellius, *N.A.* 17.4.   [6] E.g. frs. 23, 69, 91, 106 K.

[7] Compare for instance *Rud.* 414–84 (asking for water) with *Dysk.* 189–214.

[8] Sharpness: e.g. 24 K with Menander, *Kolax* 85ff., and frs. 60, 72, 83, 91, 107 K.

of this kind has two very obvious characteristics: its characters and stories offer many people an escape into a world of wish-fulfilment, a world with which they can easily identify, but neater and more entertaining than the real one often is; and secondly, there is, to a greater or less degree, an enlightening or educating influence.[1] There is, of course, a very great part of human life, even everyday life, that does not enter into Menander's portrayal of it[2] (the same is often felt about others: for instance Jane Austen). There are times when our assent is strained by the role he accords to Fortune, or Ignorance, or whatever other divine or abstract force has contributed to the fashioning of a situation.[3] There are other ways also in which he is noticeably an ancient and not a modern writer, not least in regard to his characters' behaviour, which he often accounts for very precisely (this is part of the art of dramatic structure) but in ethical, not psychological (certainly not post-Freudian) terms.[4] The test of his rating through modern eyes could easily be the passage and the play from which we began: can Polemon and Glykera still survive in modern company?

[1] Cf. Thierfelder (1956) on Roman comedy in this regard.
[2] Handley (1965a) 12f. with some further references.
[3] See Webster (1950) 198ff.; Ludwig in *Entretiens Hardt* (1970) 45–110; Bozanic (1977) 145–58; Lefèvre (1979) 320–8.
[4] Handley (1965a) 13 and n. 3; Webster (1974) 43–55.

13

HISTORIOGRAPHY

I. HERODOTUS

Herodotus of Halicarnassus (*c.* 485–425 B.C.) was the founder of ancient historiography. The paradox of his life is his dual position as a prime exponent both of Ionian story telling and, despite his use of the Ionic dialect, of Attic literature. Athens of course had attracted foreigners already in the sixth century (the Samian Anacreon is an example) and continued to do so in the fifth. But in Herodotus she acquired a writer who explained her achievements and her way of life to the Greek world at large. Like Achilles, Athens had found her Homer.

Herodotus was a descendant of an aristocratic family in Halicarnassus, which appears to have had some Carian admixture. His father's name is given as Lyxus, and the poet Panyassis, author of a poem on Heracles, was a relation; both names sound Carian. We are told by the ancient tradition, but not by Herodotus himself, that he fought the local tyrant, a descendant of Queen Artemisia, celebrated for her exploits in the Persian War, was exiled, and spent some time on Samos, with which he shows in fact a fairly close acquaintance. The ancient biography is silent about his further career except for saying that he went to the Athenian colony of Thurii in southern Italy, where his tomb was shown in the market place. This tradition is reflected in our text of the *Histories*; according to the manuscript tradition, Herodotus describes himself as a citizen of Halicarnassus in the opening sentence, but 'of Thurii' is an early variant and may well have been what Herodotus wrote. More important, he also mentions many foreign places he has visited. These references have been combined by modern scholars into a number of itineraries and arranged in chronological sequences. It is certain that he made a journey to the north, which included south Russia, and shorter trips to Babylon and Syria and Palestine, the last perhaps in connexion with his famous journey to Egypt, where he spent four months at the time of the Nile flood. A trip to Cyrenaica is perhaps to be connected with his stay in southern Italy. It is also clear from the work that he had travelled in the Aegean and on the mainland of Greece; the accuracy of his topographical descriptions (Thermopylae, Tempe, etc.) and his knowledge of local traditions (e.g. those of Sparta) are enough to establish the fact.[1]

It is surprising, then, that the most important event in Herodotus' life, his stay in Athens, is not mentioned in the work or directly in the biographical tradition. Yet it is certain. He has much local information about Athenian history and topography (as he demonstrates in the stories about the Pisistratids, Philaids, and Alcmeonids, and the descriptions of the Acropolis), and his relations with Sophocles are well attested, well enough, in fact, to furnish a date for his stay in Athens. Plutarch (*An seni* 3.785b) preserves the beginning of a poem by Sophocles addressed presumably to our Herodotus in the late 440s. Sophoclean reminiscences of the *Histories* run from *Ajax* to *Oedipus at Colonus*, among them the famous passage *Antigone* 905–12, which is here taken to be certainly genuine Sophocles and which shows knowledge of the very wording of the story of the death of Intaphernes, one of the Seven Conspirators with Darius, as preserved in our text of Herodotus.[2] Since *Antigone* is datable to the late 440s, this passage establishes not only that Herodotus was present in Athens at that time but also that the story was composed (whether orally or in writing) long before the publication of the extant work. This raises the question of the nature of Herodotus' activities during his travels and sojourns. Some modern speculation has it that he had commercial interests, but the ancients preserve a number of stories about his lecturing activities (though some of them, like the alleged decree of Anytus which authorized ten talents as reward for readings in Athens, are suspect).[3] We may perhaps classify Herodotus as a travelling intellectual, in this one aspect comparable to the sophists.

The work cannot have been published until the early years of the Peloponnesian War; some think, with less justification, that it was published during the Peace of Nicias.[4] It has been stated frequently that Aristophanes' presentation of the Persian ambassadors in the *Acharnians* of 425 reflects the publication of the work, but the parallels with Herodotus consist of some minor facts which could have been generally known in Athens; there are no verbal similarities. Yet a date around 425 or slightly earlier seems probable enough from Herodotus' references to the early events of the Peloponnesian War. There are, however, at least three reasons why this date is not especially significant: (1) the work was known in Athens prior to publication; (2) it has a long prehistory in oral composition, and conceivably in partial advance 'publication' (or better,

---

[1] The account by Jacoby (1913) 247ff. has not been superseded. Cf. also Myres (1953) and von Fritz (1967) I 104ff.

[2] Schmid–Stählin I 2, 318 n. 3; *Antigone* 909–12; Hdt. 3.119.6.

[3] Anytus: Plut. *De Herodoti malignitate* 26.862a. For evidence on lecturing, see Schmid–Stählin I 2, 590 n. 5.

[4] References to Peloponnesian War: Schmid–Stählin I 2, 590 n. 9. *Acharnians*: ibid. 591 n. 2; Wells (1923) 169–82. Peace of Nicias: see Fornara (1971a).

circulation); (3) at the time of its ultimate publication the work was something of an anachronism, for it reflected an earlier world view and style of writing. Its 'ideal' date is closer to the 440s than the 420s.

There has been much debate about the reasons for the delay in publication. Taking their cue from what to modern sensibility seems an unsatisfactory conclusion and from some gaps in the body of the work, many scholars have supposed that it is unfinished and was published after the author's death. The *Histories* end with the events of the year 479 B.C. (winter), i.e. the siege and capture of Sestos by the Athenians and the execution of Artayctes, the Persian governor of the area. This is followed by a final anecdote (9.122) in which Cyrus the Great warns the Persians of the dangers of luxury. The warning was issued at the time of the founding of the Persian empire and addressed to an ancestor of Artayctes, and thus appropriately closes off the history of Persia and the story of the Persian War (note that the account of the death of Artayctes is anticipated on the occasion of Xerxes' building of the bridges by which he crossed the Hellespont into Greece, 7.33). Herodotus is fond of placing anecdotes at the end of major accounts (compare, e.g., the story of Epizelus after the account of the battle of Marathon, 6.117.2–3, or Demaratus' message to Sparta, which is told after Thermopylae, 7.239). It is true that there is no statement here that we have come to the end of the work, except for the notation that 'nothing further happened during this year' (9.121), and that further events could easily be attached to this imperfect close. But this is probably a matter of Herodotus' style rather than of substance. As for the general contents, the year 479 has been accepted by all as the *de facto* end of the Persian Wars, which did not end *de jure* until 449 B.C. The internal gaps are similarly insufficient arguments for the incompleteness of the work as a whole. The most important are the unkept promises in 1.106 and 184 of a major Assyrian (i.e. Babylonian) excursus and the unfulfilled promise in 7.213 to tell the story of the death of Ephialtes the traitor of Thermopylae.[1]

What little we learn about Herodotus' life from the ancient sources fits the *persona* of himself which he creates in the work. He often speaks of himself, but only in his function of author, not as a private person. The key term for his intellectual activity is *historie* (1.1), investigation, which covers broadly the stories he collects about the past and about contemporary customs, buildings and geographical features. In part, Herodotus acts as a reporter who transmits what he has seen and heard, the *logoi* people tell (cf., e.g., 2.99 and 147). But *historie* also includes the exercise of judgement, first in the choice of informants: best are the local people, the *epichorioi*, and among them those that can give the best account (the *logioi andres*) such as priests and members of aristocratic families who participated in the events. Secondly, *historie* involves the compari-

<hr>

[1] See further Jacoby (1913) 373ff.

son of accounts (*symballesthai*) and the formation of judgement on the intrinsic probability of the stories told to the historian (*gnome*). He will transmit stories he does not believe to be true, and he will tell the stories as they were told to him (*legein ta legomena*, 7.152.3), but he is often selective and frequently expresses disbelief. If we are to trust his words, he relies almost entirely on oral sources. In a sense this is a fiction, for we can sometimes determine, sometimes surmise, that he relied on predecessors, e.g. Hecataeus, and other written sources, e.g. the city history of Cyrene (4.154ff.). Yet Herodotus did travel widely and relied on what he saw and heard (autopsy and *historie*) to such an extent that these features colour his whole attitude toward historical truth. Thus much of his Egyptian information came from the Egyptian 'priests' (they were not of a very high class, and thus not always well informed; and the Greek interpreters were not very accurate).[1] For historical information he went to the parties involved: in Athens a main source (though not the only one) was the family of the Alcmeonidae which no doubt included the circle of Pericles; for Persia his sources are mainly Ionian or derived from renegade Persians living in Greece.[2] What he neglects to tell us is the fact that his questions were sometimes predetermined by what he knew from earlier written sources, especially in the matter of ethnography. The work is thus a composite of information from local and general Greek traditions. It is addressed to local Greek audiences, who together form the Greek 'nation'. That Herodotus envisages a Panhellenic audience, and not merely an Athenian one, is apparent when for example he describes the Crimea first by comparison with Attica and then, for those 'who have not sailed by Attica', by comparison with the heel of Italy (4.99.3–5). But in his conception Panhellenism refers to the cultural amalgam of the individual Greek nations and not to a political unit (cf. 8.144.2). His work was composed in Athens and in Thurii. Whether he ever returned from Thurii to Athens and whether he was really buried in the new colony are questions to which we do not have the answer.

Herodotus did not invent the methods he employed. There had been travellers before him, and oral traditions had been collected by others. He himself mentions the voyage taken on behalf of Darius by Scylax of Caryanda from India to the Red Sea in the late sixth century (4.44). Other early travellers include Euthymenes of Marseilles and Hanno the Carthaginian. There must have been many nameless travellers who published no records; their interests included coastal navigation and observation of native customs. This information was soon combined with the philosophers' interest in astronomical and geographical theory. The main exponent of scientific geography was Hecataeus of Miletus whose *Circumnavigation of the known world* (*Periegesis / Periodos ges*), appeared

[1] Sourdille (1910); Heidel (1935); von Fritz (1967); Kaiser (1969); Oertel (1970).
[2] Wells (1923).

in the late sixth century and to whom Herodotus is heavily indebted. Hecataeus' work accompanied a map (perhaps an improved version of the map devised by the philosopher Anaximander) which, to judge by Herodotus' geographical statements, was of an abstract geometric shape, with the continents of Asia and Europe balancing each other. The work was in two books, which were later named *Europe* and *Asia* (Africa was considered together with Asia); it described the coast of the Mediterranean with excursions into the interior. Herodotus knew Hecataeus as a politician active during the Ionian Revolt and names him once in connexion with his own stay in Egypt (2.143); but his debt to him is much larger, for we know that he copied him outright for the descriptions of the crocodile, hippopotamus and phoenix (2.70, 71, 73), was influenced by his definition of Egypt as the Delta, and in all probability also by his descriptions of Scythia and north Africa.[1]

In any case, Herodotus' true relation to Hecataeus and other predecessors is best judged from his numerous polemics against the 'Greeks' or the 'Ionians', which are frequently based on what he himself has seen. While he generally follows the patterns of early geography and ethnography, he claims to have better information and to be able to correct the excessive schematization of the old geographers by empirical observation and the refusal to speculate where evidence does not exist. For example, he argues against the theory that Europe and Asia plus Africa are of equal size by saying that Europe is larger (4.36.2 and 42.1). Yet he too believes in geographical balance in some respects; thus the Danube balances the Nile, and the seasons in the centre of the world are in balance with the extremities.[2] Such correspondences have for him a moral and metaphysical significance: they guarantee world order. Similar is Herodotus' attitude toward order in diversity within the realm of ethnography. Here too he follows traditional schemes in reporting on foreign peoples (country; customs, first religious, then secular, with funerary customs paramount; food).[3] While he often judges customs by their social or political effect, he basically allows that each custom is valid within a specific cultural context. The diversity of customs establishes order in the world in that it both supports and limits the aspirations of each nation. Thus geography and ethnography are fundamental to Herodotus' perception of the historical process.

Herodotus' predecessors collected oral traditions for geographic and ethnographic treatises. Similar procedures were no doubt employed by his predecessors in the field of history, but here our information is very defective. Mythographers and genealogists had already turned epic material into prose and had thus codified and rationalized the legendary history of Greece. Here again Hecataeus is the foremost exponent. His mythographic *Genealogies* prob-

---

[1] Jacoby (1912) 2676ff. and *FGrH* 1; Nenci (1954); Drews (1973).
[2] Immerwahr (1966) 316.   [3] Trüdinger (1918).

ably appeared in the early fifth century and was a systematic work, which did not, however, cover historical events that fell within living memory. Its importance for Herodotus lay mainly in the concept of generations common to the two writers. But Herodotus may draw on a broader and more strictly historical tradition when he uses fixed patterns for historical events such as the chronicle of kings in his accounts of Lydia, Media and Persia, or for battle descriptions and certain types of historical anecdotes; he is unlikely to have invented all this material. One probable predecessor of Herodotus is Dionysius of Miletus, of whose *Persica* we know next to nothing. Less shadowy, but of uncertain date, are the three main historians of foreign peoples in this period, Charon of Lampsacus (*Persica*), Hellanicus of Lesbos (*Persica*), and Xanthus of Lydia (*Lydiaca*).[1] Jacoby thought that these books came later than Herodotus, but recently his dating has been challenged, and the ancients may have been right in placing them earlier. Whatever the precise dates, these works suggest that, in writing eastern history, Herodotus is not alone. The situation differs, however, for Greek history. Here Jacoby has demonstrated that (despite Charon's history of Lampsacus and the history of Cyrene, which we know from a later inscription) local chronicles and lists of officials (such as the list of Olympic victors and of various city officials) did not enter the mainstream of historical writing until after Herodotus.[2] In Greek history, Herodotus' inclusion of Greek oral traditions within the larger framework of oriental history is a new departure.

But even for eastern history, Herodotus does not follow previous written sources to any great extent. The historical accounts, like the ethnographic, are based largely on *historie*. There is thus no fundamental difference between his practice in ethnography and history. In fact Herodotus combined both disciplines in some of his accounts of foreign peoples, especially in the great Egyptian excursus (Book 2), which contains both ethnography and history. We shall discuss the precise relation of these elements when we come to describe the structure of the *Histories*.

If the early prose geographers and historians were influential in the formation of Herodotus' methodology, the scientific aspects of his work as it were, they alone did not make him an historian. Value judgements and historical interpretation came to him from poetry. The idea that history must have a great subject and that great subjects call forth great works, is Homeric (cf. the comparison of Xerxes' campaign with the Trojan War in 7.20). Herodotus established the concept of monumental history, which was continued by Thucydides and revived by the Alexander historians, Polybius, Livy and others. The heroic

[1] Jacoby (1913) 393 and 405 (Dionysius). See *FGrH* 262 (Charon); 765 (Xanthus) and 90 (Nichol. Dam.); Pearson (1939) chs. 3 and 4; von Fritz (1967), text volume, 519ff. (Charon) and 88ff. (Xanthus); Drews (1973) *passim*.
[2] Jacoby (1949) 54–60.

personality, the core of the Homeric epic, is developed by Herodotus in such figures as Leonidas and Themistocles, perhaps after the models of Ajax and Odysseus. The concept of fame as proclaimed by the historian is evident in Herodotus' first sentence; one of his aims is that 'of preventing the great and wonderful actions of Greeks and Barbarians from losing their due meed of glory' (tr. Rawlinson). A third element derived from epic is the frequent use of speeches in set scenes, especially in the account of the Persian Wars.

From lyric poetry and the popular literature on the Seven Sages (of whom Herodotus mentions Solon, Thales, Bias and Pittacus) derives the emphasis on Greek citizen morality, the *arete* of the citizen soldier, and the concept of divine justice exercised in the rise and fall of prosperous states and individuals, as adumbrated in the prooemium (1.5.4) and exemplified in the Solon–Croesus story. But the pattern by which balance is maintained in the world of conflicting forces is that often found in Attic tragedy, which was perhaps a greater influence on Herodotus than any other form of literature. The dependence is both formal and philosophical. Certain stories in Herodotus are composed in set dramatic scenes which combine to form the patterns of tragedy. In the story of Gyges and Candaules' wife, for example, (1.8–13) we have a conversation between king and retainer in which the plot is hatched; the bedchamber scene in which Gyges sees the queen naked and is in turn observed by her; the conversation of queen and retainer; the murder of the king and the accession of Gyges with the Pythia's prediction of vengeance for the death of Candaules in the fifth generation. A Hellenistic poet of sorts perceived the dramatic possibilities and wrote a play on Gyges, of which we have a fragment.[1] Other dramatic stories are the Death of Atys, son of Croesus (1.34–45), the Croesus story itself, parts of the Birth and Death of Cyrus the Great (1.107–13 and 201–14), the Rise and Fall of Polycrates of Samos (3.39–43 and 120–5), stories which prepare the way for the great tragedy of Xerxes in Books 7–9.

Thus the tragic pattern is fundamental for the understanding of the Persian Wars. Herodotus' acquaintance with the *Persae* of Aeschylus is proved by a number of passages, among them the famous epigram that at Salamis the defeat of the navy caused the defeat of the land army (Hdt. 8.68c ~ *Pers.* 728). But Herodotus did not use the play as a factual source, no doubt because his own *historie* furnished him with what he considered to be better information. The similarity of the *Persae* and Herodotus' account consists primarily in the interpretation of the events and is particularly evident on the religious plane. As the ghost of Darius explains in the play, the gods punished the young king's overbearing pride by using the rashness of his nature against him (*Pers.* 742) and thus prevented the excessive growth of Persia (759ff.).

[1] Many think that the play is early and a source for Herodotus' story. See Page (1951c). But cf. Lesky, *TDH* 536–7.

This belief in the balanced order of the universe as exemplified in history is the credo of Herodotus. He places his tragic stories not arbitrarily where they would most appeal to the audience, but at significant historical points, such as the downfall of a dynasty and the rise of another, or the punishment of a ruler. His tragic characters each have a definite function in the overall historical development, and they frequently come together in groups in which each member represents a different aspect of the historical process (Candaules, the last king of the old dynasty; Gyges, the beginning of the new; the queen who causes the shift). Connexions between the separate tragic stories are not infrequent, as for example the oracle's prediction that vengeance for the crime of Gyges would come in the fifth generation (the time of Croesus) and the references to Cyrus the Founder in the account of the campaign of Xerxes (7.8a.1; 11.2; 18.2, etc.; see above, on 9.122). Though Herodotus uses devices we associate with tragedy, such as oracles and omens, speeches and vivid conversations, and though the subtlety of his psychology may make the reader forget the historical significance of his scenes, his dramatic stories are not (as has been claimed) summaries of actual plays, nor is their impact principally moral and theological. They are rather meant to explain the major changes in the power and prosperity of individual rulers and thus to exemplify his dictum that 'human prosperity never remains in one place' (1.5.4). The emphasis on man's fate rather than on theological explanation places Herodotus close to his friend Sophocles, especially in those plays in which several persons are seen to interact, as in *Antigone*. Among the Sophoclean plays the most Herodotean is *Trachiniae* with its emphasis on life stories stretching over considerable periods of time and on the interconnexion of separate individual destinies. It has also been observed that the lost plays of Sophocles contain more geographical allusions than the extant ones.[1] Perhaps there existed a type of tragedy which drew its interest as much from stories set in far away places as from the delineation of individual character. This is in part what we find in Herodotus, for whom tragedy showed the position of man in the order of history. The demonstration of such order is his principal aim.

Herodotus' intentions appear most clearly in the overall organization of his work, which reveals greater subtlety than do his own general statements. In the latter he is much concerned with his methods in an attempt to establish his credibility. In the first sentence of the work he mentions two purposes: the preservation of the record (*ta genomena ex anthropon*) and, as stated earlier, glorification of great achievement (*erga megala te kai thomasta*). He often remarks on the marvellous nature of the monuments, customs and events he describes, but he is not merely a chronicler of marvels (*thomata*). His frequent departures from straight chronological order have earned him a reputation as

[1] Bacon (1961) 94–101.

433

a mere story teller. Yet he is often quite selective, and his technique of fitting things together reveals much about his aims.

The main portion of the work tells the story of four Persian kings: Cyrus, the Founder, and Cambyses, his son; Darius (in his view) a usurper, and his son Xerxes. But of the last he tells little except his invasion of Greece. It has frequently been claimed, therefore, that the story of the first three kings was originally planned as a history of Persia, while the Xerxes story is really a history of the Persian Wars.[1] This theory of a change in plan is often combined with the further hypothesis that Herodotus started as a geographer before he became a historian; thus all three phases of his development would be combined in the present work. But the genetic explanation largely ignores the unifying element of the three parts: the expansion of the Persian empire, which was stopped in the wars with Greece. Herodotus begins the Persian history with the story of Cyrus' birth, exposure and accession; he then selects three major campaigns, those against Ionia and the Asia Minor coast, against Babylon, the centre of wealth, and against the far-off Massagetae, among whom Cyrus is killed. The rise and fall of Persian ambition is here prefigured, as is the conflict of Persia and the Greeks. Cambyses' story is that of the conquest of Egypt, the failure of his attack on Ethiopia, the wilful destruction of his succession in madness, and his death. Darius comes to power in a conspiracy against the Magi; under him the empire reaches its zenith of wealth and organization. His numerous campaigns are successful in Asia (in particular those directed against the revolts of Babylon and the Ionian cities in Asia Minor), but in Europe they fail in large part. While he established a friendly regime on Samos, gained a foothold on the European side of the Hellespont, and subdued Thasos, Darius failed to conquer the Scythians (the first European power to be attacked by the Persians), and his forces suffered reverses in the expedition, which was wrecked at Mt Athos, and in the campaign at Marathon. Darius' European campaigns were motivated mainly by his desire for expansion, but partly also by vengeance for Athenian and Eretrian assistance to the Ionian rebellion; hence Herodotus describes the Ionian Revolt as the direct cause of the Persian Wars. In addition, Darius demanded the submission of all Greek states by asking for the gift of earth and water, but Sparta and Athens refused. Darius was thus unsuccessful in expanding his empire to include Europe (just as a Persian campaign into Africa had only temporary success); the same fate befell his son Xerxes when he attempted to continue his father's policies. The imperialist policy of Persia had four phases according to Herodotus: Cyrus consolidated a unified Asiatic kingdom; Cambyses conquered Egypt; Darius and then Xerxes attempted the conquest of Europe and thus Greece became involved. It is a highly schematic view and is based on the geographers' three-continent theory.

[1] Jacoby (1913) 347ff.; Powell (1939) chs. 2–4; von Fritz (1967) I 104ff.; Fornara (1971b) ch. 2.

One of Cyrus' conquests, in which he combined eastern and western Asia into a unified empire, has been omitted from this outline. Cyrus' campaign against Croesus of Lydia was taken by Herodotus from its natural context and placed at the beginning of the work. The gain was immense: the Croesus story became an independent unit with the history of the Lydian dynasty as its introduction, and it could serve as a paradigm for the rise and fall of all dynasties and rulers. Two additional reasons for the shift were that Croesus, not Cyrus, was the aggressor who tried to enlarge his empire and thus caused his own defeat; and that by conquering the Greek cities in Asia Minor Croesus had been the first of the eastern despots to subdue Greeks (Hdt. Preface, 1.5.3). The conflict of Greece and the Orient is thus seen as the inevitable result of despotic imperialism.

Herodotus prefixed to his work a lengthy prooemium (1.1–5) in which the author's statements frame a 'Persian story' to which is appended a 'Phoenician' variant. The form of this introduction was later imitated by Thucydides (1.1–23) and other historians. Herodotus begins, as we have seen, by justifying the publication of his research (*histories apodexis*). He adds that he will explain the reason (*aitie*) for which Greeks and barbarians came to engage in war – a clear, if vague, reference to the Persian Wars and their antecedents. The Persian story answers the question of responsibility (for this is what *aitie* means to Herodotus) by blaming the Greeks for taking vengeance, in the Trojan War, for the rape of a mere woman. The story demonstrates how a long-lasting hostility was built up between Europe and Asia over the centuries. (The Phoenician variant concerns a minor point about the earlier rape of Io.) Herodotus rejects this explanation, in part because it concerns the mythological period, and substitutes Croesus' attacks as the ultimate *historical* cause. Finally he points to the universal character of his work by saying that after Croesus he will describe large and small cities alike, because of the instability of human fortune. He then begins with Croesus and the Lydian dynasty.

Thus the *Histories* are based on two kinds of interaction: vengeance for prior injustices and imperialism which makes no claim to justification. Both require the historian to go deeply into the antecedents of the Persian Wars. The vengeance theme requires the history of all interactions between Greeks and barbarians, and the theme of imperialism, the history of the origins and development of the eastern monarchies. Herodotus adapted the chronicle of kings to his new purpose. In the same way he adapted the ethnographic material to the aim of describing the character and history of the peoples with whom the Persians came in contact. The ethnographic accounts are mostly placed at points in the narrative where this contact occurred, and their historical portions (the addition of history was probably his own invention) are carried to the point where the country loses its independence. In this way we get accounts of Lydia, Babylon, the Massagetae, Egypt, Ethiopia, India, Scythia, Cyrene, Libya, and other barbarian peoples of lesser significance, in the first half of the work. Marvel at the diversity of human existence is, to be sure, natural to this genre. But the function of the ethnographic accounts is to present the diverse nations as so many obstacles to imperialism: diversity of custom (*nomos*) and way of life (*ethos*) show the futility of world rule. The paradigm for this view is Darius' Scythian campaign (4.1–142), which is in many ways the hinge joining the two parts of the work together and in which the idea of European freedom is made explicit for the first time.

The main obstacle to Persian world rule was the Greeks. Here Herodotus was faced with the difficulty that Greek history was not yet a developed literary genre.[1] He solved the problem by treating Greek history in separate accounts which are somewhat analogous to the ethnographic accounts. Thus separate *logoi*, especially concerned with Athens and Sparta, but also with other states, are inserted at points when the Greeks came in contact, either friendly, or, more often, hostile, with the eastern powers. The history of Pisistratus and the early history of Sparta is inserted at the moment when Croesus seeks to make an alliance with the most powerful Greek state (1.59–68); the Cleisthenic revolution and further history of the Spartan kings comes at the point when Aristagoras of Miletus seeks mainland alliances against the Persians (5.39–48 and 55–96); the history of the Spartan kings is resumed at the point when Sparta collects hostages from Aegina, which had submitted to Darius (6.56–60). Other portions of Greek history are subordinated to Persian campaigns, e.g. the history of Ionia and some Ionian cities occurs in the section on the Persian subjugation of Ionia under Cyrus the Great (1.142ff.); the city history of Cyrene, in the African campaign under Darius (4.145–67). The life story of Miltiades is given in separate sections at the time of the Scythian campaign of Darius (4.137–8), the Ionian revolt (6.34–41), and Marathon (6.103ff. and 132–40). It is only in the last three books that we get a continuous Greek narrative. The technique suitably represents the subsidiary role played by the Greeks in the history of the rise and fall of the eastern dynasties prior to the Persian Wars.

Herodotus' style has been admired since antiquity even by those who do not admire his manner of writing history. Dionysius of Halicarnassus (*De Thuc.* 23) praises the charm (χάρις) and sweetness (ἡδονή) of his style. Herodotus used the Ionic dialect as the standard prose dialect of his time (it was also in use in his native Halicarnassus, as we know from inscriptions), but he modified it by the introduction of Homeric and other forms. He still shows the influence of the simple paratactic narrative and descriptive style which we see practised by such authors as Hecataeus. This gives his work a deceptive simplicity which is useful to him in establishing credibility. In fact, there are many complex sentences in

---

[1] The date of Charon's *Horoi Lampsakenon* is uncertain; see von Fritz (1967) 519ff.

his work, both in the narrative and in the speeches, especially at moments of dramatic impact.[1] The most famous, perhaps, of these dramatic statements occurs at the end of the story of the accidental killing of Croesus' son Atys by Adrastus, the 'man who cannot escape' (his fate): 'Adrastus the son of Gordias, the son of Midas – he who had become the murderer of his brother, and the destroyer of him who had cleansed him – when the tomb (of Atys) had been deserted by the people, slew himself over it in the knowledge that of all humans he knew he was the most unfortunate' (1.45.3). The style changes also according to the period Herodotus is narrating. In the early books, the conversations of wise men and rulers follow the patterns of early wisdom literature, for example in the Solon–Croesus story where we have the questions and answers on the topic: Who is the happiest, the second happiest, and so on. In the narrative of the Persian Wars we find long speeches constructed according to the rules of rhetoric as practised in Herodotus' life-time, and even rhetorical debates. The narrative, too, moves from greater reliance on anecdotes to more realistic descriptions of historical settings and events. Most important is Herodotus' use of certain simple stylistic devices to achieve narrative structure. From Homer on, the principle of so-called 'ring-composition' had been useful in this respect. By this device a story can be introduced and closed off by the repetition of the same sentence, or the same idea in similar words. Such repetition allows Herodotus to set his stories clearly apart and to guide the reader's understanding.[2] The resulting organization consists of a number of accounts which we may call '*logoi*' and which in turn consist of series of smaller *logoi* in a kind of chinese-box technique. It is these *logoi* which are arranged ultimately in the overall pattern of the rise and fall of Lydia and Persia. This organization has little to do with the division into nine books (each named after one of the Muses) which was made in the Hellenistic period.

An overall judgement of the achievement of Herodotus as the 'father of history' (according to a *bon mot* of Cicero's: *De legibus* 1.1.5) must begin and end with the realization that he has a unified conception of history and in particular of the period he deals with, and that this is reflected in the unified structure of his work. This is true despite the vast variety of experience embodied in it and the many types of stories he incorporated. Herodotus included in his work all forms of literary discourse that the Greeks had practised before him. In this sense his work is, if not universal, at least catholic in outlook. But the stories are not included because he happened to enjoy them or because he had at an earlier time been a practitioner of ethnography and oriental history (although this may well have been the case), but because he used them as building blocks for his description of the world of human history. The diversity of human existence and the rise and fall of great power demonstrated the

---

[1] Denniston (1960) 7–8.   [2] Immerwahr (1966) ch. 2.

permanence of the historical process as such. The work, then, is both specific (a history of the tragedy of the east) and universal (a demonstration of order in history). This perception is unique to Herodotus and puts him on a par with Homer and the tragedians rather than with his successors.

More specifically historical is his attempt to unify his work by a concept of causation, which has often been overlooked. He asks throughout the fundamental historical question (in Toynbee's phrase): 'How did this come out of that?' The basic answer, of course, lies in his account of the antecedents of the Persian Wars. In addition he has an informal, but comprehensive, causal scheme which assigns reasons to specific events. He is quite aware of the existence of economic, social and other causes that may lead to wars and other actions, but these do not play a very large part for him. Greek literature had developed, from Homer on, the concept of 'double motivation' by which events could be caused by divine and human agency simultaneously. This scheme was useful to Herodotus, for it allowed him to postulate an abstract anger of 'the divine' or even a mere 'necessity' in explanation of tragic actions such as Xerxes' invasion of Greece (cf. the dreams of Xerxes, 7.12–18). It allowed him at the same time to give human reasons for the same events, among them especially vengeance, in this case for the Persian defeat at Marathon. Thus there are three levels of causation, metaphysical, generally human, and particular. Whether we like it or not, there is in Herodotus a definite metaphysical element which is called upon to show that the things that have happened 'had to happen', which means that they had a function in the maintenance of world order.

At the same time men are entirely responsible for their actions; moral judgement is frequently given and more frequently implied. The praise of Leonidas and the condemnation of the traitor Ephialtes are important aspects of the description of Thermopylae. Herodotus' work has not only a scientific function, but also an educational one. It explains to the Greek audience the standards by which they have lived and the standards by which they must live. This element of historiography in Herodotus is not a consciously formulated one, but it came naturally to one who believed that Greek values were in fact in harmony with the natural order, whereas certain eastern values were not. Herodotus' work is thus patriotic history in a sense, although he does not denigrate barbarians as later authors were apt to do (an exception are some uncomplimentary remarks by Pausanias, king of Sparta, after the battle of Plataea, 9.79.1).

Herodotus' philosophy, like all Presocratic philosophy, is based on empirical observation; his claim is to report the traditions, supplemented by his own observations, of what has happened in history. The key term here is the word *atrekeie*, exactitude, and his favourite metaphor is that of the road travelled to true 'existence' (*ho eon logos*, e.g. 1.95.1). His reputation has not always lived up to his own estimate of his achievement. Thucydides probably had him in mind when he spoke critically of those who composed stories for the pleasure of the audience (1.21.1; 22.4). The opinion that Herodotus told fanciful tales runs through all of antiquity: Cicero while calling him the 'father of history' says in the same sentence that in his work are contained *innumerabiles fabulae* (*De legibus* 1.1.5).[1] In addition he was accused of partiality, especially in Plutarch's notorious work *On the malignity of Herodotus*. These criticisms must be seen in perspective: for Herodotus remained a widely read author whose work was fundamental for knowledge of the Persian Wars.

The reputation of Herodotus has similarly fluctuated in modern times. The problem has its roots no doubt partly in his own claim to report oral information and in his failure to distinguish between fact and bias in the reports he received. In the last hundred years, the book on Egypt has been the object of controversy, since it contains much that is clearly false. Sayce, in his commentary on Books 1–3 (1883) attacked the credibility of Herodotus while Spiegelberg and other Egyptologists tried to rescue Herodotus' reputation by citing supporting Egyptian evidence, and where that failed, by putting the blame for error on the inadequacy of his informants. The matter seemed to come to rest with Jacoby's analysis of Herodotus' sources, which he declared to be largely oral, with a preference for interrogation of the local inhabitants (*epichorioi*).[2] But recently, the Egyptian account has again been attacked, and an extreme theory postulates that Herodotus' statements on sources are all fictitious and part of his literary technique.[3]

Some source citations in Herodotus are in fact hard to understand. In his comparison of the Colchians on the Black Sea with the Egyptians he says that he had formed the opinion that the Colchians were Egyptians before he interrogated both peoples (2.104). Elsewhere in the second book he attributes his version of the story of Helen in Egypt to Egyptian sources (2.112ff.), and at the beginning of his work he attributes the story of the rapes of women, which is based on Greek rationalistic critique of Greek mythology, to the Persians (1.1–5). When speaking of the mythical phoenix in Egypt, a story we know to have been lifted from Hecataeus, he cites not his great predecessor, but 'the Heliopolitans' (2.73). These are not isolated instances; yet other statements involve more recent events, and people who would know when Herodotus was lying. Of this kind is the assertion of 'the Athenians' that the Corinthians did not participate in the battle of Salamis, an assertion denied by 'the Corinthians' and 'the rest of Hellas' (8.94). It is clear that Herodotus' criteria for citing his sources differ from those of a modern historian. In addition to their documentary value, they have for him also a rhetorical significance. Herodotus cites his sources only at special points in his narrative where he wants to stress either his

---

[1] Momigliano (1966) 127ff.   [2] Jacoby (1913) 392ff. and 419ff.
[3] Fehling (1971).

agreement or disagreement with what people say. He does not reproduce the actual course of his enquiries, but at times attributes certain statements to specific sources where he may have had the information only indirectly and even where he merely surmises that such and such was the view of his informants. Sometimes, he tells us only that part of the tradition which fits into the picture he has formed in his own mind. A suspicion arises that he may even attribute stories to certain sources because the bias of the account as he knew it would have been appropriate to the source. It may be that Herodotus applied to his reconstruction of events principles not so dissimilar from Thucydides' reconstruction of speeches. Both historians strive after authenticity for the purpose of persuasion and not only as an element of accurate reporting.

As an example we may cite Herodotus' account of Darius' accession to power as the leader of the Conspiracy of the Seven (3.67ff.). After the death of Cambyses a magus came to the throne and assumed the identity of Cambyses' brother, his legitimate successor, whom Cambyses had murdered. The impersonation was discovered by a Persian nobleman, Otanes, who formed a conspiracy of six which was joined by Darius as the seventh. They entered the palace and murdered the magus. These events are reported in great detail in a straight dramatic narrative, but without any mention of sources. Afterwards, the conspirators held a council on the form of government Persia was to receive; on this occasion, Otanes suggested democracy, another conspirator oligarchy, and Darius, royalty. Herodotus introduces the council by saying that 'speeches were made which some Greeks do not believe in, yet they were made' (3.80.2). He does not tell us what his sources were for this emphatic statement, but we can reconstruct them from his own words later on. At the end of the Ionian revolt Mardonius, the son of one of the conspirators, established democracies in the Ionian cities, 'a very great marvel to those who do not accept that Otanes had proposed to the Seven that Persia should become a democracy' (6.43.3). Wherever Herodotus got his knowledge of these speeches, he believed in their authenticity by a process of reasoning based on information about Mardonius' actions. This information no doubt came to him from Ionia, the interested party. The account of the conspiracy itself, which gives no sources, can be compared with Darius' own account in the Behistun inscription, which is in close, but not perfect, agreement with Herodotus in the names of the conspirators and the importance of what Darius in the inscription calls 'the lie in the land'. This concept is implied in Herodotus in the story of the discovery of the magus, and perhaps alluded to when Darius, before the murder of the magus, discusses lying at some length: 'where a lie must be spoken, let it be spoken. For liars and those who make use of the truth have the same aim. The first lie when they think to profit by deception, the others tell the truth in order to gain from truth and to be trusted more' (3.72.4). This sounds like a Greek perversion of a topic known in the tradition to have been associated with Darius. It is to be sure speculation, but a reasonable one, that this story also has Ionian sources based on Persian propaganda. A third section of this account deals with Darius gaining the kingship (3.85–7). It is a piquant anecdote, in which the person whose horse first neighs at sunrise, will be chosen as king. This is achieved by Darius' groom by exciting the stallion with the smell of a mare. A source for this story is given only when Herodotus mentions two versions of the specific manipulation by which this result was achieved: 'for the Persians tell it both ways' (3.87). It would be naive to give too much credence to this statement, attached as it is to a typical folk tale; the mention of the source here has primarily a literary function in that it gives support to an interesting anecdote. Herodotus handles source statements with considerable variety and freedom, although this does not make him a writer of fiction. The traditions he collected were no doubt partly fanciful, and he sometimes oversteps the border of what a modern historian would allow as accurate reporting.

2. THUCYDIDES

Thucydides, the first truly Athenian historian, differs from Herodotus in three major respects: (1) he dealt with the history of his native city; (2) an intellectual of the new school, much influenced by rhetoric and sophistic, he wrote contemporary history; (3) exiled in 424/3 B.C. after his disastrous generalship, he came to the writing of history as a man of action. The evidence about his life comes principally from his own statements, but antiquity also knew of his burial near the Cimonian tombs (with inscriptions, Marcell. 16 and 55; *Vita* 10) and of a decree by one Oinobios (Paus. 1.23.9) which recalled Thucydides after the end of the Peloponnesian War.[1] Thucydides was a grown man when the war broke out in 431 (1.1.1 and 5.26.5) and thus was probably born in the early 450s (before 454, if he was at least 30 at the time of his generalship in 424). The son of Olorus of the deme Halimus, Thucydides was without question of the Philaid clan, and it is an attractive hypothesis that he was a relative of Thucydides son of Melesias, the great antagonist of Pericles who was ostracized in 443.[2] By family tradition he was a conservative, though an admirer of Pericles. He had some connexion with the Thracian gold mines (4.105.1), which may explain why he was stationed as admiral in that region in 424. Exiled, perhaps justly, for failure to relieve Amphipolis from Brasidas' attack, he tells us only that this enabled him to get information from both sides (5.26.5). He probably died in Athens soon after 399 and was buried there. There is, however, wide ancient

---

[1] This decree should be dated in 404 or 403 because Thucydides tells us that his exile lasted twenty years (5.26.5).

[2] Wade-Gery (1932) 205–27.

speculation on the place and manner of his death. He says that he was engaged in the composition of his work from the very beginning of the war (1.1.1) and clearly indicates that he was still writing after 404 (2.65.12; 5.26.1; 6.15.3). The work ends abruptly in 411, in the middle of a sentence; it was continued by a number of later historians, Cratippus and Theopompus, whose work is lost, and Xenophon, whose extant *Hellenica* begins where Thucydides leaves off.

When Thucydides' *History* breaks off in 411, a remark is added in many manuscripts to indicate that the account of that year is not complete, though Thucydides clearly intended to carry his narrative to the end of the war in 404 (see especially 5.26). It is therefore legitimate to ask how far the work is finished *internally*. The question is complicated by Thucydides' statement that he began to write (not just to take notes) as soon as the war broke out. The comparison of this passage with others which clearly imply a knowledge of the outcome of the war has led scholars to look for other passages demonstrably written either early or late, in an attempt to understand the stages of composition through which the work went. This is not the place to give complete lists,[1] but some clues to early composition may be cited, such as the statement that Oropus was Attic (2.23.3), which it was not after 412 B.C., or the assessment of the Spartan invasions of Attica in 2.57.2 and 3.26.3, which ignores the invasion that led to the occupation of Decelea in 413. These may be merely early notations of no great significance, but the general statement that the plague did more damage to Athenian power than anything else (3.87.2, cf. 1.23.3) can apply only to the Archidamian War of 431–421 and is contradicted by the account of the Sicilian expedition and by statements about the causes of Athens' defeat (2.65). Hence there is some justification for the theory of Ullrich, propounded in 1845–6 and still held by many, that Thucydides originally composed a history of the Archidamian War and continued it when he saw that the Peace of Nicias in 421 was a peace in name only, as he eloquently explains in the so-called second proem of the work (5.26). It must be emphasized, however, that many of the passages cited as early are not necessarily so, or can be interpreted in other ways. This is especially true of the repeated references in Books 1–4 to 'this war' which in many, though not all, instances are applicable to both the 10-year war and the 27-year war. It is true that Thucydides does not indicate in these books (except for 2.65 which can be considered a late addition) how long the war was going to last, but this can be explained by the tendency of early writers, such as Homer and Herodotus, to refer in the opening of their works only to the beginning of the series of events which are to be covered. Thus, when Thucydides says at the beginning of the war (2.1.1) that 'now the war of the Athenians and the Peloponnesians and their allies began, which they . . . fought continuously' this can refer only to the Archidamian War, but it may have been written either

---

[1] Patzer (1937) and Luschnat (1971).

early or late. The case for a separate edition of the history of the Archidamian War, while not without foundation, is not very strong.

The same uncertainty does not exist for the recognition of passages which are demonstrably written late, either after the end of the war or at least during the Decelean War (413–404). The most famous passage of this sort is the so-called *Pentecontaetia* (1.89–118) which gives the history of the period 479–431 B.C. and was composed after the appearance of Hellanicus' *Atthis*, a work which was probably published after 407/6 and to which Thucydides refers in 1.97.2. The *Pentecontaetia* is largely an account of the growth of power of imperial Athens and thus presupposes the notion that the true cause of the Peloponnesian War was Sparta's fear of that power. This analysis also underlies certain speeches in the early books and is made explicit in the prooemium, at 1.23.6. Scholars have accordingly assigned such passages to a later stage in the composition than the more factual passages which give details of the immediate complaints leading to the war, such as the accounts of the incidents at Corcyra and Potidaea. Other scholars go further and assume that Thucydides' thought underwent a significant development during the period of the composition and revision of the *History*. Thus Schwartz (1919) postulated a development from factual historian to apologist for Periclean *Machtpolitik* under the impact of Athens' downfall, Schadewaldt (1929) traced a development from scientific historian to philosopher of history, and Andrewes recently suggested that the concept of ultimate causation represents a late stage in Thucydides' thought.[1] Against this stands a unitarian tradition beginning with Krüger in 1832 and in our time most forcefully represented by H. Patzer (1937) and J. H. Finley (1940 and 1942). The discussion by both camps has contributed much to the understanding of Thucydides, even though no definite solution has been reached.

One further element in this discussion is the question of the extent to which Books 5 and 8 are unfinished. Book 5 deals essentially with the events connected with the Peace of Nicias and the subsequent uneasy peace down to the destruction of Melos. Book 8 covers the after-effects of the Sicilian expedition and the beginning of the Decelean War down to the year 411, where it breaks off. In both there are unusual features: neither contains direct speeches (with the exception of the Melian Dialogue in 5, which is however unique in its dramatic form and may be an independent composition) and 5 cites documents verbatim, a practice which Thucydides normally avoids; in addition, both books exhibit some flaws in fitting the separate sections together. Although attempts have been made to explain these peculiarities,[2] it is not unreasonable to surmise that the whole work does consist of several parts: (1) the Archidamian War, Books 1–5.24; (2) the Peace of Nicias (5.25–84.1); (3) the Melian Dialogue (5.84.1–116), perhaps to be connected with (4) the Sicilian Expedition (Books 6–7);

---

[1] Andrewes (1959) 223–39.   [2] Luschnat (1971) 1115ff.

and (5) the beginning of the Decelean War (Book 8). In this scheme sections 1, 3 and 4 are fully elaborated, with 2 and 5 more sketchily executed. Nevertheless, the five sections have a great deal in common both thematically and philosophically.[1] Despite some inconsistencies, the separate parts of the work have enough elements in common to allow us to reconstruct a unified picture of Thucydides' thought.

In some respects Thucydides' conception of writing history differs so radically from that of all other ancient historians that scholars have not sufficiently observed the large debt he owes to his predecessors, especially to Herodotus. Instead they have been unduly influenced by his critical remarks about the inadequacies of prior historical research (1.20–2). Herodotus is clearly included in this critique; Thucydides corrects two small facts found in Herodotus (1.20.3) without mentioning his predecessor. Likewise, his scathing judgement on the 'logographers' who compose with a view to impressing the audience rather than to truth (1.21.1) and his admission that the lack of stories (1.22.4) will make his own work less pleasing are no doubt directed against Herodotus among others. But these remarks, which are influenced mainly by his consciousness of the novelty of his method, must not be allowed to hide his real relationship to his predecessor.

In the first place, Thucydides follows the same tradition of monumental history and establishes his position by comparing the greatness of the Peloponnesian War with the Persian Wars (1.23.1). In the historical sketch of the early history of Greece he omits all details of the Persian Wars, presumably because they had already been dealt with. He begins the history of the 'fifty years' at the exact point where Herodotus leaves off, the capture of Sestos in the winter of 479 B.C. (1.89.2). He also seems to agree with Herodotus on the contribution made by the Athenians to the national cause during the invasion of Xerxes – at least he reports the Athenian opinions in speeches (1.74 and 91) – and on the origin of the Delian League, formed by request of the allies (1.75.2 and 96; compare Hdt. 8.3).[2] His version of the murder of Hipparchus by Harmodius and Aristogeiton in 514 B.C. is close to that of Herodotus and contradicts Athenian popular tradition (1.20.2 and 6.54ff.; Hdt. 5.55 and 6.123.2). The well-known biographical sketches of Pausanias and Themistocles in Book 1 (128.3ff. and 135.2ff.) complete Herodotus' accounts and recall his style.[3] It is thus legitimate to compare the two historians with a view to tracing features in Thucydides' work back to his great predecessor. Some outstanding examples are Thucydides' dependence on Herodotus for his summer and winter chronology, the use of speeches, and in certain respects even his concept of power.

[1] de Romilly (1963).
[2] Pohlenz (1937) 170–1, after Krüger, seems to me correct.
[3] Cf. now Westlake (1977).

Two other historians have been cited as sources of Thucydides, but the relation here is not as widely significant. The history of the Greek foundations in Sicily (6.1–6) is often thought to be based on the history of Sicily by Antiochus of Syracuse which ended in 424 B.C.[1] Of greater consequence is Thucydides' dependence on Hellanicus, the great fifth-century chronographer. In the second half of the century chronology had come of age, as is shown by the Olympic victor list made by the sophist Hippias, the anonymous list of Athenian archons inscribed on stone about 425 B.C., and the works of Hellanicus, especially his *Priestesses of Argos*, which was intended to furnish a chronological framework applicable to all of Greek history.[2] When Thucydides dates the beginning of the Peloponnesian War by the priestess at Argos, the Spartan ephor, and the Athenian archon (2.2.1) he is synchronizing local chronology with a general Hellenic one. At the beginning of the account of the 'fifty years' he mentions Hellanicus by name and says that in his 'Attic monograph' he had dealt with the period only briefly and with inaccurate chronology (1.97.2). The criticism hides the fact that Thucydides is indeed influenced by the most recent chronological methodology.

We may then distinguish in Thucydides, as we did in Herodotus, a scientific method and a concept of historical interpretation, but the division cannot be made so neatly in the case of Thucydides. The effect of his scientific bent is felt throughout the *History*, not only in his attitude to the collection of evidence, but also in his abstract style and his theory of causation. Thucydides is the child of the sophistic movement in both its philosophical and its rhetorical branches, and because of the nearly total loss of the works of the sophists he is in a sense its major surviving representative.[3] Certain specific influences have been noted: the distinction of synonyms recalls Prodicus, the use of certain linguistic devices, the technique of Gorgias. But these are surface parallels. Fundamentally sophistic are Thucydides' deliberate restriction of history to observable phenomena of human conduct and the exclusion of metaphysical and religious explanations, his analysis of human progress in the 'archaeology' (1.2–19), and his identification of human reason with the art of persuasion. As has recently been shown, Thucydides' interest in the *logos* finds expression not only in the numerous set speeches, for which his work is famous, but also in frequent reports of speeches and conversations in indirect discourse, and the inclusion of letters and documents.[4] Particularly illuminating is the stylistic similarity between the speeches and Thucydides' own reasoning, especially in his analysis of the causes of civil strife on the occasion of the revolution in Corcyra (3.70–83; 84 is probably spurious).

[1] von Fritz (1967) I 507ff.
[2] Hippias: *FGrH* 6 F 2. Archon list: Meiggs and Lewis (1969) no. 6. *Priestesses of Argos*: *FGrH* 4 F 74–84.
[3] Guthrie (1969) 84ff. and 223–4.
[4] Luschnat (1971) 1146ff. and (1974) 764.

The speeches in Thucydides have antecedents both in Homer and Herodotus and are thus part of a developing historiographical tradition. From Homer they derive in particular the concept of fame as we see it developed in several speeches of Pericles (2.41.4 and 42, 43; 2.64.3–4), while Herodotus' later books offered Thucydides a model for the arrangement of set speeches in groups, such as those delivered in the Persian council before Xerxes' invasion (Hdt. 7.8–11) and the negotiations in Athens in the winter of 480/79 (Hdt. 8.140–4). Yet the Thucydidean development could not have taken place without the influence of rhetoric. The sophistic element appears in the statement in the proem that 'my habit has been to make the speakers say what was in my opinion demanded of them by the various occasions, of course, adhering as closely as possible to the general sense of what they really said' (1.22.1, tr. Crawley).[1] This statement should be read in the context of Thucydides' claim to accuracy (*akribeia*), an accuracy from which the speeches constitute an unavoidable departure. It is not necessarily a full description of what Thucydides actually does with speeches in the different parts of his work. But the reference to the reconstruction of speeches presupposes a theory of the *logos* as the common characteristic of all human intelligence, a system of thought and speech patterns shared by Thucydides, his audience, and his speakers when practising persuasive discourse. The foremost rhetorical pattern in Thucydides is that of 'probability' (*to eikos*), which is derived especially from judicial speeches. Thucydides has one example of this genre in the speeches of Plataeans and Thebans before the Spartans who act as judges (3.53–67) and one example of the epideictic genre in Pericles' Funeral Oration (2.35–46). The dialogue between Athenians and Melians derives its structure from Protagorean *antilogiai*, of which an extant example is the late fifth-century pamphlet, 'Double arguments' (*Dissoi logoi*).[2] But most of the formal speeches are of the deliberative genre, although they are not as rigid in form as later examples of the genre in the fourth-century Attic orators. The orations are frequently arranged in antithetical pairs and thus become arguments in which a situation is analysed. They are authentic in an ideal sense only and their arguments and style are very similar to those of Thucydides' own argumentative passages.

Finally, Thucydides' famous scheme of historical causation must be mentioned here. In 1.23.6 he mentions two kinds of causes for the Peloponnesian War: the quarrels with Sparta's allies, which led to specific accusations, and the 'truest motive', Sparta's fear of the growing power of Athens. It is quite clear that the second is a more fundamental cause than the first. It has been claimed that Thucydides derived his distinction between exciting and true causes from medical writing, but this theory has lately lost favour.[3] Herodotus too knew the

---

[1] Luschnat (1971) 1162ff. and (1974) 764ff.; W. C. West III in Stadter (1973) 124ff.
[2] DK 90.   [3] Cochrane (1929); Weidauer (1954); Pearson (1952) and (1972).

distinction between fundamental and ephemeral causes; a certain connexion between the two historians can be seen here. The novelty in Thucydides lies in the fact that he omits metaphysical causes entirely and that both surface and true causes are principally psychological. The interest in motivation is also characteristic of rhetoric. Thucydides no longer appears to us as the lonely thinker he was for a more romantic age.

To turn now to the interpretation of history in Thucydides, it is evident that the scientific aspect cannot explain all elements found in the work. The influence of poetry upon Thucydides is less easily grasped than his intellectual antecedents, but it exists nevertheless. We have already referred to the influence of Homer, despite the critique of Homer's accuracy in the 'archaeology' (1.9.4 and 10.3). The concept of the Peloponnesian War as the greatest war after the Trojan and the Persian Wars puts Thucydides in a direct line of succession from Homer, as does the emphasis on fame and reputation in the behaviour of the warring states. More profound, however, is Thucydides' dependence on contemporary tragic ideas, although he does not, as did Herodotus, imitate tragic plots as such. This dependence was noted long ago by Cornford (1907) in a famous and controversial book in which he made a comparison of Thucydides with Aeschylus and developed a tragic pattern in which Hybris is destroyed by False Hope, Deception and Fortune. This picture is not supported by Thucydides' vocabulary and is also historically unsound. Yet there are two aspects of the *History* which can be considered tragic. One is the defeat of Athens in its glaring contrast with the confidence of the Athenians and of Pericles in Book 1 and the early part of Book 2, prior to the plague. The other is the element of suffering experienced. by powerful and weak cities alike during the war. The much criticized passage in the proem, in which Thucydides speaks of suffering and disasters caused by the length of the war (1.23.1–3) finds its continuation in numerous climactic statements in which the historian speaks of an event as representing a high point of suffering ('*pathos*-statements', e.g. 3.49.4; 3.113.6; 7.30.3; 87.5–6). The work thus follows a tragic pattern in which a hero (Athens) is brought down by a number of factors (overconfidence, miscalculation, fortune), and it expresses a general tragic feeling for the human situation of man in an uncontrollable environment. Here the idea that suffering elevates the sufferer to tragic dignity is clearly Euripidean.[1]

The contradiction between scientific and dramatic principles in Thucydides shows itself in the very structure of the *History*. His insistence on an accurate chronology furnishes the basic organization of the work. Beginning in Book 2, he recounts the war by summers and winters (and subdivisions thereof), and at the end of each year he numbers the years consecutively in concluding statements, in many of which he also names himself. He is justly proud of the accuracy

[1] Tragedy of Athens: Immerwahr in Stadter (1973) 16–31. Tragedy of humanity: Stahl (1966).

of this system as compared to dating by city officials (see 5.20), but he did not invent it, for Herodotus had already followed a (less precise) summer and winter chronology for the last two years of the Persian Wars (480 and 479). The strict adherence to this system forces Thucydides to break apart actions stretching over several years and to intersperse important actions with short notations of minor events. Even more serious is the difficulty the reader sometimes experiences in judging the importance of events until he has pieced together the different sections pertaining to the same theatre of war. The Archidamian War in particular consisted of many isolated actions with frequently inconclusive results. The effect can be an overemphasis on precision in the description of minor engagements and on the haphazard nature of the conduct of war. But when the narrative reports a few major, but related, activities Thucydides' method triumphs; this is the case especially in the great Sicilian Expedition of 415–413 (Books 6–7).

On this skeleton outline Thucydides superimposed a dramatic structure by means of a number of devices, especially the elaboration of certain selected incidents with narrative detail and speeches. It is in these 'ornate' sections that his real purposes become most apparent. The first 'unit of narrative' (if that term is appropriate) in the account of the war deals with its beginning (2.1–25). The common opinion at that time was that the war began with the first invasion of Attica by the Spartans, but Thucydides saw the actual beginning of hostilities in an unsuccessful Theban attack on Plataea, which was allied with Athens, in time of peace (2.2–6). The story does not only mark the beginning of the war; it is also the opening scene in the tragedy of the Plataeans, which is told in three further instalments and ends with the total destruction of the city (2.71–8; 3.20–4; 52–68). It further presents us with Thucydides' view of the conflict between human planning and the irrationality of war, a fundamental theme of the *History* as a whole.[1] The Plataean incident in Book 2 was elaborated for dramatic reasons as much as for its historical significance. It is succeeded by the preparations of the major powers with an emphasis on their enthusiasm for war (2.7–8), a list of the allies on both sides (2.9), the first Spartan invasion of Attica, the sending of heralds to Athens, and a full account of the movement of the Athenians into the city and the effect this had on their spirit. This is followed by the first circumnavigation of the Peloponnese by the Athenian navy in accordance with Pericles' strategic planning (2.24, cf. 1.143.3). This also has a dramatic purpose, for Pericles' policy was later abandoned, a fact which contributed decisively to the defeat of Athens (2.65). It is clear from the beginning, then, that Thucydides' concern is only partially with historical 'fact' *per se*, or with causality in the modern sense.

At the end of the first year of the war we find Pericles' Funeral Oration,

[1] Stahl (1966) 65ff.

which is placed emphatically at the very end of the year (2.34–47.1). Pericles seeks to encourage the Athenians by presenting an idealized picture of Athenian democracy; the speech serves to explain the tenacity shown by the Athenians during the course of the war in defending their country. It also stands in dramatic contrast with the account of the plague, which struck Athens in the following year (2.47–54); that description centres on the plague's psychological effect on manners, morals and the Athenian will to fight. The people turned against Pericles, who defended himself by attempting again to inspire courage in the Athenians (2.59–65.4). To this speech is attached, on the occasion of Pericles' death, Thucydides' famous judgement on Pericles' leadership and the reasons for Athens' defeat (2.65.5–13). There is thus no real break between the first and second years of the war: 2.1–65 form an introduction to the themes that will be paramount in the *History*'s account of the war: the strategic plans on both sides and their abandonment by Athens; the pathology of democratic imperialism; the conflict between prudence and irrational commitment; and the irrational power of circumstance.

Another major unit is the sequence of three episodes in Book 3, the Surrender of Mytilene (3.27–50, preceded by the Revolt, 3.2–18), the Fall of Plataea (3.52–68), and the Revolution in Corcyra (3.69–85; years 4–5, 428/7 and 427/6 B.C.). Of these incidents only the first was of some consequence for the conduct of the war, but here too the elaborate treatment centres not so much on the historical significance as on the moral question of how to treat the captured Mytileneans, with the famous pair of speeches by Cleon and Diodotus and the reversal of the inhuman decree that the population be annihilated. Plataea was strategically insignificant (therefore the Athenians sent no help), and the number of those killed was small, since half of the defenders had previously escaped. But the Spartan execution of all remaining Plataeans forms a pendant to what had almost happened at Mytilene and is also elaborated by two speeches, delivered by the Plataeans and Thebans. The Corcyraean account concerns the break-up of a city's social fabric under outside pressure and leads to an overall judgement on the dehumanizing effect of war.

The remainder of the third book describes the beginnings of Athenian involvement in Sicily (3.86, etc.) and, in a more elaborate narrative, Demosthenes' disastrous defeat in Aetolia followed by his successes in Acarnania (3.94–8; 105–14). In the fourth book (year 7, 425/4 B.C.) some of these strands come together in the skilful narrative composition which combines the capture of Pylos with certain events in the so-called first Sicilian expedition (4.1–48, etc.).[1] Here the factual connexion is brought out in numerous ways, for the Athenian fleet was on its way to Sicily when Demosthenes detained it at Pylos, motivated in part by the shame of his defeat in Aetolia. But the main connexion between

[1] On Pylos see de Romilly (1956a) 129–31 and Stahl (1966) 140ff.

the Messenian and Sicilian actions lies in the emphasis on planning and fortune: the Athenians are made overconfident by their successes at Pylos (compare the speech of the Spartan envoys, 4.16–20). After the rejection of a Spartan peace-offer things go badly for the Athenians, especially at Corinth (4.44), in Sicily (4.58–65, speech of Hermocrates) and at Megara (4.66–74). Confident that they will always be victorious, the Athenians blame the Athenian generals for the failure in Sicily and punish them severely (65). Thucydides' chronological structure is here a help rather than a hindrance to historical interpretation.

Brasidas first comes to notice at Pylos and Megara. His northern campaigns form a contrast with Demosthenes' disaster at Delium in Boeotia (4.76–116; 120–35). A similar balance is achieved in the contrasting portraits of Cleon and Brasidas at the time of their deaths at Amphipolis (5.2–13; year 10, 422/1), which made possible the Peace of Nicias (5.14–24). These sections are elaborated by speeches, especially those of Brasidas in the northern cities, by dramatic incidents such as the negotiations after the battle of Delium (4.97–8), and by the account of the battle of Amphipolis. Everything here is pointed toward the conclusion of the peace: Demosthenes' ill-success at Delium as well as the successes of Brasidas changed the fortunes, and thereby the confidence, of the two belligerents. Yet the account of the peace (with two documents, 5.18 and 23) makes it clear that this was not the end of the war. This is the underlying assumption of the major dramatic elaborations, from the Funeral Oration on. Whenever these were written (or added), the work as it now stands leaves no doubt from the beginning that the war in fact continued through the period of peace (421–413 B.C.).

The so-called second proem (5.26) furnishes the link between the two parts of the war; it was written after the fall of Athens. The major part of Book 5 gives an account of the uneasy peace from 421 to 417 (5.27–83); here Alcibiades is first introduced (5.43). The year 416 is mainly given over to the Athenian expedition against Melos with the famous debate between the Athenians and Melians before the wilful destruction of the latter (5.84–116; year 16). This is in a very different style from the rest of Book 5; it looks back to the other great rhetorical debates at the beginning of the work and forward to the Sicilian expedition. For the portrayal of the extreme imperialism of the Athenians when directed against a helpless enemy finds its analogy in the grandiose scheme to conquer Sicily. Books 6 and 7 are almost entirely confined to an account of this expedition, a masterful combination of annalistic with dramatic narrative, punctuated by speeches at the most important points. The account begins without much reference to the preceding history except for the acknowledgement that the expedition was a second attempt, with a greater force, at the subjugation of Sicily (6.1). But at the end the factual connexion is made quite clear when it is shown that the Sicilian disaster was responsible for the final phase of the

Peloponnesian War (8.1–2). This would not have been possible without the recall and defection of Alcibiades at the beginning of the expedition (6.60–1; 88.9–93). But the factual connexion does not explain why Thucydides described the expedition in such detail. Given the central position which they were to occupy in the complete work, the Sicilian books may indeed be seen as a paradigm for the account of the Peloponnesian War as a whole. Thus they begin with a meeting of the Athenian assembly (6.8–27) with speeches by proponents and opponents, a meeting which calls to mind the assembly at Sparta in Book 1 (1.67–88). The description of the enthusiasm at Athens recalls the eagerness of the belligerents in Book 2 (2.7–8). At the end, therefore, we are entitled to see in the description of the disaster a foretaste of the final defeat of Athens in 404 B.C.; the account of this was never written by Thucydides, but we can find a pale reflection of it in Xenophon's *Hellenica* (2.2.3, 10, 23). The basic analysis of imperialism, its strengths and weaknesses, is a model for the war as a whole: the Sicilian alliances merely furnish excuses for the expansionism of Athens; the total commitment to country and empire causes misjudgement of fact; and the irrational nature of war increases the risks. Athens could have won in Sicily as she could have won the Peloponnesian War. In each case, the Athenians and their leaders themselves brought about the catastrophe by faulty judgements, in one case by recalling Alcibiades, in the other by ignoring Pericles' moderate policy (cf. the warning in 1.144.1 with 2.65.11). The judgement in 2.65.11–12, is however, not the only reason for the Sicilian disaster as described in Books 6–7. As at Pylos, the Athenians' basic error was overconfidence when faced with the unknown vicissitudes of war: they did not know the real strength of the Sicilians nor what to expect from other imperial powers such as Syracuse; they left the command in the hands of Nicias, an opponent of the war; and they got caught in the trap of neglecting their ships in the siege of Syracuse. Athens need not have lost the campaign, but the Athenians were not equal to the risks involved.

We have only an incomplete narrative of the succeeding years in Book 8, the style of which differs in many respects from that of previous books, but principally in the fact that speeches are reported in indirect discourse and thus as part of the narrative. The book consists of a number of interlocking actions: the revolt of the Ionian members of the empire; Alcibiades' machinations with Sparta and Persia; the oligarchic revolution in Athens and its overthrow; Alcibiades' return to Athens. The general drift of this fragmentary account seems to be to demonstrate how the Athenians, despite their reverses, continued to hold out, contrary to their own and the enemy's expectations (8.1–2; 96, the disaster of Euboea).

It is thus beyond question that the account of the Peloponnesian War was planned by Thucydides as a unified dramatic structure, in which the Sicilian

Expedition had a central position.[1] Similar conclusions can be drawn from Book 1, which forms a general introduction to the whole war. The structure of this book differs fundamentally from the chronological structure of the war itself, for it is an *argument* which proceeds in historical phases not organized by years. The phases are as follows:

(1) Early history of Greece (1.2–19).
(2) Military events at Corcyra and Potidaea, which led to accusations that the treaty of 446 B.C. had been broken (1.24–65).
(3) Assembly at Sparta and Spartan decision to declare war (1.66–88).
(4) History of the 'fifty years', 479–431 B.C. (1.89–118). Chronologically out of order.
(5) Meeting of Peloponnesian League and decision to declare war (1.119–25).
(6) First embassies between Athens and Sparta (1.126–8.1).
(7) The later careers of Pausanias and Themistocles, heroes of the Persian Wars (1.128.2–38). Chronologically out of order.
(8) Further Spartan embassies to Athens, and Athenian decision to resist (1.139–45).

Seen from this point of view, the first book contains the antecedents of the Peloponnesian War presented on a large scale in a manner reminiscent of Herodotus. Overlaid is an organization by arguments. The first of these appears in the prooemium (1.1–23), which uses history as proof for two contentions: (1) the Peloponnesian War was the greatest ever fought, and (2) Thucydides' reliability was to be established by his being a *contemporary* historian. The first is justified by the demonstration that concentration of power (*dynamis*) increased steadily throughout history (1.2–19) and by the consequent length of the war and increased suffering (1.23.1–3). Thucydides' competence is argued both at the beginning and the end of the prooemium in the chapters where he discusses his new method for the analysis of contemporary sources (1.20–2). The combination of power and suffering furnishes the main theme of the *History*, the tragedy of Athens and the tragedy of humanity in war.

The second argument concerns the causes of war, which Thucydides, as we have seen, divides into the accusations levelled by Sparta's allies and the more fundamental 'truest motive', Sparta's fear of Athens' growing power. The distinction is maintained throughout the first book by ring-composition (1.23.6; 66; 88; 89.1; 97.2; 118.2; 146; for the term, see above, p. 437). The true motive, Sparta's fear of the growing power of Athens, derives of course directly from the main theme of the proem. The affairs of Corcyra and Potidaea are a selection of *casus belli* (others are mentioned briefly in 1.67.2–4); their importance lies in the breaking of the treaty of 446 with Sparta, and the effect they had on Corinth, the prime mover for war. The debate of Corcyraeans and Corinthians

[1] See now Rawlings (1981).

sheds light on the motives of the Athenians in making alliances, with self-interest winning out over observance of the treaty (1.44); these speeches are thus a part of the intellectual analysis of the causes of the war.

The great debate of the Corinthians, Athenians, King Archidamus, and the ephor Sthenelaidas before the Spartan assembly (1.66–88) is also placed under the rubric of the 'true motive', for it furnishes a picture of Athenian imperialism seen from both sides. At the same time, Archidamus advises against the war by citing the limited capabilities of Sparta. The *Pentecontaetia* (1.89–118) is placed after the account of this assembly as proof that the Spartan estimate of the situation was correct. The meeting of the allies at Sparta (1.119–25) shifts the subject under discussion from the decision to fight to an estimate of capabilities and strategy in the speech of the Corinthians, which bears comparison with the speech of Archidamus. This speech is answered at the end of the book by a speech in which Pericles links acceptance of war with an estimate of strategy (1.140–4). The story of the embassies, with the digressions on Pausanias and Themistocles, is not so easily reconciled with this logical scheme except perhaps as a contrast between the politicians of the Persian Wars and contemporary figures.

Thus the first book is primarily an investigation of the reasons for war and the attitude of the belligerents, and only secondarily an account of the antecedents. It sets up the concept of power as the main idea of the work, but the tragic implications of power will become apparent only in the course of the war itself. History is presented here primarily as proof of certain contentions of the author and not, as in the following books, for its own sake.

This outline of the work as a whole may convey the impression that Thucydides wrote first a bare chronicle of events in which he elaborated certain sections by turning them into intellectual arguments or dramatic accounts. The error of such a view can be seen from a study of the minor actions and short chapters which are numerous in the *History*. Few of them are mere chronicle. The mention of an eruption of Mt Etna (3.116) or of tidal waves (3.89) belong in a category of disasters (*pathemata*) which is mentioned prominently in the proem (1.23.3). Many events acquire significance by repetition, such as the invasions of Attica, the Athenian circumnavigations of the Peloponnese, the activities of the ships sent out by Athens to collect tribute. Others are germinal for major events, in particular the many short mentions of Athenian activities in Sicily prior to the Sicilian expedition (e.g. 5.4–5, 422 B.C.) Frequently short accounts have a paradigmatic significance. A brief mention of a battle between Mantinea and Tegea during the armistice of 423/2 illustrates the confusion reigning in the Peloponnese (4.134); the account of the murder of Spartan envoys to Persia by the Athenians and of Spartan atrocities against Athenian citizens (2.67) contains in brief the elements of the Mytilenean and Plataean incidents; the story of the destruction of the peaceful Boeotian town of Mycalessos by

Thracian mercenaries illustrates the corruption of humanity in war time (7.29). The minor accounts are frequently informed by the same principles as the major ones.

Unlike Herodotus, Thucydides subjected historical experience to a single style of reporting. He does not report what others have said directly, but through the mirror of his own thought. The reader is guided not so much by the sequence of *logoi* as by the uniformity of thought-patterns in both narrative and speeches. A strong abstract conceptual framework of antitheses serves to impart meaning to the recording of historical fact. The most general is the antithesis of *logos* (representing human activity) and *ergon* (representing outside forces[1]); more specifically he speaks of *gnome*, intelligence, and *tyche*, chance. Such terms are representative of clusters of ideas (*techne, tropoi, nomos* [skill, character, custom]) against *physis* and *ho paralogos* (the last a Thucydidean coinage for the irrational) which use history as proof (*tekmeria, semeia*) for the antithetical picture of the conflict of man and his environment.[2] But the human mind, in addition to its rational element, contains also the irrational element of passion (*orge, tolma*). Human nature (*anthropeia physis, to anthropeion*), which is principally confined to the irrational element, thus acts, like *tyche* (luck), as a blind and uncontrollable force. The vocabulary of power and empire (*dynamis* and *arche*) partakes of both the rational and irrational: rational is the fear (*deos*) of the loss of security (*kindynos*) and the concentration of power (*paraskeue*) required to avoid it. Irrational are the commitment (*eros*) to empire and the desire for more (*pleonexia*) which resulted in Athens' defeat. A similar dichotomy occurs also in the technical descriptions of warfare, especially naval warfare, which is based on experience and training (*empeiria* and *melete*) as opposed to luck (*tyche*).

This analysis, which comes out strongly in the speeches and in Thucydides' own observations, is the intellectual ('scientific') corollary to the dramatic narrative of events. It raises the question of the purpose of Thucydides' work, which is considered by some a treatise in political science rather than pure history. This interpretation is reinforced by Thucydides' own remarks in the proem's section on method (1.22.4):

καὶ ἐς μὲν ἀκρόασιν ἴσως τὸ μὴ μυθῶδες αὐτῶν ἀτερπέστερον φανεῖται· ὅσοι δὲ βουλήσονται τῶν τε γενομένων τὸ σαφὲς σκοπεῖν καὶ τῶν μελλόντων ποτὲ αὖθις κατὰ τὸ ἀνθρώπινον τοιούτων καὶ παραπλησίων ἔσεσθαι, ὠφέλιμα κρίνειν αὐτὰ ἀρκούντως ἕξει. κτῆμά τε ἐς αἰεὶ μᾶλλον ἢ ἀγώνισμα ἐς τὸ παραχρῆμα ἀκούειν ξύγκειται.

and the absence of the story element in my work will perhaps make it rather unpleasant in recitation; but I shall be satisfied if those will judge it useful who

[1] See Parry (1981).
[2] Schmid–Stählin 1 5, 30ff.; Edmunds (1975).

454

will desire to obtain a real understanding both of past events and of those future events which because of the human condition will be similar or nearly so. My work is composed as a possession for ever rather than as a prize composition to be heard for the moment.

Here almost every word is debatable (and the translation is based on certain assumptions). Some have supposed that Thucydides subscribes to a cyclical theory of history from which knowledge of past events can be used to predict (and therefore avoid) the future. Others claim that Thucydides (as a political philosopher) merely furnishes understanding of history, but that this can have no practical effect. The solution is to be found in sophistic ideas on the nature of reality and knowledge. Thucydides does not believe in exact repetition in history, but in a similarity of observed phenomena based on the constancy of the human situation. History gives an understanding of these elements which can be used for the analysis of subsequent events, but not to predict the future. The utility of history (a fundamental criterion in later historians, which Thucydides was the first to mention)[1] consists in furthering understanding, which is of real practical importance. To the sophists the distinction between theory and practice did not exist. The citizen and the politician learn from history, as Pericles says Greece may learn from Athenian democracy (2.41.1).

It would be erroneous, however, to confine the meaning of the work to those factors which Thucydides himself mentions in the proem, for he deals there with a restricted number of topics. As has been mentioned previously, Book 1 also sets the stage for the drama of the war. Although Thucydides eliminates metaphysical causation and thus the Herodotean 'necessity' of history, he nevertheless shows from the beginning the *likelihood* of disaster. The first book is to be read with a knowledge of Athens' defeat. This raises the question of Thucydides' attitude toward empire and power in general and toward Athens and the Athenian empire in particular. Thucydides gives much scope to statements hostile to the Athenian empire (cf. the speech of the Mytileneans at Olympia, 3.9–13) and he stresses the effects of power politics on weak nations (cf. the Melian debate), but he also presents imperialism as practically unavoidable (in Pericles' speeches) and shows admiration for the perseverance of Athens (8.1.3). The idealized picture of democratic Athens in the Funeral Oration affects the reader's judgement here regardless of the opinions Thucydides may have held on democracy as a form of government (see his potentially critical remarks in 2.65.8–9 and 8.97.2). A similar ambiguity exists with respect to Thucydides' moral judgements. It is often asserted that he passes no moral judgements in his work; but the description of the degeneration of morals as the result of the plague (2.53) and of party strife in the cities (3.83) presuppose approval of common Greek morality in time of peace. We must be guided in all these questions by the impact

[1] de Romilly (1956*b*).

of the narrative and not simply by the presence or lack of specific statements by Thucydides.

The credibility of Thucydides has not been questioned to the same degree as that of Herodotus. As a source for modern historians he is unquestionably far superior, since he deals in great detail with contemporary history. Yet this confidence in Thucydides is in part misplaced. We have seen that the elaboration of incidents is not always based on their significance for the course of the war. His view of what was relevant in the account of a war is excessively narrow; Herodotus' concept of history is very much broader. Thus Thucydides was led to omit a number of facts we consider crucial: among them are the peace of Callias, the tribute assessment of 425 B.C., and the relations of Athens and Melos before the Melian expedition of 416. His use of documents is superficial; his work is based principally on oral sources.[1] The narrative is exceedingly accurate, of course, but the detail it gives is not always relevant from our point of view. It has been said that Thucydides describes warfare from the point of view of the lower commissioned ranks; this is perhaps unfair, since the purpose of such detail is frequently dramatic. But most troubling to readers and commentators alike is the style of the speeches: magnificent as they are as complex analyses of military and political problems, they require a degree of concentration no popular audience, ancient or modern, could muster. It is hard to believe that admirals would encourage their crews in the words Thucydides gives to the Peloponnesian commanders before the battle of Rhium in which they were facing the Athenian navy, a much more experienced enemy. The commanders were attempting to counteract the fear caused by a previous defeat:

> 'It was not through our own cowardice that we were defeated, nor is it right that that part of our resolve which was not completely crushed, but has within it an answer [to the enemy], should be blunted by the result of a chance event, but we must believe that men may fail as the result of fortune, while remaining steadfastly brave in their resolve, and that when bravery is present they cannot use inexperience as an excuse for becoming cowards on any occasion.' (2.87.3)

The basic idea of the sentence is simple enough, but its cramped style is Thucydides' own. The words do not reproduce a speech actually delivered, as is indicated by their being attributed not to one speaker, but to all three commanders. As it stands, the speech is more an analysis of the importance of courage in a specific situation than an inspiring exhortation.

3. COMMON ELEMENTS OF FIFTH-CENTURY HISTORIOGRAPHY

With Herodotus and Thucydides, the fifth century saw the creation of historiography as a separate form of intellectual and artistic activity which could hold

---

[1] Gomme (1945–70) I 1ff.

its own against poetry on the one hand and philosophy on the other. To be sure, a sense of history had existed in Greece since the time of Homer, and poetry, philosophy and science contributed decisively to the formation of the new genre. But the catalysts that transformed these endeavours into something new were the experience of the Persian Wars and the vicissitudes of the Athenian empire; both heightened the sense of the importance of the past for the present and also the sense of the tragic limitation of human action. History was born out of the spirit of tragedy.

One feature of history is its monumentality: history was to deal with great subjects and each subject would have its own historian. This makes the historian's assertion of competence more than a scientific claim: what the Muse (i.e. poetic tradition) was to Homer, *historie* was to Herodotus and Thucydides. The claim that the historian is superior to the poet by stricter criteria of truth is also made by both historians, by Herodotus in the distinction between legendary times and the more recent period of which we have 'knowledge' (e.g. 1.5.3), by Thucydides in his disparagement of poets and 'logographers' in the chapters on method. The truthfulness of the historian is essential to the acceptance of his interpretations and value judgements by the audience. In these lies the real function, or 'utility', of history. In Herodotus, utility is not yet a conscious concept, as it is in Thucydides, but his *Histories* clearly seek to create a patriotic and moral impact; they contribute to the maintenance of social values by an understanding of the past. From the beginning, then, ancient historiography is not confined to the preservation of the record, but aims also at an influence on the audience through example. The nature of that audience differs for the two authors: Herodotus addresses himself to all Greeks, Thucydides to a more specifically intellectual audience. Both writers write patriotic, not merely objective, history.

The close association of history and literature produced a distinctive manner of presentation which creates difficulties for anyone who tries to use the ancient historical works as source materials. Especially through the influence of epic and drama Herodotus and Thucydides set a style followed by almost all ancient historians, which may be called mimetic, that is, they write as if they had been present at the events they describe. (An exception is the Oxyrhynchus historian who aims at a more dispassionate narrative.) When Herodotus describes the conversations between Gyges and Candaules or the feelings of Xerxes after Salamis we can hardly believe that this is based on evidence; it is rather an imaginative, 'poetic', reconstruction aiming at authenticity in an idealized sense. The same is true of Thucydides when he supplies motives for actions by delving, so to speak, into the minds of the participants (e.g. the feelings of Cleon and the assembly in the discussion of Pylos, 4.27ff.) without mentioning his informants. The use of speeches is only the most obvious device of the mimetic method;

it reaches into the smallest narrative details and tends to destroy the distinction between 'fact' and interpretation. This factor, more than any other, gives ancient historiography its unique character.

4. HISTORICAL WRITING IN THE FOURTH CENTURY AND IN THE HELLENISTIC PERIOD

Thucydides' uncompleted *History* soon found continuators and imitators. Xenophon's *Hellenica* begins almost exactly where Thucydides left off; another contemporary, Cratippus,[1] wrote a similar continuation of the *History*; from Oxyrhynchus have come fragments of a historian of considerable quality which deal with the events of 396–395 B.C. The Oxyrhynchus Historian (*FGrH* 66) cannot be identified with any known writer, but appears to have followed in Thucydides' footsteps. The indebtedness of subsequent historians to Thucydides can also be seen in the way they used him as a standard for the writing and assessment of historical works. His influence is not often acknowledged, but it can be traced in many writers, even those who make no mention of him, who rejected his stylistic idiosyncrasies and who were unable or unwilling to attempt his penetrating analysis of historical cause. Consciously or unconsciously they reflected his preference for constant features of civilization, his exclusion of many features of economic, social and cultural life. In antiquity (and it is still true in modern times) there was a constant temptation to judge historical writers by the extent to which they conformed to Thucydidean standards.

At first sight this emphasis on Thucydides would seem a productive way to approach the historians of the fourth century and the Hellenistic period. Xenophon and Polybius, the two historians from these periods whose work is most fully preserved, are each in some sense 'Thucydidean' (Madame de Romilly has even called Polybius a 'faux Thucydide').[2] Yet these two authors are by no means representative of the range and variety of historical writing in these periods, a variety of which the ancient lists of 'canonical' historians are a useful reminder. They regularly included Xenophon as well as Herodotus and Thucydides. Polybius was often excluded, probably because of his inelegant style. More frequently admitted were Theopompus, Ephorus, Philistus and other writers whose approaches differed sharply from that of Thucydides. Felix Jacoby's superb collection of the fragments of the Greek historians (*FGrH*) now makes it easy to appreciate the great extent and diversity of historical writing; though still incomplete, it contains over 850 entries, a large percentage of them from writers of the fourth century and the Hellenistic period.

[1] On Cratippus' dates see Gomme (1954a) and Bloch (1940) 316 n. 4.
[2] de Romilly (1956b) 57. Of the original thirty-nine books of Polybius' narrative 1–5 survive substantially complete, the rest in fragments and excerpts, often extensive.

Some of these authors are little more than names; others can be dismissed as trivial. But among them are also to be found practitioners of important types of history quite unlike those produced by Herodotus, Thucydides, Xenophon or Polybius. Local chronicles, for example, best attested in the *Atthides* of Androtion (*FGrH* 324) and Philochorus (*FGrH* 328), were a major form of historical writing for the Greeks, and had some influence on the development of annalistic history among the Romans. Similarly, the popular form of foundation stories (*ktiseis*: legends about the foundation of cities, etc.) was taken over and developed by Cato in his *Origines*.

This complex variety of historical writing is not however a development confined to the later period; in recent years we have come to suspect that many types of literature best attested for the fourth and later centuries were already present, at least in embryo, in the fifth century. Ethnographic and travel literature, often embellished with much anecdotal material as in the case of Ion of Chios' *Epidemiae* (*FGrH* 392), discussions of constitutions, real and ideal, reports of wondrous events and strange happenings, and biographical literature, had all developed by the end of Thucydides' lifetime. Against this background Thucydides' rigorous focus on political and military history appears anomalous. It is clear from the fragments of his near contemporary Ctesias of Cnidus (*FGrH* 688) that Thucydides' exclusions were not universally adopted. Ctesias' work was much quoted and excerpted in late antiquity and was undoubtedly popular precisely for the story-telling element (τὸ μυθῶδες) which Thucydides repudiated. It is full of fanciful details, pathetic episodes elaborately narrated, elements of biography and romance side by side with political and military narrative. These elements continue to be found in the work of many Greek historical writers and remind us how dangerous it is to make our assessments solely by Thucydidean standards.

One line of historians, to be sure, attempted to follow Thucydides' lead. Among them are to be numbered, with some qualifications, Xenophon of Athens, Hieronymus of Cardia, Timaeus of Tauromenium and Polybius of Megalopolis. Xenophon's *Hellenica*, probably written in several stages during his long life (c. 428–354 B.C.), is an effort to practise what he understood as Thucydidean historiography; it is contemporary, political and austere. But the result is far from successful. From time to time, as in the story of Theramenes' condemnation under the Thirty Tyrants, it is remarkably powerful and vivid (*Hell.* 2.3.15–55). Throughout there are flashes of psychological perception. Yet the work as a whole seems to be a loosely strung narrative of the wars that Greece experienced from 411 to 362. There is no rigorous unity of subject or theme, but rather a *historia perpetua* that could be continued beyond Xenophon's stopping point; as the last sentence of the work puts it, 'the events after these will perhaps be the concern of another' (*Hell.* 7.5.27, tr. Brownson).

Most remarkable are the exclusions from the work. Throughout the *Hellenica* Xenophon is concerned about what it is appropriate to include in a narrative of this sort. Among the exclusions some, such as the failure to mention the foundation of the second Athenian naval confederacy, are most likely the result of carelessness or oversight. Others reveal the limits and weaknesses of his criteria for selecting material, and result in a very narrow and restricted narrative. One example is especially revealing: for Xenophon himself the activities of Socrates were clearly of prime importance and most historians today could not write the history of the late fifth century without some discussion of them. But Xenophon apparently believed that such material had no place in a narrative such as the *Hellenica*.[1] Although he reports Socrates' political activity, his refusal to allow an illegal indictment of the commanders at Arginusae in 406, he makes no mention of his trial and condemnation in 399, developments which from the point of view of a modern historian would be among the major events of the year. Instead Socrates' activities are relegated to a separate treatise and to a quite different type of narrative, the *Memorabilia*, a collection of notable sayings and actions.

Thus Xenophon's attempt to write a Thucydidean political-military history resulted in a sharp differentiation of literary forms. The material excluded from the *Hellenica* appears in other works, autobiographical memoir, biographical essay, collections of notable sayings and deeds, constitutional disquisitions and historical romance: the *Anabasis*, the *Agesilaus*, the *Memorabilia*, the *Cyropaedeia* and the *Politeia of the Lacedaemonians*. The *Cyropaedeia*, for example, contains elements of folk-tale, biography and romance that coexist with political and military narrative in Ctesias and to some extent in Herodotus. In Xenophon, the two types of narrative have been differentiated.

The *Hellenica* also pays little attention to differences in constitutional and civic form – *politeia* – among the various states that figure in his story. Herodotus' ethnographic interests encouraged the inclusion of such material in his work and Thucydides found important thematic material in the contrast between the relatively open, innovative and adventurous society of Athens and the more closed and conservative ways of the Spartans. Xenophon, in the *Hellenica*, again takes a narrow definition of his task. There is nothing to correspond to the debate about constitutional forms in Herodotus 3.80–4 nor to the interplay of real and ideal elements in the Periclean Funeral Oration of Thucydides' second book. A process of differentiation of literary forms is again at work, and Xenophon's interest in constitutional topics appears in separate monographs such as the *Hiero* and the *Politeia of the Lacedaemonians*. The first of these is a discussion of the moral and psychological implications of tyranny; the second an exploration of the sources of Spartan greatness – and decline.

[1] *Hellenica* 2.3.56; 4.8.1; 5.1.4.

Composed sometime in the first three decades of the fourth century, the *Politeia of the Lacedaemonians* is an example of a literary form – the *Politeia* – which had already been developed by Xenophon's day, and which continued its literary career for several centuries. The sophists showed considerable interest in forms of civic life, as Critias' *Politeiai* (DK 86 B 6–9 and B 31–8), Thrasymachus' speech *Peri politeias* (DK 85 B 1) and Protagoras' *Antilogies* (DK 80 B 5) show.[1] Hippodamus of Miletus and Phaleas of Chalcedon also wrote treatises on forms of civic life.[2] Xenophon carried on this interest using a form that seems to have been popular in the late fifth and early fourth centuries – an essay of moderate length, usually written in an unpretentious prose style. The early examples of this form seem to have been argumentative and speculative, and to have stressed the originality of the writer and the unusual features of civic life in a single city, real or imagined. Although the essays sometimes seem to describe rather than to evaluate, the author's point of view is made clear, frequently by first-person assertions or by answers to imagined objections (*hypophora*). They thus share a polemical tone with some of the proposals for governmental reform and with the discussions of the ancestral constitution that can be detected behind some sections of the Aristotelian *Athenaion politeia*. But if they are in some ways related to the shadowy and sub-literary pamphlet literature of the late fifth and early fourth centuries, the *Politeiai* are of greater and more lasting interest and influence.

Xenophon's *Politeia of the Lacedaemonians* probably attracted to the Xenophontic corpus another example of this form, the *Politeia of the Athenians*. Scholars disagree about the date of composition, although of late sentiment seems to be growing for a setting in the first years of the Peloponnesian War, i.e. 431–424 B.C. The author, almost certainly not the historian Xenophon, is sometimes called 'The Old Oligarch', although his age and identity are quite unknown and his political views are not those of the conventional oligarch. The work shows great hostility to Athenian democracy, and indeed deplores many of the features commended in the Periclean Funeral Oration in Thucydides,[4] but the object of its attack is not so much the claims of the democrats as the belief of some critics of democracy that this form of government will swiftly pass away. The author of the treatise points to the consistency of policy and the social coherence of Athenian democracy and exposes thereby the naivety of the view that it will soon disintegrate. Politically, then, the work

---

[1] The *Peri politeias*, ascribed to Herodes (Atticus?) but often thought to belong to the fifth century, is a speech with only a few words about civic form. Wade-Gery (1945) made a strong case for Critias as author, but caution is needed; see Albini (1968).

[2] Hippodamus: Aristotle, *Politics* 2, 1267b22–69a27. The fragments ascribed to a Hippodamus in Stobaeus, *Anthologium* 4.1.93–5 (Henge IV 28ff.) are often thought to belong to a later period; see Delatte (1922) 125–60. Phaleas of Chalcedon: *Politics* 1266a39–b21.

[3] The evidence is set forth in Treu (1966) 1947–1962. See also Bowersock (1971).

[4] de Romilly (1962).

belongs to the reaction against the Athenian democracy; intellectually, it reflects sophisticated doubts about the premiss, expressed in Xenophon, *Memorabilia* 2.6.19 and 24, that the *poneroi* (people of low quality/low class) should be unable to form lasting associations.

The pseudo-Xenophontic *Politeia of the Athenians* focuses on the alleged practices of contemporary Athens. The essays by Phaleas of Chalcedon and Hippodamus of Miletus were, however, constructions of imaginary ideal states. Even Xenophon's *Politeia of the Lacedaemonians* is primarily an idealizing speculation about the Lycurgan system into which his comments about the degeneracy of fourth-century Sparta (ch. 14) intrude and inevitably startle the reader. Later Aristotle transformed the *Politeia* into a more descriptive form. His *Politeia of the Athenians*, the only surviving example of the 158 *Politeiai* compiled in his school, begins with a historical survey of the development of the Athenian constitution and concludes with a description of how the constitution functioned in history. Earlier *Politeiai* seem largely to have been speculations about the ideal rather than discussions of the actual and practical.[1]

In the period before Aristotle, the closest relatives of the *Politeiai* are to be found not in historical writing or political analysis but in the literature of escape. Disillusionment with practical politics in Athens during the Peloponnesian War, especially in intellectual circles, coincided with an economic and military situation that encouraged dreams of ideal worlds and of golden ages returned. In comedy Aristophanes' *Birds* is perhaps the best example of this tendency, but the *Ecclesiazusae*, with its emphasis on communism of property and of women, is closer to the themes of some of the *Politeiai*. Indeed, it is so close, especially to Plato's *Republic*, that many have suspected contact between the authors or a common source for the two works, e.g. Protagoras' *Antilogies* (DK 80 B 5) which Aristoxenus (fr. 67 Wehrli) claimed was the source for Plato's ideal state. But this charge is 'not reconcilable with Aristotle's statement [*Pol.* 2.1266b34]...that no one...apart from Plato, has ever proposed community of women and children'.[2] Indeed, there is little need to search for a specific literary connexion when the explanation of the similarities may lie in a common situation rather than in a common source.[3] The prominence of the *Politeia* as a literary form and even the content of many of the examples are surely in large measure due to the rapid social and economic changes affecting the Greeks of the late fifth and fourth centuries. Many of these changes conflicted with ideals and expectations inherited from earlier periods of Greek history, for example with the ideal of equality of land holdings, so often reflected in the arrangements for the establishment of colonies. In most Greek cities

---

[1] It is precisely to this that Aristotle objects in *Politics* 4, 1288b37f.
[2] Dover (1972) 201.
[3] Pečírka (1963) 215–19; (1976) 5–29; and above, p. 407.

before the late fifth century, it was unusual, it appears, for land to leave the family. After the Peloponnesian War, the alienation of land became much more common and as a result in some states a few citizens acquired disproportionate holdings. The concentration of land ownership stimulated not only revolution-ary programmes for land reform but also, especially among more conservative thinkers, dreams of societies that could escape such distressing changes. These speculations did not commonly lead to practical application, although they did focus attention on fundamental issues within Greek society, such as the distribu-tion of wealth, the regulation of dowries, the status of women and the nature of citizenship. Only in rare cases – Plato's involvement in Sicily, or Alexarchus' foundation of Ouranopolis – were attempts made to put theory into practice.[1] The social revolutions of the fourth and third centuries meantime went on largely untouched by such theorizing, unless one wishes to see behind the revolution of Agis and Cleomenes in Sparta the philosophical ideas of the Stoic Sphaerus.[2] The main effect, in any event, was surely on literature, not on life. The fantasies of escape long present in political theorizing blended with the romantic fictions of the geographical literature of the Hellenistic age. The most famous example of the fusion is undoubtedly Euhemerus' *Hiera anagraphe* or *Sacred narrative* (*FGrH* 63) written c. 300 B.C. and combining a description of imagined isles in the east, a theory of the origin of the gods and a sketch of a utopian society. Several of these elements had already been brought together in Theopompus' *Philippica* (*FGrH* 115 F 75) but Alexander's conquests enriched and stimulated the Greek imagination of the east. Even ostensibly factual historical narrative resembles romance or fantasy literature when the subject matter concerns the east, for it is the east, not Magna Graecia, Italy, Africa or the lands of the Hesperides and Hyperboreans that is the fantasy world for Greek narrative. Inhabited by huge snakes, strange tribes, exotic animals, real or imagined, ascetics and Gymnosophists, it provided the setting for the most fanciful narratives of the historians. These elements are conspicuous in the works of Alexander's contemporaries Megasthenes (*FGrH* 715), Nearchus (*FGrH* 133) and Onesicritus (*FGrH* 134). The reason for this romantic treat-ment of the east is of course in part the nature of the orient itself, but it may also be that the east was associated with narratives which emphasized the unknown or unverified and exploited their emotional effects. Our knowledge of the influence of Near-Eastern forms of narrative on Greek writing is still insufficient, but from time to time there are traces of what may be indigenous narrative patterns. A comparison of Ctesias' tale of Semiramis (Diodorus 2.14) to some of the stories about Alexander is instructive, and suggests that some of the latter may have been modelled on old Near-Eastern narratives. The elaborate treat-

---

[1] Ferguson (1975) 108–10; Tarn (1933), esp. 141–4.
[2] Ferguson (1975) 132–5.

ment given by many historians to his journey to the shrine of Zeus Ammon or Callisthenes' tale that the Pamphylian sea made way before him (*FGrH* 124 F 31) should perhaps be related to these narratives rather than seen simply as attempts at ingenious flattery.[1]

Ephorus and Theopompus, pupils of Isocrates who came to be two of the most influential historians of antiquity, also rejected the narrow 'Thucydidean' criteria for the selection of subject matter. Ephorus (*FGrH* 70) turned from a single contemporary action to a comprehensive narrative of the growth and activities of the cities of Greece and Asia Minor from the time of the return of the Heraclidae to *c.* 340 B.C. Included were myths, cult and foundation legends, geographical and ethnographic material as well as a political and military narrative. This clear and polished account became virtually the standard history for the periods that it covered. The work was a 'universal history' – that is, one that brought together widely scattered events in Greek history into a single narrative, and even found space for reference to barbarian affairs – Persian, Egyptian and Carthaginian – which had a bearing on events in Greece.

His contemporary Theopompus (*FGrH* 115) began his historical career with works that followed closely in the footsteps of his great predecessors. His lost *Epitome* of Herodotus was apparently an early work, and it appears from the fragments that his *Hellenica* is a continuation of Thucydides down to the battle of Cnidus in 394 B.C. But in his *Philippica* he breaks new ground. This huge work, of whose fifty-eight books very little remains, incorporated an immense range of material, anecdotal, fabulous, discursive, rich with digressions on wondrous happenings (the Thaumasia, FF 64–76), the demagogues of Athens (FF 85–100) etc.; and it was explicit about his willingness to include myth (F 381). But its real innovation was its focus on a single great personality, 'for Europe has never brought forth a man such as Philip the son of Amyntas' (F 27). Biographical elements were present in Herodotus' work, and not totally eliminated by Thucydides. But Theopompus took the step of using a single man, Philip II of Macedon, as the core of his history around which was organized the immense and rich material of the *Philippica*. Philip, moreover, is not only a convenient organizational device but a paradigm whose success reveals much about the nature of power and morality.[2] The result is a quite new type of history, a work which had no real successor in antiquity but was almost as much used and cited as Ephorus' History.

Ephorus and Theopompus each produced original types of history and their works are quite dissimilar. Yet there is a common denominator – rhetoric. The emergence of a systematic rhetoric in the fifth century B.C. and the increasing

---

[1] Cf. Nearchus, *FGrH* 133 F 3. Ptolemy, normally a very restrained and reliable historian, tells a very fanciful story of Alexander's visit to Ammon's shrine: *FGrH* 138 F 8.

[2] Connor (1967).

emphasis on rhetoric in the training of Greek political elites inevitably meant that history would be affected and that the two major prose forms of the Greeks, history and oratory, would show similarities. The affinities, however, lie deeper. Isocrates' Panhellenism undoubtedly encouraged the historians to select subject matter that emphasized the common elements in Greek history. More important, the treatment of events is shaped by a concern with the assessment, often a highly moral assessment, of the actions and the actors. This is less evident and perhaps still controversial in the case of Ephorus,[1] but Theopompus' case is clearer, as an ancient critic testifies:

> The crowning accomplishment of his works is the distinctiveness which no one either before or after has so thoroughly or movingly accomplished. Of what does it consist? It is to see and express in each action not only the things that are clear to all observers but to examine also the hidden motives of actions and actors...and to reveal all the mysteries of seeming virtue and undiscovered vice. Indeed...the fabled examination in Hades...is not so exacting as that in the writing of Theopompus. (Dionysius of Halicarnassus, *Ad Pompeium* 6.7f. = *FGrH* 115 T 20)

To a modern reader this often appears as no more than the substitution of moral censure for Thucydidean analysis of events. But many ancient writers, even Polybius at times, thought that the function of history was the proper allotment of praise and blame. Since this was the primary purpose of ceremonial or display speeches, history had close links with epideictic oratory.[2] Stylistic affinities between the two genres resulted, and some writers, for example Theopompus, won distinction in both epideictic and historical work. The connexion of course went deeper than style and directed the historian's attention to the search for subject matter suitable for enkomion or censure. This epideictic tendency in history was thus compatible with the biographical interest that characterizes much of fourth-century literature and it persisted to some degree in almost all later Greek historical writing, sometimes in the form of laudatory treatments of great men and great deeds, sometimes in the form of severe criticisms of actions and motives, sometimes in lurid descriptions of vice and depravity.

The close tie to oratory which is evident in Ephorus and Theopompus becomes a persistent factor in later historiography and equally persistent is the discussion of the problem it raised – the relationship between history and rhetoric. Polybius says (12.28.10f.) that Ephorus dealt with this problem in a remarkably persuasive way, but the substance of Ephorus' comments can only be conjectured.[3] Whatever he said, his remarks did not close the question. History was constantly in danger of absorption by rhetoric, and the ancient

---

[1] Walbank (1955) 7 questions Barber's views (1935), esp. 78f. and 151f.
[2] Compare Polybius 2.61.6; 10.21.8 and 1.14.5 with Aristotle, *Rhet.* 1.3.3 (1358b12).
[3] See the commentary on *FGrH* 70 F 111.

writers were well aware of the problem. The danger was especially acute when the actions of a great man or powerful king were under consideration; it was easy then for history to resemble panegyric. Even Polybius felt that his separate monograph on Philopoemen demanded a defence of the hero with rhetorical *auxesis* (amplification) of his accomplishments (10.21.2 = *FGrH* 173 T 1). But continuous political-military history demanded a sterner devotion to the truth.

Among modern critics of ancient historiography it has become almost a cliché that history lost its autonomy and became a mere branch of oratory. Certainly historical writers applied their extensive rhetorical training to the problems of narrative, and it has also been shown that the rules and procedures of Hellenistic historiography derive largely from rhetoric.[1] But it is important not to be misled by these facts, nor by certain passages in Cicero that seem to imply a subordination of history to rhetoric.[2] Cicero's own view is not fully consistent, and he well knew that while it was allowed to rhetoricians to lie in their narrations (*historiae*), the highest duty of a real historian was to the truth.[3] Pliny (*Epist.* 5.8.9) was perhaps more accurate in his comment that history and oratory had much in common but many differences even in those features which seemed to have most in common. Thus history and oratory existed in mutual tension and mutual exploitation, orators adapting exempla from history, historians using the stylistic devices of oratory to produce a sustained and appealing narrative. Since rhetoric had a dominant position in the educational system, history was constantly threatened, yet it maintained a precarious autonomy and even made its own claims for the training of elites:

> ...all historians, one may say without exception, and in no half-hearted manner, but making this the beginning and end of their labour, have impressed upon us that the soundest education and training for a life of active politics is the study of History... (Polybius 1.1.2, tr. Paton)

History was also influenced by, and threatened by, poetry. Some critics viewed it, as Quintilian (10.1.31) later did, as a sort of unversified poem whose goal was emotion rather than truth. Such a view was perhaps implicit in the work of Ctesias and other writers; Thucydides and Ephorus (*FGrH* 70 F 42) seem to be rejecting just such an approach. In Duris of Samos (*FGrH* 76), however, a pupil of Theophrastus writing in the late fourth or early third century B.C., the emphasis on pleasure as a goal of historical narrative received new impetus and a more explicit articulation. His first fragment criticizes Ephorus and Theopompus for failing to attain *mimesis* (representation) and pleasure; they were concerned only with writing (αὐτοῦ...τοῦ γράφειν), i.e. with style rather than the full emotional effect of their subject matter. His own works,

---

[1] Scheller (1911).   [2] *Orator* 11.37, *De oratore* 2.36ff. Contrast *Orator* 20.68.
[3] Compare *Brutus* 10.42 and his letter to Lucceius (*Fam.* 5.12).

notably a chronicle of Samos and a history of Greek affairs from 370 to *c.* 280, were criticized for stylistic laxity but were remarkable for colourful depictions (F 70), vivid descriptions of costumes and dress (F 14), derogatory tales about the great (F 10, F 78) and sensational and emotion-charged stories such as his tale of Pericles' crucifixion of Samian trierarchs (F 67).

The distinctive features of Duris' work can perhaps best be seen by contrasting him with his near contemporary, Timaeus of Tauromenium in Sicily (*FGrH* 566, *c.* 356–260 B.C.). Cicero regarded Timaeus as *longe eruditissimus . . . et ipsa compositione uerborum non impolitus* 'by far the most learned [*sc.* of the major historians] and not unpolished in style' (*De oratore* 2.58). He was perhaps the first Greek writer to recognize the significance of Rome, and his works on Sicilian and related affairs became a standard source of information for the period prior to the Roman intervention in 264/3. Despite his love of rhetorical effects and despite Polybius' polemic he appears as a major historian, who set store by the accuracy of his narrative and resisted the emotionalism of Duris.

In Phylarchus of Athens, active in the mid third century, the tendencies detected in Duris of Samos emerge again with new vigour. The nature of Phylarchus' works (*FGrH* 81) can be determined with some confidence by a cautious comparison of the surviving fragments with portions of Plutarch's *Lives*, especially those of Agis and Cleomenes, which are heavily indebted to him, and by a judicious use of Polybius' critical remarks. These are admittedly suspect because of Polybius' chauvinism and his tendency (shared with so many other historians) to attempt to increase his own reputation by censure of his predecessors, but they help to confirm the picture of Phylarchus as a writer whose aim was 'to arouse pleasure through emotion by vivid detail':[1]

> In his eagerness to arouse the pity and attention of his readers he treats us to a picture of clinging women with their hair dishevelled and their breasts bare, or again of crowds of both sexes together with their children and aged parents weeping and lamenting as they are led away to slavery. This sort of thing he keeps up throughout his history, always trying to bring horrors vividly before our eyes. (Polybius 2.56.7f. tr. Paton)

Polybius goes on to suggest that this approach to history confounds its goal with that of tragedy – 'to overwhelm and master the emotions of the audience for the moment by the verisimilitude of his words'.

It has always been easy to level charges of sensationalism and emotionalism at Phylarchus. Certainly he is capable of elaborating, even fabricating, pathetic details, as in his introduction of the sons of Themistocles in a scene designed to point up the Athenians' mistreatment of their father (F 76). Yet perhaps Phylarchus has been misjudged and has done little worse than to visualize clearly and react strongly to his material, thereby increasing the intensity and

---

[1] This is the characterization of tragic history in Walbank (1955) 4.

broadening the appeal of his work. There is a freshness and vividness of feeling still detectable in the remains of his work and signs that at his best he was a very powerful writer.

The comparison with tragedy which occurs both in Polybius' critique of Phylarchus and in Plutarch's comments on Duris of Samos (F 67) has given rise to the convenient term 'tragic historiography' for this type of writing. The origin of this approach to the writing of history has been much disputed. The theory that it stemmed from Aristotelian distinctions in the *Rhetoric*, developed by Theophrastus and the Peripatetic school, is now no longer fashionable; it has been pointed out not only that many elements of tragic historiography preceded the Peripatetics but also that it was Aristotle who, in the *Poetics* (1451a26ff.), drew a sharp distinction between poetry and history.[1] How then is the apparent increase or intensification of this type of history to be explained? No answer is secure, but perhaps there is a clue in the contemporaneous growth of interest in and emphasis on Tyche or Fortune. In a world governed by an all-powerful and unpredictable Fortune, history is likely to be seen as the teacher of how 'to be able to endure with nobility Fortune's changes', as Polybius (1.1.2) phrases it. This goal requires new techniques. The full effect of rapid changes in status and of unexpected and unpredictable turns of events could be achieved only by a narrative that could bring events vividly before the reader's eyes and work on his emotions as well as on his intellect. Given this goal, the natural model was tragedy. To adapt its techniques was automatic and easy to justify. No elaborate theory was required. The writers of these histories and their audiences lived in a world of rapid change in which the locus of power had shifted to the courts of remote monarchs. The course of wisdom seemed to be to adapt to circumstances rather than to attempt a mastery of the uncontrollable. Hellenistic historical writing is thus a counterpart to those movements in Hellenistic philosophy that emphasize accommodation to Fortune or external circumstance.

Polybius sometimes seems to adopt his predecessors' views on the function of history, as when he maintains that the historian's business is to assign praise and blame (10.21.8); elsewhere he indicates that history should teach the individual how to bear changes in fortune (1.1.2). But there is a new element in his presentation. For him the familiar advice to distrust fortune is double-edged. It warns both against unwarranted confidence and against the premature conclusion that bad fortune must persist. Thus in the first book he relates the story of the Carthaginian recovery from disorder and defeat. One Xanthippus of

---

[1] A Peripatetic school of writing about Alexander was long supposed to have resulted from the Aristotelian reaction to Alexander's execution of Aristotle's relative, the historian Callisthenes. This view has now been almost universally abandoned thanks to the incisive discussions of Badian, especially his article on the eunuch Bagoas (1958). Callisthenes' intellectual ties to Aristotle and his school have recently been called into question by Bosworth (1970).

Sparta restores discipline, introduces good tactics and rapidly brings about the unexpected defeat of a large Roman force under Regulus. Part of the moral is obvious and Polybius (1.35f.) makes it explicit: 'He who so short a time previously had refused to pity or take mercy on those in distress was now, almost immediately afterwards, being led captive to implore pity and mercy in order to save his own life.' But the story is told from the Carthaginian point of view and thereby focuses attention on the means of their success. This is no reversal of blind fortune; good sense and good planning have triumphed. Fortune can to some extent at least be controlled and sound leadership is the key to success. Polybius frequently points out that disasters follow on bad leadership (e.g. 15.21.3) and that greatness is not simply the result of good luck (31.30.3).

Thus Polybius stands at a distance from some of the theories which he articulates. He shares the widespread interest in Tyche and her powers, but focuses on the way in which her effects can be controlled. His history aims at providing the training that a statesman requires. That training entailed contemplation of great successes and failures, but did not set out to overwhelm the reader with pathetic happenings (*ekplexis*) – quite the contrary it hoped to 'hand down to future generations such episodes of Fortune, that those who live after us may not, owing to entire ignorance of these incidents, be unduly terrified by sudden and unexpected' events (2.35.6). His work is thus the antithesis of the tendencies we have noted in Duris and Phylarchus.[1] It is a pragmatic history, concerned with political and military events and the lessons that can be learned from them. While it was apparently intended for a Greek audience, one suspects that it was shaped in part by Polybius' experience in Rome, as a political hostage and eventually as a friend of Roman leaders, especially Scipio Aemilianus. The viewpoint of his history is largely confident and optimistic. Its concerns are practical; its subject matter the growth of Roman power. He contends that since the 140th Olympiad (220–216 B.C.) history has become an organic unity, for 'Fortune has guided almost all the affairs of the world in one direction and has forced them to incline toward one and the same end' (1.4.1), namely the growth of Roman power. Hence a true universal history is now possible. Polybius speaks with respect of Ephorus' attempts in this direction, but claims to write a different type of universal history. He is not attempting to synchronize and integrate the acts of various Greek city states but to write a history unified by theme and action and by its enquiry into the causes of Roman success.

The exploration of cause receives in Polybius an attention not readily paralleled in Greek historiography since the time of Thucydides. Polybius is perhaps not a deeper thinker on the problems of causation than his predecessors

---

[1] For tragic elements in Polybius, however, see Walbank (1938).

but he recognizes their importance and attempts to deal with them. Most of his predecessors had been concerned with the events themselves and their proper presentation and evaluation. There was after all little reason why these writers should emphasize cause, since their concern was largely with how to respond to situations rather than with how to shape them. But for Polybius 'the mere statement of what has happened has emotional effect (ψυχαγωγεῖ) but is not beneficial; add the cause and the practice of history becomes fruitful' (12.25b.2). To be sure, Polybius' analysis of cause is often far from profound and his thought is frequently mechanical, for example in his treatment of the Roman constitution. Walbank has pointed out that this portion of Book 6 suggests that he was 'better at interpreting the more mechanical aspects of the constitution than he was at understanding the basic unwritten customs, such as patronage and clientship and the obligations they imposed, which together determined the way the Roman nobility made the constitution work'.[1]

Polybius' attainments often fail to match the claims, explicit and implicit, which he makes for his work. Yet his history is based upon a wealth of practical experience, from his earliest days in a family much engaged in Achaean politics, during his service in 170/69 at roughly the age of thirty as a hipparch of the Achaean confederacy, through his travels to Rome and Carthage and even on a voyage of exploration into the Atlantic, and through his lifelong and perceptive involvement in public affairs. His history reached the year of the fall of Corinth and of Carthage, 146 B.C. It lacks the range of interest and the wit of Herodotus, the intensity and analytical force of Thucydides, the stylistic and rhetorical polish of Theopompus, the emotive force of Phylarchus. But it treats perhaps the most important topic of classical history with intelligence and lucidity and shows a vigour and engagement with the material that have given it continued life. His work was carried on by the Stoic Posidonius (*FGrH* 87) as far as the dictatorship of Sulla, and was much utilized by Roman historians, not least by Livy. In resisting the excesses of the rhetorical and poetic influences on history and in reasserting the importance of practical experience, direct observation and an attempt at the analysis of cause, he did much to preserve the often threatened autonomy of this form of writing.

In the late classical and Hellenistic periods history often seems to have been a beleaguered literary form. The most original and creative minds were often attracted to other disciplines. The monarch of Hellenic education, rhetoric, exerted a strong and not always beneficent sway. But historical writing showed persistent vigour and appeal. It was perhaps the most widely practised and abundantly produced form of literature in these periods. It is hard at our remove to comprehend the surprising number, volume and variety of the works produced or to imagine their audience and its reactions. Though history sometimes

---

[1] Walbank (1972) 8.

professed to be a training for an intellectual and political elite, its appeal was also felt, Cicero tells us, by men *infima fortuna, nulla spe rerum gerendarum, opifices denique* 'of lowest fortune with no hope of a political career, even the working class' (*Fin.* 5.19.51f.). If it never fully attained the lofty role sometimes claimed for it – 'the interpreter of truth and source of all philosophy (which) can lead to perfection of character' (Diodorus 1.2, tr. Oldfather) – it was at least a form of perennial richness and of enduring interest.

14

SOPHISTS AND PHYSICIANS OF THE GREEK ENLIGHTENMENT

The century following the Persian Wars has often been referred to as the age of the Greek enlightenment, for some of its leading thinkers demonstrate a rationalism in viewing man and his world and an enthusiasm for intellectual experiment suggestive of the eighteenth century. The heady victory of civilization over barbarism doubtless contributed to this, for it heightened hopes that the world was not an unreasonable place and that man could develop within it new institutions of government and society and new forms of thought and art to fit his needs. The so-called sophists were spokesmen for this intellectual position.[1] Sophist basically means wise man and is the word used by Herodotus of Solon and Pythagoras, but when Hermes hurls it at Prometheus it has already an ironic force, and the presence of sophistic concepts and catchwords in *Prometheus vinctus* suggests that the movement was already well under way at least by the early 450s.[2] In the later fifth century, however, sophist might often be translated 'expert' and was the accepted title of those professors of eristic, rhetoric and civics who travelled to the leading Greek cities giving exhibitions of their mental and verbal cleverness. Attendance on the sophists was fashionable and exciting. It was also expensive, and their followers were often the younger members of wealthy families, not always to the delight of older and conservative relations.

The sophists were members of a profession rather than a political, philosophical, or literary school, but in professing to teach anyone public speaking and *arete*, or effectiveness in civic life, sophists seemed anti-aristocratic, while their pursuit of success in argument at the expense of consistent propagation of metaphysical or moral values inculcated a scepticism which threatened Greek traditions of religion and philosophy. Aristophanes presents sophists as charlatans, and Plato's abhorrence of sophistic relativism has given the word a permanent pejorative colouring. Yet the sophists had considerable impact on philosophy, which is outside of our concern here, and on literature, rhetoric

---

[1] The account given here is strongly influenced by Guthrie (1969). Other important discussions are those of Jaeger (1939) 286–331, Solmsen (1975) and Kerferd (1981).

[2] Cf. Herington (1970) 94–7, and above, p. 288 n. 2.

and philology.[1] They developed the concepts and categories of the parts of speech, moods, genders and diction; they contributed to the artistic qualities of literary prose; they elaborated paradoxes and commonplaces useful to dramatists and other writers; they sharpened logical reasoning, and they laid a foundation for literary criticism. Sophistry in this form proved a permanent attraction to the Greeks, continuing in evidence through the fourth century B.C. and reappearing in the second, third and fourth centuries after Christ.

Among major sophists, only Critias was an Athenian, but Athens, and to a lesser extent the Panhellenic shrines, became the chief forum of sophistry. A vivid, and perhaps not entirely unfair, picture of the sophists is to be found in Plato's *Protagoras*, set in the house of Callias which is mobbed by admirers of Protagoras, Prodicus and Hippias (compare pp. 482f.).

Protagoras, the oldest and first sophist to claim the title, came from Abdera in Thrace, where he may have known Democritus. He visited Athens repeatedly, became a friend of Pericles and Euripides, and was asked by the Athenians to draw up the law code for the new colony at Thurii in Italy. That he was later exiled from Athens and his books burned is also reported but less often believed.[2] Plato is more respectful to Protagoras than to other sophists, and the style and manner given to Protagoras in the dialogue which bears his name may have some authenticity, while the myth he expounds about the origin of human society and the gift of Prometheus certainly reflects his interests. As in the case of other sophists and philosophers of the time, we hear of numerous works by Protagoras, but these may in fact be parts of a few, larger, loosely constructed treatises.

One of Protagoras' major treatises was entitled *Aletheia* (*Truth*) or *Kataballontes* (*Refutations*). It opened with the ringing words πάντων χρημάτων μέτρον ἐστὶν ἄνθρωπος, τῶν μὲν ὄντων ὡς ἔστιν, τῶν δὲ οὐκ ὄντων ὡς οὐκ ἔστιν 'Man is the measure of all things, of the things that are that they are, and of the things that are not that they are not'.[3] Protagoras' exact meaning here has been much discussed, but probably he intended to say that there is no absolute reality, no difference between appearing and being, and that each man is the judge of what is true for himself. A second treatise, *Antilogiai* (*Contradictory arguments*), illustrated Protagoras' contention that there are two opposite arguments on every subject. He was apparently the first to claim to be able through art to make the weaker cause the stronger. He is also known to have

---

[1] The most philosophical treatment of the sophists is probably that of Untersteiner (1954). On the sophists as philologists cf. Pfeiffer 16–56, as rhetoricians Gomperz (1912) and Kennedy (1963) 26–70.

[2] Cf. Dover (1976) 34–7.

[3] From Sextus Empiricus, *Adv. math.* 7.60. This is the translation and interpretation of Guthrie (1969) 183f.

adopted an agnostic position on the existence and nature of the gods and to have shared with other sophists an interest in grammar and in criticism, examining, for example, the dramatic function of episodes in the *Iliad*.

Prodicus of Ceos visited Athens frequently where he offered students a choice of his one-drachma or his fifty-drachma lecture. Presumably the basic outline was much the same, but the more expensive lecture illustrated and amplified the text in development of the full potential of the method. Since attendance on the sophists was a social fad, Prodicus may have capitalized on the prestige offered to those who subscribed for the more expensive lecture. He was much interested in language, especially in fine distinctions of meaning between apparent synonyms, and he rationalized the gods as concepts developed from man's awareness of the benefits of nature. The most influential single passage in Prodicus' works has surely been his account of the Choice of Heracles, best known to us from Xenophon's *Memorabilia*.[1] Other typical sophists were the polymath Hippias of Elis, who often undertook embassies for his native city and was celebrated for his memory, and Thrasymachus of Chalcedon. Plato in the first book of *The republic* takes Thrasymachus as the spokesman for the extreme view that might makes right, and Aristotle in the *Rhetoric* refers to his writings as early examples of rhythmical prose.[2]

The long-lived[3] Gorgias of Leontini represents a somewhat different tradition among the sophists: he was probably influenced by Corax and Tisias, the 'inventors' of rhetoric in Sicily (compare p. 498), and perhaps by Empedocles; he presented himself chiefly as a teacher of rhetoric, including invention and style; and his favourite literary form was epideictic oratory. We have two short examples, the *Encomium of Helen* and the *Defence of Palamedes*. Both illustrate the logical technique of exhausting alternatives as well as the bizarre prose style which made a sensation when Gorgias came to Athens on an embassy in 427 B.C. This style is basically an adaptation of poetic devices of sound to highly antithetical prose, and it produced what came to be known as the Gorgianic figures, including *homoeoteleuton*, or the use of rhyming words at the end of successive clauses, and *parison*, or the juxtaposition of clauses with a similar or (*isocolon*) identical number of syllables. A celebrated example of both, as well as of Gorgias' impact on other writers of his time, is Thucydides' sentence in the Periclean funeral oration: φιλοκαλοῦμέν τε γὰρ μετ' εὐτελείας καὶ φιλοσοφοῦμεν ἄνευ μαλακίας 'We are beauty-lovers with plainness and wisdom-lovers without weakness'.[4]

Something of Gorgias' attitude toward his art may be deduced from the passage in the *Helen* which describes the irrational domination of the soul by artistic speech, 'a powerful lord who by means of the finest and most

---

[1] 2.1.21–34.   [2] *Rhet.* 3.1409a2, discussing the paean.
[3] Reports of his age vary from 105 to 109 years.   [4] 2.40.

invisible body effects the divinest works', and goes on to list the effects of speech on the audience in ways which may foreshadow Aristotle's discussion of pity and fear in the *Poetics*.[1] Another aspect of art which interested Gorgias was ὁ καιρός, or the crucial moment of time, a concept important equally in politics, tactics and medicine.[2]

An abstract of Gorgias' *On the nonexistent or on nature* is preserved by Sextus Empiricus.[3] Here he argues that nothing exists, that even if it does exist it cannot be apprehended by man, and even if it were apprehended it would be incapable of being expressed or explained. The proof again takes the form of outlining the possibilities and refuting each in turn. Presumably the argumentative technique was Gorgias' major interest, but he clearly did not find the philosophical implications repugnant.

Other than those of Gorgias, few sophistic writings survive from the fifth century. Fragments of a treatise *On truth* are preserved on papyrus and attributed to an Antiphon who may be identified with the orator and oligarchic statesman, though the work asserts definitively the equality of all men.[4] There survives also a little work on political *arete* and law, whose author is known as Anonymus Iamblichi, and an anonymous work in Doric, *Dissoi logoi* (*Twofold arguments*), which illustrates differentiation or identification of such concepts as good and bad, seemly and disgraceful, just and unjust, and true and false, and discusses other topics of interest to the sophists including the teachability of *arete*, the disadvantages of choosing officials by lot, the utility of rhetoric and the art of memory.

The sophists exploited and taught certain ideas and catchwords, many of which they derived from earlier poets and philosophers. Heraclitus, who conceived the universe as a conflict of opposites, identified *physis* with *logos*, and interested himself in language, is a particularly clear forerunner. Often it is impossible to identify the exact source of a concept which the sophists took up, a good example being the *logos–ergon*, or word–deed, contrast which was probably known to every educated Greek in Gorgias' time: although he greatly exploited it, it was certainly not his invention. Yet we may easily collect a group of interrelated ideas or concepts and identify them as especially characteristic of the sophists.

For most sophists a crucial matter was the teachability of *arete*. This is, however, an aspect of a wider issue, the contrast between *physis* and *nomos*: the inherent *v.* the acquired, or nature *v.* custom, or natural *v.* written law, or even self-interest *v.* civil justice. Protagoras stressed the possibility of human moral and political progress and inclined toward giving greater weight to *nomos* than to *physis* in the process. His views may be paralleled in all three

[1] Cf. Segal (1962) 99–155.   [2] Discussed by Pohlenz (1933) 53–92.
[3] *Adv. math.* 7.65–87.   [4] Cf. Morrison (1961) 49–58.

of the tragedians.[1] On the other hand, Antiphon's *On truth* seems to reflect the view that *nomos*, in the form of morality imposed by law or convention, is an infringement of nature,[2] and Hippias apparently thought that *physis* could destroy the barriers between men which *nomos* created.

In the epistemological sense the *physis–nomos* opposition shows up as the contrast between the real and the apparent, or being and seeming, or knowing and believing, or proving and persuading. These concepts are important not only for the sophists' own logic, but for Greek oratory, where demonstrations of proof or probability found practical application. *Physis* and *nomos* categories could even be applied to etymology: do words have their meaning by nature or do they acquire it from convention and usage? The question of being and seeming in turn may be said to raise the problem of the validity of traditional belief and thus such matters as the existence, nature and knowability of the gods. The sophists as a group were doubtful about the possibility of theological knowledge and communicated their agnosticism to others. Reaction was sharp, and among the victims was Socrates. The somewhat subtle distinction which Plato drew between Socrates' role and teaching and those of the sophists escaped some contemporaries and was distorted by others who resented or feared him.

These ideas were among the most controversial which the sophists discussed, but other aspects of their teaching were at least as great a permanent contribution to Greek intellectual history. High on the list must be put the awareness of art, *techne*. It was in the time of the sophists that the Greeks became self-conscious about their own language, including its vocabulary, its grammar, its stylistic and logical possibilities, theoretical and practical, both in poetry and in prose. On the one hand a process of conceptualization occurred which is analogous to the increasing sophistication of philosophical definition and discussion and which made possible the science of grammar and the art of textual and literary criticism in the following centuries. On the other hand, the self-consciousness which the sophists created was not one of embarrassed silence, but of artistic creativity and exuberant, even excessive excitement about the mind and the word. These things mattered to them and they set them forth for the edification and delight of their students. They are, in a sense, the fathers of higher education, certainly the precursors of Isocrates and the schools of the fourth century, and in their rivalries and their obsession with verbal subtlety they are also the first outcropping in history, for better or worse, of the academic mind.

A second important group of thinkers in the Greek enlightenment were the

---

[1] Cf., e.g., Aesch. *P.V.* 442–68; 478–506; Soph. *Ant.* 332–71; Eur. *Suppl.* 201–13.
[2] This is less specifically echoed in the poets. Guthrie (1969) 113–14 cite sEuripides, fr. 920 and passages which imply the popularity of the view by refuting it.

physicians, who shared certain characteristics with the sophists: they often travelled from city to city treating patients and lecturing, though they did not acquire such a popular following; they too had a profound interest in *physis*,[1] and, like the sophists, they too departed from received tradition, particularly in rejecting the supernatural as a basis for explaining disease. For example, the treatise *On the sacred disease*, which may be as early as the fifth century and shows the stylistic influence of the sophists, argues that epilepsy is no more (and no less) sacred than any other disease, but the result of natural causes. This work is part of the *Hippocratic corpus*, a collection of professional writings, semi-popular lectures, collections of data (*hypomnemata*), and philosophical disquisitions, some parts of which date from the fifth century B.C. After centuries of controversy it seems clear that none can be attributed with any confidence to Hippocrates himself, or even to his circle of associates, since the doctrines set forth vary enormously, but the collection may have originated in the library of Hippocrates' school on Cos.[2] He is said to have been a contemporary of Socrates and an Asclepiad, that is, a member of a medical guild, analogous to the guild of professional bards, the Homerids. Such guilds perhaps began as families which adopted promising students.[3] According to Plato (*Phaedrus* 270c) Hippocrates taught that an understanding of the body cannot be had without an understanding of nature as a whole, a doctrine not presented in detail in any surviving treatise.

The literary significance of the *Hippocratic corpus* is limited. The treatises are all in Ionic and thus of some linguistic interest, especially for the development of technical terminology. Some of this terminology was known to Thucydides, whose account of the plague at Athens is the one piece of a major fifth-century author which has direct connexions with medicine.[4] The treatise *On airs, waters and places*, which deals with the effects of climate on health and character, is of value to students of Greek town-planning and may have some connexion with remarks in Herodotus on the characteristics of various peoples. A number of the treatises illustrate the Greek proclivity for philosophical hypothesis in preference to empirical observation, and some of them can be associated with the views of specific philosophers: *On nutriment*, for example, with Heraclitus. The Hippocratic writings are, however, an important product of the Greek mind; they illustrate its powers of generalizing and reasoning, and they had great influence on Plato and Aristotle as well as in the history of medicine.[5]

[1] Jaeger (1945) 6 thinks the awareness of *physis* developed from the Ionian philosophers to the medical teachers to the sophists and Thucydides.

[2] Cf. Kühn (1956) and Diller (1959) 271–87.   [3] Cf. Jones (1923) I xliv–xlvi.

[4] Cf. Page (1953) 97–115 and Gomme (1956) on Thucydides 2.48.3.

[5] The text of this chapter was written in 1975.

15

PLATO AND THE SOCRATIC WORK
OF XENOPHON

1. XENOPHON

The striking and unusual personality of Socrates attracted much attention among the Athenians of the later fifth century, and brought him many admirers. But his influence was exerted by his conversation, not by any writing, so that posterity knew him only through the literature that sprang up, as enemies attacked him and friends attempted, often using dialogue form, to present the man they had known. Of this literature the work of Plato and Xenophon is all that survives, apart from some fragments of Aeschines of Sphettus. Plato, it is certain, made Socrates express philosophic views he never held; at times he became Plato's mouthpiece. Xenophon's Socrates, on the other hand, is hardly a philosopher at all; he gives good practical advice and sets an inspiring example of personal conduct. Plato and Xenophon may have developed different sides of their hero; but, unlike Plato, Xenophon was unable to paint a portrait that could explain the fascination which he had undoubtedly exerted.

There is nothing to show that the young Xenophon knew Socrates well before he joined the expedition of Cyrus in 401. Nor can it be said when he began to write of him; presumably this was not before returning to Greece in 394. His first contribution to Socratic literature was *Socrates' defence* (*Apology*). Earlier writers, he says, agreed that at his trial (399 B.C.) Socrates took a high or haughty line, but they failed to explain that he did this to secure his own conviction, knowing that death was better than the deterioration that age must bring. He alleges that Socrates had expounded this to a friend named Hermogenes, from whom he had also received a report of part of the speech delivered in court: Socrates had there rejected the accusation of disbelieving in the gods, defended his 'divine sign' as parallel to accepted forms of prophecy, and boasted of his own morality, wisdom, and success as an educator. This bragging hardly rings true, put in the mouth of one who was a by-word for self-depreciation; it is what Xenophon, convinced of Socrates' piety and goodness, would have said on his behalf; perhaps he even persuaded himself that this is how his hero must have spoken. It is equally hard to believe in the account given of Socrates' conduct after the verdict: he refuses to allow his friends to suggest any alternative to the death-penalty, declares the injustice of the sentence, and prophesies a bad end for the son of his accuser Anytus.

Such disregard for fact is strange to a modern reader. But even by 394 very varied accounts of Socrates' trial must have been current; memory is often weaker than imagination. If evidence conflicted, Xenophon would choose that account which best suited his conception of Socrates, or even use his fancy to invent something suitable. The methods of his time would encourage him, the methods indeed of the ancient world, for whose historians it was not a duty to give a faithful record of the speeches they claimed to report. Even Thucydides declares in an elusive phrase (1.22.1) that he gave what 'needed to be said', while holding 'as close as possible' to the speaker's general purport. Xenophon may therefore have mixed invention and evidence, and a clear line cannot be drawn. Nor is this a difference between truth and falsehood, for evidence may be untrue and guesses correct. Yet he must have been aware that 'Hermogenes' report' was his own fiction; did he intend his readers to recognize it as such, or did he hope that even half-believed it would add weight to his story?

Memorabilia or *Recollections of Socrates* opens by expressing surprise at his condemnation on charges of impiety and corruption of the young; it goes on to give a long reply to an 'accuser', plausibly identified with Polycrates, who around 390 published a speech put in the mouth of the prosecutor Anytus. Xenophon next undertakes to demonstrate Socrates' usefulness, putting down 'such conversation as he remembers', and concludes the fourth and final book by reiterating belief in his value to others and in his piety. The work has the limited purpose of showing Socrates to have been a god-fearing man, profitable to others by his practical advice and moral influence; it does not pretend to be a complete account of him. At a few of the recorded conversations Xenophon says he was present, a claim beyond disproof yet suspect because he also makes a similar but chronologically impossible assertion about his *Symposium*. Many modern scholars see these 'Recollections' as predominantly inventions that drew on the Socratic literature now lost; others believe with less probability that Xenophon 'wrote up' notes taken in his youth and consulted others for their reminiscences. Perhaps he invented sometimes, and sometimes reported. There are some conversations in which it is hard to find even a kernel of truth. Who can have heard the long reproof for ingratitude to his mother that Socrates is alleged to have given his son (2.2)? Once doubt begins it is easy to find grounds for extending it to many of the longer talks at least. The ideals of Xenophon's Socrates have a remarkable likeness to Xenophon's own. But how much did Xenophon learn from Socrates?

In *Oeconomicus* Socrates begins by praising agriculture as pleasant, profitable, and good for the physique, as fitting men for war, teaching justice and generosity, and encouraging the crafts; then he reports a talk with Ischomachus, a wealthy landowner, who had told him how he had discussed household management with his young wife, how success came from piety, honesty, keeping fit by riding, running, and walking about his farm, and helping friends as advocate or conciliator, and how a slave-foreman should be chosen and instructed; finally Socrates repeats his detailed instructions on farm-work. Ischomachus, who dominates the greater part of the dialogue, is clearly Xenophon in disguise, and Socrates is represented as showing an uncharacteristic interest in the technical side of agriculture.

The banquet (Symposium), probably subsequent to Plato's Symposium, pictures a less philosophical party, with musicians, acrobatic dancers, and a mime of Dionysus and Ariadne; an uninvited 'funny man' does something to set the tone of the earlier part, marked by paradox and somewhat tedious raillery, in which Socrates takes his share. Gradually the speeches become longer and more serious, until finally Socrates delivers an extended sermon on (homosexual) love; he sharply distinguishes love which aims at physical gratification, to be absolutely condemned as ugly and useless, from a noble kind where the lover's concern is to encourage all that is best in the beloved, while making himself worthy of the younger's man's admiration. No doubt many of Xenophon's contemporaries accepted this dichotomy; Plato, with better understanding of psychology, recognized in Phaedrus (253e–256e) that the two kinds could co-exist in the same person.

Xenophon's Socratic writing is of interest because it provides much evidence about views and assumptions common in his time. He attempted to be critical of them, but he was a superficial thinker, whose criticisms did not cut deep; he remained an enlightened and well-intentioned exponent of current ideas. But writing easily in a full, clear, and unpretentious style, he averts possible tedium by the variety of his subject matter.

2. PLATO

To treat of Plato as a writer without mentioning his philosophy would be as helpful as to describe a lion by an account of its skin. Yet his philosophy cannot be reduced to a few paragraphs, all for which this book could have room. So what will be said of it will be simplified and selective, the minimum needed to explain the form and nature of his writings; for their content the reader must go to the works themselves and modern commentators on them.

The main evidence for Plato's early formative years is given by the seventh of a collection of thirteen Letters ascribed to him. Of these, long condemned en masse as forgeries, some are undoubtedly spurious, but VI, VII, and VIII have in this century found many defenders. VII, which purports to be addressed to his friend Dion's associates after his death, is a long manifesto (twenty-eight pages of Stephanus' edition) recording Plato's aims and experiences in Sicily, where he had tried to educate and influence Dion's brother-in-law, the young Dionysius II, tyrant of Syracuse. It gives an account of his youthful attempts to play a part in political life at Athens and of the disappointments he suffered, his disillusion with the dictatorial regime of the Thirty, whom he originally supported, and his consternation at the condemnation of Socrates under the restored democracy:

> It was impossible to act without friends or associates who could be trusted; and it was not easy to find such among my acquaintance...nor was it possible to acquire new ones with any ease. Written law and old custom were being destroyed; deterioration was proceeding with surprising rapidity; so that I, who had originally been brimming with eagerness to take part in public life, ended by feeling dizzy as I watched the universal collapse. I did not abandon my enquiry how all this, and in particular how the whole structure of the state, could be amended, and all the time I was waiting for opportunities to act. In the end I came to see that all states of today without exception have bad constitutions...and was driven to affirm in praise of true philosophy that it alone is the standpoint from which one can always discern what is right whether for society or for private individuals, and that the people of mankind will therefore never see an end of their troubles until the true and genuine lovers of wisdom (*philosophoi*) come to hold power in the state, or those who dominate their cities become by some divine dispensation real lovers of wisdom. (325d–326b)

In style this letter closely reproduces Plato's manner at the supposed time of writing; nevertheless its genuineness has recently been once more under attack, mainly on the ground that it contains factual errors. A long section on metaphysics has also been criticized, not for the first time, as un-Platonic; others defend its authenticity. It certainly is a surprising piece to have been inserted by the political propagandist whom sceptical critics suppose to have forged the letter soon after Plato's death; yet he was, if he existed, an impostor of unusual skill and ingenuity.

If a propagandist's exercise, the letter becomes a less trustworthy source for Plato's biography. Yet even if he wrote it himself, an old man's memories, tinged with a desire for self-justification, may be less reliable than we like to assume. Nevertheless an early involvement in public life goes well with the recurring concern that his writings show regarding problems of social and political organization. The letter disregards, however, presumably as alien to its theme, what must have been a simultaneous early interest in current philosophical questions; and although it speaks movingly of Socrates' character and death, it makes no attempt to estimate his intellectual influence.

Plato's chosen form: dialogue

Plato's works, apart from the *Apology* and any genuine *Letters*, are all dialogues, in none of which is he himself a speaker. But there is widespread agreement that 'Socrates' often expresses his views, and the 'Visitor from Athens' of *The laws* is a thin disguise. It is more doubtful whether the 'Visitor from Elea' in *The sophist* and *The statesman* and 'Timaeus' in *Timaeus* can be exactly identified with him. By this manner of writing he did not commit himself to the truth of the conclusions or the validity of the arguments; nor did he need to be exhaustive, as in a treatise; it was enough to be suggestive. Yet one should not too readily assume that when 'Socrates' uses fallacious arguments, Plato always knew them to be such, or that he was even aware of all the questions to which some modern scholars attempt to supply his answers.

Dialogue had the advantage of easily reflecting the exploratory and critically destructive procedures of philosophic enquiry. It was reminiscent, too, of the historical Socrates, who had introduced the method of question and answer, welcomed by Plato because the assent of the respondent guaranteed in some measure the correctness of each step in the argument. To the modern reader, accustomed to continuous exposition, the replies 'Certainly', 'Indeed', 'Quite right', 'Yes', 'Of course', 'Clearly', etc. may seem otiose, and Plato knew that they could become tedious. His 'Socrates' often alleges that he cannot make the long speeches which were the forte of contemporary sophists; nevertheless many of the dialogues avoid inartistic monotony by allowing him to alternate between the method of question and answer and that of unbroken exposition. A third reason for writing dialogues was that it was something he could do so well. He enjoyed contrasting Socrates with the sophists and relished the battle of argument in which Socrates overcame his opponents. At the same time it amused him to draw slightly ridiculous pictures of famous men who had been Socrates' contemporaries and to compose delicate parodies of their literary styles.

Most frequently he used the simplest form, that which gives nothing but the words of the participants, providing a conversational drama which could be performed, and conceivably was performed on occasion. Another variety, a conversation reported, usually by Socrates himself, in a monologue (sometimes following an introductory duologue), allows of action and comment, which can articulate the argument. But sometimes action and background seem to be there for their own sake; the method is that later to be used by novelists. Thus in *Protagoras* Socrates, meeting a friend by chance, reveals that he has encountered the great sophist. Made to sit down and tell his story, he recounts how before dawn that morning his young friend Hippocrates had burst into his house and groped his way to the bedside; he had been too excited by the prospect of meeting the famous Protagoras to wait until daybreak. Socrates had restrained his excessive haste, but put some questions as they walked up and down in the courtyard. Soon there was light enough to see the young man blush when forced to concede that what Protagoras could teach him was to be a sophist. Eventually they had gone to the house where Protagoras was staying, and as they stood in the doorway, finishing a discussion,

> I believe the porter, a eunuch, overheard us, and it seems likely that the crowd of sophists had put him in a bad temper with visitors. At any rate when we knocked on the door, he opened it, saw us, and said: 'Ha! Sophists! He's busy'. And he slammed the door to as hard as he could, with both hands. (315c–d)

But at last they were admitted and Socrates describes the great gathering inside: Protagoras walking up and down followed by a train of admirers who parted when he turned and fell in again behind him, Hippias on a high chair, answering questions on astronomy, while the deep voice of Prodicus issued in an unintelligible booming from the pantry where he had been lodged.

Two other dialogues are strangely elaborate. *A symposium* is a report at second hand and *Parmenides* at third hand. Plato's motives for this procedure are obscure; a desire to explore the technique involved may have been one of them. In *Parmenides* one of the intermediaries for the record of a discussion which is never easy and finally needs close attention and verbally accurate reporting is a man described as mainly interested in horses. This improbable informant may be intended as a humorous warning against taking the dialogue to have any historical truth, but when the narrator of *A symposium* insists that he had checked the details again and again with his informant, the object must be to suspend the reader's scepticism.

As time went on Plato became less of a dramatist, more of a philosopher. In *The republic* he deprecates poets who depict men's failings, and thereafter immoralist and conceited characters disappear from his own work. With *Phaedrus* and *Theaetetus* he reverts to the plain pattern of speeches without a framework. In his later writing dialogue becomes largely a matter of form and characterization is minimal. In *Timaeus* and *Critias* after the introduction one of the speakers holds the floor, and in *The laws* the visitor from Athens at times makes long speeches, for example the whole of Book 5, without any interruption from his companions.

This renunciation – or was it this decay? – of original dramatic gifts rouses feelings of regret in the modern reader, but it accorded with Plato's philosophy. Although he deeply felt the charm of Homer, he banished him and with him all writers of tragedy and of comedy from his ideal state. The only forms of poetry he would allow were hymns to the gods and encomia of noble men. He believed one was necessarily assimilated to the characters one represented;

not only the actors, but also the audience, encouraged to sympathize with the failings and distresses of imperfect persons portrayed in epic or on the stage, would be morally harmed by their participation. The transient world, moreover, which the poet 'imitates' is itself no more than an image of true reality, from which his work must be at two removes.

Yet much as Plato distrusted poets, as men who understood neither what they were doing nor how to exert a wholesome influence on their hearers, he saw that they derived their power from some mysterious irrational source:

> If any man comes to the door of poetry untouched by the madness of the Muses but convinced that technical skill will make him an adequate poet, then will neither he nor any of his works ever be effectual: the verse of a mind that is sound is nowhere, but eclipsed by that of the madmen. (*Phaedrus* 245a)

In *Phaedrus* 'Socrates' depreciates the value of all written work; it will not, he says, be with serious intent that a man who has knowledge will

> 'write in water' or that black fluid we call ink, using his pen to sow words that cannot speak in their own defence or present the truth adequately...He will sow his seed in literary gardens and write, when he does write, by way of pastime, collecting a store of refreshment for his own memory, against the day 'when age oblivious comes', and for all such as tread in his footsteps. (276c–d)
> (Tr. R. Hackforth, with trivial changes)

There may here be an element of irony, for much of Plato's writing is deeply serious; yet he saw written philosophy, necessarily static and incomplete, as a feeble instrument compared with the protracted oral communion of sympathetic souls, which alone could lead to the vision of the highest truths. But the written word would provide an introduction to that better way, none the worse for being sometimes enigmatic and tantalizing.

Plato's characters

'Socrates' of the dialogues is from the first a literary creation, although he must retain many features of the historical personage. These include the denial that he possesses knowledge, the destructive criticism of other men's views, the habit of arguing by analogy, and a belief in the supreme value of moral goodness, which he sees as a function of knowledge, so that vice must be due to ignorance. Some incidents, too, will be historical; it is likely enough that the real Socrates refused an offer of rich friends to arrange his escape from prison (*Crito*), although it need not follow that he did so on the ground that a citizen has accepted a contract to obey the laws as they stand. But with time the picture changes: 'Socrates' becomes more and more positive, more and more didactic, and puts forward as certainties beliefs which no competent scholar would now allow the historical character to have held.

The crucial instance is the metaphysical doctrine of Forms, of which Plato was at one time convinced and which he perhaps never abandoned. According to this the sensible world is dependent on a transcendent unchanging world of true Being; for example, all beautiful things are beautiful because they share in or are modelled on the eternal Form of Beauty or what is just Beauty, uncluttered by association with anything transient. The immortal soul has seen these forms in an existence in that other world, and may be reminded of them and recapture their memory. The doctrine, hinted at in *Meno*, is first explicitly expressed in *Phaedo* and *The republic*, and then in *Parmenides* put forward by a youthful 'Socrates', who proves unable to answer the objections raised by the Eleatic philosopher. Scholars disagree over the force of these objections; some think that Plato could not see satisfactory solutions, although convinced that they must exist, while others believe that he was deliberately propounding fallacies for his readers to detect.

If 'Socrates' is a literary creation, using some traits taken from life, it must be wrong to suppose that the other characters are intended as true portraits. They too are required to play the parts that Plato has written for them in his philosophic dramas. Ion may not have been as imbecile as 'Ion', or Gorgias as unwilling to argue as 'Gorgias'. Did Alcibiades ever attempt to seduce Socrates, and confess his failure to others? Or is this Plato's story (*Symposium* 217a–219c), devised to illustrate Socrates' self-control and defend his memory against calumnies of having 'corrupted the young'?

Similar doubts apply to the *Apology*, or *Socrates' defence*. As with Xenophon's work of the same title, it is uncertain how much is based on memory of the speech made by Socrates at his trial. No one can doubt that the language is Plato's; the sentences have an elegant simplicity combined with artistic construction and balance that grip and charm the reader. What of the matter? It is noteworthy that little attention is paid to refuting the indictment, and Socrates may indeed have preferred to concentrate on other things, to say that the comic poets had given him a bad name, to explain that Apollo had laid on him the service of exposing the ignorance of the self-satisfied, to insist that death was not to be feared, but only wrong-doing. But to many readers it seems more likely that it was Plato who made him talk thus, to create an image of the man and his relation to Athenian society.

The earlier dialogues

Plato began with dialogues which are often labelled 'aporetic', because they lead to an *aporia*, an impasse, a failure to answer the question set. In several instances Socrates asks: What is X?; his respondents first reply by giving instances of X, and when shown that that is not what is demanded, prove incapable of finding any satisfying common characteristic. Thus *Euthyphro* asks what piety is, *Charmides* what *sophrosyne* (self-control, temperance, sound-mindedness) is, *Lysis* what friendship is, *Laches* what bravery is. Nevertheless these dialogues are not purely negative; they illustrate the way in which a philosopher should operate, they contribute to the picture of Socrates, and they introduce some of Plato's basic beliefs about ethics. *Laches*, one of the more elaborate, shows this well.

Although in the latter part of this work Socrates diverts the discussion into an unsuccessful attempt to discover what bravery is, this arises from a wider initial question, namely how to educate our sons, a matter on which Lysimachus and Melesias seek the advice of Nicias, a respected figure in public life, and Laches, an eminent soldier. Socrates, when drawn in, points out that we must first determine the aim of education: it is excellence of mind and character; but a man cannot teach goodness unless he knows what goodness is. Plato here expresses what he regards as fundamental truths. But he also uses the dialogue to present Socrates as a man possessed of qualities that were admired in Athenian society: he behaves modestly and politely, encouraging his elders to have their say. Laches and Nicias both express surprise that Lysimachus had never consulted him and agree that talking with Socrates is the best education their sons can enjoy. Laches twice praises his conduct on the field of battle, with the implication that spirit does more than technique to make a good soldier.

Intellectually Socrates is clearly in a different class from the others, over whom Plato allowed his gifts as a dramatist full play. The well-meaning naive Lysimachus and his tongue-tied friend Melesias are contrasted with Nicias and Laches, who are in their turn opposed; Nicias speaks *a priori* in favour of lessons in armed combat, while the practical experience of Laches shows that when it comes to the real thing the professional fails ridiculously. The latter then delivers an amusingly pompous speech about his willingness to learn, after which Nicias and he enjoy one another's discomfiture in their attempts to define bravery.

Dialogues of the middle period

Gorgias, probably written about the time of Plato's original visit to Syracuse, is the first dialogue that is predominantly positive; it is contrived to contrast rhetoric and philosophy, the pursuit of political power and that of knowledge, wrong-doing and morality. Socrates has three respondents. First is Gorgias, the famous old teacher of rhetoric, pompous and muddle-headed, but treated politely. Then the young Polus intervenes, a conceited champion of hypocrisy; he is dealt with firmly but with repeated declarations of friendliness, and forced to admit, with comparative good grace, the truth of the Socratic paradoxes. Finally Callicles, a more redoubtable opponent, has reflected more deeply on morality and determined that right is to be identified with might and self-gratification. He condescendingly despises Socrates' way of life and mode of argument, and when defeated in discussion relapses into a rude refusal to answer. Socrates presses home his intellectual victory by describing the life he believes to await the soul after death, subjected in nakedness to unerring judgement, condemned to punishment, reformative or deterrent, for its crimes, or rewarded for its goodness by residence in the Isles of the Blest.

This passage is the precursor of the eschatological stories or 'myths' which end *Phaedo*, *The republic*, and the first section of *Phaedrus*. These are much more elaborate, and fascinate by the vividness of their imaginative setting; some scholars have even been led by this to see seriously-meant geography in *Phaedo*. The other, incorporeal world must be described symbolically in our language, which has been formed to fit our physical life; Plato did not believe it to have real earthly meadows or material rivers of fire.

> Then all together they journeyed to the Plain of Forgetfulness through terrible burning heat and suffocation; for it was bare of trees and all the plants of the earth. And so, as night came on, they encamped by the River Careless, the waters of which will leak through any receptacle. Now all must needs drink a measure of that water, but those whom wise understanding does not preserve drink more than the measure, and each and every man who drinks forgets everything. And when they had fallen asleep and the hour of midnight had come, there was thunder and a quaking of the earth and suddenly thereafter they were carried up to birth, this way and that, in the manner of shooting-stars.

This concluding scene from the myth of *The republic* (621a–b) is a poet's truth, not the literal truth of a scientist.

But for Plato these stories were essentially true. He came to believe that he could prove their basic assumptions, immortality and reincarnation; his faith that everything was divinely ordered and therefore as well ordered as possible implied a general outline for the life of the disembodied soul; only the details were to be supplied by his imagination and could be no more than 'something like' the reality. Some of these details are allegorical, but these eschatological myths must not be confused with pure allegories like the cave and its prisoners or the ship and its crew in *The republic* (514a–517a; 488a–489a). Those do not describe anything outside experience in this world; they are similes for what does happen or could happen on this earth, and although the simile may help understanding of the events, its main purpose is to involve the reader's emotions as well as his intellect.

Phaedo intertwines many threads, the imperturbability of Socrates faced with the necessity of ending his own life, the devotion of his friends, the immortality of the soul, the shackles of the body, philosophy as a way of escape from the senses to the pure and untainted activity of the mind. Plato acknowledges the Pythagorean inspiration for much of this by making Phaedo report Socrates' last day on earth to a Pythagorean, Echecrates, and by causing Socrates to converse on that occasion with Simmias and Cebes, two young men from Thebes, where they had met Philolaus, a Pythagorean refugee from Italy. Socrates is to be represented as expressing his most deeply felt beliefs: Simmias and Cebes are not intimates of long standing and will find them new. They are ideal listeners, intellectually active, sympathetically sceptical, whose convictions are as yet unformed. Socrates is an old man, about to die: they have their life before them.

Formally the central part of the dialogue is an attempt to prove the immortality of the soul. But this attempt is inextricably mixed with eloquent passages which preach the faith that this soul, which, when combined with body, makes a living being, is essentially intellectual and that to cultivate the intellect is the only road to true morality and to happiness, whether in this world or in a hereafter where we shall enjoy the care of the gods.

The approach to the question of immortality is gradual. Socrates begins by defending his statement that the philosopher is ready to die; he declares a belief that his soul will survive and achieve that escape from the senses for which his life has been a training; he continues by contrasting the morality of the philosopher, who understands the rightness of his actions, with that of all other men, who are 'moral' immorally: fear makes them brave and desire for pleasure makes them self-controlled. Cebes demands proof that the soul does survive. This brings the first argument for immortality: life and death form one unending cyclical process; life must come from death, if life is not to be exhausted. Moreover all learning is recollection: for example, the sight of apparently and temporarily equal physical objects reminds us of the 'Form of Equality', or Equality itself, absolute, incorporeal and immutable; we must therefore have seen it in a previous existence. This, combined with the cyclical process, establishes, so it is claimed, the immortality of the soul and its continued consciousness after what we call death (76c–77d).

This 'proof' is put in what purports to be a logical step-by-step argument, but Plato probably recognized that it was not satisfactory, for he makes the Thebans remain unconvinced that the soul is not dispersed at death. (Yet they accept its pre-existence, which suggests that he believed he had established the premiss that learning is recollection.) Socrates' attempt, by way of reply, to show that when a man dies his soul does not break up is emotion masquerading as logic; it makes easy reading, probably in deliberate contrast with what preceded. Souls and Forms, he says, are akin; both are non-composite and invisible; souls will, like the forms, be indestructible. The section ends with an eloquent passage in which Socrates paints the progress of the philosopher as he frees himself from the toils of the body and prepares himself to meet the divine reality of the other world (82c–83b).

But there is a dramatic reversal. Simmias points out that the attunement of a lyre is invisible but is destructible; may not the soul be a destructible attunement of bodily constituents? Cebes argues in turn that the soul might be like a weaver who makes himself a series of cloaks that wear out before he does, yet he will die before the last cloak is worn through. So the soul might survive several bodies, but yet be perishable in the end. These objections strike the company with consternation. Echecrates, equally affected, interrupts Phaedo's narrative (88c); this marks the new turn that has been taken; from now on the argument becomes more sustained and more exact; modern analysis may find flaws in it, but they are no longer easy to detect.

Simmias' theory that the soul is an attunement is disposed of by three arguments, a complex one flanked by two that are easy. To deal with Cebes Socrates says that he must examine the whole problem of coming-to-be and perishing (95e). This is a sleight-of-hand excuse to introduce a hint of what Plato saw as philosophy's central task. Socrates begins with an account of his experiences when studying 'natural sciences' as a young man. The upshot had been to discover that science could tell how things happen, but not their purpose. So he has fallen back on a second-best course, which explains that things have their qualities by sharing in a Form. An obscure account of logical method follows; probably Plato thought that, applied to the Forms, it would bring the answer to the baffling question, Why?[1]

Another brief intervention by Echecrates (102a) marks a return to the immediate subject. An elaborate argument, which has given rise to much discussion in modern times, purports to show that soul cannot admit death and is therefore immortal. All are convinced, which suggests that Plato also was satisfied by the reasoning, but Socrates reinforces the conclusion by an imaginative myth that symbolically emphasizes the difference between the two orders of reality and stresses the significance for present conduct of an after-life, where there will be punishments and rewards, and where those purified by philosophy will be transported to the fairest of homes. The dialogue concludes with a deeply moving account of the events in Socrates' last hours, so vivid that it is hard to remember that Plato had not himself been present.

A symposium, close in time to *Phaedo*, is a contrast and a complement. Socrates is a guest in a varied company met to celebrate the victory of the

---

[1] The answer was to be given in *The republic*, where it is asserted that all Forms are hierarchically derived from the Form of the Good. Plato fully recognized the prevalence in this world of error and vice and disease but he believed that in the nature of things the Forms could not be fully or perfectly embodied in it. From them it had a measure of goodness; much in it served a purpose. But perfection was to be found only in the ideal world of thought, an unchanging world in which he found the only true reality.

dramatist Agathon in a contest for tragedians. After dinner it is agreed that each member should praise Eros. After a number of clever but artificial speeches by others Socrates recounts what he alleges he had heard from a prophetess Diotima. Eros is not a god but an intermediary between the human and the divine. Love of beauty is not love merely of bodily beauty, but also of that of the soul, and lovers try to beget excellence in their beloved. Some men, the philosophical, see that there is a common factor in everything we call beautiful and they slowly come to contemplate Beauty itself, 'pure, clean, uncontaminated, not infected with human flesh and hues and all other mortal nonsense, but the divine simple Beauty itself' (211e). Here Alcibiades, flushed with wine, bursts in and soon embarks on an encomium of Socrates, who is as ugly as Silenus but lovable for a character of surpassing beauty; this is illustrated by the story mentioned above of the attempt to seduce him and by reminiscences of his endurance as a soldier in the cold of Thrace and of his bravery in the retreat from Delium. The irruption of a second group of revellers puts an end to all order in the party.

Nowhere does Plato show greater skill as a writer. Unforgettable incidents make the setting vivid and at the same time characterize the actors: Socrates' fit of abstracted thought before entering Agathon's house, Aristophanes' attack of hiccups caused by over-indulgence in food and drink, the entry of Alcibiades, who with drunken self-confidence assumes charge, humoured by the others; finally Socrates, the only man left sober, argues Agathon and Aristophanes under the table, forcing them to agree against all contemporary experience that the same man would know how to write both tragedy and comedy. The earlier speeches are written each in its own manner, not without touches of parody: Phaedrus is an illogical traditionalist, Pausanias a sophistical and sensual hypocrite, Eryximachus a pompous and pedantic scientist, Aristophanes an imaginative entertainer, Agathon a follower of Gorgias, using words for their sound more than for their meaning. Socrates' speech is on a higher intellectual level and effective by eloquence free of all affectation; the motives for ascribing its matter to a prophetess have been variously explained; they may have been more than one; but the result is to surround it with an aura of revelation and authority.

Style shows that *Republic* 1, even if it has been slightly adapted to fit its present position, was begun some years before the rest; it was to be a typical 'aporetic' dialogue; Socrates forces a rude and evasive opponent, the sophist Thrasymachus, to concede that it is better to be just than unjust, but depreciates the conclusion by a reminder that they have failed to define what justice is. (The Greek word (δικαιοσύνη) covers all correct conduct in so far as it affects others.)

Republic 2 makes a new start: Plato's brothers Glaucon and Adimantus demand proof that to be just is the better course, even if it leads to disaster and injustice is crowned with success. Socrates, suggesting that it will be easier to recognize justice writ large in the state, builds an imaginary society: first an idyllic primitivism, marked by a strict division of labour, a principle preserved in the complicated but ordered society which follows. In this there will be three divisions, two constituted by the 'guardians', who form a professional defence force; from these soldiers are chosen 'guardians' in a narrower sense, who rule society by virtue of their knowledge and understanding. The third division perform all other functions in the community. The human soul is divided in a similar way: it is part reasoning, part spirited, part appetitive. A just society is one in which each division does its own part, and a just man one in whom each portion of the soul does what is proper to it. Men differ: the majority, who constitute the third division of society, will be driven by desire for acquisition and pleasures; this must be controlled by the other elements in them, which are to be fostered by education. The soldiers are moved by their spirit and love of distinction, the rulers by intellect and love of truth; in both these orders appetite must be diverted from sensual gratification to honour and knowledge; they will be allowed no material possessions, care for which would take them from their proper tasks.

Now Socrates has to meet a triple wave of problems: (i) among the guardians women must do everything that men do; (ii) among them the family must be abolished, to avoid a conflict of loyalties; (iii) how can such a society be possible? The reply, that it is only possible if rulers are philosophers, answers a question hitherto evaded, namely how can the guardians *know* what measures to take. The philosopher proceeds from the changing sensible world to an apprehension of the immutable Forms, and will finally grasp the Form of the Good, from which all others can be deduced. A man who knows what Good is will always know what is good. On this metaphysic not only the possibility but also the rightness of Plato's state depends. Accordingly it fills the central books. The next, 8 and 9, are the counterpart of 2–4, which sketched the formation of an ideal society. They give a brilliant picture, not historical but full of details suggested by history, of the ideal state's decay through 'aristocracy' or the self-interested rule of the best men, oligarchy, and democracy to tyranny or despotism. Corresponding types of men are vividly described; the lowest, the 'tyrannical', ruled by a dreadful monster of desires, enjoys brief illusory pleasures amidst unremitting fear, whereas the just man is orderly, and by obeying reason has the truest possible pleasure. So Socrates answers the original challenge, but there is another book to come, balancing the first but more profound.

After a return, now based on his metaphysic, to an earlier attack on current literature, Socrates uses a novel argument to show the soul to be immortal;

he can therefore be confident that justice will be rewarded and injustice punished in the next world. A long concluding story told by an imaginary visitor to that world reinforces this claim and insists on the responsibility of the soul for its own character and for many of the circumstances it is destined to meet on earth.

The republic is a work of astounding richness; it raises and connects fundamental questions concerning society, psychology, education, and metaphysics; its treatment of them shows great variety and imagination within its clear and balanced structure. Memorable passages abound; for example, the question who would be just if he had Gyges' ring, which could provide invisibility (359d), the criticism of contemporary medicine for coddling useless invalids (406b–d), or the discovery that no existing state is a single state, but two at least, the rich and the poor (422e). Particularly striking is the prevalence of imagery, ranging from simple comparisons like that of democracy to a fancy cloak embroidered with every kind of flower (557c) to fully worked-out pictures like that of the ship of state with its quarrelsome and ignorant crew, concerned only to win the favour of its noble but myopic owner (488a–e), or of the cave with its prisoners who see only shadows cast by models of the animals that live in the world outside (514a–517a). Today some of Plato's answers seem false and some of his consequent recommendations repulsive, but they issue a challenge to discover where he went wrong; they do not provide a reason for neglecting the wealth of true observations, constructive proposals, and seminal ideas which he offered.

The later dialogues

Theaetetus is the first of a series of dialogues more interesting as philosophy than they are as literature. Although they still contain memorable analogies and images, the tone is now less varied and the writing becomes progressively more mannered. Whereas in the earlier dialogues there is an art which conceals art, giving the reader the illusion that he is overhearing the spontaneous talk of educated men, in these later works there is much that is obviously calculated in the order of words and the structure of sentences. An artificiality surely unsuited to dialogue first appears in *The sophist*: Plato began to avoid hiatus, that is he shunned placing a word which ended with an unelidable vowel before another word which began with a vowel; this was an elegance he did not disdain to learn from Isocrates.

The sophist and *The statesman* show another change in that Socrates no longer leads the discussion; that part is taken by an uncharacterized 'visitor from Elea', the home of metaphysics and dialectic. One can do no more than guess who would have had the leading role in *The philosopher*, a concluding dialogue which Plato once intended but never wrote, although there is reason for believing that it would have been Socrates, who is once again dominant in *Philebus*, a dialogue concerned to define pleasure and its relations to intelligence and the good. Here, although only a shadow of his old self and speaking in a highly artificial style, he is still recognizably Socrates.

If the majority view is correct, after abandoning *The philosopher* Plato embarked on another scheme destined not to be completed, a trilogy, *Timaeus*, *Critias*, and *Hermocrates*. *Critias* was begun: it was to tell a story of how a primitive Athens, organized like the ideal state of *The republic*, had defeated an invasion from Atlantis, an island of great wealth and military power; but both had then perished in a natural cataclysm. *Hermocrates* was never written, but it has been guessed that like *Laws* 3 it would have dealt with the historic growth of a new civilization and perhaps suggested reforms possible in the setting of Plato's own time. *Timaeus* remains, an account of the physical universe within which man must live and construct his societies. Timaeus, probably an invented person, is a philosopher and statesman from Locri in Italy, apparently used to put forward Plato's own views or guesses, which could not appropriately be placed in the mouth of Socrates. He declares that what he says is no more than 'a likely story': no accurate scientific account of the physical world can be given, since it is always changing, a shifting reflection of another world of permanent being, and is apprehensible only by our unreliable senses. His story is cast in the form of a cosmogony: the world had been made by a divine crafts-man, working from the eternal model. But according to the tradition of the Academy, this was only a device of exposition:[1] the world had had no beginning, and the craftsman must be interpreted as the mythical representation of the rationality and goodness to be found in it.

Timaeus is a work of outstanding imaginative power; one may instance its analysis of the factors underlying the material world and the account of the human body and its influence on the operations of the human soul.

> When in any man the acid or salt phlegms and all bitter and bilious humours, wandering about the body, find no vent but are constricted within and blend their vapour in mixture with the soul's motion, they create in the soul all sorts of sickness, greater and less in degree and in extent, and carried to the three seats of the soul they produce in wide variety, according to the regions they severally attack, every different sort of discontent and despondency, of rashness and cowardice, of forgetfulness and slowness to learn. Moreover, when men are thus ill-constituted and their societies are evil, when in their cities evil discourse is spoken in public as in private, and the lessons they learn from childhood upward are in no way of a kind to provide any remedy, that is how all of us who are bad become bad, through two causes that could not be more involuntary than they are. Responsibility for these must always lie with the begetters rather than the begotten and with those who provide upbringing rather than with those

[1] Aristotle, *De caelo* 279b32; Proclus, *in Timaeum* 84 E ff.

who receive it; yet a man must endeavour in every way he can, by means of upbringing, pursuits and learning to escape from badness and to lay hold on its opposite. (86e–87b)

The language of *Timaeus*, although not simple, is clear and effective; any obscurity is due to the subject matter rather than the style. The book had great influence throughout antiquity and, through Chalcidius' Latin version of the first part, in the Middle Ages.

The laws, also a popular work with later Platonists, suffers comparative neglect today. There are obstacles to its appreciation. Still unrevised at Plato's death, it is too long and too repetitive; an artificial word-order, often designed to emphasize particular words, becomes as irritating as the constant use of italics in a modern book, and is no less tiresome when employed to bring about the juxtaposition of two or three different grammatical forms of the same word. It is often difficult to determine the meaning behind a cloud of verbiage or to follow the course of a meandering discussion. Nevertheless *The laws* contains matter of great and varied interest, as Plato displays not only his prejudices but also the fruits of his long experience and his most essential beliefs; moreover it illuminates many of the problems that confronted fourth-century society.

The dialogue is set in Crete, as the participants, three elderly men, walk from Cnossus to a sacred cave. They are a visitor from Athens, a Spartan, and a Cnossian who is one of ten men chosen to form a constitution for a city-state to be established on a deserted tract of land. This duty is not revealed until a quarter of the dialogue has passed; thereafter the trio concern themselves with the laws that shall govern the new community. Only a small part of these are set out in the form they might take as statutes; usually the Athenian, who dominates the conversation, merely describes their content, with more or less of detail, embedding this in a wide-ranging account of the purposes of the laws, seen as devoted to the stability of the state and the moral goodness of its citizens.

A few features of this state have an appeal today: a sharp limitation on wealth, and the same education for boys and girls; men and women are to share all pursuits. But all menial work or manual craft, any full-time occupation like teaching in a school, is to be performed by underprivileged aliens or severely disciplined slaves. The citizens manage their farms but spend much time in military training or physical exercise with an eye to war. The unceasing fighting among fourth-century Greeks made it clear that a state must defend itself to survive, but it was more important to Plato that this training could develop self-control and disregard of physical pleasures and pains. He was aware that societies change, but regretted it; 'change is always highly perilous' (797d), and so every effort was required to limit it: 'tradition and good custom are the rivets of society' (793d); even children's games are to be stabilized. Unnecessary foreign travel is forbidden, and literature strictly censored; but the so-called Nocturnal Council, a body of fifty or more who meet before dawn, are informed of the practices of foreign countries and may introduce any good innovation these may suggest. There is an elaborate structure of magistracies and committees to preserve order, but they are chosen by a system in which popular election and the use of the lot play a genuine part; the citizens are strictly controlled, but they themselves impose that control.

Plato as a literary author

The philosophical dialogue may have been Plato's invention; it was certainly he whose example made it an established literary form; and no one has ever rivalled his use of it. His successors in antiquity tended to make it a frame for set speeches, sometimes opposed to one another, like those of advocates in a court of law, sometimes exploring different facets of a problem, a method which Plato had himself initiated in the first part of his *Symposium*. He had indeed in his later writings reduced the variety of those means which give so much charm to the works of the earlier period; but he did not abandon them entirely, nor were they entirely neglected by dialogue writers after him.

Plato's skill with language was admired by ancients as well as moderns. He could write in a manner which has the appearance or the illusion of everyday educated speech, using an unpretentious vocabulary, numerous particles, and realistic anacolutha. Dionysius of Halicarnassus thought he detected in it an element of archaism (*Ad Gnaeum Pompeium* 2.4); if he was right, Plato could have justified it, for his characters belonged to a generation earlier than his own. From this level the style could rise, sometimes by hardly perceptible stages, to a poetic prose, in which elevated vocabulary, periphrasis, metaphor, and above all simile, played their parts. Some ancient critics, of whom Dionysius was not the first, objected to this, attaching importance to the conventional distinction between genres and their appropriate styles. Their criticisms are blunted by an intermittent insensitivity. 'Golden wealth' is not just a precious synonym for 'gold' (*The laws* 801b, 'Longinus' *Subl.* 29) but has a derogatory flavour, and some passages of *Phaedrus* which they condemn as 'dithyrambic' were intended to raise a smile. It is not for using devices familiar in poetry to amuse his readers or to enrich his meaning that Plato should be blamed, but for the mannerisms which infect his later work, as he plays with words for the sake of the game.

A striking feature of Plato's vocabulary is the sparing use of technical terms. He wrote Greek, not philosophers' Greek. For establishing conclusions this has disadvantages, since the ambiguity of common words often leaves doubt about what exactly he was trying to say; on the other hand the ambiguity, if recognized, is an excellent means of provoking thought, an object often as important to him as imparting his own ideas.

At the same time Plato's vocabulary is not just that of ordinary Attic speech or Attic prose. This becomes more noticeable as he grew older. There are words from poetry, compounds and derivatives which he may have invented himself, and words which he may have learned from non-Attic friends or writers (a simple example is the phrase τί μήν;, expressing emphatic assent, which may have been picked up in Sicily). This richness of vocabulary and the absence of jargon are two virtues of style which make the reading of Plato both easy and attractive even to the tiro in philosophy.

Ease of reading is also promoted by the striking and memorable illustrations and analogies that Plato found for his views; an image from the sensible world aids the reader to understand the immaterial. Examples are numerous: the comparison of the soul to a charioteer driving two ill-matched horses (*Phaedrus* 253c–254e), the attempt to explain error by the image of the bird-cage (*Theaetetus* 197d–200c), or the comparison of the effect of Socrates' conversation to the numbness caused by a sting-ray (*Meno* 80a). From *The republic* comes the story of the earth-born men with gold, silver, and bronze within, which illustrates the reality and importance of genetic differences (414d–417b), or the strange animal, part human, part lion, part many-headed monster, that represents the soul of man (588c–589b). Even more frequently he gives vivid instances to exemplify generalizations; these make one feel that his philosophy is firmly rooted in experience.

Another common device is the introduction of an imaginary speaker, who raises objections or expresses views that Socrates' respondents could not have raised or expressed, or puts a difficulty which the respondent hopes can be overcome, as when Cebes in *Phaedo* sees that Socrates' argument can be threatened by the analogy of a weaver and his cloaks to the soul and its body. But when in *Crito* the personified Laws argue that the citizen owes them obedience until they are changed the cause gains emotional backing because it comes from such a revered source, and in *The laws* Book 10 the argument against atheism is shown to be of immediate practical importance by being directed towards an imaginary youth who has adopted the atheist's view.

A prominent feature of the earlier dialogues in particular is irony. In the narrow sense of the Greek word *eironeia* this is self-depreciation. 'Socrates' disowns knowledge and often claims to be baffled or alarmed by the problem before him. When he then passes on to find even a partial solution, there is a sense of excitement, of discovery and final triumph. This initial self-depreciation can be combined with an ascription of wisdom or some other ability to the respondent. Clearly 'Socrates' is then to be thought of as speaking with his tongue in his cheek, which suggests that his own self-depreciation is not to be seen as entirely genuine either. The respondent confidently accepts the flattering estimates of his capacity, and his discomfiture can be enjoyable when he proves to be clay in the other's hands.

If irony is understood in the wider sense of saying with a straight face what is not to be taken seriously, that also appears. For example, in *The republic* there is the mathematical mystery which determines the number that is in some unexplained way the key to correct mating (546a–d), or the proof that the true king's life is 729 times more pleasant than that of the tyrant (587e). *Menexenus* is the most puzzling of Plato's works. The greater part is a funeral speech, composed for delivery in 386, in honour of the Athenian war dead; following the traditional pattern, it sketches and exaggerates the glories of Athens' history to that year and ends with exhortations to the living to be worthy of their heritage. But the enclosing dialogue puts it in the mouth of Socrates, who alleges that he had just heard it from Pericles' mistress Aspasia. The historical Socrates died in 399; what was Plato up to? To say that he was parodying the orators is not quite sufficient. Parody there undoubtedly is, both in matter and in the style, although if Cicero's text is to be trusted, it was not observed in antiquity: the speech was in his time annually recited at Athens (*Orator* 151), and its later part contains nothing but admirable, if conventional, sentiments. Perhaps Plato wished to suggest that admirable sentiments were hollow if recommended by falsehoods and flattery. The philosopher must distance himself from the methods of the orator, and the undoubted irony of the introductory dialogue must be intended to make more intelligent readers treat the speech with critical caution.

The reader of Plato, if his concern is for truth, should never forget critical caution. 'Socrates' is not Socrates, but neither is he Plato; even in the later dialogues, where most of what he says would have Plato's full approval, he may utter what the latter knew to be fancies, or on the other hand he may fail to reveal or even hint at the depths of Plato's thought. The reader who is prepared to neglect such problems can at least enjoy the enchantment of the writing as it builds up the character of an idealized Socrates and exposes the foibles or inadequacy or corruption of his opponent. He can be carried along by the inventive variety of treatment, as the conversation takes new and unexpected turns, as humour alternates with seriousness, and elevated language with the colloquial. He will enter a poet's imagined world, strange and unfamiliar in some respects, yet inviting and accessible and full of delight.

16

ORATORY

Discourse appears in Greek literature from the very beginning as a characteristic feature of Greek life. The debates of *Iliad* 1 and 2, the embassy of *Iliad* 9, and the pathetic appeal of Priam in *Iliad* 24 were often cited by later rhetoricians, while the comparison in the *Iliad* (3.212–24) of the oratory of Odysseus and Menelaus shows a critical awareness of style and delivery at the dawn of European literature. The poets continued to include speeches in their works. Important stages in rhetorical history are the *Homeric Hymn to Hermes*, which has apparently the earliest instance (line 265) of argument from probability, the major logical tool of Greek oratory, and the trial scene in Aeschylus' *Eumenides*, which reflects judicial procedure in Athens just before the emergence of literary oratory.

In the second half of the fifth century oratory became a literary genre in its own right. We have orations by Gorgias, Antiphon and Andocides and testimony from Thucydides, Aristophanes, Plato and other writers. In order, however, to understand literary oratory it is necessary first to review the developing role of public speaking in fifth-century political and intellectual life.[1]

Both Greek rhetorical theory and self-conscious techniques of oratory seem to be a product of democracy as it developed in Athens after the Persian Wars, especially after the reforms of Ephialtes (462 B.C.), and in Syracuse when democracy replaced tyranny (467 B.C.). According to tradition,[2] rhetoric was 'invented' by a Sicilian named Corax who taught Syracusans involved in litigation before democratic courts how to argue from the probabilities of their situation. He was followed by Tisias, who may have composed a small rhetorical handbook illustrating such argumentation and explaining how to present the facts and proof effectively in a simple standardized structure. This structure became the four usual parts of the classical judicial oration: *prooemion*, or

---

[1] General discussions are those of Blass (1887) 1 1–46, Jebb (1893) 1 cvi–cxxxiii, Navarre (1900) 3–77, and Kennedy (1963) 26–70.
[2] Cf. Radermacher (1951) 11–35.

introduction, aimed at securing the attention, interest and good will of the jury; *diegesis*, or narration, presenting the background and facts in a clear and rapid summary; *pistis*, or proof of the contention of the speaker; and *epilogos*, or conclusion, in which the speech is summarized and often an attempt is made to arouse the emotions of the jury on behalf of the speaker. Although argumentation may take its premises from the testimony of witnesses or other direct evidence, it is characteristic of Greek oratory to prefer arguments based on the probability of human conduct: to adopt the traditional example,[1] a small man accused of starting a fight would argue that it is improbable that he would initiate action against a larger and stronger man. At an early date it was realized that a counter-argument exists for the bigger man who can claim that it is unlikely he would initiate anything when, because of his size, he would immediately be accused of starting the fight. Such argumentation seems to have appealed to the Greeks as essentially rational. It relates a specific occasion to the nature of man and his situation and it can be reduced to a system which can be taught, learned and applied. Conversely, the Greeks tended to distrust the testimony of witnesses or documents, primarily because these could often be secured by force or bribery.

A characteristic of Greek democracy, especially at Athens, was the egalitarian assumption that every man should speak on his own behalf before a court. If a person inexperienced in public speaking was accused of a crime or expected to become involved in litigation, he had basically three choices: he could study the system (*techne*) of a rhetorician like Tisias or his numerous successors, either in person or through buying a written copy of a handbook, also called a *techne*; or he could turn to a skilled speech writer (*logographos*) and buy from him a speech or part of a speech which he might then memorize and try to deliver himself; or he could appear and try to stammer through some explanation as well as possible and then introduce a *synegoros* or advocate, either a friend or in some cases a professional orator, who then testified to his character and advanced arguments in his behalf. If the litigant was a minor, an alien, or a woman, he or she had no choice but to entrust the whole affair to an advocate. Occasionally there was a supplementary speech (*epilogos*), a short speech delivered by a friend after the litigant's. Obviously these possibilities were capable of various combinations,[2] but the professional logographer rarely developed, as a modern observer might expect, into a professional legal adviser. It should be pointed out that the work of a logographer was possible chiefly because most of the facts of a case were brought out and the evidence taken down in a preliminary hearing before a magistrate. What the jury heard,

---

[1] Cf. Plato, *Phaedrus* 263bdff. and Aristotle, *Rhet.* 2.1402a17ff.

[2] Lavency (1964) examines in detail the roles of logographer, *synegoros* and client in the fifth and fourth centuries B.C.

and what a logographer provided, was a speech selecting and arranging this evidence in the best interests of the litigant. There was little cross-examination,[1] and there was no instruction from the judge or conference among the jury members. Each voted in secret on the basis of his impression of the two speakers.

A distinctive feature of Athenian juries was their size, a minimum of 201 jurymen with 501 being common and larger juries not unheard of.[2] A democratic audience of this size, lacking specialized legal training or interest, encouraged the development of oratory which put more emphasis on the presentation of character or the arousing of emotion than on technical argument about the details of law. Such oratory was inherently artistic and its emergence into a literary form is thus not surprising. Artistic judicial oratory had its deliberative counterpart in speeches in the democratic assembly. Although other states imitated Athenian democracy, it is clear that artistic, literary oratory, both judicial and deliberative, was an Athenian phenomenon. Even Syracuse did not continue a significant tradition after the time of Tisias.

Aristotle and his successors divide oratory into three kinds: *symbouleutic* or deliberative, basically concerned with predicting the expediency of future action; *dicanic* or judicial, basically concerned with assessing the justice of past action; and *epideictic*, the oratory of praise and blame or of sophistic display, often delivered at a public ceremony (*panegyris* hence 'panegyric'). Epideictic oratory of the fifth century is represented today by Gorgias' *Encomium of Helen* and the *Defence of Palamedes*[3] and by fragments of his other speeches quoted by later writers. Most epideictic speeches were not composed for specific occasions, but were delivered by the sophist as a display, possibly in different forms at different times. Some dealt with serious issues, but others were *paignia*, or *jeux d'esprit*, in which entertainment was combined with an exposition of argument and style. Editing and publication of speeches as literary documents was perhaps intended to advertise the abilities of the sophist and to furnish his students with models of his technique. Thus, in Plato we meet Phaedrus studying the text of a *paignion* by Lysias. Among the speeches of Gorgias was an *epitaphios* or funeral oration, one of the most characteristic of Athenian oratorical forms. Actual speeches of this sort were intended for delivery not at the funeral of an individual, as is the case with Roman and Christian funeral oratory, but at annual public funerals for those killed in battle during the preceding year. The form probably originated early in the fifth century and served as a conspicuous expression of Athenian patriotic myths, usually arranged

[1] In the late fifth and early fourth century a litigant occasionally insists on a right to question his opponent, cf. Plato, *Apology* 24c; Lysias 12.25 and 22.5.

[2] Cf. Bonner and Smith (1930) 1 223ff.

[3] Cf. above, ch. 14; Radermacher (1951) 52–66; Sprague (1972) 40–63.

in chronological order, followed by a consolation. The most famous such speech is of course that attributed by Thucydides to Pericles, but a more typical example is the second speech found among the works of Lysias, composed early in the fourth century. Another characteristic epideictic form is illustrated by the fragmentary *Olympic oration* of Gorgias, an early expression of that Panhellenic sentiment which was to be extensively developed in the speeches of Isocrates in the fourth century. As noted in our discussion of the sophists, Gorgias' flamboyant prose style gave a permanent stamp to epideictic oratory and exerted some influence as well on other manifestations of rhetorical prose.

Antiphon

Judicial oratory before 404 B.C. is best represented today by six works of Antiphon, known to history as a leader in the oligarchic revolution of 411 B.C., which cost him his life. Thucydides describes him as the real intelligence behind the movement and an outstanding orator, but one who kept in the background because he was suspect to the *demos* for his cleverness, 'the one adviser most able to help those involved in actions both in the law courts and in the assembly' (8.68). He was thus a logographer, of the sort described above, doubtless using his 'help' as a way of enhancing his political support. (It is possible, but not certain, that Antiphon the orator is identical with Antiphon 'the sophist', author of *On truth*.)[1] Three of Antiphon's speeches written for homicide cases survive (*Orations* 1, 5 and 6). Reasons for the preservation and publication of these and subsequent judicial speeches can only be guessed: perhaps Antiphon himself wished to advertise his skill as a speech writer; perhaps he or someone else wished to furnish students of rhetoric with models; or perhaps preservation of some speeches is owed to clients who bought and kept them.

In terms of content and technique the most significant aspect of Antiphon's speeches is the conflict evident in them between direct evidence and argumentation, what Aristotle was later to call non-artistic and artistic proof. Antiphon can equally make use of evidence or argue against it.[2] Although from the point of view of a modern reader many factual and legal questions are left unanswered, in the limited areas with which they deal the speeches have considerable shrewdness. In the first speech, a prosecution of a stepmother on the charge of poisoning the speaker's father some time before, the central argument involves the refusal of the defendants to allow the household slaves to be tortured, the only way they could give evidence under Attic law. This is taken as showing that the defendants do not want the truth to come out. In the sixth speech the speaker, who had served as *choregos*, is accused of responsibility for the death of one of

[1] Cf. Sprague (1972) 108–11.   [2] Cf. Solmsen (1931).

the boys in his chorus; he makes use of the opposite argument, that the failure of the opponents to take advantage of an offer to allow cross-examination and torture shows their indifference to the truth. The longest, most vivid, and probably best speech is the fifth, *On the murder of Herodes*. Here again the speaker is attempting to counteract evidence, in this case two witnesses and a letter.

These three speeches are probably to be dated in the period between 420 and 413 B.C., though the evidence is controversial in each case.[1] They certainly seem to be intended for delivery in real trials, but we do not know the outcome. The other three extant works (*Orations* 2–4) are called 'Tetralogies'; each consists of two short speeches for the prosecution and two for the defence in a homicide case. There are no names or other identifications and the speeches are presumably intended as model treatments of three interesting situations. In the first the major interest is the use of argument from probability for and against an 'enemy' of a man found murdered in the road. In the second and third the question is one of legal responsibility rather than of fact, for example in Tetralogy 2 the issue is the responsibility for the death of a boy who runs into the path of a javelin in a gymnasium. Plutarch (*Pericl.* 36.3) reports that Pericles and Protagoras had discussed such a case. The Tetralogies differ somewhat in style, structure, and treatment from the other three speeches of Antiphon and their authenticity has been questioned. A probable answer, however, is that they are genuine, but considerably earlier in date of composition, possibly even as early as the late 440s.[2]

Hellenistic editors often grouped the works of orators by legal genre. Thus we are told that the extant speeches of Antiphon are part of a collection of fifteen speeches in homicide cases. Caecilius of Calacte, a rhetorician of the first century B.C., accepted the authenticity of these and twenty additional speeches in other kinds of cases. The best known was doubtless that in Antiphon's own defence in 411 B.C., so much admired by Thucydides (8.68). We have what seem to be a few lines of it, preserved on a Geneva papyrus, in which the orator argues forcefully that the oligarchic revolution was not in his personal interest, but it is not certain how this related to the argument of the speech as a whole.

Although Antiphon is significant historically and in the development of rhetorical technique, he has as well a literary importance. From the point of view of posterity he and Thucydides, his younger contemporary (and according to tradition his student), created literary Attic prose, which was to lead to the artistic achievements of Plato, Isocrates and Demosthenes and the whole tradition of Attic eloquence as it survived throughout the Roman Empire and even the Byzantine period. Presumably what really took place was an act of synthesis: the styles and ideas of Gorgias and other sophists and perhaps of

---

[1] Cf. Dover (1950) 44–60.   [2] Cf. Zuntz (1949) 100–3.

Ionian historians and philosophers came together, under the influence of the Athenian intelligence, with the language of the people of Attica. The context was the tension between democrats and oligarchs with its continuing need for persuasive exposition and also the mounting litigation in the courts under the democratic conditions we have described. The artistic importance of the development was clearly recognized by Greek critics like Dionysius of Halicarnassus who began the history of prose with Antiphon and Thucydides, grouped together as examples of the 'austere' or rugged style. The austere style, Dionysius says,

> wishes its separate words to be planted firmly and to have strong positions, so that each may be seen conspicuously; it wishes its separate clauses to be well divided from each other by sensible pauses. It is willing to admit frequently rough and direct clashing of sounds, meeting like the bases of stones in loose wall-work, which have not been squared or smoothed to fit each other, but which show a certain negligence and absence of forethought. It loves, as a rule, to prolong itself by large words of portly breadth...In whole clauses it shows these tendencies no less strongly...It wishes them to bear the stamp of nature rather than of art, and to stir feeling rather than reflect character. It is fanciful in imagery, sparing of copulas, anything but florid; it is haughty, straightforward, disdainful of prettiness, with its antique air and its negligence for its beauty.[1]

Fifth-century deliberative oratory is less well known than either epideictic or judicial. We have only the briefest fragments of the original eloquence of Pericles, Nicias, or Alcibiades, and thus we know the political oratory of Athens chiefly from the splendid speeches with which Thucydides illuminates the pages of his history.[2] Some speeches in Sophocles or Euripides taken together with Thucydides and what ancient critics say suggest qualities which we might guess from Gorgias or Antiphon: a sense of structure, adaptation of commonplaces (*topoi*) to varied content, more emphasis on pathos than on ethos, fondness for antithesis, argument from probability, utilization of ideas expounded by the sophists and of the patriotic traditions of Athens.[3] Preservation and publication of deliberative oratory did not occur regularly until the mid-fourth century when it was used to create a kind of pamphlet literature. Dionysius of Halicarnassus quotes a piece of a speech of Thrasymachus of Chalcedon and a longer piece of a speech which Lysias wrote for a speaker in the assembly in 403,[4] but otherwise our best evidence for deliberative oratory of the late fifth and early fourth century is in the works of Andocides.

[1] Translated by Jebb (1893) 1 22–3 from Dion. Hal. *De comp. verb.* 22.
[2] Cf. Stadter (1973).
[3] For an attempt to reconstruct the style current in the fifth century cf. Finley (1938).
[4] Cf. Radermacher (1951) 73–4 and Lysias 34.

Andocides

Andocides was probably born shortly before 440 B.C. of an aristocratic family. The major incident of his career was the bizarre profanation of the mysteries and mutilation of the herms in Athens on the eve of the departure of the Sicilian expedition in 415 B.C. By his own admission he had some knowledge of the incident of the herms, though he denies participating personally. To save the life of his father, implicated in the case of the mysteries, he claims to have turned state's evidence. This led to his exile from 415 until 403, chiefly in Cyprus, but he returned briefly in 411 and again later, perhaps in 409/8, when he failed to regain his civil rights by delivering before the assembly the speech *On his return*, which is still extant. The general amnesty after the expulsion of the Thirty Tyrants made his return possible, but he continued to be hounded by personal and political enemies and was forced to defend himself again in 399, the year of the trial of Socrates. The sixth speech in the corpus of Lysias is apparently part of the prosecution. Andocides replied with his finest speech, *On the mysteries*.[1] A third speech deals with an embassy to Sparta in 392/1. It was a failure and led to his second exile, during which he disappears from history. A fourth speech attributed to Andocides purports to be an attack on Alcibiades at a meeting of the assembly in 415, but is probably a political pamphlet or literary exercise of somewhat later date and unknown authorship.

Andocides' major significance is as an eyewitness source for a very interesting period of Athenian history. He does, however, provide us with our earliest examples of speeches before the assembly, and in style and technique he makes a sharp contrast with Antiphon. He had certainly heard the sophists and rhetoricians and occasionally tries to imitate Gorgianic figures rather crudely, but usually his language illustrates what pure Attic prose would be like if the sophists had never lived. His structure and argumentation are not products of the rhetorical schools, but he learned through practice to manipulate his material effectively. *On the mysteries* is a persuasive defence by an intelligent man of broad culture. It contains some striking narrative and a fine emotional peroration, all successfully obscuring the political motives of the conspiracy and any real involvement by the speaker.

Oratory was to become one of the greatest artistic achievements of Greek literature. Fifth-century orators like Gorgias, Antiphon and Andocides contributed to its elegance of style, force of thought and subtlety of content. It is likely that without them Lysias (whose earliest work falls at the end of the fifth century), Isocrates and Demosthenes could not have achieved what they did and that artistic Greek prose would have developed, if ever, in a very different form.

[1] MacDowell (1962).

2. ORATORY IN THE FOURTH CENTURY

Oratory as a tool for moving men's minds in the Greek democracies may have reached its fullest development in the fifth century; as a literary genre it is chiefly a phenomenon of the fourth and of Athens. Although the Athenians themselves realized this,[1] the concept of 'Attic' oratory was more extensively developed by rhetoricians, grammarians and lexicographers of the first century B.C. and later in an attempt to rescue Hellenistic Greek prose from the pretensions associated with the orators of Asia Minor and from the banality of the market-place. In their search for models these critics developed a canon of ten orators, probably based chiefly on those whose works had been collected in Alexandria. Two of these Attic orators have already been discussed: Antiphon and Andocides. The others worked chiefly or entirely in the fourth century: Lysias, Isaeus and Isocrates; Demosthenes and Aeschines; Hyperides, Lycurgus and Dinarchus. Other powerful orators of the fourth century, such as Callistratus and Demades, did not publish their speeches and are little more than names to us, while the works of Demetrius of Phalerum are lost. Indeed, only in the case of Isocrates, Demosthenes and Aeschines do we have a reasonably complete collection of published works.

By the end of the fourth century rhetoric became the basis of secondary education, which it remained throughout antiquity, but the quarrel between rhetoric and philosophy, which broke out repeatedly later, had its start at the highest educational levels in the early fourth century. About 393 B.C. Isocrates, abandoning the writing of judicial speeches, opened a school, perhaps first on Chios, but later at Athens, to teach what he called philosophy, but what others might choose to label rhetoric. This was soon followed by the foundation of Plato's Academy, where rhetoric was discussed, rejected, or reformed. Plato was, however, himself a consummate rhetorician: the *Apology* is not the least among Greek orations and even the *Menexenus* had its ancient admirers. Aristotle, apparently to counter the influence of Isocrates, gave lectures on rhetoric as an extra subject in the afternoon, perhaps while still a member of the Academy. From these lectures, after some years of revision, emerged his *Rhetoric*, whose relationship to Attic oratory is similar to the relationship of the *Poetics* to Greek tragedy: a theoretical statement of the greatest critical acumen, but an uncertain guide to analysis of specific works. Closer to the real forms of the fourth-century orators is the treatise of Anaximenes of Lampsacus commonly known as the *Rhetoric to Alexander*.

[1] Cf., e.g., Isoc. *Antid.* 295–6.

Judicial oratory

The heart of Attic oratory is the judicial branch and the heart of Attic judicial oratory is logography. Certain features stand out.[1] The logographer remained a speech writer, not a lawyer, though some developed special competences. His clients came to him, he composed a speech, or perhaps sometimes part of a speech, they paid him and did with it what they would. Occasionally a speech writer might appear as a *synegoros* for a client unable to deliver his own speech. We must not expect to learn anything certain about the political, moral, or even legal views of a speech writer from his speeches. The better he was, the more he submerged himself in his client's role. Nor can we expect to be able to judge the truth of the case; internal consistency in presenting one side of the matter is the ordinary standard of logography. It has recently been claimed that, still worse, we can rarely even be certain of the author, since the speeches we have may represent varying degrees of collaboration between the writer and his client,[2] but few scholars have agreed. In fact, the opposite may be true; that is, many speeches may be the work of a logographer with little guarantee that the client used them in their present form. Dionysius of Halicarnassus, with more complete evidence at hand, had no doubt of his own ability to recognize the magic of Lysianic *charis*, or charm, and Demosthenic *deinotes*, or forcefulness. In the case of Lysias 34, Dionysius says that he does not know whether Lysias' client ever actually made use of the deliberative speech Lysias had written, and there is a famous story that Lysias offered Socrates a ready-made defence, which the philosopher declined to employ, as well as other evidence for speeches which were never delivered.[3] What we have are certainly not records of what was spoken in court; Attic oratory as we know it consists of artistic works preserved by a literary tradition.

Lysias

In the first century B.C., 425 surviving speeches were attributed to Lysias, about half of the total corpus of the Attic orators as then known. Of these Caecilius accepted only 233 as genuine. Modern texts usually contain thirty-five speeches or parts of speeches. Thirty of these are judicial speeches, written for clients except in the case of the twelfth, which is Lysias' own prosecution of Eratosthenes, one of the Thirty Tyrants.[4] Most of the speeches were composed in the period 403–388 B.C. when Lysias lived in Athens as a metic. His father had moved from Syracuse at the suggestion of Pericles and became a friend of

---

[1] Cf. Lavency (1964). [2] Dover (1968*b*). In reply Usher (1976).
[3] Dion. Hal. *Lysias* 32 and Cic. *De or.* 1.231.
[4] 6, 9 and 20 may not be genuine; 11 is an abstract of 10; in 4, 18 and 21 Lysias apparently only composed a portion of a speech; 5, 25 and 26 are incompletely preserved.

Socrates. (Indeed, the setting of *The republic* is old Cephalus' house at Piraeus.) Lysias himself lived for a while at Thurii, but then returned to join the family business. This was confiscated by the Thirty, a financial loss which probably led him to turn to speech writing as a career.

Against Eratosthenes combines private and public issues into an unforgettable presentation of life in Athens under the arbitrary rule of the tyrants. Lysias probably felt that as a known speech writer he did not need to disguise his rhetorical powers as he did in writing for a client. Though the diction is simple, the style and argument are more varied and adventurous than is usual: not only antithesis, but other more flamboyant Gorgianic figures occur, and in the emotional parts there is considerable amplification. The structure conforms to Lysias' usual practice, but is, again, amplified. A brief prooemium is followed by vivid narration of Lysias' arrest, his attempt to bribe his way to freedom, his chance escape, and the arrest, execution and burial of his less fortunate brother, Polemarchus. Then comes the long proof that the responsibility for that death must lie with Eratosthenes. Lysias' major problem is to show that bygones should not be allowed to be bygones, that Eratosthenes is a wicked and dangerous man, and that to let him slip by would be a dangerous precedent. Eratosthenes' defence was that he had in fact opposed the arrests, but when out-voted had little choice but to execute the will of the others, unjust as that might be. Lysias replies, not entirely convincingly, that it is not in accord with probability that a man who opposed an arrest would have been ordered to execute it, that one of the Thirty cannot be allowed to excuse himself as having been ordered by the Thirty, and that Eratosthenes had an opportunity to let Polemarchus slip away, but failed to take it. Men must be judged on the basis of their actions not their words.

The refutation of Eratosthenes' plea is completed by the end of section thirty-six. The remaining two-thirds of the speech is devoted to the larger matter of the ethos of Eratosthenes, his past actions as evidence of his true character, and his claim that he supported Theramenes and thus belonged to the less radical group of tyrants. The attack on Theramenes, which is the central panel in this second part of the work, constitutes almost a speech within a speech with its own prooemium, argument and epilogue. Especially striking is the contrast between Theramenes and Themistocles. After disposing of Theramenes, Lysias returns to a contrast between Eratosthenes' plight and that of those he killed, he refutes Eratosthenes' character witnesses, and he concludes with an appeal to the two political groups which emerged from the revolution. The conviction of Eratosthenes is in the interests of all. The last words of the speech are celebrated: 'You have heard, you have seen, you have suffered, you have the guilty. Judge' (ἀκηκόατε, ἑοράκατε, πεπόνθατε, ἔχετε· δικάζετε). We do not know how the jury decided.[1]

---

[1] Lysias 10.31 has been taken to indicate that Eratosthenes escaped conviction, but the evidence is very tenuous.

In Lysias' logographic speeches the qualities which posterity has most admired are the effective simplicity of the style, which seems clear and artless, but is in fact almost inimitable, and the way the written words bring out a sympathetic, but realistic portrait of the litigants. The former is the source of the *charis* which Dionysius attributed to Lysias as his unique charm, and is perhaps best seen in the narrative portions of speeches where Lysias sketches the situation and the characters with great vividness. His works are as a result among our best sources for the private life of Athenians in the classical period. We cannot of course accept the detail of the cases in exactly the terms Lysias gives us, but we can be sure that Lysias is presenting a consistent picture credible to his contemporaries and we thus gain an impression of life in the early fourth century as it was viewed by a man of experience, culture and perception.

The other pre-eminent Lysianic quality, the portrayal of the personality of his clients, has been known since Dionysius of Halicarnassus as *ethopoeia*. This is not a matter of diction or of specific description, but a capturing of the mode of thought of the speaker and his view of himself. It usually emerges immediately in the prooemium. The most famous instances are those in which Lysias takes qualities of a speaker which might render him unpleasing to a jury and so presents them as to make the speaker seem convincingly candid. Thus the speaker in the third oration gains some credit by the way he admits to a possibly shameful love affair. The farmer accused of uprooting an olive stump in *Oration* 7 is a brusque, unsociable type who has made enemies, but seems an unlikely deceiver. Mantitheus in *Oration* 16 is a self-confident aristocrat. He knows some may resent his long hair, but he wins our confidence. Most celebrated of all is the cripple of *Oration* 24, a sardonic small businessman who is shrewdly trying to hold on to his pension and has won the grudging admiration of readers for nearly twenty-five centuries.

The speeches of Antiphon (see pp. 501ff.) reveal clearly an effort to apply systematic methods to individual cases. Lysias works with similar techniques of structure, commonplaces and arguments, but his methods are subtler. By constant surface variation he manages to conceal the system, and he consistently emphasizes character and personality, so that each case seems unique. There is less tension between direct evidence and argument than in Antiphon; what evidence is presented becomes the basis of comparison, antithesis and hypothesis in argument from probability. On the other hand, it has been remarked that 'Lysias' arguments usually cluster together like little piles of stones, and unity is simply the extrinsic one of association'.[1] Argumentation is not Lysias' greatest skill and he does not achieve the integrated logic of Isocrates or Isaeus.

[1] Bateman (1962) 160.

Isaeus

Isaeus, the third of the fourth-century logographers, is described by Jebb as 'perhaps the earliest Athenian type of a professional man'.[1] The reference is to Isaeus' special competence in inheritance cases as seen in the eleven extant speeches. These may well be his best work and Isaeus may have been the exception who went beyond speech writing to become a kind of legal adviser, but in fact he handled other cases as well. Dionysius preserves part of an excellent speech in a matter of civil rights. Isaeus' speeches are of great historical interest for what they tell about Attic inheritance law, procedure and custom and about Greek family relationships and attitudes.[2] Their literary significance, both in the judgement of Dionysius and in that of modern scholars, is chiefly in their relationship to the work of other orators. Isaeus resembles Lysias without the *ethopoeia* and charm, but with a greater emphasis on logical reasoning and demonstration. He may have been an early student in the school of Isocrates and shows Isocrates' stylistic influence in an increasing avoidance of hiatus. And most important of all, he not only is said to have been the teacher of Demosthenes, but is clearly his precursor in the cultivation of a forcefulness of style and treatment. This includes a tendency toward personal abuse of the opponent which becomes a notable feature of Greek judicial oratory.[3]

In terms of style, Isaeus shares many qualities with Lysias: his diction is as pure, his composition overall simple, but he is less fond of antitheses than is Lysias, and thus another step away from the style of the fifth century. He is also more willing to experiment with figures of thought, which he often finds convenient in urging his argument. Dionysius claims (*Isaeus* 16) that Isaeus' arguments are presented not only as 'enthymemes,' like those of Lysias, but as 'epicheiremes'. He means by this that Isaeus often goes through the full reasoning process rather than assuming some of his premises. The result is a greater sense of grappling with the opponent, a greater vehemence, and a corresponding lack of charm, even a kind of petulance.[4] It is the manner which Demosthenes cultivated to an even greater extent.

Isocrates

Isocrates' long life bridges the age of Pericles and that of Philip of Macedon. He was a major educator, he claimed to be a philosopher, and though he was not a public speaker, he worked in all major oratorical forms. The six logographic

---

[1] Jebb (1893) II 273.
[2] Wevers (1969) 94–121.
[3] Cf., e.g., 5.34ff.
[4] A good example is the passage cited by Dion. Hal. *Isaeus* 12, translated by Jebb (1893) II 306.

speeches, dating from the 390s, are his earliest surviving works.[1] They are quite good examples of their genre and represent a variety of interesting cases. One was composed for the younger Alcibiades, whom two of Lysias' clients helped prosecute on another occasion; another is a prosecution of the banker Pasion, well known from Demosthenes; *Oration* 21 is the prosecution in a case where Lysias seems to have written for the defence. The most admired has been the *Aegineticus*, a claim to an inheritance on Aegina which is the only extant Greek judicial speech of the classical period written for a non-Athenian court. The style of all these speeches is more comparable to that of Lysias or Isaeus than to the later epideictic and political works of Isocrates.

In addition to speeches intended for delivery in the lawcourts, fourth-century orators composed, and sometimes delivered, other kinds of works, which can be classified in different ways. Epideictic, the oratory of praise and blame, is represented by *epitaphioi logoi*, real or imaginary speeches for the traditional state funerals. These include a fine example attributed to Lysias, a rather poor example attributed to Demosthenes, the *Menexenus* of Plato (possibly a satire, but more likely a strangely inept attempt to demonstrate the possibilities of philosophical rhetoric), and finally and best, the speech of Hyperides on the dead in the Lamian War, which departs from the traditions of the genre by singling out the deeds of the general Leosthenes. Also within the general conception of epideictic is a group of works in the tradition of the sophists. Among the successors of Gorgias (who survived until about 376 B.C.) was Alcidamas, whose little treatise *On those writing written speeches*, or *On the sophists*, is part of the literary and philosophical dispute over the conflicting virtues and dangers of written *v.* oral composition. Other surviving examples of fourth-century sophistic discourse include an *Ajax* and an *Odysseus* attributed to Antisthenes, the erotic speeches in Plato's *Phaedrus*, an *Eroticus* in the Demosthenic corpus, and two, at least, among the works of Isocrates, the encomiastic *Helen* and *Busiris*.

The literary genre of Isocrates' major treatises is not epideictic, but deliberative, or, in the case of the *Antidosis*, judicial. What makes him an epideictic orator is that he is the prime example of a writer of 'written' discourses, of carefully elaborated and polished speeches intended to be circulated in written form or to be read aloud to small groups. These discourses, although they have significant political contents and are the vehicle of the philosophical, political, or social views of the writer, are also 'demonstrations' of his literary and rhetorical skill and models for his students to imitate. It is true of course that earlier sophists combined an interest in what they were saying with a demon-

---

[1] Isocrates implies that he did not write for clients, *Ant.* 36, and his son expressly denied that he ever did so, Dion. Hal. *Isoc.* 18, but Aristotle, *Rhet.* 2.1392b11, mentions one of the speeches as by Isocrates and subsequent ancient and modern critics have generally accepted their authenticity.

stration of how to say it – Gorgias' *Olympic* discourse would be a good example – but Isocrates developed the form on a vast scale. Unlike the earlier sophists he was an Athenian citizen, deeply interested in his city, and he had strong views about her society and her international role. He also had a weak voice and he lacked nerve and poise in delivery; thus he felt forced to present his views in written form, integrating them into his activities as a teacher of rhetoric, and circulating them as pamphlets.

When approached through his own career and writing Isocrates can seem pompous, tiresome and superficial, and these epithets are not entirely unfair. He is doubtless the wordiest Greek writer of the classical period, though hardly a match for Aelius Aristides and later sophists. His contemporaries and successors regarded him as an important literary figure, though it is difficult to estimate his political influence. His achievement can perhaps best be appreciated if we view his works in comparison with the two other greatest writers of his time, Plato and Demosthenes.

Isocrates shared with his slightly younger contemporary Plato a reverence for Socrates, a scorn for the claims of mercenary sophists, a conviction that education was essential to a virtuous society, a distrust of the Athenian democracy on the basis of its record in the later fifth century, and a highly developed interest in prose style. Both claimed to teach philosophy and to expound 'ideas'. But these similarities only served to sharpen their differences as the leaders of the two major academic institutions of Athens in the decades after 390. Although Isocrates mentions his philosophy and his school in almost all his works, his educational programme is described at greatest length in the early fragmentary treatise *Against the sophists* and in his later apology, the *Antidosis*. Plato's opposition to this programme is evident in the *Gorgias* and in the *Phaedrus*, where towards the end (278e) Socrates is made to mouth an ironic compliment to the future achievements of the young Isocrates.

Against the sophists pictures Isocrates' school as a thoughtful middle course between hypocritical teachers of eristic, on the one hand, who claim to teach men how to be happy, and professional teachers of oratory on the other, who try to reduce art to rule. His own school teaches philosophy. The students must have an aptitude to start with; they are then able to learn from the teacher about the various 'ideas', by which he means forms of speech; finally, they practise the use of these. Isocrates asserts that there is no art of *dikaiosyne*, or just living, which can be taught to students, but he does think that the study of political discourse helps to develop character. Plato's response in the *Gorgias* was to call into question whether such a study had in fact a legitimate and definable subject matter, taking Gorgias and Gorgias' pupils as characters in the discussion. He divided the arts involving the soul into legislation and justice and those of the body into gymnastic and medicine. Corresponding to these are a group of sham arts or flatteries: sophistry and rhetoric for the soul, cosmetics and cookery for the body (cf. *Gorgias* 463aff.).

In the mid-350s Isocrates was the object of a suit challenging him to undertake certain public duties at his own expense or to exchange property with the citizen who had been assigned the liturgy in the first place (an *antidosis* suit). This opened his eyes to the widespread misunderstanding of his school and to the popular feeling that he was acquiring great wealth from it. He lost the suit and bore the expense; he also composed for publication an extensive defence of his life and thought known as the *Antidosis*, which is filled with reminiscences of Socrates' *Apology*. It does not attack Plato by name, but he and his followers are clearly in the writer's mind in some passages. Isocrates describes the genre of his own political writings and quotes passages from them. He describes his students, of whom the most famous was Timotheus. And he describes the teaching of his school, which is much the same as that pictured in *Against the sophists*. The course took three or four years, he says (*Antid.* 87). He agrees that there are arts of body and soul: the former is *paidotribike* and intended to produce athletes; the latter is *philosophia* which is intended to produce orators, taken as the best civic type. Eristic, as taught by his opponents, is a kind of gymnastic of the mind, good enough as an introductory exercise, but not of practical application. Philosophy as he understands it, the writing of serious political discourse, is admittedly in the realm of opinion, not scientific knowledge, but people can become better and worthier by practising to speak well (*Antid.* 274–5). Isocrates' elevation of rhetoric into general education for the leaders of society was permanently influential. It stands behind Cicero's *De oratore* and Quintilian and the whole concept of later classical education.

We have a stately succession of the political discourses to which Isocrates refers, carefully revised by himself and tested on his students. The *Panegyricus* is the first and best and the one in which his characteristic prose style is most smoothly polished. Caecilius remarked that it took him longer to compose the *Panegyricus*, calling for a campaign against Persia, than it took Alexander to carry out the campaign.[1] Smoothness is the dominant quality of the diction and in the flow of the thought. Harsh combinations of sounds are carefully avoided; hiatus between words in a clause is almost totally prevented, sometimes by elision or crasis, but more fundamentally by a subtle choice or arrangement of words so that juxtaposition of vowels does not result. There is no sudden jumping from thought to thought, no break in construction, no rapid staccato effect; rather, each concept is fully developed, fully expressed in terms of its conditions, its results, its purposes, and often for the sake of amplification one alternative will be denied side by side with the assertion of its positive antithesis.[2]

[1] Cf. 'Longinus', *Subl.* 7.
[2] On the combination of parataxis and hypotaxis in the style of Isocrates cf. Usher (1973).

Antithesis, as well as occasional *parison*, *homoeoteleuton*, and the like, proclaim the influence of Gorgias, but the total effect is very different, for Gorgias worked with small units, Isocrates with the paragraph. His great periods were meant to caress the ear rhythmically, not to be shouted with gestures. The result is of course lack of vigour, though in an extended passage Isocrates, like Brahms, achieves and sustains intensity of emotion. The avoidance of hiatus was widely influential and characterizes all good Greek prose from the mid-fourth century on. Demosthenes often observes it; he too composes with great care and precision, and he can achieve periods of Isocratean dignity, but Demosthenes' style is much more varied and often much more rapid.

The contrast between Isocrates and Demosthenes in thought is as great as in style. Indeed, they share little but a love for Athens and some of her traditions. Isocrates is a closet orator; Demosthenes a fighter in the courts and the assembly. Isocrates' works tend to respond to long-term trends; he had witnessed much of Greek history. Demosthenes reacts to the needs of the hour. Thus Isocrates stresses the unity of Greek culture, with Athens as its leader, but includes within its pale such diverse figures as Dionysius of Syracuse, King Archidamus of Sparta, the Thessalian tyrants, the rulers of Cyprus and Philip of Macedon. To him the opponent of Hellenism remained consistently the Persian king, a view with which Demosthenes, looking at the specific threats to Athens after the mid-350s, fundamentally disagreed. Isocrates' noblest expression of his ideal is probably the celebrated words in the *Panegyricus*:

> Our city has so surpassed the rest of mankind in thought and speech that her pupils have become the teachers of others, she has made the name of the Hellenes seem no longer that of a race, but of an intelligence, and those are called Hellenes who share our culture rather than those who share our blood. (*Paneg.* 50)

The major expositions of Isocrates' political thought begin around 380 with this speech, calling for Athens and Sparta to cooperate, under Athenian hegemony, in a common Panhellenic programme and to undertake a campaign against the barbarian which would yield land and money. The theme was of course a traditional one in epideictic oratory, seen in works of Gorgias and Lysias, but Isocrates applies it to the specific circumstances of his time and his ideas may have had some influence. There followed in the 370s exhortations *To Demonicus* and *To Nicocles* on the duties of a monarch and the *Nicocles* on the duties of citizens. The *Plataicus* is a declamation on the destruction of Plataea by Thebes in 373; the *Archidamus*, in the person of the Spartan king, discusses peace proposals in 366. Then come *On the peace*, the *Areopagiticus*, and from 346 the *Philippus* which renews the Panhellenic hopes of the *Panegyricus*, but this time with Philip of Macedon as *hegemon*. Last is the *Panathenaicus*, an attempt at a final justification and synthesis of the orator's views when he was around ninety-eight years old. Although the details of treatment vary with the historical situation, Isocrates remains consistently committed to the anti-imperialist views of traditional Athenian conservatives.[1] There are also a number of letters, of which the most remarkable is the *Second letter to Philip*, congratulating him on his victory at Chaeronea and surely inconsistent with the rather romantic view of later writers that 'the old man eloquent' died in distress at hearing of Athens' defeat.

The interest of Isocrates is greatly increased by the enormous length of his life and the contacts and diversity of activity it allowed him to pursue. His influence on Greek prose style was great, and though Demosthenes is in theory the favourite model of later centuries, Isocrates' spirit hovers over the writers of the Second Sophistic. His appeal to historians derives from his apparent understanding of the fatal weakness of the Greek city states: their petty differences, their constant warfare.[2] He does indeed, more consistently and more clearly than any other Greek, call upon them to rise to their potential of cultural unity.

Demosthenes

Not counting several letters,[3] we have sixteen deliberative, two epideictic, and forty-two judicial speeches attributed to Demosthenes. Of the judicial speeches perhaps ten are cases, some public, some private, in which he was himself involved, whereas the rest were composed for another speaker. Fifteen or more of these are not Demosthenic in any sense and have been wrongly included among his works, often because of some mistaken association of individuals or subjects. Of the spurious speeches six or seven are often attributed to Apollodorus,[4] and a few others have been thought by some scholars to be works of Dinarchus. Demosthenes probably owed his reputation as a speech writer to the impression made on the public by his prosecution of his guardians and the resulting effort on his part to use his ability to help restore his own finances. In this he was successful enough to be able to afford heavy private expenditures on public duties within a few years. Many of the speeches in private cases cannot be dated with certainty, but it is clear that they are not all early works. He wrote for clients throughout his career. On the other hand, we are told that he did not appear in court in private cases after entering public life, that is, he did not act as a *synegoros* in private cases after the late 350s (30.32). Aeschines in his speech *Against Timarchus* repeatedly refers to Demosthenes as a teacher of rhetoric, one who even brought his students to court with him. It is likely enough. One of his pupils is supposed to have been Cineas who was sent by Pyrrhus on an

---

[1] Cf. Bringmann (1965).
[2] Cf., e.g., *Paneg.* 167–8.
[3] Letters 1–4 are probably genuine; cf. Goldstein (1968).
[4] Cf. Pearson (1966).

embassy to Rome.[1] A collection of prooemia may be associated with Demosthenes' teaching activities, but like Cicero he found them convenient to have at hand in his own work and used them himself.

When Demosthenes was seven his father died leaving an estate in the hands of three guardians. When this estate was turned over to him at the age of eighteen its value was drastically reduced. According to tradition as preserved by Plutarch (*Dem.* 5) and others he spent two years studying rhetoric with Isaeus and preparing his case until 364 B.C., when, in his twenty-first year, he instituted a series of prosecutions. The best of the five inheritance speeches is probably the first speech *Against Aphobus*, which brings Demosthenes on the stage of history in a very personal way. It already shows signs of what become his great characteristics: a powerful intellectual drive, full control of the facts (or the absence of them) and an ability to turn the question as the speaker sees it into the real issue of the case and to override the views of his opponents as irrelevant or misleading. Although, as usual in Greek oratory, the proof is one of probability and involves accepting the speaker's explanation of motivation, a proliferation of direct evidence in this speech gives a sense of substance to Demosthenes' claims. There is further a rather imperious ethos, serious and self-confident, which becomes a permanent feature of the orator's work. Predictably, the style has not yet developed into the subtle tool it was to become; there is not yet the devastating force of metaphor or the diabolical changes in tone and mixture of styles which later play upon the minds of the audience, nor is there quite the precision of the later style, though word choice and arrangement are coolly deliberate. The working of Blass's law (that Demosthenes tended to avoid three or more successive short syllables or more than six long ones) is first evident in *Against Aphobus* 3.[2]

Forcefulness and variety characterize all of Demosthenes' work, a fact stressed already in antiquity by critics such as Cicero, Dionysius of Halicarnassus and Hermogenes, who all regarded Demosthenes as in most respects an adequate model for all oratorical virtues. These qualities are not lacking in his logographic speeches. He seems to have been able to manage any kind of case, including inheritance cases, and to adapt his skills to almost any client. He gave less attention to *ethopoeia* of the client than did Lysias, but was capable of it when he considered it an important persuasive tool, as in the case of the exasperated young farmer who pleads *Against Callicles*. He has been especially praised for the way he can give life to ordinary oratorical conventions by vivid touches,[3] for example the realistic details in the scenes of military life and brawls in *Against Conon* which help make the speaker's arguments convincing.

Among the private orations of Demosthenes the most interesting and most often read is possibly that *For Phormio*, composed around 350. The case is a

---

[1] Cf. Plutarch, *Pyrrhus* 14.1.   [2] Cf. Adams (1917).   [3] Mathieu (1948) 21.

paragraphe, a peculiarly Greek action in which a defendant brings a countersuit against a plaintiff alleging that the plaintiff's suit is illegal. This reverses the whole procedural relationship between the two. Phormio could not speak good Attic and was represented by a *synegoros* who some editors have tried to claim is Demosthenes, though there is no evidence to that effect and considerable probability against it. The success of the speech, which relates largely to the banking business of the same family we meet in the *Trapeziticus* of Isocrates, comes in large part from the picture of the conduct and character of the two contenders. Phormio is made out to be an intelligent, hardworking and faithful freedman whom his late master rightfully left in charge of the business, while the elder son of the family, Apollodorus, is presented as a litigious, extravagant, self-indulgent opportunist who now, years after the matter seemed settled, is trying to extract some additional funds from Phormio. The importance of the speech relates not only to Demosthenes' technique and to the information on fourth-century economics which it contains, but to what it reveals about Athenian social history, especially Athenian attitudes toward slaves and former slaves.

Democratic juries which had heard a good speech were not always interested in due process. In this case Apollodorus was condemned without being allowed to reply, and his original suit had to be abandoned. But if juries were impetuous, the nerves of a litigious Greek were strong and Apollodorus did not hesitate to try again. If he could invalidate one of Phormio's witnesses, even on a minor matter, he could then accuse Phormio of suborning perjury and could reopen the whole case. He thus attacked a certain Stephanus who had testified for Phormio. In the Demosthenic corpus we have two speeches for Apollodorus against this Stephanus in precisely this case. The second of these exhibits Apollodorus' usual level of mediocre confusion and may be regarded as his own effort. The first is an able, quite Demosthenic speech with a vigorous and very nasty attack on poor Phormio. Plutarch says (*Dem.* 15) that Demosthenes, as a professional speech writer, furnished speeches to both sides. Aeschines, who was a contemporary and anxious to see as much evil as possible in Demosthenes, only accuses him of writing a speech for Phormio and then showing it to Apollodorus before the trial (2.166). It has often been thought that political considerations were involved and that Apollodorus at this time undertook to make the dangerous proposal to convert the theoric fund to military uses, a policy which Demosthenes urged in the first and third *Olynthiacs*. The combined evidence may be taken to suggest that Demosthenes, for the sake of what may have seemed the greater public interest, in some sense either betrayed a trust or broke what was regarded by some of his contemporaries as the usual code of conduct. He was to do so again in the Harpalus incident.

The private speeches represent only one level of Demosthenes' complex activities. In the mid-350s he became associated with others in a political action group of financially conservative property owners. The kaleidoscope of Athenian politics is exceedingly difficult to hold in focus, but Aristophon and Androtion were among the influential people whom Demosthenes opposed and it is possible that Eubulus was one of those with whom he associated himself.[1] The new party, if terms may be stretched to that extent, were well aware of Demosthenes' rhetorical abilities and called upon him to write speeches in their interest. We have, of course, logographic speeches in public cases by earlier orators, but all suggest a much greater personal interest on the part of the speaker, whereas here the legal actions may involve deliberate matching of a man thought to be an effective speaker with a text commissioned from a clever speech writer.

The earliest of Demosthenes' public cases (355) is a prosecution for illegal motion against Androtion, a well known figure who later was to write a history of Attica. Androtion's rather routine proposal to award crowns to members of the outgoing council is branded as illegal, since the council had been unable to complete its duty to build ships. There were two prosecutors, Euctemon, the author of whose speech is unknown, and Diodorus, for whom Demosthenes wrote. Both seem to have been chosen as respectable average citizens who would appeal to the democratic jury. Why did Demosthenes himself not speak? He may have been regarded as suspect because of political connexions or his wealth or his speech writing activities, but it is also possible that he may not yet have seemed to be a powerful enough speaker. He clearly achieved effectiveness in delivery only gradually and after Herculean efforts with the actor Satyrus, before a mirror with pebbles in his mouth, or in other ways as described by Plutarch (*Dem.* 6.3), who also says that his attempts in the preceding years to get the assembly to listen to him were failures. Diodorus may have been a rather average citizen, but the opponents of Androtion clearly regarded him as able to present effectively a long and complicated oration, presumably from memory. He may well have been a natural actor. The situation in *Against Timocrates* (353), where Diodorus was again the speaker, and in *Against Aristocrates* (352) may have been similar, and it is possible that there were additional cases not now known to us. The programmed aspect of the trials may be seen in some similarities of treatment. *Against Timocrates* even repeats verbatim a long passage from the earlier speech *Against Androtion*.

That Demosthenes was interested in participating more directly in public trials is likely enough. As a boy he had been smuggled into a courtroom to hear a great speech by Callistratus which Plutarch claims was a permanent influence on him. That he did succeed in improving his delivery is certain. The story was commonly told among later rhetoricians that Demosthenes, when asked what was the most important factor in oratory, replied 'delivery'; and

[1] Jaeger (1938) 57ff.

when asked the second most important factor, said 'delivery'; and when asked the third, said 'delivery'.[1] In assessing the artistic achievement of Demosthenes we can only guess at the visual and oral effects he achieved on the basis of our observations of his sentence structure, sound patterns, rhythms, changes of tone and use of 'audience contact' words such as particles, rhetorical questions and especially oaths, which are commoner in his work than in the other orators.

Demosthenes may, however, have fulfilled his wish to speak in a political case as early as 354 B.C. The plaintiff in *Against Leptines* is the young son of the late general Chabrias, and according to Plutarch and the *hypothesis* found in manuscripts of the speech Demosthenes spoke the oration as a *synegoros*. Werner Jaeger believed that the ethos of the speaker of *Against Leptines* could be used as a way of perceiving Demosthenes' conception of himself at this period:[2] a man from the upper circles of Athens who speaks without stormy passion, but with dignified reserve, good social form and great self-assurance. Jaeger compared him to one of the nobler characters in Menander. *Against Leptines* was always a favourite in the rhetorical schools and even if the personality portrayed is posed for effect rather than drawn from life, it shows the ability of the writer to portray character.

The other speech of most interest in this group is *Against Aristocrates*. It is our major source of information about the complicated affairs in Thrace in the mid-fourth century, including the activities of Cersobleptes and Charidemus, and it is also probably the best single source of information on Attic homicide law. The speaker is an otherwise unknown Euthycles, who must have been a very competent orator.[3] A final public case of some interest is that *Against Meidias*, a prosecution of a political opponent who slapped Demosthenes' face when he was performing an official function at a festival. It is one of Demosthenes' more unrelenting invectives, but was apparently never delivered: the case was settled out of court.

The public speeches which we have been considering represent a second level of Demosthenes' achievement. A third may be said to be the deliberative oratory which he first began to practise in the mid-350s. Outside of those speeches of Isocrates which take a deliberative form, the oratory of political harangue in fourth-century Athens is represented by the first seventeen works in the Demosthenic corpus. Of these, the speech *On Halonnesus* is generally attributed to Hegesippus and the *Reply to Philip's letter* may be taken from Anaximenes' *History*, while three others are by unknown writers. The spurious speeches are undistinguished from a literary point of view. Demosthenes himself in three

---

[1] Cf., e.g., Cic. *De or.* 3.213.

[2] Jaeger (1938).

[3] In section 19 he gives the court its choice of the order in which he will deal with topics. Of course this may not represent a real choice and the text may have been edited for publication.

speeches from the mid-350s and in the *Philippics* brought the deliberative genre to a high state of artistic development.[1] It seems likely that he published a collection of his deliberative speeches as political pamphlets; we can see some signs of the editing in the third and the fourth *Philippics*.

On the symmories, *On the Megalopolitans* and *On the liberty of the Rhodians* are beautiful examples of classical deliberative oratory: artistic exposition of reasoned views with grace and economy. All three are short, compressed, to the point. Political issues are presented in terms of policy, and personalities are totally avoided. *On the symmories*, delivered in 354 B.C., is earliest; modern critics have agreed with Dionysius (*De Thuc.* 34) that in style it shows the influence of Thucydides. Subsequent speeches are less consistently antithetical in expression as well as more flexible in the arrangement of narrative and argument. Demosthenes presents himself here as a practical man who is not going to praise the past like other speakers, but will say what ought to be done now. He then describes the danger of the proposed war with Persia, in the centre of the speech he states his proposal for reform of the system of liturgies, he next reviews the financial needs, and he concludes with an epilogue which takes up the theme of the prooemium. The structure is thus generally symmetrical with the main idea in the centre of the speech, an arrangement typical of Demosthenes' deliberative oratory. Also typical is the synthesis of arguments from expediency, justice and honour.[2] There is remarkably little adornment or metaphor, but some of Demosthenes' sarcastic force breaks out: 'Somebody proposes a two per cent tax? And what is this to the 1,200 camels which they say come bringing money to the Great King!' (14.27).

The term *Philippic* is applied to the four orations bearing that name or more widely to all of Demosthenes' deliberative speeches warning of the dangers from Philip. These include the first *Philippic*, the three *Olynthiacs*, *On the peace*, the second *Philippic*, *On events in the Chersonese*, the third *Philippic* and the fourth *Philippic*. The time of composition is the decade from 351 B.C., when Demosthenes became aware of Philip's growing power, through the Peace of Philocrates, to the events which renewed war with Philip and led to the battle of Chaeronea, but despite this lapse of time, the style and spirit of the works are remarkably consistent. Throughout, Demosthenes' problem is to arouse Athenian alarm at Philip's actions, and thus to induce counteractions, without suggesting that it is too late, or that Philip is irresistible, or that Athens has sunk too far into decline to be able to meet the challenge. His chief tools are his moral earnestness, his avoidance of personal incriminations against other Athenians, his own practical military and financial proposals, his ability to

[1] On Demosthenes' prose style cf. Ronnet (1951). On the development of Demosthenes' deliberative technique cf. Pearson (1964).
[2] Kennedy (1959).

integrate Athens' traditions and true present interest, and perhaps most of all his striking portrait of Philip. The latter emerges as a figure of incredible energy and ambition, driven on by hubris, like some kind of aberrant disaster of nature, who can, however, be stopped once and for all when his opponents realize how shallow is his base and how slender his support. There are many splendid brief glimpses of Athenians or of Philip, suddenly brought before the mind: in the first *Philippic*, for example, reports of Philip's death have falsely encouraged Athenians. Is Philip dead? No, somebody replies, but he is sick. What difference does it make? Athens as she now exists would create another Philip in his place (11). The Athenians are like an untrained boxer: their arms always move to the spot where Philip has hit rather than where he is going to hit (40–1). The third *Philippic* deals extensively with the question of Athens' decline: freedom of speech has slipped into complacency and flattery, the moral spirit of the people has ebbed away, Greece is diseased, but still something can be done. Philip is no true Greek, but an illegitimate child claiming an inheritance to which he has no right (30–1). The device of question and answer is frequently employed to give vigour to the delivery and thought; as in Demosthenes' earlier speeches there is a synthesis of argument, but leading this time to the single over-riding question of survival; as in his public judicial orations there is a constant taking up of ideas and motifs, but integrated into a complex mosaic of invention.

A fourth level of Demosthenes' achievement is reached in the two great courtroom speeches, both public cases but highly personal, in which he defends his own career and attacks that of Aeschines: *On the false embassy* and *On the crown*. In both cases we have a version of Aeschines' opposing speech to compare with Demosthenes' remarks. All four orations are on a vast scale of artistic development, over three times as long as Lysias' *Against Eratosthenes*, twice as long as *Against Leptines*.

In 346 Athens made a treaty with Philip II of Macedon which ended nearly ten years of war between the two states. The treaty is known as the Peace of Philocrates, but Demosthenes and Aeschines were also among the ambassadors who negotiated it. Aeschines clearly became convinced that Athens could not stop Philip militarily, but that negotiations and cooperation could secure some measure of safety and independence. He tended to trust Philip's assertions of good intentions and made himself the spokesman for them in Athens. Demosthenes believed that Philip must be resisted in every possible way, he distrusted Philip's promises and saw his suspicions confirmed by Philip's actions, and he regarded Aeschines as a tool of Macedon. He consistently claims that Aeschines had been bribed by Philip, but he does not prove the claim and most historians have believed that Aeschines was taking what he regarded as the only practical course for Athens.

In the embassy trial of 343 B.C. Demosthenes accused Aeschines of making untruthful reports, of disobeying instructions, of dragging his feet and of being bribed during negotiations for the Peace of Philocrates. Aeschines was acquitted by thirty votes. The Peace lasted until 340 when hostilities were resumed. Demosthenes played an effective role in uniting Thebes with Athens against Philip, but the Greek allies were decisively defeated at Chaeronea in 338, a date usually taken as the end of independence for the Greek city states. In fact, Athens retained control of her internal affairs, and Demosthenes kept out of the hands of Philip and helped prepare Athens against the possibility of siege. In 336 one Ctesiphon proposed that the assembly vote Demosthenes a crown because of his continued patriotism and recent services. This was of course a highly political proposal, though there was nothing unusual in the award of a crown. Aeschines immediately charged that the proposal was illegal. The trial was delayed by public events, including the assassination of Philip, Alexander's imposition of his authority, and the preparation for the invasion of Asia, but in 330 B.C. when the time seemed propitious, Aeschines resumed his suit. Ctesiphon replied briefly, and Demosthenes then took over as Ctesiphon's *synegoros*, delivering what has always been regarded as one of the greatest speeches of all time. It was decisively successful. Aeschines failed to get one fifth of the votes, could not pay the penalty which this incurred, and left Athens for ever.

On the false embassy is essentially a narrative, rather than an argumentative work. Demosthenes describes in considerable detail, though perhaps not entirely accurately, the various embassies and debates, seeking throughout to develop a characterization of Aeschines which will lead to the conviction that he must have been bribed even though no witnesses confirmed it. The speech has a remarkable sustained force, though it never achieves the pathos of *On the crown*, and it is less tightly structured than most of Demosthenes' speeches. Many parts are vivid, such as the picture of Philocrates ridiculing Demosthenes from the *bema*: 'He drinks water, I drink wine' (46). The second half of the speech is a greatly amplified collection of miscellaneous topics which Demosthenes plays upon as variation on his main ethical theme. Among the techniques used is a favourite one with Demosthenes, employed in some degree in most of his public orations, a kind of running dialogue with himself, here on the question of why he had undertaken the prosecution. Such passages help make the mental processes of the speaker real and relieve tedium by bringing the jury into the orator's confidence. Another source of vigour is the attack on the life and character of Aeschines. Personal invective only gradually appears in Greek oratory; it is almost unknown in Lysias, more prominent in Isaeus, fully developed by both Aeschines and Demosthenes, but a feature of judicial, not of deliberative oratory as it is in Rome. Toward the end of the speech we are treated to a nasty picture of young Aeschines, a good deal of satire on his career as an actor, and a comparison of him with Solon, a comparison at which a stronger man than Aeschines might flinch. In these passages Demosthenes reveals his ability to vary the tone with great versatility, and we must assume that his oral delivery further sharpened this tool to his purpose of undermining his opponent's credibility.

On the crown is equally personal in its invective against Aeschines, but achieves a much nobler overall effect, primarily from the pathos of patriotism and the success of Demosthenes' portrayal of his own ethical integrity. He will not admit he failed or was wrong in his policies, though fate chose to let Philip triumph in the war. He continually returns to the question 'What else could I have done?' The pathos is thus further deepened by the tragedy of a lost, noble cause: Greek freedom.

The emotional high point of the speech is the context surrounding the oath by those who fell at Marathon (206–10). The difficulties of delivery of this section, with its continually heightening tone, must have been considerable:

εἰ γὰρ ὡς οὐ τὰ βέλτιστ' ἐμοῦ πολιτευσαμένου τουδὶ καταψηφιεῖσθε, ἡμαρτηκέναι δόξετε, οὐ τῇ τῆς τύχης ἀγνωμοσύνῃ τὰ συμβάντα παθεῖν. ἀλλ' οὐκ ἔστιν, οὐκ ἔστιν ὅπως ἡμάρτετ', ἄνδρες Ἀθηναῖοι, τὸν ὑπὲρ τῆς ἀπάντων ἐλευθερίας καὶ σωτηρίας κίνδυνον ἀράμενοι, μὰ τοὺς Μαραθῶνι προκινδυνεύσαντας τῶν προγόνων, καὶ τοὺς ἐν Πλαταιαῖς παραταξαμένους, καὶ τοὺς ἐν Σαλαμῖνι ναυμαχήσαντας καὶ τοὺς ἐπ' Ἀρτεμισίωι, καὶ πολλοὺς ἑτέρους τοὺς ἐν τοῖς δημοσίοις μνήμασιν κειμένους ἀγαθοὺς ἄνδρας, οὓς ἅπαντας ὁμοίως ἡ πόλις τῆς αὐτῆς ἀξιώσασα τιμῆς ἔθαψεν, Αἰσχίνη, οὐχὶ τοὺς κατορθώσαντας αὐτῶν οὐδὲ τοὺς κρατήσαντας μόνους.

For if, on the ground that I was a political failure, you condemn Ctesiphon here [with a wave of the hand at the poor victim of high politics], you [a pointing finger?] will seem to admit being in the wrong [stressed] rather than to have suffered what befell you by the harshness of fate. [Then in heightened tone:] But it cannot be, it cannot be [repetition is a favourite Demosthenic device of emphasis] that you are in the wrong, o men of Athens [giving audience contact and allowing the previous clause to sink into the mind], undertaking danger for the liberty and safety of all [repeated cretics in the rhythm and the emotional word 'liberty' heighten the tone still more]. I swear it BY THOSE AT MARATHON who fought in the forefront of our forefathers [the alliteration – of p in the original – adds another burst of intensity], those who stood in the ranks at Plataea and those at Salamis who fought at sea and those off Artemisium and many others lying in public tombs, good men, whom all alike the city has thought worthy of an honourable burial, Aeschines [a sudden turn from the jury and the pathos becomes bitter], not only those who were successful and prevailed.

On the crown surpasses Demosthenes' early public cases in pathos and in the ethos of the characters – Demosthenes himself, the innocent Ctesiphon, the disgusting Aeschines, the barbaric Philip, the jury constantly turning from one to the other – but it is also strong in argument and arrangement. Aeschines argued that Ctesiphon's motion was illegal for three reasons: it provided for crowning Demosthenes in the theatre, which was forbidden; Demosthenes at the time was still liable to an audit for the office he held; and the claim that Demosthenes was a patriot was untrue. In his prosecution he stressed his legal arguments, which were probably technically valid. Demosthenes' 'rhetorical challenge' was to get the jury to consider the broader issue, where he had some hope of counteracting Aeschines. Such an approach not only was prudent, but was congenial to him. Legal trivia did not interest him; in his speeches he seeks consistently for the basic issues and takes a broad view of his subject and of the political life of Athens. In the case of *On the crown* he insists near the outset on taking up some matters to which Aeschines had referred and which gave him an opportunity to picture briefly his public activities in the years between the Peace of Philocrates and Chaeronea. Then he very briefly touches on the two legal arguments and plunges with full vigour into his subsequent actions and those of Aeschines, which are compared unfavourably at every possible point. The effect is completely to overshadow the legal technicalities. *On the crown* does not build up to a final great climax. It ebbs and flows like the tide of a great sea, reaching full flood about two thirds of the way through, and gradually withdraws into a more philosophical tone in picturing the tragic confrontation between Demosthenes' personal fortune and that of Aeschines. And it ends as it begins, with a prayer.

The great subsequent event of Demosthenes' life, the Harpalus incident when he was accused of accepting a bribe from the fugitive treasurer of Alexander, was an occasion for oratory, but Demosthenes' speeches have not survived. Demosthenes clearly ranks with Plato as one of the two greatest Greek prose stylists and with Cicero, who owed much to him, as one of the two greatest orators of antiquity. In the subsequent history of Greek prose down into the Byzantine period Demosthenes and Plato remain the chief influences. Study of Hellenistic rhetoric shows that in fact Demosthenes' influence was always strong, but Dionysius of Halicarnassus and Hermogenes contributed to its increase. Both saw in him a combination of all literary virtues, a never failing object of imitation, and the most forceful artisan of the spoken word. His works were regularly studied in schools, commentaries on them and replies to them were composed by sophists and rhetoricians, and Demosthenes remained 'the orator' for the ages.

Aeschines

Of Demosthenes' opponents in court the one best known to us, and perhaps the ablest, is Aeschines. He seems to have been a logographer and claims in the opening of his speech *Against Timarchus* that up to that time (345 B.C.) he had not engaged in political prosecutions. Like Andocides, he was more a talented amateur than a professional orator. To judge from Demosthenes' personal attacks on him, after initially assisting in his father's school, he became a minor government clerk and had a career as an actor before becoming involved in the highest levels of politics. After his defeat in the trial of Ctesiphon, however, he retired to Asia Minor and to Rhodes and taught rhetoric. Philostratus regarded him as the founder of the Second Sophistic, not only as a teacher, but because of his ability at extemporization when he allowed himself to be carried away by a kind of enthusiasm. The best known example of this was his speech at Delphi in 339 B.C., which he himself presents as having saved the situation for Athens and which Demosthenes regarded as the act of a paid agent of Philip.[1]

We have three speeches by Aeschines. All are flamboyant, readable, amplified and unscrupulous in their use of personal attack. Critics over the centuries have usually admired their verve and cleverness, but felt something like embarrassment at their gaucherie, particularly at Aeschines' fondness for showing off his culture. There are many instances of this, but the appeal at the end of *Against Ctesiphon* to the Earth, the Sun, Virtue, Knowledge and Paideia is a convenient example. The earliest of Aeschines' speeches, and the least read, is his prosecution of Timocrates to prevent him from joining with Demosthenes in a prosecution of Aeschines after the Peace of Philocrates. The argument is that Timocrates was ineligible to speak in the assembly or the courts because of immorality. The speech is a good source of information about male prostitution in Greece, about the procedures in the assembly, and about the opposition's view of Demosthenes in this period. Very little is said about the political background of the trial; indeed, Aeschines' work as a whole is characterized by an avoidance of the deeper issues and by attempts to divert attention to details. In this he is of course in complete contrast to Demosthenes. In part the difference is one of personality, but in part it results from the political position of the two orators. Demosthenes, as an idealist, a conservative, an old-fashioned patriot, wants confrontation and has everything to gain from thorough analysis of the machinations of Philip and of those in Athens who cooperated with him; Aeschines, whose sincerity we have no real reason to dispute, had the difficult task of supporting a cause that recognized the power of Philip, thought that the only realistic goal was one of *entente*, and needed to play down fears of appeasement and radical change. He is most successful at this in his second speech, *On the embassy* (343 B.C.), in which he replied to Demosthenes' prosecution *On the false embassy*, carefully setting out the narrative detail in order to show what was done day by day and assuring the Athenians that nobody was bribed. The third speech, *Against Ctesiphon*, attempts similar tactics, but this time Aeschines was overwhelmed by the much greater moral force of Demosthenes.

[1] Aeschin. 3.107–24 and Dem. *On the crown* 149–50.

Hyperides

The subject matter of judicial oratory brings it at times into close association with comedy. This could be illustrated from works of Lysias or Demosthenes, but is most noticeable in the speeches of Hyperides. He is the wittiest of the orators, he did not hesitate to take on sensational cases which he treated in imaginative ways, and his standards of diction, less austere than those of his predecessors, enriched his language with words from comedy and everyday life. Ancient critics represent him as the pentathlete among the orators, second only to Demosthenes as an all-round speaker: a versatile logographer, an effective political prosecutor, for example of Philocrates in 343 B.C., and a leading spokesman in the assembly for the anti-Macedonian party. Remarkably, he seems to have avoided the personal abuse to which his competitors often resort. His career is parallel to that of Demosthenes and for much of the time the two were in general agreement, but in later years they parted company and Hyperides joined with others in the prosecution of Demosthenes for taking the gold of Harpalus. We have fragments of a speech on this subject, as well as his logographic speech *For Euxenippus* (which deals with the unusual matter of temple incubation), much of his funeral oration for the dead in the Lamian War, and portions of three other judicial speeches. All come to us from papyri discovered since 1847. A little is known about other works, the most celebrated being the defence of the courtesan Phryne where Hyperides sought to show the irrelevance of the prosecution's lurid moral pictures of the tortures of the wicked in the underworld by exclaiming 'Why is Phryne to blame if a stone hangs over the head of Tantalus?' Finally, he resorted to extra-rational persuasion by dramatically undraping to the jury the fair bosom of his client. Dionysius of Halicarnassus thought Hyperides matched Lysias in style and surpassed him in invention and arrangement. He is particularly good at weaving arguments into a consistent whole, something which Lysias never mastered, he is less rigid in treating the traditional parts of the judicial oration, and he has considerable skill at *ethopoeia*, approaching that of Lysias: *Against Athenagoras* has a vivid collection of unseemly characters, including the speaker, who are worthy of Menander.

Lycurgus and Dinarchus

The two remaining judicial orators in the canon are Lycurgus and Dinarchus. Lycurgus belonged to the anti-Macedonian faction, was celebrated for his integrity and rescued Athenian finances in the years after Chaeronea. He was not a logographer, but undertook many prosecutions of corrupt opponents. We have one speech, a strident prosecution of Leocrates for treason. Dinarchus was a metic and second-rate logographer of whom three speeches survive, including an indifferent prosecution of Demosthenes in the Harpalus case.

We have only a small portion of published Greek oratory and must exercise some caution, as we must in the case of tragedy or comedy, in making generalizations about its history. It does seem, however, to have arisen out of political, legal and social conditions of the mid-fifth century and to have developed first a series of conventions of arrangement and topics. This was followed in the early fourth century by an increased artistry in the portrayal of character, including the presentation of the character of the speaker, and in the subtlety of argument. From the mid-fourth century we have examples of large-scale speeches in public cases which utilize bitter personal invective, inspired by sharp political differences. After the Lamian War political oratory had little scope in Athens and judicial speeches gradually fell back into a sub-literary form which ceased to attract the effort of first-rate minds, but the educational system remained focused on rhetoric, and oratory re-emerged as a major genre in the second century after Christ.[1]

[1] The text of this chapter was written in 1975.

17

ARISTOTLE

For the history of Greek literature, philosophy, from Aristotle onwards, is important in at least three different ways. First, style and genre: the literary presentation of philosophy, sometimes within the same writer, varies on a scale which may range from what is little more than technical shorthand to highly polished prose. Some philosophers of the Hellenistic period even present their ideas in verse, and quotations, especially from the most famous poets, are not uncommon.

Secondly, literary theory: Aristotle himself, and some later Greek philosophers, made fundamental contributions to the theory of rhetoric and to literary criticism. Much of their work in this field was taken over by later classical writers, especially the Roman rhetoricians, and it has had a continuing influence.

Thirdly, thought. This must be considered when it directly influences the subject matter of literature. In this respect Aristotle is much less significant than the Stoics and Epicureans. The philosophy of Epicurus is Lucretius' theme and Lucretius is a poet of comparable genius to Virgil. But Lucretius is only the most notable of many poets and other writers whose work was strongly influenced by Epicureanism or Stoicism. Today that influence looks decidedly more marked on Roman literature than on Greek. But this is due, at least in part, to the loss of nearly all Greek literature from the last three centuries B.C. There can be little doubt that Stoicism and Epicureanism had a pervasive influence on later Greek culture.

I. HIS LIFE AND WRITINGS

Aristotle began his philosophical career as a member of Plato's Academy at Athens in 367 B.C. Unlike Plato he was not an Athenian citizen. His father, Nicomachus, was the court doctor to Amyntas, king of Macedonia, and it was no doubt at Nicomachus' suggestion that the seventeen-year-old Aristotle joined the Academy in order to get 'the best education that Greece could offer'.[1] Aristotle remained a pupil and close associate of Plato until 347, when Plato died. Whether any of his surviving writings date from this period it is

---

[1] Ross (1923) 2.

impossible to say. But we may be confident that this long membership of the Academy was the strongest of all influences on Aristotle's philosophical development. His own work, though often critical of Plato, continuously makes explicit or implicit reference to the older philosopher's writings, and in certain works, notably the *Topics*, Aristotle is almost certainly reflecting discussions and methods of argument which were practised orally in the Academy. But none of this casts any doubt upon Aristotle's originality as both thinker and researcher. The range of his interests was enormous and he had a passion, apparently not shared by Plato, for the most painstaking collection and classification of facts, whether in biology, natural science, or the history of political constitutions. Moreover, Aristotle established methods of analysis and positive theories about the nature of things which are often not only an advance on Plato but deserve to be called original in the highest degree. This is most conspicuously true of his logic, both in its formal systematic presentation in the *Analytics*, and as a methodology for philosophical argument in general. But in all the subjects he treated, metaphysics, ethics, politics, philosophy of mind, and natural science, Aristotle demonstrated powers of sustained analytical thought which are nothing less than amazing.

After Plato's death Aristotle left Athens, returning to the city twelve years later in 335. The years of his 'travels' were spent in various cities, first in Asia Minor then later in Macedonia. Modern research has provided strong reasons for dating Aristotle's developing interest in biology to this period of his life,[1] and the years 343/2–340 are important for quite another reason. During this time Aristotle was employed by Philip of Macedon as tutor to Alexander, then a boy in his mid-teens. It is likely enough that Aristotle attempted to interest the young Alexander in some of the more elementary work of the Academy, but from what we know of master and pupil neither of them significantly influenced the other. One of Aristotle's most remarkable silences in his political writings is the complete absence of any reference to the profound changes then taking place in the Greek world, which were a direct consequence of Alexander's campaigns and imperialist ambitions.

Aristotle's official relationship with Alexander seems to have ended in 340, but the philosopher remained in Macedonia until Alexander succeeded Philip five years later. He then returned to Athens, but not to the Academy. Having now acquired, we may assume, a considerable reputation as a philosopher, Aristotle established his own circle of friends and pupils in the Lyceum, a grove sacred to Apollo just outside Athens itself, which had become a public exercise ground with a gymnasium building. The Lyceum (or Peripatos), as Aristotle's school came to be called, at first had no premises of its own but was housed in public buildings, where Aristotle was permitted by the civic authorities to

[1] Cf. Lee (1948).

teach.[1] Subsequently his successor, Theophrastus, acquired property near the Lyceum, which he made available to the school and bequeathed to his philosophical associates (Diog. Laert. 5.52). It is clear that Aristotle saw himself during these later years in Athens as an independent philosopher, directing research, lecturing, and refining his own ideas. His personal and scholarly influence on his followers was strong enough to inspire a most fruitful continuation of studies after his death. This occurred in 322, at Chalcis (Euboea) where Aristotle had retired, under the pressure of an anti-Macedonian revolution at Athens after Alexander's death was announced.

Aristotle's philosophy and the nature of his writings must be discussed together. From later antiquity up to recent times Aristotle was regarded as a systematic philosopher *par excellence*. Werner Jaeger's work on the history of Aristotle's development (1923) initiated a fundamental reassessment of this view. We now recognize that, for all Aristotle's positive views about the world and their mutual coherence, he was primarily a researcher, a poser of problems and solutions to them, only secondarily a system-builder. His writings present us with a mind which is continuously engaged upon a dialogue with itself, taking due account of established theories or empirical evidence and shaping its thought by means of clearly defined conceptual categories. The impression of a self-contained Aristotelian system, though partly true, is due in part to the commentators of later antiquity and their medieval successors. It is also due to the manner in which Aristotle's writings have been transmitted to us.

For Plato the dialogue was the literary medium of philosophy. Whatever its origins may have been, as a representation of actual Socratic discourse, Plato's dialogues are not simply a dramatic device. Their fundamental characteristic is question and answer between at least two people, and for Plato the approved method of doing philosophy, at any rate in written form, is this style of 'dialectical' exchange, conducted according to certain self-evident, though not strictly formal, principles of logic and criteria of truth. In the *Letters*, some of which are probably genuine (see pp. 480f.), and in certain passages of his dialogues, especially the later ones, extensive exposition of views by a single speaker is common enough. But apart from the debatable 7th *Letter*, Plato did not offer a written account of his own philosophy in the first person.

So far as we can judge, Plato's dialogues were unique in Greek literature. Other philosophers, including Aristotle, sometimes used the dialogue form, but not as the fundamental method of writing philosophy. The continuous prose treatise was well established for technical writing by the middle of the fifth century, and we should not regard Plato's dialogues as an interruption of that tradition. They are explicable by reference to Plato's relation to Socrates and his own philosophical methodology.

[1] Lynch (1972) 68–154.

ARISTOTLE

Like Plato Aristotle wrote works which were designed for the general educated reader, but our knowledge of these is fragmentary.[1] He himself distinguished between *logoi exoterikoi*, works intended for reading outside the school, and *logoi kata philosophian*, works of a technical philosophical nature (*Eth.Eud.* 1, 1217b22) written as lectures or for study within his own circle. It is the latter set of works which forms the extant Aristotelian corpus. Often known as 'Aristotle's lecture notes', a misleading description, the surviving treatises have certainly undergone reorganization and editing since Aristotle's death. Our own texts probably go back to an edition which was made by Andronicus of Rhodes before the middle of the first century B.C.[2] It is virtually certain that he undertook to edit a substantial set of Aristotle's own manuscripts which had been out of circulation from the death of Theophrastus (288/4) until they were recovered by an Athenian bibliophile, Apellicon, in the early first century B.C.[3] This is not important simply as bibliographical history. To Andronicus can be assigned the ultimate responsibility for the present arrangement of Aristotle's works, including the division into books and at least some titles, and his own philosophical preconceptions probably led him to give a more systematic organization to the material than Aristotle would have used himself.[4] Furthermore there is good reason to think that at least some of the texts in Andronicus' edition had not been available even in libraries after being taken to Asia Minor by Neleus of Scepsis early in the third century B.C. This does not mean that nothing of Aristotle's philosophy was known in the intervening years. His more popular writings were available, and the Alexandrian Library seems to have possessed a very large number of his works.[5] Certain texts may have been known elsewhere, but the story that our own Aristotelian writings were temporarily lost gains some support from the absence of clear references to them in the literature of the period from about 270 to 40 B.C.

'All men have a natural desire for knowledge.' This compelling statement is the first sentence of Aristotle's *Metaphysics*, and the traditional arrangement of his works is based upon a classification of knowledge or sciences which he himself recognized: theoretical, practical and productive (*Metaph.* E 1025b25). To these must be added the logical treatises, which stand first in the corpus and which Aristotle himself regarded not as parts of any one science but as a method of argument which is applicable to all sciences. Given these four divisions of Aristotle's work, the largest single part of his writings falls under 'theoretical

[1] Cf. Lesky 621–4.
[2] Ancient evidence on Andronicus' work is collected in Düring (1957) 412–25. For detailed discussion cf. Moraux (1973) who gives strong arguments for dating Andronicus' activity before the death of Cicero (pp. 45–58).
[3] Strabo (13.1.54) purports to tell the history of these texts up to their coming into the hands of Andronicus.
[4] Düring (1966) 41–2.
[5] Düring (1966) 37.

530

knowledge'. This embraces his investigations of nature, both at the level of general principles of movement and change (*Physics, On coming to be and passing away, On the heavens*) and in biology; it also includes what he calls 'first philosophy' or 'theology' (*Metaphysics*) the subject matter of which is the first principles of reality or the primary objects of scientific knowledge. His writings on *Ethics* and *Politics* are examples of 'practical knowledge' with the *Poetics* (and in some sense the *Rhetoric*) an instance of knowledge which is 'productive'. One work which falls outside this classification is the *Constitution of Athens*, the sole surviving example of a massive investigation of Greek city states which Aristotle directed, though he himself can hardly have written more than a fraction of the 158 treatises which were reputedly composed.

Aristotle was highly regarded as a stylist in antiquity. Cicero speaks of his *flumen orationis aureum* (*Acad.* 2.119) 'his golden stream of eloquence', and Quintilian repeats this, *eloquendi suauitas* (10.1.83) his 'sweetness of style'. Both critics must have had Aristotle's literary works in mind, and the remains of these are much too defective for us to corroborate such judgements. But there is little reason to doubt them. Literary artifice and elegant periods are not features of our Aristotelian corpus, for these works were not written to charm the ear. (Philodemus' comment on Aristotle's literary 'stammer', *Rhet.* II p.51, 36.11 Sudhaus, is probably a reference to the technical treatises.) Much of Aristotle's philosophy is technical and calls for familiarity with special terminology and formal argument. But although there are some passages which are condensed, or disturbed by transmission, to the point of deep obscurity, Aristotle is not consistently difficult to read for those who have thoroughly acquainted themselves with his style and language. The chief difficulties in Aristotle lie in the nature of the problems with which he grappled, and it is a measure of his distinction that he frequently found a means for expressing the most abstract thought clearly and coherently.

Moreover, even in his extant works he shows on occasions touches of that *flumen orationis aureum*. The introduction to the *Metaphysics* is one example; another is a passage from *On the parts of animals* (1.5) which reveals the aesthetic pleasure of the scientific researcher: 'Even in the study of animals which cause no delight to the senses, nature in her craftsmanship provides irresistible pleasures for those capable of recognizing causes and for the natural lovers of wisdom.' Or, when writing of the purely contemplative life, he describes this as

> superior to human nature; for such a life will not belong to man as such, but to something present in him which is divine...yet one should not follow the advice of those who bid man think human thoughts...but practise immortality to the limit of one's powers and do everything to live under the direction of what is the best in oneself. For even if it is small in bulk, in power and value it far exceeds everything else. (*Eth.Nic.* 10, 1177b26–1178a2)

Even at his driest Aristotle succeeds in conveying his own passion for knowledge, and no one has more consistently expressed the satisfaction of the completely dedicated intellectual life.

It is difficult to generalize briefly about Aristotle's methodology as a philosophical writer, but certain points must be mentioned. Unlike Plato, Aristotle likes to begin the consideration of a problem with a survey of existing views on the subject. This may be done without reference to individuals, but more often he gives a detailed account and criticism of earlier philosophers, making such use of their theories or concepts (as interpreted by him) as suits his own philosophical purpose. Two notable examples are the first book of *Metaphysics* and that of the work *On the soul*. Aristotle (in such passages) is not so much a historian of philosophy as a critic who views his predecessors through his own categories of thought.[1] But he is a fundamental source of knowledge about early Greek philosophy.

A second characteristic of his philosophical style is the quest for definitions of central concepts and the elucidation of what we would call different usages of a term, which Aristotle calls 'the different ways in which a thing is said'. Thus the first chapter of *Physics* 2 is devoted to an analysis of *physis* 'nature', which he considers to have two uses, according as we refer to the *matter* of something or its *form*. *Matter* and *form* are two fundamental Aristotelian conceptual categories which he uses in the analysis of all manner of different things. Other such concepts are *potentiality* and *actuality*, *necessary* and *contingent*, *being* and *becoming*, though the Greek terms which these words translate possess connotations which can only be partially rendered in English. Having defined the entity with which he is concerned, it is characteristic of Aristotle to discuss specific details, which not only elucidate the definition but may cause it to be modified. He repeatedly interrupts his main exposition of a subject to consider an *aporia*, a specific problem, which a modern writer might place in a footnote and which he himself may leave unresolved. It is sometimes impossible to say whether a particular *aporia* is part of his original text or something which he, or even an editor, has added later. But there can be no doubt that the majority are part of his own philosophical presentation.

Naturally the methodology varies greatly with the subject matter. In the *Analytics*, which sets out the formal principles of deductive (syllogistic) reasoning, the language is consistently technical, and the style comparable to that of a modern textbook on logic. The *Ethics*, on the other hand, is written in a plain but admirably clear Greek, and a number of moral points are illustrated by quotation from the poets. Like all educated Greeks Aristotle must have known

[1] Aristotle's reliability as an historian of philosophy was fundamentally challenged by Cherniss (1935). His argument was not seriously undermined by Guthrie (1957) as Stevenson points out (1974).

vast quantities of Homer and other poets by heart, and his interest in literature was by no means purely one of pleasure. His writings included six books of Homeric Problems,[1] a subject later treated by Zeno the Stoic and by many others. He compiled, or organized the compilation of, records of the victors and their plays at the Athenian dramatic festivals,[2] and his surviving works include two studies which are of especial literary interest, *Rhetoric* and *Poetics*. These, particularly the second, must be discussed in some detail.

2. RHETORIC

Aristotle's *Art of rhetoric*, as we have it, is in three books. As a contribution to literary theory the last of these is the most interesting, and it may have been incorporated with Books 1 and 2 by an editor after Aristotle's death. In the first two books Aristotle is explicitly concerned with 'discovering the possible means of persuasion on every subject' (1.2). He lays this down as the function of rhetoric, but because the orator seeks to *prove* his points to his audience, rhetoric is treated by Aristotle as an art which requires its practitioners to understand certain rules of reasoning or logic. Much of Books 1 and 2 is taken up with analysis of the 'enthymeme' or 'rhetorical syllogism' and the kinds of propositions which orators can expect to be effective as constituents of their arguments. Like Plato (*Phdr.* 266c–269c) Aristotle is strongly critical of existing rhetorical handbooks, and his stress on the logical element of rhetorical argument would have gained Plato's sympathy. But whereas for Plato the true orator must be a philosopher, possessing knowledge in the fullest sense, Aristotle's *Rhetoric* shows 'how to be a good orator without being a philosopher'.[3] Not that he neglects the moral and emotional aspects of rhetoric. The would-be orator, in his view, needs to understand ethical concepts and he also needs enough psychology to know what will move an audience's emotions. The second book sets out to explain how the orator must obtain the goodwill of his audience, and for this purpose, he must be a competent judge of the emotions which different situations and types of behaviour arouse.

In the third book Aristotle turns to 'style', that is: the orator's need to know 'how he should speak'. He nominates 'clarity' as the specific virtue of good prose style, and also emphasizes 'appropriateness' to the subject matter (2.1). Both of these qualities are partly elucidated by contrasting prose with poetry. The elevated language of poetry is much less suitable for prose, which should avoid rare words and be sparing in its use of similes. But metaphors are wholly appropriate to prose, 'since everyone uses them in conversation' (2.6), and Aristotle devotes much space to analysis of metaphor and its value. He argues that witty remarks are largely derived from metaphor and from misleading the

[1] Cf. Pfeiffer 69–74.   [2] Cf. *DFA* 71.   [3] Grube (1965) 93.

listener (11.6). Grammatical accuracy, avoidance of ambiguity, the proper use of connectives, and specific rather than generic terms are laid down as the constituents of 'Hellenism' – the Queen's English, as we might say (5.1).

Aristotle in this book also discusses the use of circumlocutions, prose rhythm, and the structure of periods. He stresses the importance of antithetical or balanced periods on aesthetic and logical grounds (9.8). Early Greek prose, with its liking for a string of coordinated sentences, is inferior, in his view, to the periodic style, and he cites the historian Herodotus as an example of the former. Throughout this book Aristotle is discussing rhetorical prose, and he relates his general criterion of 'appropriateness' to the different kinds of rhetoric (12.1). Political speeches call for a different style from those written as legal briefs or as ceremonial orations (*epideiktike lexis*). He also draws an interesting distinction between prose which is written to be read and speeches intended for delivery – the first should be the more precise, the second the more histrionic.

It is impossible to say how much these stylistic comments owe to earlier investigators. But we can fairly credit Aristotle with some originality, particularly on metaphor, and an admirably clear exposé of many ingredients of good writing, which exercised considerable influence on rhetorical theorists in later antiquity.

3. POETICS

If Aristotle's *Rhetoric* is now of largely historical interest, the fortunes of his short essay on poetry have been very different. *On the art of poetry*, conventionally called the *Poetics*, has enjoyed and continues to enjoy a remarkable reputation among books of literary criticism. It can fairly be judged the most influential of all such works, and, not surprisingly, nothing that Aristotle wrote is more widely studied and quoted. Yet Aristotle himself, and his contemporaries, might have been surprised by its later success. There is nothing to suggest that he regarded the *Poetics* as one of his greater achievements, which might be placed in the same company as his work in logic, metaphysics, and biology. The *Rhetoric* is a much more detailed study than the *Poetics*, even when we allow for the fact that the latter work, which is also the later, has been preserved in an incomplete form. It is probably correct to say that Aristotle was more interested in rhetorical technique and argument than in the nature of poetry.

Such an attitude on Aristotle's part would help to explain some of the deficiencies of the *Poetics*: he dealt with the subject selectively without aiming to produce a complete theory of literature. Moreover, the *Poetics*, in its present form, is so condensed that we have every reason to regard it as a treatise designed for study within the Aristotelian school rather than a book in the normal sense. It is also virtually certain that the original text has been modified by ancient editors in various places. But, for all its difficulties, the *Poetics* deserves its high reputation. It illuminates the understanding of Greek tragedy and it establishes critical tools of literary analysis which are of lasting importance.

In approaching the *Poetics* we need to take account of many historical data. First, the cultural circumstances of Aristotle's time. The second third of the fourth century B.C. was a period of decline and transition in Greek poetry. Tragedy in particular, Aristotle's main subject in the *Poetics*, produced no out-standing dramatist after Sophocles and Euripides, but the dramatic festivals continued as before, with new plays and sometimes revivals of old ones. Every schoolboy learnt his Homer, and in general, poetry remained a fundamental element of education and culture in the widest sense.

Secondly, the influence of Plato. As a close associate of Plato for twenty years, Aristotle could not fail to react to the older philosopher's views. His definition of poetry as an *imitative* art (*mimesis*) comes straight from Plato, and Aristotle also followed Plato in according great importance to the effect of poetry upon the emotions. But he shared none of Plato's censorious attitudes towards the poets. Ethical concepts play an important part in the *Poetics*, but the aim of the work is not to tell poets what they ought to say, in any moral sense. Part of the importance of the *Poetics* is its treatment of poetry as a valid activity in its own right, which needs to be analysed and understood within its own terms of reference.

Thirdly, Aristotle's methodology and conceptual categories. The *Poetics* is one of Aristotle's later works. By the time of its composition, he had already established methods of analysis and terminology which could be applied to the discussion of all kinds of different subjects. The division of poetry into 'species', the distinction between 'universal' and 'particular', the distinction between 'simple' and 'composite' – these are examples of analytical devices in the *Poetics* which occur in all of Aristotle's writings. Furthermore, certain terms in the *Poetics*, notably *praxis* – action, *ethos* – (moral) character, *hamartia* – error, are all illuminated by points discussed in his *Ethics*.

The structure of the *Poetics*, as we have it, is as follows: in chapters 1–5 Aristotle elucidates the nature of poetry in general; chapters 6–22 deal with tragedy, 23–6 with epic and a comparison of the two genres. The last sentence in our manuscripts rounds off the treatment of tragedy and epic. It is virtually certain that the *Poetics* continued with a treatment of comedy,[1] promised in 1449b21. The fourth 'species' of poetry which Aristotle mentions, 'dithyramb' (choral lyric), is nowhere discussed in detail, and there is no means of knowing whether he examined it and any other 'species' of poetry, for instance personal lyric, elsewhere.

For all their brevity, the introductory chapters are of fundamental importance.

---

[1] See Cooper (1922).

Having defined poetry as 'an imitative art', Aristotle elucidates the meaning of 'imitation' for the individual species of poetry. Poets imitate 'men acting' (1448a1), a statement which shows that Aristotle is now thinking of drama and epic. Since human agents differ in their moral character, one criterion for differentiating species of poetry is ethical: tragedy represents people as superior to men as they are, comedy as inferior (1448a17). Aristotle does not mean that the subjects of tragedy are paragons of virtue. His ethical criterion here is partly, if not mainly, a way of distinguishing the noble and heroic from the humdrum and insignificant. Another method of distinguishing between different forms of poetry is their use of narrative, drama, or both. Aristotle sees Homer as both a narrative and a dramatic poet, no doubt because the epic makes such important use of speeches.

His remarks about the 'natural' origin of poetry deserve to be quoted in full: 'the act of imitating is an integral part of human nature from childhood onwards; and man differs from other creatures in being the animal most given to imitation, and it is through imitation that learning is first achieved; furthermore all men take pleasure in the products of imitation' (1448b5–9). Poetry then, for Aristotle, is both a natural and a pleasurable constituent of human life. At no point in the *Poetics* does he suggest that the poet is a teacher or purveyor of some special kind of truths. When writing of tragedy however, Aristotle specifies certain qualities needed in a poet. He should be a man of talent rather than someone subject to inspiration (1455a32), and Aristotle seems to say that men who can be described in either of these ways are those most capable of feeling the passions which they represent in poetic form.

Aristotle's notion of 'imitation' or 'representation' (*mimesis*) is not equivalent to simple reproduction or copying. It is his way of saying that poetry is a particular kind of creative act. We should not suppose that imitation is opposed to imagination, but rather to what is purely fantastic or impossible. The poet's task is to represent human actions and life, but not necessarily life here and now. Though likened to a painter (for painting too is a species of *mimesis*), the poet may represent things as they were, or as they are, or as they are said and thought to be, or as they ought to be (1460b10). Moreover, poetry differs from history, according to Aristotle, in writing of the 'universal' rather than 'the particular' (1451b6).[1] History narrates what an individual person did or experienced. But poetry – and here Aristotle is thinking chiefly of tragedy – represents 'things of a certain kind' being done or said by 'someone of a certain kind' such that the relation between the agent and what he says or does is 'credible or necessary'. In these difficult words, Aristotle is not only contrasting tragedy with history but saying something of great importance about poetry as a genre. It must be a representation which has *general* significance and coherence, so that we are

[1] On Aristotle's distinction between poetry and history cf. Gomme (1954b).

moved to respond: yes, that is what someone like this would say or do in this sort of situation.

The 'universality' of poetry is placed within Aristotle's detailed analysis of tragedy, and it is this part of the *Poetics*, its largest section, which has rightly been praised most highly. He begins with a general definition: 'tragedy is an imitation of action which commands serious attention, and which is complete and possesses magnitude; in discourse that is made attractive...employing dramatic not narrative form, and by means of pity and fear producing the purgation (*katharsis*) of such emotions' (1449b24).

No part of the *Poetics* has stimulated more discussion than the last section of this definition. Aristotle makes no further reference to *katharsis*, but in later chapters he gives some elucidation of the 'tragic' emotions, pity and fear. They are aroused in particular, he tells us, by a change in the knowledge or fortunes of a character (1452a38). More specifically, pity is evoked by undeserved misfortune, and fear by the sufferings of 'those like [ourselves]' (1453a5). It follows that tragedies which are to be successful, in Aristotle's opinion, should seek to rouse the audience's emotions in these ways. It is difficult to know how far Aristotle's words lend themselves to the idea of feeling sympathy for the characters.[1] Some sense of feeling for others is clearly implied by pity, and Aristotle also refers to 'fellow feeling', *philanthropon*. But we should not take him to be thinking of a Romantic self-identification with the protagonist and his sufferings.[2] Both pity and fear have self-regarding connotations for Aristotle – we are moved by the thought that we too might suffer such pain. Most interesting of all is his remark that 'the poet should produce the *pleasure* which arises through mimesis from pity and fear' (1453b11). In the previous sentence he has spoken of the 'pleasure peculiar to tragedy', and this is then analysed as a product of pity and fear, as represented dramatically.

Aristotle fully recognized that pity and fear are painful (*Rhet.* 2.8). But it is not contradictory of him to speak of their causing pleasure in a tragic audience. For we do enjoy tragedy and the interesting question is why. Although any statement about *katharsis* in the *Poetics* is hazardous, Aristotle's further remarks about pity and fear strongly suggest that the *katharsis* of these and similar emotions, if not itself the pleasure in tragedy, is a process which turns what in real life would be painful experience into something pleasurable. The point seems to be that it is pleasurable to have these emotions roused and relieved by art. Aristotle says as much in the *Politics* (8.7), when writing of 'enthusiastic' music, and there is every reason to relate his remarks there to the *Poetics*.[3]

---

[1] House (1956) 102f.

[2] Jones (1962) 39f.

[3] He refers in the *Politics* passage to a 'clearer account of *katharsis* which we shall give when we come to speak of poetry'. But our text of the *Poetics* does not fulfil this prediction.

Is it the rousing of the emotions in a dramatic context that constitutes the *katharsis*? The answer is probably yes. Aristotle appears to be saying that the experience of tragedy releases our feelings in such a way that we gain emotional balance and stability.[1] Possibly we should see his notion of emotional therapy as a positive claim for the value of tragedy, defending it against the strictures of Plato.[2] But this is to base a lot on a little. It is better to relate Aristotle's view of emotional pleasure in tragedy to his general conception of man as a creature that enjoys 'imitation'. Pity, fear, and their *katharsis*, explain what the tragedian must aim to produce if the audience is to enjoy this particular species of imitation.

Less controversy surrounds the earlier parts of Aristotle's definition of tragedy. In seeking to explain these himself, he draws the conclusion that tragedy consists necessarily of six constituent elements: story or plot (*mythos*), characters, thought, diction, visual appearance, and song (1450a9). His discussion of the last three elements, though not without interest, is perfunctory and will not be examined here. The best and longest part of his treatment of tragedy is devoted to *mythos*.

By *mythos* Aristotle means 'the construction of the events' (1450a4). This, above all other concepts, elucidates the kind of mimesis which tragedy is. 'Tragedy is a mimesis not of men but of actions and life...so that they [*sc.* actors] act not in order to represent the characters, but they include the characters for the sake of the actions; hence actions and *mythos* are the goal of tragedy, and the goal is the most important of all things' (1450a15).

It is characteristic of Aristotle's approach to the explanation of an activity to look for its 'goal', and his choice of plot (the nearest English equivalent of *mythos*) or action as the goal of tragedy means that he sees these as its fundamental determining elements. In laying such stress upon action (*praxis*), Aristotle is not saying that tragedy should be packed with events, active as opposed to static. An action on his analysis is a unitary experience or set of events, e.g. Oedipus' discovery of his identity, or the murder of Agamemnon. When giving advice to the would-be dramatist (1455b2), Aristotle suggests that he should begin with a 'generalized' conception of a play, to which proper names and 'episodes' are added later. The action is both the logical and chronological starting-point, as it is also the goal. Character is subordinate to plot, not as being dispensable or normally independent of the action but because it stands to plot as the colour of a painting to a monochrome sketch (1450a39).[3] This interesting comparison shows that for Aristotle character in tragedy is regarded not as

---

[1] Since the work of Bernays (1853) a medical interpretation of *katharsis* has been favoured; thus Aristotle would be treating the purgation of the emotions as a process analogous to the effect on the body of aperients, which restores the right balance of humours. Recent critics (e.g. House (1956) and Lucas (1968)) have sought to broaden the meaning by reference to Aristotle's own concept of the ethical mean (House 108) or to ritual celebrations (Lucas 284).
[2] House (1956) 100.   [3] Cf. Jones (1962) 31.

something autonomous but as a 'colouring' of the action. If this seems to us unduly restricted, we must recognize that 'character' in his usage means moral disposition, not a broad spectrum of individual traits. Moreover, as he insists repeatedly in the *Ethics*, it is action which reveals character, a point which shows that it is mistaken to find in the *Poetics* a simple disjunction between plot and character.

Among Aristotle's most significant contributions to aesthetic theory is his insistence upon the 'organic unity' of tragic action. A tragedy, as his definition posits, must possess 'a certain magnitude', but more particularly, it must be the mimesis of an action which is 'whole and complete' (1450b24). The plot must be one in which the play develops and comes to its conclusion through a natural (necessary or credible) sequence of events. Of the 'three unities', so important in later criticism, action is the only one on which Aristotle himself laid stress. Nor did he confine its scope to tragedy. The epic poet too should aim at a similar unity of action, which Aristotle thinks Homer achieved, unlike the majority of epic poets. He was right not to treat the whole Trojan war, a theme suitable for history but too extensive for epic (1459a30).

Aristotle follows his general discussion of plot with a consideration of many of its details. The action which is represented must contain a 'change' (*sc.* of fortune), whether from good to bad or the opposite (1451a13). There is no necessity, in Aristotle's view, for a tragedy to end unhappily, though this is the 'change' he prefers, and happy endings are not uncommon in the extant plays of Sophocles and Euripides. Less useful is his distinction between 'simple' and 'complex' plots. A complex plot is one in which the change of fortune is accompanied by 'reversal', *peripeteia*, or 'recognition', *anagnorisis*, or both of these. By 'reversal' Aristotle means 'a change of the action in the opposite direction', and he exemplifies this by the Corinthian messenger in Sophocles' *Oedipus tyrannus* whose news, intended to gladden Oedipus, had the opposite effect. 'Recognition' is 'a change from ignorance to knowledge, either towards friendship (including kinship) or enmity' (chapters 10–11). 'Reversal' and 'recognition' are not themselves 'the change of fortune' but dramatic devices which may be used in its representation. Aristotle judges them to be parts of the best tragedy.

Like the structure of the plot, the change of fortune and the character of the protagonist admit of variations. Aristotle claims that a tragedy will be most effective in arousing pity and fear, if it represents the change from good to bad fortune of a famous man who is conspicuous neither for virtue nor vice, and whose downfall is the result not of wickedness but of error, *hamartia* (1453a7). By *hamartia* he does not mean a gross flaw of character, for this would contradict the denial of wickedness. The change of fortune is of someone 'better rather than worse'. Aristotle does not offer any analysis of *hamartia* in the *Poetics* but his general use of the word covers both intellectual and moral error. The rationalist tradition of Greek ethics, which Aristotle himself inherited and adapted, drew no sharp distinction between moral and intellectual failings, and the modern tendency to interpret *hamartia* as 'ignorance of some material fact'[1] seems to be unduly restrictive. Aristotle was quite capable of distinguishing between venial mistakes due to ignorance of facts and culpable error which fell short of wickedness. His analysis fits many more Greek tragedies (e.g. *Antigone* or *Persae* or *Prometheus vinctus*) if *hamartia* can include moral error. The essential point is that whatever may be the *hamartia* which causes misfortune, the suffering of the protagonist is not deserved or a punishment for his failings.

Throughout this analysis Aristotle never loses sight of the goal of tragedy and its need to move the emotions of the audience. He points out that the best tragedies take their plots from a limited range of mythical families, e.g. Oedipus and Orestes, which provide material for suffering or action which is 'terrible' (1453a18). As for the characters themselves, Aristotle supplements his earlier remarks in a chapter (15) which lays down four points at which the dramatist should aim: the characters should be 'good', but good in the way determined by their sex and status; they should be 'appropriate', which means that their qualities must accord with their sex and status; they should be 'life-like', and finally 'consistent'. All these are useful observations, but the modern reader is likely to find this part of Aristotle's discussion less rewarding than his analysis of plot. It hardly helps us to grasp the complex characterization which is found in some Greek tragedies, and it has led some modern critics to ignore the psychological springs of action which are by no means absent from the work of Aeschylus, Sophocles, and Euripides.

But Greek tragedy does differ in all manner of ways from later examples of the genre. The *Poetics* has distinct value as a guide (though not an infallible one) to the interpretation of the ancient tragedians' aims, but its greatest merit is more general. Through its implicit criticism of Plato, the *Poetics* speaks for the psychological and moral value of art, untrammelled by prescriptions to the artist of things which he ought to do which have nothing to do with his art. Aristotle's approach as a critic and as an instructor is never bookish. It is intensely practical. He constantly attends to the effect of the work of literature upon its audience's sensibilities, and his concentration upon the *action* of tragedy avoids the error of treating drama as if it were philosophy or psychology or ethics. Of course, as readers we find it appropriate to consider Greek tragedy from many perspectives which Aristotle omits, and he has next to nothing to say about the chorus, not to mention other conventions of the genre. But for all its difficulty and brevity, the *Poetics* is far and away the most important Greek contribution to literary criticism.

[1] E.g. House (1956) 94.

18

HELLENISTIC POETRY

I. INTRODUCTION

The astounding growth of the Macedonian empire in the second half of the fourth century resulted in a fundamental political restructuring of the Greek world; it also promoted radical cultural changes which turned intellectual and artistic endeavour irreversibly in new directions. In the fifth century, and even in the fourth, Greek culture had been dominated by Athens: yet it was the new Egyptian city of Alexandria which, within little more than a generation after the death of Alexander the Great, became the unquestioned intellectual centre of the transformed Hellenic world. Greek Egypt achieved stability well before the other areas of Alexander's fractured empire, which were thrown into nearly half a century of turmoil by his untimely death, and Ptolemy Soter's rapid consolidation of governmental power both within Egypt and in crucial areas of the Aegean combined with Egypt's immense natural wealth to make Alexandria one of the most attractive cities of the Greek world. The new regime determined to build for themselves in Africa a way of life which was powerfully and essentially Greek, and huge quantities of money were poured into the construction of buildings, the establishment of Greek religious cults and festivals, and the support of almost every type of intellectual and cultural activity from scholarly and scientific research to contemporary art. To Alexandria in the fourth and early third centuries went most leading intellectuals, writers and scientists from all over the Greek world, and two hundred years later Andron of Alexandria could write: 'It was the Alexandrians who educated all the Greeks and barbarians when general culture was tending to disappear owing to the continuous disturbances in the age of the Successors to Alexander.'[1]

The main focus of intellectual and artistic activity at Alexandria was the 'Museum', perhaps the most important institution in the history of Europe for the transmission of western culture: had the Alexandrian Museum not been founded when it was, Horace would probably be the nearest that a modern reader could come to Greek lyric poetry, and we might be reduced to re-

[1] Athenaeus 4, 184b.

541

constructing Sophocles from Seneca. Of the detailed working of this institution we know little, but the nature of its activities is clear: 'Museum' denoted not, as nowadays, a place to house articles for display, but 'a place for the Muses', a centre for all the kinds of intellectual activity which require imaginative inspiration (Aristotle's Lyceum at Athens was established by Theophrastus in a grove sacred to the Muses). The Alexandrian Museum was an academy, situated in the precincts of the royal palace, devoted to creative work (in both arts and sciences), to research, learning and scholarship and with some emphasis too on education. Membership of the Museum seems to have been exclusive to royal appointees, who enjoyed the privileges of a guaranteed living, many professional and social facilities, and in particular the use of a unique library – for one of the Museum's major activities in its early years was the assembling of texts of all known Greek authors, past or present.

Two points need to be appreciated about this immense book-collecting operation: first, the mere process of acquiring any given text might be extremely lengthy and problematic. The invention of printing has made possible the dissemination of texts in modern times at a level of organization unimaginable to the earlier book-trade: when Plato at Athens wanted a full copy of the poetry of Antimachus of Colophon, Heraclides had to fetch the work personally from Asia Minor.[1] Secondly, although some individuals had collected books before (most notably Aristotle), the enterprise of assembling 'the writings of all men, in so far, that is, as they were worth serious attention' (as Irenaeus describes the aim of the library)[2] was unprecedented, and evidence of an extraordinarily ambitious and magnificent breadth of vision. The task of collecting was pursued with great vigour, and although many of the stories which were later told of the early history of the Museum were doubtless *ben trovati*, they none the less illustrate the energy and determination which the Alexandrians applied to their new institution and the regard in which the results were subsequently held (see p. 31).

Of the early history of the Museum we know very little, but one thing is clear: from its inception this institution and the administration of its growing collection of books played a major role in the intellectual and cultural life of Alexandria. The Librarian was tutor to the prince regent, and the many writers and poets whom royal patronage supported in the city almost all also engaged in scholarly work in the Library, whose new, and constantly increasing, acquisitions needed sorting, classifying, and in most cases extensive editing. The poetry of the Hellenistic age (for almost all the non-technical literature which survives from this period is in verse form) was in any case intensely

[1] Proclus on Plato, *Timaeus* 21c.
[2] *Adv. haer.* 3.21.2 quoted by Eusebius, *Hist. eccl.* 5.8.11; the text continues with the dramatic account of the translation of the Pentateuch into Greek.

intellectual in mood, but the involvement of most poets of this time, or their close colleagues, in professional scholarly activity gives their writing a decidedly studied and intricate quality: there is no poet of this time who is not acutely attentive to the details of presentation, and their poetry at its best is extraordinarily intelligent (if at times severely so), at its worst derivative and pedantic.

In most Hellenistic writing the tension of two fundamentally conflicting characteristics is evident in one form or another. First, the enormous political upheavals and subsequent reshaping and expansion of the Hellenic world in the fourth century gave many Greeks a sense of separation from their roots and their past, and a weakening of their identity as Greeks: their reaction was often to intensify and reaffirm traditional values, both social and cultural – and for the Alexandrian writers, of course, this coincided with their immediate scholarly concerns, to acquire and put on a sound basis the texts of the great writers from the past. Secondly, the position of the writer had changed fundamentally by the third century: poetry in particular was no longer written primarily for public performance to serve the needs of religious festivals and competitions or ceremonial occasions, and its audience no longer looked to it necessarily for the discussion of social issues and instruction as well as entertainment. Poetry now became, for the first time, properly Literature for selective private circulation, and the writer was constrained by no expectations other than those of his immediate audience: what he wrote, and how, was a matter for his own personal choice and inspiration, and he had unprecedented freedom for innovation.

To sum up, poetry had experienced a radical shift of direction by the Hellenistic period. It was now written for its own private audience, primarily a select few attached to or associated with a royal court, for which the arts were an embellishment of power: this rather rarefied audience was well educated, for the most part worldly in experience (or at least aware of the new social and geographical horizons of the expanded Greek world) and at the same time conservative in manner and taste. As is often the case with audiences of this type, Hellenistic readers had an appetite for the sensational as well as the refined, the sentimental as well as the cerebral, and were appreciative of writing which appealed to their rather knowing sense of superiority. Thus Hellenistic poetry could find constant intrinsic interest in topics and attitudes drawn from 'low' life, rural and urban, matters vulgar and even grotesque, while still preserving rigorously an archaizing style and language which were becoming more and more remote from the vernacular. Because of this studied conservatism and the patent fact that the ordinary had appeal precisely because of its remoteness from the normal experience of most Hellenistic readers, the term 'realism', which might commend itself, cannot be used of poetry of this period without considerable qualification, and 'romanticism', as will become apparent, is hardly appropriate at all. Hellenistic poetry is a complex amalgam, and although many of its most signal features are, and were, all too easily adopted by facile and pedantic mannerists, the third century B.C. was a critical period when a new poetic was founded which, through the Roman writers, had a profounder influence on European literature than any subsequent development until the Romantic movement.

The study of Hellenistic poetry is beset with practical problems. The major part of what was written in this prolific age has been lost, and we should never forget that the true historical perspective which any intelligent reader normally demands for his understanding and placing of any given text is simply out of the question. What we possess are some of the major works of some of the major authors (together with a number of other much less significant or interesting works): we are unable to read those second-rank productions which are normally so informative about the literary sensibilities of any period, let alone take account of the mediocre writers for the assumptions about their role and their audience which they generally are so useful in betraying. Furthermore much of what we do possess is in fragmentary form and requires the application of painstaking scholarly techniques for its reconstruction and full appreciation, and although almost every year of the last three-quarter century has provided us with more material and knowledge, especially from newly-found papyri, the lacunose nature of our material remains lamentable. We possess little, we know little, and much of that will doubtless be altered radically by future papyrus finds: but with that warning given, and to be borne constantly in mind, we may turn to an examination of the major Hellenistic writers.

2. PHILETAS AND OTHERS

The most important intellectual figure in the early years of the new Hellenistic world was Philetas from the east Greek island of Cos. Philetas was the first major writer who was both poet and scholar, and secured an instant reputation in both fields. We have no direct evidence that he was ever in Alexandria, and we have no record that he was ever formally associated with the Museum, but it is difficult to believe that he was not active there: the son of the first Ptolemy, Philadelphus, who was to succeed to the royal throne of Egypt, was born on Cos, and Philetas was appointed as his tutor. Alexander the Great had had Aristotle for his teacher, and the royal family of Alexander's capital city in Egypt long continued the tradition of selecting a leading intellectual to be tutor to their offspring: after Philetas the head of the Alexandrian Library generally had that duty. Philetas' appointment was thus recognition of his standing, and his influence on the development of the Museum, which Philadelphus particularly fostered, was doubtless great. As a scholar Philetas was renowned amongst his contemporaries: the comic playwright Strato could make humorous reference in Athens to Philetas' dictionary of rare or strange terms (Athenaeus 9.383a–b), and as much as one hundred and fifty years later the famous scholar Aristarchus wrote against Philetas' interpretations of Homer. The immediately succeeding generation of poets speaks warmly of Philetas' outstanding poetic achievements, and when later ages came to draw up approved lists of the major 'classic' writers in each genre (see pp. 35f.) Philetas and Callimachus were the only two Hellenistic authors to be classed in the elegiac canon, and even from the little that is still extant of his poetry Philetas' direct influence on Callimachus and Apollonius Rhodius can be clearly discerned.

At this point an important caveat has to be entered. Philetas' central importance to his contemporaries and successors is manifest, and his reputation continued for centuries: amongst the Roman poets his name is synonymous with great elegiac writing. Yet it is most improbable that any writer later than, say, the second century B.C. had read any but a few lines of Philetas' poetry: all that he wrote seems to have disappeared within two hundred years, apart from a few quotations in anthologies and scholarly commentaries and handbooks. Apart from eleven passages in the anthologist Stobaeus and two in Philetas' near contemporary Antigonus of Carystus, his poetry is cited only in brief references by later commentators on other authors, and their lexicographical successors, in order to illustrate rare names or terms: many later writers and scholars can claim to have read Antimachus of Colophon, for example (on whom see below, pp. 546f.), and critics such as Dionysius, Quintilian and Plutarch are prepared to pass extensive comment on his style (and even the emperor Hadrian read and imitated him), but of Philetas there is no trace amongst such writers, beyond a single tradition about his physical appearance and the cause of his death, and an uneasy report by Quintilian of past critical opinion (10.1.58). It is very difficult to believe that if Philetas' poetry had survived down to the Roman period such critics would have been so silent about so eminent a writer, and the routine citation of Philetas as a 'name' by the Roman elegists merely confirms our suspicions.

However, among his contemporaries and succeeding generations of writers Philetas' reputation was outstanding: his fellow-citizens on Cos erected a statue of him in characteristic pose and Theocritus and Callimachus refer to him explicitly as an acknowledged classic. And even though so little of his poetry survives that no direct critical evaluation is possible for the modern reader, we can reconstruct enough to see that Philetas was the precursor of much that came subsequently to be regarded as fundamentally characteristic of Hellenistic poetry. First, he typified the 'scholar-ethic': his near contemporaries speak of him wearing himself out with intellectual work (a theme which later biographers developed into an account of his extraordinary physical slightness which necessitated his wearing weights on his feet in strong winds), and an elegiac couplet which possibly refers to the writer himself speaks of 'one that knows poetry's fine form and understands the track of all kinds of stories, thanks to much toil' (Powell 10). Variety and refined scholarship are hall-marks of 'Alexandrianism'. His hexameter poem *Hermes* dealt with the episode of Odysseus' visit, in the course of his wanderings, to the island of Aeolus, master of the winds; the theme is explicitly picked out of Homer, but Philetas also 'interpreted' and augmented his source, and apparently focused on a new aspect of the episode, namely Odysseus' secret liaison with one of Aeolus' daughters. This regard for the Homeric poems as primary source-material for essentially non-epic treatment is to be found in most Hellenistic writers, and in offering too an account of the hero's long conversation with his host Philetas may have written a poem which resembled Callimachus' *Hecale* in emphasis, just as his handling of the girl's passion for Odysseus and her distraught reaction at his departure anticipates Apollonius' study of Medea in his *Argonautica*. The influence of this poem on later writers seems to have been considerable.

The five brief citations which survive from the elegiac *Demeter* allow us to infer almost nothing about the poem: it may have dealt with the early history of Philetas' native island, where the wandering Demeter was said to have called, and Callimachus refers to it as a work which did much to establish its author's reputation. Beyond this we cannot reasonably go, except to observe that the few surviving couplets are concise and elegant, as well as being overtly Homeric in style and referring to the earlier classic elegist Simonides.

A few other lines and phrases survive, from unknown contexts: the patchiness of our knowledge is tantalizing, and there are serious reasons even for doubting the ascription in the *Palatine Anthology* of two epigrams to this Philetas. However, although no proper critical assessment is possible, enough material survives to demonstrate Philetas' extreme historical importance: he alone of those writers who preceded the generation of Callimachus represented in almost every way the combination of qualities which we now regard as 'Hellenistic'. The only earlier writer who is sometimes claimed by modern scholars as a precursor of the Hellenistic is Antimachus of Colophon, a poet who was notoriously esteemed by Plato and whose active career probably covered the late fifth and early fourth centuries. Antimachus was variously judged by later generations and we possess very little with which to make our own critical assessment, but all ancient authorities seem agreed that he wrote in a severe and rather obscure, involved style, and his penchant for rare archaic terms (together with some editorial work on Homer) is responsible for his reputation as a *poeta doctus*. Certainly he was one of the most influential of the preHellenistic poets on some third-century writers (Apollonius Rhodius in particular, since Antimachus' *Lyde* seems to have dealt at length with the Argonautic expedition and the love of Medea and Jason), but he was thought little of by Callimachus, amongst others, and he certainly seems to have lacked that elegance and lucidity which characterize the best of Hellenistic poetry. Antimachus was a determined eccentric who impressed both the wayward and the pedantic: it is in Philetas that we first find that sophisticated ease and intellectual versatility which mark the distinctively Hellenistic.

In the early history of the Library and Museum a number of writers played an important part. The role of Demetrius of Phalerum, the eminent Athenian politician who spent his last years in exile in Alexandria as a close associate of his old friend Ptolemy I, is hardly mentioned by most of our sources, but the notorious forgery from the second century, the *Letter of Aristeas*, mentions Demetrius as a prime mover in the building up of the Library's collections: the *Letter*'s testimony is the more credible since Demetrius is mentioned only incidentally, as the instigator of the Septuagint translation, and it is difficult not to see Demetrius as a formative influence on Ptolemy's planning and policy. Demetrius had been the most renowned of the pupils of Theophrastus at Athens' Peripatetic equivalent of the Alexandrian Museum, and he was the author of a number of works whose range and variety are not untypical of later Alexandrian taste: he wrote literary-historical studies on Homer, monographs on the sayings of Aesop and the Seven Sages, as well as speeches, Socratic dialogues and ethical works.

Another major figure of this time was Zenodotus from Ephesus, a pupil o Philetas, who succeeded his teacher as royal tutor and became the first Librarian at the Museum. The Suda records that Zenodotus was a writer of epic: no trace of any verse works has survived, but the influence of Zenodotus' scholarly activities was considerable, on contemporary writers and scholars as well as on later generations. Zenodotus was the first Alexandrian to undertake the massive task of a critical edition of Homer, along with monographs on the Homeric poems and a glossography of epic and lyric poetic language. There are clear references to his editorial work in Callimachus' poetry (see fr. 12.6 Pfeiffer), while Apollonius of Rhodes, Zenodotus' successor as Librarian, specifically wrote a book 'Against Zenodotus'. Zenodotus also compiled the first critical editions of Hesiod and Pindar (and perhaps of Anacreon), and his work may have been a significant factor in the importance of these poets to writers such as Callimachus and others of that period.

The immense quantity of material which the Museum acquired for its Library had to be sorted and catalogued; the work doubtless involved many scholars and assistants whose names are permanently lost, but we know that major parts of the undertaking were assigned to three scholars who also had reputations as poets themselves, Lycophron, Alexander Aetolus and Callimachus. The first two of these were members of the so-called Pleiad (cf. p. 345) of tragic poets; Alexander Aetolus was made responsible for tragedy in the organization of the

Library, but of his own work hardly anything survives, apart from a few elegiac fragments which are stylistically neat and restrained in language, but somewhat over-intricate and undistinguished if well-turned. About Lycophron, who came from Chalcis in Euboea, we are better informed. Though he wrote many tragedies, on mostly mythological themes (the material for the majority of Hellenistic plays), the few extant fragments nearly all come from a satyr play which made fun of the contemporary philosopher Menedemus (also from Euboea) and his salon. Lycophron's main scholarly work was a large treatise on comedy, and in the organization of material for the Library it was comedy for which he was responsible. This clever writer is the earliest attested compiler of anagrams (he turned the Greek word for 'Ptolemy' (Πτολεμαῖος) into 'from honey' (ἀπὸ μέλιτος) and 'Arsinoe' ('Αρσινόη) into 'Hera's violet' (ἴον "Ηρας), and he was the author of a long, intricate and rather perverse poem, which we possess in its entirety, called the *Alexandra*. This consists of 1,474 iambic lines, reporting a supposed prophecy of Cassandra, in which Priam's daughter foresees, in appropriately riddling form, the fall of Troy and its consequences. Superficially the poem is a mythological excursus on a stock topic (Troy) cast in the favourite Hellenistic form of a declamation about the future: but in fact the poem is a virtuoso treatment in verse of another Hellenistic preoccupation, the original foundation and settlement of the civilized Greek world in the Mediterranean. The fall of Troy is only the starting point for a detailed survey of the return of the individual Greek leaders (the *Nostoi*, the *Returns*, was an old epic theme) and also, naturally, the resettlement of the refugee Trojan survivors. Lycophron pursues his puzzling theme with a vigour and sustained concision of style which commands the admiration of any reader appreciative of formal technique:

καὶ δὴ στένει Μύρινα καὶ παράκτιοι
ἵππων φριμαγμὸν ἠιόνες δεδεγμέναι,
ὅταν Πελασγὸν ἅλμα λαιψηροῦ ποδὸς
εἰς θῖν' ἐρείσας λοισθίαν αἴθων λύκος
κρηναῖον ἐξ ἄμμοιο ῥοιβδήσηι γάνος,
πηγὰς ἀνοίξας τὰς πάλαι κεκρυμμένας.   (*Alexandra* 243–8)

Now Trojan Myrina groans and now the shores
of the sea that have awaited snorting horses
when, as he plants nimble foot's Pelasgian leap
upon the last beach, the blazing wolf
shall pipe the radiance of water from the sand
opening up fountains that have long lain hid.

(The Pelasgian, i.e. Thessalian, Achilles arrived last at Troy, and where he jumped ashore a spring gushed up.) But after a while Lycophron's very insistence on the awkward as a vehicle for virtuoso performance becomes perverse, and the poem falls exhaustingly flat. (Some scholars, ancient and modern, have been troubled by the fact that Lycophron writing in the first half of the third century refers to the growing power of Rome, and have occasionally even been tempted to argue that the *Alexandra* must have been written much later than the third century; however Rome's military prowess impressed Alexandria at this time, and Lycophron's account in ll. 1226–80 (the earliest extant) of Aeneas' settlement of Latium is consonant with the interest in early Roman history to be found in other Greek writers such as Timaeus or Callimachus.)

3. CALLIMACHUS

The most outstanding intellect of this generation, the greatest poet that the Hellenistic age produced, and historically one of the most important figures in the development of Graeco-Roman (and hence European) literature, was the third writer who had particular responsibility for organizing the Museum Library, Callimachus of Cyrene. According to a tradition which we have no reason to disbelieve, Callimachus came to Alexandria first to work as a schoolmaster in the suburb of Eleusis; from there he moved to the Museum under the patronage of Ptolemy Philadelphus. His active life covered at least the period from *c.* 280 to *c.* 245, and he lived into an old age whose debilities he says he found burdensome (fr. 1.33–8). He was exceptionally prolific as a writer in all departments, and the Suda reports that he was the author of more than eight hundred books in poetry and prose. From this huge output relatively little has survived (and almost nothing of the prose works), but although much is still uncertain or even completely obscure about Callimachus' writing, enough has survived and continues to come to light for us to make a reasonable critical assessment of his poetry and of his place in contemporary literature. It is often remarked of Callimachus that he was a 'scholar-poet'; in a literal sense this term is accurate, and indeed we shall consider Callimachus' contribution to the scholarly and intellectual activities at Alexandria before examining his achievement as a poet, but we should beware of allowing the easy generalization to be a substitute for close reading and proper evaluation of his poetry. Ovid's aphoristic assessment (*Am.* 1.15.14) 'less gifted than skilled' was written by someone who knew that that judgement was in some senses more applicable to himself than to Callimachus.

Callimachus never occupied (as he was once erroneously thought to have done) the post of Librarian and Tutor at Alexandria; Zenodotus was succeeded by Callimachus' pupil Apollonius of Rhodes, and he was succeeded by Eratosthenes. However, Callimachus' contribution to the organization and study of the newly arrived (and presumably still accumulating) material was immense, and in some ways it had more influence on the history of scholarship than any other work then current. It was Callimachus who constructed the *Pinakes* ('Lists', 'Tables') 'of all those who were eminent in any kind of literature and of their writings': this was not only the main reference catalogue for any scholar working with the Library's collection, it was also a major inventory which was nothing less than an exhaustive encyclopaedic bibliography of all major Greek writers. It became the basis for all subsequent such works and is ultimately the main source of our biographical and bibliographical knowledge of the ancient world. The *Pinakes* were divided into several different sections, according to subject matter (lyric, tragedy, philosophy etc.), and in each section authors were listed alphabetically; with each name went a brief biography, and then a list of all known works, together with an 'incipit' (citation of the opening line) for each work where known. The labour needed to make such a compilation must have been huge, and will have involved systematic reading and investigative research on a scale attempted by almost no one else; the finished product occupied one hundred and twenty 'books'. And this was not Callimachus' only major scholarly undertaking: he also compiled a chronological list and register of the dramatic poets (presumably based on Aristotle's similar study), a *Collection of marvels in all the earth according to localities* (the first known paradoxography), a lexicographical study on *Local nomenclature*, and numerous antiquarian works on subjects such as *Rivers of the inhabited world* and *Foundations of islands and cities including changes of nomenclature*. Scholar, antiquarian, polymath: Callimachus was all of these, and renowned as such in his own time. The side-effects of his academic work are certainly to be detected in his poetry, but what links Callimachus' poetic writing with his scholarly activities is not simply a taste for rare words or arcane antiquarianism on points of geography or mythology. It is something central to the man: an acuteness of mind, intellectual manoeuvrability (often and most easily observable through his wit or irony), and a penetrating intelligence which set him far above any other poet of the Hellenistic period. These extraordinary qualities came to bear on creative writing at a critical moment in the tradition, with the result that we may see in Callimachus someone who changed the course even of European literature.

Most of Callimachus' poems either cannot be dated at all, or cannot be given a very reliable date, but the first 'Hymn' (six 'hymns' have been transmitted to us through the manuscript tradition) is probably to be placed in the early years of the reign of Ptolemy Philadelphus, in the 280s, which would make it one of the earliest of Callimachus' compositions which we possess. From the opening lines his taut style and sharp manner are immediately evident:

Ζηνὸς ἔοι τί κεν ἄλλο παρὰ σπονδῆισιν ἀείδειν
λώιον ἢ θεὸν αὐτόν, ἀεὶ μέγαν, αἰὲν ἄνακτα,
Πηλαγόνων ἐλατῆρα, δικασπόλον οὐρανίδηισι;

> At Zeus's libations what else rather to hymn
> than the god himself, almighty, always king,
> Pelagonian router, bringer of justice to Heaven's sons?

(The 'Pelagonians' were the Giants, representing forces of disorder, against whom Zeus had to fight on coming to the throne.) A grand ceremonial opening with hymnal epithets builds up to a weighty (and chiastically arranged) laudatory address. Then follows a standard hymnal manoeuvre: expression of the variety of the divinity's aspects in the form of a question:

> How then shall we sing of him, as lord of Dicte
> or of Lycaeum? my heart doubts
> so much – for his birth is debatable.

The procedure is standard in the hymnal tradition, but the insistence of the last line and its tonal ambivalence already disrupt the convention. For a moment balance is restored, with the traditional:

> Zeus, in Ida's mountains they say you were born,
> but also, Zeus, in Arcadia;

but at this point the hymnal vocative turns into a conversational gambit, and if this is a hymn it seems to be taking a strange new form:

> which, Father, have lied?

With the next line convention is replaced by incongruity, as Zeus enters his own hymn quoting a proverbial remark from the philosopher Epimenides:

> 'Cretans are always liars.' Yes, Lord, your tomb
> Cretans built; and you did not die – you are forever.

Zeus's observation is confirmed with a mocking comment, and just as the hymn-form seems to have been irretrievably broken it is restored with a formulaic affirmation, and the poem proceeds in regular style to an account of the divinity's birth.

This early text illustrates two fundamental aspects of Callimachus' style as a poet. First, language and presentation are sharp and concise; every word counts, and in particular the poet is alert to every nuance of his audience's expectations. Secondly, although the form and language (both 'Homeric') are those of a traditional hymn, convention has become the vehicle for something else: the opening of the *Hymn to Zeus* is nothing so crude or straightforward as burlesque, but the rapid shifts of tone indicate that its focus is unlikely to be that of the traditional hymn which it formally resembles. This reworking by Callimachus of traditional material into a contemporary mode of expression for the thoroughly post-classical Alexandrian world is a subject to which we shall return later; here it is worth observing that the *Hymn to Zeus* continues for a while as a 'hymn', with a full account of the birth and rearing of Zeus. But next to the Childhood of Zeus the King the poet places, by means of an apparent 'example', Ptolemy Philadelphus, and the poem turns into a hymn to the poet's own patron, subtly constructed to please without suggesting any actual identification of the god and Ptolemy (though a Ptolemy eager for flattery may have assumed this to be implied). The poem seems to have been successful both at the literary and at the practical level, for Theocritus alludes to it several times in his own patronage poem, the *Encomium to Ptolemy* (*Id.* 17).[1]

The *Hymn to Zeus* offers another striking illustration of Callimachus' unusually exact and low-key style. The poem describes Rhea's search in Arcadia for water in which to wash after giving birth to Zeus (15–33):

> There when she set you down from her mighty lap
> straightway your mother sought flowing water, to cleanse
> the soilure of birth away, and to wash your body.
> But Ladon was not yet in mighty flow, nor Erymanthus
> most limpid of rivers; still without water was all
> Azenis, though to be known for full abundance of water
> later. For then, when Rhea loosed her girdle
> full many oaks above ground did moist Iaon
> raise, and many carts did Melas carry,
> and above Carion for all its water many
> the snake that cast its nest, and a man could pass
> on foot above Crathis and Metope full of pebbles
> thirsty, though plentiful water lay underfoot.
> Then in helplessness spoke lady Rhea:
> 'Dear earth, you too can bear; your labours are light.'
> So saying and raising up high her mighty arm
> the goddess struck the mountain with her staff:
> it split for her right apart and poured out
> a great flood. There your body she cleansed,
> lord, swaddled and gave you to the nymph Neda...

The language of this passage is Homeric, and the goddess's solution to her problem at the climax is characteristically epic; but within the Homeric mould language and style are kept simple and direct, and the narrative procedure is far from that of the grand epic manner. The naming of the Arcadian rivers is not to be passed off as an instance of Callimachus' 'geographical scholarship', as critics are often tempted to do in commenting on passages such as this. Quite apart from the intrinsic attraction in the naming of names, these names actualize the scene with an exactness that has the same purpose as the four details with

[1] *Id.* 17: cf. 17.58–70 and Call. 1.10–63, 17.71–6 and 1.68–86, 17.77ff. and 1.85–90, 17.135–7 and 1.94–6.

which Arcadia's dryness is illustrated (oaks, cart-roads, snake-nests, a thirsty journey). These are examples which are particular and easily appreciated, for they all come from ordinary experience, and provide a fine foil for the dramatically supernatural creation by Rhea of a mountain river. This climax is powerful, and made the more so by the contrast with the simplicity of what precedes. Just what kind of a departure this poem represents from the conventional hymnal/epic manner, and how remarkable is the simplicity and control of style can be properly appreciated if we compare a similar passage from the *Argonautica* of Apollonius Rhodius, a pupil of Callimachus, who is the main Hellenistic exponent of epic writing. In Book I Jason prays to Rhea for her help in his mission for the Golden Fleece (1140–50):

> She to their pious offerings then turned her heart
> divinely respondent, and fitting signs appeared:
> trees poured fruit beyond utterance, round their feet
> of itself earth grew flowers from the soft grass,
> wild beasts their nests and thickets left behind
> and approached with tails fawning. She yet again
> wonder performed, for previously Dindymon
> flowed with no water – yet thereon
> did it gush from thirsty peak, likewise, unceasing:
> 'Jason's' then they that dwelt there called that fount.

Apollonius' language draws fully on traditional modes of expression from Homer, and the scene depends for its effect primarily on one device, accumulation. Compared with this the spareness of Callimachus' style and manner is quite extraordinary, and the technical discipline which it represents was something for which Callimachus was famous, even notorious, and for which he strenuously and controversially campaigned throughout his career. One poem above all typified the new style of writing which Callimachus represented, the *Aetia* ('Origins' or 'Causes'). This was an immensely rich and original work, in its final form representing the labour of almost the poet's whole career as a writer, and such was its influence on Callimachus' contemporaries and particularly on later writers (Roman as well as Greek) that it is hardly too much of an exaggeration to say that the *Aetia* is second in historical importance only to the Homeric poems.

The *Aetia* consisted of four books of elegiac verse, each more than one thousand lines long, dealing with legends and stories connected with the 'origins' of Greek (and also other Mediterranean) customs, religious practices, and historical (or semi-historical) events. The work was widely read and survived intact down to at least the seventh century A.D., and possibly even to the early thirteenth century, but it is no longer extant and has to be reconstructed from the many citations in ancient authors and in particular from the material provided by recent papyrological finds. Our knowledge of this poem changes and increases almost year by year, and any discussion of the text is likely to become rapidly outdated, but what we know in outline is now reasonably secure. The first two books were almost certainly written, or at least compiled, separately from the last two, from which they differ in form. At the beginning of the work the poet imagined himself as a young man transported in a dream to Mount Helicon in mainland Greece, the site where Hesiod once met the Muses when he was herding his sheep (*Theog.* 22ff.), and where he now encountered the same Muses at the spring. Poet and Muses conversed, and *Aetia* 1 and 2 are an account of the questions which Callimachus posed on numerous topics, and the answers which the Muses gave. The parallel with Hesiod is unmistakable, and indeed made quite explicit by Callimachus himself; the first *aition* of Book 1 deals with the Graces, essential companions to good poetry, just as Hesiod's first subject in the *Theogony* was the birth and arrival at Olympus of the Muses themselves. Hesiod's style is episodic, even disjointed, as against the high narrative mode of Homer, and Callimachus' explicit alignment with Hesiod is an important programmatic statement, one which was to become a central critical issue in his last works.

The second *aition* of Book 1, the first after that of the Graces, is typical of these two books. It concerns the island Anaphe which Apollo revealed to the Argonauts during a storm when they were on their way home (fr. 7.19–26):

> How is it, Muses, Anaphe greets Apollo
>   with insults, and Lindos city with blasphemy
> sacrifices...in honour of Heracles?
>   ...began Calliope
> 'First bring to mind bright Apollo and Anaphe,
>   neighbour to Spartan Thera, and the Minyans;
> start with the heroes' departure from Colchian Aeetes
>   when they sailed back to ancient Thessaly...'

and this episode continues at some length with details about the return of the Argonauts from Colchis and the dispersal of their pursuers (Apollonius Rhodius seems later to have drawn on *Aetia* 1 for his *Argonautica*). There follow similar questions which occasion stories about violent behaviour by Heracles and the reactions of Apollo and Artemis when they were treated insultingly by men. From Book 2 we have only one fragment of any substance, a discourse on the foundations of some of the major cities of Sicily; from this come some lines, supposedly spoken by the poet to the Muses, which are often cited as expressive of Callimachus' outlook (fr. 43.12–17):

> Certainly all that I then put on my head,
>   soft golden oils with fragrant garlands,

> quite expired on the instant, and of all that passed
>   inside my teeth and into my ungrateful belly
> nothing again remained for the morrow; but whatever
>   my ears received, that alone abides with me still.

The poet offers the intellectual's variation on the common proverbial 'live today, for tomorrow you are dead'.

The question-and-answer dialogue form which these Books adopt is familiar to us from later prose treatises such as Plutarch's *Greek questions*, and if the *Problemata*, which is preserved under the name of Aristotle, does have a genuine Aristotelian substrate, then the form itself is not new; but its use in verse was, so far as we know, unprecedented, and its presentation as a recollected inspirational conversation is highly ingenious. It allows very variegated, and sometimes disjointed, material to be presented episode by episode but with the semblance of an underlying framework. Until recently some scholars were tempted to look for a unity of theme to each book, but we can now see that Callimachus' design was much less simple than that, and for clear programmatic reasons: often there is a link between adjoining items in the *Aetia*, but the connexion is frequently a secondary, or even less important, motif or incidental point, and the extraordinary achievement of the poem consists precisely in the sustaining of a large-scale work through concentration on the episodic. The whole and the constituent parts stand in counterpoint to one another; the grand scale of the epic has been redirected to elegiac matters. And in Books 3 and 4 Callimachus abandoned even the semblance of narrative unity by dropping the conversational framework in favour of straightforward juxtaposition. Callimachus' success in handling such a mass of extremely disparate material within the scope of a single work had an immense impact on contemporary and later writers, and the Roman poets in particular were fascinated by the *Aetia*; Propertius in the last book of his elegies looked to *Aetia* 3 and 4, Ovid in the *Fasti* to 1 and 2.

Books 3 and 4 of the *Aetia* were probably composed, or given their final form, in the last few years of Callimachus' life, in or not long after 246. The last *aition* of Book 4 (fr. 110) was the famous 'Lock of Berenice', which is only partially known to us in Greek, but survives in the Latin elegiac version made by Catullus for a friend (poem 66). Ptolemy III came to the throne in 247, and had immediately to leave Egypt to deal with the Syrian war in the east; his new bride, Berenice, princess of the royal family of Cyrene, vowed that if her husband returned safe she would dedicate a lock of her hair to the gods. This she did, and when the lock disappeared from the temple of Arsinoe Aphrodite at Zephyrium, Conon, the court astronomer, identified it in the heavens with the star group still known as Coma Berenices; Callimachus composed an elegiac poem in which the dedicated lock itself speaks, honoured by its apotheosis but distressed at being parted from Queen Berenice. The poem is a piece of very elegant court writing, highly stylized, and presented with bizarrely mannered wit; the declaratory solemnity of ll. 47–56 is typical:

> What can we locks of hair, when mountains so to iron
>   yield? May the race of the Chalybes die
> who first revealed it rising from the earth, a plant of evil,
>   and first taught the working of the hammer.
> I was newly-shorn and my sister locks were grieving
>   when straight the brother of Aethiopian Memnon [i.e. Zephyr]
> dashed in, circling dappled wings, soft breeze,
>   steed of violet-girdled Locrian Arsinoe,
> snatched me on the wind and took me through damp air
>   to Aphrodite's breast.

(The reference in ll. 47–8 ('when mountains so to iron yield') is to the canal which Xerxes cut for his ships through the isthmus of Mt Athos.) The compliment is fine, and so perfectly turned that the result is not fulsome but entertaining. We already knew that this poem was probably composed as a separate piece and then subsequently placed as the finale to *Aetia* 4, and a substantial new papyrus find has revealed that *Aetia* 3 and 4 were probably compiled at the same time and attuned as a whole to the specific context of the accession of Ptolemy III with his wife Berenice, who came from Callimachus' native city.

A fragment of an elegiac poem celebrating a chariot-race victory at the games of Nemea was published in 1941; Pfeiffer suggested (on fr. 383.1) that the victor might be Queen Berenice. A new batch of papyri from mummy-cartonnage published in 1977 has considerably extended our knowledge of this poem and demonstrated that Berenice was indeed the victor and that Callimachus' epinikion, a very substantial one, appeared in *Aetia* 3, probably at the very beginning of the book. If this location is correct, the symmetrical arrangement of *Aetia* 3 and 4 is obvious: the new books begin with Berenice's victory and end with her Lock, the two poems forming a frame for the work as a whole. And we may wonder whether the accession of a Cyrenaic queen to the throne of Alexandria was not itself a spur for the Cyrenean Callimachus in composing, or compiling, an additional two books for his great work, which became a kind of celebration dedicated to the new queen and patron. The marriage of Ptolemy to the princess from Cyrene itself symbolized a major success in Egyptian foreign policy, for the Ptolemies had been attempting to annex that part of North Africa for the preceding half century; and Ptolemy's victory in the Syrian war and Berenice's success in the international games at Nemea were both prestigious achievements. Callimachus commemorated what must have been a memorable royal accession with a major publication in which the Muses of Books 1 and 2 were replaced by Berenice as the outwardly unifying element. Furthermore the style and presentation of the victory elegy recall Pindar (a poet whose strong individualism and linguistic waywardness constantly fascinated Callimachus) and in particular *Pythian* 4, which was written to celebrate the victory of Arcesilaus, an important earlier king of Cyrene. Callimachus opens his victory elegy, and probably his new book, powerfully and grandly (fr. 383 + *P.Lille* 82):

> To Zeus and to Nemea a grateful gift
>   I owe, lady, scion of the royal gods,
> my gift a celebration of your steeds;
>   for newly from the land of heifer-born Danaus
> to Helen's isle and to Pallene's seer,
>   shepherd of seals, there came a golden word...

('Helen's isle' is Alexandrian Pharos, where the cult of Proteus was celebrated.) The major part of the epinikion dealt with the foundation myth of the Nemean games, Heracles' killing of the lion which was ravaging Nemea. Callimachus' account was famous amongst later writers, who regularly used it and referred to it; he dealt not so much with the heroic aspects of the story as with the unexpected theme of Heracles' stay with the poor peasant-farmer of Nemea, Molorchus. Molorchus intended to kill the sole ram which he possessed to entertain Heracles, but the latter told him to keep the ram until he had tackled the lion, and to offer it to him in victory when he returned, or to the gods of the Underworld if he did not. In approach and tone this episode closely resembled Callimachus' hexameter poem the *Hecale*, which dealt with Theseus' stay with a peasant-woman on his way to fight the bull of Marathon. Both poems have their precedent in Homer, for Odysseus' visit to the hut of Eumaeus is an important and impressive episode in the *Odyssey*, but the insistent concentration on the unconventional aspect of the traditional heroic material, and on the unusually plain elements of the story, marks the introduction of a new note in the highly formalized tradition of Greek poetry. To be sure, other Hellenistic writers, including Apollonius Rhodius whose espousal of the epic medium could not have been more conventional at one level, have a taste for the unusual and unconventional too and an especial interest in social detail. These are some of the characteristic features of Alexandrianism. But Callimachus' studied insistence on examining with a shrewdly quizzical eye the very ordinary and practical aspects of the heroic and mythic material of the poetic tradition, often exploring its odder and rarer areas, was a highly individual choice and set poetry on a new direction which was to prove fruitful for centuries to come.

We do not have to rely solely on our own assessment of their poetry to establish what were the central critical issues for Callimachus and his contemporaries. Callimachus was a highly controversial figure in his own time, and literary debate, sometimes very acrimonious, seems to have accompanied his writing at all stages in his career. It was not only that institutions like the

Museum always tend to foster hot-house disputatiousness: Callimachus' style of writing and literary views patently touched on very sensitive nerves. The evidence which survives from the debate comes almost entirely from the Callimachean side, but it allows us none the less considerable insight into the main issues. When Callimachus published Books 3 and 4 of the *Aetia* he seems also to have re-edited the first two books; in spite of the fact that he was then clearly long established as a major writer his poetry was still the object of intense controversy, for he prefaced his work with a long prologue fiercely rebutting his opponents' criticism. He dubs his critics with the nickname 'Telchines', the name of a fabled goblin-race of metal-workers, skilled in magic, who inhabited some of the Greek islands and whose most renowned characteristics were jealousy, maliciousness and possession of the Evil Eye; one tradition recounted how the Telchines made Rhodes and Ceos infertile by sprinkling them with water from the Styx, and another that it was Apollo himself, god of inspiration, who took the form of a wolf and killed them. Callimachus' Prologue to the *Aetia* begins (fr. 1.1–6):

> Οἶδ' ὅτ]ι μοι Τελχῖνες ἐπιτρύζουσιν ἀοιδῆι,
> νήιδες οἳ Μούσης οὐκ ἐγένοντο φίλοι,
> εἵνεκεν οὐχ ἓν ἄεισμα διηνεκὲς ἢ βασιλ[η
> .....]ας ἐν πολλαῖς ἤνυσα χιλιάσιν
> ἢ......]ους ἥρωας, ἔπος δ' ἐπὶ τυτθὸν ἑλ[ίσσω
> παῖς ἅτε, τῶν δ' ἐτέων ἡ δεκὰς οὐκ ὀλίγη.

I know the Telchines mutter at my song –
Ignorant they are and no friends of the Muse –
because I have not composed a single continuous poem,
on glorious kings in ten thousand countless lines
or on heroes of old; but tell a tiny tale
like a child, though the decades of my years are not few.

Envy, says Callimachus, is the motive, and, with an appeal to the earlier success of the famous elegists Mimnermus and Philetas, he dismisses the grand themes of conventional epic poetry. He continues in a passage known subsequently to every Greek and Roman poet (fr. 1.17–32):

> ἔλλετε Βασκανίης ὀλοὸν γένος· αὖθι δὲ τέχνηι
> κρίνετε,] μὴ σχοίνωι Περσίδι τὴν σοφίην·
> μηδ' ἀπ' ἐμεῦ διφᾶτε μέγα ψοφέουσαν ἀοιδήν
> τίκτεσθαι· βροντᾶν οὐκ ἐμόν, ἀλλὰ Διός.
> καὶ γὰρ ὅτε πρώτιστον ἐμοῖς ἐπὶ δέλτον ἔθηκα
> γούνασιν, Ἀπόλλων εἶπεν ὅ μοι Λύκιος·
> '..........] ἀοιδέ, τὸ μὲν θύος ὅττι πάχιστον
> θρέψαι, τὴ]ν Μοῦσαν δ' ὠγαθὲ λεπταλέην·
> πρὸς δέ σε] καὶ τόδ' ἄνωγα, τὰ μὴ πατέουσιν ἅμαξαι

τὰ στείβειν, ἐτέρων δ' ἴχνια μὴ καθ' ὁμά
δίφρον ἐλ]ᾶν μηδ' οἶμον ἀνὰ πλατύν, ἀλλὰ κελεύθους
ἀτρίπτο]υς, εἰ καὶ στεινοτέρην ἐλάσεις.'
......]ν ἐνὶ τοῖς γὰρ ἀείδομεν οἳ λιγὺν ἦχον
τέττιγος θ]όρυβον δ' οὐκ ἐφίλησαν ὄνων.
θηρὶ μὲν οὐατόεντι πανείκελον ὀγκήσαιτο
ἄλλος, ἐγ]ὼ δ' εἴην οὐλαχύς, ὁ πτερόεις.

Away, Jealousy's destructive brood. Henceforth
    judge poetry by its craft and not the Persian league;
don't seek from me the thumping song:
    thunder is not my part, that is for Zeus.
The very first time I put the tablet on my knee
    Apollo said to me, the Lupine god,
'Poet, let your sacrifice be fat as you can,
    but your Muse, my friend, keep her slim.
This too I say: where the waggon does not trample
    there you should tread, not by others' common tracks
nor the broad highway, but on unworn paths –
    no matter that you take a narrower course.'
Amongst those we sing who love the clear note
    the cicada makes, not the uproar of the ass;
like the long-eared beast others may bray,
    I would be the slight, the winged one.

The gap between Callimachus and his detractors is evident from this Prologue. They criticize him for triviality, juvenility, and writing in a frivolous manner, lacking unity of theme and style. For Callimachus this has been precisely the object of his work: to avoid the hackneyed theme and the bombastic style, which is played out and sterile. And he attributes his critics' attack to the envy of poor writers at his own success. When Callimachus contrasts himself to 'Zeus' he is not just applying a rather bland image; for an Alexandrian writer the Zeus of poetry was the epicist *par excellence*, Homer – and this brings us to a central point.

For most writers of this period 'serious' poetry (outside drama) meant primarily epic. Lyric was a rare, rather strange form, all but dead, and elegy (the elegiac couplet) a common medium but one more appropriate for incidental than high poetry. Almost all epic from this period has been lost, but we know the names of many authors and titles: there was much written on old heroic themes and much 'political' (sometimes historical) epic on the achievements of recent rulers like Philip of Macedon, and from the few fragments extant much of it seems to have been of poor quality, tedious and derivative. It is a truism that for all Greek writers Homer was *the* poet, but that truism applies to no group more accurately than the post-classical epicists: and for the early Hellenistic epicists Homer was paradigm and copy-book. Callimachus had full grounds for his rejection of the empty cliché-ridden poetic stereotypes, and his assertion of a different type and level of poetry was an attempt to establish a fresh direction for vigorous creative writing. Scornful dismissal of the traditional post-Homeric epic (often called the 'Cyclic' epic) is a regular theme in Callimachus; in a famous epigram, much echoed by Latin writers, Callimachus gives the literary point a philosophical and ironical personal twist (*Ep.* 28 Pf.):

'Εχθαίρω τὸ ποίημα τὸ κυκλικὸν οὐδὲ κελεύθωι
  χαίρω τὶς πολλοὺς ὧδε καὶ ὧδε φέρει·
μισέω καὶ περίφοιτον ἐρώμενον, οὐδ' ἀπὸ κρήνης
  πίνω· σικχαίνω πάντα τὰ δημόσια.
Λυσανίη, σὺ δὲ ναίχι καλὸς καλός· ἀλλὰ πρὶν εἰπεῖν
  τοῦτο σαφῶς ἠχώ φησί τις 'ἄλλος ἔχει'.

I detest the cyclic poem, I do not like
  the path that carries many to and fro;
I hate too the roaming lover, I do not drink
  at the fountain – I loathe all common things.
Lysanias, yes fair you are, how fair – the words
  are scarcely out, says an echo 'he's another's affair'.

The imagery here is the same as in the *Aetia* Prologue: avoidance of the common path.

The public fountain has an implicit opposite, the pure source, and this antithesis is spelt out in another poem, the second Hymn, to Apollo (probably contemporary with the re-edition of the *Aetia*), whose epilogue is a vehement statement of literary principles (105–12):

ὁ Φθόνος 'Απόλλωνος ἐπ' οὔατα λάθριος εἶπεν·
'οὐκ ἄγαμαι τὸν ἀοιδὸν ὃς οὐδ' ὅσα πόντος ἀείδει.'
τὸν Φθόνον ὡπόλλων ποδί τ' ἤλασεν ὧδέ τ' ἔειπεν·
''Ασσυρίου ποταμοῖο μέγας ῥόος, ἀλλὰ τὰ πολλὰ
λύματα γῆς καὶ πολλὸν ἐφ' ὕδατι συρφετὸν ἕλκει.
Δηοῖ δ' οὐκ ἀπὸ παντὸς ὕδωρ φορέουσι μέλισσαι,
ἀλλ' ἥτις καθαρή τε καὶ ἀχράαντος ἀνέρπει
πίδακος ἐξ ἱερῆς ὀλίγη λιβὰς ἄκρον ἄωτον.'

Envy said secretly in Apollo's ear:
'I do not like the poet who does not sing like the mighty sea.'
Apollo kicked Envy off and spoke thus:
'The Assyrian river is a great stream, but much
of earth's filth and refuse does it draw on its water.
The bees bear water to Demeter not from every source,
but where rises up pure and undefiled
from holy spring a small trickle, the supremely choice.'

Purity and discrimination: the exact reference of the epilogue is lost to us (for presumably it had a particular critic or critics in mind like the *Aetia* Prologue), but the essential literary point of the imagery is clear. It is the same as Apollo's advice in the Prologue, and there the key term is the Greek word used to describe the 'slim' Muse, λεπτός: the adjective connotes fineness, sharpness and precision, and Callimachus uses it regularly to express approval, for example of Philetas, or of his own contemporary Aratus, and its opposite παχύς (in the Prologue used of the sacrifice) connotes grossness and coarseness (a term with which Callimachus dismisses Antimachus' elegiac poem *Lyde*, which many Alexandrians admired: fr. 398 'the *Lyde* is a gross and muddled work'). This was the mark of Callimachus' new style: fineness and lightness, together with clarity and disciplined craftsmanship.

The impassioned tone of the texts cited above suggests that the Alexandrian 'Battle of the Books' was wide-ranging and of long duration, and we have much evidence to corroborate this. An ancient commentary on the Prologue lists at least seven names of contemporaries supposedly meant by Callimachus' 'Telchines'; a lost poem, the *Ibis*, which Callimachus wrote attacking an adversary, is supposed according to one tradition to have been directed at Apollonius Rhodius the epicist; in Iambus 2, fr. 192, in which Callimachus satirizes his contemporaries, he objects to the garrulity and emptiness of the writers of that time in general (ll. 13–14 'all men have become full of words and garrulous'); in fr. 393 he attacks a philosopher of the Megarian school, Diodorus, nicknamed 'old fogey', for the insistent monotony with which he taught his views on dialectic and the after-life; in fr. 215 he criticizes 'the tragic muse which makes a hollow sound'; in *Ep.* 59 Pf. he complains that after writing for the theatre he feels even worse than mad Orestes, having consequently lost even his closest friends; Iambus 13, fr. 203, was a whole poem devoted to replying to critics who had attacked him for writing precisely such a *variety* of works (a charge which seems rather strange to a modern reader and which betrays some of the contemporary literary assumptions with which Callimachus had to deal); in Iambus 1, fr. 191, Callimachus speaks in the guise of the vituperative sixth-century iambographer Hipponax come back to life and admonishes his fellow Alexandrian scholars for their quarrelsomeness.

Callimachus' style of writing was controversial and his stance aggressively outspoken; in retrospect, viewing his work through the perspective of the Roman writers who demonstrated just how fruitful Callimachus' type of 'Alexandrianism' could be, it is difficult to appreciate how innovative this great poet was. But the intelligence and verve as well as sheer technical virtuosity which are evident even in very fragmentary texts are astonishing, as is his versatility and extraordinary psychological tact *vis-à-vis* his reader. One of the most famous episodes of Book 3 of the *Aetia* illustrates many of Callimachus' qualities, that which deals with the romance of Acontius and Cydippe (frs. 67–75). Ostensibly the story has a place in the *Aetia* for the early history of Ceos, which Callimachus drew from the writings of the chronicler Xenomedes, which included the genealogy of the famous Acontiad family on the island. But in fact the aetiology is only a peg on which to hang a narrative whose import is far from dry scholarship; the opening lines set the tone and direction (fr. 67.1–8):

> Love himself it was that taught Acontius the art,
>   when the boy blazed for a girl, fair Cydippe,
> (for he was no man of cunning) how to gain
>   the lifelong name of truly wedded spouse.
> Yes, Lord, he from Ioulis, she from Naxos,
>   came to your Delian sacrifice, Cynthian Apollo;
> the one of Euxantius' blood, she from Prometheus,
>   fair stars of the islands were they both.

This is to be an account of young love, its difficult path and its romantic conclusion, and the story is of an archetypal kind, but its telling is far from direct. The outline we have from a later summary: Acontius saw Cydippe at the annual Delian festival, and on falling in love with her threw to her, at the temple of Artemis, an apple inscribed with words which Cydippe in her curiosity read out: 'I swear by Artemis to marry Acontius'; when subsequently the girl's father arranged a different marriage for his daughter but found her mysteriously ill whenever he prepared the wedding, he consulted Apollo at Delphi who advised him of Cydippe's vow and recommended her marriage to Acontius – which thus was fulfilled, to the glory of Ceos. This episode was at least one hundred and fifty lines long, but, as in the introduction, it was not on the sequence of events that Callimachus' narrative focused, but on the more interesting incidentals: the extraordinary beauty of the couple, Acontius' distraught passion, Cydippe's illness, and Acontius' final delight. These are the aspects of the story central to its quality as a romance, and it is the events themselves that Callimachus reduces to incidentals. Even Apollo's reply to Cydippe's father turns a recommendation of Acontius into a sharply appreciative account of the exotic seasonal effect of the piety of the priestly family from which Acontius comes (fr. 75.30–7):

> 'I tell you that in taking Acontius you mix
>   not lead with silver but electrum with radiant gold.
> From Codrus you her father spring, the Cean
>   groom from priests of Aristean Zeus
> rain-god, whose task upon the mountain steps
>   it is to calm stern Sirius as it rises
> and beg from Zeus the breeze by which in droves
>   quails are stricken in the linen nets.'

In the *Aetia* Callimachus established an apparently minor mode of writing on seemingly incidental topics as a substantial poetic form, demonstrating that it could be as expressive as the theoretically weightier epic and could offer the new direction which Greek poetry needed; in the Hymns and the *Hecale* he expounded the new style in reverse fashion (as did also his contemporary Theocritus in some of his Idylls) by taking the traditional hexameter form and turning it into a vehicle for the refined and unconventional (perhaps developing the trend set by the older Philetas in poems such as the *Hermes*).

An anonymous ancient commentator (on *Hymn* 2.106) remarked that Callimachus was forced to write the *Hecale* in order to prove to his critics that he could compose a work of substance; this unsupported assertion sounds like a misunderstanding, for the fragments which we possess of this poem (about three hundred lines, complete and incomplete, from a whole of up to one thousand verses) show it to have been a complex, original and highly unconventional work. In writing the *Hecale* (date unknown) Callimachus may have been responding to criticism, but it was with a fine demonstration of independence that he did so, not in conformity to traditional literary values. The *Hecale*, an 'epic' poem, dealt with the heroic theme of Theseus' taming of the great bull which ravaged the country round Marathon; the actual defeat of the bull and Theseus' triumphant return with it to the city were naturally important events in the poem, but they were not its most prominent features. The poem took its title from the name of the old peasant-woman in whose hut the hero stayed overnight when caught unexpectedly in a rainstorm, and a major part of the poem seems to have consisted of an account of Hecale's hospitality and the conversation between the old woman and her young guest. Theseus' visit to Hecale had good Homeric precedent in Eumaeus' hospitality to the disguised Odysseus, and like Eumaeus Hecale was not by origin a peasant, but Callimachus' especial concentration on the rustic details of the encounter (the wood for the fire, the different coloured olives preserved in brine and the bread on which they dined, the various household implements) not only betrays the slightly sentimental taste of the sophisticated urban audience at Alexandria, it also marks the significant shift of emphasis characteristic of the new style. Not much remains of this part of the poem, but its scope and prominence can be gauged from the many imitations in later writers (for example the description of the visit by Jupiter and Mercury to the peasants Philemon and Baucis in Ovid, *Met.* 8.624–724).

In other respects too the *Hecale* was extremely unconventional: the most extensive extant fragment describes the triumphant return of Theseus with the bull (fr. 260), but forty-five lines of this passage appear to have been words spoken by a crow to another bird, probably the owl of Athena, recounting various incidents (future as well as past) in which the harbinger of bad news suffered punishment, presumably as a warning to the owl against carrying the bad news to Theseus that in his absence the aged Hecale had died (again Ovid seems to have modelled himself closely on this passage in *Met.* 2.536–632). The conclusion of the *Hecale* was an *aition*, Theseus' repayment of the hospitality he had received by the establishment of a deme in Attica named after her, and the building of a sanctuary to Zeus Hecaleius. Thus although the *Hecale* was ostensibly an epic-style poem, its heroic theme became merely the peg on which to hang the most important elements: the conversation which permitted the introduction of stories about Theseus' past and the life of Hecale and her now deceased family, the crow's warning which encompassed the myths of Erichthonius and the daughters of Cecrops and Apollo's affair with Coronis, and the detailed description of simple country life. The poem was extremely famous in antiquity, and was imitated by Greek as well as Roman writers; it survived, at least in paraphrase, down to the thirteenth century.

It is important to realize that Callimachus' concentration on the more ordinary details of his heroic material, particularly evident in parts of the *Aetia*, the *Hecale*, and some of the Hymns, was not a *diminution* of the grand themes of tradition, but rather an essential reworking of convention, and the establishing of a new realism. Callimachus takes traditional myths and writes, like his contemporaries, in a language and form which draw heavily on Homer (that is, in an archaic style remote from contemporary Hellenistic Greek), but although the forms and material are provided by the old world their manner is that of the new and their concerns are those of contemporary Alexandrian society.

A poem which demonstrates this very clearly is the sixth Hymn, which tells the story of Erysichthon. Ostensibly the hymn, whose date is unknown (though it probably predated the fifth Hymn and Apollonius' *Argonautica*), is a standard cautionary religious tale, cast in the unusual form, developed by Callimachus and Theocritus, of a 'mimetic' poem, that is one which purports to be a verbatim report of words spoken by the characters involved in a particular scene, in this case by someone addressing the waiting celebrants of Demeter's Thesmophoria after their day of fast. After introductory instructions to the celebrants and invocation of Demeter the speaker narrates Erysichthon's offence against Demeter and his consequent punishment, the narration forming the major part of the poem, which closes with a short prayer to the goddess as the procession begins. Erysichthon's offence was to try to chop down the trees in Demeter's sacred shrine to build himself a banqueting hall. This is recounted in dignified epic narrative (33–41):

> He hurried with twenty attendants, all in their prime,
> all giants of men, sufficient to lift a whole city,
> equipping them doubly with axes and with hatchets,
> and into the grove of Demeter they ran without shame.
> A poplar there was, a great tree which reached to the sky,
> at which the nymphs at noon would make their play.

This, struck first, called a miserable tune to the rest.
Demeter heard that her sacred wood was in pain,
and spoke in wrath: 'Who chops my beautiful trees?'

Disguised as her own priestess Demeter warns off Erysichthon, and when he ignores her appeal she transforms herself into her own terrifying guise and condemns the offender to permanent insatiable hunger and thirst. With this suitable contrast to the pious celebrants who will shortly break their fast the religious import of the cautionary tale is complete, after forty-eight lines; but not so Callimachus' narrative which, in as many lines again, recounts in detail the *social* embarrassment suffered by Erysichthon's parents at their son's malaise (72–83):

Neither to feast nor to banquet could they send him,
his shameful parents; every excuse was found.
There came to bid him to the games of Itonian Athena
Ormenus' sons. His mother then refused:
'He is not at home, for yesterday to Crannon he went
to recall a debt of a hundred cattle.' There came Polyxo,
Actorion's mother, preparing a wedding for her boy,
and invited jointly Triopas and his son.
Heavy-hearted the lady answered in tears:
'Triopas can come; Erysichthon was struck by a boar
in Pindus' fair vales, and nine days has he been laid up.'
Poor devoted mother, what lies did you not tell?

But the shame could be kept secret only so long, and after Erysichthon had eaten all that the household could provide, including his father's race-horse and war-horse and even the family cat,

then the king's son sat at the cross-roads
begging for crusts and the left-over refuse from the feast. (114–15)

Tradition had many more details to add to the story of Erysichthon, including that he finally resorted to autophagy. But although Callimachus' account is one of black comedy he ignores Erysichthon's death because his concern is not out-and-out drama, but the 'other' side of Greek myth: he is concerned with the ethical framework of the ordinary and mundane, and with reflecting on what might have been the practical consequences of the punishment which tradition attributed to Erysichthon.

The *Hymn to Athena*, the fifth in our collection but probably to be dated after the sixth, is also 'mimetic' evoking the festival of Athena at Argos, written in the form, experimental for a hymn, of elegiac couplets, and containing another cautionary tale which also explores parental reaction to the punishment of a child. The poem is more heavily weighted toward representation of the Argive ceremony: fifty-six lines convey with remarkable effectiveness the mounting excitement of an official assembling and addressing the women celebrants, and invoking the goddess, as they wait for Athena's statue to emerge from the temple to be taken down to the river for the annual ritual purification. The appearance of the statue is clearly to be an epiphany for these Argive women, and Callimachus' skill emerges not only in the remarkable way in which religious fervour is conveyed, but also in the stunning narrative power with which the official, warning all males to avoid contact with the ceremony, tells the cautionary tale of Tiresias and his encounter with Athena at her bath. At the end of her account the hymn closes with a greeting to Athena who is about to emerge from the temple, but for Callimachus' readers the epiphany has already been experienced vicariously through the narrative of Tiresias, and the poem is neatly closed. There is no doubt that the fifth Hymn is a purely literary text, and not a work commissioned for and actually performed at the Argive festival as some scholars once liked to think, and for his knowledge of Argive ceremonial Callimachus probably drew on the two antiquarians of the Argolid, Agias and Dercylus, as he did elsewhere in the *Aetia*; from them too he probably took the unusual account of the blinding of Tiresias. Athena and her principal attendant, the nymph Chariclo mother of Tiresias, bathe (70–82):

> There was a time they undid the pins of their robes
> at the fair-flowing spring of the horse on Helicon
>   and bathed; noon held the hill in quiet.
> Both bathed, and noon was the hour,
>   and deep quiet held that hill.
> Tiresias alone still with his dogs, his downy beard
>   just darkening, reached the sacred place.
> Thirsting terribly he came to the spring-stream,
>   poor fool; unwittingly he saw the forbidden.
> Although angered, Athena addressed him:
>   'You shall never carry your eyes away from here;
> what spirit, Eueres' son, brought you this terrible way?'
> So she spoke, and night took his eyes.

Tiresias never speaks: it is his mother who protests to Athena, agonized by her apparent betrayal, and Athena, moved to pity, explains that Tiresias' blinding is irrevocable, since divine law requires it for any mortal who sees a god unawares. But she promises as compensation the gifts for which Tiresias was famous: the power of prophecy and interpretation of signs, extreme longevity, and retained consciousness in the Underworld after death. To a modern reader the compensations seem rather inadequate for at least the mother's grief, and we should remember that to an ancient reader Tiresias' extraordinary powers will inevitably have demanded the compensatory loss of some other natural function: but Callimachus was focusing on one of the harsher areas of the morality of classic Greek belief, and although the hymn is partly aetiological it is also a powerful narrative which explores intense feelings, of group religious fervour and (in a sense its counterpart) of personal human loss, to which Callimachus offers no simple solution. The sixth and fifth Hymns above all demonstrate that Callimachus' hymns may deal with serious and at times disturbing issues, but they are not essentially religious texts; and that their form is owed to literary convention is apparent from the other four hymns which are outwardly less experimental than those to Demeter and Athena.

The second Hymn, to Apollo, is also 'mimetic': the narrator addresses the celebrants of Carneian Apollo at Cyrene, preparing them for the god's arrival, and recounts not a myth or tale but a series of Apollo's attributes and achievements and in particular his association with the founding and early history of Cyrene. The poem is very probably to be dated to the accession period of Ptolemy Euergetes from 247: the writing is taut and powerful, and although the hymn is formally fairly conventional, its dignity and poise are thoroughly appropriate for celebration of Egypt's new alliance in North Africa. About twenty-five years previously Callimachus had written another hymn to Apollo, or rather to Apollo's sacred island Delos, the fourth Hymn, and this and the third Hymn, to Artemis, of unknown date, are both long, expansive poems in the style of the ancient Homeric hymns. The *Hymn to Delos* recounts Leto's search for a hospitable place, in the face of Hera's enmity, to give birth to Apollo, and the offer of sanctuary by the small island Delos; the *Hymn to Artemis* details the goddess's early years, her achievements and attributes, her festivals and sacred places. At first both poems seem fairly conventional, but attentive reading shows that they are not simple models to a pattern, but sophisticated and rather self-conscious variations on a type which for full appreciation require considerable familiarity with the genre. The *Hymn to Delos* in particular follows closely the first part of the *Homeric Hymn to Apollo*, and Callimachus' hymn is in fact an Alexandrian up-dating of the earlier classic poem, full of wit, irony and intellectual entertainment. This makes the more effective what might otherwise have been intolerably gross flattery when the (as yet unborn) Apollo declares from his mother's womb why the island Cos is unsuitable for his own birth (165–70):

> But for her the Fates have due another god,
> most high lineage of the Saviours, beneath whose crown
> shall come, quite willing to be subject to Macedonian,
> both continents and lands set in the sea
> as far as the end of the west and whence swift horses
> carry the sun. And he shall know his father's ways.

And Apollo continues with a prophecy about the Celtic invasion which Greece experienced in the 270s. The device is almost coy, and in the late 270s Callimachus' patronage may still have been insecure, but the literary humour of the poem as a whole converts it into a rhetorical exaggeration, an Alexandrian example of the precociousness of Apollo, to outdo Homer's young Apollo or baby Hermes (the *Homeric Hymn to Hermes* was widely read and appreciated among Hellenistic writers).

In the *Hymn to Artemis*, too, Callimachus combines intricate variation on Homeric precedent (in particular the *Homeric Hymn to Apollo* again and various scenes from the *Iliad*) with the Alexandrian taste for cuteness. The poem begins with Artemis still a young girl on her father's knee begging for perpetual virginity and a band of companions with whom to hunt, and although the scene is modelled on an early Aeolic text by Sappho or Alcaeus, the emphasis on the intimacy of father and child and on the incongruity of the infant's request is specifically Hellenistic; Zeus agrees, and the hymn continues with an equally 'baroque' scene, the young Artemis' visit to the workshops of Hephaestus and his giant Cyclops helpers to secure her bow and arrows. A central 'Hesiodic' section on Artemis' manner of punishing the unjust (with plague and untimely death) and support of the just (with prosperity and harmony) gives the poem a moral seriousness technically necessary for a hymn, but the transition to Artemis' entrance and reception on Olympus returns the text to a more purely narrative tone with an account of the greedy Heracles grumbling at the meagre spoils from her hunt. The poem finishes with an elegantly virtuoso listing of Artemis' cult-centres and followers.

The hymns to Artemis and Delos are important examples of a particular type of Hellenistic writing at which Callimachus excelled, the literary display on a set traditional theme. Neither work can be properly understood without the detailed knowledge of its ancestry that could be taken for granted in the original Alexandrian audience, and both poems are full of allusions and nuances which tempt modern readers to dismiss them impatiently as unduly scholarly, in spite of the fact that many modern poets such as Pound or Eliot have often relied heavily on similarly allusive modes of writing.

Dactylic poetry was by no means the only form Callimachus used. His critics actually attacked him for his versatility, and we have fragments of lyric poems, including one in the phalaecean metre on the women of Lemnos (a theme dealt with by Apollonius Rhodius in *Argonautica* 1), a drinking song for the Dioscuri in the 'Euripidean fourteen-syllable', a *Deification of Arsinoe* (died 270) in archebouleions, and a choriambic poem on Branchus the founder of Apollo's temple and cult at Didyme. More extensive are the remains of the thirteen iambic poems in which Callimachus revived the satirical, invective style practised by Hipponax and Archilochus three centuries earlier. None of the poems can be dated, and most are too scantily preserved to allow any detailed reconstruction, but the nature of the collection, which was about one thousand lines long, is clear. Several of the poems were directed at Callimachus' fellow writers and critics in Alexandria. In Iambus 1, fr. 191, the poet addresses his colleagues in the guise of Hipponax returned from the dead, cites the story of Bathycles' gold cup which was to be given to the greatest of the Seven Wise Men, each of whom however refused to accept it, and admonishes the Alexandrians for being so quarrelsome and critical of one another. Iambus 2, fr. 192, seems to have satirized the loquaciousness of Callimachus' contemporaries by recounting the fable that the power of speech which once belonged to animals was taken from them in punishment by Zeus and transferred to men (10–14):

> so Eudemus has a dog's voice,
> Philton an ass's, the orators parrots',
> the tragedians that of sea-fish;
> all men have become full of words
> and garrulous therefrom.

Iambus 13, fr. 203, replied aggressively to critics who had attacked him for writing in such a variety of styles, and several of the Iambi were directed at individuals: 3, fr. 193, later imitated by Tibullus (1.4), criticizes one Euthydemus for being seduced away from the poet by the wealth of a rival and laments the venality of the age, and Iambus 5, fr. 195, attacked Cleon, a schoolmaster, for abusing his pupils. Others dealt with aetiologies, and the collection contained two incidental poems: Iambus 6, fr. 196, was something of a technical *tour de force* describing to a friend the statue by Phidias of Olympian Zeus at Elis. Iambus 12, fr. 202, was a unique text, a birthday poem for the daughter of a friend, Leon: the remains are fragmentary, but we can establish that Callimachus told of the divine birthday festival for Hebe, to which each of the gods brought presents, including Apollo who took a song, the most appropriate gift of all (56–68):

> Phoebus, try your skilful art,
> which shall surpass Hephaestus' beauties.
> Gold the Indian dog-like ants
> will bring up from the depths on their wings;
> and base the home it will often inhabit,
> old the ways gold will dishonour.
> Justice and Zeus mankind will kick
> with scornful foot in order to praise
> gold, an evil so honoured.
> And Athena's gift, and that of others
> no matter how finely chiselled
> the march of time shall make dim;
> but my gift is the finest of all.

Callimachus is often judged, and dismissed, as if two famous quotations from him summed up his work: fr. 612 'nothing unattested do I sing', and fr. 465 'a big book is a big misfortune'. But we have no context whatsoever for either of these lines, and Callimachus was much more than a scholar with an axe to grind. He was the poet of his age, who was able to turn an oppressively great tradition into material for a modern style of writing. He was a mercurial figure, at times even too clever, and his extreme sophistication seems sometimes to have promoted such wit and elegance that the resulting technical fluency becomes itself a kind of disengagement. But a radical challenge and reorientation were what poetry needed in the third century, and it is always easy to depreciate pioneers after others have built on their achievements. Those prepared to make the imaginative effort of reconstructing the cultural milieu of third-century Alexandria will find Callimachus a great poet in his own right, and no single writer had a more profound influence on his own contemporaries and on the direction that poetry was to take thereafter.

4. THEOCRITUS

Theocritus, son of Praxagoras and Philinna and a native of Syracuse in Sicily, came to Alexandria shortly after 275/4 when Callimachus was probably already an established member of the Museum and royal court. Alexandria seems to have been the focus of his career as a poet, though on this, as on the chronology and course of Theocritus' life and literary output, we have almost no direct testimony and have to rely almost entirely on inference and reconstruction from the poems themselves. Unlike most other poets who were prominent in Alexandrian literary circles at that time, Theocritus seems not to have participated in the scholarly work at the Museum; there is no reference in any ancient source to prose works of any kind, and his poetry, although as carefully worked as that of Callimachus or Apollonius Rhodius, is concerned with the realm of sentiments rather than that of the mind. One of the Idylls, 16, is directed at Hieron II of Syracuse who came to power in 275/4; the poem is an appeal for patronage, and in various ways it seems to allude to the early years of Hieron's reign. Since the other two datable poems, *Id.* 15 and 17, are set in Alexandria and are to be placed between about 275 and 270, scholars generally assume that after *Id.* 16 failed to elicit support from Hieron (who, unlike his namesake two hundred years earlier, was no patron of the arts), Theocritus moved to the more generous court of Ptolemy Philadelphus and found success in Egypt with his bucolic poems about the rustic world of Sicily and South Italy. Although *Id.* 16 may be a relatively early composition, and not one on which Theocritus' reputation was subsequently based, the voice and manner are in places unmistakably those which characterize the later pastoral poems; as when the poet prays for peace in Syracuse under Hieron's rule (88–99):

> Cities once more be settled by their former people,
> to which enemies' hands brought utter ruin;
> fields be worked to abundance, and beyond count
> may sheep by thousands richly fattened at grass
> bleat across the plain, while cattle herd
> farmwards and speed dusk's traveller as they go.
> May fallows be worked for seeding as the cicada
> watches shepherds at noon from high in the trees
> and chirps in the branches. Over the armour
> may spiders stretch fine their webs, while the battle-cry
> is remembered no more. And on high may singers bear
> the fame of Hieron, beyond the Scythian sea...

Id. 17 is a hymn in praise of Ptolemy Philadelphus, eulogizing his ancestry (which Ptolemy traced back to Heracles), his family and his achievements, and the tone of the whole poem, which contrasts strongly with that of *Id.* 16, suggests clearly that Theocritus now enjoyed the support of the Egyptian king. Only one other poem, *Id.* 15, is set explicitly in Alexandria; it represents the conversation and reactions of two Syracusan women as they visit Ptolemy's palace on the occasion of the Adonis festival, and is a kind of tribute, gracefully self-deprecating, from Syracuse to Ptolemaic Alexandria. None of Theocritus' other poems are so directly or explicitly Egyptian as these, but an attentive reading of the extant poems demonstrates that the new poet from Sicily found himself fairly fully involved in the literary and social life of Alexandria and its intimate, sophisticated literary circle. With the exception of four poems in Lesbian metres and dialect (28–31), Theocritus' poems are all fairly short works in hexameter verse, and although all draw extensively on Homeric poetic language and vocabulary, many are written in a predominantly Doric dialect (one of the three major dialect groups, Doric was spoken primarily in the Peloponnese and colonial areas such as Sicily and South Italy). Doric, especially in a literary context, will have been a curiosity in sophisticated Alexandria, where the essentially Attic *koine* was the *lingua franca*, and the subject matter of Theocritus' poetry was also chosen for its special appeal to his Alexandrian audience; his themes are often drawn from the world of the country and concern aspects of the lives of studiedly ordinary people. It is clear that Theocritus took advantage of his Syracusan origins to appeal to his modish Alexandrian city audience by writing of rustic themes, often in a Sicilian or Southern Italian setting, in a rather broad Doric accent. Theocritus carefully emphasizes the *foreign* origin and nature of his poetry; two idylls have as their central character the comi-tragic grotesque Cyclops, and in *Id.* 11 when suggesting music, not medicine, as the cure for love to Nicias, Theocritus notes 'at any rate this was the easiest diversion for the Cyclops, *my countryman*' (l. 7). *Id.* 4 consists in a conversation between two rustic shepherds, Battus and Corydon, about an absent friend, and the poem is heavy with country detail (calves nibbling the olive-shoots, thorns in the feet etc.) and thick with slightly self-conscious earthy conversation; the setting too is indicated by some carefully dropped geographical hints as being South Italy, near Croton (l. 17 the river Aesarus, 24 the river Neaethus, 32 Croton). However the real context in which the poem was written is given away in l. 31 when Corydon refers to a composer called Glauce. Glauce was no fiction: she was a contemporary musician who was particularly associated with Alexandria, and the supposed currency of her reputation amongst Italian shepherds is clearly a witty and elegant compliment on Theocritus' part to someone with whom he was probably acquainted in the city. And mention of the name betrays a further dimension to the context in which Theocritus was writing: one tradition reports that Ptolemy Philadelphus was himself infatuated with Glauce (Aelian, *N.A.* 8.11), and we suddenly catch sight of a royal patron in Theocritus' audience, ready to be amused by the latest work of his protégé, the singer of country songs.

Another group of texts illustrates well the perspective in which Theocritus should be read. One of the topics which Theocritus made very much his own was the love of the gauche Cyclops Polyphemus for the sea-nymph Galatea (indeed in later writers this motif came to be typical for the bucolic world: [Bion] 2.2f., [Mosch.] 3.58ff., Bion fr. 16). One of the two poems in which Theocritus represents Polyphemus singing of Galatea, *Id.* 11, is a 'letter-poem' addressed (like *Id.* 13) to a certain Nicias, a doctor and apparently a close friend, whom Theocritus consoles for being tormented by love, proposing the standard theme that for love-sickness the only remedy is poetry and music. *Id.* 11 is an attractive poem which any friend would be pleased to receive, but it certainly teases poor Nicias, comparing him implicitly to the clumsy and grotesquely unsuccessful lover Cyclops and remarking explicitly that a doctor's powers are useless in contrast to Theocritus' chosen expertise, poetry. The ancient scholia to this idyll record some important information: that Nicias (whom we know, in any case, from *Id.* 28.7 to have been a poet) wrote a poem replying to Theocritus in his own vein. We have the opening lines:

> So it was true, Theocritus: the gods of Love
> made poets out of many otherwise uninspired.

Nicias turns Theocritus' point back against him. This fragment reminds us momentarily how disastrous is the loss of the bulk of Hellenistic poetry, since it demonstrates to what degree this was a sophisticated world of educated men for whom poetry was an important common medium of conversational and intellectual exchange.

A famous epigram of Callimachus should probably be linked with the interchange between Theocritus and Nicias. In *Ep.* 46 Callimachus takes up the same theme and recounts that the Cyclops was not so simple after all since he discovered that *poetry* is the cure for the disease of love. The epigram is addressed to a certain Philip, and since the wit of the poem derives from studied use of medical terms to describe love's affliction the addressee was presumably a doctor. Scholars have generally assumed that Theocritus and Nicias met on the island of Cos where there was a famous medical school, but there is no evidence whatsoever for this and it is just as likely that their meeting place was Alexandria (where Nicias' teacher Erasistratus studied); here there may have developed a friendship between Theocritus and Callimachus and two doctors, Nicias and Philip, and Callimachus' epigram, perhaps written after *Id.* 11, may illumine how a literary expression of friendship by Theocritus could become a matter of topical discussion in Alexandrian literary circles.

The surface simplicity of the Idylls, then, is very deceptive. The directness and the apparently uncomplicated tone which give Theocritus' poems such immediacy are in fact, just like the geographical settings, the product of very artful mannerism; and it has been failure to recognize that Theocritus' naivety is not what it seems that has led so many readers, poets as well as scholars, from antiquity to the present day, to assume that a simplistic approach is adequate for understanding the Idylls, whether they are read as songs of pastoral innocence or as dense collections of symbols. In fact the Idylls are essentially fantasy, and Theocritus' central concern in almost all of his poetry is with the art of illusion and the exploration of mood.

The achievement for which Theocritus is justly famous is, of course, that he introduced the genre of pastoral to the European tradition, and Theocritus' sense of atmosphere and his ability to convey scene and setting with extraordinary concision are especially evident in the pastoral poems. *Id.* 1 begins:

ΘΥΡΣΙΣ

Ἁδύ τι τὸ ψιθύρισμα καὶ ἁ πίτυς, αἰπόλε, τήνα,
ἁ ποτὶ ταῖς παγαῖσι, μελίσδεται, ἁδὺ δὲ καὶ τύ
συρίσδες· μετὰ Πᾶνα τὸ δεύτερον ἆθλον ἀποισῇι.
αἴ κα τῆνος ἕληι κεραὸν τράγον, αἶγα τὺ λαψῇι·
αἴ κα δ’ αἶγα λάβηι τῆνος γέρας, ἐς τὲ καταρρεῖ
ἁ χίμαρος· χιμάρω δὲ καλὸν κρέας, ἔστε κ’ ἀμέλξηις.

ΑΙΠΟΛΟΣ

ἅδιον, ὦ ποιμήν, τὸ τεὸν μέλος ἢ τὸ καταχές
τῆν’ ἀπὸ τᾶς πέτρας καταλείβεται ὑψόθεν ὕδωρ.
αἴ κα ταὶ Μοῖσαι τὰν οἴιδα δῶρον ἄγωνται,
ἄρνα τὺ σακίταν λαψῇι γέρας· αἱ δέ κ’ ἀρέσκηι
τήναις ἄρνα λαβεῖν, τὺ δὲ τὰν ὄιν ὕστερον ἀξῇι.

THYRSIS Sweet the whispered music of that pine,
goatherd, by the springs, and sweetly too you
pipe; you shall have the second prize after Pan.
Should he take the horned goat the nanny is yours,
and if he has the nanny to you redounds
the kid; and a kid's flesh is good till you milk her.

GOATHERD Sweeter, shepherd, your song than that stream
resounds as it pours down from the rock on high.
Should the Muses take the ewe as their gift
the sucking lamb is your prize; and should their pleasure
be to have the lamb, you then take the ewe.

The song which Thyrsis eventually sings for the goatherd occupies more than
half the poem and consists in a lament for the dying herdsman Daphnis: the
tone is melancholic and Daphnis, for all that he is a mysterious character (see
below, p. 575), is clearly an almost archetypal representative of the pastoral
world (Thyrsis' lament is overtly characterized as typically pastoral with its
constant refrain 'Begin, dear Muses, begin the pastoral song'). As he dies
Daphnis calls on Pan (128–37):

Come, my lord, and take this honeyed pipe
with compressed wax and fair binding at the lip;
for I am drawn to Hades now by Love.
Cease, Muses, come cease the pastoral song.

Now violets grow on brambles and on thorns,
let fair narcissus bloom on juniper,
let all be changed and pine bear pears,
for Daphnis dies – let stag worry hounds,
and from the mountains let owls call to nightingales.
Cease, Muses, come cease the pastoral song.

As a whole this fine poem depends for its success on a very careful balance, in
both structure and mood. The goatherd, a piper, sings no song, but within the
poem his ecphrasis of the cup which he will present to Thyrsis is formally a
counterpart to Thyrsis' song; the competitive excellence to which both refer at
the beginning never emerges into an open singing match, such as forms the
basis of *Id.* 5, but by the end of the poem we have had performance from each
without explicit competition. The world of Thyrsis and the goatherd is made
vivid by their descriptions of the setting and given depth and real dimension
beyond the idyll itself by their references to external characters and events. This
depth is what the lament for Daphnis conveys very powerfully with its sense
that the poem begins only at the end of a life already lived; the details are in
fact loose enough to give both the landscape and the emotional world of these

two of its inhabitants a very general value – the setting is attractive but universal, and Daphnis' plaint (the background to which still mystifies modern commentators) is intense but unspecific, and powerful precisely because Daphnis is one of the classic figures of the pastoral world. Illusion is central to this type of poetry: illusion creates the sense of moment and sense of scene and allows the reader to sympathize without having to project himself into a completely alien world.

The question to what extent Theocritus was the inventor of this kind of pastoral has been much discussed since antiquity. We possess a number of ancient sources (see Appendix) which preserve early speculations on the origins of pastoral, tracing it in each case to cult practices connected with Artemis in Laconia or Sicily; these theories are unconvincing, since Artemis plays no part in Hellenistic pastoral, which seems in any case thoroughly secular, but they are important in that they take for granted that pastoral is a Doric phenomenon which has close ties with popular song. The legendary cowherd Daphnis appeared in poetry before Theocritus, notably in the Sicilian Stesichorus, and another Sicilian writer Epicharmus supposedly spoke of the cowherd Diomus as inventor of the herdsman's work-song; country song was clearly regarded as essentially a Sicilian phenomenon (the author of the *Funeral lament for Bion* even refers to pastoral simply as 'Doric song' ([Mosch.] 3.12)). Furthermore many of Theocritus' pastoral idylls purportedly present the songs of country people (most directly *Id.* 5; also *Id.* 1, 3, 6, 7, 10, 11); however much this may be in fact the poetry of Alexandrian sophistication, the very plausibility of Theocritus' stance as a purveyor of popular song is an important indication of the cultural roots of pastoral. As mentioned, other poets had touched on pastoral topics before Theocritus, and we have evidence of a general taste for bucolic subjects at this time (thus the dramatist Sositheus wrote a play on Daphnis and Lityerses, Hermesianax mentioned Daphnis as a lover of Menalcas, and Alexander Aetolus at least mentioned Daphnis as a pupil of Marsyas); however even when due allowance is made for the possibility of a long tradition in popular culture now lost to us and of pastoral material in a wider range of authors than now survives, the notable fact remains that no ancient source regarded anyone but Theocritus as the first pastoral poet, and it is Theocritean pastoral on which all subsequent bucolic poets base themselves. How much (if at all) Theocritus owed the *form* of the literary mime to predecessors such as Sophron cannot now be estimated.

Id. 7 is clearly one of the most important pastoral poems, but also the most mysterious. The poem recounts, in the first person, how one Simichidas and two friends walk on the island of Cos through the country to join a harvest festival; on the way they encounter a goatherd, Lycidas, a well-known accomplished singer, with whom, after a bantering conversation, Simichidas exchanges songs. Lycidas sings a prayer of safe voyage for his lover Ageanax on his journey, Simichidas sings a prayer for the success in love of his friend Aratus; Lycidas makes a present of a stick to Simichidas and then leaves the friends to walk to their festival. All scholars are agreed that this poem is about more than just a walk in the country, that it is a personal statement of some sort and that one of its central concerns is the writing and place of bucolic poetry. In Simichidas we may identify the voice of the poet himself, but on Lycidas there are many theories. No one today subscribes to Reitzenstein's view that this poem (like others) is a kind of allegorical product about a literary group on Cos which formed a religious fraternity, but the 'bucolic masquerade' theory is often appealed to in more dilute form when scholars suggest that behind Lycidas we should see a contemporary poet in disguise (Aratus, Callimachus, Leonidas, to mention just a few of the many who have been proposed). None of the interpretations offered along these lines has proved satisfactory, and it is doubtful if we shall properly understand *Id.* 7 so long as the import of the songs of Lycidas in particular but also of Simichidas remains so obscure. However some points may sensibly be made about the poem. First, Lycidas, whatever or whomever he represents, seems certainly to be an epiphany of some sort, and at the very least associated with Apollo, and his behaviour towards Simichidas resembles an investiture, a recognition and formal approval of the art of Simichidas, similar to that of Hesiod's symbolic acknowledgement by the Muses (*Theog.* 29–34). Simichidas twice refers to his aspirations as a poet, remarking on the extent of his fame as a writer of bucolic 'of which report seems to have reached even the throne of Zeus' (l. 93, a reference, presumably, to Ptolemy Philadelphus), but modestly depreciating himself compared with writers such as Asclepiades or Philetas (ll. 39–41). Lycidas' reply is important as an expression of Theocritus' own critical position (43–8):

> I shall give you my stick because you are
> a sapling fashioned by Zeus entirely for truth.
> For how I hate the architect who strives
> to make his house as high as Oromedon's peak,
> and cocks of the Muses that waste their toil
> crowing against Homer, Chios' bard.

These are the critical sentiments of the leader of the *avant-garde*, Callimachus, and the passage is very similar to the Prologue of the *Aetia* (see above, pp. 558ff.) where Callimachus speaks of Homer as the divine king of poetry, not to be imitated (l. 20 'thunder is not my part, that is for Zeus'); and as Theocritus compares cocks crowing and, earlier in l. 41, frogs croaking against the grasshopper, so Callimachus contrasts the braying of the ass with the clear voice of the cicada (ll. 29–32). Theocritus is clearly aligning himself with the Callimacheans in this poem and rejecting the heroic epic in favour of a less ambitious and more restrained type of writing. What is particularly important is that *Id.* 7 is no casual poem, and this passage is not just an incidental expression of support for Callimachus: the words of the epiphanic Lycidas to Simichidas have the same overall prescriptive authority as those of Apollo to Callimachus in the Prologue, and Theocritus is making a general programmatic statement about fundamental poetic principles.

The two Cyclops poems, *Id.* 6 and 11, are typical in form and tone of the new style of writing, consisting as they do of small vignettes and poems within poems; they also exhibit many of the qualities on which the unique success of Theocritean pastoral depends. *Id.* 6 has the form, once again, of an encounter between two countrymen, Daphnis and Damoetas, who exchange songs. Daphnis addresses the Cyclops (6–14):

> Galatea pelts your flock, Polyphemus,
> with apples, calls you crass in love, a goatherd;
> and you regard her not, you fool, but sit
> piping sweetly. Again, look, she pelts the dog
> which follows to guard your sheep; it looks to sea
> and barks, while the fair waves mirror it
> as it runs along the gently murmuring beach.
> Take care that it does not leap at the girl's legs
> and tear her fair skin as she comes from the sea.

After Daphnis' address Damoetas takes up Polyphemus' part, and the Cyclops declares that his insouciance is a blind to tease Galatea (29–38):

> I whistled the dog to bark; for when I was courting
> it nuzzled her and would whimper in her lap.
> Perhaps she'll see me do this often enough
> and send a message; then I'll bar my door
> till she swears to be my bed-mate on this isle.
> For my looks are certainly not poor, they do say.
> Recently I glanced in the calm of the sea
> and my beard showed up fair, and my one eye,
> so far as I could tell, and from my teeth
> the gleam was whiter than marble of Paros.

The charm of this poem (and 'charm' is surely exactly what Theocritus effects here) derives from the careful combination of attractive rural image, finely actualized (Galatea emerging from the plashing sea while the dog barks on the beach), and the sense of detached superiority which Theocritus offers his readers as the gauche Cyclops reveals how little knowledge he has of either himself or the teasing sea-nymph.

Id. 6 offers the reader a judicious balance of involvement and detachment by presenting Polyphemus and Galatea as a story played out by two country singers; *Id.* 11 has no such frame, but achieves the same effect by more extended irony. After an address to his friend Nicias and a narrative introduction describing the love-sick Cyclops ignoring his flocks as he sang of Galatea, Theocritus offers, in monologue form, Polyphemus' serenade. Theocritus is particularly adept at characterization through first person revelation, as *Id.* 2 also demonstrates. The love-song of the Cyclops is a tender but unwittingly clumsy appeal, in which Polyphemus' very reflection on his virtues demonstrates how unattractive Galatea must find him. His opening address is well-intended but full of rustic misjudgement (19–24):

> O white Galatea, why repulse your lover?
> O whiter than curd to see, softer than lamb,
> livelier than a calf, glossier than unripe grape.
> Why thus when sweet sleep takes me do you come
> and then when sweet sleep leaves me go straightway,
> and flee like a ewe that sees a grey wolf?

Later his passion projects an image which is first sadly childish, for all its fine aspirations, then portentously pathetic (54–62):

> Alas that my mother bore me not with gills,
> that I might have dived down to you and kissed your hand
> if you refused your mouth; and I would bring you
> white snowdrops or a poppy soft with scarlet petals.
> But the one grows in summer, the other in winter,
> so I could not bring you both of them together.
> But at least I shall learn at once to swim, Galatea,
> if only some stranger will sail here in his ship,
> so I may know why you like to live in the depths.

As every reader of the *Odyssey* knows, swimming was not the issue when Odysseus visited the Cyclops in his ship.

The appeal of the Cyclops as a rustic character clearly lies in his nature as a grotesque; and it is precisely the combination which this figure offers of sympathetic involvement and distance which is the key to Theocritus' pastoral and which marks him off from all subsequent writers in the genre. Theocritus constructs a world which appeals to the fantasy of a city-bred audience and yet at the same time never pretends to offer more than a momentary illusion. His pastoral world has the depth of apparent reality and engages the emotions with very human issues, but the necessary suspension of disbelief is never concealed; pastoral may be escapist, but Theocritus offers no cloying serenity or romantic illusion of unity with nature, and he uses his audience's sense of social superiority to establish a distance which becomes disengagement once each poem concludes. The balance is exact: the fantasy world deals with real issues (mostly love) and yet real people and politics never intrude sufficiently to undermine the illusion.

There is another important respect too in which Theocritus differs from the later bucolic poets. Some of the countrymen in the Idylls (notably Daphnis, but also Menalcas) belonged to the literary tradition before Theocritus, and Theocritus uses the fact of a partly pre-formed country world for his own advantage; by having a number of his characters recur in several idylls he gives added substance and the impression of depth and three-dimensionality to his own pastoral world. Amaryllis, Corydon, Daphnis and Tityrus each become familiar figures by repetition and consequently create a semi-mythical atmosphere. However it is Theocritus' successors and imitators who fully developed this device, essentially closing off membership of the pastoral world and converting it fully into a mythical 'other place'. It is partly this self-contained quality of post-Theocritean pastoral, as well as the fact that there are patently many complexities in Theocritus which we still do not fully understand, that has tempted some modern interpreters to read Theocritus' pastoral idylls as allegorical poems. Those who wish to see issues of the principles of poetic composition, or more sombre matters, symbolically concealed below the surface of country talk in Theocritus must carry the burden of proof, and it has to be said that allegorical interpretations have so far created as many problems as they purport to solve and are generally very selective, as well as over simplistic, in their handling of evidence.

Id. 3 shows the same features as the Cyclops poems, if in more muted form. A goatherd serenades his loved one, Amaryllis, in front of her cave-dwelling from which she refuses to emerge; the dramatic monologue, full of self-pity, is both comic and sad, and once again reveals all too clearly why Amaryllis should be unmoved by the speaker. The goatherd is no curious monster this time, and the world of which he talks has plenty of pastoral attractions for Theocritus' Alexandrian audience, with its cave hung with ivy and fern, its buzzing bees, its rosebuds and fragrant celery, to say nothing of country lore and superstitions; but the pleasantness of the locale is balanced by the humorous incongruity of a formal paraclausithyron (a serenade outside the house of the loved one), which was an urban custom, here transferred to a country setting. Once again the tone is ambivalent, and detached superiority is an essential component.

Id. 10 is a dialogue between two reapers, Milon and Bucaeus, who discuss the latter's inability to concentrate on his work because of love-sickness; Bucaeus sings a love-song for his girl, Milon compliments him and sings a work-song. The two workmen are far removed from Alexandrian city life, and the poem has plenty of entertaining jocularity and country idioms and proverbs; it is a neat rustic vignette, but it is also more than this, for while it conveys the sad isolation of the unrequited lover it contrasts his sensibility with the coarser, less attractive, nature of the man who has no comparable emotional experience.

Many modern readers may be surprised to learn that at this point all of the strictly pastoral poems which can be ascribed with reasonable certainty to Theocritus have been mentioned. They total eight, and are well outnumbered (and outweighed) by the non-pastoral poems in Theocritus' corpus. His great achievement historically was as a bucolic poet, but many of his other poems are equally fine in themselves, and it is a false distinction to categorize them separately from the pastoral works. Many of them are narrative in style and deal with heroic themes (what later came to be known as 'epyllia'), but several, like the pastoral poems, are 'mimetic' in form (monologue or dialogue) and focus on the vicissitudes of love or some other dramatic scene. Thus *Id.* 14 resembles *Id.* 10 in form and subject matter, with the exception that the two speakers seem to be men of the world. Aeschinas describes for his friend Thyonichus an unfortunate party at which Aeschinas' girl-friend revealed that she was in love with another man. Aeschinas' description of the scene, his feelings and the dramatic moment, is finely done, but the poem takes a different turn from *Id.* 10, and shows its Alexandrian context, when Thyonichus suggests that the disconsolate Aeschinas sign up for service abroad (the 'Foreign Legion') under Egyptian Ptolemy (59–64):

> THYON. The best paymaster is Ptolemy for a free man.
> AESCH. In other ways what's he like?
> THYON.   The very best.
> Kindly, cultured, gallant, and utterly charming;
> he knows his friend, and his enemy even more,
> is generous to many, and doesn't refuse a request,
> as befits a king – though one shouldn't ask constantly...

and Thyonichus urges Aeschinas away to Egypt. The compliment is a fine one, to a Ptolemy who doubtless sat in the audience at the poem's first recital.

A different kind of tribute to Ptolemy's Alexandria is paid by *Id.* 15, another mimetic dialogue in which two women, natives of Theocritus' own Syracuse but residents of Alexandria, go from their houses through crowded streets to observe the Adonis display and festival at the royal palace. The dialogue of this poem, presented in particularly realistic idiom and Doric dialect, skilfully recreates each scene for the reader, from the crush in the streets to the splendours of the palace, and the climax is the celebrant's ceremonial song to Aphrodite. Theocritus may, as the scholiast remarks, have been modelling himself on a lost mime by Sophron, but the skill with which the idyll creates the illusion of an actual conversation overheard and combines amusement, for the superior court audience, at the idle domestic chatter and impressionability of the two women, with presentation of a truly grand and rather exotic festival hymn – this is the characteristic art of Theocritus as evidenced by many of the other Idylls. Superficially this poem may seem to resemble a mime by Herodas (see pp. 611ff.), but *Id.* 15 far outclasses any of the latter's surviving works.

In many ways the finest of the mimetic idylls is the second, the monologue of a jilted girl, Simaetha, as she tries magic at midnight in an attempt to regain her lover. While she performs her spells and sings the incantations which run as refrains through almost the whole poem, her mind goes back to her first encounter with Delphis and we hear the history of her passionate and misguided affair. This is a poem which both recreates the particular mood of intense concentration at a witching hour (like the fifth and sixth hymns of Callimachus) and which expounds, once again through self-revelation, an anatomy of feeling. The occasion selected, midnight witchcraft, although not without precedent in earlier writers, is unique in Theocritus or any of his contemporaries, and exploration of a woman's emotions in an erotic encounter is rare;[1] but interest in the pathology of unusual occasions is characteristic of Hellenistic taste and the theme of unsatisfied or frustrated love is one to which Theocritus returns again and again throughout the Idylls. Simaetha's historical narrative closely resembles that of Aeschinas in *Id.* 14 while the expression of her despair is not dissimilar to that of the anonymous goatherd in *Id.* 3.

The narrative idylls too, although non-dramatic in form, are closely related to the pastoral poems. Thus *Id.* 13, which tells of Heracles' loss of his beloved Hylas, not only revolves once more around the theme of love lost, it also has at the centre of its narrative a strong sense of the atmosphere of the country and its strange powers. The poem has additionally a particularly important programmatic position among Theocritus' works. The story of the rape of Heracles' squire Hylas (by the nymphs) was a very rare one, but it is found again in Theocritus' contemporary Apollonius Rhodius (*Argonautica* 1.1187–357). Close similarities between the two passages have long been observed, and although some scholars still argue for the priority of Theocritus, there can be little doubt that Apollonius came first. In view of various stylistic points (see Appendix), the fact that Apollonius had a thematic reason for being interested in the connexion between Hylas and the Cians, and the further consideration that the episode which in the *Argonautica* immediately follows the Hylas incident (the boxing match between Amycus and Polydeuces, 2.1–97) is the subject of another separate Theocritean poem, *Id.* 22, the conclusion seems inevitable that after the composition of at least Books 1 and 2 of the *Argonautica* Theocritus picked up two of Apollonius' episodes and refashioned them as short idylls. The reason for this rewriting is clear: Theocritus was following the 'Callimachean' principles expounded in *Id.* 7 and demonstrating how a poet writing in the more 'refined' and 'limited' style might approach traditional epic themes. One of the most marked characteristics of Callimachean style is the studied avoidance of tradi-

[1] There is a large exception in Apollonius Rhodius' study of Medea in Book 3 of his *Argonautica*; and the so-called Alexandrian Erotic Fragment (Powell 177), composed perhaps a century after Theocritus, is the lament in lyric monologue of a woman betrayed by her lover.

tional narrative logic; interest focuses not on events themselves but on the context in which they take place, the atmosphere and their effects.

It is worth examining first a passage from Apollonius' account. Heracles, having broken his oar earlier in the day, takes advantage of a stop in Cian territory for the night to search for a replacement in the wood, while his squire Hylas takes a bronze pitcher and looks for water (1.1221–39):

> Straightway he reached a spring which is called
> Pegae by the neighbouring inhabitants. The dance
> of the nymphs was just beginning; for the care
> of all the nymphs that dwelt on that lovely peak
> was to celebrate Artemis in nightly song.
> They, all that keep the mountain heights and streams,
> that watch the woods, were filing off away;
> but newly from the fair-flowing fountain there rose
> the water's nymph. She noticed him close by
> ablaze with beauty and with sweet charms,
> for full from the heaven there shone down
> upon him the moon; and Cypris set her wits
> aflutter, nigh helpless to gather her senses.
> No sooner had he set his jug in the stream
> reaching aslant, and the water rang dreadfully
> as it swept into the sounding bronze, than straight
> she brought her left arm down around his neck,
> burning to kiss his soft lips, and with her right
> she tugged his elbow, and pulled him down in mid-stream.

This is high poetry in the Homeric manner, and the narrative proceeds in linear fashion. Hylas comes to a spring called Pegae: round it the nymphs are just beginning their dance (explanation: night celebration of Artemis). The spring nymph appears and sees Hylas: he looks extraordinarily beautiful and she falls helplessly in love. Thus it is (and the reader has been taken through the logic of the situation) that when Hylas dips his pitcher the nymph pulls him in with an embrace. This is a fine passage, a very successful example of Hellenistic epic; the occasion is religious in a familiar Homeric fashion, and like Homer Apollonius presents the narrative in a dramatic way, drawing atmosphere from the sequence of events themselves.

However Theocritus' idyll shows how conventional Apollonius is. First, the introduction (where Theocritus, unlike Apollonius, makes the erotic element explicit) summarizes in nine lines the main narrative of the Argonautic expedition (16–24); what takes two books in Apollonius is reduced to an incidental preface. When the narrative proper begins, the setting off of the Argonauts and their arrival at Cius is described in seven lines of predominantly pastoral (one might say Hesiodic) description (25–31). Then (36–54):

Blond Hylas went for water for the meal,
for Heracles and steadfast Telamon
two comrades who always feasted together,
with a bronze vessel. Soon he spied a spring,
in a low place; around grew rushes thick,
dark celandine, green maiden-hair,
thick celery and creeping dog's tooth grass.
In midst of the water the Nymphs were fashioning their dance,
the sleepless Nymphs, dread for countrymen,
Eunica and Malis, Nycheia with eyes of Spring.
Eager to dip the cavernous pitcher in water
the boy leaned out; they all clung to his hand.
Love had scattered the soft wits of them all
for the Argive boy; into the dark water
headlong he fell, as a flaming star from heaven
headlong in the sea – and a sailor tells his friends
'Lighten the tackle, boys, there's a sailing wind.'
The Nymphs held the boy upon their knees
and tried to soothe his tears with gentle words.

This passage is full of diversions from the narrative logic, with reasons for
actions given after the events. The setting of the spring has more poetic
prominence than Hylas' discovery of it, and similarly it is the unworldliness of
this magical place on which Theocritus concentrates with its terrible, restless
dancing nymphs *in* the very water. The detailing of names actualizes the dreadful
moment, and the fateful event is no human, comprehensible action, of hugging
and kissing; only afterwards are we given any explanation, that the nymphs
have, of course, fallen in love. When Hylas tumbles in we enter another diversion,
but the simile is not just an interruption of the narrative, it also prefigures the
next event in the story: in Apollonius, immediately after Heracles rushed off to
look for Hylas the other Argonauts took advantage of a fresh wind and sailed
off. Theocritus' point, that Heracles was so infatuated with his squire that he got
left behind, is compressed incidentally into the description of Hylas' fall.

Theocritus' poem is no narrative: the material may be that of conventional
epic, but it is not what happened and in what sequence that matters but the
atmosphere, the landscape, and the very strangeness of the whole episode. The
actions are almost taken for granted and emerge indirectly while the poet concentrates on other matters of mood and psychology. The magic and landscape
are thoroughly Theocritean, but the style and the manner in which the epic
material is handled is that of Callimachus; this is the non-Homeric style, the
clarity and cleanness of the cicada recommended by Apollo and by Lycidas.

The other 'narrative' idylls show similar concerns. *Id.* 22, a 'hymn' to the
Dioscuri, is a curious text which seems to have been damaged in transmission
so that no secure critical evaluation is possible, but Theocritus' emphasis is on

atmosphere and setting rather than 'story' in recounting two myths which celebrate the prowess of Polydeuces and Castor. As already mentioned, the section on Polydeuces (27–134) reshapes the version by Apollonius, making the incident much less of a conventional, rather brutish, heroic endeavour and more a conflict of moral powers on a large scale; even in the damaged section dealing with Castor's achievement it is clear that Theocritus has chosen to introduce many new aspects not found in previous writers. *Id.* 24 deals with a heroic exploit of the young Heracles who strangled two snakes sent by Hera to kill the infant hero and his brother in their cradle; the story was a well-known one and Theocritus' account is close to that of Pindar in the first *Nemean*, but although the idyll handles material from conventional myth, in tone and manner it belongs to the same genre of Alexandrian experimental poetry as Callimachus' *Hecale*. The language and style are those of high poetry, and Heracles' exploit is presented as an extraordinary feat, a preliminary to his great achievements in adulthood; at one level the poem is a semi-hymnal laudation, with its prophecy from Tiresias of a great future for Alcmena's son and the narrative description of the education of Heracles. However the narrative focuses as much on the domestic surroundings as on the infant's strangling of the snakes; Heracles' brother Iphicles kicks off his wool blanket to try to escape, the father Amphitryon sleeps soundly during the commotion, has to be woken by his wife and urged not to linger putting on his sandals, and after arriving too late to do anything goes straight back to bed. This Heracles resembles the prodigy Hermes, and the humour of Theocritus' idyll is not dissimilar to that of the *Homeric Hymn to Hermes*, always popular in Alexandria, or, amongst contemporary poems, to that of Callimachus' entertaining *Hymn to Artemis* (see above, p. 568).

Not all of the narrative poems are as extensive as *Id.* 22 and 24. The pastoral idylls are essentially vignettes, of a particular scene or occasion momentarily framed, and Theocritus extended this type into the narrative genre. *Id.* 26 presents in thirty-eight doricizing epic hexameters a brief account of the dismemberment of Pentheus by his Bacchanalian mother and her sisters; the point of view of the narrative is uncertain; and as if to underline this the poem ends with a hymnal prayer to Dionysus. *Id.* 18 is the only complete extant Greek epithalamion, a wedding song for Helen of Sparta; in an attractive poem which has many echoes of Sappho (and is said by the ancient commentators to have drawn on a work by Stesichorus) Theocritus offers, in a mixture of narrative and choral song, another dramatized illusion, the words supposedly sung by the bride's unmarried companions outside the wedding chamber of Helen and Menelaus. The construction is the familiar one of the ancient epithalamion, comprising congratulations to the groom and ribald jocularity at his expense, praise of the bride and promises never to forget her, prayers for the couple's happiness and prosperity, and a promise to return at dawn to sing another song.

The surviving scholia to many of the idylls often remark that Theocritus was drawing on earlier Sicilian or archaic writers, and in three poems he imitates Sappho and Alcaeus quite overtly. *Id.* 28, 29, 30 are in aeolic dialect and aeolic metres, and although we do not possess originals on which they were based we may presume that Theocritus was in close respects following the Lesbian poets. *Id.* 28 is a short work written to accompany the gift of a distaff which Theocritus is taking to the wife of his doctor friend Nicias in Miletus. *Id.* 29, which opens with a quotation from Alcaeus ('wine and truth, dear boy'), is addressed to a fickle young lover, urging the advantages of constancy (similar amongst the hexameter works is the uneven and puzzling *Id.* 12, a warm address to a lover who has appeared after two days' absence, prompting a prayer that their devotion to one another thenceforth might become a famous example among posterity); *Id.* 30 is in soliloquy form lamenting the affliction of love-sickness for a boy. There remain also a few fragments of lost works, including another apparently aeolic poem (31), and a hexameter work entitled *Berenice* (fr. 3).

Although it was particularly for his pastoral works that Theocritus was famous in antiquity, those poems are only a part of his achievement. The same taste and thematic concerns run through all his poetry: the strange or bizarre event and circumstance, the curiously ambivalent characters who have the power simultaneously to evoke sympathy and to arouse a sense of dispassionate superiority, whether they are outright grotesques like Polyphemus or merely temporary aberrants like Simaetha. A more constant preoccupation than pastoral is the agony of unfulfilled love and the strangely distracting and disorienting effect of love-sickness; Theocritus more than any other Hellenistic writer is the poet of love, but of love as pain rather than lyrical experience. In terms of form and style Theocritus was an experimentalist, aligned with Callimachus, and like Callimachus he wrote hymns, heroic narratives with a contemporary realistic perspective, and 'mimetic' poems (like Callimachus' hymns to Apollo, Athena and Demeter) both pastoral and non-pastoral. Through all these works runs a strong sense of, and interest in, the psychological relationship of a writer to his audience; it is this that makes Theocritus such a master at contriving illusion, the illusion of the reality of a particular scene, or set of emotions, or actual world. As already suggested, this illusion depends on an exact balance between reality and fantasy, and it is a balance which no writer after Theocritus managed to achieve again. The later Greek pastoralists exaggerate the fantasy element and produce extravagant sentimentality, while Virgil in his *Eclogues*, although providing the model for much of later European pastoral, made the fatal mistake of importing serious politics into the illusory world, with the disturbing consequence that the political elements are sentimentalized and the country reduced to trivial fiction.

5. APOLLONIUS RHODIUS

Of the many narrative epics composed in the early Hellenistic period only one has survived, the *Argonautica* of Apollonius Rhodius. The almost complete loss of what was a very extensive and popular genre is lamentable, the more so since Apollonius was clearly too distinctive a writer for us to use his work to reconstruct or characterize Hellenistic epic; but at least in the *Argonautica* we possess what was historically one of the most important poems written in third-century Alexandria as well as one of the finest failures in the whole of Greek literature.

About Apollonius himself we have very little secure information, though the ancient biographies claim to provide details concerning his life. That he was Librarian of the Museum (succeeding Zenodotus) and tutor to Ptolemy III Euergetes (who came to the throne in 247/6 B.C.) seems certain, as also that he was an associate of Callimachus (perhaps, as some sources say, his pupil); but romantic stories of an early literary failure in Alexandria with the *Argonautica*, consequent exile to Rhodes but subsequent glorious return to his native city where he was buried alongside Callimachus, are suspect. Among the early Librarians was another Apollonius (the Eidographer, succeeding Aristophanes of Byzantium) and what appear to be exact biographical details about the poet are probably fictions derived from confused attempts to explain the presence of 'Apollonius' twice in the list of Librarians. Many modern editors of Apollonius Rhodius and Callimachus write of the famous quarrel between the two poets, often describing it as a deadly feud and the principal event in the lives of both; the styles of these two writers are certainly very different from one another, but it has to be stressed that we have almost no direct evidence of such a feud and none at all that is contemporary. As has already been mentioned (above, pp. 557ff.) Callimachus was certainly involved in considerable literary controversy, and Apollonius may well have played his part in this, but the only specific evidence for a clash is a report in several late sources (none earlier than the sixth century A.D.) that Apollonius was the object of abuse in Callimachus' lost satirical poem the *Ibis*. There is also an insulting epigram against Callimachus in the Greek Anthology (*Anth.Pal.* 11.275) which is of uncertain authorship, though some sources attribute it to an Apollonius ('the Grammarian' or 'the Rhodian'). To insist on our ignorance may seem particularly unsatisfactory, since the Quarrel has come to be regarded as the archetypal literary dispute; but granting that the ancient accounts may dimly reflect actual historical circumstances, we have to remember that their connexion with the events is at best remote, and the biographical tradition is no more to be trusted on Apollonius than on any other author.

Evidence from the poems themselves is complex and suggests that the relationship between Callimachus and Apollonius, at least as writers, was close; there are constant correspondences between the *Argonautica* and the *Aetia*, *Hecale* and Hymns of Callimachus, consisting sometimes in similarities of theme and composition in a whole episode but often in more local echoes of style and phraseology. It is not always easy to determine which writer is alluding to which; the Argonautic episode in Book 1 of the *Aetia* (frs. 719–21) certainly antedated Apollonius' work, but in some of the Hymns it was clearly Callimachus who was echoing the *Argonautica*. In an environment such as the Alexandrian royal court 'publication' of a work was more indeterminate than nowadays when an author's book is mass-produced for an extensive reading public; even a long poem such as the *Argonautica* was probably published piece-meal through oral presentation and circulation of 'private' copies, and many parts of the work may well have gone through several drafts (the ancient scholia refer at six points in Book 1 to an 'earlier edition' of the *Argonautica* with readings slightly different from the text which we possess). In these circumstances interrelationships between writers who habitually cross-refer and allude to one another are likely to be complex. Many modern scholars have been tempted to assume that allusions by one poet to the other are probably hostile in intent, and that in most cases it is Callimachus who refers to Apollonius. It is true that many of the echoes and allusions involve variations of phraseology or form, but *variatio* is a fundamental characteristic of all Alexandrian poetry, and while some of the allusions may have been intended as alternative interpretations or even improvements, none is patently, and on intrinsic grounds, attributable to hostile motives. We should therefore be very wary of indulging in the biographical fallacy. More important are the fundamental differences of poetic mode and style between Apollonius and some of his contemporaries; some of these have already been touched on (in connexion with Callimachus above on p. 553, and with Theocritus on pp. 581ff.) and we now have to consider Apollonius as the exponent of that un-Callimachean form, the large-scale epic.

The story of Jason's journey in the first ship, the *Argo*, with his heroic companions the Argonauts to the outer reaches of the known world in quest of the Golden Fleece was of ancient origin, and was known in some form to the author of the *Odyssey* (12.71) and to Hesiod (*Theog.* 992ff.). The earliest complete work on the Argonautic expedition of which we hear is a sixth-century poem ascribed to Epimenides of Crete; it dates from the same period as the *Naupactia*, a catalogue of heroines (of disputed authorship) which covered much of the same material as the *Argonautica* and often served as a *point de départ* for Apollonius. Several other early authors too, poets and prose-writers, wrote on the Argonauts, and although we can no longer date many of these, some modern scholars have found attractive the observation of Strabo (1.2.38) that Homer's Circe seems to be derived from Medea, who must therefore have been a very early subject for epic poetry. In the sixth and fifth centuries many authors such as Herodorus of Heraclea, Pherecydes of Syros and Simonides of Ceos wrote on the Argonauts and are frequently cited in the ancient scholia to the *Argonautica*, and the tragedians wrote many dramas using the Argonautic legends; in the fourth century Antimachus of Colophon (above, pp. 546f.) seems to have dealt at length with the love of Jason and Medea in his elegy *Lyde*.

When Apollonius wrote his *Argonautica*, therefore, he could count on the story (and, most important, its sequel – Jason's desertion of Medea) being thoroughly well known to his audience; the familiarity of the theme explains at least in part how Apollonius could give such characteristically Alexandrian prominence in his poem to matters of geography, ethnography, anthropology and comparative religion. Earlier poets are often cited in the scholia as important influences on the *Argonautica*, from Eumelus of Corinth, Ibycus or Pindar to Antimachus and Philetas, but prose works seem to have been even more important. At times Apollonius' poem reads more like a handbook of contemporary paradoxography (accounts of marvels and peculiarities; see p. 550); the description of Circe's Plain, which Jason passes through to reach Colchis, with its account of corpses hanging from the trees wrapped in ox-hides, might have been the opportunity for a highly-charged atmospheric introduction to the hostile territory of King Aeetes, but instead it reads more like a chapter from Herodotus' *Histories* (3.194–209). Apollonius is as much the predecessor of the later romance novel as of the Virgilian epic, and throughout his poem the Alexandrian taste for the intrinsically curious and bizarre far exceeds any interest in literary symbol.

But for all its Alexandrian qualities the *Argonautica* is a full-scale epic in the traditional mode. The Argonauts are the flower of Greece from that early generation of men which included Heracles, Jason, Orpheus and Peleus, their quest and the labours which they have to endure are of heroic proportions, and their journey takes them through the major part of the known world and into much of the unknown with its collection of strange monsters and eerie, menacing places. Magic and the supernatural play no small part in the poem, and the Argonauts live in a world inhabited also by gods who participate in the action, notably Athena, Hera, Aphrodite, and, rather remotely, Apollo. The metre of the poem is the traditional hexameter, the language is elaborately Homeric with constant allusions in every line to the diction, phraseology and vocabulary of the *Iliad* and *Odyssey*, and whole episodes are shaped on precedents in the Homeric poems. The *Argonautica* even opens (1.18–233) with a lengthy catalogue in the style of Book 2 of the *Iliad*; Books 1 and 2 refer constantly to

Homeric archetypes (thus the long sojourn with Hypsipyle on Lemnos corresponds to Odysseus' stay with Circe, the consultation of the seer Phineus matches that of Odysseus with Tiresias) and Book 4 is Apollonius' *Odyssey*, reproducing the wanderings of Odysseus in his attempt to return home and even importing directly Circe, the Sirens, Scylla and Charybdis, the Planctae, Phaeacia and Alcinous and Arete. Only a visit to the Underworld is, surprisingly, omitted.

From almost every detail of the *Argonautica* it is patent that Apollonius conceived his poem as being fundamentally Homeric, though not in any way through mere repetition or imitation, for the *Argonautica* is a very complex and sophisticated work, sensitive to its own tradition. almost to the point of self-conscious mannerism. And yet for all its irony and intricate allusion the poem does mark an attempt to construct a Homeric epic for the Alexandrian world.

Superficially, at least, the theme of Jason's expedition seems very appropriate to the medium. A summary of the plot will illustrate this point. A young prince trying to regain his throne is set an almost impossible task, to travel beyond the known world to the mysterious land of Colchis and to bring back a prized golden fleece; with a band of fifty heroes Jason travels through the Aegean to the Bosphorus, on the way staying with Hypsipyle and her women on Lemnos, visiting Cyzicus and fighting local giants, and finally reaching Mysia where the young Hylas is entrapped by a nymph and his companion Heracles is left behind by the expedition as he searches desperately for his ward (Book 1). Still at the Bosphorus the Argonauts are challenged by a brutal king, Amycus, whom Polydeuces defeats in a boxing-match, and then they visit the seer Phineus, who in return for being rescued from the dreadful Harpies predicts at length the rest of Jason's journey to Colchis (in spite of being modelled in part on Odysseus' Tiresias and Circe, Apollonius' Phineus is no more than a travel agent). The *Argo* successfully passes through the terrifying Clashing Rocks at the mouth of the Black Sea, with help from Athena, and the Argonauts travel along the north coast of Asia Minor to Colchis, passing along the way Thynias, the land of the Mariandyni, the land of the Amazons, and the island of Ares, where the Argonauts meet the sons of Phrixus who originally went with the golden fleece to Colchis (Book 2). With Jason now at Colchis Athena and Hera persuade Aphrodite to arrange that the daughter of the king, Medea, shall fall in love with him, and when King Aeetes not only refuses to let the Argonauts take the golden fleece, but imposes the seemingly unattainable condition of taming the fire-breathing bronze bulls and defeating the earth-born warriors and even plans the complete destruction of the Argonauts, then Medea's love for Jason becomes crucial. As a sorceress, she has the power to make Jason invincible in performing the task; although torn with the conflict of passion and filial loyalty, Medea eventually succumbs, and Jason, after reassuring Medea with promises that extend, finally, even to marriage, obtains a magic ointment from her and successfully tames the bulls and slays the innumerable warriors sprung from the dragon's teeth which he has to sow as part of his task (Book 3). That night Medea joins the Argonauts and leads them to the forest where the fleece is kept, subduing the guardian dragon with magic; the Argonauts flee, pursued by the Colchians, along the Danube to the Adriatic, where Jason and Medea lure her brother Apsyrtus, the commander of the pursuing forces, into an ambush and murder him in order to demoralize his followers; their final route home takes them to visit Circe, who expiates the couple of their blood-guilt, past various Odyssean landmarks to Phaeacia, where Jason and Medea marry, under duress, to Libya where the Argonauts wander lost in the strange country of the misty shallows and carry their boat overland to Triton's lake, and ultimately via Crete, where they kill the bronze giant Talus, and Anaphe, where Apollo appears to them, to Aegina and then home to Thessaly (Book 4).

This is the stuff of heroic saga and Apollonius can be unambiguously grandiose in style and tone, as has already been mentioned in discussion of Callimachus and Theocritus (above, pp. 553 and 581ff.). A characteristically expansive moment is the description of Jason turning finally to meet the sown men:

> He bent his knees nimbly, and his mighty heart
> he filled with courage, eager like a boar
> which whets its teeth for the huntsmen, and all around
> foam pours to the ground from its angry mouth.
> Over all the field as a corn-crop the earth-born now
> were springing up; stout shields bristled about
> and double-gripped spears and shining helms
> in murderous Ares' precinct, and the radiance went
> blazing through the air from earth to Olympus.
> And as when, after much snow has fallen on the ground,
> winds once more disperse the wintry clouds
> in the murky night, and multitudinous appear
> all the constellations shining through the gloom –
> so they then shone as they multiplied over the earth.
> But Jason recalled the counsel of artful Medea. (3.1350–64)

Jason despatches his awesome task in the best Homeric tradition; and even if at times we sense that Apollonius feels it necessary to write things over-large because he knows that he cannot take our acquiescence in this heroic world for granted, the essential perspective of the *Argonautica* is that of the traditional epic.

Many modern scholars find Jason disconcerting as the central figure of the poem; he can be indecisive, is easily troubled and often dismayed, and in comparison with Heracles (who figures throughout Book 1) is very reliant on the resources of his companions. In what sense, then, is this character heroic? Some have suggested even that it is essentially through his sexuality that Jason attains heroic status, others that he is indeed not a hero but a representative of 'modern man'. None of these approaches is convincing, and although Jason is a very complex figure those who find him unsatisfactory are generally guilty of falsely simplistic notions as to what constitutes a hero in ancient epic. Jason is often diffident, but so are Agamemnon and Menelaus in the *Iliad*; Jason sometimes despairs and loses momentum, but so does Agamemnon; when Aeetes announces the trial Jason is quite without resource and his companions are utterly dismayed (3.422ff., 502ff.), but the Greeks react in exactly the same way when Hector challenges them to a duel (*Iliad* 7.161ff.). In the *Iliad* as a whole only one of the Greeks is a uniformly fine representative of the 'heroic code', and Ajax is a minor figure precisely because his excellence makes him ordinary; similarly the presence of Heracles in Book 1 is far from being an embarrassment to Jason, since although Heracles is never presented as an outright grotesque, his very physicality and single-mindedness are as limiting as they are impressive. Jason, by contrast (who is no more 'sexual' than Odysseus!), is undeniably successful in his enterprise and far more sympathetic and balanced a leader than Agamemnon; if he does not have the tragic dimensions of Achilles or the symbolic status of the wandering Odysseus that is because the focus of the *Argonautica* as a whole is different from that of the Homeric poems. Indeed, it is not Jason's lack of supposedly 'heroic' qualities that should occupy us, but the almost sinister aspects of his behaviour which serve his success as a heroic leader.

The encounter with Medea, which occupies most of Books 3 and 4, is where Jason's qualities emerge most clearly and also where Apollonius' most original contribution to the epic tradition lies. All previous works dealing extensively with the Argonautic expedition have been lost and we have no means of assessing how prominent was Medea's role before Apollonius, but for later writers it was his *Argonautica* which established romantic passion as a major theme for epic. Romance was nothing new, naturally – in the *Odyssey* Odysseus' relations with Calypso, Circe and Nausicaa are crucial components in his heroic quest; but Apollonius, while as concerned with traditional models here as in every other aspect of his poem, also gave the epic a radically new emphasis, different from either earlier heroine-catalogue poetry or poetry concerning the romantic wanderer. At first, it seems that Jason's encounter with Medea is to be thoroughly conventional. Book 3.1–166 describe Athena and Hera enlisting the help of Aphrodite in ensuring that Medea fall in love with Jason; the episode has a wryly entertaining humour. But once the divine action is taken the seemingly stilted procedure of Olympian intervention is set aside and the rest of the Book, the major part, examines the motivation and process of erotic passion entirely on the human level. Book 3 of the *Argonautica* is the earliest extant example in narrative poetry of an analysis of the pathology of love. The study begins as soon as Eros has shot his arrow and withdrawn to Olympus:

the arrow burned in the girl
right under her heart like a torch. And ever
she cast radiant glances at Jason; in her breast
her heart tossed quick with passion, no other
thought had she, but sweetly her soul flowed in pain.
As a woman strews twigs round a fiery brand,
a poor hand-worker whose task is the spinning of wool,
to prepare a blaze in the night beneath her roof
when she rises early; and wondrous from the small
brand it awakes and destroys all the twigs –
so twirled round her heart there quietly blazed
the destruction of love, and turned her soft cheeks
now pale, now blushing, from the troubles of her mind. (3.286–98)

The next 850 lines are largely devoted to Medea's attempt to understand her feelings and to come to terms with them; she resists them and tries to rationalize, but finally succumbs and, only half-consciously, faces the consequences of letting action flow from passion. The means which Apollonius uses for the presentation of this dramatic Medea are those of conventional epic: narrative action, high diction, imagery and simile. But the focus is new: inner feeling, and the psychology of mood. The sub-conscious becomes explicitly important. After Jason (watched by the fearful Medea) has been told by Aeetes the labour he must perform, night falls and the princess's deep sleep is troubled by dreams that the hero has come to Colchis for her, to win her as his bride, with the result that she abandons loyalty to her parents. Apollonius repeatedly uses simile to present Medea's turbulent feelings, but one passage is justifiably especially famous. Medea has temporarily rationalized her emotions and has convinced herself that she is supporting Jason only to help her sister, whose two sons by Phrixus are in danger from Aeetes. However her conscience is still torn:

Night then brought darkness upon the earth, and at sea
sailors looked to the Bear and Orion's stars
from their ships, and sleep was now the desire
of the traveller and gate-keeper, and a mother
whose children had died was wrapped in deep slumber;
dogs no longer barked through the city, no voice
sounded – silence held the blackening night.
But no sweet sleep at all took Medea.
Many cares kept her wakeful in desire for Jason,
dreading the bulls' mighty strength, by which he was likely
to perish with shameful fate in Ares' field.
Greatly the heart within her breast throbbed,
as a sunbeam quivers on the wall in a house,
coming back off water just freshly poured
in a basin or maybe a pail, and the beam wavers,

darting up and down in the quick eddy –
so in her breast trembled the girl's heart.
Tears flowed from her eyes in pity, inwardly
pain ever troubled her, smouldering through her body
and round the fine muscles to the nape of the neck,
where most grievous of all comes the pain, whenever
untiring loves drive distress on the heart.
At first she planned to give him charms against the bulls,
then to give nothing, but herself to die;
then to do neither one nor the other
but as she was endure her fate in silence. (3.744–69)

This manner of presenting inner states is new in narrative poetry, and scarcely emerges in Apollonius until the appearance of Medea in Book 3; thereafter it dominates Book 3 and radically affects the colouring of the return voyage in Book 4. When day breaks Medea prepares the charmed ointment and goes to meet Jason; the emotion so far has been all on the part of Medea, but their encounter at the temple of Hecate is suffused with the atmosphere of Medea's passion, and although in playing upon her emotions Jason had a precedent in Odysseus' approach to Nausicaa in *Odyssey* 6, Apollonius has Jason go much further than the Homeric hero. Medea has been completely distracted waiting by the temple, and when Jason does arrive he is likened to a star; but the image is ominous since it is the Dog Star which Jason resembles, the sign of summer heat and destruction for flocks (3.956–61; this contrasts with Jason's approach to his other lover Hypsipyle, at 1.774–81, where he is also compared to a star but in an image of wistful positiveness). The image has a sinister literary dimension, since the simile comes directly from *Iliad* 22.25–32, which describes how Achilles appeared to Priam before the fatal duel with Hector; Priam's reaction, terror, was more appropriate than that of Medea to Jason. The encounter seems initially to be a timeless moment of passion:

So silent and speechless they stood by one another,
similar to oak trees or tall firs
which side by side stand rooted in silence in the mountains
with no wind, but then later at the wind's onset
they stir and rustle endlessly – so then they
were to talk their fill, stirred by the breath of love.
Jason realized that she was beset by disaster
sent from heaven, and spoke these words with beguilement.

(3.967–74)

The last two lines show that Jason is presented as being fully prepared to take conscious advantage of Medea, and at several points in the encounter Apollonius has Jason speak in terms which suggest that he is either a fool or a calculating manipulator. At 3.997ff., and again at 1096ff., Jason proposes to Medea the model of Ariadne who became famous throughout Greece for her assistance to Theseus in dealing with the Minotaur; the reader (and, naturally, Jason) cannot but recall that Theseus deserted Ariadne on Naxos as soon as they had left Crete. Jason might be being disingenuous, and although at 3.1077–8 we are told that he too had fallen in love, his remarks have an extremely sinister dimension; the reader is made well aware that all will not be well with this relationship.

The repeated mention of Ariadne by Jason to Medea in Book 3 acts as a kind of commentary which once in Book 4 is elevated to the level of overt symbol. In order to lure Apsyrtus into their ambush Jason and Medea send him diplomatic gifts, among which is a cloak given to Jason by Hypsipyle but once the property of Dionysus; the cloak is still redolent with the fragrance breathed onto it by Dionysus as he lay making love to Ariadne when she had been abandoned by Theseus on Naxos (4.421–34). The imagery here is powerful and shocking, almost overwhelming, as Medea prepares for the ultimate betrayal of her family for love of a man who will himself betray her. There is scarcely any parallel in the rest of the poem for such direct symbolism, but the emergence of Jason in his dealings with Medea as a sinister personality capable of inflicting great damage on the woman who comes close to him is in fact no surprise, for it has already been foreshadowed in Book 1, in the first major episode of the Argonautic expedition, the visit to the island of Lemnos (1.609–909). Apollonius' manner of presenting Jason in this episode is characteristic and it will be illuminating to examine it in detail.

In Book 1, as Jason goes to meet Hypsipyle in her self-created isolation on Lemnos with the other women, he wears a cloak woven by Athena with scenes which embody various aspects or themes of the Argonautic expedition (1.721–67): the power of Zeus and of song, the significance of erotic passion in motivating conflict or competition or even destructive lust, and finally the golden fleece itself. To some extent this cloak is thematically prescriptive (and patently so) for the poem, but its full significance is not conveyed on the surface. Although at first sight the cloak, like the whole episode on Lemnos, looks straightforward and without much emotional import for the rest of the poem, the sequence of embroidered scenes turns out on closer analysis to have been modelled on the Catalogue of Women whom Homer's Odysseus met in the Underworld (*Odyssey* 11.225–380); when the allusion is recognized by the reader the incidents referred to on the cloak seem more ominous than heroic, for they all concern miserable relationships between men and women in which suspicion and betrayal play a dominant part. Finally, when we realize that the last woman given prominent mention in Homer's Catalogue is Ariadne, Hypsipyle's grandmother, a shadow is cast on Jason's fine cloak; Minos' daughter is not mentioned explicitly by Apollonius, but that is because she is more effectively introduced at this stage in the Argonautic expedition as a premonition. The whole episode of Jason's encounter with Hypsipyle is coloured by this preliminary allusion to the myth of Theseus and Ariadne, and although Jason's treacherous side will not become fully explicit until Books 3 and 4 when he encounters Medea, the way in which the Lemnian episode is presented in Book 1 has prepared the reader to see Jason's behaviour as following a certain pattern; this time, with Medea, the consequences will be played out to the full.

It is characteristic of Apollonius that he establishes Jason's qualities early in the poem by the indirect means of allusion to Homer; the use of suggestion rather than direct comment gives the reader a certain sense of objective detachment, and the significance of human behaviour seems thereby to be attributable as much to the events themselves as to the individuals. When Jason goes to meet Hypsipyle Apollonius implies, by having his very cloak carry such portentous signs, that it is not just Jason's attitudes or actions, but what he represents that will be so damaging to the Lemnian queen. Outwardly Jason and Hypsipyle seem to be straightforward in their dealings with one another, for they meet, negotiate (she offering him the throne, he refusing), have an affair and part without, apparently, any emotional claims or recriminations (other than tears from Hypsipyle when Jason leaves); but the lack of overt comment or a clearly stated moral framework merely makes the encounter more troubling for Apollonius' readers. Hypsipyle deceives Jason by concealing how the Lemnian women had murdered their husbands, and Jason himself, though reminiscent (as Apollonius makes plain from allusion to Homer) of Odysseus overcoming the threat of the sorceress Circe, is in fact no romantic folk-hero but a man invested with mythic symbols of treachery.

The encounter between Jason and Medea in Book 3 is quite explicitly of the same pattern as that between Jason and Hypsipyle; structural and thematic correspondences and verbal reminiscences establish the comparison clearly. But in particular any possibility that the encounter with Medea might take on an innocent romanticism is forestalled by the sinister suggestiveness of the Lemnian episode. In Book 3 the narrative now rings with repeated warnings, such as the comparison of Jason to the destructive Dog Star (3.956–61; see above, p. 593), and it is no surprise when, in Book 4, as the retreating Argonauts decide to leave Medea behind in Illyria at the Brygean islands of Artemis (4.338–49), we hear no demur from Jason, despite his public announcement earlier, in the excitement of gaining the Fleece, that he would take Medea home and marry her (4.194–7). His same self-interested compliance leads him into agreeing with Medea's suggestion that they murder her brother. Throughout his dealings with Medea, then, Jason behaves true to form.

At the beginning of Book 3 the morality of the expedition seems, along with the course of events, to have been lifted to a higher plane; for the first time in the poem we witness an epic-style 'Council of the Gods' as Hera and Athena intercede with Aphrodite to have Medea fall in love with Jason. Even though the three goddesses resemble middle-class Alexandrian housewives, performing their toilet and commiserating on the difficulty of bringing up children, the Argonautic expedition is at last, it seems, to be given a wider, more cosmic, significance. But this is so only on the surface; once again Apollonius refers to Homer in this episode, and once the references are grasped our expectations that some kind of higher moral purpose will be affirmed (even if in a fairly orthodox way) turn out to be illusory. First, as Athena and Hera approach the palace of Aphrodite her absent husband Hephaestus is referred to in terms which recall Demodocus' song in *Odyssey* 8 about Aphrodite's adultery with Ares, then her toilet is described with an allusion to the description of Hera preparing to deceive Zeus in *Iliad* 14; like Jason, Aphrodite and Hera have shady pasts, and Apollonius reminds us that these are divinities who are as prepared to use deception to promote their self-interests as any mortals. The divine conference culminates in Eros' flight down to Colchis and his shooting of the arrow at Medea (3.275–98); the description recalls Homer's account in *Iliad* 4.73ff. of how the Trojan archer Pandarus, encouraged by Athena, treacherously broke the truce between Greeks and Trojans by shooting at Menelaus.

The divine world, then, offers no better or more attractive moral code than the human; Olympus too is populated by individuals who pursue their separate ambitions and are all too ready to deceive and betray in order to realize them. The failings and limited capacities which have been constantly suggested in Books 1 and 2 as characteristic of the Argonauts are the only resources available: there is no grander scheme of things, and if Jason and his companions are unable to transcend their frail condition, then, despite isolated actions of notable grandeur, there are no true heroes or heroics. Homer's Achilles is testimony to that suprahuman strength ('force', as Simone Weil termed it) which accomplishes through an extraordinary act of integration; Apollonius, without sentimentality or cynicism, has Jason and his companions remain essentially isolated (one might even say 'alienated'), from one another and their environment – effort no longer has the power to transform, and weakness is as influential as strength.

The *Argonautica* is, indeed, very human in its orientation: mood or atmosphere, feelings and states of mind are Apollonius' constant concern. In some respects the *Argonautica* is more rationalistic than archaic epic in so far as it is less theological (in the *Naupactia*, for example, the golden fleece was kept in Aeetes' palace and after Jason had successfully tamed the bronze bulls Aphrodite sent everyone to sleep so that the Argonauts and Medea could escape), but there is constant reference also to the mysterious processes of magic and the darker aspects of human consciousness. Again and again the *Argonautica* touches on isolation or even alienation, from the inappropriateness of Heracles for the expedition in Book 1 to the eerie wanderings of the Argonauts in Book 4 through the misty Libyan wastes where they even lie down separately in the sand and wait to die (4.1228–307). In Book 4 too are images such as the monstrous horse from the sea (4.1364–79), the garden of Atlas, recently violated by Heracles (4.1396–460), the youth standing on the shore of Lake Triton who hands the Argonauts a clod of earth (4.1537–603). The mood of the poem, which some critics have described as melancholy, particularly distinguishes it from other works in the tradition. Characteristic occasions are when the spirit of the dead hero Sthenelus stands on his funeral barrow wistfully watching the Argonauts sail past (2.911–29), or when the Hesperidean nymphs in the garden of Atlas turn to dust at the approach of the Argonauts (4.1406–9).

It is worth stressing that Apollonius' sensitivity to atmosphere marks some of the most successful parts of the *Argonautica*. The poem's archaizing narrative can sometimes seem rather torpid, but Apollonius often transforms it into poetry of renewed power by his ability to present with extraordinary lyrical intensity what may be called 'the static moment', when a mood or atmosphere is exactly captured in complete suspension within the progression of the narrative. One of the finest examples is on the occasion of the *Argo*'s departure from Thessaly as dawn rises and the wind ruffles the sea:

> Now they were drawing in the cables
> and they poured wine upon the sea, but Jason
> weeping kept his eyes from his fatherland.
> And just as youths dance for Phoebus in Pytho
> or perhaps Ortygia or by Ismenus' waters
> and around the altar together to the lyre
> they harmoniously beat the ground with their swift feet –
> so they to Orpheus' lyre struck with their oars
> the sea's furious water, and the surge swept over.
> On either side the dark brine oozed with foam
> fiercely roaring at the strength of the mighty men.
> And as the ship went their arms gleamed in the sunlight
> like a flame, and ever their track was long and white,
> like a path distinct across a grassy plain.
> From the heaven all the gods gazed down that day
> at the ship and its crew of heroes, the best of men
> that were sailing the sea; and upon the topmost peaks
> the nymphs of Pelion marvelled as they watched
> the work of Itonian Athena and the men themselves
> brandishing the oars in their hands.
> Then from the mountain-top down to the sea
> came Chiron, Phillyra's son, and at the sea's grey edge
> dipped his feet, waving and urging them on,

and prayed for them to make sound journey home.
There too was his wife carrying Achilles on her arm,
displaying the son to his dear father Peleus. (1.533–58)

Modern readers still find Apollonius' epic rather puzzling, and most critics, disconcerted by the poem's apparent lack of heroic excitement, in both theme and narrative, and by its seemingly pedestrian conservative style, judge that only Book 3 redeems a poem that as a whole is a mediocre failure. But modern scholarship is just beginning to discover that the *Argonautica* is a deceptively intricate work, and that beneath the rather bland surface are complex allusions and symbols which make the *Argonautica* a very different poem from what it seems to be. Like some other ancient poets earlier this century Apollonius still has to come into his own. About the reception of the *Argonautica* amongst Apollonius' contemporaries we have little direct evidence, though Callimachus seems to have been appreciative at least in some of his works (see above, p. 587); however, papyrus fragments suggest that the *Argonautica* was increasingly widely read over the centuries, and the poem enjoyed extensive attention from commentators (the surviving scholia are some of the fullest which we possess for any ancient author). Roman writers were much influenced by the *Argonautica*, and the poem was translated into Latin as early as the first century B.C. by Varro of Atax and used heavily by Valerius Flaccus in his epic *Argonautica* in the first century A.D. But the most important testimony to Apollonius' achievement is Virgil's *Aeneid*. Virgil was fascinated by Apollonius, and the *Argonautica* was second only to Homer as a formative influence on his great work. It is not just that the *Argonautica* was historically important for the *Aeneid*: for Virgil Apollonius' mode of writing represented a kind of enabling power which created the modern, symbolic epic out of the archaic. From Hypsipyle and Medea, as well as from Calypso, Circe and Nausicaa, comes Dido, and from the Golden Fleece, as well as from Odysseus' Return, comes Rome; from Apollonius' preoccupation with deception as a motive and isolation as a condition, as well as from Homer's Achilles, comes the *Aeneid*'s insoluble conflict between society and the individual's happiness.

6. MINOR FIGURES

Apollonius' *Argonautica* is the only narrative epic to have survived intact from the Hellenistic period, and the only other major examples of epic hexameter writing are poems in the didactic tradition by Aratus and Nicander. The biographies of both authors are uncertain, but about Aratus we can make some reasonable inferences. He seems to have been a near contemporary of Callimachus, probably (at any rate according to most of our sources) rather older; he came from Soli in Cilicia and went, apparently after a period in Athens, to live and work in Pella, Macedonia, at the court of Antigonus Gonatas (ruled 276–240/239) who was a patron of the arts and himself a man of letters and philosopher. Amongst other writers at the court were the epic poet Antagoras of Rhodes, the dramatist and scholar Alexander Aetolus (above, pp. 547 f.), and the philosophers Timon of Phlius (below, p. 637) and Menedemus of Eretria.

Aratus' work seems to have included scholarly work on the *Odyssey*, but essentially he was a poet. He wrote hymns, epigrams, elegiacs, funeral dirges (all of which may have been collected under the miscellaneous heading *Catalepton*, a title used later for the collection of miscellaneous poems ascribed to Virgil), but much of his output was on scientific themes, such as the hexametrical medical poem *Iatrica*, the *Canon* (*Table*) which dealt with the harmony of the spheres, or the *Astrica* (*On stars*) which had at least five books. The most famous of his works, and the only one still extant, was the *Phaenomena*, which deals with astronomy (ll. 1–732) and meteorology (ll. 733–1154). Appropriately one of Aratus' teachers is said to have been Menecrates of Ephesus who, like Hesiod, wrote a hexameter *Works* on agricultural topics; but the most important literary context in which the *Phaenomena* has to be read is the whole tradition of didactic poetry which goes back to Hesiod. In some respects Aratus' poem, as a technical work, is less akin to the 'wisdom' poetry of Hesiod than to the later 'scientific' works of writers such as Xenophanes, Parmenides or Empedocles (see pp. 245 ff.), but there is no doubt that Aratus himself and his contemporaries saw the *Phaenomena* as a 'Hesiodic' poem (though later critics seem to have debated whether Aratus wrote more in the style of Homer or Hesiod). Others too seem to have written poetical astronomy before Aratus: Cleostratus of Tenedos, cited in ancient sources as author of an *Astrologia*, and one Sminthes, author of a *Phaenomena*, probably wrote before the Hellenistic period, and Alexander Aetolus is also said to have written a *Phaenomena* (fr. 20 Powell).

The ancient taste for poetical works such as the *Phaenomena* is difficult for modern readers to appreciate, but the success of Aratus' poem is beyond question: one of the ancient *Lives* (III) comments that although numerous poets after Aratus wrote *Phaenomena* they were (in comparison) worthless. Our sources record some twenty names of writers who subsequently wrote commentaries on Aratus or astronomical poems; a large body of commentary and interpretation in both Greek and Latin still survives, and, quite apart from the manifest influence of Aratus on Lucretius and Virgil, we possess Latin versions and adaptations by Cicero (fragmentary), Germanicus and Avienius. Although Aratus' subject was astronomy and not astrology, we do have to remember that he was appealing to something that has captivated popular imagination in all ages, the charting of the night-sky with systematic description. Aratus' poem is an elegantly written and clear treatise – it can be used as a hand-book or guide and is not to be classified with the other type of Hellenistic didactic poetry, such as Nicander's poems, whose *raison d'être* consists in literary ornamentation of the least plausible topics. To a large extent Nicander's success, in as much as that is an appropriate term, is in proportion to the grotesqueness of his material, and he stands directly in the tradition of art as perversity; Aratus, on the other hand, who relied on the specialist prose treatise of the famous fourth-century mathematician and astronomer Eudoxus of Cnidus (also titled *Phaenomena*), was making his model more available, not more obscure, by his adaptation. Some later commentators, beginning with Hipparchus in the second century B.C., argued that Aratus had done nothing but versify Eudoxus, but the blunt fact is that Aratus continued to be read and still survives whereas Eudoxus has long since disappeared. In any case Aratus' work should be considered as part of the same process of popularization as produced the calendar of Saïs, discovered in 1902 at al-Hiba in Egypt, which was compiled with an astronomical introduction around 300 B.C. by someone concerned to propagate Eudoxian principles (*Hibeh Papyri* no. 27). The last section of the poem, the *Weather signs*, seems clearly indebted to a meteorological work, but its exact relationship to the treatise *On signs* which goes under Theophrastus' name is very uncertain; it is quite possible that both works depend on a common source, now lost.

The ancient *Lives* report that Aratus studied Stoic philosophy and associate him closely with the Stoic Dionysius of Heraclea (who late in life changed to Hedonism and was nick-named 'The Turncoat'); his patron Antigonus Gonatas had strong Stoic sympathies. The *Phaenomena* is not a thoroughgoing Stoic work by any means (although Aratus' sympathies may have been a factor in the poem's popularity), but its introduction consists in a hymn to the Zeus of the Stoics, which clearly echoes the principles enunciated in the famous Hymn to Zeus of the philosopher Cleanthes (Powell 227–9, see below, p. 632):

> From Zeus let us begin whom we mortals never
> leave unmentioned; full of Zeus are all the ways,
> and all concourse of men, and full is the sea
> and the harbours. Everywhere we all need Zeus.
> For we are also his offspring. Kindly to men
> he gives fair signs, and rouses the people to work
> prompting their living, and shows when the soil is best
> for the ox and the mattock, and shows when the season is right
> to break the earth open round plants, and to sow all the seeds.
> For he himself set the heavenly bodies in the sky,
> distinguishing constellations; and conceived for the year
> the stars which would give the most constant signs
> of the seasons for men, so that all would be sure to grow. (*Phaen.* 1–13)

What follows is a mixture of nomenclature, technical observation and information about the constellations with comments on weather or seasons and, occasionally, mythology. The writing is clear and, within limitations, elegant. Typical is the section on the Charioteer:

> But if you should wish to look at the Charioteer
> and his stars, and report has come to you of the Goat
> herself or the Kids which on the darkening sea
> often watch men as they are tossed and scattered,
> you may find the whole of him lying near to the left
> of Gemini, huge, and the top of the Great Bear's head
> turns opposite; and set upon his left shoulder
> is the sacred goat, which is said to have offered its breast
> to Zeus, and his priests call it Olenian.
> The Goat is large and bright, and by the wrist
> of the Charioteer the Kids shine faint. (*Phaen.* 156–66)

But the *Phaenomena* is not essentially a technical work; although for its scientific material it looks to Eudoxus, its poetic stance is, in characteristic Hellenistic fashion, archaizing and Aratus' manner is that of Hesiod. This emerges most clearly in some of the digressions, and notably in that on the constellation Virgo (ll. 96–136). After remarking that some accounts identify Virgo with Justice (cf. Hesiod, *Works and days* 256–7), Aratus alludes, in modified form, to the Hesiodic myth of the five ages (*Works and days* 109–201) describing how in the Golden Age (which, in markedly Hellenistic fashion, was a period of work and civilization, unlike Hesiod's) Justice lived on earth with men until the coming of the new generation:

> She was there so long as earth nourished the golden race.
> But with the silver race she mixed only little and not
> quite readily, for the ways of the people of old
> she missed. Even so still in that silver age she was there;
> she would come towards evening down from the echoing hills
> by herself, and conversed with none with soothing words.
> But when she had gathered crowds to fill the great hills,
> then she would threaten, assailing their wicked ways,
> to come no more, or appear when they called.
> 'See what an inferior race your fathers left
> from the golden age, and you shall produce worse.
> Yes, and men shall have wars, I think, they shall have
> the strangeness of murder, and be pressed by miserable grief.'
> So saying she made for the mountains, and so she left
> the people all gazing after her still. (*Phaen.* 114–28)

In spite of the Hesiodic material and manner of this passage (with clear allusions to the iron age of *Works and days* 174–201), there is no mistaking the tone as that of a Hellenistic poet. Hesiod expresses the indignation of a moralist, whereas Aratus replaces social commentary with a detached romanticism in which it is the psychology of atmosphere that is central (Justice comes 'towards *evening* down from the *echoing* hills'); the wistfulness of the last lines is reminiscent of Apollonius' description of the departure of the *Argo* (above, pp. 597f.).

Aratus' *Phaenomena* was greatly admired by contemporary writers. Leonidas of Tarentum wrote an epigram (*Anth. Pal.* 9.25) praising the author for his hard work and fine conception (*leptos*, a current Callimachean term: see above, p. 561), one of the Ptolemies, possibly Philadelphus, commented in verse that of astronomy poets 'Aratus holds the sceptre of fine (*leptos*) expression' (*Life of Aratus* 1), and to Callimachus the work was an important achievement of style too: in *Ep.* 29 he remarks that 'Hesiod's is the song and his the manner', and he greets the poem as 'fine (*leptos*) writing, a mark of Aratus' sleepless nights'. We do not know if Aratus ever visited Alexandria (though the above comments of approval by writers resident in Egypt and the mention of an Aratus in Theocritus, *Idylls* 6 and 7 suggest that he did), but he was certainly conversant with the discussion of literary principles going on there. Not only does Callimachus speak of Aratus in clear programmatic terms, but Aratus himself embedded in his work an explicit endorsement of the Callimachean mode: in the meteorological section of his poem, at ll. 783–7 when describing observation of the moon as a weather determinant, Aratus not only uses the key terms of Callimachean criticism *leptos* and *pachus* (above, p. 561) but even spells out the acrostic *lepte* with the initial letters of each line. Use of the acrostic was to become a favourite technical trick amongst later writers, but this instance, the earliest extant example,[1] is worth more to the modern reader than an incidental display of virtuosity, for it shows that Aratus almost certainly saw himself, at least in his *Phaenomena*, as aligned with the *avant-garde* of Alexandrian poetry. Didactic poetry played as important a part, for Aratus at any rate, as narrative epic or elegy in the literary debate of this period.

We possess two other sizeable didactic poems in epic hexameters, the *Theriaca* and *Alexipharmaca* by Nicander of Colophon. The ancient sources are contradictory about the dates of this poet and there appear to have been three different traditions, one placing Nicander as a contemporary of Aratus in the first half of the third century, one assigning him to the early decades of the second century, and the third making him contemporary with Attalus III Philometor of Pergamum (138–133 B.C.). We have to recognize that in the present state of our evidence Nicander cannot be dated with any security, and although some parts of his poems seem to be linked to passages from the third-century writer of didactic poetry Numenius of Heracleia and to Euphorion (see below, pp. 607 ff.) we have no means of judging who is alluding to whom (only at *Ther.* 237 do the scholia specify that Nicander was adapting Numenius). Artistically Nicander represents one of the less attractive aspects of Hellenistic poetry. The *Theriaca* certainly and the *Alexipharmaca* probably were derived

---

[1] First pointed out by Jacques (1960).

from prose treatises by an early third-century writer Apollodorus (about whom we know very little), and according to the Suda (s.v. 'Nicandros') Nicander also wrote a hexameter versification of the pseudo-Hippocratic *Prognostica*; studied obscurantism does seem to have been more important to him than imaginative writing. At the end of the *Theriaca* he describes himself as 'Homeric Nicander, nurtured by Claros' snowy town' (ll. 957–8); even Nicander can have thought of himself as 'Homeric' only in so far as his language is very archaic and elaborate, full of lexical rarities from the Homeric epics (a factor which led later scholars such as Theon of Smyrna and Plutarch to write grammatical and stylistic commentaries on him). The *Theriaca* deals with snakes, spiders, scorpions and other creatures which are poisonous and describes the supposed antidotes (mostly herbal) against their bites and stings; almost all of the account is unrelievedly technical and scientific (or at least pseudo-scientific) in manner, but mixed in with the directly medicinal advice are cures of an openly superstitious nature (as in ll. 98–114 which describe a general prophylactic compounded from marrow of a freshly killed stag, rose-oil, pure oil, wax and the flesh of two snakes caught coupling at a crossroads), and when we find a number of cases where Nicander is cavalier about nomenclature (for example prescribing νῆρις 'savin' at l. 531, instead of νήριον 'oleander') it is difficult not to conclude that the author was more interested in metrical virtuosity than the scientific exactitude appropriate to his subject. At ll. 343–58 a brief narrative interlude which recounts in elaborate language the fable how the ass gave away the gift of youth to the snake contains the signature acrostic Nikandros (ll. 345–53). The *Alexipharmaca*, a shorter poem, itemizes different kinds of poisons, their physical effects and their antidotes, and although the catalogue of material is slightly less elaborate than that of the *Theriaca* the work is poetically almost as unrelieved.

The survival of the *Alexipharmaca* and *Theriaca* is doubtless owed to their sheer extraordinariness and literary perversity; the modern reader could wish that others of Nicander's works had survived in their place. Athenaeus preserves nearly one hundred and fifty lines from the hexameter work *Georgica*, a poem in two books which according to Cicero was held by the *docti* to be of some literary merit even if lacking in expert knowledge of the subject (*De orat.* 1.69) and which Quintilian suggests may have had some influence on Virgil (*Inst.* 10.1.56); the extant fragments are somewhat dry (and not easily intelligible in a number of places) and deal with vegetables, flowers, trees, kitchen recipes and the breeding of doves. The *Metamorphoses*, a hexameter work in at least four books, would be particularly interesting to possess in view of Ovid's great poem later on the same theme. For knowledge of Nicander we are indebted almost entirely to the collected prose summaries of metamorphoses by Antoninus Liberalis, who names Nicander as having dealt with twenty-two of the stories in the collection; the few verse lines extant (frs. 50, 59, 62) suggest that the writing may have been as unremittingly elaborate as in the didactic poems. Other hexameter poems seem to have included a *Europia* (at least five books), *Oetaica* (at least two books), *Sicelia* (at least eight books), *Thebaica* (at least three books); the *Cynegetica* (on hunting) and the *Ophiaca* (on snake legends) were probably in elegiacs. Works titled *Aetolica*, *Collection of cures*, *Colophoniaca*, *Melissourgica* (on apiculture), *On poets from Colophon* may have been in prose or verse. Amongst later Greek writers Oppian was much influenced by Nicander in his didactic poems (see below, pp. 653f.), and Nonnus seems to have drawn on Nicander stylistically.

The didactic tradition was rich in the Hellenistic period, but little of it remains apart from Aratus and Nicander. A writer who seems to have played an important part in its development, as in so many other areas too, was Eratosthenes of Cyrene, the great mathematician and geographer. We have no secure dates for Eratosthenes, but tradition connected him with Callimachus and the Stoics and Platonists in Athens, and placed his period of prime activity in the second half of the third century B.C. in Alexandria, where he succeeded Apollonius as Librarian and royal tutor. Much of Eratosthenes' work was in the field of science (Archimedes dedicated his book on *Method* to Eratosthenes), but his intellectual range was immense and he called himself φιλόλογος (rather than γραμματικός) in order to stress the multiplicity of his interests. Later scholars nicknamed him 'Beta' ('Second-rate') and 'Pentathlete'. Eratosthenes' scholarly and scientific works included *On Old Comedy* in twelve or more books, *Chronographiae (Annals)* which marked the first systematic exposition of historical chronology, *On the measurement of the earth* which included calculations of the earth's perimeter and the distances between places, *Geographica* in three books which covered history, mathematical geography, cartography and ethnography, philosophical works on cosmology, mathematics, harmonics, and *Catasterismoi* on the constellations and mythology associated with them. Strabo 1.2.3 cites Eratosthenes' view (in order to disagree with it) that 'every poet aims at entertainment, not instruction', but although we possess only a few fragments of his poetry it seems that the 'entertainment' of his own writing may have been at a fairly intellectual level. In his hexameter poem *Hermes* (which a recent papyrus discovery has shown to have been about 1,600 lines long (*P.Oxy.* 3000)) the god inspects the universe from the highest heavenly sphere and observes that the planets possess the same harmony as that of the lyre which he has just invented, and that the earth, at the centre of the universe, is divided into five zones in accordance with the views expounded in Eratosthenes' geographical treatises. Eratosthenes was strongly influenced by Platonic philosophy, and especially the *Timaeus* (the Suda calls him 'a second or neo-Plato'), and the *Hermes* was clearly strongly Platonist in its outlook.

Eratosthenes' other major poetic work was the elegiac *Erigone* which 'Longinus', *Subl.* 33.5 (contrasting it with the exuberant iambic poetry of Archilochus), described as 'a thoroughly faultless poem'. It seems to have been written in the tradition of Callimachus' *Hecale* (above, pp. 563f.) and the Heracles–Molorchus episode of the *Aetia* (above, p. 557), describing how Dionysus once visited the countryman Icarius and gave him a vine in return for his hospitality; when Icarius' neighbours became drunk on the wine produced they killed Icarius, leaving the body to be found in a ditch by his daughter Erigone guided by the barking of his dog. When Erigone, out of grief, hanged herself on a tree and the dog Maira also died, Zeus translated all three to the stars (as Boötes, Virgo and Sirius), and the incident led to the institution of the Attic swing festival (the Aiora). Almost nothing remains of this work, but the clear presence of Callimachean features (both of theme and of emphasis in the presentation of rustic details) accords with the spare but lucid style of the one substantial fragment of the *Hermes* extant (fr. 16), and the work seems to have had some influence later on Virgil and Nonnus; once again we note the interest in aetiology and astronomy.

Eratosthenes' work was very important for the course of later didactic poetry. Apollodorus of Athens, a major scholar of the second century B.C. who wrote treatises on Homeric geography and theology as well as comedy, was the author of a long influential poem in comic iambic trimeters, no longer extant, called *Chronica* (*Chronicle*) in four books, dedicated to Attalus II of Pergamum and covering events from the fall of Troy (then supposed as 1184/3) until ten or twenty years before the end of the second century. Much of the poem seems to have been devoted to literary history. The *Chronica* both replaced Eratosthenes' great *Chronographiae* and stimulated other similar compositions. The unknown author of a geographical guide, *Periegesis*, which survives and can be dated to around 100 B.C. and was once erroneously attributed to Scymnus of Chios, acknowledges in his elaborate prologue that Apollodorus had been his inspiration, but whereas Apollodorus enjoyed a certain reputation in antiquity and seems, from the surviving fragments, to have had some facility for putting proper names into verse, pseudo-Scymnus' 980 lines are rather clumsy and unrelieved. The tradition was continued by Dionysius son of Calliphon (of unknown date) whose short iambic *Description of Greece* survives, and in the later hexameter work at the time of Hadrian of Dionysius the Periegete (see below, p. 606). In the field of astronomy we possess two poems in undistinguished iambic trimeters on the constellations (169 lines) and the planets (13 lines) which, ascribed by the MSS to Empedocles, are by an unknown hand and undatable.[1] Alexander of Ephesus, called Lychnus, continued both the geographical and astronomical didactic traditions in the first century; his hexameter

[1] Texts in Maass (1898) 154–70.

astronomy poem, of which a surviving fragment analyses the harmony of the spheres after the model of Eratosthenes, was probably an important influence on Varro, and his geographical work, which covered Asia, Europe and Africa, seems also to have been used by Dionysius the Periegete. His work was known to his contemporary Cicero who described him as 'a tasteless versifier, and yet an ignoramus, though of some use' (*Ad Atticum* 2.20.6).

In terms of literary history Apollodorus of Athens and the other later didactic writers stand in a tradition which goes directly back to Eratosthenes, but two other scholars have to be mentioned who were equally important as intellectual predecessors even though their strictly literary output was insignificant. Aristophanes of Byzantium was, according to the ancient biographical tradition, a pupil of Callimachus, Zenodotus and Eratosthenes; he succeeded the latter as Librarian at Alexandria in the early years of the second century when he was sixty-two (and died ten years later) and was the most prodigious scholar for many generations. His editorial work on the texts of the major authors covered Homer, Hesiod, lyric poetry, the tragedians, Aristophanes the comic dramatist and possibly Menander, and was of permanent influence on the transmission of the texts of all these poets; he was the first to use accentuation (though not punctuation) and to divide lyric texts into the short metrical cola of which stanzas are constituted (instead of leaving them written out as prose). Particularly important was the huge lexicographical work full of learned discussion, *Lexeis*, which he compiled covering all prose and verse authors. Long after his death scholars who engaged in similar editorial work were known as 'Aristophaneans'. Aristophanes' pupil Aristarchus was no less prolific a scholar, and his name became a byword for the authoritative critic (Cicero, *Ad Atticum* 1.14.3, Horace, *A.P.* 450). He too became Librarian at Alexandria succeeding Apollonius the Eidographer who came after Aristophanes, though in the troubled reign of Ptolemy VIII he had to flee to Cyprus when in 145 B.C. Ptolemy expelled many of the intellectuals whom his nephew, Ptolemy VII, had patronized. Aristarchus' major work was on Homer, and later commentators have preserved substantial excerpts from his notes, but he also wrote on other epic poets, the lyricists, and the dramatists, and he was the first Alexandrian scholar to work on a prose author, Herodotus. Aristarchus was renowned as one of the most magisterial interpretative critics, and Panaetius of Rhodes even refers to him as 'a seer' (Athenaeus 14.634c), but although he was patently an interpreter of exceptional sensitivity to the process of artistic creativity he wrote no poetry himself, saying 'I do not write poetry because I cannot do it in the way I want to and I do not want to in the way that I can' (*Rhetorica ad Herennium* 4.28.39).

Of the rest of Hellenistic epic poetry too little survives for us to be able to reconstruct the course of literary history with any plausibility. We have the names of many authors and many titles, and from the latter it is clear that mythological epic continued to be written alongside historical epic, although dates can be assigned to few authors with any confidence. Thus many *Argonautica* were written, and several *Thebaids* and many Heracles poems; often these works were long – Rhianus' *Heracleia* may have comprised fourteen books, Theodorus' *Heracleia* at least twenty-one, and the *Thebaid* of one Menelaus of Aegae eleven. These are merely cases we happen to know, and although the historical epics have disappeared along with the rulers or states which they celebrated, where history has had reason to record in more detail the fortunes of particular individuals and dynasties we hear also of their epic historians. For Rome's allies the Attalids we know of the poets Leschides and Musaeus of Ephesus, for their enemies the Seleucids Simonides of Magnesia, for the notorious Cleopatra Theodorus; and the poet Archias whom Cicero defended in court at Rome in 62 B.C. celebrated the Cimbrian and the Mithridatic wars, while one Boethus of Tarsus wrote about the battle of Philippi. Historical epic, we can reasonably assume, flourished throughout the Hellenistic period.

Only two of these epic poets are much more than names for us. The first, Rhianus of Crete, who apparently flourished in the last half of the third century B.C., was scholar as well as poet, and the Homeric scholia cite more than forty of his readings in the *Iliad* and *Odyssey*. In the writing of epic he was prolific: in addition to the mythological work *Heracleia* he wrote many historical and ethnographic poems, such as the *Achaica*, the *Eliaca*, the *Thessaliaca* (at least sixteen books), and the *Messeniaca* whose contents are known since it was used as a source by Pausanias in his guidebook (4.6.1–3, 15.2). The anthologist Stobaeus quotes twenty-one hexameters from an unknown poem by Rhianus which reflect on the folly of human conduct in prosperity and adversity alike (*Flor.* 4.34); the lines are lucid but rather bland and unexcitingly conventional. Rhianus, along with Parthenius and Euphorion, was a favourite author of the Roman emperor Tiberius (Suetonius, *Tib.* 70.2).

Contemporary with Rhianus was the prolific and strange writer Euphorion of Chalcis who, although the author of books such as *On the Isthmian games* and *On lyric poets*, was primarily an epic poet. Euphorion seems to have enjoyed royal patronage, first from Alexander of Euboea and later from Antiochus the Great who appointed him Librarian at Antioch, but he was never, so far as we know, in Alexandria or extensively involved in the world of professional scholarship. According to one source he became a citizen of Athens (Helladius in Photius 279), and thus may have spent some time there. We possess twenty-two titles of poems by Euphorion, though some of them for which our evidence is very tenuous may well be sub-titles of parts of works. In spite of the frequency with which Euphorion is referred to or cited in the ancient sources we are in fact almost completely ignorant of the contents of most of his poems, and a sum total of only about one hundred and fifty complete lines actually survives, mostly as isolated short passages or even single lines at a time. The *Chiliades* (*Thousands*), one of the three titles cited by the Suda for Euphorion, was apparently a work in five books on the subject of the punishment to be suffered by those who have deprived the poet of his living; the details of the poem's contents are unknown, but it is worth noting that one of the few substantial fragments extant (fr. 11 Van Groningen) is a series of curses, illustrated by mythological precedents, against an anonymous person, and Stephanus of Byzantium (79.9) mentions a poem titled *Curses* or *The cup-stealer*. Mythological subjects predominate; we hear of a *Hyacinth* and a *Philoctetes*, the *Dionysus* seems to have dealt with the triumphal entry of the god into Greece, and the mysterious *Thrax* at least included, to judge from the extant remains, treatment of a wide range of mythological topics such as Harpalyce's serving of a meal to Clymenus consisting of their own son, the flight of Apriate from her suitor Trambelus who was killed by Achilles, and the flight of the seer Amphiaraus from Thebes. One extant fragment (24c Van Groningen) is a prayer, in a manner reminiscent of Hesiod in the *Works and days*, for the restoration of Justice, to curb the impious, children neglectful of their parents, and the inhospitable.

Some ancient authors found Euphorion difficult to read. One Cratus, in a ribald epigram exploiting gossip about Euphorion's love-life, criticized his literary taste and remarked that he wrote poetry full of *glosses* (rare, often archaic words) and was 'Homeric' (*Anth.Pal.* 11.218); Lucian (*De historia conscr.* 57) asks sarcastically how many words it would have taken to get the water to Tantalus' lips for Parthenius, Euphorion or Callimachus, and Clement of Alexandria (*Strom.* 5.8.51) similarly says that Euphorion, Callimachus' *Aetia* and Lycophron's *Alexandra* comprised a whole exercise-ground for scholarly exegesis. Cicero, writing on oracles, commented that Euphorion was excessively obscure (*De div.* 2.64.132), and eulogized Ennius 'despite the fact that he is disdained by those who sing the praise of Euphorion' ('*ab his cantoribus Euphorionis*': *Tusc.* 3.19.45). Most modern critics echo these judgements: he has been described as a 'chilly virtuoso'[1] and his work has been said to display 'the degeneration of style developed in the period'.[2] But although Euphorion's diction does show an interest in oddities, rarities and periphrases for proper names, and his subject matter often touches on the recherché or curious, common sense should prevent us from attempting a definitive judgement of works which are no longer extant. Although ancient criticism may sound consistent on Euphorion, its form suggests partiality: the association, in Lucian and Clement, with Callimachus, whose *Aetia* was the masterpiece of Hellenistic

---

[1] Pfeiffer, 150.
[2] Lesky, 756.

poetry, suggests only that for some tastes Euphorion was too 'difficult', and Cicero's remark about the *cantores Euphorionis* suggests that in first-century Rome his poetry was controversial. Controversy always has two sides, and several ancient sources report that the renowned love poet Cornelius Gallus was, like Tiberius later, a devotee of Euphorion, whom he 'rendered' into Latin (Probus, Philargyrius II and Servius on Virgil, *Ecl.* 10, Diomedes in *GLK* 1.484.21). Euphorion seems, therefore, to have been an idiosyncratic writer who, perhaps rather in the style of Callimachus, was uncompromising as well as innovative. The few extant fragments of any length confirm that he used a language rich in rare words and terms, but give the impression that he had an exceptional command of his medium and a taut and clear style, and that he experimented vigorously with traditional epic form. Typical is the passage which describes Heracles bringing back the dog Cerberus from the underworld:

οἱ δ' ὄπιθεν λασίηι ὑπὸ γαστέρι πεπ[τηῶτες
οὐραῖοι λιχμῶντο περὶ πλεύρηισι δρά[κοντες,
ἐν καί οἱ βλεφάροις κυάνω ἠστράπτετον [ὄσσε
ἤ που θερμάστραις ἤ που Μελιγουνίδι τοῖαι
μαρμαρυγαί, αἵρηισιν ὅτε ῥήσσοιτο σίδηρος,
ἠέρ' ἀναθρώισκουσι, βοᾶι δ' εὐήλατος ἄκμων,
ἤ Αἴτνην ψολόεσσαν, ἐναύλιον Ἀστερόποιο.
ἵκετο μὴν Τίρυνθα παλιγκότωι Εὐρυσθῆι
ζωὸς ὑπὲξ Ἀίδαο δυώδεκα λοῖσθος ἀέθλων·
καί μιν ἐνὶ τριόδοισι πολυκρίθοιο Μιδείης
ταρβαλέαι σὺν παισὶν ἐθηήσαντο γυναῖκες.

And from behind, under his shaggy belly
the serpents in his tail licked around his ribs,
and in his eyes there blazed a deep dark blue;
surely in the forge or on Lipara
such are the flashes, when hammers break steel,
that spring to heaven – and the well-beaten anvil rings –
or to smoky Aetna, Asteropus'[1] haunt.
He came to Tiryns, to malignant Eurystheus,
alive from Hades, his twelve labours finished;
and at the cross-roads of barley-rich Mideia
women with their children gazed in fear. (fr. 57 Van Groningen, 5–15)

One of the forms which continued with some vigour beyond the third century was that begun by Theocritus, the pastoral. Only two names of later poets in this genre are known, Moschus and Bion, but although this is often assumed to mean that bucolic poetry never enjoyed any continuity as a form, the number of poems which were spuriously ascribed in antiquity to one of its three major

---

[1] The giant Cyclops, forger of Zeus's thunderbolts.

exponents suggests that pastoral was in fact always popular. Under the name of Theocritus are several which draw heavily on his work, such as *Idylls* 8 and 9 which both present Daphnis and Menalcas competing in country song, or *Id.* 27 in which Daphnis woos a shepherdess; *Id.* 20, the complaint of a jilted country lover, resembles Theocritus' Cyclops poems *Id.* 11 and *Id.* 3 (see above, pp. 571ff.). *Id.* 21 combines the topic of Theocritus *Id.* 10 (above p. 579), a conversation between two working men, with the emphasis on the conditions of ordinary poverty first treated as a central theme in hexameter poetry by Callimachus in the *Hecale* (above, pp. 563f.); the result, a discussion by two impoverished fishermen of their tenuous hold on a livelihood and the uselessness of dreaming, is an unusual example of social realism in ancient pastoral (though sympathy for the working poor, characteristic of Menander in the fourth century, is never far from the surface in Theocritus). Included in the ancient collections of bucolic poetry were hexameter poems on pastoral or sentimentally 'domestic' aspects of lives of the heroes, such as pseudo-Theocritus, *Id.* 25 'Heracles the Lion-Killer', pseudo-Moschus, 4 'Megara', a lament by Heracles' wretched wife, pseudo-Bion, 2 'The Wedding-song of Achilles and Deidameia'; these poems belong to the tradition established by Callimachus' *Hecale* and Theocritus' narrative Idylls (above, pp. 581ff.).

Moschus of Syracuse, who enjoyed the reputation of being 'second after Theocritus' (Suda s.v. 'Moschus'), was said to have been a pupil of Aristarchus (who according to the Suda had around forty pupils); Moschus will therefore have been active about one century after Theocritus. His most substantial extant work is the *Europa*, a poem in one hundred and sixty-six hexameters which describes the rape of Europa: Zeus, disguised as a bull, carries her over the sea to Crete. The work manages to include an account of a dream, an ecphrasis (the decorated basket carried by Europa as she picks flowers), and a narrative (Europa removed from her companions) in a pastoral setting resembling the account of Persephone's rape by Pluto in the *Homeric Hymn to Demeter*. The poem is in the tradition of the narrative Homeric hymns (it also recalls the hymn to Aphrodite), but it is essentially secular in style and straightforwardly concerned with representing a rather self-contained world of charm and sentiment as a neat, smoothly written set piece. Besides the *Europa* we have a few short excerpts, all cited in Stobaeus; written in the Doric pastoral style, they deal with love and the country as it affects human emotions; all, like the *Europa*, are pleasantly written, if slight, and their mannerism makes them seem particularly appropriate for anthologizing. Moschus was not without influence on later writers: Horace, *Odes* 3.27 imitates the *Europa*, as does Nonnus in the *Dionysiaca* (especially in 1.46–137, 322–55).

Bion of Smyrna, named by the Suda (s.v. 'Theocritus') as one of the three bucolic poets, probably wrote in the late second century B.C. He is cited often in Stobaeus (sixteen excerpts), and an anonymous poem transmitted in some MSS of Theocritus, the 'Funeral Lament for Adonis', can be ascribed to him with some certainty. In this poem, which is modelled on Thyrsis' lament for Daphnis in Theocritus *Id.* 1, we are firmly in the world of post-Theocritean pastoral. Adonis has been gored to death, and with true romantic identification of sexual longing and physical violence Bion describes Aphrodite passionately imploring Adonis to stay so that she may draw away his dying breath in a final kiss; meanwhile the blood from his thigh-wound smears his white breast and drips to his navel, and the Erotes and nature sing the ritual lament over the boy-lover. The prettiness, sentimentality, and overtones of sado-masochism, however much they may affect a note of moralizing worldliness, are quite foreign to the carefully balanced world of Theocritean pastoral (see above, pp. 573ff.). In the second century we see clearly for the first time that mood of detached un-reality and witty sentimentality which has come to be regarded as characteristic of much of European bucolic poetry. The rather unimaginative 'Funeral Lament for Bion', erroneously ascribed in some MSS to Theocritus or Moschus, claims that with the death of Bion poetry itself has died and that the whole bucolic world, from Strymonian swans to the mythical Galatea, joins in lament; the poem's most interesting aspect for modern readers is its extravagant identification of the poet with his pastoral world, confirming that romantic pastoral poetry had become securely established by the end of the second century B.C.

Bucolic poetry gained clear formal recognition shortly after the time of Bion. Artemidorus, who lived in the first century B.C., claimed in an epigram (*Anth. Pal.* 9.205) to have collected the Bucolic Muses who were previously scattered and it may have been through his edition that Greek pastoral was known to Virgil. Artemidorus' son Theon may have edited Theocritus, and Asclepiades of Myrlea, also in the first century, certainly wrote on him; thereafter continued interest in pastoral is evident not only from the activities of scholars, but also from prose writers such as Lucian and Longus and the later poets like Quintus and Nonnus who allude to earlier pastoral poetry.

The tradition of iambic poetry, maintained by Callimachus in a variegated set of thirteen poems (above, pp. 568 f.), was also represented by several other Hellenistic writers. Of these the author most accessible to modern readers (thanks largely to a papyrus acquired by the British Museum in 1892) is Herodas. Herodas' dates and provenance are unknown, but he can reasonably be assigned to some time in the third century B.C. and the name may suggest a Doric origin. His work is of interest primarily for its curiosity-value, in particular because it is the only representative of a form which is otherwise lost to us, rather than for any great intrinsic literary merit. The anthologist Stobaeus, who cites seven passages from Herodas, refers to his poems as 'Mimiambi' (mime-iambics). The 'mime', a form about which we know little directly, appears to have been a staged entertainment popular from at least the classical period onwards, with spoken dialogue generally in prose, consisting in scenes from 'everyday life'; the only author whom we know previously to have written mimes as specifically literary pieces was Sophron of Syracuse in the fifth century B.C., who wrote in Doric prose. Herodas' poems were written almost certainly for presentation by a single performer at recitations and for circulation in written form, like the *Idylls* of Theocritus. He used the metre and language of the early iambic poets, especially the sixth-century Hipponax (above, pp. 158ff.), and although the subject matter and tone may give the impression of realistic colloquial Greek, his writing is in fact elaborately stylized; the language of the Mimes is 'an imperfect imitation of that spoken in Asia Minor in the sixth century'.[1] Although the personal, jaunty, abrasive tone of the Mimes is characteristic of the iambic genre, the use of the form for dramatic dialogue, instead of monologue or narrative, was, so far as we know, without precedent. The explicitly archaizing stylization betrays Herodas' treatment of his subject matter for what it is: aesthetic mannerism, not 'realism'. The Mimes offer humorous situation sketches (the characterizations hardly go beyond rather extravagant stereotypes): a courtroom speech by a pimp prosecuting a sea-captain for assaulting one of his girls (2), a visit by two impoverished women to the shrine of Asclepius (4), a scene between a jealous woman and her slave whom she accuses of having been unfaithful to her (5), discussions between two women about a skilful shoemaker's dildoes (6 and 7). The first seven mimes rely on sexual titillation, or appeals to their audience's sense of superiority, or both, and despite the vigour of the Greek and the vivacity of the dialogue the invitation to prurience and social snobbery which they convey makes them tedious; the modern reader inevitably compares Theocritus' 'mimes' (especially the 'urban' *Idylls* 14 or 15: see above, p. 580), alongside which Herodas' work seems shallow and sensationalist, even if humorous. Only Mime 8 has particular interest for the literary historian, since it recounts a poet's dream which the speaker interprets to mean that although many would criticize his poetry he would win fame by writing in the manner of Hipponax. The text is very fragmentary and the account of the dream itself tantalizingly obscure; so far as we can tell it involved a contest at a Dionysiac festival in the country. The poem may be further evidence of literary squabbling amongst poets in the third century; it is even tempting to connect the dream with Theocritus' seventh idyll, but the poet's contentiousness and his claim to be under-appreciated by his contemporaries recall Archilochus and may have been a conventional topic within the genre. Characteristic of Herodas is Mime 2.65–82. The mime is set in a law-court on

[1] Cunningham (1971) 14.

the island of Cos (which had close connexions with the Alexandrian royal family). The brothel-keeper Battarus argues his case against a sea-captain Thales who has assaulted one of his girls Myrtale.

> Here, Myrtale; your turn.
> Show everyone: don't be ashamed.
> Think of these jurymen that you see
> as your fathers and brothers. See, gentlemen,
> where he pulled out her hair down here and up here,
> this pure fellow plucked her smooth
> when he dragged her off and raped her – oh my Age,
> he should thank you since otherwise he'd have spurted out
> his blood, as Philip the boxer did in Samos.
> You laugh? I'm a faggot, I don't deny,
> and my name is Battarus and my grandfather
> was Sisýmbras, my father Sisýmbriskus [effeminate names],
> and they all kept brothels, but where strength is concerned
> I'd confidently strangle a lion, were it Thales.
> You love Myrtale perhaps. All right,
> I love my food; give the one and you'll get the other.
> Or, by Zeus, if you're rather heated up inside,
> stuff the price in Battarus' hand
> and bash your own property as much as you want.

In later times Herodas seems to have been little read: Pliny the Younger is the only author to mention him (*Epist.* 4.3.3).[1]

Although little survives of other iambographers, the form seems to have flourished as a medium for anecdotal satire and complaint, fuelled by the popularity of Cynic philosophy and the diatribe. From Phoenix of Colophon, writing in the style of Hipponax, we have fragments complaining of the folly of the rich and moralizing about the glutton Ninus. Two anonymous papyrus fragments (Powell 213ff.) inveigh against the shameless greed of the times; these poems have often been attributed to Cercidas of Megalopolis whose so-called meliambics ('lyric iambics'), of which we possess a fragmentary papyrus text, were on the same theme. Phoenix and Cercidas seem to have written in the third century B.C., and another writer of iambics from the same century was Machon, from Corinth or Sicyon, who can be dated roughly from the remark of Athenaeus (14.664a) that Aristophanes of Byzantium as a young man was keen to study with him. Machon was a writer of comedy who lived in Alexandria; the epigrammatist Dioscorides describes his plays as 'pungent-smelling thyme', the plant of Athens growing by the Nile (*Anth.Pal.* 7.708). Of Machon's plays almost nothing survives, but Athenaeus preserves 462 lines from his *Chreiai*

---

[1] Citations in Stobaeus, Athenaeus and some ancient grammarians are not evidence of popularity or influence.

('Anecdotes'), written in iambic trimeters, which tell stories, many of them
sexually risqué, involving historical personages, some of them the standard
character-types of the comic stage such as parasites, courtesans and poets,
others powerful figures such as King Ptolemy and Demetrius Poliorcetes.[1] The
style is racy, relies a lot on puns, and, unlike that of the Mimes of Herodas, is
firmly based in the language of the author's own time, but frequent witty
allusions to the fifth-century tragedians show that Machon was writing for the
entertainment of an educated audience. Machon's work can be placed in the
tradition of instructional character-studies, such as Theophrastus' *Characters* on
the one hand, or that of the biographers on the other, but his main appeal is as
a literary collector of gossip, and he helps characterize for us the world of
courtly society, and its attitudes, to which most Hellenistic writers owed their
living.

Typical of Machon are his gossipy lines on the courtesan Nico:

> The lover of Sophocles, Demophon,
> while still a lad kept Nico, 'the Goat',
> then an older woman (nicknamed 'the Goat'
> since she once devoured her wealthy lover,
> Thallus [Shoot]: he had arrived in Athens
> to buy some russet-black dried figs
> and load up on Hymettus honey).[2]
> The woman in question is said to have had
> a very beautiful bottom, which Demophon
> asked to have. She laughed 'Right, my dear,
> and you can have it to give Sophocles from me'. (18. 422–32 Gow)

Roman contact with Hellenistic culture and literature was already extensive in
the second century B.C., as is evident from the many translations and adaptations
into Latin of Greek works, and the impact on writers occasioned by the visit to
Rome in the early 160s of the Stoic Crates was notable enough to be mentioned
later by Suetonius (*De gramm. et rhet.* 2). We hear of many other Greeks visiting
and staying in Rome thereafter, and naturally the Romans came increasingly
into contact with Greek writers in the Greek world (most notably on Rhodes)
as well as Sicily and southern Italy, but the Roman conquest of Asia Minor in
the third Mithridatic war had particularly important consequences.

During this time two writers were taken captive and went to Italy, Tyrannion
(the elder) of Amisus, a pupil of Dionysius Thrax, and Parthenius of Nicaea.
Tyrannion, who wrote on Homer and on grammar, knew Julius Caesar, Cicero

---

[1] Both, presumably, safely dead before Machon wrote (though scholars have often assumed,
over-naively, that these references would be to contemporaries and can therefore be used to help
date Machon).

[2] Mention of figs and honey may be intended to be suggestive, but the extraneous details also
help establish a gossipy tone.

(whose nephews he taught) and Atticus, and we know from his pupil the geographer Strabo (13.54) that he was active in Rome. Through Varro his writings had a great influence on Roman readers, and he also helped manage the library of Theophrastus (it included many of Aristotle's MSS), which had been removed to Rome in the spoils of Sulla and Lucullus; he thus prepared the way for the publication in Italy of the writings of the Peripatetic school. Parthenius, according to the Suda, was taken captive by one Cinna but freed in Rome expressly because of his 'culture' (διὰ παίδευσιν). He wrote much elegiac poetry, and we know of titles such as the *Lament for Arete* (his wife) of which a few scraps survive (*P.Geneva* 97), the *Encomium on Arete* in three books, the *Aphrodite*, the *Delos*; there were many other works, whether in hexameters or elegiacs we do not know, on mythological themes such as *Heracles, Iphiclus* and *Metamorphoses*. Parthenius was a central figure among Roman poets, and may well have played a large part in making Hellenistic writers so well known and influential in Republican and Augustan poetry. Since only a few verses of his poetry survive we cannot estimate the impact of his writing on contemporary Romans, but Macrobius (*Sat.* 5.18) reports that Parthenius was the teacher of Virgil, the Cinna who brought him to Rome was quite possibly a relative of Helvius Cinna the poet and friend of Catullus, and we possess a collection of *Love stories* written in prose by Parthenius for the poet Cornelius Gallus to use as an *aide-mémoire* for the writing of hexameter and elegiac poetry. The collection contains thirty-six brief accounts, drawn mostly from earlier prose- and verse-writers, of primarily mythological incidents, involving the tangled, obstructed, misplaced and often disastrous emotions of love; seduction, desertion, jealousy, betrayal, illicit love and crimes of passion are the themes of this collection. The stories are concise sketches, clearly written, in elegant Greek, and include excerpts of poetry, and if their purpose as a source-book for Gallus' poetry should seem odd, we should remember that writers have often been inspired by prosaic but suggestive summary accounts of real incidents: Shakespeare, for example, wrote many of his plays from historical chronicles and Sir Thomas North's translation of Plutarch's *Lives*, and Stendhal developed *Le Rouge et le Noir* from a brief newspaper account of a trial. Parthenius is said to have lived into the reign of Tiberius, who counted him as one of his favourite poets (Suetonius, *Tib.* 70.2), Hadrian renovated his tombstone (he was presumably buried in Rome), and Nonnus alluded to his poetry at least once (*Dion.* 26. 357).

Poetry in the Hellenistic period, although often refined and lettered, certainly did not disappear from popular culture. Although our evidence is sporadic, inscriptions have preserved numerous examples of more or less amateur work: the shrine of Asclepius at Epidaurus has produced a very early Hellenistic text in mediocre trochaic, ionic and hexameter verses by Isyllus, and hymns dating from later periods; numerous paeans come from Athens (by Macedonius), Erythrae, Delphi (including one by Philodamus Scarpheus in 325–4, one by Aristonous from 222 and one by Limenius); from the Serapeum on Delos comes an Isis Aretalogy in sixty-five awkward hexameters by Maiistas in the late third century B.C.

One form, the epigram (a short poem, usually written in elegiac couplets, but sometimes in plain hexameters or in iambic or trochaic metres), was popular at all times, and at all levels of literary and sub-literary achievement, and we are fortunate enough to possess a very substantial and representative collection called the *Greek Anthology*. The *Anthology* (also known as the 'Palatine Anthology', after the tenth-century Codex Palatinus in which it is preserved) is a very large corpus of short poems, almost entirely epigrams, in fifteen books on various topics; the poems range in date from Archilochus to the later Byzantine period. The Palatine collection was based substantially on an earlier anthology compiled by Constantine Cephalas in the early tenth century, probably in Constantinople, and Cephalas in turn drew on collections compiled by, amongst others, Agathias in the sixth century A.D., Strato at the time of Hadrian, Philip of Thessalonica in the first century A.D., and Meleager of Gadara. The Palatine Anthology can be supplemented from other sources – primarily from the anthology of Maximus Planudes (who in the fourteenth century compiled, rather carelessly, a collection which was based on that of Cephalas and which contains 378 poems not found in the Codex Palatinus), but also from earlier writers such as Athenaeus, and occasionally from modern papyrus finds.

Meleager's anthology, called by him a 'Garland', was compiled in the first century B.C. (probably in the first quarter of that century, in Meleager's old age), and covered, to all intents and purposes, the Hellenistic period. We know it to have contained work by more than forty-eight poets (of whom at least four have subsequently been lost); thirty-three were Hellenistic writers.

The epigram had been a popular form from earliest times, especially for inscriptions on monuments and dedications, and in the fifth and fourth centuries B.C. many famous authors, most notably Simonides and Plato, wrote literary epigrams; but it was in the Hellenistic period that this form reached its peak of popularity and accomplishment. Inscriptions show that the epigram continued to be used widely in this as in later periods for practical purposes, and indeed the epigram is the one poetic form which had continued wide currency as a sub-literary medium; but from Philetas onwards it was also part of every poet's repertoire. The modern reader could be forgiven for thinking that at times the epigram had replaced the lyric of earlier periods, such a wide variety of themes, mostly personal, is represented; but the epigram is always particularly concerned with stock themes and variation within the genre, and even poems which strike an apparently intimate note are also written with a view to displaying a literary conceit or figure, or a witticism. For all its fecundity the epigram was never more than a minor form.

The beautiful, intense and neatly written epigrams ascribed to Plato already prefigure the best of the Hellenistic examples:

> Ἀστέρας εἰσαθρεῖς ἀστὴρ ἐμός· εἴθε γενοίμην
> οὐρανός, ὡς πολλοῖς ὄμμασιν εἰς σὲ βλέπω.

> You gaze at the stars, my star; I wish I were
> the heaven, to look at you with many eyes. (*Anth.Pal.* 7.669)

Three authors especially represent the first generation of Hellenistic writers of epigram and are known to us almost entirely through the Anthology: Asclepiades of Samos, Posidippus of Pella and Hedylus of Samos or Athens (whose mother Hedyle was also a poet). Thematically the poems of these three often interconnect, the same poem is sometimes ascribed to more than one of them, and they may even have published a joint collection. Typical is the smoothly written pair of couplets by Asclepiades on the lover Nicagoras (who is so distracted by love and drink that he lets his garland slip off):

> Οἶνος ἔρωτος ἔλεγχος· ἐρᾶν ἀρνεύμενον ἡμῖν
> ἤτασαν αἱ πολλαὶ Νικαγόρην προπόσεις·
> καὶ γὰρ ἐδάκρυσεν καὶ ἐνύστασε καί τι κατηφές
> ἔβλεπε, χὠ σφιγχθεὶς οὐκ ἔμενε στέφανος.

> Wine is the test of love. 'I'm not in love'
> Nicagoras said, but his many toasts were our proof;
> For he cried and hung his head and looked quite downcast,
> and although it was tied his garland wouldn't stay. (*Anth.Pal.* 12.135)

Asclepiades' epigram led to a more intricate poem on the same theme by Callimachus, one of the outstanding epigrammatists of any period:

> Ἕλκος ἔχων ὁ ξεῖνος ἐλάνθανεν· ὡς ἀνιηρόν
> πνεῦμα διὰ στηθέων – εἶδες; – ἀνηγάγετο,
> τὸ τρίτον ἡνίκ᾽ ἔπινε, τὰ δὲ ῥόδα φυλλοβολεῦντα
> τὠνδρὸς ἀπὸ στεφάνων πάντ᾽ ἐγένοντο χαμαί.
> ὤπτηται μέγα δή τι. μὰ δαίμονας, οὐκ ἀπὸ ῥυσμοῦ
> εἰκάζω, φωρὸς δ᾽ ἴχνια φὼρ ἔμαθον.

> Our guest was nursing a wound; how painfully
> and deeply he drew breath – did you see? –
> the third time that he drank; and the man's roses
> dropped their petals from his garland and lay on the ground.
> He's been badly burned. By the gods, it's not from his pulse[1]
> that I figure that out – set a thief to catch a thief. (*Anth.Pal.* 12.134)

[1] Following the interpretation of Luck, (1967) 58.

Here, as so often in epigrams of the Hellenistic period, the poem builds up to the dénouement: the final couplet contains an unexpected reversal and the witticism is pointedly reserved to the last few words of the line.

Epigrammatists often assume a moralizing or quasi-philosophical stance. Thus a poem ascribed variously to Posidippus, Plato the comedian, the cynic Crates and even Heraclitus, turns on a theme at least as old as Theognis (ll. 425–8):

> Which of the paths of life should we take? In the agora
>   is wrangling and tricky business, while at home
> are cares; in the country plenty of toil; at sea
>   terror; abroad, if you own anything, fear,
> or if you're destitute, distress. Are you married?
>   You'll not be unanxious. Unmarried? You'll live quite alone.
> Children are trouble, no children a disablement. Youth
>   is foolish, grey hair, on the other hand, is feeble.
> So your choice is one of two things; to be born
>   never, or to die straightway at birth. (*Anth.Pal.* 9.359)

The epigram is particularly suited to the well-turned and concise expression of sentiment, and authors from all periods composed on life's vicissitudes and in particular on death (the elegiac couplet was one of the earliest forms used for inscriptional epitaphs). The form is delicate enough to need considerable tact when the composer is handling a serious theme, and those epigrams which are not of the highest quality often seem trite or formulaic, but the best can be as moving and dignified as epic itself. Callimachus wrote of friendship and death in a poem which has become incorporated into English literature through the version by William Cory:

> They told me, Heraclitus, they told me you were dead;
>   they brought me bitter news to hear and bitter tears to shed.
> I wept, as I remember'd, how often you and I
>   had tired the sun with talking and sent him down the sky.
> And now that thou art lying, my dear old Carian guest,
>   a handful of grey ashes, long, long ago at rest,
> still are thy pleasant voices, thy nightingales, awake,
>   for Death, he taketh all away, but them he cannot take.

> (*Anth.Pal.* 7.80)

Understated emotion and restraint characterize many of the most successful poems in the Anthology, and writers of epigram often use form and convention to give the impression of control and establish a mood of pathos, as in the following 'epitaph' by Nicias (probably the friend of Theocritus: see above, p. 572):

Ἴζευ ὑπ' αἰγείροισιν, ἐπεὶ κάμες, ἐνθάδ', ὁδῖτα,
καὶ πῖθ' ἄσσον ἰὼν πίδακος ἀμετέρας,
μνᾶσαι δὲ κράναν καὶ ἀπόπροθι ἂν ἐπὶ Γίλλῳ
Σῖμος ἀποφθιμένωι παιδὶ παριδρύεται.

Sit here beneath the poplars, weary traveller,
and drink, coming closer to our spring.
Remember the fountain even when you are far away
which Simus built for Gillus his dead son. (*Anth.Pal.* 9.315)

An author who wrote almost completely on the themes of simple, often rustic life, was Leonidas of Tarentum, a third-century poet (perhaps roughly contemporary with Callimachus and Theocritus) who had considerable influence on later writers for many centuries. Leonidas writes of his own poverty (*Anth.Pal.* 6.300, 302), but we should not assume that this is any more than the conventional poet's complaint; and although his epigrams generally concern working people and the matters of daily life (scarcely ever touching on erotic themes), his style and diction are elaborate and his choice of subject matter accords with the contemporary affectation of the cultured classes for the 'ordinary'. Leonidas represented this taste for the mundane more successfully and more consistently than any other minor Hellenistic poet, and this is the reason for his continued popularity in later periods. A house in the Via Stabiana at Pompeii has a number of frescoes with inscriptions, two of which are taken from Leonidas: one, of huntsmen offering dedications to Pan, is inscribed with *Anth.Pal.* 6.13, and another of a goat nibbling a vine cites the last line of *Anth.Pal.* 9.99 which Leonidas wrote on this theme (the topic is treated also in Aesop's fables, 404 H):

The prime, well-bearded billy goat once on a time
in an orchard nibbled all the vine's tender shoots.
But she cried out to him from the ground:
'Your jaws may strip this fruitful branch of mine,
but my root is firm and will produce sweet nectar again –
enough for a libation, goat, when you're sacrificed.'

Ovid may have had Leonidas' poem in mind when he wrote *Fasti* 1.357.

Among later epigrammatists one writer stands out above all others, the anthologist Meleager himself. More than 132 epigrams ascribed to Meleager have been transmitted in the Palatine Anthology, and most exhibit the graceful, lucid and smoothly straightforward style for which he is famous. Meleager is hardly original in any fundamental sense, but in a tradition where variation and refinement were cardinal he is one of the most pleasing and impressive composers, with a wide range of themes, levels and moods. Many of his epigrams concern lovers such as Zenophila and Heliodora, and numerous boys; whether or not any of these actually existed we do not know. Characteristic of

Meleager's neat balance between sentiment and wit is *Anth.Pal.* 5.152 (which itself stands as a companion-piece to *Anth.Pal.* 5.151, addressed to mosquitoes attracted by the sleeping Zenophila):

> Πταίης μοι κώνωψ ταχὺς ἄγγελος, οὔασι δ' ἄκροις
> Ζηνοφίλας ψαύσας προσψιθύριзε τάδε·
> 'ἄγρυπνος μίμνει σε, σὺ δ' ὦ λήθαργε φιλούντων
> εὕδεις'. εἶα πέτευ, ναὶ φιλόμουσε πέτευ·
> ἥσυχα δὲ φθέγξαι, μὴ καὶ σύγκοιτον ἐγείρας
> κινήσηις ἐπ' ἐμοὶ зηλοτύπους ὀδύνας.
> ἢν δ' ἀγάγηις τὴν παῖδα, δορᾶι στέψω σε λέοντος,
> κώνωψ, καὶ δώσω χειρὶ φέρειν ῥόπαλον.

Mosquito, fly as my rapid messenger,
  brush Zenophila's ear and whisper this:
'He wakefully waits, while you forget your lovers
  and sleep.' Now fly, yes fly you lover of art;
but speak softly, don't wake her companion too
  and stir his jealous pangs against me.
If you bring the girl, I'll crown you with a lion's skin,
  mosquito, and give your hand a club to carry.

The irony which emerges in the third couplet is reminiscent of Asclepiades and Callimachus, but the incongruous (and sardonic) final comparison of the mosquito to Heracles turns the poem into a conceit. Even when Meleager writes with less extravagance and more apparent sentiment he still displays a very figured elegance:

> Εἰνόδιον στείχοντα μεσημβρινὸν εἶδον Ἄλεξιν
> ἄρτι κόμαν καρπῶν κειρομένου θέρεος·
> διπλαῖ δ' ἀκτῖνές με κατέφλεγον, αἱ μὲν Ἔρωτος
> παιδὸς ἀπ' ὀφθαλμῶν, αἱ δὲ παρ' ἠελίου.
> ἀλλ' ἃς μὲν νὺξ αὖθις ἐκοίμισεν, ἃς δ' ἐν ὀνείροις
> εἴδωλον μορφῆς μᾶλλον ἀνεφλόγισεν·
> λυσίπονος δ' ἑτέροις ἐπ' ἐμοὶ πόνον ὕπνος ἔτευξεν
> ἔμπνουν πῦρ ψυχῆι κάλλος ἀπεικονίσας.

Walking at noon down the road I saw Alexis,
  summer was just being cropped of her fruit's tresses.
Double the beams that scorched me, those of Love
  from the boy's eyes, the others from the sun.
Night has lulled the sun again, but Love
  his phantom form in my dreams makes more inflamed.
Sleep that brings others release has brought me toil
  portraying beauty as living fire in my soul. (*Anth.Pal.* 12.127)

Meleager is always stylish, and in this he is an appropriate anthologist for the Hellenistic period at a time when the course of literature was about to change fundamentally once more. For although the early Hellenistic writers, especially those of Alexandria, are extremely conscious of form, it is in the work of poets such as Meleager that we can see the increasing importance of rhetoric for its own sake. It was the rhetorical form that the earliest Roman imitators (such as Q. Lutatius Catulus, who in the second century B.C. translated Callimachus *Ep.* 41 Pfeiffer) were primarily interested in reproducing in Latin; but for the neoteric poets of the first century (*CHCL* II 178–87) the Greek elegiac was only the jumping-off point for establishing a wholly new direction in European love poetry.

19

POST-ARISTOTELIAN PHILOSOPHY

I. THE LATER ACADEMY AND THE PERIPATOS (LYCEUM)

When Theophrastus formally established the Peripatetic school or Lyceum, following Aristotle's death, Athens possessed two centres of philosophy, for the Platonic Academy, now under its third head, Xenocrates, had continued without interruption.[1] The activities of the Academy during this period are very poorly documented, but they seem to have concentrated upon systematizing Plato's thought at a time when Aristotle and his immediate successors were engaged upon new researches over a much wider front. It is possible that Xenocrates and his associates began the interpretation of Plato which, centuries later, culminated in the complex metaphysics of Plotinus. For three hundred years, following Plato, the Academy had an uninterrupted Athenian tradition, but it contributed little of substance to Greek literature. The most important Academic philosophers, Arcesilaus (died 242/1) and Carneades (died 129/8), were Sceptics who wrote nothing, though their work, especially Carneades', was well enough known at secondhand to be used by Cicero in his *Academica* and much later by Sextus Empiricus (see p. 636). Antiochus of Ascalon, in the first century B.C., turned the Academy back to a positivist philosophy, synthesized from traditional Academic teaching and Stoic views. He was known to Cicero, whose philosophical writings contain many explicit reports of his position.

Our knowledge of the early Peripatetics is much better, and certainly sufficient to show that they maintained Aristotle's own interests, including the study of literature. We are best informed about Theophrastus, a scholar of quite remarkable range and energy. His surviving work, a tiny fraction of his total output, is mainly on scientific subjects (especially botany), which he treats in very much the same manner as Aristotle. What we know of his logic and other writings suggests that his originality as a philosopher lay in the subjects he examined rather than conceptual or methodological innovation. But he was quite prepared to criticize and elaborate Aristotle's work (cf. his *Metaphysics* ch. 9), and he can more justly be called a historian of philosophy.[2] In eighteen books he put

[1] On Speusippus and Heraclides Ponticus cf. Tarán (1981) and Gottschalk (1980).
[2] Kahn (1960) 17–22.

together the *Doctrines of natural philosophers*: only one section of this collection survives in a nearly complete form (*On sense-perception*) but all later handbooks on the history of philosophy were greatly indebted to him.

Two aspects of Theophrastus' work deserve more detailed consideration here. Like other Peripatetics he wrote extensively on rhetoric. The measure of his influence on later theorists is difficult to determine precisely, since our detailed evidence for his rhetorical work is only a handful of references, mainly in Cicero, Quintilian, and Dionysius of Halicarnassus. But it is certain that Theophrastus posited four 'virtues' of style, purity (*hellenismos*, i.e. grammatical correctness), clarity, propriety (i.e. appropriateness to the circumstances of the speech) and ornamentation (Cic. *Orator* 79). Although Aristotle gave formal recognition to only one virtue of style, clarity (see p. 533), he did recognize the importance of the other qualities. Theophrastus may be assumed to have organized the treatment of style in a more systematic way and thus it was, perhaps, that his work was taken up by other writers on rhetoric.[1] He may also have stimulated an interest in labelling and identifying figures of speech, and there is some evidence for attributing to him the distinction between three styles – full, plain and middle – which was made much of by later writers on rhetoric.[2]

Theophrastus also wrote on poetry, comedy, and 'the laughable'. How he treated these subjects we do not know, but satirical humour, if not comedy, is certainly a feature of the surviving work for which he is renowned, *Characters*. This short book is one of the most fascinating items in Greek literature. It consists of thirty sketches, most of them taking up less than one printed page, in which a character trait is delineated by describing a series of actions which the bearer of the character might perform. This is an excerpt from *kolakeia* 'flattery':

> the flatterer is the sort of person who says to the man he is walking with, 'Do you realize how people are looking at you? It happens to no one in the town except you.' 'You were being praised yesterday in the Stoa'...As he says such things he is removing a thread from his companion's coat...and with a laugh he remarks, 'Why see! Just because I haven't met you for two days your beard is full of grey hairs, though your hair is remarkably black for your age'...He buys apples and pears for children, brings them in and gives them as the father is looking, and kisses the children saying, 'chicks of a splendid father'.

This combination of speech and narrative is typical of all the character sketches, which represent the trait in question purely externally, without overt reference to the agent's motives or thoughts. Theophrastus' language is colloquial, his sentences are short, and the passage from one 'characteristic' action to another

[1] Kennedy (1963) 275.
[2] Kennedy (1963) makes the positive case for this, 278ff., and cites scholars who deny it (n. 33 *ad loc.*).

is often abrupt. These features and the humour of the portraiture seem to exclude a serious ethical purpose in the *Characters*.[1] Bad though they all are in some sense, none is deplorable or wicked. As Ussher says, 'what they exhibit are social more than moral (in our sense) transgressions of the norm':[2] boorishness, superstition, meanness, talkativeness, small-mindedness etc. It is difficult to explain such a choice of qualities if Theophrastus wrote the *Characters* as an earnest contribution to philosophy. They entertain the reader and were surely designed to do so. If it is necessary to look for any didactic purpose, this can hardly be separated from entertainment, which points, as many scholars have argued, to Comedy. Ussher finds the *Characters* reminiscent of Aristophanes,[3] and thinks that Theophrastus may have wished to recommend to Menander and other poets of New Comedy a return to Aristophanic models. This seems unlikely. Menander was himself a pupil of Theophrastus, and there is some resemblance between characters in his plays and Theophrastus' characterization (e.g. in *Dyskolos*, Knemon recalls features of Theophrastus' boorish and distrustful man).[4] But nothing suggests that Menander was actually dependent on Theophrastus. Later Greek comedy provides many examples of plays whose titles are shared by or at least resemble Theophrastan *Characters*, and it seems quite credible that Theophrastus had the contemporary stage in mind.

Only a little needs to be said about other Peripatetic philosophers. Aristoxenus, an older contemporary of Theophrastus, joined the Peripatos after an early period as a Pythagorean. This may account for his interest in music. He also wrote *Lives* of philosophers, and other biographers who have connexions with the Peripatos (especially Hermippus and Satyrus) were probably influenced by him; but Momigliano has shown that 'Hellenistic biography is to be considered a Peripatetic speciality only in a limited sense'.[5]

The influence of Aristotle and his successors on the development of Alexandrian literary scholarship was also exaggerated by earlier scholars. The subject has been authoritatively studied by Pfeiffer,[6] who shows that Peripatetics, though not without importance in Alexandria, were secondary to the poets themselves in stimulating philological research. The most notable Peripatetic associated with Alexandria was Strato of Lampsacus, who succeeded Theophrastus as head of the school in about 287. Earlier he had been invited to Alexandria by Ptolemy I to assist in the teaching of his son, but he shared this work with the literary scholar, Zenodotus. It is likely that the one Peripatetic who was a notable statesman, Demetrius of Phalerum, exercised some influence on Alexandrian scholarship through his advice to Ptolemy I.[7] Demetrius made

---

[1] This was maintained by many older scholars, references in Ussher (1960) 7–9, and attempts have also been made to relate the *Characters* to textbooks on rhetoric, see Ussher (1960) 9–11.
[2] Ussher (1960) 27.   [3] Ussher (1960) 4–6.   [4] Steinmetz (1960).
[5] Momigliano (1971) 84.   [6] Pfeiffer 57–104.   [7] Pfeiffer 99–104.

the earliest known collection of Aesop's *Fables* and also put together *Sayings of the Seven Wise Men*, but his own compositions in philosophy, rhetoric and history were of no lasting importance. Literary theory was also one of the main activities of Praxiphanes, a Peripatetic whose views were opposed in a book by Callimachus. It seems probable that Callimachus set out to vindicate the principles of the new poetry, short poems rather than large organic compositions, against the insistence by Aristotle, and no doubt by his successors too, on unity, coherence and magnitude.[1]

The activities of the Peripatos after the death of Strato (269 B.C.) were less impressive. The School seems to have produced little that was significant or influential until the recovery of Aristotle's technical writings in the first century B.C. (see above, p. 530) stimulated a new interest in the systematic study of his philosophy.

2. EPICURUS AND PHILODEMUS

The scepticism of the Academy and the decline of the Peripatos were counter-balanced by the development of the two new philosophical schools at Athens, the Garden of Epicurus and the Stoa. Epicurus, and Zeno the founder of Stoicism, had begun to teach in Athens during the last decade of the fourth century. The establishment of two new philosophical movements at the same time seems to call for some explanation, and this has been sought most frequently in the social and political circumstances of the time. The effects of Alexander's conquests on the Mediterranean world were far too complex to be summed up in a word or two. But it is probably correct to suppose that, in disrupting traditional patterns of life, they made many people receptive to philosophies which stressed the self-sufficiency of the individual. Throughout the five hundred years of their vitality in the Graeco-Roman world, Stoicism and Epicureanism were rival philosophies, each offering its own account of things and its own moral system. Yet, as has often been noticed, they resemble one another in their emphasis upon the individual's responsibility for his own happiness and the importance of freeing the mind from emotional disturbance.

Thus the situation of Greece at the end of the fourth century can help to explain certain features of Stoicism and Epicureanism. But it is a mistake to regard either of these movements as merely a response to immediate social and personal needs. Such evaluations of Epicurus and Zeno have ceased to carry conviction in the light of current research, which has stressed their relationship and reaction to the Academic and Peripatetic tradition. The history of Greek philosophy has more to teach us about Stoicism and Epicureanism than we can learn from speculating about the troubles of the Hellenistic world.

The philosophy which Epicurus founded bore the stamp of his personality

---

[1] Pfeiffer 135–7.

throughout its history. For Lucretius, writing two hundred years later, Epicurus is *deus*, a 'god' (e.g. 5.8), and such veneration of their founder was characteristic among Epicureans. Its basis was the belief that Epicurus, by undermining superstition and the fear of death, could indeed be called the 'saviour' of mankind. The potency of this message as late as A.D. 200 is eloquently proved by the inscription of Diogenes discovered in 1884 at Oenoanda in central Turkey. Diogenes was a fervent Epicurean, who wished his fellow men to be able to read the details of that philosophy, and arranged for his version of them to be inscribed on a great stone wall for all to see.

Epicurus was an Athenian citizen, but it was only at the age of thirty-four that he took up permanent residence in Attica. By this time he had already attracted a following in Mytilene and Lampsacus, and in 307/6 B.C. he established his permanent home on a small estate between Athens and the Piraeus. Known as the Garden, Epicurus' home, which he shared with his closest adherents, continued as the centre of Epicureans after his death and gave its name to their philosophy.

In the strength of his personality, and in the affection he inspired among his friends, Epicurus resembles Socrates more closely than any other Greek philosopher. But Epicurus' goal of freedom from physical and mental pain (*ataraxia*) differs radically from the Socratic insistence on moral virtue as the truly human good.[1] Socrates did not formally develop his philosophy in writing and he eschewed any claims to knowledge about the physical workings of nature. Epicurus was a prolific writer (Diog. Laert. 10.26) who set out to provide a complete explanation of the world. By his recourse to atoms and void as the ultimate entities Epicurus offered a strictly mechanistic account of phenomena. The gods, in his philosophy, have no part to play in the ordinary processes of nature. Man is an impermanent compound of atoms, and his happiness depends upon tranquillity of mind, which only a proper understanding of nature can bestow.

Epicurus renounced traditional Greek education and in a fragment of a *Letter to Pythocles* he tells his disciple to 'set sail and flee from all *paideia*' (culture).[2] Lucretius, the greatest Epicurean writer, is conspicuously well read in Greek literature, and Philodemus, besides writing on rhetoric and poetry, was a graceful epigrammatist. But the official attitude of Epicureanism towards literature, especially poetry, seems to have been negative (Cic. *De fin.* 1.72). There is only one quotation from a poet in the surviving work of Epicurus (*Letter to Menoeceus* 126, from Theognis).

Even from a strictly literary point of view however, Epicurus is not an un-

---

[1] For Epicurus all pleasure is identical with good, and the greatest pleasure or good is freedom from pain, e.g. *Letter to Menoeceus* 128, 132.
[2] Arrighetti (1973) 89.

important figure. Although we possess only a small fraction of his writings, the material is sufficient to show that his presentation of philosophy was related in a most interesting way to the needs of different audiences. His major work *On nature* occupied thirty-seven books (rolls of papyrus). None of these has survived in a complete form, but substantial fragments of many carbonized rolls were discovered by the first excavators of Herculaneum in the middle of the eighteenth century. The Herculaneum papyri have been made more accessible in recent years and they repay the most careful study.[1] They are the only surviving texts by Epicurus in which he presents his views in an extended form. Many evaluations of his philosophy have been based upon material in which he is summarizing or simplifying central doctrines, or on secondary sources such as Lucretius. Such evidence could, and often did, give an impression that the system itself was lacking in philosophical sophistication.

Study of the Herculaneum texts has gone a long way towards refuting this assessment of Epicurus. *On nature* seems to have been a systematic treatment of physics and cosmology, epistemology, psychology and perhaps ethics.[2] The difficulties of working on this material are not only palaeographical. Epicurus' Greek is idiosyncratic both in vocabulary and grammar. He was capable of writing clearly and even elegantly, but the style of *On nature* is extraordinarily loose and the thought often obscure. It also makes use of a technical vocabulary, many items of which have not yet been properly understood.

If, as seems certain, Epicurus wrote *On nature* for reading and study by his closest philosophical associates, this goes some way towards explaining the obscurity of the writing. It is reasonable to compare this work with Aristotle's technical treatises, which were not designed for a public audience. We have the impression that Epicurus is using, at least for his intended readers, acceptable philosophical jargon. But, for all their crabbed Greek, the fragments of *On nature* have compensating qualities besides the interest of their content. They offer the reader a dynamic presentation of problems and ideas, and at times succeed in conveying the immediacy of philosophical life in the Garden. This is a feature of Book 28 which, though not formally a dialogue, records in the second person some views of language held by Metrodorus, Epicurus' leading follower, and Epicurus' reaction to them.

Epicurus had many adherents in different parts of the Greek world. He kept in touch with them by correspondence, and Diogenes Laertius appended to his *Life and doctrines of Epicurus* three letters which consist of summaries of his philosophy. The longest and most detailed of these, *To Herodotus*, is the most important surviving Epicurean text. It provides an 'epitome of the whole

---

[1] In 1970 the Italian Government established a *Centro Internazionale per lo studio dei papiri Ercolanesi* under the auspices of the University of Naples. It publishes an annual journal, *Cronache Ercolanesi*.

[2] Sedley (1974).

system' for 'those unable to work in detail through all that I have written about nature' (Diog. Laert. 10.35, tr. Bailey, 1926). The *Letter to Menoeceus*, which is the clearest of all Epicurus' longer writings, gives a summary of the ethical doctrine; astronomy, cosmology and meteorology are the subject of the *Letter to Pythocles*. How many philosophers besides Plato had already used the letter as a means for writing philosophy it is impossible to say. Many of Epicurus' letters, as we know from fragments, sent greetings and news to his friends. The philosophical letters were a way of keeping them abreast of his doctrines.

In these letters we observe Epicurus' desire to disseminate his philosophy and to reduce it to essentials. But he was not content with this degree of simplification. To Diogenes Laertius we also owe the survival of forty *Principal doctrines*, a set of short statements, from which two examples may be selected: 'Death is nothing to us; for what has been dissolved is insentient, and what is insentient is nothing to us' (2). 'The just man is most troublefree, the unjust man abounds in the greatest trouble' (17). As these passages show, Epicurus was quite capable of writing in a pithy, aphoristic style, and there can be little doubt that such statements were intended for learning by heart. Another set of eighty-one aphorisms, which include several of the *Principal doctrines*, was discovered in a Vatican manuscript.

Three modes of philosophical style are thus to be found in Epicurus' surviving work. If we knew more about his lost writings that might be too simple a description. Not surprisingly it is the aphorisms which are most frequently found in later writers, sometimes translated into Latin, as in many of Seneca's early *Moral letters to Lucilius*.

As a writer Epicurus is at his best in the aphorisms and in the *Letter to Menoeceus*. He has a pleasing gift for metaphor: 'friendship dances round the world, proclaiming to us all to wake up for happiness' (*Sent. Vat.* 52). 'We must set ourselves free from the prison of business and politics' (*Sent. Vat.* 58). In the letter he succeeds admirably in conveying the elegant simplicity of Epicurean ethics. His tone is positive, optimistic, even joyful, and we can well understand how joy and friendship, for Epicurus and his followers, could be matters of constant experience as well as subjects of philosophical discourse.

Little is known about the writings of Epicureans over the next two hundred years, but from the first half of the first century B.C. we have substantial fragments of the work of Philodemus. Reference has already been made (p. 627) to Herculaneum and the carbonized papyri of Epicurus which were found there. It is virtually certain that these works by Epicurus belonged to Philodemus and formed, along with the other Herculaneum papyri, parts of his own library. Philodemus spent his later years as an Epicurean teacher in Herculaneum. There he was befriended by L. Calpurnius Piso, the wealthy statesman whose administration of Macedonia was fiercely attacked by Cicero in two speeches (*De prov. cons.* and *In Pisonem*). Cicero refers to a *Graecus quidam*, an Epicurean philosopher and poet, who was Piso's intimate friend (*Pis.* 28.68–72). There can be no doubt that he means Philodemus; and it is highly probable that Piso made him a permanent resident of his own villa.

This explains the fact that the majority of book rolls discovered at Herculaneum are the writings of Philodemus himself. That they were 'published' in any quantity is most unlikely. No quotations from them occur in later writers, and we may conclude that Philodemus' work, like that of most Epicureans, circulated among a small circle of his own acquaintances with some copies being made, perhaps, for distribution to Epicureans elsewhere.

Before surveying some of his philosophical writings, a word is needed about Philodemus the poet. For the survival of thirty-five epigrams attributed to him, we have to thank not a volcanic eruption and modern excavation but Palatine and Planudean Anthologies compiled in the Middle Ages. That the author of most of these short poems in elegiac couplets was Philodemus of Gadara there is no reason to doubt. *Anth.Pal.* 11.44 is addressed to Piso, inviting the poet's patron to a plain dinner to celebrate Epicurus' birthday, a traditional monthly commemoration among Epicureans. Moreover Cicero, in his account of the Greek who must be our Philodemus, says that he *poema facit ita festiuum, ita concinnum, ita elegans, nihil ut fieri possit argutius* 'he has written a poem so witty, polished and elegant that nothing could be more brilliant' (*Pis.* 28.69). That is an ironically generous, but not unwarranted, comment on the surviving epigrams. Philodemus is one of the outstanding Greek writers of light erotic poetry. He is indeed witty, as he shows in the verses which play on his name, 'lover of people' (*demos*), where he observes with increasing irony that he has loved four girls called Demo. Some of his poems strike a tone which is romantic and almost tender. None is crudely lubricious or mordant like some examples of the genre. Two or three seem to be genuinely autobiographical; he speaks of himself as a greying thirty-seven-year-old (*Anth.Pal.* 11.41) who should be concluding his amatory 'madness', and then expresses his desire for a simpler life with a domesticated wife (*Anth.Pal.* 11.34).

The erotic epigram was well established in Philodemus' time, and he shows himself an accomplished craftsman of the genre. His prose works are strikingly different. They frequently display the crabbed qualities of Epicurus at his worst, and one can only conclude that literary elegance was the last quality expected from technical writing at this time. Enough survives from other writers to show that this was not peculiar to Epicureans, but the prose style and language of technical treatises have been so little studied that it is extremely difficult to make comparative assessments. Most of our norms for evaluating Greek prose are derived from writers whose style is highly self-conscious and artificial. In a writer such as Philodemus we are reading perhaps the ancient equivalent of what we should call sloppy academic text books. It should also be noted that his own rhetorical views, and those of Epicureans in general, favoured a *natural* use of language.[1] But 'nature' hardly justifies the obscurity that we find in much of Epicurus and Philodemus.

The two works of greatest literary interest are the *Rhetorica* and the fifth book of *On poems*. Both of these, in their surviving form, are chiefly polemic against existing critical theories, but something of Philodemus' own position also emerges. In his *Rhetorica* Philodemus accepts that there is a 'rhetorical art', but he strenuously denies that it involves any skill in politics. The scope of rhetoric is *epideixis* – verbal display – and the 'disposition of speeches' (I p. 122.25–136.20). This removes judicial and forensic oratory – Aristotle's other two genres (see pp. 533f.) – from the 'art'. Philodemus, as an Epicurean, claims that forensic oratory is dangerous to its practitioners. Much of his treatise is occupied with an insistence on the distinction between a true philosopher and a rhetorician. Beauty of discourse, he argues, belongs to philosophers, whose language, in as much as it is natural, needs no artifice.

Only the fifth book of Philodemus' treatment of poetry is preserved in an extensive form. This is a more rewarding work than the *Rhetorica* and it contains some useful information about the critical theory of other writers – first, perhaps, Neoptolemus of Parium who influenced Horace in his *Ars poetica*, later, certainly, the Stoic Ariston of Chios and the grammarian, Crates of Pergamum, who was strongly influenced by the Stoics.[2] Philodemus argues that technical treatises on poetry are of little value. It is not helpful, he holds, to set up a list of qualities which a good poem must possess (27.25ff.). What matters is rather the whole poem, which should not be assessed by a process of dissection. Furthermore, poetry should not be valued for its moral or factual utility. If beautiful poems prove to be beneficial it is not as poems that they have this effect (29.18ff.). Nor is a poem inferior because it represents the purely imaginary rather than the actual (4.6ff.). At times Philodemus seems to be adumbrating a notion of 'art for art's sake', and he has been heralded as a forerunner of nineteenth-century aesthetic theorists.[3] But it is difficult to find firm evidence in his work for anything like a general theory of literature. There is little sign that poets themselves were influenced by his critical theory, and later critics proceeded to use principles which he himself rejected. A stronger case can be made for the influence of his *Epigrams* and his treatise *On death*, on Horace especially.[4]

[1] General discussion by De Lacy (1939). For Epicurus' linguistic theory and its connexion with other aspects of his philosophy cf. Long (1971).

[2] All are discussed by Jensen in appendices to his edition (1923). He subsequently argued that the first section treated not Neoptolemus but Heraclides Ponticus, but his original view is defended by Brink (1963) 48–74.

[3] This was argued at length by Rostagni (1955) I 356–446.   [4] Cf. Gigante (1969).

Unlike Epicurus, Zeno, the founder of Stoicism (*c.* 333–261 B.C.), was not a Greek but a Phoenician. He came to Athens, perhaps as a merchant like his father, from Citium in Cyprus about 311 B.C. For the next ten years he studied with many of the leading philosophers of the time, especially the head of the Academy, Polemo. He then began to teach as a philosopher in his own right. The *Stoa Poikile* (Painted Colonnade), which he and his followers frequented, stood next to the Athenian Agora, and thus from its beginnings Stoicism was associated with the public life of the city.

The central ideas of Stoicism are so familiar a part of the western intellectual tradition that they need no detailed summary here. It was Stoicism more than any other system of Greek thought which influenced Roman literature and culture, and the Christian fathers incorporated Stoicism as well as Platonism into their interpretation of the teaching of the Church. The Stoic conception of the world, in which all events are ultimately explicable as activities of the divine *Logos*, provided a framework for moral thought that could accommodate many established attitudes. Stoic ethics, though it contains original features, has much in common with Socratic, Platonic and Aristotelian ideas. Unlike Epicurus, the Stoics found a way of interpreting the Olympian gods in their traditional form as allegorical references to divine phenomena. Yet their emphasis on a single, all-pervasive deity or *Logos* gave Christians a pagan doctrine to which they could react with some sympathy. Not centred narrowly on the values of the Greek polis, the Stoic concept of human nature and its perfectibility could appeal to men and women of all nationalities and of any status. In this respect Zeno's ethics look forward to the establishment of a common Mediterranean culture. It was a philosophy which a slave could espouse, but it did not offer a radical transformation of the world. The goods of a Stoic are all internal – virtuous states of mind, which are strictly independent of external affairs. What the would-be Stoic seeks to change is not the world but himself.

Moral idealism was the Stoa's strongest platform throughout its history. But the Stoics contributed importantly to intellectual life in general. Under Chrysippus, Stoic logic became a highly developed system, the achievements of which have been recognized only in recent years.[1] Their physics, though crude in some respects, contains ideas which are closer than Aristotle to modern theories.[2] Some Stoics also played a notable part in the development of linguistic and rhetorical study.

The historical development of Stoic philosophy is a complex subject. From the time of Zeno down to Posidonius (died *c.* 50 B.C.) the system underwent considerable refinement and modification, much of which was due to the work

[1] Mates (1953); Frede (1974).   [2] Sambursky (1959).

of Chrysippus (died 208/4 B.C.). Our knowledge of the Stoa throughout this whole period depends upon quotations and summaries by later writers, augmented by a few papyrus fragments. It is only from the first century A.D. onwards that we possess substantial work by Stoics at first hand. By this time Stoicism had ceased to be a developing philosophical system and the later Stoics, whose work is preserved, were not original thinkers. Two of them, however – Epictetus and Marcus Aurelius – are of great interest, and something must be said about their work after a survey of earlier Stoic writers.

Too little is known about Zeno to justify any general comments about his philosophical style. His most famous work was his *Politeia* (*Republic*), where he argued that a society of the wise would have no need for the conventional institutions of the Greek polis. His wholesale rejection of temples, law-courts, money and possibly marriage, was influenced by the Cynics, and later Stoics were less utopian in their political theory. In other works Zeno laid down general principles which were developed by his successors, and they also shared his interest in literature. Zeno himself wrote on Homer, claiming that his poems were quite faultless when interpreted on the assumption that Homer himself distinguished between 'truth' and 'opinion' (*SVF* 1.274). Whether or not this is to be called 'allegorizing', the Stoics in general found it possible to read allusions to their own philosophical position in the work of the poets.[1]

Zeno's successor as head of the Stoa was Cleanthes (died 232 B.C.), who came to Athens from Assos near the site of ancient Troy. Nine of his fragments are in hexameter or iambic verse, and the longest of these, the *Hymn to Zeus*, is the most eloquent Stoic statement on theology and ethics. In thirty-five lines, which draw upon much traditional poetic language and the philosophy of Heraclitus, Cleanthes expresses the power and beneficence of Zeus, 'lord of Nature, who steers all things lawfully'. The poem represents all things as compliant with Zeus, 'save what the evil accomplish in their folly'. Cleanthes concludes with a prayer: 'rescue men from wretched ignorance', and a promise that men in return will honour Zeus with praise.

Most of Cleanthes' work was in prose, but for the sake of 'clarity' he interspersed verses from time to time (Sen. *Epist.* 108.9–10). He held that poetry was better suited than prose for expressing truth about the nature of the gods (*SVF* 1.486).

Cleanthes is an attractive figure and the only early Stoic who has strong claims to literary accomplishment. He was succeeded by Chrysippus from Soli in Cilicia, whose gifts as a philosopher were not matched by elegance or fluency in writing.[2] Chrysippus did not compose poetry but he was much given to quotation, especially from Homer and the tragedians, as a means of reinforcing his own views. His intellectual energy was prodigious, and more than any

---

[1] Pfeiffer 237ff.   [2] Sandbach (1975) 112–14.

other Stoic he was responsible for the systematic development of the philosophy in a form which remained orthodox for the next four hundred years.
Although very little of Chrysippus' work survives in an unmodified form,
most of the summaries of Stoicism which were recorded by later writers of
philosophical handbooks (e.g. Arius Didymus and Stobaeus) are probably
dependent on him. It is likely that his books were studied by philosophers up to
the second century A.D. but most of them will have been too technical to have
existed in a large number of copies.[1]

Of the early Stoics three further individuals must be mentioned briefly.
Diogenes of Babylon, Chrysippus' successor, is best known for his work on
grammar, rhetoric and music. He may have been responsible for adding
'brevity' to the four virtues of style established by Theophrastus (see p. 623)
and he was highly critical of contemporary rhetoric. Diogenes visited Rome,
with other philosophers, in 155 B.C. and from this date onwards philosophy
begins to play a significant part in Roman culture. Much of the early success
of Stoicism at Rome was due to Panaetius of Rhodes (c. 185–109 B.C.), who was
a close associate for several years of Scipio Aemilianus. Panaetius' views are
best preserved in the adaptation of his work *On the appropriate* made by Cicero
in his *De officiis*. He emphasized the need to develop Stoic moral theory in a
manner which would be practically useful for those 'advancing' along the road
towards virtue. The writings of the later Stoics show more humanity and
tolerance than we find in Chrysippus, and much of this may be due to the
influence of Panaetius.

Even more regrettable than the loss of Panaetius' work is the fact that so
little survives from Posidonius (c. 135–50 B.C.). A Syrian, who established his
home in Rhodes, Posidonius made original contributions to Stoicism, especially
in ethics and psychology. But he was far from being a typical philosopher of
his time. Much of his interest lay in history and geography, and it is still a
matter of discussion how far his work in these fields was intended to link up
with Stoicism and his scientific studies. Polybius' history terminates in 146 B.C.
and Posidonius continued the story of Roman history and expansion. As a
historian, he seems to have laid particular emphasis on geographical and
ethnographical considerations. Probably less analytical than Polybius, Posidonius
can be assumed to have written in a more colourful style. The longest historical
fragment gives a lively account of a power-seeking and disreputable philosopher
– Athenion – who persuaded the Athenians to oppose Rome in the Mithridatic
wars.[2] Other writers, especially Strabo, were heavily indebted to Posidonius
but the extent of his general influence is difficult to establish with any precision.

Epictetus (c. A.D. 50–120) and Marcus Aurelius (A.D. 121–80) – the one born

[1] On Plutarch's knowledge of Chrysippus' writings cf. Babut (1969).
[2] Edelstein–Kidd F253.

a slave, the other chosen to be Roman emperor – are the two Stoics whose work is most accessible to us. Neither of them, however, was a professional writer. We owe our account of Epictetus' philosophy to one of his pupils, Flavius Arrian, the historian of Alexander the Great. In his introductory letter of dedication to Lucius Gellius, Arrian writes:

> I have not composed these *Words of Epictetus* as one might be said to 'compose' books of this kind. But whatever I heard him say I used to write down, word for word, as best I could...They are...such remarks as one man might make off-hand to another, not such as he would compose for men to read in after time. (tr. Oldfather)

The *Discourses* seem to bear out this claim by Arrian. His own style as a writer is quite different from his record of Epictetus, whose language is not literary Attic but the *koine*. It has however been argued that Arrian's own contribution was in fact so great that the *Discourses* should be regarded as his own composition, analogous to Xenophon's *Socratic Memoirs*, a model suggested elsewhere by Arrian himself.[1] Certainly the style of the *Discourses* has literary precedents but, even allowing for Arrian's artifice, it seems best to continue to treat him as Epictetus' publicist rather than his interpreter or hagiographer. We thus have every reason to speak of this work as Epictetus', even though it was not his own literary composition.

Arrian's collection consists of 95 short lectures or sermons, and the *Encheiridion* (*Manual*), which brings together 53 excerpts from the *Discourses* as a summary of Epictetus' moral teaching. Though known as the *Discourses* Epictetus' work would be better entitled by its Greek name, *Diatribes*, for it belongs to a tradition of popular preaching on moral subjects which some other Stoic philosophers used, and which began with the Cynics in the third century B.C. (see p. 638).

The subject matter of Epictetus' work is largely confined to ethics. A committed Stoic himself, he is immensely successful at expressing the self-mastery and humanity of the Stoic way of life. No ancient moralist, perhaps no writer of any period, has disseminated his teaching with greater fervour and personal feeling. Epictetus knew slavery and he constantly emphasizes that area of life in which all men are free, their attitudes of mind. His *Discourses* abound in anecdotes and imaginary conversations; their style is lively and informal. Here are two examples:

> Remember that you are an actor in a play, the character of which is determined by the playwright; if he wishes the play to be short, it is short; if long, it is long... This is your business, to play admirably the role assigned to you; but the selection of that role is another's [i.e. god's]. (*Ench.* 17, tr. Oldfather)

Here are the two principles that you ought to have ready at hand: Outside the

---

[1] Wirth (1967).

sphere of the moral purpose there is nothing either good or bad; and, we ought not to lead events, but to follow them. 'My brother ought not to have treated me so.' No; but it is for him to look to that. As for me, no matter how he behaves, I shall observe all my relations to him as I ought. (*Diss.* 3.10.18–19)

The emperor Marcus Aurelius was too young to have known Epictetus, but he thanks a friend for acquainting him with his works (1.7). As a solace from the cares of his office and as a means of self-admonition Marcus wrote a long series of *Meditations*, the title of which, in our manuscripts, is 'To himself'. It is unlikely that Marcus had any intention of publishing his thoughts in book form, and how they came to be transmitted to the Middle Ages remains a mystery. P. A. Brunt has called the *Meditations* a spiritual diary,[1] and they are certainly unique in ancient literature.

Marcus' first language was Latin, but like most educated Romans he was fluent in Greek, and this was the natural language to choose for philosophical reflections. The *Meditations*, probably composed in Marcus' last years, are arranged in twelve books. The first consists of seventeen expressions of gratitude to friends, relations and the gods – each introduced by the word 'from': e.g. 'From my father: gentleness...' The remaining books are too varied in style and subject to be summarized briefly. They contain moral homilies addressed to himself, with constant references to the power and purpose of universal Nature, the kinship of man with the totality of things, the passage of time and the flux of life. Some examples:

Journey then through this passage of time in accord with nature, and graciously depart, as a ripened olive might fall, praising the earth which produced it, grateful to the tree that made it grow. (4.48, tr. Grube)

All those who were famous of old have been surrendered to oblivion, and all those who sang their fame have vanished long ago. (7.6)

Everything came into being for a purpose, be it a horse, or a vine. Why does this surprise you? Even the Sun will say: 'I was born for a purpose.' (8.19)

Marcus used Stoicism as a framework for expressing his own reflections and beliefs rather than as a system which he set out to expound. His writings are sometimes little more than jottings and conventional moral sentiments. But much of the time the reader is made aware of a strong and sympathetic personality.

Before concluding this short treatment of the Stoics, a little must be said about ways in which they influenced literary theory. Under the general heading of 'dialectic' they included the theoretical study of language and, in particular, grammar (Diog. Laert. 7.43–4, 55–62). Their analysis of tenses, inflections of nouns and adjectives, and parts of speech was perhaps the greatest achievement of Greek grammar. Much of the credit for this work is due to Diogenes of Babylon, and Stoic influence on the earliest surviving grammatical handbook,

---

[1] Brunt (1974) 1.

by Dionysius the Thracian (second century B.C.), is very strong.[1] The names which we still use for tenses and cases are largely Latin equivalents of terms which the Stoics invented. It is no exaggeration to say that they established the basic principles of traditional descriptive grammar.

The Stoics defined rhetoric as 'knowledge of speaking well concerning subjects expressed in narrative form' (Diog. Laert. 7.42). The main lines of their system seem to have been inherited from Theophrastus,[2] but the Stoics added 'brevity' as a fifth virtue of good style, and their interpretation of 'ornamentation' (*kataskeue*) was avoidance of commonplace language rather than subtlety or artifice. As orators the Stoics were concerned with the plain truth of the case rather than with inflaming the emotions of their audience.[3] But they did not ignore stylistics; and the lists of 'tropes' which we find in Roman writers on rhetoric were probably based upon their work.[4]

4. SCEPTICS, CYNICS, AND OTHER POST-ARISTOTELIAN PHILOSOPHERS

Like Stoicism and Epicureanism, Scepticism was a development of the Hellenistic world. As has already been mentioned (p. 622), the Platonic Academy adopted Scepticism from the time of Arcesilaus in the third century B.C. and it continued in this way for the next two hundred years. But Arcesilaus and his successors were not the first Greek philosophers to profess Scepticism, though they may have been the earliest to offer a rigorous criticism of all dogmatic claims to certainty. How far they were anticipated or influenced by Pyrrho of Elis (born *c.* 365 B.C.) is a question which cannot be answered with any precision.[5] Pyrrho's Scepticism was perhaps more a means to the attainment of tranquillity (*ataraxia*) than a theoretical criticism of positivist philosophy. It is difficult to separate his own position from that of later Pyrrhonists, whose methodology is recorded in detail by Sextus Empiricus. Though not an original thinker, Sextus is an invaluable and still relatively neglected source of information about Hellenistic philosophy. The main characteristics of his work are arguments in favour of Scepticism, and criticism of the views of other philosophers from the Sceptic's point of view. He makes little attempt at literary artifice, which would be quite incompatible with the technical vocabulary and logical structure of his work.[6]

Something of Pyrrho's philosophy, however, can be recovered from the

---

[1] Pfeiffer 270.   [2] Kennedy (1963) 293–5.
[3] Kennedy (1963) 291–3.   [4] Barwick (1957) 89ff.
[5] Diogenes Laertius' *Life of Pyrrho* (9.61–108) undoubtedly incorporates much material from later Pyrrhonism. For a short survey of the evidence, which includes references to modern discussions, cf. Long (1974) 75–88.
[6] Janáček (1948) has noted some interesting stylistic differences between *Outlines of Pyrrhonism* and *Against the professors*. The latter work has a richer vocabulary and a more developed periodic style.

fragments of Timon of Phlius. Timon (*c.* 320–230 B.C.), not to be confused with the misanthrope, was best known in antiquity for his *Silloi* 'squint-eyed verses', a hexameter poem in three books, which satirized the whole range of 'dogmatic' philosophers from Thales down to the Stoics, Epicureans, and Academics of his own day. The poem had a mock-heroic style, with extensive parody of Homer, and included philosophers doing verbal battle with one another (Book 1, written in narrative) and probably a journey to the underworld (Book 2, written in dialogue), modelled on *Odyssey* 11, where Timon, under the guidance of Xenophanes, put questions to him about the shades of the philosophers. Xenophanes' doubts about human knowledge were interpreted by later writers as the beginning of philosophical scepticism (see pp. 246ff.). This explains the privileged position he holds, along with Pyrrho, in Timon's work. In following Xenophanes, the first writer of *Silloi*, Timon indicated allegiance to his predecessor.

Another poem by Timon with the strange title *Indalmoi* 'Images' probably looked at the illusory nature of knowledge. In this work, which was written in elegiacs, and in his other writings, which included prose essays and drama, Timon may be presumed to have publicized the philosophy of Pyrrho. The combination of humour or satire and popular philosophy was characteristic of Cynic literature, and Pyrrho, as well as Timon, has some affinity with the Cynics.

The Cynics never constituted a philosophical school in any formal sense. But they are of some literary importance, especially for their influence on the form and moralizing element of Roman satire. The origins of Cynicism go back to Diogenes of Sinope, a contemporary of Aristotle. Diogenes is a figure who so rapidly prompted legends and apocryphal anecdotes that his own life and achievement cannot be assessed with any measure of exactitude. If he wrote the dialogues and tragedies attributed to him (Diog. Laert. 6.80), we know nothing of their content. But it is safe to say that he made an extraordinary impact on his contemporaries. His eccentric actions were calculated to shock and to rouse people from complacent acceptance of conventional attitudes. Diogenes seems in essence to have been a passionate preacher of a life-style which ignored wealth, social status and other conventional goods. What mattered to him was one thing only, the proper use of human reason, and the stark alternative, 'Reason or a rope', probably reflects the pungent and memorable nature of his own discourse.[1]

By his teaching and example Diogenes attracted followers, the most significant of whom was Crates of Thebes (*c.* 365–285). Like Diogenes he dedicated himself to a life of rigorous simplicity; and the influence he exerted on Zeno of

---

[1] Even if none of the sayings attributed to Diogenes (Diog. Laert. 6.22–80) is genuine, which is improbable, they are rarely banal and serve to exemplify the liveliness of Cynic wit.

Citium tells us much about his moral integrity. Cynicism easily degenerated into a cult of poverty, moral posturing and insincere exhibitionism, but its best practitioners were the nearest thing in antiquity to mendicant friars.

Crates popularized the principles of Diogenes in short elegiac poems called *Paignia* 'trifles'. They expressed serious moral points in a vivid and satirical style, emphasizing the value of a simple virtuous life and contrasting this with luxury. That became the stock theme of Cynic literature. Crates seems to have readily adapted or parodied the work of famous poets including Homer (cf. fr. 6) and he also wrote tragedies, of which two fragments survive. One of these makes a satirical contrast between the high value which people set on cooks, flatterers and brothelkeepers and the little esteem enjoyed by doctors, counsellors and philosophers (fr. 13). The other says that if hunger and time fail to put an end to erotic passion, a man can always hang himself (fr. 14).

In the third century B.C. there were other Cynic poets. Cercidas of Megalopolis expressed moral sentiments in *Meliambi*. These were short lyrical poems the content of which was conversational and satirical.[1] The fragments are substantial enough to give an idea of Cercidas' style and subject matter. He argued that the unequal distribution of wealth casts doubt upon divine providence (fr. 1a) and he adapted or perverted well-known passages from the traditional poets. Fr. 3 is autobiographical and expresses tranquillity in old age. He also refers by name to Zeno of Citium, and Sphaerus, another contemporary Stoic. The dialect of the *Meliambi* is literary Doric, and they contain many new words, especially compound adjectives.

The earliest known Cynic literature was written in verse. But the literary form chiefly associated with the Cynics was the *diatribe*. This term has no pejorative sense in Greek; its primary meaning is passage of time, and as early as Plato it can be used for a speech or discourse. The Stoics, Zeno and Cleanthes, wrote works with this title and we may presume that these were short moral homilies. But the surviving Stoic examples of the genre, Epictetus' discourses recorded by Arrian (see above, p. 634), were influenced by the Cynic diatribe, which was probably first developed by a younger contemporary of Zeno, Bion of Borysthenes. Some idea of the form and content of Bion's diatribes can be recovered by reading another Cynic writer, Teles, who probably lived in the latter part of the third century.

Teles drew heavily on other writers especially Bion, to whom he frequently refers. The subjects of his diatribes are standard Cynic themes – self-sufficiency, freedom from emotional disturbances, the depreciation of pleasure. The style is simple and the moral points are made clearly, but Teles lacks the wit and bite 'for which Bion was chiefly known (Diog. Laert. 4.46–54). Horace is referring to satire when he speaks of 'a man who takes pleasure in the discourses of Bion

[1] Powell–Barber (1921) 4ff.

and sarcasm' (*Epist.* 2.2.60). Even more significant for Roman satire was Menippus of Gadara, another Cynic writer of the third century B.C. Diogenes Laertius says that he completely lacked 'seriousness' (6.99) but he was generally regarded as an exponent of *spoudogeloion* 'seriousness combined with laughter' (Strabo 16.2.29). The titles of Menippus' works show that mockery of other philosophers was one of his themes, in which he was followed much later by Lucian. His work interspersed prose and verse and became the model for Varro's *Saturae Menippeae*, Petronius' *Satyricon*, and Seneca's *Apocolocyntosis*.

Important new developments in Stoicism, Epicureanism and Scepticism, the three systems of thought which first arose in the early Hellenistic world, seem to have come to an end by the beginning of the Christian era. Philosophical writing in Greek on these subjects continued for the next two hundred years, but there are other features of Greek philosophy at this time which call for a brief mention. First, it was an age which in some respects looked back rather than forwards, and this is indicated by the popularity of handbooks recording the main tenets of different philosophers. The two most notable of such compilers are Arius Didymus (first century B.C.) and Aëtius (first–second century A.D.) whose work was excerpted by the author of the *Epitome* attributed to Plutarch and by John of Stobi (Stobaeus, fifth century A.D.). Thus at third hand we are able to recover many outlines of positions taken by Hellenistic and earlier philosophers whose own work has perished.

Secondly, it was an age of eclecticism. Philosophers borrowed from and adopted views of rival schools, and the distinguishing marks between Stoics, Platonists and Peripatetics tended to become blurred. One of the most remarkable of such eclectics was Philo of Alexandria, a Jew who represents the culmination of a long tradition of Jewish learning in Alexandria. The Alexandrian Jews spoke Greek but retained close connexions with Palestine. In the copious writings of Philo we witness an extraordinary synthesis of Greek philosophical concepts and Judaism. Philo was not an uncritical user of Greek philosophy. His use of the term *Logos*, for instance, though influenced by the Stoics, refers to the 'incorporeal' mind of God, whereas Stoic *Logos* was corporeal. For Philo Greek philosophy provided a means to interpret events and persons from the scriptures allegorically. This method of interpretation was used by him continuously: thus he explains the creation of the world in terms of Plato's *Timaeus* and claims that this was what Moses really meant. Philo used much of the standard philosophical terminology of his time and was fully conversant with a large stock of Greek philosophical writing.

Thirdly, it was an age which offered a receptive hearing to 'wisdom literature', spiritual authorities and the elevation of mind over body. These are some of the characteristics of Neopythagoreanism, a school of thought which it is notoriously difficult to define precisely. As early as the third century B.C. there was a tradition of 'Pythagorean writings', composed in literary Doric, which purported to record the life and doctrines of Pythagoras and even included fabricated works under his name.[1] The connexion between such apocrypha and the Pythagorean revival (Neopythagoreanism) of the first century B.C. is far from clear. In its beginnings Neopythagoreanism belongs more to religion and occultism than to philosophy. But in association with the revival of interest in Plato's dialogues, especially the *Timaeus*, it helped to prepare the way for the last Greek philosopher of outstanding significance, Plotinus.

The philosophy of Plotinus is ostensibly an interpretation of Plato. But if Plato's writings were his chief inspiration Plotinus, like his immediate predecessors and successors, incorporated ideas from the Stoics and Peripatetics. His philosophy is a 'comprehensive synthesis'[2] and yet at the same time a highly individual representation of reality and the place of man in the cosmos. Plotinus is both a rationalist and religious or mystical thinker, and the combination of these two attitudes of mind, which are so frequently opposed to one another, gives his writings a strangely catholic appeal. They express an intense spiritual vision, which may be appreciated on many levels, moral, religious, intellectual and aesthetic, but which is in essence a unified conception of all things as 'emanations' from a single immaterial power that so transcends everything else that it is beyond description.

The writings (*Enneads*) of Plotinus are a series of short essays in which he presents his philosophy through the investigation of specific topics, e.g. *On the movement of the heavens*, *On destiny*, *On eternity and time*. The starting point of these is often, as in Aristotle, a problem requiring solution (*aporia*) or the views which others, especially Plato, had adopted. Plotinus wrote for his own philosophical circle, and the arrangement of his work today is due to his pupil Porphyry. The title *Enneads* means 'collections of nine', and Porphyry gave this shape to Plotinus' work by arranging his writings into six books, each containing nine essays. This classification corresponds in no sense to the chronology of Plotinus' work, which Porphyry recorded in his *Life of Plotinus* (4–6). Porphyry's arrangement is broadly conceptual: human nature, ethics and aesthetics are treated in *Enn*. 1, physics and cosmology in *Enn*. 2 and 3, psychology in *Enn*. 4 and logic and metaphysics in *Enn*. 5 and 6. But each *Ennead* contains subjects which fall outside these limits.

Plotinus is difficult in style as well as in thought. His manner of writing is allusive, sometimes severely compressed, and it 'often reflects the irregular structure of oral statements'.[3] But he has a notable ability to express the mystic's longing to escape from temporality and all other limitations of earthly existence. Here is one example:

[1] For the evidence and discussion cf. Thesleff (1961 and 1965) and Burkert (1961).
[2] Dodds, *OCD* 727.   [3] Dodds, *OCD* 847.

But how shall we find the way? What method can we devise? How can one see the 'inconceivable beauty' [Plato's phrase] which stays within in the holy sanctuary and does not come out where the profane may see it? Let him who can, follow and come within, and leave outside the sight of his eyes and not turn back to the bodily splendours which he saw before. When he sees the beauty in bodies he must not run after them; he must know that they are images, traces, shadows, and hurry away to that which they image . . . we cannot get there on foot; for our feet only carry us everywhere in this world, from one country to another. You must not get ready a carriage, either, or a boat. Let all these things go, and do not look. Shut your eyes, and . . . wake another way of seeing, which everyone has but few use. (*Enn.* 1.6.8 tr. Armstrong)

20

THE LITERATURE OF THE EMPIRE

I. THE EARLY EMPIRE:
GEOGRAPHY, HISTORY, LITERARY CRITICISM

Strabo

After the defeat of Antony at Actium in 31 B.C. and the fall of Alexandria in the next year, the eastern and western parts of the Roman empire quickly recovered from the divisiveness of Rome's civil war; and with the encouragement of the heir of Caesar, soon to be named Augustus, the Graeco-Roman culture of the Mediterranean world renewed itself. Several of the major Greek writers of the Augustan age made their way to Rome in the year 30 B.C. or just a little later.

The geographer Strabo came to Rome in 29 B.C. But Strabo had been there before. Already before the murder of Caesar he had left his native Asia Minor to visit Rome; and for him, as for other Augustan Greek men of letters, Romans were to become the principal patrons. He went to Egypt in the company of the prefect Aelius Gallus, and many years later it was the emperor Tiberius whose accession impelled Strabo, for reasons still obscure, to a new burst of activity. Although Strabo boasts at one point that he has travelled widely, from the Black Sea to Ethiopia and from Armenia to Etruria, it appears that he did little more than get from one place to another without inspecting much on the way. He reveals that he stopped at the island of Gyarus off the coast of Greece, but he seems never to have set foot in Athens. Strabo was a scholar at heart, and he worked from books.

The geographer's first publication was a work of history, the *Historical commentaries*, which are now lost. The commentaries were an unbalanced kind of universal history. They occupied forty-seven books, of which all but the first four were concerned with the post-Polybian period. One of Strabo's sources was none other than his own contemporary, Timagenes of Alexandria, who must have just barely completed his own history. It looks as if Strabo, like Dionysius, Timagenes, Nicolaus of Damascus, and doubtless other Greek writers, was taking advantage of the Augustan peace to write history for the new generation of Greeks, who may still have been stunned by the speed with which the old order had changed. Like Dionysius, Strabo had educated Roman readers in mind as much as Greeks. In the preface to his *Geography* he notes that the new work is based on comparable principles to those of the *Commentaries* – moral and political usefulness – and addressed to the same class of readers, particularly those in high positions (τοὺς ἐν ταῖς ὑπεροχαῖς).

Strabo calls his *Geography* a κολοσσουργία a 'colossal work' and asks that it be judged like a colossal statue, not in detail but with a view to the overall effect. This is an odd request in regard to a book which is essentially a compilation of details and lacks any noticeable harmony of structure. Yet to judge from the opening books, with their abundant citation of literature (especially Homer) and their polemic (especially against Eratosthenes), the initial concept of the *Geography* was considerably more audacious than it became later. Strabo evidently worked on the project over a long stretch of time, perhaps from the middle twenties down to about 2 B.C. Then, mysteriously, he stopped work, leaving untouched observations that were no longer true after that date. A group of references to the early years of Tiberius' reign suggests a renewal of writing under the inspiration of the new regime. The large ambitions of Strabo's preface slipped away somehow.

Although Homer could scarcely be considered a reliable source for geography, Strabo's reliance on him is characteristic of his general predilection for written testimony. This is even the case for regions he had actually seen himself. Such a method is not, however, unusual in antiquity. Sallust, for example, in the generation before Strabo had done just the same in writing about North Africa, where he had served under Caesar. Only in his account of Egypt does Strabo draw at length on his own experiences, and this is rather in the nature of a tribute to his patron and commander, Aelius Gallus, and an explanation of the failure of Gallus' expedition to Saudi Arabia.

Strabo's wide reading and his deep interest in history, as well as his glancing allusions to contemporary people and events, make his *Geography* a much more valuable record of Greek culture under the early Principate than might at first be imagined. His reading ranged far beyond the writings of geographers; he had important friends. Without his conviction that historical geography could be a useful tool for the leading men of his time, his own work might have been very drab.

Dionysius of Halicarnassus

Dionysius arrived in Rome in about 30 B.C., not long before Strabo. He came from Halicarnassus, modern Bodrum on the west coast of Asia Minor. His education in rhetoric had given him a lasting hatred of the florid and overblown verbiage of the so-called Asianic orators, but he saw in the Romans what he considered a salutary taste for a more disciplined style. In the capital of the empire he found himself in congenial circles of other expatriate Greeks and of cultivated, Greek-speaking Romans. The environment unlocked his energies and provided the background for his entire surviving *oeuvre*.

Dionysius was both a rhetorician and a historian. It is evident that in the former capacity he instructed young Romans as well as composed didactic treatises; he did not, however, declaim. As a historian, he obliged his patrons, of whom Q. Aelius Tubero (himself a historian) was the most notable; and he interpreted the rise of Rome for Greek audiences. The two aspects of Dionysius' literary activity were complementary, since he regarded his historical work as an exemplification of his rhetorical theory. His detailed studies of the Greek orators of the classical period together with his careful analysis of Thucydides' history reveal an author uncommonly attentive to the interplay between style and history, both in the men who made history and in those who wrote it.

In his preface to the essays on the classical orators Dionysius pays a glowing tribute to the Romans for encouraging lucidity in literature rather than the dithyrambic prose of the Asianists:

> The ancient, sober Rhetoric has been restored to her former rightful place of honour, while the brainless new Rhetoric has been restrained from enjoying a fame which it does not deserve and from living in luxury on the fruits of another's labours. And this is perhaps not the only reason for praising the present age and the men who guide its culture...but equally to be commended is the rapidity with which they have brought about this change and the measure of the improvement...I think that the cause and origin of this great revolution has been the conquest of the world by Rome...And since this great revolution has taken place in so short a time, I should not be surprised if that craze for a silly style of oratory fails to survive another single generation. (*De ant. orat.* 2–3)

These remarks serve as an introduction to critical studies of the fourth-century Attic masters, Lysias, Isocrates, Isaeus and Demosthenes. Dionysius judged that his work would be useful to students of political philosophy no less than of style. For all his good intentions his treatment of the orators is nevertheless strongly affected by the frigidity of traditional rhetoric, especially in the obsession with imitation (μίμησις). It is perhaps just as well for his reputation that Dionysius' anterior work on imitation has largely been lost.

The essay on Demosthenes looks forward in one important respect to Dionysius' subsequent and more mature critical writings. It makes use of the illuminating device of recasting sentences to illustrate points of prose style. In the *Demosthenes* Dionysius revises an awkward sentence to demonstrate how it should have been written. In his treatise on word-order (*De compositione uerborum*) he employs the same device to prove the perfection of a particularly brilliant passage. Dionysius' use of recasting as an effective means of literary criticism transcends earlier work of this kind and may well have influenced the author of the essay *On the sublime* in making similar tests of Demosthenes' prose. The difficulty of reading Dionysius' treatise on word-order should not obscure the magnitude of his achievement and the sensitivity of his criticism. His perceptive analysis of the lines on Sisyphus at *Odyssey* 11.593–6 is arresting and intelligent. Dionysius gives particular attention to the emotional impact of syllable quantities and word lengths in conjunction with the sense that the words are conveying.

Dionysius' views on Thucydides have often brought him ridicule and derision, which he certainly does not deserve. It is important to recall that Thucydides was much admired in Dionysius' day, and among the Augustan philologists with whom he associated at Rome (cf. *De Thuc.* 2) there was inevitably some lack of critical judgement. Dionysius readily acknowledged Thucydides as the greatest of all historians (τὸν ἁπάντων κράτιστον τῶν ἱστοριογράφων, *De Thuc.* 2); he had no desire to diminish the historian's stature. But, as a good academic, he did not think it unbecoming to point out the faults that he observed in a masterpiece. The modern reader will naturally have more sympathy with Dionysius' criticism of Thucydides' often impenetrable Greek than with his view of the unworthiness of the subject Thucydides chose for his history. Yet even the latter criticism is comprehensible within the rhetorical system from which Dionysius never altogether freed himself, and the former is simply true. Dionysius' attack on the style of Plato in a letter to a certain Cn. Pompeius shows him taking up an equally reasonable position. For example, on Thucydides he observes:

> Whenever he uses it [his style] with controlled moderation he is superb and in a class of his own; but when he uses it excessively and in breach of good taste, without discrimination of circumstances or regard for the degree required, he deserves censure. (*De Thuc.* 51)

On Plato Dionysius is comparably balanced:

> The language of Plato, as I have said before, aspires to unite two several styles, the elevated and the plain. But it does not succeed equally in both. . . Let no one suppose that I say this in general condemnation of the ornate and uncommon style which Plato adopts. I should be sorry to be so perverse as to conceive this opinion with respect to so great a man. On the contrary, I am well aware that often and on many subjects he has produced writings which are great and admirable and of the utmost power. (*Epist. ad Pomp.* 758–61)

As a literary critic Dionysius is by no means negligible. As a historian he merits respect for his diligence in research and his fluency in exposition. The *Roman antiquities*, of which just over half survive, trace the rise of Rome from the beginnings to the First Punic War. The history is admittedly tendentious: it was to be the first full account of early Rome in Greek, 'for no accurate history of the Romans written in the Greek language has hitherto appeared'

(*Ant.Rom.* 1.54). Dionysius argued that the Romans were actually Greeks by origin, and the point was obviously useful in encouraging goodwill in the east. Dionysius also aimed at educated Roman readers, who could read Fabius Pictor in Greek and would be pleased by this account of their ancestors. Finally Dionysius saw his work as an expression of thanks to the city of Rome for all the advantages he had received there. His history is rhetorical and occasionally platitudinous, but based on important sources. It is well worth having in addition to Livy. Dionysius discharged his debt to the Romans handsomely and with dignity.

'LONGINUS' AND OTHERS

Far the best later critic is the unknown author of *On the sublime*, probably of the first century A.D. Writing with impassioned conviction and richly varied style and imagery – 'himself the great Sublime he draws' (Pope) – Longinus[1] cuts across traditional distinctions of genre and style to analyse and show how we too may attain one particular quality, sublimity or 'height', ὕψος:

> a kind of pinnacle or prominence in speech . . . the source from which the greatest poets and prose-writers have achieved supremacy and eternal fame. (1.3)

It is what makes great literature great; he finds it in Homer, Plato, Demosthenes, a love-lyric of Sappho, the Latin of Cicero and – uniquely in pagan criticism – the Creation in Genesis. What unites all instances is their impact, a violent emotional response of ecstasy: sublimity does not charm or persuade, it stuns, an irresistible force compelling us to share the author's inspiration and feel we have created what we have only heard. This is perhaps the first truly affective theory of literature, but it is not uncritical impressionism: sublimity must overwhelm the man of literary taste and experience, withstand repeated scrutiny and meet universal acclaim, 'pleasing all always' (7.3).

Longinus combines this emotive effect with a moral approach. Sublimity is achieved first and foremost from nobility of mind, a moral stature or pride. Its virtual absence explains the decline of literature in his own day (44), its presence guarantees success: ὕψος μεγαλοφροσύνης ἀπήχημα 'sublimity is the echo of a great mind' (9.2). Examples from Homer are Ajax's silence in the Underworld (*Od.* 11.563), Ajax's prayer for light when darkness prevents combat: 'be it but light, then kill us since such is thy will' (*Il.* 17.645–7), and the greater because more ethically correct scene when Homer shows the gods not in their frailties ('he makes his men like gods, his gods like men' 9.7) but in the pure godhead of Poseidon's epiphany (*Il.* 13.18ff.). In the great digression on genius (33–6), sublimity of mind is what draws us close to the divine mind and it is by innate kinship that we recognize sublimity, instinctively marvelling at mighty rivers

---

[1] For name and identity see Appendix.

and the ocean, not small streams however clear and useful – an obvious hit at Callimachus. Greatness must involve the danger of failure, but flawed genius is superior to polished mediocrity, Homer to Apollonius, Pindar to Bacchylides. Even if we mistrust the moral demand, this is an eloquent plea for boldness and breadth of vision over safe conformity.

Longinus promises to discuss in turn five sources of sublimity: nobility of thought and vehement emotion, both largely innate, and three technical sources, figures of speech, diction and word-arrangement (8). This textbook structure is mainly a convenient frame within which he considers the interplay of the first two sources with each other and with the rest, continually highlighting the author himself and the emotional continuum binding author, work and audience. Emotion, the most original source, seems to lack independent analysis, though this puzzle was presumably solved in the long lacuna after 9.4, since emotion pervades what follows. Thus Homer's decline in emotional power with age explains why in contrast to the rage of battle in the *Iliad* he is content with narrative in the *Odyssey*, like a setting sun, still impressive but without the force; intensity similarly differentiates Demosthenes and Cicero, the one a thunderbolt, the other a spreading fire; and in a detailed sensitive appreciation Sappho is praised for her distillation of the emotions of love. Not all emotions have moral stature, notably pity, grief and fear, but 'nothing is more productive of sublimity than noble passion' (8.4), nor is this surprising since it combines the first two sources.

Technique alone can create sublimity, as in Euripides' masterly word-arrangement (40), but is normally subordinate to genius. It is for example the blinding brilliance of surrounding sublimity and emotion which hides otherwise obtrusive artifice, as when Demosthenes' anger unleashes a torrent of metaphors (32). Perfection is nature aided by art, and in using a trope or figure what matters is when, where, how and why. Lurking here is the old idea of the appropriate, but Longinus breaks away from the mere matching of content and form to concentrate on the functional use of style and the purpose and mind of the author. The latter emphasis also invigorates his treatment of imitation, μίμησις (13–14), paradoxically a form of inspiration, where one mind is fired by another, the first stimulus to independent creation.

Longinus has been enormously influential, particularly among Romantic critics. In antiquity he is nowhere cited. His concern with author and effect recalls Plato, but for Plato emotion is dangerous, the poet an ignorant madman. A closer source was contemporary rhetorical theory. This distinguished literature which moves from that which delights or persuades (see, e.g., Cic. *Orator* 69) and isolated grandeur as a specific quality or type of style – though the link is in part illusory, since grandeur is associated by these theorists with richly elaborate diction. Both the theory of qualities (ἀρεταί), and the theory of styles (χαρακτῆρες) were highly influential by the first century A.D. Though formally distinct, they are closely related – the grand style, for example, is speech shaped to show the quality of grandeur in a particular and appropriate context – and it is within these two critical frameworks that Greek developed its wide technical vocabulary for delicate analysis by critics such as Longinus.

The theory of qualities elaborated Theophrastus' list of four qualities of style, correct diction, lucidity, propriety and ornamentation.[1] Brevity was added by the Stoics, and ornamentation was subdivided into a catalogue of non-essential or additional virtues, forming the three groups of charm, grandeur and force. Our main source, Dionysius of Halicarnassus, lists them rather mechanically without analysis. Thus Lysias has the essential qualities and charm but lacks grandeur and force (*Lys.* 13), Thucydides and Herodotus both possess grandeur but Thucydides has more force, Herodotus more charm (*Ad Pomp.* 3, *De Thuc.* 23). Longinus attacks those who value wide range above quality (34): Hyperides combines the qualities of Demosthenes and Lysias, but Demosthenes is more truly sublime.

Demetrius *On style* is our only surviving detailed example of the theory of styles. The early history of this theory is obscure and controversial, particularly Theophrastus' contribution, but we commonly find two styles, grand and plain, or three, grand, plain and middle or elegant.[2] Demetrius offers an otherwise unknown set of four styles, though there were other examples of four, as in the different quartet of Philodemus (*Rh.* 1.165 Sudhaus). The four styles are the grand, plain, elegant and forceful, roughly parallel to distinctions found in the theory of qualities, since the essential qualities are all that is needed in the plain style, while the additional virtues provide grandeur, charm and force. Each style is discussed under content, diction and word-arrangement, as are the corresponding faulty styles, the frigid, arid, affected and repulsive. Form and content match according to the demands of propriety: the grand style with rich diction and elaborate sentences is suited to the impressive narrative of battles and cosmic myths, the plain style to scenes of ordinary life, the forceful to anger and Cynic invective, the elegant to the poetry of Sappho, love, wedding-songs and gardens. This last style is less of a unity, since it divides into charm and wit, though admittedly graceful wit distinguished from laughter and gibes. This whole section (128–89) is one of the rare surviving accounts of wit. Unusual too is the brief but sensible appreciation of letter-writing (223–35): the letter reflects the character of the writer and must not be a pompous tract nor disjointedly conversational in the manner of a dialogue, since it is a written form and sent as a sort of gift. Demetrius is also an important source for such standard topics as metaphor and sentences; his discussion of both shows

---

[1] Cic. *Orator* 79; cf. above, p. 623, Bonner (1939) 15–21.
[2] See, e.g., Austin (1948) on Quint. 12.10.58.

Peripatetic influence. His date is uncertain but he probably reflects ideas current B.C.: thus Demosthenes is – refreshingly – not yet the supreme maestro of all styles but is virtually confined to the forceful style. The examples cover a wide range of author and genre and the comment is usually shrewd, as in the praise of Thucydides' successful use of Homer's epithet 'sea-girt' (ἀμφίρρυτος) not for decorative richness but to reinforce an argument for the unity of Sicily, a single 'sea-girt land' (113).

On style is a modest textbook, but good of its kind, unlike the mostly arid wastes of the later rhetoricians,[1] obsessed as they are with classification and terminological niceties. For a survey of the critical system familiar to the sophists we turn to Quintilian, for literary theory to minor works of the sophists themselves, e.g. Plutarch, *De audiendis poetis*, Lucian, *De historia conscribenda*, or Dio 52, a comparison of the *Philoctetes* of Aeschylus, Sophocles and Euripides. Surveying professional critics, we may note the Περὶ ἰδεῶν, *On types of style*, of the second-century Hermogenes of Tarsus, where he analyses discursively but quite sensibly a later refinement of the theory of qualities,[2] a system of seven styles with further subdivisions. More unusual are a few treatises discussing genres of epideictic oratory, one misattributed to Dionysius, two to Menander Rhetor (the first, probably incomplete, has perhaps more claim to be his). Probably third-century, they give rules and *topoi* for forms such as the *propemptikon* (good wishes to a friend for a safe journey) and the hymn, giving an interesting insight into earlier poetry[3] and new popular prose forms such as the hymn and monody.

2. POETRY

Poetic miniatures

The bulk of the surviving Greek literature of the Imperial age is in prose and implies limited interest in traditional verse forms. It is clear from surviving scraps that a certain quantity of sterile epic was being turned out but rarely with the competence of a Quintus of Smyrna or a Nonnus in late antiquity. For didactic purposes poetry could still be useful, as it was in some metrical treatises on medicine, in the fables of Babrius and in the poems on hunting and fishing ascribed to Oppian. Religion sometimes moved the pious to compose poetic celebrations of favourite deities, but even decent versifiers like Aelius Aristides preferred to write hymns in prose. Drama had all but vanished, and its place was usurped by mime and dialogue. The legacy of Callimachus and the epigrammatists who succeeded him determined the fate of Greek poetry under

---

[1] See collections in Walz and Spengel.
[2] Cf. Ps.-Aristides, *Libri rhetorici*, ed. Schmid (1926). Hermogenes is hardly original. See Hagedorn (1964).
[3] See Cairns (1972); Russell and Wilson (1981).

the Roman Empire. Brevity, allusiveness, elegance, wit were its characteristic features. The poets became workers in miniature, and much of their achieve- ment was fortunately preserved in the Greek Anthology. In the last century inscriptions and papyri have furnished some supplementary material.

The Garland of Meleager had brought together, already at the beginning of the first century B.C., a substantial collection of epigrams of the Hellenistic period. Just as Meleager's anthology can be disengaged from the late and massive repertoire of epigrams of the Greek Anthology, so too can the anthology of Meleager's successor as a collector, Philip of Thessalonica, be similarly detached.[1] In many ways the job is easier because Philip had arranged his poems in alphabetical order by the first letter of the first line, and the survival of blocks of poems in this order within the Greek Anthology guarantees their inclusion in Philip's Garland. In his prefatory poem (*Anth.Pal.* 4.2) Philip named several of his authors explicitly. Altogether thirty-nine poets can be assigned with reasonable certainty to the second major garland of epigrams. They all wrote after Meleager. Since, with the possible exception of *Anth.Pal.* 9.178 (which may have been interpolated subsequently), no poem in the Garland alludes to anything later than the reign of Gaius, it seems reasonable to assume that the collection was prepared at that time. It was dedicated to a Camillus, who has been identified plausibly with the consul of A.D. 32, L. Arruntius Camillus Scribonianus. If the identification is correct, Camillus' revolt against the emperor Claudius in A.D. 42 constitutes a firm date before which Philip's Garland must have been issued.

Of the epigrammatists in the reigns of Augustus, Tiberius and Gaius, Crinagoras is the most notable. From the aristocracy of Mytilene he passed to the inner circles of the Augustan court. Most of his poems, while lacking in metrical subtlety, are vivid and clever commemorations of important persons and events of the time. Crinagoras was a poet who wrote for occasions, like the return of the young Marcellus from Spain or the marriage of the philhellenic Juba, king of Mauretania, to Cleopatra Selene. The few poems for which precise references cannot now be discerned still await their interpreter, for there is no good reason to think that Crinagoras wrote purely epideictic epigrams. Inasmuch as he was still alive when Cleopatra Selene died in A.D. 11 (*Anth.Pal.* 7.633), this poet laureate, who once went on an embassy to Julius Caesar,[2] must have lived to an advanced age.

Argentarius is the best of the poets in Philip's garland; and if, as is likely, he is identical with the rhetorician mentioned by the elder Seneca, he belongs to the principate of Augustus and the early years of Tiberius' rule.[3] His erotic and satiric epigrams, composed in an elegant and fluent style, are virtually unique

---

[1] Gow–Page, *Garland* I pp. XI–XXI.   [2] Gow–Page, *Garland* II 211.
[3] Gow–Page, *Garland* II 166.

in this period. They anticipated and perhaps inspired the achievements of the Neronian renaissance of both Greek and Latin letters. Several of the other writers represented in the garland, including Philip himself, were practitioners of the overwrought and extravagant style associated particularly with the Hellenistic epigrammatist, Leonidas of Tarentum. Maccius, the most successful of Philip's Leonideans, composed two epigrams on the dedications of fishermen to Priapus (*Anth.Pal.* 6.33 and 89). These display the style to its greatest advantage: for example,

Αἰγιαλῖτα Πρίηπε, σαγηνευτῆρες ἔθηκαν
δῶρα παρακταίης σοὶ τάδ' ἐπωφελίης,
θύννων εὐκλώστοιο λίνου βυσσώμασι ῥόμβον
φράξαντες γλαυκαῖς ἐν παρόδοις πελάγευς,
φηγίνεον κρατῆρα καὶ αὐτούργητον ἐρείκης
βάθρον ἰδ' ὑαλέην οἰνοδόκον κύλικα,
ὡς ἂν ὑπ' ὀρχησμῶν λελυγισμένον ἔγκοπον ἴχνος
ἀμπαύσῃς ξηρὴν δίψαν ἐλαυνόμενος.

These gifts, Priapus of the beach, seine-fishers have dedicated to you for your help beside the shore, having fenced round the whirl of tunnies with the linen of well-spun nets in the grey channels of the sea: an oak-wood mixing-bowl, and a hand-made bench of heath, and a wine-welcoming cup of glass, so that you may rest your weary feet after their twisting in the dance and chase dry thirst away. (*Anth.Pal.* 6.33, tr. Gow–Page)

The epigrams of one Honestus in Philip's anthology appear to be the work of an interesting poet in the Tiberian court whose poems were discovered in modern times on statue-bases in the grove of the Muses at the foot of Mount Helicon. It may be assumed that just as with Crinagoras and Augustus, some Greek poets of the next generation owed their inspiration to imperial patronage – whether from Tiberius himself, who admired Hellenistic preciosity, or from court women, like Livia and the younger Antonia, who had a taste for Greek culture.

The reign of Nero was as fruitful in Greek literature as it was in Latin. The origins of the Second Sophistic movement can be dated to this time with the advent of Nicetes of Smyrna; and two distinguished epigrammatists known from the Greek Anthology belong to this same period. One is Lucillius, the author of some one hundred brilliant satirical epigrams which, as has long been recognized, were an important influence on Martial, the great Latin epigrammatist of the next generation. Lucillius, who is most unlikely to be identical with the long-suffering recipient of Seneca's moral letters, directed his barbs against assorted human shortcomings such as sloppy table manners, physical deficiencies, bad character, and the like. He was also a sharp parodist, as can be seen in the way he rewrote the following tribute to Myron's much admired sculpture of a cow:

Βουκόλε, τὰν ἀγέλαν πόρρω νέμε, μὴ τὸ Μύρωνος
βοίδιον ὡς ἔμπνουν βουσὶ συνεξελάσηις.   (*Anth. Pal.* 9.715)

Shepherd, move your flock farther on so you won't take along with your cows the one by Myron as if it were real.

Lucillius turned this into the following:

Βουκόλε, τὰν ἀγέλαν πόρρω νέμε, μὴ σε Περικλῆς
ὁ κλέπτης αὐταῖς βουσὶ συνεξελάσηι.   (*Anth. Pal.* 11.178)

Shepherd, move your flock farther on so Pericles the rustler won't take *you* along with your cows.

The other significant Greek poet of Nero's day was Strato of Sardis, who (though once dated to the Hadrianic age) has been conclusively shown to have been another writer to influence Martial.[1] Strato was the author of a collection of epigrams in celebration of paederasty, and his Μοῦσα παιδική occupies, together with works of others on the same theme[2] the twelfth book of the Greek Anthology. His poems, while alluding to the grossest improprieties, display an elegant and cultivated style. The nicely pointed epigram (*Anth. Pal.* 12.175) rebuking a dinner host for disapproving of amorous glances at the boy pouring wine is clearly the model for the somewhat more heavy-handed poem of Martial 9.25, which has exactly the same denouement though varying the mythological examples. Strato's poems form an apt complement to the novel by his contemporary, Petronius.

It is scarcely surprising that the next gifted miniaturist in Greek flourished under another philhellene emperor, Hadrian. He was the freedman Mesomedes, who is represented by only two poems in the Greek Anthology. Eleven more have emerged in four late medieval manuscripts, and in two of these musical notation is provided for three poems. The additional works by Mesomedes are not epigrams, as might perhaps have been supposed from the two in the Anthology, but short hymns (to the Sun, Nemesis, Physis, Isis) and virtuoso trivia (such as a description of a sponge, an address to a sundial and a brief piece on a gnat). The existence of the musical notation has raised difficult and important problems about post-Hellenistic metrics, and the metrical elucidation of the annotated hymns is still far from finished.[3] The charm and delicacy of this poet, of whose subtle talents the Greek Anthology gives no hint, serve as a constant reminder of the fragility of inferences based on the texts that happen to survive.

[1] Keydell (1952) 499–500.
[2] A few poems in *Anth. Pal.* 12 are addressed to women, apparently by an oversight on the part of the compiler.
[3] Husman (1955).

The hexameter poems ascribed to Oppian

Among the Greek poems of the Roman Imperial age are two large works, related in character and ascribed to the same author. They are both written in sophisticated dactylic hexameters that abound in the *outré* diction of Alexandrian Homerism. One, a work in five books, concerns the art of fishing and displays much learning about fish; the other, in four books and clearly composed under the influence of the poem on fishing, concerns hunting as well as the animals that are hunted. The name Oppian is attached both to the earlier work, the *Halieutica*, and to the later, the *Cynegetica*. The testimony of late antiquity speaks of one poet, but it is obvious from the poems themselves that there were two distinct poets. The author of the *Halieutica* was a Cilician, whereas the author of the *Cynegetica* was a Syrian. Internal evidence suggests, in addition, that the emperors to whom the earlier poet dedicated his verses were Marcus Aurelius and his son, whereas the later poet was writing for Caracalla.[1] It is virtually impossible to disentangle the biographical details which the confused ancient tradition has blended together, and it may well be that the error in the tradition has obliterated altogether the real name of the author of the *Cynegetica*. It is hard to believe that a poet who chose to imitate the *Halieutica* actually bore his predecessor's name, although he may perhaps have assumed it as a sign of his indebtedness and aspirations. All we can say with certainty is that the name Oppian is used to designate two poets, and it is therefore important to be precise in indicating to which author one is referring.

The *Halieutica*, a conspicuously better poem than the *Cynegetica*, still awaits a modern critical edition. It is a work of remarkable subtlety and poetic power. The author, whose zoological erudition is formidable, nevertheless maintains a flexible verse structure and a momentum in the narrative that are not unworthy of his great Homeric prototype. He manages to invest the creatures of the sea with dignity and, at times, pathos. Few who have read the *Halieutica* forget the dolphin who has strayed from his companions and become the feast of a crowd of sharp-toothed enemies.

> αἱ μὲν γὰρ λυσσηδὸν ἀολλέες ἀμφιχυθεῖσαι
> δελφῖνος μελέεσσι βίην ἐνέρεισαν ὀδόντων...
> αὐτὰρ ὁ παντοίοισι περιπληθὴς καμάτοισι
> πόντον ἐπαιγίζει, σφακέλωι δὲ οἱ ἔνδον ὀρεχθεῖ
> μαινομένη κραδίη, φλεγέθει δὲ οἱ ἦτορ ἀνίηι,
> πάντηι δὲ θρώσκει καὶ ἑλίσσεται ἄκριτα θύων,
> παφλάζων ὀδύνηισι· κυβιστητῆρι δ' ἐοικὼς
> ἄλλοτε μὲν βαθὺ κῦμα διατρέχει ἠΰτε λαῖλαψ,
> ἄλλοτε δ' ἐς νεάτην φέρεται βρύχα...   (*Hal.* 2.573–4, 582–8)

[1] See Appendix, 'The Two Oppians'.

'For furiously they fall in a body about the limbs of the dolphin and fix in him the might of their teeth...And, full of manifold distress, he rushes over the sea and his frenzied heart within him is racked with agony and his spirit is afire with pain. Every way he leaps and turns, rushing blindly in the spasms of agony. Like a diver, now he runs over the deep waves as a whirlwind, now he plunges to the nether deeps. (tr. A. W. Mair)

At the end of his poem the author describes the perilous life of the sponge fisher, who must dive to cut away his victims and who sometimes becomes, in the process, a victim himself:

> καὶ ῥ' ὁ μὲν οἷς ἑτάροισιν ἐπισείων θαμὰ δεσμὸν
> κέκλεται αὖ ἐρύειν, τὸ δὲ οἱ δέμας ἡμιδάϊκτον
> κητείη τε βίη καὶ ὁμόστολοι ἔσπασαν ἄνδρες,
> οἰκτρὸν ἰδεῖν, ἔτι νηὸς ἐφιέμενον καὶ ἑταίρων.　　　(Hal. 5.668–71)

Shaking repeatedly the rope he bids his comrades pull him up. And the mighty Sea-monster and the companions of the fisher pull at his body rent in twain, a pitiful sight to see, still yearning for ship and shipmates. (tr. A. W. Mair)

By comparison the poem on hunting is a disappointing work, and it is strange that it has received more critical attention than the *Halieutica*. Language and imagery are often forced and unconvincing. The poet's learning impinges too much; his curiosity about cross-breeding and about the hybrids that result does not add charm to his work, and his occasional similes can verge on the grotesque. Goats appear to arouse his deepest emotions, but the reader is unlikely to respond to his elaborate evocation of old men, attended by their loving children, as a parallel for old goats (*Cyn.* 2.345–51). The fourth and last book of the work ends abruptly, after some remarks on the bladder of a gazelle and the cleverness of a fox. There is no conclusion or indeed any sign that the poem has come to an end; it may therefore be conjectured that the poet had originally envisaged a fifth and final book so as to make the entire *Cynegetica* a poem in five books, exactly like the *Halieutica*.

These two poems take their place within a recognizable tradition of ancient literature, best known from Latin examples. We possess some 132 hexameter lines of the *Halieutica* wrongly ascribed to Ovid as well as the 541 hexameters of the *Cynegetica* by Grattius.[1] Bird-catching was treated in a similar manner, and it is not surprising that a lost poem on that subject was also ascribed in antiquity to Oppian. Nemesianus, a Latin writer of the late third century, wrote poems on both bird-catching and hunting. This vein of poetry represented a substantial challenge to the literary craftsmen of the Imperial age. Like all didactic verse it required a master poet to give it beauty, and we are fortunate to find one in the author of the Greek *Halieutica*.

[1] Cf. *CHCL* II 856; Ovid, *Pont.* 4.16.34.

In the second and early third centuries performing rhetoricians won unprecedented popularity and prestige through bravura declamations before large audiences. These showmen, who brought new vitality to the myths and history of the Greek past, were known as sophists. The term had been employed long before to designate Gorgias and other classical masters of verbal wizardry, and in philosophical circles it had acquired uncomplimentary connotations that called attention to the ancient rivalry between philosophers, who sought the truth, and rhetoricians, who could make anything sound like the truth. The sophists of the Roman Empire were the product of a long and unbroken tradition. The quarrels of the Hellenistic rhetoricians and the long evolution of the controversy over the relative merits of the plain 'Attic' and the orotund 'Asianic' styles illuminate the continuity in the history of rhetoric. What makes the sophists of the second and early third centuries distinctive is not that they represent anything really new in themselves but rather that they achieved such immense worldly success. Many acquired vast wealth and highly influential friends. Several were advisers and confidants of emperors. Their performances were crowded with admirers, and their schools were filled with the intellectual elite of the Greek world. This effulgence of sophistry under the emperors is commonly called the 'Second Sophistic'. The 'sophistic' of Gorgias was the first.

The term was the invention of a pupil of some of the most eminent later sophists. Philostratus, whose family came from the island of Lemnos, looked back in the reign of Severus Alexander over the whole colourful spectacle of the Imperial sophistic movement and wrote the biographies of its principal representatives. If any faith can be placed in the confused notices which the Suda lexicon offers under the name of Philostratus, the biographer was not the only member of his family to have been active in the literary milieu of the Roman Empire. Certainly his *Lives of the sophists* attest considerable first-hand knowledge of the society in which his subjects moved. At the end of his work he names three contemporary sophists who were close friends, including one Philostratus of Lemnos (presumably a relative); and from another of his writings we learn that he belonged to the salon of the Syrian empress, Julia Domna. Although Philostratus' account of the sophists is often inadequate, even injudicious, it is none the less a priceless record of the tastes of the Greek-speaking aristocracy under Roman rule.

The conventional use of the expression 'Second Sophistic' to designate the movement that gained momentum under the emperors is, however, not what Philostratus intended. He declared that the Second Sophistic was started by Aeschines in the fourth century B.C., and that it differed from the rhetoric of Gorgias by avoiding abstract philosophical themes, like courage and justice, in favour of historical topics and character analysis. While this distinction is fair enough, not even Philostratus can produce any examples of the Second Sophistic style between the fourth century B.C. and the first A.D. apart from three shadowy figures 'who showed no skill either in invention or in the expression of their ideas'. But, says Philostratus, they were much sought after 'because of the scarcity of excellent sophists' (ἀπορίαι γενναίων σοφιστῶν). It is only with Nicetes of Smyrna and Isaeus the Assyrian, in the third quarter of the first century A.D., that Philostratus' chronicle of the Second Sophistic really gets under way. The appeal to Aeschines, like the inclusion in his work of Gorgias and other sophists of the 'First Sophistic', must represent a deliberate effort to anchor the movement of the Roman period in the classical age. Greeks have always been proud of the continuity of their culture.

Philostratus fleshed out his *Lives* not only with classical sophists but also with a handful of philosophers. These were men of eloquence who, while not actually sophists, seemed to be. This category allowed Philostratus to discuss several classical figures as well as two major figures in the cultural life of the Imperial age, Dio of Prusa and Favorinus. It is obvious that Philostratus' concept of his subject was sadly deficient in theoretical precision. He was more interested in people and style. But he successfully identified and recorded an important phenomenon in later Greek rhetoric. It is ultimately immaterial whether the cumbrous phrase 'Second Sophistic' or some other is used to refer to it.

The structure of the *Lives* is peculiar, to say the least, but it may be explained by Philostratus' judgement of who was significant. The first book concludes with a long account of Polemo, whose fame and influence may be held to justify so elaborate a treatment. An intimate of Hadrian who once turned a future emperor[1] out of his house, Polemo was an expert in physiognomics no less than rhetoric; and two declamations of his as well as a treatise on physiognomy have survived (the latter only in an Arabic translation).[2] The modern reader may thus, to some extent, savour the achievement of Polemo and understand Philostratus' interest in him. The second and final book of the *Lives* opens with an even longer biography than that of Polemo. The subject is the opulent Athenian, Herodes Atticus, whose controversial grandeur is still apparent today in the monuments and inscriptions of Greece. A little piece, purporting to be a late-fifth-century B.C. treatise on constitutional matters (Περὶ πολιτείας), survives under his name and, despite the credulity of some modern historians, was probably spun out of his inventive mind.[3] He fully deserves Philostratus' attention, and yet one suspects that so ample a treatment may have another explanation. The *Lives* are dedicated to a man who, according to Philostratus

---

[1] Antoninus Pius.
[2] *Polemonis Declamationes*, ed. Hinck (1873), on the Battle of Marathon; *Scriptores Physiognomonici*, ed. Foerster, vol. 1.   [3] Περὶ πολιτείας, ed. Albini (1968).

in his preface, traced his origins from Herodes Atticus. The man was to become an emperor (either Gordian I or Gordian II). Since Philostratus evidently chose his patron with care, he presumably fashioned his set of biographies in a form that would please him.

Previously Philostratus had been under the patronage of Julia Domna, and he had done his best to oblige her as well. In the *Lives of the sophists* he makes reference to his earlier work on Apollonius of Tyana. This is a vast narrative of the life and wonders of a Cappadocian wizard who had particularly caught the interest of the empress and her son, Caracalla. Philostratus states in his life of Apollonius that he undertook the work at Julia Domna's suggestion; but since it is not dedicated to her, it was probably completed after her death in 217. Caracalla's dedication of a shrine to Apollonius at Tyana in 215 is a good illustration of the importance attached to him by the imperial family. Philostratus provided the necessary hagiography.

The Apollonius life, rich in fabulous details of exotic lands and miraculous events, bears a close resemblance to the Greek novel (though without an erotic theme) and to the fictionalized travel literature of which Lucian makes mockery in his *True history*. In its reverential account of a holy man it evokes saints' lives and the gospels. And in its vivid confrontations of nonconformist and emperor it calls to mind the *Acts of the pagan martyrs*. It is scarcely surprising that as Christianity gathered strength in the Roman Empire, Philostratus' portrait of Apollonius provided the pagans with their anti-Christ. The comparison of the miracles of Apollonius and Jesus can still be seen in Eusebius' reply to the pagan Hierocles in the early years of the fourth century.

In recent times there has been much controversy over the degree of historical veracity in the Apollonius life. Philostratus claimed to have had access to the notebooks of Damis of Nineveh, who is said to have been Apollonius' faithful companion. Yet gross errors in the material directly attributed to Damis seem to convict Philostratus of deliberately inventing his source so as to secure greater authority for the narrative. The issue continues to be in dispute. One utterly neglected item may be worth adding to this debate. A Sanskrit tradition shows two *yogins* in India called Apalūnya and Damīśa, who are associated with persons such as Ayārcya and Prāvṛti.[1] These seem to be obviously Apollonius and Damis in relations with Iarchas and Phraotes, both of whom appear conspicuously in Philostratus' account of Apollonius in India. Either the substance of Philostratus' life somehow became known in India, although there is no other evidence of this whatever (nor any indication of any translation into Sanskrit, Persian, or Arabic); or Apollonius and Damis were really there, just as Philostratus says.

---

[1] Bhattacharya (1943) lxxii–lxxiv. Thanks are due to Professor Allen Thrasher for calling attention to this evidence.

The influence of Caracalla and his mother can be seen in another of Philostratus' surviving works, the *Heroicus*. Here a Phoenician trader and a vineyard labourer hold a dialogue on the presence of the ancient heroes in the contemporary world. This remarkable testimony to the hero cults of Philostratus' day also includes considerable correction and amplification of the Homeric narratives. Similarly, the Greek version of the Trojan War ascribed to a certain Dictys of Crete shows a tendency to Homeric revisionism; and our copies of that text are dated to the Severan age.[1] Philostratus' *Heroicus* concludes with an elaborate discussion of the cult of Achilles in the Black Sea region (a cult well documented by inscriptions). It calls to mind Caracalla's visit to the tomb of Achilles in the winter of 214/15. It evokes equally Philostratus' account of the conversation which Apollonius claimed to have had with Achilles himself.

Of Philostratus' other writings that survive, there is an essay on athletics, of which both occasion and purpose remain obscure, as well as a group of love letters (largely homosexual) followed by a few chaste letters, including one addressed to Julia Domna herself. A set of verbal descriptions of paintings also survives. These ecphraseis show Philostratus himself working in one of the popular sophistic genres. It must be acknowledged that his *oeuvre*, viewed as a whole, was astonishingly varied and influential. Without his Apollonius, paganism would have made an even more feeble resistance than it did; without his biographies of the sophists, the second and third centuries would be far less comprehensible than they are; and without the patrons he tried so hard to oblige, his talents might never have been exercised on anything more interesting than word pictures and erotica.

Aelius Aristides

In the middle of the second century A.D., at the height of the great rhetorical movement known from Philostratus as the Second Sophistic and documented by inscriptions and papyri, an ailing orator of enormous gifts sought a healing at Pergamum from the god Asclepius. For ten years Aelius Aristides awaited the prescription of cures, revealed in a succession of bizarre dreams that came to him as he 'incubated' in the Asclepieum. The treatment which Aristides sought for his sickly condition brought him into contact with many of the most illustrious personalities of the Roman empire, who had come to Pergamum for the same purpose. He cherished his eminent friends; and to judge from the favours they did for him, they cherished him too. Aelius Aristides, the superstitious hypochondriac, was one of the major literary figures of his age. When Marcus Aurelius visited Smyrna in later years, he asked particularly to hear Aristides declaim, and when Smyrna was levelled by an earthquake shortly thereafter it was to oblige Aristides that Marcus saw to the rebuilding of the unhappy city.

[1] *P.Tebt.* 268; *P.Oxy.* 2539.

It is sometimes hard to credit the reputation of Aristides. He seems so eccentric a character, so self-indulgent, so unlike most literary giants. Yet the ancients held him and his work in the highest esteem. He was an important model for the Greek orators of late antiquity and the Byzantine age; his name could stand alongside that of Demosthenes. Most of his vast *oeuvre* has been preserved to the present day. In recent centuries it has constituted something of an embarrassment, for it was scarcely to the taste of nineteenth- and twentieth-century scholars. Yet Aristides was a brilliant continuator of the classical tradition of Greek oratory. He was deeply imbued with the history and literature of the fifth and fourth centuries B.C., and in the complex phrasings of a neo-Attic style – allusive and sonorous – he revolutionized Greek literature. He was indeed a giant, ugly perhaps but impressive none the less.

Some of the rhetorical writings of Aristides can easily be paralleled in other work of the Second Sophistic. His speeches in praise of civic harmony (ὁμόνοια) are reminiscent of speeches on the same theme in the corpus of Dio Chrysostom. His exercises on topics of classical history reflect the preoccupations of the schools and the tastes of his audiences. His panegyrics of cities take their place comfortably in a long encomiastic tradition. It is evident that he is, at least to some degree, a creature of his age. Philostratus included his biography without apology among the *Lives of the sophists* and excerpted his writings just as he did those of numerous others in search of notable expressions. Yet Aristides is not quite like the others. As a man of great independence of mind and of iron-willed determination, he forged a career and a literature that set him apart. He had no desire to be just another sophist, no matter how loudly applauded. He consistently refused ever to declaim extemporaneously, and he could be sharply critical of the sophists of his day. He made no concessions to philosophy or to philosophers and banished them all to a realm of useless babblers. He had no interest in civic honours and stoutly claimed his right to immunity from those costly public services by which lesser men enhanced their reputation.

In literature Aristides was equally independent and determined. His intense spiritual life, which may be described in terms of either piety or credulity (or a mixture of the two), underlies his most original and memorable works. He addressed a number of hymns to gods and goddesses. Although he makes it plain that he was fully capable of composing in verse – and some extant verses prove it – the hymns that are to be found in the transmitted corpus are all in prose. This is no accident. In his hymn to Sarapis Aristides dwells at length on the question of how best to approach a deity and argues that prose is in fact superior to verse. Poetry makes the worshipper sound prophetic and insincere. We use prose for everything else, says Aristides:

> We make enkomia at festivals, we recount men's deeds and wars, we tell stories, we plead our cases in court – in everything, so to say, prose is what we use, but

when it comes to the gods, the very ones who gave us prose, we think it altogether inappropriate to use it . . . Metre did not come first, followed by the discovery of prose discourse; nor were poets the ones who devised the words we had to use. But when words and prose expression already existed, the art of poetry came along later to exploit them in the interest of a certain grace and attractiveness. Therefore if we value what is natural, we should be valuing the very disposition and wish of the gods: and if we value what was natural previously, in an earlier time, and better according to the poets, we should be valuing it the more by addressing the gods, who established all these things, with such a mode of speech as we use without shame when we speak, free from metrical constraint, to one another. (4–8)

Aristides goes on to discuss the flexibility of prose as against the rigidity of metrical schemes, although he is far from unaware of the possibilities of rhythms in prose. His advocacy of the prose hymn is one of his most striking contributions to Greek literature.

Another is in his autobiographical narratives. The ἱεροὶ λόγοι, *Sacred Discourses*, are a kind of spiritual autobiography, unparalleled in ancient literature. They recount the inner life of the author during the extended term of his residence at the Pergamene Asclepieum. For the most part they provide detailed reports of dreams and of the measures taken in consequence of the dreams. Historical persons, places and events figure from time to time both inside and outside the dreams, so that a reading of the *Discourses* brings one immediately into the milieu of upper-class Asia Minor in the second century. Aristides' narratives evoke, in their account of the ministrations of Asclepius, the literature of aretalogy and, in their descriptions of dreams, the *Oneirocritica* of Artemidorus as well as some personal narratives on papyri. But it is the fullness of Aristides' introspection and the powerful intellect which has so clearly created this autobiography that make the *Sacred Discourses* memorable and unique.

A little more than five of the *Discourses* survive, and of these the fourth contains more solid historical material than the others. But all are fundamentally a recitation of dreams and their impact:

Each of our days, as well as our nights, has a story, if someone, who was present at them, wished either to record the events or to narrate the providence of the God, wherein he revealed some things openly in his own presence, and others by the sending of dreams, as far as it was possible to obtain sleep. But this was rare, due to the tempests of my body. Therefore, in view of this, I decided to submit truly to the God, as to a doctor and to do in silence whatever he wishes. (1.3, tr. C. A. Behr)

Of his physical condition and the dreams at each stage of his illness Aristides gives an exact account. There seems no end of perspiration, vomiting, bathing and not bathing. Asclepius' prescriptions are often such as to perplex a modern physician, but it will not be forgotten that the doctors of Pergamum assisted in carrying out the god's instructions and that Galen himself acknowledged the value of dreams in guiding him to efficacious treatment. The ambition and vanity of Aristides often irradiate his dreams, as they do those of most ambitious persons. In his nocturnal world governors, emperors, even the Parthian king pay their respects to the great orator. Furthermore, dreams afforded a supernatural means of making direct contact with the great men of the classical age. Aristides communicated in his sleep with Plato, Lysias, Sophocles and others. The fifth and fourth centuries B.C. were far from remote; they were no lost golden age, but rather a part of the present. This is an important aspect of the so-called archaism of the Greeks of the Roman Empire. The orator Polemo, an older contemporary of Aristides, dreamed of Demosthenes and in recognition of this event set up a statue with an inscription proclaiming 'Polemo set up this statue of Demosthenes, son of Demosthenes, of Paeania in accordance with a dream.'[1]

Until recently such attention as Aristides received from critics and historians was usually directed to his orations in praise of cities, and in particular to the speech on Rome. These works are excellent examples of a popular rhetorical genre. They follow the traditional categories of enkomion and include the customary complaint that no mortal could adequately enumerate the glories of the place under review. They cannot, however, serve as historical documents of importance. The speech on Rome is a *tour de force*, not an expression of the considered opinions of a typical educated Greek of the Antonine age. It is instructive to compare, for example, Aristides' speech on Rome with his *Panathenaïcus* in praise of Athens. Of Rome he declares,

> Neither sea nor intervening continent are bars to citizenship, nor are Asia and Europe divided in their treatment here. In your empire all paths are open to all. No one worthy of rule or trust remains an alien, but a civil community of the world has been established as a free republic under one, the best, ruler and teacher of order... Now all the Greek cities rise up under your leadership, and the monuments which are dedicated in them, all their embellishments and comforts, redound to your honour like beautiful suburbs. (60, 94, tr. J. H. Oliver)

Of Athens Aristides observes,

> For all the cities and all the races of mankind turned to you and your form of life, and dialect. And the power of the city is not contained in the establishment of garrisons but in the fact that all men of their own accord have chosen your ways and enrolled themselves as far as possible into the city, praying that their sons and they themselves may have a share in the beauty which is yours. And the Pillars of Hercules are no barrier, nor are these ambitions limited by the hills of Africa... (322–4, tr. C. A. Behr)

[1] Habicht (1969) 75, no. 33 (cf. Phrynichus p. 494 Rutherford).

In the Panathenaïc oration it is as if the Roman empire did not exist. Obviously Aristides' rhetoric on cities is not fiction but rather a brilliant blend of commonplaces and historical items in accordance with the principles of laudation. He is not a representative of any segment of opinion. He is a performer.

Viewed as a whole, the achievement of Aristides is prodigious. As hymnographer, diarist, panegyrist, counsellor, and declaimer, he is a pivotal figure in the transmission of Hellenism.

4. SCIENCE AND SUPERSTITION

Galen

Galen, probably the greatest physician of antiquity after Hippocrates, was also one of the most prolific Greek authors of his time. A contemporary of Aristides and Lucian, he shared with them a penchant for voluminous productivity. The collected works of Galen fill twenty-two volumes in the antiquated edition of Kühn, which has now to be supplemented by a substantial number of lost works discovered in Arabic translation. Even by the standards of the second century A.D. Galen was something of a marvel; and although his fame rests upon his medical achievements he considered himself as much a philosopher and a philologist as a doctor. His treatises were so numerous and so popular that Galen felt obliged, toward the end of his life, to prepare a register of the authentic writings (*De libris propriis*), just as the artist Claude Lorrain in the seventeenth century drew up a list of the canvases he had actually painted (the *liber veritatis*). 'In the district of Sandalarium, where most of Rome's booksellers are, I noticed some people in doubt as to whether a book that was on sale was by me or someone else', wrote Galen at the beginning of his register. The book was inscribed with the words 'Galen the doctor', but forgeries were not uncommon. The taste for Galen's disquisitions on medicine owed much to the success of his series of lectures on anatomy – with demonstrations, presented in Rome in the early part of the reign of Marcus Aurelius. No sophist ever enjoyed greater acclaim or more cultivated audiences.

Galen's father, an architect at Pergamum, was advised in a dream that the young boy should be trained in medicine as well as philosophy. Pergamum was an ideal place for such an education. A troupe of gladiators was attached to the high priest of Asia in the city (for exploitation in festival events), and a local medical school was able to flourish with the help of the readily available supply of wounds, mutilations and cadavers. Philosophers were to be found in the precinct of Asclepius, and many of the brightest students of Asia Minor sojourned in Pergamum for instruction. Galen was exposed to all four of the principal philosophical sects of the age, Platonism, Aristotelianism, Epicureanism and Stoicism. His early training encouraged an eclecticism which he maintained throughout his life. His vigorously non-sectarian approach to philosophy explains his generous estimate of the Christians, whose upright conduct brought them near, in his view, to the philosophic ideal.

In the history of Greek literature Galen must figure as a critic and a commentator. He wrote studies on the vocabulary of Euripides and Aristophanes. These are now lost but deserve attention for the choice of subject at a time when prose authors of the classical period aroused a more lively interest. It is clear from his own writing that Galen had a keen sense of style (though his mannerisms do not appeal to everyone nowadays), and the need for precision in anatomical descriptions inevitably heightened his sensitivity to diction. Whatever the technicality of his topic, Galen always remained a man of letters. His style was sufficiently distinctive for one discriminating admirer to be able to pronounce an allegedly Galenic work a forgery on the basis of the first two lines.

Galen's eye-witness accounts of two distinguished literary contemporaries serve to illuminate their surviving writings and show Galen a perceptive observer. He saw in Aristides a man whose indomitable spirit triumphed over a body that was slowly wasting away.[1] In Lucian he saw a malicious prankster who took pleasure in embarrassing serious people.[2] There can be no doubt as to which of these two authors he judged the greater man, and his judgement was identical with the judgement of the subsequent generations of antiquity. The modern admiration of Lucian, often coupled with denigration of Aristides and his imitators (like Libanius), is a grave impediment to the understanding of Greek literature under Rome and Byzantium. Galen gives the correct perspective.

The various treatises in which Galen rehearsed his past achievements comprise a kind of autobiography. Of the surviving works the two pieces on his own publications and the essay entitled 'On prognosis' (Περὶ τοῦ προγιγνώσκειν) are significant autobiographical documents and win for Galen a place, which has not always been acknowledged, in the history of ancient autobiography.[3] At least one of his principal objectives in writing about himself was self-defence in the face of what he considered envious detraction; but a certain pride and self-revelation would undoubtedly be clearer still if it were possible to study the lost treatise entitled Περὶ διαβολῆς ἐν ὧι καὶ περὶ τοῦ ἰδίου βίου 'On slander, including an account of his own life'.

Artemidorus

It is appropriate that of all the books of dream interpretation to have been written in antiquity the only one to survive virtually complete is the work by

---

[1] Fragments of Comm. on Plato's *Timaeus*, ed. Schröder (1934) 99 (Arabic).

[2] Strohmaier (1976) 118 (Arabic).

[3] As Nutton (1972) 52 has pointed out, Galen was taken into account by Misch (1950) 328–52.

Artemidorus. Writing in the middle of the second century A.D., at a time when Galen and Aristides amply attest a deeply rooted belief in the predictive and prescriptive power of dreams, Artemidorus of Ephesus undertook to establish, on the basis of extensive research, a rational system of interpretation. He rebuked his predecessors for being content to rely upon traditional literature in their interpretations, and he adopted for himself an empiricist method which took him to Asia Minor, Greece and Italy in search of informants. As he notes in the preface to Book 1, he did not disdain the company of the popular prophets of the marketplace – wizards, magicians and holy men. He kept records of the dreams of which he heard; he attended scrupulously to the aftermath of the dreams, where it could be ascertained, so as to build up an interpretation based upon documented results.

The *Oneirocritica* of Artemidorus exist in five books, of which the first two clearly comprise the original set of interpretations, to which three books were added subsequently to provide further material as well as justification of the method. The fifth book is a repertoire of the known results of real dreams. The work as a whole, with its abundance of examples of possible dreams (some quite beyond imagining), is a unique source for the attitudes and tensions of second-century society. Many of Artemidorus' interpretations turn entirely upon the social status of the dreamer in relation to that of other persons who may appear in the dream.

A once prevalent opinion that Artemidorus' work was a rare example of literature for the superstitious common man has now given way to the far more reasonable view that it is a highly sophisticated specimen of occultism for the educated upper class. For one thing, the Greek is subtle, with careful attention to nuance and distinctions in the meanings of words. It would undoubtedly have given pleasure to the honorand of the first three books, a certain Cassius Maximus, who appears from Artemidorus' tribute at the end of Book 2 to have been a philosopher or rhetor from Phoenicia. In addition, the situations envisaged in the *Oneirocritica* often reflect the milieu of educated and affluent people. Certain dreamers, identified by name, evoke the highest circles of imperial society: Cornelius Fronto, the teacher of Marcus, epistolographer, and consul of A.D. 143, or Plutarch, the moralist, who dreamed that he was being guided to heaven by Hermes.

Artemidorus claimed to enjoy the inspiration and protection of Apollo in the course of his labour on dreams, and in particular Apollo of Daldis, a small town in Lydia (2.70). Daldis was his mother's native place, and Artemidorus chose to show his grateful affection by deliberately calling himself *Daldianos* instead of *Ephesios* in the inscription of the *Oneirocritica*. Although nothing is known of his father, his son, to whom he dedicated the two final books of the work on dreams, was also apparently a professional dream interpreter. This raises the interesting possibility that a career in occultism may have been traditional in the family.

The system of Artemidorus depends upon a sharp distinction between the prophetic dream (ὄνειρος) and the non-prophetic dream (ἐνύπνιον) or simple reflection of waking anxieties. The prophetic dream, which is of course what concerns him most, can either delineate the future as it will be or suggest it through symbol or allegory. Artemidorus further identifies subdivisions of these categories. In making interpretations he says (1.9) that it is not only advantageous but necessary to know personal details about the dreamer – what he does for a living, the circumstances of his birth, the size of his fortune, his physical condition and his age. It becomes readily apparent that for Artemidorus there is no single interpretation for any dream, and the rest of his work bears this out. As a rational expert, he takes a critical view of religious dreaming and seems in 4.22 to be censuring the kind of experience to which Aristides was so devoted:

> It is pointless to investigate the instructions that gods give men for cures. For many people, in Pergamum, Alexandria and elsewhere, have been cured by instructions, and some say that medical procedures have been revealed from such instructions. But the instructions they record are ridiculous, as I think is clear to any persons with some degree of intelligence.

Here is the dream merchant condemning sophists and doctors for irrational practices. In general Artemidorus' scientific view of his own subject appears to have made him suspicious of the great literary personalities of his age. At any rate, one is surprised to discover in his account of the significance of *fellatio* (1.79) that the category of those who work with their mouths includes 'flute-players, trumpet-players, rhetors, sophists, and the like'. Professional rivalry and competition for patrons may well be inferred.

5. BETWEEN PHILOSOPHY AND RHETORIC

Plutarch

The genial and prolific Plutarch, whose vast reading, regard for the past and love of virtue have often caused him to be considered the very embodiment of Hellenism, is actually a singular figure in the history of Greek literature. As a cultivated littérateur who served on embassies and consorted with the Roman aristocracy on familiar terms, he seems to be like many a rhetor or philosopher in the era of the Second Sophistic. But he was never a sophist; and the rhetorical pieces, which he probably wrote in his younger years, are inadequate evidence that he aspired to be one. In philosophy he was remarkably well read, as in most other subjects, but he has small claim to be an original philosopher. He did not make speeches on concord and stasis in Greek cities, as Dio Chrysostom and Aristides did, although he was much concerned about these matters. He avoided living in one of the great urban centres of the Roman east, such as Athens, Ephesus or Smyrna, but preferred instead to bolster the shrinking population of an already small town, Chaeronea, in Boeotia, the proverbial home of dullards. Plutarch, who wrote the only set of parallel biographies known to western literature, belongs to no recognizable category of authors apart from that of polymath. In his unobtrusive, observant and industrious way Plutarch is unique.

The writings of Plutarch have always been cherished wherever classical studies have flourished. This is in part because he excerpts and paraphrases so much that has been lost that he thereby provides an important link between ourselves and the Graeco-Roman world. But it is principally because his interests and outlook appear to be so modern. His comparative view of history, his devotion to his family, his ideas on marriage, his open and discursive style have often been much appreciated in modern times. Plutarch's views on religion and morality, buttressed as they are by a whole system of demonology, nevertheless strike readers as sympathetic and instructive. The calm tone and fluent, earnest manner convey an impression of sagacity, somewhat pastoral in nature. There is scarcely any humour in Plutarch; few of his comments are incisive or penetrating. But spread throughout his works is a genuine and irresistible humanity, unfettered by egotism or pretence. In this respect too he is highly unusual.

If Plutarch did not actively seek preferment in the Roman Empire, his erudition and family connexions put him in close touch with consuls, governors and emperors. Not that he boasted of these things: the accolades he received from Trajan and Hadrian are imperfectly recorded in late reference works and nowhere else. An honourable office he held at Delphi is known only from the inscribed base of the statue he erected to Hadrian. Plutarch realized that his contacts were useful in the revival of culture and economy in Greece, and it is not unreasonable to assign him an important role in the well documented rejuvenation of Delphi under Hadrian. Experience had taught him to accept the Roman domination as a fact of life to which the ancient traditions of Hellenism had to be accommodated. The clarity of Plutarch's vision is almost unnerving. In his *Political precepts*, by far the most valuable surviving account of the Greek response to Roman rule, Plutarch defines the role of the statesman in civic life:

> He will instruct his people both individually and collectively and will call attention to the weak condition of Greek affairs, in which it is best for wise men to accept one advantage – a life of harmony and quiet – since fortune has left us no prize open for competition. For what dominion, what glory is there for those who are victorious? What sort of power is it which a small edict of a pro-consul may annul or transfer to another man and which, even if it last, has nothing in it seriously worth while? (824e–f, tr. H. N. Fowler)

Obviously Plutarch judged the writing of essays and biographies something that was seriously worth while, and he was right. His works reflect not only the effort of composition (his love of abstract nouns and his meandering periods will be familiar to his readers), but they reflect equally the effort of prior reading. Plutarch's citations are so wide-ranging and abundant that nineteenth-century source critics found it impossible to believe that he had plucked them all himself from a reading of the original texts. Hence there arose the myth of commonplace books, which Plutarch was supposed to have had at his disposal. It is one of the triumphs of recent research on Plutarch, which has not been in short supply, to have established conclusively the reliance of Plutarch upon the actual books from which he quotes. He was not a fraudulent scholar. He read as compulsively as he wrote; and if his memory was fallible, it was still phenomenal. There is no way of telling to what extent Plutarch took notes or made use of assistants, but the form of many quotations and the range of topics they illustrate make it certain that he often depended upon his memory.

Plutarch's taste in literature has occasionally been called into question on the basis of some naive opinions in his essay *On the malignity of Herodotus*. The modern reader is indeed caught by surprise as he reads in the opening lines,

> Not only is it the height of injustice (as Plato puts it) 'to seem just when one is not so', but it is an act of supreme malice to put on a false show of good humour and frankness which baffles detection. And this is exactly what Herodotus does, flattering some people in the basest possible manner, while he slanders and maligns others. Hitherto no one has dared to expose him as a liar. (tr. L. Pearson)

Yet it is simply Plutarch's dogged honesty in following the rhetorical conventions of propriety in narrative history that leads him into such manifest absurdities. For he is not unlike the rhetorician Dionysius of Halicarnassus in his censure of Thucydides for writing a history on an unworthy theme. Plutarch's verdict on Herodotus is not due to tough, independent thinking. It is solidly based on presuppositions common to the education of his time, and also, it must be admitted, to a certain inability to comprehend Herodotus' lighter tone. It is, however, ironic that history in the Herodotean manner, and even dialect, became very fashionable in the generation after Plutarch; and it took the pen of a Lucian to expose the affectations of this new historiography.

The monumental undertaking to write parallel lives of the great Greeks and Romans, with comparative estimates, must have arisen, at least in part, from Plutarch's substantial contact with both Greek and Roman culture. On one of his visits to Italy he inspected the battlefield of Bedriacum in the company of his friend and patron Mestrius Florus, as he records in a surviving biography (*Otho*) from his *Lives of the Caesars*. Those *Lives* preceded the *Parallel lives*, as presumably did a few other of his biographies, like the *Epaminondas*. It may be legitimately suspected that the Roman milieu made him interested in biography just as it did Suetonius, and that after trying a set of imperial biographies, like his Roman contemporary, he turned his hand to a few non-Roman subjects (including a Persian king) before conceiving the huge plan of Greek and Roman lives in parallel. A friend of the younger Pliny, Sosius Senecio, was honoured with the dedication of the *Parallel lives*. (Plutarch also dedicated to him the miscellany of learned conversations entitled *Table talk*.) The *Parallel lives*, in their conception and execution, are a product of the Graeco-Roman empire of the second century. Plutarch sees the cultures of east and west on equal terms, without prejudice to either.

In preparing the Greek and Roman lives, Plutarch's chief aim was moral edification. He is explicit on this point:

> For it is not Histories (ἱστορίας) that I am writing but Lives (βίους); and in the most illustrious deeds there is not always a manifestation of virtue or vice, nay a slight thing like a phrase or a jest often makes a greater revelation of a character than battles where thousands fall, or the greatest armaments, or sieges of cities. (*Alexander* 665 tr. B. Perrin)

It is easy and probably wrong to lay great stress on the distinction between history and biography. Plutarch certainly did have a lively interest in history, but his own view of what he was doing was no less certainly based upon his role as teacher of morality. If there is one point that emerges from the biographies, taken as a whole, it is that virtue and vice are no respecters of nationality. The same characteristics were equally well displayed in east and west. Even when, on rare occasions, Plutarch thought it would be instructive to record the lives of evil men, he matched a bad Greek, like Demetrius, with a bad Roman, like Antony. As he says in the *Demetrius*, he must not be assumed to be including such lives merely to 'divert and amuse my readers by giving variety to my writing'. He wished to illuminate morality by its opposite, and again to emphasize that various features of mankind are not confined to one nation.

There is an unmistakably personal quality about Plutarch's work. The reader draws near to the author himself. When Plutarch describes (*Demosth.* 2) his imprecise control of the Latin language, one can hear the authentic voice of a man whose experience of the world gave him an intuitive instinct in which he had justifiable confidence.

> During the time when I was in Rome and various parts of Italy I had no leisure to practise myself in the Roman language, owing to my public duties and the number of my pupils in philosophy. And here my experience was an astonishing thing, but true. For it was not so much that by means of words I came to a complete understanding of things, as that from things I somehow had an experience which enabled me to follow the meaning of words. (tr. B. Perrin)

Plutarch's devotion to the shrine at Delphi is mirrored in his three essays, *On the E at Delphi*, *On the failure of the oracles* and *On the oracles of the Pythia*.

These pieces contain much that is autobiographical and look forward to a revival at Delphi in which Plutarch was himself involved. For many readers of the non-biographical writings, known collectively as the *Moralia*, it is the Essay on Love that proves the most arresting. Plutarch knew Plato and *A symposium* very well, but he took a different view. True love was to be found in lawful marriage:

> In the case of lawful wives, physical union is the beginning of friendship, a sharing, as it were, in great mysteries. Pleasure is short; but the respect and kindness and mutual affection and loyalty that daily spring from it convicts neither the Delphians of raving when they call Aphrodite 'Harmony' nor Homer when he designates such a union as 'friendship'. (*Amatorius* 769a tr. W. C. Helmbold)

One wonders what the Middle Platonists or Aelius Aristides made of such a passage.

In his friends, in his erudition, in his style Plutarch is a man of his time. But in his literary aspirations and his personality he stands apart.

Dio of Prusa

To Philostratus, Dio of Prusa was not simply one of those philosophers dubbed sophists with whom he is grouped. He was a man of all-round excellence who defied categorization.[1] Synesius in the early fifth[2] and von Arnim in the late nineteenth centuries were less cautious. Working, it must be admitted, from claims or hints in Dio's later productions, they distinguished two periods separated by his exile: before, the sophistic career, and after, once his own experience of poverty had taught him the truth of Stoic-Cynic doctrines, an evangelical role as moralizing philosopher and philosophizing politician. But it seems that this schema was misleading. Dio's assertion of Delphic sanction for his wanderings and of a conversion to philosophy can be seen as dramatic posturing, intended to present his intellectual career in a classical mould (a collage of Socrates, Diogenes and Zeno) and distract the reader's attention from his treachery to philosophy in his youth. Some early works already show philosophic influences, while some sophistic pieces are denied a late date on insufficient grounds. In any case a number of works seem to straddle, or sometimes overflow, these two neat categories.

Dio certainly had a training in rhetoric, though we do not know who taught him, and several works show that he proceeded to public performances of the sort which attracted the title sophist. It may be this that brought him to Rome from the small town of Prusa in Bithynia and his earliest datable work (*Or.* 29) the funeral oration for Titus' boy-friend Melancomas, probably delivered in

---

[1] Philostratus, *V.S.* 1.7.487.   [2] Synesius, *Dio* esp. 37a–38b.

Naples in A.D. 70, is in the epideictic genre. It is slight but charming; and his *Praise of hair* even slighter, a mere παίγνιον or trifle. The *Tempe* or *Memnon* which aroused Synesius' qualified admiration[1] may have been grander, but for us the fortissimo sophist can only be heard in the Trojan and Olympian speeches. The *Trojan* cleverly refutes Homer's account of the war by an entertaining mixture of *ad hominem* argument and appeal to other evidence. It shows, like many of Dio's works, that he knew and – though one might not guess it from his tone – loved his Homer, but betrays no philosophical streak. An early date might, but need not, be the reason. By contrast the *Olympian* is a heavyweight synthesis of philosophy and rhetoric. Probably delivered at the Games of A.D. 97, it explores man's notions of divinity and the contribution made to them by artistic representations. Like many of Dio's speeches (as Photius observed)[2] it has a distended preface, but this helps to engage the audience's interest and sympathy, partly by references to the speaker's own experiences, before well-organized and restrained treatment of the central themes.

Such eloquence was not directed solely towards display oratory. Already in A.D. 71, doubtless at the suggestion of his Flavian patrons and his friend Cocceius Nerva who was consul that year, Dio issued a speech or pamphlet *Against the philosophers*, a vindication to the Greek intellectual world of the regime's expulsion of philosophers from Rome. Musonius, from whom Dio had learnt Stoicism in the 60s, was not expelled, and to him Dio sent what may have been a milder essay. But the extreme language of the speech, urging the banishment of Socrates' and Zeno's followers from land and sea, shows Musonius' pupil in a nasty light, however entertaining and charming it may have been as an example of sophistic rhetoric.[3] Dio also put his sophistry at the disposal of the government in a speech to the Alexandrians *c.* 72, urging them to mend their riotous ways and blaming Cynics for the turbulence associated with theatres and horse-racing. Although there are side-swipes at sophists, the speech was clearly intended to entertain an audience with an ear for good public speaking as well as to persuade them. This sophistic objective is even clearer in the *Rhodian* of the same period (*Or.* 31): the practice of re-using honorific statues – not unusual and hardly, one would have thought, a world-shaking issue – is subjected to an exhaustive array of criticisms in what is Dio's longest speech (unless, indeed, it is a combination of two orations). It does not make easy or rewarding reading, but it is valuable evidence that well before his exile Dio was drawing on philosophical arguments and appealing to Hellenic traditions in speeches that had a practical purpose as well as an eye to entertainment. Many such tedious and patronizing pleas for good conduct were delivered in Bithynian cities by Dio after his exile, and Tarsus was also favoured with Dio's advice (*Or.* 34),

---

[1] Synesius, *Dio* 39c–d.   [2] Photius, *Bibl.*, *Cod.* 209, 165b35.
[3] Synesius, *Dio* 40a–b.

perhaps before it. A second speech to Tarsus (*Or.* 33) is in a lighter vein, chiding the Tarsians for an endemic weakness – snorting (if that is what ῥέγκειν means). That Dio is both humorous and obscure may be a clue that entertainment is his primary goal, and the citizens of Tarsus may have gone away as puzzled as modern scholars as to what Dio was pretending to criticize.

The philosophy that gave body to Dio's rhetoric also generated works in conventional philosophical forms. Most are quite short dialogues or addresses, offering lucid but unoriginal discussions of topics such as *Slavery* and *Freedom* (*Or.* 14 and 15), *Beauty* (21) and *Opinion* (66). Some, like the last two mentioned, can be dated to his exile, as can the group in which Diogenes is the mouthpiece (6, 8–10). But we cannot be certain that none predates it. The most substantial (1–4) are the four works on *Kingship*. Two, at least, are intended for delivery to Trajan on Dio's ambassadorial visits to Rome in the years of his intense political activity at Prusa (100–107?). They analyse imperial virtues in such a way as to make the emperor feel complimented on their presence rather than warned to remedy their deficiency. Form and tone vary. The first is a sermon introduced by an anecdote, the third a more intimate address taking its cue from a conversation of Socrates. The others are dialogues; Alexander puts forward Dio's views in disputation with Philip (2) and Diogenes takes over that role in debate with Alexander (4). All are a serious attempt to apply Hellenistic theories of monarchy to the Roman imperial system, and in consideration of such themes as a monarch's duties to his friends show the humanity that makes so many of Dio's moral works appealing. They are not great works, but their view of the good king ruling under the guidance and protection of divinity secured them influence in Christian Byzantium. They show Dio in a much better light than the political in-fighting of the Prusan speeches with which they are contemporary, documents of the behaviour which Dio pompously criticizes as 'Greek foibles' in his speech on concord at Nicomedia (*Or.* 38.38).

Most enjoyable, however, of Dio's philosophical works are those where his literary purposes are allowed to dominate, whether to sugar the pill or (more probably) because Dio wishes to create philosophy whose claims as literature will be as compelling as the *oeuvre* of his model Plato. Not for nothing was the *Phaedo* one of the two books he took into exile (the other was Demosthenes' *On the false embassy*)[1] and the elegant *Charidemus* (30) has his master's lucidity and charm. The young eponym leaves as his deathbed testament a pair of Platonic myths presenting contrasted allegories of *la condition humaine*, the underprivileged prisoner or the over-pampered banqueter. If Charidemus is fictitious, we may suspect that the tender pathos of the introduction derives its power from the attested early death of Dio's own son. In the *Euboean* (7), however, Dio is explicit (and perhaps mendacious) in claiming personal

---

[1] Philostratus, *V.S.* 1.7.488.

experience as the basis for his idyllic depiction of a hunter's family life in the hill country of Euboea. This novelistic sequence, deservedly well known and admired, is an engaging prelude to serious proposals for improving the quality of city life.[1] It shows Dio's sophistic skill employed at once in the service of philosophy and in the creation of fiction in a manner very different from his contemporaries who wrote novels, fiction which anticipated the developments of Lucian. Even more literary are such miniature dialogues as the *Chryseis* (61).

Dio's virtuosity impressed his contemporaries and secured transmission of his works, albeit often incomplete, to admirers in late antiquity and Byzantium. Polemo travelled to Bithynia to hear him, Favorinus recognized him as his teacher. Even Trajan saw his distinction and allegedly had him with him in his chariot at his Dacian triumph (probably that of 102). But whether any of Dio's messages struck home is less certain: Trajan's remark (if authentic) might have been uttered by any of his patrons – 'I don't know what you are saying, but I love you as I love myself.'[2] His Greek audiences knew what he was saying. But they were probably less impressed by the constant appeals to Homer and Hellenic traditions (common form of the era) than by the lucid, easy-flowing and moderately Attic Greek, recalling not only Plato but also that favourite author of the period, commended by Dio in his reading-list (*Or.* 18) for an aspiring politician, Xenophon. What we may find most engaging is the sympathetic impression of his character conveyed in his moral works – sincere, patient, humane, seriously intent on the good of his listener but also capable of humour. Perhaps exile did reform him. But we should not forget the turncoat attack on philosophy or the nastiness of his earliest Prusan speech to a starving crowd of his fellow citizens (*Or.* 46). The same threats of Roman intervention loom in political speeches from his later years, and we must allow that the man whom Hellenism and philosophy marked as humane and civilized when confidently displaying his mastery of speech may have shed this veneer when he saw his own interests threatened and lost his nerve.

Maximus

Many of Dio's philosophical features reappear in a Greek from Tyre who is found lecturing in Rome in the reign of Commodus, the Platonist Maximus. Although he was no sophist (which presumably explains why he was omitted from Philostratus' *Lives*) there is ample witness to Maximus' gifts as a speaker. Forty-one sermons survive, easy on the ear and mind alike. The style aims at simplicity (ἀφέλεια), avoiding long periods; in the pursuit of elegance (κάλλος) Maximus balances short *cola* with matching sounds and rhythms; and to enliven the flow of his rhetoric he sprinkles questions, apostrophes and formulas

---

[1] Cf. Brunt (1973).   [2] Philostratus, *V.S.* 1.7.488.

marking the progress of his arguments. We may feel that in application of his stylistic canons (except, perhaps, his selection of Attic vocabulary) he goes too far. In elaboration of philosophical points, however, he does not go far enough. He is an expounder rather than a thinker, and his expositions seek to present trite themes in an interesting way, using the poets, images (εἰκόνες) from daily life and examples of classical history to illustrate philosophical truths and in turn to invite explanation by philosophy. Some addresses do indeed purport to be investigating basic problems of philosophy (*Whether virtue is a skill*, 27; *What is the goal of philosophy?* 29) or at least of Platonism (*What was Socrates' spiritual guide?* 8 and 9). Others are more straightforward moral sermons – *What marks friends from flatterers?* (14). But in all he plays the role of entertaining debater which is explicit in such pairs as 15 and 16, asserting the superiority of the practical and the theoretical life respectively. He is more valuable for his documentation of enthusiasm for Homer and Plato in himself and his audience than for any contribution to Platonism. The cultivated elite who attended the six lectures given on successive days during his first visit to Rome must have admired the rhetorical panache with which from day to day he took up different positions on the relation of pleasure to virtue (30–6). But the last day's culminating appeal to philosophy to check the warring onslaughts of hate and envy was surely treated as a stunning *tour de force* to be applauded rather than as a serious moral doctor's prescription for a quiet life.

Lucian

The common stock of rhetorical and philosophical forms and techniques was also being exploited for literary ends by a near contemporary of Maximus, likewise from the Levant, the Commagenian Lucian. But because of his predominantly satirical stance, his many-sided wit and fantasy and his effortless command of clear-flowing Greek, Lucian's works seem at first sight to come from a different world from other rhetorical *belles lettres*, just as they indisputably outclass them in quality. Yet the world is the same. Indeed Lucian's merciless exposé of his coevals opens up new if distorted perspectives on the philosophers, rhetoricians, prophets and doctors who peopled the second-century intellectual scene. He is an invaluable complement to Philostratus' *Lives of the sophists* in his documentation of the pretentious shallowness of figures whose writings alone would have us treat them as serious and dedicated missionaries of Hellenic culture. Moreover several of his own works (not the best) fall into conventional sophistic categories, and many of the remainder have demonstrably rhetorical ancestry. His style is clearly the product, however subtly engineered, of the Atticist fashions he mocks. And in his acceptance of a Hellenic frame of reference as the context of his fictions – whether it be classical Athens or timeless Olympus and Hades – Lucian shows that within literature, at least, he subscribes to many of the basic mythologies that he questions.

It is sad that a writer so eloquent on the subject of his contemporaries should tell us so little about himself, and that when he does so it is often in a way that makes biographic fact hard to distinguish from fictional posture. The only contemporary mention of him, recently noticed in an Arabic translation of a work of Galen, is a precious clue that Lucian's delight in debunking is more than a matter of literary genre. We are told that he 'discovered' a work of Heraclitus and only revealed that it was a forgery when a distinguished philosopher had been induced to equip it with a learned commentary![1] Such behaviour makes his omission from Philostratus' catalogue less puzzling: he may have got as far in a sophistic career as the second-rate Aelian, but the over-serious Philostratus cannot have approved of his unrepentant iconoclasm. As a result of his and others' silence however, only a sketchy biography and tentative chronology are possible.

Born at Samosata, the former capital of Commagene on the Euphrates, in an area where Aramaic was the language of the people and Greek the language of culture, Lucian probably went west to Ionia for his further rhetorical education. We need not take as serious autobiography the Xenophontic 'choice of Heracles' between the ladies Education (Παιδεία) and Sculpture which Lucian recalls having dreamt at the crucial moment of his family's selection of his career: this is simply a pleasant, classicizing fantasy to entertain his compatriots when he returned a great man and delivered the *Dream* ('Ενύπνιον) at Samosata. The Suda may be right to allege that he was a barrister at Antioch, but this could be a misunderstanding of Lucian's own reference to abandoning court cases, and these were almost certainly sophistic declamations. For in the other major 'autobiographic' work, *Twice prosecuted* (Δὶς κατηγορούμενος) Lucian tells us that the dreamed promises of Education (*Dream*, 11) came true. In prosecuting her now renegade disciple, Rhetoric complains that she found Lucian foot-loose in Ionia, trained him and launched him on a successful career that took him from Ionia and Greece to Italy and even Gaul (*Twice pros.* 27). Elsewhere Lucian claims success as a sophist in Gaul (*Apol.* 15), and Philostratus' silence is the only ground for doubt. This period is presumably responsible for the competent but undistinguished *Phalaris* pieces, and perhaps for some preludes (προλαλιαί) and epideictic speeches (e.g. the witty *Praise of a fly*, or the encomium of a bath constructed by Hippias). Other epideictic works (e.g. *Defending a lapse in greeting*) and preludes (*Dionysus, Heracles*) are certainly late.

If *Twice prosecuted* is taken literally, Lucian deserted Rhetoric at forty (32) and took up with Dialogue, his second accuser. But the age of forty was proverbial for maturity, and reappears in the *Hermotimus* as the age of Lycinus

[1] For Galen's recently observed mention of Lucian cf. Strohmaier (1976).

(Lucian's mouthpiece) who is already characterized as mocking philosophers (*Herm.* 13 and 51). Lucian's attachment to serious philosophy cannot have been long-lasting, and more probably never existed at all. The *Nigrinus*, a charming dialogue in which Lucian tells an interlocutor how the Platonist Nigrinus, by precept and example, opened his eyes to the emptiness of common ambitions and the rewards of simple virtue, is the nearest Lucian gets to taking philosophy seriously in a dialogue. As in the *Demonax* (in the genre ἀπομνημονεύματα, 'recollections') the sincere admiration aroused by a compelling philosophical personality may be responsible for Lucian's straight handling of the theme. But in most dialogues he commits the outrages of which Dialogue accuses him:

...τὸ μὲν τραγικὸν ἐκεῖνο καὶ σωφρονικὸν προσωπεῖον ἀφεῖλέ μου, κωμικὸν δὲ καὶ σατυρικὸν ἄλλο ἐπέθηκέ μοι καὶ μικροῦ δεῖν γελοῖον. εἶτά μοι εἰς τὸ αὐτὸ φέρων συγκαθεῖρξεν τὸ σκῶμμα καὶ τὸν ἴαμβον καὶ κυνισμὸν καὶ τὸν Εὔπολιν καὶ τὸν Ἀριστοφάνη, δεινοὺς ἄνδρας ἐπικερτομῆσαι τὰ σεμνὰ καὶ χλευάσαι τὰ ὀρθῶς ἔχοντα. τελευταῖον δὲ καὶ Μένιππόν τινα τῶν παλαιῶν κυνῶν μάλα ὑλακτικὸν ὡς δοκεῖ καὶ κάρχαρον ἀνορύξας, καὶ τοῦτον ἐπεισήγαγέν μοι... (*Twice pros.* 33)

> He took from me that tragic, restrained mask and made me put on another which was comic and satyric and all but ridiculous. Then to share my confinement he brought along jest, lampoon, cynicism; and Eupolis and Aristophanes, men with a gift for mocking what is sacrosanct and vilifying correct procedures. Finally he dug up one of the ancient cynics called Menippus, a dog with quite a bite, it turns out, as well as a bark, and brought him in beside me too...

We may reasonably doubt that Lucian was ever a committed philosopher, or that his exploitation of the dialogue form began with a new life at forty. But the schematic literary pedigree furnishes plausible data about the influences on much of Lucian's best work. Sophistic rhetoric played a part, developing the skills of anecdote, argument and illustration. Platonic dialogue provides the pattern for more than half the major works, and Plato and Xenophon are the most obvious stylistic models. The interlocutor is often Menippus, and the form of the satires written by the real-life Menippus is responsible for the occasional blend of verse and prose in Lucian just as their content offered such themes as trips to heaven or Hades or comparison of conflicting philosophic doctrines. But the earlier model of Old Comedy is important here too – Aristophanes had flights to heaven and descents to Hades, and his rich vein of fantasy reappears constantly in his imaginative reincarnation Lucian. Old Comedy, Menippean satire and Cynic diatribe must jointly be credited for the mixture of keen questioning, humorous exposure and vigorous though never vulgar abuse.

Although some dialogues may be marked off as purely sophistic there is too much in common between those of satirical, Menippean and philosophical flavours for these to be seen as separate groups (as by Helm). It is also perilous to take Lucian's repeated use of motifs as a basis for chronological proximity, still more for sequence.

Some works, however, can be grouped together and attributed to the 160s. Three have allusions to Olympia and Babylon in a context suggesting the emperor Verus' Parthian war and the Olympic games of A.D. 165 (*Twice pros.* 2; *Ship* (Πλοῖον) 32, 44; *Hermotimus* 27–8). Lucian was present at these games to see the self-immolation of the Cynic – and charlatan – Peregrinus, and this gives a date shortly after 165 for *Peregrinus* and *Runaways* (Δραπέται, cf. 7). It is safe to say that in the mid-160s Lucian was writing satirical dialogues and colouring the quasi-biography *Peregrinus* with related motifs. But Lucian's writing had not wholly deserted sophistic for satire. The dialogue form is used for encomiastic ends in both *Statues* (Εἰκόνες) and *On dancing* (Περὶ ὀρχήσεως), the former an elegant compliment to Verus' mistress Pantheia, the latter a sustained vindication of the art of the pantomime. Both are plausibly associated with Verus' presence in Antioch in the period 163–6. Conversely, satire but not dialogue characterizes the work *How to write history* (Πῶς δεῖ ἱστορίαν συγγράφειν) prompted by the pullulation of Parthian war-historians.

The age of forty assumed by *Twice prosecuted* and *Hermotimus* may be used to give a date for Lucian's birth around 120. This precarious inference may in turn allow us to put works in which Lucian claims to be an old man into the 170s. It was then that he accepted a post on the staff of the prefect of Egypt, a step towards an official career which he had no difficulty in distinguishing (in the *Apology*) from the sort of prostitution of professional talents he had previously satirized (in *On hirelings* Περὶ τῶν ἐπὶ μισθῶι συνόντων). But as far as we can tell no further promotion followed. The return to epideictic activity by the ageing (γέρων) Lucian, alluded to in *Heracles* (7), might well be a consequence. Our last fixed point is the reference to the emperor Marcus as divine in *Alexander* (48), showing that this scurrilous biography was not published until after 180, even if it may be suspected that it was composed nearer 170.

Lucian's dissemination of his satirical dialogues seems to have followed the pattern established for the display rhetoric of travelling sophists. He sometimes refers to his audiences as large (*Heracles* 7), sometimes select (*Fisherman* Ἁλιεὺς 26). *Harmonides* envisages a recitation before a single, influential patron, which corroborates its statement that Lucian is already famous (4). In the *Scythian* Lucian tells how he has sought out a father and son, a Macedonian city's political leaders, to be his patrons, and is quite unrestrained in his flattery of them (esp. 10–11). Some of these preludes (προλαλιαί) would be appropriate for sophistic performances. But *Zeuxis* implies that Lucian's entertainments are thought of as novel (1–2) and *Dionysus* that they are being underestimated as merely comic and satirical (5). Both these works must be related to the development of which *Twice prosecuted* shows Lucian to have been so proud, and seem to be preludes to an epideictic performance which is not the first the audience addressed has heard from Lucian (*Dionysus* 7; *Zeuxis* 1–2). We must thus imagine Lucian as a special sort of sophist, touring the cultural centres and arranging invitations to perform in palaces and theatres (cf. *Zeuxis* 12). Some of his documented hosts are hardly in the first league – north Italy, Macedonia, distant Thracian Philippopolis (now Plovdiv); Athens, Ephesus and Olympia are also probable, and Verus' court at Antioch almost certain.

He clearly achieved fame and acquired some important friends (like the governor of Cappadocia mentioned in *Alexander* 55), and the works he delivered must soon have been circulated in book form. Others will have been such from the start, and are sometimes addressed to a recipient – the work *How to write history* (Πῶς δεῖ ἱστορίαν συγγράφειν) to Philo, the *Peregrinus* to a Saturninus whom Lucian, breaking his own rules,[1] calls Kronios, and the *Alexander* to the Epicurean Celsus. There is little formal difference between these, the *Teacher of rhetoricians* whose addressee is unnamed, and pamphlets like the *False-speaker* (Ψευδολογιστής) where the target of the assault, whose name is apparently Timarchus (cf. 27), is directly addressed and would clearly be the last person in the world to have welcomed the dedication of such an attack. All these works are manipulating the conventional, short treatise in epistolary or near-epistolary form to marshal a series of amusing onslaughts that might equally well have been handled in dialogues.

Within the dialogues themselves there is considerable variety. The *Nigrinus* is in fact preceded by a letter to the philosopher whom it apparently eulogizes (unless he is a fiction). This suggests it was composed for reading rather than performance. The dialogue opening and close is little more than a frame for Lucian's account of his visit to Nigrinus in Rome, itself chiefly occupied by the philosopher's scornful run-down of the follies and vices of the capital. The interlocutor simply echoes Lucian's reactions of enchantment to Nigrinus and draws the reader's attention to the writer's narrative skill. In other dialogues the content is distributed more widely between the speakers, whether that content be witty but innocuous caricatures of various philosophical schools (e.g. *Lives for sale* Βίων πρᾶσις) or uncompromising debunking of human aspirations (except freedom of speech and behaviour) such as run through the Menippean works (e.g. *Charon, Menippus, Dialogues of the dead* = Νεκρικοὶ διάλογοι).

Lucian's image is that of a satirist. But like the poets of Old Comedy whom he claims as ancestors, his primary purpose is to entertain, and, although his means to that end include satire on contemporary society, they go far beyond it. The upper class audiences who laughed at his journalistic exposure of the peccadilloes and inconsistencies of philosophers and rhetoricians, or the brazen

---

[1] Cf. *How to write history*, 21, where he ridicules a historian whose Atticism led him to render the Roman names Saturninus, Fronto and Titianus as Kronios, Phrontis and Titianios.

impostures of holy men, were themselves patrons or even practitioners of these arts. Lucian will not have expected to convert them, and, like conventional sophists, he must have entertained as much by the techniques as by the content of his discourse. Not surprisingly, then, much of his satire is not directed against his contemporaries, and some of his writing is not satirical at all.

The first category is exemplified by *Dialogues of the gods* (Θεῶν διάλογοι). Here Lucian gets his laughs by the way he follows through notorious incidents in the love-lives of the Olympians as if they were contemporary bourgeois Greeks. Homeric data are cleverly exploited (e.g. Apollo's willingness to be caught in bed with Aphrodite, from *Od.* 8.334ff.) and sometimes overplayed (e.g. Hephaestus' lameness) while at the same time Lucian can take wing on novel flights of fancy as in the following hilarious characterization of Ganymede as the ingénu shepherd-lad:

ΓΑΝΥΜΗΔΗΣ Ἢν δὲ παίζειν ἐπιθυμήσω, τίς συμπαίξεταί μοι; ἐν γὰρ τῆι Ἴδηι πολλοὶ ἡλικιῶται ἦμεν.

ΖΕΥΣ Ἔχεις κἀνταῦθα τὸν συμπαιξόμενόν σοι τουτονὶ τὸν Ἔρωτα καὶ ἀστραγάλους μάλα πολλούς. θάρρει μόνον καὶ φαιδρὸς ἴσθι καὶ μηδὲν ἐπιπόθει τῶν κάτω.

ΓΑΝΥΜΗΔΗΣ Τί δαὶ ὑμῖν χρήσιμος ἂν γενοίμην; ἢ ποιμαίνειν δεήσει κἀνταῦθα;

ΖΕΥΣ Οὔκ, ἀλλ' οἰνοχοήσεις καὶ ἐπὶ τοῦ νέκταρος τετάξηι καὶ ἐπιμελήσηι τοῦ συμποσίου.

ΓΑΝΥΜΗΔΗΣ Τοῦτο μὲν οὐ χαλεπόν· οἶδα γὰρ ὡς χρὴ ἐγχέαι τὸ γάλα καὶ ἀναδοῦναι τὸ κισσύβιον.

ΖΕΥΣ Ἰδού, πάλιν οὗτος γάλακτος μνημονεύει καὶ ἀνθρώποις διακονήσεσθαι οἴεται· ταυτὶ δ' ὁ οὐρανός ἐστι, καὶ πίνομεν, ὥσπερ ἔφην, τὸ νέκταρ.

ΓΑΝΥΜΗΔΗΣ Ἥδιον, ὦ Ζεῦ, τοῦ γάλακτος;

ΖΕΥΣ Εἴσηι μετ' ὀλίγον καὶ γευσάμενος οὐκέτι ποθήσεις τὸ γάλα.

ΓΑΝΥΜΗΔΗΣ Κοιμήσομαι δὲ ποῦ τῆς νυκτός; ἢ μετὰ τοῦ ἡλικιώτου Ἔρωτος;

ΖΕΥΣ Οὔκ, ἀλλὰ διὰ τοῦτό σε ἀνήρπασα, ὡς ἅμα καθεύδοιμεν.

ΓΑΝΥΜΗΔΗΣ Μόνος γὰρ οὐκ ἂν δύναιο, ἀλλὰ ἥδιόν σοι καθεύδειν μετ' ἐμοῦ;

ΖΕΥΣ Ναί, μετά γε τοιούτου οἷος εἶ σύ, Γανύμηδες, οὕτω καλός.

GANYMEDE But what if I want to play? Who will play with me? There were a lot of us who were of my age on Ida.

ZEUS You have someone to play with here too – there's Eros over there – and lots and lots of knucklebones as well. Only you must cheer up and be a bit more pleased with life, and stop longing for things below.

GANYMEDE But how could I possibly be any use to you? Will I have to look after a flock here too?

ZEUS No, you'll pour wine, and be in charge of the nectar, looking after us at table.

GANYMEDE That's quite simple. I know how to pour milk, and hand round the milk bowl.

ZEUS There he goes again. Keeps harping on his milk! Thinks he'll be waiting on men! This is heaven, let me tell you, and, as I said just now, our drink is nectar.

GANYMEDE Is that nicer than milk, Zeus?

ZEUS   You'll know very soon, and once you've tasted it, you won't miss your milk any more.
GANYMEDE   Where shall I sleep at night? With Eros, my playmate?
ZEUS   No, that's why I carried you off up here; I wanted us to sleep together.
GANYMEDE   Can't you sleep alone? Will you prefer sleeping with me?
ZEUS   Yes, when it's with a beautiful boy like you. (*Deor. Dial.* 4, tr. M. D. Macleod)

Lucian's inventive genius is nowhere more striking than in the *True histories*. The parody of a traveller's tale, which extends over two books, must have derived much of the impact it had on its first audience from its clever development of themes from familiar narratives – Alexander-historians, Iambulus, Antonius Diogenes. But much of the fantasy is recognizably Lucianic, and even without the parodic effect *True histories* stands as a masterpiece of imaginative and witty story-telling.

The story-teller who is constantly popping up in the other works (even the small-scale preludes) is an important part of Lucian's literary personality. Two major dialogues are simply frames for a collection of stories, in *Toxaris* ten linked by the theme of friendship, in *Liars* (Φιλοψευδεῖς) nine on the supernatural and magic. It is probably correct to attribute to Lucian the *Metamorphoses* thought by Photius to be by Lucius of Patrae (which will make it the original both of Apuleius' *Golden ass* in Latin and of the Greek epitome *Lucius or the ass* transmitted among Lucian's works).[1] Although we have to rely on Photius' summary for content and his verdict for style, it is clear that the *Metamorphoses* was as accomplished as Lucian's other narrative works. It confirms the picture of a literary artist with a light touch, fertile wit and unrivalled range and versatility. It can no longer be read. But the works of Lucian that have survived are sure of a future. Their Greek will be admired so long as Greek is read, and in translation their quality persists in sufficient measure to make them classics of European literature.

Alciphron

Alciphron's personality is unknown and his date uncertain. The tradition which preserves his one hundred and twenty-three letters describes him as a *rhetor*, but that may be inference from content and style. Close similarity to Lucian in treatment of some themes which ultimately stem from New Comedy suggests that he knew and was stimulated by the satirist's work. It has also been argued that Longus and Aelian draw on Alciphron. If these relationships are accepted Alciphron must have written during the period 170–220.

The letters share many features with other literature of the time. Each implies a fourth-century B.C. Attic context and attempts to evoke a rural or urban

[1] Cf. below, p. 687; Perry (1967); Anderson (1976).

situation more familiar to readers from their acquaintance with New Comedy than from life. Alciphron entertains by presenting in sequence the varied reactions of different characters to mundane and easily imagined situations. In the letters of fishermen and farmers the chief interest lies in the contrast of temperaments – often pointed by the choice of meaningful names like Philocomus and Astyllus (2.28: 'Village-lover' and 'Towny') – or of different parties' attitudes, as in 2.24–5 where the master Gemellus complains that the slave Salaconis will not sleep with him and she in turn gives vent to her loathing for him. Meaningful names are also characteristic of the parasites' letters, whereas those of hetaerae ('tarts') exploit famous historical figures like Phryne and Praxiteles (4.1). The letters of hetaerae are also different in their occasional expansion into an ecphrasis, e.g. 4.14 with its lurid account of a sympotic orgy.

Alciphron may deserve the credit for developing the fictitious letter to serve ends similar to those pursued by Lucian in his miniature dialogues or Longus in his novel – lively and 'convincing' exchanges between characters intrinsically interesting to his readership by virtue of their very remoteness from late second-century urban intellectual life. But the game cannot sustain prolonged watching. Although letters are sometimes paired and themes contrasted the surviving corpus lacks the formal appeal of Aelian's less ambitious collection.

Aelian

Another sophist to turn his hand to entertaining literature was Aelian. No declamations survive to show whether he was right to judge himself unsuited to that genre.[1] But the Ποικίλη ἱστορία (*Historical pot-pourri*) and the similar work Περὶ ζῴων ἰδιότητος (*Animal peculiarities*) suggest he had little talent for 'history' either. The first is a hotch-potch of tales from natural, political or cultural history. Aelian tells them to astonish more often than to edify, and no principle of selection or arrangement is apparent. The work on animals is equally devoid of order, but at least has a preface. That and the epilogue show the Stoic Aelian specially concerned to document the operation of moral impulses outside the human species. Its greatest value lies in its preservation of the views of more serious writers on natural history. However Aelian often seems to have used them carelessly, and his work clearly falls in the tradition of collections of astonishing phenomena (paradoxography) – taking its cue from Herodotus and exemplified by Phlegon's *Wonders* – rather than the more serious observation of natural phenomena found in Favorinus' *Miscellany*.[2] We can only gasp when he has the arrogance to echo Thucydides in the preface

---

[1] As reported by Philostratus, *V.S.* 2.31 (624).
[2] For Phlegon's Θαυμάσια cf. *FGrH* IIB, 257 F 36. For Favorinus' Παντοδαπὴ ἱστορία cf. Mensching (1963) and Barigazzi (1966).

that advertises the *Animal peculiarities* as 'a treasure far from negligible' and claims that it will be 'profitable'.[1]

More convincing is the same preface's claim that the material has been clothed in τὴν συνήθη λέξιν 'untechnical language'. Yet the most striking feature of the style is not its lack of technicalities but its extreme Atticism in diction and simplicity of constructions. The preciosity of Aelian's short *cola*, grouped by parataxis and rarely varied by any other than participial subordination, rapidly becomes monotonous. What Philostratus praised as simple elegance (ἀφέλεια) has been fairly condemned as 'arch naïveté and nursery syntax'.[2] It is just tolerable within each entry or anecdote, but quite unsuited to continuous works of fourteen and seventeen books respectively.

The collection of twenty *Rustic letters* is much more readable. Aelian's stylistic affectations are less developed (hence the work has been thought early) and certainly less obtrusive in their miniature context. Although entitled in our tradition 'from Aelian's rustic letters' they are surely a whole as they stand. Their vignettes of rural life, starting with a roll in the hay and skilfully re-handling this theme from various viewpoints in alternation with complaints, quarrels and enkomia of rustic simplicity, build up a harmonious cycle. A letter will develop, or contrast with, themes in its predecessor, and coherence as well as variety is achieved by including two pairs (7–8; 11–12) and a quatrain (13–16). Each letter neatly portrays the country ways of the supposed writer and by economic allusions apprises the reader of the situation he must envisage. By letter 20 (a sort of postponed programmatic piece) we feel we have come to know many individuals and features of the Attic countryside; we are prepared to join the author in his praise of country ways and to concede the success of his posture as an Attic farmer:

μὴ τοίνυν γεωργῶν καταφρόνει· ἔστι γάρ τις καὶ ἐνταῦθα σοφία, γλώττῃ μὲν οὐ πεποικιλμένη οὐδὲ καλλωπιζομένη λόγων δυνάμει, σιγῶσα δὲ εὖ μάλα καὶ δι' αὐτοῦ τοῦ βίου τὴν ἀρετὴν ὁμολογοῦσα· εἰ δὲ σοφώτερα ταῦτα ἐπέσταλταί σοι ἢ κατὰ τὴν τῶν ἀγρῶν χορηγίαν, μὴ θαυμάσῃς· οὐ γὰρ ἐσμὲν οὔτε Λίβυες οὔτε Λυδοὶ ἀλλ' Ἀθηναῖοι γεωργοί.

So then do not be contemptuous of farmers; for in them too is wisdom of a sort – not elaborately expressed in speech nor decking itself out with forceful rhetoric, but conspicuous by its silence and confessing its virtue through its very life. If these written words addressed to you are too clever for the country to supply, do not marvel; for we are not Libyan nor Lydian, but Athenian farmers. (tr. Benner & Fobes)

It is, of course, a game. Aelian came from Rome and claimed never to have left Italy. His farmers draw on themes from comedy, quote or allude to many

[1] *N.A.* pref.; cf. Thuc. 1.22.4.
[2] Philostratus, *V.S.* 2.31 (624); Russell (1964) 160 on 'Longinus', *Subl.* 34.2.

classical authors and (it seems probable) plagiarize Aelian's contemporary Alciphron. But it is more important that Aelian's letters are entertaining than that they are derivative. His reputation would stand higher had they alone survived.

Athenaeus

An educated public which craved erudition in any sphere was prepared to sample it in almost any presentation – witness Aelian. But some writers faced the challenge of imposing a literary structure on the recalcitrant mass of facts: Gellius, who happens to write chiefly in Latin for his bilingual readers, and Athenaeus of Naucratis (the only Egyptian city known as a nurse of sophists) whose equally Roman readership was offered a massive work in Greek, *Dining sophists* (Δειπνοσοφισταί).

Athenaeus presents his recondite compilation of convivial material (much of it dependent on earlier catalogues and lexica) in a swollen version of a Platonic dialogue. The opening echoes that of the *Phaedo*, but the *Symposium* is the model. Plutarch's *Table talk* seems also to have been influential, and indeed among the two dozen participants appears a Plutarch of Alexandria, probably invented as a compliment to the distinguished scholar from Chaeronea. Like Plutarch, Athenaeus involves a Roman consular: the host is P. Livius Larensis, a real figure[1] of the Rome of the late second century where the banquet is set. But whereas Plutarch has us imagine that he is presenting conversations on several different occasions, Athenaeus envisages, albeit incoherently, a single banquet. Some speakers are, like Larensis, identifiable as historical and appropriate individuals: certainly Galen, and perhaps Ulpian. But enough are clearly fictional to make the identification with Ulpian uncertain, and with it the date of composition after A.D. 228 which it would imply.

Although some of the incongruities may be partly the product of our abbreviated text, it is hard to see how the original thirty books could have made any impact as a work of literature in the dialogue tradition. For contemporaries as for us their value must have been as a storehouse of learning. Pride of place is of course given to food and drink. But these topics naturally lead into Comedy. Even after the papyrus finds of the last eighty years our knowledge of New Comedy (and indeed of Middle Comedy and of Aristophanes' contemporaries) is formed largely by what Athenaeus, responsive to an age fascinated by Attic language and culture, chose to quote. He is equally important for our knowledge of historiography. These and the other branches of learning – philosophy, medicine, law – on which his diners pontificate are a fair indication of the range and coherence of the era's erudite interests. Like Lucian, Athenaeus shows us that sophists, philosophers, doctors and grammarians belonged to

[1] Cf. *CIL* VI 2126, cf. Dessau (1892).

the same world where not even the currency of two languages produced two cultures.

6. THE GREEK NOVEL

The genre

The most influential product of Graeco-Roman literary activity is also the most enigmatic; ancient literary theory finds no place for prose narrative about lovers who are separated, exposed to perils and finally reunited. Apart from two dismissive allusions in Philostratus to a work and an individual, neither certainly novelistic, only a derogatory sideswipe in Julian betrays other writers' awareness of the genre.[1] The earliest attempt to pass a constructive literary verdict is that of Photius about A.D. 855. Yet most of these works were written by men of considerable erudition, arguably for appreciation by educated readers. The extent to which some were read (and the range of the form's varieties) has been demonstrated, at least for Egypt and Antioch, by papyri and mosaics discovered over the last eighty years.[2]

Papyrus texts have also aided chronology, although there is still uncertainty about the novel's origins and development and its place in the culture of the Hellenistic world. Rohde saw the genre as a product of the Second Sophistic in which declamatory themes and techniques operated upon a hybrid of Alexandrian love-elegy and travel tales. He began the novel's development with Antonius Diogenes in the first century A.D. and ended it with Chariton in the fifth. The discovery in 1893 of the *Ninus* romance, probably composed in the first century B.C. and certainly written in a hand of the early first century A.D., undermined the general theory. Moreover Rohde's view of the novelists' order was overthrown by the publication in 1900 of a papyrus of Chariton dating from the second century A.D. Much remains disputed, but the table on p. 684 presents a provisional chronology (titles of works extant in continuous texts are in capitals, related genres in square brackets).

It would be injudicious to use the tabulation below as the basis for any general theory. We remain uncertain when the first and last of our novels was written. *Ninus* might be as early as 100 B.C.[3] and it has been argued that the *Aethiopica* belongs to the late fourth century. These dates would give a span of five centuries and ground for seeing the genre as culturally symptomatic of later

---

[1] Philostr. *V.S.* 1.22.524 to the *Araspes and Pantheia*, possibly a novel (cf. below, p. 686) and id. *Epist.* 66 to Chariton, disparaging his λόγοι: this may be the novelist; Julian, *Epist.* 89B (Bidez) 301b: ὅσα δέ ἐστιν ἐν ἱστορίας εἴδει παρὰ τοῖς ἔμπροσθεν ἀπηγγελμένα πλάσματα παραιτητέον, ἐρωτικὰς ὑποθέσεις καὶ πάντα ἁπλῶς τὰ τοιαῦτα 'We must eschew the fictions reported under the form of history by earlier writers, love stories and all that sort of stuff'.

[2] See Appendix p. 877 (General works; Texts) and p. 878 (*anepigraphi*); cf. also p. 688 n. 2.

[3] *Ninus*, Perry (1967) 153; *Joseph and Asenath*, S. West (1974) 79–81; Chariton, Papanikolaou (1973).

Hellenism.[1] But neither *Ninus* nor Chariton need antedate the first century A.D., and if Heliodorus were third-century the efflorescence would match that of Philostratus' Second Sophistic. For this a purely literary explanation is possible. The novels' rise would reflect merely the avid reading and prolific writing of the age, their demise the decline of a peaceful and cosmopolitan Greek world.

[*Alexander*-romance prototype   ? second century B.C.]

[*Nectanebus*' dream   second century B.C.]

[JOSEPH AND ASENATH   first century B.C./A.D.?]

Ninus   first century B.C.? (papyri first century A.D.)

Chariton, CHAEREAS AND CALLIRHOE   mid-first century B.C./A.D.? (papyri mid-second/ early third century A.D.)

Metiochus and Parthenope   first century A.D.? (papyri second century A.D.)

Iolaus   first century A.D.? (may influence Petronius: papyrus early second century A.D.)

[*Tefnut*   first/second century A.D.? (demotic text second, Greek text third, century A.D.)]

Sesonchosis   first/second/third century A.D.? (papyri third century A.D.)

[?Celer, *Araspes and Pantheia*   c. A.D. 150]

Xenophon of Ephesus, ANTHIA AND HABROCOMES   mid-second century? (no papyri)

Diogenes, *The incredible beyond Thule*   early/mid-second century A.D.? (parodied by Lucian in 160s: papyri late second/early third century)

Lucian(?), *Metamorphoses* A.D. 150–180 (no papyri)

Iamblichus, *Babyloniaca*   A.D. 165–180 (Photius cod. 94.10 = p.32 ed. Habrich; no papyri)

Lollianus, *Phoenicica*   mid-second century (papyrus second half of second century A.D.)

Longus, DAPHNIS AND CHLOE   late second/early third century A.D. (no papyri).

Achilles, LEUCIPPE AND CLITOPHON   late second century A.D. (papyri second century and later)

Heliodorus, AETHIOPICA   early/mid third century OR late fourth century A.D. (no papyri)

[Philostratus, APOLLONIUS   c. A.D. 230 (no papyri)]

It is uncertain what features should be seen as characterizing the genre. The five novels which survived to influence Byzantine and European readers can reasonably be seen as a coherent group,[2] each a variant on the 'ideal' romance. The plot is one element of unity. Boy and girl of aristocratic background fall in love, are separated before or shortly after marriage and subjected to melodramatic adventures which threaten their life and chastity and carry them around much of the eastern Mediterranean. Eventually love and fortune prove stronger than storms, pirates and tyrants and the couple is reunited in marital bliss. Longus offers a variation that is recognizably germane: the horizon is the Aegean off Lesbos, but the Methymnaean sportsmen can start a war, and

---

[1] As Reardon (1969) 293–4.

[2] Chariton, Xenophon, Longus, Achilles and Heliodorus: as well as the last two Photius knew Iamblichus, Antonius Diogenes and 'Lucius of Patrae'.

Daphnis and Chloe turn out to be lost aristocrats in pastoral guise. Unity can also be claimed for the genre on grounds of scale, style and treatment. Longus again diverges with four books: but Chariton and Achilles have eight, the original text of Xenophon ten,[1] as does Heliodorus. All five write careful, literary Greek, eschewing hiatus[2] and affecting particular prose rhythms, especially, it seems, in speeches. Speeches, reflections and letters are much exploited to delineate the characters' emotions, set in the foreground of the reader's attention against a backcloth of travel and adventure. These emotions and the beauties of art and nature are given a generous allocation of rhetoric by Achilles, Longus and Heliodorus (too generous, indeed, for modern taste). But even Chariton, despite his less pretentious style, loses few opportunities for emotional and rhetorically moulded outbursts, and his neglect of Atticist predilections in syntax and vocabulary is a witness to the environment in which he was educated rather than to a humbler intent.

Fragments show four other works to have been similar. In the *Ninus* the young king of Assyria is found pleading for the hand of Semiramis and later parted from her by shipwreck. Love and adventure in a Near-Eastern setting also mark the *Sesonchosis* story and Iamblichus' *Babyloniaca*. All four have stylistic pretensions and, like Chariton, envisage a specific historical context: thus *Metiochus and Parthenope* is linked with Polycrates' Samos. The reader can fancy that he is enjoying a sentimental sidelight on conventional political history. This may support the view that local history is one ancestor of the novel, although it may only be the guise under which novelists chose to masquerade, as suggested by the form of title probably current in antiquity – *Ephesiaca*, *Lesbiaca*, *Ethiopica*.

But at least one example shows that a historical context could provide a setting at a more popular level. The story of the Egyptian Asenath's love for the biblical Joseph, a love which leads to her conversion and marriage, is written in a monotonous and simple Greek close to the *koine*. Its novelistic motifs show that the author was acquainted with the genre. We do not know at what level, and it is tempting to imagine that the author knew popular examples, which preceded the development of the literary form. Indeed, some have seen Graeco-Egyptian literature as an important factor in the creation of the Greek novel.[3] But the tale of Tefnut, translated from demotic Egyptian to Greek at some time before the third century A.D., lacks *erotica*, and the dream of Nectanebus is too short to justify its classification with the novel. We need not, therefore, believe that the literary novel descended from Greek translations of Egyptian tales *via* Greek popular stories.

It might be, indeed, that less pretentious versions of the novel were written

---

[1] Bürger (1892).   [2] Reeve (1971).
[3] Barns (1956); Reardon (1969) nn. 39 and 43.

only contemporaneously with or even after the earliest literary attempts. They certainly went on being written in the novel's heyday. The *Phoenicica*, ascribed by the papyrus fragments to Lollianus, seems to fall within the boundaries of the genre. There is eroticism (but not sentimentality) and dramatic if improbable incident reminiscent of Xenophon (see below, pp. 69off.). But there is also surprising material: the seduction of the narrator Androtimus by a girl who is not the heroine (and does not seem to have the importance to the plot of Achilles' Melite or Longus' Lycaenion, cf. below, pp. 693 and 698), and a mystery ritual in which the sacrifice of a boy so that his heart can be eaten is followed by group copulation in Androtimus' presence. The style, never elevated and sometimes crude, confirms the impression that a substantial gap separates this work from the 'ideal' romance. It is hard to believe that it is by the sophist from Ephesus, P. Hordeonius Lollianus, but it may have been circulated maliciously under his name, like the *Araspes and Pantheia* published under Dionysius of Miletus' name by his enemy Celer.[1]

Three further works exemplify a type of prose fiction clearly related to the love romance but in many respects different. Antonius Diogenes' *The incredible beyond Thule* is known only in epitome. Love seems to have played but a small part, albeit pivotal: the narrator Deinias fell in love with Dercyllis in Thule. But the many adventures are as striking as the complex framework within which they are told (cf. Heliodorus, below p. 695). The first location seems to have been Thule. Deinias narrates his own journey there and then gives Dercyllis' account (complete with sub-plots) of how she and her brother fled to Thule pursued by the wizard Paapis. Deinias' narrative continues with Paapis' arrival and death. The siblings after a false death regain their native Tyre: Deinias too returns via the moon, assisted by a magic wish (cf. Lucian's *True histories* and *Wishes*). Only then do we learn that all this is being told by a Deinias living happily in Tyre with Dercyllis. The final twist is still to come; Dercyllis provides tablets for the recording of the narrative, and these, buried by the principals' graves, were discovered during Alexander's siege of Tyre and form the basis of Diogenes' book.

The 'chinese box' effect is not the only remarkable feature. Size, twenty-four books, marks it off from all the love romances save that of Iamblichus. Magic and Pythagoreanism anticipate Philostratus' work on Apollonius.[2] Furthermore Antonius claimed to be a practitioner of Old Comedy.[3] As the only claim to a literary pedigree in the novelists this merits attention, even if it only alludes to the rich vein of fantasy – humour is hard to read into the epitome! Antonius Diogenes' work does not play the vital role in the development of the genre assigned to it by Rohde, but it is a valuable index of how varied prose fiction could be.

---

[1] Philostr. *V.S.* 1.22.524.   [2] Bowie (1978) 1663ff.   [3] Photius, *Bibl.*, Cod. 166, 111a34.

Yet another sort of fiction is found in the *Metamorphoses* preserved in epitome by Photius and ascribed by him to Lucius of Patrae. It is very probably by Lucian, and the original of both the *Ass* in the Lucianic corpus (a work unlikely to be by Lucian) and Apuleius' *Metamorphoses*.[1] Erotic incident will have been treated without sentiment and simply as one of many sorts of adventure: magic, fantasy and travel provide a bridge to *The incredible* of Antonius, but the obscenity (if we trust Photius) is a differentiating ingredient.

Comedy may also have been one objective of the *Iolaus* novel, known from a recent papyrus scrap in which prose and verse are mingled. Iolaus is apparently represented learning the mysteries of the eunuch priests of Cybele in order that he may pass himself off as one and thereby seduce his boy-friend. Form and tone have suggested that the work was of the sort known to us only by the Latin *Satyrica* of Petronius.

The three works just reviewed show that prose narrative fiction could take many forms. Others are also related, though they would not merit our modern term 'novel': Dio's *Euboean*, Lucian's *True histories*, Philostratus' *Apollonius* and *Heroic tale*. Much was left to the writer's choice. Even those who selected what seems identifiable as a particular type, the ideal love romance, could exploit, develop or parody standard motifs.

The search for origins which dominated much earlier scholarship has now few practitioners. It is clear that the writers of novels were, like contemporaries in other literary fields, highly conscious of classical works. In its many facets the novel exhibits formal resemblances to the *Odyssey*, Herodotus, Thucydides and above all Xenophon's *Cyropaedia* as well as community of content with love-poetry and New Comedy. Whatever this might tell us about origins (and that is still disputed) is less important than its bearing on the writers' intentions. All these classical forms were still popular with readers, but only historiography was being written with any distinction. The others must have offered few openings, and to a man who wished to exercise his talents in writing rather than declaiming, the prose narrative form, once available, offered a challenge and a guarantee of a readership. Other motives may have operated. The novel has been seen as the Hellenistic myth, expressive of man's solitude and search for union with another being, human or divine. Such a view overplays the solitude of the central characters in novels, and we do not need to explain why the adventure plot, familiar since the *Odyssey*, continued to attract the readers of our period. Love is likewise a primary ingredient of literature which calls for no special explanation. But the combination of love and religion tells us much about the spiritual life a novelist might expect his reader to find meaningful. Religion was an increasingly prominent constituent of private and public life. That suffices to explain its role in the novel, and few scholars accept Merkelbach's ingenious

---

[1] Cf. above, p. 679 and *CHCL* II 778–85.

hypothesis that all the love romances save Chariton are mystery texts, communicating an allegory of the progress of the initiate through ordeals, death and resurrection to recognition by and union with the deity.[1] The correspondences Merkelbach noted are adequately explained by the common model of both novels and mystery ritual. That model is life, and it is about life as a Graeco-Roman reader saw it (or wished to see it) that the novelist writes.

We must assume that the writers had a better idea of their readership than we can form. Little in their erudite approach supports modern fancies that the works were intended for women or children. Like paradoxography, epistolography and the works of Lucian, the novels were more probably written as lighter reading for the intelligentsia. The preference for an Eastern setting is no guide to readership distribution, and the varied origins of the authors – Achaea, western Asia Minor, Syria and perhaps Alexandria – show the same scatter as other branches of literature. Papyri can tell us that some, but not all, were read in Egyptian towns (as well as attesting illustrated texts), and mosaics that *Ninus* and *Metiochus* were of interest to owners of villas in fourth-century Antioch.[2] Fortunately the novels were popular enough in late antiquity for the survival of several to be assured.

The surviving texts

Chariton's *Chaereas and Callirhoe*, probably the earliest of the extant group, already shows a deft mastery of the genre, to which its apparent directness and simplicity should not blind us. Chariton professes to recount a love story (πάθος ἐρωτικὸν ἐν Συρακούσαις γενόμενον διηγήσομαι) and although he tells it straight he never drops his conscious narrative role. Most striking is his preface to the eighth and last book, where, after recapitulating the lovers' adventures, he promises a happy end:

> And I also think this last chapter will give most pleasure to its readers: for it purges the grim happenings of the earlier episodes. No longer piracy and slavery and litigation and battle and endurance and warfare and capture, but now legal passions and lawful marriages. So I shall tell how Aphrodite brought the truth to light and revealed to each other the lovers each unaware of the other's identity. (8.1.4)

There are many other places, however, where the author is found to intervene in the thinly disguised *persona* of Tyche, manipulating the plot in the required direction (e.g. 4.5.3). Yet despite reminders that a story of remarkable changes of fortune is being told the reader is rarely faced with sheer improbability (unless perhaps the fortuitous capture of the pirate Theron by Syracusans

---

[1] Merkelbach (1962): for criticism cf. Reardon (1971) 393f.

[2] Illustrated texts and mosaics, Weitzmann (1959) 99f.; Maehler (1976) 2 where the appearance of a Leucippe and of an unnamed daughter of Polycrates in mime is observed.

which discloses to Chaereas his wife's fate, 3.3f.). Chariton gives his narrative just enough motivation. When the couple, married through the power of Eros, have to be separated, jealousy moves Chaereas to kick Callirhoe: taken for dead, she comes to life again in her tomb. Thence Theron hales her to Ionia and sells her to a leading Ephesian, Dionysius. She marries him when she discovers she is pregnant with a child of Chaereas, who has meanwhile pursued her to Ionia and become a slave of the satrap Mithridates. He encourages Chaereas to send Callirhoe a letter whose interception gives rise to the next journey theme; Mithridates and Dionysius are summoned before the Great King in Babylon to decide the truth of their mutual accusations. Mithridates conceals Chaereas, his trump card, until the day of the trial, so that the lovers can suddenly be confronted with each other in the court room but prevented from embracing. The legal battle now shifts to possession of Callirhoe and is protracted by the king's own passion for the lovely heroine. Decision is fore-stalled by an Egyptian revolt. The king leaves Babylon with Dionysius in his army and Callirhoe in his train. In despair Chaereas joins the rebels and leads them to the capture of Tyre and naval victory, while Dionysius' exploits in the victorious land campaign win him the title to Callirhoe. But she is with the women and baggage in Aradus, captured by Chaereas: briefly the author pro-longs the suspense in postponing recognition, then they are reunited to sail finally to Syracuse.

The narrative has linear simplicity, untrammelled by flashbacks or subplots. Other men's passions indeed complement that of Chaereas, but they are united by having the same object, Callirhoe, whose overwhelming beauty acts as a leitmotiv insistently recalling the power of Eros and Aphrodite. Beside her Chaereas is a feeble figure. We know he is handsome, but his initial and fatal jealousy is no more attractive than his recurrent despair in adversity; it is this despair and not any more positive quality which precipitates his unexpected energy and valour in the wars as he seeks that death from which a friend (created for this very purpose) has often saved him. Dionysius, on the other hand, is sympathetically drawn as an aristocrat whose impeccable behaviour derives largely from Hellenic *paideia* (1.12.6; 2.5.11; 3.2.6; 5.9.8). His thoughtful and stable character appeals strongly to the reader and seems to offer a much closer bond with Callirhoe than Chaereas' adolescent passion. For Callirhoe too is educated (1.12.9) and her strength of purpose is unintelligible to the barbarian eunuch trying to lure her to the king's bed: οὐκ ἤιδει δὲ φρόνημα Ἑλληνικὸν εὐγενὲς καὶ μάλιστα τὸ Καλλιρόης τῆς σώφρονος καὶ φιλάνδρου 'but he did not understand the noble spirit of a Greek, and particularly of Callirhoe, who was chaste and loyal to her husband' (6.4.10). Being *barbaros* does not damn the king, for he too is inhibited by *noblesse*, although his attempt to check his own infatuation by absorption in sport (6.3.8f.) predictably fails. Eros follows him into the field, and the eunuch's view is confirmed: φάρμακον γὰρ ἕτερον Ἔρωτος οὐδέν ἐστιν πλὴν αὐτὸς ὁ ἐρώμενος...ὁ τρώσας αὐτὸς ἰάσεται 'there is no other remedy for love save the beloved himself...the wounder shall himself heal' (6.3.7).[1] The king and Dionysius are both sensitive and worthy princes, but a reader who put his money on them would lose, for their outclassing by the improbable Chaereas vindicates the author's creed that love conquers all.

Chariton expects his readers not only to venerate Love but to admire his characters as larger than life. Callirhoe is often compared to, twice taken for, a goddess; Chaereas resembles Achilles, Nireus, Hippolytus or Alcibiades (! 1.1.3); and the heroic atmosphere is fostered by apt quotations from Homer.[2] Slaves (2.1.5), barbarians (cf. 6.4.10 quoted above) and the mob are deemed inferior (8.6.7) – although Plangon, the bailiff's wife charged with Callirhoe's care, is allowed a simple nobility – and echoes of classical orators and historians (especially Xenophon) show that the educated classes of the Greek East are envisaged as readers. They had the *paideia* of Dionysius and might dream of having his rank, and they would enjoy a tale in which Chaereas combined traits of culture heroes like Odysseus, Alexander and the Xenophon of the *Anabasis* with some features of the less known general Chabrias in Egypt in the fourth century B.C.[3] They would appreciate the many reflections and speeches of the characters, rhetorical (cf. 6.1.4 ἐρρητόρευον) but not excessive, and such text-book touches, blending allusion and contrast, as the comment on Chaereas' return with Persian booty: ὥστε ἐνεπλήσθη πᾶσα ἡ πόλις, οὐχ ὡς πρότερον ἐκ τοῦ πολέμου τοῦ Σικελικοῦ πενίας Ἀττικῆς, ἀλλὰ, τὸ καινότατον, ἐν εἰρήνηι λαφύρων Μηδικῶν 'And so the whole city overflowed, not, as before after the Sicilian war, with Athenian poverty, but, most strangely, in peace with Persian spoils' (8.6.12). This game played between educated author and reader makes it clear that Chariton is no popular or folk writer, and the contrast between such features and the admission to his careful prose of post-classical vocabulary and syntax condemned by Atticists forces us to attribute him to a time and place where the Atticist movement had not yet triumphed.

Xenophon's Ephesian tale of *Anthia and Habrocomes* evokes little enthusiasm among modern critics. That the surviving text in five books is an epitome of an original ten[4] may be partly to blame for maladroitness of construction and motivation as well as for the flat simplicity of a style which lacks Chariton's charm. Comparison with Chariton is inevitable, for they share many themes and details, Xenophon usually being deemed the borrower.[5] Our text has little room for close observation of human emotions (albeit speechifying is not infrequent) and throughout the action, more complex than in Chariton, divine

---

[1] An allusion to the oracle given to Telephus.
[2] Cf. Papanikolaou (1973) ch. 1.   [3] Salmon (1961).   [4] As shown by Bürger (1892).
[5] Cf. Gärtner (1967) 2080f. Merkelbach (1962) and Petri (1963) put Chariton after Xenophon.

motivation and intervention combine with melodramatic and scarcely credible incident to produce a mediocre work closer to a thriller than a novel.

Eros is seen as an active force from the start. Habrocomes, handsome, well-connected but scornful of love, is made by Eros to fall for a lovely fourteen-year-old at a procession in Ephesus. Both waste away as they try to resist their mutual passion, and the oracle at Claros obscurely enjoins a solution interpreted as marriage but predicts dreadful overseas adventures before the couple can enjoy a better fortune. Xenophon launches his pair on their travels, but they are caught, predictably, by pirates, and on the estate in Phoenicia of the pirate king Apsyrtus their beauty invites approaches to each which result in their separation. Thereafter Xenophon attempts to handle each star's fortunes alternately. Anthia's fidelity survives a marriage to a noble goatherd (his name Lampon might suggest knowledge of Longus' Lampis), a wedding to the magistrate Perilaus (eleventh-hour false death by potion which occasions a Charitonian theft of the revived heroine from her tomb), and many threats to her chastity culminating in enlistment in a brothel in Tarentum. Habrocomes' perils are chiefly to his life, and he is saved by the miraculous intervention of the Nile when he prays to Helios, as does Anthia to Isis. The pair's tribulations are recurrently linked by the person of the robber Hippothous (an aristocrat turned desperado through disaster in love); a device more ingenious than successful, for the author must ship three, not two, on separate but parallel courses from Cilicia to Egypt, thence to Italy and Rhodes for final reunion. This sometimes overtaxes his techniques of motivation; and when Hippothous captures Anthia for the second time (necessarily, to prevent her disappearance to India in the train of the tourist monarch Psammis) we are told blandly that neither recognized the other (4.3.6). The original text may have been more convincing, but in many details (e.g. Anthia shut in a ditch with two fierce dogs 4.6.3f.) the reader must have doubted if Xenophon's world were his own.

Yet realism of a sort is one of the author's objectives. His circumstantial detail about places and distances in Anatolia and his concern to give mainly realistic names to a high proportion of his characters are witnesses to that. It will not have disturbed the cultivated reader that most of these names were commoner in Athens and mainland Greece than in the Anatolian and Near-Eastern setting of the novel. This classicism is but one indication among many that the author's intentions, at least, were literary. The role of divinities is also a mark of pretensions both literary, in the line of descent from Homer and Herodotus, and realistic: prayers to gods and miraculous responses were part of the life of second-century Greeks. It is for such reasons, and not because Xenophon is himself the prophet of a religious message whether open or cryptic, that his gods are so prominent in the narrative.

It would be unjust to neglect some grounds for commendation. His prolonged separation of the lovers and the involvement of Hippothous entail more complexity than Chariton or Achilles undertake, and it pays dividends in the denouement. Tension mounts as the three converge but fail to unite in Egypt, then Sicily and Magna Graecia: from the moment Hippothous recognizes Anthia in the slave-market at Tarentum (5.9.5) the reader's excitement is constantly fuelled until the climactic scene in Rhodes when Habrocomes is told that Anthia is found and runs like a maniac through the streets (5.13.2). Hippothous himself is a far more interesting creation than Chariton's Polycharmus and Achilles' Cleinias or Menelaus: to fashion the hero's trusty companion out of a robber whose capture of the heroine is twice vital to the plot shows ingenuity, and the mixture of good and bad in his character some awareness of the danger of polarizing heroes and villains. Although no papyri have been identified the need for an epitome and its survival to the Byzantine period are testimony enough that the work found readers.

Iamblichus' *Babyloniaca* is known chiefly from Photius' epitome. A few manuscript fragments show that in details of handling and style he had fewer pretensions than Achilles, and elements of the plot put him closest to Chariton. The beautiful couple Sinonis and Rhodanes, already wed, flee the lust of the Babylonian monarch Garmus in a series of melodramatic incidents. They are separated by the jealousy of Sinonis when Rhodanes rewards a helpful country lass with a kiss, and only reunited when Garmus sends Rhodanes at the head of his army against the Syrian monarch to whom Sinonis has allowed herself to be married out of pique. Rhodanes not only wins the war and Sinonis but even becomes king of Babylon. But if the jealousy, oriental setting and military denouement recall Chariton, the succession of false deaths (demanded by the frequency with which the pursuers are on the point of seizing the fugitives) and variety of digressive material on the ways of the Orient put the author nearer to Achilles and Heliodorus. The introductory frame (comparable to Antonius Diogenes) also serves to authenticate the narrator as an authority on the arcane lore of the East (cf. pp. 2, 32 Habrich).

The eight books of Achilles Tatius' *Leucippe and Clitophon* were probably written in the last quarter of the second century A.D. Clitophon, a rich young Tyrian, falls in love with his cousin Leucippe, evacuated to Phoenicia from war-threatened Byzantium. Surprised by her mother on the point of making love they elope only to be shipwrecked in Egypt and be captured by brigands. Clitophon escapes, witnesses an apparent sacrifice of his beloved and is about to kill himself when it is revealed (to him and to the reader) that she has survived by a conjuring trick. Although reunited with Clitophon she demurs at love-making, and the dangerous attentions of the general Charmides are only frustrated by her sudden and death-like collapse. When she is cured they visit Alexandria and Pharos: here Leucippe is kidnapped by pirates and the pursuing hero again thinks he sees her die. Returning to Egypt he is cajoled into marriage, but not bed, with widow Melite: they go to her native Ephesus where Leucippe turns out to be living, but as Melite's slave. The 'widow's' husband is also alive, and unsuccessfully pursues Leucippe while Clitophon finally, but once only, succumbs to Melite. A trial and ordeal establish Leucippe's virginity and the couple can at last return to a wedding in Byzantium.

Achilles' treatment is rarely direct and vigorous. The florid, Asianic style, intent on conceits and short sentences, combines with rich elaboration of plot and incident to produce a baroque *tour de force* which sometimes cloys. Structurally it falls into pairs of books each presenting a different stage of the lovers' fortunes[1] while progress is retarded by sub-plots, descriptions of the works of man or nature, and philosophic speeches and reflections. The first pair lingers over the growth of the couple's love. Only at 2.7 does Clitophon, feigning to have been stung on the lip, deceive the shy but not unresponsive Leucippe into their first kiss by asking her to use the cure she had earlier used on her maid:

> She came close to me and put her mouth close to mine, so as to work the charm, and murmured something while she touched the tip of my lips; and I gently kissed her, avoiding all the noise of an ordinary salute, until, in the successive opening and shutting of her lips as she murmured it, she converted the charm into a series of kisses...(tr. Gaselee)

Although by the end of this book they are embarked for Egypt Clitophon is not in bed with Leucippe but debating the merits of boys and women with friends old and new, Clinias and Menelaus. The second pair of books exploits separation and danger, and adumbrates in the general Charmides the rival motif that will dominate Books 5 and 6. Their location allows digressions on the geography and beasts of the Nile, evocative of Herodotus. Within Books 5 and 6 the couples Clitophon–Melite and Thersander–Leucippe are contrasted: Book 5 culminates in the former's union, 6 in Leucippe's impassioned assertion of her virginity. The implausibility of this claim prepares the way for the trial of Clitophon and ordeal of Leucippe that are expanded to fill most of Books 7 and 8.

Within this framework sub-plots act as pendants to the love of the smitten couple and extend the range of erotic incident. The topic of *eros* is likewise pursued in many speeches and reflections exploring its psychology, physiology and analogues in nature. Although suffused with ill-concealed rhetoric these set in perspective the characters' actions and emotions: this cannot be said for the many digressions (e.g. on the discovery of purple 2.11.5, the phoenix 3.25, or the elephant 4.4) where relevance and propriety are often ignored.

There are several counts, however, on which Achilles shows advances on his predecessors. The setting is no longer historical. The contemporary world of

[1] Reardon (1971) 361.

the East Mediterranean reader is envisaged and evoked with a fair measure of consistency and realism. Only the Byzantines' Thracian war invites the reader to imagine a particular date, less probably historical[1] than invented. In 1.3 Clitophon takes over the narrative role from the first-person author to whom he tells his own story as they admire a painting at Sidon (and the *ego*-narrator is then forgotten, even at the end of Book 8). This stifles questions about the truth or morality of the tale, but carries with it the limitation that all events are seen from Clitophon's point of view – only his side of the story is continuously told. The same bias is evident in the analyses of passion and most glaringly in the acquiescence of both writer and Clitophon in the latter's seduction by Melite (a male orientation which should give pause to theories of a chiefly female readership).

The seduction of the hero is one of many reversals or over-exploitations of conventions which shows Achilles apparently playing with rather than by the rules of the game. One explanation is that he is concerned to make his characters more realistic than the distant and idealized figures of Chariton or Xenophon. But set alongside the excesses of rhetoric it has been seen as an argument that he must be parodying the genre with humorous intentions. Nevertheless, there is a fine line between wit and humour. Readers of some erudition (not all of whom need have been endowed with comparable taste or intelligence) might well have taken a pleasure in Achilles' deployment of conventions that savoured the art rather than scorned the artificiality. The audience's tastes are as enigmatic as its composition (see above, p. 688). But those who endured the rhetorical gymnastics of Aristides surely appreciated similar *techne* as displayed by Achilles, and his digressions would also entertain a generation ready to seek *paideia* in that genre of *varia historia* to which, according to the Suda, he also contributed.

Read he was, and perhaps at several levels. The names of Leucippe and Clitophon given to the parents of St Galaktion of Emesa, combined with the Suda tradition that Achilles became a bishop, show he left his mark below the upper crust of culture.[2] But it was upper-class readers such as Photius whose admiration for the sophistic style and manner of Achilles overrode disapproval of his licentious subject matter and guaranteed for him and for Heliodorus extensive readership and copying in the ninth and tenth centuries (*Bibliotheca*, *Cod.* 87).

Heliodorus' *Aethiopica* is organized in ten books, but in bulk it is more than twice the length of its nearest rival, *Leucippe and Clitophon*. The length results not from mere accumulation of incident, as in Iamblichus, but from a leisurely elaboration which is especially manifested in the construction of dramatic set-pieces. Time and trouble are applied to development of plot and delineation of character alike. The work is held by many to be the best of the extant novels.

[1] As argued by Altheim (1948) 121–4.   [2] Cf. Dörrie (1937).

Motivation is well handled, the principal characters nicely drawn, even if they may not achieve the realism of Achilles, and the sub-plots and digressions in which the sophistic author takes pleasure are carefully integrated in the story.

But it is in the story itself, and the manner in which Heliodorus unfolds its complexities, that his superiority most clearly lies. He begins with a dramatic scene of mystery and excitement: an Egyptian strand strewn with bodies. Only Theagenes and Charicleia are alive. Apprehended by robbers they follow a perilous course up-country, the heroine attracting the attentions of Thyamis, their leader. Their companion, Cnemon, has been separated from them so that he can meet the central character Calasiris and hear his story. An Egyptian priest, Calasiris had gone to Delphi and thence brought Charicleia from her adoptive father to return to her native Ethiopia, where she had been born the white daughter of black royalty and entrusted by a priest to a visiting Delphian, Charicles. Naturally the trip to Ethiopia includes Charicleia's innamorato, Theagenes, and their shipwreck is the prelude to the dramatic opening scene. Cnemon and Calasiris duly find Charicleia, and then, at Memphis, Theagenes: here Calasiris dies and Thyamis, who turns out to be his son, is installed as priest, while the lovers are captured by the Persian satrap's wife Arsace. Her lust for Theagenes precipitates their flight and eventually an Egyptian–Ethiopian war in which they are captured by the Ethiopians and taken to be human sacrifices at Meroe. There their virginity and Charicleia's identity are established in the course of the awesome ceremony that should result in their death; they are married and consecrated priest and priestess of the Sun.

Heliodorus' Odyssean plunge *in medias res* not only gives pace and tension to the story but allows the structure to be presented to the reader from different angles. At first the Delta journey seems a pointless movement south in the hands of a Thyamis whose hieratic origins are circumstantial frills no more meaningful than the aristocratic past of Xenophon's Hippothous. Calasiris' entrance (the stage metaphor is apt to the author's approach) gives an added dimension to the characters. Although Theagenes is leaving his country for a distant and exotic land, and gives a strong impression of linear progress to the story, Charicleia, we discover, has a destiny to fulfil, and her journey is the homeward and circular movement familiar from other novels. Ambiguity also pertains to the reasons for Calasiris' visit to Delphi: he alleges at different junctures a general motive of pilgrimage (2.26) and specific instructions from the Ethiopian queen (4.12f.). But Heliodorus' sleight of hand conceals the flaw (if it is such) and evokes admiration rather than suspicion for such Odyssean tales whose share of truth and falsehood is elusive.

The impression that the couple is in the hands of divinity, escorted from Apollo's Delphi to the idealized Ethiopia (where he is worshipped as Helios) by a series of priests of an ascending order of sanctity, is a mixed literary blessing. It gives added point to the lovers' chastity and the adventures which imperil it, and for a reader of the third or fourth century, with strong religious convictions and a proclivity to accept divine explanations of the world's ways, it will have charged the whole story with a deeper and more coherent significance than the more casual reference to gods or fortune in the earlier writers. But the perfection required from hero and heroine impedes realistic characterization, and the reader's conviction that they will survive their perils leaves little room for nerve-wracking suspense. Their union is threatened seriously on only two occasions – the opening episode of robbers and the passion of Arsace. When together they face death in Meroe we have little doubt that they will escape, and are best advised to admire Heliodorus' dramatic rendering of the occasion instead of nurturing pity or fear.

Many of these literary weaknesses are balanced by the religious intensity of the work, but we are not entitled to assume that this was the writer's chief concern. A religious stamp is indeed given by the role of Delphi, the priests and the traditionally pious Ethiopians, as well as the author's claim to be 'a Phoenician from Emesa, of the line of Helios, Theodosius' son Heliodorus'. But the personal link here established between the writer and Helios has also a literary purpose, as has Calasiris' flashback narrative. It is not for religious ends that Calasiris is brought on in the way he is, and the fact that so central a character is a priest tells us no more about Heliodorus' own commitment to religion than Philostratus' elaboration of the analogous ascetic Apollonius tells us about that sophist's Neopythagoreanism.

It might help to solve this problem of Heliodorus' priorities if his date were certain, for a location in the 220s or 230s would strengthen the case for linking him with the imperial house that sprang from Emesa and the religious propaganda that has been credited to it. To the present writer the preoccupations and presentation of Heliodorus seem too close to those of Achilles and Philostratus to make anything later than the 230s probable. A similarity between his siege of Syene and the historical siege of Nisibis in A.D. 351 has been alleged to prove a date later in the fourth century.[1] But the similarity is vulnerable to alternative explanations. A reader of Heliodorus should bear in mind that he *may* be dealing with a contemporary of Philostratus. Although in that age the currents of religious thought ran strongly, those of sophistic literature were equally powerful. It is as a product of the literary skills of the sophistic age operating in their most developed form upon the range of models open to writers of prose fiction that the *Aethiopica* is best seen.

The other candidate for primacy amongst extant novelists chose an utterly different approach. Instead of augmenting scale and complexity Longus in his

---

[1] For the arguments and their proponents cf. Reardon (1971) 334 n. 57; and for a refutation, Szepessy (1975).

Daphnis and Chloe presents a miniature romance, simple in its theme, construction and narration. The action does not range over half the Mediterranean but is confined to the east coast of Lesbos. The lovers meet no kings or queens but move in a world of shepherds and goatherds, a world to which they return even when they are discovered to be foundling children of city aristocrats. The narrative moves simply forward, professing to expound a painting seen by the writer in a grove of the nymphs in Lesbos, and focusing on the gradual growth of sexual awareness and experimentation in the naive couple until obstacles are overcome and they are united to live happily ever after.

Simplicity is not the only gain that is achieved by the choice of a pastoral theme. Longus can revel in pictorial descriptions (ecphraseis) of nature (indeed the whole work is a sort of ecphrasis) and use the progress of the seasons both as a framework and as a source of forward movement: spring (1.9f.), summer (1.23f.) and autumn (2.1f.) are at once a backcloth and a stimulus to the development of *eros* as Daphnis, carried by the advance of the seasons from fifteen to sixteen years, vies in naivety with a Chloe two years his junior. No journey is needed to create a story. But Longus makes it clear that his work is to be compared to the adventure-story genre. In addition to the natural agent of winter (3.3) conventional hazards are exploited to separate the couple. Tyrian (!) pirates carry off Daphnis, their ship is wrecked and he is saved by the pan-pipes of his potential rival Dorcon who is himself fatally beaten up (1.28f.). A war between Mytilene and Methymna occasions Chloe's kidnapping, wondrously terminated by Pan (2.20f.). Finally, when the older woman Lycaenion's lesson in the act of love (3.18) has supplemented that of old man Philetas in its theory (2.3f.) and ensured that Chloe's virginity will soon go the way of Daphnis', dangerous rivals are introduced to effect tension and impediment before the adolescents' recognition and marriage.

Concentration on a small and unified stage also gives Longus advantages over the other novelists. His descriptions of the rural scene at different points in the year build up a comprehensive picture in the reader's vision: we feel we are spectators of a pastoral world that is worked out and developed in all its vivid details, and only on reflection do we appreciate how selective these are, how they are sometimes less than plausible or consistent, and how many of them derive from the literary tradition of pastoral fiction, notably Theocritus, rather than from the real world they successfully suggest.

Pruning of *dramatis personae* is also an advantage: the minor figures can be picked out with small but effective touches of realism (e.g. the reluctance of the foster-parent to forego the economic gain of purloining the infant's upper-class tokens, 1.3.1). On the other hand Longus makes no great effort to develop the children's characters: they are types of artless rustic teenagers, and never become individuals. Longus examines *physis*, nature, not *ethos*, character. Indeed he sometimes carries his representation of natural artlessness too far. Chloe's uncomprehending soliloquy after seeing Daphnis bathing may strike us as implausible in a country lass: νῦν ἐγὼ νοσῶ μέν, τί δὲ ὁ νόσος ἀγνοῶ· ἀλγῶ, καὶ ἕλκος οὐκ ἔστι μοι· λυποῦμαι, καὶ οὐδὲν τῶν προβάτων ἀπόλωλέ μοι. κάομαι, καὶ ἐν σκιᾶι τοσαύτηι κάθημαι... 'Now I am sick, but of what sickness I know not; I feel pain, and I have no wound; I am distressed, and none of my flock is lost; I burn, and am resting in all this shade...' (1.14.1). Our credulity is even more severely tested when Daphnis and Chloe get as far as lying down together, as prescribed in Philetas' treatment for *eros*, but go no further εἰδότες δὲ τῶν ἐντεῦθεν οὐδέν... 'knowing nothing of what follows' (2.11.3). Yet this guileless innocence is required not only to spin out the action over Longus' four books but so that the gradual operation of *physis* can be celebrated.

For one clear objective of the writer is to hymn nature as a guide and god. It is from their goats and sheep that the foster-parents learn tenderness and pity for the foundlings (1.3.1 and 6.1), and from a dream sent by the Nymphs that they are to be consigned to Eros (1.7.1). Eros, like the Nymphs, is a manifestation of nature, as is made clear in the next stage of learning, Philetas' tale. It is indeed puzzling that nature and its rural servants are inadequate to instruct the young people in the culminating act of love, and that a city girl, Lycaenion, has to lend a hand: but even here Longus insists that *physis* is the chief agent: τὸ δὲ ἐντεῦθεν οὐδὲν περιειργάζετο ξένον· αὐτὴ γὰρ ἡ φύσις λοιπὸν ἐπαίδευσε τὸ πρακτέον 'But from then on she lavished no unfamiliar craft: for nature herself taught what was then to be done' (3.18.4).

One feature, be it noted, is very far from natural, and that is Longus' style. Eschewing subordination and long periods in favour of participial and paratactic constructions he favours simple sentences of two, three or sometimes four members, often carefully balanced in length and similar in rhythm, with an especial preference for *tricolon*, often *crescendo*. Within the limited compass and scale of the work the finite number of variants possible on these few patterns can be seen as binding the whole together: but even so they approach a mesmeric monotony, and they would not have sustained a longer story. Only one example can be given (see also above); Longus describes the spring which is to be the setting of awakening love:

ἦρος ἦν ἀρχὴ καὶ πάντα ἤκμαζεν ἄνθη, τὰ ἐν δρυμοῖς, τὰ ἐν λειμῶσι καὶ ὅσα ὄρεια· βόμβος ἦν ἤδη μελιττῶν, ἦχος ὀρνίθων μουσικῶν, σκιρτήματα ποιμνίων ἀρτιγεννήτων· ἄρνες ἐσκίρτων ἐν τοῖς ὄρεσιν, ἐβόμβουν ἐν τοῖς λειμῶσιν αἱ μέλιτται, τὰς λόχμας κατῆιδον ὄρνιθες· τοσαύτης δὴ πάντα κατεχούσης εὐωρίας οἱ' ἁπαλοὶ καὶ νεοὶ μιμηταὶ τῶν ἀκουομένων ἐγίνοντο καὶ βλεπομένων...

Spring was beginning, and all the flowers were in full bloom, in thickets, in meadows and those on the hills. By now there was the humming of bees, the calling of song birds, the gambols of the flocks' newborn young. Lambs gambolled in the hills, in the meadows the bees hummed, birds drowned the copses in song. Everything basked in these seasonable blessings, and Daphnis and Chloe, being young and tender, began to imitate what they heard and saw. (1.9.1–2)

Choice of words is also simple, poetry is drawn upon sparingly, and the range of vocabulary presents the reader with a mixture of current and classicizing usages such as he might expect in a writer of pretensions without pedantry.

The overall intent of the work must be judged in the light of this mannered simplicity as well as of the content. The preface makes a series of claims, balancing pleasure and instruction:

ἀνάθημα μὲν Ἔρωτι καὶ Νύμφαις καὶ Πανί, κτῆμα δὲ τερπνὸν πᾶσιν ἀνθρώποις, ὃ καὶ νοσοῦντα ἰάσεται, καὶ λυπούμενον παραμυθήσεται, τὸν ἐρασθέντα ἀναμνήσει, τὸν οὐκ ἐρασθέντα προπαιδεύσει.

A dedication to Eros and the Nymphs and Pan, and a pleasing possession for all men, which will heal the sick, comfort the distressed, will remind anyone who has loved and instruct anyone who has not. (pref. 3)

This is the traditional blend of objectives in Greek literature (even in the Thucydides here echoed) and it is no slight to Longus to credit him with primarily literary aims. There is indeed a stronger case for seeing religious statements here than in the other novels. The novel can be seen as allegory of love, initiating the reader in the gradual unfolding of its mystery and in the essential identity of Eros with the other divine forces of nature represented by the Nymphs, Pan, Dionysus and Demeter.[1] But we can accept the author's veneration for nature without interpreting Daphnis and Chloe's progress allegorically – it need only be a microcosmic example. He wished no doubt to express a certain sort of worship for natural forces, but that wish should probably be seen as the formal rather than the proximate cause of the work's creation. For that we should look to literary intentions, and compare *Daphnis and Chloe* with Dio's *Euboean*, Alciphron's and Aelian's rustic letters or Philostratus' *Heroic tale* rather than with Aristides' *Sacred discourses*.

7. THE FABLE

Greek popular culture, which must have underlain and fertilized the different literary genres, is on the whole inadequately represented in our texts. By their very nature such forms as folk song and folk tale were anonymous and orally transmitted, and only rarely thought worthy of preservation in written form. But the richness and sophistication of the literary tradition suggest that there was a vast penumbra of popular material from which authors could draw ideas

---

[1] Chalk (1960), endorsed by Reardon (1969) 300–2.

and stories, patterns of thought and rhetorical devices: it is hard to conceive of highly developed lyric like that of the Lesbian poets without a tradition of folk song behind it, or of the mature polish of Homeric epic without a background of widespread and long-established habits of storytelling. Comedy, elegy and iambus, and the mime as we know them in their literary forms must all have had very close links with the world of popular entertainment. It must always have been possible and natural for jokes, comic ideas, song and dance to find their way from the more or less improvised entertainment of the streets or the drinking party into self-conscious and ambitious literary genres. But it would no doubt be wrong to think in terms of a 'pure' folk culture which gave birth to a sophisticated literature and then was superseded and swept aside. A more convincing model would be one of continuing exchange between the higher and lower levels, though in some cases a literary genre might grow so influential as to stifle any independent popular activity.

There is one major exception to the general rule that Greek popular culture tends to be neglected in the written record. We have a great deal of evidence, much of it admittedly from late antiquity, for popular wisdom. Traditional sayings, whether proverbs or fables, were widely used and extremely influential in literature of all kinds. They did not in themselves originally constitute a literary genre, but served as powerful devices of rhetoric to add persuasiveness, dignity or interest to the contexts they embellished. Proverbs and (more important) reflective sayings (*gnomai*) cast in the memorable style of proverbs are to be found everywhere in Greek literature. They can be used quite casually and lightheartedly, but it is interesting that they carry no intrinsically 'low' or 'primitive' associations: indeed they are often used by tragedians to express the most profound insights into human experience.[1] Essentially the gnomic saying functions as a validating device, establishing links with an immemorial past and appealing to what society has 'always' said and believed as a criterion of truth and morality.

The fable (*ainos, mythos, logos*), itself a species of proverb, has had a particularly curious history. Like the *gnome* it is an ancient form, but the many surviving fables in our manuscripts appear in versions that are almost entirely the product of late antiquity. Being normally rather longer and more circumstantial than the simple proverb, the fable offered more scope as a potential literary form in its own right, and best of all it could be used as a very versatile educational tool, which is what guaranteed its eventual survival through the Middle Ages.

The rhetorician Theon accurately defined the fable as a 'fictitious story metaphorically representing the truth' (λόγος ψευδὴς εἰκονίζων ἀλήθειαν, *Progymnasmata* 3), the 'truth' in question being a fact of life or human behaviour,

---

[1] A famous example is 'learning by suffering' (Aeschylus, *Agamemnon* 177; cf. 250–1 and the related idea that the doer must suffer, *Ag.* 1563–4; *Cho.* 313–14).

more often a piece of worldly wisdom than a 'moral' in the ethical sense. Sometimes the point seems in any case to have been less important than the intrinsic interest or entertainment value of the story, but it is worth noting that in our earliest examples the fable is normally addressed to a particular person and is used as a means of remarking on his behaviour.[1] By the fifth century B.C. the Greeks commonly associated the fable with a Thracian 'story-maker' (λογοποιός) called Aesop, who lived in Samos in the early sixth century, and as time went on he was credited with more and more stories of the same type. But there is no doubt that the fable was a much older phenomenon than Aesop; some of the Greek examples have very close parallels in Near Eastern texts,[2] and fables are actually used in extant Greek works composed long before his time: Hesiod uses the story of the hawk and the nightingale (*Works and days* 202-12; cf. Aes. 4 Perry) and Archilochus tells 'The fox and the eagle' (frs. 174–81 West; cf. Aes. 1 Perry) and 'The fox and the monkey' (frs. 185–7 West; cf. Aes. 81 Perry), while Semonides' poem on women (cf. above, pp. 154ff.) is inconceivable without a tradition of fable behind it.

The subject matter of the fables is quite varied: often the characters are animals endowed with human intelligence and speech, as they supposedly were in mythical times, but inanimate nature, the gods, and the daily life of human beings were also favourite subjects. So alongside the beast fables we find such titles as 'Fir tree and bramble', 'Butterfly and wasp', 'Boreas and Helios', 'Hermes and Earth', 'The seer', 'The farmer's unruly sons', 'The old woman and the doctor'. A typical sample is Aes. 7 (from the so-called Augustana recension of fables, which was made sometime in the first or second century A.D. and is our earliest surviving collection):[3]

The doctor cat and the birds

A cat, hearing that the birds in a certain coop were sick, disguised himself as a doctor and went to call on them, taking the appropriate medical instruments with him. He stood outside the coop and asked how they were. 'Very well', they replied, 'if you will go away.'

Just so among mankind the wicked don't fool the wise, even if they make a great pretence of virtue.

More often than not there is a marked element of wit in the way the story is formulated, and fables were clearly used for attacking opponents as well as for light entertainment, but as with the proverb, so with the fable: this seemingly homely device could be used by serious poets to illuminate themes of the deepest significance, as in *Agamemnon* (717–36) when the Chorus tell the story of the lion cub which grows up to make havoc in the household that reared it – a

---

[1] West (1978a) 204–5.   [2] Perry (1965) xi–xxxiv; West (1978a) 28–9.
[3] Text in Perry (1952) 321–411.

motif which relates in complex ways to the whole play and indeed to the whole of the *Oresteia*.[1]

Despite its great imaginative potential, the fable remained for many centuries essentially a rhetorical device to be used in some larger context. It was slow to develop into an autonomous genre, even though collections of fables began to be published: the first we know of was compiled by Demetrius of Phalerum in the fourth or early third century B.C., presumably to serve as a handbook, just as collections of proverbs and *gnomai* were compiled as an aid to aspiring speakers and writers. But in the imperial period the fable acquired new literary status when Babrius published his *Muthiamboi Aisopeioi*, a collection (which survives in two books) of mainly traditional fables turned into scazons, the type of iambic verse commonly used in lampoons and satire (cf. above, p. 159). Babrius is a mysterious figure: his date is uncertain (second or possibly first century A.D.), and very little is known about his life, but scholars have conjectured from internal evidence that he was a Hellenized Latin speaker who may have lived in Syria.[2] His *Prologue* makes a claim for the fable as literature which seems not to have been made before in Greek (though the Roman poet Phaedrus in the first century A.D. had 'polished Aesop's material' in Latin verse):

> It was a just race of men that came first, Branchus my boy, the one they call Golden; and after that, they say, the Silver race came next; and we are third in descent: the Iron generation. In the days of the Golden race all living creatures as well as men had the power of articulate speech and understood such words as we use among ourselves, and they held their assemblies in the midst of the woods. The pine tree could talk, too, and the leaves of the laurel, and the fish that swam in the sea chatted with the friendly sailor, and the sparrows talked to the farmer in words he could understand. Everything grew from the earth without the earth's making any demands on men, and mortals and gods were on good terms. You can learn that all this was so from wise old Aesop, who has told us tales in the free form of prose. And now I shall embellish each of them with my poetic skill and offer you a honeycomb dripping with sweetness, softening the harshness of bitter iambics.

There is a certain elegance and epigrammatic simplicity about many of Babrius' poems, though they do not have the brilliance of a Lafontaine. His work was greatly admired and imitated, but the fable's survival was not dependent on his or any other author's strictly literary success: it seems to have found a secure place in the Hellenistic system of education, which set the pattern for the whole of later antiquity and the Byzantine Middle Ages. Fables were obviously appropriate reading for children at an early stage in their schooling, and we know from the rhetoricians' handbooks that the composition of a fable was one of the exercises for older students when they reached the stage of the *pro-*

---

[1] Knox (1952).   [2] Perry (1965) xlvii–lxxiii.

gymnasmata (cf. above, pp. 27f.). It is this widespread use in teaching that accounts for the proliferation of late fable collections; and the habit of treating 'Aesop' as a school text continued in western Europe during the Renaissance and after. But as stricter canons of what was 'classical' came to be accepted by scholars and teachers the texts fell out of favour. Now they are being freshly explored for what they can reveal of popular traditions, and although the sources are mainly so late they must surely include much that goes back to the earliest period of Greek literature.

8. HISTORICAL WRITING OF THE HIGH EMPIRE

Arrian

L. Flavius Arrianus is one of many Greeks who played an important part in the Roman administration as well as achieving distinction as a writer. Lucian, rarely generous with praise, calls him 'a Roman of the first rank with a life-long attachment to learning' (παιδεία).[1] He also identifies him for his readers as 'the pupil of Epictetus', and inscriptions now show that the man we think of primarily as the historian of Alexander was labelled by his contemporaries not historian but philosopher. Arrian himself claims enthusiasm from an early age for hunting, generalship and knowledge (σοφία). The work in which this remark appears, *On hunting* (1.4), corroborates the first of these, and his career and writings confirm the other two. But σοφία suggests philosophy rather than historiography, and it is unclear when he began to see himself as a historian. His claim to be a famous figure in the opening of the *Journey up-country* ('Ανάβασις) suggests maturity if not age, but when (*Anab.* 1.12.5) he boasts of his primacy in letters (λόγοι) as his ground for writing about the greatest Greek general, he does not make it clear whether that literary reputation was based on an *oeuvre* that included historiography. Most scholars, following Schwartz, have dated the *Journey up-country* and other historical works to the period after Arrian's Roman career when he is known to have been resident in Athens. This schema is precarious, as has recently been demonstrated,[2] but arguments for putting the *Journey up-country* early, before his consulship, are not conclusive. In the following sketch the traditional view is retained, but its vulnerability must be kept in mind.

Arrian's home was the Bithynian city of Nicomedia (now Ismit, in western Asiatic Turkey), his family clearly one of wealth and distinction. Education predictably took him abroad and about A.D. 108, presumably aged around twenty, he attended Epictetus' lectures at Nicopolis in north-west Greece. His enthusiastic note-taking supplied material for what may well be his earliest work, the *Discourses* (Διατριβαί) *of Epictetus*. He claims that these are a plain

---

[1] Lucian, *Alexander* 2.   [2] Bosworth (1972).

record, not literary elaboration, and that they are only being published because his notes had somehow slipped into circulation.[1] This should perhaps be discounted as a *topos* of informal philosophical writing, and if so Arrian deserves some credit for the vigour and incisiveness with which Epictetus' staccato argumentation is reported. A firm date is unattainable, but a reference to Euphrates (who died in 118 or 119) in the past tense,[2] and the recent discovery that the dedicatee, L. Gellius Menander, honoured Arrian precisely as a philosopher during the period of his Cappadocian command (131–7), can be used to put the *Discourses* in the 120s.

Arrian also wrote a handbook ('Εγχειρίδιον) to Epictetus' teaching, and the four books of *Discourses* to survive come from an original total of twelve. There may have been several philosophical works among the many now lost. Two which survive in fragments, *On the heavens* (Περὶ μετεώρων) and *On comets* (Περὶ κομητῶν) are a useful indication that Arrian tackled problems of natural as well as moral philosophy.

The publication of the *Discourses*, if it belongs to the 120s, took place when Arrian was almost certainly embarked on his senatorial career. He had already had a foretaste of administration on the advisory committee of C. Avidius Nigrinus in Greece about 110 (no doubt his philosophical interests commended him to a man whose family already had friends like Plutarch). He may have been launched on the senatorial *cursus* by Hadrian, for whom he shows both admiration and affection. But we cannot tell if he was excused junior posts, or at what age he attained the senior offices attested. These are now known to include the proconsulate of Baetica, during which Arrian had inscribed a four-line elegiac poem of dedication to Artemis. It should be shortly before his suffect consulate in A.D. 129 or 130.

The next post, as legate of Cappadocia from 131 to 137, was his most important, and it allowed him to test his military skills in successful confrontation with marauding Alans. Three minor works belong to this period. The earliest is the *Circumnavigation of the Black Sea*. It combines a report to Hadrian of a personal tour of inspection with rewriting of an earlier periegesis. In attempting to transform a Latin report (which was also sent!) into an elegant Greek epistle, Arrian alludes and refers several times to Xenophon. The *Circumnavigation* itself illustrates the fusion of practical and literary skills, as well as Anatolian interests, which was Arrian's justification for seeing himself as the new Xenophon. In the *Order of battle against the Alans*, his plan of campaign for the defensive operation of (?) 135, Arrian actually calls himself Xenophon. But although this literary nickname is implied by his references in the *Circumnavigation* to 'the older Xenophon' (12.5; 25.1), it is significant that in the prescript he simply calls himself Arrianus. This, or Flavius Arrianus, is the

---

[1] *Epist. ad Gellium* 4–5.   [2] 4.8.17.

form of his name given by inscriptions, and it is unlikely that Xenophon was ever formally a *cognomen*.

In the third surviving work from the legateship, *On tactics* (dated to 136–7) Arrian supplements a derivative account of Greek and Macedonian tactics (1–32) with his own description of Roman cavalry manoeuvres. He is impressed by Rome's readiness to adopt other nations' techniques, and commends Hadrian particularly for innovations borrowed from Armenia and Parthia and for his encouragement of native traditions within the Roman army. Appropriately he concludes with fulsome praise of Hadrian's reign (44).

We know of no post after Cappadocia. Arrian seems to have spent his fifties and later years in Athens, native city of Xenophon and in many eyes capital of Greek culture. Arrian had been given Athenian citizenship (he treats Athens as his city in the work *On hunting*, perhaps of the early 140s) and he was elected to the archonship of 145/6. It is here that Arrian is generally believed to have turned to the writing of history.

The first two historical works (as documented in the *Bithynian history*)[1] were *Lives* of Timoleon and Dion (of Syracuse), now lost. Their model may have been Xenophon's *Agesilaus*. The most important in posterity's estimation was the third, the *Journey up-country of Alexander*, in title and format recalling Xenophon's seven-book *Anabasis*. Arrian gives as his reasons for choosing this hackneyed theme both his own distinction in letters (λόγοι) – which more than his public career fit him to be Alexander's prose Homer – and Alexander's unique and inspiring deeds, ἔργα, which have not been adequately commemorated (*Anab.* 1.12.4–5). He often shows enthusiasm for his hero, but the Xenophontic restraint of the narrative is not merely stylistic. In his choice of authorities he regards as reliable (Ptolemy and Aristobulus), and in his attempt to extract corroborative material from other traditions, Arrian deserves more credit than he gets from scholars with Thucydidean standards of accuracy and modern facilities for research. His task was of course very different from that of Xenophon or Thucydides. He was almost entirely dependent on written sources. Sometimes he will confirm a point by autopsy (e.g. the statues of the tyrannicides restored by Alexander from Persepolis to Athens, *Anab.* 3.16.8). But so reliant has he become on others' accounts that he neglects opportunities for personal observation, and at one point makes a mistake that any of his Roman friends might have corrected: Lysippus' group of the horsemen killed at the Granicus, he says, stood at Dium (*Anab.* 1.16.4) – but in fact they had been moved to Rome in 148 B.C. by Metellus Macedonicus.

Mistakes of this sort, and omissions or deficiencies on other topics, limit the value of the *Journey up-country* as history. Nevertheless it has remained a standard work since Appian turned to it in the 150s, and this is due not simply

---

[1] Photius, *Bibl.*, Cod. 93, 73b3f.

to its survival. Its clarity, conciseness and readability confirm Arrian's mastery of λόγοι, and do much to compensate for his mediocrity as an investigator.

Although Arrian represented the work on Alexander as a task which fired his enthusiasm, in the *Bithynian history* – of which only fragments and a brief notice by Photius survive – he claimed that *it* had engaged his energies from the start of his literary career.[1] This does not mean that the *Journey up-country* was a merely preparatory exercise. Arrian was no doubt the sort of person who felt great commitment to the job in hand, and work on Alexander could have totally absorbed him for some period of his extended researches on Bithynia (such as an eight-book work in the Herodotean tradition would require). As it is, Arrian blamed his inadequate application to these preliminaries for the work's delay, and when it did appear he dedicated it to the native land which was no longer his residence, τῆι πατρίδι δῶρον ἀναφέρων τὰ πάτρια.[2] It is not untypical that a Greek in Roman service should continue to feel strongly about his homeland, even one who, like Arrian, had other outlets for his Hellenic enthusiasm in Athens and Alexander. It is also characteristic of the age that he devoted much of the work (whose terminus was 75 B.C.) to the remote and mythical past.

Historical works not mentioned in the *Bithynian history* are probably later. But this is hardly true of the *Indian history*, a virtuoso piece in Ionic dialect marrying some Indian ethnography with the return voyage of Nearchus. It is virtually an appendix to the *Journey up-country*, where it is twice advertised. The *Alan history* (whence the *Order of battle* possibly came) may also have been slight enough to be passed over in the preface of the *Bithynian history* (as it has by almost all our testimony) and so be earlier.

But both the *After Alexander* and the *Parthian history* (known only from fragments and from Photius' epitomes) should be late. The former is a sequel to the *Journey up-country*, but its detailed account in ten books of the tangled events of 323–2 B.C. (down to the return of Antipater to Macedon) must have been a harder theme to control, even with Hieronymus of Cardia to follow. The *Parthian history* seems to have given an equally detailed narrative of Trajan's wars, to which the last ten of the seventeen books were allocated. Arrian will have been able to draw on his experience of the Roman army at war and of the Eastern frontier, but it is not clear whether written sources or personal investigation furnished the bulk of the material.

The historical works have been taken to be late, but the view that they belong to the 120s should not be forgotten. Were it correct, there would be some truth in the tradition in Themistius and Photius that Arrian was promoted because of his learning.[3] But works and career alike demonstrate that he was no ivory-

---

[1] Photius, *Bibl.*, *Cod.* 93, 73b13f.   [2] Photius, *Bibl.*, *Cod.* 93, 73a35.
[3] Themistius, *Or.* 34.8; Photius, *Bibl.*, *Cod.* 58, 17b15f.

tower thinker. He was a man with interests in the practical and the theoretical, in both the Greek and the Roman worlds. Moreover his own life shows how Greek traditions could be given a valuable and creative role for the Graeco-Roman upper classes.

Appian

Appian of Alexandria claims that his *Roman history* treats a subject attempted by many writers, Greek as well as Roman.[1] After the Augustan writers of world histories, however – Diodorus, Nicolaus, Strabo – we know of no extended treatment of the rise of Rome in Greek apart from the lost *Greek and Italian history* of Charax of Pergamum, consul in A.D. 147.[2] Part of the story had been used in biographies (as by Plutarch) and the outlines covered in chronographic works such as that of Phlegon of Tralles.[3] But neither of these genres posed the problems which Appian saw in previous treatments of the theme and which his own approach did much to solve.

Appian complains that the annalistic framework disrupts narrative of Rome's dealings with each of the peoples she subjected and thereby impedes assessment of the weakness or endurance of the peoples and the virtue or good fortune of Rome. Accordingly he describes the rise of Rome people by people, in the order in which they fell under Roman domination. The schema cannot always be observed. The regal period has a book to itself of which only excerpts survive, as do Rome's two great foes, Hannibal and Mithridates. The civil wars are given five books, which offer our only surviving continuous narrative from the Gracchi to Actium and are chiefly responsible for modern interest in Appian. This has consequently been dominated by studies of Appian's reliability and sources to the neglect of his own interests and intentions. It is clear, however, that a major factor in his decision to offer a continuous history of the civil wars was their effect on the provinces and particularly their precipitation of Egypt's annexation after Actium. It is this rather than the drift to monarchy which caught Appian's eye, and in synchronizing the end of that process with Egypt's annexation he sees the latter as a decisive factor in establishing Augustus as *princeps*.[4] His interest in his own native land also appears in his allocation of four books whose survival would have been invaluable to the history of its dealings with Rome, his reference to the Ptolemies as 'my kings', and the misleading implication that in 31 B.C. their kingdom was the only great constituent of the empire in his own day that had not yet been absorbed.[5] The hundred years after Actium were presumably narrated with special reference to further annexations, and two of these, Dacia and Arabia, received separate treatment in the last two books.

[1] Pref. 45. [2] Bowie (1974) 178. [3] Bowie (1974) 176.
[4] Pref. 60; *Bell. Civ.* 1.5.21 and 6.24. [5] Pref. 39; *Bell. Civ.* 1.5.

Appian claimed that his novel approach would make Rome's rise easier to understand and assess. Even from the surviving portions of the history it seems that the claim is justified. He is competent in his arrangement of material, and although he is entirely dependent on earlier writers he has sought out sources both on the provinces (notably Syria) and on the civil wars to which we do not have access elsewhere and which preserve data and interpretations of great importance for political history. In particular his account of the late Republic shows awareness of the interaction of economic, social and political forces. This may be the observation of his much-disputed source, but Appian deserves some credit for choosing that source rather than another; and his own interest in financial aspects of economic history (where first-hand knowledge of the empire may have been brought to bear) emerges from more than one passage.[1]

But intelligibility was not the only aim. Two other points are important. First, as a Greek from the provinces Appian gives the first extensive assessment of Rome from the provincial viewpoint. Although he is an admirer of Rome's might and virtue he often allows the reader, himself likely to be from the provinces, to see events from the point of view of the conquered (e.g. Antiochus or Mithridates). In particular, as a Greek, Appian often offers material which a Roman historian would not – Homer's evidence on Bithynia, Mithridates' interest in Greek culture,[2] and Greek equivalences or explanations for Roman institutions. Secondly, the organization of the history around provincial annexation recalls a classical model, Herodotus. It is typical of the Graeco-Roman culture of the eastern empire that an author of the fifth century B.C. should offer a pattern for understanding and expounding the history of Rome.

Herodotus' influence has also been noted in Appian's language and style, as has that of Thucydides and Xenophon. Despite his twenty-four books (perhaps a Homeric touch) Appian sees himself treading the path of classical historians. But his style neither imitates any individual (as Arrian imitates Xenophon) nor does it adopt an extreme Atticist position. Although he draws on the classics for phraseology, continues to use the dual and shows care in avoiding hiatus, there is much influence from the *koine*, especially in his use of participles and prepositions. Worse still, the influence of Latin has been seen in his syntax, in the meanings of certain words and in his formation of compounds. He is one of the few Greek writers of any pretensions to admit Latin terms in transliteration such as λίβερτος for freedman, ἰντέρρηγα for *interrex* and ἰγκουΐλῖνον for lodger.[3] But in each case there is a good reason for giving the Latin term (much more often Appian offers a Greek equivalent or a periphrasis) and the decision is characteristic of the hard-headed barrister who understood and respected the workings of the Roman system and had no sympathy for the Cynics who,

[1] Cf. pref. 61 and Kühne (1969).   [2] *Mithr.* 1 and 550.
[3] *Mithr.* 4; *Bell. Civ.* 1.98.457; ib. 2.2.8.

especially in Alexandria, attacked it.[1] The result may be stylistically undistinguished, but it is far from unreadable. Despite unevenness of treatment the historical enquirer will learn from the work what he needs to know, and the literary reader may admire (albeit with qualifications) the speeches which form almost a tenth of the whole, and often catch the excitement with which Appian can infuse his account of critical junctures.

Pausanias

The only ancient survey of Greece and its monuments that survives from antiquity in its entirety is the *Periegesis* of Pausanias. Although generally viewed as a peripheral production of the Antonine age, it has long excited scholarly interest. In the nineteenth century critics dissected Pausanias' ten books on the various regions of Greece in search of stylistic and formal antecedents. In the twentieth century with the immense gains of modern archaeology, Pausanias has finally emerged from the mire of source-criticism as an uncommonly reliable and independent authority on the topography, sculpture and buildings of his age. His work has once again become what it was at the start: an explanatory guide-book. As such it belongs to a recognizable genre of periegetic literature that evokes the names of Hellenistic authors like Heliodorus and Polemo (not to be confused with the later novelist and rhetorician). It is evident, both from comparison with the fragments of earlier writers and from the confirmations of archaeology, that Pausanias was not much indebted to his professional predecessors for the substance of his work. He wrote from personal observation, supplemented by wide reading. But the form – a guide-book with historical, religious and mythological digressions – had been well established before him.

Books of this kind naturally have literary roots in the various other genres that correspond to the digressions, so that one should not be surprised, for example, to find reminiscences of Herodotus and Thucydides in the many historical sections of Pausanias' *Periegesis*. There has been a recent tendency to emphasize the Herodotean character of Pausanias' writing and even to allege that the opening words of the guide-book are a programmatic echo of Herodotus 4.99.[2] But the beginning of Pausanias is banal, without introduction or apology: 'Cape Sunium, in the land of Attica, juts out from that part of the Greek mainland which faces the Cyclades and the Aegean Sea.' These words scarcely sound programmatic and are most unlikely to have recalled to anyone's mind Herodotus' comparison of the Tauric Chersonese with Cape Sunium or the opening words of 4.99, 'Thrace juts out into the sea from the land of Scythia'. There is

---

[1] *Mithr.* 110.
[2] Levi (1977) 179. The translations from Pausanias are by J. G. Frazer.

perhaps a Herodotean flavour in Pausanias' first words, but nothing more portentous. The latest study of his prose detects, throughout the *Periegesis*, more signs of Thucydides' influence than any other writer's.[1]

Pausanias was not a historian, mythologist or ethnographer; nor did he claim to be, although he moved comfortably in the domains of such writers. A periegete was an antiquarian with broad interests. It has often been pointed out, however, that Pausanias appeared to take little pleasure in landscapes. Yet that is perfectly understandable since the appreciation of landscapes had never been a part of the periegetic tradition, which properly left such things to the muse of poetry.

Pausanias was not only a conventional periegete but in other respects a typical man of his time. Like other Greeks of the second century, he looked back wistfully to the great days of classical Greece, but he had no illusions about the past or regrets about the present. In 4.35.3 he remarked, 'No people ever yet, so far as we know, throve under a democracy except the Athenians; and they certainly flourished under it'. But they flourished equally under Roman rule: though suffering at the hands of Sulla, whose harshness Pausanias thought most uncharacteristic of the Romans generally (1.20.4; 9.33.4), the Athenians 'flourished again in the reign of Hadrian' (1.20.4). Just like Dio Chrysostom, Plutarch and Aristides,[2] Pausanias found no inconsistency in praising the Roman administration while censuring the imperial cult as 'the hollow rhetoric which flattery addresses to power' (8.2.5).

The audience for which Pausanias wrote was almost certainly Greek rather than Roman, and a comment like the foregoing condemned a peculiarly Greek weakness, *Graeca adulatio*. Pausanias' outlook is so close to that of the other principal writers of his age (save Lucian) that it is not unreasonable to suppose that his work was explicitly designed to introduce the literate peoples of greater Hellas – Greece and Asia Minor – to their fatherland and its treasures. For reviving a fruitful but neglected genre and directing it to the enthusiasms of the second century Pausanias deserves an honoured place in the pantheon of Greek writers of the Roman Empire.

Cassius Dio and Herodian

Of the Greek historians of the third century A.D. only two are represented today by anything more than fragments. These are Cassius Dio and Herodian, whose histories overlap for the years A.D. 180–229, through which both of them lived. Although the two historians were markedly different in background and in historical method, they nevertheless shared as a common experience the turbulent period of two of Rome's most irresponsible emperors, Commodus and Elaga-

---

[1] Strid (1976).   [2] Bowersock (1973).

balus, and two of her most effective, Septimius Severus and Severus Alexander. It was an age of rapid transformation and upheaval, of nostalgia for the golden era of the Antonines and of reluctant accommodation to new pressures at home and on the frontiers. In many ways Cassius Dio embodied the old way of life, and Herodian the new.

Cassius Dio came from a distinguished Bithynian family already possessed of the Roman citizenship as well as good contacts with the Roman upper class. He entered the senate in the reign of Commodus. He won the esteem of Septimius Severus by the composition of a timely essay on the dreams and portents that adumbrated the accession of Severus. The emperor's cordial reception of this work caused Dio to dream that a spirit advised him to compose a history of the wars and civil strife from which Severus had emerged victorious. Once he had followed this advice, the welcome accorded the history of so brief a period moved him to undertake no less a subject than the whole history of Rome from the beginning, within which the work on Severus' wars would be incorporated. As Dio set about this gigantic project, he did not abandon his career as a senator. In 229, the date at which his history finally terminated, Dio held the consulate for the second time and after service in high positions in several provinces. It is obvious that Dio chose to bring his narrative down to the point of his own most important success, the second consulate. Dio was a characteristic product of the eastern aristocracy, a man of letters naturally and easily absorbed into the Roman government. In writing about the history of Rome, he was writing about traditions and government to which he belonged.

Herodian was altogether different. It is safe to assume from his own silence that this historian was a man of no eminence or wealth. He was a man who came to Rome and to her history as an outsider, even though it is impossible to say from where. Syria is a likely place, or perhaps eastern Anatolia. The lush, ornamented rhetoric of his narrative style is far removed from the controlled gravity of Cassius Dio. Herodian claims to have held imperial and senatorial posts; but whatever they were, they were manifestly not legateships and proconsulates. There is no reason to think that Herodian was even a Roman citizen before the universal grant by Caracalla in A.D. 212. Herodian's perspective could not be more unlike Dio's. His work, in its rich detail, its obsession with description, its concentrated emotion, is a pre-echo of Byzantium. If it was composed, as has been suggested, to celebrate the Secular Games of the emperor Philip the Arab in A.D. 248, on what was by one calculation the millennial anniversary of the founding of Rome, Philip, whose very presence on the imperial throne was something of a portent, would have delighted in Herodian's prose. The times were visibly changing.

As a researcher Dio was careful and thorough. There is no sign that Herodian was either. By his own account Dio spent ten years in assembling the material for his great history and another twelve in writing it (72.23.5). The twenty-two year period must have extended at least a little beyond A.D. 229, with which the narrative ends. Dio proceeded in annalistic fashion through the years of Republic and Empire, but he occasionally grouped cohesive material together under one year when it did not all belong there; and he was not averse to intruding references to his own day to make a comparison with practices of an earlier time. In the speeches, which Dio added to his history in conformity with the old tradition of classical historiography, he allowed himself considerable freedom in both substance and rhetoric. The most famous of the speeches in his history are those assigned to Agrippa and Maecenas at the opening of the Principate. The antilogy constitutes a debate on monarchy, with Agrippa against and Maecenas in favour. Apart from the historical implausibility of Agrippa's ever having taken such a position, the strikingly pro-senatorial character of Maecenas' concept of monarchy has long elicited comment; and it is hard not to believe that Dio is making some kind of allusion to his own day, presumably the reign of Severus Alexander.

Herodian, for all his carelessness, was deeply imbued with the traditions of Greek historical writing. The opening pages of his work contain clear verbal allusions to Thucydides. Although it is evident that Herodian's commitment to ἀκρίβεια (accuracy) was not so great as that of his admired predecessor, it is unwarranted to assume that he deliberately made up his history in the manner of a novel. He fully exploited the licence of rhetoric to adorn and to develop an incident, but he does not deserve to be called the author of an 'historical novel'. He states explicitly that he is recording events he had seen or heard about (εἶδόν τε καὶ ἤκουσα), and there is some evidence that shows him in possession of the truth, presumably from autopsy, when Dio and others lack it. For the most part, however, there is no denying that Herodian can be an unreliable guide. It appears that he made use of the recent work of his older contemporary, Cassius Dio. But where these two historians are concerned, students of source criticism have still to find a consensus.

The two historians can be observed and compared with particular profit by placing together their accounts of a disreputable incident in the amphitheatre during the final year of Commodus' reign. Both authors indicate that they were present. Dio writes:

> Here is another thing that he [Commodus] did to us senators which gave us every reason to look for our death. Having killed an ostrich and cut off its head, he came up to where we were sitting, holding the head in his left hand and in his right hand raising aloft his bloody sword; and though he spoke not a word, yet he wagged his head with a grin, indicating he would treat us in the same way. (73.21.1–2, tr. H. B. Foster)

Dio goes on to confess that he chewed laurel leaves to keep from laughing at this grotesque spectacle. Contrast Herodian:

> Wild beasts were brought from all over the world for him [Commodus] to kill, species which we had admired in pictures but saw for the first time on that occasion...All of them, if any were previously unknown, were now on show for the Romans to see as they were killed by Commodus. His marksmanship was generally agreed to be astonishing. For instance, on one occasion he used some arrows with crescent-shaped heads to shoot at Mauretanian ostriches, birds that can move tremendously quickly because of the speed at which they run and because of their folded back wings. Commodus decapitated the birds at the top of their necks with his arrows, so that they went on running around as though they had not been touched, even when their heads had been cut off by the sweep of the arrow. (1.15.4–5, tr. C. R. Whittaker)

Clearly Commodus' dire gesture of warning to the senators held no interest for Herodian. He failed to notice it. Yet his observation is circumstantial and exact. While referring to himself in the first person plural, he speaks of Romans in the third. He could not be more remote from the world of the Bithynian consul, who was once with him in that amphitheatre in A.D. 192.

21

EPILOGUE

With the possible exception of Heliodorus (see above, p. 696), the active careers of the writers discussed in this volume all came to a close before the end of the third century A.D. This does not mean, of course, that Greek literary production stopped; on the contrary, expert estimates of the word-count for extant Greek literature run at about 19,000,000 for the period up to A.D. 200 and 70,000,000 for the next four centuries. But little of what was written in Greek after the middle of the third century A.D. can be considered 'classical' in any sense of that elastic term, and most of it hardly qualifies as 'literature' at all.

The middle years of the third century were a critical period in which many must have doubted that Graeco-Roman civilization could long survive.

> Between A.D. 218 and 268 about fifty usurpers assumed the imperial title, either at the capital or in some other part of the empire; and of the twenty-seven 'regular' emperors of the third century (insofar as they can be distinguished from usurpers) seventeen were killed by their own people – all but one of them by the troops – and two of the others were forced to commit suicide.[1]

The administrative, military and financial chaos which resulted from this anarchy encouraged the inroads of the barbarian peoples who had long been threatening (and infiltrating) the Roman frontier: Sassanian Persia to the east overran Roman territory as far as Antioch (and in 260 captured the Emperor Valerian), while to the north and west Goths and Franks broke the barriers of the Danube and the Rhine, to bring devastation to the Balkans, Greece, Gaul and Spain. Though the last decades of the century saw a military recovery, economic disruption, spectacular inflation and ruinous taxation impoverished the urban middle-class which had been the audience for the classical literary genres and furthered the steady depopulation of the cities which with their theatres, stoas, gymnasia and libraries had preserved for so many centuries the external aspects if not the vigorous spirit of classical Greek culture.

At the same time as the old literary forms, their possibilities exhausted and their audiences gone, were losing their vitality, a new literature, polemical and energetic, was imposing its presence. By the second half of the second century

[1] Grant (1978) 363.

the Christian apologists had made significant advances in their attempt to prove the superiority of Christian doctrine not only to pagan mythology but also to Greek philosophy; they also clothed their presentation of the Christian message in a literary style most calculated to appeal to educated pagan Greeks. Clement of Alexandria and his successor Origenes were active propagandists and teachers of the Christian faith in the late second and early third century; the force and vitality of their writing is a sharp contrast to the tired artifice of style and the emptiness of content which are all too common in the work of their pagan contemporaries. They are the spokesmen of a new age, a new world of thought and feeling; from this time on, even though Byzantine writers will try, as late as the eleventh century, to imitate the style and language of the classical models they studied at school, Greek literature is concerned with issues that have no precedent in the classical models. The works of those writers who do go on exploiting pagan themes in classical genres are for the most part antiquarian artefacts, the last irregular heartbeats of a moribund culture. Quintus Smyrnaeus, for example, about whom we know nothing except that he came from Smyrna (12.309ff.) and (from internal evidence) that he probably wrote in the fourth century A.D., carried the story of Troy on from the death of Hector to the fall of the city in 14 books of hexameter verse as full of Homeric formulas and reminiscences as they are empty of inspiration – a leaden echo of the great voice of his original. Here for example is a characteristic passage (chosen at random); it describes an attack made by the Trojan ally Eurypylus:

> τοὺς δ' ὁπότ' Εὐρύπυλος λαοσσόος εἰσενόησε
> χαζομένους ἅμα πάντας ἀπὸ στυγεροῖο κυδοιμοῦ,
> αὐτίκα κάλλιπε λαόν, ὅσον κατὰ νῆας ἔλασσε,
> καί ῥα θοῶς οἴμησεν ἐπ' 'Ατρέος υἷε κραταιώ
> παῖδά τε καρτερόθυμον 'Οιλέος, ὃς περὶ μὲν θεῖν
> ἔσκε θοός, περὶ δ' αὖτε μάχηι ἔνι φέρτατος ἦεν.   (6.513–18)

And when Eurypylus the saviour of his people saw that they were all drawing back from the hateful noise of battle, he at once abandoned the people whom he was driving to the ships and quickly rushed against the two strong sons of Atreus and the stout hearted son of Oeleus, who was the swiftest runner and also the bravest in battle.

Every word in these lines can be found in the Homeric corpus. All but three of them occur, in fact, in exactly the same grammatical form and most of them stand in the same position in the line in both poets. Quintus' lines are thoroughly predictable; what we are faced with is a kind of Homeric cento on a vast scale. Just as mechanical (though mercifully much shorter) is the *Capture of Troy* by one Triphiodorus of Egypt, which seems to have been written in the late third or early fourth century.

But classical epic poetry was to have a late and strange flowering. In the fifth century Nonnus of Panopolis in Egypt produced an epic in 48 books (a deliberate affirmation of rivalry with Homer) called *Dionysiaca*. It is an extraordinary production, which presents at inordinate length the whole story of Dionysus, from his birth at Thebes (not forgetting everything that led up to it) to his reception on Olympus after his conquest of India; his conquests in the field of love are also described with an explicitness which is unusual in Greek epic.

In passages comparable with Homer and Quintus which describe combat (Gods and Giants, Dionysus and the Indians) Homeric language predominates (though there is a generous admixture of post-Homeric compound adjectives, whether invented by Nonnus or inherited from Alexandrian epic we do not always know). But in the long stretches of the poem where Nonnus treats un-Homeric themes – the amours of Dionysus for example – the writing is as un-Homeric in vocabulary as it is in its obsession with sensuous detail. Typical of his baroque scenarios is the description of Dionysus' rape of the sleeping nymph Aura.

> καί μιν ἰδὼν Ἰόβακχος ἐπ' ἀστρώτοιο χαμεύνης
> νυμφιδίου Ληθαῖον ἀμεργομένην πτερὸν Ὕπνου,
> ἄψοφος ἀκροτάτοισιν ἀσάμβαλος ἴχνεσιν ἕρπων
> κωφὸν ἀφωνήτοιο μετήιε δέμνιον Αὔρης·
> χειρὶ δὲ φειδομένηι γλαφυρὴν ἀπέθηκε φαρέτρην
> παρθενικῆς, καὶ τόξα κατέκρυφε κοιλάδι πέτρηι,
> μή μιν ὀιστεύσειε τιναξαμένη πτερὸν Ὕπνου·
> καὶ δεσμοῖς ἀλύτοισι πόδας σφηκώσατο κούρης,
> καὶ παλάμαις ἑλικηδὸν ἐπεσφρηγίσσατο σειρήν,
> μή μιν ἀλυσκάζειεν· ἐπιστορέσας δὲ κονίηι
> παρθενικὴν βαρύυπνον ἑτοιμοτάτην Ἀφροδίτηι
> Αὔρης ὑπναλέης γαμίην ἔκλεψεν ὀπώρην.   (48. 621–32)

And Iobacchos saw her lying on the ground, no bed spread, plucking the Lethean feathers of oblivion from Sleep, her marriage maker; soundless and sandalless he crept on tiptoe to the bed which heard nothing and Aura who spoke no word. With careful hand he put away the maid's elegant quiver and her bow in the hollow rock, so that she would not shake off winged sleep and shoot him. With fetters unlooseable he clamped the girl's feet together and round her hands wound a cord to seal them, so she would not escape him. Then he laid her down in the dust, heavy with sleep and ripe for Aphrodite, and as she slept, he stole Aura's bridal fruit.

Here un-Homeric formations abound. Most of them appear for the first time in our texts in early lyric poetry and fifth-century tragedy. And the metric of Nonnus' hexameter, like his vocabulary, is post-Homeric: he adopts the whole set of constraints Callimachus had imposed on the line (refinements of the rules governing word-end position, caesura, placing of monosyllables, etc.) and even adds some subtle exigencies of his own. And yet one feature of his metric reflects the radical changes which were transforming the spoken language, changes which in most other respects he serenely ignores. By the fourth century A.D. Greek speakers had long since abandoned the musical pitch characteristic of classical pronunciation. The written language still displayed those accents devised by Aristophanes of Byzantium to indicate pitch but the syllables marked with an acute or circumflex accent now received not a higher tone but a dynamic stress. Though Nonnus managed to produce, in his *Dionysiaca*, more than twenty thousand flawless lines of quantitative verse in spite of the fact that contemporary speech made no distinction between long vowels and short, he was influenced by the new dominance of stress: in the whole of his vast poem there is not a single line which ends in a word accented on the antepenultimate syllable, a limitation unknown to Callimachus and Homer.

The main narrative of the *Dionysiaca* (Books 13–40) deals with the expedition of Dionysus to India and his defeat of the Indian king Deriades. (This name appears on a papyrus fragment (fourth century A.D.) of an epic poem on the same subject, the *Bassarica* of Dionysius, evidently one of Nonnus' sources.) Books 1–7 contain some strange mythology – the intervention of Cadmus in the struggle between Zeus and Typhoeus, for example – and lead up, through the history of the line of Cadmus, to the birth of Dionysus; 40–48 describe various amours of Dionysus and also the fate of Pentheus. Though weighed down by much undigested mythological and astrological lore, and padded with unnecessarily long rhetorical speeches, the poem is a remarkable achievement. The terms in which it portrays Dionysiac frenzy are exaggerated, at times grotesque, but this is no mere academic recreation; its vigour seems to stem from some genuinely religious awe. It is all the more remarkable, then, that this same poet produced, in similarly baroque language and Homeric hexameter, a poem over 3,500 lines long which is a poetic paraphrase of the Fourth Gospel. Here, for example, is his version of a well known scene (John 18.18):

συμμιγέες δ' ἵσταντο διάκτοροι ἀρχιερῆος
θῆτες ὁμοῦ καὶ δμῶες· ἐθερμαίνοντο δὲ κύκλωι
ἀνθρακιὴν στορέσαντες. ὑπὸ σπινθῆρι δὲ λεπτῶι
πυρσὸν ἄκαπνον ἔχουσα μαραίνετο φειδομένη φλόξ.
νὺξ γὰρ ἔην σκοτίη, δυσπέμφελος· ἑσπέριοι δὲ
γαῖαν ἐπιψύχοντες ἀνερρίπιζον ἀῆται·
δμῶες ὅθεν θάλποντο φίλωι πυρί. καὶ μέσος αὐτῶν
ἄψοφος ἵστατο Πέτρος ἔχων ἄγνωστον ὀπωπήν.   (18.83–90)

Mixed in a crowd there stood the highpriest's household,
hired men and slaves together. They warmed themselves, forming a circle
round a coal fire they had laid. The sparks were tiny

as the niggard flame, on a smokeless fire, burned low.
For the night was pitch dark, stormy. But from the westward,
freezing the ground, gale winds began to fan the flames.
And so the servants warmed themselves with the welcome fire. And in their midst
stood Peter. He made no sound and no one recognized his face.

In spite of its grandiloquence (John's original has only twenty-four words in it) and its close adherence to Homeric vocabulary (all the underlined words are found in Homer) this is no mere rhetorical exercise; it betrays, like the rest of the poem, a real conviction. Whether it is the fruit of a late conversion or, as some have proposed, an early work, or whether, as must have been the case with so many in these centuries of transition, Nonnus managed to be half Christian and half pagan, we do not know. But nothing could be a clearer indication that his *Dionysiaca* is the point of no return, the final creation of that classical literary tradition which, beginning with Homer, had lasted for more than a thousand years.

APPENDICES

INDEX TO GENERAL BIBLIOGRAPHIES

Elegy and iambus, 728

Archaic choral lyric, 735–6

Monody, 740

Early Greek philosophy, 751–2

Tragedy, 758–9

Origins of tragedy, 759

Tragedy in performance, 759–61

Minor tragic poets, 772

Satyr plays, 772–3

Comedy, 773–5

Historical writing in the fourth century and in the Hellenistic period, 786

Sophists and physicians of the Greek enlightenment, 791

Oratory, 796

Aristotle and post-Aristotelian philosophy, 805–6

Hellenistic poetry, 810–11

The Stoa and Stoic writers, 844

The literature of the Empire, 856–7

The Greek critics, 858

The novel, 877–8

The fable, 886–7

APPENDIX OF
AUTHORS AND WORKS

HOMER

LIFE

Worked probably in latter half of 8th c. B.C., but nothing plausible known about his life or background. His date depends mainly on refs. in *Il.* and *Od.* to 8th-c. practices and artefacts (e.g. hoplite-style fighting, gorgon-head brooch, tripod-cauldrons), on the probable posteriority of Hesiod, the decline of oral composition by the time of Archilochus, the appearance of epic scenes on vases etc. after 680, and on ancient opinions (esp. Herodotus (2.53) and Hesychius, citing a probably classical source on date of Arctinus (Suda s.v.)). His region is indicated by predominantly Ionic dialect of the poems, by local east-Aegean detail and colour (e.g. *Il.* 2.144–6, 459–63, 13.12–14) and by the unanimous ancient tradition, which associated him primarily with Chios and Smyrna (so e.g. Pindar according to *Vit. Thom.* 2); other *Lives* (in OCT v; mostly of Graeco-Roman date and feebly fictitious) add Cumae and Colophon, agreeing that he died on Ios. See G. S. Kirk, *The songs of Homer* (Cambridge 1962) 271–87.

WORKS

(All in hexameters except *Margites*.) (1) *Iliad* and *Odyssey*. On division of each into twenty-four books see Kirk, *Songs* 305f.; on possibility of two monumental composers, above pp. 49–51. *Odyssey* was considered by 'Longinus' (*Subl.* 9–13) to be the product of H.'s old age, a not impossible explanation for the minor stylistic and lexical differences between the two poems (excluding those caused by different subjects). (2) Erroneously attributed to H. in antiquity were: thirty-three *Hymns* (see pp. 727f.), esp. *Hymn to Apollo* (Thuc. 3.104; see l.172); *Thebais*; other parts of the Epic Cycle (see pp. 726f.) – though Herodotus thought that *Cypria* was not his (2.116f.) – and probably also *Epigoni* (4.32); even *Margites*, a trivial work in iambics and hexameters (Arist. *Poet.* 4.1486b) and *Batrachomyomachia* (see p. 110). Many of these are several centuries later than H.; see e.g. on *Hymns* p. 111 and D. B. Monro, *Homer's Odyssey* (Oxford 1901) 340–84.

HOMER

TRANSMISSION

The *Iliad* and *Odyssey* come from close to the end of the oral heroic tradition. Essentially oral in technique, their debt to writing (alphabet becoming known in Greece by mid-8th c.), either through the listing of topics or through dictation, is disputed. In any case, transmission through 7th c. must have been partly or mainly oral, primarily through rhapsodes (reciters not singers) prone to subjective choice and virtuoso embellishment (see Plato's *Ion*); their activity at Sicyon in early 6th c. is attested by Herodotus (5.67.1). The establishment of rhapsodic competitions at the Athenian Panathenaic festival necessitated both a rule that H.'s work should be recited fully and consecutively, and also, presumably, an official text to act as control (rule attributed to Hipparchus towards end of 6th c. (Ps.-Plat. *Hipparch.* 228b), less plausibly to Solon (Diog. Laert. 1.57)). Written texts seem to have proliferated from then on, esp. in Athens, although learning by heart was still widely practised; hence quotations are still inaccurate in 4th c. Systematic librarianship and scholarship in Alexandria and Pergamum from 3rd c. onwards intensified efforts to establish an accurate and agreed text. Greatest of Homeric scholars was Aristarchus of Samothrace (*c.* 215–*c.* 145 B.C.), head of the Alexandrian library. Basing his judgements both on conjecture and on the evaluation of earlier texts, he extruded certain obvious doublets and additions due to rhapsodic or learned elaboration, cast doubt on many other verses and passages, as well as discussing difficulties of grammar and sense. His text became standard to the extent of causing the disappearance of 'wild' versions, known from papyrus fragments, with many additional and palpably non-Homeric verses. H.'s popularity in the Roman period and the multiplication of copies of his work ensured his survival through the early Middle Ages; with the revival of classical studies in the 9th c. A.D. much of the best Homeric criticism was collected, excerpted and written as scholia in luxurious minuscule codices; these editions formed the basis of the first printed texts and, eventually, of the modern vulgate. See Kirk, *Songs* 301–15.

BIBLIOGRAPHY

TEXTS AND COMMENTARIES: TEXTS: *Il.*: D. B. Monro, T. W. Allen, 3rd ed. (OCT, 1920). *Od.*: T. W. Allen, 2nd ed. (OCT, 1917). LIVES: T. W. Allen (OCT, 1912: with *Hymns*, Epic Cycle etc.). COMMENTARIES: *Il.*: W. Leaf, 2 vols. (London 1899–1901). Bks 1–4: G. S. Kirk (Cambridge 1985); Bk 24: C. W. Macleod (Cambridge 1982). See also M. M. Willcock, *A companion to the Iliad* (Chicago 1976: brief comm. on R. Lattimore's tr.). *Od.*: W. B. Stanford, 2 vols., 2nd ed. (London 1959). Bks 1–4: S. West, 5–8: J. B. Hainsworth, 9–12: A. Heubeck, 13–16: A. Hoekstra (Rome 1981–4: in Italian). *Scholia. Il.*: H. Erbse (Berlin 1969–83). *Od.*: W. Dindorf (Oxford 1855: repr. Amsterdam 1962).

TRANSLATIONS. *Il.*: A. Lang, W. Leaf, E. Myers, rev. ed. (London 1892); R. Lattimore (Chicago 1951); R. Fitzgerald (Oxford 1984). *Od.*: S. H. Butcher and A. Lang (London 1921); R. Lattimore (Chicago 1965); W. Shewring (Oxford 1980).

STUDIES. (1) SURVEYS: H.-J. Mette, 'Homer 1930–56', *Lustrum* 1 (1956) 7ff., cont. in vols. 2, 4, 5, 11, 15; A. Heubeck, *Gymnasium* 58 (1951) 362ff., cont. in vols. 62, 63, 66, 71; A. Lesky, *A.A.H.G.* 6 (1953) 129ff., cont. in vols. 8, 12, 13, 17, 18; F. M. Combellack, *C.W.* 49 (1955) 17ff., 29ff., 45ff.; E. R. Dodds, L. R. Palmer, D. H. F. Gray in *FYAT* ch. 1; J. B. Hainsworth, *G.&R.* New surveys in the classics III (1969); J. Holoka, *C.W.* 66 (1973) 257–93; A. Heubeck, *Die homerische Frage* (Darmstadt 1974); D. W. Packard and T. Meyers, *A bibliography of Homeric scholarship 1930–1970*, preliminary ed. (Malibu, Calif. 1974). (2) GENERAL: C. H. Whitman, *Homer and the heroic tradition* (Cambridge, Mass. 1958); W. Schadewaldt, *Von Homers Welt und Werk* (Stuttgart 1959); G. S. Kirk, *The songs of Homer* (Cambridge 1962), abbrev. as *Homer and the epic* (Cambridge 1964); Lesky ch. III; idem, 'Homeros', *RE* suppl. XI (1968) 687ff.; C. R. Beye, *The Iliad, the Odyssey and the epic tradition* (London 1968); (ed.) F. Codino, *La questione omerica* (Rome 1976); M. I. Finley, *The world of Odysseus*, 2nd ed. (London 1977); J. Griffin, *Homer on life and death* (Oxford 1980). (3) *Iliad*: W. Schadewaldt, *Iliasstudien*, 2nd ed. (Leipzig 1943: repr. Darmstadt 1966); (ed.) P. Mazon, *Introduction à l'Iliade* (Paris 1948); H. T. Wade-Gery, *The poet of the Iliad* (Cambridge 1952); D. L. Page, *History and the Homeric Iliad* (Berkeley 1959); K. Reinhardt, *Die Ilias und ihr Dichter* (Göttingen 1961); J. M. Redfield, *Nature and culture in the Iliad* (Chicago 1975); H. van Thiel, *Iliaden und Ilias* (Basel & Stuttgart 1982). (4) *Odyssey*: W. B. Stanford, *The Ulysses theme* (Oxford 1954); D. L. Page, *The Homeric Odyssey* (Oxford 1955); B. Fenik, *Studies in the Odyssey* (Wiesbaden 1974); N. Austin, *Archery at the dark of the moon* (Berkeley 1975); E. Delebecque, *Construction de l'Odyssée* (Paris 1980). (5) LANGUAGE, FORMULAS, ORAL TRADITION: W. Arendt, *Die typischen Szenen bei Homer* (Berlin 1933); M. Leumann, *Homerische Wörter* (Basel 1950); P. Chantraine, *Grammaire homérique*, 2 vols. (Paris 1953–8); A. B. Lord, *The singer of tales* (Cambridge, Mass. 1960); B. Fenik, *Typical battle scenes in the Iliad* (Wiesbaden 1968); J. B. Hainsworth, *The flexibility of the Homeric formula* (Oxford 1968); A. Hoekstra, *Homeric modifications of formulaic prototypes* (Amsterdam 1969); D. Lohmann, *Die Komposition der Reden in der Ilias* (Berlin 1970); (ed.) A. Parry, *The making of Homeric verse* (Oxford 1971: contains all writings of Milman Parry, with introductory survey by ed.); G. P. Shipp, *Studies in the language of Homer*, 2nd ed. (Cambridge 1972); M. N. Nagler, *Spontaneity and tradition; a study in the oral art of Homer* (Berkeley 1974); G. S. Kirk, *Homer and the oral tradition* (Cambridge 1976); C. Moulton, *Similes in the Homeric poems*, Hypomnemata XLIX (Göttingen 1977); (ed.) J. Latacz, *Homer: Tradition und Neuerung*, Wege der Forschung CDLXIII (Darmstadt 1979); G. C. Horrocks, *Space and time in Homer* (New York 1981). (6) ARCHAEOLOGY, HISTORY: H. L. Lorimer, *Homer and the monuments* (London 1950); A. J. B. Wace and F. H. Stubbings, *A companion to Homer* (London 1962); E. T. Vermeule, *Greece in the bronze age* (Chicago 1965); (edd.) F. Matz and H.-G. Buchholz, *Archeologica Homerica* (Göttingen 1967–: series of monographs); G. S. Kirk, 'The Homeric poems as history', *CAH* II 2 (1975) 820–50. (7) TRANSMISSION: G. M. Bolling, *The external evidence for interpolation in Homer* (Oxford

1925: repr. 1968); H. Erbse, *Beiträge zur Überlieferung der Iliasscholien* (Munich 1960); R. A. Pack, *Greek and Latin literary texts from Graeco-Roman Egypt*, 2nd ed. (Ann Arbor 1965); S. West, *The Ptolemaic papyri of Homer* (Cologne 1967); M. J. Apthorp, *The manuscript evidence for interpolation in Homer* (Heidelberg 1980).

LEXICA: H. Ebeling, 2 vols. (Leipzig 1880–5: repr. Hildesheim 1963); (*Il.*) G. L. Prendergast, (*Od.*) H. Dunbar, both rev. B. Marzullo (Hildesheim 1962).

HESIOD

LIFE

Son of a native of Cyme in Asia Minor who emigrated to Ascra in Boeotia (*W.D.* 633–40). In conflict with his brother Perses over patrimony (if what he claims in *W.D.*, esp. at 34–9, is to be trusted). Won poetry contest at funeral games of Amphidamas at Chalcis in Euboea (*W.D.* 651–9). Scholars in antiquity disagreed over the relative chronology of Homer and H. (evidence in the *Lives*: see below). H.'s date is still disputed: Amphidamas died in the Lelantine War (Plut. *Mor.* 153f), which many scholars date to late 8th c. (see J. N. Coldstream, *Geometric Greece* (London 1977) 200–1), but others to 7th (see R. C. M. Janko, *Homer, Hesiod and the Hymns* (Cambridge 1982) 94–8). For full discussion see M. L. West, *Hesiod, Theogony* (Oxford 1966) 40–8; G. P. Edwards, *The language of Hesiod in its traditional context* (Oxford 1971) 199–206. According to legendary tales current in antiquity H. was related to Homer, was father of Stesichorus, competed with Homer and defeated him in the poetry contest, and was ultimately murdered in Locris. Later his remains were transferred to Orchomenus, where a tomb was built for him in the agora (recorded by Pausanias, 9.38.3). For *Lives* and testimonia and for text of Περὶ Ὁμήρου καὶ Ἡσιόδου καὶ τοῦ γένους καὶ ἀγῶνος αὐτῶν (= *Certamen Homeri et Hesiodi*) see U. von Wilamowitz-Moellendorff, *Vitae Homeri et Hesiodi*, Kleine Texte CXXXVII (Bonn 1916). (Texts of *Lives* also in F. Solmsen's OCT of Hesiod (1970), text and tr. of *Certamen* in H. G. Evelyn-White, *Hesiod* (Loeb, 1914).) On the legends see R. Scodel, *G.R.B.S.* 21 (1980) 301–20; M. Lefkowitz, *The lives of the Greek poets* (London 1981) ch. I. On *Certamen*: M. L. West, *C.Q.* n.s.17 (1967) 433–50; N. J. Richardson, *C.Q.* n.s.31 (1981) 1–10.

WORKS

(1) EXTANT: *Theogony, Works and days, Shield* (*Scutum*, Ἀσπίς). Only *Theog.* and *W.D.* are regarded as genuine. On *Shield* see R. M. Cook, *C.Q.* 31 (1937) 204–14. (2) FRAGMENTARY: *Catalogue of women* or *Ehoiai* (a later continuation of *Theog.* in five books), *Great Ehoiai, Marriage of Ceyx, Melampodia, Descent of Pirithous, Idaean dactyls, Precepts of Chiron, Great works, Astronomy, Aegimius* (also ascribed to Cercops of Miletus), *Caminus* or Κεραμεῖς. *Ornithomanteia* and Ἐπικήδειον εἰς

HESIOD

Βάτραχον (a lover's lament to one Batrachus) appear to be completely lost. None of these works is thought to be genuine; for other dubious or spurious fragments see R. Merkelbach and M. L. West, *Fragmenta Hesiodea* (Oxford 1967) 171–90.

BIBLIOGRAPHY

TEXTS AND COMMENTARIES: TEXTS: (1) Complete corpus. A. Rzach, ed. maior (Leipzig 1902), ed. minor, 3rd ed. (BT, 1913); F. Solmsen (*Theog., W.D., Shield*), R. Merkelbach and M. L. West (*Fragmenta selecta*) (OCT, 1970). (2) *Theog., W.D., Shield.* P. Mazon (Budé, 1928). (3) *Theogony.* F. Jacoby (Berlin 1930). (4) *Works and days.* A. Colonna (Milan 1959). (5) Fragments. R. Merkelbach, *Die Hesiodfragmente auf Papyrus* (Leipzig 1957: with notes); R. Merkelbach and M. L. West, *Fragmenta Hesiodea* (Oxford 1967); (edd.) P. J. Parsons, P. J. Sijpesteijn and K. A. Worp, *Papyri, Greek and Egyptian, in honour of E. G. Turner* (London 1981) = *P. Leiden* inv. 502–9 (*Catalogue*). COMMENTARIES: (1) *Theogony.* W. Aly (Heidelberg 1913); M. L. West (Oxford 1966). (2) *Works and days.* P. Waltz (Brussels 1909: with tr.); P. Mazon (Paris 1914); U. von Wilamowitz-Moellendorff (Berlin 1928: repr. 1962: *Works* only); T. A. Sinclair (London 1932: repr. Hildesheim 1966); M. L. West (Oxford 1978). (3) *Shield.* C. F. Russo, 2nd ed. (Florence 1965: with tr.). (4) *Catalogue.* A. Traversa (Naples 1951). Scholia. *Theog.*: L. di Gregorio (Milan 1975). *W.D.*: A. Pertusi (Milan 1955). Byzantine scholia: T. Gaisford, *Poetae minores Graeci* (Oxford 1814, Leipzig 1823).

TRANSLATIONS: (1) PROSE: A. W. Mair (Oxford 1908); H. G. Evelyn-White (Loeb, 1914: rev. 1920, 1936); W. Marg (Zurich & Stuttgart 1970: with notes); D. Wender (Harmondsworth, 1973: *Theog.* and *W.D.*). (2) VERSE: R. Lattimore (Ann Arbor 1959).

STUDIES: (1) GENERAL: P. Waltz, *Hésiode et son poème morale* (Paris 1906); A. R. Burn, *The world of Hesiod* (London 1936); F. Solmsen, *Hesiod and Aeschylus*, Cornell Stud. in Class. Phil. XXX (Ithaca, N.Y. 1949); H. Diller, 'Die dichterische Form von Hesiods Erga', *Abh. Akad. Mainz* 1962, 2; H. Fränkel, *Early Greek poetry and philosophy* (New York & London 1975) = *Dichtung und Philosophie des frühen Griechentums*, 2nd ed. (Munich 1962) ch. III; *Entretiens VII: Hésiode et son influence* (Fondation Hardt, Geneva 1962); M. Detienne, *Crise agraire et attitude religieuse chez Hésiode*, Coll. Latomus LXVIII (Brussels 1963); W. Nicolai, *Hesiods Erga: Beobachtungen zum Aufbau* (Heidelberg 1964); E. Will, 'Hésiode: crise agraire? Ou recul de l'aristocratie?', *R.E.G.* 78 (1965) 542–56; P. Walcot, *Hesiod and the Near East* (Cardiff 1966); (ed.) E. Heitsch, *Hesiod*, Wege der Forschung XLIV (Darmstadt 1967); J. Blusch, *Formen und Inhalt von Hesiods individuellem Denken* (Bonn 1970); L. Bona Quaglia, *Gli Erga di Esiodo* (Turin 1973); J.-P. Vernant, 'The myth of Prometheus in Hesiod', in *Myth and society in ancient Greece*, tr. J. Lloyd (Brighton 1980) = *Mythe et société en Grèce ancienne* (Paris 1974); P. Pucci, *Hesiod and the language of poetry* (Baltimore 1977);

M. Griffith, 'Personality in Hesiod', *Classical Antiquity* 2 (1983) 37–65. On the Hesiodic fragments: J. Schwartz, *Pseudo-Hesiodeia: recherches sur la composition, la diffusion et la disparition anciennes d'oeuvres attribuées à Hésiode* (Leiden 1960); I. Löffler, *Die Melampodie* (Meisenheim am Glan 1963). (2) LANGUAGE AND STYLE: I. Sellschopp, *Stilistische Untersuchungen zu Hesiod* (Hamburg 1934: repr. Darmstadt 1967); H. Troxler, *Sprache und Wortschatz Hesiods* (Zurich 1964); G. P. Edwards, *The language of Hesiod in its traditional context*, Philol. Soc. Publ. XXII (Oxford 1971); B. Peabody, *The winged word* (Albany 1975), reviewed by J. B. Hainsworth, *C.R.* 28 (1978) 207–8; R. C. M. Janko, *Homer, Hesiod and the Hymns* (Cambridge 1982). (3) TEXT: N. A. Livadaras, Ἱστορία τῆς παραδόσεως τοῦ κειμένου τοῦ Ἡσιόδου (Athens 1963), reviewed by M. L. West, *Gnomon* 37 (1965) 650–5; M. L. West, 'The medieval and Renaissance manuscripts of Hesiod's *Theogony*', *C.Q.* n.s.14 (1964) 165–89; idem, 'The medieval manuscripts of the *Works and Days*', *C.Q.* n.s.24 (1974) 161–85.

LEXICA: J. Paulson, *Index Hesiodeus* (Lund 1890: repr. Hildesheim 1962); M. Hofinger, *Lexicon Hesiodeum cum indice inverso* (Leiden 1973–8); W. W. Minton, *Concordance to the Hesiodic corpus* (Leiden 1976); J. R. Tebben, *Hesiod-Konkordanz: a computer concordance to Hesiod* (Hildesheim 1977).

THE CYCLIC EPICS

Many epic poems were composed in the archaic period besides the *Iliad* and *Odyssey* and the Hesiodic corpus; at an unknown date a large number were grouped into a 'cycle' in the following order (with names of poets to whom they were attributed): (1) *Theogony*. (2) *Battle of the Titans*: Arctinus of Miletus or Eumelus of Corinth. (3) Theban epics. *Oedipodeia*: Cinaethon of Lacedaemon; *Thebais*: Homer; *Epigoni*: Homer ('Antimachus' in schol. on Ar. *Peace* 1270). (4) Trojan cycle. *Cypria* (11 bks): Homer, Stasinus of Cyprus or Hegesinus of Salamis (in Cyprus); *Iliad*; *Aethiopis* (5 bks): Arctinus; *Little Iliad* (4 bks): Lesches of Mytilene or Pyrrha, Thestorides of Phocaea, Cinaethon, Diodorus of Erythrae, Homer; *Iliou persis* (2 bks): Arctinus or Lesches; *Nostoi* (5 bks): Agias or Hegias of Trozen, Eumelus(?); *Odyssey*; *Telegonia* (2 bks): Eugammon of Cyrene. Very few fragments survive; the Trojan Cycle is better attested than the rest because summaries of its contents are preserved in the *Chrestomathia* of Proclus.

Other epics not included in the Cycle: (1) *Corinthiaca* (incl. Argonautic legends): Eumelus of Corinth, 8th c. (2) Heracles epics. *Capture of Oechalia*: Homer or Creophylus of Samos; *Heraclea*: Panyassis of Halicarnassus, 5 th c. Further discussion in Rzach under *Studies* below *ad init.* and Lesky 79–84.

Mock epic: only extant example of this genre is the pseudo-Homeric *Batrachomyomachia* (*Battle of frogs and mice*); for other titles see Suda s.v. Ὅμηρος 45, 103.

BIBLIOGRAPHY

TEXTS: *EGF*; T. W. Allen, *Homeri opera* V (OCT, 1912: rev. 1946); E. Bethe, *Homer, Dichtung und Saga* II (Leipzig 1922). Proclus only: A. Severyns, *Recherches sur la Chrestomathie de Proclus* IV (Liège 1963). *Batrachomyomachia*: H. Ahlborn (Berlin 1968: with tr.). Panyassis: V. J. Matthews, *Mnemosyne* suppl. XXXIII (1974: with comm.).

TRANSLATIONS: H. G. Evelyn-White (Loeb, 1914: rev. 1920, 1936: with Hesiod).

STUDIES: A. Rzach, *RE* VIII (1913) 2146–82 ('Homeridai') and XI (1922) 2347–435 ('Kyklos'); E. Bethe, *Homer, Dichtung und Saga* II–III (Leipzig 1922–7); W. Kullmann, *Die Quellen der Ilias*, *Hermes* Einzelschriften XIV (1960); A. Severyns, *Le cycle épique dans l'école d'Aristarque* (Paris & Liège 1928); idem, *Recherches sur la Chrestomathie de Proclos* IV (Liège 1963); G. L. Huxley, *Greek epic poetry* (London 1969); M. L. West, 'Greek poetry 2000–700 B.C.', *C.Q.* n.s.23 (1973) 179–92; J. Griffin, 'The Epic Cycle and the uniqueness of Homer', *J.H.S.* 97 (1977) 39–53; W. Burkert, 'Seven against Thebes: an oral tradition between Babylonian magic and Greek literature', in (edd.) C. Brillante, M. Cantilena, C. O. Pavese, *I poemi epici rapsodici non omerici e la tradizione orale* (Padua 1981) 29–51; R. C. M. Janko, *Homer, Hesiod and the Hymns* (Cambridge 1982). *Batrachomyomachia*: H. Wölke, *Untersuchungen zur Batrachomyomachia* (Meisenheim am Glan 1978).

LEXICON: B. Snell *et al.*, *Lexicon des frühgriechischen Epos* (Göttingen 1959–).

THE HOMERIC HYMNS

At some stage in antiquity all the hexameter hymns not associated with other famous hymnodists were gathered with those specifically (but wrongly) attributed to Homer to form the corpus of thirty-three 'Homeric Hymns'. The four longest (to Demeter, Apollo, Hermes and Aphrodite; from 293 to 580 verses) probably date from between 650 and 400 B.C.; the rest (from three to fifty-nine verses) are likely to be later. Earliest allusion is Thuc. 3.104, quoting *Hymn to Apollo* 145–50.

BIBLIOGRAPHY

(See Richardson under *Commentaries* below, 86–92, and Janko (1982) under *Studies* below, 280–96.)

TEXTS AND COMMENTARIES: TEXTS: T. W. Allen, *Homeri opera* V (OCT, 1912); J. Humbert (Budé, 1936). COMMENTARIES: A. Gemoll (Leipzig 1895); T. W.

ARCHILOCHUS

Allen, W. R. Halliday, E. E. Sikes (Oxford 1936: earlier ed. of Allen and Sikes (London & New York 1904) still valuable, esp. for *Hymn to Apollo*); F. Càssola (Milan 1975: with Italian tr.); A. N. Athanassakis (Baltimore 1976: with tr.). *Hymn to Aphrodite*: P. Smith, *Nursling of mortality. A study of the Homeric Hymn to Aphrodite* (Frankfurt, Berne & Cirencester 1981). *Hymn to Demeter*: N. J. Richardson (Oxford 1974). *Hymn to Hermes*: L. Radermacher. *S.A.W.W.* 213 (1931) 1–264; L. Kahn (Paris 1978: French tr. and comm., no text).

TRANSLATIONS: H. G. Evelyn-White (Loeb, 1914: rev. 1920, 1936: with Hesiod).

STUDIES: O. Zumbach, *Neuerungen in der Sprache der homerischen Hymnen* (Zurich 1955); E. Heitsch, *Aphroditehymnos, Aeneas und Homer: sprachliche Untersuchungen zum Homerproblem*, Hypomnemata xv (Göttingen 1965); A. Hoekstra, *The sub-epic stage of the formulaic tradition* (Amsterdam 1969); L. H. Lenz, *Der homerische Aphroditehymnus und die Aristie des Aineias in der Ilias* (Bonn 1975); K. Förstel, *Untersuchungen zum homerischen Apollonhymnos* (Bochum 1979); (edd.) C. Brillante, M. Cantilena, C. O. Pavese, *I poemi rapsodici non omerici e la tradizione orale* (Padua 1981); R. C. M. Janko, *Homer, Hesiod and the Hymns* (Cambridge 1982).

ELEGY AND IAMBUS

GENERAL WORKS

Bowra, C. M., *Early Greek elegists* (London 1938: repr. Cambridge 1960)
Burn, A. R., *The lyric age of Greece* (London 1960)
Campbell, D. A., *The golden lyre: the themes of the Greek lyric poets* (London 1983)
Degani, E., *Poeti greci giambici ed elegiaci* (Milan 1977)
Fatouros, G., *Index verborum zur frühgriechischen Lyrik* (Heidelberg 1966)
Fränkel, H., *Early Greek poetry and philosophy*, tr. M. Hadas and J. Willis (New York & London 1975)
West, M. L., *Studies in Greek elegy and iambus* (Berlin & New York 1974)

ARCHILOCHUS

LIFE

(Testimonia are numbered as in Tarditi under *Texts* below.) b. in Paros, son of Telesicles (T 2), who is generally thought to have led a Parian colony to Thasos (T 116, but see A. J. Graham (*B.S.A.* 73 (1978) 72–86) who argues that Telesicles may have done no more than report the oracle that gave directions for the foundation; the colonization could have been as late as *c.* 650). According to Critias (T 46) A.'s

728

mother was a slave woman, Enipo, but this has been doubted by many scholars. His grandfather(?) Tellis was probably associated with the taking of the cult of Demeter to Thasos (T 121). A.'s links with Thasos, frequently mentioned in his poetry, are borne out by T 1, a 7th-c. inscription commemorating his friend Glaucus son of Leptines (cf. e.g. frs. 96, 105, 131). He saw military action (whether as a mercenary soldier is not clear) and was killed in battle by a Naxian called Calondas (T 141). Most scholars place his date in the first half of the 7th c.: see F. Jacoby, *C.Q.* 35 (1941) 97–109. (Fr. 19 refers to Gyges, king of Lydia *c.* 687–652; in fr. 20 the 'troubles of the Magnesians' are usually associated with the destruction of Magnesia in the late 650s; the total eclipse of the sun mentioned in fr. 122 is most likely to be that of 648.) A. was famous in antiquity for his turbulent way of life and violent attacks on others. His most notorious quarrel was with Lycambes over his daughter Neobule (frs. 30–87, 172–81, 196A). A.'s poems allegedly drove Lycambes and his daughters to suicide (testimonia in *IEG* I 15 and 63f.). See M. L. West, *Studies in Greek elegy and iambus* (Berlin & New York 1974) 25–8 for a sceptical view of the whole story. A. achieved an outstanding posthumous reputation (testimonia in Tarditi 232–8, discussion in H. D. Rankin, *Archilochus of Paros* (Park Ridge, N.J. 1978) ch. I, M. Lefkowitz, *The lives of the Greek poets* (London 1981) 25–31) and was venerated as a hero on Paros; a shrine (the Archilocheion) was built in his honour by Mnesiepes in the 3rd c. B.C., with a long inscription recording legends about A. (T 4). In the 1st c. B.C. a further inscription was set up by Sosthenes giving details (based on the work of Demeas) of A.'s doings and writings (T 5).

WORKS

Short poems in a variety of metres: elegiacs, iambic trimeters, trochaic tetrameters, and 'epodes', strophic combinations of long and short lines, usually a hexameter or an iambic trimeter followed by shorter dactylic or iambic cola (see Metrical Appendix). The fragments have been augmented in recent years by papyrus finds, but must still represent a small proportion of A.'s total output.

BIBLIOGRAPHY

(See Treu under *Commentaries* below, 142–9; D. E. Gerber, *C.W.* 61 (1967/8) 274–8 and 70 (1976/7) 84–91.)

TEXTS AND COMMENTARIES: TEXTS: Diehl I 3, 3rd ed. (1952); G. Tarditi (Rome 1968: with tr.); *IEG* I 1–108. The Cologne fragment (*P.Col.* inv. 7511 = fr. 196A West): R. Merkelbach and M. L. West, *Z.P.E.* 14 (1974) 97–113; D. L. Page, *SLG* s478, with review by R. Führer, *G.G.A.* 229 (1977) 35–44. COMMENTARIES: T. Hudson-Williams, *Early Greek elegy* (Cardiff 1926); F. Lasserre, with tr. and notes by A. Bonnard (Budé, 1958); M. Treu (Munich 1959: with tr.). Select fragments: D. A. Campbell, *Greek lyric poetry* (London 1967: repr. Bristol 1982); D. E. Gerber, *Euterpe* (Amsterdam 1970).

TRANSLATIONS: (1) PROSE: J. M. Edmonds, *Elegy and iambus* II (Loeb, 1931). (2) VERSE: R. Lattimore, *Greek lyrics*, 2nd ed. (Chicago 1960); M. Ayrton (London 1977); G. Davenport, *Archilochos Sappho Alkman* (Berkeley & Los Angeles 1980). Iambics only: Z. Franyó, B. Snell, H. Maehler, *Frühgriechische Lyriker* II (Berlin 1972); fr. 196A: M. Robertson in H. Lloyd-Jones, *Females of the species* (London 1975) 101 (see pp. 125–6).

STUDIES: F. Lasserre, *Les épodes d'Archiloque* (Paris 1950); *Entretiens X: Archiloque* (Fondation Hardt, Geneva 1964); M. L. West, *Studies in Greek elegy and iambus* (Berlin & New York 1974); H. D. Rankin, *Archilochus of Paros* (Park Ridge, N.J. 1978) with review by M. L. West, *C.R.* n.s.29 (1979) 137; B. Seidensticker, 'Archilochus and Odysseus', *G.R.B.S.* 19 (1978) 5–22; A. P. Burnett, *Three archaic poets. Archilochus, Alcaeus, Sappho* (London 1983). On fr. 196A: R. Merkelbach, *Z.P.E.* 16 (1975) 220–2; M. L. West, *Z.P.E.* 16 (1975) 217–19 and 26 (1977) 44–8. Discussion in *Museum Criticum* 8/9 (1973/4) 1–106, ed. B. Marzullo; *Poetica* 6 (1974) 468–512 (H. Flashar, T. Gelzer, L. Koenen, K. Maurer, W. Theiler, M. L. West); *Arethusa* 9.2 (1976) (J. Van Sickle, D. A. Campbell, J. Henderson, M. R. Lefkowitz, G. Nagy, L. A. Rossi); *Rh.M.* 119 (1976) 97–126 (M. Treu), 242–66 (F. Stoessl), 289–310 (W. Rösler).

CALLINUS

LIFE

From Ephesus, active in mid-7th c. B.C.: according to Strabo (14.1.40, 13.4.8) he mentioned the war between Magnesia and Ephesus (fr. 3; Magnesia was destroyed in the late 650s) and the fall of Sardis in 652 (fr. 5).

WORKS

Of his elegies only one substantial fragment (fr. 1 = twenty-one verses) and a few scraps remain. For bibliography see pp. 731–2 under Mimnermus.

TYRTAEUS

LIFE

Son of Archembrotus, active at Sparta at the time of the second Messenian War (mid-7th c. B.C.). The Suda gives his *floruit* as 640–637. Probably Laconian despite the story first mentioned in Plato (*Laws* 1.629a) that he was of Athenian origin (testimonia in Gentili and Prato under *Texts* below, nos. 43–64). According to Strabo (8.4.10) T. described himself as leading the Spartans as a general (cf. Athen. 14.630f quoting Philochorus), but this may be based on a misinterpretation (see Schmid–Stählin I 1 358 n.2).

WORKS

According to the Suda he wrote 'a constitution [or 'on government'] for the Spartans, exhortations in elegiacs, and war songs, in five books'. The genuine surviving fragments are all in elegiacs: frs. 1–4 come from a poem entitled *Eunomia* 'Good order' on the Spartan constitution; the rest mainly deal with military virtue. There is no evidence that *PMG* 856 and 857 (popular songs on military subjects) were composed by T. For bibliography see below under Mimnermus.

MIMNERMUS

LIFE

From Colophon (Strabo 14.1.4); from Smyrna according to Pausanias (9.29.4), but this could be a mistaken inference from fr. 9.3–6. Active in latter half of 7th c. B.C. (the Suda gives 632–629 as his *floruit*). See M. L. West, *Studies in Greek elegy and iambus* (Berlin & New York 1974) 72–4. Testimonia in Gentili and Prato under *Texts* below.

WORKS

Wrote either two books (Porph. on Hor. *Epist.* 2.2.101) or 'many' (Suda): elegiac collections including a long poem called *Nanno* and a *Smyrneis* on the battle between Smyrna and the Lydians under Gyges. Testimonia on these poems in *IEG* II 81–2, Most of the surviving fragments are from quotations in later authors: M. was much admired in antiquity. Some fragments of iambics are dubiously attributed to him (frs. 24–6).

BIBLIOGRAPHY

(See D. E. Gerber, *C.W.* 61 (1967/8) 265–71 and 70 (1976/7) 72–8; Gentili and Prato under *Texts* below, xiv–xxxi.)

TEXTS AND COMMENTARIES: TEXTS: Diehl I 1, 3rd ed. (1949); *IEG* II 47–50, 81–90, 149–63; B. Gentili and C. Prato, *Poetarum elegiacorum testimonia et fragmenta* (BT, 1979) 1–61. COMMENTARIES: T. Hudson-Williams, *Early Greek elegy* (Cardiff 1926); J. Defradas, *Les élégiaques grecs* (Paris 1962). Select fragments: D. A. Campbell, *Greek lyric poetry* (London 1967: repr. Bristol 1982); D. E. Gerber, *Euterpe* (Amsterdam 1970). Tyrtaeus: C. Prato (Rome 1968).

TRANSLATIONS: (1) PROSE: J. M. Edmonds, *Elegy and iambus* I (Loeb, 1931). (2) VERSE: R. Lattimore, *Greek lyrics*, 2nd ed. (Chicago 1960). Text with German tr.: Z. Franyó, B. Snell, H. Maehler, *Frühgriechische Lyriker* I (Berlin 1971).

STUDIES: C. M. Bowra, *Early Greek elegists* (London 1938: repr. Cambridge 1960); K. J. Dover, 'The poetry of Archilochos', in *Entretiens X: Archiloque* (Fondation Hardt, Geneva 1964) 188–95; H. Fränkel, *Early Greek poetry and philosophy* (New York & London 1975) ch. IV; M. L. West, *Studies in Greek elegy and iambus* (Berlin & New York 1974); E. Degani, *Poeti greci giambici ed elegiaci* (Milan 1977). Mimnermus: S. Szádeczky-Kardoss, *RE* suppl. XI (1968) 935–51.

THEOGNIS

LIFE

Late authorities (Suda etc.) place his *floruit* at various times in the period 552–541 B.C. If he was a citizen of mainland Megara, the social upheavals reflected in his poems may have been those which followed the overthrow of the tyrant Theagenes in that city: this would locate his work in the first half of the late 6th c. But there is no certainty here: West, for example (under *Studies* (1974) below), makes a case for the turbulence preceding the establishment of Theagenes' tyranny, i.e. the second half of the 6th c. According to Plato (*Laws* 630a) he was a citizen of Sicilian Megara. A scholiast on this passage refers to the long-standing controversy and asks: 'Why should he not have been born of this (i.e. mainland) Megara and then have gone to Sicily...and become a citizen of Sicilian Megara?' Most modern scholars have thought this a reasonable suggestion.

WORKS

Some 700 elegiac couplets are attributed to T. in the MSS. These include, however, verses belonging to other poets (Solon, Mimnermus, Tyrtaeus, (?)Euenus), repetitions and near-repetitions, and one passage (773–82) referring to events later than the probable date of T. See pp. 136ff.

BIBLIOGRAPHY

(See D. E. Gerber, *C.W.* 61 (1967/8) 272–4 and 70 (1976/7) 80–4.)

TEXTS AND COMMENTARIES: TEXTS: Harrison (1902) under *Studies* below; D. Young, 2nd ed. (BT, 1771); M. L. West, *IEG* I,172–241; idem, *Theognidis et Phocylidis fragmenta* (Berlin 1978). COMMENTARIES: T. Hudson-Williams (London 1910); J. Carrière, 2nd ed. (Budé, 1948). Bk 1: B. A. van Groningen (Amsterdam 1966). Select fragments: D. A. Campbell, *Greek lyric poetry* (London 1967: repr. Bristol 1982); D. E. Gerber, *Euterpe* (Amsterdam 1970).

TRANSLATIONS: (1) PROSE: J. M. Edmonds, *Elegy and iambus* I (Loeb, 1931). (2) VERSE: R. Lattimore, *Greek lyrics*, 2nd ed. (Chicago 1960: brief selections).

STUDIES: E. Harrison, *Studies in Theognis* (Cambridge 1902: incl. text); A. Peretti, *Teognide nella tradizione gnomologica* (Pisa 1953); A. Garzya, *Teognide: Elegie* (Florence 1958); A. R. Burn, *The lyric age of Greece* (London 1960) 247–64; M. L. West, *Studies in Greek elegy and iambus* (Berlin & New York 1974) 40–71, 149–67; H. Fränkel, *Early Greek poetry and philosophy* (New York & London 1975) 401–25.

SOLON

LIFE

b. *c.* 640 B.C., son of Execestides. Prominent in Athens' war with Megara for possession of Salamis, and chief archon of Athens 594/593. Allegedly travelled overseas for ten years after his reforms, returned to Athens and d. sometime after Pisistratus' usurpation of 561. He had already become a semi-mythical figure by the 5th c. B.C. – his meeting with Croesus of Lydia, one of the showpieces of Herodotus' *Histories* (1.29–33), is generally agreed, on chronological grounds alone, to be unhistorical. Plutarch's *Life* preserves the anecdotal tradition and Aristotle's *Constitution of the Athenians* (5–12) gives a late-fourth-century view of S.'s political and economic reforms. (It is also the source of the most important fragments of the poems dealing with his archonship.) See I. M. Linforth, *Solon the Athenian* (Berkeley, Calif. 1919: with text, tr. and comm. of works); K. Freeman, *The life and work of Solon* (London 1926: with tr.); J. W. Woodhouse, *Solon the liberator* (Oxford 1938); A. Masaracchia, *Solone* (Florence 1958); A. Martino, *Solone. Testimonianze sulla vita e l'opera* (Rome 1968: complete collection of the ancient sources); Gentili and Prato under *Texts* below, 61–92 (selected sources).

WORKS

According to Diog. Laert. 1.61 S. wrote 5,000 elegiac verses and also iambics and epodes: there survive 219 lines of elegiacs, some 20 of trochaic tetrameter and some 47 of iambic trimeter. Longest extant poem is fr. 13 (75 lines of elegiacs).

BIBLIOGRAPHY

(See D. E. Gerber, *C.W.* 61 (1967/8) 269 and 70 (1976/7) 78–80; also the works under *Life* above and Gentili and Prato under *Texts* below, xxxi–xxxvii.)

TEXTS AND COMMENTARIES: TEXTS: *IEG* 119–45; B. Gentili and C. Prato, *Poetarum elegiacorum testimonia et fragmenta* (BT, 1979) 93–126. COMMEN-TARIES: W. Jaeger, *Solons Eunomie, Sitz. Preuss. Ak. Wiss.* phil.-hist. Klasse, 1926; L. Massa Positano, *L'elegia di Solone alle Muse* (Naples 1947). Select fragments: D. A. Campbell, *Greek lyric poetry* (London 1967: repr. Bristol 1982); D. E. Gerber, *Euterpe* (Amsterdam 1970).

TRANSLATIONS: (1) PROSE: J. M. Edmonds, *Greek elegy and iambus* I (Loeb, 1931). (2) VERSE: R. Lattimore, *Greek lyrics*, 2nd ed. (Chicago 1960).

STUDIES: R. Lattimore, 'The first elegy of Solon', *A.J.Ph.* 68 (1947) 161ff.; H. Fränkel, *Early Greek poetry and philosophy* (New York & London 1975) 217–37.

SEMONIDES

LIFE

From Samos; led colony to Amorgos (Suda IV 363.1 and IV 360.7 (latter ref. in entry on Simmias of Rhodes, which contains material relevant to S.)). Usually dated to mid- or late 7th c. B.C.; for discussion see Lloyd-Jones under *Commentaries* below, 15–16. His name is regularly spelled Simonides in the ancient sources, but Choeroboscus (*Et.Magn.* 713, 17C) gives the correct spelling.

WORKS

At least two books of iambics, also an 'archaeology [i.e. history] of the Samians' and an elegy in two books (Suda): the two latter may be identical. Some fragments attributed to Simonides of Ceos may belong to S. (see *IEG* II 112). Apart from frs. 1 and 7 very little remains of his work.

BIBLIOGRAPHY

(See D. E. Gerber, *C.W.* 61 (1967/8) 278 and 70 (1976/7) 91–3.)

TEXTS AND COMMENTARIES: TEXTS: Diehl I 3, 3rd ed. (1952); *IEG* II 96–102. COMMENTARIES: Select fragments: D. A. Campbell, *Greek lyric poetry* (London 1967: repr. Bristol 1982); D. E. Gerber, *Euterpe* (Amsterdam 1970); H. Lloyd-Jones, *Females of the species: Semonides on women* (London 1975: with tr.). Fr. 7: W. Marg, *Der Charakter in der Sprache der frühgriechischen Dichtung*, 2nd ed. (Würzburg 1967); W. J. Verdenius, *Mnemosyne* 21 (1968) 132–58.

TRANSLATIONS: (1) PROSE: J. M. Edmonds, *Elegy and iambus* II (Loeb, 1931); Lloyd-Jones under *Commentaries* above. (2) VERSE: R. Lattimore, *Greek lyrics*, 2nd ed. (Chicago 1960).

STUDIES: P. Maas, *RE* IIIA (1929) 184–6; H. Fränkel, *Early Greek poetry and philosophy* (New York & London 1975) 200–7; M. L. West, *Studies in Greek elegy and iambus* (Berlin & New York 1974); E. Degani, *Poeti greci giambici ed elegiaci* (Milan 1977).

HIPPONAX

LIFE

There is no really reliable information; ancient notices are clearly based on deductions from the texts. According to the Suda he came from Ephesus, but lived in Clazomenae after being expelled by the tyrants Athenagoras and Comas. For story of H. and sculptors Bupalus and Athenis see Pliny, *N.H.* 36.5.11–13; same source gives H.'s *floruit* as 540–537 B.C.

WORKS

Poems in two 'books' (probably the books of the Alexandrian edition): the few remaining fragments contain iambic trimeters (mostly in the choliambic form that H. may have invented), trochaic tetrameters, hexameters and a combination of iambic trimeter with a shorter dactylic line.

BIBLIOGRAPHY

(See D. E. Gerber, *C.W.* 61 (1967/8) 278–9 and 70 (1976/7) 93–4.)

TEXTS AND COMMENTARIES: TEXTS: *IEG* I 109–71; H. Degani (BT 1983). COMMENTARIES: W. de Sousa Madeiros, *Hipponax de Efeso, Fragmentos dos iambos* (Coimbra 1961); O. Masson (Paris 1962); A. Farina (Naples 1963: with Italian tr.); W. de Sousa Madeiros, *Hipponactea* (Coimbra 1969). Select fragments: D. A. Campbell, *Greek lyric poetry* (London 1967: repr. Bristol 1982); D. E. Gerber, *Euterpe* (Amsterdam 1970); E. Degani and G. Burzacchini, *Lirici Greci* (Florence 1977).

TRANSLATIONS: A. D. Knox in *Herodes, Cercidas and the Greek choliambic poets* (Loeb, 1929: with Theophrastus' *Characters* tr. J. M. Edmonds).

STUDIES: M. L. West, *Studies in Greek elegy and iambus* (Berlin & New York 1974) 28–31, 140–9.

ARCHAIC CHORAL LYRIC

GENERAL WORKS

Bowra, C. M., *Greek lyric poetry*, 2nd ed. (Oxford 1961)
Campbell, D. A., *The golden lyre: the themes of the Greek lyric poets* (London 1983)
Färber, H., *Die Lyrik in der Kunsttheorie der Antike* (Munich 1936)
Fatouros, G., *Index verborum zur frühgriechischen Lyrik* (Heidelberg 1966)

Fränkel, H., *Early Greek poetry and philosophy*, tr. M. Hadas and J. Willis (New York & London 1975)

Gentili, B., 'Lirica greca arcaica e tardo-arcaica', in *Introduzione allo studio della cultura classica* (Milan 1972)

idem, 'Storicità della lirica greca', in *Storia e civiltà dei greci* 1 1 (Milan 1978) 383ff.

Johnson, W. R., *The idea of lyric: Lyric modes in ancient and modern poetry* (Berkeley & Los Angeles 1982)

Wilamowitz-Moellendorff, U. von, *Textgeschichte der griechischen Lyriker* (Berlin & Göttingen 1900)

ALCMAN

LIFE

Active probably in late 7th c. B.C. at Sparta, but neither his dates nor birthplace are certain. *Chronology*: three dates for his *floruit*: (1) 631–628 (Suda), synchronized also with reign of Ardys of Lydia (probably *c.* 679–630); (2) 659/8 (Eusebius); (3) 611/10 (Eusebius). The list of Spartan kings in *P.Oxy.* 2390 = fr. 5.2 col. i *PMG* favours the later date: see F. D. Harvey, *J.H.S.* 87 (1967) 69; M. L. West, *C.Q.* n.s.15 (1965) 191f. Older than Stesichorus, b. *c.* 632–629 (Suda s.v. 'Stesichorus'). Activity in last quarter of 7th c. would probably fit most of evidence. See J. A. Davison, 'Notes on Alcman', *From Archilochus to Pindar* (London 1968) 176–9; M. L. West, *C.Q.* n.s.15 (1965) 188–94; P. Janni, *La cultura di Sparta arcaica. Ricerche* 1 (Rome 1965) 96–120. *Origins*: Laconian from village of Messoa (Suda); Lydian: Ael. *V.H.* 12.50. Lively debate in antiquity as to whether he was Lydian or Laconian by birth: *PMG* 10 and 13 ('Laconian Alcman' and Aristotle's support of Lydian origin, *PMG* 13a). Lydian birth based in part on interpreting fr. 16 *PMG* autobiographically; also *Anth.Pal.* 7.18 ('strife between two continents whether he was Lydian or Laconian'); Vell.Pat. 1.18.2. See also *P.Oxy.* 2802 = *SLG* 85. Said to be a slave of Agesidas, set free because of his extraordinary gifts: Heraclides Ponticus, *Politeiai* fr. 2 = Arist. fr. 611.9 Rose.

See Davison 173–87, West, Janni (cited above) and Page under *Commentaries* below, 164–70.

WORKS

Six books of lyric poems (Suda, confirmed by *P.Oxy.* 3209), plus Κολυμβῶσαι 'Diving women', of unknown contents: see G. L. Huxley, *G.R.B.S.* 5 (1964) 26–8. Placed first in Hellenistic canon of lyric poets. Famous for love-poems, of which only a few fragments survive in quotation. Extant works include substantial fragments of two partheneia or maiden-songs (*PMG* 1 and 3), summary of a cosmogonic poem (*PMG* 5), diverse fragments on mythical subjects, food, local Laconian cults and remote peoples; recently published poem on Odysseus(?) in dactylic metre (*P.Oxy.* 2443 fr. 1+3213). Language: local Laconian dialect, with free borrowings from epic diction;

ALCMAN

fondness for rare words, some possibly of Lydian origin. See Page under *Commentaries* below, 102–63; E. Risch, 'Die Sprache Alkmans', *M.H.* 11 (1954) 20–37. Metre: dactylic, trochaic, iambo-trochaic, Aeolic. Generally fairly simple metres. Probably did not use triadic structure in choral odes; see *PMG* 14.

BIBLIOGRAPHY

(See (1936–52) G. M. Kirkwood, *C.W.* 47 (1953) 49; (1952–67) D. E. Gerber, *C.W.* 61 (1967/8) 325–7; (1967–75) idem, *C.W.* 70 (1976) 94–100; also, under *Studies* below, Calame (1977) II 179–86 and Puelma (1977) 53f.)

TEXTS AND COMMENTARIES: TEXTS: D. L. Page, *PMG*; idem, *Lyrica Graeca selecta* (OCT, 1968). COMMENTARIES: D. L. Page, *Alcman, the Partheneion* (Oxford 1951); A. Garzya, *Alcmane, I frammenti* (Naples 1954); G. Perrotta and B. Gentili, *Polinnia* (Rose 1965: does not include *Parthen.* 1); D. A. Campbell, *Greek lyric poetry* (London 1967: rpr. Bristol 1982); D. E. Gerber, *Euterpe* (Amsterdam 1970). New 'Odyssey' fragment: M. L. West, *Z.P.E.* 26 (1977) 38f.; A. L. Brown, *Z.P.E.* 32 (1978) 36–8.

STUDIES: (ed.) R. M. Dawkins, *The sanctuary of Artemis Orthia at Sparta*, *J.H.S.* suppl. V (1929); B. A. van Groningen, 'The enigma of Alcman's Partheneion', *Mnemosyne* 3.3 (1935/6) 241–61; C. M. Bowra, *Greek lyric poetry*, 2nd ed. (Oxford 1961); M. L. West, 'Three Presocratic cosmogonies', *C.Q.* n.s.13 (1963) 154–76 (154–6 on Alcman); A. P. Burnett, 'The race with the Pleiades', *C.Ph.* 59 (1964) 30–4; B. Marzullo, 'Il primo Partenio di Alcmane', *Philologus* 108 (1964) 174–210; A. F. Garvie, 'A note on the deity of Alcman's Partheneion', *C.Q.* n.s.15 (1965) 185–7; P. Janni, *La cultura di Sparta arcaica. Ricerche*, 2 vols. (Rome 1965–70); M. L. West, 'Alcmanica', *C.Q.* n.s.15 (1965) 188–202; T. G. Rosenmeyer, 'Alcman's Partheneion 1 reconsidered', *G.R.B.S.* 7 (1966) 321–59; F. D. Harvey, 'Oxyrhynchus Papyrus 2390 and early Spartan history', *J.H.S.* 87 (1967) 62–73; C. O. Pavese, 'Alcmane, il Partenio del Louvre', *Q.U.C.C.* 4 (1967) 113–33; M. L. West, 'Alcman and Pythagoras', *C.Q.* n.s.17 (1967) 1–15; J. A. Davison, *From Archilochus to Pindar* (London 1968) 146–95; M. Treu, 'Alkman', *RE* suppl. XI (1968) 19–29; M. F. Galiano, 'Iris Murdoch, Alcman, Safo y la siesta', *E.Clás.* 13 (1969) 97–107; J.-P. Vernant, 'Thétis et le poème cosmogonique d'Alcman', in *Hommages à Marie Delcourt* (Brussels 1970) 38–69, repr. in Vernant and M. Detienne, *Les ruses de l'intelligence: la Métis des Grecs* (Paris 1974) 134–64 (Eng. tr. by Janet Lloyd, *Cunning intelligence in Greek culture and society* (Hassocks 1978)); T. B. L. Webster, *The Greek chorus* (London 1970); M. L. West, 'Melica', *C.Q.* n.s.20 (1970) 205–15; B. Gentili, 'I frr. 39 e 40 P di Alcmane e la poetica della mimesi nella cultura greca arcaica', in *Studi filologici e storici in onore di V. de Falco* (Naples 1971) 59–67; A. Griffiths, 'Alcman's Partheneion: the morning after the night before', *Q.U.C.C.* 14 (1972) 7–30; J. W. Halporn, 'Agido, Hagesichora, and the Chorus', *Antidosis, Festschrift W. Kraus*, *W.S.* suppl.

v (1972) 124–38; P. E. Easterling, 'Alcman 58 and Simonides 37', *P.C.Ph.S.* n.s.20 (1974) 37–43; J. L. Penwill, 'Alcman's cosmogony', *Apeiron* 9 (1974) 3–39; B. Gentili, 'Il Partenio di Alcmane e l'amore omoerotico femminile nei tiasi spartani', *Q.U.C.C.* 22 (1976) 59–67; C. Calame, *Les choeurs de jeunes filles en Grèce archaïque* II, *Alcman* (Rome 1977) 1–55; M. Puelma, 'Die Selbstbeschreibung des Chores in Alkmans grossem Partheneion-Fragment', *M.H.* 34 (1977) 1–55; G. F. Gianotti, 'Le Pleiadi di Alcmane', *R.F.I.C.* 106 (1978) 257–71.

STESICHORUS

LIFE

Dates 632/629–556/553 B.C. (Suda), his death synchronized with that of Simonides (Cic. *Rep.* 2.20, Suda s.v. 'Simonides'). Born or active either at Himera in Sicily (Plato, *Phaedr.* 244a, Arist. *Rhet.* 2.1393b, Glaucus of Rhegium *apud* Plut. *De mus.* 7, Suda) or in Matauros, a Locrian colony of s. Italy (Steph. Byz. s.v. 'Matauros'; cf. Arist. *Rhet.* 2.1395a). Original name Teisias; called Stesichorus because he 'first set up chorus for the lyre' (πρῶτος κιθαρῳδίας χορὸν ἔστησεν, Suda); 'Stesichorus' may be a kind of professional name or title. Contemporary of Sappho, Alcaeus and Pittacus (Suda s.v. 'Sappho'). Son of Euphemus (Suda, Plato, *Phaedr.* 244a) (also Euphorbus, Hyetes, Hesiod: Suda). *Marmor Parium* 50 notices arrival of 'Stesichorus' in Greece in 485; idem 73 sets victory at Athens in 370/69; these notices presumably refer to later poets of the same name: cf. M. L. West, *C.Q.* n.s.20 (1970) 206; idem, *C.Q.* n.s.21 (1971) 302–7; J. Vürtheim, *Stesichoros' Fragmente und Biographie* (Leiden 1919) 103–5. Tomb at Himera (Pollux 9.100) or Catane (Pollux 9.7, Phot. s.v. πάντα ὄκτω, *Anth. Pal.* 7.75, Suda), where 'Stesichoreian Gate' was named after him (Suda). His exile from Pallantion in Arcadia to Catane (Suda) was possibly based on mention of Arcadian Pallantion in *Geryoneis* (Paus. 8.3.2 = fr. 182 *PMG*).

See West (1970), (1971) 302–14, Vürtheim 99–112, cited above.

WORKS

Twenty-six books, in Doric dialect (Suda), with ample borrowings from epic diction. Mainly on mythical subjects. Substantial papyrus fragments of *Geryoneis* and a poem of unknown title about the royal house of Thebes. Important fragments also of *Eriphyle, Iliou persis, Nostoi, Oresteia,* two *Palinodes.* Some works were of considerable length and unlikely to be choral: e.g. *Geryoneis* reached at least 1,500 lines. Celebrated as a love-poet (Athen. 13.601a); but the erotic works *Kalyke* and *Rhadine* are perhaps spurious, possibly the work of the 4th-c. Stesichorus. Bucolic themes in *Daphnis* (Ael. *V.H.* 10.18 = fr. 279 *PMG*), but this work too is suspect and may be the work of the 4th-c. Stesichorus: see West (1970) and Vürtheim 73–6, under *Life* above. Said to have written fables on political topics (Arist. *Rhet.* 2.1393b and 1395a) and on popular wisdom (Ael. *N.A.* 17.37, frs. 280, 281 *PMG*), of which the latter is of highly dubious authenticity. Best known for lyrical narrative of epic themes and celebrated for dignity, grandeur and Homeric spirit (*Stesichori graves Camenae*, Hor. *Odes* 4.9.8); cf. Dion. Hal. *Cens. Vet.* 2.7, 'Longinus', *Subl.* 13.3, Quint. 10.1.62. Metre: early form of dactylo-epitrite; preponderance of dactylic metres. See M. Haslam, *Q.U.C.C.* 17 (1974) 9–57; idem, *G.R.B.S.* 19 (1978) 29–57. Said to have developed triadic structure of choral ode, 'the three of Stesichorus', i.e. strophe, antistrophe, epode: Suda s.v. τρία Στησιχόρου; see M. L. West, *C.Q.* n.s.21 (1971) 312f.

BIBLIOGRAPHY

(See (1952–67) D. E. Gerber, *C.W.* 61 (1967/8) 327f.; (1967–75) idem, *C.W.* 70 (1976) 100–5.)

TEXTS AND COMMENTARIES: J. Vürtheim, *Stesichoros' Fragmente und Biographie* (Leiden 1919); D. L. Page, *PMG*; idem, *Lyrica Graeca selecta* (OCT, 1968), with Addenda for *Geryoneis*; idem, *SLG* for *Geryoneis, Iliou persis*. New poem on Theban royal house: *P. Lille* 73, 76, in *Cahiers de recherches de l'institut de papyrologie et d'égyptologie de Lille 4, Études sur l'Égypte et le Soudan ancien:* Publications de l'Université de Lille III (Lille 1977) 287ff. (*P. Lille* 76); C. Meillier, *Z.P.E.* 26 (1977) 1–5 (*P. Lille* 73); P. Parsons, 'The Lille Stesichorus', *Z.P.E.* 26 (1977) 7–36. Select fragments: D. A. Campbell, *Greek lyric poetry* (London 1967: rpr. Bristol 1982); D. E. Gerber, *Euterpe* (Amsterdam 1970).

STUDIES: J. Vürtheim, *Stesichoros' Fragmente und Biographie* (Leiden 1919); G. Vallet, *Rhégion et Zancle*, Bibl. d'Écoles françaises d'Athènes et de Rome CLXXXIX (Paris 1958) 255–86; C. M. Bowra, *Greek lyric poetry*, 2nd ed. (Oxford 1961) 74–129; L. Woodbury, 'Helen and the Palinode', *Phoenix* 21 (1967) 157–76; J. A. Davison, 'Stesichorus and Helen', *From Archilochus to Pindar* (London 1968) 196–225; M. Treu, 'Stesichorus', *RE* suppl. XI (1968) 1253–6; T. B. L. Webster, 'Stesichorus: *Geryoneis*', *Agon* 2 (1968) 1–9; M. I. Davies, 'Thoughts on the *Oresteia* before Aischylos', *B.C.H.* 93 (1969) 215–60; M. Robertson, '*Geryoneis*: Stesichorus and the vase-painters', *C.Q.* n.s.19 (1969) 207–21; M. L. West, 'Stesichorus redivivus', *Z.P.E.* 4 (1969) 135–49; A. Garzya, *La poesia lirica greca nella Magna Grecia*, Le Parole e le Idee XIII (Naples 1970) 9–14; M. L. West, 'Stesichorus', *C.Q.* n.s.21 (1971) 302–14; C. O. Pavese, *Tradizioni e generi poetici della Grecia arcaica* (Rome 1972) 239–46; D. L. Page, 'Stesichorus: the *Geryoneis*', *J.H.S.* 93 (1973) 136–54; B. Gentili, *Gnomon* 48 (1976) 745–8 (review of Page's edd., under *Texts* above); J. Bollack, P. Judet de la Combe, H. Wismann, *La réplique de Jocaste*, Cahiers de Philologie II, avec un supplément, Publications de l'Université de Lille III (Lille 1977); F. Bornmann, 'Zur *Geryoneis* des Stesichorus', *Z.P.E.* 31 (1978) 33–5.

MONODY

GENERAL WORKS

Bowra, C. M., *Greek lyric poetry*, 2nd ed. (Oxford 1961)

Burn, A. R., *The lyric age of Greece* (London 1960)

Campbell, D. A., *The golden lyre: the themes of the Greek lyric poets* (London 1983)

Degani, E. and Burzacchini, G. *Lirici Greci* (Florence 1977).

Fatouros, G., *Index verborum zur frühgriechischen Lyrik* (Heidelberg 1966)

Fränkel, H., *Early Greek poetry and philosophy*, tr. M. Hadas and J. Willis (New York & London 1975)

Kirkwood, G. M., *Early Greek monody* (Ithaca & London 1974)

Wilamowitz-Moellendorff, U. von, *Textgeschichte der griechischen Lyriker* (Berlin & Göttingen 1900)

idem, *Sappho und Simonides* (Berlin 1913)

SAPPHO

LIFE

b. probably *c.* 630 B.C. in Eresus in Lesbos; apparently lived mainly in Mytilene. Parents Scamandronymus and Cleis, brothers Charaxus (for whose affair with the courtesan Rhodopis see Hdt. 2.134), Eurygyus (or Erigyus) and Larichus, husband Cercylas (?: see p. 203), daughter Cleis. Exiled to Sicily sometime between 604/3 and 596/5. Date of death unknown. Sources (see Campbell under *Texts* below, 2–29): *P. Oxy.* 1800 fr. 1 and Suda (biographies; see also Ps.-Ovid, *Her.* 15, esp. for S.'s legendary association with Phaon and her lover's leap); *Marm. Par.* 36, Euseb. *Chron. Ol.* 45.1, Strabo 13.2.3, Athen. 13.598b–599d, Hdt. 2.134 (chronology); Suda, Strabo *loc. cit.* (birthplace); Max. Tyr. 18.9 (literary rivals).

WORKS

(For testimonia see Campbell under *Texts* below, 28–51.) Suda records nine books of lyric poems together with epigrams, elegiacs, iambics and monodies (surely another title for her lyric poems); the elegiacs and iambics do not survive, and the three epigrams attributed to her in *Anth. Pal.* (6.269, 7.489, 505) are almost certainly Hellenistic. Bk 1 contained poems in Sapphic stanzas (schol. metr. on Pind. *Pyth.* 1), Bk 2 'Aeolic dactyls' (Heph. *Ench.* 7.7), and so on: see Page under *Commentaries* below, 318–20. Metres are almost exclusively aeolic, built round choriambs ($-\cup\cup-$).

BIBLIOGRAPHY

(See D. E. Gerber, *C.W.* 61 (1967/8) 317–20 and 70 (1976/7) 106–15.)

TEXTS AND COMMENTARIES: TEXTS: E. Lobel and D. L. Page, *PLF*; M. Treu, 4th ed. (Munich 1968); D. L. Page, *Lyrica Graeca selecta* (OCT, 1968); E.-M. Voigt, *Sappho et Alcaeus* (Amsterdam 1971); D. L. Page, *SLG* (Oxford 1974) 74–6, 87–102; D. A. Campbell, *Greek Lyric* I (Loeb, 1982). COMMENTARIES: Select fragments: D. L. Page, *Sappho and Alcaeus* (Oxford 1955); D. A. Campbell, *Greek lyric poetry* (London 1967: repr. Bristol 1982); D. E. Gerber, *Euterpe* (Amsterdam 1970).

TRANSLATIONS: Campbell under *Texts* above; selections in R. Lattimore, *Greek lyrics*, 2nd ed. (Chicago 1960); W. Barnstone (New York 1965); S. Q. Groden (Indianapolis 1966).

STUDIES: (1) GENERAL: E. Lobel, Σαπφοῦς μέλη (Oxford 1925); R. Merkelbach, 'Sappho und ihr Kreis', *Philologus* 101 (1957) 1–29; E.-M. Hamm, *Grammatik zu Sappho und Alkaios* (Berlin 1957); A. W. Gomme, 'Interpretations of some poems of Alkaios and Sappho', *J.H.S.* 77 (1957) 255–66, with 78 (1958) 84–6; C. M. Bowra, *Greek lyric poetry*, 2nd ed. (Oxford 1961) 176–240; R. Bagg, 'Love, ceremony and daydream in Sappho's lyrics', *Arion* 3 (1964) 44–82; J. A. Davison, *From Archilochus to Pindar* (London 1968) 226–41; M. Treu, *RE* suppl. XI (1968) 1222–40; M. L. West, 'Burning Sappho', *Maia* 22 (1970) 307–30; H. Saake, *Zur Kunst Sapphos* (Paderborn 1971); idem, *Sapphostudien* (Paderborn 1972); M. R. Lefkowitz, 'Critical stereotypes and the poetry of Sappho', *G.R.B.S.* 14 (1973) 113–23; G. Nagy, 'Phaethon, Sappho's Phaon, and the White Rocks of Leucas', *H.S.C.Ph.* 77 (1973) 137–77; G. M. Kirkwood, *Early Greek monody* (Ithaca & London 1974) 100–49; C. Segal, 'Eros and incantation: Sappho and oral poetry', *Arethusa* 7 (1974) 139–60; A. P. Burnett, *Three archaic poets. Archilochus, Alcaeus, Sappho* (London 1983). (2) INDIVIDUAL POEMS: Fr. 1: G. L. Koniaris, *Philologus* 109 (1965) 30–8; K. Stanley, *G.R.B.S.* 17 (1976) 305–21. Fr. 2: T. McEvilley, *Phoenix* 26 (1972) 323–33. Fr. 16: E. M. Stern, *Mnemosyne* 4.23 (1970) 348–61. Fr. 31 (and Catullus 51): G. Wills, *G.R.B.S.* 8 (1967) 167–97. Fr. 94: T. McEvilley, *Phoenix* 25 (1971) 1–11. Fr. 96: T. McEvilley, *Hermes* 101 (1973) 257–78; C. Carey, *C.Q.* n.s.28 (1978) 366–71. Fr. 976 *PMG*: see under *Studies* (1) above Gomme (1957 and 1958) and Kirkwood (1974) 128, 261.

ALCAEUS

LIFE

b. in Mytilene on Lesbos *c.* 620 B.C. (perhaps as early as 630), apparently of a noble family which unsuccessfully competed for power after the Penthelidae were overthrown. Was too young to help his brothers and Pittacus in deposing Melanchrus 612–609 (fr. 75.7ff.), but old enough to fight against Athenians for Sigeum before 600 (fr. 428: threw away his armour). Allied with Pittacus against Myrsilus, but a fierce critic of Pittacus when he was tyrant 590–580. Exiled on Lesbos more than once, and is known to have gone to Egypt. Date of death unknown (but see ref. to 'grey chest' in fr. 50). Sources (see Campbell under *Texts* below, 206–19): own works *passim*, Suda, *P. Oxy.* 2307, 2506 (biographical material); Euseb. *Chron. Ol.* 45.1 (chronology); Arist. *Pol.* 1285a 35ff., Strabo 13.2.3, Diog. Laert. 1.74–5 (relations with tyrants).

WORKS

(For testimonia see Campbell under *Texts* below, 218–33.) Poems arranged according to subject-matter in at least ten books. One book contained over 1,000 lines (*Ox. Pap.* XXIII 106), and the 800th line of a book is attested (*P. Oxy.* 2295 fr. 4). For editions of Aristophanes and Aristarchus see Hephaestion pp. 73f. Consbruch. Metres mostly aeolic, built round choriambs (–∪∪–).

BIBLIOGRAPHY

(See D. E. Gerber, *C.W.* 61 (1967/68) 317–18, 322–3 and 70 (1976/7) 115–17.)

TEXTS AND COMMENTARIES: TEXTS: E. Lobel and D. L. Page, *PLF*; M. Treu, 2nd ed. (Munich 1963); W. Barner, *Neuere Alkaios-Papyri aus Oxyrhynchos* (Hildesheim 1967); D. L. Page, *Lyrica Graeca selecta* (OCT, 1968); E.-M. Voigt, *Sappho et Alcaeus* (Amsterdam 1971); D. L. Page, *SLG* 77–102; D. A. Campbell, *Greek lyric* I (Loeb, 1982). COMMENTARIES: Select fragments: D. L. Page, *Sappho and Alcaeus* (Oxford 1955); D. A. Campbell, *Greek lyric poetry* (London 1967: repr. Bristol 1982); D. E. Gerber, *Euterpe* (Amsterdam 1970).

TRANSLATIONS: Campbell under *Texts* above; selections in R. Lattimore, *Greek lyrics*, 2nd ed. (Chicago 1960); W. Barnstone, *Greek lyric poetry* (Bloomington, Indiana 1961).

STUDIES: (1) GENERAL: E. Lobel, Ἀλκαίου μέλη (Oxford 1927); E.-M. Hamm, *Grammatik zu Sappho und Alkaios* (Berlin 1957); A. W. Gomme, 'Interpretations of some poems of Alkaios and Sappho', *J.H.S.* 77 (1957) 255–66; C. M. Bowra, *Greek lyric poetry*, 2nd ed. (Oxford 1961) 130–75; M. Treu, *RE* suppl. XI (1968) 8–19; G. M. Kirkwood, *Early Greek monody* (Ithaca & London 1974) 53–99; A. P. Burnett, *Three archaic poets. Archilochus, Alcaeus, Sappho* (London 1983). (2) INDIVIDUAL POEMS: Fr. 129: A. J. Beattie, *C.R.* n.s.6 (1956) 189–91. Fr. 298: R. Merkelbach, *Z.P.E.* 1 (1967) 81–95; H. Lloyd-Jones, *G.R.B.S.* 9 (1968) 125–39; G. Tarditi, *Q.U.C.C.* 8 (1969) 86–96; R. L. Fowler, *Z.P.E.* 33 (1979) 17–28. Fr. 326: B. Marzullo, *Philologus* 119 (1975) 27–38.

IBYCUS

LIFE

b. at Rhegium, but left the West for the court of Polycrates, tyrant of Samos *c.* 533–
c. 522 (the Suda's dating of his arrival to 564–561 is normally discounted because of
discrepancies with Herodotus 3.39). Date of death unknown; buried at Rhegium.
Sources (see Edmonds under *Translations* below, 78–85): Suda (biography); Euseb.
Chron. Ol. 59.3 (chronology); Diogen. *Paroem.* 1.207 (story that I. might have been
tyrant in Rhegium, had he not left); *Anth. Pal.* 7.714 (burial).

WORKS

Seven books of poetry in the Alexandrian edition. His narrative poetry, almost
completely lost, dealt with such epic themes as the adventures of Heracles, Meleager
and the Argonauts, and the Trojan War and its sequel. For predominance of erotic
themes in his poems see Cic. *Tusc.* 4.71.

BIBLIOGRAPHY

(See D. E. Gerber, *C.W.* 61 (1967/8) 328 and 70 (1976/7) 117–19.)

TEXTS AND COMMENTARIES: TEXTS: D. L. Page, *PMG* 144–69; F.
Mosino (Reggio Calabria 1966); D. L. Page, *Lyrica Graeca selecta* (OCT, 1968) 134–
45; idem, *SLG* 44–73. COMMENTARIES: Select fragments: D. A. Campbell, *Greek lyric
poetry* (London 1967: repr. Bristol 1982); D. E. Gerber, *Euterpe* (Amsterdam 1970).

TRANSLATIONS: J. M. Edmonds, *Lyra Graeca* II (Loeb, 1924); selections in
R. Lattimore, *Greek lyrics*, 2nd ed. (Chicago 1960); W. Barnstone, *Greek lyric poetry*
(Bloomington, Indiana 1961).

STUDIES: D. L. Page, 'Ibycus' poem in honour of Polycrates', *Aegyptus* 31 (1951)
158–72; C. M. Bowra, *Greek lyric poetry*, 2nd ed. (Oxford 1961) 241–67; J. P. Barron,
'The sixth-century tyranny at Samos', *C.Q.* n.s.14 (1964) 210–29; F. Sisti, 'L'ode a
Policrate', *Q.U.C.C.* 4 (1967) 59–79; J. P. Barron, 'Ibycus: to Polycrates', *B.I.C.S.*
16 (1969) 119–49; M. L. West, 'Melica', *C.Q.* n.s.20 (1970) 206–9; M. Robertson,
'Ibycus: Polycrates, Troilus, Polyxena', *B.I.C.S.* 17 (1970) 11–15.

ANACREON

LIFE

b. *c.* 570 B.C. in Teos in Asia Minor. After Persian attack on Greek coastal cities sailed with Teians to Thrace, where they founded Abdera *c.* 540. Invited to court of Polycrates of Samos (ruled *c.* 533–*c.* 522), on whose murder he was brought to Athens by Pisistratus' son Hipparchus. After Hipparchus' assassination in 514 he either remained in Athens or went to Thessaly (cf. frs. 107, 108D). If he did go to Thessaly, he returned to Athens and may have spent much of later life there. d. *c.* 485 B.C. Sources (see Edmonds under *Translations* below, 120–37): Suda (biography); Eusebius, *Chron. Ol.* 61.1, Ps.-Lucian, *Macr.* 26, schol. on Aesch. *P.V.* 128 (chronology); Himerius, *Or.* 28.2, 29.24 Colonna, Strabo 14.1.16, Ael. *V.H.* 9.4, 12.25, Paus. 1.2.3, Hdt. 3.121 (connections with Polycrates); Ps.-Plato, *Hipparch.* 228b–c, Plato, *Charm.* 157e, Himerius, *Or.* 39.11 Colonna (activity at Athens).

WORKS

Only a few complete poems survive. A.'s work was edited by Aristarchus (Hephaestion p. 68.22, 74.11–14 Consbruch), possibly in five books arranged on metrical principles: see Crinagoras, *Anth. Pal.* 9.239. Most of the surviving poems and fragments are in lyric metres, especially anacreontics and glyconics linked with pherecrateans, but he also wrote elegiacs (some are preserved in *Anth. Pal.*) and iambics (388 is the most substantial extant example). He may have written maiden-songs (see Page, *PMG* 500–1).

BIBLIOGRAPHY

(See D. E. Gerber, *C.W.* 61 (1967/8) 323–4 and 70 (1976/7) 119–22.)

TEXTS AND COMMENTARIES: TEXTS: B. Gentili (Rome 1968); D. L. Page, *PMG* 172–235; idem, *Lyrica Graeca selecta* (OCT, 1968) 148–66; idem, *SLG* 103–4. COMMENTARIES: Select fragments: D. A. Campbell, *Greek lyric poetry* (London 1967: repr. Bristol 1982); D. E. Gerber, *Euterpe* (Amsterdam 1970).

TRANSLATIONS: J. M. Edmonds, *Lyra Graeca* II (Loeb, 1924); selections in R. Lattimore, *Greek lyrics*, 2nd ed. (Chicago 1960); W. Barnstone, *Greek lyric poetry* (Bloomington, Indiana 1961).

STUDIES: (1) GENERAL: K. Latte, *Gnomon* 27 (1955) 495–7 (review of *Ox. Pap.* XXII, edd. Lobel and Roberts); B. Gentili, 'I nuovi frammenti papiracei di Anacreonte', *Maia* n.s.8 (1956) 181–96; D. L. Page, *C.R.* n.s.9 (1959) 234–7 (review of Gentili's edition); C. M. Bowra, *Greek lyric poetry*, 2nd ed. (Oxford 1961) 268–307; M. H. da

744

Rocha Pereira, 'Anakreon', *Das Altertum* 12 (1966) 84–96; M. Treu, *RE* suppl. XI (1968) 30–7; M. L. West, 'Melica', *C.Q.* n.s.20 (1970) 209–10; G. M. Kirkwood, *Early Greek monody* (Ithaca & London 1974) 150–77. (2) INDIVIDUAL POEMS: Fr. 348: D. Page, in *Studi in onore di L. Castiglioni* (Florence 1960) 661–7. Fr. 358: L. Woodbury, *T.A.Ph.A.* 109 (1979) 277–87 with bibliography. Fr. 388: W. J. Slater, *Phoenix* 32 (1978) 185–94.

SKOLIA

A collection of twenty-five 'Attic skolia' (drinking-songs) is preserved by Athenaeus 15.693f–695f. Majority were completed late 6th or early 5th century in four-line stanzas in Aeolic rhythm. Athenaeus mentions Alcaeus, Anacreon and Praxilla as writers of skolia. See also schol. on Ar. *Wasps* 1216ff.; schol. on Plato, *Gorg.* 451e; Plut. *Quaest. conv.* 1.1.5.

BIBLIOGRAPHY

TEXTS AND COMMENTARIES: TEXTS: D. L. Page, *PMG* 472–8; idem, *Lyrica Graeca selecta* (OCT, 1968) 238–45. COMMENTARIES: Selection in D. A. Campbell, *Greek lyric poetry* (London 1967: repr. Bristol 1982).

TRANSLATIONS: J. M. Edmonds, *Lyra Graeca*, 2nd ed., III (Loeb, 1940) 560–75; selection in R. Lattimore, *Greek lyrics*, 2nd ed. (Chicago 1960).

STUDIES: R. Reitzenstein, *Epigramm und Skolion* (Giessen 1893) 3–44; C. M. Bowra, *Greek lyric poetry*, 2nd ed. (Oxford 1961) 373–97; A. J. Podlecki, 'The political significance of the Athenian 'Tyrannicide'-Cult', *Historia* 15 (1966) 129–41.

CHORAL LYRIC IN THE FIFTH CENTURY
(for *General works* see pp. 735-6)

SIMONIDES

LIFE

b. 557/6 B.C. at Iulis in Ceos. Invited by Hipparchus to Athens before 514. Commissioned by Scopadae in Thessaly and survived collapse of their palace 514. Active in Athens in 490s; defeated Aeschylus in competition for epigram on the fallen at Marathon. Invited to Syracuse *c.* 476 and mediated between Hieron, his host, and

Theron of Acragas. d. in Sicily and buried in Acragas 468. Inventor of a mnemonic technique. Sources: fr. 77 D, Strabo 10.486, Suda (birth and background); fr. 88 D, Ps.-Plato, *Hipparch.* 228c, *Vit. Aesch.* 4, Plut. *Them.* 5, Cic. *Fin.* 2.32.104 (Athens); Call. fr. 71, Cic. *De or.* 2.86.353, schol. on Theocr. *Id.* 16.36f., Simon. fr. 510 P (Thessaly); Ps.-Plato, *Epist.* 2.311a, Athen. 14.656d, Ael. *V.H.* 9.1, Timaeus *apud* schol. on Pind. *Ol.* 2.29d (Sicily); Cic. *De or.* 2.87.357 (mnemonics); *Marm. Par.* 73 (death). See J. M. Edmonds, *Lyra Graeca* II (Loeb, 1924) 246–73.

WORKS

(1) LYRIC: Hymns, paeans, dithyrambs (fr. 79 D commemorates fifty-six victories), encomia, epinicia, dirges (especially famous; see Quint. 10.1.64, Cat. 38.8), skolia (drinking-songs). No complete work survives, and only two fragments exceed twenty-five lines (542–3 *PMG*). (2) ELEGIES AND EPIGRAMS, many of doubtful authenticity.

BIBLIOGRAPHY

(See (1949–68) P. A. Bernadini, *Q.U.C.C.* 8 (1969) 140–68; (1952–75) D. E. Gerber, *C.W.* 61 (1967/8) 328–9 and 70 (1976/7) 122–5.)

TEXTS AND COMMENTARIES: TEXTS: Diehl II (1925) 61–118; *PMG* 238–323 (lyrical frs. only). COMMENTARIES: D. A. Campbell, *Greek lyric poetry* (London 1967: repr. Bristol 1982: selection).

TRANSLATIONS: J. M. Edmonds, *Lyra Graeca* II (Loeb, 1924) 273–417.

STUDIES: U. von Wilamowitz-Moellendorff, *Sappho und Simonides* (Berlin 1913) 137–209; D. L. Page, 'Simonidea', *J.H.S.* 71 (1951) 133–42; A. W. H. Adkins, *Merit and responsibility: a study in Greek values* (Oxford 1960) 165–6, 196–7, 355–9; C. M. Bowra, *Greek lyric poetry*, 2nd ed. (Oxford 1961) 308–72; B. Gentili, 'Studi su Simonide', *Maia* n.s.16 (1964) 278–306; M. Detienne, *Les maîtres de vérité dans la Grèce archaïque* (Paris 1967) 105–23; P. E. Easterling, 'Alcman 58 and Simonides 37', *P.C.Ph.S.* n.s.20 (1974) 37–43; H. Fränkel, *Early Greek poetry and philosophy*, (New York & London 1975) 303–24; J. Svenbro, *La parole et le marbre* (Lund 1976) 141–72.

PINDAR

LIFE

b. 522 or 518 B.C. at Cynoscephalae in Boeotia; member of aristocratic clan of Aegeidae. Trained in Athens (tutor Lasos of Hermione); won dithyrambic victory there 497/6. Secured early commissions for aristocratic families of Thessaly (*Pyth.* 10, 498), Sicily

(*Pyth.* 6 and 12, 490) and Athens (*Pyth.* 7, 486). Fined by Thebes for composing dithyramb for Athens at time of Persian war. Visited courts of Hieron of Syracuse and Theron of Acragas 476. d. in Argos sometime after 446 (latest dated poem *Pyth.* 8), perhaps in 438. Sources: fr. 183 Bo = 193 Sn, *Pyth.* 5.75f. with schol. *ad loc.*, Suda (birth and background); *Vit. Amb.* p. 1.11ff. (training); *P. Oxy.* 2438.9f. (victory); fr. 64 Bo = 76 Sn, *Vit. Ambr.* p. 1.15ff., Isoc. *Antid.* 166, Paus. 1.8.4. (fine); *Ol.* 1–3 (Sicily); *Vit. Metr.* p. 9.21 (death; cf. *Vit. Thom.* p. 7.11f., *P. Oxy.* 2438.6ff.). Ancient *Lives* (*Ambrosiana, Thomana, Metrica*) in Drachmann's ed. of scholia (see below) 1 1–11; see M. Lefkowitz, *The lives of the Greek poets* (London 1981) ch. VI.

WORKS

(1) EXTANT: Four books of epinician *Odes*: *Olympian* (14), *Pythian* (12), *Nemean* (11), *Isthmian* (8: incomplete). *Pyth.* 3 and *Nem.* 11 are not epinicia. *Ol.* 5 may be spurious. (2) LOST OR FRAGMENTARY: One book each of encomia, hymns, paeans, dirges; two each of dithyrambs, hyporchemata (dance-songs), prosodia (processionals); three of partheneia (maiden-songs).

BIBLIOGRAPHY

(See D. E. Gerber, *A bibliography to Pindar, 1513–1966, A. Ph. A.* monographs XXVIII (1969); M. Rico, *Ensayo de bibliografía pindarica*, Manueles y anejos de *Emerita* XXIV (Madrid 1969); E. Thummer, *A.A.H.G.* 11 (1958) 65–88; 19 (1966) 289–322; 27 (1974) 1–34; (1967–75) D. E. Gerber, *C.W.* 70 (1976/7) 132–57.)

TEXTS AND COMMENTARIES: TEXTS: C. M. Bowra, 2nd ed. (OCT, 1947); A. Turyn, 2nd ed. (Oxford 1952); B. Snell, 10th ed. rev. H. Maehler (BT, 1971–5). COMMENTARIES: (1) Complete. A. Boeckh (comm. on *Nem.* and *Isth.* by L. Dissen), 2 vols. in 4 (Leipzig 1811–21: with Latin tr.: vol. II 2 repr. Hildesheim 1963); L. R. Farnell, 3 vols. (London 1930–2: with tr.). (2) Individual works. *Ol.* and *Pyth.*: B. L. Gildersleeve, 2nd ed. (New York 1890: repr. Amsterdam 1965). *Nem.*: J. B. Bury (London & New York 1890). *Isth.*: E. Thummer, 2 vols. (Heidelberg 1968–9: with German tr.). (3) Selections. G. Kirkwood, *A.Ph.A.* Textbook Series (Chico, Calif. 1982); C. Carey, *A commentary on five odes of Pindar* (New York 1981). *Scholia.* A. B. Drachmann, 3 vols. (BT, 1903–27: repr. Amsterdam 1964).

TRANSLATIONS: C. M. Bowra (Harmondsworth, 1969); F. J. Nisetich, *Pindar's victory songs* (Baltimore & London 1980).

STUDIES: (1) GENERAL: U. von Wilamowitz-Moellendorff, *Pindaros* (Berlin 1922); W. Schadewaldt, *Der Aufbau des pindarischen Epinikion* (Halle 1928); G. Norwood, *Pindar* (Berkeley & Los Angeles 1945); F. Schwenn, 'Pindaros', *RE* XX.2 (1950) 1606–97; J. Duchemin, *Pindare, poète et prophète* (Paris 1955); E. L. Bundy, *Studia Pindarica* (Berkeley & Los Angeles 1962); C. M. Bowra, *Pindar* (Oxford 1964); A.

Köhnken, *Die Funktion des Mythos bei Pindar* (Berlin & New York 1971); J. Peron, *Les images maritimes de Pindare* (Paris 1974); H. Fränkel, *Early Greek poetry and philosophy*, tr. M. Hadas and J. Willis (New York & London 1975) 425–504; G. F. Gianotti, *Per una poetica pindarica* (Turin 1975); K. Crotty, *Song and action: the victory odes of Pindar* (Baltimore & London 1982). (2) INDIVIDUAL WORKS: R. W. B. Burton, *Pindar's Pythian Odes* (Oxford 1962); D. C. Young, *Three odes of Pindar*, Mnemosyne suppl. IX (1968: *Pyth.* 3, 11, *Ol.* 7); idem, *Pindar Isthmian 7, Myth and example*, *Mnemosyne* suppl. XV (1971); C. Carey, 'Three myths in Pindar: *Nem.* 4, *Ol.* 9, *Nem.* 3', *Eranos* 78 (1980) 143–62. (3) MISCELLANIES: (edd.) W. C. Calder and J. Stern, *Pindaros und Bakchylides*, Wege der Forschung CXXXIV (Darmstadt 1970). (4) MSS: A. Turyn, *De codicibus Pindaricis* (Cracow 1932); J. Irigoin, *Histoire du texte de Pindare* (Paris 1952).

LEXICON: W. J. Slater (Berlin 1969).

BACCHYLIDES

LIFE

b. *c.* 510 B.C. at Iulis in Ceos; nephew of Simonides, contemporary and rival of Pindar. Early activities unknown. Invited by Hieron to Syracuse mid-470s and celebrated his host's Olympian victory of 468 (*Ode* 3). Exiled from Ceos to Peloponnese, perhaps in 460s (possible date of *Ode* 9 and *Dith.* 20). Composed *Odes* 1 and 2 between 464 and 454, 6 and 7 (latest dated poems) in 452. d. *c.* 450 (despite Euseb. *Chron. Ol.* 87.2). Sources: Suda, *Et. Magn.* 582.20, Strabo 10.486, *Chron. Pasch.* 162b, Euseb. *Chron. Ol.* 78.2, 82.2 (dates and antecedents); Ael. *V.H.* 4.15 (Sicily); Plut. *De exil.* 14.605c–d (exile); schol. on Pind. *Ol.* 2.154ff., *Pyth.* 2.97, 131a, 132c, 163b, 166d, *Nem.* 3.143 (rivalry with Pindar; cf. 'Longinus', *Subl.* 33.5); *IG²* XII 5 608 = Dittenberger *SIG³* 1057; *P. Oxy.* 222 (dated poems). See J. M. Edmonds, *Lyra Graeca* III (Loeb, 1927) 80–6; A. Severyns, *Bacchylide. Essai biographique* (Liège & Paris 1933).

WORKS

(1) EXTANT: Substantial papyrus fragments of *Epinicia* and *Dithyrambs*, several between 100 and 200 lines long and virtually complete; two dedicatory epigrams (*Anth. Pal.* 6.53 and 313). Three poems (13, 5, 4) celebrate same victories as odes of Pindar (*Nem.* 5, 485 or 483; *Ol.* 1, 476, *Pyth.* 1, 470). (2) LOST: Hymns, paeans, prosodia (processionals), partheneia (maiden-songs; Ps.-Plut. *De mus.* 17.1136f.), hyporchemata (dance-songs), encomia, erotica.

BIBLIOGRAPHY

(For 1952–75 see D. E. Gerber, *C.W.* 61 (1967/8) 384–6 and 70 (1976/7) 125–30.)

TEXTS AND COMMENTARIES: TEXTS: B. Snell, 10th ed. rev. H. Maehler (BT, 1970: with bibliography and *index verborum*). COMMENTARIES: F. G. Kenyon (London 1897); R. C. Jebb (Cambridge 1905); D. A. Campbell, *Greek lyric poetry* (London 1967: repr. Bristol 1982: selection); H. Maehler, with German tr. (Leiden 1982).

TRANSLATIONS: R. Fagles (New Haven 1961).

STUDIES: A. Körte, 'Bacchylidea', *Hermes* 53 (1918) 113–47; idem, 'Bakchylides', *RE* suppl. IV (1924) 58–67; B. Gentili, *Bacchilide. Studi* (Urbino 1958); A. Parry, 'Introduction' in Fagles under *Translations* above; G. M. Kirkwood, 'The narrative art of Bacchylides', in (ed.) L. Wallach, *The classical tradition: literary and historical studies in honor of Harry Caplan* (Ithaca, N.Y. 1966) 98–114; (edd.) W. M. Calder and J. Stern, *Pindaros und Bakchylides*, Wege der Forschung CXXXIV (Darmstadt 1970); M. Lefkowitz, *The victory ode* (Park Ridge, N.J. 1976); C. Segal, 'Bacchylides reconsidered: epithets and the dynamics of lyric narrative', *Q.U.C.C.* 22 (1976) 99–130; J. Peron, 'Les mythes de Crésus et Méléagre dans les Odes III et V de Bacchylide', *R.E.G.* 91 (1978) 307–39; C. Segal, 'The myth of Bacchylides 17: heroic quest and heroic identity', *Eranos* 77 (1979) 23–37.

CORINNA

LIFE

According to Suda a pupil of Myrtis and contemporary of Pindar, whom she defeated five times, b. in Thebes or Tanagra. Date in 5th c. much contested: not mentioned before second half of 1st c. B.C. (Antipater of Thessalonica, *Anth. Pal.* 9.26), nor in the Alexandrian canon of lyric poets; late authors and scholia add her as a tenth. To Propertius (2.3.19–21) she is *antiqua Corinna*, vaguely associated with Sappho; but Statius (*Silv.* 5.3.156–8) brackets her with Callimachus and Lycophron (though also Sophron): *tenuisque arcana Corinnae*. In fr. 664a *PMG* she criticizes Myrtis for vying with Pindar, but this need not mean she is contemporary with either. The orthography of the longest fragment, the Berlin Papyrus (654 *PMG*; see under *Works*) belongs to the latter part of the 3rd c. B.C. Either C. wrote then or else her poems, if she wrote in the 5th c., were transliterated then into the current spelling. Sources: brief biography in Suda; fr. 655.3 *PMG*, Paus. 9.22.3, Ael. *V.H.* 13.25, Plut. *Glor. Athen.* 4.347f., schol. on Ar. *Ach.* 720 (Tanagran citizenship, relationship to Pindar); schol. on Pind. *proem.* 1.11.20ff. Drachmann, Tzetzes, *Prol. ad Lycophron.* p. 2.3ff. Scheer, *CGF* 35.19.22 (added to canon of lyric poets).

WORKS

Five books (Suda), possibly called Ϝεροῖα 'Tales' or 'Narratives' (cf. D. L. Clayman, *C.Q.* n.s.28 (1978) 396f.): frs. 655.ii, 656, 657 *PMG*. Titles of other works on mythical subjects, mainly Boeotian, including *Seven against Thebes*, *Iolaus*, perhaps *Orestes* (690 *PMG*). Main texts: 654 *PMG* (*P. Berol.* 284): two long narrative fragments, one on a singing contest between Helicon and Cithaeron, the other on the daughters of Asopus; 655 *PMG* (*P. Oxy.* 2370): some twenty lines, perhaps from the Ϝεροῖα (line 2), a first-person description of her poetry. Dialect: the artificial literary language common to Greek lyric, but with an admixture of Boeotian vernacular. Metres: choriambic dimeter, glyconic, pherecratean, of rather simple type, rather more characteristic of Hellenistic than of archaic style: see Page under *Commentaries* below, 61f., 87f. For other indications of possible later date in prosody see E. Lobel, *Hermes* 65 (1930) 362f.

BIBLIOGRAPHY

(See D. E. Gerber, *C.W.* 61 (1967/8) 329–30 and 70 (1976/7) 130.)

TEXTS AND COMMENTARIES: TEXTS: *PMG*. COMMENTARIES: D. L. Page (London 1953: repr. 1963); D. A. Campbell, *Greek lyric poetry* (London 1967: repr. Bristol 1982) 103–6 and 408–13; D. E. Gerber, *Euterpe* (Amsterdam 1970) 391–400.

STUDIES: U. von Wilamowitz-Moellendorff, *Die Textgeschichte der griechischen Lyriker*, *Abh. Göttingen* phil.-hist. Klasse n.s.4.3 (1900) 21–3; P. Maas, *RE* XI.2 (1922) 1393–7; E. Lobel, 'Corinna', *Hermes* 65 (1930) 356–65; C. M. Bowra, 'The daughters of Asopus', *Problems in Greek poetry* (Oxford 1953) 54–65; D. L. Page, *Corinna* (London 1953: repr. 1963); A. E. Harvey, 'A note on the Berlin papyrus of Corinna', *C.Q.* n.s.5 (1955) 176–80; G. M. Bolling, 'Notes on Corinna', *A.J.Ph.* 77 (1956) 282–7; K. Latte, 'Die Lebenszeit der Korinna', *Eranos* 54 (1956) 57–67; P. Guillon, 'Corinne et les oracles béotiens: la consultation d'Asopus', *B.C.H.* 82 (1958) 47–60; idem, 'À propos de Corinne', *Annales de la Faculté de Lettres d'Aix* 33 (1959) 155–68; C. M. Bowra, *Pindar* (Oxford 1964) 279–81; Lesky 178–80; M. L. West, 'Corinna', *C.Q.* n.s.20 (1970) 277–87; A. Allen and J. Frel, 'A date for Corinna', *C.J.* 68 (1972) 26–30; G. M. Kirkwood, *Early Greek monody* (Ithaca, N.Y. & London 1974) 185–93, 278–80; C. P. Segal, 'Pebbles in golden urns: the date and style of Corinna', *Eranos* 73 (1975) 1–8; D. L. Clayman, 'The meaning of Corinna's Ϝεροῖα', *C.Q.* n.s.28 (1978) 396–7; J. Ebert, 'Zu Korinnas Gedicht vom Wettstreit zwischen Helikon und Kithairon', *Z.P.E.* 30 (1978) 5–12.

EARLY GREEK PHILOSOPHY

GENERAL WORKS

Standard text of all authors discussed in this chapter and numbering of fragments is by DK = H. Diels and W. Kranz, *Die Fragmente der Vorsokratiker* I–II, 6th ed. (Berlin 1951–2) and later editions; this includes German translation and extensive testimonia. Vol. III is a comprehensive word index. Fragments in this edition are translated into English by K. Freeman, *Ancilla to the Pre-Socratic philosophers* (Oxford 1956).

STUDIES

(1) Books which include general appraisals or comprehensive studies of authors discussed in the chapter.

Barnes, J., *The Presocratic philosophers*, 2 vols. (London 1979)

Burnet, J., *Early Greek philosophy*, 4th ed. (London 1930)

Gigon, O., *Der Ursprung der griechischen Philosophie*, 2nd ed. (Basel & Stuttgart 1968)

Guthrie I (Cambridge 1962: Xenophanes and Heraclitus); II (Cambridge 1965: Parmenides to Democritus)

Hussey, E., *The Presocratics* (London 1972)

Kirk, G. S., Raven, J. E., and Schofield, M. *The Presocratic philosophers*, 2nd ed. (Cambridge 1983: incl. principal texts and tr.)

Zeller, E., *Die Philosophie der Griechen* I 1, 7th ed. (Leipzig 1923: Xenophanes and Parmenides); I 2, 6th ed. rev. W. Nestle (Leipzig 1920: Heraclitus to Democritus)

idem and Mondolfo, R., *La filosofia dei Greci nel suo sviluppo storico* I 3, *Gli Eleati*, ed. G. Reale (Florence 1967); I 4, *Eraclito*, ed. R. Mondolfo (Florence 1961); I 5, *Empedocle, Atomisti, Anassagora*, ed. A. Capizzi (Florence 1969)

(2) Books which include specialized discussions of all or most authors.

Allen, R. E. and Furley, D. J. (edd.), *Studies in Presocratic philosophy*, 2 vols. (London 1970–5)

Fränkel, H., *Wege und Formen frühgriechischen Denkens*, 2nd ed. (Munich 1960)

Hölscher, U., *Anfängliches Fragen* (Göttingen 1968)

Mourelatos, A. P. D. (ed.), *The Pre-Socratics* (New York 1974)

(3) Background studies and books which deal with particular aspects.

Cornford, F. M., *Principium sapientiae* (Cambridge 1952)

Dodds, E. R., *The Greeks and the irrational* (Berkeley & Los Angeles 1951)

Fränkel, H., *Early Greek poetry and philosophy*, tr. M. Hadas and J. Willis (New York & London 1975)

Jaeger, W., *The theology of the early Greek philosophers* (Oxford 1947)

Kahn, C. H., *Anaximander and the origins of Greek cosmology* (New York 1960)

idem, *The verb 'Be' in ancient Greek* (Dordrecht 1973)

Lloyd, G. E. R., *Early Greek science from Thales to Aristotle* (London 1970) idem, *Polarity and analogy. Two types of argumentation in early Greek thought* (Cambridge 1966)

Lloyd-Jones, H., *The justice of Zeus* (Berkeley & Los Angeles 1971)

Nilsson, M. P., *A history of Greek religion*, 2nd ed. tr. F. J. Fielden (New York 1964)

Sambursky, S., *The physical world of the Greeks* (London 1956)

Snell, B., *The discovery of the mind: the Greek origins of European thought*, tr. T. G. Rosenmeyer (Oxford 1953)

West, M. L., *Early Greek philosophy and the Orient* (Oxford 1971)

XENOPHANES

LIFE

b. *c.* 570 B.C., son of Dexius or Orthomenes, at Colophon on the Ionian mainland. After Cyrus' conquest of Lydia 545 lived an itinerant life in various cities, incl. Zancle and Catana in Sicily, for at least another sixty-seven years. Regarded in antiquity as founder of Eleatic philosophy and as teacher of Parmenides. d. *c.* 470 B.C. Sources: frs. 1–3, 8; Diog. Laert. 9.18–21; Clem. Alex. *Strom.* 1.64; Plato, *Soph.* 242d; Arist. *Metaph.* A5, 986b18; others in DK 21A.

WORKS

About 120 verses preserved. Over half are elegiacs and one poem (fr. 1) may be complete. Others, apart from one iambic trimeter (fr. 14.1), are hexameters. Some of these are quoted from the *Silloi* (squint-eyed verses) or *Parodies*, and by late antiquity at least five books of *Silloi* were credited to him (fr. 21a); Proclus says that they were directed 'against all philosophers and poets' (DK 21A 22; cf. Diog. Laert. 9.18). The other extant lines may also come from this work, although certain fragments may belong to a poem entitled *On nature* in Hellenistic period (for this view see H. Diels, *A.G.Ph.* 1897, 530–5 and K. Deichgräber, *Rh.M.* 87 (1938) 1–31; against, under *General works* (1) and (3) for 'Early Greek Philosophy', Burnet 115f. and Jaeger 40, n.11, 210). X. is also said to have written 2,000 verses on the foundations of Colophon and Elea (Diog. Laert. 9.20). Views attributed to X. by author of *On Melissus, Xenophanes, Gorgias* (in Aristotelian corpus) were probably compiled 1st c. B.C. and are generally discredited as a source.

BIBLIOGRAPHY

(For 1957–70 see J. Wiesner, *A.A.H.G.* 30 (1972) 1–15.)

TEXTS AND COMMENTARIES: TEXTS: Diehl I, 3rd ed. (1954) 63–74; *IEG* II 163–70; J. M. Edmonds, *Elegy and iambus* I (Loeb, 1931) 182–215. COMMENTARIES: M. Untersteiner (Florence 1955: with Italian tr.).

STUDIES: (1) GENERAL: C. M. Bowra, *Early Greek elegists* (London 1938) 105–36; K. von Fritz, *RE* IXA.2 (1967) 1541–62. (2) MORE SPECIALIZED: C. M. Bowra, 'Xenophanes on songs at feasts', in *Problems in Greek poetry* (London 1953) 1–14 and 'Xenophanes and the Olympic games', ibid. 15–37; J. Defradas, 'Le banquet de Xénophane', *R.E.G.* 75 (1962) 344–65; E. Heitsch, 'Das Wissen des Xenophanes', *Rh.M.* 109 (1966) 193–235; P. Steinmetz, 'Xenophanes-Studien', ibid. 13–73; D. Babut, 'Xénophane critique des poètes', *A.C.* 43 (1974) 83–117. See also *General works* for 'Early Greek Philosophy'.

PARMENIDES

LIFE

b. *c.* 515 B.C., son of Pyres, at Elea in southern Italy. Probably a wealthy man of noble birth who had some association in his youth with Xenophanes and with Ameinias, a Pythagorean, in whose honour he built a shrine. Is said to have acted as legislator for Elea (Speusippus fr. 1). d. *c.* 449–440 B.C. Sources: Diog. Laert. 9.21–3; Suda; Plato, *Parm.* 127a–c; others in DK 28A.

WORKS

Hexameter poem of which 154 lines survive, the longest continuous section through a single quotation by Simplicius in his commentary on Arist. *Phys.* (144.26). The work had three parts: a prooemium of thirty-two lines (all but last two quoted by Sext. Emp. *Adv. math.* 7.111ff.); the 'Way of truth' (seventy-six lines survive, perhaps nine-tenths of original); the 'Way of seeming' (forty-four complete lines attested, six in Latin version by Caelius Aurelianus; perhaps only a tenth of original). Whole poem entitled *On nature* in later antiquity and the description may be P.'s own (see Hölscher under *Texts* below, 68).

BIBLIOGRAPHY

(For 1957–70 see H. Schwabl, *A.A.H.G.* 30 (1972) 15–43.)

TEXTS AND COMMENTARIES (all with tr.): J. Zafiropulo, *L'école éléate* (Paris 1950); M. Untersteiner (Florence 1958); L. Tarán (Princeton 1965); U. Hölscher (Frankfurt am Main 1969); K. Bormann (Hamburg 1971).

STUDIES: H. Diels, *Parmenides' Lehrgedicht* (Berlin 1897); W. J. Verdenius, *Parmenides: some comments on his poem* (Groningen 1942); K. Reinhardt, *Parmenides und die Geschichte der griechischen Philosophie*, 2nd ed. (Frankfurt 1959); G. E. L. Owen, 'Eleatic questions', *C.Q.* n.s.10 (1960) 84–102, repr. in Allen and Furley II, under *General works* (2) for 'Early Greek Philosophy'; J. Mansfeld, *Die Offenbarung des*

Parmenides und die menschliche Welt (Assen 1964); A. P. D. Mourelatos, *The route of Parmenides* (New Haven & London 1970); J. Jantzen, *Parmenides zum Verhältnis von Sprache und Wirklichkeit* (Munich 1976). See also *General works* for 'Early Greek Philosophy'.

EMPEDOCLES

LIFE

b. *c.* 492 B.C., son of Meton, a wealthy aristocrat, at Acragas in Sicily. Probably associated with Pythagoreans whose doctrines, together with Parmenides', were the most decisive influence on his thought. Supported democracy at Acragas and declined offer of the kingship. Enjoyed great reputation as orator, doctor, and wonder-worker. Sources: frs. 112–14; Diog. Laert. 8.51–77 (citing many Hellenistic sources); Suda; Arist. *Metaph.* A3, 984a11; others in DK 31A.

WORKS

Fragments from two poems preserved, *On nature* (3 bks) and *Purifications* (2 bks; see M. L. West, *Maia* 20 (1968) 199), which together comprised 5,000 lines. All the fragments (about 450 lines) belong to one or the other poem (van der Ben under *Texts* below, 7–9). In 1901 Diels assigned about 100 lines of the surviving material to the *Purifications*, and his attributions have largely been accepted. But only seventeen lines (frs. 112–14) certainly belong to this poem and van der Ben has argued that the other fragments so assigned by Diels form part of the prooemium to *On nature*. It is too soon to judge the effects of this radical view, but it must be said that the tone and subject of the traditional *Purifications* fragments are markedly different from the material previously assigned to *On nature*. For lost and spurious works see Guthrie (1965) under *General works* (1) for 'Early Greek Philosophy', 135 n.1.

BIBLIOGRAPHY

(Up to 1965 see D. O'Brien, *Empedocles' cosmic cycle* (Cambridge 1969) 337–402.)

TEXTS AND COMMENTARIES (all with tr.): E. Bignone (Turin 1916); J. Bollack, 3 vols. in 4 without as yet the *Purifications* (Paris 1965–9); M. R. Wright (New Haven & London 1981); N. van der Ben, *The proem of Empedocles' Peri physeos. Thirty-one fragments* (Amsterdam 1975). Ed. of *Purifications* only by G. Zuntz in *Persephone* (Oxford 1971).

STUDIES: C. M. Millerd, *On the interpretation of Empedocles* (Chicago 1908); A. Traglia, *Studi sulla lingua di Empedocle* (Bari 1952); D. J. Furley, 'Variations on themes from Empedocles in Lucretius' proem', *B.I.C.S.* 17 (1970) 55–74; C. H. Kahn,

'Religion and natural philosophy in Empedocles' doctrine of the soul', in Mourelatos under *General works* (2) for 'Early Greek Philosophy', 426–56; A. A. Long, 'Empedocles' cosmic cycle in the sixties', ibid. 397–425. See also *General works* for 'Early Greek Philosophy'.

HERACLITUS

LIFE

b. *c.* 540 B.C., son of Bloson (or Herakon), at Ephesus. Surrendered his right to hereditary 'kingship' to his brother. His writings prove he had the greatest contempt for the Ephesians. Alleged to have withdrawn from society out of misanthropy. This and most other anecdotes about him are probably inferences from his own words. d. *c.* 480 B.C. Sources: Diog. Laert. 9.1–17; Suda; Strabo 14 pp. 632–3C; others in DK 22A.

WORKS

Collection of about 120 short apophthegms, quoted particularly by writers of Christian era. From Aristotle onwards (*Rhet.* 1407b11) reference is made to the 'writings' or 'book' of H., but it has been suggested that this was a collection of oral statements compiled after his death (so Kirk under *Commentaries* below, 7). Even if H. wrote down his sayings in their extant form, his book is likely to have been a series of pithy statements, only loosely linked together. Fr. 1 has a complex periodic structure and was probably designed as an introduction to the individual statements.

BIBLIOGRAPHY

(See E. N. Roussos, *Heraklit Bibliographie* (Darmstadt 1971).)

TEXTS AND COMMENTARIES (all with tr.): TEXTS: I. Bywater (Oxford 1877). COMMENTARIES: G. S. Kirk, *Heraclitus: the cosmic fragments*, corrected repr. (Cambridge 1962); M. Marcovich (Mérida 1967); J. Bollack and H. Wismann, *Héraclite ou la séparation* (Paris 1972); R. Mondolfo and L. Tarán, *Eraclito. Testimonianze e imitazioni* (Florence 1972); C. H. Kahn, *The art and thought of Heraclitus* (Cambridge 1979).

STUDIES: G. Vlastos, 'On Heraclitus', *A.J.Ph.* 76 (1955) 337–68, repr. in part in Allen and Furley under *General works* (2) for 'Early Greek Philosophy', I 413–29; C. Ramnoux, *Héraclite ou l'homme entre les choses et les mots* (Paris 1959); K. Axelos, *Héraclite et la philosophie* (Paris 1962); C. H. Kahn, 'A new look at Heraclitus', *American Philosophical Quarterly* I (1964) 189–203; M. Marcovich, *RE* suppl. X (1965) 246–320. See also *General works* for 'Early Greek Philosophy'.

ANAXAGORAS

LIFE

b. *c.* 500 B.C., son of Hegesibulus, at Clazomenae on the Ionian coast. Spent about thirty years in Athens, probably between 480 and 430. Friend of Pericles, and perhaps also acquainted with Euripides. Prosecuted for impiety by Cleon *c.* 433–430 and left Athens for Lampsacus, where he d. *c.* 428 B.C. Sources: Diog. Laert. 2.6–15; Suda; Plato, *Phdr.* 270a; Plut. *Per.* 4.4, 8.1, 16.5–7; others in DK 59A.

WORKS

A 'single treatise' (so Diog. Laert. 1.16), known later as *On nature.* Sixteen passages from its 'first book' are quoted by Simplicius, all but one in his commentary on Aristotle's *Physics;* other writers preserve a few further lines. The whole work could be bought for a drachma in 399 (Plato, *Apol.* 26d), and a substantial part of its opening is probably contained in the extant fragments. The lost books attributed to A. on squaring the circle, on scene-painting and perspective, and on problems (DK 59A 38–40), may all be spurious.

BIBLIOGRAPHY

(Up to 1970 see C. J. Classen, *RE* suppl. XII (1970) 28–30.)

TEXTS AND COMMENTARIES: D. Lanza (Florence 1966: with Italian tr.)

STUDIES: K. Deichgräber, 'Hymnische Elemente in der philosophischen Prosa der Vorsokratiker', *Philologus* 88 (1933) 347–61; O. Gigon, 'Zu Anaxagoras', *Philologus* 91 (1936) 1–41; J. Zafiropulo, *Anaxagore de Clazomène* (Paris 1948); G. Vlastos, 'The physical theory of Anaxagoras', *Ph.R.* 59 (1950) 31–57; J. A. Davison, 'Protagoras, Democritus, and Anaxagoras', *C.Q.* n.s.3 (1953) 33–45; M. C. Stokes, 'On Anaxagoras', *A.G.Ph.* 47 (1965) 1–19, 217–50; W. Burkert, 'La genèse des choses et des mots. Le papyrus de Derveni entre Anaxagore et Cratyle', *E.Ph.* 25 (1970) 443–55; M. Schofield, *An essay on Anaxagoras* (Cambridge 1980). See also *General works* for 'Early Greek Philosophy'.

MELISSUS

LIFE

b. *c.* 485 B.C., son of Ithagenes, at Samos. Statesman and admiral of that city, defeating Athenians in naval battle 441/40. Pupil or follower of Parmenides. Sources: Diog. Laert. 9.24; Suda; Plut. *Per.* 26–8.

DEMOCRITUS

WORKS

A book entitled, according to Simplicius (DK 30A 4), 'On nature or On what is'. Eight passages are quoted by Simplicius, all but one in his commentary on Aristotle's *Physics*. Further evidence about M. in pseudo-Aristotelian treatise, *On Melissus, Xenophanes, Gorgias*.

BIBLIOGRAPHY

TEXTS AND COMMENTARIES: G. Reale (Florence 1970: with tr.).

STUDIES: See *General works* for 'Early Greek Philosophy'.

DEMOCRITUS

LIFE

b. *c.* 460 B.C., son of Hegisistratus (or Athenocritus or Damasippus), at Abdera in Thrace. Follower of Leucippus and possibly associate of Anaxagoras. Travelled widely, probably to Egypt and perhaps as far as India. Known in Roman world as 'the laughing philosopher'. Date of death unknown. Sources: Diog. Laert. 9.34–49 (incl. catalogue of writings); Suda; others in DK 68A.

WORKS

Over sixty titles attested in Diog. Laert. 9.46–8, most arranged under following headings (classification attributed to Thrasyllus, Librarian at Alexandria early 1st c. A.D.): ethical, physical, mathematical, musical (includes poetry), and technical. A representative sample of titles: *On good humour, On the planets, On colours, Causes concerning sounds, On irrational lines and solids, On poetry, On painting*. No book survives, and number of certain fragments is very small. Most are ethical maxims, preserved in the anthology of Stobaeus who records about 130 under D.'s name. A further eighty-six short aphorisms (many the same as in this anthology) are listed in two MSS of Stobaeus as 'The golden sayings of Democrates the philosopher'. Transmission of these is independent of Stobaeus himself (see DK 11 154) and it has been widely assumed that Democrates equals D. On authenticity of ethical fragments see Guthrie (1965) under *General works* (1) for 'Early Greek Philosophy', 489ff. and bibliography cited there; M. L. West, *C.R.* n.s.19 (1969) 142. Aristotle is the best source for D.'s philosophy.

BIBLIOGRAPHY

TEXTS AND COMMENTARIES: S. Luria (Leningrad 1970: in Russian).

STUDIES: P. Natorp, *Die Ethica des Demokrits* (Berlin 1893); C. Bailey, *The Greek Atomists and Epicurus* (Oxford 1928); E. A. Havelock, *The liberal temper in Greek politics* (Cambridge, Mass. 1962) 125–54; T. Cole, *Democritus and the sources of Greek anthropology* (Cleveland, Ohio 1967); D. J. Furley, *Two studies in the Greek Atomists* (Princeton 1967); H. Steckel, *RE* suppl. XII (1970) 191–223. See also *General works* for 'Early Greek Philosophy'.

TRAGEDY

GENERAL WORKS

(1) Bibliography

Lesky, *TDH*

Webster, T. B. L., *G.&R.* New surveys in the classics v (1971)

(2) Tragedy in general

Baldry, H. C., *The Greek tragic theatre* (London 1971)

Buxton, R. G. A., *Persuasion in Greek tragedy* (Cambridge 1982)

von Fritz, K., *Antike und moderne Tragödie* (Berlin 1962)

Garton, C., 'Characterization in Greek tragedy', *J.H.S.* 77 (1957) 247–54

Gould, J., 'Dramatic character and "human intelligibility" in Greek tragedy', *P.C.Ph.S.* n.s.24 (1978) 43–63

Jones, J., *On Aristotle and Greek tragedy* (London 1962)

Kitto, H. D. F., *Greek tragedy*, 3rd ed. (London 1961)

idem, *Form and meaning in drama* (London 1956)

Knox, B. W. M., *Word and action: essays on the ancient theater* (Baltimore 1979)

Lattimore, R., *The poetry of Greek tragedy* (Baltimore 1958)

idem, *Story patterns in Greek tragedy* (London 1964)

Lesky, A., *Greek tragedy*, 2nd ed. (London 1967)

idem, *TDH*

Lloyd-Jones, H., *The justice of Zeus* (Berkeley & Los Angeles 1971)

Lucas, D. W., *The Greek tragic poets*, 2nd ed. (London 1959)

Pohlenz, M., *Die griechische Tragödie*, 2nd ed. (Göttingen 1954)

de Romilly, J., *L'évolution du pathétique d'Éschyle à Euripide* (Paris 1961)

eadem, *Time in Greek tragedy* (Ithaca, N.Y. 1968)

eadem, *La tragédie grecque* (Paris 1970)

Seeck, G. A. (ed.), *Das griechische Drama* (Darmstadt 1979)

Snell, B., *Scenes from Greek drama* (Berkeley & Los Angeles 1964)

Steidle, W., *Studien zum antiken Drama* (Munich 1968)

Taplin, O. P., *Greek tragedy in action* (London 1978)

Vernant, J.-P. and Vidal-Naquet, P., *Mythe et tragédie en Grèce ancienne* (Paris 1973), English tr. by J. Lloyd (Brighton 1981)

Vickers, B., *Towards Greek tragedy* (London 1973)

Yale Classical Studies 25 (1977) ed. T. F. Gould and C. J. Herington

(3) Text, form, metre

Dale, A. M., *The lyric metres of Greek drama*, 2nd ed. (Cambridge 1968)

eadem, *Metrical analyses of tragic choruses*, fasc. I, *B.I.C.S.* suppl. XXI.1 (1971); fasc. II, *B.I.C.S.* suppl. XXI.2 (1981)

Duchemin, J., L'ἀγών *dans la tragédie grecque* (Paris 1945)

Jackson, J., *Marginalia scaenica* (Oxford 1955)

Jens, W. (ed.), *Die Bauformen der griechischen Tragödie* (Munich 1971)

Kranz, W., *Stasimon* (Berlin 1933)

Kraus, W., *Strophengestaltung in der griechischen Tragödie*, *S.A.W.W.* 231.4 (1957)

Nestle, W., *Die Struktur des Eingangs in der attischen Tragödie* (Stuttgart 1930: repr. Hildesheim 1967)

Page, D. L., *Actors' interpolations in Greek tragedy* (Oxford 1934)

Schadewaldt, W., *Monolog und Selbstgespräch* (Berlin 1926)

ORIGINS OF TRAGEDY

BIBLIOGRAPHY

(1) GENERAL: *DTC* (1st *and* 2nd edd.); H. Patzer, *Die Anfänge der griechischen Tragödie* (Wiesbaden 1962); G. F. Else, *The origin and early form of Greek tragedy* (Cambridge, Mass. 1965); A. Lesky, *Greek tragedy*, 2nd ed. (London 1967) chs. II–III; W. Burkert, 'Greek tragedy and sacrificial ritual', *G.R.B.S.* 7 (1966) 87–121; H. Lloyd-Jones, 'Problems of early Greek tragedy: Pratinas, Phrynichus, the Gyges fragment', *Estudios sobre la tragedia griega*, Cuaderno de la Fundación Pastor XIII (Madrid 1966); Lesky, *TDH* chs. I–III; F. R. Adrados, *Festival, comedy and tragedy: the Greek origins of theatre* (Leiden 1975). (2) THESPIS: *DTC* 69–89; Lesky, *TDH* 49–56. (3) PRATINAS, PHRYNICHUS: *DTC* 63–8; M. Pohlenz, 'Das Satyrspiel und Pratinas von Phleius', *Kleine Schriften* II (Hildesheim 1965) 473; Lesky, *TDH* 57–64. (4) GYGES FRAGMENT: E. Lobel, 'A Greek historical drama', *P.B.A.* 35 (1950) 3–12; D. L. Page, *A new chapter in the history of Greek tragedy* (Cambridge 1951): for bibliography see Lesky, *TDH* 536 n.30; R. A. Pack, *Greek and Latin literary texts from Graeco-Roman Egypt*, 2nd ed. (Ann Arbor 1965) 97 (on no. 1707).

TRAGEDY IN PERFORMANCE

BIBLIOGRAPHY

(1) GENERAL: *DFA*; R. C. Flickinger, *The Greek theater and its drama*, 4th ed. (Chicago 1936); A. W. Pickard-Cambridge, *The theatre of Dionysus in Athens* (Oxford 1946); A. Spitzbarth, *Untersuchungen zur Spieltechnik der griechischen*

Tragödie (Zurich 1946); M. Bieber, *The history of the Greek and Roman theater*, 2nd ed. (Princeton 1961); N. C. Hourmouziades, *Production and imagination in Euripides* (Athens 1965); T. B. L. Webster, *Monuments illustrating tragedy and satyr play*, 2nd ed., *B.I.C.S.* suppl. xx (1967); idem, *Greek theatre production*, 2nd ed. (London 1970); H. C. Baldry, *The Greek tragic theatre* (London 1971); E. Simon, *Das antike Theater* (Heidelberg 1972), tr. C. E. Vafopoulou-Richardson (London 1982); N. G. L. Hammond, 'The conditions of dramatic production to the death of Aeschylus', *G.R.B.S.* 13 (1972) 387–450; S. Melchinger, *Das Theater der Tragödie* (Munich 1974); P. Walcot, *Greek drama in its theatrical and social context* (Cardiff 1976); H.-D. Blume, *Einführung in das antike Theaterwesen* (Darmstadt 1978). (2) FESTIVALS: *DFA* 25–125; H.-J. Mette, *Urkunden dramatischer Aufführungen in Griechenland* (Berlin 1977); H. W. Parke, *Festivals of the Athenians* (London 1977) 104–6, 125–35. (3) THEATRE BUILDING: W. Dörpfeld and E. Reisch, *Das griechische Theater* (Athens 1896); Pickard-Cambridge, *Theatre* 1–74, 134–68; W. B. Dinsmoor, 'The Athenian theater of the fifth century', in *Studies presented to D. M. Robinson* I (St Louis 1951) 309–30; A. M. Dale, 'An interpretation of Aristophanes, *Vesp.* 136–210 and its consequences for the stage of Aristophanes', *J.H.S.* 77 (1957) 205–11 = *Coll. Papers* (Cambridge 1969) 103–18; A. von Gerkan and W. Müller-Wiener, *Das Theater von Epidauros* (Stuttgart 1961); P. Arnott, *Greek scenic conventions in the fifth century B.C.* (Oxford 1962) 1–43; K. J. Dover, 'The skene in Aristophanes', *P.C.Ph.S.* 192 (1966) 2–17; J. Travlos, *Pictorial dictionary of ancient Athens* (London 1971) 537–52; Melchinger, *Theater* 3–49, 82–111, 126–37. (4) STAGE MACHINERY: Pickard-Cambridge, *Theatre* 100–22; Arnott, *Conventions* 72–88; Hourmouziades, *Production* 93–198, 146–69; Melchinger, *Theater* 191–200. (5) PROPERTIES: J. Dingel, *Das Requisit in der griechischen Tragödie* (diss. Tübingen 1967). (6) SCENERY: H. Bulle, *Eine Skenographie*, 94th Winckelmannsprogramm (Berlin 1934); Pickard-Cambridge, *Theatre* 30–74, 122–7; Arnott, *Conventions* 91–106; Hourmouziades, *Production* 35–57; Simon, *Theater* 31–40; Melchinger, *Theater* 162–4. (7) ACTORS: J. B. O'Connor, *Chapters in the history of actors and acting in ancient Greece* (Chicago 1908); B. Hunningher, *Acoustics and acting in the theatre of Dionysus Eleuthereus* (Amsterdam 1956); *DFA* 126–76; P. Ghiron-Bistagne, *Recherches sur les acteurs dans la Grèce antique* (Paris 1976). (8) COSTUMES, MASKS, FOOTWEAR: *DFA* 177–209; Simon, *Theater* 17–31; Melchinger, *Theater* 201–16. (9) PRONOMOS VASE: P. E. Arias, M. Hirmer, B. B. Shefton, *A history of Greek vase painting* (London 1962) 377–80; F. Brommer, 'Zur Deutung der Pronomosvase', *A.A.* 1964, 110–14; E. Simon, 'Die "Omphale" des Demetrios', *A.A.* 1971, 199–206; H. Froning, *Dithyrambos und Vasenmalerei in Athen* (Würzburg 1971) 5–15. (10) ACTING AND PRODUCTION: K. Reinhardt, *Aischylos als Regisseur und Theologe* (Berne 1949); W. Steidle, *Studien zum antiken Drama* (Munich 1968); A. M. Dale, 'Seen and unseen on the Greek stage', *W.S.* 69 (1956) 96–106 = *Coll. Papers* 119–29; eadem, 'Interior scenes and illusion in Greek drama', *Coll. Papers* 259–71; O. P. Taplin, 'Significant actions in Sophocles' *Philoctetes*', *G.R.B.S.* 12 (1971) 25–44; D. Bain, *Actors and audience: a study of asides and related conventions in Greek drama* (Oxford 1977); O. Taplin, *The stagecraft of Aeschylus: observations on the dramatic use of exits and entrances in Greek tragedy* (Oxford 1977); D. J. Mastronarde, *Contact and discontinuity: some conventions of speech and action on the Greek tragic stage* (Berkeley & Los Angeles 1979); D. Bain, *Orders, masters and servants in Greek tragedy* (Manchester 1981).

AESCHYLUS

LIFE

b. 525/4 B.C. (?) at Eleusis, of eupatrid family. Fought at Marathon 490 and probably at Salamis; perhaps too at Plataea. Began competing at tragic festivals early in 5th c. and was first victorious in 484. Visited Sicily some time between 472 and 468 (revived *Persae*, produced *Aetnaeae*) and again in 458 or later. d. at Gela 456/5. May have been initiated into Eleusinian mysteries. Total no. of victories given as twenty-eight (Suda) or thirteen (*Life*). Sources: *Marm. Par.* 59 (birth); ibid. 50, *Life* (OCT 331–3), Suda s.v. 'Pratinas' (literary career); *Marm. Par.* 48, schol. on Aesch. *Pers.* 429, Paus. 1.14.5, *Life* 331.10–13 (military career). On his initiation see Lesky, *TDH* 65f., B. M. W. Knox, *The heroic temper* (Berkeley & Los Angeles 1964) 174 n.82; on Sicilian visits C. J. Herington, *J.H.S.* 87 (1967) 74–85; on political sympathies K. J. Dover, *J.H.S.* 77 (1957) 230–7 (*Eum.*); E. R. Dodds, *P.C.Ph.S.* n.s.6 (1960) 19–31 (*Oresteia*); A. J. Podlecki, *The political background of Aeschylean tragedy* (Ann Arbor 1966), reviewed by R. P. Winnington-Ingram, *Gnomon* 39 (1967) 641–6.

WORKS

Suda gives total no. of plays as ninety. A list in the MSS of A. (OCT 335) contains seventy-three titles but is demonstrably incomplete. Eighty-one (perhaps eighty-three) titles survive, but some may be duplicates. Numerals in the *Life* are probably corrupt. (1) EXTANT: Seven tragedies: *Persae* (produced 472), *Septem contra Thebas* (467), *Supplices* (460s: see H. Lloyd-Jones, *A.C.* 33 (1964) 356–74; Garvie, under *Studies* (2) below), *Oresteia* (*Agamemnon, Choephori, Eumenides*: 458), *Prometheus vinctus* (see Griffith, under *Studies* (2) below, 9–13). (2) LOST OR FRAGMENTARY (alphabetical by Greek titles, as in *TGF*: for the satyr plays see D. F. Sutton, *H.S.C.Ph.* 78 (1974) 123–30). *Athamas, Aegyptii, Aetnaeae, Alexander* (sat.? see Sutton 128–9), *Alcmene, Amymone* (sat.), *Argei, Argo, Atalanta, Bacchae, Bassarai* 'Bacchants', *Glaucus* (*pontios* 'of the sea' (sat.?) and *Potnieus* 'the Potnian'), *Danaides*, '*Dikē* play' (sat.), *Dictyulci* 'Net-drawers' (sat.), *Dionysou trophoi* 'Nurses of Dionysus' (sat.?), *Hektoros lytra* 'Ransom of Hector' or *Phryges, Eleusinii, Epigoni, Edoni, Heliades, Heraclidae, Thalamopoioi* 'Bride-chamber builders' (sat.?), *Theoroi* 'Spectators' or *Isthmiastae* 'Those who went to the Isthmia' (sat.), *Threissae, Hiereiai* 'Priestesses', *Ixion, Iphigenia, Cabiri, Callisto, Cares* or *Europa, Cercyon* (sat.), *Kerykes* 'Messengers' (sat.), *Circe* (sat.), *Cressae, Laius, Lemnii, Leon* (sat.). *Lycurgus* (sat.), *Memnon, Myrmidones, Mysi, Neaniskoi* 'Youths', *Nemea, Nereides, Niobe, Xantriai* 'Wool-carders', *Oedipus, Ostologoi* 'Gatherers of bones' (sat.), *Hoplon krisis* 'Judgement of the arms', *Palamedes, Pentheus, Perrhaebides, Penelope, Polydectes, Prometheus* (*lyomenos* 'unbound', *pyrphoros* 'the fire-bearer' and (sat.) *pyrkaeus* 'the fire-kindler'), *Propompoi* 'Escorts', *Proteus* (sat.), *Salaminiae, Semele* or *Hydrophoroi* 'Water-carriers', *Sisyphus* (*drapetes* 'the fugitive' (sat.?) and *petrokylistes* 'the stone-roller' (sat.), *Sphinx* (sat.), *Telephus, Toxotides* 'Archeresses', *Hypsipyle* (sat.?), *Philoctetes, Phineus, Phorcides, Psychagogoi* 'Necromancers', *Psychostasia* 'Weighing of lives', *Orithyia*. For an attempt to group these into trilogies and tetralogies see Mette under *Texts and commentaries* below.

BIBLIOGRAPHY

(See A. Wartelle, *Bibliographie historique et critique d'Éschyle et de la tragédie grecque 1518–1974* (Paris 1978).)

TEXTS AND COMMENTARIES: TEXTS: H. Weil (BT, 1903); U. von Wilamowitz-Moellendorff (Berlin 1914: repr. 1958); H. W. Smyth (Loeb, 1922–6: II rev. H. Lloyd-Jones 1957 to incl. principal papyrus fragments); D. L. Page (OCT, 1972). COMMENTARIES: (1) Complete. P. Groeneboom (Groningen 1928–52: lacks *Supp.*); H. J. Rose, 2 vols. (Amsterdam 1957–8). (2) Individual plays. *Oresteia*: G. Thomson (Cambridge 1938: with tr. and incl. work of W. G. Headlam: rev. ed. Prague 1966, without tr. but with scholia). *Ag.*: E. Fraenkel, 3 vols. (Oxford 1950: with tr.); J. D. Denniston and D. L. Page (Oxford 1957). *Cho.*: U. von Wilamowitz-Moellendorff, *Aischylos Orestie* II (Berlin 1896); T. G. Tucker (Cambridge 1901). *Pers.*: H. D. Broadhead (Cambridge 1960). *P.V.*: G. Thomson (Cambridge 1932: repr. New York 1979); M. Griffith (Cambridge 1983). *Sept.*: T. G. Tucker (Cambridge 1908); G. Italie (Leiden 1950). *Supp.*: J. Vürtheim (Amsterdam 1928); H. Friis Johansen and E. W. Whittle, 3 vols. (Gyldendalske Boghandel 1980). *Dictyulci*: M. Werre deHaas (Leiden 1961). *Fragments. TGF* 3–128; Lloyd-Jones in Loeb II; H.-J. Mette, *Die Fragmente der Tragödien des Aischylos* (Berlin 1959); idem, *Der verlorene Aischylos* (Berlin 1963); idem, *Lustrum* 13 (1968) 513–34 and 18 (1975) 338–44. *Scholia*. O. L. Smith (BT: I, *Oresteia* and *Supp.*, 1976; II 2, *Sept.*, 1982); idem, *Studies in the scholia on Aeschylus. I: The recensions of Demetrius Triclinius, Mnemosyne* suppl. XXXVII (1975). *Pers.*: O. Dähndardt (BT, 1894); (Triclinian scholia) L. Massa Positano (Naples 1948). *P.V.*: C. J. Herington, *Mnemosyne* suppl. XIX (1972).

TRANSLATIONS: (1) PROSE: W. G. and C. E. Ş. Headlam (Bohn, London 1909). *Oresteia*: H. Lloyd-Jones, 3 vols. (Englewood Cliffs, N.J. 1970: with notes: repr. London 1979). *Pers.*: A. Podlecki (Englewood Cliffs, N.J. 1970: with notes). *Sept.*: C. M. Dawson (Englewood Cliffs, N.J. 1970: with notes). (2) VERSE: P. Vellacott (Harmondsworth 1956–61); (ed.) W. Arrowsmith, *The Greek tragedy in new translations* (Oxford: pubd so far: *P.V.*, J. Scully 1975; *Sept.*, A. Hecht and H. H. Bacon 1974; *Supp.*, J. Lembke 1975). *Oresteia*: R. Lattimore (Chicago 1953); R. Fagles (Harmondsworth 1977). *Ag.*: L. MacNeice (London 1936).

STUDIES: (1) GENERAL: U. von Wilamowitz-Moellendorff, *Aischylos Interpretationen* (Berlin 1914); G. Murray, *Aeschylus, the creator of tragedy* (Oxford 1940); G. Thomson, *Aeschylus and Athens* (London 1941); F. Solmsen, *Hesiod and Aeschylus* (Ithaca, N.Y. 1949); K. Reinhardt, *Aischylos als Regisseur und Theologe* (Berne 1949); E. T. Owen, *The harmony of Aeschylus* (Toronto 1952); J. de Romilly, *La crainte et l'angoisse dans le théâtre d'Éschyle* (Paris 1958); R. D. Dawe, 'Inconsistency of plot and character in Aeschylus', *P.C.Ph.S.* n.s.9 (1963) 21–62; C. J. Herington, 'Aeschylus: the last phase', *Arion* 4 (1965) 387–403; H. D. F. Kitto, *Poiesis* (Berkeley & Los Angeles 1966) 33–115; (ed.) M. H. McCall, *Aeschylus: a collection of critical essays* (Englewood Cliffs, N.J. 1972); P. E. Easterling, 'Presentation of character in Aeschylus', *G.&R.* 20 (1973) 3–19; (ed.) H. Hommel, *Aischylos*, 2 vols., Wege der Forschung LXXXVII and CDLXV (Darmstadt 1974); M. Gagarin, *Aeschylean drama* (Berkeley & Los Angeles 1976); O. Taplin, *The stagecraft of Aeschylus: observations on the dramatic use of exits and entrances in Greek tragedy* (Oxford 1977); V. di Benedetto, *L'ideologia del potere e la tragedia greca* (Turin 1978); (ed.) E. G. Schmidt, *Aischylos und Pindar: Studien zu Werk und Nachwirkung* (Berlin 1981); T. G. Rosenmeyer, *The art of Aeschylus* (Berkeley, Los Angeles & London 1982); R. P. Winnington-Ingram, *Studies in Aeschylus* (Cambridge 1983). (2) INDIVIDUAL PLAYS: *Oresteia*: H. D. F. Kitto, *Form and meaning in drama* (London 1956) chs. I–III; E. R. Dodds, 'Morals and politics in the *Oresteia*', *P.C.Ph.S.* n.s.6 (1960) 19–31; A. Lebeck, *The Oresteia: a study in language and structure* (Washington 1971); C. W. Macleod, 'Politics and the *Oresteia*', *J.H.S.* 102 (1982) 124–44. *Cho.*: on *kommos* see W. Schadewaldt, *Hermes* 67 (1932) 312–54; A. Lesky, *S.A.W.W.* 221.3 (1943). *Eum.*: A. L. Brown, 'Some problems in the *Eumenides* of Aeschylus', *J.H.S.* 102 (1982) 26–32. *Pers.*: K. Deichgräber, *N.A.W.G.* 1941; idem, *Der listensinnende Trug des Gottes* (Göttingen 1952); R. Lattimore, 'Aeschylus on the defeat of Xerxes', *Classical studies in honor of W. A. Oldfather* (Urbana, Ill. 1943) 82–93; R. P. Winnington-Ingram, 'Zeus in the *Persae*', *J.H.S.* 93 (1973) 210–19; G. Paduano, *Gli Persiani di Eschilo* (Rome 1978). *P.V.*: C. J. Herington, *The author of the Prometheus Bound* (Austin, Texas 1970); E. R. Dodds, 'The *Prometheus vinctus* and the progress of scholarship', *The ancient concept of progress* (Oxford 1973) 26–44; M. Griffith, *The authenticity of the Prometheus Bound* (Cambridge 1977); idem, 'Aeschylus, Sicily and Prometheus', in (edd.) R. D. Dawe et al., *Dionysiaca* (Cambridge 1978) 105–39; M. L. West, 'The Prometheus trilogy', *J.H.S.* 99 (1979) 130–48; D. J. Conacher, *Aeschylus' Prometheus Bound: a literary commentary* (Toronto 1980). *Sept.* (see Lesky, *TDH* 88 n.23; R. P. Winnington-Ingram, *Y.Cl.S.* 25 (1977) 1–45): K. Wilkens, *Die Interdependenz zwischen Tragödienstruktur und Theologie bei Aischylos* (Munich 1974); W. G. Thalmann, *Dramatic art in Aeschylus' Seven against Thebes* (New Haven & London 1978). On authenticity of closing scene see H. Lloyd-Jones, *C.Q.* n.s.9 (1959) 80–115; E. Fraenkel, *M.H.* 21 (1964) 58–64; R. D. Dawe, *C.Q.* n.s.17 (1967) 16–28; idem, in (edd.) Dawe et al., *Dionysiaca* (Cambridge 1978) 87–103. *Supp.*: R. P. Winnington-Ingram, 'The Danaid trilogy of Aeschylus', *J.H.S.* 81 (1961) 141–52; A. F. Garvie, *Supplices: play and trilogy* (Cambridge 1969). (3) STYLE: C. F. Kumaniecki, *De elocutionis Aeschyleae natura* (Cracow 1935); J. Dumortier, *Les images dans la poésie d'Éschyle* (Paris 1935: repr. 1975); W. B. Stanford, *Aeschylus in his style* (Dublin 1942); F. R. Earp, *The style of Aeschylus* (Cambridge 1948); O. Hiltbrunner, *Wieder-holungs- und Motivtechnik bei Aischlos* (Berne 1950); A. Sideras, *Aeschylus Homericus*, Hypomnemata XXXI (Göttingen 1971); E. Petrounias, *Funktion und Thematik der Bilder bei Aischylos* (Göttingen 1976). (4) TEXT AND TRANSMISSION: A. Turyn, *The manuscript tradition of the tragedies of Aeschylus* (New York 1943); R. D. Dawe, *The collation and investigation of manuscripts of Aeschylus* (Cambridge 1964); idem, *A repertory of conjectures on Aeschylus* (Leiden 1965); A. Wartelle, *Histoire du texte d'Éschyle dans l'antiquité* (Paris 1971). (5) METRE: O. Schroeder, *Aeschyli cantica* (Leipzig 1907).

LEXICA: G. Italie, 2nd ed. (Leiden 1964: addenda by S. Radt); H. Holmboe, 6 vols. (Akademisk Boghandel 1971–3: lacks *Eum.*); H. E. Edinger, *Index analyticus Graecitatis Aeschyleae* (Hildesheim 1981).

SOPHOCLES

LIFE

b. 497/6 or 496/5 B.C. (*Marm. Par.* 56, *FGrH* 239) at Colonus, son of Sophillus. As a boy led paean of celebrations after Salamis. First competed at tragic festival in 468: won 1st prize with Triptolemus, beating Aeschylus (Plut. *Cimon* 8.8). Served as *hellenotamias* 443/2 (*IG* I² 202.36), as *strategos* with Pericles 441/0 (Androtion *FGrH* 324 F 38, Ion of Chios *FGrH* 392 F 6), possibly also with Nicias later (Plut. *Nicias* 15.2); *proboulos* 412/11 (Arist. *Rhet.* 1419a26–31, unless Arist. refers to a different Sophocles). Won 1st prize in 409 with Philoctetes (2nd *Hypoth.*). d. after Dionysia of 406 (*Vit. Eur.* 135.42ff.) and before Lenaea of 405 (Ar. *Frogs* 787ff.). Won eighteen victories at Dionysia = seventy-two plays (*IG* II² 2325). Total no. of victories (i.e. including some at Lenaea) was either twenty (*Life* 8) or twenty-four (Suda). Never placed lower than second. Served on embassies and was prominent in Athenian religious life, esp. in cult of Asclepius (*IG* II² 1252–3). Given posthumous hero cult under name of Dexion (*Et. Magn.* 256.6). Family: wife Nicostrate, son Iophon (tragic poet), concubine Theoris, son Ariston, grandson Sophocles (tragic poet). Sources: S. Radt, *Tragicorum Graecorum fragmenta* IV (Berlin 1977) 29–95. For S.'s political career see V. Ehrenberg, *Sophocles and Pericles* (Oxford 1954); L. Woodbury, *Phoenix* 24 (1970) 209–24; H. C. Avery, *Historia* 22 (1973) 509–14; for the *Life* see J. A. Fairweather, 'Fiction in the biographies of ancient writers', *Anc. Soc.* 5 (1974) 231–75; M. Lefkowitz, *The lives of the Greek poets* (London 1981) 75–87.

WORKS

Suda gives total no. of plays as 123; titles of some 118 are known. (1) EXTANT: Tragedies: *Ajax*, *Antigone* (produced *c.* 442?), *Trachiniae*, *Oedipus tyrannus* (after 429?), *Electra*, *Philoctetes* (409), *Oedipus Coloneus* (posthumously prod. by grandson Sophocles 401). For problems of dating see Lesky, *TDH*, on individual plays; H.-J. Newiger, *G.G.A.* 209 (1967) 175–94. Also K. Schefold, *A.K.* 19 (1976) 71–8 (on *Ajax*); (ed.) P. E. Easterling, *Trachiniae* (Cambridge 1982) 19–23. Satyr play: *Ichneutae* 'Searchers' (substantial fragments). (2) LOST OR FRAGMENTARY (alphabetical by Greek titles, as in *TGF* and Pearson: for the satyr plays see D. F. Sutton, *H.S.C.Ph.* 78 (1974) 130–40). *Admetus* (sat.), *Athamas* A & B, *Ajax Locrus*, *Aegeus*, *Aegisthus*, *Aethiopes*, *Aichmalotides* 'Captives', *Acrisius*, *Aleadae*, *Alexander*, *Aletes*, *Alcmeon*, *Amycus* (sat.), *Amphiaraus* (sat.), *Amphitryon*, *Andromache* (?), *Andromeda*, *Antenoridae*, *Atreus* or *Mycenaeae*, *Achaion syllogos* 'Gathering of the Achaeans', *Achilleos erastai* 'Lovers of Achilles' (sat.), *Daedalus* (sat.), *Danae*, *Dionysiscus* (sat.), *Dolopes*, *Helenes apaitesis* 'Demand for Helen', *Helenes gamos* 'Marriage of Helen' (sat.), *Epigoni* (= *Eriphyle?*), *Eris*, *Hermione*, *Eumelus*, *Euryalus*, *Eurypylus*, *Eurysaces*, *Heracleiscus* (sat.), *Heracles* or *Heracles at Taenarum* (= *Cerberus?*) (sat.), *Erigone*, *Thamyras*, *Theseus*, *Thyestes* A & B, *Iambe* (sat.), *Iberes*, *Inachus* (sat.), *Ixion*, *Iobates*, *Hipponous*, *Iphigenia*, *Camici*, *Cedalion* (sat.), *Clytemnestra*, *Colchides*, *Creusa* (= *Ion?*), *Krisis* (sat.), *Kophoi* 'Dullards' (sat.), *Lacaenae*, *Laocoon*, *Larisaei*, *Lemniae*, *Manteis* 'Seers' or *Polyidus*, *Meleager*, *Momus* (sat.), *Musae* (?), *Nauplius* (*katapleon* 'ashore' and *pyrkaeus* 'the fire-kindler'), *Nausicaa* or *Plyntriai* 'Washerwomen', *Niobe*, *Odysseus akanthoplex* 'wounded by the prickle' or *Niptra* 'Footwashing', *Oecles*, *Oeneus* or *Schoeneus* (sat.: on authorship see p. 772), *Oenomaus*, *Palamedes*, *Pandora* or *Sphyrokopoi* 'Hammerers' (sat.), *Peleus*, *Poimenes* 'Shepherds', *Polyxena*, *Priamus*, *Procris*, *Rhizotomoi* 'Herbalists' or 'Sorcerers', *Salmoneus* (sat.), *Sinon*, *Sisyphus*, *Scythae*, *Scyrii*, *Syndeipnon* 'Banquet' (sat.), *Tantalus*, *Teucer*, *Telephus* (see Sutton 138), *Tereus*, *Triptolemus*, *Troilus*, *Tympanistai* 'Drummers', *Tyndareus*, *Tyro* A & B, *Hybris* (sat.), *Hydrophoroi* 'Water-carriers', *Phaeaces*, *Phaedra*, *Phthiotides*, *Philoctetes at Troy*, *Phineus*, *Phoenix*, *Phrixus*, *Phryges*, *Chryses*. Also paeans (Suda): a fragment is preserved (*PMG* 737). Elegy to Herodotus (Plut. *Mor.* 786b). Prose work *On the chorus* (Athen. 13.603ff.).

BIBLIOGRAPHY

TEXTS AND COMMENTARIES: TEXTS: A. C. Pearson (OCT, 1924: corr. 1928); A. Dain and P. Mazon (Budé, 1955–60); R. D. Dawe (BT, 1975–9). COMMENTARIES: (1) Complete. L. Campbell, 2 vols. (I, 2nd ed., Oxford 1879; II, Oxford 1881); R. C. Jebb (Cambridge 1883 onwards, with tr.: *Aj.* 1896; *Ant.*, 3rd ed., 1900; *El.* 1894; *O.C.*, 3rd ed., 1900; *O.T.*, 3rd ed., 1893; *Phil.*, 2nd ed., 1898; *Tr.* 1892); F. Schneidewin and A. Nauck, rev. E. Bruhn (Berlin: *O.T.* 1910; *El.* 1912; *Ant.* 1913) and L. Radermacher (*O.C.* 1909; *Phil.* 1911; *Aj.* 1913; *Tr.* 1914). (2) Individual plays. *Aj.*: W. B. Stanford (London 1963); J. C. Kamerbeek, 2nd ed. (Leiden 1963); J. de Romilly (Paris 1976). *Ant.*: G. Müller (Heidelberg 1967). *El.*: G. Kaibel (Leipzig 1896); J. H. Kells (Cambridge 1973); J. C. Kamerbeek (Leiden 1974). *O.C.* idem (Leiden 1984). *O.T.*: idem (Leiden 1967); O. Longo (Florence 1972); R. D. Dawe (Cambridge 1982). *Phil.*: T. B. L. Webster (Cambridge 1970); J. C. Kamerbeek (Leiden 1980). *Tr.*: idem (Leiden 1959); O. Longo (Padua 1968); P. E. Easterling (Cambridge 1982). *Ichneutae*: V. Steffen (Warsaw 1960). *Inachus*: D. F. Sutton (Meisenheim am Glan 1979). *Fragments*. *TGF* 131–360; A. C. Pearson, 3 vols. (Cambridge 1917); D. L. Page, *Select papyri* III (Loeb, 1941) 12–53; R. Carden, *The papyrus fragments of Sophocles* (Berlin & New York 1974); S. Radt, *Tragicorum Graecorum fragmenta* IV (Berlin 1977). W. Willige, *Sophokles. Tragödien und Fragmente* (Munich 1966) gives a German tr. of the fragments. *Scholia*. W. Dindorf (Oxford 1852); P. N. Papageorgius (BT, 1888). *Aj.*: G. A. Christodoulou (Athens 1977). *O.C.*: V. de Marco (Rome 1952). *O.T.* (Byzantine scholia): O. Longo (Padua 1971).

TRANSLATIONS: (1) PROSE: *El.*: W. Sale (Englewood Cliffs, N.J. 1973: with notes). *O.T.*: T. Gould (Englewood Cliffs, N.J. 1970: with notes). (2) VERSE: E. F. Watling (Harmondsworth 1947–53); (edd.) D. Grene and R. Lattimore, in *The complete Greek tragedies* (Chicago 1959); R. Fagles and B. M. W. Knox, *Sophocles: the three Theban plays* (New York & London 1982); (ed.) W. Arrowsmith, *The Greek tragedy in new translations* (Oxford: pubd so far: *Ant.*, R. E. Braun 1974; *O.T.*, S. Berg and D. Clay 1978; *Tr.*, C. K. Williams and G. W. Dickerson 1978). *Tr.*: Ezra Pound (London 1956: repr. 1969); R. Torrance (Boston 1966).

STUDIES: (1) SURVEYS: H. Friis Johansen, *Lustrum* 7 (1962) 94–288; (ed.) H. Diller, *Sophokles* (Darmstadt 1967) 537–46 (Literatur-Übersicht); Lesky, *TDH* 169–274; H. Strohm, *A.A.H.G.* 24 (1971) 129–62; 26 (1973) 1–5; 30 (1977) 129–44; R. G. A. Buxton, *G.&R.* New surveys in the classics XVI (1984). (2) GENERAL: T. von Wilamowitz-Moellendorff, *Die dramatische Technik des Sophokles* (Berlin 1917); G. Perrotta, *Sofocle* (Milan 1935: repr. Rome 1963); C. M. Bowra, *Sophoclean tragedy* (Oxford 1944); K. Reinhardt, *Sophokles*, 3rd ed. (Frankfurt am Main 1947), English tr. by H. M. and F. D. Harvey (Oxford 1979); A. J. A. Waldock, *Sophocles the dramatist* (Cambridge 1951); C. H. Whitman, *Sophocles: a study of heroic humanism* (Cambridge, Mass. 1951); G. M. Kirkwood, *A study of Sophoclean drama* (Ithaca, N.Y. 1958); H. Diller, W. Schadewaldt, A. Lesky, *Gottheit und Mensch in der Tragödie des Sophokles* (Darmstadt 1963); A. Maddalena, *Sofocle*, 2nd ed. (Turin 1963); B. M. W. Knox, *The heroic temper* (Berkeley & Los Angeles 1964); R. M. Torrance, 'Sophocles: some bearings', *H.S.C.Ph.* 69 (1965) 269–327; (ed.) T. Woodard, *Sophocles, a collection of critical essays* (Englewood Cliffs, N.J. 1966); (ed.) H. Diller, *Sophokles*, Wege der Forschung XCV (Darmstadt 1967); T. B. L. Webster, *An introduction to Sophocles*, 2nd ed. (London 1969); W. Schadewaldt, *Hellas und Hesperien* I (Zurich & Stuttgart 1970) 369–434; G. H. Gellie, *Sophocles: a reading* (Carlton, Victoria 1972); R. W. B.

Burton, *The chorus in Sophocles' tragedies* (Oxford 1980); R. P. Winnington-Ingram, *Sophocles: an interpretation* (Cambridge 1980); C. Segal, *Tragedy and civilization: an interpretation of Sophocles* (Cambridge, Mass. 1981); A. Machin, *Cohérence et continuité dans le théâtre de Sophocle* (Quebec 1981); D. Seale, *Vision and stagecraft in Sophocles* (London 1982). (3) INDIVIDUAL PLAYS: *Aj.*: B. M. W. Knox, 'The *Ajax* of Sophocles', *H.S.C.Ph.* 65 (1961) 1–37; M. Simpson, 'Sophocles' Ajax: his madness and transformation', *Arethusa* 2 (1969) 88–103; P. Burian, 'Supplication and hero cult in Sophocles' *Ajax*', *G.R.B.S.* 13 (1972) 151–6; M. Sicherl, 'The tragic issue in Sophocles' *Ajax*', *Y.Cl.S.* 25 (1977) 67–98. *Ant.*: R. F. Goheen, *The imagery of Sophocles' Antigone* (Princeton 1951); D. A. Hester, 'Sophocles the unphilosophical', *Mnemosyne* 24 (1971) 11–59; H. Rohdich, *Antigone: Beitrag zu einer Theorie des sophokleischen Helden* (Heidelberg 1980). *El.*: H. Friis Johansen, 'Die *Elektra* des Sophokles: Versuch einer neuen Deutung', *C.&M.* 25 (1964) 8–32; C. P. Segal, 'The *Electra* of Sophocles', *T.A.Ph.A.* 97 (1966) 473–545; H.-J. Newiger, 'Hofmannsthals *Elektra* und die griechische Tragödie', *Arcadia* 4 (1969) 138–63. *O.C.*: I. M. Linforth, 'Religion and drama in "Oedipus at Colonus"', *Univ. of Calif. Publ. in Class. Phil.* 14.4 (1951); P. E. Easterling, 'Oedipus and Polynices', *P.C.Ph.S.* 13 (1967) 1–13; P. Burian, 'Suppliant and saviour: *Oedipus at Colonus*', *Phoenix* 28 (1974) 408–29. *O.T.*: B. M. W. Knox, *Oedipus at Thebes* (New Haven & London 1957); E. R. Dodds, 'On misunderstanding the *Oedipus Rex*', *G.&R.* 13 (1966) 37–49; A. Cameron, *The identity of Oedipus the king* (New York 1968); (ed.) M. J. O'Brien, *Twentieth-century interpretations of Oedipus Rex* (Englewood Cliffs, N.J. 1968). *Phil.*: O. P. Taplin, 'Significant actions in Sophocles' *Philoctetes*', *G.R.B.S.* 12 (1971) 25–44; P. Vidal-Naquet, 'Le *Philoctète* de Sophocle', in J.-P. Vernant and P. Vidal-Naquet, *Mythe et tragédie en Grèce ancienne* (Paris 1973) (Eng. tr. by Janet Lloyd, *Myth and tragedy in ancient Greece* (Brighton 1980)); J. U. Schmidt, *Sophokles Philoktet: eine Strukturanalyse* (Heidelberg 1973); P. E. Easterling, '*Philoctetes* and modern criticism', *I.C.S.* 3 (1978) 27–39. *Tr.*: P. E. Easterling, 'Sophocles' *Trachiniae*', *B.I.C.S.* 15 (1968) 58–69; C. P. Segal, 'Sophocles' *Trachiniae*: myth, poetry, and heroic values', *Y.Cl.S.* 25 (1977) 99–158. (4) STYLE: L. Campbell, *Sophocles* I, 2nd ed. (Cambridge 1879) 1–107; E. Bruhn, *Sophokles erkl. von Schneidewin/Nauck, Anhang* (Berlin 1899: repr. 1963); F. R. Earp, *The style of Sophocles* (Cambridge 1944); A. A. Long, *Language and thought in Sophocles* (London 1968); A. C. Moorhouse, *The syntax of Sophocles* (Leiden 1982). (5) METRE: O. Schroeder, *Sophoclis cantica* (Leipzig 1908); H. Pohlsander, *Metrical studies in the lyrics of Sophocles* (Leiden 1964); A. M. Dale, *Metrical analyses of tragic choruses*, fascs. I and II, *B.I.C.S.* suppl. XXI.1 (1971) and XXI.2 (1981). (6) TEXT: A. Turyn, *Studies in the manuscript tradition of the tragedies of Sophocles* (Urbana, Illinois 1952); R. D. Dawe, *Studies on the text of Sophocles*, 3 vols. (Leiden 1973–8).

LEXICON: F. Ellendt, 2nd ed. rev. H. Genthe (Berlin 1872: repr. Hildesheim 1958).

EURIPIDES

b. 485/4 or 480 B.C., son of Mnesarchus (or Mnesarchides), of the deme of Phyle. d. 406 in Macedonia; his last years, 408–406 (?), were spent at the court of Archelaus in Pella. Competed at Dionysia on twenty-two occasions (first in 455), but won first prize only four times, the last time posthumously for the group of plays which included *Bacch.* and *I.A.* Apparently took no active part in public life (unlike Sophocles). Sources: ancient *Life* (ed. E. Schwartz, *Scholia in Euripidem* I (Berlin 1887) 1–8) and fragments of a *Life* by Satyrus (ed. G. Arrighetti (Pisa 1964)); Arist. *Rhet.* 2.6.20 with schol., Plut. *Nic.* 17 (alleged visit to Syracuse, elegy on those who died there); see P. T. Stevens, 'Euripides and the Athenians', *J.H.S.* 76 (1956) 87–94; M. Lefkowitz, 'The Euripides *Vita*', *G.R.B.S.* 20 (1979) 188–210. What biographical material we possess is unreliable: most of it obviously stems from comic travesties; cf. M. Lefkowitz, *The lives of the Greek poets* (London 1981) 88–104. There may be some truth to the Aristophanic hint (*Frogs* 1048) that he was unfortunate in his marriage, and it is certain that one of his sons (or perhaps a nephew), Euripides by name, was also a tragic poet. The one item of the anecdotal tradition which may have a basis in fact is the picture of E. as an intellectual recluse, the possessor of a large library (cf. Ar. *Frogs* 943 and 1409).

Life gives total no. of plays as ninety-two, Suda as seventy-eight; latter figure probably represents no. of plays still available to Alexandrian scholars. (1) EXTANT: Tragedies (when approximate dates are given, these are based on the metrical criteria proposed by T. Zieliński, *Tragodoumenon libri tres* II (Cracow 1925)): *Alcestis* (produced 438: prosatyric), *Medea* (431), *Heraclidae* (*c.* 430), *Hippolytus* (428), *Andromache* (*c.* 425), *Hecuba* (*c.* 424), *Supplices* (*c.* 424), *Ion* (*c.* 418/17), *Electra* (417: perhaps 413), *Hercules furens* (*c.* 417), *Troades* (415), *Iphigenia in Tauris* (*c.* 413), *Helen* (412), *Phoenissae* (after 412, before 408), *Orestes* (408), *Bacchae* and *Iphigenia in Aulide* (both prod. posthumously, probably 405). Also *Rhesus* (if the extant play is by E., his earliest surviving work). Satyr play: *Cyclops*: see D. F. Sutton, *The date of Euripides' Cyclops* (Ann Arbor 1974). (2) LOST OR FRAGMENTARY (alphabetical by Greek titles, as in *TGF*: for the satyr plays see D. F. Sutton, *H.S.C.Ph.* 78 (1974) 140–3). *Aegeus, Aeolus, Alexander, Alcmeon through Corinth, Alcmeon through Psophis, Alcmene, Alope* or *Cercyon, Andromeda, Antigone, Archelaus, Auge, Autolycus,* (sat., possibly A & B: see D. F. Sutton, *Eos* 62 (1974) 49–53), *Bellerophon, Busiris* (sat.), *Danae, Dictys, Epeus, Erechtheus, Eurystheus* (sat.), *Theristai* 'Reapers' (sat.), *Theseus, Thyestes, Ino, Ixion, Hippolytus, Cadmus, Cresphontes, Cressae, Cretes, Lamia, Licymnius, Melanippe* (*hē sophē* 'the wise' and *hē desmotis* 'the prisoner'), *Meleager,*

EURIPIDES

Mysi, Oedipus, Oeneus, Oenomaus, Palamedes, Peliades, Peleus, Plisthenes, Polyidus
or *Glaucus, Protesilaus, Stheneboea, Sisyphus* (sat.), *Sciron* (sat.), *Scyrii, Syleus* (sat.),
Telephus, Temenidae, Temenus, Hypsipyle, Phaethon, Philoctetes, Phoenix, Phrixus,
Chrysippus. Attributed by Alexandrians to Critias: *Pirithous, Rhadamanthus, Tennes*
(see p. 341).

BIBLIOGRAPHY

(See C. Collard, *G.&R.* New surveys in the classics XIV (1981).)

TEXTS AND COMMENTARIES: TEXTS: R. Prinz and N. Wecklein (Leipzig
1877–1902); G. Murray (OCT, 1902–9); L. Méridier, L. Parmentier, H. Grégoire,
F. Chapoutier (Budé, 1926–: lacks *I.A.* and *Rhes.*); BT (1964–: *Alc.*, A. Garzya 1980;
And., idem 1978; *Hec.*, S. G. Daitz 1973; *Hel.*, K. Alt 1964; *Heraclid.*, A. Garzya
1972; *Ion*, W. Biehl 1979; *I.T.*, D. Sansone 1981; *Or.*, W. Biehl 1975; *Tro.*, idem
1970); J. Diggle (OCT, 1981–). COMMENTARIES: (1) Complete. F. A. Paley (London
1857–74). (2) Selection. H. Weil (Paris 1905: *Hipp.*, *Med.*, *Hec.*, *I.A.*, *I.T.*, *El.* and
Or.). (3) Individual plays. *Alc.*: A. M. Dale (Oxford 1954). *And.*: P. T. Stevens
(Oxford 1971). *Bacch.*: E. R. Dodds, 2nd ed. (Oxford 1960); J. Roux, 2 vols. (Paris
1970–2). *Cyc.*: N. Wecklein (Leipzig 1903); J. Duchemin (Paris 1945); V. de Falco
(Naples 1966); R. G. Ussher (Rome 1978). *El.*: J. D. Denniston (Oxford 1939: repr.
1954). *Hel.*: A. M. Dale (Oxford 1967); R. Kannicht, 2 vols. (Heidelberg 1969).
H.F.: U. von Wilamowitz-Moellendorff (Berlin 1895: repr. Darmstadt 1959); G. W.
Bond (Oxford 1981). *Hipp.*: W. S. Barrett (Oxford 1964). *Ion*: U. von Wilamowitz-
Moellendorff (Berlin 1926: repr. 1969); A. S. Owen (Oxford 1939). *I.A.*: E. B. England
(London 1891: repr. New York 1979). *I.T.*: M. Platnauer (Oxford 1938: repr. 1952).
Med.: D. L. Page (Oxford 1938). *Or.*: W. Biehl (Berlin 1965); V. di Benedetto
(Florence 1965). *Phoen.*: A. C. Pearson (London 1909: repr. New York 1979). *Supp.*:
C. Collard, 2 vols. (Groningen 1975). *Tro.*: K. H. Lee (London 1976). *Fragments.*
TGF 363–716; H. von Arnim, *Supplementum Euripideum* (Bonn 1913); B. Snell,
Supplementum (Hildesheim 1964); C. Austin, *Nova fragmenta Euripidea in papyris*
reperta (Berlin 1968); (edd.) G. A. Seeck *et al.*, *Euripides, Sämtliche Tragödien und*
Fragmente VI (Munich 1981: with German tr. of the fragments). Bibliography: H.-J.
Mette, 'Die Bruchstücke', *Lustrum* 12 (1967); 13 (1968) 284–403 and 569–71; 17
(1973–4) 5–26; 23–4 (1981–2). Discussion: H. van Looy, *Zes verloren Tragedies van*
Euripides (Brussels 1964); T. B. L. Webster, *The tragedies of Euripides* (London 1967).
Fragmentary plays (editions and discussions). *Aeolus*: S. Jäkel, *G.B.* 8 (1979) 101–18.
Alexander: B. Snell, *Hermes* Einzelschriften V (1937); R. A. Coles, 'A new Oxyrhyn-
chus papyrus: the hypothesis of Euripides' *Alexandros*', *B.I.C.S.* suppl. XXXII (1974).
Antiope: J. Kambitsis (Athens 1972); B. Snell, *Scenes from Greek drama* (Berkeley &
Los Angeles 1964) 70–98. *Cresphontes*: O. Musso (Milan 1974). *Cretans*: R. Cantarella
(Milan 1963). *Erechtheus*: P. Carrara (Florence 1977); A. M. Diez (Granada 1975).
Hypsipyle: G. W. Bond (Oxford 1963). *Phaethon*: J. Diggle (Cambridge 1970).
Telephus: E. W. Handley and J. Rea, *B.I.C.S.* suppl. V (1957). *Scholia*: E. Schwartz

(Berlin 1887–91); O. L. Smith, *Scholia metrica anonyma in Euripidis Hecubam Orestem Phoenissas* (Copenhagen 1977); S. G. Daitz, *The scholia in the Jerusalem palimpsest of Euripides* (Heidelberg 1979).

TRANSLATIONS: (1) PROSE: *Alc.*: C. R. Beye (Englewood Cliffs, N.J. 1974: with notes). *Bacch.*: G. S. Kirk (Englewood Cliffs, N.J. 1970: with notes: repr. Cambridge 1979). *Ion*: A. P. Burnett (Englewood Cliffs, N.J. 1970: with notes). *I.A.*: K. Cavander (Englewood Cliffs, N.J. 1973: with notes). (2) VERSE: P. Vellacott (Harmondsworth, 1953–72: lacks *I.A.* and *Cyc.*); D. Grene and R. Lattimore, *The complete Greek tragedies* (Chicago 1953–72); (ed.) W. Arrowsmith, *The Greek tragedy in new translations* (Oxford: pubd so far: *I.T.*, R. Lattimore 1973; *Hipp.*, R. Bagg 1973; *Alc.*, W. Arrowsmith 1974; *Rhes.*, R. E. Braun 1978; *I.A.*, W. S. Merwin 1978; *Hel.*, J. Michie and C. Leach 1981; *Heraclid.*, H. Taylor and R. A. Brooks 1981; *Phoen.*: P. Burian and B. Swann 1981).

STUDIES: (1) GENERAL: G. Murray, *Euripides and his age* (London 1913); E. R. Dodds, 'Euripides the irrationalist', *C.R.* 43 (1929) 97–104; G. M. A. Grube, *The drama of Euripides* (London 1941); E. M. Blaiklock, *The male characters of Euripides* (Wellington, N.Z. 1952); W. H. Friedrich, *Euripides und Diphilos* (Munich 1953); L. H. G. Greenwood, *Aspects of Euripidean tragedy* (Cambridge 1953); G. Zuntz, *The political plays of Euripides* (Manchester 1955); H. Strohm, *Euripides: Interpretationen zur dramatischen Form* (Munich 1957); J. Jones, *On Aristotle and Greek tragedy* (London 1962) sect. IV; N. C. Hourmouziades, *Production and imagination in Euripides* (Athens 1965); F. Jouan, *Euripide et les légendes des chants cypriens* (Paris 1966); D. J. Conacher, *Euripidean drama* (Toronto 1967); H. Rohdich, *Die euripideische Tragödie* (Heidelberg 1968); W. Steidle, *Studien zum antiken Drama* (Munich 1968); R. P. Winnington-Ingram, 'Euripides *poietes sophos*', *Arethusa* 2 (1969) 127–42; A. P. Burnett, *Catastrophe survived* (Oxford 1971); G. Zuntz, 'Contemporary politics in Euripides', *Opuscula selecta* (Manchester 1972) 54–61; C. H. Whitman, *Euripides and the full circle of myth* (Cambridge, Mass. 1974); C. Collard, 'Formal debates in Euripides' drama', *G.&R.* 22 (1975) 58–71; A. Rivier, *Essai sur le tragique d'Euripide*, 2nd ed. (Paris 1975). (2) COLLECTIONS: *Entretiens VI: Euripide* (Fondation Hardt, Geneva 1960); (ed.) E. Segal, *Euripides: a collection of critical essays* (Englewood Cliffs, N.J. 1968); (ed.) E. R. Schwinge, *Euripides*, Wege der Forschung LXXXIX (Darmstadt 1968). (3) INDIVIDUAL PLAYS: *Alc.*: K. von Fritz, 'Euripides' *Alkestis* und ihre modernen Nachahmer und Kritiker', *A.&A.* 5 (1956) 27–70; (ed.) J. Wilson, *Twentieth-century interpretations of Euripides' Alcestis* (Englewood Cliffs, N.J. 1968); H. Erbse, 'Euripides' *Alkestis*', *Philologus* 116 (1972) 32–52. *And.*: A. Lesky, 'Der Ablauf der Handlung in der *Andromache* des Euripides', *A.A.W.W.* 84 (1947) 99–115 = *Ges. Schrift.* 144; H. Erbse, 'Euripides' *Andromache*', *Hermes* 94 (1966) 276–97; P. D. Kovacs, *The Andromache of Euripides: an interpretation* (Chico, Calif. 1980). *Bacch.* R. P. Winnington-Ingram, *Euripides and Dionysus* (Cambridge 1948: repr. Amsterdam 1969); J. de Romilly, 'Le thème du bonheur dans les *Bacchantes*', *R.E.G.* 76 (1963) 361–80; C.

Segal, *Dionysiac poetics and Euripides' Bacchae* (Princeton 1982). *El.*: K. Matthiessen, *Elektra, Taurische Iphigenie und Helena* (Göttingen 1964); M. J. O'Brien, 'Orestes and the gorgon: Euripides' *Electra*', *A.J.Ph.* 86 (1964) 13–39. *Hec.*: G. Kirkwood, 'Hecuba and Nomos', *T.A.Ph.A.* 78 (1947) 61–8; W. H. Adkins, 'Values in Euripides' *Hecuba* and *Hercules Furens*', *C.Q.* n.s.16 (1966) 193–219. *Hel.*: F. Solmsen, 'Onoma and Pragma in Euripides' *Helen*', *C.R.* 48 (1934) 119–21; A. P. Burnett, 'Euripides' *Helen*: a comedy of ideas', *C.Ph.* 55 (1960) 151–63; C. Segal, 'The two worlds of Euripides' *Helen*', *T.A.Ph.A.* 102 (1971) 553–614. *H.F.*: H. H. O. Chalk, 'Arete and Bia in Euripides' *Herakles*', *J.H.S.* 82 (1962) 7–18; J. C. Kamerbeek, 'Unity and meaning of Euripides' *Heracles*', *Mnemosyne* n.s.4.19 (1966) 1–16. *Heraclid.*: J. W. Fitton, 'The *Suppliant Women* and *Herakleidae* of Euripides', *Hermes* 89 (1961) 430–61; A. Lesky, 'On the *Heraclidae* of Euripides', *Y.Cl.S.* 25 (1977) 227–338; P. Burian, 'Euripides' *Heraclidae*: an interpretation', *C.Ph.* 72 (1977) 1–21. *Hipp.*: B. M. W. Knox, 'The *Hippolytus* of Euripides', *Y.Cl.S.* 13 (1952) 3–31 = *Word and action* (Baltimore 1979) 205–30; R. P. Winnington-Ingram, '*Hippolytus*: a study in causation', in *Entretiens VI: Euripide* (Fondation Hardt, Geneva 1960) 171–97. *Ion*: C. Wolff, 'The design and myth in Euripides' *Ion*', *H.S.C.Ph.* 69 (1965) 169–94; B. M. W. Knox, 'Euripidean comedy', *Word and action* (Baltimore 1979) 250–74. *I.A.*: D. L. Page, *Actors' interpolations in Greek tragedy...with special reference to Euripides' Iphigeneia in Aulis* (Oxford 1934). *I.T.*: G. Zuntz, 'Die *Taurische Iphigenie* des Euripides', *Die Antike* 9 (1933) 245–54. *Med.*: P. E. Easterling, 'The infanticide in Euripides' *Medea*', *Y.Cl.S.* 25 (1977) 177–91; B. M. W. Knox, 'The *Medea* of Euripides', *Y.Cl.S.* 25 (1977) 193–225 = *Word and action* (Baltimore 1979) 295–322. *Or.*: N. A. Greenberg, 'Euripides' *Orestes*: an interpretation', *H.S.C.Ph.* 66 (1962) 157–92; E. Rawson, 'Aspects of Euripides' *Orestes*', *Arethusa* 5 (1972) 155–67; W. Burkert, 'Die Absurdität der Gewalt und das Ende der Tragödie: Euripides' *Orestes*', *A.&A.* 20 (1974) 97–109. *Phoen.*: H. D. F. Kitto, 'The final scenes of the *Phoenissae*', *C.R.* 53 (1939) 104–11; E. Fraenkel, 'Zu den *Phoenissen* des Euripides', *S.B.A.W.* 1963, 1; J. de Romilly, 'Les Phéniciennes d'Euripide', *R.Ph.* 39 (1965) 28–47; E. Rawson, 'Family and fatherland in Euripides' *Phoenissae*', *G.R.B.S.* 11 (1970) 109–27. *Rhes.*: W. Ritchie, *The authenticity of the Rhesus of Euripides* (Cambridge 1964); H. D. F. Kitto, 'The *Rhesus* and related matters', *Y.Cl.S.* 25 (1977) 317–50. *Tro.*: T. C. W. Stinton, *Euripides and the judgment of Paris* (London 1965); G. L. Koniaris, '*Alexander, Palamedes, Troades, Sisyphus* – A connected tetralogy? A connected trilogy?', *H.S.C.Ph.* 77 (1973) 87–124; R. Scodel, *The Trojan trilogy of Euripides* (Göttingen 1980). (4) TEXT AND TRANSMISSION: A. Turyn, *The Byzantine manuscript tradition of the tragedies of Euripides* (Urbana 1957); G. Zuntz, *An inquiry into the transmission of the plays of Euripides* (Cambridge 1965); V. D. di Benedetto, *La tradizione manoscritta euripidea* (Padua 1965); S. G. Daitz, *The Jerusalem palimpsest of Euripides* (Berlin 1970); K. Matthiessen, *Studien zur Textüberlieferung der Hekabe des Euripides* (Heidelberg 1974); J. Diggle, *Studies on the text of Euripides* (Oxford 1981). (5) STYLE: W. Breitenbach, *Untersuchungen zur Sprache des euripideischen Lyrik* (Stuttgart 1934: repr. Hildesheim 1967); W. Ludwig, *Sapheneia: ein*

Beitrag zur Formkunst im Spätwerk des Euripides (Tübingen 1954); E. R. Schwinge, *Die Verwendung der Stichomythie in den Dramen des Euripides* (Heidelberg 1968); S. A. Barlow, *The imagery of Euripides* (London 1971); K. H. Lee, *Index of passages cited in Breitenbach, etc.* (Amsterdam 1979).

CONCORDANCE: J. H. Allen and G. Italie (Berkeley & Los Angeles 1954), supplemented by C. Collard (Groningen 1971).

MINOR TRAGIC POETS

LIVES, FRAGMENTS, INDEXES

The ancient testimonia are assembled in B. Snell, *Tragicorum Graecorum fragmenta* I (Göttingen 1971). This volume also contains the fragments themselves, thus replacing Nauck's *TGF* 719–833. Snell's volume has no *index verborum*: for Nauck's edition there is an index to the whole, *Tragicae dictionis index spectans ad Tragicorum Graecorum Fragmenta* (Petersburg 1892: repr. Hildesheim 1962). Discussion and bibliography in Lesky, *TDH* 523ff.; B. Snell, *Szenen aus griechischen Dramen* (Berlin 1971); G. Xanthakis-Karamanos, *Studies in fourth-century tragedy* (Athens 1980).

INDIVIDUAL AUTHORS

Achaeus: C. Drago, 'Achaeo: un satirografo minore del V secolo', *Dioniso* 5 (1936) 231–42. Agathon: P. Leveque, *Agathon* (Paris 1955). Chaeremon: C. Collard, 'On the tragedian Chaeremon', *J.H.S.* 90 (1970) 22–34. Critias: D. F. Sutton, 'Critias and atheism', *C.Q.* 31 (1981) 33–8. Ezechiel: H. Jacobson, *The Exagoge of Ezekiel* (Cambridge 1983). Ion of Chios: A. von Blumenthal, *Ion von Chios. Die Reste seiner Werke* (Stuttgart & Berlin 1935).

SATYR PLAYS

WORKS

Euripides' *Cyclops*: see D. F. Sutton, *The date of Euripides' Cyclops* (Ann Arbor 1974). Considerable papyrus fragments of Aeschylus' *Dictyulci*, 'Dikē play' and *Theoroi* or *Isthmiastae*, Sophocles' *Ichneutae* and *Inachus*, and anonymous *Oeneus* or *Schoeneus* (Sophoclean authorship made more likely by *P. Oxy.* 2453; cf. introd. to Page, under *Commentaries* below). Hypotheses of Euripidean satyr plays in *P. Oxy.* 27.2455. For lost plays see *Appendix* entries for Aesch., Soph. and Eur.; also D. F. Sutton, 'A handlist of satyr plays', *H.S.C.Ph.* 78 (1974) 107–43. Bibliographical refs. in R. A. Pack, *The Greek and Latin literary texts from Graeco-Roman Egypt*, 2nd ed. (Ann Arbor 1965) s.v. 'satyr play' and individual authors.

BIBLIOGRAPHY

(See Schmid–Stählin I 2 79–86 and individual authors; Guggisberg (1947), under *Studies* (1) below.)

TEXTS AND COMMENTARIES: TEXTS: W. Steffen *Satyrographorum Graecorum fragmenta* (Poznań 1952). COMMENTARIES: As for tragedians. Papyrus texts (often abbrev.) with tr. and comm. in H. Lloyd-Jones, *Aeschylus* II (Loeb, 1957) and D. L. Page, *Select papyrii* III (Loeb, 1941).

MONUMENTAL EVIDENCE: F. Brommer, *Satyrspiele*, 2nd ed. (Berlin 1959); T. B. L. Webster, *Monuments illustrating tragedy and satyr play*, 2nd ed., *B.I.C.S.* suppl. xx (1967) 148; A. D. Trendall and T. B. L. Webster, *Illustrations of Greek drama* (London 1971) ch. II.

STUDIES: (1) GENERAL: W. Aly, 'Satyrspiel', *RE* IIA.2 (1925) 235–47; W. Süss, *De Graecorum fabulis satyricis* (Dorpat 1929); L. Campo, *I drammi satireschi della Grecia antica* (Milan 1947); P. Guggisberg, *Das Satyrspiel* (Zurich 1947); L. E. Rossi, 'Il drama satiresco attico', *D. Arch.* 6 (1972) 248–302; N. C. Hourmouziades, *Satyrika* (Athens 1974); B. Seidensticker, 'Das Satyrspiel', in (ed.) G. A. Seeck, *Das griechische Drama* (Darmstadt 1979) 204–57; W. Steffen, *De Graecorum fabulis satyricis* (Wrocław 1979); D. F. Sutton, *The Greek satyr play* (Meisenheim am Glan 1980); idem, 'Satyr plays and children in the audience', *Prudentia* 13 (1981) 71–4. (2) AESCHYLUS: A. Setti, 'Eschilo satirico', *A.S.N.P.* 17 (1948) 1–36; R. G. Ussher, 'The other Aeschylus', *Phoenix* 31 (1977) 287–99. (3) SOPHOCLES: W. N. Bates, 'The satyr-dramas of Sophocles', in *Classical studies presented to Edward Capps* (Princeton 1936) 14–23; W. Steffen, 'De Sophoclis indagatoribus quaestiones aliquot', *Poznańskie Towarzystwo Przyjaciół Nauk* 11 (1949) 83–112. (4) EURIPIDES: W. Wetzel, *De Euripidis fabula satyrica quae Cyclops inscribitur cum Homerico comparata exemplo* (Wiesbaden 1965); A. P. Burnett, *Catastrophe survived* (Oxford 1971), index s.v. 'satyric motifs'; L. E. Rossi, 'Il *Ciclope* di Euripide come *Komos* mancato', *Maia* 23 (1971) 10–38; W. Steffen, 'The satyr-dramas of Euripides', *Eos* 69 (1971) 203–26.

GREEK COMEDY

GENERAL WORKS

(1) List of poets (259 in all)
Austin, C., *Z.P.E.* 14 (1974) 201–25
(2) Fragments
Austin, *CGFPap*
Austin, C. and Kassel, R., *Poetae comici Graeci* IV, *Aristophon–Crobylus* (London & New York 1983)

Edmonds, J. M., *Fragments of Attic comedy*, 3 vols. (Leiden 1957–61: with tr.: much speculative restoration)

Kaibel, *CGF* (Epicharmus and other Doric writers)

Kock, *CAF*, with J. Demiańczuk, *Supplementum comicum* (Cracow 1912)

Meineke, A., *Fragmenta comicorum Graecorum*, 5 vols. (Berlin 1839–57: history of comedy vol. I, word index by H. Iacobi vol. v)

Olivieri, A., *Frammenti della commedia greca e del mimo. . .*, 2 vols., 2nd ed. (Naples 1946: Epicharmus etc., with comm.)

(3) Inscriptional records

Geissler, P., *Chronologie der altattischen Komödie* (Berlin 1925: repr. with addenda 1969)

Mette, H.-J., *Urkunden dramatischer Aufführungen in Griechenland* (Berlin & New York 1977)

Pickard-Cambridge, *DFA* 101–25

(4) Other archaeological material (representations of scenes, actors, masks etc.)

Bieber, M., *The history of the Greek and Roman theater*, 2nd ed. (Princeton 1961: 870 illustrations)

Brea, L. Bernabò, *Menandro e il teatro greco nelle terracotte liparesi* (Genoa 1981)

Pickard-Cambridge, *DFA*

idem, *DTC* (origins)

Seeberg, A., *Corinthian komos vases*, *B.I.C.S.* suppl. XXVII (1971: origins)

Trendall, A. D., *Phylax vases*, 2nd ed., *B.I.C.S.* suppl. XIX (1967)

Webster, T. B. L., *Monuments illustrating Old and Middle Comedy*, 3rd ed. by J. R. Green, *B.I.C.S.* suppl. XXXIX (1978)

idem, *Monuments illustrating New Comedy*, 2nd ed., *B.I.C.S.* suppl. XXIV (1969)

(5) Ancient and medieval writings on comedy

Kaibel, *CGF*

Koster, W. J. W., *Scholia Graeca in Aristophanem* I 1 a (Groningen 1975)

(6) History

Herter, H., *Vom dionysischen Tanz zum komischen Spiel* (Iserlohn 1947: origins)

Lesky 233–40, 417–52, 633–7, 642–65

Meineke, A., under (2) above

Pickard-Cambridge, *DTC* (origins)

Schmid, W., in Schmid–Stählin IV 2 (1946) 1–470 (5th c.)

Webster, T. B. L., *Studies in later Greek comedy*, 2nd ed. (Manchester 1969: 4th c. to Menander)

(7) Special studies

Arnott, W. G., 'From Aristophanes to Menander', *G.&R.* 19 (1972) 65–80

Berk, L., *Epicharmus* (Groningen 1964: see also *DTC* 230–90)

Bonnanno, M. G., *Studi su Cratete comico* (Padua 1972)

Breitholz, L., *Die dorische Farce* (Stockholm 1960)

Descroix, J., *Le trimètre iambique des iambographes à la comédie nouvelle* (Mâcon 1931)

Dohm, H., *Mageiros* (Munich 1964)

Fraenkel, E., *De media et nova comoedia quaestiones selectae* (Göttingen 1912)

Gil, L., 'Comedia ática y sociedad ateniese', *Estudios clásicos* 18 (1974) 61–82, 151–86; 19 (1975) 59–88

Hofmann, W. and Wartenberg, G., *Der Bramarbas in der antiken Komödie, Abh. Ak. Wissenschaften DDR* 1973, 2

Hunter, R. L., *Eubulus: the fragments* (Cambridge 1983)

Oeri, H.-G., *Der Typ der komischen Alten* (Basel 1948)

Pieters, L., *Cratinus* (Leiden 1946)

Schwarze, J., *Die Beurteilung des Perikles durch die attische Komödie* (Zurich 1936)

Sifakis, G. M., *Parabasis and animal choruses* (London 1971)

Wehrli, F., *Motivstudien zur griechischen Komödie* (Zurich 1936)

White, J. W., *The verse of Greek comedy* (London 1912)

Wiemken, H., *Der griechische Mimus: Dokumente zur Geschichte des antiken Volkstheaters* (Bremen 1972)

(8) Surveys

Dover, K. J., in *FYAT* (on comedy generally, c. 1900–68)

Kraus, W., *A.A.H.G.* 24 (1971) 161–80 (Old Comedy and Epicharmus)

idem, *A.A.H.G.* 28 (1975) 1–18 (4th c. comedy excluding Menander)

Murphy, C. T., *C.W.* 49 (1956) 201–11, 65 (1972) 261–73 (Aristophanes and Old Comedy)

ARISTOPHANES

LIFE AND WORKS – EXCURSUS

Aristophanes, son of Philippus, of the deme Kydathenai in Athens (Kirchner, *Prosop. Att.* 2090), was probably in his late 'teens when his first play, the lost *Daitales* ('Banqueters'), was staged in 427 B.C.; his birth-date is accordingly put at about 445 (*Clouds* 528–31 and schol.; Anon. *De com.* II 43f. Kaibel, III 38 Koster). The play was well received, and took second prize; in the next year *Babylonians* (also lost) won a first, and more firsts came in the two following years with *Acharnians* and *Knights* (for sources see *General works* for 'Greek Comedy' under (3) 'Inscriptional records'). This was a brilliant start, and when the selection of the eleven plays that survive was made, five were chosen from the first seven years of A.'s career: they are *Acharnians*, 425; *Knights*, 424; *Clouds*, 423; *Wasps*, 422; *Peace*, 421.

Like some of his contemporaries, A. sometimes gave plays to other people to produce. He is defensive about this in *Knights*, which was his first independent production (512ff.); the practice is reflected in the joke that he was 'born on the fourth', like Heracles, to toil for others (Ameipsias, fr. 28 K *et al.*; cf. Plato com. frs. 99–100 K with *P. Oxy.* 2737 fr. 1 ii 10ff. = *CGFPap* 56, 44ff.). None the less, when Cleon, who was his fellow-demesman, took offence at the political content of *Babylonians*, it seems likely to have been A. himself and not his producer Callistratus who was brought before the Council by the offended politician and denounced for 'slandering the city in front of foreigners' (that is, in a play produced at the Dionysia; cf. *Ach.* 377–82, 502ff., 630ff. with schol. on 378, 503; *Wasps* 1284–91 and schol.).

By the time of his references to the affair in *Acharnians*, A. was already working on his all-out attack on Cleon in *Knights*, apparently with some collaboration with his rival and close contemporary Eupolis, over which the two exchanged hard words (*Ach.* 300ff.; *Clouds* 553f. with schol., quoting Eupolis, *Baptai* (78 K); *Knights* 1288ff. with schol.); for what it is worth, Cratinus, who had been written off by A. in the *Knights* as an old drunkard who was once supremely powerful and popular, appears in this matter to have sided with Eupolis (*Knights* 526ff. with schol. on 531).

These personal references perhaps have their nearest modern counterparts in the world of the revue theatre or of the satirical magazine. No doubt they reflect some of the pressures that were felt by a writer of topical comedy competing for production and success at one of the two annual festivals in Athens; but just how deep the feelings were is hard to say. Two of his rivals' jokes (that he was going bald and that he was of suspect Athenian status because of a connexion with Aegina) A. ingeniously tries to neutralize by adopting them (*Clouds* 540, *Knights* 550, *Peace* 767ff., *Ach.* 653f.). The other side of the early success-story is to be seen in his disappointment over *Clouds*, which came third to the play *Pytine* ('Wine-flask') by Cratinus and the *Konnos* of Ameipsias, which (gallingly) brought in Socrates, like the *Clouds* (*Wasps* 1043ff.; *Clouds* 530ff.; Cratinus, *Pytine* frs. 181–204 K; Ameipsias, *Konnos* frs. 7–12 K).

The passage of *Clouds* just cited comes from a part of the play composed for a revised edition, which is the one that survives, probably not long before 417. There A. looks back with pride to the *Knights*, and criticizes his rivals for the sameness of their repeated attacks on Hyperbolus, by contrast with his own ventures into new fields. The death of Cleon and the ending of the war in 421 had certainly changed the scene in which A. had his early thrills and spills by removing two of his main pre-occupations. But, little as we know about his personal circumstances in earlier times, we now know less, since, whether speaking with the voice of a character or that of a chorus in a parabasis, he has less to say for himself. The plays which survive from his 'middle period', 420–400, from about age 25 to about 45, are *Birds* (414), *Lysistrata* (411), *Thesmophoriazusae* (411) and *Frogs* (405); and though Euripides is a character in the last two of these (as earlier in *Acharnians*) we have no outside information about their personal relationship, if any existed.

Beneath all the variety of theme in the plays there are trends which show the direction in which comedy was developing. There is less immediate political engagement, and a growing social interest; lyric still flourishes, but largely above and beyond its traditional function in epirrhematic syzygies and other patterned sequences of scenes; but if we argue from these trends to changes in A.'s personal attitude to politics and music, we are merely arguing in circles. There are still, as earlier, passages which show that he was eminently conscious of the comic tradition in which he worked and of his own competitive position (e.g. *Second Thesmophoriazusae* (prob. 407/6) frs. 333–4 K; *Frogs* 1–14). Whether he had, or expressed, strong theoretical views on playwriting we have no way to tell: when Plato in the *Symposium* has Socrates attempt to question Agathon and A. about the writing of tragedy and comedy, it is at the end of a very long party, and A., amusingly enough, is the first to fall asleep (*Symp.* 223d); perhaps the practical criticism of the second half of *Frogs* was nearer to his own temperament.

From the twenty years between *Frogs* and the presumed date of A.'s death in the mid-380s we have two plays, *Ecclesiazusae* (393 or 392?) and *Plutus* (388), which are conspicuous by their diminution of the role of the chorus and their turn away from the lively topicalities of the fifth-century plays to a less colourful style and a more generalized approach to the affairs of the time. A. had sons who were comic poets, Philippus (*Prosop. Att.* 14460), Araros (*Prosop. Att.* 1575)) and possibly another (?Philetaerus, *Prosop. Att.* 14253; ?Nicostratus, *Prosop. Att.* 11038). It is an interesting reflection of his continuing status as a comic writer that later critics could see in his last two plays, the lost *Kokalos* and *Aiolosikon*, what they recognized as anticipations of Middle and New Comedy (Platonius, I 31f. Kaibel, I 29f. Koster; *Vit. Ar.* XI 69f. D.–D., XXVIII 54f. Koster); it is also interesting that these plays by a man nearing 60 with a long career behind him could be handed over for production to someone of the next generation, his son Araros, with a view to increasing his standing with the public (*Plut.* arg. III Coulon = IV Dübner, *et al.*). The Alexandrian Library catalogued forty-four plays in all, of which four were thought doubtfully authentic or spurious (Anon. *De com.* II 47f. Kaibel, III 41 Koster, *et al.*).

Sources: Cantarella's edition of A. sets out most of the relevant texts in the Prolegomena, I 135ff.; for some friends of A. see Sterling Dow, *A.J.A.* 73 (1969) 234–5, discussing *IG* II² 2343; for portraits G. M. A. Richter, *Portraits of the Greeks* I (London 1965) 140, with T. B. L. Webster, *Monuments illustrating Old and Middle Comedy*, 3rd ed. by J. R. Green, *B.I.C.S.* suppl. XXXIX (1978), under AS1.

BIBLIOGRAPHY

TEXTS AND COMMENTARIES: TEXTS: F. W. Hall and W. M. Geldart (OCT, 1906–7: with fragments); V. Coulon and H. van Daele (Budé, 1923–30 and later corrected reprints); B. B. Rogers (Loeb, 1924: with verse tr.); R. Cantarella (Milan 1949–64: with prolegomena and Italian prose tr.); A. Sommerstein (London 1980–3: *Ach.*, *Knights*, *Clouds*, *Wasps*, with parallel tr. and short notes). COMMENTARIES: (1) The eleven plays. B. B. Rogers (London 1902–16: with verse tr. as Loeb); J. van Leeuwen, 12 vols. incl. prolegomena (Leiden 1893–1906). (2) Individual plays. *Ach.*: W. W. Rennie (London 1909); W. J. M. Starkie (London 1909: with parallel tr.). *Knights*: R. A. Neil (Cambridge 1901). *Clouds*: W. J. M. Starkie (London 1911: with parallel tr.); K. J. Dover (Oxford 1968). *Wasps*: W. J. M. Starkie (London 1897); D. M. MacDowell (Oxford 1971). *Peace*: H. Sharpley (London 1905); M. Platnauer (Oxford 1964). *Birds*: T. Kock and O. Schroeder (Leipzig 1927); P. I. Kakrides (Athens 1974: in Greek). *Lys.*: U. von Wilamowitz-Moellendorff (Berlin 1927). *Frogs*: T. G. Tucker (London 1906); L. Radermacher, *S.A.W.W.* 1921, 2nd ed. by W. Kraus (Vienna 1954); W. B. Stanford, 2nd ed. (London 1963). *Eccl.*: R. G.

Ussher (Oxford 1973). *Plut.*: K. Holzinger, *S.A.W.W.* 218.3 (1940). *Fragments.* See *General works* under 'Greek Comedy'. For *Daitales* ('Banqueters') see A. C. Cassio, *Banchettanti: i frammenti* (Pisa 1977). *Scholia.* W. Dindorf and F. Dübner (Paris 1842 and reprints: obsolete, but not yet replaced for all plays); W. J. W. Koster *et al.* (in progress: Groningen 1960–). *Birds*: J. W. White (Boston & London 1914). *Lys.*: G. Stein (Göttingen 1891). Also G. Zuntz, *Die Aristophanes-Scholien der Papyri*, 2nd ed. (Berlin 1975); W. G. Rutherford, *A chapter in the history of annotation* = *Scholia Aristophanica* III (London 1905). See further T. Gelzer, *Gnomon* 33 (1961) 26–34, and for work on the scholia and the textual transmission generally idem under *Studies* (1) below, *Aristophanes der Komiker* 1548–63.

TRANSLATIONS: W. Arrowsmith, D. Parker *et al.*, *The complete Greek comedy* (Ann Arbor 1961–: *Ach.* 1961; *Clouds* 1962; *Wasps* 1962; *Birds* 1961; *Lys.* 1964; *Frogs* 1962; *Eccl.* 1967); D. Fitts (New York 1962: *Birds, Lys., Thes., Frogs*); D. Barrett (*Wasps, Birds, Thes., Frogs, Eccl.*) and A. Sommerstein (*Ach., Knights, Clouds, Peace, Lys., Plut.*) (Harmondsworth, 1964–78); P. Dickinson, 2 vols. (Oxford 1970).

STUDIES: (1) SURVEYS: K. J. Dover, *Lustrum* 2 (1957) 52–112; T. Gelzer, *Aristophanes der Komiker* (Stuttgart 1971) = *RE* suppl. XII 1391–1570; R. G. Ussher, *G.&R.* New surveys in the classics XIII (1979); see *General works* (8) under 'Greek Comedy'. (2) GENERAL: C. Pascal, *Dioniso: saggio sulla religione e la parodia religiosa in Aristofane* (Catania 1911); W. Süss, *Aristophanes und die Nachwelt* (Leipzig 1911); G. Murray, *Aristophanes, a study* (Oxford 1933); Q. Cataudella, *La poesia di Aristofane* (Bari 1934); V. L. Ehrenberg, *The people of Aristophanes*, 2nd ed. (London 1951: 3rd ed. New York 1972: reprints); W. Süss, 'Scheinbare und wirkliche Inkongruenzen in den Dramen des Aristophanes', *Rh.M.* 97 (1954) 115–59, 229–54, 289–316; H.-J. Newiger, *Metapher und Allegorie* (Munich 1957); T. Gelzer, *Der epirrhematische Agon bei Aristophanes* (Munich 1960); E. Fraenkel, *Beobachtungen zu Aristophanes* (Rome 1962); C. F. Russo, *Aristofane, autore di teatro* (Florence 1962); P. Händel, *Formen und Darstellungen in der aristophanischen Komödie* (Heidelberg 1963); C. H. Whitman, *Aristophanes and the comic hero* (Cambridge, Mass. 1964); J. Taillardat, *Les images d'Aristophane*, 2nd ed. (Paris 1965); P. Rau, *Paratragodia* (Munich 1967); K. J. Dover, *Aristophanic comedy* (London 1972); G. E. M. de Ste Croix, *The origins of the Peloponnesian war* (London 1972) App. xxix 'The political outlook of Aristophanes'; J. Sánchez Lasso de la Vega, 'Realidad, idealidad y politica en la comedia de Aristofane', *C.F.C.* 4 (1972) 9–89; A. Sommerstein, 'On translating Aristophanes', *G.&R.* 20 (1973) 140–54; E. S. Spyropoulos, *L'accumulation verbale chez Aristophane* (Thessaloniki 1974); J. Henderson, *The maculate muse: obscene language in Attic comedy* (New Haven & London 1975); B. A. Sparkes, 'Illustrating Aristophanes', *J.H.S.* 95 (1975) 122–35; C. W. Dearden, *The stage of Aristophanes* (London 1976); W. Kraus, 'Aristophanes und Sokrates', *Sprachwissenschaftliche Beiträge zur Literaturwissenschaft* (Öst. Akad. der Wissenschaften) 7 (1976) 161–79; H. Schareika, *Der Realismus der attischen Komödie* (Frankfurt am Main, Berne & Las Vegas 1978); F. Heberlein,

Pluthygieia: zur Gegenwelt bei Aristophanes (Frankfurt am Main 1980). (3) INDIVIDUAL
PLAYS: *Knights*: M. Pohlenz, *N.A.W.G.* 1952 = *Kl. Schr.* II 511ff.; O. Navarre, *Les
cavaliers d'Aristophane: étude et analyse* (Paris 1956); M. Landfester, *Die Ritter des
Aristophanes* (Amsterdam 1967). *Wasps*: U. von Wilamowitz-Moellendorff, *S.D.A.W.*
1911 = *Kl. Schr.* I 284ff.; G. Paduano, *Il giudice giudicato: le funzioni del comico nelle
Vespe di Aristofane* (Bologna 1974). *Birds*: E. Fraenkel, *Kleine Beiträge* (Rome 1964)
427–67 with *Beobachtungen zu Aristophanes* (Rome 1962) 58–99; H. Hofmann,
Mythos und Komödie (Hildesheim 1976) 70–229. *Thes.*: H. Hansen, 'Aristophanes'
Thesmophoriazusae: theme, structure, production', *Philologus* 120 (1976) 165–85. (4)
METRICAL STUDIES: Descroix and White in *General works* (7) under 'Greek Comedy'.
P. Pucci, 'Aristofane ed Euripide', *M.A.L.* ser. 8 x.5 (1961) 273–423; C. Prato, *I
canti di Aristofane* (Rome 1962); A. M. Dale, *Lyric metres of Greek drama*, 2nd ed.
(Cambridge 1968) and (1969) under (5) below; T. McEvilley, 'Development in the
lyrics of Aristophanes', *A.J.Ph.* 91 (1970) 257–76; E. Domingo, *La responsión
estrofica en Aristofane* (Salamanca 1975). (5) COLLECTED STUDIES (items in these
collections are *not* listed separately above; the obelus indicates that all or much of the
material is reprinted from elsewhere). Κωμωδοτραγήματα: *studia Aristophanica in
honorem... W. J. W. Koster* (Amsterdam 1967: a miscellany); † (ed.) D. J. Littlefield,
Twentieth-century interpretations of the Frogs (Englewood Cliffs, N.J. 1968); A. M.
Dale, *Collected papers* (Cambridge 1969: see esp. nos. †3, †8, †9, †11, †14, †15, 21–5,
mainly on staging and on the nature of verse); † (ed.) H.-J. Newiger, *Aristophanes
und die alte Komödie* (Darmstadt 1975: with introd. and long bibliography, 487–510);
(ed.) J. Henderson, *Aristophanes: Essays in interpretation*, *Y.Cl.S.* 26 (1980).

LEXICA: O. J. Todd (Cambridge, Mass. 1932: based on OCT: corrections by
W. K. Pritchett, *C.Ph.* 51 (1956) 102); H. Dunbar, new ed. by B. Marzullo (Hildesheim
1973).

MENANDER

LIFE AND WORKS–EXCURSUS

Menander, son of Diopeithes, of the deme Kephisia (Kirchner, *Prosop. Att.* 9875),
was born in 342/1 B.C.; he died in 292/1 or a neighbouring year (*IG* XIV 1184 and
other sources; but there are conflicts of evidence). He was remembered as having been
a pupil of Theophrastus, Aristotle's successor as head of the Peripatetic School
(Diog. Laert. 5.36), and also as a contemporary of Epicurus, who, though born in
Samos, did his military service in Athens and was in the same ephebe class as M.
(Strabo 14.638). It may have been through Theophrastus and his circle that M. came
into contact with a somewhat older contemporary, Demetrius of Phalerum, and
formed a friendship which is said to have put him in peril at the time of Demetrius'
overthrow from his governorship of Athens in 307 (Diog. Laert. 5.79). M. thus seems
to have moved in the higher circles of Athenian intellectual and political life; but we

do not know of any political engagement or activity on his part, nor of intellectual interests outside his writing for the theatre. Like Aristophanes and other comic poets, he began early; and he had early successes. In spite of disagreements between sources, we can probably say that his first production came in 321 with the lost play *Orge* ('Anger') and that it won a first (Jerome, *Chron.* 1696; Anon. *De com.* II 69ff. Kaibel, III 57ff. Koster). It is not certain what lies behind the tradition that associates M. with Alexis (who was producing comedies in Athens at least as early as the 350s). They are thought of as nephew and paternal uncle (Suda, s.v. Ἄλεξις, at the same time describing Alexis as from Thurii in south Italy); or as pupil and master (Anon. *De com.*, *loc. cit.*): some critics presumably saw a special affinity in their work.

M. is variously credited with 105, 108 and 109 plays (Aulus Gellius 17.4.4 knows of all three figures); nearly all of these are now known at least by title, though the existence of alternative titles complicates the reckoning now as (no doubt) in antiquity. Dating is difficult because we have few firm records, and there are problems both in translating what may seem to be logical sequences of literary development into a chronological sequence and in trying to use as evidence for precise dating events mentioned in the plays as part of the background of fictional characters' lives. Apart from the (probable) initial success of *Orge* in 321, *Dyskolos* (*or Misanthrope*) won first prize at the Lenaean festival in 316 (production notice in the Bodmer codex), and an unidentified play at the Dionysia in the next year (*Marm. Par. B* ep.14). M.'s total of eight victories in thirty years (Gell. *loc. cit.*) is an eminently respectable, though not spectacular score, and there must have been many disappointing occasions. One of these was in 312, when his *Heniochos* ('Charioteer') came fifth (*IG* II² 2323a, 36f.); by 301, when a production of the *Imbrians* had to be postponed, the number of his plays was reckoned in the seventies (*P. Oxy.* 1235, 103ff.). Soon after his death, if not within his lifetime, a portrait statue by the sons of Praxiteles, Cephisodotus and Timarchus, was set up in the theatre of Dionysus; only its inscribed base now survives (*IG* II² 3777), but the influence of this work on the numerous later portraits appears to have been considerable.

M.'s plays became classics of the theatre within a generation or so of his death; and from 240 B.C. onwards Latin comedies adapted from him and other fourth-century playwrights were being performed at festivals in Rome. He was a much-favoured author throughout the Hellenistic age and later antiquity, as can be seen from numerous references to him and from the frequency of fragmentary copies of the plays in collections of excavated papyri. M. was still being read and copied in the sixth, perhaps the early seventh century (*P. Berol.* 21199), but after the Byzantine Dark Ages is only known from quotations and from Latin versions (at least eight plays by Plautus and Terence are based on him) until his renaissance in modern times. Our knowledge of his work has been transformed by the progressive recovery of new texts in the 19th and 20th centuries, most notably from the Cairo codex (*P. Cair.* J 43227), published in 1907, and from the Bodmer codex (1959, 1969). Studies and commentaries written before or between the stages of rediscovery have useful material and valuable insights, but will inevitably mislead if used without forethought.

MENANDER

Sources: most of the relevant texts are set out in the Testimonia at the beginning of vol. II of Koerte–Thierfelder's BT ed.; for portraits see G. M. A. Richter, *Portraits of the Greeks* (London 1965) with S. Charitonidis, L. Kahil, R. Ginouvès, *Les mosaïques de la maison du Ménandre à Mytilène*, *A.K.*, Beiheft VI (1970) 27–31, E. Lissi Caronna, *B.A.* 52 (1967) 41–2 and B. Ashmole, *A.J.A.* 77 (1973) 61.

BIBLIOGRAPHY

TEXTS AND COMMENTARIES: TEXTS: Collected plays and fragments: A. Koerte (BT: I, *Reliquiae in papyris et membranis vetustissimis servatae*, 3rd ed. 1938, repr. with addenda 1955, 1957; II, *Reliquiae apud veteres scriptores servatae*, rev. and augmented by A. Thierfelder, 2nd ed. 1959); D. del Corno, vol. I (Milan 1967: contents similar to Koerte I, but without *Samia* and 'Com. Flor.' = *Aspis*: with Italian prose tr.); J.-M. Jacques (Budé: I 1, *Samia*, 1971: I 2, *Dyskolos*, 2nd ed., 1976); F. H. Sandbach, *Reliquiae selectae* (OCT, 1972: omits shorter quoted fragments: corrected repr. 1976); W. G. Arnott, vol. I (Loeb, 1979: *Aspis–Epitrepontes*). See also *CGFPap. Sententiae*: W. Görler, Μενάνδρου Γνῶμαι (Berlin 1963); S. Jaekel (BT, 1964) with D. Hagedorn and M. Weber, *Archiv für Papyrusforschung* 3 (1968) 15–50 and R. Führer, *Zur slavischen Übersetzung der Menandarsentenzen* (Königstein 1982). COMMENTARIES: A. W. Gomme and F. H. Sandbach (Oxford 1973: goes with OCT). One or more plays: *Aspis* and *Samia*: C. Austin, 2 vols. (Berlin 1969–70: I, text with app. crit. and indexes; II, *Subsidia interpretationis*); F. Sisti (Rome: *Aspis*, 1971; *Samia*, 1974). *Dyskolos*: E. W. Handley (London & Cambridge, Mass. 1965); J. Martin, *L'atrabilaire*, 2nd ed. (Paris 1972). *Epitrepontes*: U. von Wilamowitz-Moellendorff, *Das Schiedsgericht* (Berlin 1925); V. de Falco, 3rd ed. (Naples 1961). *Hydria*: K. Gaiser, *A.H.A.W.* 1977, I (conjectural reconstruction from *CGFPap* adesp. nov. 244 and other sources). *Misoumenos*: E. G. Turner, *The lost beginning of Menander, Misoumenos* (London 1978) = *P.B.A.* 73 (1977) 315–31, and *P. Oxy.* 48 (1981) and 3368–71 (new text of lines 1–100). *Phasma*: E. G. Turner, *G.R.B.S.* 10 (1969) 307–24. *Samia*: see above with *Aspis*; D. M. Bain (Warminster 1983). *Sikyonios*: R. Kassel (Berlin 1965: critical ed.).

TRANSLATIONS: L. Casson (New York 1971); P. Vellacott, 2nd ed. (Harmondsworth 1973: includes select shorter fragments: with Theophrastus, *Characters*). *Epitrepontes, Perikeiromene* (reconstructed versions in verse): G. Murray, *The arbitrants* (London 1942), *The rape of the locks* (London 1945). *Samia* (version for broadcasting: blank verse): E. G. Turner (London 1972).

STUDIES: (1) SURVEYS: A. Koerte, *RE* XV.1 (1931) 707–61, with H.-J. Mette, *RE* suppl. XII (1970) 854–62; H.-J. Mette, *Lustrum* 10 (1965) 5–211; 11 (1966) 139–49; 13 (1968) 535–68; W. G. Arnott, 'Menander: discoveries since the *Dyskolos*', *Arethusa* 3 (1970) 49–70; idem, 'Menander, Plautus, Terence', *G.&R.* New surveys in the classics IX (1975); W. Kraus, *A.A.H.G.* 26 (1973) 31–56; E. W. Handley, 'Recent papyrus finds: Menander', *B.I.C.S.* 26 (1979) 81–7; W. Luppe, 'Literarische Texte: Drama', *Archiv für Papyrusforschung* 27 (1980) 233–50. (2) GENERAL: C. Préaux, 'Ménandre et la société athénienne', *C.E.* 32 (1957) no. 63, 84–100; eadem, 'Les fonctions du droit dans la comédie nouvelle', *C.E.* 35 (1960) no. 69, 222–39; T. B. L. Webster, *Studies in Menander*, 2nd ed. (Manchester 1960); A. Dain, 'La survie de Ménandre', *Maia* 15 (1963) 278–309; A. Barigazzi, *La formazione spirituale di Menandro* (Turin 1965); K. Gaiser, 'Menander und der Peripatos', *A.&A.* 13 (1967) 8–40; P. Flury, *Liebe und Liebesprache bei Menander, Plautus und Terenz* (Heidelberg 1968); A. Blanchard, 'Recherches sur la composition des comédies de Ménandre', *R.E.G.* 73 (1970) 38–51; T. B. L. Webster, *Studies in later Greek comedy*, 2nd ed. (Manchester 1970); W. T. MacCary, 'Menander's soldiers: their names, roles and masks', *A.J.Ph.* 93 (1972) 279–98; J. S. Feneron, 'Some elements of Menander's style', *B.I.C.S.* 21 (1974) 81–95; N. Holzberg, *Menander: Untersuchungen zur dramatischen Technik* (Nürnberg 1974); T. B. L. Webster, *An introduction to Menander* (Manchester 1974); D. del Corno, 'Alcuni aspetti del linguaggio di Menandro', *Studi classici e orientali* 24 (1975) 13–48; A. G. Katsouris, *Linguistic and stylistic characterization: tragedy and Menander* (Ioannina 1975); M. G. Ferrero, 'L'asindeto in Menandro', *Dioniso* 47 (1976) 82–106; K. Treu, 'Die Menschen Menanders', in (ed.) R. Mueller, *Mensch als Mass aller Dinge* (Berlin 1976) 399–421; M. Marcovich, 'Euclio, Knemon and the Peripatos', *I.C.S.* 2 (1977) 192–218; S. M. Goldberg, *The making of Menander's comedy* (London, Berkeley & Los Angeles 1980); E. G. Turner, 'The rhetoric of question and answer in Menander', *Themes in drama* 2 (1980) 1–23. (3) INDIVIDUAL PLAYS: *Adelphoi II*: O. Rieth, *Die Kunst Menanders in den Adelphen des Terenz* (Hildesheim 1964). *Aspis*: H. Lloyd-Jones, *G.R.B.S.* 12 (1971) 175–95. *Dis exapaton*: E. W. Handley, *Menander and Plautus* (London 1968 and – in German – as Wege der Forschung CXXXVI (1973): deals with the text corresponding to Plautus, *Bacchides* 494ff.); K. Gaiser, *Philologus* 114 (1970) 51–87; V. Pöschl, *S.H.A.W.* 1973, 4. *Dyskolos*: A. Schäfer, *Menanders Dyskolos: Untersuchungen zur dramatischen Technik* (Meisenheim am Glan 1965). *Hypobolimaios*: M. Kokolakis, *Athena* 66 (1962) 9–114. *Misoumenos*: T. B. L. Webster, 'Woman hates soldier: a structural approach to Greek comedy', *G.R.B.S.* 14 (1973) 287–99. *Samia*: H.-D. Blume, *Menanders Samia: eine Interpretation* (Darmstadt 1974); H. Lloyd-Jones, *Y.Cl.S.* 22 (1972) 119–44. *Sikyonios*: H. Lloyd-Jones, *G.R.B.S.* 7 (1966) 131–57 (quotes the Greek extensively). *Theophoroumene*: E. W. Handley, *B.I.C.S.* 16 (1969) 88–101 (quotes extensively). (4) SOME SHORTER GENERAL DISCUSSIONS: G. Murray, *Aristophanes* (Oxford 1933) 221–63; A. W. Gomme, *Essays in Greek history and literature* (Oxford 1937) 249–95; L. A. Post, *From Homer to Menander* (Berkeley, Cal. 1951); E. Lefèvre, 'Menander', in (ed.) G. A. Seeck, *Das griechische Drama* (Darmstadt 1979) 307–53. Webster (1974) 111–93, under (2) above, gives 'summary reconstructions of all the plays of which anything useful can be said'. (5) PRODUCTION AND COSTUME: See *General works* (4) under 'Greek Comedy' and add: T. B. L. Webster, 'The masks of Greek comedy', *Bull. John Rylands Library* 32 (1949) 97–136; idem, 'Menander: production and imagination', *Bull. John Rylands Library* 45 (1962) 235–72; Charitonidis *et al.* under

Life and works above *ad fin.* (6) COLLECTED STUDIES: C. Corbato, *Studi Menandrei* (Trieste 1965); F. Zucker, *Menanders Dyskolos als Zeugnis seiner Epoche* (Berlin 1965); (ed.) E. G. Turner, *Entretiens XVI: Ménandre* (Fondation Hardt, Geneva 1970).

INDEXES (partial coverage only): Koerte, BT ed. II, supplemented (mainly from *Dysk.*) by H.-J. Mette, *ed. Dysk.*, 2nd ed. (Göttingen 1961). *Aspis* and *Samia*: Austin I, under *Commentaries* above. *Dysk.*: H. Lloyd-Jones, *ed. Dysk.* (OCT, 1960). *Mis.* (most of), *Sik.* and some other pieces: *CGFPap. Sententiae*: Jaekel, BT ed.

HISTORIOGRAPHY

HERODOTUS

LIFE

b. *c.* 485 B.C. at Halicarnassus in Caria, of aristocratic family; related to epic poet Panyassis. Exiled after fighting against local tyrant Lygdamis and resident for a time in Samos. Extensive travels: north as far as south Russia; Babylon, Syria, Palestine; Egypt, Cyrenaica; Aegean and mainland Greece, incl. Athens. Acquainted with Sophocles. Settled in Thurii (founded 444/3), where perhaps he d. and was buried *c.* 425 B.C. Sources: Dion. Hal. *Thuc.* 5, Gell. 15.23 (dates); Luc. *Herod.* 1–2, Plut. *De Herod. malign.* 26.862b (recitations); Plut. *An seni* 3.785b (Sophocles); Steph. Byz. s.v. 'Thurii' (epitaph); his own works, Suda, s.v. 'Herodotus' and 'Panyassis'. On travels see F. Jacoby, *RE* suppl. II (1913) 247ff.

WORKS

Histories (9 bks) on origins and events of Persian War to 479 B.C.; probably in circulation at least in portions during 440s (no refs. later than 430), but not pubd until early years of Peloponnesian War. On question of completeness see above p. 428.

BIBLIOGRAPHY

(See L. Bergson, *Lustrum* 11 (1966) 71–138 (for 1937–60); P. MacKendrick, *C.W.* 47 (1954) 145–52, 56 (1963) 269–75 (for 1954–63), 63 (1969) 37–44 (for 1963–9); G. T. Griffiths, *FYAT* 183–8, 227–9; (ed.) W. Marg, *Herodot: eine Auswahl aus der neueren Forschung*, 2nd ed. (Munich 1968).)

TEXTS AND COMMENTARIES: TEXTS: H. Stein (Berlin 1869–71); A. D. Godley, 2nd ed. (Loeb, 1922–38); C. Hude, 3rd ed. (OCT, 1927); P.-E. Legrand, 2nd ed. (Budé, 1955: with *index analytique*). COMMENTARIES: H. Stein, 5 vols. in 7,

4th–6th ed. (Berlin 1893–1908: repr. 1962–3); W. W. How and J. Wells, 2 vols., 2nd ed. (Oxford 1928). Bks 1–3: A. H. Sayce (London 1883). Bks 4–6: R. W. Macan, 2 vols. (London 1895). Bks 7–9: R. W. Macan, 2 vols. in 5 (London 1908). Bk 2: A. B. Lloyd (Leiden: I Introduction, 1975; II Commentary 1–98, 1976).

TRANSLATIONS: G. Rawlinson, 4 vols., 4th ed. (London 1880: with comm. and appendices), rev. ed. W. G. Forrest (London 1966); J. E. Powell, 2 vols. (Oxford 1949); A. de Sélincourt, rev. with introd. by A. R. Burn (Harmondsworth, 1972).

STUDIES: (1) GENERAL: A. Hauvette, *Hérodote, historien des guerres médiques* (Paris 1894); F. Jacoby, *RE* suppl. II (1913) 205–520; W. Aly, *Volksmärchen, Sage und Novelle bei Herodot und seinen Zeitgenossen* (Göttingen 1921: repr. 1969); J. Wells, *Studies in Herodotus* (Oxford 1923); M. Pohlenz, *Herodot, der erste Geschichtsschreiber des Abendlandes* (Berlin 1937); J. E. Powell, *The history of Herodotus* (Cambridge 1939); J. L. Myres, *Herodotus, father of history* (Oxford 1953); H. R. Immerwahr, *Form and thought in Herodotus* (Cleveland 1966); K. von Fritz, *Griechische Geschichtsschreibung* I (Berlin 1967) 104–475; H.-F. Bornitz, *Herodot-Studien: Beiträge zum Verständnis der Einheit des Geschichtswerks* (Berlin 1968); C. W. Fornara, *Herodotus: an interpretative essay* (Oxford 1971). (2) HISTORICAL: G. B. Grundy, *The great Persian war and its preliminaries* (London 1901); A. R. Burn, *Persia and the Greeks; the defence of the West, c. 546–478 B.C.* (London 1962); A. T. Olmstead, *History of the Persian empire, Achaemenid period* (Chicago 1948); C. Hignett, *Xerxes' invasion of Greece* (Oxford 1963). (3) DIALECT: M. Untersteiner, *La lingua di Erodoto* (Naples 1949); H. B. Rosen, *Eine Laut- und Formenlehre der herodotischen Sprachform* (Heidelberg 1962).

LEXICON: J. E. Powell (Cambridge 1938).

THUCYDIDES

LIFE

b. in Athenian deme of Halimus, possibly before 454 B.C.; perhaps related to Thucydides son of Melesias (H.-T. Wade-Gery, *J.H.S.* 52 (1932) 210–11). Survived Athenian plague of 430–427. As *strategos* in 424 failed to relieve Amphipolis from Brasidas' attack and lived in exile for twenty years; returned to Athens and probably d. there soon after 399; buried in Cimon's family vault. Possessed right of working goldmines in Thrace. Sources: own work, esp. 2.48.3 (plague), 4.105.2 (mines), 5.26 (Amphipolis and exile), two *Lives* (in OCT ed. I), Dion. Hal. *Thucydides*, Plut. *Cimon* 4, Pausanias 1.23.9.

WORKS

Unfinished *History* (8 bks) of Peloponnesian War, projected to 404 (5.26.1); narrative breaks off in 411. Begun in 431 (1.1.1) and still in progress after 404 (2.65.12, 6.15.3). Continued in lost works of Cratippus and Theopompus, in Oxyrhynchus *Hellenica* (on authorship see *FYAT* 192–4), and in Xenophon's *Hellenica*.

BIBLIOGRAPHY

(See. F. M. Wassermann, *C.W.* 50 (1956/7) 65–7, 89–101 (for 1942–56), cont. by M. Chambers, *C.W.* 57 (1963/4) 6–14; H.-P. Stahl, *Thukydides* (Munich 1966) 172–9; G. T. Griffith, *FYAT* 188–92, 229–32; O. Luschnat, *RE* suppl. xii (1970) 1323–38; K. J. Dover, *Thucydides*, *G.&R.* New Surveys in the classics vii (1973); on speeches 1873–1970 see W. C. West in Stadter (1973), under *Studies* (2) below, 124–61.)

TEXTS AND COMMENTARIES: TEXTS: C. Hude, editio maxima (Leipzig 1898–1901); idem, editio maior, 2nd ed. (BT, 1913–25); C. F. Smith, 2nd ed. (Loeb, 1928–35); H. S. Jones and J. E. Powell, 2nd ed. (OCT, 1942); L. Bodin, J. de Romilly, R. Weil (Budé, 1953–); O. Luschnat, 2nd ed. (BT, 1960: Bks 1–2). COMMENTARIES: E. F. Poppo and M. Stahl, 4 vols. 2nd–3rd ed. (Leipzig 1886–9); J. Classen and J. Steup, 8 vols., 3rd–5th ed. (Berlin 1900–22: repr. with appendix and bibl. by R. Stark 1963); A. W. Gomme, A. Andrewes, K. J. Dover, 4 vols. (Oxford 1945–70: Bks 1–7). *Scholia.* C. Hude (BT, 1927).

TRANSLATIONS: T. Hobbes (London 1629: ed. D. Grene, 2 vols., Ann Arbor 1960); B. Jowett, 2 vols. (Oxford 1881: text and notes); R. Crawley (London 1910); R. Warner (Harmondsworth, 1954).

STUDIES: (1) GENERAL: F. W. Ullrich, *Beiträge zur Erklärung des Thukydides*, 2 vols. (Berlin 1845–6); E. Meyer, *Forschungen zur alten Geschichte* ii (Halle 1899); F. M. Cornford, *Thucydides mythistoricus* (London 1907); J. B. Bury, *The ancient Greek historians* (New York 1909) ch. iii; E. Schwartz, *Das Geschichtswerk des Thukydides* (Bonn 1919); G. F. Abbott, *Thucydides: a study in historical reality* (London 1925); C. N. Cochrane, *Thucydides and the science of history* (London 1929); W. Schadewaldt, *Die Geschichtsschreibung des Thukydides* (Berlin 1929); H. Patzer, *Das Problem der Geschichtsschreibung des Thukydides und die thukydideische Frage* (Berlin 1937); J. H. Finley, *Thucydides* (Cambridge, Mass. 1942); W. Jaeger, *Paideia: the ideals of Greek culture* i, 2nd ed. tr. G. Highet (New York 1945) 382–411; G. B. Grundy, *Thucydides and the history of his age*, 2 vols., 2nd ed. (Oxford 1948); A. W. Gomme, *The Greek attitude to poetry and history* (Berkeley 1954); J. de Romilly, *Histoire et raison chez Thucydides* (Paris 1956); eadem, *Thucydides and Athenian imperialism*, tr. P. Thody (Oxford 1963); F. E. Adcock, *Thucydides and his history* (Cambridge 1963); H.-P.

Stahl, *Thukydides: die Stellung des Menschen im geschichtlichen Prozess* (Munich 1966); J. H. Finley, *Three essays on Thucydides* (Cambridge, Mass. 1967); K. von Fritz, *Griechische Geschichtsschreibung* I (Berlin 1967) 523–823; (ed.) H. Herter, *Thukydides*, Wege der Forschung XCVIII (Darmstadt 1968); H. D. Westlake, *Individuals in Thucydides* (Cambridge 1968); V. Hunter, *Thucydides the artful reporter* (Toronto 1973); O. Luschnat, *RE* suppl. XII (1970) 1085–1134 and XIV (1974) 760–86; A. G. Woodhead, *Thucydides on the nature of power* (Cambridge, Mass. 1970); H. R. Rawlings, *The structure of Thucydides' history* (Princeton, N.J. 1981). (2) SPEECHES: R. C. Jebb in (ed.) E. Abbott, *Hellenica* (London 1880); A. W. Gomme, *Essays in Greek history and literature* (Oxford 1937); (ed.) P. A. Stadter, *The speeches in Thucydides* (Chapel Hill 1973). (3) HISTORICAL: B. W. Henderson, *The great war between Athens and Sparta: a companion to the military history of Thucydides* (London 1927); D. Kagan, *The outbreak of the Peloponnesian War* (Ithaca 1969); idem, *The Archidamian War* (Ithaca 1974); J. B. Wilson, *Pylos 425 B.C.* (Warminster, Wilts. 1979); D. Kagan, *The Peace of Nicias and the Sicilian Expedition* (Ithaca 1981). (4) TEXT: A. Kleinlogel, *Geschichte des Thukydidestextes im Mittelalter* (Berlin 1965).

LEXICA: E.-A. Bétant, 2 vols. (Geneva 1843: repr. Hildesheim 1961); M. H. N. von Essen (Berlin 1887).

HISTORICAL WRITING IN THE FOURTH CENTURY AND IN THE HELLENISTIC PERIOD

GENERAL WORKS

For text and commentary on authors in this section whose work survives in fragments see *FGrH* = F. Jacoby, *Die Fragmente der griechischen Historiker* (Leiden 1923–).

STUDIES

Fritz, K. von, *Die griechische Geschichtsschreibung* (Berlin 1967–)
Jacoby, F., *Atthis* (Oxford 1949)
idem, *Abhandlungen zur griechischen Geschichtsschreibung* (Leiden 1956)
Momigliano, A., *Contributi alla storia degli studi classici* (Rome 1955–75)
idem, *The development of Greek biography* (Cambridge, Mass. 1971)
Strasburger, H., *Die Wesenbestimmung der Geschichte durch die antike Geschichtsschreibung*, 2nd ed. (Wiesbaden 1966)

INDIVIDUAL AUTHORS

ALEXANDER HISTORIANS: L. Pearson, *The lost histories of Alexander the Great* (New York 1960), with review by E. Badian, *Studies in Greek and Roman history* (Oxford 1964) 250ff.

ALEXANDER ROMANCE: R. Merkelbach, *Die Quellen des griechischen Alexander-Romans*, Zetemata IX (Munich 1954).

CLITARCHUS: T. S. Brown, *A.J.Ph.* 71 (1950) 134–55.

DIODORUS: E. Schwartz, *RE* v (1905) 663–704.

DURIS: R. B. Kebric, *In the shadow of Macedon: Duris of Samos* (Wiesbaden 1977).

EPHORUS: G. L. Barber, *The historian Ephorus* (Cambridge 1935).

HIERONYMUS: T. S. Brown, *American Historical Review* 52 (1946/7) 684–96.

NEARCHUS: E. Badian, *Y.Cl.S.* 24 (1975) 147–75.

ONESICRITUS: T. S. Brown, *Onesicritus*, University of California publications in history XXXIX (Berkeley 1949).

OXYRHYNCHUS HISTORIAN: Texts in V. Bartoletti (BT, 1959); additional fragment in G. A. Lehmann, *Z.P.E.* 26 (1977) 181–91. See I. A. F. Bruce, *An historical commentary on the Hellenica Oxyrhynchia* (London 1967). Bibliography on question of identity by G. T. Griffith, *FYAT* 214–15 nn.43–57.

PHYLARCHUS: T. W. Africa, *Phylarchus and the Spartan revolution*, University of California publications in history LXVIII (Berkeley 1961).

POSIDONIUS: K. Reinhardt, *RE* XXII (1953) 558–826; H. Strasburger, 'Poseidonius on problems of the Roman empire', *J.R.S.* 55 (1965) 40–53.

PTOLEMY: H. Strasburger, *Ptolemaios und Alexander* (Leipzig 1934).

THEOPOMPUS: K. von Fritz, *American Historical Review* 46 (1941) 765–87; W. R. Connor, *Theopompus and fifth-century Athens* (Washington 1968).

TIMAEUS: A. Momigliano, 'Atene nel III secolo a.c. et la scoperta di Roma nelle storie di Timeo di Tauromenio', *R.S.I.* 71 (1959) 529–56, variously reprinted including a translation in *Essays in ancient and modern historiography* (Middletown, Conn. 1976).

XENOPHON

LIFE

b. *c.* 428 B.C. Participated in expedition of Cyrus to Persia 401. Joint leader of Greek forces on retreat to Black Sea and Thrace 401–399. Joined Spartan king Agesilaus; with him against Athens at Coronea 394. Banished for treason; set up estate at Scillus in Elis, where he farmed, hunted and wrote. Expelled after Spartan defeat at Leuctra 371 and retired to Corinth; rights at Athens restored. d. *c.* 354 B.C. Sources: Xen. *Anab.* passim; Diog. Laert. 2.48–59; Suda; Pausanias 5.6.5–6 (Scillus); Dio Chrys. 8.1 (exile). See E. Delebecque, *Essai sur la vie de Xénophon* (Paris 1957).

WORKS

(1) SOCRATIC: *Apology* (between 394 and 387): thought by some to precede, by others to follow Plato's *Apology*. On authenticity see (for) M. Wetzel, *Neue Jahrbücher f. d. klass. Altertum* 5 (1900) 389–405; O. Immisch, ibid. 405–15; H. Gomperz, ibid. 29 (1924) 129–73; A. Busse, *Rh.M.* n.s.79 (1930) 215–29; (against) U. von Wilamowitz-Moellendorff, *Hermes* 32 (1897) 99–106; K. von Fritz, *Rh.M.* n.s.80 (1931) 36–68. Wilamowitz later undecided, *Platon* II (Berlin 1909) 50. *Memorabilia Socratis* (4 bks): subsequent to *Apology* (4.8.4–10); replies (1.1–2) to Polycrates (394–388); if 3.5.4 reflects conditions of 360s, composed over long period. *Oeconomicus. Symposium*: probably later than Plato's *Symposium*, with which many points of contact: dramatic date 421. (2) HISTORICAL etc. (for evidence on dates see Breitenbach (1966) under *Studies* (1) below and Lesky 616–23): *Agesilaus*: biographical essay on Spartan king who d. 360. *Anabasis* (7 bks): account of expedition of Greek forces under Cyrus and their return 401–399. *Cynegeticus*: treatise on hunting. *Cyropaedeia* (8 bks): historical novel, centred round Cyrus, on the education of statesmen. *Hellenica* (7 bks): history of Greece from 411 to 362, probably written in several stages. *Hiero*: dialogue on tyranny between Hiero of Syracuse and poet Simonides of Ceos. *Hipparchicus*: on duties of a cavalry commander. *On horsemanship. On the revenues*: on economic conditions in Athens; presupposes situation in 355. *Politeia of the Lacedaemonians*: account of Spartan constitution, composed sometime in first three decades of 4th c. Spurious: *Politeia of the Athenians*: account of Athenian constitution, probably set in first years of Peloponnesian War (431–424); identity of author, sometimes called 'The Old Oligarch', unknown. See M. Treu, *RE* IXA (1966) 1928–82; G. W. Bowersock, *Gnomon* 43 (1971) 416–18.

BIBLIOGRAPHY

(See Bursian 100 (1899), 117 (1903), 142 (1909), 178 (1919), 203 (1925), 230 (1931), 251 (1936), 268 (1940).)

TEXTS AND COMMENTARIES: TEXTS: E. C. Marchant (OCT, 1900–10); G. W. Bowersock, C. L. Brownson, E. C. Marchant, W. Miller, O. J. Todd (Loeb, 1914–68). COMMENTARIES: *Apology* and *Symposium*: F. Ollier (Budé ,1961). *Hellenica*: G. E. Underhill (Oxford 1906: repr. New York 1979). *Hipparchicus*: E. Delebecque (Paris 1950). *Memorabilia Socratis*: (Bks 1–2) O. Gigon (Basel 1953–6); (Bk 3) A. Delatte (Liège & Paris 1933). *Oeconomicus*: P. Chantraine (Budé, 1949); K. Meyer (Marburg 1975). *On the revenues*: P. Gauthier (Geneva & Paris 1976). *Politeia of the Lacedaemonians*: F. Ollier (Lyons & Paris 1934: with tr.: repr. New York 1979). *Symposium*: see under *Apology*. *Politeia of the Athenians*: E. Kalinka (Leipzig 1913); H. Frisch (Copenhagen 1942: with tr.); see also commentaries on Aristotelian *Ath. Pol.* by J. E. Sandys (London 1912) and P. J. Rhodes (Oxford 1981).

TRANSLATIONS: R. Warner *et al.* (Harmondsworth, 1966–72: *Anab.*, *Hell.*, *Mem. Socr.*, *Symp.*).

STUDIES: (1) GENERAL AND HISTORICAL: J. Luccioni, *Les idées politiques et sociales de Xénophon* (Paris 1947); H. R. Breitenbach *RE* IXA.2 (1966) 1571–2052; W. P. Henry, *Greek historical writing* (Chicago 1966: on *Hellenica*); J. K. Anderson, *Xenophon* (London 1974); W. E. Higgins, *Xenophon the Athenian* (New York 1977); R. Nickel, *Xenophon* (Darmstadt 1979). (2) SOCRATIC: K. Joel, *Der echte und der xenophontische Socrates*, 2 vols. (Berlin 1893–1901); J. Burnet, *Plato's Phaedo* (Oxford 1911) xii–xxiii; A. Diès, *Autour de Platon* (Paris 1927) 127–55, 218–44; E. Edelstein, *Xenophontisches und platonisches Bild des Sokrates* (Berlin 1935); R. Simeterre, *La théorie socratique de la vertu-science selon les 'Mémorables' de Xénophon* (Paris 1938); V. Longo, ΑΝΗΡ ΩΦΕΛΙΜΟΣ (Genoa 1959); H. Erbse, 'Die Architektonik im Aufbau von Xenophons *Memorabilien*', *Hermes* 89 (1961) 257–87. (3) LANGUAGE, TEXT, INFLUENCE: L. Gautier, *La langue de Xénophon* (Geneva 1911); A. W. Persson, *Zur Textgeschichte Xenophons* (Lund 1914); K. Munscher, *Xenophon in der griechischen-römischen Literatur*, *Philologus* suppl. XIII.2 (1920); J. Bigalke, *Einfluss der Rhetorik auf Xenophons Stil* (Greifswald 1933).

LEXICON: F. W. Sturz, 4 vols. (Leipzig 1801–4: repr. Hildesheim 1964).

POLYBIUS

LIFE

b. *c.* 200 B.C. at Megalopolis, son of statesman Lycortas. Carried ashes of Philopoemen to burial 182 and was appointed envoy to Egypt 180 (embassy cancelled). Served as hipparch of the Achaean confederation 170/69. One of 1,000 Achaeans deported to Rome after conquest of Macedonia 168; befriended by Scipio Aemilianus, whom he probably accompanied to Spain 151 and Africa; witnessed destruction of Carthage 146.

POLYBIUS

Acted as mediator after sack of Corinth 146/5. Travelled extensively (the Atlantic, Alexandria, Sardis; perhaps Numantia 133). d. after 118 from a riding accident. Sources: see Walbank under *Commentaries* below, I 1–6.

WORKS

Histories (39 bks, plus a chronologically arranged résumé): bks 1–5 survive substantially complete, the rest in fragments and excerpts; originally designed to cover period 220–168, later extended down to 146. Lost are a panegyric on Philopoemen (Polyb. 10.21.5–8), a history of the Numantine war (Cic. *Fam.* 5.12.2), and works on military tactics (Polyb. 9.20.4; Arr. *Tact.* 1; Ael. *Tact.* 1, 3.4, 19.10) and the equatorial region (Geminus 16.12).

BIBLIOGRAPHY

(See Walbank under *Commentaries* below, I–III.)

TEXTS AND COMMENTARIES: TEXTS: T. Büttner-Wobst (BT, 1889); W. R. Paton (Loeb, 1922–7); P. Pédech *et al.* (Budé, 1961–77). COMMENTARIES: F. W. Walbank, 3 vols. (Oxford 1957–79).

STUDIES: K. Ziegler, *RE* XXI (1952) 1440–1578 (*q.v.* for earlier bibliography); K. von Fritz, *The theory of the mixed constitution in antiquity* (New York 1954); M. Gelzer, 'Die pragmatische Geschichtsschreibung des Polybius', *Festschrift für Carl Weickert* (1955) = *Kleine Schriften* III (Wiesbaden 1964) 155–60; F. W. Walbank, 'Polemic in Polybius', *J.R.S.* 52 (1962) 1–12; idem, 'Polybius and Rome's Eastern policy', *J.R.S.* 53 (1963) 1–13; J. M. Moore, *The manuscript tradition of Polybius* (Cambridge 1965); G. Lehmann, *Untersuchungen zur historische Glaubwürdigkeit des Polybios* (Münster 1967); P. Pédech, *La méthode historique de Polybe* (Paris 1969); F. W. Walbank, *Polybius* (Berkeley 1972); G. Schepens, 'The bipartite and tripartite division of history in Polybius', *Ancient Society* 5 (1974) 277–87; K. Meister, *Historische Kritik bei Polybios* (Wiesbaden 1975); K. S. Sachs, 'Polybius' other view of Aetolia', *J.H.S.* 95 (1975) 92ff.,; P. S. Derow, 'Polybius, Rome and the East', *J.R.S.* 69 (1979) 1–15; K. S. Sachs, *Polybius on the writing of history*, University of California publications in classical studies XXIV (Berkeley 1981).

LEXICON: A. Mauersberger (Berlin 1956–75).

SOPHISTS AND PHYSICIANS
OF THE GREEK ENLIGHTENMENT

GENERAL WORKS

For texts of the sophists see DK = H. Diels and W. Kranz, *Die Fragmente der Vorsokratiker* II, 6th ed. (Berlin 1952); L. Radermacher, *Artium scriptores* (Vienna 1951). The fragments are translated in R. K. Sprague, *The older sophists. A complete translation by several hands* (Columbia, S.C. 1972). For texts of the Hippocratic corpus see edition by E. Littré (Parts 1839–61); for a translation of selected works see W. H. S. Jones and E. T. Withington (Loeb, 1923–31).

STUDIES

Gomperz, H., *Sophistik und Rhetorik* (Leipzig 1912)

Guthrie III

Jaeger, W., *Paideia. The ideals of Greek culture*, tr. G. Highet, I (New York 1945) 286–331

Kennedy, G., *The art of persuasion in Greece* (Princeton 1963) 26–70

Kerferd, G. B., *The sophistic movement* (Cambridge 1981)

Kühn, J. H., 'System- und Methodenprobleme in Corpus Hippocraticum', *Hermes* Einzelschriften XI (1956)

Lloyd, G. E. R., *Magic, reason and experience. Studies in the origin and development of Greek science* (Cambridge 1979)

Pfeiffer 16–56

Smith, W. D., *The Hippocratic tradition* (Ithaca 1979)

Solmsen, F., *Intellectual experiments of the Greek enlightenment* (Princeton 1975)

Untersteiner, M., *The sophists*, tr. K. Freeman (Oxford 1954)

INDIVIDUAL SOPHISTS

PROTAGORAS OF ABDERA (*c.* 490–*c.* 420 B.C.): Testimonia indicate his major works were called: *Truth* or *Refutations*; *On being*; *The great speech*; *On the gods*; *Contradictory arguments*. Texts in DK II 253–71. See A. Capizzi, *Protagora* (Florence 1955).

GORGIAS OF LEONTINI (*c.* 480–*c.* 375 B.C.): Extant are the *Encomium of Helen* and *Defence of Palamedes*; an outline of *On the nonexistent or on nature* is preserved by Sext. Emp. *Adv. math.* 7.65–87. Texts in DK II 271–307; Radermacher B VII; edition of *Helen* by O. Immisch (Berlin & Leipzig 1927). See J. de Romilly, *Magic and rhetoric in ancient Greece* (Cambridge, Mass. 1975).

PRODICUS OF CEOS (*c.* 465–?400 B.C.): Testimonia indicate his major works were called *Horai* or *Seasons*, and *On nature*. Texts in DK II 308–19; Radermacher B VIII.

THRASYMACHUS OF CHALCEDON (*fl. c.* 427 B.C.): Testimonia indicate his major works were speeches, including *On the constitution* and *For the Larisaeans*, and the *Long textbook*. Texts in DK II 319–26; Radermacher B IX.

HIPPIAS OF ELIS (*fl. c.* 430 B.C.): Composed speeches, elegies, a list of Olympic victors, a nomenclature of tribes, and other works. Texts in DK II 326–34; Radermacher B XI.

CRITIAS OF ATHENS (*c.* 460–*c.* 403 B.C.): Composed hexameter and elegiac verse, several constitutions, aphorisms, lectures, *On the nature of desires or of virtues*, and may have written dramas including a *Sisyphus*. Texts in DK II 371–99; Radermacher B XVII.

ANTISTHENES OF ATHENS (*c.* 455–*c.* 360 B.C.): Founder of Cynicism. Two extant declamations are attributed to him, *Ajax* and *Odysseus*; also lost dialogues. Texts in Radermacher B XIX.

ALCIDAMAS OF ELEA (*fl. c.* 390 B.C.): Extant are a work *On those writing written speeches* or *On the sophists*, and (spurious) a declamation, *Odysseus*. Texts in Radermacher B XXII.

ANAXIMENES OF LAMPSACUS (*c.* 380–*c.* 320 B.C.): Extant is the *Rhetorica ad Alexandrum*: edition by M. Fuhrmann (BT, 1966); translation by H. Rackham in *Aristotle. Problems* II (Loeb, 1937). Additional fragments in Radermacher B XXXVI; fragments of historical works in *FGrH* II A 112–30.

PLATO AND THE SOCRATIC WORK OF XENOPHON

XENOPHON

See pp. 788–9.

PLATO

LIFE

b. 427 B.C. in Athens, son of Aristo, who traced descent from kings of Athens, and Perictione, sister of oligarchic politician Charmides; cousin of Critias who, like Charmides, belonged to 'The Thirty'. Visited Italy (Archytas at Tarentum) and Sicily (met Dion with Dionysius I at Syracuse) 388. After return to Athens founded

PLATO

'Academy', a society of men studying philosophy, mathematics and political science. In Syracuse 367–366 and 361–360 (attempts to influence Dionysius II). d. in Athens 348. Sources: Plato, *Letters* 7 and 8; Philodemus, *Acad. ind.* col. x 5ff.; Nepos, *Dion* 2–3; Plut. *Dion* 5, 17, 20; Diog. Laert. 3.1–9, 18–46; Apuleius, *De Platone* 1.1–4; Olympiodorus, *Vita Platonis* (in A. Westermann, *Vitarum scriptores Graeci minores* (Brunswick 1845) 382ff.).

WORKS

(1) *Apology* (*Socrates' defence*). Perhaps after 394. (2) DIALOGUES: (*a*) *Genuine*, listed in approximate order of composition. (Order determined mainly by stylometry, with the results of which apparent philosophical development on the whole accords. Stylometry least effective for arranging supposed earlier part of group (i), but order from *Gorgias* onwards plausible, unless *Symposium* preceded *Phaedo*. Group (iii) marked by avoidance of hiatus. Uncertain when P. began to compose his dialogues; if living characters could by convention not be used, after 399. Dialogues may have been revised over fairly long periods, which would make stylometry less effective. See R. Simeterre, *Introduction à l'étude de Platon* (Paris 1948) 72–41 (summary, with bibliography); idem, *R.E.G.* 58 (1945) 146–62; W. D. Ross, *Plato's theory of ideas* (Oxford 1951) 1–10; A. Diaz Tejera, *Emerita* 29 (1961) 241–86; H. Thesleff, *Studies in the style of Plato* (Helsinki 1967) 8–25; idem, *Studies in Platonic chronology* (Helsinki 1982: reviews earlier work).) (i) *Ion, Laches, Crito, Charmides, Euthyphro* (placed later than *Meno* by K. Reich, *Euthyphron* (Hamburg 1968) and E. Kapp, *Ausgewählte Schriften* (Berlin 1968) 61; than *Gorgias* by K. H. Ilting, *Gnomon* 44 (1972) 382), *Hippias minor, Protagoras, Lysis, Cratylus* (date uncertain: see M. Warburg, *Zwei Fragen zum 'Kratylos'* (Berlin 1929) 31–61; J. V. Luce, *A.J.Ph.* 85 (1964) 136–54), *Gorgias, Meno, Euthydemus, Menexenus* (? 386; not before 390, cf. 245e), *Phaedo, Symposium* (? after 385; cf. 193a and K. J. Dover, *Phronesis* 10 (1965) 2–20), *Republic* (10 bks; 1 earlier in style than 2–10). (ii) *Parmenides, Phaedrus, Theaetetus* (? after 369; cf. 142a). (iii) *Sophist, Statesman* (*Politicus*), *Timaeus* (placed before *Parmenides* by G. E. L. Owen, *C.Q.* n.s.3 (1953) 79–95; but see e.g. H. Cherniss, *A.J.Ph.* 78 (1957) 225–66), *Critias, Philebus, Laws* (12 bks, unfinished in 348; said to have been 'transcribed', perhaps prepared for publication, by Philippus of Opus). (*b*) *Doubtfully genuine. Hippias major* (For: G. M. A. Grube, *C.Q.* 20 (1926) 134–48; idem, *C.Ph.* 24 (1929) 369–75; M. Soreth, *Der platonische Dialog Hippias maior* (Munich 1953); Friedländer under *Studies* (1) below, II 105–16; others. Against: Wilamowitz-Moellendorff under *Studies* (1) below, II 327–8; D. Tarrant, *C.Q.* 42 (1948) 28–34; others), *Alcibiades I* (For: Friedländer under *Studies* (1) below, II 231–43. Against: Wilamowitz-Moellendorff under *Studies* (1) below, II 326–7; R. S. Bluck, *C.Q.* n.s.3 (1953) 46–52; most scholars), *Clitopho* (For: G. M. A. Grube, *C.Ph.* 26 (1931) 302–8; H. Kesters, *De authenticiteit van den Kleitophoon* (Louvain 1935). Against: most scholars), *Epinomis* (For: J. Harward, *The Epinomis of Plato* (Oxford 1928) 26–58; É. des Places, Budé ed. (1956). Against: 'some say that *Epinomis* is the work of Philippus of Opus' (Diog. Laert. 3.37, cf. Suda s.v. φιλόσοφος); G. Müller, *Studien zu den*

793

platonischen Nomoi (Munich 1951). (*c*) *Spurious*. (i) Included in canon of Thrasyllus (d. A.D. 36), who arranged P.'s work into tetralogies: *Theages, Alcibiades II, Erastae, Hipparchus*. (ii) Not included by Thrasyllus: *Alcyon* (= Ps.-Lucian, *Alcyon*), *Axiochus* (post-Epicurus), *De iustitia, De virtute, Demodocus, Eryxias* (? 3rd c.), *Sisyphus*. (iii) Lost: *Cimon* (Athen. 506d), *Midon* (?), *Phaeacians, Chelidon, Hebdome, Epimenides* (Diog. Laert. 3.62). See W. A. Heidel, *Pseudo-Platonica* (Baltimore 1896: repr. New York 1976). (3) Thirteen *Letters*, mostly spurious: 7 and 8 have best claim to be genuine. R. Hackforth, *The authorship of the Platonic Epistles* (Manchester 1913) accepts 3, 4, 7, 8, 13; G. Pasquali, *Le Lettere di Platone* (Florence 1938) accepts 6, 7, 8; G. R. Morrow, *Plato's Epistles* (Indianapolis 1962) accepts 4, 6, 7, 8, 10. No. 7 defended by K. von Fritz, *Phronesis* 11 (1966) 117–53 and *Platon in Sizilien* (Berlin 1968) 5–62; rejected by G. Ryle, *Plato's progress* (Cambridge 1966) 55–89; L. Edelstein, *Plato's seventh Letter* (Leiden 1966), but see F. Solmsen, *Gnomon* 41 (1969) 29–34); M. Levison, A. Q. Morton, A. D. Winspear, *Mind* 77 (1968) 309–25, but see L. Brandwood, *Revue pour l'étude des langues anciennes par co-ordinateur* 4 (1969) 1–25; N. Gulley, *Entretiens XIV: Pseudepigrapha* (Fondation Hardt, Geneva 1971) 105–43. No. 8 defended by G. J. D. Aalders, *Mnemosyne* 4.22 (1969) 233–57; see also J. Souilhé, *Platon, Lettres* (Paris 1926). (4) Epigrams. *Anth. Pal.* 5.77–80; 6.1, 43; 7.99–100, 217, 256, 259, 265, 268–9, 669–70; 9.3, 39, 44–5, 51, 506, 747, 823, 826–7; *Anth. Plan.* 13, 160–1, 210; Olympiodorus, *Vita Platonis* 1 p. 384 W. Perhaps none is authentic; some have alternative ascription. See W. Ludwig, *G.R.B.S.* 4 (1963) 59–82. (5) Some 200 spurious *Definitions*: see J. Souilhé, Budé ed. XIII 3.153–9.

BIBLIOGRAPHY

(See C. Ritter, Bursian 220 (1929) 37–108 and 225 (1930) 121–68; E. de Strycker, *Études classiques* 4 (1935) 219–36; idem, *A.C.* 4 (1935) 227–43; T. G. Rosenmeyer, *C.W.* 50 (1957) 173–201, 209–11; H. Cherniss, *Lustrum* 4 (1960) 1–316 and 5 (1961) 321–648; Guthrie IV and V; J. B. Skemp, *Plato, G.&R.* New surveys in the classics X (1976); L. Brisson, *Lustrum* 20 (1977).)

TEXTS AND COMMENTARIES: TEXTS: J. Burnet, 1st–2nd edd. (OCT, 1903–15); R. G. Bury, H. N. Fowler, W. R. M. Lamb, P. Shorey (Loeb, 1914–35); L. Bodin, E. Chambry, M. and A. Croiset, L. Méridier, É. des Places, A. Diès, A. Rivaud, L. Robin, J. Souilhé (Budé, 1921–56). COMMENTARIES (AND DISCUSSIONS): *Apology*: J. Burnet (Oxford 1924: with *Euthyphro, Crito*); E. Wolf (Berlin 1929); R. Hackforth (Cambridge 1933); T. Meyer (Stuttgart 1962). *Axiochus*: E. H. Blakeney (London 1937). *Charmides*: T. G. Tuckey (Cambridge 1951); B. Witte, *Die Wissenschaft von Guten und Bösen* (Berlin 1970). *Cratylus*: V. Goldschmidt (Paris 1940). *Crito*: see under *Apology*. *Epinomis*: F. Novotny (Prague 1960); L. Tarán, *Academica* (Philadelphia 1975). *Euthydemus*: H. Keulen (Wiesbaden 1971); R. S. W. Hawtrey (Philadelphia 1981). *Euthyphro*: see under *Apology*. *Gorgias*: E. R. Dodds (Oxford

1959); T. Irwin (Oxford 1980: with tr.). *Hippias major*: D. Tarrant (Cambridge 1928); P. Woodruff (Oxford 1982: with tr.). *Laws*: E. B. England, 2 vols. (Manchester 1921); G. R. Morrow, *Plato's Cretan city* (Princeton 1960). *Letters*: F. Novotny (Brno 1930): R. S. Bluck (Cambridge 1947: 7–8 only); G. R. Morrow (Indianapolis 1962: with tr.). *Menexenus*: C. H. Kahn, *C.Ph.* 58 (1963) 220–34; E. F. Bloedow, *W.S.* n.s.9 (1975) 32–48. *Meno*: R. S. Bluck (Cambridge 1961). *Parmenides*: F. M. Cornford (London 1939: with tr.). *Phaedo*: J. Burnet (Oxford 1911); R. Hackforth (Cambridge 1955: with tr.), R. S. Bluck (London 1955: with tr.); D. Gallop (Oxford 1975: with tr.). *Phaedrus*: R. Hackforth (Cambridge 1952: with tr.); G. J. de Vries (Amsterdam 1969). *Philebus*: R. G. Bury (Cambridge 1897); R. Hackforth, *Plato's examination of pleasure* (Cambridge 1945: with tr.); J. C. B. Gosling (Oxford 1975: with tr.). *Politicus*: J. B. Skemp (London 1952: with tr.). *Protagoras*: F. Dirlmeier and H. Scharold Munich 1959); C. C. W. Taylor (Oxford 1976: with tr.). *Republic*: J. Adam, 2 vols. (Cambridge 1920–1: 2nd ed. rev. D. A. Rees 1963); R. C. Cross and A. D. Woozley (London 1964). *Sophist*: F. M. Cornford, *Plato's theory of knowledge* (London 1935: with Theaetetus and tr.). *Symposium*: R. G. Bury (Cambridge 1909: 2nd ed. 1932). *Theaetetus*: see under *Sophist*; J. McDowell (Oxford 1973: with tr.). *Timaeus*: F. M. Cornford, *Plato's cosmology* (London 1937: with tr.). *Scholia*. W. C. Greene (Haverford 1938).

TRANSLATIONS: B. Jowett, 4 vols. (Oxford 1871: 4th ed. rev. D. J. Allan and H. E. Dale, Oxford 1953); W. K. C. Guthrie, W. Hamilton, H. D. P. Lee, T. J. Saunders, H. Tredennick, 6 vols. (Harmondsworth, 1951–71: *Apology, Critias, Crito, Euthyphro, Laws, Meno, Phaedo, Protagoras, Republic, Symposium, Timaeus*); (edd.) E. Hamilton and H. Cairns (Princeton 1961: with *Letters*).

STUDIES: (1) GENERAL (very selective): U. von Wilamowitz-Moellendorff, *Platon*, 2 vols. (Berlin 1918–19), esp. II 323–33, 411–28; P. Friedländer, *Plato*, 2 vols. (Berlin & Leipzig 1928–30: 2nd ed. Berlin 1954–60: 3rd ed. 1964–75), expanded version tr. H. Meyerhoff (London & New York 1958–69); G. M. A. Grube, *Plato's thought* (London 1935); I. M. Crombie, *An examination of Plato's doctrines*, 2 vols. (London 1962–3). (2) MORE LIMITED (also selective): P. Frutiger, *Les mythes de Platon* (Paris 1930); R. Schaerer, *La question platonicienne* (Neuchâtel 1938: repr. 1970); R. Robinson, *Plato's earlier dialectic* (Oxford 1941: 2nd ed. 1953); V. Goldschmidt, *Les dialogues de Platon* (Paris 1947: repr. 1963); K. R. Popper, *The open society and its enemies* I (London 1947); G. J. de Vries, *Spel bij Plato* (Amsterdam 1949); A. de Marignac, *Imagination et dialectique* (Paris 1951); R. B. Levinson, *In defence of Plato* (Cambridge, Mass. 1953); J. Andrieu, *Le dialogue antique* (Paris 1954) 284–6, 288–9, 304–8, 316; D. Tarrant, *J.H.S.* 75 (1955) 82–9; R. K. Sprague, *Plato's use of fallacy* (London 1962). (3) LANGUAGE: H. C. Baldry, *C.Q.* 31 (1937) 141–50 (technical terms); D. Tarrant, *C.Q.* 40 (1946) 109–17 and n.s.8 (1958) 158–60 (colloquialisms etc.), 42 (1948) 28–34 and n.s.1 (1951) 59–67 (use of quotations), n.s.5 (1955) 222–4 (extended *oratio obliqua*), *C.R.* n.s.2 (1952) 64–6 (metaphors in *Phaedo*); H. Thesleff, *Studies in the style of Plato* (Helsinki 1967: with bibliography); idem, *Arctos* 7 (1972) 219–27. (4) MS TRADITION: H. Alline, *Histoire du texte de Platon* (Paris 1915); E. Bickel, *Rh.M.* 92 (1944) 97–159; N. G. Wilson, *Scriptorium* 16 (1962) 386–95; J. A. Philip, *Phoenix* 24 (1970) 296–308. (5) ANCIENT LITERARY CRITICISM: Dion. Hal. *Pomp.* 1–2, *De comp. verb.* 208–9; Quint. 10.1.81; 'Longinus', *Subl.* 4, 28, 29, 32.

LEXICA: D. F. Ast, 3 vols. (Leipzig 1835–8); É. des Places, 2 vols. (Budé, 1964); L. Brandwood (Leeds 1976).

ORATORY

GENERAL WORKS

TEXTS
Baiter, J. G. and Sauppe, H., *Oratores Attici* (Zurich 1850: with scholia and frs.)

STUDIES
Blass, F., *Die attische Beredsamkeit*, 3 vols. (Leipzig 1887–93)

Bonner, R. J. and Smith, G., *The administration of justice from Homer to Aristotle*, 2 vols. (Chicago 1930–8)

Bruns, I., *Das literarische Porträt der Griechen im fünften und vierten Jahrhundert vor Christi Geburt, die Persönlichkeit in der Geschichtsschreibung der Alten. Untersuchungen zur Technik der antiken Historiographie* (Berlin 1896: repr. Hildesheim 1961)

Jebb, R. C., *The Attic orators*, 2 vols. (London 1893)

Kennedy, G., *The art of persuasion in Greece* (Princeton 1963)

Lausberg, H., *Handbuch der literarischen Rhetorik. Eine Grundlegung der Literaturwissenschaft* (Munich 1960)

Lavency, M., *Aspects de la logographie judiciaire attique* (Louvain 1964)

Navarre, O., *Essai sur la rhétorique grecque avant Aristote* (Paris 1900)

Norden, E., *Die antike Kunstprosa* (Leipzig 1923)

ANTIPHON

LIFE

b. *c.* 480 B.C. Teacher of rhetoric and professional speech-writer in Athens. Champion of oligarchic revolution 411; tried and executed the same year. Often identified, perhaps rightly, with Antiphon the sophist; see discussion and bibliography in R. K. Sprague, *The older sophists* (Columbia 1972) 108–11. Sources: Thuc. 8.68 and 90; Ps.-Plut. *Vit X or.* 832c–4b; Philostr. *V.S.* 1.15; Plato, *Menex.* 236a.

ANDOCIDES

WORKS

(1) Three *Tetralogies*, each comprising two speeches apiece for prosecution and defence; composed as exercises sometime between 440s and 420s. On date and authenticity see G. Zuntz, *M.H.* 6 (1949) 100–3. (2) Three homicide speeches: *On the choreutes* (419/18), *Against the stepmother* (c. 417), *On the murder of Herodes* (c. 415); on dates see K. J. Dover, *C.Q.* 44 (1950) 44–60. (3) Fragments of other speeches (incl. his own defence of 411) and of a manual *On the art of public speaking*.

BIBLIOGRAPHY

TEXTS AND COMMENTARIES: TEXTS: F. Blass and T. Thalheim (BT, 1914); L. Gernet (Budé, 1923: with Antiphon the sophist); K. J. Maidment, *Minor Attic orators* I (Loeb, 1941). COMMENTARIES: *Tetralogies*: F. D. Caizzi (Milan 1969: with Italian tr.).

TRANSLATIONS: K. Freeman, *The murder of Herodes and other trials from the Athenian law courts* (New York 1963).

STUDIES: F. Solmsen, *Antiphonstudien. Untersuchungen zur Entstehung der attischen Gerichtsrede* (Berlin 1931); U. Schindel, *Der Mordfall Herodes; zur 5. Rede Antiphons* (Göttingen 1979); B. Due, *Antiphon, a study in argumentation* (Copenhagen 1980); E. Heitsch, *Recht und Argumentation in Antiphons 6. Rede* (Wiesbaden 1980).

INDEX: F. L. van Cleef (New York 1895).

ANDOCIDES

LIFE

b. c. 440 B.C. of aristocratic family. Turned state's evidence after involvement in mutilation of Hermae 415, but was barred from Athenian temples and agora; withdrew into exile and traded as merchant. After unsuccessful attempts in 411 and c. 408 (*On his return*), regained civil rights 403. Successfully defended himself against attempt to subject him to the decree of Isotimides 399 (*On the mysteries*). Ambassador to Sparta 392 and advocate of peace-terms rejected by Athenians (*On the peace*); exiled. Date of death unknown. Sources: his first two speeches; Ps.-Lysias, *Against Andocides* (part of prosecution of 399); Thuc. 6.60 (Hermae); *FGrH* 328 F 149 (peace of 392).

WORKS

The three speeches named under *Life* above. The speech *Against Alcibiades*, set in Athenian assembly of 415, is spurious; see Dalmeyda under *Texts* below, 103–10.

LYSIAS

BIBLIOGRAPHY

TEXTS AND COMMENTARIES: TEXTS: F. Blass and C. Fuhr (BT, 1913); G. Dalmeyda (Budé, 1930); K. J. Maidment, *Minor Attic orators* I (Loeb, 1941). COMMENTARIES: *Return* and *Peace*: U. Albini (Florence 1961–4). *Mysteries*: D. M. MacDowell (Oxford 1962).

STUDIES: G. A. Kennedy, 'The oratory of Andocides', *A.J.Ph.* 79 (1958) 32–43; I. Opelt, 'Zur politischen Polemik des Redners Andocides', *Glotta* 57 (1979) 210–18.

INDEX: L. L. Forman (Oxford 1897: with Lycurgus, Dinarchus).

LYSIAS

LIFE

b. in Athens, perhaps in 444 B.C., son of a metic from Syracuse. Moved to Thurii *c.* 429, but was expelled after failure of Athenian expedition to Sicily 415–413. Returned to Athens and prospered as manufacturer of shields. Much of his property confiscated by Thirty Tyrants 404; his brother put to death. Escaped to Megara and espoused cause of Athenian democrats; on return to Athens was briefly granted full rights of citizenship. Conducted a school (perhaps 403–401) and supported himself as speechwriter. d. *c.* 375. Sources: his speech *Against Eratosthenes*; *P. Oxy.* 1606; Dion. Hal. *Lysias*; Ps.-Plut. *Vit X or.* 835c–6d; Cic. *Brut.* 48.

WORKS

233 speeches accepted as genuine in antiquity; thirty-five survive (some only in part). All, apart from one epideictic speech and the *Funeral oration*, are judicial. Nos. 6, 8 and 20 are probably spurious. Only *Against Eratosthenes* (403) and probably *Olympiacus* (388) were delivered by L. himself. Speech attributed to L. in Plato's *Phaedrus* is a parody; see bibliography in G. Kennedy, *The art of persuasion in Greece* (Princeton 1963) 134 n.23.

BIBLIOGRAPHY

TEXTS AND COMMENTARIES: TEXTS: K. Hude (OCT, 1912); T. Thalheim (BT, 1913); L. Gernet and M. Bizos (Budé, 1924–6); W. R. M. Lamb (Loeb, 1930). COMMENTARIES: E. S. Shuckburgh (London 1882: selection).

STUDIES: W. Motschmann, *Die Charactere bei Lysias* (Munich 1906); O. Buechler, *Die Unterscheidung der redenden Personen bei Lysias* (Heidelberg 1936); J. J. Bateman,

'Some aspects of Lysias' argumentation', *Phoenix* 16 (1962) 155–77; K. J. Dover, *Lysias and the corpus Lysiacum* (Berkeley 1968).

INDEX: D. H. Holmes (Bonn 1895: repr. Amsterdam 1962).

ISAEUS

LIFE

b. *c.* 420 B.C. in Athens or Chalcis. Pupil of Isocrates and teacher of Demosthenes; activities limited to writing speeches for others. Earliest extant speech (5) belongs to 390/89, latest (12) to 344/3. Date of death unknown. Sources: Dion. Hal. *Isaeus*; Ps.-Plut. *Vit. X or.* 839e–f.

WORKS

Fifty speeches accepted as genuine in antiquity. Twelve survive, eleven on testamentary cases and one (preserved in part by Dion. Hal. *Isaeus* 17) on civil rights. Ps.-Plut. also mentions a treatise on rhetoric.

BIBLIOGRAPHY

TEXTS AND COMMENTARIES: TEXTS: T. Thalheim (BT, 1903); P. Roussel (Budé, 1922); E. S. Forster (Loeb, 1927). COMMENTARIES: W. Wyse (Cambridge 1904).

STUDIES: R. F. Weavers, *Isaeus. Chronology, prosopography and social history* (The Hague 1969: bibliography 122–3); R. R. Renehan, 'Isocrates and Isaeus', *C.Ph.* 75 (1980) 242–53.

INDEX: J.-M. Denommé (Hildesheim 1968).

ISOCRATES

LIFE

b. 436 B.C. in Athens, of wealthy family. Taught by Prodicus, Gorgias (in Sicily), Tisias and Theramenes; acquainted with Socrates. After working as speech-writer, opened a school of rhetoric *c.* 393; historians Ephorus and Theopompus, orators Hyperides and Isaeus among his pupils. Never active as orator or politician, but published most of his orations as pamphlets. Starved himself to death 338. Sources: own works, esp. *Antidosis*; Dion. Hal. *Isocrates*; Ps.-Plut. *Vit X or.* 836e–9d; Cic. *Or.* 176. On opening of school see G. Kennedy, *The art of persuasion in Greece* (Princeton 1963) 176; on involvement with Theramenes, P. Cloché, *L.E.C.* 5 (1936) 394–484.

DEMOSTHENES

WORKS

(1) Orations. Dion. Hal. accepts twenty-five as genuine; twenty-one survive. (*a*) Logographic. *Or.* 16–21, pubd in 390s; but cf. *Antid.* 36ff. and 49, Dion. Hal. *Isocr.* 18. (*b*) Encomia. *Busiris* and *Helen* (370?). (*c*) Educational. *Antidosis* (353), *Against the sophists* (392?). (*d*) Political. *Panegyricus* (380, calling for campaign against Persia), *Plataicus* (on destruction of Plataea 373), *To Demonicus* and *To Nicocles* (370s; on duties of a monarch), *Nicocles* or *Cyprians* (*c.* 368), *Archidamus* (on peace proposals of 366), *Evagoras* (*c.* 365), *Areopagiticus* (357; see W. Jaeger, *H.S.C.Ph.* suppl. 1 (1941)), *On the peace* (355), *Philippus* (346), *Panathenaicus* (completed 339; comparison of Athens and Sparta). (2) Nine *Letters* to various addressees, incl. Dionysius I of Syracuse and Philip of Macedon; on authenticity see bibliography in Kennedy under *Life* above, 191 n.97. (3) A manual on rhetoric. Surviving fragments are doubtfully genuine: see Kennedy 70–4.

BIBLIOGRAPHY

(See Mikkola (1954) under *Studies* below, 297f.; U. Albini, *A.&R.* 6 (1961) 193–210.)

TEXTS AND COMMENTARIES: TEXTS: G. E. Benseler and F. Blass (BT, 1879); E. Drerup, vol. 1 (Leipzig 1906); G. Norlin and L. Van Hook (1928–45). G. Mathieu and E. Brémond (Budé, 1928–62). COMMENTARIES: *Cyprians*: E. S. Forster (Oxford 1912). *Panegyricus*: P. Treves (Turin 1932). *Philippus*: P. Treves (Milan 1933); M. L. W. Laistner (New York 1927: with *Peace*). *Trapezeticus* (*Or.* 17): J. C. A. M. Bongenaar (Utrecht 1933). *Scholia*. W. Dindorf (Oxford 1852, repr. Hildesheim 1970: with Aeschines).

STUDIES: W. Jaeger, *Paideia* III (New York 1945) 46–155; E. Mikkola, *Isocrates, seine Anschauungen im Lichte seiner Schriften* (Helsinki 1954); E. Buchner, *Der Panegyricus des Isokrates: eine historisch-philologische Untersuchung* (Wiesbaden 1958); M. A. Levi, *Isocrate: saggio critico* (Milan 1959); P. Cloché, *Isocrate et son temps* (Paris 1963); K. Bringmann, *Studien zu den politischen Ideen des Isokrates* (Göttingen 1965); S. Usher, 'The style of Isocrates', *B.I.C.S.* 20 (1973) 39–67; E. Rummel, 'Isocrates' ideal of rhetoric', *C.J.* 75 (1979) 25–35; R. R. Renehan, 'Isocrates and Isaeus', *C.Ph.* 75 (1980) 242–53.

INDEX: S. Preuss (Leipzig 1904: repr. Hildesheim 1963).

DEMOSTHENES

LIFE

b. 384 B.C. in Athens. Studied rhetoric under Isaeus and prosecuted his guardians for embezzling his inheritance 364 (speeches *Against Aphobus* and *Against Onetor*).

DEMOSTHENES

Earliest public speech *Against Androtion* 355; earliest extant deliberative speech *On the symmories* 354. Subsequently pursued increasingly anti-Macedonian policy, acquiescing only in the Peace of Philocrates 346. Delivered funeral oration after defeat of Athens at Chaeronea 338. Defended his career against prosecution of Aeschines in *On the crown* 330. Was heavily fined on conviction of a bribery charge 324, but escaped into exile. Recalled on death of Alexander, but condemned to death after defeat of Greeks in Lamian war 322; fled to island of Calauria, and poisoned himself the same year. Sources: own works, esp. *Against Aphobus* and *On the crown*; Aeschines *passim*; Ps.-Plut. *Vit X or.* 844a–8d; Plut. *Dem.*; Dion. Hal. *Amm.* 1, *Dem.*; 'Longinus', *Subl.* 12 (comparison of D. and Cicero). On development of his policies see G. L. Cawkwell, *R.E.G.* 73 (1960) 416–38; 75 (1962) 453–9; *C.Q.* n.s.12 (1962) 122–41; n.s.13 (1963) 120–38; *J.H.S.* 83 (1963) 47–67; *Philip of Macedon* (London 1978).

WORKS

Corpus contains sixty-three works. (1) Deliberative speeches. *On the symmories* (354), *For the Megalopolitans* (353), *Philippics* 1–4 (1, 351; 2, 344; 3, 341; 4, 340; on authenticity of 4 see C. D. Adams, *C.Ph.* 33 (1938) 129–44), *On the liberty of the Rhodians* (351), *Olynthiacs* 1–3 (349), *On the peace* (346), *On the Chersonese* (341). (2) Other public speeches. *Against Androtion* (355), *Against Leptines* (354), *Against Timocrates* (353), *Against Aristocrates* (352), *Against Meidias* (348: not delivered), *On the crown* (330). (3) Private speeches. Some twenty are genuine. (4) Six *Letters*, of which four (1–3, 6) may be genuine; see J. A. Goldstein, *The letters of Demosthenes* (New York 1968). (5) Dubious or spurious. Nos. 46–7, 49–50, 52–3, 59 (perhaps by Apollodorus), 58 (Dinarchus), 7 (Hegesippus), 13, 17, 26, 40, 42–4, 48, 56 (unknown authors), 11 (perhaps from Anaximenes' *History*) and 12 (*Philip's letter*). *Funeral oration, Erotic essay* and *Prooemia* (though the latter, a collection of introductions to speeches, may be associated with D.'s teaching activities; cf. Aesch. *Tim.* 117); see introductions by Clavaud (Budé) under *Texts* below.

BIBLIOGRAPHY

(For 1915–65 see D. F. Jackson and G. O. Rowe, *Lustrum* 14 (1969).)

TEXTS AND COMMENTARIES: TEXTS: S. H. Butcher and W. Rennie (OCT, 1903–31); C. Fuhr and J. Sykutris (BT, 1914–37: 1–26 only); J. H. Vince *et al.* (Loeb, 1926–49); M. Croiset *et al.* (Budé, 1954–74). COMMENTARIES: H. Weil, *Plaidoyers politiques de Démosthène*, 2 vols., 2nd ed. (Paris 1881–3); idem, *Harangues de Démosthène*, 3rd ed. rev. G. Dalmeyda (Paris 1912). Individual works. (1) Public speeches. *Androtion* and *Timocrates*: W. Wayte, 2nd ed. (Cambridge 1893). *On the crown*: W. W. Goodwin (Cambridge 1901); P. Treves (Milan 1933); G. Ballaira (Turin 1972); H. Wankel (Heidelberg 1976). *On the false embassy*: R. Shilleto (London 1894). *Leptines*: J. E. Sandys (Cambridge 1890). *Megalopolitans*: W. Fox (Freiburg im Breisgau 1890).

Meidias: J. R. King (Oxford 1901); W. W. Goodwin (Cambridge 1906). *Philipp.*, *Olynth.*, *Peace, Chersonese*: J. E. Sandys, 2 vols. (Cambridge 1897–1933). (2) Private speeches. F. A. Paley and J. E. Sandys, 2 vols., 2nd ed. (Cambridge 1886: selections); L. Pearson, *Six private speeches* (Norman, Oklahoma 1972); S. Isager and M. H. Hansen, *Paragraphe-speeches in the Corpus Demosthenicum* (nos. 32–38; 56) (Odense 1975). *Scholia*. W. Dindorf, 2 vols. (Oxford 1851); M. L. Dilts (BT, 1984–).

TRANSLATIONS: C. R. Kennedy, 5 vols. (London 1892–5); A. W. Pickard-Cambridge, 2 vols. (Oxford 1912: public speeches only); A. N. W. Saunders, *Greek political oratory* (Harmondsworth 1970: selection).

STUDIES: (1) GENERAL: A. Schaefer, *Demosthenes und seine Zeit*, 3 vols., 2nd ed. (Leipzig 1885–7); A. W. Pickard-Cambridge, *Demosthenes and the last days of Greek freedom* (London 1914); C. D. Adams, *Demosthenes and his influence* (London 1927); W. Jaeger, *Demosthenes: the origin and growth of his policy* (Berkeley 1938); G. Mathieu, *Démosthène. L'homme et l'oeuvre* (Paris 1948); G. Ronnet, *Étude sur le style de Démosthène dans les discours politiques* (Paris 1951); L. Pearson, *The art of Demosthenes* (Meisenheim am Glan 1976). (2) INDIVIDUAL WORKS: W. Schwann, *Demosthenes gegen Aphobus: ein Beitrag zur Geschichte der griechischen Wirtschaft* (Leipzig 1929); R. Chevalier, 'L'art oratoire de Démosthène dans le discours sur la couronne', *B.A.G.B.* 4 (1960) 200–16; J. R. Ellis and R. D. Milns, *The spectre of Philip. Demosthenes' first Philippic, Olynthiacs and speech On the peace; a study in historical evidence* (Sydney 1970).

INDEX: S. Preuss (Leipzig 1892).

APOLLODORUS

b. in Athens 394 B.C. Co-operated with Demosthenes on occasion in early 340s; Demosthenes subsequently wrote for him the first speech *Against Stephanus*. Six other speeches in Demosthenic corpus (46, 49–50, 52–3, 59) were spoken by A., and are generally attributed to him. Dem. 47 may also be his. Texts as for Demosthenes.

HEGESIPPUS

Dates *c*. 390–325 B.C. Supporter of Demosthenes. According to Libanius' *hypothesis* he was the author of Dem. 7, *On Halonnesus*. Texts as for Demosthenes.

AESCHINES

LIFE

b. 390 B.C. or earlier in Athens. Early career as hoplite, minor government clerk and actor. Made his first known public speech in 348, supporting Eubulus' plan for a common peace against Macedon. Ambassador to Arcadia same year and, with Demosthenes, to Philip in 346; indicted for treason by Timarchus and Demosthenes, but successful both in his counter-indictment *Against Timarchus* and in his defence *On the embassy*. Delegate to Amphyctionic council 339 and peace ambassador after Athenian defeat at Chaeronea 338. In 336 opposed Ctesiphon's motion to confer crown on Demosthenes, but defeated by the latter's speech *On the crown* in 330. Retired into exile, perhaps as teacher of rhetoric on Samos and Rhodes.; date of death unknown. Sources: own speeches (esp. *Tim.* 49 for birth; but cf. D. M. Lewis, *C.R.* n.s.8 (1958) 108); Ps.-Plut. *Vit. X or.* 840–1a; Philostr. *V.S.* 1.18; Plut. *Dem.* 24 (exile). Other *Lives* in Blass (BT) under *Texts* below.

WORKS

(1) GENUINE: Three speeches: *Against Timarchus* (345), *On the embassy* (343), *Against Ctesiphon* (330). (2) SPURIOUS: Twelve *Letters*: see Martin and de Budé under *Texts* below, II 121–43.

BIBLIOGRAPHY

TEXTS AND COMMENTARIES: TEXTS: F. Schultz (BT, 1865: with scholia); F. Blass and C. Fuhr (BT, 1908). C. D. Adams (Loeb, 1919); V. Martin and G. de Budé (Budé, 1927–8). COMMENTARIES: *Ctes.*: G. A. and W. H. Simcox, *The orations of Demosthenes and Aeschines on the crown* (Oxford 1872); T. Gwatkin and E. S. Schuckburgh (London & New York 1890). *Scholia*. W. Dindorf (Oxford 1852: repr. Hildesheim 1970: with Isocrates).

STUDIES: M. Heyse, *Die handschriftliche Überlieferung der Reden des Aeschines* (Ohlau 1912); A. Diller, 'The manuscript tradition of Aeschines' orations', *I.C.S.* 4 (1979) 34–64.

INDEX: S. Preuss (Leipzig 1896).

HYPERIDES

LIFE

b. 390 B.C. in Athens. Studied under Plato and Isocrates. A professional speech-writer and politician, he supported Demosthenes' anti-Macedonian policies (successfully prosecuted Philocrates 343), but was one of Demosthenes' prosecutors in 324. Delivered funeral oration after Lamian war of 322; executed at the order of Antipater the same year. Sources: *IG* II 941 (birth); Ps.-Plut. *Vit. X or.* 848d–50b; Athen. 8.342c (tutors).

WORKS

Ps.-Plut. (above) attributes seventy-seven speeches to him. From papyri there survive one complete speech, *For Euxenippus* (between 330 and 324), and considerable portions of five others, including his speech against Demosthenes (324) and his *Funeral oration* (322). His defence of the courtesan Phryne was his most famous work; see Colin under *Texts* below, 10ff.

BIBLIOGRAPHY

(See G. Bartolini, *Iperide: Rassegna di problemi e di studi* (1912–1972) (Padua 1972).)

TEXTS AND COMMENTARIES: TEXTS: F. G. Kenyon (OCT, 1907); C. Jensen (BT, 1917); G. Colin (Budé, 1946); J. O. Burtt, *Minor Attic orators* II (Loeb, 1954). COMMENTARIES: *For Euxenippus* and *Against Athenogenes*: V. de Falco (Naples 1947).

STUDIES: U. Pohle, *Die Sprache des Redners Hypereides in ihren Beziehungen zur Koine* (Leipzig 1928); T. B. Curtis, *The judicial oratory of Hyperides* (Chapel Hill 1970).

INDEX: H. Reinhold (in BT ed.).

LYCURGUS

LIFE

b. *c.* 390 B.C. of distinguished Athenian family. Generally supported policies of Demosthenes. Held important post in controlling Athenian finances after Chaeronea 338–326, and responsible for many laws and public works. d. 324. Sources: Ps.-Plut. *Vit. X or.* 841a–4a; Libanius' *hypothesis* to Dem. 25; *IG* II 457, 1627, 1672; *SIG* 218.

DINARCHUS

WORKS

One speech survives (*Against Leocrates*) out of fifteen accepted as genuine in antiquity.

BIBLIOGRAPHY

TEXTS: F. Blass (BT, 1899); F. Durrbach (Budé, 1932); J. O. Burtt, *Minor Attic orators* II (Loeb, 1954).

INDEX: As for Andocides (p. 798).

DINARCHUS

LIFE

b. *c.* 360 B.C. at Corinth. Professional speech-writer (tutors Theophrastus and Demetrius of Phalerum) in Athens. His three extant speeches were written for clients during prosecution of those alleged to have been bribed by Harpalus 324. Prospered under Cassander's oligarchy 322–307, but withdrew to Chalcis on liberation of Athens by Demetrius Poliorcetes. Returned in 292 and d. at unknown date. Sources: Dion. Hal. *Dinarchus* (tr. G. Shoemaker, *G.R.B.S.* 12 (1971) 393–409); Ps.-Plut. *Vit. X or.* 850b–e; other testimonia in Conomis under *Texts* below, 1–10.

WORKS

Dion. Hal. credits him with 160 speeches (incl. Dem. 58). Three survive: *Against Demosthenes, Against Aristogeiton, Against Philocles* (all delivered 324/3 B.C.).

BIBLIOGRAPHY

TEXTS: J. O. Burtt, *Minor Attic orators* II (Loeb, 1954); N. C. Conomis (BT, 1975: with bibliography ix–xv).

INDEX: As for Andocides (p. 798).

ARISTOTLE AND POST-ARISTOTELIAN PHILOSOPHY

GENERAL WORKS

Armstrong, A. H. (ed.), *The Cambridge history of later Greek and early medieval philosophy* (Cambridge 1967)

Bréhier, E., *Histoire de la philosophie* I (Paris 1926)

Dillon, J., *The Middle Platonists* (London 1977)

Dodds, E. R., *The Greeks and the irrational* (Berkeley & Los Angeles 1951)

Dudley, D. R., *A history of Cynicism* (London 1937)

Ferguson, W. S., *Hellenistic Athens* (London 1911)

Fraser, P. M., *Ptolemaic Alexandria*, 3 vols. (Oxford 1972)

Grube, G. M. A., *The Greek and Roman critics* (London 1965)

Kennedy, G., *The art of persuasion in Greece* (Princeton 1963)

Kneale, W. and M., *The development of logic* (Oxford 1962)

Krämer, H.-J., *Platonismus und hellenistische Philosophie* (Berlin & New York 1972)

Lloyd, G. E. R., *Early Greek science: Thales to Aristotle* (London 1970)

idem, *Greek science after Aristotle* (London 1973)

Long, A. A., *Hellenistic philosophy* (London 1974)

Nilsson, N. M. P., *Geschichte der griechischen Religion* II, 2nd ed. (Munich 1961)

Pfeiffer, R., *A history of classical scholarship* I (Oxford 1968)

Steinthal, H., *Geschichte der Sprachwissenschaft*, 2 vols., 2nd ed. (Berlin 1890–1)

Susemihl, F., *Geschichte der griechischen Literatur in der Alexandrinerzeit*, 2 vols. (Leipzig 1891–2)

Tarn, W. W., *Hellenistic civilisation*, 3rd ed. rev. G. T. Griffith (London 1952)

Wallis, R., *Neoplatonism* (London 1972)

Zeller, E., *Die Philosophie der Griechen* (Leipzig: II 2, 3rd ed. 1879; III 1, 4th ed. rev. E. Wellmann 1909; III 2, 4th ed. 1889)

ARISTOTLE

LIFE

b. 384 B.C. at Stagira; son of Nicomachus, friend and doctor of Amyntas II of Macedonia. Worked with Plato in the Academy 367–347. Spent next five years first at Assos (near ancient Troy), then at Lesbos. Married Pythias, niece of Hermias, ruler of Atarneus and Assos. Returned to Macedonia 343/2; remained there until 335 serving, during part of this time, as tutor to Alexander. Then returned to Athens where he worked and taught with a group of followers in the Lyceum. On death of Pythias lived with Herpylis and had a son, Nicomachus. Left Athens 323 and d. 322 in Chalcis. Sources: Diog. Laert. 5.1–11 (life), 12–21 (will and sayings), 22–7 (list of works), 28–34 (philosophy); Philodemus, *Acad. ind.* col. 6.28ff. and *Rhet.* 2 p. 50 Sudhaus (A., Speusippus and Academy; views on rhetoric and politics); Dion. Hal. *Amm.* 723, 727, 733 (life; controversy over date of *Rhetoric*); Plut. *Alex.* 7–8 (A. and Alexander), *Adv. Col.* 1115a–c (A.'s opposition to Plato's theory of forms); Pliny, *N.H.* 8.44 (zoological researches); *Lives* in Greek, Latin, Arabic and Syriac (I. Düring, *Aristotle in the ancient biographical tradition* (Göteborg 1957) for text and comm., with many other testimonia).

WORKS

Three ancient catalogues of A.'s writings preserved: Diog. Laert. 5.22–7, perhaps based on inventory of Alexandrian library (Düring (1966) under *Studies* (1) below, 37); list appended to anonymous *Life* (*Vita Menagiana*), probably by Hesychius; catalogue of one Ptolemy, transcribed in Arabic by Ibn al Qifti (1172–1248) in his *Chronicle of wise men*. For texts and discussion see P. Moraux, *Les listes anciennes des ouvrages d'Aristote* (Louvain 1951).

(1) GENUINE: (*a*) Logical works. *Categories* (chs. 10–15 probably a late addition), *De interpretatione*, *Prior* and *Posterior analytics* (2 bks each), *Topics* (8 bks), *On sophistical refutations* (= *Top.* 9). (*b*) Philosophy of nature. *Physics* (8 bks), *On the heavens* (4 bks), *On coming to be and passing away* (2 bks), *Meteorology* (4 bks; 4th may be spurious), *On the soul* (3 bks), nine short works known collectively as *Parva naturalia* (*On sense and sensible objects*, *On memory and recollection*, *On sleep and waking*, *On dreams*, *On prophecy in sleep*, *On length and shortness of life*, *On youth and old age*, *On life and death*, *On respiration*), *Inquiry into animals* (*Historia animalium*, 10 bks; 10 is spurious, 7 and 9 doubtful), *On the parts of animals* (4 bks), *On the motion of animals*, *On the progression of animals*, *On the generation of animals* (5 bks). (*c*) *Metaphysics* (collection of 13 bks composed at different periods). (*d*) Other works. *Nicomachean ethics* (10 bks), *Politics* (8 bks), *Rhetoric* (3 bks), *Poetics* (incomplete), *Constitution of Athens* (incomplete).

(2) PROBABLY GENUINE: *Eudemian ethics* (For: C. J. Rowe, *P.C.Ph.S.* suppl. III (1971); A. Kenny, *The Aristotelian Ethics* (Oxford 1978). Against: L. Spengel, *A.B.A.W.* 3.2 (1841), 3.3 (1843); Jaeger under *Studies* (2) below, 228–58.)

(3) PROBABLY SPURIOUS: *Magna moralia* (2 bks) (For: F. Dirlmeier, *Aristotelis Magna moralia*, 2nd ed. (Berlin 1966), recanting on views in *Rh.M.* 88 (1939) 214–43; Düring (1966) under *Studies* (1) below, 438ff. Against: e.g., D. J. Allan, *J.H.S.* 77 (1957) 7–11 and *Gnomon* 38 (1966) 142–4.)

(4) SPURIOUS: *On the universe* (*De mundo*), *On breath*, *On colours*, *On audible objects*, *Physiognomica*, *On plants* (2 bks), *On wondrous rumours* (*De mirabilibus auscultationibus*), *Mechanics*, *On indivisible lines*, *Locations and names of winds*, *On Melissus, Xenophanes, Gorgias*, *Problems* (30 divisions), *On virtues and vices*, *Economics* (2 bks), *Rhetoric addressed to Alexander*.

(5) PRINCIPAL FRAGMENTARY WORKS: (*a*) Dialogues. *Eudemus* (on psychology; see O. Gigon in (edd.) I. Düring and G. E. L. Owen, *Aristotle and Plato in the mid-fourth century* (Göteborg 1960) 19–34), *Protrepticus* (see W. G. Rabinowitz, *Aristotle's Protrepticus and the sources of its reconstruction* (Berkeley 1957); I. Düring, *Aristotle's Protrepticus, an attempt at reconstruction* (Göteborg 1961)), *On philosophy* (see P. Wilpert in *Autour d'Aristote. Recueil d'études...offert à Mr A. Mansion* (Louvain 1955) 99–116 and *J.H.S.* 77 (1957) 155–62), *On justice* (see P. Moraux, *À la recherche de l'Aristote perdu; le dialogue Sur la justice* (Louvain 1957)). (*b*) Other works. *On ideas* (see P. Wilpert, *Zwei aristotelische Frühschriften über die Ideenlehre* (Regensberg

1949); G. E. L. Owen, *J.H.S.* 77 (1957) 103–11), *On the Pythagoreans* (see P. Wilpert, *Hermes* 75 (1940) 371ff.; W. Burkert, *Weisheit und Wissenschaft* (Nürnberg 1962)), *On wealth* etc. (see P.-M. Schuhl *et al.*, *De la richesse, De la prière, De la noblesse, Du plaisir, De l'éducation* (Paris 1968)).

(6) POEMS: Diog. Laert. 5.7 and 27; Olympiodorus, *In Gorg.* pr. 41.9. Cf. W. Jaeger, *C.Q.* 21 (1927) 13–17; C. M. Bowra, *C.Q.* 32 (1938) 182–9.

CHRONOLOGY OF WORKS: It is impossible to establish precise dates for any of A.'s writings, and firm evidence of their relative chronology is slight. Some of the larger works, e.g. *Physics* and *Metaphysics*, give clear indications of combining earlier and later books into a loosely unified whole, which may be due to editors after A.'s death. Some books certainly presuppose a knowledge of others (e.g. *Met.* A of *Physics* 1–2). On the assumption (not universally accepted) that A.'s earliest writings were those most strongly influenced, positively or negatively, by Plato, it is plausible to suggest that the dialogues, e.g. *Eudemus* and *On philosophy*, and the criticism of the Platonic theory of forms in *On ideas* were some of the earliest works. It is likely that the *Topics* was A.'s earliest contribution to logic, and that his first biological writings date from the years when he left the Academy in 347 for Asia Minor. Cross-references, an assumed familiarity with terms and concepts, and a different treatment of the same problem are further criteria which can be used to arrive at a hypothetical order of the works. Certain books of *Metaphysics* (notably Zeta), the research into constitutions, *Politics* (apart from bks 7–8), *Nicomachean ethics* (apart from bks 5–7, common to *Eudemian ethics*), *Poetics* and *Rhetoric* are probably among his latest works.

BIBLIOGRAPHY

(See selective general bibl. by Düring (1966) under *Studies* (1) below, 623–40, with details of earlier surveys; (ed.) P. Moraux, *Aristoteles in der neueren Forschung* (Darmstadt 1968); (edd.) J. Barnes, M. Schofield, R. Sorabji, *Articles on Aristotle*, I *Science* 194–205, II *Ethics and politics* 219–33, III *Metaphysics* 178–97, IV *Psychology and aesthetics* 177–92 (London 1975–9).)

TEXTS AND COMMENTARIES: TEXTS: Complete works ed. I. Bekker (Berlin 1831–70: incl. Latin tr., scholia, frs., and index by H. Bonitz). Most works in BT and Budé editions, a large number in OCT; Loeb edition lacks only vol. III of *Historia animalium* and fragments. For texts and testimonia of fragments see V. Rose (Leipzig 1866); W. D. Ross (Oxford 1955); M. Plezia (Warsaw 1961: letters). See also under *Works* (5) above. COMMENTARIES: *An. pr.* and *An. post.*: W. D. Ross (Oxford 1949). *An. pr.*: M. Mignucci (Naples 1969: with Italian tr.). *An. post.*: J. Barnes (Oxford 1975: with tr.). *Ath. pol.*: J. E. Sandys, 2nd ed. (London 1912); P. J. Rhodes (Oxford 1981). *Cael.*: O. Longo (Florence 1962: with Italian tr.). *Cat.* and *Int.*: J. L. Ackrill (Oxford 1963: with tr.). *De an.*: R. D. Hicks (Cambridge 1907: with tr.); W. D. Ross (Oxford 1961). Bks 2–3: D. W. Hamlyn (Oxford 1968: with tr.). *Eth. Eud.*: F. Dirlmeier, 2nd ed. (Berlin 1962: with German tr.). Bks 1–2, 8: M.

Woods (Oxford 1982: with tr.). *Eth. Nic.*: J. A. Stewart, 2 vols. (Oxford 1892); J. Burnet (London 1900); R. A. Gauthier and J. Y. Jolif, 3 vols., 2nd ed. (Louvain 1970: with French tr.); H. H. Joachim, ed. D. A. Rees (Oxford 1951). *Gen. an.*: H. Aubert and F. Wimmer (Leipzig 1860: with German tr.). Bk 1 (with bk 1 of *Part. an.*): D. M. Balme (Oxford 1972: with tr.). *Gen. corr.*: H. H. Joachim (Oxford 1922); W. J. Verdenius and J. H. Waszink, 2nd ed. (Leiden 1966); C. J. F. Williams (Oxford 1982: with tr.). *Hist. an.*: H. Aubert and F. Wimmer (Leipzig 1868: with German tr.). *Incess. an.*: M. C. Nussbaum (Princeton 1978: with tr.). *Mag. mor.*: F. Dirlmeier, 2nd ed. (Berlin 1966: with German tr.). *Mem.*: R. Sorabji (London 1972: with tr.). *Metaph.*: W. D. Ross, 2 vols. (Oxford 1924); G. Reale, 2 vols. (Naples 1968: with Italian tr.). Bks Γ, Δ and E: C. Kirwan (Oxford 1971: with tr.). Bks M and N: J. Annas (Oxford 1976: with tr.). Bk Z: M. F. Burnyeat *et al.* (Oxford 1979). *Mete.*: J. L. Ideler, 2 vols. (Leipzig 1834–6: with Latin tr.). Bk 4: I. Düring (Göteborg 1944). *Part. an.*: W. Ogle (London 1882); I. Düring (Göteborg 1943). *Parv. nat.*: W. D. Ross (Oxford 1955). *Ph.*: W. D. Ross (Oxford 1936). Bks 1–2: W. Charlton (Oxford 1970: with tr.). *Poet.*: I. Bywater (Oxford 1909); A. Gudeman (Berlin 1934); A. Rostagni, 2nd ed. (Turin 1945); G. F. Else (Cambridge, Mass. 1957: with tr.); D. W. Lucas (Oxford 1968); L. J. Potts (Cambridge 1968). *Pol.*: W. L. Newman, 4 vols. (Oxford 1887–1902). Bks 3–4: R. Robinson (Oxford 1962: with tr.). *Rhet.*: E. M. Cope, rev. J. E. Sandys, 3 vols. (Cambridge 1877); R. Kassel (Berlin & New York 1976).

TRANSLATIONS: (edd.) J. A. Smith and W. D. Ross, 12 vols. (Oxford 1908–52). *Pol.*: T. A. Sinclair, rev. T. J. Saunders (Harmondsworth 1981).

STUDIES: (1) GENERAL: H. Cherniss, *Aristotle's criticism of Presocratic philosophy* (Baltimore 1935); J. le Blond, *Logique et méthode chez Aristote* (Paris 1939); H. Cherniss, *Aristotle's criticism of Plato and the Academy* I (Baltimore 1944); (edd.) I. Düring and G. E. L. Owen, *Aristotle and Plato in the mid-fourth century* (Oxford 1960); (ed.) P. Moraux, *Aristote et les problèmes de méthode* (Louvain 1961); M. Grene, *A portrait of Aristotle* (London 1963); I. Düring, *Aristoteles. Darstellung und Interpretation seines Denkens* (Heidelberg 1966); G. E. R. Lloyd, *Aristotle: the growth and structure of his thought* (Cambridge 1968); D. J. Allan, *The philosophy of Aristotle*, 2nd ed. (London 1970); J. L. Ackrill, *Aristotle the philosopher* (Oxford 1981); A. Edel, *Aristotle and his philosophy* (Chapel Hill 1982).

(2) DEVELOPMENT OF THOUGHT AND CHRONOLOGY OF WRITINGS: W. Jaeger, *Aristotle*, tr. R. Robinson from *Aristoteles, Grundlegung einer Geschichte seiner Entwicklung* (Oxford 1934); W. D. Ross, 'The development of Aristotle's thought', *P.B.A.* 43 (1957) 63–78; G. E. L. Owen, 'The Platonism of Aristotle', *P.B.A.* 50 (1965) 125–50.

(3) ESSAYS ON INDIVIDUAL WORKS: *Ath. Pol.*: J. H. Day and M. Chambers, *Aristotle's history of Athenian democracy* (Berkeley & Los Angeles 1962). *De an.*: (edd.) G. E. R. Lloyd and G. E. L. Owen, *Aristotle on mind and the senses* (Cambridge 1978). *Eth. Eud.*: (edd.) P. Moraux and D. Harlfinger, *Untersuchungen zur Eudemischen Ethik* (Berlin 1972); A. Kenny, *The Aristotelian Ethics* (Oxford 1978). *Eth. Nic.*: (ed.) A. O.

Rorty, *Essays on Aristotle's Ethics* (Berkeley & Los Angeles 1980). *Poet.*: H. House, *Aristotle's Poetics* (London 1956). *Pol.*: R. Stark *et al.*, *La Politique d'Aristote* (Geneva 1965). *Rhet.*: W. M. A. Grimaldi, *Studies in the philosophy of Aristotle's Rhetoric* (Wiesbaden 1972). *Top.*: (ed.) G. E. L. Owen, *Aristotle on dialectic. The Topics* (Oxford 1968); J. D. G. Evans, *Aristotle's concept of dialectic* (Cambridge 1977).

(4) LITERARY THEORY: F. Solmsen, 'The origins and methods of Aristotle's *Poetics*', *C.Q.* 29 (1935) 192–201; E. Olson, 'The Aristotelian tradition in ancient rhetoric', *A.J.Ph.* 62 (1941) 35–50, 169–90; J. Jones, *On Aristotle and Greek tragedy* (London 1962); G. M. A. Grube, *The Greek and Roman critics* (London 1965); (ed.) E. Olson, *Aristotle's Poetics and English literature* (Chicago 1965); J. M. Bremer, *Hamartia. Tragic error in the Poetics and in Greek tragedy* (Amsterdam 1968); (ed.) R. Stark, *Schriften zur aristotelischen und hellenistichen Rhetorik* (Hildesheim 1968); B. R. Rees, 'Pathos in the *Poetics* of Aristotle', *G.&R.* 19 (1972) 1–11; T. C. W. Stinton '*Hamartia* in Aristotle and Greek tragedy', *C.Q.* n.s.25 (1975) 221–54.

(5) STYLE: R. Eucken, *De Aristotelis dicendi ratione* (Göttingen 1866: on particles); idem, *Über den Sprachgebrauch des Aristoteles* (Berlin 1868: on prepositions); K. von Fritz, *Philosophie und sprachlicher Ausdruck bei Demokrit, Plato und Aristoteles* (New York 1938); G. Morpurgo-Tagliabue, *Linguistica e stilistica di Aristotele* (Rome 1967).

(6) ORGANIZATION OF SCHOOL AND TRANSMISSION OF TEXTS: J. P. Lynch, *Aristotle's school* (Berkeley & Los Angeles 1972); P. Moraux, *Der Aristotelismus bei den Griechen* 1 (Berlin & New York 1973); F. Grayeff, *Aristotle and his school. An inquiry into the history of the Peripatos* (London 1974).

(7) ANCIENT LITERARY CRITICISM: Cic. *Acad.* 2.119, *Brut.* 121, Dion. Hal. *De imit.* 2.4, Quint. 10.1.83.

INDEX: H. Bonitz, in Bekker under *Texts* above (repr. Graz 1955). Subject index: T. W. Organ (Princeton 1949).

HELLENISTIC POETRY

GENERAL WORKS

Fraser, P. M., *Ptolemaic Alexandria*, 3 vols. (Oxford 1972)

Körte, A. and Händel, P., *Die hellenistische Dichtung* (Stuttgart 1960)

Pfeiffer, R., *History of classical scholarship: from the beginnings to the end of the Hellenistic age* (Oxford 1968) (= Pfeiffer)

Susemihl, F., *Geschichte der griechischen Literatur in der Alexandrinerzeit*, 2 vols. (Leipzig 1891–2)

Tarn, W. W. and Griffith, G. T., *Hellenistic civilisation*, 3rd ed. (London 1952)

Wilamowitz-Moellendorff, U. von, *Hellenistische Dichtung*, 2 vols. (Berlin 1924)

In addition to the works listed under individual authors below two collections contain many of the poets whose works survive only, or largely, in fragmentary form:

Powell, J. U., *Collectanea Alexandrina: reliquiae minores poetarum Graecorum aetatis Ptolemaicae 323–146 A.C.* (Oxford 1925) (= Powell)
Parsons, P. J. and Lloyd-Jones, H., *Supplementum Hellenisticum* (Berlin & New York 1983) (= *SH*)

PHILETAS

LIFE

b. on Cos, lived at time of Alexander the Great and Ptolemy I. Tutor to Ptolemy Philadelphus and reportedly teacher of Hermesianax, Theocritus and Zenodotus.

WORKS

Hermes (hexameters), *Demeter* (elegiacs), paegnia (elegiacs), epigrams; Ἄτακτοι γλῶσσαι 'Unarranged glosses' a lexicographical compilation of rare and technical expressions and terms (Athen. 9.383a–b).

BIBLIOGRAPHY

TEXTS: G. Kuchenmüller (diss. Berlin 1928: with testimonia and comm.). Poetical fragments only: Powell 90–6. Additional fragment: *P. Oxy.* 2260 i 1ff., *P. Oxy.* 2258 A fr. 2(c); see *SH* 673–5.

STUDIES: A. von Blumenthal, *RE* XIX (1938) 2165–70.

ANTIMACHUS

LIFE

Apparently active before death of Lysander (395 B.C.; Plut. *Lys.* 18) and admired by Plato (Heraclides Ponticus fr. 6 Wehrli, Cic. *Brut.* 191). A native of Colophon.

WORKS

Fragments survive of *Thebaid* (hexameters) and *Lyde* (elegiacs: at least 2 bks); almost nothing is known of two other works, *Artemis* and *Delti*. 'Edited' Homer.

BIBLIOGRAPHY

TEXTS: B. Wyss (Berlin 1936). Additional fragments: *P. Oxy.* 2516, 2518, 2519(?). *SH* 52–79.

DEMETRIUS

LIFE

b. *c.* 350 B.C. at Phalerum. Governor of Athens for Macedonia 317–307. Pupil and friend of Theophrastus. Fled from Athens on its capture by Demetrius Poliorcetes and spent his later years as member of Ptolemy I's court in Alexandria, where he probably helped to organize the Library (Pfeiffer 99ff.). Expelled from court on accession of Ptolemy Philadelphus and d. in Upper Egypt *c.* 280 (supposedly bitten in his sleep by an asp). Sources: Diog. Laert. 5.78–83; Suda; Athen. 12.542 (D.'s profligacy); Diodorus 19.78, 20.45 (sack of Athens).

WORKS

According to Diog. Laert. 5.80–1 titles of forty-five works known, including writings on philosophy (*Socrates, On dreams*), Athenian law and constitution (*On the legislation of Athens, On the constitutions of the Athenians*), his own regime (*On the ten years, On the constitution*), chronology (*The register of archons*) and poetry (commentative works on the *Iliad* and *Odyssey*). Edited collections of Aesop's *Fables* and the sayings of the Seven Wise Men. For the treatise *On style*, attributed to D. by MSS and now universally regarded as spurious, see pp. 648–9, 859–60.

BIBLIOGRAPHY

TEXTS: F. Wehrli, *Die Schule des Aristoteles* IV, *Demetrios von Phaleron*, 2nd ed. (Basel 1968); *FGrH* 228.

STUDIES: E. Martini, *RE* IV (1901) 2817–41; W. S. Ferguson, *Hellenistic Athens* (London 1911); E. Bayer, *Demetrios Phalereus*, Tübinger Beiträge zur Altertumswissenschaft XXXVI (Tübingen 1942); F. Wehrli, *RE* suppl. XI (1968) 514–22.

ZENODOTUS

LIFE

From Ephesus; pupil of Philetas. First Librarian at Alexandria, tutor to the royal family (children of Ptolemy I); Aristophanes of Byzantium may have been among his pupils.

WORKS

Produced the first major, and very influential, critical edition (διόρθωσις) of Homer; also of Hesiod's *Theogony* and Pindar, and perhaps of Anacreon; format is uncertain, but appears to have involved extensive annotations (Z. was probably the inventor of the obelus as a critical sign; see pp. 31f.). Compiled an alphabetically arranged *Glossary* (Γλῶσσαι) of which a few quotations survive (referring to epic and lyric poetry); may also have written monograph 'On the number of days in the *Iliad*' and a Life of Homer. The Suda (s.v. 'Zenodotus') records that he wrote epic poetry, but nothing of this survives.

BIBLIOGRAPHY

TEXTS: There is no adequate modern text. See H. Düntzer, *De Zenodoti studiis Homericis* (Göttingen 1848); for the Hesiod edition see schol. on Hes. *Theog.* 5, 116; for the Pindar edition see schol. on Pind. *Ol.* 2.4, 6.55 and *P. Oxy.* 841, *P. Oxy.* 2442; for Anacreon see schol. on Pind. *Ol.* 3.29.

STUDIES: See K. Nickau, *RE* XA (1972) 23–45; Pfeiffer 105–19; K. Nickau, *Untersuchungen zur textkritischen Methode des Zenodotus von Ephesos* (Berlin 1977). Also A. Römer, 'Über die Homerrezension des Zenodot', *Abhandlungen der philos.-philol. Classe der Königliche Bayer. Akademie der Wissenschaften* 17 (1886) 641–722; H. Pusch, 'Quaestiones Zenodoteae', *Dissertationes Philologicae Halenses* 11 (1890); M. van der Valk, *Researches on the text and scholia of the Iliad* 11 (Leiden 1964) 1–83; cf. E. G. Turner, *Greek papyri* (Oxford 1968, 1980) 100–24.

ALEXANDER AETOLUS

LIFE

From Pleuron; worked in Alexandria under Ptolemy Philadelphus, and was invited to the Macedonian court by Antigonus Gonatas (ruled 276–240/39 B.C.) along with the poet Aratus and others.

WORKS

Renowned writer of tragedy (member of Pleiad), but only one title (*The dice-players*) survives; at the Alexandrian Library had charge of classification of tragedy and satyr plays. A few fragments remain of his epics (*The sailor*, about Glaucus' search for a plant of immortality, and *Circa*, whose authorship was already doubted in antiquity), of elegy (*Apollo*, *Muses*) and epigrams: A. is also said to have written a *Phaenomena*, perhaps under the influence of Aratus, and scatological ionics in the manner of Sotades before him.

BIBLIOGRAPHY

TEXTS: Powell 121–30; F. Schramm, *Tragicorum Graecorum Hellenisticae quae dicitur aetatis fragmenta* (diss. Monast. 1929) 40–2; Snell 1 278–9.

STUDIES: A. Meineke, *Analecta Alexandrina* (Berlin 1843) 215–51.

LYCOPHRON

LIFE

From Chalcis in Euboea. Said to have enjoyed the hospitality in Eretria (along with Aratus and others) of the philosopher Menedemus whom he mocked in a satyr play; wrote a tragedy commemorating the foundation of Cassandreia (Potidaea) in Macedonia by Cassander (316 B.C.); worked in Alexandria. Ovid (*Ibis* 531–2) implies that he was killed by an arrow.

WORKS

A prolific writer of tragedy and a member of the Pleiad: the Suda cites twenty titles which comprise both traditional mythological themes and rare mythical and even historical topics, while Tzetzes (see Scheer under *Texts* below, II p. 4) says that he wrote either forty-six or sixty-four tragedies: only one fragment, from a *Pelopidae*, survives (Stobaeus 119, 113). Wrote a satyr play *Menedemus*, of which some fragments survive (Diog. Laert. 2.140, Athen. 2.55d, 10.419f.). In charge of classifying comedy at the Alexandrian Library and wrote a treatise *On comedy* in at least nine books (Athen. 11.485d). The author of anagrams on the names of the Alexandrian royal family. The date (and therefore authorship) of the long iambic poem *Alexandra* has been disputed (since ancient times: see schol. on Lyc. 1226), primarily on account of the references to the power of Rome in ll. 1226ff. and 1446ff.; but most modern Hellenistic scholars accept the traditional attribution to Lycophron of Chalcis.

BIBLIOGRAPHY

TEXTS AND COMMENTARIES: TEXTS: *Alexandra*: E. Scheer, I text (Berlin 1881), II scholia (Berlin 1908); A. W. Mair (Loeb, 1921: with Callimachus and Aratus); L. Mascialino (Leipzig 1964). Drama: F. Schramm, *Tragicorum Graecorum Hellenisticae quae dicitur aetatis fragmenta* (diss. Monast. 1929) 25–40; Snell I 273–8. COMMENTARIES: *Alexandra*: C. von Holzinger (Leipzig 1895).

STUDIES: In general see K. Ziegler, *RE* XIII (1927) 2316–81; St. Josifović, *RE* suppl. XI (1968) 888–930. On the dating of the *Alexandra* see A. Momigliano, *Secondo contributo alla storia degli studi classici* (Rome 1960) 431–43, 446–52; on its sources see St. Josifović, *Zur Quellenkunde von Lykophrons Alexandra* (Novi Sad 1960).

LEXICON: M. G. Ciani (Hildesheim 1975).

CALLIMACHUS

LIFE

From Cyrene; grandson of a Cyrenean general of the same name. (Refers to himself in *Ep.* 35 as Battiades, which might indicate that his family traced their descent back to the legendary founder of Cyrene, but which may also have been just a nickname; the Suda's assertion that his father's name was Battus is only an inference from this epigram.) Married the daughter of a Syracusan and had a nephew, also named Callimachus, who was a writer of epic. Apparently worked as a schoolteacher in Eleusis, suburb of Alexandria, before being appointed to work in the Museum and its Library. Author of the Library's catalogue, but never librarian (assertions that he was are derived from a mistranslation of Tzetzes by an anonymous fifteenth-century Italian humanist in MS Vat. Lat. 11469, ed. by F. Ritschl, *Opuscula* I (1866) 5); seems to have spent his career entirely in Alexandria connected with the court and Museum (fr. 178.27 ff., if taken as strictly autobiographical, suggests that C. had never been to sea, and earlier attempts to have him studying at Athens, for example with Praxiphanes, were probably misplaced). The Suda states that he survived into the reign of Ptolemy Euergetes (accession in 247/6), and this is confirmed by the *Lock of Berenice* (fr. 110) and the Victory of Berenice which is now known to have opened Book III of the *Aetia*; otherwise no works are accurately datable (frs. 378–9 the *Galatea* must be dated after 278, Hymn 4 and fr. 228 the *Deification of Arsinoe* must postdate 270, Hymn 2 was probably written at the time of Euergetes). Among his pupils are said to have been Apollonius Rhodius, his fellow-Cyrenean Eratosthenes, and Aristophanes of Byzantium.

WORKS

A prolific writer, said by the Suda to have been the author of more than 800 works. (1) Poetry. Most significant was the elegiac *Aetia*, at least 4,000 lines long, of which Books I and II were in the form of a conversation with the Muses, while Books III and IV, in the form of juxtaposed discontinuous episodes, were compiled separately, or at least re-edited and revised, after 247/6; the whole was re-edited, with a new preface (fr. 1), late in C.'s life in a Collected Works which also included at least the Iambi. Thirteen poems in various iambic metres were contained in the collection; we do not know when they were written, nor whether singly or as a complete group, and only fragments survive. Sparse fragments of four lyric poems survive, including the *Deification of Arsinoe*. The *Hecale* was a hexameter work on Theseus and the bull of Marathon; fragments and titles remain of other hexameter (*Galatea*) and elegiac (*Grapheion, The victory of Sosibius*) works. Sixty-three epigrams and several fragments are preserved in the *Palatine Anthology* and elsewhere, though the authorship of some is disputed. The Suda's ascription to C. of satyr plays, tragedies and comedies has often been discounted, but needlessly in view of *Ep.* 59. Of the 'obscure and abusive poem' (Suda) *Ibis* nothing whatsoever is known beyond that it attacked an enemy; Ovid's elegiac poem of the same name is apparently only in the same style (*Ib.* 55–6) and not a direct imitation (cf. *Ib.* 447–50). Six hymns have been transmitted directly, five in hexameters (to Zeus, Apollo, Artemis, Delos and Demeter), one in elegiacs (to Athena). (2) Prose. *Pinakes*: a bio-bibliography in 120 books of all important Greek writers and writings which served as the catalogue for the Museum Library; *A collection of wonders of the world geographically arranged* (the earliest known paradoxography); *A table and register of dramatic writers in chronological order from the beginning* (partially preserved in the fragments of three wall inscriptions in Rome: *IG* XIV 1098a, 1097, 1098). Numerous monographs, including: *On games, On winds, Non-Greek customs, Local nomenclature, Local month-names, On nymphs, On birds, On the rivers of the Greek world, Against Praxiphanes.*

BIBLIOGRAPHY

(See H. Herter, Bursian 255 (1937) 65 ff. 'Literatur zur hellenistischen Dichtung aus den Jahren 1921–1935', 82–217 'Kallimachos'; idem, *RE* suppl. v (1931) 386–452 and suppl. XIII (1973) 184–266.)

TEXTS AND COMMENTARIES: TEXTS: R. Pfeiffer (Oxford 1949–53). Hymns and Epigrams: A. W. Mair, rev. ed. (Loeb, 1955). Fragments: C. A. Trypanis (Loeb, 1958); *SH* 238–308. COMMENTARIES: Hymns: E. Cahen (Paris 1930). Hymn 1: G. R. McLennan (Rome 1977). Hymn 2: F. J. Williams (Oxford 1978). Hymn 3: F. Bornmann (Florence 1968). Hymn 5: A. W. Bulloch (Cambridge 1985). Hymn 6: N. Hopkinson (Cambridge 1984). Iambi: C. M. Dawson, *Y.Cl.S.* 11 (1950). Epigrams: Gow–Page, *Hell. Ep.* 1035–1348.

STUDIES: (1) GENERAL: E. Cahen, *Callimaque et son oeuvre poétique* (Paris 1929); E. Howald, *Der Dichter Kallimachos von Kyrene* (Erlenbach and Zurich 1943); B. Snell, *The discovery of the mind* (Harvard 1953: English tr.) ch. XII. (2) ON INDIVIDUAL WORKS AND VARIOUS PROBLEMS: (ed.) A. Skiadas, *Kallimachos* (Darmstadt 1975: collection of some of the most important recent articles with an extensive bibliography 401–18). Hymn 2: H. Erbse, *Hermes* 83 (1955) 411–28; P. von der Mühll, *M.H.* 15 (1958) 1–10. Hymn 3: H. Herter, 'Kallimachos und Homer', *Xenia Bonnensia* (Bonn 1929) 57–76 = *Kleine Schriften* (Munich 1975) 377–92. Hymn 5: H. Kleinknecht, 'ΛΟΥΤΡΑ ΤΗΣ ΠΑΛΛΑΔΟΣ', *Hermes* 74 (1939) 300–50. Hymn 6: K. J. McKay, *Erysichthon: a Callimachean comedy*, *Mnemosyne* suppl. VII (1962); H. Gundert, 'Erysichthon' *Forschungen zur röm. Literatur. Festschrift...K. Büchner* (Wiesbaden 1970) 116–24; A. W. Bulloch, 'Callimachus' *Erysichthon*, Homer and Apollonius Rhodius', *A.J.Ph.* 98 (1977) 97–123. *Aetia*: P. J. Parsons, *Z.P.E.* 25 (1977) 1–50. *Pinakes*: Pfeiffer 126–34. E. Eichgrün, *Kallimachos und Apollonios Rhodios* (diss. Berlin 1961). (3) NACHLEBEN:

W. Wimmel, *Kallimachos in Rom*, *Hermes* Einzelschriften XVI (1960); W. Clausen, 'Callimachus and Roman poetry', *G.R.B.S.* 5 (1964) 181–96.

THEOCRITUS

LIFE

From Syracuse, Sicily; his parents were probably called Praxagoras and Philinna. Appealed to Hieron II of Syracuse (275/4–215 B.C.) for support (*Id.* 16), but an encomium to Ptolemy Philadelphus (*Id.* 17) and several eulogistic references to him and his family (*Id.* 7.93, 14.59–64, 15.46–9, 94–5), as well as the Alexandrian setting of *Id.* 15, suggest that he enjoyed the patronage of the Egyptian royal family (in addition, various poems have connections with the works of Callimachus and Apollonius Rhodius). Few dates are known: *Id.* 15 and 17 mention Arsinoe as bride of Ptolemy and are therefore to be dated before her death in 270. He may have been familiar with Cos; among his friends was the doctor Nicias who practised in Miletus (*Id.* 28, *Ep*, 8) and wrote poetry (*Id.* 11 and schol.).

WORKS

Extant works ascribed to T. are: a collection comprising twenty-seven hexameter poems and three poems in Aeolic dialect and metres; twenty-four epigrams; a technopaegnion called *Syrinx* (a poem in the shape of a pan-pipe); five lines from a hexameter poem *Berenice*; scrappy papyrus fragments of another apparently Aeolic poem. The authenticity of many of the poems in the collection is doubted by modern scholars (esp. *Id.* 8, 9, 19–21, 23, 25, 27); the 'traditional' order of the poems in modern editions dates back only to Stephanus' edition of 1566. The Suda reports that some also ascribed to T. *Proitos' daughters, Hopes, Hymns, Heroines, Dirges, Lyrics, Elegies, Iambi, Epigrams*; but these titles bear almost no relation to what we know otherwise of T.'s writings. T. seems not to have published a collected edition of his own works; the earliest editor of whom we know is Artemidorus in the 1st c. B.C. (cf. *Anth. Pal.* 9.205).

BIBLIOGRAPHY

TEXTS AND COMMENTARIES: TEXTS: A. S. F. Gow, *Bucolici Graeci* (OCT, 1952). COMMENTARIES: A. S. F. Gow, 2 vols., 2nd ed. (Cambridge 1952). Select poems: K. J. Dover (London 1971). *Scholia*. C. Wendel (Leipzig 1914: incl. collection of ancient sources on the origins of pastoral).

STUDIES: (1) GENERAL: P. E. Legrand, *Étude sur Théocrite* (Paris 1898); E. Bignone, *Teocrito: studio critico* (Bari 1934); B. A. van Groningen, 'Quelques problèmes de la poésie bucolique grecque', *Mnemosyne* 11 (1958) 293–317 and 12 (1959) 24–53; W.

Meincke, *Untersuchungen zu den enkomiastischen Gedichten Theokrits* (diss. Kiel 1965); U. Ott, *Die Kunst des Gegensatzes in Theokrits Hirtengedichten*, Spudasmata XXII (Hildesheim & New York 1969); T. G. Rosenmeyer, *The green cabinet: Theocritus and the European pastoral lyric* (California 1969); G. Serrao, *Problemi di poesia alessandrina* I, *Studi su Teocrito*, Filologia e critica VIII (Rome 1971); A. Horstmann, *Ironie und Humor bei Theokrit* (Meisenheim am Glan 1976); F. T. Griffiths, *Theocritus at court*, Mnemosyne suppl. LV (1979); S. F. Walker, *Theocritus*, Twayne's world author series DCIX (Boston 1980); C. Segal, *Poetry and myth in ancient pastoral* (Princeton 1981). (2) ON INDIVIDUAL WORKS AND VARIOUS PROBLEMS: For articles down to 1950 see Gow under *Commentaries* above, II 565–89, 594; for later works see bibliographies in works under (1) above and also: S. Nicosia, *Teocrito e l'arte figurata* (Palermo 1968); E. L. Brown, 'The Lycidas of Theocritus' *Idyll 7*', *H.S.C.Ph.* 85 (1981) 59–100; A. Kurz, *Le Corpus Theocriteum et Homère*, Publications universitaires européennes. Série XV philologie et littérature classiques XXI (Berne 1982). (3) CONNECTIONS WITH OTHER AUTHORS AND NACHLEBEN: R. T. Kerlin, *Theocritus in English literature* (Lynchburg, Virginia 1910); G. Schlatter, *Theokrit und Kallimachos* (diss. Zurich 1941); Köhnken, *Apollonios Rhodios und Theokrit*, Hypomnemata XII (Göttingen 1965). (4) TEXT-HISTORY: U. von Wilamowitz-Moellendorff, *Die Textgeschichte der griechischen Bukoliker*, Philologische Untersuchungen XVIII (Berlin 1906).

LEXICON: I. Rumpel (Leipzig 1879).

NICIAS

LIFE

b. in Miletus, where he lived with his wife Theugenis and practised as a doctor. A man of letters and friend of Theocritus, who addressed *Idylls* 11 and 13 to him, and wrote *Epigram* 8 (an inscription for an Asclepius statue) for him and *Idyll* 28 for his wife. Said to have been a fellow-student of Erasistratus, probably at medical school in Alexandria (there is no evidence for the common assumption that they were students on Cos).

WORKS

A poet (Theocr. 11.6, 28.7) who wrote epigrams and at least one work in continuous hexameters (schol. on Theocr. *Id.* 11).

BIBLIOGRAPHY

TEXTS AND COMMENTARIES: Gow–Page, *Hell. Ep.* ll. 2755–86.

APOLLONIUS OF RHODES

LIFE

b. in Alexandria, son of Silleus, in the tribe Ptolemais, but generally called 'Rhodian'. Poet and writer, apparently a pupil of Callimachus; Librarian at Alexandria (before Eratosthenes) and tutor to the royal family. Our evidence is too meagre and unreliable to date his activity as a writer, but the *Argonautica* shows the influence of Callimachus throughout and in turn clearly influenced some of the works of Callimachus and Theocritus. (Reports in the two *Lives* of Apollonius and the Suda s.v. 'Callimachus' that (*a*) A. and Callimachus quarrelled, (*b*) A.'s *Argonautica* was a failure when first published in Alexandria, causing A.'s withdrawal to Rhodes, but (*c*) A. subsequently returned in triumph to Alexandria and was even buried alongside Callimachus, are too questionable to be of any value as evidence; many modern scholars acknowledge the flimsiness of these accounts but inconsistently still try to use them to support their own reconstructions of A.'s career.)

WORKS

(1) POETRY: *Argonautica* (4 bks), *Foundations* (apparently a collection of hexameter poems each devoted to a Greek city); *Canobus*, a work in choliambics probably on the town of the Nile delta and its mythological eponymous hero; of the *Epigrams*, mentioned by Pamphilus (Antonin. Lib. *Met.* 23), none survives (*Anth. Pal.* 11.275, sometimes ascribed to the Rhodian, is of uncertain authorship). (2) PROSE: *Against Zenodotus* (on Homeric topics); *On Archilochus*; wrote on Hesiodic matters in a work containing at least three books (title unknown). (A supposed work *On Antimachus* was based on an incorrect supplement to the Berlin papyrus of Antimachus, fr. 158 Wyss; works on the trireme and symposia, mentioned by Athenaeus 3.97 and 5.191, are by unidentifiable authors named 'Apollonius'.)

BIBLIOGRAPHY

(See H. Herter, Bursian 275 (1944–55) 213ff.; idem, *RE* suppl. XIII (1973) 15–56.)

TEXTS AND COMMENTARIES: TEXTS: H. Fränkel (OCT, 1961); F. Vian (Budé, 1974–81). COMMENTARIES: G. W. Mooney (London & Dublin 1912); H. Fränkel, *Noten zu den Argonautika* (Munich 1968). Bk 1: A. Ardizzoni (Rome 1967). Bk 3: M. M. Gillies (Cambridge 1928); A. Ardizzoni (Bari 1958); F. Vian (Paris 1961); M. Campbell (Hildesheim 1983). Bk 4: E. Livrea (Florence 1973). *Scholia.* C. Wendel (Berlin 1935).

STUDIES: (1) GENERAL: K. W. Blumberg, *Untersuchungen zur epischen Technik des Apollonios von Rhodos* (diss. Leipzig 1931); F. Stoessl, *Apollonios Rhodios* (Berne &

Leipzig 1941); P. Händel, *Beobachtungen zur epischen Technik des Apollonios Rhodios*, Zetemata VIII (Munich 1954); A. Hurst, *Apollonios de Rhodes, manière et cohérence*, Bibl. Helvetica Rom. VIII (Rome 1967); G. Paduano, *Studi su Apollonio Rhodio*, Filologia e critica X (Rome 1972). (2) ON VARIOUS ISSUES: E. Delage, *La géographie dans les Argonautiques d'Apollonios de Rhodes* (diss. Paris 1930); L. Klein, 'Die Göttertechnik in den *Argonautika*', *Philologus* 40 (1931) 18–51, 215–57; H. Fränkel, 'Apollonius as narrator in the *Argonautica*', *T.A.Ph.A.* 83 (1952) 144–55; idem, 'Das Argonautenepos des Apollonios', *M.H.* 14 (1957) 1–19; idem, 'Ein Don Quixote unter den Argonauten des Apollonios', *M.H.* 17 (1960) 1–20; G. Lawall, 'Apollonius' *Argonautica*: Jason as antihero', *Y.Cl.S.* 19 (1966) 119–69; C. R. Beye, 'Jason as love hero in Apollonios' *Argonautika*', *G.R.B.S.* 10 (1969) 31–55; D. N. Levin, *Apollonius' Argonautica re-examined* I, *The neglected first and second books*, Mnemosyne suppl. XIII (1971); M. R. Lefkowitz, *The lives of the Greek poets* (London 1981) ch. XI 'Hellenistic poets'. (3) CONNECTIONS WITH OTHER AUTHORS AND NACHLEBEN: F. Mehmel, *Virgil und Apollonios Rhodios*, Hamburger Arbeiten zur Altertumswiss. 1 (Hamburg 1940); J. Carspecken, 'Apollonius Rhodius and the Homeric epic', *Y.Cl.S.* 13 (1952) 33–143; M. Hügi, *Vergils Aeneis und die hellenistische Dichtung*, Noctes Romanae IV (Berne & Stuttgart 1952); E. Eichgrün, *Kallimachos und Apollonios Rhodios* (diss. Berlin 1961); A. Köhnken, *Apollonios Rhodios und Theokrit*. Hypomnemata XII (Göttingen 1965); M. Campbell, *Echoes and imitations of early epic in Apollonius Rhodius*, Mnemosyne suppl. LXXII (1981). (4) TEXT HISTORY: C. Wendel, *Die Überlieferung der Scholien zu Apollonios von Rhodos*, Abhandlungen der Gesellsch. der Wiss. zu Göttingen phil.-hist. Klasse 3.1 (Berlin 1932); H. Fränkel, *Einleitung zur kritischen Ausgabe der Argonautica des Apollonios*, Abhandlungen der Akademie der Wiss. in Göttingen phil.-hist. Klasse 3.55 (Göttingen 1964).

INDEX: In A. Wellauer, *Apollonii Rhodii Argonautica* (Leipzig 1828), repr. as separate *Index verborum* (Hildesheim 1970); M. Campbell (Hildesheim 1983).

ARATUS

LIFE

From Soli in Cilicia; son of Athenodorus and Letophila. A contemporary of Callimachus; active at the Macedonian court of Antigonus Gonatas (276–240/39 B.C.), who is said to have summoned him there; may have spent some time also at the court of Antiochus I in Syria. Said to have been a pupil of Menecrates of Ephesus, Timon of Phlius and Menedemus of Eretria. Influenced by Stoicism.

ANTAGORAS OF RHODES

WORKS

(1) DIDACTIC POEMS: *Phaenomena, Canon, Astrica* (a title which may have included the *Phaenomena* and *Canon*), *Iatrica* (also possibly the title of a collection). (2) NON-DIDACTIC POEMS: Hymn to Pan (apparently celebrating Antigonus' victory over the invading Celts at Lysimacheia in 277), Funeral Laments (*Epicedeia*), elegies, epigrams. Smaller works were possibly collected under the title *Catalepton*. Testimonia and fragments in *SH* 83–120. Prepared an edition of the *Odyssey*, and was supposedly asked by Antiochus to edit the *Iliad*.

BIBLIOGRAPHY

TEXTS AND COMMENTARIES: TEXTS: E. Maass (Berlin 1893: with *index verborum*); G. R. Mair (Loeb, 1921: with Callimachus and Lycophron tr. A. W. Mair). COMMENTARIES: J. H. Voss (Heidelberg 1824); J. Martin (Florence 1956). *Scholia, ancient commentaries, Lives etc.* E. Maass, *Commentariorum in Aratum reliquiae* (Berlin 1898); J. Martin, *Scholia in Aratum vetera* (Stuttgart 1974).

STUDIES: E. Maass, *Aratea*, Philologische Untersuchungen XII (Berlin 1892); J. Martin, *Histoire du texte des Phénomènes d'Aratos*, Études et commentaires XXII (Paris 1956: see ch. IV for discussion of the ancient biographies); W. Ludwig, 'Die *Phainomena* Arats als hellenistische Dichtung', *Hermes* 91 (1963) 425–9; M. Erren, *Die Phainomena des Aratos von Soloi. Untersuchungen zum Sach- und Sinnverständnis* (Wiesbaden 1967). NACHLEBEN: in addition to the material in Maass under *Scholia* above see V. Buescu, *Cicéron: les Aratea* (Paris & Bucharest 1941); D. B. Gain, *The Aratus ascribed to Germanicus Caesar* (London 1976).

ANTAGORAS OF RHODES

LIFE

A contemporary of Aratus, and like him active at the Macedonian court of Antigonus Gonatas (276–240/39 B.C.), who is said to have summoned him there. Diogenes Laertius (4.26 and 2.133) connects him with the philosophers Crantor and Menedemus, and his epitaph for Crates and Polemo (*Anth. Pal.* 7.103) associates him with the Academy at Athens. (Polemo died in 270 or 266/5; *Anth. Pal.* 9.147 was written for a bridge built in 321/20, but need not have been written at the time of construction.)

WORKS

Thebaid, To Eros (hexameter work of unknown length), epigrams.

BIBLIOGRAPHY

TEXTS AND COMMENTARIES: TEXTS: Powell 120–1. COMMENTARIES: P. von der Mühll, *M.H.* 19 (1962) 28–32; Gow–Page, *Hell. Ep.* II 29–31.

MENECRATES OF EPHESUS

LIFE

Said to have been a teacher of Aratus (Suda s.v. 'Aratus').

WORKS

Works, on agriculture and in at least two books (cf. *Et. Magn.* s.v. ἠθμός): according to Varro, *R.R.* 1.1.9 M. wrote 'ut Hesiodus Ascraeus'. A *Melissourgica* (on apiculture) is an assumption by modern scholars: Varro, *R.R.* 3.16.18 and Pliny, *N.H.* 11.17 suggest only that M. mentioned bees somewhere in his writings, as schol. on Eur. *Rhes.* 529 suggest that he mentioned the constellations, and these topics could well have occurred in a Hesiodic *Works*.

BIBLIOGRAPHY

TEXTS: H. Diels, *Poetarum philosophorum fragmenta* (Berlin 1901) 171–2. See also *SH* 542–50.

NICANDER

LIFE

From Claros in Asia Minor, close to Colophon; the son of Damaeus (if fr. 110 is autobiographical: the Suda names his father as Xenophanes). Ancient sources differ on his dates: *Lives* of Theocritus, Aratus and Lycophron make him a contemporary of those poets, other *Lives* of Aratus put him in the late 3rd c., and the *Life* of Nicander and the Suda put him in the reign of Attalus III of Pergamum (138–133).

WORKS

Alexipharmaca, *Theriaca*; lost hexameter poems: *Europ(i)a* (at least 9 bks), *Georgica* (2 bks), *Metamorphoses* (5 bks), *Oetiaca* (at least 2 bks), *Prognostica*, *Sicelia* (at least 7 bks), *Thebaica* (at least 3 bks); lost elegiac poems: *Cynegetica* (or *Thereutica*), *Ophiaca*; works of indeterminate form: *Aetolica* (at least 2 bks), *Cimmerii*, *Collection of cures, Colophoniaca, Hyacinthus* (?), *Lithica, Melissourgica, On oracles* (at least 3 bks), *On poets from Colophon*; epigrams. Prose work: *Glosses*.

BIBLIOGRAPHY

TEXTS: O. Schneider (Leipzig 1856: with scholia); *FGrH* 271–2; A. S. F. Gow and A. F. Scholfield (Cambridge 1953: with tr.). *Scholia. Theriaca*: A. Crugnola, Testi e documenti per lo studio dell'antichità XXXIV (Milan 1971). *Alexipharmaca*: M. Geymonat, Testi e documenti per lo studio dell'antichità XLVIII (Milan 1974). For possible additional fragments see *SH* 562–3A.

STUDIES: W. Kroll, *RE* XVII (1936) 250–65; H. Schneider, *Vergleichende Untersuchungen zur sprachlichen Struktur der beiden erhaltenen Lehrgedichte des Nikander von Kolophon*, Klass.-Philol. Studien XXIV (Wiesbaden 1962).

NUMENIUS

LIFE

From Heracleia. According to Athenaeus 1.5a a pupil of the doctor Dieuches, hence datable to the 3rd c. B.C. (According to schol. on Nicander, *Ther.* 237 Nicander imitated a line of N.)

WORKS

Halieuticon (hexameters), *Theriacon* (hexameters), *Deipnon* (metre unknown). Celsus 5.18.35 and 21.4 refers to medical prescriptions of N.

BIBLIOGRAPHY

TEXTS: T. Birt, *De Halieuticis Ovidio falso adscriptis* (Berlin 1878) 126–30. See also schol. on Nicander, *Ther.* 237, 257 (cf. on 519, 637), *SH* 568–96.

ERATOSTHENES

LIFE

From Cyrene, the son of Aglaos. Dates uncertain, but according to the Suda b. in 276–273 B.C., d. at age 80, and was summoned (from Athens) to Alexandria by Ptolemy III Euergetes (246–221). Succeeded to headship of the Library after Apollonius Rhodius; said to have been a pupil of Callimachus, the grammarian Lysanias, and the philosopher Ariston of Chios, and the teacher of Aristophanes of Byzantium. Nicknames: Beta, Plato Jr, Pentathlete.

WORKS

(1) PROSE: *Architectonicus* (lexicography), *Arsinoe*, *Catasterismoi* (astronomy etc.), *Chronographiae* (chronology), *Geographica*, *On the measurement of the earth*, *Olympic victors*, *On good and evil*, *On Old Comedy*, *On wealth and poverty*, *Platonicus* (mathematics), *Sceuographicus* (lexicography), and various other treatises. (2) POETRY: *Erigone* (elegiacs), *Hermes* (hexameters).

BIBLIOGRAPHY

TEXTS: G. Bernhardy, *Eratosthenica* (Berlin 1822); C. Robert, *Eratosthenis Catasterismorum reliquiae* (Berlin 1878); H. Berger, *Die geographischen Fragmente des Eratosthenes* (Leipzig 1880); K. Strecker, *De Lycophrone, Euphronio, Erastosthene comicorum interpretibus* (diss. Greifswald 1884); Powell 58–68; *FGrH* 241. Additional fragment: *P. Oxy.* 3000; see *SH* 397–9.

STUDIES: F. Solmsen, 'Eratosthenes as Platonist and poet', *T.A.Ph.A.* 73 (1942) 192–213; idem, 'Eratosthenes' *Erigone*', *T.A.Ph.A.* 78 (1947) 252–75; E. P. Wolfer, *Eratosthenes von Kyrene als Mathematiker und Philosoph* (Groningen 1954); Pfeiffer ch. IV (152–70); G. Dragoni, 'Introduzione allo studio della vita e delle opere di Eratosthene', *Physis* 17 (1975) 41–70.

APOLLODORUS OF ATHENS

LIFE

According to Ps.-Scymnus, *Periegesis* 16–49 (C. Müller, *Geographi Graeci minores* I (Paris 1855) 196ff.), b. at Athens, and a pupil of the Stoic Diogenes of Babylon (d. *c.* 151); for a long time 'studied with' Aristarchus; dedicated his *Chronicle* to Attalus Philadelphus (of Pergamum), probably after fleeing Alexandria when Ptolemy VIII exiled many intellectuals. Possibly extended his *Chronicle* in a fourth book which went down to 120/19, or 110/9.

WORKS

(1) POETRY: *Chronica* (*Chronicle*: 4 bks in iambic trimeters). (2) PROSE: *Etymologies*, *On Athenian courtesans*, *On the catalogue of ships* (12 bks), *On Epicharmus* (10 bks), *On the gods* (24 bks), *On Sophron* (at least 4 bks). (The *Bibliotheca* ascribed to A. is generally agreed to be a work of the 1st or 2nd c. A.D. and not by A. of Athens.)

BIBLIOGRAPHY

TEXTS: *FGrH* 244. Additional fragments: *P. Oxy.* 2260 (see R. Merkelbach, *Archiv für Papyrusforschung* 16 (1956) 115ff.), *P. Oxy.* 2426(?), C. Theodoridis, *Glotta* 50 (1972) 29–34, *Rh.M.* 122 (1979) 9–17, *P. Köln* 5604 (ed. L. Koenen and R. Merkelbach in *Collectanea Papyrologica* I, *Papyrologische Texte und Abhandlungen* 19 (Bonn 1976) 3–26).

STUDIES: E. Schwartz, *RE* I (1894) 2855–86; F. Jacoby, *Apollodors Chronik*, Philologische Untersuchungen XVI (Berlin 1902); A. A. Mosshammer, 'The Apollodoran *Akmai* of Hellanicus and Herodotus', *G.R.B.S.* 14 (1973) 5–13; idem, 'Geometrical proportion and the chronological method of Apollodorus', *T.A.Ph.A.* 106 (1976) 291–306.

DIONYSIUS SON OF CALLIPHON

LIFE

Identity known only from the acrostich in ll. 1–23 of his poem; generally considered to be of 1st c. B.C. His work is dedicated to a Theophrastus.

WORKS

Description of Greece in iambic trimeters (the section describing the Peloponnese is lost).

BIBLIOGRAPHY

TEXTS: C. Müller, *Geographi Graeci minores* I (Paris 1855) 238–43.

ALEXANDER OF EPHESUS

LIFE

An orator who was also statesman, historian and didactic poet. Apparently a contemporary of Cicero, who sent for his works in 59 B.C. and wrote of them dismissively (*Att.* 2.20.6, 22.7). Nickname: Lychnus 'Lamp'.

WORKS

Phaenomena (twenty-six lines preserved in Theon of Smyrna p. 138 H), and a geographical poem divided into three sections: Europe, Asia, Africa (cited several times by Stephanus of Byzantium and Eustathius on Dionysius the Periegete).

BIBLIOGRAPHY

TEXTS: A. Meineke, *Analecta Alexandrina* (Berlin 1843) epimetrum ix (371–7). Cf. G. Knaack, *RE* i (1894) 1448; Powell 129 (Alexander Aetolus fr. 20); W. Burkert, *Philologus* 105 (1961) 32–43; *SH* 19–39.

ARISTOPHANES OF BYZANTIUM

LIFE

Son of Apelles, a military officer. Said to have studied when young with Zenodotus, Callimachus and Machon, amongst others. Became Librarian at age 62 (probably succeeding Eratosthenes) and d. aged 77; said once to have planned to flee Alexandria for Pergamum, but to have been imprisoned. Reported to have exposed plagiarists at a poetry festival thanks to his extensive scholarship and remarkable memory (Vitruvius 7 praef. 5–7).

WORKS

Edited Homer (said to have regarded *Od.* 23.296 as the end of the poem), Hesiod, Alcaeus, Anacreon, Pindar, and possibly other lyric poets; his work on colometry formed the basis of all subsequent metrical work until the nineteenth century. Worked on drama, including Aristophanes and Menander (whom he admired second only to Homer: *IG* xiv 1183c); compiled important Introductions (*Hypotheseis*), many of which survive. Composed *Lexeis*, a very wide-ranging lexicographical work. Monographs included *On Athenian courtesans, On masks, Metrical proverbs, Unmetrical proverbs, On animals*.

BIBLIOGRAPHY

TEXTS: A. Nauck, *Aristophanis Byzantini grammatici Alexandrini fragmenta* (Halle 1848). *Lexeis*: E. Miller, *Mélanges de littérature grecque* (Paris 1868) 427–34; A. Fresenius, *De λέξεων Aristophanearum et Suetonianarum excerptis Byzantinis* (Wiesbaden 1875); L. Cohn, 'De Aristophane Byzantino et Suetonio Tranquillo Eustathii auctoribus', *Jahrbücher für class. Philologie* suppl. xii (1881) 283ff. *On animals*: S. P. Lambros, *Supplementum Aristotelicum* i 1 (Berlin 1885); A. Roselli, *Z.P.E.* 33 (1979) 13–16. *Hypotheseis*: T. O. H. Achelis, *Philologus* 72 (1913) 414–41, 518–45 and 73 (1914–16) 122–53.

STUDIES: Pfeiffer ch. v (171–209); W. J. Slater, *Phoenix* 30 (1976) 234–41; idem, *C.Q.* 32 (1982) 336–49.

ARISTARCHUS

LIFE

Son of Aristarchus; b. on Samothrace, but adopted Alexandrian citizenship. Pupil of Aristophanes, lived during the reign of Ptolemy Philometor (180–145 B.C.), whose brother and sons he tutored. Said to have had *c.* forty pupils, among them Moschus, Ammonius, Apollodorus of Athens, Dionysius Thrax and Aristonicus. Became Librarian after Apollonius the Eidographer (who succeeded Aristophanes). Withdrew to Cyprus where he died of dropsy, aged 72. In later generations his name was a by-word for penetrating criticism (Panaetius *ap.* Athen. 14.634c, Cic. *Att.* 1.14.3, Hor. *A.P.* 450).

WORKS

Said to have compiled more than 800 commentaries. Was particularly concerned with interpretation of Homer, attempting to establish Homeric practice and usage; worked also on Hesiod, Alcman, Alcaeus, Anacreon, Pindar, Bacchylides, the dramatists (according to Dionysius Thrax he could quote the whole of tragedy by heart: *Grammatici Graeci* I 3 160.32–4), and Herodotus.

BIBLIOGRAPHY

TEXTS: K. Lehrs, *De Aristarchi studiis Homericis* (1st ed. 1833, 3rd ed. rev. A. Ludwich, Leipzig 1882); A. Ludwich, *Aristarchs homerische Textkritik* (Leipzig 1884–5).

STUDIES: L. Cohn, *RE* II (1895) 862–73; A. Römer, *Aristarchs Athetesen und die Homerkritik* (Leipzig & Berlin 1912); idem (ed. E. Belzner), *Die Homerexegese Aristarchs in ihren Grundzügen dargestellt*, Studien zur Geschichte und Kultur des Altertums XIII (Paderborn 1924); H. Erbse, 'Über Aristarchs Iliasausgaben', *Hermes* 87 (1959) 275–303; M. van der Valk, *Researches in the text and scholia of the Iliad* II (Leiden 1964) 84ff.; Pfeiffer ch. VI (210–33); H. Erbse, 'Zur normativen Grammatik der Alexandriner', *Glotta* 58 (1980) 236–58.

RHIANUS

LIFE

From Crete (Bene or Ceraea); said to have been a slave (custodian of a gymnasium) before receiving an education and becoming a scholar. A contemporary of Eratosthenes. The extant fragments of his poetry show him to have been influenced by Callimachus.

EUPHORION

WORKS

Epics: mythological: *Heracleia* (4 bks, on Heracles); historical: *Achaeaca* (at least 4 bks), *Eliaca* (at least 3 bks), *Messeniaca* (at least 6 bks), *Thessaliaca* (at least 16 bks). Epigrams. Edited the *Iliad* and *Odyssey*.

BIBLIOGRAPHY

TEXTS AND COMMENTARIES: TEXTS: J. la Roche, *Die homerische Textkritik im Altertum* (Leipzig 1866) 43–9; Powell 9–21; *FGrH* 265. Additional fragments: *P. Oxy.* 2463, 2522, 2883; see *SH* 715–16. COMMENTARIES: Gow–Page, *Hell. Ep.* II 503–8.

STUDIES: A. Meineke, *Analecta Alexandrina* (Berlin 1843) 171–212; C. Mayhoff, *De Rhiani Cretensis studiis Homericis* (Leipzig 1870); W. Aly, *RE* IA (1914) 781–90.

EUPHORION

LIFE

From Chalcis in Euboea, the son of Polymnestus. Studied under the philosophers Prytanis and Lacydes (head of the Academy 241/40–216/15 B.C.) and the poet Archebulus of Thera. Said to have been favoured by Nicia, wife of Alexander the ruler of Euboea, and then transferred to the court of Antiochus the Great (224/3–188/7) in Syria, where he became head of the Library. Buried in Apamea or Antioch. (The Suda gives 275 as the year of his birth.)

WORKS

(1) POETRY: Hexameters: *Alexander, Anius, Apollodorus, Artemidorus, Chiliades, Cletor, Crane, Curses* (also titled *The cup-thief*), *Demosthenes, Dionysus, Dionysus gaping, Hesiod, Hippomedon the Greater, Histia, Hyacinth, Inachus, Lament for Protagoras, Mopsopia, Philoctetes, Polychares, Reply to Theodoridas, Xenius*; epigrams. (2) PROSE: *Historical commentaries, Language of Hippocrates* (6 bks), *On the Aleuads, On the Isthmian Games, On lyric poets.*

BIBLIOGRAPHY

TEXTS AND COMMENTARIES: TEXTS: F. Scheidweiler (diss. Bonn 1908); Powell 28–58; D. L. Page, *Select papyri* III, *Literary papyri* (Loeb, 1942) 488–98; R. J. D. Carden, 'P. Schubart 7', *B.I.C.S.* 16 (1969) 29–37; L. A. de Cuenca (Madrid

MOSCHUS

1976); *SH* 413–54. COMMENTARIES: Gow–Page, *Hell. Ep.* II 284–6; B. A. van Groningen (Amsterdam 1977), cf. H. Lloyd-Jones, *C.R.* 29 (1979) 14–17.

STUDIES: A. Meineke, *Analecta Alexandrina* (Berlin 1843) 1–168; K. Latte 'Der Thrax des Euphorion', *Philologus* 90 (1935) 129–55 = *Kleine Schriften* (Munich 1968) 562–84; B. A. van Groningen, 'La poésie verbale grecque', *Mededeelingen d. kon. Nederl. Akad. van Wetensch. Afd. Letterk.* 16.4 (Amsterdam 1953) 189–217.

MOSCHUS

LIFE

From Syracuse, Sicily. Scholar and poet; an acquaintance or pupil (γνώριμος) of Aristarchus (hence belongs to 2nd c. B.C.). Said by the Suda to be 'the second (bucolic) poet after Theocritus'.

WORKS

Bucolica, Eros the runaway slave, Europa; epigram. Nothing is known of any prose works. The *Epitaph for Bion* and *Megara* were incorrectly ascribed to M. by Fulvio Orsini in the sixteenth century.

BIBLIOGRAPHY

TEXTS AND COMMENTARIES: TEXTS: A. S. F. Gow, *Bucolici Graeci* (OCT, 1952). COMMENTARIES: W. Bühler, *Die Europa des Moschos, Hermes* Einzelschriften XIII (1960); Gow–Page, *Hell. Ep.* II 416–17. *Epitaph for Bion*: V. Mumprecht (diss. Berne, Zurich 1964).

STUDIES: NACHLEBEN: L. Raminella Marzo, 'Mosco attraverso i secoli', *Maia* 2 (1949) 14–29.

BION OF SMYRNA

LIFE

From Phlossa near Smyrna. Named by the Suda s.v. 'Theocritus' as the third, and last, bucolic poet. The anonymous *Epitaph for Bion* (earlier ascribed to Moschus) speaks of B. as having been poisoned (ll. 109–12), but this may be hyperbolic imagery.

WORKS

Bucolica (apparently a collection of works: surviving fragments deal mostly with Eros and erotica, but include works on Hyacinth and Polyphemus), *Epitaph for Adonis* (transmitted anonymously but attributable to B. from the Pseudo-Moschus *Epitaph for Bion*). The *Epithalamion for Achilles and Deidameia* was incorrectly ascribed to B. by Fulvio Orsini; see preceding entry on Moschus under *Works*.

BIBLIOGRAPHY

TEXTS: A. S. F. Gow, *Bucolici Graeci* (OCT, 1952).

STUDIES: U. von Wilamowitz-Moellendorff, 'Adonis', *Reden und Vorträge* I (Berlin 1925) 292–305; M. Fantuzzi, 'Bionis Adonis Epitaphium: contesto culturale e tipologia testuale', *Philologus* 125 (1981) 95–108. NACHLEBEN: I. Cazzaniga, 'La tradizione poetica ellenistica nella favola Ovidiana di Giacinto', *P.P.* 13 (1958) 149–65.

HERODAS

LIFE

External evidence tells us nothing of H.'s life. Internal evidence suggests that he wrote in the first half of the 3rd c. B.C., and *Mim.* 1.23–5 in praise of Egypt and Ptolemy suggests a link with Alexandria. (Nothing can be inferred from the settings of *Mim.* 1 (Cos) and *Mim.* 6 and 7 (Ionia).) On his name see Lesky 747 n. 3.

WORKS

Mimiambs (eight more or less complete; short fragments of at least three others).

BIBLIOGRAPHY

TEXTS AND COMMENTARIES: R. Meister, *Abhandlungen der kgl. sächs. Ges. der Wiss. XXX* phil.-hist. Klasse 13 (Leipzig 1893); W. Headlam and A. D. Knox (Cambridge 1922: with tr.); A. D. Knox (Loeb, 1929: with Theophrastus' *Characters* tr. J. M. Edmonds); I. C. Cunningham (Oxford 1971).

STUDIES: O. Crusius, *Untersuchungen zu den Mimiamben des Herondas* (Leipzig 1892); V. Schmidt, *Sprachliche Untersuchungen zu Herondas*, Untersuchungen zur antiken Literatur und Geschichte 1 (Berlin 1968).

PHOENIX OF COLOPHON

LIFE

Only information is that he wrote a lament for Colophon after it was sacked by Lysimachus and its inhabitants transferred to Ephesus (287–281 B.C.: Paus. 1.9.7).

WORKS

Poems (at least 2 bks) in choliambics on ethical themes and *Koronistai* 'Singers of the crow-song', a poem in the same metre based on a traditional kind of begging song.

BIBLIOGRAPHY

TEXTS: Powell 231–6; A. D. Knox (Loeb, 1929: with Theophrastus' *Characters* tr. J. M. Edmonds); Diehl III, 3rd ed. (1952) 124–30.

STUDIES: G. A. Gerhard, *Phoinix von Kolophon* (Leipzig 1909); Powell–Barber (1921) 12–16; G. Wills, 'Phoenix of Colophon's ΚΟΡѠΝΙΣΜΑ', *C.Q.* 20 (1970) 112–18.

CERCIDAS

LIFE

b. at Megalopolis, apparently of a prominent family. *c.* 226 sent by Aratus of Sicyon to negotiate with Antigonus Doson. Commanded one thousand men from Megalopolis before battle of Sellasia 222. Had reputation as 'excellent' lawgiver.

WORKS

Meliambi: poems in lyrical iambics on Cynic themes. Papyrus fragments first pubd by A. S. Hunt in *P. Oxy.* 8 (1911) 1082, 20–59. Other short fragments survive, including one choliambic line cited by Athenaeus (12.554d) from C.'s *Iambi*. It is possible, but not provable, that certain papyrus fragments of choliambics should be attributed to C.; see A. D. Knox, *The first Greek anthologist* (Cambridge 1923); Powell 213–19.

BIBLIOGRAPHY

TEXTS: Powell 201–19; A. D. Knox (Loeb, 1929: with Theophrastus' *Characters* tr. J. M. Edmonds); Diehl III, 3rd ed. (1952) 141–52.

STUDIES: G. A. Gerhard, *Phoinix von Kolophon* (Leipzig 1909); idem, *RE* XI.1 (1921) 294–308; Powell–Barber (1921) 2–12; D. R. Dudley, *A history of Cynicism* (London 1937) 74–84; M. Gigante, *Ricerche filodemee* (Naples 1969) 122–30.

MACHON

LIFE

From Sicyon or Corinth. Put on his comedies in Alexandria, where he enjoyed a considerable reputation and where Aristophanes of Byzantium studied comedy under him. Said to have been a contemporary of Apollodorus of Carystus (first half of 3rd c. B.C.). According to the epitaph of Dioscorides (*Anth. Pal.* 7.708) he was an old man when he died.

WORKS

Comedies (incl. *Auge, Ignorance, The letter*), *Chreiai* (*Anecdotes*).

BIBLIOGRAPHY

TEXTS AND COMMENTARIES: A. S. F. Gow, Cambridge classical texts and commentaries I (Cambridge 1965).

TYRANNION OF AMISUS

LIFE

From Amisus in Pontus; son of Epicratides and Lindia (from Alexandria). Originally named Theophrastus, but renamed by his teacher Hestiaeus because of his oppressive behaviour towards his peers. Pupil of Dionysius Thrax. Captured by Lucullus in the third Mithridatic war in Pontus (71 B.C.) and taken to Rome, where he was freed. There he became eminent and rich and a friend to Caesar, Atticus and Cicero, who particularly prized him and engaged him to work on his library; amassed a huge library. Helped retrieve and arrange the library of Theophrastus (incl. works of Aristotle) which had fallen into neglect after Sulla's plundering of it in 84. d. an old man in 26/5 B.C.

WORKS

Most titles are lost, being confused in the Suda in the list of works by Tyrannion the Younger. Wrote *On the amphibrach metre* for Caesar, dedicated a book on prosody and accents to Atticus (bef. 46 B.C.: Cic. *Att.* 12.6.2), wrote on Homer and grammar.

BIBLIOGRAPHY

TEXTS: Testimonia in H. Funaiolo, *Grammaticae Romanae fragmenta* (Stuttgart 1907) xv–xvii (no. 26).

STUDIES: C. Wendel, *RE* VIIA (1948) 1811–19.

PARTHENIUS

LIFE

From Nicaea; son of Heracleides and Eudora. Taken prisoner in the third Mithridatic war and sent to Rome, where he was freed and had a strong influence on Roman poetry. Dedicated his *Erotica pathemata* to Cornelius Gallus, and was said to have been the teacher of Virgil (Macr. *Sat.* 5.18).

WORKS

(1) POETRY: Elegiacs: *Aphrodite, Bias, Crinagoras, Delos, Encomium on Arete* (his wife: in 3 bks), *Lament for Archelais, Lament for Arete, Leucadiae*; unknown metre: *Anthippe, Eidolophanes, Heracles, Iphiclus, Lament for Auxithemis, Metamorphoses, Propempticon.* (2) PROSE: *Erotica pathemata* (*Love stories*).

BIBLIOGRAPHY

TEXTS: A. Meineke, *Analecta Alexandrina* (Berlin 1843) 255–338; S. Gaselee (Loeb, 1929: with Longus tr. G. Thornley rev. J. M. Edmonds). *Erotica pathemata*: P. Sakolowski in E. Martini, *Mythographi Graeci* II (Leipzig 1896). *SH* 605–66.

STUDIES: R. Pfeiffer, 'A fragment of Parthenios' *Arete*', *C.Q.* 37 (1943) 23–32 = *Ausgewählte Schriften* (Munich 1960) 133–47; W. V. Clausen, 'Callimachus and Roman poetry', *G.R.B.S.* 5 (1964) 181–96; T. P. Wiseman, *Cinna the poet, and other Roman essays* (Leicester 1974); N. B. Crowther, 'Parthenius and Roman poetry', *Mnemosyne* 29 (1976) 66–71; R. O. A. M. Lyne, 'The neoteric poets', *C.Q.* 28 (1978) 167–87.

ISYLLUS

LIFE AND WORKS

Author of an inscription recording the institution of a procession for Apollo and Asclepius sometime in the latter part of the 4th c. B.C.

BIBLIOGRAPHY

TEXTS: Powell 132–6.

STUDIES: U. von Wilamowitz-Moellendorff, *Isyllos von Epidauros*, Philologische Untersuchungen IX (Berlin 1886).

PAEANS

TEXTS: Powell 136–71.

STUDIES: Powell–Barber (1921) 41–9 and (1929) 60–1.

MAIISTAS

TEXTS: Powell 68–71.

GREEK ANTHOLOGY

For text, introduction, commentary and biographies for all individual Hellenistic authors in Meleager's *Garland* see Gow–Page, *Hell. Ep.* Subsequent volumes deal with the remainder of the collection down to A.D. 50: Gow–Page, *Garland*; D. L. Page, *Further Greek epigrams* (Cambridge 1981). Other texts: W. R. Paton (Loeb, 1916–18); H. Beckby (Munich 1957–8). Texts of authors from Archilochus to Meleager: D. L. Page, *Epigrammata Graeca* (Oxford 1975).

STUDIES: In addition to works cited by Gow and Page see: D. H. Garrison, *Mild frenzy: a reading of the Hellenistic love epigram*, Hermes Einzelschriften XLI (1978); S. L. Tarán, *The art of variation in the Hellenistic epigram*, Columbia studies in classical tradition IX (Leiden 1979). NACHLEBEN: J. Hutton, *The Greek Anthology in Italy to the year 1800*, Cornell studies in English XXIII (New York 1935); idem, *The Greek Anthology in France and in the Latin writers of the Netherlands to the year 1800*, Cornell studies in classical philology XXVIII (New York 1946).

POST-ARISTOTELIAN PHILOSOPHY

THE LATER ACADEMY AND
THE PERIPATOS (LYCEUM)

(For *General works* see pp. 805–6.)

XENOCRATES

LIFE

b. *c.* 396 B.C., son of Agathenor, at Chalcedon. Came to Athens as young man and joined the Academy. Left Athens with Aristotle after Plato's death 347. Succeeded Speusippus as head of Academy 339. d. 314 B.C. Sources: Diog. Laert. 4.6–15; others in Heinze under *Texts* below.

WORKS

Seventy-five titles listed by Diog. Laert. 4.11–14, but surviving evidence extremely fragmentary. X. wrote copiously on logic and on style.

BIBLIOGRAPHY

TEXTS AND COMMENTARIES: R. Heinze (Leipzig 1892).

STUDIES: E. Zeller, *Geschichte der griechischen Philosophie* II 1, 4th ed. (Leipzig 1889) 1010–32; H. Cherniss, *The riddle of the early Academy* (Berkeley & Los Angeles 1945); P. Merlan, *From Platonism to Neoplatonism*, 2nd ed. (The Hague 1960); H.-J. Krämer, *Der Ursprung der Geistmetaphysik* (Amsterdam 1965); J. Dillon, *The Middle Platonists* (London 1977) 22–39.

ANTIOCHUS

LIFE

b. *c.* 125 B.C. at Ascalon. Joined sceptical Academy at Athens, directed by Philo of Larisa, but subsequently abandoned scepticism for system which he claimed to be the teaching of the Old Academy. Closely acquainted with Lucullus and Cicero, who

THEOPHRASTUS

attended his lectures in Athens. d. *c.* 68 B.C. Sources: Cic. *Acad.* 1.13–14, 2.11–18; others in Luck under *Texts* below.

WORKS

Two titles known, *Sosus* (probably book on which Cicero drew heavily in his *Academica*) and *Criteria* (*Kanonika*). Frequent refs. to A. in Cic. *Fin.* 4 and 5.

BIBLIOGRAPHY

TEXTS AND DISCUSSION: G. Luck, *Der Akademiker Antiochus* (Berne & Stuttgart 1953).

STUDIES: E. Zeller, *Die Philosophie der Griechen* III 1, 4th ed. rev. E. Wellmann (Leipzig 1909) 618–30; J. Glucker, *Antiochus and the later Academy* (Göttingen 1978); J. Dillon, *The Middle Platonists* (London 1977) 52–105.

THEOPHRASTUS

LIFE

b. 372/370 B.C. at Eresos in Lesbos, son of Melantes whose substantial property he inherited. Originally named Tyrtamus and called Theophrastus by Aristotle because of 'his divinely sweet style'. Probably a member of Platonic Academy but may have first encountered Aristotle at Assos. Spent time in Macedonia and perhaps also in Egypt and Cyrene. Succeeded Aristotle as head of Peripatos 322 and provided it with buildings which he bequeathed to his successors. Allegedly freed Eresus twice from tyrants. Friend of Demetrius of Phalerum. d. in Athens 288/286 B.C. Sources: Diog. Laert. 5.36–41 (life; 38 for name), 42–50 (writings), 51–7 (will); Plut. *Adv. Col.* 1126f. (tyrants).

WORKS

Over 220 titles recorded by Diog. Laert.; following survive in complete or extended form. *Enquiry into plants* (9 bks), *On the causes of plants* (6 bks), *On sensation, On stones, On fire, On odours, On winds, On weather signs, On weariness, On vertigo, On perspiration, Metaphysics, Characters.* Principal fragmentary works are *On piety, On style, Doctrines of natural philosophers* and *Laws. On colours,* attributed to Aristotle, may be T.'s; see H. B. Gottschalk, *Hermes* 92 (1964) 59–85.

BIBLIOGRAPHY

(See O. Regenbogen, *RE* suppl. VII (1940) 1354–1562.)

836

TEXTS AND COMMENTARIES: TEXTS: (1) Complete. J. G. Schneider (Leipzig 1818–21); F. Wimmer (Leipzig 1854–62: with incomplete collection of frs. and Latin tr.). (2) Individual works. *Enquiry into plants, On odours, On weather signs*: A. F. Hort (Loeb, 1916). *On the causes of plants*: B. Einarson and G. K. K. Link (Loeb, 1976). *On fire*: A. Gercke (Greifswald 1896). *Characters*: H. Diels (OCT, 1910); J. M. Edmonds (Loeb, 1929). *Doctrines of natural philosophers*: H. Diels, *Doxographi Graeci* (Berlin 1879) 473–527. COMMENTARIES: *On sensation*: G. M. Stratton, *Theophrastus and the Greek physiological psychology before Aristotle* (London 1917: with tr.). *On stones*: E. R. Caley and J. F. C. Richards (Columbus, Ohio 1956: with tr.); D. E. Eichholz (Oxford 1965). *On fire*: V. Coutant (Assen 1971: with tr.). *On winds*: V. Coutant and V. L. Eichenlaub (Notre Dame, Indiana 1975: with tr.). *Metaphysics*: W. D. Ross and F. H. Fobes (Oxford 1929: with tr.). *Characters*: R. G. Ussher (London 1960); P. Steinmetz, 2 vols. (Munich 1960–2); W. Anderson (Ohio 1970: with tr.). *On piety*: W. Poetscher (Leiden 1964: with German tr.). *On style*: A. Meyer (Leipzig 1910). *Laws*: H. Hager, *Journal of Philology* 6 (1876) 1–27. A complete edition of the fragments is being prepared by 'Project Theophrastus' under the direction of W. W. Fortenbaugh (Rutgers University, New Brunswick, U.S.A.).

TRANSLATIONS: *Characters*: P. Vellacott, 2nd ed. (Harmondsworth 1973).

STUDIES: (1) LITERARY THEORY: J. Stroux, *De Theophrasti virtutibus dicendi* (Leipzig 1912); G. M. A. Grube, 'Theophrastus as a literary critic', *T.A.Ph.A.* 83 (1952) 172–83; idem, 'Thrasymachus, Theophrastus and Dionysius of Halicarnassus', *A.J.Ph.* 73 (1952) 251–67; G. Kennedy, 'Theophrastus and stylistic distinctions', *H.S.C.Ph.* 62 (1957) 93–104; A. Michel, *Rhétorique et philosophie chez Cicéron* (Paris 1960); G. Kennedy, *The art of persuasion in Greece* (Princeton 1963) 273–84; G. M. A. Grube, *The Greek and Roman critics* (London 1965) 103–9. (2) OTHER SPECIFIC TOPICS: I. M. Bochenski, *La logique de Théophraste* (Fribourg 1947); J. B. McDiarmid, 'Theophrastus on the Presocratic Causes', *H.S.C.Ph.* 61 (1953) 85–156; G. Senn, *Die Pflanzenkunde des Theophrast von Eresos, seine Schrift über die Unterscheidungsmerkmale der Pflanzen und seine Kunstprose*, ed. O. Gigon (Basel 1956); A. E. Raubitschek, 'Theophrastus on ostracism', *C.&M.* 19 (1958) 77–109; P. Steinmetz, 'Menander und Theophrast', *Rh.M.* 103 (1960) 185–91; idem, *Die Physik des Theophrastos von Eresos* (Berlin 1964); K. Gaiser, 'Menander und der Peripatos', *A.&A.* 13 (1967) 8–40; (ed.) I. Düring, *Naturphilosophie bei Aristoteles und Theophrast* (Heidelberg 1969); C. B. Schmitt, 'Theophrastus in the Middle Ages', *Viator* 2 (1971) 251–70; H. B. Gottschalk, 'Notes on the wills of the Peripatetic Scholarchs', *Hermes* 100 (1972) 314–42; A. Graeser, *Die logischen Fragmente des Theophrast* (Berlin 1973). (3) MS TRADITION: J. B. McDiarmid, *A.G.Ph.* 44 (1962) 1–32 (*On senses*); N. G. Wilson, *Scriptorium* 16 (1962) 96–102; W. Burnikel, *Textgeschichtliche Untersuchungen zu neun Opuscula Theophrasts* (Wiesbaden 1974); B. Einarson, *C.Ph.* 71 (1976) 67–76 (*Enquiry into plants*.) (4) ANCIENT LITERARY CRITICISM: Cic. *Or.* 62, Quint. 10.1.83, Sen. *N.Q.* 6.13.

ARISTOXENUS

LIFE

b. *c.* 370 B.C. at Tarentum, son of Spintharus, a musician. At Athens was first the pupil of Xenophilus, a Pythagorean, and later an associate of Aristotle. Suda reports that he hoped to succeed Aristotle as head of Peripatos. d. at unknown date after 322 B.C. Sources: Suda; Cic. *Tusc.* 1.18, 41, *Att.* 13.32; Apollonius, *Hist. mirab.* 49.

WORKS

453 works accredited by Suda, many on music, subject for which A. is chiefly known. Principal surviving work the *Elements of harmony* in three books, which are probably incomplete sections from two independent treatises combined and abridged in antiquity. Bk 2 of *Elements of rhythm* is partially preserved. Titles of lost works include *Lives* (e.g. Pythagoras and Socrates), *Pythagorean maxims*, *Educational laws*, *Political laws*, *Historical memoirs*.

BIBLIOGRAPHY

TEXTS AND COMMENTARIES: *Harmony* and *Rhythm*: R. Westphal, 2 vols. (Leipzig 1883–93: repr. Hildesheim 1965). *Harmony*: H. S. Macran (Oxford 1902: with tr.); R. da Rios (Rome 1954). *Fragments*. F. Wehrli, *Die Schule des Aristoteles* II, *Aristoxenos*, 2nd ed. (Basel 1967).

STUDIES: E. Zeller, *Die Philosophie der Griechen* II 2, 3rd ed. (Leipzig 1879) 881–9; L. Laloy, *Aristoxène de Tarente et la musique de l'antiquité* (Paris 1904); F. Wehrli, *RE* suppl. XI (1968) 336–43; A. Momigliano, *The development of Greek biography* (Cambridge, Mass. 1971) 73–89; A. Barker, 'Music and perception. A study in Aristoxenus', *J.H.S.* 98 (1978) 9–16.

STRATO

LIFE

b. *c.* 328 B.C. at Lampsacus, son of Arcesilaus. Before succeeding Theophrastus as head of Peripatos 288/285 taught Ptolemy Philadelphus in Alexandria. Directed Peripatos for eighteen years. d. 270/267 B.C. Sources: Diog. Laert. 5.58 (life), 59–60 (writings), 61–4 (will); Suda; Cic. *Acad.* 1.34.

PRAXIPHANES

WORKS

Forty-six titles listed by Diog. Laert.; none of these works survives. S. chiefly re-nowned for his physics, the part of his work best represented in extant fragments. He may be author of the work *On audible objects*, transmitted in Aristotelian corpus; see H. B. Gottschalk, *Hermes* 96 (1968) 435–60.

BIBLIOGRAPHY

TEXTS AND COMMENTARIES: F. Wehrli, *Die Schule des Aristoteles* v, *Straton von Lampsakos*, 2nd ed. (Basel 1969); H. B. Gottschalk, 'Strato of Lampsacus: some texts', *Proceedings of the Leeds Philosophical and Literary Society*, Lit. and Hist. Section 11.6 (1965) 95–182.

STUDIES: E. Zeller, *Die Philosophie der Griechen* II 2, 3rd ed. (Leipzig 1879) 897–921; W. Capelle, 'Straton der Physiker', *RE* IVA (1932) 278–315; M. Gatzemeier, *Die Naturphilosophie des Straton von Lampsakos. Zur Geschichte des Problems der Bewegung des frühen Peripatos* (Meisenheim am Glan 1970).

DEMETRIUS OF PHALERUM

(See p. 812.)

PRAXIPHANES

LIFE

Approximate contemporary of Theophrastus, b. in Mytilene and joined Peripatos in Athens. Later worked in Rhodes. Chiefly known for his work on literature and grammar. Sources: Strabo 14 p. 655 C; *CIG* XI 4, 613.

WORKS

Few traces survive. Wrote a work on friendship (some frs. in *P. Herc.* 1027), *On poets* (dialogue between Plato and Isocrates; Diog. Laert. 3.8), *On poems* and *On history*. Callimachus wrote a book *Against Praxiphanes* (fr. 460 Pfeiffer).

BIBLIOGRAPHY

TEXTS AND COMMENTARIES: F. Wehrli, *Die Schule des Aristoteles* IX, *Phainias von Eresos. Chamaileon. Praxiphanes*, 2nd ed. (Basel 1969).

STUDIES: C. O. Brink, 'Callimachus and Aristotle: an inquiry into Callimachus Πρὸς Πραξιφάνην', *C.Q.* 40 (1946) 11–26; W. Aly, *RE* XXII.2 (1954) 1769–84; Pfeiffer 135–6.

EPICURUS AND PHILODEMUS

(For *General works* see pp. 805–6.)

EPICURUS

LIFE

b. 341 B.C. at Samos, son of Neocles, a schoolmaster and Athenian citizen. Spent 323–321 on compulsory military and civilian service. Learnt about Democritean atomism from Nausiphanes of Teos, and established his own philosophical circles in Mytilene and Lampsacus. Returned to Athens 307/6 and bought a house with a garden, which became both his home and the centre of his school of philosophy. Bequeathed this estate to his successor Hermarchus. d. in Athens 271 B.C. Sources: Diog. Laert. 10.1–28; Suda; Epicurus, *Letter to Herodotus* 35–7, *Letter to Pythocles* 84–5, fragmentary *Letters* (40–133 Arrighetti); Plut. *Mor.* 1086c–1107c (*That Epicurus makes a pleasant life impossible*); Sext. Emp. *Adv. math.* 1.3–4.

WORKS

(1) COMPLETE. *Letters to Herodotus, Pythocles* and *Menoeceus* (on authenticity of *Pyth.* see Arrighetti under *Commentaries* below, with bibl.), recorded in Diog. Laert. 10.35–135. Forty *Principal doctrines* (*Kuriai doxai*), short aphorisms recorded in Diog. Laert. 10.139–54. Eighty-one further *Aphorisms* (incl. thirteen of known *Principal doctrines* and some sayings attributed to E.'s followers) transmitted in Vatican MS of 14th c. (*Gnomologium Vaticanum*) (2) FRAGMENTARY. On Herculaneum papyri, parts of *On Nature* (originally 37 bks) bks 2, 11–12, 14–15, 28, 32, 35, and some parts from books of unknown numbers. Best preserved are parts from 11 (cosmology), 14 (polemic against Platonic theory of elements), 28 (language and epistemology) and Arrighetti 34 (causes of human action). Many fragments from other works survive; titles of certain works in Diog. Laert. 10.26–8.

BIBLIOGRAPHY

(See P. de Lacy, *C.W.* 48 (1954/5) 169–77 (for 1937–54); W. Schmid, *RAC* v (1961) 681–819; H. Steckel, *RE* suppl. XI (1968) 579–652; Rist (1972) under *Studies* (1) below, 177–82.)

TEXTS AND COMMENTARIES: TEXTS: H. Usener (Leipzig 1887: repr. Stuttgart 1966: with large selection of secondary sources but excl. frs. from Herculaneum papyri). *Letters* and *Principal doctrines*: P. von der Mühll (BT, 1922); H. S. Long, *Diogenis Laertii Vitae philosophorum* II (OCT, 1964). COMMENTARIES (all with tr.): C. Bailey (Oxford 1926: excl. papyri); E. Bignone (Bari 1930); G. Arrighetti, 2nd ed. (Turin 1973: incl. most previously pubd frs. from Herculaneum); C. Diano (Florence 1974: incl. comm. but no tr. of ethical writings, comm. and tr. of fragmentary *Letters* preserved in Philodemus' Πραγματεῖαι). *Letter to Herodotus*: J. and M. Bollack, H. Wismann (Paris 1971). *Letter to Menoeceus* and *Principal doctrines*: J. Bollack (Paris 1975). *Letter to Pythocles*: J. Bollack and A. Laks (Lille 1978). *Life* in Diog. Laert. 10.1–34: A. Laks, *Cahiers de Philologie* I (Lille 1976) 1–118. *Fragments*. A. Vogliano, *Epicuri et Epicureorum scripta in Herculanensibus papyris servata* (Berlin 1928); W. Schmid, *Ethica Epicurea. Pap. Herc. 1251* (Leipzig 1939); G. Arrighetti, 'Il libro "Sul Tempo" (PHerc. 1413)', *Cron. Erc.* 2 (1972) 5–46; D. Sedley, 'Epicurus On nature book xxviii', *Cron. Erc.* 3 (1973) 5–83; (on bk 15) C. Millot, *Cron. Erc.* 7 (1979) 9–39.

STUDIES: (1) GENERAL: C. Bailey, *The Greek Atomists and Epicurus* (Oxford 1928); N. W. De Witt, *Epicurus and his philosophy* (Minneapolis 1954); J. M. Rist, *Epicurus. An introduction* (Cambridge 1972); A. A. Long, *Hellenistic philosophy* (London 1974) 14–74. (2) MORE SPECIALIZED (for critical discussion of recent work and collection of papers on many aspects of Epicureanism see *Actes du VIIIe Congrès Association Guillaume Budé* (Paris 1969)): H. Widmann, *Beiträge zur Syntax Epikurs* (Stuttgart & Berlin 1935); E. Bignone, *L'Aristotele perduto e la formazione filosofica di Epicuro*, 2 vols. (Florence 1936); P. de Lacy, 'The Epicurean analysis of language', *A.J.Ph.* 60 (1939) 85–92; A. J. Festugière, *Epicurus and his gods*, tr. C. W. Chilton (Oxford 1955); C. Brescia, *Ricerche sulla lingua e sullo stilo di Epicuro*, 2nd ed. (Naples 1962); D. J. Furley, *Two studies in the Greek Atomists* (Princeton 1967); A. A. Long, 'Aisthesis, prolepsis and linguistic theory in Epicurus', *B.I.C.S.* 18 (1971) 114–33; G. Arrighetti, 'L'opera "sulla natura" di Epicuro', *Cron. Erc.* 1 (1971) 90–111 and 5 (1975) 39–51; D. Sedley, 'The structure of Epicurus' On nature', *Cron. Erc.* 4 (1974) 89–92; idem, 'Epicurus and the mathematicians of Cyzicus', *Cron. Erc.* 6 (1976) 23–54; (edd.) J. Bollack and A. Laks, *Études sur l'Épicurisme antique, Cahiers de Philologie* I (Lille 1976); M. Gigante, *Scetticismo e Epicureismo* (Naples 1981).

INDEX: H. Usener, *Glossarium Epicureum*, ed. M. Gigante and W. Schmid (Rome 1977).

DIOGENES OF OENOANDA

LIFE

b. *c.* A.D. 150/160 at Oenoanda. May have belonged to one of leading Lycian families, and served as Lyciarch. Set up at own expense a large stone inscription, towards end of his life, which recorded main principles of Epicureanism for benefit of his fellow citizens; see *IGR* III 500 (*Denkschrift Akad. Wien* 45 (1897) 41ff.), although this does not certainly refer to the Diogenes of the inscription. Sources: frs. 2.ii, vi; 50–3 Chilton.

WORKS

Account of Epicureanism inscribed on stone; fragments first discovered 1884.

BIBLIOGRAPHY

TEXTS AND COMMENTARIES: TEXTS: C. W. Chilton (BT, 1967). COMMENTARIES: J. William (Leipzig 1907); A. Grilli (Milan 1960); C. W. Chilton (London 1971: with tr.). New fragments: M. F. Smith, *A.J.A.* 74 (1970) 51–62 and 75 (1971) 357–89; *C.Q.* n.s.22 (1972) 159–62; *J.H.S.* 92 (1972) 147–55; *Thirteen new fragments of Diogenes of Oenoanda, Denkschrift akad. Wien* 117 (1974); *Hermathena* 118 (1974) 110–29; *A.S.* 28 (1978) 39–92 and 29 (1979) 69–89; *Prometheus* 8 (1982) 193–212; *Cahiers de Philologie* I (Lille 1976) 281–318; A. Laks and C. Millot, 'Réexamen de quelques fragments de D. sur l'âme, la connaissance et la fortune', ibid. 321–57.

PHILODEMUS

LIFE

b. *c.* 110 B.C. at Gadara. Studied under the Epicurean Zeno of Sidon at Athens. Came to Italy before 70 and befriended there by L. Calpurnius Piso who probably owned the villa at Herculaneum, discovered in 1750, where many carbonized papyri were found. This may have been P.'s home during his later life. Along with the Epicurean Siro, P. was probably known to Virgil and Horace. Some have detected Republican sympathies in his work. d. *c.* 40/35 B.C. Sources: *Anth. Pal.* 5.112, 11.34, 41 and 44; W. Crönert, *Kolotes und Menedemos* (Leipzig 1906) 126–7, 163; Cic. *Pis.* 68–72; Strabo 16 p. 759 C.

WORKS

(1) EPIGRAMS: *Palatine anthology* attributes thirty-five to P.; *Planudean anthology* adds one more, omitting eleven of *Palatine* collection. Not all are genuine; see Gow–Page,

Garland II 371. (2) PROSE WRITINGS: Substantial fragments from many philosophical works on Herculaneum papyri; transcribed in *Herculanensium voluminum quae supersunt, Collectio prior* (Naples 1793–1855) and *Collectio altera* (Naples 1862–76). Not all these texts are available in modern editions. For lists of works and early bibliography see D. Comparetti and G. de Petra, *La villa ercolanese dei Pisoni e la sua biblioteca* (Turin 1883); W. Crönert, *Memoria Graeca Herculanensis* (Leipzig 1903).

BIBLIOGRAPHY

TEXTS AND COMMENTARIES: (1) EPIGRAMS: Gow–Page, *Garland*. (2) FRAGMENTARY PROSE WRITINGS: *Rhetoric*: S. Sudhaus (Leipzig 1892–6). Bks 1–2: F. Longo Aurrichio (Naples 1977). Bk 5: M. Ferrario, *Cron. Erc.* 10 (1980) 55–124. *Against the sophists*: F. Sbordone (Naples 1947). *On anger*: C. Wilke (Leipzig 1914). *On conversation*: F. Amoroso, *Cron. Erc.* 5 (1975) 63–76. *On economy*: C. Jensen (Leipzig 1906). *On flattery*: T. Gargiulo, *Cron. Erc.* 11 (1981) 103–28. *On free speech*: A. Olivieri (Leipzig 1914). *On gods* bks 1 and 3: H. Diels, *Abh. Preuss. Akad. Wiss.* 1915–16 (Berlin 1916–17). *On music*: J. Kemke (Leipzig 1884). Bk 1: G. M. Rispoli in Sbordone 1 below and *Cron. Erc.* 4 (1974) 57–87. *On poems*: (ed.) F. Sbordone, *Ricerche sui papiri ercolanesi*, 2 vols. (Naples 1969–76: with Italian tr.); J. Heidmann, *Cron. Erc.* 1 (1971) 90–111. Bk 2: A. Hausrath, *Jahrb. für class. Philol.* suppl. XVII (Leipzig 1890). Bk 5: C. Jensen (Berlin 1923: with German tr.). *On (?) providence*: M. Ferrario, *Cron. Erc.* 2 (1972) 67–94. *On signs*: P. and E. de Lacy, *Philodemus: On methods of inference* (Philadelphia 1941: with tr.). *On the good king according to Homer*: A. Olivieri (Leipzig 1909). *On vices*: C. Jensen (Leipzig 1911). Other fragmentary works in A. Vogliano, *Epicuri et Epicureorum scripta in Herculanensibus papyris servata* (Berlin 1928); M. Gigante, *Ricerche filodemee* (Naples 1969).

TRANSLATIONS: *Rhetoric*: H. M. Hubbell (New Haven 1920).

STUDIES: (1) LITERARY THEORY: A. Rostagni, *Scritti minori* I (Turin 1955) 356–446; C. O. Brink, *Horace on poetry, Prolegomena to the literary Epistles* (Cambridge 1963) 48–74; G. M. A. Grube, *The Greek and Roman critics* (London 1965) 193–206. (2) OTHER STUDIES: R. Philippson, *RE* XIX.2 (1938) 2444–82; O. Murray, 'Philodemus on the good king according to Homer', *J.R.S.* 55 (1965) 161–82; A. Henrichs, 'Towards a new edition of Philodemus' treatise on poety', *G.R.B.S.* 13 (1972) 69–98; idem, 'Die Kritik der stoischen Theologie in PHerc. 1428', *Cron. Erc.* 4 (1974) 5–32; idem, '*De pietate* als mythographische Quelle', *Cron. Erc.* 5 (1975) 5–38; M. Gigante, '"Philosophia medicans" in Filodemo', *Cron. Erc.* 5 (1975) 53–62; T. Dorandi, 'L'Omero di Filodemo', *Cron. Erc.* 8 (1978) 38–51.

INDEX: C. J. Vooys and D. A. Krevelen (Purmerand, Amsterdam 1934–41).

THE STOA AND STOIC WRITERS

GENERAL WORKS (see also pp. 805–6)

No complete book survives by any Stoic who wrote before the Christian era. Evidence for Stoics from Zeno of Citium to Boethus of Sidon (2nd c. B.C.) in SVF = H. von Arnim, *Stoicorum veterum fragmenta*, 4 vols. (Leipzig 1903–24: repr. Stuttgart 1964). The work of Stoics from this period and later is discussed in the following:

Arnold, E. V., *Roman Stoicism* (Cambridge 1911)
Edelstein, L., *The meaning of Stoicism* (Cambridge, Mass. 1966)
Hicks, R. D., *Stoic and Epicurean* (New York 1910)
Long, A. A. (ed.), *Problems in Stoicism* (London 1971)
idem, *Hellenistic philosophy* (London 1974)
Pohlenz, M., *Die Stoa*, 3rd ed. (Göttingen 1964)
Rist, J. M., *Stoic philosophy* (Cambridge 1969)
idem (ed.), *The Stoics* (Berkeley & Los Angeles 1978)
Sambursky, S., *The physics of the Stoics* (London 1959)
Sandbach, F. H., *The Stoics* (London 1975)
Schofield, M., Burnyeat, M., Barnes, J. (edd.), *Doubt and dogmatism* (Oxford 1980)
Watson, G., *The Stoic theory of knowledge* (Belfast 1966)
Zeller, E., *Die Philosophie der Griechen* III 1, 4th ed. rev. E. Wellmann (Leipzig 1909)

ZENO

LIFE

b. *c.* 332 B.C. at Citium in Cyprus. Came to Athens, perhaps as a merchant like his father, *c.* 311. Studied with Cynic, Megarian and Platonist philosophers. Began teaching in his own right in the Painted Colonnade (*Stoa Poikile*) *c.* 300. Declined offer of Athenian citizenship. Honoured by Athenians with golden crown, tomb and inscriptions set up in Academy and Lyceum. d. *c.* 261 B.C. Sources: Diog. Laert. 7.1–34 (life and writings), 38–160 (philosophy, incl. much from later Stoics); others in SVF I 9–44.

WORKS

Twenty titles recorded in Diog. Laert. 7.4. Very few genuine fragments survive. Subjects apart from philosophy included 'style', 'Homeric problems', 'the reading of poetry' and 'rhetoric'. Best known work was *Republic*, his first book, strongly influenced by Cynic doctrines.

BIBLIOGRAPHY

TEXTS AND COMMENTARIES: TEXTS: *SVF* I 45–332. COMMENTARIES:
A. C. Pearson, *The fragments of Zeno and Cleanthes* (London 1891).

STUDIES (see comprehensive treatment and bibl. by K. von Fritz, *RE* suppl. XA
(1972) 83–126). C. O. Brink, 'Theophrastus and Zeno on nature and moral theory',
Phronesis I (1955) 123–45; H. C. Baldry, 'Zeno's ideal state', *J.H.S.* 79 (1959) 3–15;
A. Graeser, *Zenon von Kition, Positionen und Probleme* (Berlin & New York 1975).

CLEANTHES

LIFE

b. *c.* 332 B.C. at Assos near ancient Troy. Came to Athens as young man and became
follower of Zeno, whom he succeeded as head of Stoa *c.* 261. d. 232 B.C. Sources:
Diog. Laert. 7.168–76 and others in *SVF* I 464–80.

WORKS

Fifty titles recorded in Diog. Laert. 7.174–5, mostly ethical topics but including 'two
books on Zeno's natural philosophy', 'four expositions of the teaching of Heraclitus'
and works on logic. Much of surviving material deals with physics and theology. C.
interspersed some of his prose writings with verse. His surviving poems are in hexameters or iambic trimeters; most substantial the *Hymn to Zeus* (35 hexameters). Four
iambic lines (*SVF* I 570) are a dialogue between Reason and Passion.

BIBLIOGRAPHY

TEXTS AND COMMENTARIES: TEXTS: *SVF* I 483–619. COMMENTARIES:
A. C. Pearson, *The fragments of Zeno and Cleanthes* (London 1891).

STUDIES: (1) *Hymn to Zeus.* E. Neustadt, *Hermes* 66 (1931) 387–401; G. Zuntz,
H.S.C.Ph. 63 (1958) 289–308; M. Marcovich, *Hermes* 94 (1966) 245–50; M. Dragona-
Monachou, *Philosophia* I (1971) 339–78; Meerwaldt under (2) below. (2) Others. G.
Verbeke, *Kleanthes von Assos* (Brussels 1949); J. Meerwaldt, 'Cleanthea I', *Mnemo-
syne* 4 (1951) 40–69 and 'Cleanthea II', ibid. 5 (1952) 1–12; F. Solmsen, *Cleanthes or
Posidonius? The basis of Stoic physics* (Amsterdam 1961); A. A. Long, 'Heraclitus and
Stoicism', *Philosophia* 5–6 (1976) 133–56.

CHRYSIPPUS

LIFE

b. *c.* 280 B.C. at Soli in Cilicia. On coming to Athens studied first with Arcesilaus at the Academy and then became follower of Cleanthes whom he succeeded as head of Stoa 232. d. *c.* 206 B.C. Sources: Diog. Laert. 7.179–202 and others in *SVF* II 1a–12, 19–34.

WORKS

161 titles listed in incomplete catalogue of Diog. Laert. 7.189–202, but only quotations by later writers and a few badly damaged papyri survive. Most of extant titles refer to writings on logic. Many aspects of C.'s philosophy can be reconstructed in some detail from the criticism of Plutarch and Galen.

BIBLIOGRAPHY

TEXTS: *SVF* II and III 1–768. No annotated edition exists. J. B. Gould, *The philosophy of Chrysippus* (Leiden 1970) studies some of the texts.

STUDIES: M. Pohlenz, 'Zenon und Chrysipp', *N.G.G.* phil.-hist. Kl. n.s.2 (1938) 173–210; E. Bréhier, *Chrysippe et l'ancien stoïcisme*, 2nd ed. (Paris 1951); B. Mates, *Stoic logic* (Berkeley & Los Angeles 1953); D. Babut, *Plutarque et le stoïcisme* (Paris 1969) esp. 32f.; M. Frede, *Die stoische Logik* (Göttingen 1974).

DIOGENES OF BABYLON

LIFE

b. *c.* 240 B.C. at Seleucia adjacent to ancient Babylon. Known as the 'Babylonian' in antiquity. Succeeded Zeno of Tarsus as head of Stoa. Visited Rome 155 as ambassador along with Carneades and Critolaus. His lectures there aroused Roman interest in Stoicism. d. *c.* 152 B.C. Sources in *SVF* III 210–12.

WORKS

Some fragments preserved from following: *On the art of speech, On the dialectical art, On the governing principle of the soul, On Athena, On divination, On noble birth, On laws, On music, On rhetoric.* No complete list of titles survives and some fragments belong to unnamed books. His views on music and rhetoric are recoverable in some

PANAETIUS

detail through criticized comments in Philodemus' fragmentary books on these subjects; see A. J. Neubecker, *Die Bewertung der Musik bei Stoikern und Epikureern. Eine Analyse von Philodems Schrift De Musica* (Berlin 1956).

BIBLIOGRAPHY

TEXTS: *SVF* III 212–43.

STUDIES: A. Bonhöffer, 'Die Telos Formel des Stoikers Diogenes', *Philologus* 67 (1908) 582–605; M. Pohlenz, *Die Stoa* I, 3rd ed. (Göttingen 1964) 180–90; A. A. Long, 'Carneades and the Stoic Telos', *Phronesis* 12 (1967) 59–90; F. H. Sandbach, *The Stoics* (London 1975) 115–17.

PANAETIUS

LIFE

b. *c.* 185 B.C., son of Nicagoras, at Rhodes. Studied with Diogenes of Babylon at Athens. Chosen by Rhodians of Lindos to be priest of Poseidon Hippios *c.* 149. Probably a little later came to Rome and became intimate friend of Scipio Africanus. Accompanied him on embassy to Egypt 140/39 and up to 129 lived alternately in Rome and Athens. In that year succeeded Antipater of Tarsus as head of Stoa. d. *c.* 109 B.C. Sources: Suda; *Stoic. index Herc.* cols. 55–77; others in van Straaten under *Texts* below, 1–32.

WORKS

Virtually nothing survives in P.'s own words, but his three books *On the appropriate* were Cicero's main source for *De Officiis* 1–2 (*Att.* 16.11.4, *Off.* 3.7–10). He also wrote *On providence, On cheerfulness, On magistracies* (Cic. *Leg.* 3.13–14), *On philosophical sects, On matters concerning Socrates*. No complete list of works survives. In *Stoic. Index Herc.* col. 61 he is called 'strongly pro Plato and Aristotle'.

BIBLIOGRAPHY

TEXTS: M. van Straaten, 3rd ed. (Leiden 1962).

STUDIES: B. N. Tatakis, *Panétius de Rhodes* (Paris 1931); M. van Straaten, *Panétius, sa vie, ses écrits et sa doctrine avec une édition de ses fragments* (Amsterdam 1946); M. Pohlenz, *RE* XVIII.3 (1949) 418–40.

POSIDONIUS

LIFE

b. *c.* 135 B.C. of wealthy family at Apamea in northern Syria. Pupil of Panaetius at Athens. Subsequently settled in Rhodes where he acquired citizenship and held office of *prytanis*. Served as ambassador to Rome 87/6, and at some period travelled extensively over Mediterranean world. Was visited in Rhodes by Cicero and Pompey. d. *c.* 55 B.C. Sources: Suda; Cic. *Att.* 2.1.2, 14.11.4, *Tusc.* 2.61; Strabo 3 p. 175 C, 6 p. 277 C and (*prytanis*) 7 p. 316 C; Plut. *Marius* 45.4 (embassy); others in T1a-72 Edelstein–Kidd.

WORKS

Thirty certain titles known (complete list in Edelstein–Kidd under *Texts* below, v–vi); only fragments survive. Most substantial material comes from the *History* (52 bks) and from a work *On passions* quoted and discussed at length by Galen in *On the opinions of Hippocrates and Plato* 4 and 5. P.'s writings covered all conventional subjects of Greek philosophy and much of his scientific work was excerpted by Strabo.

BIBLIOGRAPHY

TEXTS AND COMMENTARIES: J. Bake (Leiden 1810); L. Edelstein and I. G. Kidd, vol. I (Cambridge 1972: vol. II of commentary by Kidd forthcoming); W. Theiler (Berlin and New York 1982). Historical fragments in *FGrH* II 87.

STUDIES: K. Reinhardt, *Poseidonios* (Munich 1921); L. Edelstein, 'The philosophical system of Posidonius', *A.J.Ph.* 57 (1936) 286–325; K. Reinhardt, *RE* XXII.1 (1953) 558–826; A. D. Nock, 'Posidonius', *J.R.S.* 49 (1959) 1–15; M. Laffranque, *Poseidonius d'Apamée* (Paris 1964); H. Strasburger, 'Poseidonius on problems of the Roman empire', *J.R.S.* 55 (1965) 40–53.

EPICTETUS

LIFE

b. *c.* A.D. 55, son of a slave woman, at Hierapolis in Phrygia. Owned and later liberated by Epaphroditus, Nero's freedman and secretary. Attended lectures of Musonius Rufus in Rome and became a Stoic philosopher in his own right. Banished, with other philosophers, by Domitian in about 92–3 and settled in Nicopolis in Epirus where he continued to lecture and attracted many followers. These included the historian

Arrian, who recorded the discourses he heard. d. *c.* A.D. 120. Sources: own works, esp. *Diss.* 1.7.32, 1.19.19, 2.6.20; Suda; Gell. 2.18.10 and (expulsion) 15.11.5; Macr. 1.11.45; others in Schenkl under *Texts* below, I xiv–xxiii.

WORKS

Four books of *Discourses* survive out of eight pubd by Arrian. The *Manual* (*Encheiridion*) is also preserved, comprising fifty-three short extracts from the *Discourses* selected by Arrian; Simplicius' commentary on this survives, ed. J. Schweighäuser (Leipzig 1800).

BIBLIOGRAPHY

(See W. A. Oldfather, *Contributions towards a bibliography of Epictetus* (Illinois 1927), supplementary ed. *with a preliminary list of Epictetus' manuscripts* by W. H. Friedrich and C. U. Faye (Illinois 1952).)

TEXTS: H. Schenkl, 2nd ed. (BT, 1916); W. A. Oldfather (Loeb, 1925–8); J. Souilhé (Budé, 1943–65). Text, tr. and comm. on *Diss.* 3.22: M. Billerbeck, *Epiktet vom Kynismus* (Leiden 1978).

TRANSLATIONS: G. Long (London 1877); P. E. Matheson (Oxford 1916).

STUDIES: A. Bonhöffer, *Epiktet und die Stoa* (Stuttgart 1890); idem, *Die Ethik des Stoikers Epiktet* (Stuttgart 1894); T. Colardeau, *Étude sur Épictète* (Paris 1903); A. Bonhöffer, *Epiktet und des Neue Testament* (Giessen 1911); F. Millar, 'Epictetus and the imperial court', *J.R.S.* 55 (1965) 140–8; T. Wirth, 'Arrians Errinerungen an Epiktet', *M.H.* 24 (1967) 149–89, 197–216; J. Xenakis, *Epictetus, philosopher-therapist* (The Hague 1969); P. A. Brunt, 'From Epictetus to Arrian', *Athenaeum* 55 (1977) 19–48; P. A. Stadter, *Arrian of Nicomedia* (Chapel Hill 1980); A. A. Long, 'Epictetus and Marcus Aurelius', in (ed.) J. Luce, *Ancient writers* (New York 1982) 985–1002.

MARCUS AURELIUS

LIFE

b. A.D. 121, son of Annius Verus. Adopted by Antoninus Pius as his successor along with L. Verus. Became Roman emperor 161. Spent most of the years 170–80 defending Danube frontier against barbarian invasions. Taught rhetoric by M. Cornelius Fronto, with whom he corresponded in later life. d. A.D. 180. Sources: his *Letters* and *Meditations*; Dio Cassius bks 71–2; *Historia Augusta* 4.1.

WORKS

One genuine work in Greek preserved, twelve books (division certainly made by 10th c.; see Suda) of *Meditations* ('To himself'). Earliest reference to it is by Themistius in A.D. 364 (*Or.* 6 p. 81c). On transmission of text see Farquharson under *Commentaries* below, I xiii–lxxiv. Some *Letters* in Latin also survive in fragmentary correspondence of M. Cornelius Fronto discovered in Milan in 1815 by Cardinal Mai.

BIBLIOGRAPHY

(See Klein (1971) under *Studies* below.)

TEXTS AND COMMENTARIES: TEXTS: *Meditations*: H. Schenkl (BT, 1913); C. R. Haines (Loeb, 1916); A. L. Trannoy, 2nd ed., with preface by A. Puech (Budé, 1953); W. Theiler (Zurich 1951: with German tr.). *Letters*: C. R. Haines (Loeb, 1919–20). COMMENTARIES: *Meditations*: A. S. L. Farquharson, 2 vols. (Oxford 1944: with tr.).

TRANSLATIONS: *Meditations*: G. M. A. Grube (Indianapolis & New York 1963); M. Staniforth (Baltimore 1964).

STUDIES: G. C. Thomes, *Per la critica di Marco Aurelio* (Turin 1955); A. Birley, *Marcus Aurelius* (London 1966); (ed.) R. Klein, *Marc Aurel*, Wege der Forschung DL (Darmstadt 1971); P. A. Brunt, 'Marcus Aurelius in his *Meditations*', *J.R.S.* 64 (1974) 1–20; A. A. Long, 'Epictetus and Marcus Aurelius', in (ed.) J. Luce, *Ancient writers* (New York 1982) 985–1002.

SCEPTICS, CYNICS AND OTHER POST-ARISTOTELIAN PHILOSOPHERS

(For *General works* see pp. 805–6.)

SEXTUS EMPIRICUS

LIFE

Probably b. in second half of 2nd c. A.D. (but F. Kudlien, *Rh.M.* 106 (1963) 251–4 suggests an earlier date), perhaps at Chaeronea. Taught by one Herodotus who may be identical to a doctor who lived at Rome (Gal. 13.788, 801, 8.751 Kühn), where S. himself may have lived for a time. Certainly a physician (*Pyrrh.* 2.238, *Adv. math.* 1.260), but his membership of the 'empirical' school of doctors depends on external evidence (Diog. Laert. 9.117; Gal. 14.683 Kühn). Other sources: Suda s.v. 'Sextus of Chaeronea'; Diog. Laert. 9.116–17.

WORKS

(1) EXTANT: *Outlines of Pyrrhonism* in three books: bk 1 presents arguments for scepticism, bks 2–3 a summary criticism of dogmatic philosophers. *Against the professors* (*Adversus mathematicos*) in six books: against 1 the grammarians, 2 the rhetoricians, 3 the geometers, 4 the arithmeticians, 5 the astrologers, 6 the musicians.

Five further books against philosophers, generally entitled *Against the professors* bks 7–11: against 7–8 the logicians, 9–10 the physicists, 11 the moralists. Much of the series *Against the professors* seems to be a more detailed treatment of material presented in *Outlines of Pyrrhonism* 2–3. (2) LOST: *Medical memoirs* (*Adv. math.* 7.202) and a work *On soul* (*Adv. math.* 6.55, 10.284). For other possible lost works see Brochard (1887) under *Studies* (1) below, 319–20.

BIBLIOGRAPHY

TEXTS: H. Mutschmann, J. Mau, K. Janáček (BT, 1912–62); J. B. Bury (Loeb, 1933–49).

TRANSLATIONS: Selected texts in P. Hallie and S. Etheridge, *Scepticism, man and god* (Middletown, Connecticut 1964); M. Hossenfelder, *Sextus Empiricus. Grundriss der Pyrrhonischen Skepsis* (Frankfurt 1968).

STUDIES: (1) GENERAL: V. Brochard, *Les sceptiques grecs*, 2nd ed. (Paris 1887); M. Patrick, *Sextus Empiricus and Greek Scepticism* (Cambridge 1899); C. L. Stough, *Greek Skepticism* (Berkeley & Los Angeles 1969); M. dal Pra, *Lo Scetticismo greco* II, 2nd ed. (Rome & Bari 1975). (2) MORE SPECIALIZED: W. Heintz, *Studien zu Sextus Empiricus* (Halle 1932); K. Janáček, *Prolegomena to Sextus Empiricus* (Olomouc 1948); J. Blomquist, 'Textkritisches zu Sextus Empiricus', *Eranos* 66 (1968) 73–100 and 69 (1971) 12–24; K. Janáček, *Sextus Empiricus' sceptical methods* (Prague 1972); A. A. Long, 'Sextus Empiricus on the criterion of truth', *B.I.C.S.* 25 (1978) 35–49.

INDEX: Janáček in BT ed. IV.

TIMON

LIFE

b. *c.* 320 B.C., son of Timocrates, at Phlius. After working as a dancer became follower first of Stilpo at Megara and then of Pyrrho at Elis. Spent period as sophist in Chalcedon where he earned enough money to support himself in Athens from *c.* 275. Was acquainted with Antigonus Gonatas, Ptolemy Philadelphus and Alexandrian poets. d. *c.* 230 B.C. Sources: Diog. Laert. 9.109–15; Suda; Aristocles *ap.* Eusebius, *Praep. ev.* 14.18, 1–30.

WORKS

(1) POETRY: Surviving fragments belong mainly to the *Lampoons* (*Silloi*: frs. 1–66 Diels) in hexameters. A few lines of the *Indalmoi* (*Images*) in elegiacs are also preserved (frs. 67–70 Diels). T. is also reputed to have written epics, sixty tragedies, satyr plays, thirty comedies, and *Kinaidoi* (pornographic poems). (2) PROSE: *Against the natural philosophers* (frs. 75–6 Diels), *On sensation* (fr. 74 Diels), *Pytho*, a conver-

sation between Pyrrho on a journey to Delphi and Timon (frs. 77–81 Diels), *The funeral feast of Arcesilaus* (fr. 73 Diels).

BIBLIOGRAPHY

TEXTS: C. Wachsmuth, *Sillographorum Graecorum reliquiae* (Leipzig 1885) 89–187; *PPF* 173–206.

STUDIES: Wachsmuth (above) 8–50; V. Brochard, *Les sceptiques grecs*, 2nd ed. (Paris 1887) 79–91; W. Nestle, *RE* VIA.2 (1937) 1301–3; M. dal Pra, *Lo Scetticismo greco* I, 2nd ed. (Rome & Bari 1975) 83–111; A. A. Long, 'Timon of Phlius: Pyrrhonist and satirist', *P.C.Ph.S.* 204 (1978) 68–91.

CRATES OF THEBES

LIFE

b. *c.* 365 B.C., son of Ascondas, at Thebes. Came to Athens as young man and became Cynic philosopher under influence of Diogenes of Sinope. Allegedly renounced wealth and was given free entry to any Athenian home (Diog. Laert. 6.87–8; Apuleius, *De mag.* 22, *Flor.* 2.14). Acquainted with Demetrius of Phalerum and Zeno of Citium who wrote a lost book of *Memoirs of Crates* (Diog. Laert. 7.4). d. *c.* 285 B.C. Sources: Diog. Laert. 6.85–93; Teles p. 28.5, 35.4, 38.3 Hense; Suda; Julian, *Or.* 6 (probably based on lost life by Plutarch).

WORKS

(1) POETRY: *Trifles* (*Paignia*) in elegiacs, *Parodies* of epic on contemporary life, and tragedies; these genres represented in the few preserved fragments, which also include some lines in hexameters about Pera, a Cynic utopian city. (2) PROSE: Philosophical *Letters* (no genuine example survives), Platonic in style (Diog. Laert. 6.98).

BIBLIOGRAPHY

TEXTS: C. Wachsmuth, *Sillographorum Graecorum reliquiae* (Leipzig 1885) 192–200; *PPF* 207–23; Diehl I, 3rd ed. (1958) 120–6.

STUDIES: G. A. Gerhard, *Phoinix von Kolophon* (Leipzig 1909); D. R. Dudley, *A history of Cynicism* (Cambridge 1937) 42–53; R. Höistad, *Cynic hero and cynic king* (Uppsala 1948).

CERCIDAS

(See pp. 831–2.)

BION OF BORYSTHENES

LIFE

b. *c.* 335 B.C., son of a freedman and of a former prostitute, at Borysthenes (Olbia). His family was enslaved because of fraud committed by his father. B. was brought up by a rhetorician and inherited his property. Came to Athens and associated with various philosophers, especially Crates the Cynic. Travelled widely in Greek world lecturing on Cynic themes in a vivid style. Patronized by Antigonus Gonatas at Pella. d. *c.* 246 B.C. Sources: Diog. Laert. 4.46–57.

WORKS

Discourses (Diatribes) on Cynic moral themes and Homeric parody (Diog. Laert. 4.52 for two hexameters). Little survives in his own words, but he is the principal source of Teles' *Diatribes*.

BIBLIOGRAPHY

TEXTS AND COMMENTARIES: TEXTS: C. Wachsmuth, *Sillographorum Graecorum reliquiae* (Leipzig 1885) 73–7, 201–2; O. Hense, *Teletis reliquiae*, 2nd ed. (Tübingen 1909). COMMENTARIES: J. F. Kindstrand (Uppsala 1976).

STUDIES: R. Heinze, *De Horatio Bionis imitatore* (Bonn 1889); H. von Arnim, *RE* III.1 (1897) 483–5; D. R. Dudley, *A history of Cynicism* (London 1937) 62–9.

TELES

LIFE

Probably lived in mid 3rd c. B.C.

WORKS

Cynic *Discourses (Diatribes)*. Seven are preserved in Stobaeus' *Anthology*, mediated through an epitome made by one Theodorus.

BIBLIOGRAPHY

TEXTS: U. von Wilamowitz-Moellendorff, *Der kynische Prediger Teles* (Berlin 1881); O. Hense, *Teletis reliquiae*, 2nd ed. (Tübingen 1909).

TRANSLATIONS: W. Capelle, *Epiktet, Teles und Musonius* (Zurich 1948); L. Paquet, *Les Cyniques grecs* (Ottawa 1975).

MENIPPUS

LIFE

b. a slave early 3rd c. B.C. at Gadara. Acquired sufficient wealth to be granted citizenship at Thebes. Became a Cynic philosopher, probably under influence of Metrocles of Maroneia. Alleged to have worked as money-lender and to have committed suicide. Sources: Diog. Laert. 6.95, 99–101.

WORKS

Six titles recorded by Diog. Laert. 6.101 who also refers to doubt about their authenticity. Other titles in Athenaeus 14.629f (*Symposium*), 14.664e (*Arcesilaus*) and Diog. Laert. 6.29 (*Sale of Diogenes*). One of the two extant fragments (Athen. 1.32e) is part of an apparently original hexameter line. It is impossible to assess precisely Lucian's indebtedness to M.; see *Dialogues of the dead* 1.1, 10.11, *The twice accused* 33, *Menippus* 1, *Icaro-Menippus* 15–16, *The fisherman* 26.

BIBLIOGRAPHY

TEXTS: C. Wachsmuth, *Sillographorum Graecorum reliquiae* (Leipzig 1885) 78–85.

STUDIES: D. R. Dudley, *A history of Cynicism* (London 1937) 69–74; D. McCarthy, 'Lucian and Menippus', *Y.Cl.S.* 4 (1954) 1–55; R. Helm, *Lucian und Menipp*, 2nd ed. (Hildesheim 1967); L. Giangrande, *The use of spoudaiogeloion in Greek and Roman literature* (The Hague & Paris 1972).

PHILO OF ALEXANDRIA

LIFE

b. c. 30 B.C. of Jewish parents at Alexandria. Represented Jewish community there on an embassy to Rome A.D. 39. d. c. A.D. 45. Sources: Philo, *Against Flaccus* and *On the embassy to Gaius*.

WORKS

Majority of surviving works have their own title but form parts of three large works on the Pentateuch. (1) *Questions and solutions* (see Eusebius, *Praep. ev.* 7.13) is largely fragmentary but four books on Genesis and two on Exodus are in Armenian translation. (2) *Allegories of the sacred laws*, a commentary on Genesis 2–4, with which other works on later passages of Genesis (e.g. *On agriculture*, Gen. 9.20f.) are to be associated. (3) A series of expositions of the Mosaic Law, including *Lives* of Abraham and Joseph as exemplars of virtue. (4) A group of miscellaneous works.

BIBLIOGRAPHY

(See H. L. Goodhart and E. R. Goodenough in Goodenough's *The politics of Philo Judaeus* (New Haven 1938); L. H. Feldman, *Scholarship on Philo and Josephus* 1937–62 (New York 1962).)

TEXTS AND COMMENTARIES: TEXTS: L. Cohn, P. Wendland, S. Reiter (Berlin 1896–1930: with index by H. Leisegang); F. H. Colson, G. H. Whitaker, R. Marcus (Loeb, 1929–62); R. Arnaldez, J. Pouilloux *et al.* (Paris 1961–). COMMENTARIES: *Against Flaccus*: R. Box (Oxford 1939). *On the embassy to Gaius*: E. M. Smallwood, 2nd ed. (Leiden 1970). *Fragments*. J. R. Harris (Cambridge 1886).

STUDIES: H. A. Wolfson, *Philo*, 2 vols. (Cambridge, Mass. 1948); E. Bréhier, *Les idées philosophiques et religieuses de Philon d'Alexandrie*, 2nd ed. (Paris 1950); E. R. Goodenough, *An introduction to Philo Judaeus*, 2nd ed. (Oxford 1962); I. Christiansen, *Die Technik der allegorischen Auslegungswissenschaft bei Philon von Alexandrien* (Tübingen 1969); A. Maddalena, *Filone alessandrino* (Milan 1970); S. Sandmel, *Philo of Alexandria : an introduction* (Oxford 1979).

INDEX: G. Mayer (Berlin & New York 1974).

PLOTINUS

LIFE

b. *c.* A.D. 205 in Egypt. From *c.* 232–43 studied under Ammonius Saccas at Alexandria. In 243 joined expedition of Gordian III against Persians in the hope of learning about eastern thought. Came to Rome 244 where he became leading figure of an intellectual group which included senators among its members. From 253 began to write a series of philosophical essays. Left Rome for Campania shortly before his death in A.D. 270. Sources: Porphyry, *Vita Plotini*; Suda; others in H.-R. Schwyzer, *RE* XXI (1951) 471ff.

WORKS

Six sets of nine essays (*Enneads*) edited by Porphyry and pubd by him *c.* 301–5. Another edition of P.'s work by a further pupil, Eustochius, has not survived beyond a few traces (Schwyzer under *Life* above, 488–90).

BIBLIOGRAPHY

(Up to 1949 see B. Mariën in Italian tr. of P. by V. Cilento III 2 (Bari 1949); cf. also J. Trouillard, *La purification plotinienne* (Paris 1955); Rist (1967) under *Studies* (3) below, 270–5.)

TEXTS AND COMMENTARIES: TEXTS: E. Bréhier (Budé, 1924–38); P. Henry and H.-R. Schwyzer, editio maior (Paris, Brussels and Leiden 1951–73), editio minor (OCT, 1964–82); A. H. Armstrong (Loeb, 1966–84: 1–5, with 6–7 forthcoming). COMMENTARIES: R. Harder *et al.*, 5 vols. in 11 (Hamburg 1956–67).

TRANSLATIONS: S. MacKenna, 3rd ed. rev. B. S. Page (London 1962).

STUDIES: (1) STYLE: Bréhier under *Texts* above, I xiv–xxxix; H.-R. Schwyzer *RE* XXI (1951) 512–30. (2) IMAGES: E. Bréhier, *Études de philosophie antique* (Paris 1955) 292–307; R. Ferwerda, *La signification des images et des métaphores dans la pensée de Plotin* (Groningen 1965). (3) GENERAL: W. R. Inge, *The philosophy of Plotinus*, 3rd ed. (London 1929); H.-R. Schwyzer, *RE* XXI (1951) 471–592; E. R. Dodds, 'Tradition and personal achievement in the philosophy of Plotinus', *J.R.S.* 50 (1960) 1–7; M. de Gandillac, *La sagesse de Plotin*, 2nd ed. (Paris 1966); J. M. Rist, *Plotinus: the road to reality* (Cambridge 1967); (ed.) A. H. Armstrong, *The Cambridge history of later Greek and early medieval philosophy* (Cambridge 1967) 195–263; H. J. Blumenthal, *Plotinus' psychology: his doctrines of the embodied soul* (The Hague 1971); R. T. Wallis, *Neoplatonism* (London 1972); G. O'Daly, *Plotinus' philosophy of self* (Shannon 1973).

THE LITERATURE OF THE EMPIRE

GENERAL WORKS

Bowersock, G. W., *Greek sophists in the Roman empire* (Oxford 1969)
idem (ed.), *Approaches to the second sophistic* (Pennsylvania 1974)
Bowie, E. L., 'Greeks and their past in the Second Sophistic', *P.&P.* 46 (1970) 1–41; repr. in (ed.) M. I. Finley, *Studies in ancient society* (Cambridge 1974) 166–209
idem, 'The importance of sophists', *Y.Cl.S.* 27 (1982) 29–59

STRABO

Flashar, H. (ed.), *Entretiens XXV: Le classicisme à Rome aux Iers siècles avant et après J.C.* (Fondation Hardt, Geneva 1979)
Kennedy, G., 'The age of the sophists', in *The art of rhetoric in the Roman world* (Princeton 1972) 553–613
Lesky 829–45, 'The Second Sophistic'
Palm, J., *Rom, Römertum und Imperium in der griechischen Literatur der Kaiserzeit* (Lund 1959)
Reardon, B. P., *Courants littéraires grecs des IIe et IIIe siècles après J.C.* (Paris 1971)
Sandbach, F. H., 'Atticism and the Second Sophistic movement', *CAH* XI 678–90
Schmid–Stählin II 2 688–828, 'Der neue oder zweite Sophistik'

STRABO

LIFE

b. *c.* 64 B.C.; from influential and wealthy family of Amaseia in Pontus. Studied as a young man at Nysa with Aristodemus. Went to Rome before 44 B.C.; still there in 35 B.C. but left before 29 B.C., when he stopped at Gyarus on his way back to the city. Accompanied Aelius Gallus, prefect of Egypt, *c.* 26–24 B.C. Returned later to Italy, perhaps Naples. d. after A.D. 24. Sources: his *Geography* (refs. as in Casaubon's pagination) 10.477, 11.499, 12.557 (background; see *RE* IVA.1 76–7 for birth-date); 14.650 (study); 12.568, 6.273, 10.485 (Rome); 17.804ff. (Egypt; cf. 2.118); 5.246 (Naples); 17.828 (latest datable ref.; cf. 17.576).

WORKS

(1) *Geography* (17 bks): on time and place of composition see E. Pais, *Ancient Italy* (Chicago 1908) 379–428; J. G. C. Anderson in *Anatolian studies presented to Ramsay* (Manchester 1923) 1–13. (2) Lost history (Ἱστορικὰ ὑπομνήματα) in forty-seven books; all but first four dealt with history after Polybius (*Geog.* 11.515); fragments in *FGrH* IIA 91.

BIBLIOGRAPHY

(See Diller (1975) under *Studies* below, 167–79.)

TEXTS AND COMMENTARIES: TEXTS: G. Kramer (Berlin 1844); A. Meineke (Berlin 1852); H. L. Jones (Loeb, 1917–32); G. Aujac and F. Lasserre (Budé, 1966–: 1–12 only). Bks 1–4: W. Aly (Bonn 1968–72). Bks 1–6: F. Sbordone (Rome 1963–70). Palimpsest of parts of *Geog.*: W. Aly (Rome 1956).

STUDIES: M. Dubois, *Examen de la Géographie de Strabon* (Paris 1891); W. Aly, *Untersuchungen über Text, Aufbau und Quellen der Geographica: Strabonis Geographica*

857

IV (Bonn 1957); A. Diller, *The textual tradition of Strabo's Geography* (Amsterdam 1975); R. Baladié, *Le Péloponnèse de Strabon* (Paris 1980).

DIONYSIUS OF HALICARNASSUS

LIFE

Dates of birth and death unknown. Came to Italy 30 B.C. and had been in Rome twenty-two years when he wrote preface to *Ant. Rom.* Teacher of Latin and associate of eminent Romans. Mentioned by Strabo (14 p. 656 C) as a contemporary historian. Sources: *Ant. Rom.* 1.7–8, Phot. *Bibl. Cod.* 83, Suda.

WORKS

(1) Ῥωμαϊκὴ ἀρχαιολογία, known as *Antiquitates Romanae*, history down to outbreak of first Punic war in twenty books; just over first ten survive. (2) Treatises on rhetoric and literary criticism. *Ad Ammaeum 2, Ad Cn. Pompeium, De imitatione 3* (mostly lost), *De antiquis oratoribus* (Lysias, Isocrates, Isaeus, Demosthenes), *De compositione verborum, De admiranda vi dicendi in Demosthene, De Dinarcho, De Thucydide.* (3). Lost. *Chronica* (*Ant. Rom.* 1.74, Clem. Alex. *Strom.* 1.21, 102, 1, Suda s.v. 'Euripides') and abridgement of *Ant. Rom.* in five books (Phot. *Bibl. Cod.* 84, Steph. Byz. s.v. Ἀρικία and Κορίολλα).

BIBLIOGRAPHY

TEXTS AND COMMENTARIES: TEXTS: C. Jacoby, H. Usener, L. Radermacher (BT, 1885–1929); E. Cary, S. Usher (Loeb, 1937–). COMMENTARIES: *Amm.* and *Pomp.*: W. Rhys Roberts (Cambridge 1901: with tr.). *De comp. verb.*: W. Rhys Roberts (Cambridge 1910: with tr.). *Thuc.*: W. K. Pritchett (Berkeley 1975: with tr.).

STUDIES: S. F. Bonner, *The literary treatises of Dionysius: a study in the development of critical method* (Cambridge 1939); E. Noè, 'Ricerche su Dionigi d'Alicarnasso', *Ricerche di Storiografia Antica* 1 (Pisa 1979) 21–116.

THE GREEK CRITICS

GENERAL WORKS

Grube, G. M. A., *The Greek and Roman critics* (Toronto 1965)
Russell, D. A. and Winterbottom, M., *Ancient literary criticism. The principal texts in new translations* (Oxford 1972: with brief surveys and bibliographies)
Russell, D. A., *Criticism in antiquity* (London 1981)
Spengel, L., *Rhetores Graeci* (BT, 1853–6)

LONGINUS

LIFE

Name and dates unknown. Called Longinus from manuscript attribution to 'Diony-sius or Longinus' and 'Dionysius Longinus', but unlikely to be 3rd-c. A.D. Cassius Longinus. Refers to Augustan critics Caecilius and Theodorus, and probably lived 1st c. A.D. when discussion of decline of literature (44) was commonplace (e.g. Tacitus' *Dialogus*). Rhetorician, tutor or associate of Roman addressee, Postumius Terentianus. Greek (12.4), with possible Jewish links (9.9).

WORKS

On the sublime (Περὶ ὕψους: about a third lost from six large lacunae). Lost: *On Xenophon, On word-arrangement* in 2 bks (8.1, 39.1); cf. also promised *On emotions* (44.12) and refs. to 'elsewhere' (9.2, 23.3).

BIBLIOGRAPHY

TEXTS AND COMMENTARIES: D. A. Russell (Oxford 1964).

TRANSLATIONS: N. Boileau-Despréaux (Paris 1674); W. H. Fyfe (Loeb, 1927: with Arist. *Poet.* and Demetrius, *On style*).

STUDIES: W. Bühler, *Beiträge zur Erklärung der Schrift vom Erhabenen* (Göttingen 1964).

DEMETRIUS

LIFE

Dates and real name unknown; called Demetrius from mistaken attribution to Deme-trius of Phalerum. Later than *c.* 275 B.C., probably 1st c. B.C. or A.D. Has Peripatetic sympathies.

WORKS

On style (Περὶ ἑρμηνείας).

BIBLIOGRAPHY

TEXTS AND COMMENTARIES: TEXTS: L. Radermacher (BT, 1901: repr. 1966). COMMENTARIES: W. Rhys Roberts (Cambridge 1902).

TRANSLATIONS: W. Rhys Roberts (Loeb, 1927: with Arist. *Poet.* and 'Longinus' tr. W. H. Fyfe); G. M. A. Grube, *A Greek critic: Demetrius on style* (Toronto 1961: with introd. and notes).

STUDIES: Grube under *Translations* above, 3–56; D. M. Schenkeveld, *Studies in Demetrius on style* (Amsterdam 1964).

HERMOGENES

LIFE

c. A.D. 160–*c.* 225, from Tarsus, youthful prodigy admired by Marcus Aurelius but indifferent adult orator; influential rhetorician. Sources: Philostr. *V.S.* 2.7, Syrianus, Suda.

WORKS

Treatises *On types of style* (Περὶ ἰδεῶν: 2 bks) and *On issues* (Περὶ στάσεων). Lost: commentaries on Demosthenes, Περὶ εὑρέσεως, Περὶ κοίλης Συρίας (2 bks). Spurious: *Progymnasmata*, Περὶ εὑρέσεως (4 bks), Περὶ μεθόδου δεινότητος.

BIBLIOGRAPHY

TEXTS: Spengel II 131–456; H. Rabe (BT, 1913).

STUDIES: D. Hagedorn, *Zur Ideenlehre des Hermogenes* (Göttingen 1964).

MENANDER RHETOR

LIFE

From Laodicea; rhetorician, probably 3rd c. A.D. and later than Minucianus of mid-3rd c. See Suda.

WORKS

Two treatises *On epideictic oratory* (Περὶ ἐπιδεικτικῶν) survive under his name, almost certainly by different hands, the first perhaps by M. Lost: commentaries on Minucianus, Hermogenes, Aristides and Demosthenes; prose-hymns and probably declamations. Presumably overlapping with the preceding, at least in part, Τέχνη, Μέθοδοι, Ἐγκώμια (*P. Berol.* 21849).

BIBLIOGRAPHY

TEXTS AND COMMENTARIES: TEXTS: Spengel III 329–446. COMMENTARIES: D. A. Russell and N. G. Wilson (Oxford 1981: with tr.).

STUDIES: C. Bursian, *Der Rhetor Menandros und seine Schriften*, *A.B.A.W.* 16.3 (1882); J. Soffel, *Die Regeln Menanders für die Leichenrede* (Meisenheim am Glan 1974).

POETIC MINIATURES

BIBLIOGRAPHY

GENERAL: C. Cichorius, 'Römisches aus der griechischen Anthologie', *Römische Studien* (Stuttgart 1961) 294–375; H. Beckby, *Anthologia Graeca* (Munich 1964); Gow–Page, *Garland*.

CRINAGORAS: TEXTS AND COMMENTARIES: M. Rubensohn (Berlin 1888); Gow–Page, *Garland* I 199–231, II 210–60. STUDIES: C. Cichorius, *Rom und Mytilene* (Leipzig 1888); G. W. Bowersock, 'Anth. Pal. VII 638 (Crinagoras)', *Hermes* 92 (1964) 255–6.

HONESTUS: TEXTS AND COMMENTARIES: W. Peek, Γέρας 'Αντωνίου Κεραμοπούλλου (Athens 1953) 609–34; Gow–Page, *Garland* I 268–79, II 301–9. STUDIES: C. P. Jones, 'The epigram of Honestus concerning a Σεβαστή', *H.S.C.Ph.* 74 (1970) 249–55.

LUCILLIUS: TEXTS AND COMMENTARIES: H. Beckby, *Anthologia Graeca* III (Munich 1964) 550–751, 830–49; B. J. Rozema, *Lucillius the epigrammatist* (diss. Wisconsin 1971). STUDIES: A. Linnenkugel, *De Lucillio Tarrhaeo* (Paderborn 1926: identification of epigrammatist with grammarian from Tarrha should not be accepted); A. Garzya, 'Lucillio', *G.I.F.* 8 (1955) 21–34; L. Robert, 'Les épigrammes satiriques de Lucillius sur les athlètes: parodie et réalités', *Entretiens* XIV: *L'épigramme grecque* (Fondation Hardt, Geneva 1968) 181–291.

MESOMEDES: TEXTS AND COMMENTARIES: E. Heitsch, *Die griechischen Dichter-fragmente der römischen Kaiserzeit* I (Göttingen 1964) 24–32. STUDIES: K. Horna, 'Die Hymnen des Mesomedes', *S.A.W.W.* 207 (1928) 1–40; H. Husman, 'Zu Metrik und Rhythmik des Mesomedes', *Hermes* 38 (1955) 231–6.

STRATO: TEXTS AND COMMENTARIES: H. Beckby, *Anthologia Graeca* IV (Munich 1964) 8–145, 515–27. STUDIES: R. Aubreton, 'Le livre XII de l'Anthologie palatine: la Muse de Straton', *Byzantion* 39 (1969) 35–52; P. G. Maxwell-Stuart, 'Strato and the *Musa puerilis*', *Hermes* 100 (1972) 215–40; W. M. Clarke, 'The manuscript of Straton's *Musa puerilis*', *G.R.B.S.* 17 (1976) 371–84; idem, 'Problems in Straton's Παιδική Μοῦσα', *A.J.Ph*, 99 (1978) 433–41.

STRATO AND RUFINUS: TEXTS AND COMMENTARIES: D. L. Page, *The epigrams of Rufinus* (Cambridge 1978). STUDIES: A. Cameron, 'Strato and Rufinus', *C.Q.* n.s.32 (1982) 162–73; L. Robert, 'La date de l'épigrammatiste Rufinus. Philologie et réalité', *C.R.A.I.* 1982, 50–63.

THE TWO OPPIANS

LIFE

Oppian, author of the *Halieutica*, was a Cilician (*Hal.* 3.7–8 and 206–9), probably from Corycus (Suda s.v. 'Oppian', Κίλιξ ἀπὸ Κωρύκου πόλεως; cf. *Hal.* 3.209). *Halieutica* was addressed to a Roman emperor, an Antoninus, and his son (1.3, 66, 78; 2.41, 683; 4.4–5). These are probably Marcus Aurelius and Commodus, between A.D. 176 and 180 (cf. Suda, γεγονὼς ἐπὶ Μάρκου Ἀντωνίνου βασιλέως). Athenaeus 13b mentions Oppian the Cilician, author of *Hal.* as being a little before his own time. The author of the *Cynegetica* dedicated his poem to the emperor Caracalla (*Cyn.* 1.3–4); he was a native of Apamea in Syria (*Cyn.* 2.127 and 157). The Suda entry ascribes both *Hal.* and *Cyn.* to the Cilician Oppian, clearly in error. *Lives* attached to the poems in various manuscripts speak of but one poet named Oppian, from either Anazarbus or Corycus in Cilicia, who was exiled by Septimius Severus and restored to Rome by Caracalla. If the story of exile contains any truth at all (which is unlikely), it must reflect episodes in the life of the Syrian poet.

WORKS

Oppian of Cilicia: *Halieutica* (5 bks). The Syrian poet called Oppian: *Cynegetica* (4 bks). The Suda, making the two poets one, states that he was also the author of *Ixeutica* in two books. Such a work does not exist, but a prose paraphrase by Eutecnius (*Ixeutica*) does. The authorship of the lost original is uncertain.

BIBLIOGRAPHY

TEXTS AND COMMENTARIES: TEXTS: *Hal.* and *Cyn.*: J. G. Schneider (Strasburg 1776 and Leipzig 1813); A. W. Mair (Loeb, 1928). *Cyn.*: P. Boudreaux (Paris 1908). COMMENTARIES: *Cyn.* 1: W. Schmitt (Münster 1969).

STUDIES: H. Köchly, *Coniectanea in Apollonium et Oppianum* (Leipzig 1838) = (edd.) G. M. Thomas, G. Kinkel, E. Böckel, *Opuscula philologica: gesammelte kleine philologische Schriften* I (Leipzig 1881) 300–37; O. Schmidt, *De elocutione Oppiani Apameensis* (Leipzig 1866); A. Ausfeld, *De Oppiano et scriptis sub eius nomine traditis* (Leipzig 1876); G. Bürner, *Oppian und sein Lehrgedicht vom Fischfang* (Bamberg 1912); O. Rebmann, *Die sprachlichen Neuerungen in der Kynegetika Oppians von Apamea* (Basel 1918); M. L. West, 'On Nicander, Oppian, and Quintus of Smyrna', *C.Q.* 13 (1963) 57–62; A. W. James, 'The Honey on the Cup in Oppian and others', *P.C.Ph.S.* n.s.12 (1966) 24–6; A. S. F. Gow, 'On the Halieutica of Oppian', *C.Q.* 18 (1968) 60–8; P. Hamblenne, 'La légende d'Oppien', *A.C.* 37 (1968) 589–619; F. Fajen, *Überlieferungsgeschichtliche Untersuchungen zu den Halieutika des Oppian* (Meisenheim am Glan 1969); G. Giangrande, 'On the Halieutica of Oppian', *Eranos* 68 (1970) 76–94; A. W. James, *Studies in the language of Oppian of Cilicia* (Amsterdam 1970); idem, *Index in Halieutica Oppiani Cilicis et in Cynegetica poetae Apameensis* (Hildesheim 1970); G. Giangrande, 'On the text of ps.-Oppian, *Cynegetica*', *G.R.B.S.* 13 (1972) 489–96; idem, 'Metodi di lettura: la lingua di Oppiano', *Museum philol. Lond.* I (1975) 127–35.

PHILOSTRATUS (FLAVIUS PHILOSTRATUS)

LIFE

b. probably in reign of Marcus Aurelius (A.D. 161–80), on Lemnos. Sometimes called Philostratus II because Suda mentions an earlier 'first' Philostratus; also 'Philostratus the Elder' to distinguish him from author of second set of *Imagines*, who was clearly a younger writer named Philostratus. Pupil, either in Athens or Rome, of Antipater of Hierapolis, who also taught the sons of Septimius Severus. Also studied with Herodes Atticus' pupils, Proclus of Naucratis and Hippodromus of Larissa, and with Damian of Ephesus. Belonged to circle of Julia Domna. Taught at Athens at same time as Apsines of Gadara. Married Aurelia Melitine. Athenian citizen; hoplite general at Athens c. 205. Dedicated *V.S.* to Antonius Gordianus, ὁ λαμπρότατος ὕπατος and ἄριστος ἀνθυπάτων (*V.S. ad init.*). d. under Philip the Arab (244–9). Sources: Eunap. *V.S.* 454, Synes. *Dio* 1 (birthplace; cf. Philostr. *V.S.* 2.27, *Vit. Apoll.* 6.27, *Epist.* 70); Philostr. *V.S.* 2.24 (Antipater), 2.21 (Proclus), 2.27 (Hippodromus), 2.23 (Damian); *Vit. Apoll.* 1.3 (Julia Domna); Suda (dates), ibid. s.v. Φρόντων Ἐμισηνός (Apsines; cf. Philostr. *V.S.* 2.33); *SIG*³ 878 (citizenship) and 879 = *IGR* IV 1544 (marriage). For generalship see B. D. Meritt and J. S. Traill, *The Athenian Agora XV: Inscriptions – the Athenian councillors* (Princeton 1974) nos. 447–9 (pp. 313–15).

WORKS

(1) EXTANT: Romantic biography of Apollonius of Tyana (called by P. not βίος but τὰ ἐς Ἀπολλώνιον, *V.S.* p. 570) in eight books. *Lives of the Sophists* (Βίοι σοφιστῶν) in two books, written after 222 (see *V.S.* p. 625). *Heroicus*, dialogue on the heroes of

the Trojan war. *Gymnasticus* (Περὶ γυμναστικῆς), treatise on athletics, sometimes credited with little reason to another Philostratus. Seventy-three *Letters* ('Επιστολαί) including many of erotic character. The earlier group of surviving *Imagines* (Εἰκόνες) or word-pictures ascribed to a Philostratus is probably the work of this author (see Men. Rhet. 390.2–3 Sp.). (2) DUBIOUS: Two Διαλέξεις in Kayser's edd.; P. did write such works acc. to Suda. Some ascribe Ps.-Luc. *Nero* to P. because of parallels in bks 4 and 5 of *Vit. Apoll.*, but Suda ascribes a work of same name to an earlier Philostratus. (3) LOST: An essay on the flute entitled Αἶγες, epigrams and declamations (Suda).

BIBLIOGRAPHY

TEXTS AND COMMENTARIES: All surviving works in *Corpus Philostrateum* in edd. by C. L. Kayser (Zurich 1853 with valuable notes, and BT, 1871: repr. 1964). TEXTS: F. C. Conybeare, W.C. Wright, A. Fairbanks, A. R. Benner, F. H. Fobes (Loeb, 1912–49: *Letters* with those of Alciphron and Aelian). *Heroicus*: L. de Lannoy (BT, 1977). COMMENTARIES: *Life of Herodes* (in *V.S.*): I. Avotins, unpublished Harvard diss. (see résumé in *H.S.C.Ph.* 73 (1969) 305–7). *Gymnasticus*: J. Jüthner (Leipzig 1909: repr. Amsterdam 1969). *Imagines*: F. Jacobs and F. T. Welcker (Leipzig 1825); E. Kalinka and O. Schoenberger (Munich 1968: with German tr.). *Letters of Apollonius*: R. J. Penella (Leiden 1979).

TRANSLATIONS: *Vit. Apoll.*: J. S. Phillimore, 2 vols. (Oxford 1912); C. P. Eels (Stanford 1923); C. P. Jones, with notes by G. W. Bowersock (Harmondsworth 1970).

STUDIES: (1) P.'s LIFE AND WORKS: K. Münscher, 'Die Philostrate', *Philologus* suppl. x (1907) 469–558; F. Solmsen, 'Some works of Philostratus the Elder', *T.A.Ph.A.* 71 (1940) 556–72; T. D. Barnes, 'Philostratus and Gordian', *Latomus* 27 (1968) 581–97; G. W. Bowersock, 'The biographer of the sophists', in *Greek sophists in the Roman empire* (Oxford 1969) 1–16; V. Nutton, 'Herodes and Gordian', *Latomus* 29 (1970) 719–28; G. Kennedy, *The art of rhetoric in the Roman world* (Princeton 1972) 556–65; C. P. Jones, 'The reliability of Philostratus', in (ed.) G. W. Bowersock, *Approaches to the Second Sophistic* (Pennsylvania 1974) 11–16; K. D. Grasby, 'The age, ancestry and career of Gordian I', *C.Q.* n.s.25 (1975) 123–30. (2) *Vit. Apoll.*: E. Meyer, *Hermes* 52 (1917) 371–424; T. Hopfner, *Seminarium Kondakov* 4 (1931) 135–64; F. Grosso, 'La vita di Apollonio di Tiana come fonte storica', *Acme* 7 (1954) 333–532; F. Lo Cascio, *La forma letteraria della Vita di Apollonio Tianeo* (Palermo 1974); J. Palm, *Om Filostratus och hans Apollonios-Biografi* (Uppsala 1976). See also F. Lo Cascio, *Sulla autenticità delle epistole di Apollonio Tianeo* (Palermo 1978); E. L. Bowie, 'Apollonius of Tyana: tradition and reality', *ANRW* II 16.2 (1978) 1652–99. (3) *Vit. Soph.*: G. W. Bowersock and C. P. Jones, 'A guide to the sophists in Philostratus' *Vitae sophistarum*', in (ed.) G. W. Bowersock, *Approaches to the Second Sophistic* (Pennsylvania 1974) 35–40 (cf. J. and L. Robert, *Bull. Épig.* 1974, 74); I. and M. M. Avotins, *An Index to the Lives of the Sophists of Philostratus* (Hildesheim 1978); I. Avotins, 'The date and recipient of the *Vitae sophistarum* of Philostratus', *Hermes* 106 (1978) 242–7. (4) *Heroicus*: H. Grentrup, *De Heroici Philostratei fabularum fontibus* (diss. Münster 1914); E. Bethe and F. Huhn, 'Philostrats *Heroicus* und Diktys', *Hermes* 52 (1917) 613–24; T. Mantero, *Ricerche sull'Heroikos di Filostrato* (Genoa 1966). (5) *Letters*: G. Anderson, 'Putting pressure on Plutarch: Phil. *Epist.* 73', *C.Ph.* 72 (1977) 43–5.

ARISTIDES (P. AELIUS ARISTIDES THEODORUS)

LIFE

b. A.D. 117 at Hadrianutherae in Mysia. Pupil of Alexander of Cotiaeum; student at Athens and Pergamum. Early travels to Egypt (perhaps via Rhodes), Cyzicus, and Rome 144. Ten-year illness. Evaded posts of high priest and tax-collector at Smyrna, and of irenarch at Hadrianutherae. Immunities guaranteed by emperors Marcus and Lucius. Secured help from emperor for Smyrna after devastating earthquake 178. Lived into reign of Commodus. Sources: own works, esp. (refs. to Keil's ed.) 50.57 (birth; see C. A. Behr, *A.J.Ph.* 90 (1969) 75–7; for birthplace see *M.D.A.I.(A.)* 29 (1904) 280); 32 (student; also Philostr. *V.S.* 2.9, Suda; cf. Aristid. 51.64); 36 (Egypt; cf. 24.3, 63; also Philostr. *V.S.* 2.9, Aristid. 25 (if genuine)); 27 (Cyzicus); 26 (Rome); 47–52 (illness); 50.63–102 (evasions; 50.74 for immunity); 19 (earthquake); *OGIS* 709 (full name; cf. Aristid. 21).

WORKS

Hymns to deities, as well as to the Asclepiads, Aegean sea and spring of Asclepius; panegyrics addressed to cities and the water of Pergamum; advice to cities; declamations on topics from the classical past, from Homer to 4th c. B.C.; polemical speeches, including justifications of his refusal to declaim *ex tempore*; miscellaneous speeches for special occasions (celebrations, lamentations); six *Sacred discourses*. All these prose-works survive (nos. 25 and 35 often considered spurious), as do some fragments of verse.

BIBLIOGRAPHY

(see Behr (1968) under *Studies* below, 296–306.)

TEXTS AND COMMENTARIES: TEXTS: W. Dindorf (Leipzig 1829: repr. 1964: with scholia); B. Keil (Berlin 1898: repr. 1958: 17–53 only); C. A. Behr and F. W. Lenz, fasc. 1–4 (Leiden 1976–80: 1–16 only); C. A. Behr (Loeb, 1973: 1–2 only). Dedications by A.: L. Robert, *Études anatoliennes* (Paris 1937) 207–22; C. P. Jones, *Phoenix* 32 (1978) 231–4. Poems by A. as quoted by him: E. Heitsch, *Die griechischen Dichterfragmente der römischen Kaiserzeit* II (Göttingen 1964) 41–2.

Autobiographical poem by A.: C. Habicht, *Die Inschriften des Asklepieions: Altertümer von Pergamon* VIII 3 (Berlin 1969) 144–5, no. 145. Another dedication by A.: *Bull. Épigr.* 1970, 422 no. 33. COMMENTARIES: C. A. Behr (Leiden 1981: nos. 17–53, tr. with notes). *Roman oration*: J. H. Oliver, *The ruling power* (Philadelphia 1953: with tr.). *Panathenaic discourse*: J. H. Oliver, *The civilising power* (Philadelphia 1968: with tr.). *Hymn to Dionysus*: W. Uerschels (Bonn 1962). *Hymn to Serapis*. A. Höfler (Stuttgart 1935). *Hymn to Zeus*: J. Amann (Stuttgart 1931).

STUDIES: A. Boulanger, *Aelius Aristide et la sophistique dans la province d'Asie au IIe siècle de notre ère* (Paris 1923); U. von Wilamowitz-Moellendorff, 'Der Rhetor Aristides', *S.P.A.* 1925, 333–53; C. A. de Leeuw, *Aelius Aristides als Bron voor de Kennis van zijn Tijd* (Amsterdam 1939); F. W. Lenz, *The Aristeides prolegomena*, *Mnemosyne* suppl. V (1959); idem, *Aristeidesstudien*, *S.D.A.W.* 40 (1964); C. A. Behr, *Aelius Aristides and the Sacred Tales* (Amsterdam 1968); A. J. Festugière, 'Sur les "discours sacrés" d'Aelius Aristide', *R.E.G.* 82 (1969) 117–53; C. P. Jones, 'Aelius Aristides, *Eis basilea*', *J.R.S.* 62 (1972) 134–52.

GALEN

LIFE

b. Aug./Sept. A.D. 129 in Pergamum, of wealthy family. No ancient authority for the *nomen* Claudius. Student at Smyrna, Corinth and Alexandria. Doctor for gladiators of high priest of Asia in Pergamum 157–61. In Rome 162–6; five anatomical demonstrations there. Visited Lemnos, Cyprus, and Syria Coele at uncertain dates. Returned to Rome via Balkans winter 168–9. Went to Marcus and Lucius at Aquileia, then to Rome after Lucius' death; doctor to Commodus there. Many of his books and medicines destroyed by fire 192. d. c. 199. Confrontation between G. and Alexander of Aphrodisias probably an invention of Arabic writers based on Alexander's attacks on G.'s views (Ibn abī 'Uṣaibi'a, '*Uyūn al-anbā*). Sources: own works, esp. (refs to Kühn's ed.) 13.599, 19.15 (birth); 2.217–18 (student); 13.599–600, 18 B.567 (doctor in Pergamum); 19.15 (Rome; cf. 14.608, 647, 649); 2.215, 218, 14.611–13, 626–9 (demonstrations); 12.171 (travels); 14.649–50, 19.14, 17–18 (Marcus, Lucius, Commodus); 2.216, 13.362, 14.60, 19.19–21 (fire); Suda (death). On early career see V. Nutton, *C.Q.* n.s.23 (1973) 158–71.

WORKS

Complete list in Schubring (under *Texts* below) vol. XX. Over 120 medical and philosophical works survive; some may be forgeries. G.'s own register of his genuine works: *De libris propriis* (vol. XIX K). Some lost works survive in Arabic translation; see ed. by M. Lyons (Berlin 1969: selected treatises, with tr.), and G. Bergsträsser, *Abhandlungen für die Kunde des Morgenlandes* 17.2 (1925).

BIBLIOGRAPHY

TEXTS AND COMMENTARIES: TEXTS: Complete. C. G. Kühn (Leipzig 1821–33) rev. K. Schubring (Hildesheim 1965). Selections. J. Marquardt and I. Müller (BT, 1884–1908); *Corpus medicorum Graecorum* (Leipzig 1914–), see esp. v 8.1 (1979), *De praecognitione*, ed. V. Nutton. COMMENTARIES: See Schubring vol. xx and the following. *De captionibus*: R. B. Edlow (Leiden 1977). *Institutio logica*: J. S. Kieffer (Baltimore 1964). *De usu partium*: M. T. May, 2 vols. (Ithaca 1968). *Scholia*. F. R. Dietz (Königsberg 1834: repr. Amsterdam 1966).

TRANSLATIONS: See G. Sarton, *Galen of Pergamum* (Kansas 1954) 101–7; J. Scarborough, *Roman medicine* (London 1969) 165–6.

STUDIES: J. Ilberg, 'Über die Schriftstellerei des Klaudios Galenos', *Rh.M.* 44 (1889) 207–39; 47 (1892) 489–514; 51 (1896) 165–96; 52 (1897) 591–623; idem, 'Aus Galens Praxis', *N.J.A.* 15 (1905) 276–312, repr. in H. Flashar, *Antike Medizin* (Darmstadt 1971) 361–416; R. Walzer, *Galen on Jews and Christians* (Oxford 1949); G. Strohmeier, 'Eine bisher unbekannte Galenschrift', *Helikon* 6 (1966) 259–66; V. Nutton, 'Galen and medical autobiography', *P.C.Ph.S.* n.s.18 (1972) 50–62; P. L. Donini, 'Motivi filosofici in Galeno', *P.P.* 194 (1980) 330–70; (ed.) V. Nutton, *Galen: problems and prospects* (London 1981).

ARTEMIDORUS

LIFE

Date of birth unknown; lived in 2nd c. A.D. Came from Ephesus, but called Daldianus after his mother's city (Daldis in Lydia). Travelled extensively. Friend of Cassius Maximus, a Greek rhetor from Phoenicia (identified by some scholars with Maximus of Tyre). Sources: own work 1.1, 2 *ad fin.*, 3.66. Mentioned in Ps.-Luc. *Philopatris* 21; perhaps Galen 15.444 K.

WORKS

(1) EXTANT: *Oneirocritica* (5 bks; only four according to Suda), on interpretation of dreams. (2) LOST: *Oionoskopika*, on augury from birds, and *Chiroskopika*, on palmistry (Suda).

BIBLIOGRAPHY

(See Pack (BT) under *Texts* below, xviii–xxiii.)

TEXTS: R. Hercher (Leipzig 1864: repr. 1964); R. A. Pack (BT, 1963).

TRANSLATIONS: R. White (New Jersey 1975); A. J. Festugière (Paris 1975); T. Fahd, *Le livre des songes d'Artémidore d'Éphèse* (Damascus 1964: newly discovered Arabic tr. of much of the *Oneirocritica*).

STUDIES: C. Blum, *Studies in the dream-book of Artemidorus* (Uppsala 1936); R. A. Pack, 'Artemidorus and the physiognomists', *T.A.Ph.A.* 72 (1941) 321–34; idem, 'On Artemidorus and his Arabic translator', *T.A.Ph.A.* 98 (1967) 313–26; A. S. Osley, 'Notes on Artemidorus' *Oneirocritica*', *C.J.* 59 (1963/4) 65–9.

PLUTARCH (MESTRIUS PLUTARCHUS)

LIFE

b. in A.D. 40s at Chaeronea. Travelled to Alexandria, Achaea (as ambassador), Delphi (with Ammonius when Nero was in Greece), and Rome and Italy on many occasions. Saw cities of north Italy with Mestrius Florus, through whom either he or his father received citizenship, since his Roman name was Mestrius Plutarchus. In Rome *c.* 92/3. Permanent priest at Delphi. Friend of Q. Sosius Senecio (cos. II 107), to whom he dedicated his *Quaestiones convivales* (*Table talk*) and *Parallel lives*. Perhaps received *ornamenta consularia* from Trajan. Epimelete of Delphic Amphictyony. Perhaps appointed nominal procurator of Greece by Hadrian. Married, probably young, with both sons and daughters. Sources: own works, esp. 391e (birth; cf. 385b); 678c ff., 816c f., 385b ff., *Vit. Dem.* 2.2 (travels); *Vit. Otho* 14.1–2, 18.1, *Vit. Mar.* 2.1 (north Italy); 632a, 522d–e (Rome); *SIG*³ 829A (citizenship, priesthood (cf. 700e, 792f.), epimelete); Suda (honoured by Trajan); Euseb. *Chron.* p. 415 Helm (procurator); *Amat.* 749b ff. (marriage).

WORKS

Parallel lives of Greeks and Romans: forty-four biographies arranged in pairs; on date see C. Stoltz, *Zur relativen Chronologie der Parallelbiographien Plutarchs* (Lund 1929). *Lives of the Caesars*: only *Galba* and *Otho* survive. Biographies of Artaxerxes and Aratus. *Moralia*: name given to seventy-eight works on moral, political, philosophical or scientific topics in essay or dialogue form (some twelve are considered spurious); see annotated list in Russell (1973) under *Studies* below, 164–72. A late antique catalogue, known as the Catalogue of Lamprias, registers 227 works by P., including well over a hundred now lost but omitting some that survive. On chronology of above works see C. P. Jones, *J.R.S.* 56 (1966) 61–74.

BIBLIOGRAPHY

(See R. Flacelière, *Actes du VIIIe Congrès de l'Association Guillaume Budé* (Paris 1969) 481–594.)

TEXTS AND COMMENTARIES: TEXTS: D. Wyttenbach (Oxford 1795–1830: with lexicon and partial comm.); B. Perrin, F. B. Babbitt *et al.* (Loeb, 1914–76); C. Lindskog, K. Ziegler, W. R. Paton *et al.* (BT, 1925–); R. Flacelière, J. Defradas *et al.* (Budé, 1957–). COMMENTARIES (full list in Russell (1973) under *Studies* below, 167–74): *Lives: Alexander*: J. R. Hamilton (Oxford 1969). *Aristides*: I. C. Limentani (Florence 1964). *Caesar*: A. Garzetti (Florence 1954). *Cicero*: D. Magnino (Florence 1962). *Moralia: Roman questions*: H. J. Rose (Oxford 1924: with tr.). *Greek questions*: W. R. Halliday (Oxford 1928: with tr.). *Pythian oracles, On the Delphic E, On the failure of the oracles, Dialogue on love*: R. Flacelière (Paris 1937–53). *Virtues of women*: P. A. Stadter (Cambridge, Mass. 1965).

STUDIES: M. Peter, *Die Quellen Plutarchs in den Biographieen der Römer* (Halle 1865: repr. Amsterdam 1965); R. Volkmann, *Leben, Schriften und Philosophie des Plutarch von Chaeroneia* (Berlin 1869); F. Leo, *Die griechisch-römische Biographie* (Leipzig 1901: repr. Hildesheim 1965); R. Hirzel, *Plutarchos* (Leipzig 1912); C. Theander, *Plutarch und die Geschichte* (Lund 1951); W. C. Helmbold and E. N. O'Neill, *Plutarch's quotations* (Baltimore 1959); K. Ziegler, *RE* XXI.1 (1951) 636–962 (rev. 1964); D. Babut, *Plutarque et le stoicisme* (Paris 1969); C. P. Jones, *Plutarch and Rome* (Oxford 1971); D. A. Russell, *Plutarch* (London 1973); B. Scardigli, *Die Römerbiographien Plutarchs: ein Forschungsbericht* (Munich 1979).

INDEX: See Wyttenbach under *Texts* above.

DIO OF PRUSA
(T. FLAVIUS (?) COCCEIANUS DIO)

(The name Chrysostom is first attested in Menander, Spengel III 390.)

LIFE

Birth-date unknown, probably *c.* A.D. 40. Father Pasicrates, a rich Bithynian from Prusa; mother from Apamea already a Roman citizen. Education in rhetoric perhaps initially in Bithynia. Philosophical training by Musonius Rufus (Fronto, *Epist.* 133.9 van den Hout = 2.50 Haines) probably in Rome *c.* 62–5 or Asia 60–2 (cf. Tac. *Ann.* 14.59). Flavian friendship by 69 implied by unreliable Philostr. *V.A.* 5.27f., supported by *Or.* 29 = funeral speech for Melancomas, boyfriend of Titus (Themist. 10.211.9f. Downey), of 70 or possibly 74. Supported Flavian expulsion of philosophers in 71 by vituperative *Against the philosophers* and presumably milder *To Musonius*, arguably now acquiring Roman citizenship and *cognomen* from *consul ordinarius* M. Cocceius Nerva. In East for *Alexandrian* (dated *c.* 72 by Jones (1973), *c.* 108–12 by von Arnim (1898) 435f. and Kindstrand (1978) under *Studies* below: likewise backing government and attacking Cynics) and *Rhodian* (early 70s) speeches (*Or.* 32 and 31); the *Tarsians* (*Or.* 33–4) and speech at Celaenae (*Or.* 35) could also as well be Flavian as Trajanic. Friendship with disgraced member of imperial house (probably T. Flavius Sabinus, cos. 82; cf. von Arnim (1898) under *Studies* below, 228–31) caused exile from Italy and Bithynia in which he visited Borysthenes (Olbia) and Getae (Dacians) on Danube frontier. Here (Viminiacium?) he repressed mutinous soldiery on news of Domitian's death (Philostr. *V.S.* 1.7.488): old links with Nerva secured return to Prusa for which he won privileges from Trajan, thought to be addressed on visits to Rome in two of the works on *Kingship* (*Or.* 1–4). Prusan speeches of 96/7–105/6 (*Or.* 40, 42–5, 47–52) document difficulties with governors and with Apamea and opposition to Dio's urban developments involving a colonnaded street: another project, a library in which his wife and son were buried, was administered by Dio, and his *cura* questioned by his enemy Archippus – Trajan's instruction to Pliny to elicit accounts (Pliny, *Epist.* 10.81–2) in 111 is our last evidence.

WORKS

A surviving corpus of eighty works (at least three spurious) is supplemented by several titles of lost works in Philostratus, Synesius and the Suda. They may be grouped (though categories overlap) as (*a*) philosophical discourses, sometimes partly or wholly in dialogue form: 1–10, 13–28, 30, 36, (?) 42, 54–6, 62–74, 76–80 and the lost *Is the universe perishable?* and *To Musonius.* In form some (esp. 13, *On exile*, 36, *Borysthenite*; presumably *Against the philosophers*) approach rhetoric, as does (differently) the *Euboean* (7). Others have part-literary themes, e.g. 18, a reading list for an orator, 55, *Homer and Socrates*, and the (lost) four books *Defending Homer against Plato*, linking with (*b*) mythological miniatures: 52–3; 57–61. Many of (*a*) and (*b*) show affinities with (*c*) epideictic rhetoric: 11–12 (*Trojan* and *Olympian*), 29 (*epitaphios* for Melancomas), 75–6 (*Law* and *Custom*), *Praise of Hair* (Synesius 64d–65d), and the lost *Tempe, Memnon, Praise of the parrot, Praise of the gnat, Praise of Heracles and Plato*; (*d*) political speeches: delivered in Rhodes (31), Alexandria (32), Tarsus (33–4), Celaenae (35), Nicomedia (38), Nicaea (39), Apamea (41) and Prusa (40, 42–51), the first three very sophistic in structure and tone, and all in varying degree marked by philosophical thought; (*e*) quasi-historical works: *Getic history; On the virtues of Alexander* in eight books (both lost and probably moralistic). Assessment is impeded by high proportion of apparently disturbed and certainly unfinished works.

BIBLIOGRAPHY

(See Desideri (1978), Jones (1978) and Salmeri (1982) under *Studies* below.)

TEXTS: H. von Arnim (Berlin 1893–6); G. de Budé (BT, 1916–19); J. W. Cohoon and H. L. Crosby (Loeb, 1932–51). A Budé is announced. Fragments of 15, 14 and a lost work, perhaps *Against the philosophers*, in a 4th-c. codex: J. G. Milne, *J.E.A.* 16

(1930) 187–92. No proper commentaries: for 32 see E. Wilmes, *Beiträge zur Alexandrinerrede* (*Or.* 32) *des Dion Chrysostomos* (Bonn 1970).

TRANSLATIONS: G. de Budé (Corbeil 1927); W. Elliger (Zurich & Stuttgart 1967). *Or.* 7 (*Euboean*) in M. Hadas, *Three Greek romances* (New York 1953).

STUDIES: W. Schmid, *Der Atticismus* I (Stuttgart 1887); H. von Arnim, *Leben und Werke des Dio von Prusa* (Berlin 1898); H. Dessau, 'Zum Leben Dios von Prusa', *Hermes* 34 (1899) 81–7; L. Lemarchand, *Dion de Pruse. Les oeuvres d'avant l'exil* (Paris 1926); V. Valdenberg, 'La théorie monarchique de Dion Chrysostome', *R.E.G.* 40 (1927) 142–62; C. Vielmetti, 'I discorsi bitinici di Dione Crisostomo', *S.I.F.C.* 18 (1941) 89–108; R. Höistad, *Cynic hero and cynic king* (Uppsala 1948); A. D. Momigliano, rev. Wirszubski, 'Libertas', *J.R.S.* 41 (1951) 149–53 = *Quinto contributo* (Rome 1976) 966–74; E. D. Phillips, 'Three Greek writers on the Roman empire', *C.&M.* 17 (1957) 102–19; J. Palm, *Rom, Römertum und Imperium in der griechischen Literatur der Kaiserzeit* (Lund 1959); B. F. Harris, 'The Olympic oration of Dio Chrysostom', *J.R.H.* 2 (1962) 85–97; A. D. Momigliano, 'Dio Chrysostomus', *Quarto contributo* (Rome 1969) 257–69; G. Kennedy, *The art of rhetoric in the Roman world* (Princeton 1972) 566–82; F. Trisoglio, 'Le idee politiche di Plinio il Giovane e di Dione Crisostomo', *P. Pol.* 5 (1972) 1–43; C. P. Jones, 'The date of Dio of Prusa's Alexandrian oration', *Historia* 22 (1973) 302–9; P. A. Brunt, 'Aspects of the social thought of Dio Chrysostom and the Stoics', *P.C.Ph.S.* n.s.19 (1973) 9–34; G. Highet, 'The huntsman and the castaway', *G.R.B.S.* 14 (1973) 35–40; J. F. Kindstrand, *Homer in der zweiten Sophistik* (Uppsala 1973); F. Jouan, 'Les thèmes romanesques dans l'*Euboicos* de Dion Chrysostome', *R.E.G.* 90 (1977) 38–46; P. Desideri, *Dione di Prusa. Un intellettuale greco nell'impero romano* (Messina & Florence 1978); C. P. Jones, *The Roman world of Dio Chrysostom* (Harvard 1978); J. F. Kindstrand, 'The date of Dio of Prusa's Alexandrian oration: a reply', *Historia* 27 (1978) 378–83; J. L. Moles, 'The career and conversion of Dio Chrysostom', *J.H.S.* 98 (1978) 79–100; M. H. Quet, 'Rhétorique, culture et politique. Le fonctionnement du discours idéologique chez Dione de Pruse et dans les *Moralia* de Plutarque', *Dial. d'hist. et arch.* 4 (1978) 51–117; G. Salmeri, *La politica e il potere. Saggio su Dione di Prusa*, Quaderni del Siculorum Gymnasium IX (Catania 1982); E. Berry, 'Dio Chrysostom the moral philosopher', *G.&R.* 30 (1983) 70–80.

MAXIMUS

LIFE

Birth-date unknown. From Tyre, hence usually identified with Cassius Maximus to whom Artemidorus dedicated his *Oneirocritica*, and not as by Eusebius (*Ol.* 232) with the Stoic teacher of Verus, Claudius Maximus. Eusebius' date of 152 may also be wrong for his *floruit*: Suda asserts Roman visit under Commodus (180–92) and visits to Rome are corroborated by the MS superscription (cf. Mutschmann (1917) and Koniaris (1982) under *Studies* below). By the time of 1.9b (to Greek audience) he was both rich and famous though still young.

WORKS

There survive forty-one short lectures. The principal MS (R) distinguishes dubiously between six Διαλέξεις and thirty-five pieces given the more general title Φιλοσοφούμενα.

BIBLIOGRAPHY

TEXTS: F. Dübner (Paris 1840); H. Hobein (BT, 1910: Hobein did not realize that R. was a 9th-c. MS and ancestor of all other MSS and departed from its (traditional) order of the works: his edition is nevertheless the most useful available and his numeration is cited throughout). New texts are announced by G. L. Koniaris and by J. Puiggali (Budé). No proper commentary exists but for 30–5 cf. Mutschmann (1917) and Koniaris (1982) under *Studies* below; for 2 cf. U. von Wilamowitz-Moellendorff, *Griechisches Lesebuch* II 2 (Berlin 1909) 212–13.

TRANSLATIONS: T. Taylor, 2 vols. (London 1804).

STUDIES: H. Hobein, *De Maximo Tyrio quaestiones philologae selectae* (Göttingen 1895); K. Dürr, *Sprachliche Untersuchungen zu den Dialexeis des Maximus von Tyrus*, *Philologus* suppl. VIII.1 (1899) 1–156; K. Meiser, 'Studien zu Maximos Tyrios', *S.B.A.W.* 1909, 6; H. Hobein, 'Zweck und Bedeutung der ersten Rede des Maximus Tyrius', Χάριτες...*F. Leo* (Berlin 1911) 188–219; H. Mutschmann, 'Das erste Auftreten des Maximos in Rom', *Sokrates* 5 (1917) 185–97; G. Soury, *Aperçus de philosophie religieuse chez Maxime de Tyr, platonicien éclectique* (Paris 1942); J. F. Kindstrand, *Homer in der zweiten Sophistik* (Uppsala 1973); G. L. Koniaris, 'On Maximus of Tyre: Zetemata (1)', *Class. Ant.* 1 (1982) 87–121 (further studies forthcoming).

LUCIAN

LIFE

Birth-date unknown, probably *c.* A.D. 120. From Samosata (modern Samsat) in Commagene. Sophistic career, starting in Antioch or Ionia, took him to Italy, Gaul (perhaps only Cisalpine), Achaea, Macedonia and Thrace. His feud with Alexander occasioned visit to Abonouteichos while travelling with his father and family (including perhaps, the son of *Eunuch* 13) to Amastris (from Samosata during Parthian wars?); cf. *Alex.* 55f. Attended three Olympic festivals before that of 165 at which he witnessed death of Peregrinus, so first visited Greece no later than 153 (*Peregr.* 35). Much of active life may have been at Athens, but he visited Rome (*Nigrinus*) and probably Antioch during Verus' presence there 162–5. Already old (*Apol.* 4) when appointed to post on staff of prefect of Egypt. Last datable work is *Alexander*, pubd after Marcus' death (*Alex.* 48); Suda's dating to 'Trajan and his successors' may be as unfounded as its tale that L. was killed by dogs and assertion that he would burn in hell for slandering Christ (in *Peregr.* 11 and 13). On identity of Egyptian post, probably *archistator*, see H. Pflaum, *Mél. de l' École française de Rome* 71 (1959) 281–6; Egyptian prefect argued to be C. Calvisius Statianus by Schwartz (1968) under *Studies* below, 11–14, giving a date of 170–5.

WORKS

Seventy-one prose pieces survive; a mock tragedy (*Podagra*) in iambics and other metres; and a collection of epigrams some of which may be L.'s. The *Metamorphoses* exists only in Photius' epitome (*Bibl. Cod.* 129). L.'s MSS also offer some ten demonstrably spurious works. Prose works comprise four sophistic declamations (*Phalaris* 1 and 2, *Tyrannicide, Disinherited*); nine Προλαλιαί (*Dionysus, Electrum, Harmonides, Heracles, Herodotus, Prometheus in words, Scythian, Thirsters, Zeuxis*); five epideictic pieces (*Hippias, The house, Praise of fatherland, Praise of the fly, Defending a lapse in greeting*); seventeen narrative or argumentative pieces in epistolary or pamphlet form; thirty-six dialogues.

BIBLIOGRAPHY

(See under *Studies* below Bompaire (1958), Betz (1961), Anderson (1976) *Theme and variation*...; also V. Fumarola, *A.&R.* 9 (1964) 97–107.)

TEXTS AND COMMENTARIES: TEXTS: C. Jacobitz (Leipzig 1836–41: repr. Hildesheim 1966: with scholia and word index); idem (BT, 1851); N. Nilén (BT, 1906–23: fasc. 1–2 only); A. M. Harmon, K. Kilburn, M. D. Macleod (Loeb, 1913–67); E. Steindl, *Scytharum colloquia* (BT, 1970); M. D. Macleod (OCT, 1972–). COMMENTARIES: Apart from notes in Loeb ed. only modern commentaries are as follows. *Toxaris*: C. G. Jacob (Halle 1825). *Podagra and Ocypus*: J. Zimmermann (Leipzig 1909). *On the Syrian goddess*: H. A. Strong and J. Garstang (London 1913); C. Clemen, *Der alte Orient* XXXVII 3–4 (Leipzig 1938). *Philopseudeis* 'Liars': L. Müller, *Eos* suppl. 13 (1932); J. Schwartz, 2nd ed. (Paris 1963: with *Peregr.*). *True histories*: C. S. Jerram (Oxford 1936); F. Ollier (Paris 1962). *How to write history*: H. Homeyer (Munich 1965). *Lives for sale*: T. Beaupère (Paris 1967). *Ship*: G. Husson (Paris 1970). *Zeus tragodos*: J. Coenen (Meisenheim am Glan 1977). *Scholia*. H. Rabe (BT, 1910).

TRANSLATIONS: H. W. and F. G. Fowler (Oxford 1905). Selections: P. Turner (Harmondsworth 1961); B. P. Reardon (New York 1965).

STUDIES: W. Schmid, *Der Atticismus* I (Stuttgart 1887); R. Helm, *Lucian und Menipp* (Leipzig 1906); E. J. Putnam, 'Lucian the sophist', *C.Ph.* 4 (1909) 162–77; H. Piot, *Les procédés littéraires de la seconde sophistique chez Lucien: l'ecphrasis* (Rennes 1914); A. R. Bellinger, 'Lucian's dramatic technique', *Y.Cl.S.* I (1928) 3–40; B. P. McCarthy, 'Lucian and Menippus', *Y.Cl.S.* 4 (1934) 3–58; M. Caster, *Lucien et la pensée religieuse de son temps* (Paris 1937); idem, *Études sur Alexandre ou le faux prophète de Lucien* (Paris 1938); F. W. Householder, *Literary quotation and allusion in Lucian* (New York 1941); J. Bompaire, *Lucien écrivain* (Paris 1958); H. Betz, *Lukian von Samosata und das Neue Testament* (Berlin 1961); B. Baldwin, 'Lucian as a social satirist', *C.Q.* n.s.11 (1961) 199–208; idem, *Studies in Lucian* (Toronto 1973); J. Schwartz, *Biographie de Lucien de Samosate*, Coll. Latomus LXXXIII (Brussels 1968); G. Anderson, *Studies in Lucian's comic fiction* (Leiden 1976); idem, *Lucian. Theme and variation in the Second Sophistic* (Leiden 1976); G. Strohmaier, 'Übersehenes zur Biographie Lukians', *Philologus* 120 (1976) 117–22; C. Robinson, *Lucian and his influence in Europe* (London 1979); G. Anderson, 'Lucian: a sophist's sophist', *Y.Cl.S.* 27 (1982) 61–92; J. Hall, *Lucian's satire* (New York 1981); C. P. Jones, *Culture and society in Lucian* (forthcoming).

ALCIPHRON

LIFE

No ancient evidence except label ῥήτωρ in MSS tradition and Tzetzes, *Chil.* 8.895. Allusions have been taken as evidence for Syrian origin, and common themes link him with Lucian, Longus and Aelian. Priority is disputed, but use of Lucian by A. and of A. by Longus and Aelian is probable; see Loeb introd. 6ff. and B. E. Perry, *The ancient romances. A literary–historical account of their origins* (Berkeley & Los Angeles 1967) 350–1.

WORKS

123 *Letters* purporting to be written by fishermen, farmers, parasites and courtesans in Attica of the 4th c. B.C.

BIBLIOGRAPHY

(To 1949 see Loeb introd. 1ff. and 32ff.)

TEXTS: M. A. Schepers (BT, 1905); A. R. Benner and F. H. Fobes (Loeb, 1949: with letters of Aelian and Philostratus).

TRANSLATIONS: F. A. Wright (London & New York 1923).

STUDIES: K. Meiser, 'Über die Briefe des Rhetors Alkiphron', *S.B.A.W.* 1904; C. Bonner, 'On certain supposed literary relationships', *C.Ph.* 4 (1909) 32–44 and 276–90; C. N. Jackson, 'An ancient letter-writer – Alciphron', *Harvard essays on classical subjects* (Boston 1912) 67–96; L. Previale, 'L'epistolario di Alcifrone', *M.C.* 2 (1932) 38–72; G. Carugno, 'Alcifrone nei suoi rapporti con Longo e il mondo bucolico', *G.I.F.* 8 (1955) 153–9; idem, 'Intrighi familiari, inesperienza ed ignoranza dei contadini nelle "Epistole Rustiche", di Alcifrone', *G.I.F.* 13 (1960) 135–43; F. Conca, 'Osservazioni intorno allo stilo di Alcifrone', *R.F.I.C.* 102 (1974) 418–31; A. S. Gratwick, 'Sundials, parasites, and girls from Boeotia', *C.Q.* 29 (1979) 308–23.

AELIAN (CLAUDIUS AELIANUS)

LIFE

Birth-date unknown, probably *c.* A.D. 165, since d. at over 60 between 222 and composition of Philostr. *V.S.*, a childless bachelor. He himself regards Rome as his *patria*, as does Philostratus, and Suda alone specifies Praeneste and alleges he held a priesthood there. Pupil of Pausanias of Caesarea and admirer of Herodes. Declaimed in Rome but despite title sophist abandoned declamation for writing as more suited to his talents. Claimed never to have left Italy but asserts having seen a five-footed ox at Alexandria (*N.A.* 11.40 – a paradoxographer's convention?). Herms of Homer and Menander inscribed with elegiac poems (one by Antipater of Sidon, *Anth. Pal.* 7.6 = *Hell. Epigr.* 224–7, the others presumably by A.) ἕνεκ' Αἰλιανοῦ, and found Alle Tre Fontane outside Porta S. Paolo, may mark his *villa suburbana*; cf. *IG* XIV 1168 and 1183. Sources: own works, esp. *V.H.* 2.38, 12.25, 14.45 (Rome), Philostr. *V.S.* 2.31, Suda.

WORKS

Animal peculiarities (Περὶ ζῴων ἰδιότητος, *De natura animalium*) in seventeen books. *Historical pot-pourri* (Ποικίλη ἰστορία, *Varia historia*) in fourteen books, complete to 3.12 and thereafter only in excerpt. Twenty *Rustic letters* (Ἀγροικικαὶ ἐπιστολαί). Poems (?), see under *Life*. Works *On providence* (Περὶ προνοίας) and *On divine manifestations* (Περὶ θειῶν ἐναργείων), illustrating the gods' punishment of wickedness (fragments). A declamation against Elagabalus (after his death) entitled Κατηγορία τοῦ Γύννιδος (lost).

BIBLIOGRAPHY

TEXTS: *De natura animalium*: R. Hercher (BT, 1864); A. F. Scholfield (Loeb, 1958–9). *Varia historia, Epist., Fragmenta*: R. Hercher (BT, 1866). *Varia historia*: M. R. Dilts (BT, 1974). *Epist.*: A. R. Benner and F. H. Fobes (Loeb, 1949: with letters of Alciphron and Philostratus).

TRANSLATIONS: *Varia historia*: T. Stanley (London 1665).

STUDIES (see bibl. in edd. of Scholfield, Dilts, and Benner and Fobes under *Texts*): W. Schmid, *Der Atticismus* III (Stuttgart 1893); C. Bonner, 'On certain supposed literary relationships', *C.Ph.* 4 (1909) 32–44; G. Carugno, 'Il "misantropo" nelle Epistole rustiche di Eliano', *G.I.F.* 1 (1948) 110–13; I. L. Thyresson, 'Quatre lettres de Claude Elien inspirées par le *Dyscolos* de Ménandre', *Eranos* 62 (1964) 7–25; J. Richmond, *Chapters on Greek fish-lore*, *Hermes* Einzelschriften XXVII (1973).

ATHENAEUS

LIFE

From Naucratis in Egypt, birth-date unknown. Writing after Commodus (d. A.D. 192) whose mention at 537f indicates a dramatic date for the *Deipnosophistae* in his reign, and perhaps after 228 if the character Ulpianus of Tyre is modelled on the jurist and praetorian Ulpianus murdered in that year. The Roman setting and allusions suggest the author was for some time resident in Rome.

WORKS

Dining sophists (Δειπνοσοφισταί) in thirty books; survives in fifteen (first two and part of third in excerpt only) and in an epitome. A history of *The kings of Syria* (211a) and a work on a passage of Archestratus' *Fishes* (329c) are lost.

BIBLIOGRAPHY

TEXTS AND COMMENTARIES: TEXTS: G. Kaibel (BT, 1887–90); C. B. Gulick (Loeb, 1927–41); A. M. Desrousseaux and C. Astruc (Budé, 1956–). Epitome ed. S. P. Peppink (Leiden 1937–9). COMMENTARIES: J. Schweighäuser (Strasburg 1801–7).

STUDIES: G. Kaibel, *De Athenaei epitome* (Rostock 1883); F. Rudolph, 'Die Quellen und die Schriftstellerei des Athenaios', *Philologus* suppl. VI (1891) 109–62; K. Mengis, *Die schriftstellerische Technik in Sophistenmahl des Athenaeus* (Paderborn 1920: reviewed by A. Rostagni, *R.F.I.C.* 49 (1921) 120–2); L. Nyikos, *Athenaeus quo consilio quibusque usus subsidiis Dipnosophistarum libros composuerit* (Basel 1941).

THE NOVEL

GENERAL WORKS

(1) TEXTS

Hercher, R., *Erotici scriptores Graeci*, 2 vols. (Leipzig 1858–9)

Hirschig, G. A., *Erotici scriptores, Graece et Latine* (Paris 1856)

Lavagnini, B., *Eroticorum Graecorum fragmenta papyracea* (Leipzig 1922)

Pack, R. A., *The Greek and Latin literary texts from Graeco-Roman Egypt*, 2nd ed. (Ann Arbor 1965) nos. 2271 (?), 2468, 2616–41

Zimmermann, F., *Griechische Romanpapyri und verwandte Texte* (Heidelberg 1936: comm. and bibl.)

A complete edition of fragments of ancient Greek novels, with tr. and comm., is being prepared by J. Winkler and S. Stephens.

(2) STUDIES (For 1945–60 see O. Mazal, *Jahrb. d. Öst. Byz. Gesell.* 11–12 (1962–3) 7–55; 13 (1964) 29–86; 14 (1964) 83–124; for 1950–70 see G. N. Sandy, *C.W.* 67 (1974) 321–59)

Anderson, G., *Studies in Lucian's comic fiction* (Leiden 1976)

idem, *Eros sophistes. Ancient novelists at play* (Chico 1982)

Braun, M., *Griechischer Roman und Hellenistische Geschichtsschreibung* (Frankfurt am Main 1934)

Gärtner, H., 'Xenophon von Ephesos', *RE* IXA.2 (1967) 2055–89

Hägg, T., *Narrative technique in ancient Greek romances* (Stockholm 1971)

idem, *The novel in antiquity* (Oxford 1983)

Haight, E. H., *Essays on the Greek romances* (New York 1943) and *More essays on the Greek romances* (New York 1945)

Heiserman, A., *The novel before the novel* (Chicago 1977)

Kerenyi, K., *Die griechisch-orientalische Romanliteratur in religionsgeschichtlicher Beleuchtung* (Tübingen 1927: repr. Darmstadt 1962)

Ludvikovsky, J., *Le roman grec d'aventures* (Prague 1925: French summary 147–58)

Merkelbach, R., *Roman und Mysterium in der Antike* (Munich & Berlin 1962)

Perry, B. E., *The ancient romances. A literary-historical account of their origins* (Berkeley and Los Angeles 1967)

Rattenbury, R. M., 'Traces of lost Greek novels', in Powell–Barber III 211–57

Reardon, B. P., *Courants littéraires grecs des IIe et IIIe siècles après J.-C.* (Paris 1971) 309–403

idem, 'The Greek novel', *Phoenix* 23 (1969) 55–73

Reitzenstein, R., *Hellenistische Wundererzählungen* (Leipzig 1906)

Rohde, E., *Der griechische Roman und seine Vorläufer*, 3rd ed. (Leipzig 1913: repr. 1960)

Rommel, H., *Die naturwissenschaftlich-paradoxographischen Exkurse bei Philostratos, Heliodoros und Achilleus Tatios* (Stuttgart 1923)

Schissel von Fleschenberg, O., *Entwicklungsgeschichte des griechischen Romans im Altertum* (Halle 1913)

Schwartz, E., *Fünf Vorträge über den griechischen Roman* (Berlin 1896)

Scobie, A., *Studies in the ancient romance and its heritage* (Meisenheim am Glan 1969) and *More studies in the ancient romance and its heritage* (Meisenheim am Glan 1973)

Sinko, T., 'De ordine quo erotici scriptores Graeci sibi successisse videantur', *Eos* 41 (1940–6) 23–45

Todd, F. A., *Some ancient novels. Leucippe and Clitophon. Daphnis and Chloe. The Satyricon. The Golden Ass* (Oxford 1940)

Weinreich, O., *Der griechische Liebesroman* (Zurich 1962)

Weitzmann, K., *Ancient book illustration* (Cambridge, Mass. 1959) 99–111

Zimmermann, F., 'Zum Stand der Forschung über den Roman in der Antike', *Forsch. und Fortschritte* 26 (1950) 59–62

An alphabetical keyword-in-context concordance to the Greek novelists has been published in microfiche by the *Thesaurus Linguae Graecae*, *TLG* Publications VIII (Irvine 1980).

ANEPIGRAPHI

TEXTS AND STUDIES: *Iolaus*: P. J. Parsons, 'Narrative about Iolaus', *P. Oxy.* 42 (1974) no. 3010, 34–41, cf. idem, 'A Greek Satyricon?', *B.I.C.S.* 8 (1971) 53–68; Anderson (1976) under *General works* for 'The Novel', 106–8. *Joseph and Asenath*: M. Philonenko (Leiden 1968: introd., text, Fr. tr., notes and *index verborum*); S. West, *C.Q.* 24 (1974) 70–81. *Metiochus and Parthenope*: Lavagnini (*General works*) 21–4; Zimmermann (*General works* (1)) nos. 6A and B (but not 6C, 62–3); H. Maehler, *Z.P.E.* 23 (1976) 1–20. *Nectanebus' dream*: Lavagnini (*General works*) 37–42. *Ninus and Semiramis*: S. Gaselee, in Gaselee and J. M. Edmonds, *Daphnis and Chloe* etc. (Loeb, 1916); Lavagnini (*General works*) 1–5; Zimmermann (*General works* (1)) no. 1, 13–35; M. Norsa and G. Vitelli, *P.S.I.* 13 (Florence 1939) no. 1305, 82–6; F. Zimmermann 'Das neue Bruchstück des Ninos-Romans (*P.S.I.* 1305)', *W. Z. Rostock* 1953–4 175–81; C. Wehrli, 'Un fragment du roman de Ninos', *Z.P.E.* 6 (1970) 39–41. *Sesonchosis*: B. P. Grenfell and A. S. Hunt, *P. Oxy.* 15 (1922) no. 1826; Zimmermann (*General works* (1)) no. 2, 36–40; S. West, 'Addendum to P. Oxy. 2466: 'Sesonchosis romance', *P. Oxy.* 47 (1980) no. 3319, 11–19; J. N. O'Sullivan and W. A. Beck, *Z.P.E.* 45 (1982) 71–83. *Tefnut*: R. Reitzenstein, *S.H.A.W.* 1923, suppl. 2; S. West, 'The Greek version of the legend of Tefnut', *J.E.A.* 55 (1969) 161–83. *Tinouphis*: M. W. Haslam, 'Narrative about Tinouphis in prosimetrum', *P. Turner* (1981) no. 8, 35–45.

LOLLIANUS

LIFE

Identification with the Philostratean sophist (*V.S.* 1.23) who flourished under Pius is unlikely in view of stylistic crudity of the papyrus, but its date puts the author no later than mid-2nd c. A.D. A work maliciously circulated under L.'s name by a rival might explain the phenomena (cf. the *Araspes and Pantheia* apparently pubd as a work of Dionysius of Miletus by his enemy Celer, Philostr. *V.S.* 1.22.524).

WORKS

Phoenicica, whose hero was probably Androtimos; only fragments survive.

BIBLIOGRAPHY

TEXTS: A. Henrichs (Bonn 1972), editing and discussing *P. Col.* inv. 3328 of second half of 2nd c. A.D. (giving subscription and fragments of Bk 1 and fragments spanning junction between two other books).

STUDIES: G. Sandy, 'Notes on Lollianus' *Phoinicica*', *A.J.Ph.* 100 (1979) 367–76; J. J. Winkler, 'Lollianus and the desperadoes', *J.H.S.* 100 (1980) 155–81; C. P. Jones, 'Apuleius' *Metamorphoses* and Lollianus' *Phoenikika*', *Phoenix* 34 (1980) 243–54; J. N. O'Sullivan, *Z.P.E.* 50 (1983) 7–11.

ANTONIUS DIOGENES

LIFE

Unknown. *Nomen* excludes Photius' Hellenistic dating, and within 1st c. and first half of 2nd c. A.D. a date near to the parody in Lucian's *Verae historiae* (160s?) is probable, unless there is also parody in Petronius' *Satyrica*.

WORKS

Τὰ ὑπὲρ Θούλην ἄπιστα 'The incredible beyond Thule' (24 bks), extant only in Photius' epitome and papyrus fragments.

CHARITON

BIBLIOGRAPHY

TEXTS: No attempt to combine epitome and fragments exists. *Epitome*: Photius, *Bibliotheca*, ed. R. Henry, vol. 2 (Paris 1960) *Cod.* 166, 140–9. *Papyri*: C. Bonner, 'A papyrus describing magical powers', *T.A.Ph.A.* 52 (1921) 111–18, demonstrated as novelistic by E. R. Dodds, 'A fragment of a Greek novel (P. Mich. inv. no. 5)', in *Phoenix* suppl. II (1952) 133–8, and claimed for D. by K. Reyhl, *Antonios Diogenes* (diss. Tübingen 1969); G. Vitelli, *P.S.I.* 10 (1932) no. 1177 (cf. F. Zimmermann, 'Die stumme Myrto', *Ph.W.* 55 (1935) 474–80 and idem, 'Die ἄπιστα des Antonius Diogenes im Lichte des neuen Fundes', *Hermes* 71 (1936) 312–20); P. J. Parsons, *P. Oxy.* 42 (1974) no. 3012; C. Gallavotti, 'Frammento di Antonio Diogene?', *S.I.F.C.* 8.4 (1930) 247–57 (*editio princeps* of *P.S.I.* 1177) improbably suggests that *P. Dublin* C3 (Lavagnini 16 and Zimmermann no. 8, under *General works* (1) for 'The Novel') also belongs to D. *Quoted fragments*: Porphyrius, *Opuscula selecta*, ed. A. Nauck (Leipzig 1886), *Vita Pythagorae* sections 10–17, 32–47, 54–5 (see Reyhl, under *Papyri* above); Lydus, *De mens.*, ed. R. Wünsch (Leipzig 1898) 3.5, 4.42 (with specific ref. to Bk 13).

STUDIES: K. Reyhl, *Antonios Diogenes* (diss. Tübingen 1969); G. Anderson, *Studies in Lucian's comic fiction* (Leiden 1976) 1–7.

CHARITON

LIFE

Claims (1.1.1) to be from Aphrodisias and secretary to rhetor Athenagoras, perhaps truthfully (see *CIG* 2782–3; 2846 for these names there). Possibly addressed in Philostr. *Epist.* 66. Earliest papyrus (Michaelides) mid-2nd c. A.D. but style (see Papanikolaou (1973) under *Studies* below) might suggest date as early as 1st c. B.C.

WORKS

Τὰ περὶ Χαιρέαν καὶ Καλλιρόην ἐρωτικὰ διηγήματα 'The love stories of Chaereas and Callirhoe' (8 bks).

BIBLIOGRAPHY

TEXTS: W. E. Blake (London 1938); D. S. Crawford, *Papyri Michaelidae* (Aberdeen 1955) no. 1; G. Molinié (Budé, 1979).

TRANSLATIONS: W. E. Blake (London 1939); G. L. Schmeling (New York 1974).

STUDIES: S. Heibges, *De clausulis Charitoneis* (Halle 1911); A. Calderini, *Caritone di Afrodisia* (Turin 1913); B. E. Perry, 'Chariton and his romance from a literary point of view', *A.J.Ph.* 51 (1930) 93–134; W. Bartsch, *Der Charitonroman und die Historiographie* (Leipzig 1934); T. W. Lumb, 'Charito', *G.&R.* 4 (1935) 83–91; P. Salmon, 'Chariton d'Aphrodisias et la révolte égyptienne de 360 avant J.C.', *C.E.* 36 (1961) 365–76; R. Petri, *Über den Roman des Chariton* (Meisenheim am Glan 1963); J. Helms, *Character portrayal in the romance* (The Hague & Paris 1966); A. D. Papanikolaou, *Chariton-Studien* (Göttingen 1973); B. P. Reardon, 'Theme, structure and narrative in Chariton', *Y.Cl.S.* 27 (1982) 1–27.

XENOPHON

LIFE

According to Suda an ἱστορικός (probably on sole basis of works cited) from Ephesus; both name and origin are doubted. His mention of the office of irenarch (2.13.3, 3.9.5) gives a *terminus post quem* of Trajan but hardly (as Moreschini (1970/1) under *Studies* below) an *ante quem* of Marcus (cf. *Dig.* 48.13.4.2), although mid/late 2nd c. A.D. is likely. See H. Gärtner, *RE* IXA.2 (1967) 2057–8.

WORKS

Τὰ κατὰ ᾽Ανθίαν καὶ ᾽Αβροκόμην ᾽Εφεσιακά 'The Ephesian history of Anthias and Habrocomes' in 10 bks (Suda); our text in five is an epitome. Other works are alleged by Suda but only *On the city of Ephesus* named. Few accept Merkelbach's view that the epitomator was converting an Isis into a Helios mystery-novel (see Gärtner under *Life* above, 2074–80).

BIBLIOGRAPHY

TEXTS: G. Dalmeyda (Budé, 1926); G. Miralles (Barcelona 1967); A. D. Papanikolaou (BT, 1973).

TRANSLATIONS: M. Hadas, *Three Greek romances* (New York 1953).

STUDIES: E. Mann, *Über den Sprachgebrauch des Xenophon Ephesius* (Progr. Kaiserslautern 1895–6); K. Bürger, 'Zu Xenophon von Ephesus', *Hermes* 27 (1892) 36–67; O. Schissel von Fleschenberg, *Die Rahmenerzählung in den Ephesischen Geschichten des Xenophon von Ephesus* (Innsbruck 1909); H. Henne, 'La géographie de l'Égypte dans Xénophon d'Ephèse', *R.H.Ph.* n.s.4 (1936) 97–106; F. Zimmermann, 'Die ᾽Εφεσιακά der sog. Xenophon von Ephesos', *W.J.A.* 4 (1949/50) 252–86; A. D. Papanikolaou, 'Chariton and Xenophon von Ephesos: zur Frage der Abhängigkeit',

Fests. Vourvéris (Athens 1964) 305–20 (cf. review by K. Nickau, *Gymnasium* 53 (1966) 543–5); T. Hägg, 'Die *Ephesiaka* des Xenophon Ephesios – Original oder Epitome?', *C.&M.* 27 (1966) 118–61; H. Gärtner, *RE* IXA.2 (1967) 2055–89; C. Moreschini, 'Un ipotesi per la datazione del romanzo di Senofonte Efesio', *S.C.O.* 19/20 (1970/1) 73–5; T. Hägg, 'The naming of the characters in the romance of Xenophon Ephesius', *Eranos* 69 (1971) 25–59; A. M. Scarcella, 'Les structures socio-économiques du roman de Xénophon d'Éphèse', *R.E.G.* 90 (1977) 249–62; G. L. Schmeling, *Xenophon of Ephesus* (Boston 1980).

INDEX: Papanikolaou (BT ed.) 73–117.

IAMBLICHUS

LIFE

Claims Syrian birth and mother-tongue (Aramaic) and to have predicted Verus' Parthian victory, giving a *floruit* in the 160s A.D.: he presumably learned *magice*, as he said he did Babylonian, from his tutor (*tropheus*), a 'Babylonian' captured in Trajan's Parthian wars who allegedly furnished I. with his tale (see pp. 2 and 32 Habrich). Photius' belief that I. was himself a Babylonian is probably a misunderstanding.

WORKS

Babyloniaca or Τὰ κατὰ Σινωνίδα καὶ 'Ροδάνην 'The history of Sinonis and Rhodanes', in 39 bks (Suda). Photius, *Bibl. Cod.* 94 *ad fin.*, 78b44 (68.15 Habrich), seems to have a complete text in 16 bks, either (if both numerals are sound) an epitome or an alternative edition.

BIBLIOGRAPHY

TEXTS: E. Habrich (BT, 1960).

STUDIES: A. Borgogno, 'Qualche suggerimenti per la ricostruzione delle storie babilonesi di Giamblico', *R.F.I.C.* 102 (1974) 324–33.

ACHILLES TATIUS

LIFE

A rhetor from Alexandria; probably late 2nd c. A.D., if the βουκόλοι of Cassius Dio 72.4.1 (A.D. 172) lie behind those of 3.9.2f. Earliest papyrus (Vogliano under *Texts* below) is 2nd c., and has suggested that our MS tradition experienced a 4th-c. revision (Reardon (1971) under *General works* for 'The Novel', 334 n.56). The Suda tradition that he became a bishop may be affected by that on Heliodorus. Sources: Eustathius on Hom. *Od.* 14.350, Thomas Mag. s.v. ἀναβαίνω (profession; latter perhaps on inference not evidence); Suda and MSS (birthplace).

WORKS

Τὰ κατὰ Λευκίππην καὶ Κλειτοφῶντα 'The history of Leucippe and Cleitophon' in 8 bks (original title Φοινικικά? See A. Henrichs, *Die Phoinikika des Lollianos* (Bonn 1972) 206). Suda also credits him with works *On the sphere*, *Etymologies* and a *Miscellaneous history of many great and remarkable men*: only the first survives (if the Achilles is the same) in extracts; see E. Maass, *Commentariorum in Aratum reliquiae* (Berlin 1898) 27–85.

BIBLIOGRAPHY

TEXTS AND COMMENTARIES: TEXTS: S. Gaselee (Loeb, 1917); A. Vogliano, 'Un papiro di Achille Tazio', *S.I.F.C.* 15 (1938) 121–30; W. Schubart, *Griechische literarische Papyri* (Berlin 1950) nos. 30, 59–60; E. Vilborg (Stockholm 1955: with full bibl.); A. Henrichs, 'Achilleus Tatios aus Buch III (P. Col. inv. 901)', *Z.P.E.* 2 (1968) 211–26. COMMENTARIES: E. Vilborg (Stockholm 1962). Bk 3: T. F. Carney (Salisbury 1961).

STUDIES (pre 1955 see Vilborg above): C. F. Russo, 'Pap. Ox. 1250 e il romanzo di Achille Tazio', *R.A.L.* 8.10 (1955) 397–403; idem, *Gnomon* 30 (1958) 585–90 (review of Vilborg); D. Sedelmeier, 'Studien zu Achilleus Tatius', *W.S.* 72 (1959) 113–43; M. Hikichi, 'Eros and Tyche in Achilles Tatius', *J.C.S.* 13 (1965) 116–26; J. Schwartz, 'Quelques observations sur les romans grecs', *A.C.* 36 (1967) 536–62.

LEXICON: J. N. O'Sullivan (Berlin & New York 1980).

HELIODORUS

LIFE

Claims (10.41.4) to be a Phoenician from Emesa, of the line of Helios, Theodosius' son Heliodorus. Socrates (*H.E.* 5.22) identifies him with bishop of Tricca who introduced celibacy in the church of Thessaly (cf. Phot. *Bibl. Cod.* 73 *ad fin.*, 51b40–1). The 4th- or early 5th-c. date this would entail is not corroborated by marginal note at end of Vat. Gr. 157 (11th c.) locating him under Theodosius the Great (379–95), almost certainly a false interpretation of the paternity asserted by Heliodorus. Van der Valk (1941) and Colonna (1950), under *Studies* below, argue that the siege of Syene 9.3f. is modelled on that of Nisibis as described by Julian (*Or.* 1 and 3) and corroborated by St Ephraim of Nisibis (*Carmina Nisibena*, ed. G. Bickell (Leipzig

1886) 71f.); this would set the work after A.D. 357 (Julian, *Or.* 3). But Szepessy (1976), under *Studies* below, has now demonstrated that Ephraim's account diverges and that Julian is dependent on Heliodorus, who can thus belong to the 3rd c. as similarities with Achilles and Philostratus suggest. Identity with Heliodorus Arabs of Philostr. *V.S.* 2.32 or with T. Aur. Heliodorus Antiochi f. Hadrianus of Palmyra (*IG* XIV 969–71) has been proposed: Ἀράβιος for an Emesene is odd, but not impossible as is Παλμυρηνός.

WORKS

Αἰθιοπικὰ τὰ περὶ Θεαγένην καὶ Χαρίκλειαν 'The Aethiopian history of Theagenes and Charicleia' (10 bks).

BIBLIOGRAPHY

TEXTS: R. M. Rattenbury, T. W. Lumb, J. Maillon (Budé, 1935–43: 2nd ed. 1960); A. Colonna (Rome 1938: but see Budé ed. III, pref.).

TRANSLATIONS: M. Hadas (Ann Arbor 1957); W. Lamb (London 1961).

STUDIES: J. W. H. Walden, 'Stage-terms in Heliodorus' *Aethiopica*', *H.S.C.Ph.* 5 (1894) 1–43; M. Oeftering, *Heliodor und seine Bedeutung für die Literatur* (Berlin 1901); J. Fritsch, *Der Sprachgebrauch des griechischen Romanschriftsteller Heliodor und sein Verhältnis zum Atticismus*, 2 vols. (Kaaden 1901–2); C. W. Keyes, 'The structure of Heliodorus' *Aethiopica*', *S.Ph.* 19 (1922) 42–51; D. Baumgarten, 'Quid Xenophonti debeat Heliodorus Emesenus', *Stud. Leopol.* 4 (Lvov 1932) 1–36; M. van der Valk, 'Remarques sur la date des *Éthiopiques* d'Héliodore', *Mnemosyne* 9 (1941) 97–100; F. Altheim, 'Helios und Heliodor von Emesa', *Albae Vigiliae* 12 (Amsterdam 1942) = *Literatur und Gesellschaft im ausgehenden Altertum* II (Halle 1951) 94–124; A. Wifstrand, *Eikota V: zu den Romanschriftstellern* (Lund 1944–5) 36–41; V. Hefti, *Zur Erzählungstechnik in Heliodors Aethiopika* (Wien 1950); A. Colonna, *Athenaeum* 28 (1950) 79–87 and *M.C.* 18 (1951) 153–9 (on H.'s chronology); T. Szepessy, 'Die *Aethiopika* des Heliodoros und der griechische sophistische Liebesroman', *A. Ant. Hung.* 5 (1957) 241–59; T. R. Goethals, *The Aethiopica of Heliodorus. A critical study* (diss. Columbia 1959 microf.); E. Feuillâtre, *Études sur les Éthiopiques d'Héliodore* (Poitiers 1966); R. Keydell, 'Zur Datierung der *Aethiopika* Heliodors', in *Polychronion: Fests. Dölger* (Heidelberg 1966) 345–50; D. Kövendi, 'Heliodors *Aithiopika*. Eine literarische Würdigung', in (edd.) F. Altheim and R. Stiehl, *Die Araber in der alten Welt* III (Berlin 1966) 136–97; M. D. Reeve, *C.Q.* n.s.18 (1968) 282–7 (bibl. of textual articles); C. Lacombrade, 'Sur l'auteur et la date des *Éthiopiques*', *R.E.G.* 83 (1970) 70–89; A. M. Scarcella, 'Testimonianze della crisi di un'età nel romanzo di Eliodoro', *Maia* 24 (1972) 8–41; T. Szepessy, 'Le siège de Nisibe et la chronologie d'Héliodore', *A. Ant. Hung.* 24 (1976) 247–76; J. R. Morgan, 'History, romance and realism in Heliodorus', *Class. Ant.* 1 (1982) 221–65; J. J. Winkler, 'Heliodorus' *Aithiopika*', *Y.Cl.S.* 27 (1982) 93–158.

LONGUS

LIFE

Dates and birthplace unknown. His familiarity with Lesbos is asserted only by the text (*pref.* 1); it is not refuted by elements drawn from literary tradition which sometimes submerge realism, but his residence on the island is disputed. For support of the name and late-2nd-c. A.D. date see *IG* XII 2 249 from Thermi (cf. *IG* XII suppl. p. 76 and F. Hiller von Gaertringen, *N.G.G.* 1936, 111–16). But although a date in second half of 2nd or first half of 3rd c. is probable, the earlier date depends on accepting imitation by Alciphron (see Dalmeyda, pref. xvii, and Schönberger, introd., under *Texts* below; Perry under *General works* for 'The Novel', 350–1), often doubted (e.g. by Dörrie (1936) under *Studies* below).

WORKS

Ποιμενικὰ τὰ κατὰ Δάφνην καὶ Χλόην 'The pastoral history of Daphnis and Chloe' (4 bks).

BIBLIOGRAPHY

TEXTS: J. M. Edmonds and G. Thornley (Loeb, 1916); A. Kairis (Athens 1932); G. Dalmeyda (Budé, 1934); O. Schönberger, 2nd ed. (Berlin 1973); M. D. Reeve (BT, 1982).

TRANSLATIONS: J. Lindsay (London 1948); P. Turner (Harmondsworth 1956); W. E. McCulloh (New York 1970).

STUDIES: H. Reich, *De Alciphronis Longique aetate* (Königsberg 1894); C. Cichorius, *Römische Studien* (Leipzig 1922) 323; G. Valley, *Der Sprachgebrauch des Longus* (Uppsala 1926); L. Castiglioni, 'Stilo e testo del romanzo pastorale di Longo', *R.A.L.* 61 (1928) 203–23; E. Vaccarello, 'L'eredità della poesia bucolica nel romanzo di Longo', *M.C.* 5 (1935) 307–25; H. Dörrie, *G.G.A.* 198 (1936) 345–50 (review of Dalmeyda); G. Rohde, 'Longus und die Bukolik', *Rh.M.* 86 (1937) 23–49; M. P. Nilsson, *Opuscula selecta* II (Lund 1952) 524–41; H. H. O. Chalk, 'Eros and the Lesbian pastorals of Longus', *J.H.S.* 80 (1960) 32–51; P. Turner, '*Daphnis and Chloe*: an interpretation', *G.&R.* 7 (1960) 117–23; M. C. Mittelstadt, *Longus and the Greek love romance* (diss. Stanford 1964); idem, 'Longus, *Daphnis and Chloe* and Roman narrative painting', *Latomus* 26 (1967) 752–61; M. Berti, 'Sulla interpretazione mistica del romanzo di Longo', *S.C.O.* 16 (1967) 343–58; A. M. Scarcella, *Struttura e tecnica narrativa in Longo sofista* (Palermo 1968); idem, *La Lesbo di Longo sofista* (Rome 1968); idem, 'Realtà e letteratura nel paesaggio sociale ed economico del romanzo di Longo sofista', *Maia* 22 (1970) 103–31; M. C. Mittelstadt, 'Bucolic-lyric motifs and dramatic narrative in Longus' *Daphnis and Chloe*', *Rh.M.* 10 (1970) 211–27; idem, 'Love, Eros and poetic art in Longus', in *Saggi...d'Agostini* (Turin 1971) 305–32; A. M. Scarcella, 'La tecnica dell'imitazione in Longo sofista', *G.I.F.* 23 (1971) 134–59; idem, 'La donna nel romanzo di Longo sofista', *G.I.F.* 24 (1972) 63–84; F. C. Christie, *Longus and the development of the pastoral tradition* (diss. Harvard 1972); S. Deligiorgis, 'Longus' art in brief lives', *Ph.Q.* 53 (1974) 1–9; A. Geyer, 'Roman und Mysterienrituel, *W.J.A.* n.s.3 (1977) 179–96; L. R. Cresci, 'Il romanzo di Longo sofista e la tradizione bucolica', *A.&R.* n.s.26 (1981) 1–25; B. Effe, 'Longos. Zur Functionsgeschichte der Bukolik in der römischen Kaiserzeit', *Hermes* 110 (1982) 65–84; R. L. Hunter, *A Study of Daphnis & Chloe* (Cambridge 1983).

THE FABLE

The fable must be a very ancient form; it is used by early writers such as Hesiod and Archilochus and had no doubt been in existence in Greece and the Near East long before their time. The Greeks associated their traditional fables with Aesop, a Thracian slave who lived in Samos in the 6th c. B.C., but many fables ascribed to him must have come from different sources. A collection of 'Tales of Aesop' (*logoi Aisopeioi*, Diog. Laert. 5.80) was made by Demetrius of Phalerum in the late 4th or early 3rd c. B.C. (see B. E. Perry, 'Demetrius of Phalerum and the Aesopic fables', *T.A.Ph.A.* 93 (1962) 287–346), but the earliest surviving recension, the so-called Augustana, dates from the 1st or 2nd c. A.D., and the others from late antiquity and the middle ages. The other great name in the Greek tradition is that of Babrius, who wrote fables in verse, as Phaedrus had in Latin (*CHCL* II 624–6). He may have been a Hellenized Latin speaker who lived in Syria; his date is uncertain, perhaps 2nd c. A.D. Both Babrius and 'Aesop' were popular texts, widely used in schools until the end of antiquity and beyond. The ancient biographical traditions about Aesop attest the interest he aroused; for testimonia and texts of the *Lives* see B. E. Perry, *Aesopica* I (Urbana, Illinois 1952).

BIBLIOGRAPHY

TEXTS AND COMMENTARIES: TEXTS: Aesop and the corpus ascribed to Aesop: E. Chambry (Budé, 1927); B. E. Perry, *Aesopica* I (Urbana, Illinois 1952); A. Hausrath, 2nd ed. rev. H. Hunger (BT: I 1, 1970; I 2, 1959). Babrius: B. E. Perry (Loeb, 1965: with Phaedrus). COMMENTARIES: Babrius: W. G. Rutherford (London 1883).

TRANSLATIONS: Aesop: S. A. Handford, 2nd ed. (Harmondsworth 1964). Babrius: (verse) D. B. Hull (Chicago 1960); (prose) B. E. Perry (Loeb, 1965). H. S. Schnur, *Fabeln der Antike* (Munich 1978: text and German tr.: includes Aesop and Babrius).

STUDIES: A. Hausrath, *RE* VI (1909) 1704–36 ('Fabel)'; B. E. Perry, *Studies in the text history of the life and fables of Aesop* (Haverford, Penn. 1936); idem, 'Fable', *Stud. Gen.* 12 (1959) 17–37; idem, introduction to *Babrius and Phaedrus* (Loeb, 1965); M. Nøjgaard, *La fable antique*, 2 vols. (Copenhagen 1964–7); M. L. West, 'Near Eastern material in Hellenistic and Roman literature', *H.S.C.Ph.* 73 (1969) 113–34; F. R. Adrados, *Historia de la fábula greco-latina* I (Madrid 1979).

ARRIANUS, LUCIUS FLAVIUS

LIFE

b. A.D. 85–90 at Nicomedia (mod. Ismit), where educated and later priest of Demeter and Kore (Phot. *Bibl. Cod.* 93, 73a37–b3). Heard Epictetus at Nicopolis *c.* 108 (F. Millar, *J.R.S.* 55 (1965) 142) and served on *consilium* of C. Avidius Nigrinus in Achaea, probably before 110 (A. Plassart, *Fouilles de Delphes* III (4) (1970) 38f., nos. 290 and 294; cf. A. B. Bosworth, *C.Q.* 22 (1972) 184 n.2). Proconsul of Baetica late 120s (?), as attested by an epigram from Cordoba; cf. Oliver (1982) under *Studies* below for text and bibl. to date. Consul *suffectus* 129 or 130. *Legatus Aug. pro. pr.* of Cappadocia 131–7; cf. Roos–Wirth (1968) under *Texts* below, *test.* 8–17. Retired to Athens where archon 145/6 (*IG* II² 2055) and honoured as consular and philosopher (ὑπατικὸν φιλόσοφον, *A.A.A.* 3 (1970) 377–80): he had already been labelled φιλόσοφον by L. Gellius Menander at Corinth *c.* 131 (cf. G. W. Bowersock, *G.R.B.S.* 8 (1967) 279–80).

WORKS

Much of his considerable output (cf. Phot. *Bibl. Cod.* 58, 17b21–2, Suda) is lost. (*a*) Philosophical. Lectures of Epictetus in twelve books, of which four, entitled Διατριβαί, survive: four of the remaining eight may have been Διατριβαί or Διαλέξεις, and the final four Ὁμιλίαι; cf. H. Schenkl, *Epicteti dissertationes* (BT, 1894) xi f. *On the heavens* (Περὶ μετεώρων) and *On comets* (Περὶ κομητῶν) were perhaps part of one work: fragments in Roos–Wirth (1968) under *Texts* below, 186–95. (*b*) Historical etc. *Circumnavigation of the Black Sea* (Περίπλους Εὐξείνου Πόντου) *c.* 132 (17.3); *On tactics* (Τέχνη τακτική) 136/7 (cf. 44); *Order of battle against the Alans* ("Εκταξις κατὰ 'Αλανῶν) after *c.* 135 and perhaps part of the *Alan history* ('Αλανική) now lost. Lives of *Timoleon* and *Dio*, lost, which with the *Journey up-country of Alexander* ('Ανάβασις 'Αλεξάνδρου) in seven books (plus an appendix in Ionic, the *Indian history*, 'Ινδική) preceded the *Bithynian history* (Βιθυνιακά), in eight books (lost), cf. Phot. *Bibl. Cod.* 93, 73a31f. This sequence, usually put after 137, is argued to precede the consulship by A. B. Bosworth, 'Arrian's literary development', *C.Q.* 22 (1972) 163–85. The life of Tillorobos (cf. Lucian, *Alex.* 2) is undatable. The *Successors of Alexander* (Τὰ μετὰ 'Αλέξανδρον) in ten books (lost) and *Parthian history*

APPIANUS

(Παρθικά) in seventeen books (lost) are agreed to be late. *On hunting* (Κυνηγετικός) probably belongs to the retirement in Athens.

BIBLIOGRAPHY

TEXTS AND COMMENTARIES: TEXTS: (*a*) Philosophical. H. Schenkl, 2nd ed. (BT, 1916); W. A. Oldfather (Loeb, 1925–8); J. Souilhé, A. Jagu (Budé, 1943–65). (*b*) Historical etc. A. G. Roos, G. Wirth, I *Alexandri Anabasis*, II *Scripta minora et fragmenta* (BT, 1967–8: bibliographies I lvi–lxiv, II xlvi–liii). *Anabasis* and *Indike*: P. A. Brunt (Loeb, 1976–). *Indike*: P. Chantraine, (Budé, 1927). Fragments: *FGrH* no. 156. COMMENTARIES: Apart from notes in Loeb, Budé and *FGrH* there are only: G. Marenghi, *Arriano, Periplo del Ponto Eusino* (Naples 1958); D. B. Hull, *Hounds and hunting in ancient Greece* (Chicago 1964) 161–4 (tr. and brief comm. on *Cynegeticus*); H. T. Hutzel, *From Gadrosia to Babylon. A commentary on Arrian's Anabasis 6.22–7.30* (diss. Indiana 1974); A. B Bosworth, *A historical commentary on Arrian's History of Alexander* I, *Commentary on Books i–iii* (Oxford 1980).

TRANSLATIONS: Complete: E. J. Chinnock in (ed.) F. R. B. Godolphin, *Greek historians* (Toronto 1942). *Anabasis*: A. de Sélincourt, rev. ed. with a new introd. and notes by J. R. Hamilton (Harmondsworth 1971).

STUDIES: E. Schwartz, *RE* II 1230–6 = *Griechische Geschichtsschreiber* (Leipzig 1957) 130–40; F. Reuss, 'Arrian und Appian', *Rh.M.* 45 (1899) 446–65; G. Wirth, 'Anmerkungen zur Arrianbiographie: Appian–Arrian–Lukian', *Historia* 13 (1964) 209–45; P. A. Stadter, 'Flavius Arrianus, the new Xenophon', *G.R.B.S.* 8 (1967) 155–61; G. Schepens, 'Arrian's view of his task as an Alexander-historian', *Anc. Soc.* 2 (1971) 254–68; A. B. Bosworth, 'Arrian's literary development', *C.Q.* 22 (1972) 163–85; idem, 'Arrian in Baetica', *G.R.B.S.* 17 (1976) 55–64; P. A. Stadter, 'Xenophon in Arrian's *Cynegeticus*', *G.R.B.S.* 17 (1976) 157–67; P. A. Brunt, 'From Epictetus to Arrian', *Athenaeum* 55 (1977) 19–48; P. A. Stadter, *Arrian of Nicomedia* (Chapel Hill 1980); idem, 'Arrian's extended preface', *I.C.S.* 6 (1981) 157–71; J. H. Oliver, 'Arrian in two roles', *Hesperia* suppl. XIX (1982) 122–9; R. Syme, 'The career of Arrian', *H.S.C.Ph.* 86 (1982) 181–211.

APPIANUS

LIFE

b. *c.* A.D. 96 (at latest: he seems to be an adult by 115–17, the date of the incident of fr. 19, and is an old man by the 150s, see below), presumably in his *patria* Alexandria, where he had a distinguished career. His skill in forensic oratory took him to Rome, where he pleaded cases before emperors and was eventually (after at least two requests from his friend Fronto to Pius) made *procurator Augusti* (*pref.* 62; Fronto, *Epist. ad Ant. Pium* 9.2–3.162 van den Hout), probably a titular appointment. Fronto's letter may refer to his own refusal of the proconsulship of Asia, *c.* 158 (so C. R. Haines, *Fronto* I (Loeb, 1919) 263, rejected by E. Champlin, 'The chronology of Fronto', *J.R.S.* 54 (1974) 149), but its date is usually fixed by reference to A.'s preface, written 900 years after Rome's foundation (34–5), suggesting *c.* 150, and 200 years after the principate was established (23–4), so *c.* 152 if Caesar is taken as the founder (as by Gabba) or *c.* 169 if A. was counting from Actium (as his own distinctions in *pref.* 22–3 and 60 rather support). The latter date might be supported by A.'s claim to have been procurator of *emperors* (σφῶν, *pref.* 62): either Pius and the succeeding régime of Marcus and Lucius Verus, and in any case after 161. The date of the preface should also be *before* 163 (Gabba 1967) under *Commentaries* below, x). By the time it was written A. was old and childless (Fronto, *Epist.* 9.2–3) and had already published an autobiography (*pref.* 62). Only seventeen of the twenty-four books of the history seem to have been completed when the preface was written (Viereck–Roos under *Texts* below, pref. vi–vii).

WORKS

Autobiography (lost). Letter to Fronto (van den Hout p. 227; Viereck–Roos I 537). Roman history in twenty-four books, of which thirteen (square brackets) survive only in fragments or Photius' epitome (*Bibl. Cod.* 57): [1: Kings. 2: Italy. 3: Samnium. 4: Gaul. 5: Sicily.] 6: Spain. 7: Hannibal. 8: Carthage [& Numidia. 9: Macedon] & Illyria. 10: Greece [& Asia.] 11: Syria. 12: Mithridates. 13–17: Civil Wars in five books. [18–21: Egypt in four books. 22: the first century of empire. 23: Dacia. 24: Arabia.]

BIBLIOGRAPHY

TEXTS AND COMMENTARIES: TEXTS: H. White (Loeb, 1912–13); P. Viereck, A. G. Roos, E. Gabba, *Appiani Historia Romana* I (BT, 1962); L. Mendelssohn, P. Viereck, *Appiani Historia Romana* II (BT, 1905). COMMENTARIES: *Bell. Civ.* 1: E. Gabba, 2nd ed. (Florence 1967). *Bell. Civ.* 5: E. Gabba (Florence 1970: both with Italian tr.).

STUDIES: J. Hering, *Lateinisches bei Appian* (diss. Leipzig 1935); E. M. Sanford, 'Contrasting views of the Roman empire', *A.J.Ph.* 58 (1937) 437–56; E. Gabba, *Appiano e la storia delle Guerre Civili* (Florence 1956); idem, 'Sul libro Siriaco di Appiano', *R.A.L.* 8.12 (1957) 337–51; T. J. Luce, *Appian's exposition of the Roman constitution* (diss. Princeton 1958); E. Gabba, 'Storici greci da Augusto a Severo', *R.S.I.* 71 (1959) 361–81; P. Jannacone, 'Appunti per una storia della storiografia retorica nel secondo secolo', *G.I.F.* 14 (1961) 289–307; H. J. Kühne, 'Appians historiographische Leistung', *W.Z. Rostock* 18 (1969) 345–77; I. Hahn, 'Papyrologisches zum Namen Appians', *Philologus* 117 (1973) 97–101.

PAUSANIAS

LIFE

b. in first or second decade of 2nd c. A.D.; probably came from Asia Minor, perhaps Lydia. Was writing the Περιήγησις under Marcus Aurelius. Had visited Asia Minor, Greece, Macedonia, Syria, Palestine, Egypt and Rome (see Heberdey (1894) under *Studies* below). Sources: own work, esp. 8.9.7 (birth; P. did not see Antinous, with an implication that a reader might imagine he had); 5.13.7 (birthplace; παρ' ἡμῖν suggesting origin at Magnesia ad Sipylum); 5.1.2 (date of Περιήγησις; foundation of Roman Corinth dated 217 years before the time of writing, which for that passage is therefore 173) and 10.34.5 (ref. to invasion of Greece by Costoboci 170 or 171).

WORKS

Guide to Greece (Περιήγησις τῆς Ἑλλάδος) in ten books.

BIBLIOGRAPHY

TEXTS AND COMMENTARIES: TEXTS: F. Spiro (BT, 1903); W. H. S. Jones, H. A. Ormerod, R. E. Wycherley (Loeb, 1918–35); M. H. Rocha-Pereira (BT, 1973–81). COMMENTARIES: H. Hitzig and H. Blümner, 3 vols. (6 half-vols.) (Berlin & Leipzig 1896–1910); J. G. Frazer, 6 vols., 2nd ed. (London 1913): N. Papachatzis, 4 vols. (Athens 1963–75); P. Levi, 2 vols. (Harmondsworth 1971). Selections: E. Meyer, *Beschreibung Griechenlands* (Zurich 1954: with tr.): G. Roux, *Pausanias en Corinthie* (2.1–15) (Paris 1958).

STUDIES: A. Kalkmann, *Pausanias der Perieget* (Berlin 1886); W. Gurlitt, *Über Pausanias* (Graz 1890); R. Heberdey, *Die Reisen des Pausanias* (Vienna 1894); C. Robert, *Pausanias als Schriftsteller* (Berlin 1909); G. Pasquali, 'Die schriftstellerische Form des Pausanias', *Hermes* 48 (1913) 161–223; F. A. Trendelenburg, *Pausanias in Olympia* (Berlin 1914); L. Deicke, *Quaestiones Pausanianae* (Göttingen 1935); G. Daux, *Pausanias à Delphes* (Paris 1936); A. Diller, 'The manuscripts of Pausanias', *T.A.Ph.A.* 88 (1957) 169–88; R. E. Wycherley, 'Pausanias in the Agora of Athens', *G.R.B.S.* 2 (1959) 21–44; J. Hejnic, *Pausanias the periegete and the archaic history of Arcadia* (Prague 1961); R. E. Wycherley, 'Pausanias at Athens II', *G.R.B.S.* 4 (1963) 157–75; M. Marinescu-Himu, 'Les sources d'inspiration de Pausanias dans le livre IV de la Périégèse', *Actes de la XIIe conférence internationale d'études classiques: Eirene*, Cluj-Napoca 1972 (Amsterdam 1975) 251–7; M. Jost, 'Pausanias en Megalopolitide', *R.E.A.* 75 (1973) 241–67; idem, 'Sur les traces de Pausanias en Arcadie', *Rev. Arch.* (1974) 179–86; O. Strid, *Über Sprache und Stil des Periegeten Pausanias* (Uppsala 1976); J. Heer, *La personnalité de Pausanias* (Paris 1979).

890

CASSIUS DIO
(CLAUDIUS CASSIUS DIO COCCEIANUS)

LIFE

Date of birth unknown. From Nicaea in Bithynia. Accompanied father Apronianus when legate of Cilicia. Senator at Rome under Commodus. Honoured by Pertinax A.D. 193 and designated praetor. Consul for first time as suffect under a Severus in unknown year, perhaps 205 (under Septimius Severus) or 223 or 224 (under Severus Alexander). At Nicomedia with Caracalla 214–15. Appointed by Macrinus *curator* of Pergamum and Smyrna; there in winter 218/19. In Asia *c.* 221. Served in Africa (223) as legate or proconsul, then *legatus Augusti pro praetore* of Dalmatia (224–5) and Upper Pannonia (226–8). Consul for second time, as colleague of emperor, A.D. 229. Sources: own work, esp. 75.15.3 (background; cf. Phot. *Bibl. Cod.* 71, Suda); 72.7.2 (Cilicia); 72.4.2 (Commodus; cf. 72.16.3, 20.1, 21.1); 73.12.2 (praetor); 76.16.4, 80.2.1 (consul; cf. *fasti*); 77.17–18, 78.8.4 (Nicomedia); 79.7.4 (*curator*); 79.18.3 (Asia); 49.36.4, 80.1.2–3 (Africa, Dalmatia, Pannonia); *Bull. Épig*, 1971, 454 no. 400 ('Claudius' among his names).

WORKS

(1) EXTANT: *Roman history* down to A.D. 229, in 80 books; twenty-two years spent in preparation and composition (72.23.5). Bks 36–54 survive in full, 55–60 in substantial fragments, 79–80 in part. Epitomes of Xiphilinus (11th c.) and Zonaras (12th c.) valuable for lost parts of original. (2) LOST. Biography of Arrian (Suda; see G. Wirth, *Klio* 41 (1963) 221–33); treatise on dreams and prodigies for Septimius Severus at beginning of his reign (Dio 72.23.1). Suda erroneously mentions two works by Dio called *Persica* and *Getica*; error best explained by confusion of names; Dinon of Colophon wrote the former, Dio of Prusa (Dio Chrysostom) the latter.

BIBLIOGRAPHY

TEXTS: U. P. Boissevain (Berlin 1895–1931: with *index verborum* by W. Nawijn); E. W. Cary (Loeb, 1914–27: with brief notes).

STUDIES: E. Gabba, 'Sulla storia romana di Cassio Dione', *R.S.I.* 67 (1955) 289–333; J. Bleicken, 'Der politische Standpunkt Dios gegenüber der Monarchie', *Hermes* 90 (1962) 444–67; F. Millar, *A study of Cassius Dio* (Oxford 1964); F. Kolb, *Literarische Beziehungen zwischen Cassius Dio, Herodian und der Historia Augusta* (Bonn 1972); C. Letta, 'La composizione dell'opera di Cassio Dione: cronologia e sfondo storico-politico', *Ricerche di Storiografia Antica* 1 (Pisa 1979) 117–89.

HERODIAN

LIFE

Not from Italy; probably of eastern origin. Lived during period about which he wrote (A.D. 180–238). Held unidentified imperial and public posts. Sources: his *History* 1.2.5, 2.11.8, 2.15.7.

WORKS

History (8 bks) from death of Marcus to accession of Gordian III.

BIBLIOGRAPHY

(See Whittaker (Loeb ed.) under *Texts* below, lxxxix–xcv.)

TEXTS: L. Mendelssohn (BT, 1883); K. Stavenhagen (BT, 1922); F. Cassola (Florence 1968); C. R. Whittaker (Loeb, 1969: with full notes).

STUDIES: F. Cassola, 'Sulla attendabilità dello storico Erodiano', *A.A.P.* n.s.6 (1956/7) 195ff.; F. J. Stein, *Dexippus et Herodianus rerum scriptores quatenus Thucydidem secuti sint* (Bonn 1957); W. Widmer, *Kaisertum, Rom und Welt in Herodians* Μετὰ Μᾶρκον βασιλείας ἱστορία (Zurich 1967); G. Alföldy, 'Zeitgeschichte und Krisenempfindung bei Herodian', *Hermes* 99 (1971) 429–49; idem, 'Herodians Person', *Anc. Soc.* 2 (1971) 204–33; F. Kolb, *Literarische Beziehungen zwischen Cassius Dio, Herodian und der Historia Augusta* (Bonn 1972); G. W. Bowersock, 'Herodian and Elagabalus', *Y.Cl.S.* 24 (1975) 229–36.

METRICAL APPENDIX[1]

(1) BASIC PRINCIPLES

(A) STRESSED AND QUANTITATIVE VERSE

In metres familiar to speakers of English, rhythm is measured by the predictable alternation of one or more stressed syllables with one or more unstressed syllables (distinguished by the notation – and ◡, or ′ and ×). Consequently, it is word-accent that determines whether or not a word or sequence of words may stand in a certain part of the verse. Thus the word *Hellenic* may occupy the metrical unit represented by the notation ◡–◡ by virtue of the stress imparted to its second syllable in everyday pronunciation. In contrast, the rhythms of classical Greek metres are measured by the predictable alternation of one or more 'heavy' syllables with one or more 'light' syllables (defined below, and distinguished by the notation – and ◡), so that in the construction of Greek verse the factor of primary importance is not word-accent but syllabic 'weight'. Thus the word Ἑλλήνων, although accented in normal speech on the second syllable, consists for metrical purposes of three heavy syllables, and for this reason can only occupy the metrical sequence –––. Verse constructed upon this principle is conventionally designated *quantitative*: it should be emphasized that this term refers to the quantity (or 'weight') of syllables, and that throughout this account such quantity is described by the term 'heavy' and 'light' to distinguish it from the intrinsic length of vowels; unfortunately, both syllabic weight and vowel-length are still generally denoted by the same symbols, – and ◡.

(B) SYLLABIFICATION

A syllable containing a long vowel or diphthong is heavy (e.g. the first syllables of δῶρον and δοῦλος).

A syllable containing a short vowel is light if it ends with that vowel (e.g. the first syllable of θέρος), but heavy if it ends with a consonant (e.g. the first syllable of θέρμος).

---

[1] References by name only are to bibliography under (4) below.

To decide whether or not a short-vowelled syllable ends with a consonant (and thus to establish its quantity), the following rules should be observed:[1] (i) word-division should be disregarded; (ii) a single consonant between two vowels or diphthongs belongs to the succeeding syllable (thus λέγω → *lĕ–go*; πάθεν ἄλγεα → *pă–thĕ–nal-ge–a*); (iii) of two or more successive consonants, at least one belongs to the preceding syllable (thus λέμμα → *lēm–ma*; φίλτατε ξένων → *phĭl–ta–tēk–se–non*).

Note: the rough breathing does not count as a consonant (except in the case of ῥ, which normally makes the preceding syllable heavy; see West 15–16); ζ, ξ and ψ count as two (*ʒd*, *ks* and *ps*).

To (iii) there is an important exception. In the case of the combination of a plosive and a liquid or nasal consonant (πβφ, τδθ, κγχ followed by λ or ρ, or by μ or ν), the syllabic division may be made either between the consonants (e.g. πατρός → *pāt–ros*) or before them (e.g. *pă–tros*), resulting in *either* a heavy *or* a light preceding syllable. However, when two such consonants belong to different parts of a compound or to two different words, the division is always made between them, giving a heavy preceding syllable e.g. ἐκλέγω → *ēk–le–go* not *ĕ–kle–go*; ἐκ λόγων → *ēk–lo–gon*, not *ĕ–klo–gon*). Lastly, when, after a short final vowel, these consonants begin the next word, the division is nearly always (except in epic) made before them, giving a light preceding syllable (e.g. ὁ κλεινός → *hŏ–klei–nos*).

See further West 15–18.

(C) ACCENT

The accent of ancient Greek was basically one of pitch (i.e. 'tonal'). It had a negligible influence on the construction of recited verse (though it clearly affected the melody of the spoken line), and in lyric verse was completely subordinate to the requirements of the musical accompaniment. Whether there was also an element of stress in the accentuation of classical Greek (either related to the tonal accent or independent of it), and, if there was, whether it had any significant effect on the construction of recited verse, are matters of debate: see Allen (1973) 274–334, (1974) 120–5, 161–7 (with bibliography 161; see also M. L. West, *Gnomon* 48 (1976) 5–6).

A fundamental change in accentuation took place by gradual stages in later antiquity. By the latter part of the 4th c. A.D. the tonal accent had been replaced by a 'dynamic' one: i.e. the accented syllable was no longer differentiated by variation of pitch but by stress. This change was reflected in the structure of verse, which ceased to be quantitative and came to be based on the opposition of stressed and unstressed syllables; see Allen (1974) 119–20, West 162–4.

---

[1] The resulting division is practical only; for the difficulties involved in an absolute definition of the syllabic unit see Allen (1973), esp. 27–40.

(2) TECHNICAL TERMS

Anceps ('unfixed'): term used to describe a metrical element which may be represented by either a heavy or a light syllable. The final element of many Greek metres is regularly of this nature, but not in certain lyric metres in which there is metrical continuity (*synaphea*) between as well as within lines. In this account the convention is followed of marking final anceps as heavy.

Antistrophe: see *Strophe*.

Aphaeresis: see *Synecphonesis*.

Arsis: see *Thesis*.

Caesura ('cutting') and *diaeresis*: division between words within a verse is traditionally termed *caesura* when occurring inside a foot or metron, and *diaeresis* when occurring at the end of a foot or metron (but cf. M. L. West, *C.Q.* n.s.32 (1982) 292–7). The varied distribution of these plays an important part in avoiding monotony in the construction of verse; in particular, the caesura prevents a succession of words coextensive with the feet or metra of a line.

Catalexis: the truncation of the final syllable of one colon or metron in relation to another (e.g. the pherecratean is the catalectic form of the glyconic; see under (3b) below).

Contraction: the substitution of one heavy syllable for two light ones.

Correption: see *Elision*.

Crasis: see *Synecphonesis*.

Diaeresis: see *Caesura*.

Elision and *hiatus* ('cleft'): a short final vowel is generally suppressed or *elided* when immediately preceding another vowel. When it is not elided in these circumstances it is said to be in *hiatus*; by the process of *correption* (commonest in early epic and elegy) a long vowel or diphthong in hiatus (either within a word or at word-juncture) may be scanned short to make a light syllable. See further West 10–15.

Epode: (1) A two-line period in which a short line follows a longer line (e.g. Archilochus uses iambic trimeter plus dactylic hemiepes, hexameter plus iambic dimeter etc.). (2) See *Strophe*.

Prodelision: see *Synecphonesis*.

Responsion: see *Strophe*.

Resolution: the substitution of two light syllables for a heavy one.

Strophe: metrical structure used by the dramatists and lyric poets, made up of one or more periods and recurring in the same form either once (when the second strophe is called the *antistrophe*) or more often. *Triadic structure* denotes the scheme in which two strophes (strophe and antistrophe) are followed by a third of different metrical form (*epode*); the scheme may be repeated *ad lib.*

Synaphea: see *Anceps*.

Synecphonesis: the merging into one syllable either of two vowels within a word (e.g. θεός as a monosyllable) or of a final diphthong or long vowel (or ὁ, ἁ, τό, τά) and an initial vowel; when the second word begins with ε (generally ἐστι) this is known as *prodelision* or *aphaeresis* (e.g. ποῦ 'στιν). According to whether or not the synecphonesis is indicated in writing, it is sometimes termed *crasis* (e.g. καὶ ἐγώ→κἀγώ) or *synizesis* (e.g. ἢ οὐ as a monosyllable).

Synezesis: see *Synecphonesis*.

Thesis and *arsis*: terms used originally to designate those parts of Greek verse accompanied by the setting down and raising of the foot (i.e. the down beat and up beat). Since the terms are now generally used in the opposite of their original meanings, West recommends abandoning them and using substitutes such as *ictus* for the down beat.

Triadic structure: see *Strophe*.

Units of analysis:

Period: metrical structure, sometimes extending over many written lines (e.g. the Sapphic strophe), (i) whose boundaries do not cut into a word, (ii) within which there is metrical continuity (synaphea), and (iii) whose final element is anceps.

Colon: single metrical phrase of not more than about twelve syllables (e.g. the glyconic); generally cola are subdivisions of periods, though some may be used as short periods in themselves.

Metron: the rhythm of some verse is regular enough to be divided into a series of identical or equivalent units known as metra, and the period may be described according to the number of metra it contains (dimeter, trimeter, tetrameter, pentameter, hexameter = metron × 2, 3 etc.).

Foot: metrical unit which is identical with the metron in some types of verse (e.g. dactylic), a division of it in others (e.g. in iambic, trochaic and anapaestic verse there are two feet in each metron).

(3) COMMON METRES

For the sake of simplicity only the most basic characteristics of each metre are given here. For the numerous divergencies regarding anceps, resolution, position of caesura etc., see Dale, Raven and West. The notation used below is basically that of West: − = heavy, or final anceps; ∪ = light; × = anceps; ⌣ = usually heavy; ⌣ = usually light; ∪∪ = resolvable heavy; ∪∪ = contractible pair of lights).

(a) Stichic verse (constructed by repetition of same metrical line; chiefly intended for recitation or recitative, though some stichic metres were sung)

Iambic tetrameter catalectic:

$$× -∪-|\ ×\ -∪-|×\ -∪-|∪--$$

(very common metre of comedy, used mainly for entries and exits of chorus and in contest scenes)

Iambic trimeter:

$$\times -\cup- | \times -\cup- | \times -\cup-$$

(principal metre of dramatic dialogue; used by iambographers as an 'informal' metre for satirical and abusive poetry; used by Archilochus in alternation with a shorter line (hemiepes, iambic dimeter etc.) to form an epode)

Choliambus or scazon:

$$\times -\cup- | \times -\cup- | \times ---$$

(= iambic trimeter with heavy in place of final light; used for satirical and scurrilous poetry (Hipponax, Callimachus, Herodas), for philosophical invective (Timon) and for fable (Babrius))

Trochaic tetrameter catalectic:

$$-\cup-\times | -\cup-\times | -\cup-\times | -\cup-$$

(apparently (Arist. *Poet.* 1449a21) the original metre of tragic dialogue, but in extant tragedy (where it is associated with scenes of heightened tension) far less common than the iambic trimeter; very common in comedy, particularly in the epirrhemes of the parabasis (see pp. 358ff.))

Dactylic hexameter:

$$-\cup\cup | -\cup\cup | -\cup\cup | -\cup\cup | -\cup\cup | --$$

(regular metre for epic, pastoral and didactic poetry; also used for oracles, riddles, hymns and laments; occasionally found in drama; used by Archilochus in alternation with a shorter line (hemiepes, iambic dimeter etc.) to form an epode)

Dactylic 'pentameter' (properly = hemiepes × 2):

$$-\cup\cup-\cup\cup- | -\cup\cup-\cup\cup-$$

(almost invariably following the hexameter to form the elegiac couplet, which is regarded as an entity and hence as stichic (or 'distichic'); used for a wide variety of themes (sympotic, military, historical, descriptive, erotic) and the standard metre for epigram)   .

Anapaestic tetrameter catalectic:

$$\cup\cup-\cup\cup- | \cup\cup-\cup\cup- | \cup\cup-\cup\cup- | \cup\cup--$$

(dignified metre, very common in comic dialogue)

(b) Non-stichic verse (constructed by combination and expansion of different metrical cola and metra; chiefly intended for singing, either solo (monody) or choral, to the accompaniment of music and/or dance)

The principal units may be classified as follows (though n.b. units from different categories are frequently found in combination):

Iambic: based on metron ×‒◡‒; commonest sequences are of dimeters and trimeters; often combined with other cola.

Trochaic: based on metron ‒◡‒×; commonest sequences are of dimeters and trimeters; often combined with other cola.

lekythion:	‒◡‒◡̄|‒◡‒	(= catalectic dimeter)
ithyphallic:	‒◡‒◡|‒‒	
scazon:	‒◡‒×|‒◡‒×|‒◡‒×|‒‒‒	

Dactylic: based on metron ‒◡◡; commonest sequences are of from two to six metra; often combined with iambics and trochaics.

hemiepes:	‒◡◡‒◡◡‒

Dactylo-epitrite: based on the hemiepes (‒◡◡‒◡◡‒) and cretic (‒◡‒), which may be preceded, separated or followed by an anceps which is normally heavy (epitrite = ‒◡‒‒; for the terminology see West 70); particularly common in Pindar and Bacchylides.

Anapaestic: based on metron ◡◡‒◡◡‒; traditionally a marching metre, and particularly associated with parts of drama where movement takes place on stage; commonest sequence is of dimeters, often ending in a paroemiac (◡◡‒◡◡‒\|◡◡‒‒ = catalectic dimeter).

Dochmiac: based on metron ◡‒‒◡‒; associated with scenes of great excitement; very common in tragedy, rare in comedy except in parodies; commonest sequences are of metra and dimeters; often combined with iambics, cretics and bacchii (= ◡‒‒).

Cretic: based on metron ‒◡‒ or ‒◡◡◡ ('first paeon') or ◡◡◡‒ ('fourth paeon'); common in comedy, rare in tragedy; commonest sequences are of dimeters, trimeters and tetrameters.

Ionic: based on metron ◡◡‒‒ (minor ionic) or ‒‒◡◡ (major ionic); associated with cult, and with the exotic and barbaric; commonest sequences are of dimeters and trimeters; often found in combination with the anacreontic = ◡◡‒◡‒◡‒‒.

Aeolic: term sometimes used to include other cola of asymmetrical length, but here restricted to those containing as a nucleus the choriamb (‒◡◡‒):

glyconic:	××|‒◡◡‒|◡‒
pherecratean:	××|‒◡◡‒|‒
telesillean:	×|‒◡◡‒|◡‒
reizianum:	×|‒◡◡‒|‒
hipponactean:	××|‒◡◡‒|◡‒‒
hagesichorean (or enoplian):	×|‒◡◡‒|◡‒‒
aristophanean:	‒◡◡‒|◡‒‒
dodrans:	‒◡◡‒|◡‒
adonean:	‒◡◡‒|‒

Some Aeolic cola are used as periods in themselves; more often they are used to form longer periods, (i) by combination with other cola (Aeolic or otherwise), (ii) by the addition of prefix or suffix (e.g. addition of bacchius to glyconic gives the phalaecian = ×× |–∪∪–|∪–∪––), or (iii) by dactylic or choriambic expansion from within (e.g. choriambic expansion of glyconic gives the lesser asclepiad = ×× |–∪∪––∪∪–|∪–). Two common Aeolic strophes based on Aeolic cola are the Sapphic (= –∪–× |–∪∪–| ∪–– (three times) plus –∪∪–|– = adonean) and the Alcaic (= × –∪–× |–∪∪–|∪– (twice) plus × –∪–× –∪–– plus –∪∪–∪∪–|∪––); for different analyses of these strophes see West 32–3, Raven 77–9, *OCD* 683.

(4) BIBLIOGRAPHY

Allen, W. S., *Accent and rhythm* (Cambridge 1973)

idem, *Vox Graeca*, 2nd ed. (Cambridge 1974)

Dale, A. M., *The lyric metres of Greek drama*, 2nd ed. (Cambridge 1968)

eadem, *Metrical analyses of tragic choruses*, fasc. I, *B.I.C.S.* suppl. XXI.1 (1971); fasc. II, *B.I.C.S.* suppl. XXI.2 (1981)

Maas, P., *Greek metre*, tr. H. Lloyd-Jones (Oxford 1962)

Raven, D. S., *Greek metre*, 2nd ed. (London 1968)

Sommerstein, A. H., *The sound pattern of ancient Greek* (Oxford 1973)

West, M. L., *Greek metre* (Oxford 1982)

White, J. W., *The verse of Greek comedy* (London 1912)

Wilamowitz-Moellendorff, U. von, *Griechische Verskunst* (Berlin 1921)

WORKS CITED IN THE TEXT

Adams, C. D. (1917). 'Demosthenes' avoidance of breves', *C.Ph.* 12: 271–94.

Adkins, A. W. H. (1960). *Merit and responsibility*. Oxford.

Adrados, F. R. (1978). 'Propuestas para una nueva edición et interpretación de Estesícoro', *Emerita* 46: 251–99.

Albini, U. (1968). [Erode Attico] ΠΕΡΙ ΠΟΛΙΤΕΙΑΣ. Florence = Biblioteca nazionale, Serie dei classici greci e latini. Testi con commento filologico VIII.

Allen, T. W. (1912). *Homeri opera* v. OCT.

Allen, T. W., Halliday, W. R. and Sikes, E. E. (1936). *The Homeric Hymns*. Oxford.

Altheim, F. (1948/1950). *Literatur und Gesellschaft im ausgehenden Altertum*. Halle/Saale.

Anderson, G. (1976). *Studies in Lucian's comic fiction. Mnemosyne* suppl. XLIII. Leiden.

Andrewes, A. (1956). *The Greek tyrants*. London.

(1959). 'Thucydides on the causes of war', *C.Q.* n.s. 9: 223–39.

Arnim, H. von (1913). *Supplementum Euripideum*. Bonn.

Arnott, W. G. (1975). *Menander, Plautus, Terence. G. & R.*, New surveys in the classics IX.

(1979). *Menander* I. Loeb. London & Cambridge, Mass.

Arrighetti, G. (1973). *Epicuro opere*. 2nd ed. Turin.

Austin, M. M. (1970). *Greece and Egypt in the archaic age. P.C.Ph.S.* suppl. II.

Austin, R. G. (1948). *Quintiliani Institutionis Oratoriae Liber XII*. Oxford.

Babut, D. (1969). *Plutarque et le stoïcisme*. Paris.

Bacon, H. (1961). *Barbarians in Greek tragedy*. New Haven.

Badian, E. (1958). 'The eunuch Bagoas', *C.Q.* n.s. 8: 144–57.

Bailey, C. (1926). *Epicurus. The extant remains*. Oxford.

Baldry, H. C. (1953). 'The idler's paradise in Greek comedy', *G. & R.* 22: 49–60.

Barber, G. L. (1935). *The historian Ephorus*. Cambridge.

Barigazzi, A. (1966). *Favorino di Arelate*. Florence.

Barlow, S. A. (1971). *The imagery of Euripides: a study in the dramatic use of pictorial language*. London.

Barns, J. W. B. (1956). 'Egypt and the Greek romance', *Akten des VIII Kongress für Papyrologie*, 29–36. Vienna.

Barrett, W. S. (1964). *Euripides, Hippolytos*. Oxford.

Barwick, K. (1957). *Probleme der stoischen Sprachlehre und Rhetorik*. Abhand. zu Leipzig, Phil.-hist. Kl. XLIX 3. Berlin.

Bateman, J. J. (1962). 'Some aspects of Lysias' argumentation', *Phoenix* 16: 155–77.

Beck, F. A. G. (1975). *Album of Greek education*. Sydney.

Bernays, J. (1853). *Grundzüge der verlorenen Abhandlung des Aristoteles über Wirkung der Tragödie*. Breslau.

Berthiaume, G. (1982). 'Les rôles du *mágeiros*: étude sur la boucherie, la cuisine et le sacrifice dans la Grèce ancienne', *Mnemosyne* suppl. LXX.

Bhattacharya, V. (1943). The *Āgamaśāstra of Gauḍapāda*. Calcutta.

Bieber, M. (1961). *The history of the Greek and Roman theater*. 2nd ed. Princeton, N.J.

Björck, G. (1950). *Das alpha impurum und die tragische Kunstsprache*. Uppsala.

Blanchard, A. (1970). 'Recherches sur la composition des comédies de Ménandre', *R.E.G.* 83: 38–51.

Blass, F. (1887). *Die attische Beredsamkeit*. Leipzig.

Bloch, H. (1940). 'Historical literature of the fourth century', *H.S.C.Ph.* suppl. I, 302–76.

Blum, R. (1977). *Kallimachos und die Literaturverzeichnung bei den Griechen*. Frankfurt am Main.

Boegehold, A. L. (1963). 'Toward a study of Greek voting procedure', *Hesperia* 32: 366–74.

Bollack, J., Judet de la Combe, P. and Wismann, H. (1977). *La réplique de Jocaste*, *Cahiers de Philologie*, II, *avec un supplément*, Publications de l'Université de Lille III. Lille.

Bolling, G. M. (1956). 'Notes on Corinna', *A.J.Ph.* 77: 282–7.

Bonanno, M. G. (1972). *Studi su Cratete comico*. Padua.

Bonner, R. J. and Smith, G. (1930). *The administration of justice from Homer to Aristotle*. Chicago.

Bonner, W. S. (1939). *The literary treatises of Dionysius of Halicarnassus*. Cambridge.

Bosworth, A. B. (1970). 'Aristotle and Callisthenes', *Historia* 19: 407–13.

(1972). 'Arrian's literary development', *C.Q.* n.s. 22: 163–85.

Bowersock, G. W. (1969). *Greek sophists in the Roman empire*. Oxford.

(1971). Review of M. J. Fontana, *L'Athenaion Politeia*, *Gnomon* 43: 416–18.

(1973). 'Greek intellectuals and the Imperial Cult in the second century A.D.', *Le culte des souverains dans l'empire romain*, *Entretiens Hardt* 19: 179–212. Geneva.

Bowie, E. L. (1974). 'Greeks and their past in the Second Sophistic', in M. I. Finley, ed., *Studies in ancient society*, 166–209. London (= *Past and Present* 46 (1970) 3–41).

(1978). 'Apollonius of Tyana: tradition and reality', *ANRW* II.xvi.2 1652–99.

Bowra, C. M. (1964). *Pindar*. Oxford.

Bozanic, N. (1977). 'Structure, language and action in the comedies of Menander'. Diss. London.

Brillante, C., Cantilena, M. and Pavese, C. O. (1981). (edd.). *I poemi epici rapsodici non omerici e la tradizione orale*. Padua.

Bringmann, K. (1965). *Studien zu den politischen Ideen des Isokrates*. Hypomnemata XIV. Göttingen.

Brink, C. O. (1963). *Horace on poetry. Prolegomena to the literary epistles*. Cambridge.

Brown, A. L. (1978). 'Alkman, P. Oxy. 2443 Fr. 1 and 3213', *Z.P.E.* 32: 36–8.

Browning, R. (1960). 'Recentiores non deteriores', *B.I.C.S.* 7: 11–21.

(1969). *Medieval and modern Greek*. London. (2nd ed. Cambridge 1983.)

Bruns, I. (1896). *Das literarische Porträt der Griechen im fünften und vierten Jahrhundert vor Christi Geburt*. Berlin.

Brunt, P. A. (1973). 'Aspects of the social thought of Dio Chrysostom and of the Stoics', *P.C.Ph.S.* n.s. 19: 9–34.

(1974). 'Marcus Aurelius in his *Meditations*', *J.R.S.* 64: 1–20.

Bundy, E. L. (1962). *Studia pindarica*. Univ. of Calif. Studies in Classical Philology XVIII.1 and 2. Berkeley & Los Angeles.

Bürger, K. (1892). 'Zu Xenophon von Ephesus', *Hermes* 27: 36–67.

Burkert, W. (1961). 'Hellenistische Pseudopythagorica', *Philologus* 105: 16–43; 226–46.

(1977). 'Le mythe de Géryon: perspectives préhistoriques et tradition rituelle', in B. Gentili and G. Paioni (ed.), *Il Mito Greco, Atti del Convegno Internazionale* (Urbino 7–12 maggio 1973) 273–83. Rome.

Burnett, A. P. (1964). 'The race with the Pleiades', *C.Ph.* 59: 30–4.

Burnyeat, M. F. (1977). 'Socratic midwifery, Platonic inspiration', *B.I.C.S.* 24: 7–16.

Butcher, S. H. (1891). *Some aspects of the Greek genius*. London.

Cairns, F. (1972). *Generic composition in Greek and Roman poetry*. Edinburgh.

Calame, C. (1977). *Les choeurs de jeunes filles en Grèce archaïque*, II, *Alcman*. Rome.

Campbell, D. A. (1967). *Greek lyric poetry*. London & New York.

Cassio, A. C. (1977). *Aristofane, Banchettanti: i frammenti*. Pisa.

Chadwick, J. (1973). 'The Berezan lead letter', *P.C.Ph.S.* n.s. 19: 35–7.

(1976). *The Mycenaean world*. Cambridge.

Chalk, H. H. O. (1960). 'Eros and the Lesbian pastorals of Longus', *J.H.S.* 80: 32–51.

Charitonidis, S., Kahil, L. and Ginouvès, R. (1970). *Les mosaïques de la maison du Ménandre à Mytilène. Antike Kunst*, Beiheft 6. Bern.

Cherniss, H. (1935). *Aristotle's criticism of presocratic philosophy*. Baltimore.

Cochrane, C. N. (1929). *Thucydides and the science of history*. London.

Coffey, M. (1976). *Roman satire*. London.

Cole, T. (1967). *Democritus and the sources of Greek anthropology*. Cleveland, Ohio.

Coleman, R. G. G. (1972). 'The role of the Chorus in Sophocles' *Antigone*', *P.C.Ph.S.* n.s. 18: 4–27.

Conacher, D. J. (1967). *Euripidean drama*. Toronto.

Connor, W. R. (1967). 'History without heroes: Theopompus' treatment of Philip', *G.R.B.S.* 8: 133–54.

(1971). *The new politicians of fifth-century Athens*. Princeton, N.J.

Constantinides, E. (1969). 'Timocles *Ikarioi satyroi*: a reconsideration', *T.A.Ph.A.* 100: 49–61.

Cook, R. M. (1937). 'The date of the Hesiodic *Shield*', *C.Q.* 31: 204–14.

Cooper, L. (1922). *An Aristotelian theory of comedy*. New York.

Cornford, F. M. (1907). *Thucydides mythistoricus*. London.

Cousin, J. (1935). *Études sur Quintilien* I. Paris.

Cunningham, I. C. (1971). *Herodas*. Oxford.

Dain, A. (1963). 'La survie de Ménandre', *Maia* 15: 278–309.

Dale, A. M. (1954). *Euripides, Alcestis*. Oxford.

(1959). 'The Hoopoe's song', *C.R.* 9: 199–200 = *Collected papers* (1969) 135–6.

Davies, M. I. (1969). 'Thoughts on the Oresteia before Aischylos', *B.C.H.* 93: 214–60.

Davison, J. A. (1968). *From Archilochus to Pindar*. London. (= *Phoenix* 16 (1962) 219–22)

Dawe, R. D. (1972). 'Stesichorus, frag. 207 P', *P.C.Ph.S.* n.s. 18: 28–30.

Dawkins, R. M. (1929). (ed.). 'The Sanctuary of Artemis Orthia at Sparta', *J.H.S.* suppl. v. London.

Dawson, C. M. (1966). '*Spoudaiogeloion*: random thoughts on occasional poems', *Y.Cl.S.* 19: 39–76.

Deichgräber, K. (1933). 'Hymnische Elemente in der philosophischen Prosa der Vorsokratiker', *Philologus* 88: 347–61.

Delatte, A. (1922). *Essai sur la politique pythagoricienne*. Liège.

Delorme, J. (1960). *Gymnasion*. Paris.

Denniston, J. D. (1960). *Greek prose style*. Oxford.

Denniston, J. D. and Page, D. L. (1957). *Agamemnon*. Oxford.

Dessau, H. (1892). *Inscriptiones Latinae Selectae* I. Berlin.

Detienne, M. (1967). *Les maîtres de vérité dans la Grèce archaïque*. Paris.

Devereux, G. (1976). *Dreams in Greek tragedy*. Oxford.

Dickie, Matthew (1978). 'The argument and form of Simonides 542 *PMG*', *H.S.C.Ph.* 82: 21–33.

Diller, H. (1959). 'Stand und Aufgaben der Hippocrates-Forschung', *Jahrb. der Acad. der Wiss. und der Lit. Mainz* 271–87.

Dittenberger, W. (1915–24). *Sylloge Inscriptionum Graecarum*. 3rd ed. Leipzig.

Dodds, E. R. (1929). 'Euripides the irrationalist', *C.R.* 43: 97–104.

(1951). *The Greeks and the irrational*. Berkeley & Los Angeles.

(1960). *Euripides, Bacchae*. 2nd ed. Oxford.

Dohm, H. (1964). *Mageiros*. Zetemata XXXII. Munich.

Dörrie, H. (1973). 'Die griechischen Romane und das Christentum', *Philologus* 93: 273–6.

Dover, K. J. (1950). 'The chronology of Antiphon's speeches', *C.Q.* 44: 44–60.

(1954). 'Greek comedy', in *FYAT*.

(1964). 'The poetry of Archilochos', in *Entretiens Hardt* 10: 181–212. Geneva.

(1968*a*). *Aristophanes' Clouds*. Oxford.

(1968*b*). *Lysias and the corpus Lysiacum*. Berkeley.

(1972). *Aristophanic comedy*. London.

(1976). 'The freedom of the intellectual in Greek society', ΤΑΛΑΝΤΑ 7: 24–54.

Drews, R. (1973). *The Greek accounts of eastern history*. Washington, D.C.

Düring, I. (1957) *Aristotle in the ancient biographical tradition*. Stud. Graeca et Latina Gothoburgensia v. Göteborg.

(1966). *Aristoteles. Darstellung und Interpretation seines Denkens*. Heidelberg.

Dziatzko, K. (1899). 'Buchhandel', *RE* III 973–85.

Easterling, P. E. (1973). 'Presentation of character in Aeschylus', *G. & R.* 20: 3–19.

(1974). 'Alcman 58 and Simonides 37', *P.C.Ph.S.* n.s. 20: 37–43.

(1978). 'The second stasimon of *Antigone*', in R. D. Dawe, J. Diggle, P. E. Easterling, ed. *Dionysiaca*. Cambridge.

Ebert, J. (1978). 'Zu Corinnas Gedicht vom Wettstreit zwischen Helikon und Kithairon', *Z.P.E.* 30: 5–12.

Edmunds, L. (1975). *Chance and intelligence in Thucydides*. Cambridge, Mass.

Edwards, G. P. (1971). *The language of Hesiod*. Publications of the Philological Society XXII. Oxford.

Ehrenberg, V. L. (1951). *The people of Aristophanes*. 2nd ed. Oxford. (3rd ed. New York 1962.)

Eliot, T. S. (1926). Introduction to *Savonarola: a dramatic poem*, by Charlotte Eliot. London.

Else, G. F. (1965). *The origin and early form of Greek tragedy*. Cambridge, Mass.

Entretiens Hardt (1970). *Ménandre: Entretiens* 16. Geneva.

Erbse, H. (1969–83). *Scholia graeca in Homeri Iliadem*. 6 vols. Berlin.

Fehling, D. (1971). *Die Quellenangaben bei Herodot*. Berlin.

Fenik, B. C. (1968). *Typical battle scenes in the Iliad*. *Hermes* Einzelschriften XXI.

Ferguson, J. (1975). *Utopias of the classical world*. Ithaca.

Finley, J. H. jr. (1938). 'Euripides and Thucydides', *H.S.C.Ph.* 49: 23–68.

(1940). 'The unity of Thucydides' history', *H.S.C.Ph.* Suppl. Vol. I. 255–97.

(1942). *Thucydides*. Cambridge, Mass.

Finley, M. I. (1956). *The world of Odysseus*. London. (2nd ed. London 1977.)

Fornara, C. W. (1971*a*). 'Evidence for the date of Herodotus' publication', *J.H.S.* 91: 25–34.

(1971*b*). *Herodotus: an interpretative essay*. Oxford.

Forrest, W. G. (1968). *A history of Sparta, 950–192 B.C.* London.

Fraenkel, E. (1922). *Plauteinisches im Plautus*. Berlin. (Revised as *Elementi plautini in Plauto*, Florence 1960.)

(1950). 'Some notes on the Hoopoe's song', *Eranos* 48: 75–84 = *Kleine Beiträge* I (1964) 453–61.

Fränkel, H. (1961). 'Schrullen in den Scholien zu Pindars Nemeen 7 und Olympien 3', *Hermes* 83: 385–97.

(1962). *Dichtung und Philosophie des frühen Griechentums*. 2nd ed. (Engl. tr. as Fränkel 1975.)

(1975). *Early Greek poetry and philosophy*. New York & London. (Tr. of Fränkel 1962.)

Fraser, P. M. (1972). *Ptolemaic Alexandria*. 3 vols. Oxford.

Frede, M. (1974). *Die stoische Logik*. Göttingen.

Fritz, K. von (1967). *Griechische Geschichtsschreibung* I. Berlin.

Furley, D. J. (1973). 'Notes on Parmenides', in G. Vlastos, ed., *Exegesis and argument: Studies in Greek philosophy presented to Gregory Vlastos*, 1–15. Assen.

Galinsky, G. K. (1969). *Aeneas, Sicily, and Rome*. Princeton, N.J.

Garrod, H. W. (1920). 'The hyporcheme of Pratinas', *C.R.* 34: 129–36.

Gärtner, H. (1967). 'Xenophon von Ephesos', *RE* IXA.2 2055–89.

Garvie, A. F. (1965). 'A note on the deity of Alcman's Partheneion', *C.Q.* n.s. 15: 185–7.

(1969). *Aeschylus' Supplices: play and trilogy*. Cambridge.

Garzya, A. (1954). *Alcmane. I frammenti*. Naples.

Gelzer, T. (1956). 'Aristophanes und sein Sokrates', *M.H.* 13: 65–93.

(1960). *Der epirrhematische Agon bei Aristophanes*. Zetemata XXIII. Munich.

(1976). 'Some aspects of Aristophanes' dramatic art in the *Birds*', *B.I.C.S.* 23: 1–14.

Gentili, B. (1958). *Bacchilide. Studi*. Urbino.

(1971). 'I frr. 39 e 40 di Alcmane e la poetica della mimesi nella cultura greca arcaica', in *Studi filologici e storici in onore de V. de Falco*, 59–67. Naples.

(1972). 'Lirica greca arcaica e tardo-arcaica', in *Introduzione allo studio della cultura classica*. Milan.

(1976). Review of D. Page, *PMG*, *LGS*, *SLG*, in *Gnomon* 48: 740–51.

Gerber, D. E. (1967/8). 'A survey of publications on Greek lyric poetry since 1952, III', *C.W.* 61: 373–85.

(1970). *Euterpe, an anthology of early Greek lyric and iambic poetry*. Amsterdam.

(1975/6). 'Studies in Greek lyric poetry: 1967–75', *C.W.* 70: 66–154.

Ghiron-Bistagne, P. (1976). *Recherches sur les acteurs dans la Grèce antique*. Paris.

Giannini, A. (1960). 'La figura del cuoco nella commedia greca', *Acme* 13: 135–216.

Gianotti, G. F. (1975). *Per una poetica pindarica*. Torino.

(1978). 'Le Pleiadi di Alcmane', *R.F.I.C.* 106: 257–71.

Gigante, M. (1969). *Ricerche Filodemee*. Naples.

Goldstein, J. A. (1968). *The letters of Demosthenes*. New York.

Gomme, A. W. (1938). 'Aristophanes and politics', *C.R.* 52: 97–119. (Repr. in D. A. Campbell, ed., *More essays in Greek history and literature* (Oxford 1962).)

(1954a). 'Who was "Kratippos"?', *C.Q.* n.s. 4: 53–5.

(1954b). *The Greek attitude to poetry and history*. Berkeley & Los Angeles.

(1956). *A historical commentary on Thucydides* II. Oxford. (See also Gomme *et al.* (1945–70).)

(1957). 'Interpretations of some poems of Alkaios and Sappho', *J.H.S.* 77: 255–66.

Gomme, A. W. *et al.* (1945–70). *A historical commentary on Thucydides*. Oxford.

Gomme, A. W. and Sandbach, F. H. (1973). *Menander: a commentary*. Oxford.

Gomperz, H. (1912). *Sophistik und Rhetorik*. Leipzig.

Gostoli, A. (1978). 'Some aspects of the Theban myth in the Lille Stesichorus', *G.R.B.S.* 19: 23–7.

Gottschalk, H. B. (1980). *Heraclides of Pontus*. Oxford.

Grant, M. (1978). *History of Rome*. New York.

Griffin, J. (1977). 'The Epic Cycle and the uniqueness of Homer'. *J.H.S.* 97: 39–53.
(1980). *Homer on life and death*. Oxford.

Griffith, J. G. (1968). 'Early lyric poetry', in *FYAT*, ch. 2. Oxford.

Griffith, M. (1977). *The authenticity of Prometheus Bound*. Cambridge.

Griffiths, A. (1972). 'Alcman's Partheneion: The morning after the night before',
Q.U.C.C. 14: 7–30.

Grube, G. M. A. (1965). *The Greek and Roman critics*. London.

Guarducci, M. (1974). *Epigrafia Greca* III. Rome.

Guillon, P. (1958). 'Corinne et les oracles béotiens: la consultation d'Asopos', *B.C.H.*
82: 47–60.

Guthrie, W. K. C. (1957). 'Aristotle as a historian of philosophy', *J.H.S.* 77: 35–41.
(1962–80). *A history of Greek philosophy*. 6 vols. Cambridge.
(1962). *A history of Greek philosophy* I. Cambridge.
(1965). *A history of Greek philosophy* II. Cambridge.
(1969). *A history of Greek philosophy* III. Cambridge.

Habicht, C. (1969). *Die Inschriften des Asklepieions: Altertümer von Pergamon* VIII 3.
Berlin.

Hagedorn, D. (1964). *Zur Ideenlehre des Hermogenes*. Göttingen.

Halporn, J. W. (1972). 'Agido, Hagesichora, and the chorus (Alcman 1.27ff. PMG)',
Antidosis, Festschrift für Walter Kraus, *W.S.* Beiheft V 125–38.

Hamilton, R. (1974). *Epinikion*. The Hague.

Hamm, E.-M. (1958). *Grammatik zu Sappho und Alkaios*. Berlin.

Händel, P. (1963). *Formen und Darstellungen in der aristophanischen Komödie*. Heidelberg.

Handley, E. W. (1953). 'XOPOY in the *Plutus*', *C.Q.* n.s. 3: 55–61.
(1959). Review of H. J. Newiger, *Metapher und Allegorie*, in *J.H.S.* 79: 166–7.
(1965 a). *The Dyskolos of Menander*. London & Cambridge, Mass.
(1965 b). 'Notes on the *Sikyonios* of Menander', *B.I.C.S.* 12: 38–62.
(1968). *Menander and Plautus: a study in comparison*. (Inaugural lecture) London.
(1969). 'Notes on the *Theophoroumene* of Menander', *B.I.C.S.* 16: 88–101.
(1973). 'The poet inspired?', *J.H.S.* 93: 104–8.
(1975 a). 'Plautus and his public: some thoughts on New Comedy in Latin',
Dioniso 46: 117–32.
(1975 b). 'Some new fragments of Greek comedy', *Proc. xiv int. congr. papyrologists, 1974*, 133–48.
(1977). '*P. Oxy.* 678: a fragment of New Comedy', *B.I.C.S.* 24: 132–4.
(1979). 'Recent papyrus finds: Menander', *B.I.C.S.* 26: 81–7.
(1982 a). '*P. Oxy.* 2806: a fragment of Cratinus?', *B.I.C.S.* 29: 109–17.
(1982 b). 'Aristophanes' rivals', *Proc. Class. Ass.* 79: 23–5.

Handley, E. W. and Rea, J. R. (1957). *The Telephus of Euripides. B.I.C.S.* suppl. v.

Harrison, E. B. (1976). 'The Portland Vase: thinking it over', in L. Bonfante and H.
von Heintze, edd., *Essays in memoriam Otto J. Brendel*. Mainz.

Harvey, F. D. (1964). 'The use of written documents in the business life of classical Athens', *Pegasus* 2: 4–14.

(1966). 'Literacy in the Athenian democracy', *R.E.G.* 79: 585–635.

(1967). 'Oxyrhynchus Papyrus 2390 and early Spartan history', *J.H.S.* 93: 62–73.

(1978). 'Greeks and Romans learn to write', in *Communication arts in the ancient world*, 63–78. New York.

Haslam, M. W. (1974). 'Stesichorean meter', *Q.U.C.C.* 17: 9–57.

(1978). 'The versification of the new Stesichorus (P. Lille 76 abc)', *G.R.B.S.* 19: 29–57.

Havelock, E. (1963). *Preface to Plato*. Cambridge, Mass.

(1976). *Origins of Western literacy*. Toronto.

Heidel, W. A. (1935). 'Hecataeus and the Egyptian priests in Herodotus, Book II', *Memoirs of the Am. Academy of Arts and Sciences* XVIII.2 53–124.

Henderson, J. (1975). *The maculate muse: obscene language in Attic comedy*. New Haven.

Herington, C. J. (1970). *The author of the Prometheus Bound*. Austin, Texas.

Heubeck, A. (1979). *Schrift* in *Archaeologica Homerica* III, ch. X. Göttingen.

Hirmer, M. and Arias, P. E. (1962). *A history of Greek vase painting*. London.

Hodgart, M. (1969). *Satire*. London.

Hofmann, H. (1976). *Mythos und Komödie*. Spudasmata XXX. Hildesheim.

Hofmann, W. and Wartenberg, G. (1973). 'Der Bramarbas in der antiken Komödie', *Abh. der Akad. der Wiss. der DDR*, 1973.2.

Horrocks, G. C. (1981). *Space and time in Homer*. New York.

House, H. (1956). *Aristotle's Poetics*. London.

Hunter, R. L. (1979). 'The comic chorus in the fourth century', *Z.P.E.* 36: 23–38.

Husman, H. (1955). 'Zu Metrik und Rhythmik des Mesomedes', *Hermes* 83: 231–6.

Hussey, E. (1972). *The Presocratics*. London.

Huxley, G. L. (1962). *Early Sparta*. London.

(1964). 'Studies in early Greek poets II: Alcman's *Kolymbōsai*', *G.R.B.S.* 5: 26–8.

Immerwahr, H. R. (1964). 'Book rolls on Attic vases', in *Classical, medieval and renaissance studies in honor of Berthold Louis Ullman* I. Rome.

(1966). *Form and thought in Herodotus*. Cleveland.

(1973). 'More book rolls on Attic vases', *Antike Kunst* XVI.2 143–7.

Irigoin, J. (1962). 'Survie et renouveau de la littérature antique à Constantinople', *C.C.M.* 5: 287–302.

Jacoby, F. (1912). 'Hekataios', *RE* VII 2666–2769. (Reprinted in Jacoby (1956) 185–237.)

(1913). 'Herodotos', *RE* suppl. II 247ff. Stuttgart. (Reprinted in Jacoby (1956) 7–164.)

(1941). 'The date of Archilochus', *C.Q.* 35: 97–109.

(1949). *Atthis: the local chronicles of ancient Athens*. Oxford.

(1956). *Griechische Historiker*. Stuttgart.

Jacques, J. M. (1960). 'Sur un acrostiche d'Aratos (*Phén.* 783–7)', *Revue des Études Anciennes* 62: 48–61.

Jaeger, W. (1923). *Aristoteles, Grundlegung einer Geschichte seiner Entwicklung*. Berlin. 2nd ed. tr. R. Robinson (1948). *Aristotle: fundamentals of the history of his development*. Oxford.

(1938). *Demosthenes. The origin and growth of his policy*. Berkeley.

(1939). *Paideia: the ideals of Greek culture* I, tr. G. Highet. Oxford.

(1945). *Paideia: the ideals of Greek culture* III, tr. G. Highet. Oxford.

(1947). *The theology of the early Greek philosophers*. Oxford.

Janáček, K. (1948). *Prolegomena to Sextus Empiricus*. Olomouc.

Janko, R. (1982). *Homer, Hesiod, and the Hymns*. Cambridge.

Janni, P. (1965, 1970). *La cultura di Sparta arcaica. Ricerche* I, II. Rome.

Jebb, R. C. (1893). *The Attic orators*. London.

Jeffery, L. H. (1961). *The local scripts of archaic Greece*. Oxford.

Jensen, C. (1923). (ed.) *Philodemos Über die Gedichte Buch 5*. Berlin.

Jones, A. H. M. (1940). *The Greek city from Alexander to Justinian*. Oxford.

(1963). 'The Greeks under the Roman empire', *D.O.P.* 17: 3–19.

Jones, J. (1962). *On Aristotle and Greek tragedy*. London.

Jones, W. H. S. (1923). *Hippocrates I*. Loeb. London & Cambridge, Mass.

Kahn, C. H. (1960). *Anaximander and the origins of Greek cosmology*. New York.

Kaiser, M. (1969). 'Herodots Begegnung mit Ägypten', in Morenz, S. *Die Begegnung Europas mit Ägypten*, 243–65. Zurich.

Kapsomenos, S. G. (1964). 'The Orphic papyrus roll of Thessalonica', *Bulletin of the American Society of Papyrologists* 2: 3–14.

Kennedy, G. (1959). 'Focusing of arguments in Greek deliberative oratory', *T.A.Ph.A.* 90: 131–8.

(1963). *The art of persuasion in Greece*. Princeton, N.J.

Kerferd, G. B. (1981). *The sophistic movement*. Cambridge.

Kern, O. (1922). *Orphicorum fragmenta*. Berlin.

Keydell, R. (1952). 'Bemerkungen zu griechischen Epigrammen', *Hermes* 80: 499–500.

Kirk, G. S. (1962). *The songs of Homer*. Cambridge.

(1976). *Homer and the oral tradition*. Cambridge.

(1977). In *Archilochos* by Michael Ayrton. London.

Kirk, G. S. and Raven, J. (1957). *The Presocratic philosophers*. Cambridge.

Kirkwood, G. M. (1953/4). 'A survey of recent publications concerning Classical Greek lyric poetry', *C.W.* 47: 51–4.

(1974). *Early Greek monody*. Cornell Studies in Classical Philology XXXVII. Ithaca & London.

Kleberg, T. (1967). *Buchhandel und Verlagswesen in der Antike*. Darmstadt.

Knox, B. M. W. (1952). 'The lion in the house', *C.Ph.* 47: 17–25. (= *Word and action* (Baltimore 1979) 27–38.)

(1964). *The heroic temper*. Berkeley & Los Angeles.

(1968). 'Silent reading in antiquity', *G.R.B.S.* 9.4: 421–35.

(1976). 'Euripides' Medea', *Y.Cl.S.* 25: 193–206.

Koenen, L. (1979). *The Cairo codex of Menander (P. Cair. J 43277)*. A photographic edition prepared under the supervision of Henry Riad and Abd el-Kadr Selim, with a preface by L. Koenen. London, Institute of Classical Studies.

Köhnken, A. (1971). *Die Funktion des Mythos bei Pindar*. Berlin & New York.

Körte, A. (1893). 'Archäologische Studien zur alten Komödie', *J.D.A.I.* 8: 61–93.

Krüger, K. W. (1832). *Untersuchungen über das Leben des Thukydides*. Berlin.

Kühn, J. H. (1956). 'System- und Methodenprobleme im Corpus Hippocraticum', *Hermes* Einzelschriften XVI.

Kühne, H. J. (1969). 'Appians historiographische Leistung', *W. Z. Rostock* 18: 345–77.

Labarbe, J. (1948). *L'Homère de Platon* (= Bibliothèque de la Faculté de Philos. et Lettres de l'Université de Liège, fasc. CXVII).

De Lacy, P. H. (1939). 'The Epicurean analysis of language', *A.J.Ph.* 60: 85–92.

Lang, M. (1976). *The Athenian Agora* XXI. *Graffiti and dipinti*. Princeton. B1, B2, C5.

Lasserre, F. and Bonnard, A. (1958). *Archiloque, Fragments*. Paris.

Lattimore, R. (1958). *The poetry of Greek tragedy*. Baltimore.

Lavency, M. (1964). *Aspects de la logographie judiciaire attique*. Louvain.

Lee, H. D. P. (1948). 'Place-names and the date of Aristotle's biological works', *C.Q.* 42: 61–7.

Lefèvre, E. (1979). 'Menander', in G. A. Seeck, ed., *Das griechische Drama*, 307–53. Darmstadt.

Lefkowitz, M. R. (1968). 'Bacchylides' *Ode* 5: imitation and originality', *H.S.C.Ph.* 73: 45–96.

(1975 a). 'The influential fictions in the scholia to Pindar's *Pythian* 8', *C.Ph.* 70: 173–85.

(1975 b). 'Pindar's Lives', in *Classica et Iberica*, a Festschrift in Honor of the Rev. J. M. F. Marique, S.J., ed. P. T. Brannan, S.J., Institute for Early Christian Iberian Studies (Worcester, Mass.), 71–93.

(1978). 'The poet as hero: fifth-century autobiography and subsequent biographical fiction', *C.Q.* n.s. 28: 459–69.

Lemerle, P. (1969). 'Elèves et professeurs à Constantinople au Xe siècle', *C.R.A.I.* 576–87.

(1971). *Le premier humanisme byzantin*. Paris.

Leo, F. (1895). *Plautinische Forschungen*. 2nd ed. 1912. Berlin.

Levi, P. (1977). Review of O. Strid, *Über Sprache und Stil des Periegeten Pausanias*, in *C.R.* 27: 178–80.

Lewis, N. (1974). *Papyrus in classical antiquity*. Oxford.

Lloyd-Jones, H. (1956). 'Zeus in Aeschylus', *J.H.S.* 76: 55–67.

(1957). *Aeschylus* II. 2nd ed. Loeb.

(1966). 'Problems of early Greek poetry', in *Estudios sobre la tragedia griega*, *Cuadernos de la Fundación Pastor* XIII 11–33.

(1971). *The justice of Zeus*. Berkeley & Los Angeles.

(1973). 'Modern interpretation of Pindar: the Second Pythian and Seventh Nemean Odes', *J.H.S.* 93: 109–37.

(1975). *Females of the species: Semonides on women*. London.

Lobel, E. (1925). Σαπφοῦς μέλη. Oxford.

(1927). Ἀλκαίου μέλη. Oxford.

Long, A. A. (1968). *Language and thought in Sophocles*. London.

(1971). 'Aisthesis, prolepsis and linguistic theory in Epicurus', *B.I.C.S.* 18: 114–33.

(1974). *Hellenistic philosophy*. London.

(1976). 'Heraclitus and Stoicism', *Philosophia* 5–6: 134–56.

Lucas, D. W. (1968). *Aristotle, Poetics*. Oxford.

Luck, G. (1967). Review of Gow–Page, *Hellenistic Epigrams*, *G.G.A.* 219 (1967) 23–61.

Ludwig, W. (1970). 'Die plautinische Cistellaria und das Verhältnis von Gott und Handlung bei Menander', in *Entretiens Hardt* 16: 43–110.

Luppe, W. (1980). *Literarische Texte: Drama. Archiv für Papyrusforschung* 27: 233–50.

Luschnat, O. (1971). 'Thukydides', *RE* suppl. XII 1085–1354.

(1974). 'Thukydides (Nachträge)', *RE* suppl. XIV.

Lynch, J. P. (1972). *Aristotle's school*. Berkeley, Los Angeles, London.

Maass, E. (1898). *Commentariorum in Aratum reliquiae*. Berlin.

MacDowell, D. (1962). *Andocides. On the mysteries*. Oxford.

(1971). *Aristophanes, Wasps*. Oxford.

McKay, K. J. (1974). 'Alkman Fr. 107 Page', *Mnemosyne* 4.27: 413–14.

Maehler, H. (1976). 'Der Metiochos-Parthenope-Roman', *Z.P.E.* 23: 1–20.

(1980). 'A new method of dismounting papyrus cartonnage', *B.I.C.S.* 27: 120–2.

Marrou, H.-I. (1965). *Histoire de l'éducation dans l'antiquité*. 6th ed. Paris.

Marzullo, B. (1964). 'Il primo Partenio di Alcmane', *Philologus* 108: 174–210.

Mates, B. (1953). *Stoic logic*. Berkeley & Los Angeles.

Mathieu, G. (1948). *Démosthène. L'homme et l'oeuvre*. Paris.

Mazon, P. (1904). *Essai sur la composition des comédies d'Aristophane*. Paris.

(1948). (ed.) *Introduction à l'Iliade*. Budé. Paris.

Meiggs, R. and Lewis, D. M. (1969). *A selection of Greek historical inscriptions to the end of the fifth century B.C.* Oxford.

Meillier, C. (1976). 'Callimaque (P.L. 76 d, 78 abc, 82, 84, 111 c) Stésichore (?) (P.L. 76 abc)', *Cahiers de recherche de l'Institut de Papyrologie et d'Égyptologie de l'Université de Lille* IV: 255-360.

Mensching, E. (1963). *Favorin von Arelate. Der erste Teil der fragmente*. Berlin.

Merkelbach, R. (1962). *Roman und Mysterium in der Antike*. Munich & Berlin.

(1974). 'Epilog des einen der Herausgeber', in R. Merkelbach and M. West, 'Ein Archilochos-Papyrus', *Z.P.E.* 14: 97–113.

Mette, H. J. (1959). *Die Fragmente der Tragödien des Aischylos*. Berlin.

Millar, F. (1977). *The emperor in the Roman world*. London.

Milne, J. G. (1908). 'Relics of Graeco-Egyptian schools', *J.H.S.* 28: 121–32.

Misch, G. (1950). *History of autobiography in antiquity*. London.

Momigliano, A. D. (1966). 'The place of Herodotus in the history of historiography', in *Studies in historiography*. London. 127ff.

(1971). *The development of Greek biography*. Cambridge, Mass.

(1975). *Alien wisdom*. Cambridge.

Moraux, P. (1973). *Der Aristotelismus bei den Griechen* I. Berlin, New York.

Morrison, J. S. (1961). 'Antiphon', *P.C.Ph.S.* n.s. 7: 49–58.

Mourelatos, A. P. D. (1970). *The route of Parmenides: a study of word, image, and argument in the fragments*. New Haven & London.

Murray, G. (1933). *Aristophanes: a study*. Oxford.

Muscarella, O. W. (1974). *Ancient art: The Norbert Schimmel Collection*. Mainz.

Mussche, H. F. and others (1965). *Thorikos* III. Brussels.

Myres, J. L. (1953). *Herodotus father of history*. Oxford.

Nagy, G. (1973). 'On the death of Actaeon', *H.S.C.Ph.* 77: 179–80.

Navarre, O. (1900). *Essai sur la rhétorique grecque avant Aristote*. Paris.

Nenci, G. (1954). *Hecataei Milesii fragmenta*. Florence.

Nestle, W. (1901). *Euripides. Der Dichter der griechischen Aufklärung*. Stuttgart.

Newiger, H.-J. (1957). *Metapher und Allegorie: Studien zu Aristophanes*. Zetemata XVI. Munich.

Norman, A. F. (1960). 'The book trade in fourth-century Antioch', *J.H.S.* 80: 122–6.

Norwood, G. (1931). *Greek comedy*. London.

(1945). *Pindar*. Berkeley & Los Angeles.

Nutton, V. (1972). 'Galen and medical autobiography', *P.C.Ph.S.* n.s. 18: 50–62.

Oeri, H. G. (1948). *Der Typ des komischen Alten: seine Nachwirkungen und seine Herkunft*. Basel.

Oertel, F. (1970). *Herodots Ägyptischer Logos und die Glaubwürdigkeit Herodots*. Bonn.

Ohly, K. (1928). *Stichometrische Untersuchungen = Zentralblatt für Bibliothekswesen*, Beiheft 61. Leipzig.

Owen, A. S. (1936). 'The date of the Electra of Sophocles', in *Greek poetry and life, Essays presented to Gilbert Murray*, ed. C. Bailey and others. Oxford.

Owen, G. E. L. (1960). 'Eleatic questions', *C.Q.* n.s. 10: 84–102; repr. with additional notes in D. J. Furley and R. E. Allen, eds. (1975) *Studies in presocratic philosophy* II 48–81. London.

Page, D. L. (1942). *Greek literary papyri*. London.

(1951a). *Alcman: The Partheneion*. Oxford.

(1951b). 'Simonidea', *J.H.S.* 71: 133–42.

(1951c). *A new chapter in the history of Greek tragedy*. Cambridge.

(1953). 'Thucydides' description of the great plague at Athens', *C.Q.* n.s. 3: 97–115.

(1955). *Sappho and Alcaeus*. Oxford.

(1956). 'Greek verses from the eighth century B.C.', *C.R.* n.s. 6: 95–7.

(1959). *History and the Homeric Iliad*. Berkeley & Los Angeles.

(1964). 'Archilochus and the oral tradition', in *Entretiens Hardt* 10: 117–63. Geneva.

(1973*a*). 'Stesichorus: The Geryoneis', *J.H.S.* 93: 136–54.

(1973*b*). 'Stesichorus: The "Sack of Troy" and "The Wooden Horse" (P. Oxy. 2169 and 2803)', *P.C.Ph.S.* n.s. 19: 47–65.

Panofsky, D. and E. (1962). *Pandora's box.* 2nd ed. Princeton, N. J.

Papanikolaou, A. D. (1973). *Chariton-Studien.* Hypomnemata XXXVII. Göttingen.

Parry, A. (1971). (ed.) *The making of Homeric verse* (collected works of Milman Parry with an introduction by Adam Parry). Oxford.

(1981). *'Logos' and 'Ergon' in Thucydides.* New York.

Parsons, P. J. (1977). 'The Lille "Stesichorus"', *Z.P.E.* 26: 7–36.

Patzer, H. (1937). *Das Problem der Geschichtsschreibung des Thukydides und die thukydideische Frage.* Berlin.

Pavese, C. O. (1967). 'Alcmane, il Partenio del Louvre', *Q.U.C.C.* 4: 113–33.

(1972). *Tradizione e generi poetici della Grecia arcaica.* Rome.

Payne, H. (1931). *Necrocorinthia.* Oxford.

Pearson, L. (1939). *Early Ionian historians.* Oxford.

(1952). 'Prophasis and aitia', *T.A.Ph.A.* 83: 205–23.

(1964). 'The development of Demosthenes as a political orator', *Phoenix* 18:95–109.

(1966). 'Apollodorus, the eleventh Attic orator', *The classical tradition. Literary and historical studies in honor of Harry Caplan*, pp. 347–59. Ithaca.

(1972). 'Prophasis: a clarification', *T.A.Ph.A.* 103: 381–94.

Pečirka, J. (1963). 'Aristophanes' Ekklesiazusen und die Utopien in der Krise der Polis', *Wissenschaftliche Zeitschrift der Humboldt Universität, Berlin: Gesellschaft. u. sprach.* 12: 215–19.

(1976). 'The crisis of the Athenian Polis in the fourth century', *Eirene* 14: 5–29.

Penwill, J. L. (1974). 'Alcman's Cosmogony', *Apeiron* 8: 13–39.

Perrotta, G. and Gentili, B. (1965). *Polinnia.* Messina & Florence.

Perry, B. E. (1952). *Aesopica* I. Urbana, Illinois.

(1965). *Babrius and Phaedrus.* Loeb. London & Cambridge, Mass.

(1967). *The ancient romances. A literary-historical account of their origins.* Berkeley & Los Angeles.

Petri, R. (1963). *Ueber den Roman des Chariton.* Meisenheim am Glan.

Pfohl, G. (1968). (ed.) *Das Alphabet.* Wege der Forschung LXXXVIII. Darmstadt.

Philippson, R. (1932). 'Sokrates' Dialektik in der Wolken', *Rh.M.* 81: 30–8.

Pickard-Cambridge, A. W. (1946). *The theatre of Dionysus at Athens.* Oxford.

Podlecki, A. J. (1971). 'Stesichoreia', *Athenaeum* 49: 313–27.

Pohlenz, M. (1933). 'To prepon. Ein Beitrag zur Geschichte des griechischen Geistes', *N.G.G.* 1933: 53–92.

(1937). *Herodot der erste Geschichtsschreiber des Abendlandes.* Berlin.

Pollitt, J. J. (1974). *The ancient Greek view of art: criticism, history and terminology.* New Haven & London.

Pouilloux, J. (1964). 'Archiloque et Thasos: histoire et poésie', in *Entretiens Hardt* 10: 1–27. Geneva.

Powell, J. E. (1939). *The history of Herodotus.* Cambridge.

Privitera, G. A. (1965). *Laso di Ermione nella cultura ateniese e nella tradizione storiografica.* Rome.

Puelma, M. (1977). 'Die Selbstbeschreibung des Chores in Alkmans grossem Partheneion-Fragment', *M.H.* 34: 1–55.

Radermacher, L. (1951). 'Artium scriptores. Reste der voraristotelischen Rhetorik', *S.A.W.W.* 227: 3.

Rau, P. (1967). *Paratragodia: Untersuchung einer dramatischen Form des Aristophanes.* Zetemata XLV. Munich.

Rawlings, H. R. (1981). *The structure of Thucydides' history.* Princeton, N.J.

Reardon, B. P. (1969). 'The Greek novel', *Phoenix* 23: 55–73.

(1971). *Courants littéraires grecs des IIe and IIIe siècles après J.C.* Paris.

Reeve, M. D. (1971). 'Hiatus in the Greek novelists', *C.Q.* n.s. 21: 514–39.

Reinhardt, K. (1916). *Parmenides und die Geschichte der griechischen Philosophie.* Bonn.

(1947). *Sophokles.* 3rd ed. Frankfurt am Main.

Reynolds, L. D. and Wilson, N. G. (1974). *Scribes and scholars,* 2nd ed. Oxford.

Richardson, N. J. (1974). *The Homeric Hymn to Demeter.* Oxford.

Robert, C. (1911). *Die Masken der neueren attischen Komödie.* Hallisches Winckelmannsprogr. XXV. Halle a. S.

Robert, L. (1935). 'Notes d'épigraphie hellénistique', *B.C.H.* 59: 421–5 (= *Opera minora selecta* I (1969) 178–82. Amsterdam).

(1968). 'De Delphes à l'Oxus. Inscriptions grecques nouvelles de la Bactriane', *C.R.A.I.* 421–57.

Roberts, C. H. (1953). 'Literature and society in the papyri', *M.H.* 10: 264–79.

(1954). 'The codex', *P.B.A.* 40: 169–204.

(1970). 'Books in the Graeco-Roman world and in the New Testament', *Cambridge History of the Bible* I, 48–66. Cambridge.

Roberts, C. H. and Skeat, T. C. (1983). *The birth of the codex.* British Academy publications. Oxford.

Robertson, M. (1969). 'Geryoneis: Stesichorus and the vase-painters', *C.Q.* n.s. 19: 207–21.

de Romilly, J. (1956a). *Histoire et raison chez Thucydide.* Paris.

(1956b). 'L'utilité de l'histoire selon Thucydide', in *Entretiens Hardt* 4. Geneva.

(1962). 'Le pseudo-Xénophon et Thucydide', *Revue de Philologie* 36: 225–41.

(1963). *Thucydides and Athenian imperialism,* tr. P. Thody. Oxford.

Ronnet, G. (1951). *Étude sur le style de Démosthène dans les discours politiques.* Paris.

Rose, H. J. (1932). 'Stesichorus and the Rhadine-Fragment', *C.Q.* 26: 88–92.

Rosenmeyer, T. G. (1966). 'Alcman's *Partheneion I* reconsidered', *G.R.B.S.* 7: 321–59.

Ross, W. D. (1923). *Aristotle.* London.

Rostagni, A. (1955). *Scritti minori.* 3 vols. Turin.

Russell, D. A. (1964). *Longinus on the sublime.* Oxford.

(1973). *Plutarch.* London.

Russell, D. A. and Wilson, N. G. (1981). (edd.). *Menander Rhetor, On epideictic oratory.* Oxford.

Russell, D. A. and Winterbottom, M. (1972). *Ancient literary criticism*. Oxford.

de Ste Croix, G. E. M. (1972). *The origins of the Peloponnesian War*. London.

Salmon, P. (1961). 'Chariton d'Aphrodisas et la révolte égyptienne de 360 avant J.-C.', *Chronique d'Égypte* 36: 365–76.

Sambursky, S. (1959). *The physics of the Stoics*. London.

Sandbach, F. H. (1975). *The Stoics*. London.

Sayce, A. H. (1883). *Herodotos I–III*. London.

Schadewaldt, W. (1928). *Der Aufbau des Pindarischen Epinikion*. Schriften der Königsberger Gelehrten Gesellschaft. Geisteswiss. Klasse v.3. Halle.

(1929). *Die Geschichtsschreibung des Thukydides*. Berlin.

Scheller, P. (1911). *De hellenistica historiae conscribendae arte*. Leipzig.

Schlesinger, E. (1968). 'Zu Pindar, Pyth. 12', *Hermes* 96: 275–86.

Schmid, W. (1926). (ed.) *Ps-Aristides, Libri rhetorici*. BT. Leipzig & Stuttgart.

(1948). 'Das Sokratesbild der Wolken', *Philologus* 97: 209–28.

Schröder, H. O. (1934). *In Platonis Timaeum commentariorum fragmenta*. BT. Leipzig & Stuttgart.

Schwartz, E. (1919). *Das Geschichtswerk des Thukydides*. Bonn.

Schwarze, J. (1971). *Die Beurteilung des Perikles durch die attische Komödie und ihre historische und historiographische Bedeutung*. Zetemata LI. Munich.

Sedley, D. N. (1974). 'The structure of Epicurus On Nature', *Cronache Ercolanesi* 4: 89–92.

Seeberg, A. (1971). *Corinthian Komos vases*. *B.I.C.S.* suppl. XXVII.

Segal, C. P. (1962). 'Gorgias and the psychology of the logos', *H.S.C.Ph.* 66: 99–155.

(1975). 'Pebbles in golden urns: the date and style of Corinna', *Eranos* 63: 1–8.

(1976). 'Bacchylides reconsidered: epithets and the dynamics of lyric narrative', *Q.U.C.C.* 22: 99–130.

(1977). 'The myth of Bacchylides 17: heroic quest and heroic identity', *Eranos* 74: 23–37.

Seidensticker, B. (1978). 'Archilochus and Odysseus', *G.R.B.S.* 19: 5–22.

Severyns, A. (1933). *Bacchylide, Essai biographique*. Liège & Paris.

(1963). *Recherches sur la Chrestomathie de Proclos* IV (= Bibliothèque de la Faculté de Philos. et Lettres de l'Université de Liège, fasc. 170).

Shackleton Bailey, D.R. (1966). *Cicero's letters to Atticus* v. Cambridge.

Sifakis, G. M. (1971). *Parabasis and animal choruses*. London.

Simon, E. (1971). 'Die "Omphale" des Demetrios', *A.A.*: 199–206.

(1972). *Das antike Theater*. Heidelberg. (Tr. C. E. Vafopoulou-Richardson (1982) London.)

Sisti, F. (1965). 'Le due Palinodie di Stesicoro', *Stud. Urb.* 39: 303–13.

Skeat, T. C. (1956). 'The use of dictation in ancient book production', *P.B.A.* 42: 179–208.

Smith, A. H. (1898). 'Illustrations to Bacchylides', *J.H.S.* 18: 267–80.

Smyth, H. W. (1900). *The Greek melic poets*. London.

Snell, B. (1953). *The discovery of the mind: the Greek origins of European thought*, tr. T. G. Rosenmeyer. Oxford.

Snell, B. and Maehler, H. (1975). *Pindari carmina cum fragmentis*. BT. Leipzig & Stuttgart.

Solmsen, F. (1931). 'Antiphonstudien. Untersuchungen zur Entstehung der attischen Gerichtsrede', *Neue philologische Untersuchungen* VIII. Berlin.

(1961). 'Greek philosophy and the discovery of the nerves', *M.H.* 18: 169–97.

(1975). *Intellectual experiments of the Greek enlightenment*. Princeton, N.J.

Sourdille, C. (1910). *La durée et l'étendue du voyage d'Hérodote en Égypte*. Paris.

Spiegelberg, W. (1929). *The credibility of Herodotus' account of Egypt*. Tr. A. M. Blackman. Oxford.

Sprague, R. K. (1972). *The older sophists*. Columbia, South Carolina.

Stadter, P. A. (1973). (ed.) *The speeches in Thucydides*. Chapel Hill.

Stahl, H.-P. (1966). *Thukydides; die Stellung des Menschen im geschichtlichen Prozess*. Munich.

Steinmetz, P. (1960). 'Menander und Theophrast', *Rh.M.* 103: 185–91.

Stern, J. (1967). 'The structure of Bacchylides' Ode 17', *R.B.Ph.* 45: 40–7.

Stevenson, J. G. (1974). 'Aristotle as historian of philosophy', *J.H.S.* 94: 138–43.

Strid, O. (1976). *Über Sprache und Stil des Periegeten Pausanias*. Uppsala.

Strohmaier, G. (1976). 'Übersehenes zur Biographie Lukians', *Philologus* 120: 117–22.

Sutton, D. F. (1974a). *The date of Euripides' Cyclops*. Ann Arbor.

(1974b). 'A handlist of satyr plays', *H.S.C.Ph.* 78: 107–43.

Svoboda, K. (1952). 'Les idées de Pindare sur la poésie', *Aegyptus* 32: 108–20.

Szepessy, T. (1975). 'Die "Neudatierung" des Heliodorus und die Belagerung von Nisibis', *Eirene* (= Actes de la XIIe conférence internationale d'études classiques). Amsterdam.

Taplin, O. (1975). 'The title of Prometheus Desmotes', *J.H.S.* 95: 184–6.

Tarán, L. (1981). *Speusippus of Athens: a critical study with a collection of the related texts and commentary*. Leiden.

Tarditi, G. (1968). *Archiloco*. Rome.

Tarn, W. W. (1933). 'Alexander the Great and the unity of mankind', *Proceedings of the British Academy* 19: 123–66.

Thayer, H. S. (1975). 'Plato's quarrel with poetry: Simonides', *J.H.I.* 36: 3–26.

Thesleff, H. (1961). *An introduction to the Pythagorean writings of the Hellenistic period*. Acta Academiae Aboensis, Humaniora XXIV.3. Åbo.

(1965). *The Pythagorean texts of the Hellenistic period*. Acta Academiae Aboensis, Humaniora Ser. A. XXX.1. Åbo.

Thierfelder, A. (1956). 'Römische Komödie', *Gymnasium* 63: 326–45.

Thummer, E. (1968–9). *Pindar, Die Isthmischen Gedichte*. 2 vols. Heidelberg.

Tigerstedt, E. N. (1965). *The legend of Sparta in classical antiquity*. Lund.

Torrance, R. M. (1965). 'Sophocles: some bearings', *H.S.C.Ph.* 69: 269–327.

Trendall, A. D. (1967). *Phlyax vases*. 2nd ed. *B.I.C.S.* suppl. XIX.

Trendall, A. D. and Webster, T. B. L. (1971). *Illustrations of Greek drama*. London.

Treu, M. (1966). 'Pseudo-Xenophon ΠΟΛΙΤΕΙΑ ΑΘΗΝΑΙΩΝ', *RE* IXA.2 1928–1982. Stuttgart.

  (1968*a*). 'Alkman', *RE* suppl. XI 19–29.

  (1968*b*). 'Stesichoros', *RE* suppl. XI 1253–6.

Trüdinger, K. (1918). *Studien zur Geschichte der griechisch-römischen Ethnographie.* Diss. Basel. Leipzig.

Turner, E. G. (1952). *Athenian books in the fifth and fourth centuries.* Inaugural lecture. 2nd ed. 1978. London.

  (1965). 'Athenians learn to write: Plato's *Protagoras* 326a', *B.I.C.S.* 12: 67–9.

  (1968). *Greek papyri.* Oxford.

  (1971). *Greek manuscripts of the ancient world.* Oxford.

  (1973). *The papyrologist at work. G.R.B.S.* monograph VI.

  (1976). 'A fragment of Epicharmus? (or Pseudoepicharmea?)', *W.S.* 89: 48–57.

  (1978). 'The lost beginning of Menander, *Misoumenos*', *Proc. Brit. Acad.* 73: 315–31.

  (1980). 'The rhetoric of question and answer in Menander', *Themes in Drama* 2: 1–23.

Untersteiner, M. (1954). *The sophists*, tr. K. Freeman. Oxford.

Usher, S. (1973). 'The style of Isocrates', *B.I.C.S.* 20: 39–67.

  (1976). 'Lysias and his clients', *G.R.B.S.* 17: 31–40.

Ussher, R. G. (1960). *The Characters of Theophrastus.* London.

  (1973). *Aristophanes, Ecclesiazusae.* Oxford.

Vallet, G. (1958). *Rhégion et Zancle.* Bibl. d'Écoles françaises d'Athènes et de Rome CLXXXIX. Paris.

Van Groningen, B. A. (1935/6). 'The enigma of Alcman's Partheneion', *Mnemosyne* ser. III, 3: 241–61.

van Groningen, B. A. (1963). *Traité d'histoire et de critique des textes grecs.* Amsterdam.

Vermeule, E. (1966). 'The Boston Oresteia Krater', *A.J.A.* 70: 1–22.

Vernant, J.-P. (1980). *Myth and society in ancient Greece*, tr. J. Lloyd. Brighton.

Vernant, J.-P. and Detienne, M. (1974). *Les ruses de l'intelligence. La métis chez les grecs.* Paris. (Engl. tr. *Cunning intelligence in Greek culture and society* (1978) Hassocks.)

Vickers, B. (1973). *Towards Greek tragedy.* London.

Voigt, E.-M. (1971). *Sappho et Alcaeus.* Amsterdam.

Vürtheim, J. (1919). *Stesichoros' Fragmente und Biographie.* Leiden.

Wace, A. J. B. and Stubbings, F. H. (1962). (edd.). *A companion to Homer.* London.

Wade-Gery, H. T. (1932). 'Thucydides the son of Melesias', *J.H.S.* 52: 205–27.

  (1945). 'Kritias and Herodes', *C.Q.* 39: 19–33.

  (1952). *The poet of the Iliad.* Cambridge.

Walbank, F. W. (1938). ΦΙΛΙΠΠΟΣ ΤΡΑΓΩΙΔΟΥΜΕΝΟΣ, *J.H.S.* 68: 55–68.

  (1955). 'Tragic history: a reconsideration', *B.I.C.S.* 2: 4–14.

  (1972). *Polybius.* Berkeley & Los Angeles.

Webster, T. B. L. (1950). *Studies in Menander.* 2nd ed. 1960. Manchester.

(1952). 'Chronological notes on Middle Comedy', *C.Q.* n.s. 2: 13–26.

(1959). *Greek art and literature, 700–530 B.C.* London.

(1965). 'The poet and the mask', in M. J. Anderson, ed., *Classical drama and its influence: essays presented to H. D. F. Kitto*, 3–13. London.

(1967). *The tragedies of Euripides.* London.

(1968). 'Stesichoros: Geryoneis', *Agon* 2: 1–9.

(1969). *Monuments illustrating New Comedy.* 2nd ed. *B.I.C.S.* suppl. xxiv.

(1970a). *The Greek chorus.* London.

(1970b). *Studies in later Greek comedy.* 2nd ed. Manchester.

(1974). *Menander: an introduction.* Manchester.

Webster, T. B. L. and Green, J. R. (1978). T. B. L. Webster, *Monuments illustrating Old and Middle Comedy*, 3rd ed. rev. and enlarged by J. R. Green. *B.I.C.S.* suppl. xxxix.

Wehrli, F. R. (1948). *Motivstudien zur griechischen Komödie.* Zurich & Leipzig.

Weidauer, K. (1954). *Thukydides und die Hippokratischen Schriften; der Einfluss der Medizin auf Zielsetzung und Darstellungsweise des Geschichtswerkes.* Diss. Heidelberg.

Weitzmann, K. (1959). *Ancient book illumination.* Cambridge, Mass.

(1970). *Illustrations in roll and codex*, 2nd ed. Princeton, N. J.

Welles, C. B., Fink, R. O. and Gilliam, J. F. (1959). *The excavations at Dura-Europos, Final report V, part 1. The parchments and the papyri.* New Haven.

Wells, J. (1923). 'The Persian friends of Herodotus', in *Studies in Herodotus*, 95–111. Oxford.

West, M. L. (1963). 'Three Presocratic cosmologies', *C.Q.* n.s. 13: 154–76 (154–6 on Alcman).

(1965). 'Alcmanica', *C.Q.* n.s. 15: 188–202.

(1966). *Hesiod, Theogony.* Oxford.

(1967). 'Alcman and Pythagoras', *C.Q.* n.s. 17: 1–15.

(1969). 'Stesichorus Redivivus', *Z.P.E.* 4: 135–49.

(1970a). 'Melica', *C.Q.* n.s. 20: 205–15.

(1970b). 'Corinna', *C.Q.* n.s. 20: 277–87.

(1971a). 'Stesichorus', *C.Q.* n.s. 21: 302–14.

(1971b). 'Further light on Stesichorus' Iliu Persis', *Z.P.E.* 7: 262–4.

(1974). *Studies in early Greek elegy and iambus.* Berlin & New York.

(1975). 'Cynaethus' Hymn to Apollo', *C.Q.* n.s. 25: 161ff.

(1977). 'Notes on Papyri', *Z.P.E.* 26: 38–9.

(1978a). (ed.). *Hesiod, Works and days.* Oxford.

(1978b). *Theognidis et Phocylidis fragmenta.* Berlin.

West, S. (1967). *The Ptolemaic papyri of Homer.* (Papyrologica Coloniensia iii). Cologne & Opladen.

(1974). '*Joseph and Asenath*: a neglected Greek romance', *C.Q.* n.s. 24: 70–81.

Westlake, H. D. (1977). 'Thucydides on Pausanias and Themistocles. A written source?', *C.Q.* n.s. 37 (1977) 93–110.

Wevers, R. F. (1969). *Isaeus. Chronology, prosopography, and social history.* The Hague·
Wilamowitz-Moellendorff, U. von (1903). *Timotheos: Die Perser.* Leipzig.
    (1925). *Menander: Das Schiedsgericht.* Berlin.
    (1962). *Kleine Schriften* IV. Berlin.
Wilson, A. M. (1974). 'A Eupolidean parallel for the rowing scene in Aristophanes'
    Frogs', *C.Q.* n.s. 24: 250–2.
Wilson, N. G. (1975). 'Books and readers in Byzantium', *Byzantine books and bookmen.*
    Dumbarton Oaks.
Wind, R. (1971–2). 'Bacchylides and Pindar: A question of imitation', *C.J.* 67: 9–13.
Winnington-Ingram, R. P. (1948). 'Clytemnestra and the vote of Athena', *J.H.S.* 68:
    130–47.
    (1965). 'Tragedy and Greek archaic thought', in M. J. Anderson, ed., *Classical
    drama and its influence.* London.
Wirth, T. (1967). 'Arrians Erinnerungen an Epiktet', *M.H.* 24: 149–89, 197–216.
Wolke, H. (1978). *Untersuchungen zur Batrachomyomachia.* Meisenheim am Glan.
Woodbury, L. E. (1967). 'Helen and the Palinode', *Phoenix* 21: 157–76.
    (1976). 'Aristophanes' *Frogs* and Athenian literacy: *Ran.* 52–53, 1114', *T.A.Ph.A.*
    106: 349–57.
    (1979a). 'Gold hair and grey, or the game of love: Anacreon fr. 13: 358 *PMG*, 13
    Gentili', *T.A.Ph.A.* 109: 277–87.
    (1979b). 'Neoptolemus at Delphi: Pindar, *Nemean* 7.30ff.', *Phoenix* 33: 95–133.
Young, D. C. (1964). 'Pindaric criticism', *Minnesota Review* IV 584–641; repr. in
    W. M. Calder III and J. Stern, edd. (1970) *Pindaros und Bakchylides*, 1–95.
    Darmstadt.
Zalateo, G. (1961). 'Papiri scolastici', *Aegyptus* 41: 160–235.
Zieliński, T. (1885). *Die Gliederung der altattischen Komödie.* Leipzig.
Zuntz, G. (1949). 'Once again the Antiphontean Tetralogies', *M.H.* 6: 100–3.
    (1955). *The political plays of Euripides.* Manchester.
    (1971). *Persephone.* Oxford.

INDEX

Academy, Academics, 622–5 *passim*, 835–40 *passim*; Antagoras and, 821; Aristotle and, 505, 527–8; in comedy, 408; and cosmogony, 493; foundation of, 505; *mouseia* at, 29; Polemo at, 631; and Scepticism, 622, 636; Timon of Phlius and, 637; Zeno's inscription to, 844; *see also* Arcesilaus, Carneades, Plato

Achilles Tatius, 682, 684, 685, 686, **692–4**, 696, *882–3*, 884

Acts of the pagan martyrs, compared with Philostratus on Apollonius, 657

Aelian (Claudius Aelianus), **680–2**, *875–6*; and Alciphron, 679, 874; compared with Lucian, 674; and Longus, 699; on Ptolemy II and Glauce, 572; on Stesichorus, 192 & n. 6, 738–9; cited, 168, 186, 218 n. 2

Aeschines, 505, **523–4**, *803*; and Demosthenes, 514, 516, 520–4 *passim*, 801, 803; invective in, 521; and Second Sophistic, 655, 656; on Solon's education laws, 6

Aeschines of Sphettus, follower of Socrates, 478

Aeschylus, **281–95**, *761–4*; life and career, 281–3, *761*

works, *761–2*; *Persae*, 258, 263, 268, 272, 273, 279, 281, 282, **283–4**, 297, 339, 367–8, 432, 540, *761*; *Septem*, 8, 273, 282, 283–4, 291, 292–3; *Supplices*, 8, 273, 282, **284–6**, 292, 349; *Oresteia*, 196–7, 268, 271, 273, 274, 275–6, 282, 284, 285, **286–8**, 292–3, 294–5, 297, 324, 331–2; (*Agamemnon*), 107, 191, 258, 270, 272, 275–6, 284, 285, 286–7, 289, 290–1, 292, 293–4, 295; (*Choephori*), 40, 270, 271, 287, 288, 291, 292, 294, 338, 410 & n. 5; (*Eumenides*), 8, 282, 285, 287, 288, 291, 292, 498; *Prometheus*, 8, 265, 271, 274, 282, 284, 288–90, 295, 344, 472, 476 n. 1, 540; lost or fragmentary, 36, 258 n. 4, 273, 281–4

passim, 291, 295, 297, 333, 342 n. 1, 347–8, 349, 350, 351, 370, 649, *761–2*, 772

character of drama, 281–95 *passim*; actors, 258, 274, 276, 280, 281, 297; chorus and choral lyric, 258, 259, 268, 285, 291, 338; fable in, 701; freedom and compulsion in, 294; *gnomai* in, 700; gods and religion, 289, 290–5 *passim*, 324; imagery, themes and symbols, 233, 291–2; language, 271, 290, 313; and origins of tragedy, 258, 262; politics, 282, 285–6, 293; psychology and character, 284, 291, 314, 326, 540; settings, 283; single plays, 297; trilogies, 258 n. 4, 273, 282 & n. 4, 283–4; trimeter, 337; use of props, 270–2, 273, 278; visual effect and spectacle, 291

reputation, influence and popularity, 35, 42, 216, 339, 342, 343, 344; in Aristophanes, 9, 35, 319, 329, 337, 371, 386–7, 389, 390, 406; Aristotle on, 258, 540; Athenaeus on, 298; and Euripides, 324, 331–2, 339; and Simonides, 745; and Sophocles, 296, 297, 299, 313, 314; and Thucydides, 447; and Tynnichus of Chalcis, 222

Aesop, 156, 192, 547, 619, 625, 701, 702, 812, *886*

Aëtius, compiler of philosophic handbook, 639

Aethiopis, 107, 726

Agathias, 616

Agathon, tragic poet, 11, 340, 341–2, 343

Agias, antiquarian of Argolid, 566

Agias (Hegias?) of Trozen, epic poet, *726*

Aï Khanoum, finds at, 25

Alcaeus, 202, **209–14**, 222, *741–2*; Alcaic stanza, 213; and Anacreon, 218, 219; audiences for, 214; Bacchylides and, 236; and Callimachus, 568; choral works, 166; on friendship, 221; on Helen, 191; and Hesiod, 105 n. 1, 156; Homeric language, 190; love

Alcaeus (*cont.*)

songs, 213–14; preservation and scholarship on, 4, 5, 826, 827; skolia, 220, 745; and Stesichorus, 186; and Theocritus, 585; use of dialect, 169

Alcibiades: Andocides' attacks, 504; in Aristophanes, 395; Euripides' epinikion for, 242; in Plato, 485, 490; in *Poetics*, 413; in Thucydides, 450, 451, 503

Alcidamas of Elea, rhetorician and sophist, 510, *792*

Alciphron, **679–80**, 682, 699, *874–5*, 885

Alcmaeon of Croton, natural scientist, 255

Alcman, 5, 130, **168–85**, *736–8*; Aristarchus on, 827; and choral lyric, 165; composing for local festivals, 223; and dance, 166; horse imagery, 217; Laconian dialect, 166; monodic poems, 166; Philochorus on, 30; and Stesichorus, 186; on *Tekmor* and *Poros*, 96, 179; theological and cosmological speculation, 179–80, 247

Alcmeonids, Herodotus and, 427, 429

Alexander Aetolus, 31, 547–8, 575, 599, *813–14*

Alexander of Aphrodisias, 866

Alexander of Cotiaeum, 23

Alexander of Ephesus ('Lychnus'), 605, *825–6*

Alexander of Euboea, patron of Euphorion, 607

Alexander the Great: and Alexandria, 544; and Aristotle, 528, 544, 806; conquests of, 463, 512, 625; death of, 529; in Dio of Prusa, 671; historians of, 431, 463–4, 679, 703, 705, 706; and Peripatetics, 468 n. 1

Alexander-romance, 684

Alexandria, Library, Museum and scholarship at, 5 & n. 2, 20, 23, 29, 30–6 *passim*, 37, 40, **541–2**, 547, 570, 586, 606, 722, 777, 812, 813, 816, 819, 823, 826, 827; scholars and writers: Alexander Aetolus, 548, 813; Apollonius Rhodius, 586; Aratus, 602; Aristophanes of Byzantium, 826, 832; Callimachus, 549, 550, 558, 563, 568, 569, 815, 816; Eratosthenes, 823; Lycophron, 548, 814; Machon, 832; Peripatetics, 624; Philetas, 544; Theocritus, 570, 571, 573, 579, 580; subjects of study: Aeschylus' *Prometheus* plays, 288; Alcaeus, 213; Archilochus, 128; Aristophanes, 417, 777; Aristotle, 530, 807; biography, 236; canon of poets, 240; Corinna, 240; epics, 109; Euripides, 336, 769; geography, 463; Greek theatre, 264; Hipponax, 158, 735; Homer, 42, 111; Ibycus, 743; lyric poets, 749; orators, 502; Sappho, 203; Theognis, 158; *see also under individual authors*

Alexandrian Erotic Fragment, 581

Alexarchus, foundation of Ouranopolis, 463

Alexis, comic poet, 13, 365 n. 5, 395 n. 3, 399, 408 n. 3, 413, 780

Ameipsias, comic poet: *Komastai*, 382; *Konnos*, 388, 776; *Sappho*, 203 n. 1; cited, 775

Ammonius, scholar, 827

Amphis, comic poet, 408 & n. 3

Amyntas of Macedon, 527

Anacreon of Teos, 5, 166, n. 2, 174, 177, 202, 214, **216–20**, 222, 247, 426, 547, *744*, 745, 812, 826, 827

Ananius, choliambic poet, 368

Anaxagoras, 8, 10, **253–5**, 255–6, *756*, 757

Anaxandrides, comic poet, 399, 404, 413

Anaximander, 179, 245, 253, 255; map of, 430

Anaximenes of Lampsacus, historian and rhetorician, 505, 518, *792*, 801

Anaximenes of Miletus, philosopher, 245, 255

Andocides, 498, 503, **504–5**, 523, *797–8*

Andron of Alexandria, on Alexandria, 541

Andronicus of Rhodes, Peripatetic philosopher, 530 & nn. 2, 3

Androtion, atthidographer, 459, 517

Anonymus, *De comoedia* 393 nn. 2, 3, 399, 413, 780

Anonymus Iamblichi, 475

Antagoras of Rhodes, poet, 599, *821–2*

Antigonus of Carystus, 111, 545

Antigonus Gonatas, 599, 600, 813, 820–1, 851, 853

Antimachus of Colophon, poet and scholar, 542, 545, 546–7, 561, 588, *811*, 819

Antioch: intelligentsia of, 40; library of, 607

Antiochus of Ascalon, head of Academy, 622, 635–6

Antiochus the Great: and Euphorion, 607, 828

Antiphanes, comic poet, 243, 399, 408 n. 5, 410 n. 5, **411–13**, 417 n. 6

Antiphon, 475, 476, 498, **501–3**, 504, 505, 508, *796–7*

Antisthenes of Athens, philosopher, 510, *792*

Antonia the Younger, and Greek culture, 651

Antoninus Liberalis, mythographer: prose summary of Nicander, 603–4

Antonius Diogenes, 679, 683, 686, 687, 692, *879*

Antony (Marcus Antonius), 642

Apellicon, Athenian bibliophile, 530

Apollodorus, orator, 514, 801, *802*

Apollodorus, prose author, 603

Apollodorus of Athens, scholar, 605, 606, *824–5*, 827; cited, 170 n. 2, 235 n. 1

Apollodorus of Carystus, comic poet, 418, 424 n. 3

Apollonius the Eidographer, 586, 606, *827*

Apollonius Rhodius, 33, 35, **586–98**, *819–20*; 'Against Zenodotus', 547; Antimachus of Colophon and, 546; Aratus and, 602; and Callimachus, 549, 553, 554, 557, 561, 564, 568, 586, 587, 598, 815, 819; and epic, 557; and Eumelus, 108; as librarian, 547, 549, 604; 'Longinus' on, 647; Medea of, 546, 581 n. 1; and Philetas, 545, 546; scholia on, 108; and Theocritus, 570, 581–4 *passim*, 817, 819; on women of Lemnos, 568

Apollonius of Tyana, *see* Philostratus

Appian, 705, 707–9, *888–9*

Apuleius, original of *Golden ass*, 679, 687

Aratus, 561, 576, **598–602**, 604, 813, 814, *820–1*, 822

Arcesilaus, Academic philosopher, 622, 636, 846

Archebulus of Thera, poet, 828

Archestratus, *Fishes*, 876

Archias, poet, 607

Archilochus of Paros, **117–28**, 616, 701, *728–30*; Callimachus and, 568; and Callinus, 129; in Cratinus' *Archilochoi*, 385; dithyrambs and paeans of, 166; emperor Julian on, 158; and Herodas, 612; and Homer, 129, 158, 190; invective of, 123–7; life and career, 117–18, 728–9; and literacy, 3–4, 45, 105, 128; 'Longinus' on, 605; metres, 120, 128, 129, 133, 151, 153, 159, 259, 897; and monody, 202; and origins of comedy, 363, 393; personae, 118–19, 121, 127; and sack of Cimmerians, 129; and Semonides, 156; social and political aspects, 121–2; as soldier, 121, 410 & n. 5; style, 119–28 *passim*, 568; use of fable, 886

Archimedes: dedicates book to Eratosthenes, 604

Archippus, comic poet, 395 n. 2

Arctinus of Miletus, 721, *726*

Argentarius, epigrammatist, 650–1

Arion of Methymna, 168, 182, 202, 260–1

Aristarchus of Samothrace, scholar, 27, 32–3, 34, 545, 606, 610, 722, 742, 744, 824, *827*, 829

Aristeas, Letter of, 547

Aristeas of Proconnesus, poet: *Arimaspeia*, 183

Aristides (P. Aelius Aristides Theodorus), 511, 649, **658–62**, 663, 664, 665, 666, 669, 694, 699, 710, 860, *865*; Ps. Aristides, 649 n. 2

Aristobulus, Alexander historian: as source for Arrian, 705

Aristomenes, comic poet, 10

Ariston of Chios, philosopher, 630, 823

Aristonicus, grammarian, 827

Aristonous, writer of paeans, 616

Aristophanes: life and career, 355, 400 n. 2, *775–7*

works, 417, *775–7*; *Acharnians*, 270, 279, 301, 340, 355, 356, 357, 359, 360 & n. 3, 361, 369, 373, 374, 376, 377, 378, 381 n. 2, 384, 385, 387, 390, 395, 397, 400, 403, 410, 427, 472, 775, 776; *Birds*, 242, 263, 360, 364 & n. 2, 371, 379–80, 380–2, 384, 395, 407, 408 n. 4, 462, 776; *Clouds*, 9, 356, 357, 359–60, 361, 370, 375–6, 380, 381, 385, 387, 388–90, 392–3, 407, 408 & nn. 2–4, 775, 776; *Ecclesiazusae*, 278 n. 1, 358, 360, 361, **399–402**, 405, 406–7, 409, 411, 415, 462, 777; *Frogs*, 9, 35, 243, 278 n. 1, 319, 328, 329, 330, 337, 338, 340, 341–2, 356, 357, 359 n. 1, 360, 365, 370–1, 371–2, 376, 379, **383–4**, 385, 389, 394, 400, 403, 406, 776, 777; *Knights*, 11, 355, 357, 359–60, 361, 364 n. 2, 372, 373, 375 & n. 3, 377 n. 3, 378, 380, 385, 390, 393 n. 1, 395 nn. 2, 4, 408 n. 5, 412 n. 1, 775, 776; *Lysistrata*, 278 n. 1, 357, 360, 376, 377, 378, 383, 395 n. 4, 395–6, 397 & n. 1, 407 & n. 2, 776; *Peace*, 271, 359–60, 361, 372, 376, 377, 378, 379, 388, 397, 403, 414–15, 775; *Plutus*, 356, 358, 360, 361, 379, 384–5, 398, 399–402, 403, 405, 406, 407, 777; *Thesmophoriazusae*, 40, 270, 319, 329, 332, 338, 356, 360, 373, 379, 381 n. 2, 382, 384, 385, 386, 387–8, 393 n. 1, 395–6, 397 n. 1, 776; *Wasps*, 11, 220, 221, 263, 340, 356, 359–60, 366 & n. 2, 368 n. 3, 372, 375, 379, 390, 392, 395, 397, 410 n. 2, 775; lost or fragmentary, 11, 220, 242, 349, 364 n. 2, 374, 375, 377 & n. 2, 387, 400, 403, 417, *775–7*

character of drama: *agon*, 361, 420 n. 3; chorus and lyric, 169, 357, 358–60 *passim*, 364 & n. 2, 378, 380, 399–400, 400–1, 412, 776–7; Cleon in, 357, 372–8 *passim*, 406, 776; dialects in, 395; idealism and conservatism, 379; intellectualism, 379; language, 217, 357–8, 394–5, 418, 663; literary allusion and parody, 242, 373; (Euripides), 9, 243, 279, 319, 328, 329, 331, 332, 338, 373, 374, 379, 381 n. 2, 384–5, 386, 387, 394, 403, 406, 776; metres, 358–61; monsters, 370–2; music, 406; opinions, 379, 390–1, 397, 776; and oratory, 498; origins in ritual, 357; patterns and themes, 356, 358–60; personification, 357; phallus in, 357; *pnigos*, 361; political aspects, 374–8 *passim*, 404–5, 406–7; realism and fantasy in, 356–7, 379–80, 391–2, 394; and stage devices, 270, 271, 278 & n. 1; Socrates in, 357, 373, 375–6, 381, 388–9, 407, 408, 776; and sophists, 472; visual effects, 357; on war and peace, 369, 377, 378, 397; on women, 395–6, 397 n. 1

reputation, influence and popularity, 39, 777; Aristophanes of Byzantium on, 606, 826; Galen on, 663; Lucian on, 675; and

Aristophanes (*cont.*)
  Menander, 414–15, 418, 420 n. 3; and Plato, 375–6, 407, 462, 490, 776–7; and Plautus, 402; and Theophrastus' *Characters*, 624 sons of, 777
Aristophanes of Byzantium, **32**, 33, 34, 35, 586, **606**, 613, 717, 742, 812, 815, 823, *826*, 827, 832
Aristophon, 517
Aristophon, comic poet, 408 n. 4
Aristotle, 468 n. 1, **527–40**, 622–5 *passim*, *806*–10; life and career, 527–9, 544, 622, *806*
  works, 530–1, *807–8*; *Analytics*, 532; *On coming to be and passing away*, 531; *Constitution of Athens*, 22, 36, 266, 461, 462, 531, *733*; *On the heavens*, 493 n. 1, 531; *Homeric problems*, 533; *Metaphysics*, 13, 246, 254, 530, 531, 532; *Nicomachean Ethics*, 531, 535, 539, 542; *On the parts of animals*, 531; *Physics*, 531, 532; *Poetics*, 13–14, 36, 250, 258, 258–62 *passim*, 264, 272, 274, 280, 297, 298, 299, 318, 362–4, 366–7, 369, 398, 401, 412 n. 2, 413, 475, 505, 531, 533, **534–40**, 625, 897; *Politics*, 461 n. 2, 462, 531, 537 n. 3, 742; *Problems*, 555; *Rhetoric*, 398 n. 3, 468, 474, 499 n. 1, 505, 531, **533–4**; *On sophistical refutations*, 13; *On the soul*, 532; *Topics*, 13, 528; in Aristotelian corpus, 752, 757, 836, 839
  philosophy and opinions, **527–40**; on Archilochus, 118, 127; on Anaxagoras, 254; on Carcinus and Chaeremon, 343–4; on comedy, 355, 362–4, 366–7, 369, 370, 393, 404, 413, 550; on cyclic poems, 107–8; and definition, 532; on Empedocles, 250; on Heraclitus, 253, 755; on Herodotus, 534; and Hippocratic writings, 477; as historian of philosophy, 532; and Homer, 42, 250, 533, 536, 539; on iambic trimeter, 401; on Isocrates, 14, 505, 510; on making extracts, 14–15; manuscripts of, 530, 615; and Plato, 462, 527–8, 532, 533, 535, 538, 540, 806, 808; on poetry and history, 413, 468; as researcher, 256, 529; on rhetoric, 500, 505, 830; on Solon, 150–1; on Stesichorus, 192, 738; on style, 623; as stylist, 531; technical works, 627; on Theognis, 139, 158; on tragedy, 236 n. 1, 258–62 *passim*, 264, 272, 274, 280, 297, 298, 299, 312, 318, 326, 331, 332, 337, 339, 341, 342, 362, 412 n. 2, (*katharsis*), 537 & n. 3, 550; on types of proof, 501; on Xenophanes, 246; on Zeno of Elea, 255
  influence and heritage, 30, 299, 529, 624; and Aristoxenus, *838*; and book collecting, 13–14, 29, 542; and Epicurus, 627; and Galen, 662; and Lyceum, Peripatos, 542,

622–5 *passim*; and Panaetius, 847; and Plotinus, 640; and Stoicism, 631; and Theophrastus, 622, 836
  cited, 13–14, 93, 137 n. 1, 138, 398 n. 3, 461 n. 2, 474, 721, 736, 738, 742
Aristoxenus of Selinus, iambic poet, 368
Aristoxenus of Tarentum, Peripatetic philosopher and biographer, 462, 624, *838*
Arrian (L. Flavius Arrianus), 634, 638, **703–7**, 849, *887–8*
Artemidorus, editor of Theocritus, 611, 817
Artemidorus of Ephesus, 660, **663–5**, *867–8*, 871
Asclepiades of Myrlea, scholar, 611
Asclepiades of Samos, epigrammatist, 576, 617, 620
Asianic style, 505, 643, 644, 655, 693
Astydamas, tragic poet, 342, 343; Astydamas Minor, *Heracles satyricus*, 354
Atellan farce, 346
Athenaeus, 409–10, **682–3**, *876*; citations, views and quotations, 9 (Euripides' books), 16 (comedy), 185 (Alcman), 186 (Sacadas of Argos and Xanthus of Lydia), 193 (Stesichorus), 211 (Alcaeus), 216 (Critias on Anacreon), 218 n. 2 (Polycrates), 227 (Pindar), 298 (Aeschylus), 343 (Theodectas), 354 (Astydamas Minor), 354 (Timocles), 363 n. 4 (Sosibius and Semus on ithyphalloi), 392 (titles of comedies), 395 n. 3 (Alexis), 399, 403, 409–10 (comedy), 541 (Andron of Alexandria), 545 (Strato on Philetas), 603 (Nicander), 606 (Panaetius on Aristarchus), 613 n. 1 (Herodas), 613–14 (Machon), 613 (Aristophanes of Byzantium), 730 (Tyrtaeus), 738 (Stesichorus), 740 (Sappho), 823 (Numenius), 831 (Cercidas), 854 (Menippus), 862 (Oppian); and *Greek Anthology*, 616; preserves Attic skolia, 221, 745
Athenion, philosopher, 633
Attalids: poets of, 607
Attalus II, 605, 824
Attalus III, 602
Atthides, Atthidographers, 30; *see also* Androtion, Philochorus
Attic dialect, 148, 151, 158, 259, 571
Attic style, Atticism, 28, 505, 655, 659, 673, 677 n. 1, 681, 690, 708
Atticus, 615, 832, 833
Augustus, emperor, 642, 650, 651, 707
Aurelianus, Caelius: Latin version of Parmenides, 753
Aurelius, Marcus, 253, 632, 633–5, 653, 658, *849–50*, 860, 862
Avienus: translation of Aratus, 599

Babrius, 649, 702, *886*, 897

Babylonian literature: and Hesiod, 101

Bacchylides, 36, 222, **235–9**, 242, 243, 244, *748–9*; Aristarchus on, 827; compound adjectives, 189, 241; direct discourse in, 189; dithyrambs of, 243 & n. 2; 'gnomic bridge passages', 171; at Hiero's court, 367; 'Longinus' on, 340, 647; metre, 898; pessimism of, 144; and Pindar, 232; and Simonides, 223, 235, 748; and Stesichorus, 187, 200, 201

Basil, St, 38

Battle of frogs and mice (*Batrachomyomachia*), 39, 110, 721, 726

Battle of the Titans, 106, 108, 726

Berenice, wife of Ptolemy III, 555–6

Bias, 432

Bible, 37, 40; *see also* Genesis, gospels, Septuagint

Bion of Borysthenes, 638–9, *853*

Bion, Funeral lament for, 575, 611, 830

Bion of Smyrna, 572, 609, 610–11, *829–30*; Ps. Bion, 572, 610

Blass's law, 515

Boethus of Sidon, Stoic, 844

Boethus of Tarsus, poet of Philippi, 607

Byzantium, Byzantine culture: administration, 41; Aelius Aristides and orators of, 659; and Archilochus, 128; character of literature, 39–40, 663, 715; and Dio of Prusa, 672; education, 23, 25, 38–9, 41, 128; and Euripides, 316; and *Greek Anthology*, 39–40, 616; and novel, 684; and Pindar, 227; political theory, 671; and Theognis, 136, 142 n. 1, 158; and tragedy, 340; and Xenophon of Ephesus, 692

Caesar, Julius: and Crinagoras, 650; and Sallust, 643; and Tyrannion, 614, 832, 833

Caecilius of Calacte, rhetorician, 502, 506, 512

Caecilius Epirota, Augustan critic, 859

Callimachus, **549–70**, *815–17*; works, 36, **550–70**, *815–16*; *Aetia*, 35, 136 & n. 2, **553–9**, 561–3, 564, 566, 586, 815; *Hecale*, 40, 546, 557, 563–4, 584, 586, 605, 610, 815; *Hymns*, **550–3**, 560, 563, 564–8, 584, 586, 816; *Ibis*, 561, 816; *Pinakes*, 32, 550, 816; fragments, 556–7, 568–9, 815–16; elegiacs, 556–7; epigrams, 560, 561, 573, 617–18; hexameter verse, 716, 717; iambic verse, 158, 545, 561, 568–70, 897; lyric metres, 568–9
  style, view of poetry and literary activities, **550–70**, 581–2, 602, 625; on Antimachus of Colophon, 547; and Apollonius Rhodius, 549, 553, 554, 557, 561, 564, 568, 586, 587, 598, 815, 819; on Aratus, 602; and Aristophanes of Byzantium, 606; and Eratosthenes,

604, 605, 823; and Euphorion, 608, 609; and Hipponax, 158, 561, 568–9; on Homer, 576; and Library, 549, 570; and Meleager, 620; on Mimnermus, 136 & n. 2; on Praxiphanes, 625, 839; and Philetas, 545, 546, 558, 561, 563; and Roman history, 549; and Theocritus, 552, 563, 564, 570, 573, 576–7, 581–2, 583, 584, 585, 817; on Zenodotus, 547
  influence and reputation, 545, 549–50, 553, 555, 564, 570, 608, 621, 647, 649–50, 716, 717, 827

Callimachus, epic poet (nephew of preceding), 815

Callinus, 47, 128, 130, 132, 158, *730*

Callisthenes: on Alexander, 464; execution of, 468 n. 1

Callistratus, orator, 505, 517

Camillus, L. Arruntius, 650

Capture of Oechalia, 108–9, 236, 726

Caracalla, emperor, 653, 658, 862

Carcinus, tragic poet, 342, 343

Carneades, Sceptic, 622, 846

Catalogue of Women, see under Hesiod

Cato: *Origines*, 459

Catullus, 119, 124, 173, 183, 224, 555, 615

Catulus, Q. Lutatius, 621

Celer: *Araspes and Pentheia*, 684, 686, 879

Celsus the Epicurean, 677

Cephalas, Constantine, 616

Cercidas of Megalopolis, 613, 638, *831–2*

Cercops of Miletus, 724

Chaeremon, tragic poet, 13, 343–4

Chalcidius: Latin version of *Timaeus*, 494

Chalcocondyles, Demetrius: text of Homeric hymns, 111

Charax of Pergamum: *Greek and Italian history*, 707

Chariton, 683 & n. 1, 684, 685, 688, **688–90**, *880–1*; and Achilles, 694; and Iamblichus, 692; and Xenophon of Ephesus, 690, 691, 692

Charon of Lampsacus, historian, 431

Chionides, comic poet, 355, 363, 367

Choerilus, epic poet, 13

Choerilus, playwright, 262

Choeroboscus: on name of Semonides 153 n. 1, 734

Christianity, Christians, the Church: and codex, 18; funeral oratory of, 500; Galen on, 663; and Greek culture, 23, 37–9, 715; and Greek language, 23; and Hipponax, 158; and Nonnus, 718; poems in *Greek Anthology*, 39–40; political theory, 671; and Rome, 37–8, 657; and Stoicism, 631; *see also* Byzantium, gospels, Jesus

Chrysippus, 631, 632, **632–3**, 633 n. 1, *846*

Cicero: adaptation of Panaetius, 633, 847; on

Cicero (*cont.*)
 Alexander of Ephesus, 616, 825; on
 Anacreon, 216; on Antiochus of Ascalon,
 622, 835–6; and Archias, 607; on Aristarchus,
 606; on Aristotle, 531; and Carneades, 622;
 on circulation of works, 13; on Democritus,
 257; and Demosthenes, 515, 518 n. 1, 523;
 and Ennius, 608; on Epicureanism, 626; on
 Euphorion, 608–9; on Herodotus and history,
 437, 439, 466 & nn. 2 & 3, 467, 471; on
 Ibycus, 743; 'Longinus' on prose of, 646,
 647; on Lysias, 506 n. 3; on Nicander's
 Georgica, 603; on Philodemus, 629; on
 Plato, 257, 467; and Posidonius, 848; on
 recitation of *Menexenus*, 497; on rhetoric,
 512, 623, 647; on Simonides, 225; on style,
 648 n. 1; on Theophrastus, 623; translation
 of Aratus, 599; and Tyrannion, 614, 832
Cinaethon, epic poet, 726
Cinesias, dithyrambic poet, 242
Cinna, Helvius, 615
Claudius, emperor, 650
Cleanthes the Stoic, 252, 253, 257, 354, 600,
 632, 638, *845*, 846
Clearchus, Peripatetic philosopher, 25
Clement of Alexandria, 38, 253, 608, 715
Cleon: and Aristophanes, 357, 372–8 *passim*,
 406, 776; in Thucydides, 457
Cleonymus, 382
Cleopatra, 607
Cleostratus of Tenedos, author of *Astrologia*,
 599
Clonas of Thebes (Tegea), 169
Codex Palatinus of the *Greek Anthology*, 616
Comedy: Old, 355–98 *passim*, 682, 686, *see
 also* Aristophanes; Middle, 354, 395, **399–
 414**, 414–25 *passim*, 682, 777; New, 336,
 356, 362, 403, 410, **414–25**, 624, 679, 680,
 682, 687, 777; *see also* Menander
Constantinople, 40, 41; *see also* Byzantium
Constitution of Athens, *see under* Aristotle
Coptic, 38
Corax, rhetorician, 474, 498
Corinna of Tanagra, 239–41, *749–50*
Corinthiaca, 108
Cory, William: version of Callimachus'
 Heraclitus poem, 618
Counsels of Wisdom, 101
Crantor, philosopher, 821
Crates, comic poet, 355, 369, 380, 393, 395 &
 n. 3, 404
Crates of Pergamum, grammarian, 630
Crates the Stoic, 614
Crates of Thebes, Cynic, 252, 618, 637–8, *852*,
 853
Cratinus, comic poet, 5 n. 2, 354, 355, 357,
 359, 367, 372 & n. 1, 378, 379, 383–4, 385,

388, 393, 400, 776
Cratippus, historian, 442, 458, 785
Cratus, epigrammatist, 608
Creophylus of Samos, epic poet, 109, *726*
Crinagoras, 650, 651, 744
Critias of Athens, sophist and tragic poet, 117,
 137, 216, 252, 340–1, 344, 461 & n. 1, 473,
 728–9, 769, 792
Critolaus, 846
Ctesias of Cnidus, 459, 460, 463, 466
Ctesiphon, 521, 522, 523, 524
Cyclic epics, 44, 47, 106–10, 167, 258, 560,
 721, 726–7
Cynaethus of Chios, rhapsode, 115
Cynics, Cynic philosophy, 637–9, 850–4;
 Antisthenes and, 792; Appian and, 708–9;
 Cercidas and, 831; diatribe, 634, 675; Dio of
 Prusa and, 669, 670; invective, 648; and
 Peregrinus, 676; and Pyrrho and Timon,
 637; satire and parody, 248, 613; and Zeno's
 Stoicism, 632, 844
Cypria, 107, 109, 236, 721, 726

Damis of Nineveh, 657
Deinolochus, comic poet, 370
Delphic maxims, 25
Demeas: on Archilochus, 729
Demetrius, *On style*, 346, 648, *859–60*
Demetrius of Phalerum, 12 n. 1, 30, 505, 547,
 624–5, 702, 779, 805, *812*, 836, 852, 859,
 886
Democritus, 256–7, 473, *757–8*, 840
Demon, Atthidographer, 30
Demosthenes, **514–23**, *800–2*; and Aeschines,
 516, 520–3, 523–4, 801, 803; affinity to
 comedy, 525; and Apollodorus, 801, 802;
 attacked by Timocles, 405; in canon, 505;
 compared with Aristides, 659; on Artists of
 Dionysus, 398 n. 3; *On Crown*, 522–3; Dio of
 Prusa on, 671; Dionysius of Halicarnassus
 on, 506, 644; *Eroticus* (?), 510; funeral
 oration, 510; and Hegesippus, 802; and
 Hyperides, 525, 804; influence of fifth-century
 orators on, 504; Isaeus and, 509, 515, 799,
 800; and Isocrates, 511, 513, 514; 'Longinus'
 on, 646, 647, 648; Lucian on, 22; and
 Lycurgus, 804; and Antiphanes, 399;
 Menander Rhetor on, 860; opposition view of,
 524; and Pasion, 510; Polemo and, 661; prose
 of, 502; prosecuted by Dinarchus, 526; on
 Solon, 147, 419
Dercylus, antiquarian of Argolid, 566
Derveni, papyrus from, 15, 17
Dicaearchus, scholar: on *Frogs*, 376 & n. 1
Didymus, Arius, 34, 129 n. 1, 633, 639
Dieitrephes, 382
Dinarchus, orator, 505, 514, 525–6, 801, *805*

Dinon of Colophon, author of *Persica*, 891

Dio Cassius (Claudius Cassius Dio Cocceianus), 710–13, 882, *891–2*

Dio of Prusa (Dio Chrysostom, T. Flavius (?) Cocceianus Dio), 21, 191, 649, 656, 659, 665–6, **669–72**, 687, 699, 710, *869–71*, 891

Diodorus, Megarian philosopher, 561

Diodorus of Erythrae, *726*

Diodorus Siculus, 20, 92, 170 n. 2, 463, 471, 707

Diogenes, novelist, 684

Diogenes of Apollonia, 389

Diogenes of Babylon, Stoic, 633, 635, 824, *846–7*

Diogenes of Oenoanda, 626, *842*

Diogenes of Sinope, 637–8, 669, 671, 852

Diogenes Laertius: citations, views and quotations, 12 (Protagoras' books), 13 (Satyrus, Speusippus), 21 n. 3 (copyists), 29 n. 2 (*mouseia*), 146, 722, 733 (Solon), 210 (Alcaeus on Pittacus), 245 (Anaximenes), 246, 752 (Xenophanes), 254, 255, 756 (Anaxagoras), 255 (Alcmaeon of Croton 'hears' Pythagoras), 256 (Leucippus, Epicurus), 298 (Polemo on Sophocles), 354 (satyr play on Cleanthes), 408 n. 3 (comic poets on Plato), 529, 779, 836 (Theophrastus), 626, 627–8, 840 (Epicurus), 635 (Stoics and grammar), 636 (Stoics and rhetoric), 637 (Diogenes of Sinope), 638 (Bion of Borysthenes), 639 (Menippus), 742 (Alcaeus), 757 (Democritus), 779 (Menander), 807 (Aristotle), 812 (Demetrius of Phalerum), 821 (Antagoras of Rhodes), 839 (Strato), 844 (Zeno), 845 (Cleanthes), 846 (Chrysippus), 854 (Menippus)

Dionysius son of Calliphon, 605

Dionysius of Halicarnassus, **643–6**, *858*; on Alcaeus, 209; on Antimachus of Colophon, 545; on books, 14, 21 n. 4; on Demosthenes, 506 & n. 3, 515, 519, 523; on Dinarchus, 805; on Herodotus, 436; on Hyperides, 525; on Isocrates, 14, 510 n. 1, 800; on Lysias, 503, 506, 508, 525; misattributed treatise on oratory, 649; on Plato, 12, 495; preserves Isaeus, 509, 799; on Sappho, 203–4; on Simonides, 224, 225–6; on Stesichorus, 188, 195–6, 739; and Strabo, 642–3; on style, 503, 648; on Theophrastus and rhetoric, 623; on Theopompus, 465; on Thrasymachus of Chalcedon, 503; on Thucydides, 503, 519, 667

Dionysius of Heraclea, Stoic poet, 600

Dionysius of Miletus, historian, 431

Dionysius of Miletus, sophist, 686, 879

Dionysius the Periegete, 605, 606, 717

Dionysius Thrax, 27, 614, 636, 827, 832

Dionysus, Artists of, 398 n. 3

Dioscorides, epigrammatist, 354, 613, 832

Diphilus, comic poet, 203, 392, 417, 418, **424** & nn. 3, 4

Dissoi logoi, 446, 475

Doric dialect, 166–7, 186, 188, 370, 385, 395, 398, 571, 575, 580, 610, 611, 612, 638, 640, 738

Duris of Samos, 466–7, 468, 469

Ecphantides, comic poet, 366 n. 2

Egyptian didactic works, 101

Eleatic movement in philosophy, 246; *see names of individual philosophers*

Eliot, T. S.: allusiveness, 568; on drama, 315–16; and Heraclitus, 253

Empedocles, 245–6, **249–52**, 253, 256, 474, 599, 605, *754–5*

Ennius: Cicero on, 608

Enuma Elish, 179

Ephorus, 28, 458, **464–5**, 466, 468, *787*, 799

Ephraim of Nisibis, St, 883–4

Epic Cycle, *see* Cyclic epics

Epicharmus, 13, 252, 363 & n. 3, 365 & n. 5, 367, 370, 371, 385, 391, 398, 402, 575; Ps. Epicharmus, 370 n. 1

Epicrates, comic poet, 408

Epictetus, 632, 633–5, 638, 703–4, *848–9*, 887

Epicurus, Epicureanism, Epicureans, **625–30**, *840–1*; and Democritus, 256, 257; Galen and, 662; Lucretius and, 250, 527; and Menander, 779; and Scepticism, 636; and Stoicism, 631; Timon of Phlius on, 637

Epigoni, 106 n. 1, 109, 721, 726

Epimenides of Crete, religious teacher and philosopher, 108, 551, 587

Erasistratus of Ceos, physician, 818

Eratosthenes, 33, 549, **604–6**, 643, 815, *823–4*

Eubulus, comic poet, 365 n. 5, 401, 403, 404 n. 1

Eudoxus of Cnidus, mathematician, 600, 601

Euenus of Paros, poet and sophist, 12, 137–8 n. 1

Eugammon of Cyrene, epic poet, 726

Euhemerus: *Hiera anagraphe*, 463

Eumelus of Corinth, 108, 168, 588, 726

Euneidai, professional chorus, 165 n. 1

Euphorion of Chalcis, 602, 607–9, *828–9*

Euphron, comic poet, 370

Euphronius, 32 n. 3

Eupolis, 9, 187, 343 n. 1, 349, 354, 355, 357 n. 1, 360 & n. 2, 366 n. 2, 378 & n. 1, 379, 381, 383, 384, 388, 393, 397–8, 408 & n. 5, 675, 776

Euripides, **316–39**, *768–72*; life and career, 9, 12, 341, 473, 756, 768
  works, *768–9*, 772; *Alcestis*, 270, 297 &

Euripides (*cont.*)
n. 2, 316, 318, 326, 346, 348, 352; *Medea*, 270, 274, 311, 316, 317, 318, 327, 329–30, 330–1, 339; *Heraclidae*, 316, 318, 333–4; *Hippolytus*, 16, 275, 316, 318, 319, 321–2, 323, 324, 325, 327, 328–9, 329–30, 340; *Andromache*, 271, 316, 323, 327, 329; *Hecuba*, 316, 318, 323, 328, 334, 338, 348, 349 & n. 1, 350, 353; *Supplices*, 316, 318, 333, 344, 476 n. 1; *Ion*, 265, 271, 281, 316, 318, 323, 338, 369–70, 401; *Electra*, 271, 272, 275, 279, 310, 316, 318, 323, 327, 328, 332, 337, 338, 339; *Hercules furens*, 270–1, 316, 321, 322; *Troades*, 272, 281, 316, 318, 321, 325, 328, 334–5, 338, 339, 342; *Iphigenia in Tauris*, 316, 318, 323, 332–3, 338, 348, 352; *Helen*, 191, 274, 279, 281, 316, 318, 321, 332–3, 338, 348, 352, 386; *Phoenissae*, 199, 316, 318, 320–1, 323, 342; *Orestes*, 265, 272, 281, 316, 318, 328, 331–2, 338, 348; *Bacchae*, 275, 311, 316, 318, 321, 323–4, 325, 327, 338, 339, 340, 344, 371, 768; *Iphigenia in Aulide*, 316, 318, 326–7, 335–6, 348, 768; *Rhesus*, 342–3; *Cyclops*, 346, 347, 348, 349 & n. 1, 350, 351, 352, 353; lost or fragmentary, 5 n. 2, 8, 9, 11, 22, 36, 316, 318, 319–20, 322–3, 328, 329, 332, 334–5, 336, 340, 348, 350, 351, 352, 361, 384, 386, 403–4, 649, 768–9, 772; epinikion for Alcibiades, 242
character of drama: and acting style, 281; actor-arias and monodies, 276, 338; and Aeschylus, 324, 331, 332; character and psychology, 274, 298, 311, 317, 325–7, 328–9, 331, 336–7, 339, 540; chorus, 243, 268, 338–9; and comic poets, 320; (Aristophanes), 9, 35, 271, 279, 319, 328, 329, 330, 331, 332, 337, 338, 341, 342, 361, 371, 373, 374, 379, 384, 385, 386, 387, 389, 390, 394, 395–6, 403, 406, 768; (Cratinus), 379 n. 1; (Eubulus), 403; 'decadence' and subversiveness, 42, 299, 319; development, 318–19; domestic realism and comedy, 311, 318, 330–2, 337 & n. 1, 413; god from machine in, 332; gods, prophecy and religion, 317, 318, 319, 321–5 *passim*, 338; happy endings, 539; human suffering in, 339, 447; humanism, 305; 'irrationalism', 317, 323–7 *passim*, 329; *kommos*, 338; 'light', 'social' aspects, 335; on love, 329; music, 337–8; nostalgia for escape in, 181; patriotism, attitude towards Athens, 318, 333–4, 335; pictorial aspects, 338–9; poetry, 243, 337–8, 568; politics, political argument, 319–20, 320–1, 334–5; rags, 279; 'rationalism' and intellectualism 317, 319, 322–4, 325, 379; revenge in, 318; rhetoric and speeches, 317–18, 327–9, 329–30, 339, 503; 'romantic' element, 318, 332–3,

338; sophism, 12, 317, 319–21, 328, 329, 337, 473; and Sophocles, 297, 298, 299, 305, 310, 311, 313, 324, 331; stage devices, props, etc., 270–2 *passim*, 332; style, 336–7; trimeter, 337, 342, 345; vocabulary, 337 & n. 1, 663; on war, 318, 334–5; and women, 274, 318, 329–30
reputation, influence and popularity, 5 n. 2, 35, 36, 299, 316, 317, 318, 337, 339, 342; Aristotle on, 318, 331, 332, 337, 339; Galen on, 663; 'Longinus' on, 647; Menander and New Comedy, 318, 335–6, 401, 406; and Seneca, 339
Eusebius: on Arion, 168; on Jesus and Apollonius, 657; cited, 542 n. 1 (Irenaeus on library), 736 (dates), 740 (Sappho), 742 (Alcaeus), 743 (Ibycus), 744 (Anacreon), 871 (Maximus of Tyre)
Eustochius, pupil of Plotinus, 856
Eutecnius; paraphrase of Oppian's *Ixeutica*, 862
Euthycles, orator, 518
Euthymenes of Marseilles, traveller, 429

Fabius Pictor, 646
Favorinus, 656, 672, 680
Flaccus, Valerius, 598
Florus, Mestrius, 667
Fronto, Marcus Cornelius, 664, 849–50, 889

Gaius, emperor, 650
Galen, **662–3**, **866–7**; in Athenaeus, 682; on Chrysippus, 846; on circulation of works, 20; on Democritus, 257; on dreams, 661, 664; influence of education on, 27; on Lucian, 674; on Posidonius, 848; on Ptolemies collecting texts, 31
Gallus, Aelius, 642, 643, 857
Gallus, Cornelius, 609, 615, 833
Gellius, Aulus, 280, 424 n. 5, 682
Gellius, Lucius, 634
Genesis: 'Longinus' on, 646
Germanicus, Julius Caesar: translation of Aratus, 599
Glaucus of Rhegium, scholar, 738
Gorgias of Leontini, 11, 12, 445, **474–5**, 485, 490, 498, 500, 501, 502, 503, 504, 507, 510, 511, 511–12, 513, 655, 656, *791*, 799
gospels, 657
Grattius, Augustan poet: *Cynegetica*, 654
Great works (*Megala erga*), 109
Greek Anthology (*Palatine Anthology*), 39–40, 546, 586, 608, 611, **616–21**, 629, 650–2, 740, 743, 744, 794, 834, 842; *see also names of individual poets*
Gyges, play on, 432

Hadrian, emperor: on Antimachus of Colophon,

Hadrian (*cont.*)
545; and Arrian, 704, 705; and Parthenius, 615; as philhellene, 652; and Plutarch, 666, 868; and Polemo, 656
Hanno the Carthaginian, 429
Hecataeus of Miletus, 429–30, 430–1, 436, 439
Hedyle, poetess and mother of following, 617
Hedylus of Samos (Athens?), 617
Hegesinus of Salamis, epic poet, 726
Hegesippus, Athenian statesman and orator, 518, 801, *802*
Hegias of Trozen, *see* Agias
Heliodorus, 683, 684, 685, 686, 692, **694–6**, 714, *883–4*
Heliodorus, periegetic author, 709
Helladius: on Euphorion, 607
Hellanicus of Lesbos, 431, 436 n. 1, 443, 445
Hephaestion, metrist, 369 n. 3, 740, 742, 744
Heraclea (Panyassis), 109, 726
Heraclides Ponticus, 630 n. 2, 736
Heraclitus, Homeric scholar: on Alcaeus, 210
Heraclitus of Ephesus, 5, 13, 139, 229, 245, 246, **252–3**, 475, 477, 618, 632, 674, *755*
Heraclitus of Rhodiapolis, 23
Hermarchus, Epicurean, 840
Hermesianax of Colophon, poet, 575, 811
Hermippus, comic poet, 378 & n. 1
Hermippus of Smyrna, biographer, 624
Hermogenes of Tarsus, rhetor, 188, 515, 523, 649, *860*
Herodas, 369, 370, 580, **611–13**, 614, *830*, 897
Herodes Atticus, 461, 656–7, 863, 875
Herodian, 710–13, *892*
Herodorus of Heraclea, 588
Herodorus of Susa, 23
Herodotus, **426–41**, *783–4*; life and career, 426–9, *783*; and Panyassis, 109, 783; and Sophocles, 260, 427, 433, 783
  History: conception of causation, 438, 447, 452–3, 455; conception of history, 428–9, 431, 433, 438, 456, 457; date of, 427–8; on forms of constitution, 460; and Hippocratic writings, 477; influence of poetry, 431–2, 432–3, 457; organization and narrative, 433–4, 442, 457, 464; patriotism, 438, 457; philosophy, 438–9; style, 436–7; system of chronology, 448; use of sources and predecessors, 429–31, 439–41
  citations, testimony and opinions: 6 (schools), 47, 96, 721 (Homer and Hesiod), 153, 472, 733 (Solon); 161 (*bekos*), 168 (early hymns), 168, 260 (Arion), 208 (Sappho), 260 (Cleisthenes and tragic choruses), 262 (Phrynichus' *Capture of Miletus*), 263 n. 2 (Gyges), 278 (*kothornos*), 306 (Apollo's oracle to Croesus), 366

(Hippoclides' dance), 472 (Pythagoras), 722 (rhapsodes)
  influence, assessments, scholarship and comparisons, 8, 437, 438–9, 456, 458, 588, 606, 827; and Aelian's paradoxography, 680; Aelius Theon and, 28; and Appian, 708; Aristarchus on, 33; Aristotle on, 534; and Arrian, 706; Cicero on, 437, 439; Dionysius of Halicarnassus on, 648; and novel, 687, 693; and Pausanias, 709; and Polybius, 470; Plutarch on, 667; and Theopompus, 464; and Thucydides, 438–9, 441, 444, 445, 446, 447, 448, 452, 454, 455, 456, 457; and Xenophon, 460; and Xenophon of Ephesus, 691
Hesiod, 92–105, *724–6*; life and career, 47, 93, 104, 106, *724*; literacy, 3, 92, 104–5
  works, 109, 175, *724*; *Theogony*, 3, 8, **94–7**, 98, 101, 102, 104, 109, 122, 226, 240, 248, 287, 372, 812; *Works and days*, 3, 92, 93–4, **97–103**, 104–5, 109, 111, 145, 148, 211, 250; *Shield*, 94, 102 n. 2, **103–4**; *Catalogue of women* (*Ehoiai*), 96, 101, 103, 109, 115, 191 & n. 1; cosmogony of, 179, 180; fable in, *886*; and Homer, 96, 97, 99, 100, 102, 103, 104, 158, 721, 724; interpolation in, 96, 99, 100, 103; language, 104–5, 156; on life of countrymen, 99; mode of composition, 104–5, 106; oriental influence, 92–3, 97, 101; on poetry as illusion, 226; style, 101–5, 148; theology, 96–8, 247, 262, 289, 293; traditional tales in, 97, 701; values, 131; on women, 99–100, 154, 155–6, 184
  influence, assessments and scholarship, 13, 32, 118, 547, 606, 826; and Alcaeus, 211; and Alcman, 179, 180, 184; and Apollonius of Rhodes, 819; and Aratus, 599, 601–2; on archaic poets, 105 & n. 1; and Archilochus, 118, 122; and Argonautic story, 587; Aristarchus on, 827; and Aristophanes, 372; and Bacchylides, 236; and Callimachus, 554, 568; and choral poetry, 167; and Corinna, 240; in Cratinus' *Archilochoi*, 385; and Cyclic poems, 109; and didactic poetry, 599; as educator, 13, 246; Empedocles on, 245–6, 250; Euphorion and, 608; Heraclitus on, 246; Herodotus on, 47, 96; and Homeric hymns, 111, 115; and Ionian philosophy, 245; Parmenides and, 245–6, 248, 249; Pausanias and, 5, 94; and Semonides, 154, 155–6; and Solon, 148; and Stesichorus, 189, 191, 197, 724, 738; and Theocritus, 576, 582–3; and tragedy, 262; and Tyrtaeus, 131, 133; Xenophanes on, 245–6, 247, 252; Zenodotus on, 812
Hesychius, 181, 721, 807
Hierocles: Eusebius' reply to, 657

Hieron II of Syracuse: Theocritus and, 570, 571, 817
Hieronymus of Cardia, 459, 706
Himerius: on Alcaeus, 213; on Anacreon, 744; on Sappho, 207
Hipparchus, astronomer: on Aratus, 600
Hippias of Elis, 11, 12, 445, 473, **474**, 476, 483, 792
Hippocrates, Hippocratic writings, 477, 603, 662
Hippodamus of Miletus, author of work on civic life, 461 & n. 2, 462
Hippolytus, Roman presbyter: on Xenophanes, 247 n. 3
Hippon of Samos, natural philosopher, 388
Hipponax, 123, 124, 151, 153, 154 n. 3, **158–64**, 561, 568–9, 612, *735*, 897
Hölderlin: influence of Pindar on, 227
Homer, **42–91**, *721–4*; identity and date, 3, 49–51, 72, 104, 191–2
  works, 721–2; *Iliad*, **52–74**, 266 (Shield of Achilles), 368–9 (bk 10), 591 (characters of Agamemnon and Menelaus); *Odyssey*, **74–91**, 282–3 (Menelaus and Helen in Egypt), 347, 352–3 (Cyclops), 368 (bk 12), 588 (Circe); falsely attributed works, 39, 109, 721, 726, 727; book division, 55–6; comparison of *Iliad* and *Odyssey*, 49–51, 73, 74–5, 79–81, 85, 353; context of composition, 3, 44–8, 92, 104, 721; and Cyclic epics, 106–7, 108, 721, 726; debates, speeches and oratory in, 73, 75, 76, 102, 498; ethos and values, heroic ideal, 62, 71, 73, 74, 75–6, 77, 78, 79–80, 83, 89, 91, 119, 122, 131, 133, 135, 432; formulae, conventional epithets, 43, 50, 54, 56, 65, 66, 75, 77, 80, 85, 104, 106, 141, 165, 176, 188–9; gods in, 51, 53–4, 57, 73, 74, 81, 96, 97, 324; Hades in, 88; hexameter, 717; and Homeric hymns, 11, 115, 721, 727; humour, 73, 80; language and style, 48–51, 56, 65–6, 74, 75, 77, 79, 80, 85, 104; martial interest, 66, 74, 78, 79, 133, 334; as oral literature, 3, 42–51, 55, 63, 76, 80, 84–5, 88, 721–2; on poetry and rhapsodes, 76, 187 n. 3, 226; prayer in, 205; ring-composition, 291, 437; similes, 58, 65–6, 69–70, 74, 77–8, 83, 129, 135, 156, 157, 207, 237; and storytelling, 700; themes, 85–9; view of human condition, 266
  influence, popularity, assessments and allusions, 23, 42, 118, 181, 298, 658, 722; and Aelian, 875; and Aelius Theon, 28; and Alcman, 176, 180–1, 182; allegorical interpretation of, 38; and Anaxagoras, 255; and Apollonius Rhodius, 582, 588–9, 591, 593, 594, 595, 596; and Appian, 708; and Aratus, 599; and Archilochus, 119, 122, 190;

Argonautic story, 587; Aristides on, 865; Aristophanic allusions to, 385; Aristotle on, 250, 533, 536, 539; and Astydamas, 342; and Bacchylides, 236, 237, 238; St Basil on, 38; and Callimachus, 551, 552, 554, 557, 559, 563, 564, 568, 576; and Chariton, 690; and choral lyric, 165–6, 167; Chrysippus quotes, 632; Cratinus and, 385; Demetrius on, 649; and Democritus, 257; and Dio of Prusa, 670, 672; Dionysius of Halicarnassus on, 645; and drama, 258–9, 342, 352–3, 363; in education, 11, 13, 28, 37, 40, 42, 246, 387, 535; and elegists, 129–30, 133, 134, 135, 136, 141, 148, 151, 156, 158, 164; and Empedocles, 245–6, 250–1; Epicharmus and, 368–9; Euphorion and, 608; Euripides and, 324, 342; and Hellenistic poets, 546, 559; Heraclitus and, 246; and Herodotus, 47, 96, 431, 432, 436, 438, *721*; and Hesiod, 97, 99, 100, 102, 103, 104, 721, 724; and historiography, 431, 432, 457; Horace on, 188; and Ionian philosophy, 245; 'Longinus' on, 646–9, 721; Lucian and, 678; and Maximus, 673; and Nicander, 603; and Nonnus, 716, 718; and novel, 687; and Oppian, 653; and Parmenides, 245–6, 248, 249, 250; parodies of, 248, 637, 638, 853; performances of Homeridae, 47, 48, 115, 280, 477, 722; and Philetas, 545, 546; and Pindar, 721; Plato and, 108, 483; Plutarch and, 669; Praxilla and, 241; Protagoras on, 474; and Quintus of Smyrna, 715; Rhianus of Crete and, 607, 828; and Sappho, 190, 207; and Simonides, 187, 224; Stesichorus and, 187, 188–90, 191, 193–5, 199, 201, 739; Strabo and, 588, 643; and Theocritus, 571, 576, 578; and Thucydides, 446, 447; and Virgil, 598; Xenophanes on, 245–6, 247; and Xenophon of Ephesus, 691; Zeno the Stoic on, 533, 632
  scholarship, commentaries, textual study, 11, 29, 31, 33, 34, 39, 111, 257, 607, 722; Antimachus of Colophon, 546, 811; Apollodorus of Athens, 605; Apollonius Rhodius, 819; Aratus, 599, 821; Aristarchus, 33, 34, 545, 606, 827; Aristophanes of Byzantium, 32, 606, 826; Aristotle, 250, 533, 536, 539; Demetrius of Phalerum, 547, 590, 812; Philetas, 545, 546; Rhianus, 828; Tyrannion, 614, 833; Zenodotus, 31, 547, 812–13
Homeric Hymns, 3, 47, 95, **110–16**, 133, 166, 167, 182, 212–13, 350, 498, 567, 568, 584, 610, 721, 727
Homeridae, 47, 477
Honestus of Corinth, epigrammatist, 651
Horace: *Ars Poetica*, 129, n. 1 (inventor of

Horace (*cont.*)
elegy), 259 (Thespis), 278 (Aeschylus and *kothornos*), 375 (transformation of comedy by legislation), 630 (Neoptolemus of Parium); and Alcaeus, 209, 211, 213–14; and Archilochus, 126; on Bion of Borysthenes, 638–9; and Greek lyric poetry, 541; on Homer, 188; and Moschus, 610; and Philodemus, 842; and Pindar, 227; and Stesichorus, 87–8, 739

Hyginus, 349

Hymns, Homeric, *see Homeric Hymns*

Hyperides, 36, 405, 505, 510, **525**, 648, 799, *804*

Iamblichus, 684, 685, 686, 692, 694, *882*

Iambulus, 679

Ibsen, 329

Ibycus of Rhegium, 5, 166 n. 2, 174, 185, 192, 202, **214–16**, 218, 222, 588, *743*

Iliad, Little, 107, 726

Iliou persis, 107, 726

Instructions of Ninurta, 101

Instructions of Šuruppak, 101

Iolaus, 684, 687

Ion of Chios, 8, 137, 242, 247, 296, 340, 459

Ionian philosophy, 96, 245–55 *passim*, 477 n. 1, 503

Ionic dialect, 151, 158, 161, 169, 186, 202, 259, 426, 436, 477, 706, 721

Iophon, son of Sophocles, 341

Irenaeus: on Alexandrian library, 542

Isaeus, 505, 508, **509**, 510, 515, 521, 644, *799*, 800

Isaeus the Assyrian, 656

Isis Aretalogy (Maiistas), 616

Isocrates, 13, 14, 465, 476, 501, 502, 504, 505, 508, **509–14**, 516, 518, 644, *799–80*; pupils of, 464, 799, 804; cited, 12 (on treatise on salt), 140 (Theognis), 191 (blindness of Stesichorus), 227 (Pindar), 405 (comic poets and criticism)

Isyllus of Epidaurus, poet, 616, *834*

Jesus, 657

Jews: in Alexandria, 639; education, 37; *see also* Aristeas, Bible, Septuagint, Philo

John's Gospel: Nonnus and paraphrase of, 717–18

Joseph and Asenath, 684, 685

Julia Domna, 655, 657, 658, 863

Julian, emperor, 158, 683, 883–4

Juvenal: on women, 155

ktiseis (foundation stories), 459

Lacydes, head of Academy, 828

Lafontaine, 702

Lasus of Hermione, poet, 222, 261, 746

Leo the Philosopher, 41

Leonidas of Tarentum, 576, 602, **619**, 651

Lesbian poets, 158, 191, 202, 218, 700; *see also* Alcaeus, Arion, Sappho, Terpander

Lesches of Mytilene, epic poet, 726

Leschides, epic poet, 607

Leucippus, 256, 757

Libanius, 663, 804

Library of Alexandria, *see under* Alexandria

Licymnius of Chios, dithyrambic poet and rhetor, 12, 14, 243

Limenius, author of paean, 616

Linear A, 1–3

Linear B, 1–3, 46, 48

Little Iliad, see *Iliad, Little*

Livy, 368 n. 1, 431, 470, 646

Lollianus, novel writer, 684, 686, *879*

'Longinus', **646–9**, *859*; influence of Dionysius of Halicarnassus on, 644–5; judgements, 51, 721 (*Odyssey*), 188, 201, 739 (Stesichorus), 205–6 (Sappho), 225 (Simonides and Sophocles), 227, 235, 340 (Pindar), 235, 340 (Bacchylides), 296 n. 1, 340 (Sophocles), 340 (Ion of Chios), 495 (Plato), 512 n. 1 (Isocrates), 605 (Eratosthenes and Archilochus), 644–5 (Demosthenes)

Longinus, Cassius, 859

Longus, 611, 679, 680, 684, 685, 686, 691, **696–9**, 874, *885–6*

Lorrain, Claude, 662

Lucian of Samosata, **673–9**, 684, 687, *872–4*; and Alciphron, 679, 680, 874; and Antonius Diogenes, 684, 686, 879; on Arrian, 703; and Athenaeus, 682; audience of, 688; on books, 21–2; and Dio of Prusa, 672; Galen on, 663; on history, 649, 667; influence of education on, 27; language of, 23; and Menippus, 854; on Parthenius, Euphorion and Callimachus, 608; and pastoral, 611; and Pausanias, 710; on philosophers, 639; on Semonides' *bête noire*, 154; on travel literature, 657; on Timon, 383; Ps. Lucian, 744, 864

Lucillius, epigrammatist, 651–2

Lucius of Patrae, 679, 684 n. 2, 687

Lucretius: and Aratus, 599; and Empedocles, 250, 251, 252; and Epicurus, Epicureanism, 527, 626, 627; and Greek literature, 626

Lyceum, 528–9, 542, 547, 622; *see also* Peripatos

Lychnus, *see* Alexander of Ephesus

Lycophron, 31, 191 n. 1, 345, 354, 547, **548–9**, 608, *814*

Lycurgus, orator, 132, 505, 525, **804–5**

Lysanias, grammarian, 823

Lysias, **505–6**, *798–9*; affinity to comedy, 525; Aristides and, 661; deliberative oratory of, 503; and Demosthenes, 515, 520; Dionysius of Halicarnassus on, 503, 506, 525, 644, 648; ethopoeia of, 515, 525; as evidence for cross-questioning, 500 n. 1; funeral oration, 501, 510; and Hyperides, 525; influence of fifth-century orators on, 504; invective in, 521; and Isaeus, 508, 509; and Isocrates, 510; 'Longinus' on, 648; panhellenism of, 513; in *Phaedrus*, 12, 500; and prosecution of Andocides, 504; and Socrates, 506; unity of arguments, 525

Maccius, epigrammatist, 651
Macedonius, author of paeans, 616
Machon, iambic poet, 613–14, *832*
Macrobius: on Parthenius' influence on Virgil, 615
Magnes, comic poet, 355, 357 & n. 2, 363, 364, 367
Maiistas: Isis Aretalogy of, 616, 834
Margites, 109–10, 721
Marmor Parium, 187, 192, 366, 367 n. 1, 738, 740, 780
Martial: on *Batrachomyomachia*, 39; and Lucillius, 651; and Strato of Sardis, 652
Maximus of Tyre, 216, **672–3**, 740, 867, *871–2*
Maximus, Cassius, 664, 867, 871
Maximus, Claudius, 871
Megasthenes, Alexander historian, 463
Melanippides, dithyrambic poet, 242, 243, 281
Melanthius, Atthidographer, 30
Meleager of Gadara, 616, 619–21, 650, 834
Melissus of Samos, philosopher, 255–6, *756–7*
Menander, 36, 39, 42, 356, 358, 404, 410, 411, **414–15**, *779–83*; *Aspis*, 343, 395, 413, 416 & n. 4, 420, 422; *Dis exapaton*, 416, 418; *Dyskolos*, 362, 383, 401, 408 n. 6, 416, 417 n. 3, 419–20, 422–3, 424, 624; *Epitrepontes*, 336 & n. 2, 404, 415, 420; *Heros*, 415; *Misoumenos*, 408 n. 6, 416, 420–2, 423; *Orge*, 415; *Perikeiromene*, 336, 373, 401, 414, 415, 423; *Samia*, 392, 405, 409, 415, 416 & n. 4, 424 n. 4; *Sikyonios*, 416, 420–1, 423; *Synaristosai*, 392, 417; other works, 417; acts in, 400; Aelius Theon on, 28; and Alexis, 399; and Aristophanes, 400, 418; chorus in, 399, 401; and comedy of manners, 414; and Demosthenes, 518; design predominating over language, 418; and Euripides, 318, 335–6; as evidence for idiom, 394; herm of, at Aelian's villa, 875; and Philemon, 424; plot and character, 419; Plutarch on, 39; on poor, 610; rape and recognition in, 403; scholarship of Aristophanes of Byzantium, 606, 826; social comment, 405;

and Theophrastus' *Characters*, 624
Menander Rhetor, 649, *860–1*
Menecrates of Ephesus, didactic poet, 599, 820, 822
Menedemus, Cynic philosopher, 548, 814, 821
Menedemus of Eretria, philosopher, 599, 820
Menelaus of Aegae, 607
Menippus, 639, 675, 677, *854*
Mesomedes, poet, 652
Metiochus and Parthenope, 684, 685, 688
Metrocles of Maroneia, Cynic, 854
Metrodorus, follower of Epicurus, 627
Metrophanes of Eucarpia, 23
Milesian philosophy, 179, 246, 247, 252, 255; see also *names of philosophers*
Mimnermus, 5, 128, 134–6, 137, 153, 156–7, 158, 558, *731–2*, 732
Minucianus, 860
Mnesiepes, inscription of, 117
Morsimus, tragic poet, 340
Morychus, tragic poet, 340
Moschion, tragic poet, 344–5
Moschus of Syracuse, 609, 610, *829*; Ps. Moschus, 572, 575, 610, 611, 830
Musaeus of Ephesus, 607
Museum, *see under* Alexandria
Musonius Rufus, 670, 848, 869
Myrtilus, comic poet, 366 n. 2
Myrtis of Anthedon, Boeotian poetess, 239, 241

Naupactia, 587, 596
Nausiphanes of Teos, Atomist, 840
Nearchus, Alexander historian, 463, 464 n. 1
Nectanebus' dream, 684, 685
Neleus of Scepsis: and texts of Aristotle, 530
Nemesianus, didactic poet, 654
Neoptolemus of Parium, 630
Neopythagoreanism, see Pythagoras, Pythagoreans
neoteric poets, 621
Nero, emperor: Greek renaissance under, 651–2
Nicander of Colophon, 598, 600, **602–4**, *822–3*
Nicetes of Smyrna, 651, 656
Nicias, doctor and man of letters, 572, 618–19, *818*
Nicolaus of Damascus, 642, 707
Nicomachus, father of Aristotle, 527
Nicophron, 10
Nigrinus the Platonist, 675
Ninus romance, 683, 684, 685, 688
Nonnus of Panopolis, 604, 605, 610, 615, 649, 716–18
Nostoi, 107, 726
Numenius of Heracleia, 602, *823*

Oedipodeia, 106, n. 1, 726

Oeneus, 347, 350
'Old Oligarch' (Ps. Xenophon, *Politeia of the Athenians*), 375 & n. 2, 461–2, *788*
Old Testament, 40; *see also* Bible, Genesis, Septuagint
Olen of Lydia, writer of hymns, 168
Olympus of Phrygia, inventor of musical scale, 168
Onesicritus, Alexander historian, 463
Onitadai, professional chorus, 165 n. 1
Oppian, 604, **653–4**, *862–3*
Origenes, 715
Orpheus, 13; Orphism, Empedocles and, 251–2
Ovid, 549, 555, 563, 603, 619, 654, 740, 814, 816
Oxyrhynchus historian, 457, **458**, 785

Palatine Anthology, see Greek Anthology
Pamphilus of Alexandria, lexicographer, 819
Pamphos of Lycia, writer of hymns, 168
Panaetius of Rhodes, 606, 633, *847*, 848
Panyassis of Halicarnassus, 109, 426, *726*
Parian Chronicle, *see Marmor Parium*
Parmenides, 245–6, 248–9, 250 & n. 1, 252, 253, 255, 256, 599, 752, *753–4*
Parthenius of Nicaea, 608, 609, 614, 615, *833*
Pausanias, **709–10**, *890*; citations, remarks, etc., 5, 94, 100, 724 (Hesiod), 6 (schools), 108 (*Corinthiaca*), 115 (temple of Trophonius and Agamedes), 159 (Bupalus), 169 (Alcman), 170 n. 2 (Heracles and Spartan kingship), 195 (Pallanteum), 197 (Iphigenia), 207 (Sappho), 213 (Alcaeus), 240, 241 (painting of Corinna and Pindar), 266 & n. 2 (theatre of Epidaurus), 441 (Thucydides), 607 (Rhianus' *Messeniaca*)
Peisander of Rhodes, epic poet, 109
Pentateuch, *see* Bible, Old Testament, Septuagint
Peregrinus of Parium, Cynic, 676
Pericles: Duris of Samos on, 467; and Herodotus, 429; and Lysias' father, 506; and Protagoras, 473, 502; in Thucydides, 446, 448–9, 451, 453, 455, 460, 461, 474, 501, 503
Peripatos, Peripatetics, 29, 30, 468 & n. 1, **622–5**, 639, 640, 649, 836, 859; *see also* Aristotle, Lyceum, Theophrastus
Pergamum, 23, 29, 33, 35, 42
Petronius: Hipponax as model, 163; influence of *Iolaus*, 684, 687; and Menippus, 639; parody of Antonius Diogenes, 879; and Strato of Sardis, 652
Phaedrus, composer of verse fables, 702, 886
Phaleas of Chalcedon, 461 & n. 2, 462
Pherecrates, comic poet, 242, 383, 392, 392–3, 395, 410 n. 2, 467 n. 2

Pherecydes of Syros, prose writer: on Argonauts, 588
Philemon, comic poet, 336, 418, 424 & nn. 3, 4
Philetas of Cos, 30–1, **544–7**, 558, 561, 563, 576, 588, 616, *811*, 812
Philieus, tragic poet, 345
Philip of Macedon: Aristotle and, 528; Demosthenes and, 519–22, 524; in Dio of Prusa, 671; Theopompus on, 464
Philip of Thessalonica, 616, 650, 651
Philippi: poetry of, 607
Philippus of Opus, mathematician and astronomer, 793
Philistus of Syracuse, historian, 28, 458
Philo of Alexandria, 639, *854–5*
Philo of Larisa, head of Academy, 835
Philochorus of Athens, Atthidographer, 30, 459, 730
Philodamus Scarpheus, author of paean to Dionysus, 616
Philodemus, 531, 626, **628–30**, 648, *842–3*, 847
Philolaus of Croton, 13, 255
Philostratus, Flavius ('the Elder'), 524, **655–8**, 659, 669, 672, 673, 680 n. 1, 681, 683, 684, 686, 687, 696, 699, *863–5*, 875, 880, 884
Philostratus of Lemnos, 655
Philoxenus of Cythera, dithyrambic poet, 242, 243, 401
Philyllius, comic poet, 403, 404 n. 1
Phlegon of Tralles, historian, 680, 707
Phoenix of Colophon, iambic poet, 613, *831*
Phormis, Syracusan writer of comedy, 363 n. 3, 370
Photius, 41, 365 n. 3, 607, 670, 679, 683, 684, 687, 692, 694, 706, 738, 873, 879, 882, 889
Phrynichus, comic poet: *Monotropos*, 382–3
Phrynichus, tragic poet, 262–3, 263 n. 2, 285
Phrynis, poet and musician, 242
Phylarchus of Athens, historian, 467–8, 469, 470
Pindar, 222, 223, **226–35**, 242, 243, 244, *746–8*; works, 227, *746–7*; *Olympians*, (1), 227, 228, 236; (2), 227, 251; (3), 227; (6), 225; (9), 226; (13), 196; *Pythians*, (1), 177, 223, 224, 228–31; (2), 224; (4), 223, 232, 330, 557; (7), 226; (8), 244; *Nemeans*, (1), 225, 584; (7), 191, 232 n. 1, 239; *Isthmians*, (7), 177; (8) 225; *Paean 6*, 191, 232 n. 1; Aeolic forms in, 167; allegorization, 231–2; and Alcman, 171, 172, 176–7; on Archilochus, 123, 368 n. 3; and Bacchylides, 235, 236, 237, 238–9, *748*; and Corinna, 240, 241, 749; dramatic use of direct discourse, 189; Empedocles and, 251; formulas in, 231; 'gnomic bridge passages', 171; and Hiero, 224, 238, 367–8; on Homer, 721; on

INDEX

Pindar (*cont.*)

Homeridae, 47 n. 3; imagery, figures
of speech, 177, 228, 233, 236, 237, 290; and
Ibycus, 216; 'kenning' of, 177; and literacy,
8; on man, 172, 239; metre, 898; morality,
171, 172; and myth , 171, 251; and
Neoptolemus story, 191; religious element,
167, 234, 239, 251; ring composition in, 291;
and Simonides, 223, 225, 226, 233–4; on
Spartan choruses, 169; and Stesichorus, 187,
188, 195, 196, 200; and symbolism of gold,
176; unity of odes, 227–8; view of poetry,
185, 226, 231, 233–4, 238–9, 243

influence, reputation, assessments and
scholarship, 40, 227; and *Argonautica*, 588;
Aristarchus on, 827; Aristophanes of
Byzantium on, 826; Callimachus and, 556–7;
'Longinus' on, 235, 340, 637; Quintilian on,
188; Theocritus and, 584; Zenodotus and,
547, 812

Piso, L. Calpurnius, 628–9, 842

Pittacus, 432

Planudean Anthology: and Philodemus, 616,
629, 842

Planudes, Maximus, 616

Plato, **480–97**, *792–6*; life and career, 340,
408 n. 3, 463, **480–1**, 542, *792–3*

works, *793–4*; *Apology*, 375–6, 388, 389,
482, 500 n. 1, 505, 512, 756, 788; *Charmides*,
340–1, 486, 744; *Critias*, 340, 483, 493; *Crito*,
484; *Epinomis*, 257; *Euthyphro*, 486;
Gorgias, 244, 251, 320 nn. 1 & 2, 485,
486–7, 511; *Hermocrates*, 493; [*Hipparchus*],
722, 744; *Ion*, 7, 222, 280, 485, 722; *Laches*,
486; *Laws*, 14 n. 3, 244, 257, 405, **494–5**;
Letters, 480–1, 482, 483, 493, 494–5, 496,
529; *Lysis*, 11, 486; *Menexenus*, 497, 505,
510; *Meno*, 485, 496; *Parmenides*, 483, 485;
Phaedo, 10, 251, 253, 254, 485, **486–9**, 496,
671, 672, 682; *Phaedrus*, 12, 191, 477, 480,
483, 484, 486, 495, 496, 499 n. 1, 500, 510,
511, 533, 798; *Philebus*, 493; *Philosopher*,
492, 493; *Protagoras*, 11, 12, 388, 473, 482–3;
Republic, 7, 16, 251, 320 & n. 2, 407, 462,
474, 483, 486, 489 n. 1, **490–2**, 493, 496, 497,
507; *Sophist*, 482, 492; *Statesman*, 482, 492;
Symposium, 12, 341, 376, 480, 483, 485, **489–
90**, 495, 669, 682, 776–7, *788*; *Theaetetus*,
367, 483, **492**, 496; *Timaeus*, 255, 482, 483,
493–4, 604, 639, 663 n. 1; epigrams,
616–17; and Anaxagoras, 253, 254, 255, *756*;
audience of, 530; and comedy, 375–6, 407,
408–9, 462; and Democritus, 257; and
diatribe, 638; *eironeia*, 496–7; and
Empedocles, 251; on Forms, 489, 491; on
Heraclitus, 253; and Hippocrates, 477; and
Homer, 37, 42, 108, 191–2, 280, 722; and

Isocrates, 511, 512; and letter form, 628; on
literature, 7, 244, 405, 483–4, 535, 538;
medium of dialogue, 12–13, 482–4, 529;
myths, 251, 487; on oratory, 498, 533; on
Orphic books, 16; as rhetorician, 505; on
schools, 11; on Socrates, 253, 254, 375–6,
389, 476, 478, 481–3, 484–5, 497, 512, 529;
on Solon, 153; on sophists, 12, 319, 472,
473, 476, 482; on Stesichorus, 191–2; style
and literary characteristics, 337, 394, 484–5,
495–7, 502, 523; on Theognis, 138, 139, 145,
158; on Tyrtaeus, 130; as visionary, 235; on
Xenophanes, 246

influence, assessments, interpretations,
reputation: and Academy, 13, 505, 527, 622;
and Aelius Theon, 28; and Antimachus of
Colophon, 542, 546, 811; Aristides and, 661;
and Aristotle, 462, 527–8, 532, 533, 535, 538,
540, 806, 808; Athenaeus and, 682; Cicero
on, 257; Dio of Prusa and, 671, 672;
Dionysius of Halicarnassus on, 645; and
Eratosthenes, 604; and Hyperides, 804; and
Lucian, 675; and Panaetius, 847; and Philo,
639; and Plotinus, 640; Plutarch quotes,
667; cited, 730, 732, 738, 744

Platonism, Platonists, 494, 604, 631, 639, 662,
669, 672, 673, 675, 844; *see also* Academy

Plato the comic poet, 369 n. 1, 376, 395, 618

Plautus, 39, 373, 392, 402, 404, 408 n. 6, 410,
413, 416, 417 & n. 3, 418, 420, 423, 424, 780

Pleiad, 345, 547, 813, 814

Pliny the Elder: on Hipponax, Bupalus and
Athenis, 159, 735; on Menecrates, 822; on
papyrus, 19 n. 1

Pliny the Younger: and Herodas, 613; on
history and oratory, 466; Trajan and, 870;
friend of, 668

Plotinus, 622, **640–1**, *855–6*

Plutarch, 27, 555, 615, 639, 649, 664, **665–9**,
682, 704, 707, 710, *868–9*; citations and comments, 6, 11 (schools), 15 (texts of tragedy),
29 n. 1 (Museum), 38, 418 (Menander), 146,
147, *733* (Solon), 226 (Simonides), 240
(Corinna and Pindar), 242 (Philoxenus of
Cythera), 273 n. 1 (painter Agatharchus),
274 (actors), 296 (Sophocles), 298
(Sophocles and Aeschylus), 337 (recitations
of Euripides), 342 (Astydamas' Hector), 372
(satires on Pericles), 395 n. 2 (Alcibiades),
427, 439 (Herodotus), 468 (Duris), 467
(Phylarchus), 502 (Pericles), 515, 516, 517,
518 (Demosthenes), 545 (Antimachus of
Colophon), 603 (Nicander), 633 n. 1, 846
(Chrysippus), 707, 710 (Rome); Ps.-
Plutarch, 168, 169, 799, 804

Polemo of Athens, head of Academy, 298, 631,
821

Polemo, Marcus Antonius, orator, 656, 661, 672
Polemo of Ilium, Stoic geographer, 709
Polus: rhetorical handbook of, 12
Polybius, 40, 243, 431, 458 & n. 2, 459, 465 &
    n. 2, 466, 467, **468–70**, 633, *789–90*
Polycrates, author of speech for Anytus, 479
Polymnastus of Colophon, poet and musician,
    169
Porphyrio, Pomponius, scholar, 213
Porphyry, scholar: and Plotinus, 640, 856
Porson's law, 346
Posidippus of Pella, epigrammatist, 617, 618
Posidippus, comic poet, 417 n. 6
Posidonius, 256, 470, 631, **633**, *848*
Pound, Ezra: allusiveness of, 568; influence of
    Pindar on, 227
Pratinas of Phlius, playwright, 242, 260, 262
Praxilla of Sicyon, poetess, 239, 241
Praxiphanes, Peripatetic philosopher, 625,
    815, *839–40*
Precepts of Chiron, 109
Proclus, 106, 107, 257, 493 n. 1, 726, 752
Prodicus of Ceos, 11–12, 321, 445, 473,
    474, 483, *792*, 799
Propertius, 134, 555, 749
Protagoras of Abdera, 11–12, 446, 461, 462,
    473–4, 475–6, 502, *791*; *see also under* Plato
Prytanis, philosopher, 828
Ptolemies, 23, 26, 29, 544; *see also* Alexandria
Ptolemy I Soter, and Demetrius of Phalerum,
    30, 547, 624, 812; as historian, 464 n. 1, 705;
    and literature, 29; and Machon, 614; and
    Strato, 624; and Zenodotus, 812
Ptolemy II Philadelphus: and Alexander
    Aetolus, 813; and Alexandrian Museum,
    29 n. 1, 544; and Aratus, 602; and Athenian
    gymnasium, 24; and Callimachus, 549, 550,
    552; and Philetas, 30–1, 544, 811; and
    Strato, 838; and Theocritus, 570, 571, 572,
    576, 580, 817; and Timon, 851
Ptolemy III Euergetes I, 31, 555–6, 567, 586,
    823
Ptolemy VI Philometor, 827
Ptolemy VII Neos Philopator: and patronage,
    606
Ptolemy VIII Euergetes II: and expulsion of
    intellectuals, 33, 606, 824
Ptolemy: and Aristotle catalogue, 807
Pyrrho of Elis, 636, 637, 851
Pyrrhonists, 636
Pythagoras, 247, 252, 255, 472, 640, 838
Pythagoreans, 13, 255, 409, 488, 624, 640, 686,
    753, 754, 838; Neopythagoreans, 639–40, 696
Pythangelus, tragedian, 342
Python, playwright, 354

Qifti, Ibn al, 807

Quintilian, 188, 196, 199, 225, 466, 512, 531,
    545, 603, 623, 649, 739
Quintus Smyrnaeus, 649, 715, 716

Racine: *Phèdre*, 329
Rhetorica ad Herennium, 606
Rhianus of Crete, 607, *827–8*
Rhinthon of Syracuse (Tarentum?), 370 & n. 2
Rome, Romans: and annalistic history, 459; and
    Argonautica, 598; and Callimachus' *Aetia*,
    553, 556, 560, 561, 564; and Christianity,
    37; and comedy, 780; and elegiac metre,
    128; and Epicureanism, 527; and Greek
    language, 635; and Greek literature, 37, 614;
    imitations of Hellenistic poetry, 621;
    libraries and books at, 37; literature of
    Empire, **642–718**; Lycophron on, 549; and
    Parthenius, 615, 833; and patronage, 33;
    and Philetas, 545; and philosophy, 633;
    Polybius and, 469, 470; and rhetoric, 500,
    527, 636; satire, 637; scholarship on Greek
    theatre, 264; and Stoicism, 527, 631, 846;
    tragedy, 346; translations of Greek works,
    614

Sacadas of Argos, musician and poet, 169, 186,
    187
saints' lives, 657
Saïs, calendar of, 600
Sallust, 643
Sappho, 166, 167, 169, 185, 190, 191, **202–9**,
    218, *740–1*; and Archilochus, 122–3; and
    Bacchylides, 236; and Callimachus, 568; and
    Corinna, 749; Demetrius on, 648; and
    Hipponax, 164; and Ibycus, 214; 'Longinus'
    on, 646, 647; and Mimnermus, 134; Sapphic
    stanza, 213; and Stesichorus, 186; text, 4, 5;
    and Theocritus, 584, 585
Satyrus, actor, 517
Satyrus, biographer, 13, 624, 768
Sceptics, Scepticism, 636–7, 850
Schoenus, 347, 350
Scipio Aemilianus, 469
Scipio Africanus, 847
Scylax of Caryanda: voyages of, 429
Scymnus of Chios, prose author: work
    erroneously attributed to, 605, 824
Seleucids: poets of, 607
Semonides of Amorgos, **153–7**, *734*; and
    Homer and Hesiod, 47, 105 n. 1, 156, 157,
    518; iambic trimeter, 151; on life of man,
    136, 157; and Simonides, 153 & n. 1, 154,
    157, 734; on women, 99, 151, 154–6, 701
Semus of Delos, antiquarian, 363 n. 4
Seneca, 339, 542, 628, 632, 639, 651
Seneca the Elder, 650
Septuagint, 542 n. 2, 547

INDEX

Sesonchosis, 684

Seven Sages, 432; Demetrius of Phalerum's work on, 547, 625, 812

Sextus Empiricus, 473 n. 3, 475, 622, 636, 753, 791, *850–1*

Shakespeare: *Othello*, 329; and Plutarch, 615; *Timon*, 383

Shield of Heracles (*Scutum*, *Aspis*), 94, 102 n. 2, 103–4

Silloi, 246; of Xenophanes, 247

Simon, cookery author, 13

Simonides of Ceos, 222, **223–6**, *745–6*; on Argonauts, 588; and Bacchylides, 235, 236, 748; conception of poetry, 226, 233, 243; condemned by Phidippides in *Clouds*, 387; and elegiac couplet, 137; and epigram, 616; and Hiero, 367, 788; on life of man, 136, 157; and Philetas, 546; and Pindar, 233; and Semonides, 153–4, 157, 734; and Stesichorus, 186–7, 200

Simonides of Magnesia, 607

Simplicius, 246, 255, 753, 756, 757, 849

Siro, Epicurean, 842

skolia, 220–1, 745

Sminthes, author of *Phaenomena*, 599

Socrates: and Anaxagoras, 253; Aristoxenus on, 838; in comedy, (Aristophanes) 357, 373, 375–6, 381, 388–9, 407, 408, 776; (Ameipsias and Eupolis), 388, 776; Demetrius of Phalerum's dialogues, 547; Dio of Prusa and, 669, 670, 671; and Epicurus, 626; and Isocrates, 511–12, 799; and Lysias, 506, 507; Plato and, 253, 254, 375–6, 389, 476, 478, 481–5 *passim*, 497, 512, 529; and sophists, 476, 482; and Stoic ethics, 631; and Xenophon, 460

Socrates, Church historian, 883

Solon of Athens: life, 6, 146–7, 382, 432, 472, 521–2, *733–4*; works, 5, 15, 136, 137, **146–53**, 157, 158, 226, 236, 246, 259, 260, 262, 292, 732, *733–4*

sophists, sophistic movement, 8, 9, 11–12, 223, 226, 319, 320, 321, 328, 329, 343, 388, 427, 461, **472–6**, 477, 482, 500, 502, 503, 504, 510–11, 655; and Euripides, 317, 319–21, 328, 329, 337; and Thucydides, 441, 445, 455; *see also* names of sophists

Sophistic, Second, 24, 27–8, 514, 524, 651, **655–62**

Sophocles, **295–316**, *764–7*; life and career, 260, 272, 295–7, 297, 316, 340, 427, 433, *764* works, *765*; *Ajax*, 270, 271–2, 296, 300–2, 310, 311, 312, 313–14, 315, 427; *Antigone*, 242, 284, 296, 305, **307–9**, 310, 311, 312, 313–14, 344, 353, 427, 433; *Trachiniae*, 274, 275, 296, 297 & n. 2, 302, 303–4, 305, 310–11, 312, 313, 314, 315, 433; *Oedipus*

tyrannus, 36, 87, 107, 275, 296, 299, **303–9**, 315, 340, 539; *Electra*, 271–2, 273, 275, 280, 296, 303, 305, 310–12, 313, 314, 315; *Philoctetes*, 265, 271–2, 296, 310, 311, 312, 313, 314, 315, 348, 649, 764; *Oedipus Coloneus*, 144, 225, 269–70, 275, 296, 302, 303, 305, 307, 309–10, 312, 315, 339, 427; lost or fragmentary, 8, 242, 274, 311, 342 n. 1, 347–51, 352, 417, 433, 764, 765, 772

character of drama, 265, 268–76 *passim*, 280, 298, 312; character and psychology, 298, 310–11, 312, 314, 326, 540; compared with Aeschylus, 285, 296, 297–8, 313, 764; compared with Euripides, 297 & n. 2, 298, 310–11, 313–14, 324, 331, 339; crime and punishment, 309–10; entrances and exits, 315; *hamartia*, 540; happy endings, 539; irony, 304, 309; language and poetry, 313, 314, 317, 338, 503; manipulation of inconsistency, 314; treatment of tragic issues, 299–300; musical element, 315; *peripeteia* in, 539; pessimism, 144, 305–6; prophecy, gods, fate, 304–10, 321, 324; props, 314; realism, 310–11, 315–16; single plays, 297; and fifth-century intellectual controversies, 313, 319, 503; use of chorus, 268, 297, 299, 765; use of actors, 258, 274, 275, 297, 315, 362 & n. 1; view of man, 299–300; visual element, 271–3, 297, 314–15

reputation, influence and popularity, 35, 36, 243, 297, 298, 299, 326, 339, 340, 341, 342, 417, 539, 540, 661

Sophron, 369, 370, 575, 580, 612

Sosibius, scholar, 170 n. 2, 363 n. 4, 365 n. 4

Sositheus, playwright, 350, 354, 575

Sosius Senecio, 668

Sotades, poet, 813

Speusippus, 13, 753

Sphaerus the Stoic, 463, 638

Stasinus of Cyprus, epic poet, 726

Statius: on Corinna, 749

Stendhal: *Le Rouge et le Noir*, 615

Stephanus of Byzantium, 608, *738*, *826*

Stesichorus of Himera, 5, 166, 181, **186–201**, 214, 222, 223, 235, 236, 259, 575, 584, 724, 736, *738–9*

'Stesichorus' (4th-century poet), 186 n. 3, 192, 738

Stesimbrotus, biographer, 8

Stobaeus, 154 (Semonides on women), 343 (Theodectas), 461 n. 2 (Hippodamus), 545 (Philetas), 607 (Rhianus), 610 (Moschus), 611 (Bion), 611–12, 613 n. 1 (Herodas), 633 (philosophical handbook), 639 (Aëtius), 757 (Democritus), 853 (Teles)

Stoics, Stoicism, 527, 625, 630, **631–6**, 844–50; in Academy, 622; Aelian and, 680; Aratus

934

Stoics (*cont.*)
and, 600, 820; and diatribe, 638; Dio of
Prusa and, 669, 670; and Eratosthenes, 604;
Galen and, 662; and Heraclitus, 253; and
logos, 639; at Pergamum, 33; Plotinus and,
640; on style, 648; Timon of Phlius on, 637
Strabo of Amasia, 23, 27, **642–3**, 707, *857–8*;
13, 30 (Aristotle), 20 (copyists), 162
(Hipponax), 342 (Theodectas), 588 (Circe
and Medea), 604 (Eratosthenes), 633,
848 (Posidonius), 639 (*spoudogeloion*), 730
(Callinus, Tyrtaeus), 731 (Mimnermus), 779
(Menander and Epicurus), 858 (Dionysius of
Halicarnassus)
Strato, comic playwright, 544–5
Strato of Lampsacus, Aristotelian philosopher,
624, 625, *838–9*
Strato of Sardis, poet and anthologist, 616, 652
Strattis, comic poet, 405 n. 2
Strindberg, 329
Sublime, On the, see 'Longinus'
Suetonius: compared with Plutarch, 668; on
Crates' visit to Rome, 614; on Tiberius, 607,
615
Susarion, comic poet, 366–7
Synesius, 669, 670, 870

Tacitus: *Dialogus*, 859
Tefnut, 684, 685
Telegonia, 107, 726
Teles the Cynic, 638–9, *853–4*
Telesilla of Argos, poetess, 239, 241
Terence, 39, 392, 409, 416, 417, 418, 424, 780
Terpander of Lesbos, 168, 169, 182, 202, 243
Thales, 179, 432, 637
Thaletas of Gortyn, 169
Thebais, 106 n. 1, 109, 721
Theban epics, 106 & n. 1, 726
Themistius: on Arrian, 706
Theocritus, 173, 182, 243, 339, 367 & n. 2,
369, 370, 552, 563, 564, **570–86**, 609, 610,
611, 612, 618, 697, *817–18*, 818, 819; and
Aratus, 602; and Callimachus, 552, 563, 564,
570, 576–7, 581, 583; and Philetas, 545, 811
Theodectas, tragic poet and orator, 11, 343
Theodorus, epic poet of Cleopatra, 607
Theodorus of Byzantium: rhetorical handbook,
12
Theodorus of Gadara, rhetor and critic, 859
Theognis, 15, **136–46**, 149, 158, 236, 246, 340,
618, 626, *732–3*
Theogony (from Cyclic epics), 106, 109, 726
Theon, Aelius, 28, 700
Theon of Alexandria, son of Artemidorus, 611
Theon of Smyrna, 602, 603, 825
Theophrastus, 530, **622–5**, *836–7*; on
Anaximander, 245; *Characters*, 614, 623–4;

dedication of work to, 825; and Demetrius
of Phalerum, 812, 836; and Democritus, 256;
library of, 615, 832; and Lyceum, 529, 542,
547, **622**; and Menander, 779; pupils of, 466,
547, 805; on qualities of style, 633, 648; and
Stoic rhetoric, 636; and tragic history, 468;
on Xenophanes, 246; Ps. Theophrastus: *On
signs*, 600
Theopompus, 10, 28, 442, 458, 463, **464–5**,
466, 470, 785, 799
Thespis, 259, 262, 366
Thestorides of Phocaea, epic poet, 726
Thrasycles the Athenian, tragic poet, 345 n. 1
Thrasyllus, Alexandrian librarian, 757, 794
Thrasymachus of Chalcedon, 12, 461, 474, 490,
503, *792*
Thucydides, **441–56**, *784–6*; on Antiphon, 501,
502; on assassination of Hipparchus, 218; on
Athens, 455, 460; on campaigns of archaic
Greece, 93; on causation, 446–7, 455, 469;
chronology of, 445, 447–50; compared with
Arrian, 705; compared with Polybius, 470;
composition and structure of history, 442–4,
447–8, 450; conception of history, historical
methodology, 8–9, 431, 444, 445, 447, 452,
454–5, 456, 457, 458, 459, 464, 465, 466;
continuators of, 458, 459–60, 464, 785;
criticisms of other historians, 438–9, 444,
457, 459; Dionysius of Halicarnassus on,
503, 519, 644, 645, 648, 667; and Herodotus,
435, 438–9, 441, 444, 445, 446, 447, 448, 452,
454, 455, 456, 457; and Homer, 111, 114,
446, 447; influence of poetry on, 447, 457;
influence of history, 22, 519 (Demosthenes),
28 (Aelius Theon), 458, 459–60, 464 (in
fourth century), 680 (Aelian), 687 (novel),
699 (Longus), 708 (Appian), 709–10
(Pausanias), 712 (Herodian); life, 441–2; and
medical writers, 477; moral judgements,
455–6; Pentekontaetia, 443, 452, 453; on
Pericles, 375 n. 4, 378 n. 3 (*see also under
speeches*); Plutarch on, 667; and rhetoric,
328 n. 1, 498, 503; on schools, 6; and
sophism, 445; speeches in, 147, 329, 440,
445–6, 456, 457–8, 460, 461, 474, 479, 501,
503; style of, 502, 503
Tiberius, emperor, 607, 609, 615, 642, 643,
650, 651
Tibullus, 569
Timaeus, 459, 467, 549
Timagenes of Alexandria, 642
Timocles, playwright, 354, 405
Timon of Athens, 382–3, 411 n. 1
Timon of Phlius, 246, 248, 252, 599, 637, 820,
851–2, 897
Timotheus, dithyrambic poet, 15, 165, 242,
243, 281, 337–8

Timotheus, son of Conon, 512
Tisias of Syracuse, teacher of rhetoric, 12, 22, 474, 498–9, 500, 799
Trajan, emperor: and Arrian, 706; and Dio of Prusa, 671, 672, 870; and Plutarch, 666, 868
Triphiodorus of Egypt, epic poet, 715
Trojan cycle, 726; *see also Cypria*
Tubero, Q. Aelius, 644
Tynnichus of Chalcis, poet, 222
Tyrannion (the elder) of Amisus, scholar, 614–15, *832–3*
Tyrtaeus, 5, 15, 105 n. 1, 128, 129, 130, 135, 136, 137, 141, 143, 147, 158, 169, *730–1*, 732
Tzetzes, John, Byzantine polymath, 30, 31 n. 1, 163, 814, 815, 874

Ulpian, 682

Varro, 19, n. 2, 606, 615, 639, 822
Varro of Atax, 598
Velleius Paterculus, 736
Virgil, 37, 99, 190, 296, 527, 585, 588, 598, 599, 603, 605, 611, 615, 833, 842
Vitruvius: on Aeschylus and scene-painting, 273

Weil, Simone, 596

Xanthus of Lydia, 186, 187, 431
Xenocles, tragic poet, 341–2
Xenocrates, head of Academy, 622, *835*
Xenocritus of Locri, 169
Xenomedes, chronicler, 562
Xenophanes, 96, **245–8**, 252, 254, 255, 599, 637, *752–3*, 753
Xenophilus, Pythagorean, 838
Xenophon, 9, 10, 11, 14, 28, 243, 268 & n. 1, 278, 410, 442, 451, **458–62**, 474, **478–80**, 485, 634, 672, 675, 687, 704–5, 708, 785, *788–9*; Ps. Xenophon, 375 & n. 2; *see also* 'Old Oligarch' (*Politeia of the Athenians*)
Xenophon of Ephesus, 684, 685, 686, **690–2**, 694, 695, *881–2*

Zeno of Elea, 255
Zeno of Citium, 23, 533, 625, 631, 637–8, 669, 670, *844–5*, 845, 852
Zeno of Sidon, Epicurean, 842
Zenodotus of Ephesus, scholar, 31, 547, 549, 586, 606, 624, 811, *812–13*, 813
Zeuxis, 243
Zoroastrian myths: and Hesiod, 101